MW00776562

Fairy Tales,

PATRIOTISM & THE NATION-STATE

The Rise of the Modern West and the Response of the World
(with parallel Google Earth folder for each chapter)

— J. Brown

Kendall Hunt

publishing company

Cover images
© J. Brown
© Shutterstock, Inc.

Kendall Hunt
publishing company

www.kendallhunt.com
Send all inquiries to:
4050 Westmark Drive
Dubuque, IA 52004-1840

Copyright © 2014 by J. Brown

ISBN 978-1-4652-4604-2

Kendall Hunt Publishing Company has the exclusive rights to reproduce this work,
to prepare derivative works from this work, to publicly distribute this work,
to publicly perform this work and to publicly display this work.

All rights reserved. No part of this publication may be reproduced,
stored in a retrieval system, or transmitted, in any form or by any
means, electronic, mechanical, photocopying, recording, or otherwise,
without the prior written permission of the copyright owner.

Printed in the United States of America
10 9 8 7 6 5 4 3 2 1

Contents

Foreword p. xi

Introduction p. xiii

PART ONE: THE RISE OF THE MODERN WEST.........................**1**

CHAPTER 1   The Rise of European Technological Power.............................**3**

Chapter outline and where it fits in the whole (3) — PART ONE: EUROPEAN MARITIME TECHNOLOGY circa 1300–1500 (4) — The compass (4) — Sails, hulls and armament (5) — A way to determine latitude, but not longitude (5) — Two kinds of maps (5) — The Starfinder (6) — The *Reconquista* (8) — Portugal takes shape (8) — Portuguese leadership in the explorations (9) — Borrowed sails, borrowed hulls (10) — Understanding Trade Winds, Westerlies, and the North Atlantic gyre (10) — A new way of finding latitude; educated guessing about longitude (11) — Bartolomeu Dias turns the Cape (12) — Vasco da Gama and the first Portuguese trade with India (14) — Albuquerque's "closing" of the Indian Ocean (14) — The Italian Renaissance context of it all (16) — The Renaissance quickly defined (17) — Florence: eye of the storm (18) — The link between war and art (20) — PART TWO: SCIENTIFIC REVOLUTION circa 1500–1700 (21) — The Reformation and Counter-Reformation context of it all (21) — Protestant university reform; Catholic response (22) — The solution of the Problem of Motion (23) — Copernicus (24) — Brahe and Kepler in Prague (24) — Galileo (25) — Huygens, Gilbert, and Newton (26) — Navigation transformed (26) — Holland's Glorious Century (27) — American footnote: the Dutch in New Amsterdam, the Pilgrims in Leiden (28) — PART THREE: INDUSTRIAL REVOLUTION, IMPERIAL POWER circa 1700–1900 (29) — Why Britain? (29) — Textiles (30) — Steam (31) — Metallurgy (32) — The Crystal Palace (33) — *Tools of Empire, Tentacles of Progress* (33) — Gunboats (34) — Rifles and machine guns (36) — Imperial botany (37) —"Industrial" quinine (39)—Conclusion and advertisement (40) — Endnotes (41)

CHAPTER 2   *"Enfants de la Patrie":* Political Nationalism in the Enlightenment and French Revolution..**43**

The heart of the matter (43) — A nod to the French language (45) — A quick sketch of the topography and texture of the land of France (46) — Early history: Celts, Romans & Germans (48) — Feudalism, the 100 Years War and the legacy of Joan of Arc (49) — The absolutism of Louis XIV (51) —The Enlightenment: origins and overview (52) — The Enlightenment's progression of ideas (53) —Montesquieu (53) — Diderot's "Supplement to the Voyage of Bougainville" (54) — Rousseau's General Will (56) — Turgot, the last hope for reform from above (59) — The coming of the Revolution (60) —At Versailles (61) — Fall of the Bastille (61) — The "Great Fear" (62) —

The August 4 Assembly and the end of feudalism (63) — The Constitution of 1791 (64) — The radical phase (65) — The Committee of Public Safety and the year of "The Terror" (66) —The draft army (67) — Napoleon: the early years (68) — Napoleon: the glory days (69) — The Code Napoléon (71) — The Grand Empire and the satellites (71) — End game (72) —The legacy of it all (73) — Endnotes (74)

CHAPTER 3   "A New Binding Tie": Cultural Nationalism in Germany 75

The heart of the matter (75) — A quick look at the German language (77) —Some common German place names (78) —Topography and texture of the land (78) — The Germanies in the time of Napoleon (80) —The Prussian Reforms (82) —*The Juniper Tree* (83) — Romanticism, Herder, and the "Folk" (84) —Fichte and Jahn (86) —The lives of the Brothers Grimm (87) — The Grimms and the "organic" idea (89) — The Model of Cultural Breakdown (90) — The *Eddas* and Old Norse Mythology (91) — European discovery of the *Rigveda* (93) — The invention of philology (94) — Jacob Grimm's *Teutonic Mythology* (95) — Wagner's opera (97) —The Congress of Vienna (99) — The Age of Metternich, 1815 to 1848 (101) — List's economic nationalism (101) — Growing unrest (102) — The Revolutions of 1848 (103) — The Frankfurt Assembly (104) — Austria vs. Prussia (104) — Otto von Bismarck (105) — Kaiser William I (106) — Bismarck's creation of the German Empire (106) — The Seven Weeks War, 1866 (107) — Franco-German War, 1870 (108) — Bismarck's domination of world diplomacy (109) — William II and Germany's "Place in the Sun" (111) —World War I (113) — Weimar Republic and revolution (115) — Versailles Treaty (116) — The political structure of Weimar (117) — Culture and economics in Weimar Germany (118) — Hitler and the NSDAP (119) — Beer hall putsch (121) — The Third Reich (123) — Philosophical asides (125) — Friedrich Meinecke's look back (126) — Endnotes (127)

CHAPTER 4   "The Socialist Fatherland": Socialism in Russia 129

The heart of the matter (129) — Introduction to the Russian language (130) — Topography and texture of the land (133) — Kievan Russia (136) — The rise of Muscovy (137) — The Romanov dynasty (138) — Imperial Russia (140) — *Natasha's Dance*: Romantic nationalism in Russia in the nineteenth century (142) — Meanwhile, Western and Central European socialism (145) — Herzen and the birth of *narodnichestvo* (146) — The Reform Era of Alexander II (146) — "What is to be done?" (147) — Reaction and Russification (148) — Karl Marx (149) — Classical Marxism (150) — Its strengths (151) — Its weaknesses (152) — The first Russian Marxists (154) — Nicholas II (155) — Lenin and the St. Petersburg Group (155) — The "short, victorious war" and the Revolution of 1905 (157) — Stolypin's necktie, and his "wager on the strong" (158) — Russia's side of World War I (159) — The March (February, old-style) Revolution, 1917 (161) — The Dual Government (162) — The "Great October Revolution" (163) — R.S.F.S.R. and SOVNARKOM (164) — War Communism (165) — *The ABCs of Communism* (166) — The NEP (167) — Stalin's power base (168) — Collectivization and industrialization (169) — Kirov's assassination and the purges (170) — Stalin and Hitler (171) — World War II (172) — Tehran, Yalta, and Potsdam (174) —Beginnings of the Cold War (175) —Korean War (176) —Solzhenitsyn's judgment (177) — The succession; Khrushchev (178) — Cold War in Africa, beginning with Ghana (181) — Cold War in the Mideast, beginning with Egypt (181) — Cold War in Southeast and South Asia, beginning with Vietnam (182) — Cold War in Latin America, beginning with Cuba (183) — The Soviet system stagnates (184) — Czechoslovakia, Poland, and Afghanistan (185) — Gorbachev: the system dismantled (185) — Failure of the August Coup (187) — End of the Cold War (189) — Lessons learned (189) — Endnotes (190)

CHAPTER 5   "Racy of the Soil": Ireland. 191

The heart of the matter (191) — Introduction to the Gaelic (Irish) language (192)   Topography and texture of the land (194) — Legends, folklore, and early history (196) — The three most important dates in Irish history: 1171, 1533, 1610 (197) — Puritan Revolution and aftermath (198) — The Penal Laws and the "Protestant Ascendancy" (200) — Impact of the American and French Revolutions (201) — The Irish Rebellion of 1798 (201) —"The Counselor" and Catholic Emancipation (203) —Young Ireland (203) — Potato Famine (204) — "My Mother, Mary Kelly" (205) — The Ordnance Survey in Ireland (206) —Irish Republican Brotherhood and Fenians (206) — Michael Cusack and the Gaelic Athletic Association (207) — Parnell and Gladstone (208) — Irish literary revival and the Gaelic League (209) — The Home Rule Movement Before WW I (211) — The Irish Orange (212) — Easter Rising 1916 (212) — The partitioning of Ireland (216) — De Valera shapes the Republic of Ireland (216) — The Troubles (217) — The Good Friday Agreement and since (219) — Final musings on nationalism and socialism (220) — Endnotes (221)

CHAPTER 6   "Land of Heroes": Finland. 223

The heart of the matter (223) — A quick introduction to Finnish (224) — Topography and texture of the land (224) — The step-children of Scandinavia (225) — The Kingdom of Sweden and the Reformation (227) — Mikael Agricola (227) — Sweden as the local great power: The Thirty Years' War (228) — Russia replaces Sweden as the local great power: The Great Northern War (229) —The Fennophiles (230) —Napoleonic wars and Russian control (231) — The Turku Romantics (232) — The freshman class of 1822: Runeberg, Snellman, and Lönnrot (233) — Defense of the *Kalevala* (234) — Russian imperial politics (235) — Sibelius (236) — War and Revolution (237) — Baron Mannerheim (238) — Independence (239) — The Winter War (240) — The "Continuation War" (240) — Since (240) — Endnotes (241)

CHAPTER 7   *Ma Vlast* ("My Fatherland"): Czechs, Czechoslovakia, and the Bratislavan Lesson 243

The heart of the matter (243) — Some introduction to the Czech language (244) — Topography and texture of the land (245) — Prehistory and early history (246) — Foundations of a Bohemian/ Moravian state: two golden ages (247) — The life and times of Jan Hus (John Hus) (249) — The Hussite Wars (251) —Another defenestration, another decades-long war (252) — Roots of the Czech national renaissance (253) — Ideal patterns of cultural nationalism (253) — The forerunners (255) — The Slav Congress in Prague in 1848 (257) — The nationalist composers: Smetana and Dvořak (258) — Sokol (260) — *Budweisers into Czechs and Germans* (260) — Inside the Dual Monarchy's Cisleithania (261) — Count Taaffe's "Iron Ring" (262) — The Budweis/Budějovice Compromise (263) — World War I (264) — Tomáš Masaryk and independence (264) — The Third Reich and German ascendancy (265) — Eduard Beneš and the assassination of Heydrich (266) — In the wake of WW II (267) — Inside the Soviet Bloc (267) —Velvet revolution, velvet divorce (268) — The Bratislavan lesson (270) — General lessons learned about modern European social mobilization (270) — Endnotes (271)

PART TWO: THE RESPONSE OF THE WORLD **273**

CHAPTER 8   "Strengthening Devotion to Patriotic Symbols":
The Veracruz-to-Mexico City Corridor of Latin America 275

The heart of the matter (275) — Introduction to area languages: Spanish (276) — Introduction to area languages: Náhuatl (277) — SECTION A: TOPOGRAPHY AND TEXTURE OF THE LAND (278) — From the coast to the crest of the Sierra Madre Oriental (278) — The altiplano, the volcano La Malinche, and the Sierra de Tláloc (281) — The Valley of Mexico (282) — SECTION B: "FIRST NATIONS" AND THE SPANISH INVASION (283) — Before the Aztecs (283) — The Mexica (284) — Cortés and the Spanish invasion (286) — SECTION C: THE COLONIAL ERA, 1521–1810 (289) — Colonial institutions take shape: encomienda and repartimiento (289) — Christianity and Church institutions (290) — The founding of Puebla (291) — The Virgin of Guadalupe (291) — Fr. Sahagún and the Indian-Spanish honeymoon (292) — The hacienda (293) — Commerce on rival roads (294) — Royal fairs, royal convoys, and the Bourbon Reforms (295) — SECTION D: INDEPENDENCE AND INTERVENTIONS (295) — Beginnings of the independence movement (295) — Ideas in the air (297) — The "Interventions": foreign invasions of Mexico (298) — Santa Anna (298) — The main U.S. invasion (299) — Benito Juárez, the Liberal Reforms, and the Civil War (301) — The French invasion and Maximilian (302) — SECTION E: THE PORFIRIATO AND THE REVOLUTION (304) — The Porfiriato (304) — The coming of the Revolution (305) — Revolution: The military phase 1910–1920 (307) — Revolution: The cultural phase 1920–1940 (311) — SECTION F: SINCE THE REVOLUTION (313) — The era of World War II (313) — 1968, Olympic Games and politics (313) — Fidel Castro and Che Guevara in the Valley of Mexico (314) — Liberation Theology (315) — NAFTA and immigration (316) — Lessons learned (316) —Endnotes (317)

CHAPTER 9   "The Only Antidote to Foreign Rule and Modern Imperialism":
The Durban-to-Pretoria Corridor of Sub-Saharan Africa. 319

The heart of the matter (320) — SECTION A: SOME INTRODUCTION TO AREA LANGUAGES AND THE TOPOGRAPHY AND TEXTURE OF THE LAND (321) — The Click languages of the Khoisan (321) — Bantu languages in Southern Africa: Sotho/Tswana and Nguni (321) — A few Portuguese linguistic survivals (322) — From Dutch to Cape Dutch to Afrikaans (323) — General geography (323) — The Durban-to-Pretoria corridor (324) — SECTION B: PRE- AND EARLY HISTORY (329) — The rock art of the Khoisan (329) — *The Abundant Herds* (330) — Halfway to Java (331) — SECTION C: THE BRITISH ARRIVAL, THE ZULU CRUSHING, THE GREAT TREK, AND NATALIA (333) — British takeover (333) — Zulu power and the Mfecane/Difaqane (333) — The fate of the refugees (336) — The Great Trek and its legacy (336) — SECTION D: BRITISH DOMINANCE, THE ZULU WAR AND THE BOER WARS (338) — The British in Natal (338) — Xhosa tragedy (339) — The growth of British Natal by 1850 (339) — Bushman raiders of the Drakensberg (340) — Shepstone, the N.N.P., and the "barrier locations" (340) — Langalibalele of the Hlubi (341) — The Colensos and English liberalism (341) — Lord Carnarvon's federation idea (343) — Cetshwayo and the Zulu revival (343) — The Anglo-Zulu War of 1879 (343) — *King Solomon's Mines* (346) — Dismembering the Zulu state (347) — The Boer republics and the Anglo-Boer wars (348) — The first Anglo-Boer War (349) — Diamonds at Kimberley; gold on the Rand (350) — The railroads to Jo'burg (351) — Cecil Rhodes (351) — Jameson's Raid (352) — The Second Anglo-Boer War (353) — The "concentration" camps (355) — The Union of South

Africa, 1910 (355) — SECTION E: CULTURAL NATIONALISM AMONG THE AFRIKANERS (356) — The first voices (356) — The *Broederbond* (357) — *Die Tweede Trek* ("The Second Trek") (358) — *Cry, the Beloved Country* (359) — Instituting apartheid, 1948–50 (359) — SECTION F: AFRICAN CULTURAL NATIONALISM (360) — Early civil rights struggle part one: Gandhi in South Africa (360) — Early civil rights struggle part two: J. L. Dube (363) — The Bambatha (Zulu) rebellion of 1906 (364) — Dube, the African National Congress, and the Native Lands Act (364) — Nelson Mandela (365) — Albert Luthuli (366) — The P.A.C. and the Sharpeville massacre (367) — Steve Biko and "Black consciousness" (368) — The Soweto riots (368) — *July's People* (369) — Buthelezi and Inkatha (370) — Desmond Tutu and the Truth and Reconciliation Commission (370) — The current state of affairs, post-apartheid, and lessons learned (372) — Endnotes (373)

CHAPTER 10 "To Create a New State": The Damascus-South-to-Water Corridor
of the Mideast 375

The heart of the matter (376) — SECTION A: LANGUAGE AND TOPOGRAPHY (377) — A brief introduction to Hebrew and Arabic (377) — Topography and texture of the "Damascus south to water" corridor (381) — A word on climate, and especially the availability of water (385) — A "fruit ladder" of traditional routes across the land (387) — SECTION B: BACKGROUND OF THE MODERN STATE OF ISRAEL (388) — Beginnings (388) — Greeks and Romans (388) — Diaspora (389) — Ashkenazi Jews: the European settlement (390) — Enlightenment and Haskalah (391) — The closing of the doors (392) — Zionism: a quick definition (392) — Ben-Yehuda and the rebirth of spoken Hebrew (393) — The First Aliyah (394) — Theodor Herzl and the Zionist Congresses (394) — *The Fiddler on the Roof* (396) — Ahad Ha'am (396) — The Second Aliyah (397) — Manya Shochat (398) — A. D. Gordon (398) — David Ben–Gurion (399) — Chaim Weizmann and the Balfour Declaration (399) — World War I in the region (400) — Massive Arab backlash (401) — Vladimir Jabotinsky and the Jewish Legion (402) — BETAR and Irgun (403) — British policies in the last years of the mandate (404) — Independence (405) — Politics and the "Ingathering of the Exiles" (406) — SECTION C: BACKGROUND OF MODERN ARAB NATIONALISM IN GENERAL (407) — The last chapters of Imperial Roman rule (408) — The glory days of Arabic poetry (409) — The life of Muhammad (409) — Muslim expansion AD 632–732 (410) — The Arab kingdoms (411) — Invasion from west and east: Crusaders and Mongols (411) — *The Arabian Nights' Entertainment,* or the *1001 Nights* (412) — Ottoman rule (413) — The pilgrimage road (414) — The challenge of the West (415) — Muhammad Ali and Ibrahim Pasha (416) — Protestant mission schools and the Arab Awakening (417) — Reform and Reaction: from Tanzimat to Abdul Hamid II (419) — Young Turks, Sharif Hussein, and "Lawrence of Arabia" (419) — From the Sykes-Picot Agreement to the Hashemite Kingdoms (421) — SECTION D: MODERN PALESTINIAN NATIONALISM IN THE LARGER CONTEXT OF ARAB, MUSLIM, AND WORLD EVENTS (422) — How Tanzimat ("The Reforms") worked out in Palestine (422) — The Afula land transfer of 1910 (423) — World War I and the first years of the mandate: intellectuals "imagining" the community (424) — The Arab Revolt and World War II (424) — *Al-Nakba*, the Catastrophe (425) — The rise of Egypt's Gamal Abdal Nasser (426) — Yasser Arafat, *al-Fatah*, and the P.L.O. (428) — From the Ramadan/Yom Kippur War to the Camp David Accords (429) — "Outside" and "Inside": from the *Intifada* to the Oslo Accords (429) — Palestinians, Israelis, and the U.S. in the Arab Spring (431) — Final musings on nationalism (433) — Endnotes (433)

CHAPTER 11 "The Idolatry of Nation":
The Grand Trunk Road Corridor of South Asia 435

The heart of the matter (435) — SECTION A: LANGUAGE, TOPOGRAPHY, AND THE TEXTURE OF THE LAND (436) — Spoken languages and language families of South Asia (436) — Written languages (436) — Hindi: the (very) short course (437) — Topography and texture (440) — The Grand Trunk Road, northwest to southeast (442) — SECTION B: ANCIENT RELIGIOUS HISTORY (444) — Historical geography of the *Mahabharata* and *Ramayana* (444) — Indian origins of Buddhism (446) — SECTION C: CLASSIC DYNASTIES (448) — Mauryans (448) — Ashoka (448) — Guptans (449) — Mughals (449) — Babur (450) — The great road of Sher Shah Surii (451) — Akbar (452) — Jahangir and Nur Jahan (453) — Shah Jahan (454) — Aurangzeb (456) — A word on non-Muslim religious developments in Mughal times (457) — SECTION D: WESTERN INTRUSION (458) — The century of "John Company" rule, 1757–1857 (459) — Sepoy Mutiny/First War of Independence (460) –SECTION E: THE RAJ (461) — The manner of British control (462) — Gandhi returns to India: the highlights (464) — Bengali Renaissance (466) — Hindu nationalist manifestations from elsewhere in British India (468) — The Muslim response (470) — Gandhi in deeper context (471) — SECTION F: INDEPENDENCE (473) — Partition (473) — Kashmir (475) — The new Pakistan (475) — The Republic of India (476) — India's new linguistic states (477) — Nehru's economic development plans (477) — Indira Gandhi (478) — Babri Musjid/Ram Mandir (479) — Revenge & reconciliation (480) — Endnotes (480)

CHAPTER 12 "True Love of the Soil of Indonesia": Southeast Asia's Java Roads 483

The heart of the matter (483) —A brief introduction to the languages of Java and environs (484) — TOPOGRAPHY AND TEXTURE OF THE JAKARTA-TO-SURABAYA CORRIDOR (485) — Setting in Southeast Asia and Indonesia (485) — The Wallace Line (486) — Views along one road (488) — PREHISTORY AND EARLY HISTORY: JAVANESE KINGDOMS AND RELIGIONS (489) — Prambanan and Borobudur (489) — The Pasisir and the Muslim Kingdom of Demak (490) — The Sultanate of Mataram (491) — Legacies of the Javanese kingdoms: the *priyayi* and the Alus Art complex (491) — DEVELOPMENT OF THE DUTCH EAST INDIES (493) — Jan Pieterzoon Coen, "the Butcher of Banda" (494) — The erosion of Mataram (495) — VOC administration of Java (495) — Gov.–Gen. Daendals and the *Grote Postweg* (496) — British interlude (497) — The Java War (498) — The Cultivation System (498) — *Max Havelaar* (499) — The "Liberal Policy" and neo-colonialism (500) — The Ethical Policy (500) — ROOTS OF INDONESIAN NATIONALISM (501) — *Letters of a Javanese Princess* (501) — Sarekat Islam (501) — The creation of Bahasa Indonesia (502) — The young Sukarno (503) — Japanese occupation (504) — INDEPENDENCE (505) — Establishing the Republic (505) — The Bandung Conference (506) — "Guided Democracy" (507) — *The Year of Living Dangerously* (507) — General Suharto's New Order (509) — Pramoedya reflects on the Great Post Road and the New Order (510) — The author reflects on Pramoedya (511) — Endnotes (511)

CHAPTER 13 "Against Foreign Imperialist Oppression": East Asia I 513

The heart of the matter (514) — Introduction to the Chinese language (514) — SECTION A: GENERAL GEOGRAPHY; TOPOGRAPHY AND TEXTURE OF THE YANGTZE VALLEY CORRIDOR IN PARTICULAR (519) — The Middle Kingdom (519) — Three river systems (519) — Mountains (520) — The corridor of special focus: the Yangtze River Valley (521) — The Jiangnan (521) — The middle Yangtze (523) — The three gorges (524) — Sichuan's purple bowl (524) — Mountains, some with pandas (525) — Commodities that shaped the traditional life cycle, and the landscape (525) — Traditional river transportation (527) — SECTION B: PRE- AND EARLY HISTORY (529) — "Dragon bones" (529) — Confucius (530) — Warring States and the "First Emperor" (531) — The sensuous and dangerous South (531) — All Rivers' Weir (532) — Miracle Canal (533) — The Han Dynasty (533) — Three Kingdoms, Six Dynasties (534) — SECTION C: CLASSIC DYNASTIES circa 600–1900 (535) — Buddhism enters China (535) — A reunited China and a grand canal: the Sui-Tang Dynasties (536) — The perfecting of the civil service (536) — Commerce and culture in the Song Dynasty (537) — The northern nomads (537) — The Southern Song Dynasty (538) — Mongol conquest and the Yuan Dynasty (538) — The Ming and Qing Dynasties (539) — Traditional Chinese novels (539) — SECTION D: WESTERN INTRUSION AND CHINESE RESPONSE (544) — The Ming voyages vs. contemporary western explorations (544) — Matteo Ricci and the Jesuits (545) — The "Canton System," the Opium Wars, and the Unequal Treaty (545) — Treaty port life (546) — Heavenly Kingdom of the Great Peace (547) — The "Ever-Victorious Army" (548) — "Self-strengthening" (549) — The Jiangnan arsenal (550) — Rong Hong's educational missions (551) — The Dowager Empress (551) — War with Japan (551) — The "Scramble for Concessions" (552) — Kang Youwei and the 100 Days of Reform (552) — "Righteous, Harmonious Fists" (553) — Sun Yatsen and "Double Ten" (553) — May 4, 1919, and the New Culture Movement (554) — Chinese Communist Party formation, Shanghai (555) — SECTION E: FROM THE NORTHERN EXPEDITION TO THE PRESENT (556) — Chiang Kai-shek, the early years (556) — The Northern Expedition (557) — The Nationalist decade, 1928–1937 (558) — Mao Zedong, the early years (559) — Mao's "peasant Marxism" and the Jiangxi Soviet (560) — Encirclement (561) — The Long March (562) — The Xian Incident (563) — World War II: Chiang's conventional war (563) — World War II: Mao's guerrilla war (564) — *Wei Qi, Xiang Qi,* and end game (564) — Governance: "expert" vs. "red" (565) — The "Great Leap Forward" and the "Great Proletarian Cultural Revolution" (566) — *The Last Emperor* and the Tiananmen Square Massacre (567) — The 2008 Olympics and the foreseeable future (568) — Endnotes (569)

CHAPTER 14 "The Era of Patriotism Has Come": The Kyoto-to-Tokyo Corridor of East Asia . . . 571

The heart of the matter (571) — Introduction to the Japanese language (572) — Some common Japanese place names (573) — The four main islands and the Inland Sea (574) — *Tokaido* and *Nakasendo* (574) — Topography and texture of the corridor (575) — Samples of folklore and legend from our corridor (576) — Archaeology and prehistory (577) — Shinto and the Ise Shrines (578) — Borrowing from China (579) — The imperial Age of Heian (580) — *Tales of the Heike* (581) — The Kamakura Shogunate (581) — Japanese feudalism compared with European feudalism (582) — *Zen in the Art of Archery* (584) —

"Divine Winds" (585) — The feudal wars of the late 1500s (585) — Statler's *Japanese Inn* (586) — Tokugawa Ieyasu (587) — The Battle of Sekigahara (588) — Will Adams (588) — "Alternate Residence" and the formalizing of the Tokaido (588) — Engelbert Kaempfer's 1691 trip on the Tokaido (589) — The affair of the 47 Ronin (590) — Basho (590) — Chikamatsu (591) — Hiroshige's "53 Stages of the Tokaido" (591) — Roots of modern cultural nationalism (592) — Commodore Perry and the Unequal Treaty (592) — Meiji Restoration (594) — Westernization, Japanese style (595) — Sino-Japanese War and the Heian Jingu Shrine (597) — Russo-Japanese War (597) — The "21 Demands" and the Kwantung Army (598) — *Nashonarizumu*: State Shinto and rising militarism (599) — Prince Saionji and Japanese Liberalism (600) — World War II (600) — Damage on our corridor (601) — The legacy of imperialism (602) — *The Chrysanthemum and the Sword* (602) — General Douglas MacArthur, S.C.A.P. (603) — "Japan, Inc." (604) — The 1964 "coming out" party: the Olympics and the *Shinkansen* (604) — Yukio Mishima (605) — "Prudent nationalism?" (605) — Endnotes (606)

Foreword

For every history book that really is "innovative," "trend-setting," "unprecedented," "one-of-a-kind," "a must read," "explores new terrain," there are dozens that make such claims falsely. Jim Brown's modern world history is all it claims to be and more. In order to fulfill promises made in the claims, writers have to cross both national and disciplinary boundaries. They cannot rest secure in the neat categories of social, political, military, economic, cultural, or religious history that have long prevailed nor even reside intellectually on one continent. They must find common ground, intersections containing "aha" moments where the familiar makes sense in an entirely different way because the angle of approach is so new and different.

This is precisely what Jim Brown has done in *Fairy Tales, Patriotism, and the Nation-State*. In order to pull this off, he has mastered history, folk ways, and geography, using the most modern technical assets. This book is Google-come-to-the-Grimms-brothers. Although the book may seem like the gestation of many specialists who must have lived several lifetimes struggling with sources and technology, it is more accurately the product of a superb teacher (one of the best I have ever known) whose half century university teaching career at a fine liberal arts university required him to teach nearly every course in the history curriculum and also gave him license to teach in interdisciplinary honors classes, teachers' institutes, special January term courses in the Amazon basin, Bhutan, China, Britain, and elsewhere. There was no time for narrow specialization or tedious monographs that were remaindered almost on the day of publication. Having been unofficially proclaimed by students during the past half century as the most challenging and intellectually stimulating professor they ever had is something few of us obtain and even fewer deserve. But having read his work and directed graduate programs at another university attended by many of his undergraduate students, I can affirm what they told me both about his range of thought and the quality of his teaching.

Most importantly, this mastery (from the rise of national states with a fascinating pattern of replication, to the determinant role of geography with its trails, paths, valleys, mountain chains, and trade routes) does not so much refute or even challenge traditional understanding of historical patterns as simply move underneath and beyond them. This book will challenge even the best informed historians, geographers, and folklorists by its connections, and it will intrigue casual readers by its breath. This is simply a treasure for students, faculty, and informed citizens worldwide, quite literally a new kind of history.

Dr. Wayne Flynt

Distinguished University Professor Emeritus, Auburn University,
former head of the History Department and past President, Southern Historical Association

Introduction

This book is written particularly for American college students, though I hope it will find a wider audience in the reading American public as well. It assumes the sort of general familiarity with U.S. history that most Americans get in elementary and secondary school and just by growing up here. It assumes at least a smattering of English history from the Norman Conquest to Winston Churchill and the latest doings of the royal family. It assumes a reader has heard of Socrates, Alexander the Great, Julius Caesar, and Pilate. And it assumes the sort of geographic knowledge of the world that's based on international conflicts involving the U.S. over the last century or so—the Western Front of WW I, the Normandy landings of WW II, North vs. South Korea, Vietnam, Afghanistan, Iraq. As the wicked one-liner goes, "War is God's way of teaching Americans geography."

It seems to me that the big story of world history in the last 500 years is this: (a) with unprecedented new power, Europe (and later Europeanized countries, including the U.S.) explored and then conquered most of the rest of the world; and (b) then the rest of the world fought back to win its independence, though in part by borrowing some of those new sources of European strength and becoming somewhat Europeanized in the process. So that's the way the book is structured, a first half on the rise of European power and a second half on the response of the rest of the world.

For the first half, the European advantage in technology may be the first thing to come to mind, and in fact it is the main subject of the first chapter. It is relatively easy to see and measure: telescopes and good clocks ("chronometers") making precise calculations of longitude possible; numbers of steam engines generating so many horsepower in a given year of the industrial revolution; the accurate range of the single-shot, bolt-action, brass-cartridge, smokeless powder Martini-Henry rifle . . . .

But I will argue (and every history book is to some extent a personal argument, whether it admits it or not) that the most powerful of the new European strengths, though harder to see and measure, came from the world of ideas. Political nationalism, cultural nationalism, and socialism in particular—these are weightless, intangible, ephemeral ideas, and yet they mobilized the energy of Europeans sufficiently to make this smallish continent the dominant continent of the modern world, at least until quite recently. And so the second chapter deals with the Enlightenment and the Revolution in France, to get at this new political nationalism. The third chapter focuses on the Germanies from the Brothers Grimm to Hitler for an understanding of this new cultural nationalism, an even stronger force. The fourth chapter tackles socialism by focusing on the intersection of Russian history and Marxism up to the dissolution of the Soviet Union in 1991. These three chapters (2, 3, and 4) together are also designed to give a fairly good summary of European history from the 1700s to 1991, a backdrop against which much of modern world history plays out. Three shorter European chapters follow, dealing with smaller European groups—the Irish, the Finns, and the Czechs—as they were transformed by these ideologies of political and cultural nationalism and socialism, against the backdrop of major power politics.

The second half of the book, also of seven chapters but considerably longer (because in general we Americans know less about the non-European world) tries to show the response of the rest of the world to this new European power, and among other things how "exportable" those new ideologies of political and cultural nationalism and socialism turned out to be. For each of six world regions, a key transportation corridor (two for East Asia) will be explored as a sort of "history in microcosm." The aim is to get at important regional developments while still keeping history at a personal level, so that it's still about interesting individual human stories.

○ For Latin America it will be the Veracruz-to-Mexico City corridor;

○ for Africa it will be the Durban-to-Johannesburg and Pretoria corridor;

- ○ for the Mideast it will be the network of roads from Damascus south to water (Gulf of Aqaba; Nile Delta);
- ○ for South Asia it will be the Grand Trunk Road from Kolkata (Calcutta) to Lahore and on to the Khyber Pass;
- ○ for Southeast Asia it will be Java's network of roads from Jakarta to Surabaya;
- ○ and for East Asia it will be China's transportation corridor on and along the Yangtze River (Chang Jiang);
- ○ and then Japan's Tokaido and Nakasendo ("East Sea Road" and "Central Mountain Road") corridor from Tokyo to Kyoto.

A brief introduction to important local language(s) will begin each chapter, and a longer introduction to the topography and texture of the country or corridor will follow that. Hopefully this will serve as a visual stage set on which the history of that corridor of the last 500 years can be played out.

Someone once said that the best way to educate yourself in the Humanities and the Arts, in cultural history broadly speaking, is to "read, travel, read, travel, and repeat." It's not the only way; Thoreau once wrote that he had "traveled widely in Concord." But in general there's a lot of truth in that "read, travel, and repeat" formula. If you read about a place before you go, you will "see" things while there that you otherwise would not; and once having been to a place you're usually much more interested in what has been written about it, and prepared to understand a higher level of writing about it. As a European historian by specialist training, I have spent a good bit of time in the European countries under discussion. Over the course of my teaching career, however, as I gradually became more of a generalist in world history, I made it a point to "work" almost all of these seven "corridors" of the non-European world with camera, GPS unit, and interpreters. Most of these seven non-European "corridor" chapters also explore one interesting artistic aspect of the culture, used to illustrate its history: for example, South Asia's imperial Mughal architecture, in which the ruling philosophy of the seven key Mughal Emperors can be seen to a nicety; China's six famous traditional novels that quickly get you beyond the conventional Confucian face of society; Japan's landscape art in woodblock prints, especially of the Tokaido just before it was transformed by western intrusion; Java's ancient shadow puppet plays so loved by Sukarno.

The GIS Angle of the Textbook

Finally, my history classes have been visually transformed in the past fifteen years by the new computerized mapping programs ("Geographic Information Systems," or GIS) that make possible a kind of virtual travel—for me and my students. Based on that, I've prepared parallel GIS "chapters" for each of the fourteen chapters of the book in one of these systems, still a free download as of this writing: Google Earth. These Google Earth folders (or .kmz files) are freely distributed separate from this text, in keeping with the spirit of Google Earth. You can find them posted on the Google Earth Community site, chapter by chapter:

- ○ On the web, go to "Google Earth Community—Google Groups"
- ○ Then choose "Education"
- ○ Then choose "Educators"
- ○ Then scroll down to "Fairy Tales, Patriotism, and the Nation-State"

Download the folder for the chapter that you need (they'll be out of numerical order, because each time one is edited it has to be removed from the list, and when added back it appears at the end).

I hope the textbook can be read and understood on its own, but if you will take a few minutes to learn how to use these Google Earth folders, it will go a long way towards fulfilling the "travel" part of that "read, travel, etc." advice. Google Earth offers a new visuality to the setting of historical events, available to anyone with a computer and a fairly good Internet hookup. It offers hundreds of thousands of embedded photographs (Panoramio icons for simple photographs, 360 Cities icons into which you can "fly" and look all around) at historical sites all over the world. And my better students have quickly gotten into a self-education cycle of going from Google Earth to a web search for information, whether it be a quick search of Wikipedia or a more detailed one in the Encyclopedia Britannica or scholarly journals, and back again—that is, they will see something while exploring the Google Earth (virtual) surface and go to the web to find out what it is, or they will read about some place or building and then go hunt it up on the Google Earth surface, building up a pattern of where things happened geographically and a fund of visual images of buildings, monuments, landscapes, and such.

Google Earth Terminology and History

In general GIS uses a layering technique, the way one might stack transparencies atop one another, each with its own data set. There are many different such systems, from very expensive and difficult to master but very accurate ones, down to ones that are less accurate but free and much easier to use. In the United States, for example, the governments of most cities and towns of any size use the California-based E.S.R.I. ArcWorld or ArcMap suite of software for city planning and data management. You could imagine there is one basic layer for the electrical grid, one for property boundaries, one for political boundaries, and so on. Many businesses are beginning to use it too, as a help in planning distribution of products, or where to put a new store. But ArcWorld is very expensive, and takes months if not years of training to master, and E.S.R.I.'s freeware has little of its capability. Google Earth is on the other end of the spectrum—not as precise, but much, much easier to use even in its basic free version. The terrain can be viewed in 3-D almost effortlessly, and a combination of the mosaic of aerial photos and the more intimate Panoramio and 360 Cities images gives it a visuality none of the other GIS programs can match, at least as of this writing.

Google Earth uses .kml and .kmz files, and a nutshell history of Google Earth can help explain what those are. A firm called Keyhole, Inc., was formed in 2001 ("keyhole" apparently in reference to some earlier military "spy in the sky" satellites), with a project of "draping" aerial photos over an underlying digital 3-D structure representing terrain. Its use in television news coverage of the 2003 Gulf War popularized it, and Google bought it the next year. It was first called "Keyhole Earth Viewer," and a .kml file just stood for "keyhole markup language," and a .kmz file for "keyhole markup zip," a way of sending a compressed version of the file. By 2005 the whole was renamed simply Google Earth (though the basic files are still named .kml and .kmz).

How to Get Google Earth on Your Computer

In going through installation and tips on use given below, remember that Google Earth takes a live Internet hookup to work—and the faster your computer and Internet hookup, the better. At least as of this writing, it doesn't really work on a tablet or a smartphone.

The basic version of Google Earth is a free download. Go to earth.google.com and begin the process by clicking on "Download Google Earth." It works equally well with either PC or Mac, and the download program will know which one you have. Uncheck Google Chrome if you do not want that automatically installed as your web browser, then "Agree and Download." "Run" the file (if you are on a Mac, drag Google Earth to the Applications folder on your hard drive to install). On either PC or Mac you should now have an icon that looks like a blue marble with three white, wavy stripes. Click on it to open the program.

Basic Screen Layout

When Google Earth opens, most of the screen will be taken up with a map in which the whole globe appears, with North America front and center. But also take notice of the Legend, or Table of Contents, down the left-hand side of the screen. At top left is a Search box, at middle left is a Places box (which should be mostly empty at this point), and at bottom left is a Layers box. This Layers box has all the basic, automatically available layers that Google Earth provides (as opposed to ones you may create yourself later and store in the Places box). To begin with, just check one of these basic layers—"Borders and Labels," at the top of the list. This "Borders and Labels" layer gives you national borders and names in yellow, state borders and names in white, and county borders and labels in green. It also gives city and town names, smaller ones appearing as you zoom in towards the earth's surface.

Navigating in the Map Part of Google Earth

First, here is how to navigate the slow, mouseless way. At the top right of the map screen you will see the outline of a set of navigational tools. Moving the computer cursor over any of them causes them to light up. Experiment with them from bottom to top:

❍ The slide bar at bottom is the zoom tool; you can either click and drag on the oval at the bar's midpoint, or click on the plus or minus sign at either end. Try clicking on the oval at midpoint and moving it upwards to zoom in—you should zoom right on down to somewhere in Lawrence, Kansas, right? Then zoom back out until you can see Kansas and all the states around it, including Missouri. While you do this, notice the "Eye Altitude" number in the bottom right-hand corner of the map screen; it reads your apparent altitude in miles down to about ten miles from the surface, and then changes to feet.

❍ The middle tool, a white disc with a hand in the middle and four outward pointing arrows, takes you North, East, South, West (NESW) or any point of the compass between two of them. Place cursor somewhere on that circle and click and hold on it, and your view will shift in that direction. The farther towards the circumference of the disc you click, the faster the view will change, and conversely the closer to the center (the hand) you click, the slower it will move. With Kansas and neighboring states showing, center Missouri's dark green Ozark Mountains in your screen with that middle North-East-South-West tool (you can also use the four directional arrows on your keyboard to do this NESW movement). Then use the bottom tool again to zoom right down into those green hills—zoom in until the "Eye altitude" number in bottom right corner of map screen reads 5,000 ft, more or less.

❍ The top symbol is really two tools in one. The outer ring with the N on it is for spinning the view—just click and drag the ring around. Then simply tapping once on the N itself restores the view to the conventional "north up" map view.

❍ Then experiment with the white disc inside the ring, the disc with the stylized eye at center and four outward pointing arrows. This is a tilt-and-spin tool. First click and hold near the top of the disc, and the earth's surface will tilt away from you. Click the bottom edge of the disc to restore a view looking straight down. With view tilted as much as you want, say approximately 45 degrees, click either side of disc to spin the view, keeping that same angle of view from the vertical. This really lets you appreciate how the aerial photographs are "draped" over an underlying 3-D structure that represents the terrain.

But with a mouse you can navigate in Google Earth about five times as fast! Here's how to do almost all the navigation shown above:

❍ Zoom in and out using the roller button on the mouse.

❍ For NESW navigation, left-click some point on the screen where your cursor is, hold it down and drag the screen over; release and repeat.

❍ To tilt the view, depress the roller button on mouse, and while keeping it depressed pull the whole mouse towards you. The view will tilt towards horizontal. Pushing the mouse away from you with roller button depressed gradually restores the view to vertical. Moving the mouse from side to side or circling it, still with roller button depressed, spins the view, and in fact with some practice you can turn it into a real joystick.

The only thing you can't do with a mouse that the "hard, mouseless" way does is to automatically restore North up. So if you're working on a mouseless computer, and plan on doing much with the Google Earth layers in this book, go buy yourself a mouse and save yourself a lot of tedious maneuvering with those upper-right-corner navigation icons!

Finally, as you are navigating around in the map screen, there is some important information available to you, in white print, along the very bottom. You have already used the "Eye altitude" information at bottom right. Just left of that is the elevation of the land immediately under your cursor. Just left of that is the latitude (degrees north or south of the equator) and longitude (degrees east or west of the Prime Meridian through Greenwich, England). Run your cursor around the screen a bit and watch these numbers change. And last, just left of that, is the date the aerial photo for that part of the earth's surface was taken; it can be from very recent to several years in the past. This might be a good time to say that these aerial photos come in two different resolutions—a coarse, fuzzy resolution with pixels perhaps twenty yards square that show fields but not small buildings, and a crisper, finer resolution with pixels perhaps two feet square, that show automobiles but not persons. More and more of the earth's surface is under the finer resolution these past few years, and presumably it all will be.

Now you have all the Google Earth operating skills you need to explore the textbook proper. When you begin a new chapter, just open the matching Google Earth folder (.kmz file). Footnotes in the text will each have their matching number as a Google Earth layer—so when you get to a footnote in the book (or e-book), glance at it and then go to that matching layer in Google Earth. Typically you will work from left to right within a given layer:

1.   Check square box at left (left-click inside it) to turn it on;
2.   Double-click (two fast left-clicks) on layer icon to "fly" to framed or pre-set view;
3.   Click (left-click) on any title that is blue to open up what is embedded there.

Sometimes further instructions will appear in those layers, often advice to click on a certain Panoramio or 360 Cities icon in the view so you can explore a real photograph of a site, not just a virtual reconstruction. If you have the time, doing some exploring of the Google Earth surface near sites marked in this way can often be very interesting, and you will be beginning that "read, travel, read, travel," educational cycle spoken of earlier.

At times the Panoramio or 360 Cities icon may not immediately appear beneath a Placemark pointer, because of different computer settings or screen resolution. In that case zooming in or out a bit will often cause it to appear. But occasionally a photograph will have been withdrawn by its poster, and just won't be there. In that case, sometimes you can explore nearby icons and find a similar view, but otherwise you'll just have to do without that particular visual.

With every new piece of computer hardware or software, of course, there comes a learning curve, some more aggravating than others. If you're like me, sometimes you feel that life's just too short for all this. But I think you'll find using Google Earth to explore history and historical sites well worth the trouble. I will try to be especially clear about using the Google Earth folder (.kmz file) and its sub-layers early in the upcoming Chapter 1, so that even if you've never used Google Earth before, you can quickly catch on to it. By Chapter 2 you should be an old hand! Various other bells and whistles of the Google Earth software will be introduced and explained at times in the text itself.

Finally, Debts of Gratitude

This modern world history textbook evolved over four decades and more of teaching, and I owe debts of gratitude to more people than I can name here. But here's a good start:

Thanks to Jeff Northrup, departmental colleague for twenty-seven years and fellow traveler to East Asia, for a preliminary editing of the manuscript, including every one of the thousands of Google Earth layers.

Most recently history professors Tennant McWilliams (former Dean of A&S at the University of Alabama in Birmingham) and Carolyn Johnston (Professor of American Studies, Eckerd College) took a keen interest in it and gave me the renewed courage to finish it. History Professor Bob England (and Program Director, Outdoor Leadership at Northwest-Shoals Community College) encouraged me over the years with stories of his teaching success with "the J. Brown model of nationalism."

Thanks to Bob Taylor for his support of the History Department through the years, and most recently for his donation to the department designated "for the finishing of J. Brown's book."

My appreciation to professors in the World Languages department here at Samford—to Heather West, Millicent Bolden, and others, and to linguistically talented colleagues such as David Johnson and old friends such as Najwa Bateh, for help with languages I either didn't know, or didn't know as well as I thought I did.

From 2001 to 2005 I was the only historian in a grant-writing "gang of five," otherwise of scientists—my Geography colleagues Max Baber and Eric Fournier, and my Biology colleagues Bob Stiles and Paul Blanchard—that won a $200,000 NSF grant (AEGIS) to integrate GIS into the general education curriculum here at Samford University.

Most of the GIS-based teaching techniques in this book grew out of discussions with them and in the practice of the grant-writing and grant-carrying-out.

Two former students and now good friends, who have both gone far beyond me in scholarship and achievement—Douglass Sullivan-González (History professor and currently Dean of the Sally McDonnell Barksdale Honors College at Ole Miss) and Michael Johnson (international lawyer, and currently Honorary Consul of Germany for the State of Alabama and lead instrumentalist/vocalist in the best Cajan band outside Louisiana)—served as interpreters and guides for me on the Veracruz-to-Mexico City and the Durban-to-Pretoria corridors.

In and around 1989–90, at a time when I was head of our university's Honors program, the Samford University administration took advantage of a new opportunity to turn the regular regional accreditation process into a rethinking of general education as a whole. Small teams of professors and top students got travel money to explore exceptional university curricula nationwide. The result was the Cornerstone curriculum, my corner of which was an integrated sequence of history, literature, philosophy, art, and music, called Cultural Legacies. The vision was truly world class. The first year was Western Civ in two halves, from the Greeks to Shakespeare, and from Shakespeare to the present. The second year began with a semester on Africa/Mideast and ended with one on Monsoon Asia. The third year began with a semester on Latin America and ended with one on the history of the United States. Each week featured a Monday lecture, Wednesday reading quiz and discussions, and some Friday hands-on activity (trying to make a simple Japanese-style woodblock print; learning the rules to Chinese "courtier chess" and "encirclement chess" and wondering how they related to Chinese history from Sunzi to Chiang Kai-shek). It was an Honors program in all but name, attracting about 10 percent of entering freshmen; and it only lasted seven years—the university would have had to change the way it recruited faculty, among other things, to have sustained it. But it was the most exciting, rewarding, and educational curriculum I've ever been associated with, and I owe a debt to those students (especially those in its chaotic first year!) who participated, and especially to those full- or part-time faculty who ran the show or worked closely with me—to Professor Myralyn Allgood, chair of World Languages, and her trusty and unflappable administrative assistant Martha Thompson, to Janet Keyes, Jeff Northrup, Lowell Vann, Mark Baggett, Dean Rod Davis, and a dozen more.

Somewhere here I need to recognize a debt owed to all of the History Dept. chairs, Arts & Sciences deans, and VPAAs and provosts at Samford University over the years who recommended or approved me for five successive Sabbatical leaves to work on this textbook, even though no finished book-length publication immediately resulted from any of them.

A special word of thanks to Bob Stiles, Samford Biology professor emeritus and extraordinaire, with whom I traveled and taught "culture and environment" courses in the Peruvian Amazon, in Kenya, in the UK, in China, in Russia and Uzbekistan—and in various parts of the South. He won't have to read this book; I've hashed most of it out with him in our forty-year-long professional and personal time together.

And way back in the 1970s, when I was first discovering the link between folklore and political history worldwide, a remarkable pulse of undergraduate students—Mark Gooch, Cathy Hanby, Mary Thompson, and others—played a significant role in it all. In that time and context, fellow history professor Wayne Flynt, who was just getting his teeth into his life's work with poor whites in American history, helped me to a new understanding of folklore as we jointly led the creation of a minor field in it here at Samford. And more recently, of course, my appreciation to Wayne for the Preface to this book, which may praise it too highly.

I've appreciated family support for this whole project over the years—my children's bemused interest in a project that's gone on much of their lifetime, my parents' encouragement, and my sister's willingness to read sample text. I dedicate this book to my wife Linda Faye, center of my world for fifty years. She made it all possible, and remains my single best coach in understanding basic human nature, and in what's right and what's wrong in how we all treat each other.

J. Brown

Samford University
Spring 2014

Part One

THE RISE OF THE MODERN WEST

Chapter One

The Rise of European Technological Power

CONTENTS

Chapter outline and where it fits in the whole—PART ONE: EUROPEAN MARITIME TECHNOLOGY circa 1300–1500—The compass—Sails, hulls and armament—A way to determine latitude, but not longitude—Two kinds of maps—The Starfinder—The *Reconquista*—Portugal takes shape—Portuguese leadership in the explorations—Borrowed sails, borrowed hulls—Understanding Trade Winds, Westerlies, and the North Atlantic gyre—A new way of finding latitude; educated guessing about longitude—Bartolomeu Dias turns the Cape—Vasco da Gama and the first Portuguese trade with India—Albuquerque's "closing" of the Indian Ocean—The Italian Renaissance context of it all—The Renaissance quickly defined—Florence: eye of the storm—The link between war and art—PART TWO: SCIENTIFIC REVOLUTION circa 1500–1700—The Reformation and Counter-Reformation context of it all—Protestant university reform; Catholic response—The solution of the Problem of Motion—Copernicus—Brahe and Kepler in Prague—Galileo—Huygens, Gilbert, and Newton—Navigation transformed—Holland's Glorious Century—American footnote: the Dutch in New Amsterdam, the Pilgrims in Leiden—PART THREE: INDUSTRIAL REVOLUTION, IMPERIAL POWER circa 1700–1900—Why Britain?—Textiles—Steam—Metallurgy—The Crystal Palace—*Tools of Empire, Tentacles of Progress*—Gunboats—Rifles and machine guns—Imperial botany—"Industrial" quinine—Conclusion and advertisement

Chapter outline and where it fits in the whole

The basic story of the modern world as told in this book, as was explained in the Introduction, is of two main developments: first, the rise of European power that let Europeans explore and then dominate the rest of the world; and second, the reaction of the rest of the world to that domination, fighting back to regain their independence though in part by borrowing some of those new European power ideas.

In a rising Europe's relationship with the rest of the world, it is the growing scientific and technological advantage that shows up first. Besides, beginning with that subject in this very first chapter guarantees some general coverage of the European intrusion into the rest of the world.

So a sampling of European technological and scientific development it is, here in this first chapter, in three 200-year-long chunks of time.

○ Part One will discuss the development of maritime technology (traveling on the oceans, applying power at end of travels) from about 1300–1500. It will feature the Portuguese voyages of exploration, and their deeper emotional setting in the context of the Christian reconquest of Iberia and their deeper intellectual setting in the context of the Italian Renaissance.

○ Part Two will deal with the "Scientific Revolution" from about 1500–1700. It will focus on the solution of the age-old problem of motion, and show it in its deeper setting of the Protestant-Catholic religious struggle of the times. This includes the emergence of Protestant Holland that quickly seized world trade from Catholic Portugal.

○ Part Three will at least sketch in the main developments of the Industrial Revolution as it emerged in Britain from about 1700–1900, and talk particularly about its implications for military power.

Not to give the ending away, but while in 1300 Europeans were inferior in both destructive and productive technology to several other parts of the world, by 1900 their power peaked, relative to the rest of the world, so much so that the process called "neo-imperialism" (including such major happenings as the carving up of China and the partitioning of Africa) was done with relative ease.

The deeper emotional and intellectual setting of this new industrialism and imperial power, as the text slows down and deals in more detail with the last few centuries, will come in Chapters 2, 3, and 4; Chapter 2 on the political nationalism that emerged during the Enlightenment and French Revolution; Chapter 3 on the cultural nationalism that developed during the Romantic Era and later especially in the Germanies, and Chapter 4 on nationalism and its relationship to socialism, particularly Marxism, as it worked out in modern Russia and the Soviet Union. But first let's explore the rise of European technology.

PART ONE: EUROPEAN MARITIME TECHNOLOGY circa 1300–1500

One of the most remarkable developments in all of recorded history was the European seaborne exploration of these couple of centuries, with the power necessary to force their way into regional trading networks and even to conquer land bases worldwide. As of 1300, it would have seemed improbable, so limited was the scientific knowledge and technological know-how of this very small continent.[GE¹] Here's a quick list of what they had to work with.

The compass

Europeans had the compass by this time (the Crusaders learned about it from the Arabs, who had it from the Chinese, who invented it). It was primitive, a small magnetized needle balanced on the point of a sharpened nail driven into the center of a little block of wood with N-S-E-W written around the edges. The needle wibbled and wobbled, and from it you could tell magnetic north within 5° or so. But they had no idea that the magnetic north and south poles were hundreds of miles from the geometric poles (true center of axis of earth's spin),[GE²] or that iron-rich parts of the earth's crust could skew the compass reading by 20° or even 30°. It was a neat device, for sure, but as Europeans sailed out farther and farther from known waters it had the potential to mislead them as much as lead them.

---

1. Please open the Google Earth Folder (.kmz file) titled "Chpt 01 Technology." It should show up in your Places box at left center of screen. Open, the way you would any computer file, by clicking on the little box at left of layer title with the plus in it. The layers inside are numbered to match these footnotes in the text. Begin, then, by opening sub-folder A titled "Maritime Technology," and then open GE Layer 1 which matches this first footnote, titled "Europe in (half of) a wide world," by turning it on (clicking in box at left of layer title), and then "flying" to pre-set view (by double-clicking on the layer icon, in this case a pushpin Placemark icon). Notice how Europe is dwarfed by both Africa and the part of Asia you can see in the half of the globe shown, not to mention North and South America, not much of which show in this view. In your basic "Layers" box at bottom left of Google Earth screen, you only need two layers turned on at this point: the "Borders and Labels" one and the "Photos" one.

2. GE Layer 2 is a Folder titled "North Poles." Turn it on by left-clicking in the box at left of layer title, then double-click on Folder icon to both "fly" to pre-set view and open the Folder. Then turn on each of the three Placemarks, in turn—the first is Polar, or geometric, north; the other two are where the "geomagnetic" north poles were as of 2000 and 1900—they wander a bit. To measure the distance between them, select "measure" tool (ruler symbol in top drop-down menu); make sure the main tab is on Line instead of Path, and that you are measuring in miles. Then click once at Polar North, and again near the two magnetic north icons—over 700 miles apart, right? Close measure box to clear screen.

Sails, hulls and armament

On the well-known waters of the Mediterranean, naval warfare in these centuries was still done largely by galleys—giant rowboats often with more than one bank of oars, and not all that much changed from when the Greek navy led by Athens fought the Persian navy at Salamis back in 480 BC[GE[3]] But galleys wouldn't do outside the Mediterranean, in the great "ocean-sea." The true sea-going ships on the Atlantic coast of Europe as of 1300 or so had only two virtues—they were big, in terms of cargo space, and with their square-rigged sails could sail at various angles downwind fairly well. "Square-rigged" means generally hanging a rectangular sheet down from a horizontal boom, with each such boom fastened to a vertical mast. While this lets you put a lot of square-footage of sail in the air, square-rigged ships had trouble sailing across the wind, and could not tack up at an angle into it at all. No sailing ship can sail directly into the wind, but the longer and stiffer the leading edge of a sail, the closer you can come. Do you know the expression "by and large"? It's an old sailors' phrase that means how a sailing ship handles in general—both when the wind is "large," with the ship going any angle downwind, or when the ship is sailing "by" the wind, angling as close as it can to upwind. In this sense the ocean-going European ship of 1300 was a fair sailer going "large," but—especially with its rounded hull which drifted sideways easily (making considerable "leeway")—could hardly sail "by" the wind at all. If you tried to angle the vertical edges of those square-rigged sails into the wind, they just folded up and pushed you back downwind.

As for naval arms, in 1300 they were mostly bows, crossbows, and hand-held bladed weapons of various sorts. Firearms—invented in China and transmitted to the West by the Arabs, like the compass and so many other major inventions—didn't appear in Europe until around 1325. Before that, it was typical of two opposing ships to close and grapple (throw huge treble hooks on ropes to hook onto the other ship, and drag them together), and then fight a miniature land battle on the decks of the ships.

A way to determine latitude, but not longitude

In 1300 Europeans had one way to find latitude (distance north or south of the equator measured in 90° arcs—the equator being 0°, the North Pole being 90° N, the South Pole being 90° S): wait for a clear night, and measure the angle between the North Star and the horizon with a protractor or some segment of it such as a quadrant or sextant. That was all well and good until they sailed south across the Equator, at which point the North Star disappeared behind them beneath the waves and they were on their own in a very wide and directionless world.

As to longitude—how far around the earth east to west they were from some chosen north-south line (which would be 0° longitude), to 180° W and 180° E (both of which would be the same north-south line on the opposite side of the globe)—in 1300 Europeans out of sight of known shores could not even make an educated guess.

Two kinds of maps

In 1300 Europeans had two sorts of maps relevant to the problem of maritime exploration.

The first kind of map was called a *portolan*—a practical sailing chart made by sailors (particularly in Lisbon, Barcelona, and Naples) for other sailors to use. The word came into English from the Italian *portolano* (the *Oxford English Dictionary*, which specializes in word origins and evolution, says it originally had the sense of "port superintendent," a map approved by the port authority).[1] At any rate, these *portolani* dealt with relatively small pieces of the earth's surface, and were not to any regular mathematical projection (the solid geometry problem of how to represent part of a spherical surface on a flat piece of paper). These maps paid a

---

3. GE Layer 3 references a Photos icon in Barcelona's Maritime Museum, titled "Барселона. Морской музей, галера," a Russian photographer's picture of the stern of the flagship galley that fought at Lepanto in 1571. Click on it to open a good photo of a huge galley that fought in the Mediterranean Sea battle of Lepanto in 1571. Clicking on the nearby 360 Cities icon (red and brown square, or a sphere if close in) gives you an interactive 3-D view. Click "Exit Photo" to exit 360 Cities views.

lot of attention to shoreline features, usually indicated the prevailing winds, and often had lines radiating from several points to help a navigator lay out a rough course to a given place. In a word, they were locally useful, but didn't help you get anywhere new.

The second kind of map was Ptolemy's world map dating from the Roman Empire of about AD 150. Well, his actual map itself had not survived, but his description of how to make it had, in Greek, in the *Geographia*. By about 1400 this was translated into Latin by a Florentine scholar. Then, according to instructions in the text to show lines of latitude as concentric circles and longitude as radial lines, Ptolemy's locations numbered by latitude and longitude could be plotted in and thus the map reconstructed. Ptolemy's map only showed a fourth or so of the globe. It did a good job with the Mediterranean, a fair job with the Red Sea and Persian Gulf, a poor job with India, and had only the haziest of notions about East and Southeast Asia. It presented the Indian Ocean as landlocked, like the Mediterranean. It underestimated the size of the earth by a considerable fraction, and of course had no clue about the Americas, Australia, Antarctica, and such.

Compounding the limitations of each kind of map, generally speaking the sailors who knew about the portolani didn't know about Ptolemy's world map, and the scholars who knew about the world map didn't know about the portolani.

The Starfinder

A last piece of maritime technology that Europeans had in 1300, and by far the most interesting of all, was the *astrolabe*—literally "the starfinder." It was worked out by Hellenistic intellectuals in Egypt during the second century BC, when the library at the lighthouse at Alexandria had the greatest collection of books and scholars in the world. The astrolabe was a device of real genius, the laptop computer for everything navigational for about 2000 years. Time of day, day of the year, position of the sun or any bright star in the sky—if you knew any two, you could calculate the third, and you could do this for the past, present, or future. As a bonus, knowing the position of any single star (or the sun) automatically gave you the position of all the rest at that same instant, whether they were above or below your horizon!

In brief, what these late classical Greek scholars did was superimpose three different sets of data on a single globe (it helps to think of this globe as transparent, when trying to visualize it all):

○ The first set of data is simply the North Pole, the Equator, and the Tropics of Cancer and Capricorn (at about 23½° N. & S. of the Equator; tropic means a turning, as when the sun reaches its maximum latitude in respective summers and then turns back towards the Equator).

○ The second set of data—harder to envision—is a view of the sky from where you stand (or float!) somewhere in the northern hemisphere. Imagine a night sky, and draw a bright, imaginary line all around the horizon. Then raise your angle 10° and draw another circle around the sky there, then draw one at 20° and so on with smaller circles up to 80°, and finally, at the point straight over your head, put a dot for 90°. Now pull all of that down to your (transparent) globe, so that the 90° point straight overhead comes to earth where you are standing, and the big circle around the horizon comes to earth halfway around the world from you, with all the other circles fitting on the globe in-between—like a "cap" of circular lines that now covers exactly half the globe.

○ The third set of data is the star (and eventually sun) data. Every star, and every constellation, has its own unchanging latitude, a place on the earth's surface where it will pass directly overhead. Shrink them all down to the surface of the earth: the North Star will come to rest on the North Pole of your transparent globe; the Big Dipper will come down to between 50 to 70 North Latitude; Orion will straddle the Equator, etc. But this third layer of data, the star field, must be able to spin around once a day, pivoting on the North Pole.

Now all they needed was a way to put all this data on a flat surface (*planisphere*, another name for the astrolabe, just means "flattened sphere"). These Hellenistic Greek inventors of sophisticated solid geometry simply said, put your eye at the South Pole of your transparent globe, and look directly at the North Pole, and see how it all looks from there. They did it with mathematical projection (though taking a photograph with a fisheye lens at the South Pole of such a transparent model would yield a "plansiphere," except that the star field data set wouldn't be able to spin!). Once you have flattened out your three sets of data, you can insert a perfect circle into the star field to symbolize the yearly movement of the sun against the background of the fixed stars. The star field rotates clockwise once a day, and the sun position goes counter-clockwise around that perfect circle once a year. Finally, add a pointer pivoted on the center of the planisphere, at the North Pole/North Star. You can align it with any object represented in the sky (or below the horizon!) and read the sun time on the 24-hour sun dial on the outer edge.[GE⁴]

If you were indeed able to understand all that in your first reading of the two paragraphs above, drop out of whatever school or job you're in now and immediately apply to Harvard to teach solid geometry there. The main historical point to pursue here, I suppose, is that Europeans had lost the knowledge of the astrolabe with the decline and fall of Rome, and only rediscovered it from Arab scholars much later. Some proof of that is that we still call dozens of major stars by their Arabic names—for example, Rigel, from the Arabic word for "foot" (of the giant, Orion), *rijl*; Betelgeuse, from the Arabic for "shoulder of the giant," *bi't al-jauza*; Vega, from the Arabic for "stooping" or "diving" (eagle or vulture), *al Waqi;* and most any star name that begins with *al*, the Arabic article: Altair (*al-ta'ir*, "the flier"), Aldeboran (*al'dabaran*, "the follower"). These came into Latin (and later English) about the same time as knowledge of the astrolabe, and probably in association with it. Chaucer's *Treatise on the Astrolabe* of 1391 was the very first technical manual in English on any device or process; he was writing for a (presumably very bright) ten-year-old boy who hadn't been to his Latin "grammar" school yet. Chaucer's material came, one step removed, from an Arab source. The Arabs, in fact, seem to have geared the parts of the astrolabe together as early as AD 900, and powered the whole to create the first modern clocks. Very old European clocks, such as Prague's famous town hall one from 1410,[GE⁵] still look like (and are indeed) astrolabes. The familiar dial and hour hand of a traditional circular clock are just remnants of the geared and powered astrolabe, with a 12-hour dial instead of the original 24-hour one.

Genius navigational device that it was, however, the astrolabe didn't work south of the Equator, and European scholars of this 1300–1500 period had not quite the skill or understanding to make a matching astrolabe for the southern hemisphere.

---

4. GE Layer 4 is a Placemark referencing Alexandria, Egypt. Turn the layer on, and "fly" to the pre-set view by double-clicking on the layer's Pushpin icon. Click on the blue layer title to open it, and follow instructions that tell you to click on the Photos icon titled "Old Lighthouse of Alexandria " for a view of the (reconstructed) lighthouse at Alexandria's eastern harbor.

But the real reason for this footnote and Google Earth layer is to embed a website with a good photo of a working astrolabe:

http://www.puzzlering.net/astrolabe.html

The website is an advertisement—which I'm not pushing!—but the top left picture shows the parts of the astrolabe more clearly than any other image I can find on the web. The outer rim is both a 24-hour clock and a sun dial; the pointer pivots on the center (North Star/North Pole). The spidery looking silver structure is the third set of data talked about in the text above, the star field (the irregularly located little spikes represent bright stars, and the perfect circle embedded in it is the sun's yearly path through those stars). Underneath everything else is the Plate, on which are engraved the first two sets of data The whole Plate shows the first set of data—North Pole at center, then three circles representing Tropic of Cancer, Equator, and, almost to outer edge, Tropic of Capricorn. The dense network of lines in top half or so of Plate is the second set of data, the sky visible from where observer stands.

For a very visual working model, see the "electric astrolabe" website: http://www.astrolabes.org/pages/electric.htm

5. GE Layer 5 is a Placemark referencing a Panoramio icon from Old Town Prague with a picture of the old astrolabe/clock ("Prague astronomical clock").

The *Reconquista*

Much of the original European exploration of the globe was based in the Iberian peninsula, today's Spain and Portugal.[GE6] In many respects it was just a continuation of the Christian reconquest of Iberia that began in the 700s and went on for centuries. Here's some background.

One wing of the remarkable Muslim conquests in the century after Mohammand's death in AD 632 had swept westwards through Egypt, along the Mediterranean coast of North Africa, and crossed the Straits of Gibraltar[GE7] in 711. Gibraltar,[GE8] as in the rock of, was named for the leader of that crossing, Tarik (if you say "Jebel Tarik," meaning in Arabic "Tarik's Mountain," for a few centuries it comes out "Gibraltar"). The Muslim push north conquered almost all of Iberia in just twenty years, and the final thrust was only blunted by Charlemagne's grandfather in 732 at the Battle of Tours,[GE9] another 300 miles on up into what is today France. But along the Atlantic coast of northern Iberia, where the rugged Cantabrian Mountains front the Bay of Biscay,[GE10] some small Christian communities held out. When the Muslim advance had exhausted itself, the little Christian states began to expand south. Unlike the lightning Muslim advance north, this was a process that would take over 700 years. Granada, the last Muslim state in the extreme south of Iberia, only fell to a newly unified Spain in 1492, a date every American knows because it freed up some royal money to sponsor a visionary Italian's plans to sail west to Asia. The whole centuries-long process was called in mostly Christian Europe the *Reconquista*, the "re-conquest" of these lands by Christendom.

One site in particular in northeastern Iberia came to be associated with the whole movement. In 813, in response to a vision experienced by a local Christian, the remains of the apostle James (the James who was the son of Zebedee and brother of John) were claimed to be miraculously found at the place called ever since Santiago de Compostela—St. James of the Field of Stars.[GE11] It became a spiritual rallying point for Christians throughout the Reconquista. During the Middle Ages it was the third most popular site of Christian pilgrimage in the world, after Jerusalem and Rome (and is still important today in that regard). As you'll see in a later chapter, Cortés and his Spanish armies fought the Aztecs in 1520 with the traditional cry of "St. James and at them!" and *Matamoros* ("Death to Moors") would be easily replaced with *Mataindios* in the New World. But it would be Portugal more than Spain that led in the greatest of the explorations, including the development of the scientific and technological breakthroughs it took to make them.

Portugal takes shape

As the little Christian states of the Reconquista gradually lengthened southwards, some combined and some new ones were born. Portugal as an independent state only took shape in the 1100s, when a local ruler—after a smashing victory over the Moors—claimed to be an independent king and was so recognized by the ruler of the larger Iberian state of Castile and, more importantly, by the Pope. This was the great century of the Western European crusades aimed at recovering Jerusalem for Christendom (First Crusade 1096–99; Second Crusade 1144–55; Third Crusade 1187–92). Crusading monastic orders of fighting men were common, and such orders

---

6. GE Layer 6 is a Placemark framing an overview of the Iberian peninsula. Double-click on the Placemark icon at left of layer title to "fly" to pre-set view.

7. GE Layer 7 is a Placemark framing a view of the Strait, about nine miles across.

8. GE Layer 8 is a Placemark framing a view of Gibraltar itself. Notice that the layer title is blue, meaning something is embedded in it. Click once on that blue layer title to open text; it tells you to click on Panoramio icon underneath Pushpin symbol, titled "Gibraltar–Panorama," for view of this impressive natural fortress. To close picture, click anywhere on map screen off picture itself.

9. GE Layer 9 shows approximate battle site of Tours (sometimes also called the battle of Poitiers) with red Pushpin symbol and layer title near top of framed view.

10. GE Layer 10 is a Placemark framing a view of the Cantabrian Mountains; the province of Asturias was at the heart of the original whole resistance.

11. GE Layer 11 is a Placemark referencing the Cathedral of Santiago de Compostela, with dozens of Photos icons to explore. Pilgrims walking the paths to it can still often be identified by their walking sticks hung with scallop shells.

also fought in the Portuguese expansion. In a little over a century the new Portuguese state, expanding southwards along the Atlantic coast in a band averaging a hundred miles wide,[GE12] simply ran out of land to conquer when the Atlantic coast turned eastwards at a sharp angle—essentially completing Portugal's borders. The last Moorish stronghold in the territory of present-day Portugal, Silves,[GE13] was captured in 1249, almost two and a half centuries before Spain (Castile plus Aragon) captured its last Moorish stronghold, Granada, in that most famous 1492. By some standards Portugal was the first modern European state to take shape.

Portuguese leadership in the explorations

Portuguese naval exploration was at first mainly a continuation of the Reconquista by water. A vigorous new dynasty, the Aviz, came to the throne in 1383 in the person of King John I (João I). In 1415 the Portuguese took their first step into Africa by capturing Ceuta[GE14], a fortified peninsula just across the Straits of Gibraltar. John then gave the place to be administered by his third son, Prince Henry the Navigator (1394–1460), then only 21 years old. Prince Henry would spend most of his life in the fortified seaside city of Sagres[GE15] on the extreme southwest point of Portugal, directing the Portuguese explorations from that base. Five years later that same prince was named head of the Order of Christ, a very wealthy crusading order based in Tomar,[GE16] that was a successor to the Knights Templar who had guarded Jerusalem. This gave him substantial financial resources to use to sponsor explorations down the African coast in the remaining 40 years of his life. At this point economic motives for the explorations began to be as important as Christian crusading—the search for the source of West African gold, and for slaves as well. Ceuta as a port was an important northern terminus of the overland gold route that came up through the Sahara desert, and Prince Henry reasoned, and correctly, that by circling around West Africa by sea the Portuguese could tap the flow of gold nearer to its source. So he began to send out small exploring fleets of a few ships each, down the southwest-trending Atlantic coast of today's Morocco.[GE17] The first fruits of that were the discovery and claiming of the Canaries, Madeira, and the Azores (though the Canaries were inhabited, and the inhabitants fought back fiercely enough to delay Portuguese conquest and let the Spanish edge in).[GE18]

The move southwest, however, was held up by Cape Bojador,[GE19] literally "the Bulging Cape." Almost 900 miles from the Straits of Gibraltar, it was the first and perhaps greatest obstacle in the whole Portuguese expansion. Viewed in Google Earth in the context of the entire coastline of what is today Morocco and Western Sahara, it seems harmless and nondescript enough, just one little cape of many along the coast. The problem was that with existing sail and hull design, and with the prevailing currents and winds that from here on southwest down the coast run strongly towards the southwest (more in a minute), it was virtually impossible for ships to return along the same coast. So for a time Cape Bojador acquired a fearsome reputation with Portuguese sailors as a place from beyond which no ship ever returned.

---

12. GE Layer 12 is a Placemark framing a view of Portugal, geographically complete in its modern form by 1259.

13. GE Layer 13 is a Placemark referencing Silves, the last Muslim stronghold. Click on Panoramio icon under pointer, titled "Silves—A Xelb muçulmana vista de norte," for nice view of hilltop fort.

14. GE Layer 14 is a Placemark referencing Ceuta, about 15 miles south of Gibraltar. Click on Panoramio icon under pointer, titled "Camino alrededor de la Fortaleza Hacho," for view of old fortress wall.

15. GE Layer 15 is a Placemark framing Sagres in relationship to south Portugal.

16. GE Layer 16 is a Placemark referencing the Convento de Cristo (Monastery of Christ) in Tomar.

17. GE Layer 17 is a Placemark framing a view of today's Atlantic coast of Morocco. It is 1200 miles of southwest-trending coast, more and more desolate towards the southwest.

18. GE Layer 18 is a Folder titled "Island Groups," that contains three Polygons—one each circling the Madeiras (in red), the Canaries (in orange), and the Azores (in yellow). Zoom out to see general relationships to Europe, Africa; zoom in to explore each. Frame and then tilt the view for Madeira, then Tenerife, then Gran Canaria to see impressive relief. Highest point of Tenerife more than 12,000' elevation, key to combing moisture out of Trade Winds.

19. GE Layer 19 is a Placemark referencing Cape Bojador. Put your mouse cursor on it and notice that it's about 26° N. Latitude, the importance of which will appear soon in the text.

Borrowed sails, borrowed hulls

You'll remember that the European ocean-going ships, mainly because of their square-rigged sails, found it difficult to sail at any angle upwind. But there were ships as near as the eastern Mediterranean and above all in the Arabian Sea and Indian Ocean that could do it well, using a completely different type of sail. Feluccas on the Nile River and dhows on the Indian Ocean used a lateen rig[GE20]—a short, stumpy vertical mast that held up a long, angled boom which supported a triangular sail (point of the triangle forward, as in today's sailboard or little Sunfish sailboat). The stiffer the leading edge of a sail, the better angle upwind you can achieve, right? It's hard to get much stiffer than a long boom of teakwood.

In the course of the 1400s, Europeans led by the Portuguese "married" the technology of the dhow to that of their own, larger square-rigged ships. Such a hybrid ship might have a mast amidships that was still square-rigged for driving power when sailing large, but fore and aft of that would be lateen-rigged masts for sailing by the wind. The hulls, again borrowing from the dhow, got a little more pronounced "V" to keep leeway (slipping downwind) to a minimum. Before the end of the century, then, this fully decked "lateen caravel" had become the most sea-worthy, maneuverable ship in the world. Backed by less maneuverable but enormous floating fortresses and storehouses called carracks, they would take the Portuguese literally to the ends of the (watery) earth.[2]

This technology was sufficiently incorporated by the Portuguese by 1434 as to enable them to successfully turn (and return by!) Cape Bojador. It paid off in just a few years. In 1441 the first gold and slaves came back from further down the West African coast, and in 1445 and 1446 they reached the mouths of the Senegal[GE21] and Gambia Rivers[GE22]. By the end of Prince Henry's life in 1460, his captains had discovered the Cape Verde Islands[GE23], to add to Portuguese holdings in the Madeira and the Azores islands groups further north.

By this time the first modern world maps had begun to appear, fitting discoveries as described on new portolani into position on truly global maps. By this time, too, the compass had been made larger, with a compass card that could show directions such as SSW and even one degree of a 360° circle. Its magnetized needle had been damped down in a glass container of some light liquid, such as alcohol, that steadied its movement. The whole thing was mounted on gimbals, weighted U-shaped brackets that kept it level whether the ship was rolling side to side or pitching fore and aft. It wasn't exactly rocket science, just tinkering with a major invention made elsewhere, but it made of the compass a much more valuable tool.

The reign of King John II (1481–1495) was even more impressive in terms of maritime expansion. Before his accession to the throne the Portuguese had made it around the western bulge of Africa. In the first full year of his reign John II had built (on today's Ghana coast) the fortress called São Jorge da Mina—St. George of the Mine, meaning the source of gold. [GE24] Portuguese ships returning from there figured out a much better way to get back home than beating up the coast in the teeth of the prevailing winds and current. In the process they had to learn about the basic winds and currents of the North Atlantic, which would probably be good for us to do too, at this point.

Understanding Trade Winds, Westerlies, and the North Atlantic gyre

The Portuguese understood from early on, while challenging Cape Bojador, that the prevailing winds there blew towards the southwest. They found those same winds lasting down to about 5° North Latitude. They knew from back home (the Portuguese coast is from 37° to 41° North Latitude) that the prevailing winds there came

---

20. GE Layer 20 is a Folder with seven Placemarks referencing Panoramio icons of lateen-rigged sailing boats and ships, including Nile feluccas and East African coastal dhows.

21. GE Layer 21 is a Path symbolizing the Senegal River as an aqua line.

22. GE Layer 22 is a Path symbolizing the Gambia River in aqua.

23. GE Layer 23 is a Polygon symbolized as a green line circling the Cape Verdes. By this time the Spanish had edged in and gotten the Canaries.

24. GE Layer 24 is a Placemark referencing the old Portuguese fort, São Jorge da Mina, at today's Elmina, Ghana.

from the west or southwest, the opposite direction. What they had found were the Trade Winds of the low latitudes, blowing towards the southwest, and the Westerlies further north, blowing northeast.

The physical reason for theses prevailing winds probably deserves just a word of explanation. Because of the power of the sun at the equator, hot air rises there, and in the northern hemisphere a bit cooler air is sucked generally southwards along the surface to replace it. The hot air circles north, at altitude, and somewhere short of about 30° North Latitude it comes back down to the surface and heads south to complete the convection cycle. But the moving air along the surface doesn't come straight south because of the "Coriolis Effect," which is how inertia plays out on a spinning sphere. The air coming south towards the Equator to replace the rising hot air there has been spinning around (with the whole earth) at a slower speed than the air at the Equator— simply because the circumference of the earth is less as you go north from the Equator. As it moves south it appears to slow down relative to the earth's surface, which is spinning to the east, and manifests itself as a wind blowing in a southwest direction.[GE25] Another vertical cell of convection rotation, going the opposite way, accounts for the Westerlies, which blow generally towards the northeast.[GE26] Between these two sets of usually reliable winds is a band of variable winds called the Horse Latitudes (behind which name are many intriguing theories—such as having to throw all your horses overboard when becalmed for weeks—but no consensus!). It is these two sets of prevailing winds that create the great clockwise gyre of the North Atlantic.[GE27] The Trades push water into the Caribbean Sea, which pushes it into the Gulf of Mexico, which shoots it out between Cuba and the Bahamas on the southeast side and the tip of Florida on the northwest side as the famous Gulf Stream. It leaves the U.S. coast about North Carolina's Outer Banks, and becomes the eastern-moving North Atlantic Drift. The Westerlies in those latitudes encourage it eastwards, and even send a branch of it northeast, to warm up northern Europe more than its high latitude otherwise deserves, but the main current circles down by the coast of southern Europe and North Africa and heads west towards the Caribbean again, as the North Equatorial Current, to complete the loop.

With today's technology, especially remote sensing, it is all easy enough to see and understand. The Portuguese had to learn it by trial and error—a sort of Darwinian "survival of the fittest navigator" process. Knowing about the Trades, the Westerlies, and at least the current of the eastern side of the Atlantic Ocean gyre, Portuguese navigators developed the neat trick called the *volta da Mina*, the "return from the mine" (São Jorge da Mina, today's Elmina, Ghana).[GE28] Instead of trying to beat up into the prevailing winds and currents along the western and northwestern side of Africa, they would sail far west—hundreds of miles west—and then angle northwest and then north with the Trades on their starboard beam or at a broad angle upwind. They would work north across the Horse Latitudes (the least predictable part of the trip), and at the latitude of the Azores and southern Portugal—where they picked up the Westerlies—they would turn due east for home, sailing large on those winds blowing towards the northeast.

A new way of finding latitude; educated guessing about longitude

As the Portuguese pushed on south, they crossed the Equator, at which point the North Star sank in the sea behind them and they had no way to determine their latitude (there is no South Polar star, inconveniently). So in 1484 the Portuguese government, in an early think-tank development, enlisted the university mathematicians

---

25. GE Layer 25 is a Folder titled "North Atlantic Trades." First go to the View drop-down menu at top of the Google Earth screen, and inside it turn on the "Grid" layer; it should show you the Equator and Tropic of Cancer in bright yellow lines, and other lines of latitude and longitude in white. Then simply turn on the whole Folder, which has a set of green arrow-shaped Paths showing the usual direction and position of the trades. They shift a bit northwards during the northern hemisphere's summer and southwards during winter. If the Grid layer begins to clutter the screen unduly, turn it back off by same process—drop down View—then uncheck Grid.

26. GE Layer 26 is a Folder titled North Atlantic Westerlies; turning on the entire folder will show a set of orange arrows representing the Westerlies.

27. GE Layer 27 is a Folder titled "North Atlantic Gyre." Constricted parts of the generally circular current, as between the Yucatan peninsula and Cuba, or again between Cuba and Florida, can run 7 or 8 knots.

28. GE Layer 28 is a Path, symbolized as a broad yellow line, showing a typical "Volta da mina," a "return from the mine" (today's Elmina, Ghana).

in the overall project. They reported back that it was all just a matter of solid geometry, and compiled for the navigators a book of tables based on the angle of the sun above the horizon at mid-day. Just take the angle between the horizon and the sun's peak altitude, the navigators were told, and as long as you knew what day of the year it was, the little book of tables should give you your latitude north or south of the Equator. A fleet was sent down around the bulge of West Africa just to try it out, taking the decreasing altitude of the North Star on clear nights and on clear days the sun's altitude at high noon as interpreted by the tables. They both logically worked down to zero, the latitude of the Equator, and afterwards the sun's altitude as converted to latitude in the tables picked up logically enough, little by little.

Finding a way to measure exact longitude would take Europeans another couple or three hundred years. It had to await one of two things, or preferably both: (a) very accurate clocks (chronometers), or (b) a much more sophisticated knowledge of astronomy (which would require telescopes, knowledge of the movements of the Galilean moons of Jupiter, and such). By the mid-1400s, however, Portuguese navigators could make an educated guess at their longitude, by keeping good records of speed and direction of sailing. The "log" book was named for keeping records of the log, a block of wood tied onto a string with knots at regular intervals: it was thrown overboard and timed (the later British navy used a 28-second sand glass, for example), and how many "knots" you were making was entered every hour or so in the logbook (today we've pegged the nautical knot at 1.1 m.p.h., incidentally). That was speed through the water, of course, not "speed over ground" (SOG, as a modern nautical GPS unit has it). And if you happened to be sailing against the main currents of one of those ocean gyres (the Gulf Stream, for instance), you could be making a respectable seven knots, water speed, but actually going backwards because the current against you was eight knots, or if you were going with the current, a blazing 15 knots. It helped to know about those great ocean gyres, and the Portuguese were learning fast.

Not far down the African coast below the Equator, between 5° and 10° South Latitude, the Portuguese encountered a cold water current coming north (the Benguela Current, named for the coastal Angolan town) [GE[29]], and prevailing winds blowing towards the northwest. At this point they began to guess that the South Atlantic had mirror images of the Trades, Westerlies, and gyre of the North Atlantic's.[GE[30]] This guess was confirmed by one of the most famous voyages of exploration of all time.

Bartolomeu Dias turns the Cape

In the fall of 1486, a small but well-supplied three-ship fleet—two lateen caravels and a less maneuverable but bigger square-rigger for a supply ship—left Lisbon heading south. The fleet commander was Bartolomeu Dias, and he was charged with finding a way around southern Africa. They stopped for resupply at the Cape Verdes and then El Mina. Then the little fleet struggled down the coast south of the Equator, against the Benguela Current and the prevailing wind. Around Walvis Bay,[GE[31]] however, partly helped by a storm, Dias stood out to sea going southwest, until they caught the steady Westerlies of the Roaring 'Forties latitudes, and ran east for a time. Finally turning north, they hit land in February of 1488 (still summer in southern Africa) around Mossel Bay.[GE[32]] Going on east along the coast another 260 miles, they got almost as far as the mouth of the Bushman River, where they put up a memorial on an isolated headland.[GE[33]] With the coast definitely trending northeast, Dias knew he had turned the tip of Africa and badly wanted to go on to India. A rebellious crew encouraged him otherwise, and on the return trip, staying in close to the coast, he actually saw Cape Agul-

29. GE Layer 29 is a Placemark referencing Benguela, Angola. Zoom out for perspective.

30. GE Layer 30 is a Folder titled "South Atlantic winds, currents." It contains three Folders, one for the Trades, one for the Westerlies, and one for the main parts of the generally circular South Atlantic currents, all of which are symbolized to match the colors in their North Atlantic parallels.

31. GE Layer 31 is a Placemark referencing Walvis Bay of today's Namibian coast.

32. GE Layer 32 is a Placemark referencing Mossel Bay.

33. GE Layer 33 is a Placemark referencing the Dias pillar. Click on Panoramio icon under pointer, titled "diaz cross from the air," for one nice view. Zoom out for perspective of coast.

has,[GE34] the southernmost point of Africa at 34° 50' S. Latitude, and then the dramatic rocky cape near today's Cape Town. Dias wanted to call it the Cape of Storms, after all he'd been through. Probably with an eye to public relations, the Portuguese government insisted on "Cape of Good Hope."[GE35]

In parallel with the Bartolomeu Dias fleet, the Portuguese government sent an exploring party to spy out the Indian trade another way, via the eastern Mediterranean Sea. It was led by the equally remarkable Pêro da Covilhão, who numbered Arabic among the several languages he spoke fluently. In Cairo he joined a group of Muslim merchants heading east down the Red Sea coast of Arabia, and eventually sailed on the monsoon winds to the southwest coast of India, exploring from Calicut [GE36] up through Goa.[GE37] Upon return to the east African coast, he went as far down the coast as Sofala,[GE38] the southernmost east African port served by the annual monsoon winds that dominate the Indian Ocean.

"Monsoon" comes from the Arabic word *mausim,* meaning "seasonal." The Indian Ocean has no gyre to speak of, and no Trade Winds, but it does have these regular "seasonal winds." It's as if Asia, the largest of continents, breathes in and out once a year. In summer, the land heats up long before surrounding oceans. The hot air rises there, pulling in cooler air from the southwest and southeast—air full of moisture from its time over the ocean, that falls as the torrential "monsoon rains." In winter the process reverses; the land cools down, the air over it becomes relatively cold and dense and pushes southeast and southwest. It was a totally different wind pattern than in either North or South Atlantic, but unlike them had been sailed in for thousands of years by pilots who knew it well. And now Pêro da Covilhão knew it too.

He made it back to Cairo, and passed along all his information to other Portuguese agents he met there— including information on the Indonesian spices that were traded at Calicut. He himself never made it back to Portugal. He went to the Coptic Christian kingdom of Ethiopia to make contacts there for Portugal, and was deemed so valuable to the government there that they never allowed him to leave. But by 1488, with this price-less new information from Covilhão and the new Bartolomeu Dias sea route around the Cape, Portugal was primed to make a bold move towards India itself. First, however, the Portuguese were in for a bit of a shock.

Cristoforo Colombo (1451–1506), an Italian from the city of Genoa whose name has been anglicized as Christopher Columbus and hispanicized as Cristóbal Colón, was for a time in his life a sea captain in the employ of the Portuguese. As such he had made the trip from Lisbon to São Jorge da Mina and back (the *volta da mina*), years before his famous 1492 voyage of discovery for Spain. He knew about the Trades and the West-erlies and the eastern half of the North Atlantic gyre, and rightly calculated he could use them to get a long, long way west and back home again. When he got back in 1493 from the first of his four major voyages, he claimed he had reached Asia going west (which he believed until he died, which is why the Americas are not named the Columbias). The Portuguese didn't really believe it, but called on the Pope to divide the Portuguese sphere of influence (Africa and India to the east) from the Spanish (western lands just found). In 1494 the Treaty of Tordesillas (a town in eastern Spain where negotiators met to hammer out terms) set the north-south dividing line "370 leagues west of the Cape Verde Islands."[GE39] There was argument later over just exactly where that meridian was (45° W? 47° W? something in-between?), but either way, you will notice, the treaty lines cross a considerable bulge of South America, which hadn't yet been discovered—the importance of which will appear shortly.

---

34. GE Layer 34 is a Placemark referencing Agulhas.

35. GE Layer 35 is a Placemark framing a view of the Cape of Good Hope that runs south from the vicinity of today's Cape Town.

36. GE Layer 37 is a Placemark referencing Calicut, today's Kozhikode.

37. GE Layer 37 is a Placemark referencing Goa's Fort Aguada. Zoom out a bit to see (white) outlines of the Goa administrative region. We'll do a bit more with Goa later when we get to Alfonso d'Albuquerque.

38. GE Layer 38 is a Placemark referencing Sofala.

39. GE Layer 39 is a Folder titled "Treaty of Tordesillas Line(s)." It has two lines, one a 45° West Latitude and one at 47°, which fairly well covers the range of territory argued over later.

Vasco da Gama and the first Portuguese trade with India

There was a short delay in sending the next Portuguese fleet south around Africa. Some scholars have speculated that they spent the first few years after Columbus's 1493 announcement in exploring a route around or through South America's Cape Horn instead—but in strictest secrecy because of the Treaty of Tordesillas.[3] Then in the summer of 1497 the Portuguese sent a four-ship fleet, captained by Vasco da Gama, to India. Technically speaking, it was more of "an armed commercial embassy"[4] than an exploration (though it did sail along over a thousand miles of southwest African coast no European had ever seen, between the spot where Dias had turned back and Sofala, the port opposite Madagascar that had been visited by Covilhão).

At the southern limits of the northern Trades, around today's Sierra Leone, the fleet headed south out into the open ocean instead of turning in along the African coast towards Elmina. For three months they sailed out of sight of land—across the Equator, down through the southern Trades, then catching the Westerlies and riding them due east down the 34° line of latitude to landfall near the southern tip of Africa. By mid-December they passed the easternmost spot reached by Bartolomeu Dias, and the day before Christmas they pulled into a sheltered bay to fish and rest. They named it "Natal," Portuguese for Christmas; today it is the harbor of the city of Durban,[GE[40]] in a state of South Africa still called (KwaZulu-)Natal. On the way north they touched at ports on the coast of today's Mozambique, Tanzania, and southern Kenya (including Mombasa), but—because of inferior trade goods, or attitude, or religion—were nowhere much welcomed until they got to Malindi[GE[41]] on today's central Kenyan coast. Here da Gama hired a pilot to take the fleet over to Calicut; they landed there in May of 1498, some ten years after Pêro da Covilhão had scoped it out.

The local king was unimpressed by the gifts da Gama brought from the Portuguese king, but he did allow da Gama to trade locally. Da Gama filled up with Indonesian spices, and against the advice of his pilot headed back southwest across the Indian Ocean before the monsoon winds had reversed. It had taken him just over three weeks to cross the Indian Ocean to Calicut, but it took him over four months to re-cross it, beating up into contrary winds. He lost two of his four ships on the way home, and a good many of his sailors died of the vitamin deficiency called scurvy. But when he sailed back into Lisbon in September of 1499, his cargo sold for fifty times what the whole expedition had cost, and he got a hero's welcome.

From the capture of Ceuta in 1415 to the last months of 1499—eighty-five years—Portugal had consistently pushed this ocean-borne exploration, including working up the scientific and technological developments it required. In the next 15 years it would pay off beyond the dreams of the most ambitious Portuguese king, and this little European state would drastically change the course of history of several regions of the world.

Albuquerque's "closing" of the Indian Ocean

In 1500 the second Portuguese fleet to India discovered the western tip of Brazil—on the Portuguese side of the Treaty of Tordesillas line—before it ever left the Atlantic Ocean. This is why a good half of all Latin Americans speak Portuguese today. The populating of Brazil by the Portuguese, though, would be a comparatively long, slow process. A more dramatic short-term development was the conquest of virtually all of the Indian Ocean from the coast of east Africa to the Straits of Malacca.

By this time the Portuguese had done the same thing with firearms that they had done earlier with the compass. From crude handguns they evolved huge deck-clearing shotguns, with a flange to hang over a rail so they wouldn't knock the shooter down. Small wooden forts began to grow up on the very bows and sterns of the ships, so as to get the drop on the enemy (*focsle,* the English word for the platform at the bow of a sailing ship, comes from saying "fore castle" for hundreds of years). Soon brass and then iron swivel cannons were mounted on the tops of high platforms fore and aft, and the heavier they got, the more problem ships had with toppling over, not a good thing for a ship to do. So the heavier guns were stepped back down, to the main deck, and then also to sub-decks equipped with porthole covers to keep the water out when sailing. By the end of the 1400s

---

40. GE Layer 40 is a Placemark referencing today's Durban Harbor.

41. GE Layer 41 is a Placemark referencing the Vasco da Gama pillar at Malindi; click on Panoramio icon under pointer titled "Monumento di Vasco De Gama a Malindi."

Europeans had invented the "broadside." With perhaps eight substantial cannons to a side, later twelve, and so on, they no longer had to grapple, but could sink enemy ships at distance before they could ever get close enough to grapple. By 1500 one state-of-the-art European warship, especially a huge Portuguese carrack built of thick oak beams and planks that would hold up under their cannon's powerful recoil, could neutralize the entire navy of a non-European power, and even blow away most any coastal fort. It was unprecedented new power, and the Portuguese were not shy about using it. One of the best scholars of this time and place says the Portuguese broke into the Indian Ocean "with complete ruthlessness and astonishing speed."[5] For ruthlessness, here's a sample to stand for the whole: when Vasco da Gama captured a shipload of Muslim pilgrims to Mecca, he had them all driven below decks and the ship burned.

As for speed, in about fifteen years the Portuguese conquered the whole Indian Ocean coast and points beyond. From 1505 to 1507 they built a chain of forts up the east African coast—one at Sofala, that southernmost port affected by the trades, one at the little island city Mozambique,[GE42] and one at Kilwa[GE43] to support their base farther north in Malindi. In 1507 they conquered the Omani capital of Muscat[GE44] at the entrance of the Persian Gulf, though Hormuz at the straits, the real choke point of the Gulf, successfully resisted them for a few years more. Their single biggest military victory was the Battle of Diu[GE45] in 1509, where the Portuguese destroyed the combined fleets of the two strongest rulers of western India—the Zamorin of Calicut and the Sultan of Gujarat, plus the two major powers of the eastern Mediterranean—the Mamluks of Egypt and the Ottoman Empire. The battle was fought close in to the port, the defenders hoping to be sheltered by the fort's guns. They hoped in vain, and the Portuguese victory at Diu gave them control of the Indian Ocean for a century.

The new Portuguese governor of Asia in the wake of the battle of Diu was Alfonso de Albuquerque. No stranger to the Indian Ocean, he had fought around the coast of east Africa, Arabia, and western India since 1503. Now he did two things that clinched Portuguese control. First, he seized Goa[GE46], a 60-mile-long territory on the west Indian coast, to be the central Portuguese capital of Asia. Second, he nailed shut as best he could the (oceanic) doors into the Indian Ocean. In 1511 he took the city of Malacca[GE47] that controlled the straits of that name, and thus almost all trade with Southeast and East Asia (defeating a Javanese fleet in 1513 that came to try to take it back). He finally conquered Hormuz[GE48] in 1515, choking off the Persian Gulf. He never quite managed to nail shut the door to the Red Sea, failing to capture Aden and having to make do with a base on the island of Socotra.[GE49] Overall, however, Albuquerque was so successful that every ship sailing in the Indian Ocean had to have a Portuguese license issued from Hormuz, Malacca, or Goa itself. So Portugal got rich two ways—by controlling the Europe-Asia trade particularly in spices, and by taking over the inter-Asia trade itself.

By 1515 the Portuguese had made it to the Moluccas (in the eastern part of today's Indonesia), then the only source of cloves and nutmeg. In 1517 they sailed into Guangzhou/Canton, south China's biggest city (causing panic when they shot off a salute with their cannon, not a particularly good omen for future east-west relations). By 1543 they had landed in Japan. Soon they were the middlemen of the Java and South China Seas, as they had become earlier in the Indian Ocean. They faced some challenge from the Spanish, who in 1520 were led by a Portuguese navigator (Magellan), apparently using a Portuguese map, through the straits at the

---

42. GE Layer 42 is a repeat of the Placemark icon referencing the island of Mozambique; for which the later state was named. See Fortaleza de Sao Sebastoa on the little island's northern end.

43. GE Layer 43 is a Placemark referencing Kilwa. Though it has just an Omani top from later centuries, it is still called the Arab Castle. Click on Panoramio icon under pointer titled "Kilwa kisiwani."

44. GE Layer 44 is as Placemark referencing Muscat; click on Panoramio icon titled "Jalaly fort" for one good view. Zoom out for general bearings.

45. GE Layer 45 is a Placemark referencing Diu; the fort is very well preserved and obviously much photographed.

46. GE Layer 46 is a Placemark referencing Goa.

47. GE Layer 47 is a Placemark referencing Malacca. Zoom out for larger perspective.

48. GE Layer 48 is a Placemark referencing the Portuguese fort on the northern tip of the little island of Hormuz, just over 4 miles off the Iranian/Persian mainland.

49. GE Layer 49 is a Placemark referencing Socotra.

bottom tip of South America that now bear his name.[GE50] Naming, and sailing across the Pacific (by rightly understanding the Westerlies, Trades, and gyres of the South and North Pacific to be similar to those in the Atlantic), Magellan let the Spanish eventually get hold of the Philippines. But that was only a minor irritant in the century-long Portuguese maritime domination of South, Southeast, and East Asia, where the great majority of the world's population lived. It lasted until the Dutch showed up around 1600 and blew them out of key forts from West Africa to East Indonesia, wielding the next level of European power.

Portugal today is still a small state, with something like eleven million people—not much more than the population of greater Houston, Texas. It left huge legacies, however, most obviously in a quarter-billion people in Lusophone (Portuguese-speaking; *Lusitania* was the Roman name for Portugal) countries, most notably Brazil with 200 million, and Angola and Mozambique with over twenty million each. It left romantic ruins, from Fort Jesus in Mombasa[GE51] to the facade of the great cathedral of St. John in Macau.[GE52] Portuguese place names are scattered all over the world. Bombay (now Mumbai), came from the Portuguese *bom baim*, the "good bay." Formosa, the common name for the island of Taiwan used for centuries, was the Portuguese word meaning the "beautiful" island. Some significant Portuguese outposts lasted down to very modern times. Goa was only taken by India in 1962, 15 years after the creation of the modern Indian state and 450 years after its seizure by Albuquerque. Macau, an hour's hydrofoil ride across the Pearl River estuary from Hong Kong, only went back to China in 1999, 50 years after the creation of the People's Republic of China and over 420 years after its establishment. These are all reminders that the chief Portuguese legacy was this opening wedge of exploration that began the modern European domination of much of the rest of the world.

The Italian Renaissance context of it all

This entire A.D. 1300–1500 couple of centuries was southern Europe's shining hour. Portugal you've seen in some detail, and Spain's role has appeared on the margins—but all of this new military power and maritime exploration really happened in the deeper context of the Italian Renaissance. It brought sharp new attention to bear on the physical world, including the world beyond Europe. Three Italian cities in particular were important in this regard. Two of them were the great seaports of Genoa and Venice, at the top left and top right, respectively, of the Italian Peninsula (Genoa at the head of the Ligurian Sea, and Venice at the head of the Adriatic Sea). Each had a huge Mediterranean trade network, and they were often rivals. The third key city, Florence, was curiously enough fifty miles inland from the closest salt water.[GE53]

Genoa's most famous explorer was of course Columbus, but the city's exploring tradition was centuries older. In 1291 the city's Vivaldi brothers set off down the coast of Morocco in a small but well-supplied fleet with the ultimate ambition of circling Africa (they were never heard of again). In 1312 it was Genoa's Lancellotto Moballo who discovered (and gave his name to) Lanzarote, one of the Canary Islands. He headed up a settlement there for twenty years or so, until evicted by a revolt of the native Guanches. It was the Genoese captain of one ship and the Venetian captain of another ship, both sailing for the Portuguese Prince Henry the Navigator, who in 1455 found the mouth of the Gambia River. It was a Genoese navigator who a few years later discovered the Cape Verdes on behalf of Portugal, and actually governed it for a time. The real name of John Cabot, the explorer who in 1497 famously found and claimed for England the North American coast in the vicinity of what today is Canada's Cape Breton Island and Nova Scotia, was Giovanni Caboto. He seems to have been born in Genoa, and by his teens was living in Venice.

Venice's most famous explorer—and maybe the most famous of all time—was Marco Polo. His travels from 1271–1295 through Mongol lands, including China, and back by sea through the Straits of Malacca and

50. GE Layer 50 is a Path showing the Straits of Magellan as a blue line.

51. GE Layer 51 is a Placemark referencing Fort Jesus, Mombasa. Click on Panoramio icon under pointer, titled "Fort Jesus."

52. GE Layer 52 a Placemark referencing the remaining facade of St. Paul's Cathedral, Macau.

53. A GE Layer 53 is a Folder containing, and framing a view of, Placemarks for each of the three cities. In the case of Genoa and Florence, general Renaissance walls/boundaries show as red lines. Venice is of course an island; see its famous S-shaped Gran Canal.

around the Indian coast, were truly epic. Nearing home after nearly a quarter-century on the road, he was captured by the Genoese, currently at war with Venice, and he dictated an account of his travels to a fellow prisoner in a Genoese prison. He finally got back home to Venice in 1299, ne'er to roam again; but his accounts set the tone for the exploring age to come. Over a century later the Venetian Niccolo de' Conti came close to duplicating his travels, coming back in 1439 by sea from South China. In the paragraph above on Genoa a couple of the many Venetian navigators working for Prince Henry the Navigator were mentioned. And Venice supplied more than navigators. In the 1450s the Portuguese government commissioned one of the first of the new world maps, fitting the growing portolani information into Ptolemy's general global framework, from the great Venetian map maker Fra Mauro.

As you saw earlier, it was a Florentine who translated Ptolemy from Greek into Latin about 1400 and so put Ptolemy's globe in the hands of the whole scholarly community. From Florence came Amerigo Vespucci, who was on, and eventually in charge of, the Portuguese voyages exploring the South American coast from 1499–1502 (he was with Cabral when Brazil was discovered in 1500). His reports apparently convinced map makers that this was indeed a new continent. "America," the name of which appeared on maps as early as 1507, is a version of Amerigo. The Florentine Giovanni da Verrazano sailed for the French, becoming the first European to explore from North Carolina's Cape Fear up to Rhode Island's Narragansett Bay (including the Verrazano Narrows just seawards of present-day Manhattan).

The Renaissance quickly defined

Renaissance—a French word meaning "rebirth"—was a concept popularized in the nineteenth century to describe what began in the states of Italy from the late 1300s to the early 1500s. It is a less popular term with historians today than it used to be. The more the era and those before and after it have been studied in detail, the less it appears to be a decisive break with the past. But for the quick overview of European history at hand, it may still be a valuable concept. It was described most brilliantly in 1860 by the Swiss historian Jakob Burckhardt in his *The Civilization of the Renaissance in Italy.* Looking for the spirit that informed the age, he boiled it down to three main themes—the revival of antiquity, the development of the individual, and "the state as a work of art."[6]

The revival of antiquity meant, first, new attention to Rome, and not the Rome of the Papacy and Christianity as much as the Rome of the Republic and pre-Christian Roman Empire. To study this in any depth, one had to learn Latin and Greek to tap the primary sources, and then Arabic and Hebrew, since so much of classical antiquity was only preserved in Arabic, and most of the interpreters of it were Jewish. A "humanist" originally simply meant one who had learned those four languages in a quest for learning from the classical European past. As early as the 1300s the city fathers of Florence aspired to build a dome as great as had imperial Rome in Hadrian's Pantheon, but by 1440 had only the foundations of a new cathedral (*Santa Maria del Fiore,* St. Mary of the Flowers) without much idea how to do the dome itself. Filippo Brunelleschi won the competition to do it, and build it he did by 1461.[GE54] Thus Florence got the first great Renaissance building to equal and in some ways surpass its classical Roman inspirations.

In the dog-eat-dog warfare between Italian states, says Burckhardt, no mediocre leaders survived—only those of talent, ambition, and strength of character. They were proud going on vain, and tended to celebrate themselves in what might be a short time in power. They surrounded themselves with talented egos much like themselves, and so a new kind of individualism—the first concerned with modern fame—percolated down through society. The development of the individual produced what we still call a "Renaissance" person—deeply as well as broadly educated in many fields, an artist and a practical engineer, so valuable as to find shelter and employment anywhere. Leon Battista Alberti (1404–1472), Genoese-born of a Florentine businessman and a prototypical Renaissance man, said, "Only he who has learned everything is nowhere a stranger; robbed of his fortune and without friends, he is yet the citizen of every country." Leonardo da Vinci (1452–1519) and Michelangelo Buonarroti (1475–1564), both Florentines, were to Alberti as experts to a beginner in this development of the individual.

---

54. GE Layer 54 is a Placemark referencing Brunellischi's great dome.

"The state as a work of art" was the gradual working out of the idea that statecraft had a logic of its own, a sort of game theory of state formation and preservation. Instead of simply running the state by tradition, the way your grandfather had run it, you as a ruler needed to learn this logic if you were to survive the warfare between Italian states. It came to be called *ragione di stato*, or as it is mainly known to scholars today, by its French equivalent *raison d'état*, literally "reason of state," and less literally as the "right" or "logic" of the state. It first emerged clearly in the 1454 Peace of Lodi masterminded by Florence's Cosimo de' Medici, as I'll explain below. It got its classical statement of all time in the Florentine Niccolò Machiavelli's *The Prince*, written from internal exile shortly after the Florentine Republic for which he had worked for fourteen years was crushed in 1512. Leaving morality aside, said he, let me show you what works in domestic and foreign policy, and in what kinds of states.

Florence: eye of the storm

Florence was the heart and soul of what Italians call the Quattrocento (QWA-tro-CHEN-to), or '400s, (the 1400s) until Rome hijacked the Renaissance in the next century. Why Florence? Historians have described a political and military "perfect storm" that swirled around it from around 1385 to 1454 and even later. It created a new level of political involvement called "civic humanism" that was an important precursor of modern nationalism.[7]

Here's the setting. In Italy in the mid-1300s there were five major territorial states. Each had a different sort of government, and four of them were different from the fairly broad Republic of the city–state of Florence. From weakest to strongest, they were:

a. The Papal states, capital city Rome.[GE55] This was of course a theocracy where the religious ruler was also the political ruler. The Papal States cut Italy in half; the Papacy was an institution with international power—but during this crucial century it was divided and generally paralyzed, a passive player instead of a real actor. The northern extension of the Papal States, generally called the Romagna, was virtually independent for much of this time. Bologna, the famous university city there, would usually figure as a key ally of Florence.

b. The Kingdom of Naples-Sicily, capital city Naples.[GE56] Potentially a strong power, during much of our century it was paralyzed by Spanish or French occupation. Twice it would break out of that, though, and threaten to conquer the rest of Italy, from south to north.

c. The Duchy of Lombardy, capital city Milan.[GE57] It was the dominant state of the largest productive plain in Italy, the Po River Valley. Perhaps the strongest power of the whole peninsula when the century started, it was a very active player, and—from the point of view of Florence—generally the villain. The Visconti family provided strong ducal leadership to this state in Lombardy for two centuries, and they felt it their destiny to unite Italy—as France and Spain had been united.

d. The island state of Venice (which you've already seen), a very limited Republic. At the start of our key century, Venice had a huge maritime empire but no real interest in the mainland. Its government was set up to let the wealthiest merchants run the show, with a strong executive called the Doge (Duke) running a council of key businessmen. In the first half of our key century, it was passive; in the second half, very active.

---

55. GE Layer 55 is a Folder containing a red Polygon showing the extent of the state, a white Placemark showing the capital city Rome, and a blue Path showing the main Tiber River.

56. GE Layer 56 is a Folder containing an orange Polygon showing the extent of the state, and a white Placemark locating the capital Naples.

57. GE Layer 57 is a Folder titled Lombardy, Milan, River Po. It shows Lombardy as a purple Polygon, Milan as a white Pushpin, and the River Po and a key tributary, the Secchia River, as blue Paths.

e. Last, the Republic of Florence, located in, but not in control of, Tuscany.[GE58] It was a broader Republic than Venice, its government machinery devised to let middle-class and the wealthy direct politics. But there was nothing much in the way of idealistic loyalty to the Republic; the government was just a practical way to let the wool merchants and bankers run the show. Florence, although just a single city, did have a defensive alliance with other Tuscan cities such as Pisa and Siena, and even cities such as Bologna on the other side of the rugged Apennine mountains that run down the spine of Italy.

What happened in Italy from 1385 to 1454 has been described as a four-part drama.

Act I. Duke Giangaleazzo Visconti of the Duchy of Milan, perhaps the strongest of the whole Visconti line, opened a campaign to capture Tuscany in 1385, undoubtedly with an eye to capturing all Italy in due course. With a standing army and enough money to bribe city governments by the dozen, he slowly (just campaigning in summers, generally) ate into Florence's defensive alliance until by 1402 only Florence and Bologna were left. Later that year even Bologna fell, and Florence was put under deadly siege. Then Florence was saved by what looks very much like an historical accident: the plague broke out in Giangaleazzo's army, killed him and many of his troops, and the Milanese army ended the siege and went back home. But here the myth was born in Florence that Florence had saved Italy from tyranny.

Act II. A decade later the Kingdom of Naples-Sicily, temporarily free from foreign entanglements, decided its mission was to unite Italy from south to north. It pushed north through the helpless Papal States, and plowed into Tuscany. By 1414, all that was left of the Florentine defensive alliance was Bologna, and it was under siege. Then suddenly, through no fault of the Florentines, the King of Naples-Sicily died and his army retreated home to influence the succession. It had only been twelve years since the 1402 defense against Giangaleazzo, and the myth that Florence had saved Italy from tyranny got a shot in the arm. Florentines began to compare themselves with the Roman Republic of classical times.

Act III. Giangaleazzo's son, Filippo Maria Visconti, by 1420 had reorganized the Duchy of Milan and was prepared to reassert his father's old plans. In a more sophisticated attack, he launched a pincer movement southwards, the western wing taking Genoa and coming on down the west coast, and the eastern wing coming down across the Po River valley and into the Romagna on the east coast. This time, you'll be glad to hear, Florence didn't just sit there and wait to be saved by a miracle. Florence rushed troops to the Romagna to help defend their allies there such as Bologna. But they were poorly-trained civilian troops, and unfortunately for them were generally routed by the more professional Milanese. But then Florence was saved, albeit indirectly, by its own efforts. Venetians had been reading the celebration of Republican-ness the Florentines had been writing, and as a fellow Republic joined the war on the side of Florence. That quickly rolled up the eastern flank of the Duke of Lombardy's military, and by 1425 the third crisis was over.

Act IV. In 1447 Duke Filippo Maria Visconti died, and for the first time in two centuries a Visconti duke left no male heir. A mercenary soldier (*condottiere*) named Francesco Sforza took over the government, and although he tried to legitimize himself by marrying a daughter of the last Visconti duke, he sat very unsteadily on the ducal throne. Milan, from being the strongest state in the peninsula, had become one of the weakest. Now Venice (from Florence's point of view!) became the villain, having developed a taste for mainland Italian territory. It conquered the eastern third of northern Italy (thereafter generally called the Venezia or just the Veneto),[GE59] and by 1450 had begun to eat into the Lombardy itself.

At this point the wily and fabulously wealthy banker Cosimo de' Medici, the real controller of city government in Florence though mostly choosing to rule from behind the scenes, transformed the situation by allying with Florence's traditional enemy Lombardy. His logic—*ragione di stato*—was clear: if Milan falls, we're next,

---

58. GE Layer 58 is a Folder titled "Florence, Tuscany, Arno River, allied cities." Notice that Pisa controls the mouth of the Arno River, Siena the heart of Tuscany, and Bologna is in the sometimes independent Romagna just across the Apennine Mountains from Florence.

59. GE Layer 59 is a Placemark framing a view of the Veneto (today's state defined by white lines).

so it's better to help Milan survive even given our history of hostility. What resulted was a two-on-two war, with Florence and Milan fighting Venice and Naples-Sicily. Then in 1454 Cosimo de' Medici again transformed the situation by opening negotiations with Naples-Sicily. Although there's no historical record of it, I expect the dialogue went something like this:

> **Cosimo:** King, we're at war.
> **King of Naples:** I know.
> **Cosimo:** Although we and Milan have interior lines of communication, you and Venice are the stronger side; your odds on winning are probably 70–30.
> **King:** I agree, pretty good odds for my side.
> **Cosimo:** Then what happens?
> **King:** Hmmm. I guess in a few years I'll have to go to war with Venice for control of the whole peninsula.
> **Cosimo:** That's the way I've got it figured, too, and your odds of winning that war are probably only about 40–60. So King, your five-year survival odds are 70% × 40% = 28%.
> **King:** (moment of silence) Do that again.
> **Cosimo:** (does it again).
> **King:** Not good odds. What can I do about it?
> **Cosimo:** Drop out of the war, join us, and we'll force Venice to a peace treaty that respects all the different states as they now exist.
> **King:** OK.

The upshot (whether there was any such dialogue or not!) was the 1454 Peace of Lodi, the first modern treaty. The traditional medieval idea was that there should be one world ruler. This Peace of Lodi assumed that different sorts of states could co-exist, and concerned itself with the balance of power between them. It wouldn't be echoed by Europe at large until almost two centuries later with the 1648 treaty that ended the Thirty Years' War. It fairly well kept the peace in Italy for forty years, and even then it was great power invasion from outside that broke it.

All this time civic humanism grew in Florence, a celebration of the city's past and accomplishments. Cosimo fed it with his money, grooming artists to celebrate the city and its heritage. He influenced the choice of Brunelleschi to build the cathedral dome, for example. His grandson Lorenzo, who died in that famous Columbus discovery year of 1492, was the greatest of the patrons of art celebrating the city. Lorenzo's court included Leonardo da Vinci and Michelangelo. The link between art and politics was very close indeed in the Florentine Renaissance.[GE60]

The link between war and art

The link between war and politics may have been even closer than the link between art and politics, and the third side of the triangle—the connection between war and art, or at least artists—shows up dramatically in the greatest artists of the Renaissance. Here's how.

The "gunpowder revolution" that slowly transformed European warfare after 1325 wasn't uniquely Italian. First, the English, then the French, then the Spanish and the southern Germans developed good artillery. But the fortification response to artillery <u>was</u> particularly Italian. At the very end of the Quattrocento, in 1494, the French invaded Italy with fast horse-drawn bronze cannon, firing cast iron balls with gunpowder of sophisticated chemistry and grain size (which affects burn rate). They set about breaching traditional vertical stone city and fortress walls in record speed. In hurried trial and error response, two things were found to work against an artillery attack. First, instead of a vertical stone wall that cannon could quickly knock down, make fortress walls lower, and put a sloping ramp (*glacis*) in front of them to absorb the cannon balls, with a trench behind as first line of defense against invaders tempted to run up the slope. Second, instead of square or round fortress

---

60. GE Layer 60 is a Folder showing the centrality of Florence to the early Renaissance, generally showing birthplaces and migrations of some of the most famous "Renaissance men" to the city.

walls, all of which have "dead" zones where opposing infantry can only be fired on straight down, give forts projecting polygons, so that every piece of wall is covered by its defenders from at least two oblique angles. So was born the "star fort," or what the French called the *trace italienne*, translating roughly as the "Italian shape" fort. Leonardo da Vinci, who always seemed happiest when he had a position that let him be both artist and engineer, made star forts for Cesare Borgia in 1502–3 in Imola (near Bologna, in the Romagna just over the Apennines from his hometown of Florence). In 1504 the Florentine city government, Leonardo's next employer, pulled him off work painting a famous historical battle on the interior of city hall and sent him to supervise the modernization of fortifications at the Tuscan port of Piombino. The younger Michelangelo in his turn helped his beloved hometown of Florence with star-shaped fortifications in 1528–29. As early as 1521 the great Florentine historian Guicciardini could see that these star forts had turned the tide in siege warfare, the advantage going back to the defender.[8] You've already seen such "Italian shape" star forts built by the Portuguese—Elmina in Ghana, Fort Jesus in Mombasa, the castle at Hormuz, one of the castles in Goa—from the later 1500s. You'll see them as well in this text in the hands of the Spanish at Veracruz, the Dutch at Cape Town, and the British at Calcutta, and lots more. This is part of the reason Europeans were as formidable defensively as they were offensively vis-a-vis the non-European world. For the next few centuries, their artillery could destroy most any non-European fort, and their fortresses could survive most any non-European assault.

In a word, from 1300–1500 Europeans proved to be gifted technicians, tinkering with basic inventions from more sophisticated Middle Eastern or Eastern cultures or the classical European past. In the next couple centuries they would forge ahead in the world of ideas as well, breaking new intellectual ground—which would add to their growing relative power.

PART TWO: SCIENTIFIC REVOLUTION circa 1500–1700

The Reformation and Counter-Reformation context of it all

The general setting of this "scientific revolution" was, curiously enough at first glance, western and central Europe's fiercest religious wars. A rebellion against the authority of the western Christian Church in Rome and what critics of the Church said was its non-scriptural claims of power had threatened to break out for centuries (and had indeed already done so in the Hussite Wars of the 1400s, as you'll see in detail in a later chapter). The "Reformation" proper is most often dated to Martin Luther's nailing a list of ninety-five subjects for debate on the door of the castle church in the Elbe River [GE61] city of Wittenberg, a university town in Saxony,[GE62] on Halloween day, 1517. The success of the Reformation was in part owing to some very non-religious factors, as well. A wave of inflation swept east across Europe as Aztec gold flooded in through Spain, hitting the agricultural sector of local economies hardest. And local rulers, especially in northern Europe, were looking for any excuse to get out from under Papal control.

The central figure who had to organize a response to all this was his most Catholic majesty Charles V (1500–1559), Holy Roman Emperor. He had made interesting choices of parents and grandparents. When his father died in 1506 he became (child) ruler of the Burgundian Netherlands—much of today's eastern France and almost all of today's Belgium and Holland. In 1516 his grandfather Ferdinand of Aragon died, and left him Spain and its new American colonies (which in five years would include the entire Aztec Empire and in twenty years the entire Inca Empire). Then at age nineteen, in 1519, he inherited from his other grandfather the title and lands of the Holy Roman Empire. At this point he owned close to half of western and central Europe, including some of its richest lands. Contemporaries probably expected him and his advisors to make short work of "this pesky monk" in Saxony. But the Empire proved too big and too varied to manage, and the "Protestant" emotions were stirred too hot. In 1555 a tired Charles V and a rival group of Lutheran princes signed a document agreeing in essence that the religion of the local ruler would be the official religion of each governing area—*cujus regio, ejus religio* ("whose the region, his the religion"). This so-called Peace of Augsburg

---

61. GE Layer 61 is an aqua Path representing the Elbe River, flowing northwest across modern Germany.

62. GE Layer 62 is a Placemark referencing the Castle Church at Wittenberg; click on Panoramio icon under pointer for night view.

recognized that northern Europe (though not Ireland!) was mostly Protestant, while the south generally remained Catholic.

It was only a truce, however, and violence between Catholics and Lutherans (and Calvinists, and other Protestant denominations that spun off later) flared up during the following century. Most Americans will know how it marked England, where Henry VIII created the independent Church of England, his daughter Mary (from his first wife Catherine of Aragon) as Queen tried to take England back to Catholicism, and his daughter Elizabeth (from his second wife Anne Boleyn) as Queen took England permanently in a Protestant direction. The English defeat of the Spanish Armada in 1588 was an important punctuation of this Protestant-Catholic warfare. In 1572 there were the St. Bartholomew's Day massacres of Protestants in France, an all-out religious war that threatened to destroy France as a state. It only ended (again, temporarily) in 1589 when the one surviving claimant to the throne, the Protestant Henri IV, agreed at least nominally to become Catholic to meet a condition for being French king. "Paris is worth a mass," said he, and became Catholic, but it was obvious to all there would be no persecution of Protestants (*Huguenots*, they were called in France) on his watch. His "Edict of Nantes" of 1598 gave Huguenots all but full civil rights. But he was assassinated in 1610 by a Catholic extremist.

The Thirty Years' War of 1618–1648 was started by Protestants in Prague who threw Catholic officials out the town hall windows to their deaths. It drew Catholic armies from the south and Protestant armies from as far north as Sweden to battle in what is today Germany. Even though the shrewd Cardinal Richelieu of France supported the northern Protestant powers with money so as to weaken France's main rival the (fellow Catholic) Holy Roman Empire, domestically he made war on France's own Protestants. In 1627–28 he personally watched over the siege and eviction of French Protestants based at La Rochelle.[GE63] In 1685 the great "Sun King" of France, Louis XIV, evicted all Protestants from France in his "Revocation of the Edict of Nantes."

Protestant university reform; Catholic response

As the Reformation that Martin Luther (1483–1546) led succeeded in northern Europe, for a time he was content to let the old universities—home of much of the scholasticism that had buttressed the Catholic Church's claim to authority—languish. As a university professor himself, however, he soon decided there was a need for a reformed sort of higher education, and assigned his close friend and fellow Reformation leader Phillip Melanchthon to undertake such reform, beginning with the University of Wittenberg itself. It was a movement that would favor "sciences that had practical value." That included medical astrology, in the views of the day, which in turn took some astronomy to accurately measure the "aspects" of the planets (the angles between them) at certain times. Tycho Brahe and Johannes Kepler, two big names on the list of those who solved the problem of motion (discussed below), between them trained in the northern European universities of Copenhagen, Leipzig, and Tübingen[GE64] under first or second generation Melanchthon scholars.[9]

In this whole process the Catholic Church for its part was also to some extent transformed, in what is often called the "Counter-Reformation" or "Catholic Reformation." There was some attention to undeniable institutional abuses highlighted by Protestants, but also a rallying to the defense of Catholic tradition and church authority. Most famous of the new institutions of the Counter-Reformation was the Society of Jesus, the Jesuit Order, founded by Ignatius Loyola (1491–1556). He was a Spanish nobleman who, while recuperating from serious battlefield wounds received when he was thirty years old, had a religious awakening and developed a disciplined meditation he later described in *The Spiritual Exercises*. In 1539 he and his followers were formally recognized as the Society of Jesus, to serve as missionaries and defenders of what they believed was the true faith directly under the Pope. Besides the three vows of poverty, chastity, and obedience required of ordered priests, the Jesuits also took a fourth vow directly to the Pope. The Society's organization was of military strictness and its claims of loyalty were total; Loyola would be appointed its first "Father General." Jesuit missionaries were soon in the forefront of the European exploration of the world. Americans will probably be familiar

---

63. GE Layer 63 is a Placemark referencing La Rochelle.
64. GE Layer 64 is a Folder containing red pushpin Placemarks for the three universities.

with the Jesuit Father Jacques Marquette's exploration of the Mississippi River in 1673, and there were South American and Asian explorations even more dramatic.

It was the Jesuits, too, who led the intellectual struggle with the rising Protestant universities. Their key institution was the Roman College (*Collegio Romano*) that Ignatius Loyola set up in 1551.[GE⁶⁵] It was lavishly endowed by Pope Gregory XIII (elevated to the papacy in 1572, died 1585). By 1600 there were over 200 Jesuit colleges throughout Catholic Europe. One thing that won Jesuit missionaries unusual acceptance in even sophisticated civilizations elsewhere in the world, including the court of the Emperor of China, was their intellectual training in this cutting-edge new European math, astronomy, map-making, and navigational techniques. The one great visual reminder of the scientific sophistication of Catholic institutions of the late 1500s may be Pope Gregory XIII's map gallery in the Vatican, seen by perhaps a million visitors a year. Between the Vatican museum of antiquities tucked away in the northern corner of Vatican City, and the Sistine Chapel nestled close to St. Peter's Basilica itself, tourists walk a 375-yard-long corridor, part of which includes 40 huge wall maps of parts of Italy, some of them of sophisticated aerial views that in this time before aircraft had to be imagined. It was for Gregory XIII that brilliant Catholic mathematicians and astronomers modernized the old Julian calendar, and this "Gregorian" calendar was gradually adopted all over the world.

The solution of the Problem of Motion

In the setting of this fierce Protestant-Catholic struggle, then, consider one of the most remarkable intellectual breakthroughs made by European intellectuals, the solution of the "problem of motion"—why and how things move. Since the time of Aristotle there had been a general understanding that one set of laws and substances operated on earth, and a different set operated in the heavens. Here is the short course in each: Terrestrial Mechanics 101, and Celestial Mechanics 102 (tuition included in price of this book).

On earth everything was made up of just four elements in various mixes—earth, water, air, and fire. In a perfect world they would have existed in perfectly nested spheres—an inner one of earth, a shell of water around that, air around that, and an outer one of fire. The world was less than perfect—maybe good for us in that there's some earth above the water to live on, and some fire down from the outer sphere to warm by—but each element obviously sought its own rightful place. The natural motion of anything earthly was straight line down towards the center of the earth. Why? Because all earthy matter longs to be part of a sphere, the perfect shape. Things went faster the farther they dropped because they were "jubilant" at approaching the earth sphere. This sounds funny, until you stop and think "what makes gravity work, anyway?" It's a question almost none of us ask these days. Any other kind of earthly motion was unnatural motion, requiring a mover to remain in motion. To explain the movement of an arrow through the air, for example, it was clear to them that the bowstring propelled it the first couple or three feet. They knew medium affected motion—an arrow shot through water behaved differently than one shot through air—so they figured the medium was agitated by the arrowhead, and rushed around behind the arrow to push it out of that particular area. Eventually friction robbed the arrow of its speed, the medium ceased to be agitated, and even an arrow shot high in the air sooner or later turned abruptly downwards and came to earth.

Heavenly matter—the sun, moon, stars, planets, comets—obviously obeyed different rules, because it didn't fall down towards the center of the earth. Natural motion in the heavens was curved, unlike the straight-line-down natural motion on earth. The sun and moon and fixed stars rose in the east and arched over to the west (well, the stars close to the North Star just spun around it in circles without ever quite setting or rising). And where there was motion, everyone knew, there had to be a mover—so it must be that invisible spheres (made up of a magical "quintessence," a fifth kind of substance) surrounded the earth. The sun was a bright spot on one such sphere, and since round things naturally turn, the sun described an arc. The moon was a less bright spot on a sphere within that, and the fixed stars bright spots on a sphere outside the sun sphere. So far so good, but the planets gave them troubles. Moving generally in the ecliptic (the band of sky traversed by the sun and moon), they sometimes rushed ahead, did little loops and then appeared to move backwards in what was known as retrograde motion. It was Ptolemy—he of the world map/globe, the Greek scholar in second

---

65. GE Layer 65 is a Placemark referencing the Collegio Romano (today's Pontifical Gregorian University).

century AD Roman Egypt—who figured out that if you had several nested crystalline spheres per planet, the planet could ride on one for awhile, then kick over to another, and so on. By one version of this system, it took some eighty-two nested crystalline spheres to explain heavenly motion. Things might change on the imperfect earth, but the heavens were perfect and changeless.

All this may sound strange to us today, but such was the integration of philosophy, religion, ethics, aesthetics, and science in this admiration of the sphere and circular motion, that the real solution of the problem of motion defeated the best intellects for centuries. The break-through in understanding, in fact, took a full century and a half of our 1500–1700 period. The key names in the sequence are Copernicus, Brahe, Kepler, Galileo, and Newton.

Copernicus

Nicholas Copernicus (1473–1543) was born in the Prussian state in what is today Poland. He spoke German and Polish (in addition to Italian, Latin, and Greek), and is claimed as a native son by both linguistic groups today. He was educated in part in Italy, but also in Krakow in the spirit of Renaissance humanism that was radiating up from Italy. The year of his death, 1543, also saw the publication of his great work that argued for a sun-centered universe. Among other things, the book argued that the earth went around the sun and not vice-versa. This was generally right, of course, but part of his motivation was a conservative defense of Aristotle's idea of the simple, uniform motion of things. He thought Ptolemy had cheated when applying Aristotle to planetary motion—with his little off-center places to explain the little loops they made. Copernicus discovered if he put the sun at the center of planetary motion he could make more nearly circular paths out of planetary orbits, and reduce the number of crystalline spheres by over half. The idea of the earth as a sphere, spinning once a day on its axis and rotating once a year around the sun, was dynamite, and of course set a lot of other thought in motion. But Copernicus always thought natural motion was circular, and when asked to explain heavenly movements—such as why didn't the spinning earth fly apart from centrifugal force—came up with no better explanation than that round things naturally turned, and in doing what came naturally no harm could befall them . . . .

Brahe and Kepler in Prague

Tycho Brahe (1546–1601) was a Danish nobleman of some wealth, and he supplemented his astronomical researches with grant money from the Danish king. A couple of night sky happenings in the 1570s really piqued his interest. In 1572 an extremely bright star suddenly appeared, a nova (from the Latin *stella nova*, "new star") that was the fourth brightest thing in the sky (after the sun, moon, and Venus), and then in 1577 a spectacular comet came through. All of a sudden the heavens seemed not so changeless. Brahe was a superb technician, and put together a first rate astronomical institute on Hven Island in the Øresund channel off Copenhagen.[GE66] Although he had no telescope (because it wouldn't be invented until 1608 in Holland), he did have devices for recording exactly where and when planets were against the background of the fixed stars. Though it was beyond his mathematical capabilities to make sense of it all, he tried to harmonize the philosophy/theology of the day that made the earth the center of the universe with Copernicus's sun-centered view of things. Brahe's system had the observable five planets circling the sun, but the sun itself circling the earth. This way, however, the supposed crystalline spheres on which the heavenly bodies rode would have had to go through the sun, and each other, which after awhile made Brahe doubt their whole existence. When he measured the altitude of the 1577 comet above the earth (by taking its angle at different times of day, and therefore at different places around the spinning earth at that latitude), he found it to be way up in the heavens, and not an "exhalation of earth's vapors" at all. It, too, had to be cutting across those supposed crystalline spheres.

---

66. GE Layer 66 is a Placemark generally locating the site of Brahe's institute and observatory. The castle garden is still recognizable.

Tycho Brahe spent his last years in Prague[GE67] as royal astronomer to the current Holy Roman Emperor, Rudolph II. Rudolph was a famous patron of the arts, and of scientists, too. Nominally Catholic, in practice he was "non-observant," and welcomed both Protestants and Jews to his late-Renaissance style court. He built an observatory a little more than twenty miles northeast of Prague[GE68]—even then "light pollution" from urban areas may have been a factor! Late in life Brahe read some works by the younger scholar Johannes Kepler (1571–1630). Admiring his mathematical brilliance, but having a thing or two to teach him about the accuracy of measurements, Brahe invited Kepler to Prague. Kepler visited early in 1601 and moved there later in the year, the same year Brahe died. Rudolph II appointed Kepler to the now-vacant post of royal astronomer.

Kepler (1571–1630) found pattern in the three decades' worth of data on planetary motion collected by Brahe. He discovered three major things. First, planets moved in ellipses (not circles), with the sun at one of the foci of the ellipse. The ellipse is not quite as "perfect" as a circle, but it's not bad. You can describe it with a simple x-y formula of Cartesian geometry, or you can nail two nails in a board, make a loop of string just larger than distance between the two nails, and force a pencil outwards and around in the loop to draw one mechanically. And the sun would be at one of the nail holes. Second, planetary speed was not uniform, but was faster in close to the sun and slower away from it. But if you drew a line from the planet to the sun at one point and another line from the planet to the sun thirty days later, the area of the arc swept out by the line from one to the other would be equal in area for that of any thirty-day period on the planet's path. And third and last, Kepler found mathematical regularity between the fast years of the inner planets, and the slower and slower years of the outer planets. The square of the period of the orbit (the number of earth days in the year of any planet, times itself) is proportional to the cube of the mean distance from the sun (the average distance from the sun, times itself, and times itself again): for all planets it made exactly the same fraction! But Kepler to the end of his life believed that natural motion in the heavens was curved, and when asked why the planets kept circling (elipticing?) the sun, his answer was that there were some "fibers" coming out of the sun that moved them around their orbits.

Galileo

Galileo Galilei (1564–1642) was from Tuscany (born in Pisa, though from a Florence-based family). He lived in Florence himself as a young man working in art and design. But it was as a scientist that he really put an end to the notion of separate earthly and heavenly motion. He could roll cylinders down planks in his backyard and think about Jupiter's motion in that context. He was conservative in that he thought planetary motion was circular, not elliptical. But in 1609—after reading a description of an "optical tube" made in Holland in 1608—he made his first good telescope (maybe the first good telescope ever, 30 power magnification and better) and began looking at the night skies. So far as we know, he was the first person to see the mountains on the moon, the rings around Saturn, and the four biggest moons of Jupiter (which he wanted to call the Medician moons, for his patrons of the de' Medici family, but which we now call the Galilean satellites, after him).

In 1632 he wrote one of his most important books, *Dialogue on the Two Chief Systems of the World*. To arguments against the earth's daily rotation and yearly circling of the sun—"if we're going around at a speed of 20,000 miles/day, why isn't my hair ruffled?"—he countered with the example of a ship's cabin. There, since everything was moving in the same direction and the same speed, the captain could have a quiet bowl of soup because cabin, soup, spoon, and captain were all moving at the same speed and there was no sense of motion. It was a great teaching tool. But his ultimate proof, so he thought, was his explanation of the tides. Consider the ship, rocked by the waves and the soup sloshing a bit in the bowl—behold, the tides, as the earth's oceans rocked in their basin as the world bumbled through the forces of space. Wrong. He had nothing here about the differential gravitational attraction of water on the earth's surface versus the center of the planet. To the end of his days Galileo thought natural motion was curvilinear. But even so, he got in major trouble with the Catholic Church for not having the earth at the center of the universe. He was tried for heresy in 1633 and put under

---

67. GE Layer 67 is a Placemark referencing Brahe and Kepler's palace location on the "Prague Castle" side of town.

68. GE Layer 68 is a Placemark titled "Observatory at Benatky nad Jizerou," referencing the hilltop castle of the town.

virtual house arrest the last decade of his life.[GE69] About this time Copernicus' book on heliocentricity was placed on the Catholic index of prohibited books and stayed there until 1835, two full centuries more. It put something of a damper on subsequent Catholic scientific investigation.

Huygens, Gilbert, and Newton

While the Jesuits spread the "Brahe system" that had the planets circling the sun but the sun circling earth, the Protestants, with apologies for the pun, generally proceeded to eclipse them scientifically. Christiaan Huygens in the new Protestant state of Holland (on which more in a minute) worked out the math of centrifugal force: if a 2 lb. rock on a 3 ft. string spins once a second, what is the pull on the string? While doing so he invented the pendulum clock. William Gilbert in England figured out that electricity (he invented the word, which means "amber-like" in Greek) and magnetism were different things. He worked out the mathematics of attraction in a gravitational field—an interesting model that might help suggest a gravitational field. There were even suggestions that centrifugal force held the planets away from the sun, and some mysterious force X held them in.

Still, it took a brilliant twenty-four-year old, Isaac Newton (1642–1727), to have the ultimate insight that all motion could be explained by two concepts: *inertia* (a mass at rest stays at rest unless acted on by a force; a mass in motion goes in straight line at uniform speed unless acted on by a force) and *gravity* (masses attract proportional to their mass and inversely proportional to their distance apart). The place was Trinity College, Cambridge, [GE70] in the corner of England most impacted by Dutch Protestantism and Dutch science, on which more below. The year was 1666, and—whether or not he was inspired by a falling apple—he was young enough to still be flexible and old enough to have mastered the math and science of the day. Newton built the first reflecting telescope, mainly as an offshoot of his work with optics. He made some detailed observations of Halley's Comet in 1680–81. But his real contribution to astronomy was this theory of universal gravitation, famously published in 1687 in *Philosophiae Naturalis Principia Mathematica* (*The Mathematical Principles of Natural Philosophy*). It took him some twenty years from the original insight to write it up because among other things he had to invent calculus—which lets one compute the area under any regular curve—to prove his point. In so doing, he made solar system astronomy explainable by physics, and physics explainable by math.

Navigation transformed

Europeans could measure latitude to a nicety, north or south of the Equator. An exact reckoning of longitude was what was missing for truly scientific navigation. It promised great commercial wealth and an edge in naval warfare, and governments began to take an active interest. France set up the Paris Observatory in 1660;[GE71] Britain built the Greenwich (rhymes with "spinach") Observatory[GE72] just down the Thames from London in 1675. By century's end the Greenwich Observatory was making precision instruments that were being bought by observatories all over Europe. In the competition between states all over the world to establish the "Prime Meridian" (from which all longitude would be measured) through their capital, Britain eventually won, hence "Greenwich Mean Time." Calculating exact longitude required either such accurate astronomical prediction that one could use the heavens as a clock, or developing a super-precise clock (a chronometer) that wouldn't lose accuracy on a pitching, rolling ship. Both of those would happen in the 1700s. Back in 2003–6 we in the U.S. celebrated the bicentennial of the Lewis & Clark expedition, and many of us read in whole or part their journals. I remember reading about one or the other of them sitting patiently somewhere in the Rocky Mountains with a telescope trained on Jupiter, watch in hand to note just when a certain moon of Jupiter would

---

69. GE Layer 69 is a Placemark referencing the neighborhood of Arcetri, location of Galileo's villa where he spent the last eight years of his life under virtual house arrest. It's within a mile of the famous Boboli Gardens of south bank Florence's Pitti Palace.

70. GE Layer 70 is a Placemark generally framing a view of Trinity College buildings and greens.

71. GE Layer 71 is a Placemark referencing the Paris Observatory; click on Panoramio icon under pointer for one view of observation dome.

72. GE Layer 72 is a Placemark referencing the Greenwich Observatory.

appear from behind the planet—and thus giving both the precise time and a measure of the accuracy of the watch. It may have taken a Sacajawea to guide them there, but with a sequence of latitude-longitude pairs of figures they could allow anyone with the same technology to guide themselves there. It was a kind of power the rest of the world didn't yet have, and just one of the powers unleashed by that basic 1500–1700 period.

Holland's Glorious Century

One small Protestant state, forged in the crucible of these religious wars, would impact the world in the 1600s as dramatically as Portugal had impacted it in the 1500s. This was the United Netherlands, often just called Holland after one of its largest parts. It has crept into the narrative above with the Dutch "optic tube" of 1608 and Huygens' math of centrifugal force and the pendulum clock. Now it needs a little dedicated space of its own in this narrative.

Philip II, the son of Charles V, was King of Spain, and Portugal, and Naples-Sicily, from 1559–1598. For a time he was also king of "The Seventeen Provinces," today's Belgium, Luxemburg, the Netherlands, and bits of northern France and western Germany. In 1567 he sent a Spanish officer, the Duke of Alba, into these Seventeen Provinces to deal with unrest there—rebellion mainly coming from Protestant elements unhappy with Spain politically and Catholicism religiously. The Duke of Alba immediately set up a tribunal to take care of such rebels, and over the next decade executed an average of about a thousand people a year. The Prince of Orange, known as William the Silent, became the leader of the rebellion (the reason Dutch national soccer teams wear orange uniforms today, incidentally). He had been summoned to appear before the Duke's tribunal, but refused to appear. He represented many of those in the Lowlands who resented Spanish rule and who were concerned about the persecution of Protestants, and he was already a famous administrator. By 1568 he was leading an armed uprising against the Spanish that generally counts as the beginning of the "80 Years' War." Although his armies found it hard to maintain themselves against the huge Spanish military machine, soon Protestant refugees calling themselves "The Sea Beggars" manned a fleet that actually defeated the local Spanish fleet. In 1572 the Beggars captured their first mainland base, not far from Rotterdam, and raised the flag of the House of Orange. A general rising of the northern part of the seventeen provinces elected him "Stadtholder." He led a desperate defense of the maritime provinces of Zeeland and Holland for the next four years, and by 1579 (in the Union of Utrecht) an independent republic had begun to come into being. William the Silent was assassinated by a Catholic in 1584, but his second son became Stadtholder after him, and consolidated his hold on all those territories north of the main mouths of the River Rhine. The Dutch call this "the closing of the garden;" by 1587 the United Netherlands had taken final shape.[GE73] Meanwhile England had oscillated from Protestant to Catholic and back to Protestant in the Tudor Dynasty, from Henry VIII to his daughter Mary to his daughter Elizabeth. In 1588, of course, a now firmly Protestant England (and the weather) destroyed Philip II's enormous Spanish Armada, and Protestant Europe, including Holland, got some time to establish itself.

Supporting all the Dutch military activity, and in parallel with it, was a remarkable economic expansion. The Dutch had always been important in the shipping and fishing part of the seventeen Provinces, but now Amsterdam totally eclipsed Antwerp, which had been the major regional port. So many political and religious refugees from Antwerp settled in Amsterdam that it was called half-jokingly "New Antwerp." With gang saws (multiple saws) run by those famous Dutch windmills, they could ripsaw logs into planks for ship construction much, much faster than the Portuguese could "rive" (split out and then plane) their planks. Dutch ships and the coastal "flyboats" looked slow, with their bluff bows, but they were extremely cheap to make, more seaworthy than they looked, and were manned by some of Europe's best sailors. Soon the Dutch were carrying the lion's share of coastal European trade.

With independence, small groups of (Protestant) Dutch businessmen immediately began challenging the (Catholic) Portuguese hold of trade routes east. In 1602 the Dutch government insisted that these Dutch firms

---

73. GE Layer 73 is a Placemark framing a view of today's Netherlands. Although there was a good bit of border changing from 1579 to today's borders—sometimes larger, sometimes smaller—the present borders are a reasonable approximation of those of the original United Netherlands.

quit competing with each other and unite as one government-protected monopoly called the VOC, from *Vereenigde Oostindische Companie*, or United East-India Company.[GE74] Some economists call this the world's first real joint stock company: investors committed to the entire enterprise for a five-year term, not just to a single ship or a single trading voyage. Presided over by a board of directors called the Gentlemen Seventeen (*Heeren XVII*), the VOC spearheaded Holland's "Glorious Century."

In 1596 the Dutch had made their first successful trading voyage to the "spice islands" (generally today's eastern Indonesia). After 1602 they systematically began to blow the Portuguese out of key forts. They took Ambon,[GE75] which controlled the whole nutmeg and clove trade of the spice islands, in 1605, and captured Batavia,[GE76] to be their main base on Java, in 1619. They captured Elmina (St. George of the Mine),[GE77] as you've seen the key Portuguese fort on the coast of today's Ghana, in 1637. They took the fort of Malacca[GE78] that controlled the strait of Malacca from the Portuguese in 1641. That same year they won from the Japanese, alone of all Europeans, the rights to a trading station in Japan (the little peninsula of Deshima[GE79] in Nagasaki harbor). They captured Colombo[GE80] and many other major coastal forts on the great island of Sri Lanka in the 1650s. The one great navigational trick they added to the general Portuguese repertoire was to sail "under the monsoon" when going east from Africa's Cape of Good Hope. It let them run in the generally reliable Westerlies, or Roaring 'Forties latitudes, no matter which way the monsoon winds were blowing in the Indian Ocean north of them. Plus, at 40 degrees or more south latitude, a degree of longitude was only three-fourths as long (in miles) as at the Equator, meaning they could "run off" their easterly longitude more quickly. All they had to do was ride those southern hemisphere Westerlies to just short of Australia's west coast, then turn north for the Sunda Strait[GE81] that separates Sumatra from Java. That put them in the Java Sea, where they could head east to the Spice Islands or north to China and Japan.

A century of virtually total domination of inter-European trade, European-Asian trade, and inter-Asian trade—most of the world's trade!—generated incredible wealth. That in turn supported the fabulous Dutch artistic renaissance associated with Vermeer and Rembrandt, and the scientific and intellectual developments associated with Leeuwenhoek and Huygens and with the persecuted foreign intellectuals who found shelter there, such as Descartes and Spinoza (the latter born in Amsterdam, though his parents were Jewish refugees from the Inquisition in Portugal).

American footnote: the Dutch in New Amsterdam, the Pilgrims in Leiden

All this had a direct bearing on American history, of course. In 1609, the Englishman Henry Hudson, sailing for the Dutch, discovered the river that bears his name. By 1623 the Dutch had built Fort Orange (today's Albany), a trading post 150 miles up the Hudson, and in 1625 they built the substantial "Fort Amsterdam" on lower Manhattan Island. In a few decades they had a thriving colony here in "New Amsterdam" (today's Wall Street is named for the northern wall of the settlement).

In 1608, the year before Hudson discovered his river, Leiden, Holland,[GE82] was a university town of 40,000 or so, open-minded on religion and ethnicity even by Holland's generally tolerant standards. In that year about 400 extreme English Puritans, known as Separatists for their refusal to be part of the official Church of

---

74. GE Layer 74 is a Placemark referencing the old VOC headquarters in Amsterdam, today a living historical museum mainly dedicated to the VOC.

75. GE Layer 75 is a Placemark referencing Ambon.

76. GE Layer 76 is a Placemark referencing Batavia (today's Jakarta).

77. GE Layer 77 is a Placemark referencing Elmina.

78. GE Layer 78 is a Placemark referencing Malacca (today's Melaka).

79. GE Layer 79 is a Placemark referencing the original site of Deshima.

80. GE Layer 80 is a Placemark referencing Colombo.

81. GE Layer 81 is a Path marking the Sunda Strait with a red line.

82. GE Layer 82 is a Placemark referencing the famous University of Leiden (Leyden). It was established in 1575 by Stadtholder William of Orange because the northern provinces, breaking away as a separate Protestant state, had no university of their own.

England under James I, came there to settle. They did find general freedom of worship there, and lived in a fairly tight-knit community. A decade later, however, these rural and small-town English folk were still not used to the fast-paced commercial life of the Dutch city, which meant dawn to dusk employment six days a week, fifty-two weeks a year. The current truce with Spain was due to expire soon, and it was possible war would devastate the city once again. Perhaps worst of all, they could see their children gradually becoming Dutch. So in July of 1620 most of these English Separatists in Leiden uprooted themselves yet again. They sailed from nearby Delfshaven in a misnamed little ship called the *Speedwell*, to rendezvous on the south coast of England with a larger ship their agents had hired called the *Mayflower*. The two started off across the Atlantic several times, but came back to the southern shore of England either because of headwinds or to deal with leaks in the *Speedwell*. The last time was at Plymouth, fifty miles west of Dartmouth, where they decided *Speedwell* just couldn't make the trip, and so crowded as many as they could on the *Mayflower*. They were heading for Hudson's river, but made landfall on Cape Cod and didn't have supplies enough to sail on south. By year's end they were ashore in mainland Massachusetts, advance guard of the Puritan tide that would flow in strongly from 1629–1641 to escape King Charles I's Long Parliament and purge of Puritans from the Anglican Church.[10] The rest, as they say, is history. I wonder if we Americans, in our democratic proceedings that partly began with the Pilgrims, still say "all opposed by *nay*" because that's the pronunciation of the Dutch word for "no."

But to end this subchapter on a more relevant note, what happened in the Protestant-Catholic rivalry of these two centuries from 1500–1700 was that Europe generally forged into the intellectual leadership of the world. I know, for example, that my own field of history was transformed by this rivalry. The early Protestants began attacking the Catholics historically, asking what was the source of the institutional power claimed by the Catholic Church. It took Catholics awhile to recognize the direction of this new attack, but when they did, they had all the resources of the Vatican Library to work with. This period, with both Protestant and Catholic scholars, is where careful modern textual criticism and some of the greatest collection of historical documents originated. In general, such intellectual leadership in many fields also made for the growth of European power, as in navigation or the casting of cannon.

PART THREE: INDUSTRIAL REVOLUTION, IMPERIAL POWER circa 1700–1900

Why Britain?

Around or about 1780 in Great Britain the gently rising graph of human production of goods over the preceding centuries rather suddenly took a steep upward turn, which we're still riding in the twenty-first century. Why in Britain, and why then? We know the classical Romans had model steam engines. Was slave labor just so cheap for them they didn't need to develop the real things?

One ingredient you've just seen: by the 1700s the British (with Isaac Newton spectacularly leading the way) were at the cutting edge of world scientific development. There are some other interesting factors that all came together in Britain, many of them surely coincidental. A second ingredient is that the Brits were among the first Europeans to use up their forests, and be driven to use coal, of which they had lots. Coal is bulky, and cries out for new forms of transport. Ground water tends to seep into coal mines the deeper one digs, and a new coal-fired power source (how convenient) could assist in pumping it out. The way charcoal, made from the partial burning of wood, burns hotter than wood itself, so coke burns hotter than its parent coal, and a lot hotter than charcoal, which opens up interesting avenues for transforming metals. Third, the weather for farming in the mid-1700s in Britain was excellent, and the bigger farmers had savings put away that could be used for buying Jamaican sugar plantations and the slaves to work them, or for, say, backing some crazy new idea for production or transportation involving steam and iron. Fourth, the Dissidents (Protestants outside the official state Church of England) were frozen out of many traditional routes of high advancement, including attending the Oxford or Cambridge colleges, and perhaps as a result tended to get into more innovative enterprises. Fifth, by the 1750s the British East India Company had gained control of a sizeable block of South Asia, mostly in today's eastern India and Bangladesh—which in the coming decades meant upwards of 100,000,000 customers under wraps if British manufacturers could just find something they wanted. Coincidental many of these elements all may have been, but coming together they transformed not just Britain but the world.

One way to get a quick handle on major developments of the Industrial Revolution might be to use a "successive bottleneck" approach. Often some obstacle to development becomes clear to most everyone, and fame and fortune await whosoever solves it. Today, for example, arguably the greatest obstacle to economic development is cheap, clean energy. Fossil fuels are finite and burning them adds to greenhouse gases. Nuclear energy of the fissionable kind that we now use is generally solidly reliable but not cheap, is potentially deadly in its waste by-products, and is subject to catastrophic failure in case of earthquake, tsunami, or terrorism. Wind, tidal, and other "renewable" sources of power are not available everywhere, can't just be turned on when we need them, and don't store well. Nuclear fusion, however, which releases power but no radioactive by-products, would seem to fit the bill, so "room-temperature fusion" is the holy grail of today's energy search. Take a day or so off from school or work, brainstorm and solve the problem; you'll be a billionaire in a year and on the cover of news magazines worldwide. Now take this model back to history of the Industrial Revolution. In hindsight, at least, it's fairly easy to identify such critical bottlenecks and their solution. They more or less spiraled up through three parallel and closely interconnected fields—textile manufacture, steam power, and metallurgy.

Textiles

South Asians loved cotton cloth, naturally enough since they were the ones who had domesticated cotton around 4,000 years ago. Many common English names for types and patterns of such cloth come to us directly or indirectly from South Asia—for example, *calico* from the port of Calicut, *madras* from port of Madras, *chintz* from the Hindi word for variegated (complex colors and pattern), *muslin* from the Tigris River city of Mosul in today's Iraq, but for cloth that came through there from South Asia. The British knew something about making woolen cloth, but there was no—repeat, no—market for wool in Calcutta, which can hit 115° F. on a good May day. So they went to work with cotton cloth, in the weaving of which generally speaking there were four processes: carding the cotton (combing the fibers straight and making them into long, thin hanks called "rovings"); a first "soft" spinning of the rovings to make thread; a second much tighter "hard" spinning to make a stronger thread, and then weaving it on a loom. All they needed to do was do one or more of those things more cheaply than the abundant hand labor of South Asia, including the transportation costs of the cotton from wherever it grew (not in Britain!) and of the cloth itself to South Asia.

The first to fame and fortune was Richard Arkwright. In the mid-1760s he developed a machine that carded, produced a continuous "rovings" of carded fibers, and spun soft thread from it all at the same time. It was a marvel, but it took such power that humans and soon even horses were not enough to revolve all the complicated machinery. So in 1771 he and a partner built what seems to have been the first water-powered textile mill in the world at Cromford, on the little Derwent River in Derbyshire.[GE83] Most of England's water power, to forecast a bit, would come like Cromford Mill's from streams running off the Pennine mountains. [GE84] Arkwright added the "hard" spinning that made the thread strong enough for the warp threads of a loom (weft threads woven through the warp can be much weaker). He went on to build dozens of mills in England and Scotland, and from these and his patents he amassed a huge fortune and got himself knighted in 1786. He died in 1792 at age 59, awaiting the completion of a castle he had ordered up and for which he probably paid cash (this—the castle, not the relatively early death—to inspire you in your quest for room-temperature fusion).

James Hargreaves built his first "spinning jenny" just when Arkwright got started, in the mid-1760s. At first it spun eight threads at once. A workman would pull a few feet of rovings out with a bar, then set all the spindles in motion, and when he thought the eight parallel threads were twisted enough, slow the spindles to wind that few feet of thread on them, pull a few more feet of rovings out, and so on. The thread that resulted

83. GE Layer 83 is a Placemark titled "Cromford Mill," referencing the historic buildings; several interesting Photos icons to explore. The Derwent River runs across the top of the view, and Cromford Canal heads from the mill buildings towards lower right of screen.

84. GE Layer 84 is a Folder titled "The Pennines." It contains a Polygon in bright green outline generally encompassing the Pennine mountains, and a Path in purple marking the general route of today's famous hiking trail, The Pennine Way. Turn on the whole folder at once. Zooming in on the southern end of the Pennines will pop up some famous industrial towns: Manchester, Stoke-on-Trent, Sheffield, Leeds.

was not strong—only suitable for weft—but the jenny was amazingly productive, especially when the original eight simultaneously-revolving spindles became over a hundred. By 1779 Arkwright's device and Hargreaves' "jenny" had been combined into a "mule." The first dramatic bottleneck—fast and cheap production of cotton thread—had been broken through.

Now everybody was waiting on the weavers, while the spools of thread piled up. In 1784 Edmund Cartwright, a country clergyman, visited one of Arkwright's factories and was inspired by seeing the spinning machines there to invent a weaving machine, a power loom. He did indeed, though he never really solved some of the basic problems—how the warp threads continually tighten as the weft is woven in, when tension needs to remain the same for the cloth to be uniform, for example—and didn't become rich in actual business. But he did become famous, and in 1809 a grateful British Parliament voted him a tidy £10,000 for having started this whole power loom business. His prototype may have been crude, but it had proven capable of almost infinite refinement, over time.

Steam

By 1712 there was a functioning steam engine, albeit primitive, called the Newcomen engine. A large cast iron cylinder fitted with a piston had steam injected into it, which pushed the piston, which pushed whatever the piston was attached to (usually a lever for hoisting water out of a mine). Then the steam inside the cylinder slowly cooled, and the piston slowly, slowly returned to the base of the cylinder. Then and only then was a new burst of steam introduced, and the piston pushed up again. It was a steam engine, but it wasn't until James Watt got hold of it that you really got the age of steam. Not for nothing is our basic unit of (electrical) power, worldwide, called a "watt."

James Watt was a Scot, and a good bit of the science of "thermodynamics" (heat transfer) came from Scotland. Quick answer, now: what is Scotland's most famous commodity export? If you said tartans, plaids, tam o'shanters or bagpipes, I suppose it would be an understandable mistake, but the correct answer of course is Scotch, a specialized kind of whiskey. Every second town in Scotland seems to have its own distillery. The distillation process involves taking the product of some natural fermentation, such as beer, and then boiling the whole mixture in a closed container with a copper pipe leading out of it. With its low boiling point the alcohol boils off first, and is condensed in the copper pipe which is immersed in cold water (I write these lines from my present location at the southern end of the Appalachians, where Scots-Irish-inspired stills were once common and still turn up occasionally). It takes a lot of heat to do such boiling. Fuel is at a premium in Scotland, and the people in this picturesque but generally bare and windswept land are famously frugal. So it was Scots, inspired in part if not mainly by the whiskey business, who first carefully measured heat transfer (which is why the rest of us still buy our air conditioners by BTUs, British Thermal Units).

James Watt (1736–1819) was taught house and ship construction by his father and math and Greek by his mother. He went for a time to Glasgow and then London to learn how to be a scientific instrument maker (of compasses, quadrants, balances, and such). When he was twenty-one he set up shop in Glasgow, mainly making instruments for the faculty of the university there.[GE[85]] In 1764, while repairing a Newcomen engine for one of the university labs, it hit him that you could exhaust the steam to a separate condenser instead of waiting for it to cool down inside the cylinder. This not only meant you could immediately start another piston stroke, but that you didn't waste all that heat each time by having the cylinder cool down. With help from one of the university's professors, he built a model of such a steam engine and in 1769 took out a patent on it. Nothing much came of it at first, partly because Watt had embarked on a new career as land surveyor. But Matthew Boulton, a metal manufacturer in Birmingham, bought into Watt's sagging business and pumped new energy into it and James Watt, too. At his urging Watt invented a rotary engine, turning the linear movement of the piston into circular motion. Watt also invented the process of injecting steam on both sides of the piston, alternately, radically increasing both its speed and its power. This last invention was patented in 1781, as good as any a year to pinpoint the take-off of the industrial revolution.

---

85. GE Layer 85 is a Placemark referencing Glasgow University. Zoom out to see relationship to downtown, Clyde River.

It came at a good time, because Britain had just about used up every site suitable for water-run mills, along those little rivers that ran off the north-south Pennines. With a steam engine you didn't need a white-water river, just a fuel source, and the orders for them piled up. By 1790 James Watt too was a very wealthy man.

Metallurgy

Metallurgy has already begun to seep into this narrative, as with Matthew Boulton's partnering with Watt. But let's go back a little earlier.

The Darbys were a family of English Quakers—more Dissidents, from the point of view of the Church of England. They began their metallurgical work by 1700 or so, producing cast brass cookware in Bristol, the big English port city near the estuary of the Severn River.[GE86] Their key early innovation was to smelt copper ore with the hot-burning coke, which proved both cheaper and faster than using charcoal. Within a decade they were working with cast iron the same way, at a place up the Severn River called Coalbrookdale[GE87] that had low-sulfur coal. They made a lot of cast iron cookware, but over the next few decades they also cast more than 100 Newcomen engine cylinders. In 1780 the grandson of the first metallurgical Darby built the famous Iron Bridge[GE88] across the Severn near Coalbrookdale—ever after the poster child of the Industrial Revolution.

John Wilkinson (1728–1808) was the son of a Dissident (Presbyterian) cast iron foundryman who had been one of the first to use the original Darby's coke-fired smelting of iron. By his late '20s John was a partner in his own blast furnace two or three miles south of Coalbrookdale. His famous Bersham works developed a new and more accurate way of boring the barrels of iron cannon, rotating the whole cannon instead of the borer, making for a much more uniform interior cylinder and therefore a much more accurate cannon. But the same technology benefitted the steam engine as well, since a more uniform cylinder made for much less leakage of steam. He became the main supplier of such cylinders to Boulton & Watt, and was a major supporter of the Iron Bridge built by the third Darby—so interconnected were all these strands of the developing industrial revolution. He too became fantastically rich, mainly known in his later years for surrounding himself with everything he could made of iron, including his own coffin.

All of the above both made possible and set in motion a transportation revolution. The first stage of it was the canal-building mania that began in the 1770s to haul the bulky coal and heavy iron. Even today, for a few hundred British pounds a week you can rent yourself and friends a 7' wide, 50' long canal barge, or narrowboat, and wend yourself (at a leisurely 4 m.p.h., opening canal locks on your own by hand) all over southern England, from London on up through Oxford and deep into the English Midlands.[GE89] It was state-of-the-art, horse-drawn, cheap bulk transportation in the late 1700s, but time was money as the industrial revolution progressed, which of course led to railroads and steamboats. They in turn had great appetites for coal and iron, and so the whole industrial process logically drove itself faster and faster.

There was a steam engine on wheels which ran on wrought iron rails as early as 1802. The most famous early example was the *Rocket*, winner of the 1829 contest to pick an engine for the nearly-completed Liverpool and Manchester Railway.[GE90] It had two cylinders pushing two drive wheels, and a couple of major innovations—lots of small tubes for boiling water instead of one large container, for speed of boiling, and

---

86. GE Layer 86 is a Folder titled "Bristol and the Severn River." Bristol is shown as a yellow pushpin Placemark icon, the Severn as an aqua Path.

87. GE Layer 87 is a Placemark referencing Coalbrookdale; click on Panoramio icon under pointer, with the Chamber of Commerce style title "Coalbrookdale: The birthplace of modern industry."

88. GE Layer 88 is a Placemark referencing Ironbridge; click on Photos icon under pointer of same name for good view of the carefully renovated structure.

89. GE Layer 89 is a Folder containing Paths showing in purple some of the canals that cross in and around the single Midlands city of Birmingham; zoom in on yellow pushpin icon, "Narrowboat in lock," for close-up of same (though you'll have to go to the View dropdown menu, and turn on "Historical Imagery" to use a slide bar to click back to it).

90. GE Layer 90 is a Folder titled Manchester to Liverpool. It includes a Path in purple that at least roughly symbolizes the line between Manchester and Liverpool; it's right at seventeen miles long. It also includes a Placemark at Stephenson's Bridge, one of the few still-identifiable sites (at least on the Google Earth screen!) along the old 1829 route.

shooting the cylinder exhaust up the main smokestack to create enough vacuum to suck a sharp draft of air through the firebox, which of course is why steam locomotives puff. The railway was built mainly to transport goods from mill town Manchester to Liverpool port, but when it opened in 1830 it also carried passengers—the first train with regularly scheduled departures and arrivals! By the 1840s railroad lines were pushing through the whole industrial world, and by the 1850s began to be introduced into the colonies. Creation of a railroad was of great importance on every one of the seven non-European regional transportation corridors we'll see in the second half of the book.

Steamships also originated in the first decade of the 1800s, with Fulton's *Clermont* steam-driven paddle-wheeler going up and down New York's Hudson River as early as 1807. The specific development of the river gunboat is given below, but steam power for ocean transport deserves a general word here. Given the properties of steam, as in driving a piston engine, it turns out that all the power in the steam is not used up in going through a single engine. By mid-19th century there were compound (two, at first) engines through which the steam was run, and later in the century the steam engine came to its perfection in the triple-expansion engine. First the steam was run through a small-cylinder, high-pressure engine, then through a medium-sized-cylinder, medium-pressure engine, and finally through a large-sized-cylinder, low-pressure engine—thus milking the steam of every last horsepower. With such an engine in a large ship, the energy released by burning a single sheet of notebook paper could move a ton of goods a mile.

The Crystal Palace

Taken altogether this was break-through technology, most noticeable in power generation, transportation and communication, and metallurgy. It also had behind it new ways to mobilize financial resources, usually summed up as "capitalism" (on which whole libraries have been written, but we'll just leave it at this until the Russia and Socialism chapter). Just as important was a new attitude of the British and other European governments towards the business classes, the ones using this new technology to generate amazing new wealth and reverse all balance of trade problems. In 1851 Britain staged its "Great Exhibition of the Works of Industry of all Nations" in Hyde Park, London. An iron-framed glass exhibition hall, several stories high and grandiosely called The Crystal Palace, was specially built to house it.[GE[91]] Despite the exhibition's name, it was really a celebration of British industry, with the rest of the world invited mainly to show the contrast. In this year Britain was generating approximately half the total Gross National Product of the whole world. That was close to the peak of British preeminence, because by that time France and the U.S., to be joined very soon by Germany, began to become competitive industrially. But so far as the rest of the world was concerned, that new wealth and power developed by the industrial revolution would translate very quickly into a new level of European intrusion. Half of this was the wave of inexpensive but high-quality industrial goods that would flood the world. Karl Marx, in his *Communist Manifesto* written in late 1847, had at least this part of his analysis of modern world history right:

> The bourgeoisie, by the rapid improvement of all instruments of production, by the immensely facilitated means of communication, draws all, even the most barbarian, nations into civilization. The cheap prices of its commodities are the heavy artillery with which it batters down all Chinese walls, with which it forces the barbarians' intensely obstinate hatred of foreigners to capitulate.[11]

But the other half of this power was heavy artillery (and all its technological kin) of the actual, not metaphorical, kind.

Tools of Empire, Tentacles of Progress

During the 1980s History professor Daniel Headrick wrote a couple of remarkable books, published by Oxford University Press, the full titles of which sum up, or at least broadly hint at, the whole process. First came *The*

---

91. GE Layer 91 is a Placemark referencing the location of the 1851 Crystal Palace in Hyde Park. For dozens of paintings and old photographs of the building, do a Google—Images search of "Crystal Palace."

Tools of Empire: Technology and European Imperialism in the Nineteenth Century, dealing mainly with weapons and steam transportation, Suez Canals and undersea cables—in a word, what enabled Europeans to get to and control other parts of the world. His second book of the decade was *The Tentacles of Progress: Technology Transfer in the Age of Imperialism, 1850–1940*. Here, using India for example, British-style harbors, railroad and telegraph networks, schools for technical education, and even the Calcutta sewage project came to be—in a word, how European technology was introduced into the colonies mainly for the purpose of extracting profit for the mother country. Several of the examples in the section below are drawn from those works.[12]

Gunboats

"Gunboat" in its nineteenth and early twentieth century sense meant not just any boat with guns but a shallow-draft, heavily armored river steamer. Shallow draft meant drawing only five or six feet of water when battle ready, so it could get over the shallow bars that usually form at the mouth of rivers. Water-tight steel hull construction and steel shielding above deck was a new development defensively, and offensively it was especially heavily gunned for its size. It was powered by steam (later diesel) engines, turning side-mounted paddle-wheels (later stern propellors). It was the single most powerful tool in the European conquest of virtually all of the world's navigable rivers.

The first commercially successful steamboat was probably Robert Fulton's *Clermont*, launched in 1807, that as we've seen ran up and down the Hudson River between New York City and Albany. It was noisy and clanky ("the devil on his way to Albany in a sawmill"), but it worked, against current, and wind, and tide. By the 1820s American and western European rivers were so alive with steamboats that they no longer attracted much attention. It was at the (expanding) interface between European and non-European spheres of influence that they became most dramatic game-changers, especially as ordinary river steamers evolved into gunboats.

By 1824 the British East India Company, supported more and more by the British government, had spent three-quarters of a century carving out a commercial and territorial empire in India. In that year the Company, headquartered in Calcutta/Kolkata in Bengal, went to war with the Kingdom of Burma. Although Burma was just east of Bengal, it was sheltered by mountains too rugged over which to mount much of a land offensive. The most obvious route of invasion was up the Irrawaddy River[GE92] from the seaport of Rangoon (today's Yangon)[GE93] to the capital of Ava[GE94]—some 340 straight line miles and a lot more as the river wound. Although the British had superior firepower, they were no match for the Burmese guerrilla warriors in the swamps of the delta, and lost a good fraction of their army there. On the river the Burmese war boats were 90' long, slim and fast boats with perhaps seventy paddlers. They had small cannon lashed into their bows, and could dash in and get off a shot or two and dash out again, faster than the British could sail after them. When the wind was right the Burmese would send fire ships drifting down on the British fleet, no joking matter to those on ships made mostly of wood, canvas, and tar-saturated rope.

It was the steamboat *Diana* that turned things around. Built in the Kidderpore yard adjoining Calcutta in 1823 to work as a harbor tug, she was outfitted with swivel cannon and Congreve rockets (the same as those used at Baltimore's Fort McHenry a dozen years earlier, as in "the rockets' red glare") and thus made into a primitive early gunboat, and sent to Burma in 1824. In Headrick's words, she became the star of the show: ". . . she towed sailing ships into position, transported troops, reconnoitered advance positions, and bombarded Burmese fortifications. . . ." On top of this she ran down the fast Burmese riverboats because eventually their crews would tire, whereas the steam engines would not. The *Diana* led the British fleet upriver until by February of 1826 they captured Amarapura, the closest river city to Ava, which was about five miles away from the main Irrawaddy. At this point the Burmese king sued for peace, giving Assam—the eastern third of his realm—to the East India Company. Soon even the rest of Burma would just be a province of "British India."

---

92. GE Layer 92 is a Folder called "Irrawady River and delta," which can be turned on all at once. The delta shows as a light blue wash, and the river as a darker aqua line.

93. GE Layer 93 is a Placemark referencing Rangoon/Yangon.

94. GE Layer 94 is a Placemark referencing Ava.

John and McGregor Laird were a father-son team of manufacturers, Scots who had come down to Liverpool and built the Birkenhead Iron Works.[GE95] It produced steel-hulled steamships that greatly interested the British government for use in its imperial wars. It was the Lairds who built the star of the second generation of gunboats, the *Nemesis*, launched at Birkenhead in January of 1840. It was the first true gunboat. The largest iron ship built to date, it was of 184' length, 29' beam, 11' feet deep, drawing only 5' draft in battle trim. Two 60 hp engines powered it, one to a covered paddle wheel on each side, with these side-wheels located about two-thirds of the way back towards the stern. It had heavy armament for a ship so small: two 32-pounder swivel cannon, five brass 6-pounders, ten smaller cannon, and a rocket launcher. It had seven watertight compartments, and two sliding keels. The only things wooden about it were the flooring of the deck and a mast both fore and aft for supplemental power from sails, should the wind be favorable.

The *Nemesis* left Portsmouth on England's southern shore on March 28, 1840, with a top-secret destination—which was of course correctly guessed by reporters for *The Times* of London and published a couple of days later, namely China and the Opium Wars. In brief, in the early 1800s the British had a huge balance of trade deficit with China, since they mainly imported such luxuries as tea, porcelain, silks, and lacquerware and paid for it with gold and silver. By the 1830s they had essentially solved their balance of trade problem by smuggling opium into south China. What resulted was a three-cornered trade as efficient, and at base almost as destructive, as the three-cornered industrial goods-rum-slaves trade in the Atlantic. In this new triangle industrial goods would come from England to India, opium from eastern India would be smuggled into southern China, and luxury goods from China would go to England, with a neat profit turned on every leg.

Opium took a heavy toll on the richer classes in south China, and the Chinese government—intelligently—decided to do something about it. In 1839 it sent a special governor-general down to Canton/Guangzhou to end the trade. His forces boarded western ships and seized the opium and destroyed it, which you might think the Chinese had a right to do. But a great cry went up that British territory had been violated (the decks of British ships), giving a patriotic luster to a war that was really about business profits from a very destructive trade. The resulting war, begun in that same 1839, saw the British fleet and a few thousand marines unable to make much impact on China. Until the arrival of the *Nemesis*.

The *Nemesis* was the first iron ship to steam round the Cape of Africa. She confounded all her critics who predicted she would attract lightning or boil her crew alive in the tropics. After a stop in Delagoa Bay, heading up the East Africa coast, she had a brush with a coral reef and ripped a hole in the hull—but just flooded one of the watertight compartments. The ship was careened and patched, and steamed off without other incident—to Sri Lanka by early October, and then Macau (at the lower end of the long bay with Canton at its head)[GE96] by November 25, 1840. At this point the *Nemesis* transformed the war more completely than the *Diana* had done the Burmese war. She destroyed the forts guarding the narrow Bogue (mouth)[GE97] of upper Canton bay, steamed at will in shallow waters, and actually bombarded the city from behind, where no foreign warship had ever appeared. When fire-rafts were sent downwind on the British fleet, the *Nemesis* grappled and towed them away. When there was still no sign of Chinese surrender, the *Nemesis*, towing a huge British warship, led the British fleet into the mouth of the Yangtze River.[GE98] They quickly blew away all defenses to Shanghai, and headed upriver another 180 miles or so to where the Grand Canal [GE99]—built to supply Beijing ("North Capital") with rice—crossed the Yangtze River. The *Nemesis* pulled sailing warships off sandbars, towed becalmed ships one by one to the next station upriver, and in July of 1842 reached and captured Zhenjiang,[GE100] a river town at the crossing of the Grand Canal. Nanjing, "South Capital," was just another fifty miles upriver, and the British could clearly take it in short order.

---

95. GE Layer 95 is a Placemark in the general vicinity of Birkenhead.

96. GE Layer 96 is a Placemark referencing Macau, framing a view of its relationship to the great estuary today called the Zhujiang River Estuary.

97. GE Layer 97 is a Placemark framing a view of the Bogue, the upper narrows of the bay, at lower right, and Canton (Guangzhou) city in upper left.

98. GE Layer 98 is a Path showing the Yangtze in aqua, framing a view of the lower course of the river.

99. GE Layer 99 is a Path showing the general course of the Grand Canal, and framing a view of its crossing of the Yangtze.

100. GE Layer 100 is a Placemark referencing Zhenjiang.

At this point the Chinese government in Beijing sued for peace, sending a delegation to Nanjing to negotiate and sign "The Treaty of Nanking," as the city name was transliterated in those days. It is called an "unequal treaty," and a quick list of terms reveals why:

1. Britain got Hong Kong,[GE101] an island off the northern corner of the Pearl River estuary that sheltered the best deep-water harbor in Asia. This would be the "wrist" of British control of China.
2. Britain got rights to five "treaty ports,"[GE102] from Canton in the south to Shanghai in the north; land was allotted to the British there totally under their control, with full trading rights. These were to be the "fingers" of the British grasp.
3. China agreed to a tariff—a tax on imported goods—of no more than 5 percent.
4. China agreed to give Britain "Most Favored Nation" status (MFN for short); that is, if China granted any other power any right Britain didn't already have, Britain automatically picked it up too.
5. China gave the British "extraterritoriality" (extrality for short); that is, if any Brit was accused of a crime in China, he would be tried in British law courts, not Chinese.
6. The Chinese had to pay the British an enormous indemnity—200,000 ounces of silver—to compensate the British for the cost of the war.

And of course the one thing not mentioned in this treaty that ended the Opium Wars was opium, the trade in which would still be carried on by the British to the detriment of Chinese society.

This 1842 "unequal treaty," incidentally, would be a model for European and Europeanized powers in future years. We in the U.S., along with France, demanded and got from China many of those same terms two years later in 1844, and in 1854 we of the U.S. (in the person of Commodore Perry) forced similar terms on Japan, as you'll see in detail in a later chapter.

Gunboats dominated the world's navigable rivers for the next century and more. They made it into literature; here are just a couple of examples from an extensive list. Joseph Conrad's *Heart of Darkness* was written around 1900 but based on a trip up the Congo River in 1890 on which he was reserve pilot on an armored river steamer. Most of the novel takes place on such a trip, including one particularly vivid scene of the gunboat being ambushed with arrows and spears from the forest when the channel on the outside of a curve threw the gunboat near the shore. The steel shutters came down, and the passengers opened up on that patch of forest with Winchester and Martini-Henry rifles. *Sand Pebbles*, a 1962 novel by an American author that was later made into a movie, was set aboard an American gunboat (the *San Pablo*, hence its crew's nickname the sand pebbles) on the Yangtze River on or about 1926.

Rifles and machine guns

Speaking of firearms, their quick evolution under the influence of the industrial revolution is equally striking.

For the first few decades of the nineteenth century, the common firearm of a European soldier was still the muzzle-loading musket. To reload, he had to be standing up or at least kneeling, and perform several operations including the pouring in of a measured dose of powder, and the pushing down the barrel of a patch and ball. If he could get off two shots a minute, he was a prodigy. When he did fire, smoke from the black powder (a) obscured his view, depending on the wind; and (b) showed his exact location to the enemy from great distance. Artillery was just a larger version of this.

The first regular issue breech-loader was the Dreyse needle-gun used by the Prussian army by the late 1840s. The top half of the end of the barrel nearest the shooter had been sawn away, and here a paper cartridge (containing powder, percussion cap, and bullet) could be placed, with a bolt-operated mechanism to close the firing chamber. Then, while still lying down, the soldier could fire, getting off as many as eight shots a min-

---

101. GE Layer 101 is a Polygon outline in red showing Hong Kong island (later Hong Kong) included Kowloon and the New Territories on the mainland, framed in white outline as framed in this view on Google Earth.
102. GE Layer 102 is a Folder containing Placemarks (shown as orange stars) for each of the five Treaty Ports; westerners knew them by these names in the nineteenth century: Canton, Amoy, Fuchow, Ningpo, and Shanghai.

ute—a huge jump in infantry firepower. It had some problems. The needle that plunged in through paper and powder and ignited the cap at the base of the bullet tended to burn off at the end, for one. Two, the locking mechanism didn't seal the barrel well, and especially as black powder residue fouled the barrel, sparks shot out the cracks to the extent that you could tell a good Dreyse man by scorched right eyebrow. Since flinching at the moment of squeezing the trigger is generally not good for one's aim, accuracy undoubtedly declined with fouling of the barrel.

The first really classic single-shot rifle, however, was the British Martini-Henry of the late 1860s. It was bolt action, introducing a brass cartridge housing to both seal the barrel at time of firing and keep the ammunition waterproof to a certain extent. It used smokeless powder, keeping advertisement of the shooter's whereabouts to a minimum while not obscuring his vision. Within a decade other European classics followed, including the German Mauser, probably the best of them all. And artillery followed suit, rifled for accuracy, breech-loading for speed, smokeless powder for its advantages of being able to see and not be seen.

The next major development was the so-called "machine gun." An intermediary step towards it was the "semi-automatic" rifle, one that tapped some of the gas explosion of a shot and used it to eject the empty hull and jack a new round into the firing chamber. This way every time a shooter pulled the trigger, there was a round already loaded for him, without any effort on his part. The German Ferdinand Mannlicher developed the first of these in 1885. The final step to a fully automatic weapon, or machine gun, came quickly thereafter. There had been heavy and clumsy machine guns since before the U.S. Civil War—the Gatling Gun, for example, with multiple barrels that revolved while an empty hull was ejected, a fresh round inserted, a firing phase of the cycle and then repeat. But the first true light-weight, single-barreled machine gun was patented in 1888 by the American inventor Hiram Maxim. It could get off eleven rounds a second, so close together you couldn't hear the individual explosions, just a continual roar. The U.S. army was not yet interested, so it was the British army which first contracted for and used it.

To see the impact of this first real machine gun on European versus non-European conflicts, all you have to do is compare the 1885 Battle of Khartoum and the 1898 Battle of Omdurman, fought within a few miles of each other.[GE[103]] Khartoum, the capital of today's Sudan, is where the White and Blue Niles come together. Britain got control of Egypt by 1882, and in 1885 General Charles "Chinese" Gordon took an army to Khartoum to extend British rule there. In a conflict with the religiously-inspired troops of a local leader claiming to be the Mahdi, the British were defeated and Gordon killed. In 1898 General Herbert Kitchener went back to Khartoum, with next-generation artillery, gunboats, and the new Maxim machine guns. A young Winston Churchill, who was there, described the battle:

> But at the critical moment the gunboat arrived on the scene and began suddenly to blaze and flame from Maxim guns, quick-firing guns, and rifles. The range was short; the effect tremendous. The terrible machine, floating gracefully on the waters—a beautiful white devil—wreathed itself in smoke. The river slopes of the Kerreri Hills, crowded with the advancing thousands, sprang up into clouds of dust and splinters of rock. The charging Dervishes, sank down in tangled heaps. The masses in rear paused, irresolute. It was too hot even for them.[13]

Perhaps half of the Mahdi army of 40,000 was killed; the British lost a few dozen men. It was no lack of bravery, or even of intelligent strategy, on the side of the losers; many of the British and Churchill himself were much impressed by both. It was just industrialized warfare measured against what came before.

Imperial botany

Botany may seem a strange thing to be labeled imperial or industrial, but indeed it became so. Today Europe's capital cities have wonderful botanical gardens—among them London's Royal Botanic Gardens at Kew, Amsterdam's Hortus Botanicus, the Jardin des Plantes in Paris, and Berlin's Botanische Garten und Botanische

---

103. GE Layer 103 is a Folder framing a general view of Khartoum, with two Placemarks, one each for the battles of Khartoum and Omdurman. It's just six or seven miles between them.

Museum.[GE104] They all have giant glass greenhouses, plants from literally all over the world, and miles of footpaths through greenery, much of it labeled. Their main function today seems to be serving as quiet, green retreats for big city dwellers suffering from a surfeit of asphalt, exhaust, and the din of traffic. But that's not why they were built.

The age of exploration initially produced two kinds of private gardens in Europe, the decorative and exotic, and the medicinal.

For the first, wealthy patrons supported the scientific explorations of naturalists, providing they would send back colored paintings from nature, dried and pressed specimens for their collections, and better yet, viable seeds and cuttings for their gardens. If you had more than one patron—as did Mark Catesby, in the 1720s the first good naturalist in eastern North America, for example—it was a real problem how to divide up your specimens among the sponsors. Among the wealthy it was beyond a fashion—it was a rage—to have the biggest and best "orangerie," or heated house for growing oranges and other warm-climate plants. The result was a very active exploration on world frontiers. Good examples again for North America would be the father-son team of John and William Bartram, the latter of which wrote *Bartram's Travels*, and the fact that English hedgerows today are about half made up of North American species of hawthornes.

For the medicinal gardens, this was when almost all medicines came from plants. In this light, consider Sir Hans Sloane and the Chelsea Physic Garden. Sloane (1660–1753) was born in northern Ireland of Scottish stock, but came to London to study medicine, and then did advanced study in France. When he was just twenty-seven he went to Jamaica as a physician accompanying wealthy patrons, and in a little over a year collected and then catalogued and wrote up the natural history of the island. He hated the local chocolate-plus-water drink, and apparently invented—and certainly popularized in England—the chocolate-plus-milk drink, originally for medicinal purposes. He became secretary of the Royal Society, a famous scientific body once headed by Isaac Newton and one very interested in new things and information being brought back from the explorations of the world. Sloane was one of Catesby's patrons on his travels, incidentally, and later used his position in the Royal Society to sponsor Catesby's production of his *Natural History of Carolina, Florida and the Bahamas*—hand-colored etchings on huge folio-sized paper, thus establishing a model for the works of later artistic naturalists such as Audubon.

In 1713 Sloane bought himself a manor house down in riverside Chelsea,[GE105] partly to store his huge and growing natural history collections (which upon his death in 1753 became the nucleus of the British Museum!), and partly because the land included an apothecaries' training garden—for teaching druggists to recognize and use medicinal plants. This he quickly turned into the world's best medicinal garden, the Chelsea Physic Garden. Druggists from downtown London could float up on the incoming tide with minimum effort, clip plant parts to replenish their stocks, while away a few hours waiting on the out-going tide in a next-door coffee house featuring the newest recreational drug, caffeine, and float back down to London in a heightened state of awareness.

As a result of developments such as this (and not forgetting the great Swedish organizer of it all, Carl Linnaeus), by the nineteenth century botany had been systematized, and botanists knew how to identify, collect, transport, and grow hundreds of thousands of plants. The neo-imperialism of the century would put that knowledge to use in a way that would transform much of the tropical and sub-tropical world. Daniel Headrick puts it in perspective in his *Tentacles of Progress*:

> Plants are the wealth of the tropical world and the livelihood of most of its people. It was the seductive and costly spices of the Indies that enticed Europeans to risk their lives upon the oceans. Over the centuries, as the supply of each desired crop increased to meet the demands of Western consumers, new crops stimulated new desires: sugar, coffee, and tea, then cotton, quinine, and rubber. Today's cocaine and heroin are but the latest in a long series of such cravings.[14]

---

104. GE Layer 104 Is a Folder titled "Major European botanical gardens"; it includes Placemarks for all four of these, should you wish to explore a bit.

105. GE Layer 105 is a Placemark referencing Chelsea Physic Garden.

Originally Kew was just one of many British royal family retreats up the Thames River from London. The old decorative gardens there first began to take scientific shape in the 1770s when the botanist Joseph Banks, who had gone around the world with Captain Cook, became its director. In 1841, Parliament appropriated the money to make it a truly national institution. Under the direction of Sir Joseph Dalton Hooker, friend of Charles Darwin and perhaps the best botanist of his day, it flourished. By century's end a million (!) species of plants were growing there. It worked closely with the Colonial Office on problems of economic botany, and had a network of related gardens throughout the British Empire, such as the Royal Garden at Calcutta that was even bigger than Kew Gardens.

The Dutch eventually developed their main economic and scientific botanical gardens in Java, in Buitenzorg (today's Bogor) in the forested highlands. Within seven degrees of the equator and with regular rains, it didn't take a fancy hothouse to grow tropical plants there. The French had their colonial botanical stations in what was then called French Equatorial Africa and Indochina. Germany, which got in the colonial race late, had such a station in their west African colony of Kamerun (Cameroun); in the Botanische Garten und Botanische Museum, in the Dahlem suburb of Berlin, one room still has an incredibly detailed model of a West African rubber plantation. The project of all these was the discovery of new, potentially profitable plants or strains of plants, the working out how best to grow them, and learning how to fight diseases that afflicted them.

With the rubber boom of the mid-nineteenth century, for example, the latex from the sap of the South American rubber tree (*Hevea brasiliensis*) became a most valuable commodity. Originally limited to the Spanish colonial realm in the Americas called New Spain, it was a carefully guarded monopoly. But in 1875 several thousand seeds were smuggled out to Kew Gardens. Carefully tended seedlings were then sailed to British holdings in Ceylon (Sri Lanka) and Singapore, and by the turn of the century the British were growing them in huge plantations in many parts of Malaysia.

"Industrial" quinine

Perhaps the single most dramatic chapter of this imperial botanizing was the development of quinine. Up until this time malaria was the one guardian of the tropics Europeans didn't seem to be able to fight against. There is a sort of generalized malaria worldwide, caused by *Plasmodium vivax*, and a much more deadly strain mainly in Africa called *P. falciparum*. Most Africans have some natural immunity, partly genetic and partly from frequent low-level bouts with the disease. People of European stock have none, and even today need to saturate their system with quinine or some manufactured quinine-mimic to survive anywhere the *Anopheles* mosquito carrier is. Malaria still kills more people worldwide than any other single disease, but before modern medicine the numbers were staggering. British troops in Sierra Leone and the Gold Coast (today's Ghana) in the years leading up to 1836 had a death rate per annum from disease of 483 and 668 per thousand, respectively, mostly from malaria. In 1833 McGregor Laird, he of the steamboat manufacturing company in Liverpool, led a small, armored steamboat fleet up the Niger River, hoping to found a trading station for palm oil at the junction with the Benue.[GE106] The steamers performed well, but of the forty-eight Europeans who went upriver, only nine returned alive. Laird himself was a semi-invalid the rest of his life.

Only in 1880 was the *Plasmodium* organism that causes malaria identified in the blood, and it took until 1897 for the *Anopheles* mosquito to be identified as the carrier. But a substance that could alleviate malaria was known to Europeans, mainly from Jesuit missionaries in Amazonia, from the 1600s—the ground-up bark of the cinchona tree. Here is how it was "industrialized."

In 1820 two French scientists extracted the active ingredient, an alkaloid called quinine; by 1830 it was being commercially produced in quantity. French army physicians experimented with it in malarial areas, and a break-through treatment came in the mid-1830s, at the French garrison in Bône in Algeria.[GE107] In the early 1830s every year from 60 percent to upwards of 70 percent of the garrison there was being hospitalized, and two of every seven so hospitalized died. Part of the death rate was due to treatment—treating fevers with bleedings, purgatives, and starvation diets ("feed a cold, starve a fever," conventional wisdom since the Middle Ages), and

---

106. GE Layer 106 is a Folder titled "Niger River and tributaries."
107. GE Layer 107 is a Placemark referencing Bône, today's Annaba, Algeria.

only giving malaria patients the very expensive quinine after their seventh or eighth attack of fever. In 1834 a Dr. François Maillot was stationed at Bône, and he not only fed his patients well but gave them substantial doses of quinine beginning at the first sign of fever. Only one in twenty of the patients in his ward died, and soon soldiers from other wards were escaping theirs and descending on his, even if they had to crawl there. He wrote it up for a major French medical journal and the practice quickly spread. In the 1840s British expeditions up the Niger experimented, and successfully, with the "prophylactic" use of quinine—saturating the system with it before a person ever got to malarial areas. In 1854 a British voyage of 112 days on the Niger and Benue rivers began with the fleet physician insisting that sailors begin taking quinine as soon as they crossed the bar, and keep taking it for two full weeks after leaving the Niger. The captain was also a physician, and insisted on strict observance. There was not a single death in the European crew.

Africa's last and best guardian against European intrusion was thus neutralized. From 1878 to 1914 Africa was quickly carved up among European powers (except for Liberia, technically free but in fact a U.S. colony, and the geographically isolated highland Ethiopia). In 1881 the Scientific Congress of Algiers, capital of French Algeria, honored Dr. Maillot with this: "It is thanks to Maillot that Algeria has become a French land; it is he who closed and sealed forever this tomb of Christians."[15]

Until the 1850s, all the cinchona bark in the world came from the slopes of the Andes. It was France, Holland, and Britain—the European countries with the greatest tropical holdings outside of South America—that stole it. A British-born, French-reared explorer sent some seeds to the botanical garden in Paris. In 1851 the botanical garden at Leyden, associated with Holland's most famous university, got one of the plants. In 1852 they sent a cutting to Java; it made the trip and flourished when planted there. But one plant couldn't reproduce, so a gardener from Holland's Java botanical gardens at Buitenzorg/Bogor was sent to the Andes. He secretly and illegally collected several cases of it, and by 1854 was back in Java establishing the first cinchona plantation in the world. By the early 1860s over a million cinchona trees were growing in Java.

The British too had smuggled out some cinchona plants in the 1850s, but when planted in India they all died. British deaths from malaria during the great Sepoy Mutiny/First Indian War of Independence of 1857–58, however, made this a critical matter of state. Kew Gardens agreed to build a special greenhouse, and exploring parties—at least one of which posed as examiners of Inca ruins in Peru—came back with specimens of not one but six different cinchona species. The first seeds reached Kew in 1860. A botanical garden in the southern Indian hill country station of Ootacamund[GE[108]]—chosen because its climate at 7500' elevation was much like that of the slopes of the Andes—produced over 100,000 trees in two years time. Selective breeding of strains raised the alkaloid content of the bark from 2 percent to as much as 10 percent. The British produced a generalized sort of dilute quinine (the "tonic" of Gin & Tonic, the favorite British way of taking the extremely bitter quinine). The Dutch mastered the extraction and marketing of pure quinine, having a virtual monopoly of it until WW II, when (a) the Japanese took Java away from them; and (b) a synthetic version of quinine was manufactured.

Conclusion and advertisement

The earliest Chinese novels, not far removed from street-corner storytelling, usually ended each chapter with a couplet. The first line would sum up the episode of the story the audience had just heard, and the second line would hint at exciting things to come, to try to keep the crowd around. Below, in the last paragraphs of this first chapter, is your author's attempt to do the same in a little more length.

From around 1300 to 1500 southern Europeans—the Portuguese, the Spanish, and the Italians—mainly by tinkering with other people's basic inventions, transformed maritime power. It was backed by the intellectual curiosity of the Renaissance, which revived Greek and Roman learning and open-mindedly appreciated the product of Arab and Jewish scholarship. It was also fueled by the close-minded crusading fervor of the Iberian Reconquista, along with a quest for fame and fortune. The contradiction between exporting Christianity and its general moral code, and importing slaves, bothered almost no one at the time.

---

108. GE Layer 108 is a Placemark referencing Ootacamund, today's Ooty.

From around 1500 to 1700, northern and southern Europeans—in the context of a bitter religious struggle between Catholics and Protestants in central and western Europe—became the leaders of the world in science. Breakthroughs in optics and astronomy had a power dimension in terms of what they made possible in navigation. In the 1500s, the newly transformed Lutheran universities were countered by the brilliant Jesuit colleges, though in the end the Catholic Church's rejection of the Copernican system left the major advances of the 1600s to scholars of the Protestant countries, such as Newton. Power began to shift from south to north in Europe. In the last decades of the 1500s Protestant Holland not only survived massive attacks from the Spanish Kingdom and the Austrian-based Holy Roman Empire, but by the early 1600s blew the Portuguese out of key forts all over the world, the Dutch now largely replacing them as the middleman of the Indian Ocean, Java, and South China seas. As far as the non-European world was concerned, Protestant European treatment of non-Europeans was no real improvement over the original Catholic wave of conquest (as you'll see in detail later in Indonesia with "the butcher of Banda" and other episodes).

From around 1700 to 1900, the Industrial Revolution—beginning in Britain and spreading mainly in northern Europe and the U.S.—transformed the production of goods, transportation and communication, military power, and even the management of disease. Steam engines and railroads, gunboats and machine guns, imperial botany and industrial quinine—these are just a few areas of the transformation. The whole package would hit non-European peoples with the shock of an earthquake. Assumptions about power so traditional that they were subconsciously believed would all of a sudden shift beneath their feet.

To compound the impact of this AD 1700–1900 scientific and technological wave, Europeans also tapped new power in terms of social mobilizing forces among their own citizens. More subtle and less tangible than the technological developments, it is more interesting to most historians. The most important of these were political nationalism, cultural nationalism, and socialism, which appeared in roughly that order. The following three chapters examine these in turn, attempting to give each a "face" by exploring the country where it emerged most clearly:

❍ for political nationalism, France of the Enlightenment and French Revolution;

❍ for cultural nationalism, the Germanies from the time of Napoleon through Hitler;

❍ and for socialism, Russia and the Soviet Union to its dissolution in 1991.

Overall, it ought also yield some overview of major events on the dominant continent in the world in the eighteenth, nineteenth, and early twentieth centuries, useful background for the rest of the text. The final three chapters in this first, European, half of the book will deal with smaller case studies—Ireland, Finland, and the Czech Republic—as they experienced both the dominant ideologies of the time and the military power of the states that wielded them.

Endnotes

1. See "portolan, *n.*" in *Oxford English Dictionary* (Third edition, December 2006; online version September 2011).

2. J. H. Parry (1914–1982) was a historian who wrote the foundational works on this European "age of reconnaissance," the title of one of his books. His 1981 *The Discovery of the Sea* (Berkeley: University of California Press) may still be the most readable one-volume treatment of this period of the maritime explorations.

3. C. R. Boxer, *The Portuguese Seaborne Empire 1415–1825* (New York: Knopf, 1969), p. 36.

4. *The Oxford Atlas of Exploration* (New York, Oxford University Press, 1996), p. 38.

5. Boxer, *Portuguese Seaborne Empire*, p. 46.

6. See Jacob Burckhardt, *Civilization of the Renaissance in Italy*, volume I (New York: Harper & Row, Publishers, 1958; first published in English in 1929).

7. See the two Hans Baron articles of same title—"A Struggle for Liberty in the Renaissance: Florence, Venice, and Milan in the Early Quattrocento"—in successive issues of the *American Historical Review* (vol. 58, No. 2, Jan 1953, pp. 265–289, and vol. 58, No. 3, Apr. 1953, pp. 594–570).

8. Bert S. Hall, *Weapons and Warfare in Renaissance Europe: Gunpowder, Technology, and Tactics* (Baltimore & London: The Johns Hopkins University Press, 1997), p. 161.

9. Katherine Park and Lorraine Daston (eds.), *The Cambridge History of Science*, vol. 3, *Early Modern Science*, pp. 573–578 (in Chapter 24, William Donahue's "Astronomy.").

10. See Nathaniel Philbrick, *Mayflower: A Story of Courage, Community, and War* (New York: Penguin Group, 2006).

11. Karl Marx & Friedrich Engels, *The Communist Manifesto* (London: Penguin Books, 1987), p. 84.

12. Daniel R. Headrick, *The Tools of Empire: Technology and European Imperialism in the Nineteenth Century* (New York and Oxford: Oxford University Press, 1981), and *The Tentacles of Progress: Technology Transfer in the Age of Imperialism, 1850–1940* (New York and Oxford: Oxford University Press, 1988).

13. Winston Churchill, *The Battle of Omdurman, 1898*, from the Modern History Sourcebook (for entire account see website http://www.fordham.edu/halsall/mod/1898churchill-omdurman.asp).

14. Headrick, *Tentacles of Progress*, p. 209.

15. As quoted in Headrick, *Tools of Empire*, p. 67. See generally his Chapter Three, "Malaria, Quinine, and the Penetration of Africa."

Chapter Two

"Enfants de la Patrie": Political Nationalism in the Enlightenment and French Revolution

"From this moment until that when the enemy is driven from the territory of the republic, every Frenchman is commandeered (*en réquisition permanente*) for the needs of the armies. Young men will go to the front; married men will forge arms, and carry food; women will make tents and clothing, and work in hospitals; children will turn old linen into bandages; old men will be carried into the squares to rouse the courage of the combatants, and to teach hatred of kings and republican unity."

—Decree of the Committee of Public Safety, August 23, 1793

CONTENTS

The heart of the matter—A nod to the French language—A quick sketch of the topography and texture of the land of France—Early history: Celts, Romans & Germans—Feudalism, the 100 Years War and the legacy of Joan of Arc—The absolutism of Louis XIV—The Enlightenment: origins and overview—The Enlightenment's progression of ideas—Montesquieu—Diderot's "Supplement to the Voyage of Bougainville"—Rousseau's General Will—Turgot, the last hope for reform from above—The coming of the Revolution—At Versailles—Fall of the Bastille—The "Great Fear"—The August 4 Assembly and the end of feudalism—The Constitution of 1791—The radical phase—The Committee of Public Safety and the year of "The Terror"—The draft army—Napoleon: the early years—Napoleon: the glory days—The Code Napoléon—The Grand Empire and the satellites—End game—The legacy of it all

The heart of the matter

We Americans reflect a good deal on our American Revolution, naturally enough. More than any other event it defined us as a people, even those of us who (or whose ancestors) immigrated here later and adopted its values. Worldwide, however, the French Revolution probably had more direct impact. It was a powerful and complicated upheaval that lasted from 1789 to 1799, and if you throw in Napoleon, its offspring, on down to 1815. True, it owed some inspiration to the American Revolution, but a good many world-class thinkers see in the French Revolution and not the American Revolution the beginning of modern times, for good or for ill. Hannah Arendt, the great analyst of modern totalitarianism, saw the Jacobins of the most extreme phase of the Revolution as the first modern example of the practice. Karl Marx saw in the class struggle of the French Revolution a dress rehearsal for the ultimate class struggle of the Proletarian Revolution that he so confidently predicted (though to date he seems a better historian than foreteller of the future). Many intellectuals in the world today, and most French people, probably not surprisingly, see in the French Revolution the real beginnings of modern political nationalism, which has played such a large role in creating the modern political landscape. In the run-up to the 1989 bicentennial of the outbreak of the French Revolution, there was some talk in France about celebrating the event by the launch of several highly reflective satellites into a polygon formation. Visible to most of the world several times on every clear night of the foreseeable future, it would have been a permanent reminder of the event—a highly rational geometric figure imposed on the randomness of the stars. Maybe they should have done it. World history teachers could begin every modern history course with a night session . . . .

To show just how dramatic the change was, consider French society in the 1780s, the decade just before the Revolution. In many ways it was closer to the Middle Ages of 500 years before than it was to modern western society just a few decades later.

In the countryside the local aristocratic family, by a thousand years of accumulated rights and privileges, typically owned all the forest, all the grazing lands, and much of the plow lands. The lord had a monopoly on the local wine presses, bakery ovens, and grist mills; no peasant, however enterprising, had the right to build one. The lord had all hunting and fishing rights, and if he chose to ride across peasants' gardens with forty hounds and twenty horses, so much the worse for the gardens. Travelers in the more isolated countryside still reported cases of the archaic *Droit du seigneur*, the so-called Right of the Lord, where peasant brides of the estate spent their wedding nights not with their new husbands but with the lord—truly medieval.

Society in the cities had changed much more than in the countryside. By the 1780s there was an upper-middle class that could read and write (and support professional writers) for the first time since the fall of Rome. Blue-collar workers had developed the germ of collective consciousness. The pace of commerce was beginning to quicken, with all the new international trade and with the industrial revolution kicking off in nearby Britain. But even in the French cities the old medieval framework still generally held. Craft monopolies were controlled by guilds. The royal government sold to the highest bidder the right to collect the royal taxes (and whatever else the winning bidder could collect for himself, a system the abuses of which you can imagine). Perhaps because there had been such social change below and not much change in the old restrictions from above, the cities, and Paris in particular, were restive.

But city or country, the most obvious example of how medieval things were was the Estate system. By the 1780s a person was born into either the Third Estate (commoners would be the closest English translation), or into the privileged estate of the nobility. Typically the oldest noble son inherited the main estate and the title, and younger sons became army officers or church administrators. The nobility were collectively called the Second Estate, and the clergy were the First Estate. Together they made up only 5 percent of French society, though as you'll see they had a virtual monopoly on all positions that yielded power and wealth.

In this situation, the modern sort of patriotism that we take so much for granted didn't yet exist. Suppose today, for example, you are visiting Rome, and a local asks who you are. Your first answer would probably be that you are an American (by which we mean from the USA, which causes some minor resentment among other people who live in the western hemisphere, incidentally). Now imagine some French person visiting Rome in the 1780s, and hearing the same question. His or her first answer would likely have been to give their Estate. Second Estate people in France would have had much more in common with the local nobility in neighboring states than they did with Third Estate people in France, and Third Estate people with commoners elsewhere. If the questioner had persisted, "No, I mean where are you from?," the answer would probably have been a naming of Languedoc, or Brittany, or just "The South"—the person's home province or general region. Only if the questioner continued, "No, I mean what is your <u>political</u> belonging?" would the reply have come back, "Oh, why didn't you say so? I'm a subject of the French king." To the extent that the nation was an ideal, motivating a person by duty and love to work and fight for it, only a few traditional civil service families in France had any of that.

This class system would be shattered in the French Revolution, aided by the development of modern patriotism, but only because the former had been destroyed and the latter had been created in the world of ideas in the decades before. Over and over in history you will see this pattern, that the ideas come a generation or two before they are played out in politics and warfare. This is what makes the Enlightenment, a general term for intellectual developments from the 1680s to the 1770s, so interesting. And it ought to be doubly interesting to "Americans," of course, because most of our founding ideas came from this same Enlightenment.

Before tackling the Enlightenment and Revolution in more depth, however, let's do a brief introduction to the language and then to the topography and texture of the country of France. It is the general pattern of all subsequent chapters in this text, and should help you out with your Google Earth explorations. You can of course cut straight to the (historical) chase by jumping over these sub-sections, though even a little linguistic knowledge can add depth to history, and some visual knowledge of the country is valuable—it's the 3-D and living color stage set of where the history played out.

A nod to the French language

French uses the same basic 26-letter Latin alphabet as English, but some of the letters are pronounced differently than in English and some of their vowels, especially, have strange-looking accent marks.

In terms of consonants, their letter J is pronounced like our ZH. The French CH is like our SH, so the French name *Charles* is pronounced something like "Sharl." This, incidentally, is why we spell Tchaikovsky with a T, because we got it through the French, and TCH is the way they spell the sound we spell CH. Perhaps the least used consonants in their alphabet are W and K; they only seem to be used for German and English loan words, such as *le week-end.* The K sound in French is done with a QU, as in *quiche* ("keesh"), or sometimes with a C.

French pronunciation tends to drop most final consonants that are not followed by a vowel, as in *Chevrolet,* a name of French origin. They nasalize final Ns without ever touching tip of tongue to palate (the difference between the English "John," where the final N has the front of the tongue firmly hitting the palate—try it, pronouncing it slowly and thinking about where your tongue is—and its French equivalent *Jean,* where the initial J is pronounced ZH, followed by a vowel much like the English pronunciation of the word OH, and then a very nasalized N where the tongue never quite hits the palate). Their letter R is done deep in the throat, and not with the tongue curled up towards the palate as we do it. So the world-famous museum housed in an old royal palace in Paris, the *Louvre,* is pronounced something like a stressed "loov" followed by an unstressed "ruh," where the R is done more with the very back part of the tongue, almost a soft gargle. Like English, French irrationally has the three letters C, K, and S for two sounds, and their C can be either a hard K or a soft S before the vowels A, O, and U. They show it is soft with the cedilla, a little hook under the C, as in *garçon* (boy, young man) or the name *François(e).*

In terms of vowels, their A is much like the A in the English "father." But their version of the long A, as in the English word "gate," is done with an *accent acute* over the E, as in É. So the French "flambé" (flaming, ablaze) is pronounced much like "flam-bay." The unaccented French letter E, as in *je* (meaning "I"), is pronounced like the O in "connect." There is also another pronunciation of the French letter E when it has an *accent grave* over it, È—as in *après* (French for "after)—pronounced like the E in the English word "bed." The French vowel I, as in so many European languages, is pronounced more like the English EE. This means that the French word for yes, *oui,* is pronounced much like the English "wee." Finally, there is a circumflex accent, an upside down little V, atop several vowels. Sometimes it affects the pronunciation a bit, but often it just shows that another letter, usually an S, has been omitted after the vowel. In that case it is like the apostrophe in English that shows a letter has been omitted. Knowing this makes many French words more familiar to a speaker of English. *Forêt* is obviously "forest"; *hôpital* is "hospital"; *château* becomes more obviously kin to the English "castle" (they both come from the Latin for a fortified camp, *castra*); and *île* becomes "isle," an island. Another neat trick to help recognize the English version of French words is to replace any initial É (the E with an acute accent) with an S. The French phrase for the United States, for example, is *États-Unis. Étranger* is revealed as "stranger" and *école* as school. *Étouffe* becomes "stuff," and so *étouffée*—literally "stuffed," or less literally "smothered"—means stewing something in a closed pot. This initial É to S trick doesn't always work, but is usually worth a try.

In terms of vowel combinations, the French AU is the equivalent of our long O, so the name of the great French leader of WW II and after, *Charles de Gaulle,* is pronounced "Sharl de Gole." The vowel combination OU is like our OO (as in *Louvre*); the combination OI is like our WA, as in town of *Poitiers,* "Pwah-tyay." Finally, in vowel combinations the French have a sign called the *tréma*—two dots over the second vowel—that tell a reader to separate the vowels clearly from one another, as in *Noël* and *naïve.*

French was the European universal language—not just of romance, but of diplomacy, of science, of literature—when Europe had just begun to dominate the world. Only in the past century has it been overtaken by English, and there are still parts of the world where it stands you in better stead—a good half of Africa; French Quebec (Québec, pronounced in French something like "kay-bek"); parts of South and Southeast Asia. There is still a certain *cachet* (pronounced with the stress on the last syllable "cah-shay," a French word originally meaning a stamp or signet ring but that came to mean something like original character or high quality) to knowing some French. It helps you pronounce *coup d'état* correctly ("koo day-tah"), the internationally-recognized phrase for a forcible takeover of a government. It helps one avoid personal embarrassment as when ordering red wine in a fancy restaurant and pronouncing the T in *pinot noir* (correctly pronounced something like "pee-no nwar," wherein the tongue never touches the palate on the last R). But for purposes of this text, it is mainly to help with historical terms, and with those you are likely to encounter when browsing the French part of the (virtual) earth's surface in Google Earth. Here's a quick list.

Rue is the usual word for street, and occasionally you'll see a *ruelle*, a little street. *Chemin* means "way" or "path," and is often translated into English as "road," and *boulevard* is a grand avenue. The French for railroad, *chemin de fer*, literally means "road of iron," as it does in so many other languages. *Gare* is the word for train station.

The common word for city is *ville*. A City Hall is an *Hôtel de Ville* (the beginning H is silent). An open city park of the kind we call a Square is in French a *Place*, linguistic kin to the Spanish *Plaza* and the Italian *Piazza*. *Château*, you've already seen, means castle or a grand manor house (plural *châteaux*). Cathedral (a church that is the site of a bishop's chair) is recognizable as *cathédrale*; a regular church is an *église*. Garden is *jardin*.

A large river, especially one that flows under that same name to the sea, is a *fleuve*. A smaller river or tributary is a *rivière*. Lake is *lac*; pond is *étang* or *mare*. *Canal* is the same in both English and French. Bridge is *pont*.

The overall good news is that French is one of the easiest of foreign languages for a native English speaker to learn. Like English, French has lost most of its original declension (the different endings on nouns and adjectives depending on the place of the word in sentence structure—subject, object, etc.). About all that's left, as in English, is the difference between the words for persons when they are subject and when they are object in a sentence, as *I* and *me* in English and the parallel *je* and *moi* in French. It is admittedly a bit of a nuisance that all nouns and their associated adjectives, not just animate ones, have male or female gender that just have to be memorized. And they tend to reverse what we think of as natural word order, as in *Mont Blanc*, "Mountain White." But overall, as a French teacher friend of mine says, thanks to the Norman (French) conquest of England in 1066, about 40 percent of the English language is still just badly pronounced French.

A quick sketch of the topography and texture of the land of France

Let's start with the major rivers. If you zoom in on Switzerland, mountainous source of many rivers, you can see its two biggest lakes (each about forty-five miles long)—Lake Constance on the northeast side bordering Germany, and Lake Geneva on its southwest side bordering France.[GE¹] These two give rise to the Rhine and the Rhône rivers, respectively, in many ways the mirror image of each other and a good place to anchor yourself when trying to learn basic western European geography.[GE²] Both flow west or a bit southwest for a few miles. Then the Rhine goes north, and arcs northwest, and finally west—serving as the border between France and Germany for awhile, then going through Germany proper, and spending its last 100 miles going through Holland, emptying into the Atlantic in the vicinity of Rotterdam and Amsterdam (we'll do more with the Rhine in the next chapter). Notice two important western tributaries of the Rhine that rise in France: first, the Moselle, that goes into the Rhine at Koblenz, and second the Meuse (called the Maas in Holland and northern Belgium), that enters the Rhine closer to its mouth. The Rhône, after some miles going southwest, then turns straight south and goes into the Mediterranean. It is in French territory, all but its first few miles in Switzerland. Notice that where the Rhône turns due south, it joins the Saône that is coming down from the north. At the junction is the city of Lyon (also sometimes spelled Lyons),[GE³] historically perhaps the second most important city of France.

---

1. Google Earth Layer 1 is a Folder titled "Switzerland's 2 biggest lakes." Turn on the layer by clicking in the square box at left; "fly" to pre-set view by double-clicking on the Folder icon.

2. GE Layer 2 is a Folder titled "Rhine and Rhône river systems." Turn it on, and double-click on the Folder icon to fly to framed view of both.

3. GE Layer 3 is a Placemark framing a view of the river junction in Lyon.

The other major rivers all go into the Atlantic; we'll do them north to south.

The Seine (rhymes with "Zen") River,[GE[4]] though not the biggest in France, is probably the most famous because Paris grew up around an island in it, the *Île de la Cité*. It (and its next-door smaller upstream island *Île St. Louis*) is about four miles downstream from where the Marne, a tributary almost as big as the Seine at that point, joins it.[GE[5]]

The great river of central France is the Loire.[GE[6]] Its headwaters are only one mountain ridge west of the Rhône, but it flows north instead of south, and then curves in a great arc northwest and then west, entering the Atlantic south of the Brittany peninsula. Rising in the *Massif central*, substantial highlands in south central France you'll see a map of shortly, it is France's single longest river, and is famously home to several hundred châteaux. The Loire is France's version of the Mason-Dixon line, traditionally dividing north from south. Notice that its biggest upper tributary is the Allier and the most important lower tributary is the Vienne.

Finally, and southernmost, is the big estuary called the Gironde, and the two rivers that flow into it—the larger in the south, the Garonne, and the Dordogne just to its north.[GE[7]] The Garonne runs through Toulouse, higher up, and the main town on its lower course is Bordeaux.

Now take a quick look at the mountains and uplands, starting with the southern, eastern, and northeastern perimeter of present-day France.

The southern border of France is nicely defined by the Pyrenees (French *Pyrénées*), a narrow and rugged mountain chain with peaks over 11,000'.[GE[8]] The southeastern corner of France, the chunk just east of the lower Rhône valley, is Provence and the French Alps, which end in an even more rugged mountain border with Italy and Switzerland including the highest peaks in central and western Europe.[GE[9]] The Jura (pronounced in French as with a ZH, "Zhura") are rugged mountains defining the French border with the northwest side of Switzerland and a bit of adjoining Germany.[GE[10]]

So far so good, in terms of clear and defensible borders. But just north of the Jura such clarity begins to disappear. At the northern end of the Jura is a gap before the Vosges range (pronounced something like "Vōzh"), less impressive mountains further north.[GE[11]] In that gap is Belfort, a critical fort updated and renewed by many French kings and most Republican governments since. Between the crest of the Vosges and the Rhine River paralleling it to its east is the narrow province of Alsace.[GE[12]] Today part of France, it has often been part of Germany or of some German state. It's a long-running international debate, often with guns, as to whether the Rhine River or the Vosges Mountains should be the western boundary of France in these latitudes. Turning northwest along the border a traveler comes to the Ardennes,[GE[13]] mostly in the southern tip of Belgium but spilling over into France. Hardly high enough to be called mountains, they are still rugged,

---

4. GE Layer 4 is a Folder titled "Seine (and Marne)." In addition to Paths for the Lower Seine, the upper Seine and the Marne, there is a Placemark that frames a view of the Île de la Cité and the next-door upstream island Île St. Louis.

5. GE Layer 5 is a Placemark titled "Seine-Marne junction, islands," framing a view of the junction of the Marne and Seine at lower right, and the Île de la Cité and Île Saint Louis at upper left.

6. GE Layer 6 is a Folder titled "Loire River (and Allier and Vienne)." It includes Paths for all three.

7. GE Layer 7 is a Folder containing a Polygon for the Gironde estuary, and Paths for both the Garonne and Dordogne Rivers.

8. GE Layer 8 is a Folder titled "Pyrenees Mountains." Placemarks reference a couple of selected Photos icons to explore.

9. GE Layer 9 is a Folder titled "French Alps." Placemarks reference Photos icons, beginning with Mont Blanc. At over 15,700', it's almost 2,000' taller than anything in the Rockies.

10. GE Layer 10 is a Folder titled "Jura Mountains." Double-click on the Folder itself to both open it and frame a view of the Jura.

11. GE Layer 11 is a Folder titled "Vosges Mountains." Notice that they generally show up dark green with forest cover in the Google Earth surface.

12. GE Layer 12 is a Placemark titled "Alsace," generally framing a view between the crest of the Vosges Mountains and the Rhine River, running parallel to it, east of there.

13. GE Layer 13 is a Placemark framing a view of the Ardennes, which generally shows up as dark green on the Google Earth view. Notice how the Meuse cuts through them from south to north.

mainly forested hills. Northwest of the Ardennes the terrain generally flattens out, making invasion easier and defense harder (in both directions!).

West of the Rhône valley, and source of the headwaters of the Loire and its tributaries Allier and Vienne, is the *Massif central*,[GE14] a highlands of plateaus and mountains, though lower than the Alps across the Rhône (the valley of the Rhône is so deep between the two sets of mountains that it is often called the "furrow" of the Rhône). The *Massif central* takes up perhaps an eighth of the country, France's only substantial uplands other than those perimeter mountains already described. It is something like a French version of the Appalachians, except that its tallest peaks are extinct volcanoes.

But natural features only suggest borders. It's human activity that finally determines them, over time. Here are the high points of the history of the territory that became today's France, leaping over many things but lingering on those in which a growing national consciousness can be seen. The Enlightenment and Revolution, of course, are where we'll linger most!

Early history: Celts, Romans & Germans

The eight most important years in French history may be 59–52 B.C. In those years Celtic-language-speaking Gaul—all of today's France except for a narrow strip along the Mediterranean coast that Rome already had— was conquered by Julius Caesar as a key step in his rise to power in Rome. French today is one of the five major "Romance" languages (meaning descended from Roman Latin, along with Portuguese, Spanish, Italian, and Romanian), because five centuries of the use of Latin in the military, the courts, and eventually the schools made it and not the original Celtic language the basic language of the land. This Roman heritage shows up in place names, too. *Paris* as a name comes from the Latin "Lutetia Parisiorium," the name of the fortified camp there used at times by Julius Caesar himself. *Lyon* (or *Lyons*) as a modern city name evolved from "Lugdunum," the Roman name for the fortified camp at the junction of the Rhône and Saône rivers.

Roman Gaul, along with the rest of the Roman Empire, became officially Christian in the early 300s in accordance with the Emperor Constantine's policies. Even earlier, around AD 250, a Christian bishop named Denis had based his mission work with the Parisii on the Île de la Cité.[GE15] Reputedly he angered the leaders of the local religions by the success of his conversion work, and he and two followers were beheaded on the prominent hill in Paris known ever since as Montmartre, "Mount of Martyrs."[GE16] The beheaded Denis is supposed to have walked for miles carrying his own head, and it preaching a sermon all the while—so at least he is shown in early statuary. His burial site a few miles north of the city center became a major national shrine, as you'll see.

When the western Roman Empire collapsed from around AD 450 to 520, and Germanic tribes came in to seize property and lands, there was a struggle for Roman Gaul. The winning power was a Frankish kingdom that first took shape in what is today Belgium. Its real founding figure, Clovis, in a thirty-year-long rule from around 481 to 511, expanded the kingdom south and west, eventually defeating the Visigoths near the lower Loire River. He made Paris his capital, and he converted to Catholic Christianity. That conversion apparently assured for him the support of the existing Gallo-Roman nobility. *Clovis*, in accordance with the mysterious laws of linguistic drift, morphed over time into *Louis*, ever after the most popular name for French kings.

---

14. GE Layer 14 is a Polygon titled "Massif central," showing it in a uniform green. But you can find a better presentation of its topography (and indeed all the other mountains we've discussed) on a map from the Institute géographique national at the following website:http://www.discoverfrance.net/France/DF_maps.shtml

Scroll down to the topographic map of France, and then click on it to enlarge it. The dark browns of the Spanish and Swiss borders are especially high and rugged mountains, but the reds and yellows of the *Massif central* show up well too. The two deep notches in the northern border of the *Massif central* are the valleys of the upper Loire and the Allier. Notice also the gaps north and south of the Vosges Mountains.

15. GE Layer 15 is a Placemark framing the Île de la Cité. Its most famous structure today is the Cathedral of Notre Dame, which dominates the southern corner of the island.

16. GE Layer 16 is a Placemark framing a view of Montmartre, topped by the *Basilique de Sacre Coeur*, the Basilica of the Sacred Heart, an Arabesque church built to memorialize the French shedding other French blood in the civil war of the Paris Commune on 1870.

For over a thousand years French kings would generally be crowned at Reims (also sometimes spelled Rheims),[GE17] where Clovis was baptized, and be buried at the Abbey of Saint Denis, where St. Denis was buried.[GE18]

As the Merovingian line of kings descended from Clovis decayed, important administrators called "mayors of the palace" became the real rulers of the land. This was the origin of the Carolingian dynasty of Frankish kings, so named because several of them were named *Carolus*, or Charles. Charles Martel stopped the Muslim northwards advance at Tours (or Poitiers) in 732.[GE19] His son Pepin the Short, ruler in his turn, forged a tight alliance with the Papacy in Rome. In the mid-750s he defeated the Lombards in northern Italy who were at war with the Pope, gave a band of land stretching completely across central Italy to the Papacy (the "Donation of Pepin," essentially the same as the Papal Estates of Renaissance Italy you saw in the last chapter), and in turn was anointed King of France (no longer simply Mayor of the Palace) by the Pope in a ceremony at the Abbey of Saint Denis. And Pepin's son was Charlemagne, *Carolus Magnus*, Charles the Great.

Charlemagne ruled from 768 to 814. Crowned "Roman Emperor" on Christmas day of 800, he created an empire that was short-lived but impressive in extent. With its capital at Aachen/Aix la Chapelle, it included the whole heartland of Europe, including today's France, Holland, Belgium, Germany, most of Italy.[GE20] Despite the proud title, this polity was something different from the original Roman Empire, more of a hybrid between German tribal traditions and the memory of the late, great Roman Empire. Although for a half century it seemed to submerge any potential "France" in a much larger empire, in 843 Charlemagne's three grandsons divided it among themselves. The western part would eventually evolve into France, the eastern part into Germany, with the middle part doomed in the long run to fragmentation into successor states such as Burgundy fated to be absorbed into one of its two larger neighbors. Linguists claim to see in the 843 treaty the first real early French, as opposed to late Latin, language.

Feudalism, the 100 Years War and the legacy of Joan of Arc

With the breakdown of the Carolingian Empire came feudalism, a system of loyalty and protection that linked Emperor, Kings, Dukes, Knights, and Peasants. It was an aristocracy, its most important personal building block being the armored knight — trained in combat from childhood, expensively armored and horsed, motivated by chivalry (*cheval-erie,* literally "horsery") which was about half a carefully selected Christianity (rescuing upper-class damsels, questing for the Holy Grail, going on Crusades to recover the "Holy Land" from the "Infidel," but little of the "turn the other cheek" strain of New Testament scripture, or its compassion for the poor) and half the professional code of a military caste. The territorial building block of the age was, generally speaking, a Duke who owned a castle-fortified Duchy.

This generally held in what is today France and all neighboring lands. The kings of the age were first-among-equals who led the nobility into battle, and who in cooperation with increasingly national branches of the Church administered some rudimentary justice and welfare. In this time there was some consolidation of a royal France from 900 to 1300. The University of Paris, one of the first three universities in Europe, was established around 1200 (on the Left Bank a few blocks away from the river, where it still is).[GE21] King Louis IX of the 1200s so fit the chivalric ideal that he was idealized by his own and later feudal generations, and actually

---

17. GE Layer 17 is a Placemark referencing the Cathedral of Reims.

18. GE Layer 18 is a Placemark referencing the Cathedral of Saint Denis.

19. GE Layer 19 is a Placemark referencing a historical marker at the battle site; click on Panoramio icon under pointer, "732 La bataille de Poitiers." It was fought within two or three miles of the Vienne River. Some forty-five miles south of Tours, way up north on the Loire River, and twelve miles NNE of Poitiers, it's hard to see how either town gave their name to the battle! Zooming out shows that this extended Muslim drive made it about halfway across France, south to north.

20. GE Layer 20 is a Folder containing a Polygon representing Charlemagne's empire in light purple, with a red star representing the capital Aachen/Aix-la-Chapelle.

21. GE Layer 21 is a Folder titled "University of Paris" containing a Path, showing as a yellow line the Boulevard Saint-Michel (the "Boul Mich" in local parlance) running south from the Île de la Cité, and a Placemark generally located in the Sorbonne, center of the complex of University of Paris buildings.

became a Saint (as in St. Louis, the French colonial city on the middle Mississippi named for him almost 500 years after his death).

Back in 1066 Duke William of Normandy, feudal vassal of the French king, had famously invaded England, the last successful invasion of that country to date, becoming in the process King William the Conqueror. It transformed English history, of course, among other things ensuring that our general words for meat served on a plate are Latin-French words used by the new Norman overlords who ordered it (pork/porc, beef/boeuf, and mutton/mouton) whereas the names for the same animals on the hoof, as cared for by the conquered Saxon herders, are still basically Germanic (pig, cow, sheep). But what made this so important for French history is that the Norman rulers still held lands on the continent for almost 400 years more. It all culminated in the 100 Years War, off and on warfare from 1337 to 1453 between England's royal Angevin dynasty (originally based in the French provinces of Normandy and Anjou, hence "Anjou-vin") and the Valois dynasty of France.

Years ago historian Barbara Tuchman, in her *A Distant Mirror: The Calamitous 14th Century*, followed the life of one Enguerrand de Coucy (1340–97), whose basic estate and castle were not far north of Paris. As ideal a representative of the feudal nobility as Saint Louis himself had been of the ideal feudal king, the Baron de Coucy was much written about in Froissart's famous Chronicles about the 100 Years War. Towards the end of the life of this paragon of feudalism, however, Tuchman could see him facing a choice of a new sort of loyalty, and the beginnings of his national commitment to France, the first stirrings of modern nationalism.[1]

The early decades of the 100 Years War were mostly about the last continental holdings of the Angevins in southwest France. But in 1415 England's King Henry V drove into France near the narrows of the English Channel, and at the battle of Agincourt destroyed a third or more of the nobility of France. By 1428 English armies driving in from the west met the armies of their Burgundian ally driving in from the east, together conquering almost all French territory north of the Loire. In fact, England controlled more of traditional French territory in this year than the French monarchy did, and they began a siege of Orléans, that key city on the northern side of the Loire's northernmost bend.[GE22]

Enter Jeanne d'Arc, a teenaged farm girl from a village in eastern France who in 1428 heard God's voice directing her to join the French army defending the city. In 1429 her presence and message reinvigorated the French army, which broke the English siege in a matter of days and then captured other strongholds along the Loire. The *Dauphin* of France (the French version of the British Prince of Wales, the heir to the national throne), Charles, was twenty-six years old but uncrowned because of the English occupation of Reims. Joan encouraged him to throw his forces against the English lines and make a quick march to Reims, 135 straight line miles northeast of Orléans,[GE23] to be traditionally crowned. It went off like clockwork, Charles becoming King Charles VII in the most traditional and binding of ceremonies (over 800 years after Clovis's baptism there!). The next year, 1530, the Burgundians captured Joan of Arc and sold her to the English, who tortured and burned her at the stake in 1431. All this did was give the French a martyr even more powerful in death than in life. This whole 1428–31 sequence was the turning point of the conflict. By 1453 all England had left on the continent was a little land around Calais, just opposite Dover. The memory of Joan of Arc became a key piece of the national mind-set that was to become full-blown French nationalism later.

Two centuries more of consolidation of the French monarchical state led to *Le Grand Siècle*, "The Great Century," from the early 1600s to the early 1700s when France was the most powerful country with the most influential culture in Europe. The brilliant Cardinal Richelieu, Prime Minister in all but name for a quarter century until his death in 1642, brought France to the threshold of European supremacy. He trained his own successor, Cardinal Jules Mazarin, who in turn trained the most famous French king of them all.

---

22. GE Layer 22 is a Placemark titled "Orléans," showing its general position on the northern bank of the northernmost bend of the Loire.

23. GE Layer 23 is a Polygon titled "Drive for Reims," showing the general route of the fast French march from their breakout at Orléans to Reims as an orange arrow.

The absolutism of Louis XIV

It's interesting that the Enlightenment really began in the reign of the most famous of "absolute" monarchs, Louis XIV. He was not quite five years old in 1643 when he inherited the throne of France, and was just ten years old when a Civil War (sarcastically named The Fronde, after a children's game) broke out. His life was very much in danger, and his living conditions at times miserable; many biographers attribute his firm crushing of all opposition in later years to the trauma of these few years. But his remarkable chief minister Mazarin weathered the crisis and ended the Civil War, and for most of the next decade he educated his bright royal ward in the art of war and politics, and the higher arts in general. When Mazarin died in 1661, Louis XIV was just twenty-two years old, but determined to rule in his own right. Rule he would, for the next fifty-four years until his death in 1715. It would be the single most famous royal rule in all of French history. Louis XIV's clan, the house of Bourbon, in his time surpassed the Spanish and Austrian Hapsburgs as the most powerful in Europe. His overall conception of power in the French state was brutally simple: *"L'état, c'est moi"* ("The state, it's me" is the literal translation, but it rhymes in French—something like "lay-tah say-mwah"—making it a little catchier), said he.

Colbert, his early minister of both finance and navy, built up one of the most efficient systems of taxation in Europe. He attracted new crafts to France with subsidies. As minister of the navy, he encouraged a merchant marine, and built huge new ports like Toulon[GE24] to house a big new fighting navy. With his great ability for work, he added to all of that the oversight of production of the arts and of higher education, and of Louis XIV's huge new building program. Much of what was built has been destroyed in the past 300 years, but the Château of Versailles remains as a symbol and a showpiece of that absolutism.

Roughly ten miles west-southwest of Paris, Versailles (the last syllable sounds something like "sigh") was the site of a hunting lodge and a small château of Louis XIV's father, and as a boy he had spent some time there. In 1661 when Louis XIV began ruling in his own right, he immediately began reshaping Versailles into what would become the most famous royal residence in Europe.[GE25] Entrance is by way of a grand paved courtyard. The single most famous room of the palace is the *Salle des glaces*, the Hall of Mirrors. A barrel-vaulted room 240' long, it has seventeen giant arched windows looking out over the royal gardens, each window echoed by a similarly-shaped giant mirror on the wall opposite the windows. A row of fountains slopes down away to the Grand Canal, a cross-shaped lake big enough so that today they rent you rowboats in which to tour it. Maple trees flanking the fountains are trimmed up seventy feet high. A perfectly symmetrical man-made lake just south of the Hall of Mirrors is big enough on which to water-ski (ski boats not rented, though). Smaller palaces are scattered through manicured forests elsewhere on the grounds. In a word, Louis XIV had two miles of a shallow, swampy valley sculpted and built upon by the best architects and decorated by the most famous artists of the age.

It wasn't just from love of architecture, of course. Louis XIV moved the royal government there in 1682 partly to get it away from the influence of the Paris crowds and partly to tame the independent-minded nobility. Those nobles who were willing to come live there, in a sort of gilded cage, were handsomely rewarded from the government treasury. Of those who refused, Louis XIV would sniff, "I never see him," and of course remained unsubsidized. Theatre by Molière, music by Lully, tapestry wall hangings from the Gobelins workshops, and overall the center of high society and government—Versailles gradually seduced the whole French nobility. In the reign of Louis XIV, and mainly from force of his will, they went from semi-independent feudal lords to silk hose-wearing courtiers incapable of fomenting civil wars like the Fronde of his childhood.

Foreign wars were both the glory and the ultimate weakness of Louis XIV's reign. Vauban, the minister of defense, had first showed his abilities fighting against the government in the Fronde; but he was enticed to join the royal side, and became the most famous builder, defender, and attacker of fortresses in the history of Europe. A fortress built and defended by Vauban—the perfection of those *trace Italienne* fortress talked about in Chapter 1 in Renaissance Italy—never fell, popular belief had it, and one attacked by him always did. In

---

24. GE Layer 24 is a Placemark framing a view of Toulon. Zoom out a bit to see its relationship to nearby Marseille, the lower course of the Rhône, and France in general.

25. GE Layer 25 is a Folder titled "Versailles," containing Placemarks indicating sample Photos icons of most of the things described in this paragraph.

attack he would build a circular trench just out of cannon range, and then run zigzag trenches towards it (zigzag so as to avoid enfilading fire), and built another circular trench closer, and so on, until the last was actually at the *glacis* (the sloping earthen defense of the outer walls). The whole rim of France, and especially the vulnerable northeast, is still dotted with those Vauban fortresses. Louis XIV permanently added to France the territories of Alsace and Franche-Comté, [GE26] plus scattered smaller territories in the northeast. French energy in the reign of Louis XIV helped shape things closer to home for us here in America, of course. About the same time the government was moved to Versailles, Robert de la Salle explored the part of the Mississippi River that Father Marquette hadn't gotten to a decade earlier, the southern part, and named the general territory *Louisiane* in honor of Louis XIV, a name that with a single vowel change is still very much with us.

But—as Colbert had feared before he died in 1683—the many wars of Louis XIV, not to mention the enormous expenditure on palaces such as Versailles, were a heavy drag on the economy and ultimately the power of the French state. The very military successes of the early reign of Louis XIV conjured up coalitions of enemy states against him later. And in much the same way, his absolutism in governing conjured up philosophies opposed to it. These would be an important strand of the general intellectual movement we call the Enlightenment.

The Enlightenment: origins and overview

The Enlightenment is one of those great terms for an age—like Renaissance or Reformation—that are a bit like a cloud: far away they seem well defined, but up close the boundaries (in terms time, space, and even ideology, in the case of the Enlightenment) tend to be indistinct and foggy. But literature scholars and artists and historians and political scientists still see enough truth in a unity there to keep using it, so it might be important at this point to try for a definition.

In terms of space, the Enlightenment ranged from the American colonies of Great Britain across most of Europe to Moscow. Ben Franklin was a fine representative of it, as was Mikhail Lomonosov of Russia. They both experimented with electricity (Franklin only got shocked flying kites in stormy weather, Lomonosov had a friend next to him killed). They both set up remarkable institutions of higher learning, among the first in their countries—Franklin's The University of Pennsylvania of 1743, the first real university (as opposed to schools of theology which even Harvard and Yale arguably still were then) in the American colonies, and Lomonosov's Moscow State University of 1755, still the flagship of Russian higher education. Between these western and eastern geographic extremes the Enlightenment was well represented in England and Scotland, the Low Countries, Scandinavian states, German and Italian cities. But the center of gravity of the whole Enlightenment was surely in France. Here lived its most famous writers, and here occurred the most dramatic repercussions.

In terms of time, the Enlightenment ran from the 1680s when the basic ideas were penned, through the 1770s when some of its greatest writers/propagandists worked. One of its basic causes seems to have been those European voyages of exploration talked about in Chapter 1. There were a few isolated corners of the earth Europeans hadn't gotten to yet, but in general they were the first people in the world to discover the great variety of cultures in the world. These discoveries destroyed their confidence in the traditional European definition of human nature: it was way too narrow. So the Enlightenment was as concentrated a search for what is basic human nature as you'll find anywhere in the world, anywhere in history. It had to be universal, applying to Chinese and Samoans and Iroquois as well as to Europeans. If there is a single key word to Enlightenment thought, it is "natural" or "the natural," or its American equivalents in our founding documents "inalienable" or "unalienable." That is, what is it that, if you take it away from a human being, makes that human no longer whole or complete.

Do you remember how Newton solved the whole complicated problem of motion with two simple concepts, gravity and inertia? Enlightenment thinkers consciously used this as a model (somebody should write a book on the use and abuse of scientific models in the social sciences!). If we can just find out what basic human nature is, they figured, and get down to its few essential principles, we can correctly redesign social and polit-

---

26. GE Layer 26 is a Folder containing two Polygons, one in blue showing France-Comté and another in purple showing Alsace.

ical structures to fit it and make the world a much happier place. Other key concepts are rationalism (the importance of using reason instead of emotion to analyze things, and see what really is) and individualism (educated individuals with free access to information should be able to control their own destinies). Although their writing of history expanded to include the whole world, and they were careful as best they could to separate demonstrable fact from opinion, in terms of respect for time-honored institutions Enlightenment writers were very anti-historical. No matter how old or venerable a social or political institution, if it didn't fit well with human nature it should be junked and a new one designed and set up. Does this sound, overall, like a very improbable and even dangerous quest? But think about it: the U.S. is a continuing experiment rooted in those very beliefs (still an experiment, arguably, when measured against such standards as the thousand-year-long Roman civilization).

The Enlightenment's progression of ideas

The founding ideas of the Enlightenment from the 1760s are at first glance a strange grab bag of ideas. Here are three of them.

A French priest named Richard Simon, using new methods of textual criticism, began to argue that the Old Testament was not historically reliable. The five books attributed to Moses, for example, couldn't possibly have been written by the same person. And this denial of the absolute literal accuracy of the Bible was coming from inside the official Catholic Church of France.

Across the channel in England, John Locke was up to his ears in the Glorious Revolution of 1688 that saw William and Mary replace James II and agree to parliamentary supremacy. But it was in terms of his profession as a doctor (a physician) that he asked himself where knowledge came from. The medieval answer was that it was in the mind and gradually awakened through God's agency. Locke's opposing conclusion was that at birth the mind was open and empty (*tabula rasa*, a clean slate), and that information filtered into it through the five senses. The implication of this that he—and virtually all later Enlightenment thinkers—drew, was that good environment made for good people 100 percent of the time, and bad environment made for bad people. It's not a belief that many of us today agree with as totally as they did, but it is important for us to know in understanding the age.

Pierre Bayle, back in France, was what you might almost call a professional skeptic. He was up-to-date on the new astronomical breakthroughs in England by Newton, Halley, and others, and when a rash of comets came through in the 1680s, he said to his panicky fellow Frenchmen that they should not be jumping off roofs and declaring the end of the world—comets were just on elongated ellipses, understandable material phenomena. In 1695 he published his massive *Historical and Critical Dictionary*, showing that a good bit of traditional and popular belief was so much unfounded opinion and superstition. He was not an atheist or even a deist (one who saw God only as first cause, setting up the world but not having much to do with it thereafter), but he did argue for a clear separation between rational thought and religious belief. Neither area really had anything of value to say to the other.

These three basic ideas don't necessarily have to go together, but in the late 1600s these and some others did indeed coalesce into a general system of beliefs. An optimistic search for basic universal human nature led to the belief that educated individuals could use their reason to redesign social and political institutions to fit. That was the first stage.

Later in the Enlightenment the major writers generally called themselves *Philosophes*, "Philosophers," though they were just as much publicists and propagandists. As they pursued this optimistic search for universal truths about human nature it increasingly led them to a celebration of the dignity of people—every individual, that is, not just humankind in general.

Montesquieu

The biggest name of the second generation of Enlightenment thinkers was Charles-Louis de Secondat, the Baron of La Brède and later of Montesquieu. He was born in 1689, just when the basic ideas above were coming together. His original home in La Brède[GE27], some eleven or twelve miles SSE of Bordeaux, was a wealthy noble estate known for its wines. Between Bordeaux and Paris he got the best secondary, college, and law school education money and social status could buy, and married into even more wealth. For a time it seemed he would settle contentedly into the political and legal affairs of Bordeaux, but fascination with the new breakthroughs in the sciences, including physics, geology, and even human physiology, pulled him more and more into the intellectual world. Fond of society although apparently quite shy, he became an overnight sensation in Paris in 1721 with the publication of *Persian Letters*. The satire contained letters ostensibly written from 1711 to 1720 by a wealthy Persian traveler named Usbek, by a younger friend, by some wives left behind in the seraglio (especially his favorite wife Roxanne), by the Chief Eunuch in charge of guarding the harem, and a few others. On the one hand, it is a great vehicle for criticizing western institutions. The Pope, for example, is called the "chief dervish" of the Christians; King Louis XIV (who only died in 1715) is supposed here to have a formal policy for punishing any general who succeeded so well he attracted attention away from the King's person. But in the hundreds of pages of letters there is also equal criticism of oriental institutions. In the nine years' absence of their lord, for example, the women of the Persian seraglio become more and more restive and hostile, judging by their letters and the Chief Eunuch's letters about them. Denied other pleasures of life, he reveled in his power as a jailer over the women. In the last few letters, a reader discovers that Roxanne was surprised in the arms of a young man, who was killed in a fight after wounding the Eunuch, and the single last letter, #161, is written to Usbek by Roxanne as she is dying of poison she has just taken. She never loved him, she says, and took delight in transforming his seraglio from a prison into a place of delight. Here is a key paragraph of that last letter:

> How could you think that I was such a weakling as to imagine there was nothing for me in the world but to worship your caprices; that while you indulged all your desires, you should have the right to thwart me in all mine? No: I have lived in slavery, and yet always retained my freedom: I have remodeled your laws upon those of nature; and my mind has always maintained its independence.[2]

The laws of nature talked about here is a reference to that basic universal human nature common to us all that was such a consistent quest of the Enlightenment to discover.

Montesquieu traveled widely in the 1720s, already at work on his systematic study of government, *The Spirit of the Laws,* that would be published in 1748. He was particularly impressed by British society and government, and may have done more to popularize the idea of a balance of executive, legislative, and judicial power even than John Locke. He wrote a good bit on the effect of climate on society and government. This didn't mean there was not a basic universal human nature, just that it reacted similarly to the warmth and ease of living in the tropics versus the more strenuous work needed to survive the winters of the temperate zone. He was less positive about human nature than many other Enlightenment figures, and as a result less zealous about reforms and more inclined to study them critically. He saw in monarchy a very real tendency to become despotism, and he saw in democracy a tendency towards mob rule. It was the nobility, in his mind, that was best able to insist on moderate behavior in both king and common people. In general he taught the next generation of Enlightenment thinkers to think deeply and critically of existing institutions, although they would come to a different conclusion about the worth of the institution of nobility.

Diderot's "Supplement to the Voyage of Bougainville"

Denis Diderot (1713–1784), born when Montesquieu was twenty-four, was one of the biggest names among the *Philosophes* in the third and final generation of the Enlightenment. He came from Langres,[GE28] a picturesque little hilltop town on the plateau of east central France, and like so many other *Philosophes* first planned

---

27. GE Layer 27 is a Placemark referencing the Château de La Brède, suggesting a Panoramio icon for one good aerial view. This Montesquieu family seat was about twelve miles south of the city of Bordeaux.

28. GE Layer 28 is a Placemark referencing Langres, a town which gives its name to the whole plateau thereabouts. Click on Panoramio icon under pointer, titled "tp-Foto Langres - Blick auf die Stadt," for a "view of the town" snapped by a German visitor.

and later rejected a career in the Church and eventually moved to Paris, center of the intellectual action of the age. His most important literary monument was the *Encyclopédie*, an enormous encyclopedia in twenty-seven huge volumes he edited and partially wrote from 1751–1772. The full title was *Encyclopédie, ou Dictionnnaire raisonnée des Sciences, des Arts, et des Métiers, par un société de gens des lettres* (*Encyclopedia, or Reasoned Dictionary of the Sciences, Arts and Trades, for the reading public*). As the name implies, it was an attempt to "encircle" all important knowledge, especially the new scientific and technological developments, but it was also suffused with the radical new world view of the Enlightenment. Deep in some article on a new manufacturing process, for example, might be a paragraph on why monarchy was not the ideal form of government, or criticism of the church throwing its weight behind some superstition—a real red flag to the royal censors when they finally came across it. As often happens, however, censorship actually encouraged the skills of writers challenged by it, giving wings to allusion and metaphor beyond the ken of the plodding, literal-minded censors.

There is a good illustration of that, and of the whole project of the Enlightenment, in a little 1772 pamphlet by Diderot. Called "Supplement to the Voyage of Bougainville,"[3] it is never listed among his great works (and in fact I have never been able to find a full translation in English, as famous as Diderot's writings are). It is used here just because it was such an ordinary Enlightenment work. Bougainville, the great French explorer of the world's oceans, had just published a volume of memoirs the year before, and Diderot wanted to use it as a jumping off point for some Enlightenment propaganda. His pamphlet has four acts, more or less, and he probably wrote it in a week.

The curtain opens on Guy A and Guy B sitting on a French beach talking about the weather, because a fog is rolling in. They decide to retreat from the beach and read Bougainville (I told you it wasn't great literature). Discussing it later, they eulogize Bougainville himself as a man with a taste for good living, an urge to see the world for himself, and a man with a firm intellectual foundation in the sciences, geometry, calculus, mechanics, astronomy, and natural history. Talk turns to islands he found, how they happen to have animals on them. One speculates that maybe they used to be part of the mainland. The other wonders why the people there didn't multiply until the island was as crowded as Paris. His friend replies with a crude but interesting anthropological model. In the earliest stages of human society cannibalism ensured there was no overpopulation. In a subsequent religious stage of society (Diderot, in true Enlightenment fashion, calls this the age of organized superstition), multiplication was limited by superstitious customs—tossing every tenth child into volcanoes to appease the fire god, and such, we take him to mean. Over time, a political stage of society developed, in which laws to prevent overpopulation were formulated by a government (fourth and later sons had to sail off to settle new islands, perhaps). These new governmental institutions, led by a tribal chief, and the older religious institutions, led by a tribal witch doctor, worked very closely together. A moral is drawn at this point: supernatural institutions fortify themselves in civil and national law, and civil and national institutions consecrate themselves with divine principles, a fatal cycle. Already by the end of Act I you can see that Diderot is not really talking about the Polynesian islands; the civil and national institutions he is thinking about are those of the French monarchy and aristocracy, and the supernatural institutions are those of the French Catholic church. He is just using a Pacific island setting to get around the censorship.

In the second part of the "Supplement," Diderot gets to the question of physical actions versus moral ideas. He tells the story of an old island chief who takes a French expedition to task for having destroyed the innocence of some of his people. Before the French came, says the chief, love was made in the open without reserve and was even a part of the hospitality offered strangers. The French abused the gift and inspired the women with an unknown madness. The "man of black," the robed Catholic priest, walked among them and made the men hesitate and the women blush. The sailors poisoned the loving sentiments of the girls with "unnatural" (there's that word again, or at least its opposite) acts. So the moral ideas are traditional European-Christian ideas of vice and virtue, and the physical action is in this case sexual relations. Getting more interesting, *n'est-ce pas*?

In part the third, the French priest visits the hut of the hospitable island chief. In other words, the representative of Western Civilization ca. 1772 confronts the noble savage. The priest suddenly discovers that local custom calls for him to sleep with one of the daughters or the wife of the chief. He protests that his religion and his state laws will not let him do this. The chief in his turn is angered at this impolite refusal. The next morning the priest explains to the chief his understanding of God and the place of religious and political institutions. The chief is a bit dubious about a being who made the world without tools or sweat, and is especially sarcastic about one who thought up such strange rules of social behavior. He is thankful his own fathers were not spoken to by such a one. Then he asks the key question of the pamphlet: "Tell me, do the orders of your God, your priests and your magistrates really prevent young men from ever sleeping with young girls in your country?" The priest can't deny that this occasionally happens, perhaps more often than he knows, and the chief proudly proclaims that you just can't fight the natural.

The last act returns to the dialogue of A and B. One asks how the greatest and most innocent of our pleasures became a source of guilt. The other replies that religious institutions attached the names of vice and virtue to actions not susceptible to any such morality. In fact, says one—and here is the Enlightenment in a one-sentence nutshell—the history of all misery is the conflict of natural man (and woman) with artificial institutions.

The fog lifts. One suggests they get some female company and read them the conversation between priest and chief: "What will they say about it, do you think?" "I don't know." "What will they think?" "Perhaps the opposite of what they say." On this light note the little drama ends. It is not important so much for what it says about sex—Diderot seems to have been a good deal more liberal, even libertine, on that than most of his contemporaries. It is more important in the way he goes about arguing, appealing to the natural, that is so typical of the age, and in the way he identifies a "conflict of natural man with artificial institutions."

Rousseau's General Will

This view of human nature in turn seems to have been the foundation for the final emphasis on equality you can see late in the Enlightenment. If we are all potentially good, and we are all of intrinsic value as humans, how then should we be divided into castes? Equality was a logical but really surprising result of the Enlightenment. One of the most thought-provoking ironies of the age is to think of the very aristocratic Montesquieu—a Baron, an aristocrat of aristocrats—or even the upper-middle-class and socially aspiring Voltaire, working in a movement that would pulverize the whole social stratification.

In this respect, Jean-Jacques Rousseau (1712–1778), although within a year of Diderot in age, was something of a culmination of Enlightenment thought. A concern with the goodness of "natural man" led him to an impassioned plea for the equality of all people and even beyond that, to a glimpse of a new kind of state made up just of these free and equal people—no kings, aristocrats, or even churchmen needed.

A sketch of Rousseau's life, necessary as background for his philosophy, shows some human tragedy. He was born in Geneva (the French-speaking western corner of Switzerland)[GE[29]] in 1712. His mother died a few days later. His father looked after him after a fashion until he was ten, then had to leave town because of a quarrel, so Jean-Jacques stayed a year or so with a maternal uncle. Then he was apprenticed—farmed out might be more like it—in turn to a pastor, as clerk to a notary, and as apprentice to an engraver, from whom he ran away before age sixteen. He must have been an attractive young man (although his sensitivity was beginning to slide over into paranoia even then), because he found a series of protectors and rich mistresses. One of them, with whom he lived off and on in his late teens and early twenties, was a wealthy woman some ten years his senior, who lived in Savoy (not part of France until the nineteenth century) some forty-five miles south of Geneva. She introduced him to her circle of educated friends. Yet he had little success as a tutor (in Lyon), an engraver, and a musician in roughly that order. When he was thirty he moved to Paris, hoping to make his fortune with a new system of writing music, though nothing came of it. Only at age thirty-nine or so did he begin to have any success with his writing as winner of a national essay contest. For a time he won real acceptance into the circle of *Philosophes*, but soon the peculiarities of his character turned everything sour. He eventually feuded with most of the *Philosophes* and even his closest friend among them, Diderot, and became the butt of many a sarcastic literary treatment. He lived with an uneducated girl in a common-law marriage, and as each of his five children was born he deposited it in an orphanage. What kind of father serially gives away his chil-

---

29. GE Layer 29 is a Folder titled "Sites of Rousseau's early life." The first Placemark in it references the house where he was born in Geneva, still standing, and the second is the home of the wealthy Madame de Warens, who took him in and introduced him to educated circles.

dren like this? Rousseau was a social outcast most of his life, and from that point of view wrote a bitter critique of society and social conventions. In society as it existed, he wrote over and over, a good man (meaning himself, of course) could not be content.

The genius of Rousseau is not in this self-serving negative critique, however, but in a positive, nearly utopian, vision of natural people in a naturally constructed society and government. Three of his greatest works were published within eighteen months of each other in 1761 and 1762: *Julie, or the New Helen*; *On the Social Contract*; and *Emile, or On Education*. The *Emile* especially has a modern ring to it; if you were ever attracted by the back-to-the-land movement you might really enjoy it. Rousseau's theme is the basic satisfaction of doing what comes naturally. "Fix your eyes on nature, follow the path traced by her," he says in the first few pages. He rails against habits such as confining a newborn in heavy cloths that make motion impossible, against fashionable young women ceasing to nurse their own babies, against fathers rarely spending time with their young children, and such. One by one in moving language he explains the artificiality of each situation and the resulting evil. The whole purpose of the rambling book is to describe a "natural" education for a hypothetical boy, Emile, from birth to age twenty, and shorter shrift to a hypothetical female counterpart, Sophie. A question that cries to be asked is what gave Rousseau the right to preach on child rearing, given his own life? Perhaps the pain of knowing the wrong way gave him some insights. At any rate, the *Emile* and *New Helen* got to be more than just popular books, but virtual cult items. After Rousseau, few literate French people were unaware of the artifice of sophisticated society and the basic humanness of us all. Even Marie Antoinette, raised at the brilliant formal Austrian court in Vienna and Queen of France as of 1774, may have been affected by this. Out back of her severely geometric personal little palace at Versailles, *Le Petit Trianon*,[GE30] she had *Le Petit Hameau*, the little hamlet of the Queen—built in a miniature version of the countryside where she and her ladies in waiting could play at being shepherdesses.[GE31]

Out of this view of human nature and the essential equality of people came the most important political concept of modern times, the General Will (*volonté générale*), which first appears in Rousseau's *Social Contract*. It is a delicate and almost mystical concept that Rousseau himself obviously found difficult to state precisely. He sort of walks around it like a cat around a cream pitcher, telling you first what it is not. The General Will is not necessarily majority vote, nor embodied in any set of formal written law that can be true for all time and places. That much it clearly is not. What it is, he says, is a solution to the greatest political and social dilemma of all time: namely, how to construct a government that protects the citizen and the citizen's property and at the same time costs that citizen no freedom. Now that has always been the trick, hasn't it? Law and order is not hard to achieve: Nazi Germany and Soviet Russia both had lots of order, but little of what most of us today would call freedom. The trick ever since Plato's day is how to combine law and order with individual freedom. I've got it, says Rousseau.

In the critical pages of definition near the beginning of the book, Rousseau says something transcendental and confusing about each man giving himself totally to all others, no one losing more than anyone else in the deal, yet everyone gaining more than he loses. And then Rousseau himself italicizes the following sentence:

> Each of us puts his person and all his power in common under the supreme directionof the General Will, and,
> in our corporate capacity, we receive each member as anindivisible part of the whole.[4]

The concept gets a little clearer when he continues that this act association creates a moral and collective body. So the General Will is a kind of invisible moral force for Rousseau, but very tangible and not at all abstract. If one's particular will should lead one to dispute the General Will, then one must be compelled to follow the General Will. A reader's first reaction here is probably to see this as a clear limitation of individual freedom, and to wonder about Rousseau's earlier comment on all this "costing a man no freedom." But some-

---

30. GE Layer 30 is a Placemark framing a view of Marie Antoinette's personal little palace, the *Petit Trianon*. You can explore its severe geometry in many local Photos icons.

31. GE Layer 31 is a Placemark framing a view of the Hameau in its carefully crafted non-geometric "natural" setting. Many Photos icons to explore.

how for Rousseau a person's freedom is being increased to a new level, and this makes it permissible to "force" him or her to be free.

The last resort of a teacher trying to explain a difficult and delicate concept is to retreat to a comparison, a parable. Here is one that occurred in a flash of enlightenment to this teacher. Remember that parables only work with a sympathetic audience; don't show this one to your local political science professor.

The flavor of Rousseau's meaning for General Will, freedom, particular will, etc., can be seen every fall in a home game at the University of Alabama (this teaching is being done in the state of Alabama; plug in nearest football powerhouse to you for a local translation). Imagine the eleventh game of the season, to be played against cross-state rival Auburn, which as it turns out this year will decide not only the SEC championship but also a #1 ranking in the national bowl picture. Visualize an Alabama fan who did not realize the importance of the game until late in the season, and who then bought a ticket from a scalper for $900. The fan drove two hours to the stadium, took an hour and $30 to park and half an hour to get to his or her seat, in front of an excitable drinker who sloshed the first of every beer on his or her back. Two and a half hours he sat there in an intermittent drizzle, then took fifty minutes to get to the car and an hour to leave the lot. After the game some crockery was broken at a post-game celebration, and the fan got home at 3:30 Sunday morning, weary of mind and body, and out—counting the crockery—about $1200.

Now from the point of view of an independent observer having no emotional ties to the University of Alabama, the whole thing makes no sense. There are all sorts of limitations on that fan's freedom—freedom to drive and walk in the direction and speed he or she wants, freedom to move around the crowded stands, freedom to speak his or her mind. What would happen if one shouted too vigorously for Alabama if surrounded by Auburn fans, or worse yet spoke—anywhere in the stadium—of the absurdity of twenty-two semi-professional athletes upholding the reputations of academic institutions?

But from the fan's point of view there is no loss of freedom. He or she has reached a whole new level of existence, in fact, a sense of being totally immersed in a sympathetic group consciousness. The guy spilling beer would give the fan his last brew as a fellow Crimson Tider. The fan may be hemmed in, but who wants to go? Down on the field eleven crimson-jerseyed athletes are slowly pushing back a wall of Auburn men, and the fused minds of all the Alabama supporters are willing Alabama toward the end zone like a tractor beam in a sci-fi movie. It is a time of intense belonging that might be called by Rousseau and some others a new level of freedom. The General Will of the crowd is overriding and fulfilling, submerging individual wills into a lethe of forgetfulness. For a week or so the fan forgets about being twenty pounds overweight, that a son or daughter needs $3000 worth of braces, and that if the business has two more bad months there'll be trouble with the bank. There's an old Russian proverb that says it's not the sea that drowns you, it's the puddle; that is, it's not the dramatic crises of life that break you, but the long-term daily grind. Anything that elevates your spirit above it tends to be really valuable to you as a person.

So, when Rousseau writes a convoluted phrase like this one later in the *Social Contract*:

> The undertakings which bind us to the social body are obligatory only because they are mutual; and their nature is such that in fulfilling them we cannot work for otherswithout working for ourselves. Why is it that the General Will is always in the right,unless it is because there is not a man who does not think of 'each' and meaning 'him' . . . .[5]

you ought to think of a great crowd of football fans wending their ways to bars and homes for a post-game fellowship, a brother- and sisterhood beautiful to behold. This is the kind of emotion and belonging that Rousseau coveted for the state. This was the intellectual invention of modern patriotism, as clearly as I can trace it to its source.

To jump from Rousseau straight into the Revolution might seem a little unfair; after all, he died eleven years before it broke out. About the only solid proof that he was the bridge between Enlightenment and Revolution is that his books were in the libraries of many of the revolutionaries. But a greater if less tangible proof is that the Revolution not only followed his logic, it even used his phraseology to describe what happened. Rousseau was the "antenna of the race," as Rimbaud said poets and seers must be. He enunciated the vibrations of the future when no one else was really conscious of them.

Turgot, the last hope for reform from above

In 1776—an especially easy date for most Americans to remember—the Scottish thinker Adam Smith wrote his beautifully titled *An Inquiry into the Nature and Causes of the Wealth of Nations*, the kind of inquiry more of us should interest ourselves in today. Some of his particular arguments included how specialization of labor in a pin factory could lead to a huge jump in overall production. His general argument, though, was for free trade—letting the marketplace operate on its own to solve problems, free of governmental interference. If, for example, there happened to be a shortage of shoes, and people were willing to pay more and more for a pair, some enterprising person would build a shoe factory to make big money from it. This was Smith's "invisible hand"—private ambition that made for general public welfare.

The phrase that sums all this up is *laissez faire*, (you) leave [it] to do [by itself]. We use the French phrase because there was a parallel school of thought across the channel in France of theorists who called themselves the Physiocrats, and they were using this phrase and general concept a decade or two earlier than Smith.

A key member of these French Physiocrats was Anne-Robert-Jacques Turgot (1721–1781). He (which he was, despite the Anne) was born in Paris into an old family traditionally close to the throne, educated at the Sorbonne (still the Arts & Sciences heart of the University of Paris today), and early in his career was a church-man. A talented young man speaking seven languages, but having fallen away from literal belief in much of the Bible, he switched over to government service. By the 1750s he was writing articles for Diderot's *Ency-clopédie*, and beginning to get interested in economics. He toured widely in France with his mentor, the real founder of the Physiocrats, the Intendant of Commerce Vincent de Gournay (originator of the phrase *"laissez faire, laissez passer"*). Turgot began his own innovative work by arguing that grain should not be taxed as it moved from province to province in France. If the customs barriers between provinces were removed and it was allowed to move cheaply and freely, many local famines could thus be avoided with no effort on the part of either church or state. Soon Turgot was extending this idea to many other categories of goods. By 1760 he was good friends with Voltaire, who popularized his work in progressive circles. In 1761 his reputation and connections were such that the king's government appointed him Intendant of Limoges. He spent fourteen years there trying out his theories in the real world.

The position of Intendant had been created by the brilliant Cardinal Richelieu, ruling minister a century earlier, as the central government's key man in each province. The list of responsibilities was daunting: collect-ing taxes (under an archaic and bizarre system); promoting agriculture, industry, and commerce; administering justice and keeping public order; distributing poor relief. Limoges,[GE32] where the Loire River tributary the Vienne River flows west out of the *Massif central*—for all that we associate its name with excellent china, and that "limousin" (someone or something from Limoges) today means excellence in private transportation—was then a poor province. Its biggest town was 14,000, and 85 percent of the province's people were farmers. The roads, such as they were, were maintained by the *corvée*—drafting local peasants to work on them without pay.

Turgot immediately began creating a professional civil service in the province, deposing some wealthy but venal officials who had gotten their offices through connections and were of course beholden to those who gave them the office to start with. He began the enormous job of updating the land records. To improve the roads he decided to tax everyone—including the wealthy and the nobility—and pay workers to work. Soon Limoges, this hillbilly province in central France, had the best roads in the country. He focused on jobs and food for the general population, with good effect.

So in 1774, when old Louis XV died and twenty-year-old Louis XVI inherited the throne, Turgot was called to Paris as Controller-General of France, to make the whole kingdom as efficient and equitable as Limo-ges. He arrived something of a hero to the common people and the *Philosophes* and a very real threat to the traditional privileges of the nobility. In his attempts to replicate his Limoges reforms country-wide and in a short time, he stirred up incredible opposition from the nobility, and even from the royal family. Marie Antoi-nette resented it immensely when her customary rights of dispensing grants to favorites was limited—and she was now Queen. The result of it all was the firing of Turgot in that same easy-to-remember 1776, with a return to upper-class privilege as usual. Those two turbulent years, the first two years of the well-meaning but weak

---

32. GE Layer 32 is a Placemark referencing Limoges.

Louis XVI on the throne, were probably the last realistic chance for *ancien régime* France to reform itself, from above. "Good is impossible, Turgot has been toppled, and I weep for France," wrote the thoughtful Abbé de Véri in his diary.[6] Thirteen years later basic change would come from below, in an explosion of violence.

The coming of the Revolution

The greatest irony of the French Revolution is that it was triggered by those who lost the most in it, namely the nobility. As a class they had been tamed by Louis XIV, and his famous absolutism had been built mainly at their expense. After his death in 1715, however, under weaker kings and regencies, their power soared. By the 1780s it was as great as it had been two centuries earlier. The nobility monopolized all the higher positions of state, including the diplomatic corps and the intendancies. They claimed every seat in the thirty-one top courts of France, including the *Parlement de Paris*, the Supreme Court of the land. Every single bishop in the French Catholic Church was noble. If you wanted to be even the lowest grade of officer in the army, and if you didn't have four noble grandparents, you needed not apply. The nobility paid no taxes, and from them the state required no service. It was no responsibility and virtually all privilege. All they feared was some new Louis XIV super-king figure who might arise and take those rights and privileges away, and for this reason they agitated—in a gentlemanly sort of way, of course—for a Constitution. They quoted Montesquieu and talked of truth and justice for all, when what they were really after was something that would guarantee their current rights and privileges forever.

No king in his right mind or in normal times would favor that, of course. Unfortunately for Louis XVI, however, the French state was rapidly approaching bankruptcy. In the short run France had fought one too many wars. The Seven Years War of 1756–63 had been expensive to wage and had cost France Canada and all its holdings in India, among other losses. Residual anger over that helped determine French support for Britain's rebellious American colonies from 1777–1783—support without which U.S. independence would not have happened and I would be writing for you my fellow British Commonwealth subjects a somewhat different modern world history book—but that was the straw that broke the treasury's back. In the long run, however, France—one of the richest lands in Europe—had a bankrupt government because of a taxation system under which almost no one with any money was taxed. Neither nobility nor French Catholic Church were taxed, so the *taille*, or fireplace tax, fell heaviest on the peasantry, the poor farmers.

In July of 1788 a formal deal was struck between King and nobility. The nobles would allow themselves to be taxed, moderately, and so bail the government out of its bankruptcy crisis. On his side the King would help them get their Constitution guaranteeing all the rest of their rights and privileges forever. Here is where it gets a bit complex institutionally, because the nobles didn't want the King simply to hand them a Constitution (because anything the King did today he could undo tomorrow). The deal was that the King would call an Estates General (*États généraux*), a late medieval body that had last met in 1614. It had been called in major crises, with delegates from each estate sitting in three separate houses. The First Estate, the clergy, gave any enterprise spiritual blessing and the French Catholic Church was one of the few strong national organizations. The Second Estate, the nobility, were to do the required fighting. And the Third Estate, or merchants, were to pay for it. This all made a certain sense in, say, AD 1300, and so critical national issues were decided by a vote of these three houses, 2–1 or 3–0. You can see why the nobility liked this institution. They and their kin who administered the Catholic Church could win any vote 2–1, even though they were together only 5 percent of the French population. And a formal document arrived at by the Estates General couldn't be changed by the King. So in July of 1788 the King publicly announced that 300 delegates from each estate would be elected the following spring, and that there would be meeting of such an Estates General at Versailles in May of 1789.

Louis XVI's next major mistake was to call for a public debate on how the Estates General should meet, since the last one had been 175 years before, well before living memory. This triggered a debate with elements of the Third Estate arguing that it was no longer 1614, and the Third Estate representation should at least be doubled to 600 delegates and 2 votes for its house. The proposal was quickly run through the higher courts—staffed solely by nobles, remember—and the verdict was more devious than a simple "no." The Third Estate was allowed to elect 600 delegates, but its house still got only one vote.

In January of 1789 the first signs of real revolutionary anger appeared in a famous pamphlet by the Abbé Sieyès, an abbot, a churchman and so technically First Estate, but who was elected from Paris for the Third Estate. It was titled *"Qu'est-ce que le tiers état?,"* "What is the Third Estate?" In it he talks about what makes a nation, and how the Third Estate does nineteen-twentieths of the real work of the French nation, while the privileged classes take all the plums and by so doing show that they aren't really part of the nation. That spring, as the countryside elected its delegates to the Third Estate, every village was asked to draw up a Notebook of Grievances (*Cahier de Doléances*). By the series of indirect elections being held, the odds on the delegate from any single village going to Versailles were very small, so this way each village would at least be represented by a notebook. Looking back, it was a real consciousness-raising process, with villagers in essence being invited to think and talk about the logic and origins of the present social structure. As a refrain went in an English rebellion several centuries before this, "When Adam dalfe (dug) and Eve span (spun), Who was then a gentleman?" That is, where did this aristocracy dodge come from and why do you get to be one and us not? Historians are virtually unanimous in believing that what is important in history in causing events is not what is, but what people believe at the time, and beliefs were changing fast that spring.

At Versailles

The 1200 delegates duly assembled at Versailles in May, going to the building provided for them by the King. The meeting place for the Estates was the *Salle des Menus Plaisirs*, about a third of a mile down the main approach avenue from the gates of the palace. It included a ceremonial hall big enough to hold them all in any full session of all three Estates and other rooms and courtyards for each of the three sitting separately.[GE33] The First and Second Estates got busy drafting their Constitution, but the Third Estate decided to go on a sit-down strike until they got their double vote. Led by the Abbé Sieyès, they insisted that all 1200 delegates meet together for all votes by a show of hands, which would have effectively given the Third its double representation. For six weeks things were virtually deadlocked. Then on June 13 a few priests from the First came over to sit with the Third, and got an enthusiastic reception. On June 17 the augmented Third Estate voted to call itself the National Assembly. Implicit in this was that those of the First and Second who would not come join would be disenfranchised. It was a truly revolutionary step.

When the delegates of this self-proclaimed National Assembly came back to their hall on June 20, they found it closed and guarded by order of the King. Milling around the grounds they soon found an empty squash court, what we'd call a small gymnasium,[GE34] and in an impromptu meeting inside swore to each other they would not leave Versailles until France had a Constitution—by which they meant something very different than the Constitution the nobles were working toward. This has come down in the history books as "The Tennis Court Oath." At this point the King and the First and Second Estates realized that the Third Estate was much more a danger to each of them than they were to each other. By month's end the King had ordered the assembling of the bulk of the French army, 18,000 men, in the vicinity of Versailles. He was clearly planning to put this upstart National Assembly down by force.

Fall of the Bastille

Versailles was just a one-hour pony jog or a three-hour walk from downtown Paris. The assembling of the 18,000-man army there was impossible to hide, and Parisians feared they were the ultimate target. Once a century, on average, Paris had physically rebelled against the French kings; that, in fact, is one reason Versailles was built in the first place, to remove it from the reach of Paris insurrection. So now Parisians were wondering aloud, 18,000 troops for 600 unarmed Third Estate delegates? What is this army really for? And since by the series of indirect elections a large percentage of the total delegates came from Paris—most of

---

33. GE Layer 33 is a Polygon showing in red outline the approximate location of the whole complex of the *Hôtel des Menus-Plaisirs*.

34. GE Layer 34 is a Placemark symbolized by a red Pushpin, titled "Jeu de Paume," referencing the site of the "tennis court oath" events of June 20.

them busily writing their home constituents letters as to how the King and the nobles were conspiring against them—conditions in Paris were tense indeed. In this setting all it took was one horseman, clearing the way a little too vigorously with his whip for the carriage of some noble or a member of the royal family, to turn a crowd of strangers into a mob with a single purpose.

As the Parisians tried to arm themselves against what they saw as a coming attack, they broke into arsenals for weapons. In the course of this, on July 14 a crowd gathered at the Bastille just a bit east of city center.[GE35] It was a long-out-of-date fortress, built back in the 100 Years War to anchor defense of what was then the eastern wall of Paris. In 1789 it was something like the Tower of London, used as a prison and to house a small military force. Not only did the crowd want the guns and gunpowder in it, but rumor had it that there were thousands of political prisoners locked up there. The commandant of the garrison of about 100, to overawe the crowd, rolled his cannons into sight in their embrasures. The crowd, fast becoming a mob, went to get cannons of their own. Shooting started, with dozens killed. The commandant, probably not wishing to shed more French blood, told the crowd there were no thousands of political prisoners, just a handful of common criminals, and bridged the moat so that they could send witnesses in under white flag. But more and more of the crowd poured in, and the discovery that there were no political prisoners seemed to enrage them more. The fortress was sacked, the commandant killed and his head fixed on a pike and carried in procession to City Hall, where the mayor was killed as well.[GE36] Although everybody knows about the Bastille as a building, the real significance of this day is that this mob seized control of city government, and Paris seceded from the King's France.

The "Great Fear"

These events in Paris gave the King pause, and while he hesitated to impose his army on Versailles an even more awesome violence broke out in the countryside. It is called the *Grande Peur,* literally the Great Fear, though a better name for it might be the Grand Panic.

As background, the harvest of 1788 had been marginal. In summer, just before the new harvest could come in, grain prices spiked, out of reach of many of the poor. There were rumors of coming famine, and a few elderly people still around to tell of the horrors of the last one, when people ate the bark off the trees in their desperation. Letters had been coming to the villages from Versailles delegates since early May, warning of collusion of King and nobility. Through a hungry countryside rolled grain caravans owned by the wealthy, going to where prices were high. An otherwise law-abiding French peasant woman or man with multiple mouths to feed and no money might easily have turned Robin Hood at that point. And most chilling of all came the rumor that the beggars were coming to town. Even in good times there were beggars, and homes of a certain value had to maintain shelters for them. But in bad times like these the begging armies tended to swell, wiping out whole villages and heading on for the next. In the century before, Lyon, the second biggest city in France, had to slam its doors and call out the army to hold off such a begging army estimated at 100,000. As it turned out, the beggars were not really out in force—but common belief had it so, and that played its part in the unusual tension. It was like dust in a mine or a mill, taking just a spark to set off a huge blast.

The spark was apparently word from Paris about the sack of the Bastille and the capture of city government. The historian Georges Lefebvre tells us that on or about July 20, at five spots scattered around France, ordinary events happened that in the stress of the moment were interpreted in extraordinary ways. In one town a couple of traveling salesmen appeared, and were immediately assumed to be spies for the begging army lurking outside town. They were quickly killed, a militia created of able-bodied adult males, the children, and non-combatants rounded up in a strong house in town, and word sent out to neighboring villages that the beggars were upon them. Another village saw a mysterious dust cloud, assumed the beggars were on the march,

---

35. GE Layer 35 is a Placemark referencing the site of the Bastille, and suggesting a Panoramio icon for a view of the "July Column" that now dominates the square. Doing a Google—Images search of "Bastille" will turn up lots of old paintings and drawings of the eight-towered old fort.

36. GE Layer 36 is a Placemark referencing the Hôtel de Ville, on the Right Bank of the Seine just opposite the Île de la Cité.

and behaved likewise. It was like dropping five matches into a dry field of grass. In two weeks' time, it had burned over all of France except a few areas, mostly on the periphery.[GE[37]]

In many villages, one other thing also happened. A delegation of adult farmers would visit the château, or manor house, of the local lord. If they liked him, and if he was home, they would knock politely and ask him to come outside while they burned his manor house. If they didn't like him, they just didn't knock (though many were absent, at their city homes or traveling). It was said you could follow the progress of *la Grande Peur* by the columns of smoke rising from the burning châteaux. They burned more manor houses than Sherman ever thought about marching through Georgia. Why? Partly because it was the greatest local symbol of nobility, and they had recently become more conscious of social inequities. But more tangibly, the records of the manor house were written proof that the lord owned the woods, the meadows, and most of the plow lands. They burned those deeds, and before the ashes were cool plowed themselves out a farm big enough that they could make a living on it. Land hunger: whenever you have a population that is majority agricultural, and yet they don't have enough land to live on, you have social dynamite easily set off. In later chapters you'll see it in Mexico in 1910 (and in southern Mexico as recently as 1994), in Russia in 1917, in China at the end of virtually every dynasty, and other places and times. But this one in France during the last third of July and the first few days of August, 1789, may be the most famous example of all time.

The August 4 Assembly and the end of feudalism

If the insurrection in Paris and the fall of the Bastille had been unpleasant to the nobility, these paled alongside the Great Fear. It struck at the root of French wealth and prestige: ownership of the land. More than that, it came as profound shock to many aristocrats to realize what the peasants really thought about them and their social position. On the night of August 4, a handful of noblemen came over to the meeting house of the National Assembly and made short speeches renouncing all feudal rights on their estates. The first few speeches seem to have been preplanned, but the meeting turned into something as emotional as the last night of a tent revival. So many noblemen voluntarily renounced their rights that the Assembly was encouraged to make general resolutions sweeping away the legal aspects of feudalism for all France. Within a month the Assembly issued the Declaration of the Rights of Man and Citizen. Inspired to some extent by the American Declaration of Independence, it was a step more radical. This document spoke of the natural rights of man, equality before the law, and even of the state as the expression of the General Will. Rousseau began to look more and more like a prophet.

In the next couple of months the royal government simply melted away. On October 6 the King was taken to Paris, to the Tuileries,[GE[38]] as a virtual prisoner, and the National Assembly followed him there two days later, occupying the Manège,[GE[39]] the Riding School attached to the Tuileries. In that same year the city government, the Commune of Paris, moved into the nearby Palais-Royal.[GE[40]] From here it would have been a five-minute walk to the Louvre and Tuileries palaces, and a ten-minute walk to the Manège: the Paris Commune could watch national policy very closely!

These closely-watched delegates of the National Assembly now wrestled with a dual problem: (1) the writing of a constitution which was their original mission as a constituent body, and (2) the day-to-day coping with the immediate problems of government, with a treasury still near bankruptcy. These were able men, idealistic and at the same time practical—a combination in history that is perhaps rarer than you might think. They had cut their intellectual teeth on the great philosophers of the Enlightenment, but at the same time many of them

---

37. GE Layer 37 is a Polygon showing in red the general area where the Great Fear raged from July 20 to August 4, 1789. Main source of map, Geoffregy Barraclough, editor, *The Times Atlas of World History* (Maplewood NJ: Hammond, 1985), p. 203.

38. GE Layer 38 is a Placemark referencing the Tuileries. The Palace, a western extension of the Louvre, was destroyed in the Paris Commune, a civil war of 1871; now it is a garden.

39. GE Layer 39 is a Polygon showing in red outline the approximate location of the Manège, the building taken over for use of the National Assembly.

40. GE Layer 40 is a Placemark referencing the Palais-Royal.

had a legal background and considerable experience in administrative affairs. Much of their work was brilliant, considering the circumstances, though whether for good or bad is still debated. A crushing debt still lay on the central government, and everywhere the counterrevolution was beginning to raise its voice, aided not least by the Church establishment. At a stroke the delegates attempted to "crush the infamous thing" (Voltaire's imperative against "superstitious" institutions) and invent a new money supply. They confiscated the rich lands of the French Church—some 10 percent of all the farmland of France, accumulated over the centuries through wills and tithes—and made it the backing for a paper money called the *Assignat*. "Assign the bearer of this bill X amount of land," the name meant. Does that sound strange, land as a backing for paper money? But what is behind your paper money, Dear American Reader? Gold or silver? Not for decades and decades; nothing but popular confidence. And in a nation where the majority were still farmers, land made some sense—you could see it and touch it, and you know the old saying, "Buy land; they're not making any more of it!" The Assignat would eventually inflate, and not much of it ever was actually exchanged for land, but for a few years it won the confidence of the French people and gave the government great buying power. A not inconsiderable by-product of this measure was that the government inherited all matters of health, welfare, and education from the Church, another sure sign of the coming of the modern nation-state.

The Constitution of 1791

This constitution that was finally proclaimed in September of 1791 by these same men, after more than two years of intense labor, was a great achievement. It began with that ringing Declaration of the Rights of Man and Citizen, and proceeded to set up a constitutional monarchy with a unicameral (one-house) legislature. Possibly one of the best constitutions ever written, it collapsed in a short six months. Why?

First, the king had tried to escape in June of that year and had gotten as far as Lorraine in eastern France before being caught and brought back. How could a constitutional monarchy possibly function with an unwilling monarch?

Second—and this will take a little more explaining—there had been a "Left-shift" in politics. You may be generally familiar with the terms "Left" and "Right" in politics. In the U.S., for example, the Republican Party is generally considered Right of center and the Democratic Party Left of center. In each there is a continuum, from moderates close to the center to more extreme views on either end of the spectrum. Then outside the Republic Party on the Right are more extreme groups, until out on the end of the spectrum you get survivalists, white supremacists, and some real right-wing crazies expecting black government helicopters to arrive momentarily. And outside the Democratic Party on the left come more and more radical socialist and then Marxist and Maoist parties shading off into true left-wing crazies. Some political scientists say you should bend the Left-Right continuum up into a circle so that Right- and Left-wing crazies are next to each other! This Left-Right continuum, incidentally, wasn't invented by any political scientist. In France in the mid-nineteenth century, after yet another political upheaval, elected delegates met in a wide but shallow hall. The hard-line socialists took up a position with their backs to the left-hand wall, and the die-hard monarchists had their backs to the right-hand wall, and everybody else just shuffled around until they sat next to whomever they could tolerate. I've always been tempted (but have never had the courage) to have members of a college class come up to the front of the room and form a line, and talk about hot-button issues such as abortion, global warming, balanced budget, current wars, U.S. support of Israel and whether or not to bomb Iran's nuclear program, and instruct everybody to move around in the line until they're as comfortable as they can be with their neighbors. I think we'd get a good Left-Right (or Right-Left) continuum in less than ten minutes.

Well, the whole point of this rambling explanation is that this Left-Right continuum is real world behavior, not just some intellectual construct. And one thing that always characterizes a Revolution is the speed of change of public opinion along that continuum. I was never in a Revolution proper, but I have experienced some "Movements" in my time—the "Sixties" in the U.S., the atmosphere in central China before and during the Tiananmen Square massacres of 1989, and some others. I remember in my student days that Bob Dylan would have taken some public stand considerably to my Left in politics, and somehow, six months later, I and my friends had slid over to that position. This is what happened in France from 1789 to 1792. In October of 1789 the Left-Right continuum was monarchist on the Right, constitutional monarchist in the Center, and moderate republican on the Left—and the midpoint of that continuum was what the Constitution was written to serve. But by 1792 public opinion had shifted radically Leftwards along that continuum—no monarchists left at all, a dwindling band of constitutional monarchists on the Right, moderate republicans in the Center (generally called *Girondins* because leading members were from Bordeaux and other sites around the *Gironde* estuary), and a growing force of radical republicans on the Left (most importantly the *Jacobins,* who met in the building of a former Dominican monastery on the Rue St. Jacques).[GE⁴¹] For this new Left-Right continuum the Constitution was simply unacceptable.

Third and probably most important, though, was the coming of war. Less than six months had passed under the new constitution when in April 1792 the leaders of the Convention (radical successor to the National Assembly) drifted rather lightheartedly into a war with two great powers of Europe. At that point, the pressures of foreign invasion and domestic rebellion quickly rendered the Constitution useless. Beginning with the popular insurrection in August 1792, the Revolution entered a new phase.

The kings and queens and aristocratic governments of the rest of Europe had regarded the French Revolution with some nervousness from its beginning, you might well imagine. By 1792 they had achieved a consensus of distaste for it. But war was a step the old regime foreign ministers still resisted, despite the clamor of French émigré nobles who found refuge at their courts. Then on April 20, 1792, the French revolutionary government invaded Belgium to "liberate" it from Austria. If you don't count the American invasion of Canada in our own Revolutionary war, this was the first modern "war of liberation." In immediate response, armies from the two largest German states, Austria and Prussia, destroyed the outer French armies and began a follow-up invasion aimed directly at Paris. Now the Revolution fought for its life, and in its fight—for good or ill or both—forged the modern state.

The radical phase

In the summer of 1792 Paris became a funnel for troops loyal to the Revolution who came from all across France, as they gathered here and then marched east to war. They brought new hope to the city and a new enthusiasm for the Revolution. A contagious marching song originally composed in Strasbourg (the biggest French city on the Rhine)[GE⁴²] while it awaited German invasion, was adopted by military units from Marseilles, the big Mediterranean seaport. They in turn brought it to Paris in the summer of 1792 where of course it became known as the *Marseillaise.* In its first phrase you have a clue to coming events: "*Allons! enfants de la patrie*"—"Let's go, children of the fatherland (parentland?)." A national brother- and sisterhood of Rousseauvian intensity was obviously in the making. National anthems, incidentally, almost always come from critical periods of the growth of national consciousness; watch for them throughout this modern history, in Mexico, in South Africa (two rival ones!), in Israel, in India, in Indonesia, in Japan. In this context it may be of interest that our own national anthem comes not from the War of Independence but from the War of 1812—after the French Revolution.

A quick series of events followed, here chronicled. August 1: a manifesto from the opposing army commander was published in Paris, threatening the sack of the city if the French King or Queen were in any way harmed. August 10: a Paris force of revolutionary patriots overran the Tuileries where the royal family lived, in what amounted to a major urban battle with a thousand dead. In its wake the Commune, a revolutionary new city government of Paris, forced the abandonment of the Constitution and the election of a new body based on universal manhood suffrage—the National Convention. Late August: the military situation was worse than ever with the Prussian army closing in. September 2: Georges Danton, a key revolutionary leader, organized a desperate defense by sending Paris volunteers off to the front. In the general atmosphere of panic, the "September Massacres" began. Priests and prisoners were slaughtered, rather than leave them behind in a city stripped of

---

41. GE Layer 41 is a Placemark showing the approximate location of the old Dominican order building, on the Rue St. Jacques on the Left Bank a few blocks south of the Île de la Cité, where the political club met. They got their name from the street. From this one radical club, which had been a clique even at Versailles before October 1789, budded off almost a thousand other such clubs in other neighborhoods in Paris and in the cities and larger towns of the provinces.

42. GE Layer 42 is a Placemark generally referencing Strasbourg.

troops. September 20: the National Convention first met. September 21: it was there proposed to abolish royalty in France. September 22: news arrived that the invasion had been stopped at Valmy.[GE43] Early November: intense discussions on what to do with the king. November 20: the discovery in a secret safe of the king's correspondence, which proved him to be cooperating with and encouraging the Prussian invasion. Mid-December: the king went on trial for treason. He was found guilty by a one-vote margin in the revolutionary legislature. January 21, 1793: King Louis XVI ("Citizen Louis" at his trial) was executed by the guillotine and his head shown to a cheering crowd on what is today the *Place de la Concorde*.[GE44] This translates something warm and fuzzy like "Agreement Square," but it was not named that until later. At this time (and for a bloody year and a half following) it was the Place de la Revolution. From being militarily invaded, France pushed back until by 1793 its frontiers included all of today's Belgium and Luxembourg and virtually all German territory west of the Rhine, and south of Switzerland included much of Savoy and some of the seacoast of what is today modern Italy.[GE45]

The easiest way to sum up all these spring 1792 to January 1793 events is to see them as, first, pressure from the outside, and then an unusually vigorous response from inside France. And this was simply a rehearsal for the even greater pressure and response of 1793–94.

In early March things began to go militarily wrong in Belgium again, and a new levy of troops was proclaimed. That levy, though, served as catalyst for the growing counter-revolutionary forces in parts of France, notably on the periphery. The Vendée, a generally pro-Catholic and royalist area near the mouth of the Loire, immediately exploded, and for the next few years it alternately smoldered and flared as a civil war within a revolution.[GE46] In April the famous French General Dumouriez defected, after trying to turn his army on Paris. It was as if after wintering at Valley Forge Washington had defected to the British. Once again allied armies were poised for an invasion of France. The Assignat, the paper currency, reflected a drastic loss of confidence in the government's ability to survive as it went into a tailspin in terms of buying power as early as May.

The Committee of Public Safety and the year of "The Terror"

That was the pressure. The response was quick in coming. On May 31 a mob from the Paris Commune invaded the National Convention and forced the arrest of the more moderate group there, the Girondins. That left those called *Montagnards* ("Mountaineers," because they had cliqued together in the highest seats in the back of the hall) in charge. They had earlier opposed the opening of the foreign war, but now inherited it and proceeded to prosecute it on a new level. The Convention set up a Committee of Public Safety of a dozen members, elected every month from the Convention, to provide quick and centralized direction in this national emergency. Its character emerged as early as July 1793. Marat, the most popular radical journalist, was assassinated on July 13 by a young woman who sympathized with the Girondins, and the assassination gave the Jacobins the emotional backlash they needed to capture government. By month's end the Committee of Public Safety got magnified powers, and was joined by the man who would quickly become its spokesman—Maximilien Robespierre. A lawyer from Arras,[GE47] he had been one of the original Third Estate delegates at Versailles in May of 1789. Little known at first, his writing and speaking skills brought him popularity, and he won the reputation of being impossible to bribe. He later frequented the Jacobin Club and with the election of the National Convention in September 1792, became a leading "Montagnard." Under him, beginning in July 1793, that famous committee

---

43. GE Layer 43 is a Placemark referencing a Panoramio icon at Valmy, of a statue of General François Kellerman shown at the moment when his artillery broke the Prussian charge and he took off his hat and shouted "Vive la Nation!"

44. GE Layer 44 is a Placemark referencing the Place de la Concorde.

45. GE Layer 45 is a Folder titled "French N & E frontiers 1792, 1793." The 1792 borders show as a white line, the 1793 borders as a red line.

46. GE Layer 46 is a Polygon showing in royal blue the Vendée, in rebellion against the Revolution beginning in 1793, eventually fielding armies as large as 65,000 troops.

47. GE Layer 47 is a Placemark referencing the town of Arras in northern France. Robiespierre still seems to be a popular hometown hero, the local college prep secondary school there is Lycée Robespierre.

gradually won more and more power, until by March 1794 it had the dictatorial power to suspend any public official. In less than a year this Committee of Public Safety would lead the greatest mobilization of manpower the western world had ever seen.

Fear of foreign armies, aristocratic saboteurs, spies, and a growing counterrevolution marked the birth of the Reign of Terror with emergency and panic. At the same time an enthusiasm for equality and liberty as the revolutionaries conceived them gave the Terror an equally great positive motivation. The most dramatic result of all this was the revolutionary tribunal, perhaps the only alternative to lynch law in such an atmosphere. These tribunals built to a crescendo of execution of "enemies of the people," minimum estimates running between twenty and thirty thousand for that one July 1793 to July 1794 year. The guillotine even gave it a certain mechanized style, and was accepted as a symbol for these times by the revolutionaries themselves; some wore a miniature guillotine pin on their clothes. Whether it was the best of times or the worst of times depended largely on your social background and your loyalties.

A great enthusiasm for the Revolution by its supporters shows up in names, dress, and ceremonies. There was a renaming of streets and buildings in honor of revolutionary heroes or concepts. People with the now unfortunate name of Louis or with the noble-sounding "St." or "de" in their last names tended to drop them. For French bee-keepers, the "queen" bee became the "laying" bee. Human babies were named *Constitution* or *Égalité*. Dress and hairstyles were as important in this social upheaval as in later ones. Jewelry was out; any true patriot had given it away to help the army. The aristocratic knee-breeches, or *culottes*, were decidedly out of favor: wearing them during the Terror could get you killed on the streets. The honest workingman's trousers, or *sans-culottes* ("without culottes"), were now the ideal male dress. *Sans-culottes*, in fact, came to be a description of the revolutionary crowds of Paris. There was a feeling of kinship with the ancient Roman Republic, too. Some Parisians took to wearing togas despite the generally chilly climate, and at least one political activist adopted the name Gracchus from a social reformer of the Roman Late Republic. Playing cards even replaced kings, queens, and jacks (princes) with Mr., Mrs. and Junior Citizens.

One of the most fascinating reforms was of the calendar. The revolutionaries were so convinced they were the dawn of a new historic era that they began numbering the years over again in 1792, which thus became the year 1. Seven-day weeks were replaced by ten-day decades, partly to weaken the religious role of Sundays. The months were made a uniform thirty days and given beautiful descriptive names: November became *Brumaire*, the foggy month; July became *Thermidor*, the hot month; March became *Ventôse*, the windy month. The spring months were named *Germinal*, *Floreal*, and *Prairial*. The five days left over in the yearly calendar were made into an end-of-summer festival called the "*sansculottides.*"

The economy was one of the greatest initial problems. As you saw, after several years of good performance the Assignat began to inflate sharply (a sure sign of loss of public confidence), and so the revolutionary government determined to impose controls. The first major step, in August of 1793, was called the Maximum, a ceiling put on grain prices. Since most everything else in the French economy was tied to the price of grain and therefore bread, this was much like what we today would call a wage and price freeze. Any government can declare such price controls, but it may take a Terror to effectively enforce one. Suddenly speculators and black marketeers were subject to the quick removal of their heads should they violate this decree. As early as year's end the Assignat stabilized.

By March of 1794 the government took a major step beyond that in the "Decrees of Ventôse." A list of several hundred thousand suspected "enemies of the state" was drawn up, a common denominator of those listed being their possession of considerable wealth and their opposition to the Revolution. Then an equally large list of poor but deserving revolutionary patriots was compiled and set beside it. Property, said the Decrees, was to be transferred from the number on the first list to its matching number on the second list! Although the scheme was never really carried through for lack of time, its aims are clear—a quick and permanent redistribution of the wealth of the country.

The draft army

In all these areas—the marshaling of popular enthusiasm, the direction of the economy, and the campaign against the domestic enemies of the Revolution—the revolutionary leadership made new demands for involvement by the citizens. The ultimate demand, however, was the *levée en masse* of August 23, 1793. This "rising in force" announced by the Committee of Public Safety is mainly remembered as the origin of universal military conscription, or as young people all over the world know it today, the draft. The initial decree committed the total resources of the nation, spiritual as well as material, to the war effort, in language that the historian J. M. Thompson once called "as new as it was ominous":

> From this moment until that when the enemy is driven from the territory of the republic, every Frenchman is commandeered (*en réquisition permanente*) for the needs of the armies. Young men will go to the front; married men will forge arms, and carry food; women will make tents and clothing, and work in hospitals; children will turn old linen into bandages; old men will be carried into the squares to rouse the courage of the combatants, and to teach hatred of kings and republican unity.[7]

At a stroke, nearly half a million men were added to the army, the nucleus of that military tide that would sweep across most of Europe.

The power of the new citizen-army is only evident when compared with the style of warfare of the eighteenth century. Typically, those older armies were a small proportion of the total population. The bulk of the infantry was recruited from the dregs of society, or were mercenaries from the dregs of someone else's. The next most numerous body was the blue-blooded cavalry and officer corps. The frontline soldiers were not citizen soldiers, and they were not usually overwilling to give their lives for their country. In fact, morale was so low that a casualty rate of something like 5 percent would crumple such an army, unless it was led by an unusually charismatic general or king. Some commanders kept their most loyal men in the rear with orders to shoot deserters, and then announced that to the troops. With such an army it was difficult to march at night or through thick cover: desertion rates went too high.

Now the citizen-soldiers of revolutionary France were in the first place numerous. All of a sudden the bulk of society—not just the top and bottom extremes—provided soldiers. Army size was limited only by the huge population pool of France, the largest political unit in central or western Europe. And these were patriots with a new economic and political stake in society to defend. They could go on two-week forced marches with a few days food supply. They could absorb perhaps 50 percent casualties and still march away singing the *Marseillaise* or *Ça Ira* or some other revolutionary anthem. In several battles of the first dozen years of its existence, this new army did not just win the battle, but totally destroyed the opposing army, capturing every piece of artillery on the field. It could live off the land and the debris of defeated armies, at least before it invaded Russia. In the navy, numbers of patriotic draftees were not as valuable as technical expertise, nor could they replace experienced commanders. But the French army had moved into a new dimension of warfare, and would have to be copied to ever be beaten on its own ground. As early as December of 1793 the government of the Terror held a pageant to celebrate its victories.

The Jacobin rulers of the Terror wound up threatening too many other revolutionaries, and on July 27, 1794, Robespierre was voted out of power and shortly thereafter was guillotined himself, on the same Place de la Revolution (today's Place de la Condorde) that had seen the guillotining of King Louis XVI, Queen Marie Antoinette, Georges Danton, and other notables. This was the ninth of Thermidor of the Year III on the revolutionary calendar, and since it marked a shift back towards less radical policies, it has come to be called the Thermidorean Reaction. Those legislators who had earlier voted to end the king's life were for a few years afraid for their own. They came to rely on sympathetic young army officers in times of crisis to maintain their power. The government from 1795 to 1799 was called the Directory, a two-house legislature with an executive of five Directors. It was an uninspiring government of cronies, paralyzed by Left-Right political divisions in society. It lasted for years because the army, steadily more independent, was winning territory and glory for France and paying for itself in the process. Logically enough, the force which overthrew the Directory came from that army.

Napoleon: the early years

In French his name became Napoléon Bonaparte, but when he was born in 1769 he was Napoleone Buonaparte—what we'd call today ethnic Italian (his first name from the city of Naples, *Napoli*) on the island of

Corsica.[GE48] By chance France had picked up Corsica from Genoa the year before he was born. Napoleone's father, a lawyer, had at first fought the French takeover, and then gone over to the French side. He sent his two oldest sons to school in northern France where Napoleone, only nine years old, was teased about his thick Italian accent and his fierce Corsican loyalties. He spent a little more than five years, 1779–1885, in a military academy in Brienne-le-Château,[GE49] followed by a year at the military academy in Paris. Then he was stationed in Valence,[GE50] a Rhône River city south of Lyon in southeastern France, as second lieutenant in a regiment that specialized in artillery instruction. Meanwhile his father had died, and he went back to Corsica for two years, 1786–88, functioning head of the family at just seventeen. In the summer of 1788, just as Third Estate agitation was beginning in France, he rejoined his regiment. When the National Assembly inherited government in the summer of 1789, again Napoleone's first thoughts were of Corsica. He went there to join the Corsican independence leader who had fought the French occupation for twenty years, but found him less than welcoming—son of a turncoat father, he was seen to be. So in 1791 he rejoined the French army at Valences, first lieutenant of an artillery regiment. His self-education had branched out by this time, from military strategy and tactics to a reading of the major *Philosophes*. He joined, and then headed, the local Jacobin club, speaking against the special privileges of First and Second Estates and advocating a constitutional monarchy. Three times more he left the army to try to win a position in Corsica, in late 1791, in 1792, and in early 1793, but the third time he and his whole family were put under a virtual death sentence and fled the island for good. Rejoining the French revolutionary army in June of 1793, Napoléon (as he was to be from now on, and henceforth we'll just spell it without the *e acute*, Napoleon, as is common in English) was a vocal supporter of the National Convention and the increasingly radical Jacobins, and poised for a spectacular rise.

By this time the revolutionary armies had taken over the great southern seaport of Marseille, but were stymied by royalist armies in control of Toulon and its naval base,[GE51] some 30 miles east of Marseille, where they were supported by the British navy. Through political connections and wounds that incapacitated higher officers, Napoleon became commander of artillery for the revolutionary armies, and so harassed the British fleet that they abandoned the port in mid-December, 1793, which was quickly captured. For this Napoleon was made Brigadier General. He was twenty-four years old.

Then his star, so quickly risen, seemed to fall equally fast. With the Thermidorean Reaction in July of 1794 and Robespierre's quick execution, Napoleon was so closely associated with the radical Jacobins that he lost his position and in fact had to stand trial for collusion with them. But in October of 1795 he was called on by frightened leaders of the National Convention to disperse the royalist mob in Paris that was intent on keeping members of the National Convention from succeeding themselves and thus perpetuating the Revolution. This he did, with "a whiff of grapeshot," anti-personnel rounds that exploded in the air and rained grape-sized shrapnel on the crowds. The new government, the Directory, came into power the next month. They made Napoleon commander of the army of the interior, and in 1796 commander of the army of Italy. In the next ten years, first as a general, then as Consul, and finally as Emperor, he conquered most of Europe and in the process transformed both its international boundaries and its internal political life.

Napoleon: the glory days

In a year Napoleon conquered northern Italy from Austria. Austrian resistance hinged on the great fortress of Mantua in the Po Valley,[GE52] and four Austrian armies were sent, one after another, to try to relieve its siege. When Napoleon defeated the fourth and last at Rivoli[GE53] in January 1797, Mantua capitulated shortly

48. GE Layer 48 is a Placemark referencing Ajaccio in southwest Corsica, where Napoleon was born.
49. GE Layer 49 is a Placemark that references Brienne; the actual military academy there was disbanded a few years after Napoleon's graduation from it.
50. GE Layer 50 is a Placemark referencing Valence.
51. GE Layer 51 is a Placemark framing a view that includes Marseille at center and Toulon at right. This is the same important naval base created by Colbert early in the reign of Louis XIV.
52. GE Layer 52 is a Placemark referencing Mantua, a city defensively sited on a peninsula in a natural lake.
53. GE Layer 53 is a Placemark referencing Rivoli.

thereafter and the road to Vienna was open. At this point Austria signed a treaty (directly with General Napoleon himself, not the French government!), recognizing French control of northern Italy.

In 1798 the Directory wanted him to invade Great Britain across the channel. Napoleon briefly considered it but decided it couldn't be done without naval supremacy. Instead he sailed an army across the Mediterranean and invaded Egypt, with some vague plans of threatening the British in India (though the Suez Canal wouldn't be dug for seventy more years!). His conquest of Egypt proper was impressive, but the British destroyed the French fleet in August of 1798 near Alexandria at the Battle of the Nile,[GE54] cutting the French off from supply and easy retreat. When Napoleon tried to fight his way up and around the Mediterranean coast, the Turkish army and the British navy stopped him at the Siege of Acre in May of 1799[GE55] (more on this when we get to the Mideast later in this book). Leaving his army to die on the vine, Napoleon slipped through British naval lines in a French warship and got back to France just in time to be invited into an interesting political plot.

Back in Paris our old friend the former Abbé Sieyès, who ten years before in 1789 had written "What is the 3rd Estate?" and at Versailles had lobbied for a vote of all 1200 delegates by head, was now a member of the Directory much worried about resurgent royalists taking over the government. He finally decided to recruit an important military commander to help him enforce his policies. Napoleon, he thought, was that man, even when Napoleon insisted on being the "First Consul" (out of three) with rights to appoint persons of his choosing to a huge number of executive, legislative, and judicial positions. In November of 1799 the three and their supporters carried out the *coup d'état* of *Brumaire* ("the foggy month"). It was a Triumvirate reminiscent of the one formed by Julius Caesar, Crassus, and Pompey of 60 BC in Rome, except that Napoleon was the only one with troops and the appointive rights that would enable a determined man to become sole ruler.

As a very successful and politically connected general, Napoleon had exercised a major influence on government policy since 1795. As First Consul his control was virtually dictatorial. While he is more famous with most Americans for his military successes (and towards the end, failures), his transformation of French government is at least as important in terms of its impact on history. In many respects, he was the most remarkable administrator in French history. On the one hand, not much seemed to have changed after a tumultuous ten years: France seemed to have gone full circle from Monarchy (one man rule by a king) to Consulate (one man rule by a general). Talk of rule by the "General Will" was not encouraged by Napoleon, and gradually disappeared, at least in public. But in another way he systematized and institutionalized many of the goals of the Enlightenment, and did that not just in France proper but in most of what is today Italy and western and central Germany. Napoleonic armies operated from the Atlantic Ocean to Moscow, and in the conquered areas Napoleon changed ruling persons as well as ruling institutions. This had a truly worldwide impact through the American, African, and Asian colonies held by such occupied countries as Spain and Holland. The following paragraphs are an attempt to weave together the military conquests and the governmental changes going on at the same time, and at least hint at the huge impact that they made.

By 1800 Russian and Austrian armies had successfully recaptured most of northern Italy from France, driving up the Po Valley. The Russian army withdrew, but the Austrians laid siege to Genoa. Napoleon, with a newly trained army, crossed the St. Bernard Pass through the Alps, [GE56] surprised the Austrians from behind and defeated them at the Battle of Marengo[GE57] in June of 1800. After this defeat the Austrians not only agreed to withdraw from northern Italy once more, but they recognized French control of all the territory west of the Rhine.

In that same 1800 the new First Consul sent out an administrative army led by ninety-eight Prefects—one each to the governing areas called Départements—and in short order brought local government under tighter central control than the Indendants had ever achieved, even for Louis XIV. In general, they were shrewdly chosen for their proven administrative experience, and a surprising number were men of considerable property. In the same year Napoleon engineered the creation of a national bank, the Banque de France (that still exists today). This central financial institution, coupled with a new tax code and a most efficient tax collection sys-

54. GE Layer 54 is a Placemark referencing the Battle of the Nile, or the Battle of Aboukir Bay, fought from August 1–3, 1798.

55. GE Layer 55 is a Placemark referencing Acre, today a city on the northern coast of Israel.

56. GE Layer 56 is a Placemark referencing and framing a view of the Saint Bernard Pass.

57. GE Layer 57 is a Placemark referencing the Battle of Marengo.

tem, supported many of Napoleon's later projects. One of the earliest of these was the creation of several dozen *lycées*, advanced secondary schools that might be considered a combination of a U.S. senior high school plus junior college—except that admission was by brutal competitive exam and all winners were fully supported by government scholarship. It was very centralized; Napoleon claimed he knew what every student was studying in a particular hour of a particular school day!

By 1801 Napoleon was the only Consul, having dispensed with the others. In that same year he worked out a "Concordat" with the Catholic Church. Not religious himself, apparently, Napoleon knew nonetheless that many French people still were, and moreover, some of the greatest internal and external opposition to his government came from the Church. In the deal that was struck, Napoleon's concessions were that Catholic seminaries and even primary schools could be built again, and that the French government would pay bishops and priests a salary. The Pope's concessions were to allow the First Consul to pick the bishops, and to approve—after a decade of bitterly disapproving—the French state's seizure of Church property early in the Revolution. When in 1804 Napoleon elevated himself to the position of Emperor of France, the Pope himself came to Paris to do the crowning (though in the actual ceremony Napoleon just took the crown from his hands, making it a point to put the crown on his head himself as Charlemagne had done a thousand and four years before). Many late Enlightenment thinkers would have rejected any place for the church in government, but from Napoleon's point of view this neutralized a powerful enemy and cost him little if any personal power. The Catholic Church not only recognized the French government as valid, but at least implicitly agreed that it was now a basically secular state whose citizens had free choice of religious worship.

The Code Napoléon

A modernized, unified law code had been a project of French Revolutionary governments since at least 1793, but work on it only became systematic with Napoleon's 1799 taking of the Consulship. It was finally promulgated in 1804, the same year he became Emperor, as the Civil Code of the French, or just Code Napoléon for short. It amounted to the national standardization of the law of France that was up to that point about as unstandardized as you can imagine. Legal practice in France south of the Loire was generally based on old Roman law and that of France north of the Loire generally used Germanic common law. The members of the clergy (the former First Estate), had typically been subject to church courts, not state courts, and in fact the church courts dealt with marriage and family matters for all French people. Every province had had its own tariffs (taxes on imports) and other commercial regulations.

The new law code was written in French, not Latin, in an attempt to be clear enough so that anyone could understand it. It claimed, at least, to be based on "the natural," that universal human nature the Enlightenment had so long pondered. Religious affiliation (or non-affiliation) was specifically said to have no bearing whatsoever on legal decision. Rules for civil marriage (and divorce) legally replaced Church procedures, which were now relegated to the role of cultural tradition. Ethnic belonging was also specifically excluded from having any bearing in the legal sphere, which among other things dramatically opened up careers for the Jewish minority in France. Freedom of contract freed up individuals and businesses to make agreements without so much governmental red tape. From the point of view of modern American law, it seems remarkably progressive—with a few exceptions. For example, this new equality was just for adult males; females were very much under the control of fathers and husbands. But with its overall uniformity and simple organization, it is easy to see why it was adopted by many Italian and German states, and even today (though much amended) it is the basic law code of Belgium.

The Grand Empire and the satellites

From 1804 to 1811 Napoleon's Empire almost swallowed continental Europe. The names of the key battles of 1805–7 that made it possible are still engraved on the Triumphal Arch Napoleon had built at the "Star" of twelve radiating roads in Paris.[GE[58]]

---

58. GE Layer 58 is a Placemark framing a view of *L'Étoile*, The Star, with its centerpiece the Arc de Triomphe.

In quick summary, at Ulm[GE⁵⁹] (Oct. 20, 1805) Napoleon defeated the combined Austrian and Russian armies. At Austerlitz[GE⁶⁰] (December 2, 1805), one of his most famous victories, he virtually destroyed both of those armies, capturing all the artillery on the field. By July of 1806 he had added some of western Germany to the French Empire proper, and reorganized most of central Germany into the Kingdom of the Rhineland. [GE⁶¹] On October 14, 1806, at the twin battles of Jena and Auerstät,[GE⁶²] he broke the Prussian army and shortly thereafter occupied Berlin. Four months later at Eylau[GE⁶³] (February 7–8, 1807), considerably farther east, French and Russian armies fought to a bloody draw in a snowstorm, but at Friedland [GE⁶⁴] (June 14, 1807), Napoleon badly defeated the Russians. All three of the great central and eastern European powers, Austria, Russia, and Prussia, were forced to agree to Napoleon's recreation of a Polish state, and also to join his Continental System. Britain, protected by the English Channel and the world's largest navy, was the one great power in the region that was out of Napoleon's reach. In 1805—the year of Napoleon's great victory at Austerlitz—the British had sunk the main French battle fleet off Spain's Cape Trafalgar,[GE⁶⁵] along with Napoleon's only hope for a direct invasion of Britain. Napoleon's Continental System was an attempt to starve the British into submission, by forbidding any one on the mainland of Europe from trading with them.

In 1808–9 Napoleon turned his attention to Iberia, invading Spain and Portugal, seeming to conquer both and in fact putting his brother on the Spanish throne. The British supported pockets of resistance in what they called the Peninsular Campaign. Unable to compete in face-to-face conventional war battles with Napoleon's armies, the Spanish more and more turned to "*guerrilla*" ("little war") tactics of hit-and-run, small-scale ambush, for which Napoleon's only answer was public executions, which in the long run just made the guerrilla warriors more popular.

In 1809 Austria fought Napoleon yet another time. Napoleon defeated the main Austrian army at Wagram[GE⁶⁶] on July 5–6, just across the Danube River from Vienna, and the Austrians sued for peace—but this defeat was nowhere near as crushing as Ulm and Austerlitz had been four years earlier, and the Austrian army was still a factor in the terms of the peace.

In 1811 a map of Europe that showed the extent of the French Empire and the further extent of satellite states mainly controlled by blood relatives of Napoleon and former favorite generals[GE⁶⁷] would have seemed to indicate overwhelming power. The centralized control of all this, however, would crumble surprisingly quickly in the next few years.

End game

By 1810 France was losing its grip on Iberia in the west, and in the east Emperor Alexander I of Russia was allowing his countrymen more and more to trade with Britain in violation of the Continental System, partly because the alternative was buying very expensive French products and partly because of a Russian nationalist reaction to growing French power. In 1811 Napoleon determined to invade Russia to force compliance, and began to assemble a 600,000-man army for that purpose. In May and early June of 1812, with his army ready

---

59. GE Layer 59 is a Placemark referencing Ulm.

60. GE Layer 60 is a Placemark referencing Austerlitz.

61. GE Layer 61 is a Polygon in orange-red representing the Kingdom of the Rhineland. This map based on one available online at www.zum.de/whdmla/histatlas/germany/rheinbund.gif, as modified by existing state borders that are close to outlines shown.

62. GE Layer 62 is a Folder containing Placemarks locating Jena and Auerstät, and framing a view that includes Berlin, taken by the French soon thereafter.

63. GE Layer 63 is a Placemark referencing Eylau.

64. GE Layer 64 is a Placemark referencing Friedland.

65. GE Layer 65 is a Placemark generally referencing the location of the battle of Trafalgar.

66. GE Layer 66 is a Placemark referencing Wagram.

67. GE Layer 67 is a Folder titled "Napoleonic Control 1811." Inside are two Polygons, one in a 60 percent red wash titled "French Empire proper," and another also in 60 percent red wash titled "empire plus satellite states." Turn on the first, take a look at the map, and then turn on the second.

to march, he spent six fruitless weeks in negotiation—six weeks he would bitterly regret that coming October—before finally launching an invasion straight towards Moscow. The Russians, relying on the age-old Scythian tactics of withdrawal and scorched earth, fought one major battle against the French at Borodino,[GE68] (September 7, 1812) seventy miles west of Moscow. By this time the French advance army was down to around 200,000 men, and the Russian army numbered around 150,000. "The most terrible of all my battles," Napoleon called it later; he held the field at the end of the day but lost 50,000 men he could not replace. One week later the French army entered the west gate of Moscow as the Russian army withdrew by the southeast gate. The mainly wooden city burned that night, each side blaming the other. And there in the ashes Napoleon sat for a month waiting for the Russians to surrender. When he finally decided to leave, encouraged by the earliest winter in years, the Russian army came out of retreat and forced him back into that same scorched earth track. They so harried the French army and cut off its foragers that only 20,000 French re-crossed the border at the Berezina River.

Napoleon rushed back to France to raise a new army, realizing that a snowball of enemies was rolling down on him from the east. The critical battle came at Leipzig[GE69] (October 18, 1813), the so-called Battle of Nations. There the main French army was broken. Napoleon fought a rear-guard action as best he could, winning a battle against Prussian and Russian troops in Brienne, the town of his old military academy, as late as January 1814. But the allied drive on Paris was inexorable, and Napoleon surrendered and was exiled to the island of Elba,[GE70] between the Tuscan coast and Corsica. In the spring of 1815, to bad British jokes about his lack of "Elba room," Napoleon escaped, landed in southern France, recruited supporters and marched to Paris for a three-months-long postscript to his reign called the 100 Days. It ended at Waterloo[GE71] (June 18, 1815).

The legacy of it all

And so Napoleon was gone, exiled to the lonely island of St. Helena in the south Atlantic from which he would never return. The Napoleonic Empire was no more, with French borders moved back to their 1792 lines. The House of Bourbon was back on the throne. But the Code Napoléon was there (and in many other French-speaking lands) to stay. The equality of all (males, at least) before the law was challenged somewhat by the returned monarchs and the returned émigré nobles, but the challenge was feeble and faded away in the nineteenth century. The *lycée* system remained intact. The Bank of France, the rational system of ministries, and the role of Prefects in Départements was in general permanent.

The personal impact of Napoleon's policies and wars will reverberate throughout much of the rest of this textbook. In Chapter 3 we'll explore in more detail the threat he was to Germans in general, and how in reaction to Napoleonic occupation they began to forge their modern national consciousness. For the Russians in Chapter 4, the French burning of Moscow and the Russian occupation of Paris a few years later—the whole *War and Peace* subject of Tolstoy's novel—were also key building blocks of modern national self-image. Napoleonic plans or threats played a smaller but still important role in the modern national histories of Ireland, the Czech Republic, and Finland dealt with in Chapters 5, 6, and 7. Even in the non-European world history topics dealt with in the second part of the book there are critical passages associated with Napoleon. The Mexican independence movement discussed in Chapter 8 began in 1810 in large part because of Napoleon's occupation of Spain and claiming of all Spanish overseas territory. In Chapter 10 you'll see how Napoleon's brief occupation of the Nile Delta in 1798 set in motion the creation of the modern Egyptian state. In Chapter 9 you'll see a British fleet occupy Cape Town in South Africa in 1806 to forestall a possible Napoleonic fleet landing there (in possession of Holland, Napoleon also claimed all of the Dutch overseas empire). In Chapter 12 you'll see in 1808–9 how the Dutch governor-general of the Dutch East Indies, at Napoleon's orders, built

---

68. GE Layer 68 is a Placemark referencing Borodino, with Moscow, seventy miles east, also in the framed view. Better coverage in Chapter 4.

69. GE Layer 69 is a Placemark referencing the Battle of Leipzig.

70. GE Layer 70 is a Placemark generally framing a view of Elba.

71. GE Layer 71 is a Placemark referencing the Battle of Waterloo.

with draft labor a great Postal Road from one end of Java to the other, transforming communications there but at terrible human cost, and how the British temporarily occupied the island in 1811 to counter French influence.

On the surface of history, then, Napoleon left his personal fingerprints far and wide. But I would argue that the greater impact of the French Enlightenment and Revolution on the rest of the world came with two pre-Napoleonic developments. First is the late Enlightenment's truly utopian vision of free and equal men and women ruling themselves, without kings, aristocrats, or churchmen from any established church, in peace, harmony, true human fulfillment and a tight-knit brother- and sisterly love. Second is the draft army of the *levée en masse* of August 23, 1793: every man a free citizen with a stake in society—with the vote and land enough to farm or a job free of guilds and royal monopolies—and every citizen a patriotic soldier. These ideals and ideas so motivated people to action that they transformed the world.

Endnotes

1. Barbara W. Tuchman, *A Distant Mirror: The Calamitous 14th Century* (New York: Alfred A. Knopf, 1978).

2. Charles Louis, Baron de Montesquieu, *Lettres Persanes* trans. John Davidson, in *Persian and Chinese Letters* (Washington and London: M. Walter Dunne, Publisher, 1901), p. 289.

3. The full text of Denis Diderot's "Supplément au voyage de Bougainville" is available on the web, courtesy of Project Gutenberg, at the following site: http://www.archive.org/stream/8spvb/8spvb10u.txt

   See especially the paragraph that begins: *Voulez-vous savoir l'histoire abrégé de presque toute notre misère? La voici. Il existait un homme naturel . . . .* ("Would you like to know the brief history of almost all our misery? Here it is. There was a natural man . . . .")

4. *Jean Jacques Rousseau, The Social Contract and Discourses* (trans. G. D. H. Cole), New York: E. P. Dutton, 1950), p. 15.

5. Ibid., p. 29.

6. Daniel Roche, *France in the Enlightenment,* trans. Arthur Goldhammer (Cambridge, MA: Harvard University Press, 1998), p. 475.

7. J. M. Thompson, *The French Revolution* (Oxford: Basil Blackwell, 1962), p. 424.

Chapter Three

"A New Binding Tie": Cultural Nationalism in Germany

"There remains nothing for [a nation so ruined] but to find an entirely different and new binding tie that is superior to fear and hope."
—Johann Gottlieb Fichte, from the first of his 14 *Addresses to the German Nation,* 1807–8[1]

CONTENTS

The heart of the matter—A quick look at the German language—Some common German place names—Topography and texture of the land—The Germanies in the time of Napoleon—The Prussian Reforms—*The Juniper Tree*—Romanticism, Herder, and the "Folk"—Fichte and Jahn—The lives of the Brothers Grimm—The Grimms and the "organic" idea—The Model of Cultural Breakdown—The *Eddas* and Old Norse Mythology—European discovery of the *Rigveda*—The invention of philology—Jacob Grimm's *Teutonic Mythology*—Wagner's opera—The Congress of Vienna—The Age of Metternich, 1815 to 1848—List's economic nationalism—Growing unrest—The Revolutions of 1848—The Frankfurt Assembly—Austria vs. Prussia—Otto von Bismarck—Kaiser William I—Bismarck's creation of the German Empire—The Seven Weeks War, 1866—Franco-German War, 1870—Bismarck's domination of world diplomacy—William II and Germany's "Place in the Sun"—World War I—Weimar Republic and revolution—Versailles Treaty—The political structure of Weimar—Culture and economics in Weimar Germany—Hitler and the NSDAP—Beer hall putsch—The Third Reich—Philosophical asides—Friedrich Meinecke's look back

The heart of the matter

The preceding chapter on the Enlightenment and French Revolution was intended to convince a reader that political nationalism—with its draft armies, anthems, and new political participation of the masses—is a fairly recent thing, just over two hundred years old. This chapter on Germany, while incidentally providing some background on major developments of the nineteenth and twentieth centuries, is primarily designed to demonstrate the final logic of nationalism. With the Romantic age in general and German thinkers in particular, patriotism takes on a whole new cultural dimension. The modern German experience is one of the first and best illustrations of this new sort of national self-consciousness. It was cultural nationalism that transformed the Germanies into a Germany and led it twice to the verge of world domination.

We as Americans, because of our founding ideals and language, have some familiarity with the political nationalism produced by the Enlightenment. But while this cultural nationalism from the Romantic age may work with some American ethnic groups (the self-consciousness of American Indians, African-Americans, Hispanic-Americans, for example), it doesn't really work with American patriotism as a whole. As a result it is not a pattern we intuitively grasp, though it is more common worldwide than our own pattern of development and really important for Americans to understand. As with Germany, most national independence movements and nation-states have come into being since the French Revolution and most of those have come about by some version of the following five-step model. I call it "the J. Brown paradigm of national development" (paradigm meaning not much more than model, or best model, but sounding much more sophisticated; correctly pronouncd "pair-a-dime," so if you pronounce it "pair-a-diggum" you lose sophistication points).

Step One: To get a really fiery patriotism and eventually an independent state, you must begin with an *identifiable group* of people. Language is usually the best group identifier, followed by religion as a close second. Minor group identifiers can be occupation, kinds of food eaten or games played, or skin color, or costume, though these are mainly indicators of different origin and culture. The more things that set a cultural group apart from its neighbors, the better nationalism one can reasonably expect in the long run. "Nation" is used here not in the political sense, but in the old-fashioned way my grandmother used to say "a nation of buffalo," or "a nation of Indians," just meaning lots and lots of things alike.

Step Two: To the group must be applied a *negative stimulus*. This can be invasion, threat of conquest, oppression, loss of civil rights, or any variety of being treated as an inferior group. This is the only really complicated step, because for a fiery nationalism to develop, the negative stimulus needs to be neither too great nor too little. If the negative stimulus should be so overwhelming that it destroys the group either by extermination or cultural assimilation, obviously there would be no group left to create a nation-state. On the other hand, the negative stimulus must be grave enough to be a real, lasting danger or unpleasantness to every member of the group. No matter how good-looking, intelligent, and hard-working you are, you come in for your share of scorn from those who look down on your whole cultural group. That is psychologically necessary to generate step three.

Step Three: Some intellectuals of the oppressed group, stung by being treated as cultural inferiors, begin to argue that they are simply culturally different, and not inferior at all. They react by stressing their unique cultural heritage in a process that might be called *cultural nationalism*. This usually involves reviving the language, if language is one of the key group identifiers, or religion, or customs. In general this phase is marked by an intense concern with early history and past eras of greatness, and almost always celebrates the folk culture carried on by the common people.

Step Four: When this cultural nationalism spreads to enough people, the movement becomes a political force. Radicals of the oppressed group who have become most conscious of their cultural uniqueness begin to say, "why then shouldn't we have our own state?" At this point, cultural nationalism has developed into *political nationalism*, but a political nationalism now grounded in cultural pride. The elite, oppressing group usually responds to this with condescending humor at first, and then with absolute resistance. Patriotic organizations begin to experiment with non-violent and then violent ways of overcoming that resistance. Nation-states are customarily born, then, in revolutions and wars. National movements not numerous or concentrated enough to achieve political independence smolder and flare in periodic terrorist/freedom fighting activity.

Step Five: If a successful revolt indeed establishes a new nation-state, its citizens tend to develop an elite nationalism of their own which demands that all other ethnic or religious minorities lay down their cultural heritage and embrace that of the new ruling group. Having fought so hard against their oppressors, and having gotten so emotionally high on their own real or imagined virtues, they now find it difficult to recognize the aspirations of other groups. Their own uniquenesses, in this state of extreme nationalism, have in their minds been translated into superiorities. In its most extreme form this final step becomes *integral nationalism*—patriotism when it has become the ultimate measurement of a person's worth, and has eclipsed all other ethical, religious, or philosophical standards.

Notice that "nation" is used here and throughout the book in the sense of a cultural group and not a polity, and that "nation-state" is used to mean a political unit based mainly on a single cultural group. And this five-step paradigm is only an abstract: any real world human experience is more richly varied. The process of national development tends to be gradual instead of clearly separated into steps. There seems to be an especially strong resonance and feedback cycle between cultural and political nationalism, over time. Any model has value to the degree that it gives a user a quick handle on, or an immediate insight into, some complicated process. By the same token, when a rigidly applied model forces all facts into the same Procrustian bed, perhaps it has outlived its usefulness. The logic abstracted in this model, though, is arguably to be seen in the creation of most of the world's national independence movements since the French Revolution, and is certainly the key to understanding the rest of this book! So remember the progression of **identifiable group, negative stimulus, cultural nationalism, political nationalism,** and **integral nationalism** as we look at the modern German experience.

A quick look at the German language

First, German uses almost exactly the alphabet that English does. There are a couple of obvious exceptions. An *Umlaut*—two dots over a vowel—tells you the vowel is modified by the letter after it. For example, the umlaut-less "au" in *Umlaut* or in *Frau* (woman or wife) is pronounced to rhyme with "how," but with an umlaut over the "-a" the first syllable of *Fräulein* (Miss or girl) is pronounced to rhyme with "boy." In a word like *schön* (beautiful), the umlauted "o" is pronounced something like the English "er," as in "shern." Sometimes the umlaut gets transliterated into English as the umlauted vowel, minus the dots, with an -e after it; so the German word for the color green, *grün*, is also often transliterated *gruen*. The second difference in our alphabets is that German has one letter for "ss" when it comes at the end of a syllable, looking something like a cursive capital B in English—ß. The German word *Fluß* (meaning river), then, would be written in our alphabet as "fluss."

In terms of pronouncing consonants in German, a handful that come later in the alphabet are pronounced differently than ours. When their "s" starts a syllable, it is usually pronounced "sh" (so *Stein*, stone or rock, is pronounced more like "shtine"). Their "v" is like our "f" (*von*, meaning "from," is pronounced as "fon"). Their "w" is pronounced the way our "v" is (the German word for white, *Weiß*, is pronounced "vice"), and their "z" is pronounced something like our "ts."

Single vowels are often fairly close in pronunciation to English, but vowel combinations have tricky pronunciations. The German "ie" is our long "e," and their "ei" is our long "i" (just remember to pronounce these two like the last letter in the combination). Their "au," you've already seen in *Frau*, is like our "ow" when it has no umlaut (as in the Audi brand of car), and like our "oy" when the "au" has an umlaut. The vowel combination "eu" is also pronounced "oy," so the German word *neu*, meaning new, is pronounced "noy." The German "oo" is pronounced like an English long "o," not like the "oo" in our "boo" (so the German *Boot*, meaning boat, is pronounced much like the English word "boat").

And, you may have already noticed, all nouns in German are always capitalized, no matter where they appear in a sentence.

In one sense it's not far from English to German: after all, the English language is about 40 percent German-based, courtesy of the Anglo-Saxon invaders of Roman Britain around AD 500 (to go with that 40 percent that is Latin-based, courtesy of the Norman-French invaders of England in 1066 that we talked about in the last chapter, which leaves about 20 percent odds and ends from other languages). But modern German (not to mention Russian, and classical Greek and Latin) is tougher for most native English speakers to learn than a Romance language such as French or Spanish, because modern English like the Romance languages has all but lost its original "declension"—those modified forms of nouns and adjectives whose forms depend on their qualities and how they are used. All we have left in modern English is the difference between *I* and *me*, *she* and *her*, *he* and *his*, the ever-confusing *who* and *whom*, and the like. German declension of nouns, for example, depends on the gender of the noun (masculine, feminine, or neuter), AND on its number (singular or plural) AND on which of four "cases" it is, meaning its function in a sentence (Nominative, Genitive, Dative, or Accusative). Really complicated, no? On the other hand, we English-speakers accomplish most of that business with prepositions, which are used so irregularly as to be a real problem for non-English-speakers trying to learn them—*on* the train but *in* the car, and hundreds of other such illogicalities. Once, when the author was a poor-as-a-church-mouse graduate student, a Russian-language professor offered any of us in his class a thousand dollars if we could come up with a simple set of rules for the use of English prepositions. None of us, even with the wolf at the door, succeeded.

German verbs are a simpler problem. As with most European languages, the good news is that most verb conjugations (the endings for 1st, 2nd, and 3rd persons singular and plural, and the different kinds of past, present, and future tenses) are done according to a couple of regular patterns. The bad news is that it is usually the most common verbs that are irregular.

Hopefully this will help a little with German words that will show up in the history to come in a bit, and in the map work immediately following.

Some common German place names

In wandering through a map of today's Federal Republic of Germany (and also Austria and the northern half of Switzerland, two other places where German is the common language) you'll find that a good many place names include words for common geographic features. *Berg* is the German word for mountain or hill (we get "iceberg" straight from the German *Eisberg*, meaning "ice mountain"). *Gebirge*, meaning mountains or a mountain range, comes from that same root. A *Tal* (sometimes *Thal*) is a valley (so Neanderthal just means the Neander Valley, where some interesting old humanoid bones were found). *Bach* means brook or stream. *Fluß*, you've already seen, means river. *See*, the same basic word as the English "sea," is a common geographic name in German too; used as *Der See* (masculine) it has the sense of a big lake, but used as *Die See* (feminine) it means ocean. *Wald* means woods or forest. Color words show up fairly frequently: *schwarz* means black (so *Schwarzwald* is the Black Forest); *grün*, you've already seen is green; *weiß* is white. Kinds of trees show up as frequently in German place names as in American English ones: their *Linden* are what we call basswood trees, so *Lindental* would be just Basswood Valley. *Stein* is stone or rock.

There are also some common words for human features of the landscape. *Stadt* means city or town (not what we mean by "state" in English), and *Dorf* means village. *Bad* means bath or health resort (or what is often called a "spa" after the hot-water springs town of that name in Belgium). *Feld* is a cognate for our "field." *Brücke* is bridge. *Schloß* is castle. *Garten* is garden (*Kindergarten* we get straight from the German, literally "Children's Garden").

Finally, there are lots of place names based on simple relationships. *Ober* means upper and *unter* means lower, or below; *klein* means small and *groß* means big. *An* means at, and *am* is a contraction for *an dem*, meaning "at the"; so *Frankfurt-am-Main* means the city "Frank Ford at the Main (River)"—the ford obviously being the reason for the city being there to begin with. *Alt* is old, and *neu*, you've seen, is new, so the famous Bavarian castle of *Neuschwanstein* is pronounced "Noy-shvahn-shtine" and means "New Swan Rock." You may already have noticed from this and other examples that, in written German, words which we English speakers might write separately are often glued together ("agglutinative" is the word linguists use). If you take a complex-looking place name such as *Ruhrtalbrücke*, to give another example, and tease it apart into its components, it comes out simply the "Ruhr Valley Bridge."

Topography and texture of the land

Today's Germany is a north-to-south slice of north-central Europe about 525 miles from top to bottom. It is surprisingly far north: in terms of latitude its southernmost point is almost 150 miles north of Minneapolis, and its northernmost point is almost 100 miles north of Edmonton, Alberta.[GE[1]] It might also strike American viewers as seeming rather small, especially when compared with its huge role in modern history.

In general, elevations are highest in Germany in the south, dropping somewhat to the Central German uplands, and then are finally lowest in the North German plain. The Bavarian Alps get to over 9,700', and are

---

1. GE Layer 1 is a Folder titled "Germany from space" that includes two Polygon layers. Open the folder. For a view of today's Germany as seen from approximately 3,000' altitude, turn on the first polygon layer titled "Germany," and double-click polygon icon to "fly" to pre-set view. Then do the same with the second polygon layer, which will "fly" you to a map of Germany, correct as to size and to latitude, but spun around the globe in longitude so that it is superimposed on a view of the U.S. and Canada. After viewing, and musing thereon, turn off this GE Layer 1.

famed for their rugged beauty,[GE²] though the country generally flattens out fairly quickly further north. One way to organize it mentally might be to turn to the network of rivers.

The Rhine River (German *Rhein*) dominates the west of the country, running west along the Swiss border and then north along the French border before coming into the German "Rhineland" proper.[GE³] On its banks in this stretch are the major cities of Mainz, Kolblenz, Bonn, Cologne (*Köln*, in German), and Düsseldorf, before the river turns west into Holland and hits the ocean at the great Dutch ports of Rotterdam and Amsterdam. The stretch of river below Mainz, from Bingen down to about Koblenz, is the most scenic and famous part of the Rhine, with castles on every steep hill. A tourist highlight of this stretch is the 400'-high Lorelei rock that dangerously narrows the channel; wrecks at this spot were in olden days attributed to ghostly Rhine maidens singing sailors to their deaths.[GE⁴] One of the Rhine's tributaries, the Main River, has something of the reputation that the Mason-Dixon Line has in the U.S., it separates northern Germany (just less than of 60 percent of the country) from southern Germany (a little over 40 percent).[GE⁵] The most famous city on its banks is the afore-mentioned Frankfurt am Main, about 20 miles up the Main River from where it flows into the Rhine.

The other big river, dominating the northeast of Germany, is the Elbe.[GE⁶] It breaks through the Ore Mountains from the Bohemian Plain of today's Czech Republic at something over 400' elevation, and begins its majestic sweep northwest. Important cities along it include Dresden, Wittenberg (not a big city, but where Luther famously nailed up the 95 Theses), Magdeburg, and Hamburg.

Between the Rhine and the Elbe is the smaller Weser,[GE⁷] still large enough to support a port city the size of Bremen. East of the Elbe River, the smaller Oder River today makes up much of the eastern border of Germany (with Poland, in which the headwaters of the river rise).[GE⁸] And in the south, especially in Bavaria, is the upper Danube (*Donau*, in German).[GE⁹] Almost all the other rivers in Germany flow north or west or some

---

2. GE Layer 2 is a Folder entitled "Berchtesgaden views" that has views of the *Obersee* ("Upper Lake") and from Hitler's "Eagle's Nest" built on a spur of one of the highest peaks. The lakes are about 2,000' elevation, and the Eagle's Nest about 6,000'. Make sure you have just two Google Earth basic layers (at bottom left of screen) turned on: Borders and Labels, and Photos. Instead of opening the Berchtesgaden folder by clicking on small square box at left, try double-clicking on the folder icon proper. This not only opens it, but should "fly" you to pre-set view. Single-click blue layer to read text, then click somewhere off text box on map to close text. Then turn on Placemark layer named Obersee, double-click Pushpin icon to fly to framed view, and single-click on blue label "Obersee" to bring up text box with pointer—asking you to open the Photos icon of same name. Click somewhere off photo to close it, do same with "Eagle's New view" Placemark.

3. Open the Folder titled "Major Rivers." Turn on GE Layer 3, a Path representing the course of the Rhine River in aqua, and double-click on Path icon for framed view of river's overall course.

4. GE Layer 4 is a Folder titled "Rhine river views." Open the folder, and then highlight the first layer in the folder, a Path titled "Rhine gorges," by single-clicking on the name of the layer. Before you now "fly" yourself down the Rhine gorges, first go to the Tools drop-down menu at top left of Google Earth screen, choose Options, and then the Touring tab. Change "Camera Tilt Angle" to 65 degrees; change "Camera Range" to 4000 m, and change "Speed" to 1000; and then hit "Apply" and then "OK" buttons, which gets you back to regular Google Earth map screen. Now turn off "Photos" basic layer, to keep those square photo icons from cluttering screen. Now for the actual flying: with the "Rhine gorges" Path layer highlighted, click on small right-facing black triangle in Path icon box at extreme bottom right of Places box. If all has gone well, you should be "flying" down the gorge, in the same direction as the river flows. The "flight" down to Koblenz will take about two minutes, and give you a great view of the gorges and surrounding countryside. When finished, turn off the "flying" feature by clicking the x in the little black bar at bottom left of map screen. Turn "Photos" basic layer back on. Then turn on and fly to each of the two Placemarks included in the folder, "Castle Rheinstein" and "Lorelei" for views of some scenery there.

5. GE Layer 5 is a Path representing the course of the Main River. Turn on the layer, double-click Path icon to frame the river. Do same with the four below.

6. GE Layer 6 is a Path representing the German section of the Elbe River.

7. GE Layer 7 is a Path representing the Weser River.

8. GE Layer 8 is a Path representing the Oder River.

9. GE Layer 9 is a Path representing the German part of the upper Danube River. Expand view for view of entire course of river.

angle between them; the Danube by contrast is just setting off on its long course east. After it leaves Germany it either borders or goes through eight countries, and four of them have their capitals on it (Austria's Vienna, Slovakia's Bratislava, Hungary's Buda on one side and Pesht on the other, and Serbia's ancient Beograd, or Belgrade.

In aerial photos (including the Google Earth surface, which is a composite of such photos), the forests of Germany generally show up as dark green patches. Usually they are limited to mountainous regions, as in the Black Forest (*Schwarzwald*), the Palatinate Forest (*Pfälzerwald*), the *Odenwald*, and the *Harz* mountains. The *Spreewald* with all its canals and rivers, southeast of Berlin, is by contrast a low-lying forest.[GE10]

Germans call the sea west of the Jutland (the peninsula that becomes part of Denmark further north) the North Sea (*Nordsee)*, and the sea east of it, which we call the Baltic, they call the East Sea (*Ostsee*). These northern sea coasts are mostly flat and sandy with strings of barrier islands,[GE11] though an occasional headland confronts the sea.[GE12] The northern coasts have always been popular vacation spots, even though the latitudes there approximate those of the southern shore of Hudson Bay!

You've now been shown the stage set; the curtain is about to rise on the drama.

The Germanies in the time of Napoleon

The time is that of Napoleon's rise to power, around 1800. The place is Germany, only keep in mind that "Germany" was not a nation-state but just a geographic expression for the general area where people who spoke German lived. In fact, there were upwards of three hundred German states, from the two biggest, Austria (which included many more non-Germans than Germans)[GE13] and Prussia,[GE14] down through half-a-dozen middle-sized states such as Bavaria, Baden, Hanover, Saxony, Mecklenburg, and the Hesses[GE15] to postage-stamp kingdoms such as Liechtenstein[GE16] (still its own country today, by a quirk of history, though hardly a nation-state).

In international affairs "Germany" was weak, and had been since the heyday of the Holy Roman Emperors. To recap a thousand years of complex history in one paragraph, let's begin with the fact that Charlemagne claimed to have recreated the Roman Empire in the year 800.[GE17] By 843 his three grandsons divided it into a western part that gradually morphed into France, and eastern part that became known as German lands, and

10. GE Layer 10 is a Folder titled "Major forests." Don't turn the Folder on, but open it and then turn on each of the five Polygon layers at a time. There is one each for the *Schwarzwald, Pfälzerwald, Odenwald, Harz,* and *Spreewald*. With the "Photos" basic layer turned on, a viewer can zoom into each of these (sometimes patchy) forests and find interesting Photos icon views.

11. GE Layer 11 is a Placemark referencing a Panoramio icon titled "Mönchgut, Luftbild," with an aerial view of typical flat coast. The bright yellow patches are probably fields of rapeseed, common in much of northern Europe.

12. GE Layer 12 is a Placemark referencing a Panoramio icon titled "Kreideküste bei Saßnitz" ("Chalkcoast near Sassnitz") showing such a headland in Rugen, like a small version of the white cliffs of Dover.

13. GE Layer 13 is a Polygon giving approximate boundaries of Hapsburg Empire in 1795. Turn on layer, double-click polygon icon to frame view. Based mainly on map on pp. 438–9 of John Gagliardo's *Germany Under the Old Regime 1600–1790* (London and New York: Longman, 1991), as modified by existing boundaries as in Google Earth when they seem to approximate the map overlay.

14. GE Layer 14 is a Polygon giving approximate boundaries of the Prussian state as of 1795. Turn on, frame view.

15. GE Layer 15 is a Folder titled "Mid-sized states." Open the folder without turning it on, and then turn on each of the Polygon layers giving general boundaries of Baden, Bavaria, Hessen-Kassel, Saxony, and Mecklenburg as of 1803. Source mainly historical map, "Germany and Italy in 1803 after Principal Decree of the Imperial Deputation" from following website: http://www.rootsweb.ancestry.com/~wggerman/map/germanyitaly1803.htm.

16. GE Layer 16 is a Placemark framing a view of Liechtenstein, tucked up against the Swiss border—a surviving fragment of a fragmented Germany still independent. Now turn off GE Layers 12 through 16.

17. GE Layer 17 is a Folder titled "Charlemagne's empire & capital city." "Fly" to pre-set overview by double-clicking Folder icon, and then turn it on. The pink Polygon represents the Carolingian Empire about the time of his death in 814, and a red star Placemark locates its capital Aachen, or Aix-la-Chappelle, today the most western of German cities. Now turn off this folder to clear the map screen for later layers of history.

a middle part that was fated to be torn between them. By the twelfth century the generally German east was being called the "Holy" Roman Empire, or *Reich* (though historians have joked it was neither holy nor Roman nor empire); the "holy" claim probably grew out of the Empire's complicated rivalry with the Papacy. It became a tradition that seven rulers of states within the Reich, called "electors," would choose each new Emperor, or *Kaiser* (closer to the pronunciation of the original Latin word "Caesar" than is our English word). The Hapsburg dynasty took root in and around today's Austria by 1250, and in 1438 the title of Emperor went permanently to these Hapsburg rulers based in Austria. By 1521 one individual, Charles V, by careful choice of grandparents, had inherited Spain (the newly united Aragon and Castile) and all its American conquests, the southern half of Italy, the Low Countries and Burgundy—AND the Hapsburg lands in and around Austria. But as you saw in the first chapter it was too big to hold together, especially as the Protestant Reformation broke out just when his reign began and northern Europe generally broke away from southern Europe. By the early 1700s the Hapsburg dynasty was back in Vienna, all of its ties with Spain and its American Empire now broken. It addition to lands owned directly by the Hapsburgs, the dynasty had only a loose suzerainty over the "Holy Roman Empire"[GE18] that roughly approximated German-speaking central Europe.[GE19]

In general, the growth of large nation-states around German-speaking territory—first Poland and then Russian in the east, and France in the west—had hurt it badly. A good deal of what is today eastern France used to be western Germany. As you saw in the last chapter, the "Sun King" Louis XIV chopped off piece after piece in the late 1600s, and he was only the best at it, not any exception to the general rule. What meager fame Germany had in international affairs was derived from three dubious distinctions: (a) that German-speaking territory often served as battleground for rival armies in major European wars; (b) that it supplied mercenary soldiers to other countries' armies (witness Hessians in the American Revolutionary War); and (c) that there was a huge pool of royal mates for kings and queens of larger countries to be found here, owing to the large number of small states each with a royal family. Because of this last factor, European royal dynasties from Britain to Russia tended to become genetically German, though that proved to be of no real benefit to the Germanies. Overall, German lands were physically inferior mainly because they were not united.

Add to this an intellectual inferiority complex of considerable weight. The 1700s was the age of the Enlightenment, and its most famous writers (at least as judged at the time) were French. If one aspired to be an intellectual or to high society in one of the German countries, one learned French. And native German-speakers were aware of and vaguely uneasy about books on questions such as why German was a much less expressive language than French, and on how France descended from the Roman Empire but the Germans only came from the barbarians, so what could you expect of them in the way of modern civilization?

Then on top of all this came Napoleon. He picked on a lot of people, from the Spanish to the Russians to the Egyptians; but his greatest impact was on the German states. You've seen how in 1797, as a mere general, he defeated Austria and forced a treaty on it that took away its territories in northern Italy. As Emperor, in 1805 at Austerlitz[GE20] he not only defeated the combined Austrian-Russian armies but utterly destroyed them. It took Austria and Russia two years to rebuild their armies, and meantime Napoleon occupied Vienna, the Austrian capital, and declared the end of the Holy Roman Empire. In 1806 he broke half the Prussian army at Jena and the other half at Auerstedt.[GE21] Fugitives from the battles retreated to Berlin, but the French took the Prussian capital two weeks later. The slice of German-speaking territory next to France was added to the French Empire. Central Germany was carved up into puppet kingdoms for Napoleon's relatives and favorites to admin-

---

18. GE Layer 18 is a Polygon that shows as a red outline around the Holy Roman Empire as of 1795.

19. GE Layer 19 is a Polygon that shows as a white area that (roughly!) represents German-speaking central Europe approximately 1800. Leave preceding Layer 18 on for comparison. To see how much of the Austria Empire was NOT German speaking, turn on GE Layer 13 again. Now turn off all these Polygons to clear the map screen again.

20. GE Layer 20 is a Placemark referencing the Austerlitz memorial for the battle with several interesting Photos icons in the view. The village after which battle was named is about five miles east, today called Slavkov n Brna.

21. GE Layer 21 is a Folder referencing the battle of Jena; it includes Placemarks referencing a Panoramio icon titled "Jena from the west (autumn)," and some nearby Photos icons showing several modern battle re-enactment scenes.

ister, as "The Confederation of the Rhine," or *Rheinbund*.[GE22] Finally, the two big states of the east, Austria and Prussia, were made not so big by having their western territories lopped off, and held their independence only precariously. Napoleon was so much the arbiter of Germany after 1806 that over half the Great Army of France that invaded Russia in 1812 was drawn from the German population by the French draft. What an inconceivable catastrophe, to discover oneself a native speaker of German in these years. What a time of soul-searching, especially among the political and intellectual leaders of the Germanies.

The Prussian Reforms

The first visible reaction to the French conquest was the desperate attempt by the remaining German states to reform. The lesson of 1805–6 was crushing and simple: German states could not compete on the battlefield with the French draft army. This lesson was learned in a particularly painful way by Prussia, as its army was decimated and Berlin made a French garrison center. Napoleon demanded an enormous indemnity from Prussia, and said if Prussia failed to pay up that he would take the province of Silesia. In the wake of the 1806 battles of Jena and Auerstadt, the Prussian king sanctioned a reform program sponsored by the "patriotic party"—men such as Gerhard von Scharnhorst (of Hanover) and August von Gneisenau (of Saxony) in the military and Karl vom Stein (of Nassau) and Karl von Hardenberg (of Brunswick and Hanover) in the government. They were all non-Prussians who had been attracted or driven to Prussia as the German state that remained most free of French control. Now these brilliant non-Prussians would guide the famous "Prussian Reforms" of 1807–1813.

Question: how could they tap the reserves of strength the French had tapped in the French draft army? Answer: systematically stage the French Revolution in Prussia, but from the top down, in a controlled and socially limited way. Karl von Hardenberg, soon to become prime minister of the state, clearly stated the plan in his 1807 suggestions to King Friedrich Wilhelm (Frederick William) III:

> The French Revolution, of which the current wars are an extension, has brought the French people a wholly new vigor, despite all their turmoil and bloodshed. All their sleeping energies have awakened; their miseries and languors, their obsolete prejudices and infirmities, have been extinguished, inclusively, let us admit it freely, with much that was good. Those who stood in the path of the torrent, those who were overborne, have been swept away . . . .
>
> It is an illusion to think that we can resist the Revolution effectively by clinging more closely to the old order, by proscribing the new principles without pity. This has been precisely the course which has favored the Revolution and facilitated its development. The force of these principles is such, their attraction and diffusion is so universal, that the State which refuses to acknowledge them will be condemned to submit or perish . . . .
>
> Thus our objective, our guiding principle, must be a revolution in the better sense, a revolution leading directly to the great goal, the elevation of humanity through the wisdom of those in authority and not through a violent impulse from within or without. Democratic rules of conduct in a monarchical administration, such is the formula, it appears to me, which will conform most perfectly to the spirit of the age.[2]

Within a month of the suggestion above, Prussia abolished serfdom and most legal distinctions between classes. The second major step—educating a class of patriotic civil servants to administer the state—followed soon after. The University of Berlin was designed in 1807 and opened its doors in 1810 as the capstone of a whole new educational establishment just for this. The third and critical step was to translate all this to the battlefield, despite a limit of 42,000 placed on the Prussian army by Napoleon (he knew the power of the draft army—possibly better than anyone else in the world—and was trying to ensure that Prussia did <u>not</u> create one). Here occurred one of the most brilliant of the reforms, the modern reserve system being created to allow Prussia to field nearly three hundred thousand well-trained, patriotic soldiers by 1813. This was von Scharnhorst's idea, his so-called "shrinkage system" (*Krümpersystem*), in which a small number of officers would give some-

---

22. GE Layer 22 is a Polygon representing the Kingdom of the Rhine, based mainly on map available online at www.zum.de/whdmla/histatlas/germany/rheinbund.gif. Again, double-click on Polygon icon to frame view, then turn the layer on.

thing like a one-year-long Berlitz course in war to tens of thousands of draftees, then "retire" them to the reserve so they were not technically in the army anymore, and train tens of thousands more the next year. It was this new Prussian draft army under General von Blücher that held the center at the crucial battle of Leipzig in October of 1813, "the Battle of Nations" that sealed Napoleon's fate[GE23], and that same Prussian army that showed up just in time to rescue Wellington at Waterloo[GE24] in June 1815 (after Napoleon had escaped from the island of Elba and came back to France to try to rebuild his Empire in the so-called "100 Days").

So, although the Prussian King Frederick William III never created the representative assembly urged on him by vom Stein and von Hardenberg, the Prussian reforms overall were an explosive success, and Napoleon was beaten. The most famous German medal of honor, the Iron Cross, dates from that period: the silver-bordered black iron came from melted-down French cannon. On the primary side at the top was a crown, below which were the letters FW (for King Frederick William III); at the middle, branching out onto all arms of the cross, was an oakleaf cluster (logo of the royal house of Hohenzollern), and at the bottom was the date 1813. [GE25] Then as suddenly as the reforms had been initiated, they were halted. The king and other conservatives now felt that the need for change was gone, so why continue to destroy the social fabric needlessly and risk a real French-style Revolution by allowing a popular assembly to get its foot in the door? In effect, a Prussian state had been born that was capable of leading a German national unification; but after 1813 it appeared still-born.

The Juniper Tree

There was another movement afoot in the Napoleon-dominated Germanies after 1806, although at first glance it seems almost silly to put in on the same level of importance as the Prussian Reforms. Perhaps its first great symbol came in December of 1812 with the publication of a little volume of folktales called *Kinder- und Hausmärchen* (*Children and Household Folktales*). Collected and edited by the Brothers Grimm, in expanded form this collection of 210 tales has come to be known in English-speaking lands as *Grimms' Fairy Tales*, and by variations on that title, all over the world. The tales have elements of mystery, violence and sexual overtones that in Walt Disney versions are mostly edited out—mutilations, successfully hidden incest, raw sibling rivalry tucked away into stories the reader may not have been read as a child, as in "Manyfur" or "Fitcher's Feathered Bird."

If you think these folktales of the Grimms are primarily for children, try this experiment. Imagine yourself wanting to read a bedtime story to a five-year-old, that a handy copy of *Grimms' Fairy Tales* has just fallen open in your hands to "The Juniper Tree,"[3] and that you've settled comfortably down to a "long ago and far away" opening. A rich man and his wife had always wanted to have children, but never had any (if your five-year-old asks why, you probably won't want to talk about it). One day the woman was peeling apples in the snow under a juniper tree when she cut her finger, saw the red drops of blood on the snow, and made a wish she could have a child "white as that snow and red as that blood." And something about making the wish under the juniper made it come true. Upon the child's birth—and it was a little boy, white as snow and red as blood, the storyteller assures us—she looked at the baby and was so happy that she died and was buried under the juniper tree (and this would probably be the first time you would look inquiringly at your five-year-old, to see how he or she took this news). Her husband married again, and he and his new wife had a little girl named Marlene, the only one named in the story. The new wife, the little boy's stepmother, is a classic fairy tale stepmother, full of hate for the child not her own. She invited him to take an apple out of the apple chest, slammed

---

23. GE Layer 23 is a Placemark framing a view of the Battle of Nations monument just southeast of Leipzig; lots of Photos icons to explore.

24. GE Layer 24 is a Placemark framing a view of the Battle of Waterloo monument. The huge, perfectly conical memorial hill shows up clearly in any aerial view.

25. GE Layer 25 is a Placemark framing a view of Burg Hohenzollern, the South German castle dating from the eleventh century that was the original family home of the Prussian royal house, rebuilt—romantically—by Frederick William IV after 1846. A Wikipedia article has a picture of this side of the Iron Cross, at http://en.wikipedia.org/wiki/Prussian_Army; none were available on an Image search in Google. You'll need to scroll down about three screens to see Iron Cross photograph. If you look at it closely you can see the FW and the 1813 date.

the lid and heavy iron lock down on his neck so that his head was cut off and rolled in among the apples. She sat the body up in a chair, tied the head back on with a cloth, put an apple in the hand of the recently deceased and went back to her housework. She made Marlene think she had killed her older brother, and then they diced the boy's body up in the soup (perhaps the second good place to look inquiringly at your five-year-old audience). When the husband came home, his wife made up a lie about where the little boy had gone. The husband ate all the soup, threw the bones on the floor, and Marlene, not quite knowing why, gathered them up in a little cloth and wandered out to sit beneath the juniper tree. All of a sudden the branches of the tree moved and parted and a bird with red, green and gold feathers flew out of it, and the story for awhile follows the bird. It flew to a goldsmith's shop, perched on the roof, and sang something like this:

> My mother she killed me
> My father he ate me
> My sister Marlene collected my bones
> Tied them up in a silken cloth, under the juniper
> Tweet tweet what a beautiful bird I am

The goldsmith came out, asked for another singing of what was obviously a powerful magical song, and the bird said, no, the goldsmith had to give it something. So the goldsmith threw up a golden chain he'd just made, the bird clutched it in a claw and sang again. To make a long story shorter, the bird sang at the cobbler's house and got a pair of red leather shoes, and at the miller's and got a huge millstone that it flew down to, stuck its head through and—being magic—flew off with.

Meanwhile, back at the ranch, things had gone from bad to worse; it was gloomy and everybody felt terrible. Then the magic bird arrived, singing the same song. The father went out to hear it, and got a golden chain tossed down around his neck. Marlene went out to hear it, and got a pair of red leather shoes just her size. The wicked stepmother went out to hear it, and got squashed by a millstone that sent up flames and smoke when it landed. When Marlene and her father went out to see what had happened, there was no evil stepmother, no golden bird, but there stood the little boy, white as snow and red as blood, and he went in to eat with his father and his half-sister. And for all a reader knows, they may have lived happily ever after. But you've got to wade through considerable violence and gore, and maybe some sexual innuendo at the story's start, and perhaps come back to visit the child to whom you read during his or her subsequent nightmares.

And "Juniper Tree" is not all that unusual among the tales in the collection. There is "Fitcher's Feathered Bird" with a silver cauldron just brimming with blood and body parts. Here too are some old stand-bys that fit right in. Everybody knows "Rapunzel" (Miss Piggy on Sesame Street did a classic version). "Rapunzel" turns out to be an archaic word for an onion-like vegetable. A barren wife craves the witch's onions, shall we say; the husband steals them for her repeatedly, and when the witch catches him, the magically-conceived child must be named "Onion" and promised to the witch. Remember that "Hansel and Gretel" has rather brutal family relations and attempted cannibalism. "Cinderella" in the original Grimms' version translates literally "Ashen Slut," and in it the stepsisters actually cut off toes and heels to get the glass slipper to fit. Cinderella's mother has been buried in the garden, and a bird sits in the tree growing out of her grave and sings to the passing Prince, "Look in the shoe, there's blood in the shoe, this is not the one for you," or some such rhyme in archaic German.

The point of all this was to convince you, dear reader, that it was not altogether for children that the Grimms collected these fascinating tales.[4] To explain more fully, a cameo biography of the Bros. Grimm is in order shortly. First, however, the spirit of the age in which they lived and worked needs some describing.

Romanticism, Herder, and the "Folk"

The backdrop for the whole scene staged here is the Romantic Era. "Romanticism" with a capital R is, for most artists, literary scholars, philosophers, and historians, the age that follows hard on the heels of the "Enlightenment." Like the Enlightenment, the Romantic Age is hard to pin down chronologically, any more generally than to say that it peaked in the first half of the 1800s. If the key words of the Enlightenment were "reason" and "the natural" (in that they were going to take a clear-eyed look at how social and political institutions were and very logically change them to fit universal human nature), then perhaps the one key concept of the Romantic Age was "organic." Nature was almost a fetish for the Romantics, and their Mother Nature was not simply "the natural" universal human nature of the Enlightenment, but all of the Natural world wild and stormy and untrimmed. "Organic" refers to the process of live things growing, and the concept was used as a real rebellion against the Enlightenment's "rational" tinkering with society. If tulips developed according to a tulip pattern inherent in the bulb, and if oaks grew according to an oak pattern inherent in the acorn, did it make sense to cut a tulip off and try to graft on an oak top? If human institutions indeed had life cycles analogous to plants, did it make sense to cut off German culture in 1789 and graft on a French top? The Romantic Age is important from Russia in the east to Ireland and even to the young U.S.A. in the west, but it was nowhere more important than in the Germanies.

To understand cultural nationalism among the Germans (says the historian, whose only real insights into things arise from watching how they come into being), one must go back and watch it develop—the same way any serious understanding of the early French Revolution of 1789–94 requires some knowledge of Rousseau's works of 1761–62. As you've seen, important ideas seem to take a generation or two to spread and be worked out in politics and society. What Rousseau was to the French Revolution, Johann Gottfried von Herder (1744–1803) was to German cultural nationalism. Like Rousseau, he built on earlier foundations; but also like Rousseau, his ideas were original and powerful enough to move people into new patterns of behavior.

The geographic pattern of Herder's life is interesting, limited to a long but fairly narrow corridor from northeast to southwest from what is today Latvia to eastern France.[GE26] He was born in East Prussia (in a small town in today's Poland); educated in philosophy and theology at the University of Königsberg (today's Kaliningrad in Russia) where Emmanual Kant was the university president and dominant intellectual influence, and then from 1764–69 he preached and taught at Riga (then in the Russian Empire, now in Latvia). At Strasbourg, the easternmost city of France (where lots of German was still spoken) he was introduced to the teen-aged Goethe, and apparently fired the younger man's imagination with his ideas on folksongs, classic literature, and Shakespeare. Herder's mature works began to appear during 1771–76 when he was court preacher at Bückeburg in lower Saxony. In 1776 Goethe invited Herder to join him at the small but brilliant court at Weimar, which became the intellectual capital of the Germanies in the late 1700s and early 1800s. As Goethe's fame rose to surpass Herder's, relations between the two cooled; but Herder's greatest writing was still produced here at Weimar—chief among his books being his *Ideen zur Philosophie der Geschichte der Menschheit (Reflections on the Philosophy of the History of Mankind)* that appeared serially from 1784 to 1791.

Herder was a passionate reader of the travel literature pouring in from European explorers of the world. In this sense he was a true child of the Enlightenment: he was trying to work out a new definition of human nature common to all places and times. But Herder saw culture and not politics as the primary creation of humankind. Almost every people in every time and place was interesting and valuable, thought he, be they tiny American Indian tribes or massive oriental kingdoms. Anything such a group did to contribute to *Humanität (*literally "humanity")—which Herder seemed to measure by richness of human expression, including music, art, lore, and literature—made it worth study and contemplation. Any group was a "people," or *Volk*, if it had lived together for enough centuries to have a shared language and a shared mythology or religion.

Every *Volk*, or folk group, was according to Herder formed by the interaction of a certain group of people and a certain land area back in a "form-giving" period. So every folk group has its unique genius from the beginning, the way a seed has in it a growth pattern. "Primitive" is not a bad word in Herder's thought, as a result: sometimes "primitive" means something is closer to the first flowering of a folk culture. About the nomadic Arab, he said: ". . .his tent still preserves the wisdom of his forefathers." Trying to explain the importance of the oral literature of "uncultivated" cultures to his audience of proudly literate Europeans, Herder argued:

---

26. GE Layer 26 is a Folder titled "Life of Herder." In the folder are Placemarks referencing important venues of his life. Turning the whole folder on will show you the pattern of his life in white pushpin icons; you can explore each Placemark as it is mentioned in the text above, should you wish.

. . . most national fictions spring from verbal communications, and are instilled in the ear. The ignorant child listens with curiosity to the tales, which flow into his mind like his mother's milk, like the choice wine of his father, and form its nutriment. They seem to him to explain what he has seen: to the youth they account for the way of life of his tribe, and stamp the renown of his ancestors. The man they introduce to the employment suited to his nation and climate, and thus they become inseparable from his whole life. The Greenlander and the Tungus see in reality all their lives only what they heard of in their infancy, and thus they believe it to be evidently true.

This is an illustration of the sort of thing Herder meant by "humanity"—those things people do to explain the world to themselves and increase the degree of community with each other. In Herder's glossary "humanity" is something humans at their best have and animals don't; he seems to use it much the way a modern anthropologist might use the word "culture."

In Herder's worldview, finally, no folk group can ever be static. They are living entities, always changing, that sometimes flourish and that usually die sooner or later. Some that become so rigidly attached to older forms of society are for Herder the living dead; they survive as a shell but have no true life within.

The excitement most readers find in Herder is in his sensitive insights into cultures everywhere, and in his feeling that virtually all individuals and cultures are capable of wonderful things. It makes a reader proud to be a member of the species. But there is an unease most modern readers feel about Herder, too. Despite the picture he draws of a balanced world made up of a mosaic of rich cultures, like a stained glass window, he is the father of an idea that indirectly, at least, produced Hitler and the Holocaust. Even knowing that it is a danger to evaluate a life in terms of later events, it is hard not to think about events that happened 150 years after Herder wrote these words about Jews:

. . . parasitical plants on the trunks of other nations; a race of cunning brokers, almost throughout the whole world; who, in spite of all oppression, have never been inspired with the ardent passion for their own honor, for a habitation, for a country, of their own.[5]

There was anti-Semitism in central and eastern Europe long before Herder—Martin Luther's writings come to mind in this regard—but in Herder it now found a new philosophical foundation in this whole "organic" conception of human culture. And of course in the second half of the book you will indeed see the development among European Jews of a most "ardent passion" for a country of their own!

Fichte and Jahn

A quotation from Johann Gottlieb Fichte's *Addresses to the German Nation* headed up this chapter. In the winter of 1807–8 a French army of occupation was still in Berlin, having overrun virtually all the Germanies. This may have been the low point in German fortunes in the last five hundred years. Even in 1945, with Berlin in ruins and Hitler committing suicide in the bunker, there was little doubt that a Germany (or two) would continue to exist. In 1807, however, the future existence of any German state or states was very much in doubt. In this depressed setting, this well-known philosophy professor gave a series of fourteen lectures at the Academy in Berlin to rally not just Prussians, but Germans generally.

Fichte began with Herder's view of culture as the product of one people and one land, but he found modern German culture superior, and not just one of many valuable cultures. According to Fichte's impassioned argument, Germans (he included Danes, Swedes, and Norwegians here) alone among modern European peoples remained in their original lands, and kept up the life force of the nation by so doing. The Franks, those early Germans who had wandered west and picked up a Latin language, were rootless and superficial by comparison. They had broken the all-important ties to original language and land, and were without depth or staying power even in modern guise as Napoleon's France. The way early German tribes eventually beat off the Roman challenge to their independence, so now modern Germans would beat off the Latinized French.

Fichte then took Herder's primacy-of-culture argument and politicized it. First, he argued that a true culture deserved a state: ". . . wherever a separate language is found, there a separate nation exists, which has the right to take independent charge of its affairs and to govern itself." Second, he called for a new sort of state, one in which "this love of fatherland must itself govern the state and be the supreme, final, and absolute authority." Think about that phrase a minute: he is arguing that patriotism is the only real standard by which to judge a person, more important than any ethical or religious standard. Fichte outlined a demanding educational structure designed to produce citizens of this future state, which outline later got him the job of philosophy professor at and, briefly, of Rector (President) of the University of Berlin.[GE²⁷] In 1808 he closed his fourteenth and final lecture with this line on the importance of German response to French military occupation: ". . .if you go under, all humanity goes under with you, without hope of any future restoration."⁶

One interesting character who frequented high schools and colleges in and around Berlin around this time was Friedrich Ludwig Jahn (1778–1852). Considerably older than the young people who clustered round him, he was nicknamed "Turnvater" ("gymnastics father") or just "Father" Jahn. *Turn* is a word he took from the medieval "tournaments" (apparently named for the turning, or wheeling, involved in the jousts) which he saw as embodying the true German spirit. He either invented or introduced into Germany almost the whole paraphernalia of modern gymnastics—the rings, the high bar, the parallel bars, the pommel horse—all in the name of patriotism. The idea was to prepare young bodies physically for a coming war of liberation against the French army of occupation. Father Jahn set up the first of his formal gymnastics training clubs in 1811 in the outskirts of Berlin. He and his young disciples were so caught up in this new cultural nationalism as to be outspoken Francophobes: "If you let your daughter learn French you might just as well teach her to become a whore," said he.⁷ There was a new democratic leveling spirit here; whether of aristocratic, middle-class, or working-class origin, they all called each other *Du* (not the formal "You" but "Thou," the intimate second person singular in German). The German Empire that Friedrich Jahn envisioned included even Denmark and Switzerland, and he spoke in ringing language of the necessary union of folk and state: "A state is nothing without a *Volk*—a soulless artifact. A *Volk* is nothing without a state—a bodiless phantom, like the wandering gypsies and Jews. Only the unity of state and *Volk* makes a *Reich*."⁸

Heady stuff, this. Receptive Germans listening to Fichte and Jahn were transformed in their own minds from unimportant pawns in a civilization being crushed under Napoleon's feet to potent bearers of the future of the world. There was an upsurge of pride and self-confidence that it must have been exciting to have been part of. By this time, however, respect such as Herder had had for most other cultures had all but evaporated from this nationalist ideology, and claims of Germanic superiority had appeared that sound ominous to those who know what happened in Germany in the 1930s and 1940s.

The lives of the Brothers Grimm

To continue one story already started, consider the lives of Jacob and Wilhelm Grimm. They were Hessians, from one of the medium-sized states in the heartland of Germany.[GE²⁸] They were the closest of brothers, born only a year apart in 1785 and 1786, working together in high school and rooming together at college. After their student days Wilhelm got married, but Jacob lived with him and his tolerant, supportive, folktale-collecting wife. The great works one or the other of the brothers signed were most often collaborations between them.

Their father, a lawyer, died when they were twelve and eleven. The bereaved family then faced a dozen years of real financial woes, although they were helped some by an aunt who had a position at the court at Kassel. She took them in so they could attend the local lycée (college-prep secondary school) there. Perhaps driven by their poverty, the brothers became outstanding students. Jacob was described as plodding but very disciplined, Wilhelm as sensitive and intuitive but less disciplined. They went on to the premier college of the Hesses, the University of Marburg.[GE²⁹] Here they studied law, partly, one suspects, because of memories of

---

27. GE Layer 27 is a Placemark locating the main entrance to what is today known as Humboldt University of Berlin. Dozens of Photos icons plus a Cities 360 icon to explore.

28. GE Layer 28 is a Placemark referencing a Panoramio icon titled "Wilhelm Jacob Grimm statue in Kassel." It stands, logically enough, on Brüder Grimm Platz (Brothers Grimm Square).

29. GE Layer 29 is a Placemark referencing a Panoramio icon titled "Universität, Marburg/Lahn"; it is a view of old bridge over the Lahn and the old university campus beyond. Photos icons located across the river, at least two titled "Alte Universität" or "Old University," have close-up views of some of the older buildings. Marburg is about forty-five miles southeast of Kassel.

their father. Then, too, law was not taught in universities as most law schools teach it today, with emphasis on technique and practice; it was rather a course of studies in the evolution and philosophy of law, more a branch of cultural history.

By 1805 Jacob Grimm had grown very close to a remarkable young Marburg professor interested in Roman law and how it had been modified over the centuries by Germanic common law. This was Friedrich Karl von Savigny, who had been profoundly impressed by Herder, as is clear in this passage he wrote in 1814:

> But this organic connection of law with the being and character of the people, is also manifested in the prog-
> ress of the times; and here, again, it may be compared with language. For law, as for language, there is no
> moment of absolute cessation; it is subject to the same movement and development as every other popular
> tendency; and this very development remains under the same law of inward necessity, as in its earliest stages.
> Law grows with the growth, and strengthens with the strength of the people, and finally dies away as the
> nation loses its nationality.[9]

It was in Savigny's library that Jacob first read the old German minnesingers and other early German texts, trying to understand the medieval German culture that was "organically connected" with the law. So close was this friendship between graduate student and professor that in 1805 Jacob was invited to help Savigny do research in the *Bibliothèque Nationale* in Paris—the French national library that because of Napoleon's looting of central Europe had more medieval German materials than any library in German lands.[GE[30]] He accepted enthusiastically, and for a year soaked up medieval manuscripts the way a dry sponge soaks up water.

Back in Hesse-Kassel in 1806, Jacob had trouble finding satisfactory work. Then in November the situation was transformed: Hesse-Kassel, along with most of the Germanies, was occupied by Napoleonic troops. The Grimms' homeland was reorganized into the "Kingdom of Westphalia" (the capital of which was actually in the city of Kassel), ruled by Napoleon's frivolous youngest brother, Jérôme. Wilhelm was by now desperately ill, and Jacob was without work for some critical months. But Napoleon intended this Kingdom of Westphalia to be the model French-dominated German state of the whole Confederation of the Rhine, so for a few years there was lots of money for things cultural. In 1808 Jacob was awarded a job directing King Jérôme's private library (at the palace of Wilhelmshöhe—temporarily renamed Napoleonshöhe—about three miles west of downtown Kassel). It was a plum job, really a court post that required little work, but he apologized to Savigny about having to take a job with the French conquerors.

It is an interesting coincidence, if it is coincidence, that the Brothers Grimm really began their life's work with this French occupation of their homeland. Wilhelm immersed himself in Scandinavian literature in general and Old Norse mythology in particular, and Jacob began an exhaustingly thorough study of medieval German epics and hero stories. In the words of one biographer, "the Grimms turn to older German literature and history was at once an escape from the depressing contemporary political situation and an attempt to find solace in the ancient glories and achievements of their nation."[10]

In 1809–1810 Austria raised the hopes of many Germans in its latest war with Napoleon. When Austria lost again, Jacob was crushed. He told his brother that he was so depressed by life in Kassel that he would leave it if his mother's grave were not still fresh there. In 1811 and early 1812, when Napoleon began to concentrate his Great Army in the Germanies to threaten Russia, the low point of Germany's fortune was reached.

But by this time Jacob had edited the oldest lays and epics of Germany and Wilhelm had mastered Norse mythology. Then came the time when they began to see a link between the two, some hints that Germany's ancient mythology was identical to, maybe part of, the Norse. In particular, Jacob Grimm was the first to discover that the oldest surviving German sagas, though they had always been translated as prose works, in fact shared the alliteration and meter of the old Scandinavian sagas. Beyond that, the brothers had a glimmer of an idea that the surviving epics and folktales of Germany were simply relics of a powerful religion and culture from much earlier times.

---

30. GE Layer 30 is a Placemark referencing Panoramio icon titled "Cours–Bibliothèque Nat.," with a photograph of the central building of the French National Library, France's version of our Library of Congress or the British Library of the British Museum.

On Christmas day of 1812, out of the Grimms' patriotic fervor, came the famous *Children and Household Folktales*, first edition, a collection of their first fifty tales. It was for adults as well as children (the earliest known folktales collected by Jacob Grimm are seven he sent in 1808 to Professor von Savigny—and to Savigny's three-year-old daughter; one of them was a version of "The Juniper Tree!"). The following paragraph is from the Grimms' preface to the original 1812 edition:

> When a storm or some other misfortune sent by Heaven has knocked the crops to the ground, we find that in some low hedge or bushes which stand by the road, a small spot has remained intact along with individual ears of fruit. If the sun then shines again they continue to grow, quietly and unnoticed. No premature sickle cuts them for the big storehouses, but in the late summer, when they have become ripe and full, there come poor and pious hands to seek them, and when they are bound carefully ear to ear, they are carried home with more respect than whole sheaves would be, and all winter long they provide nourishment, perhaps also the only seed for the future. Thus it is when we look at the wealth of German poetry in early time and then see that of so much nothing has remained alive, even the memory of it has been lost and only folk songs and these innocent household fairy tales are all that is left. The places at the stove, the kitchen hearth, the attic steps, the festivals still celebrated, the meadows and woods in their silence, and above all the undimmed sense of imagination have been the hedges which protected them and handed them down from one age to another . . . . [11]

The collection of folktales was part of the Grimms' work with mythology and the German language, a demonstration of the German mind and the high antiquity of German culture. It was to preserve what was uniquely German if Germany should die under Napoleon, but more immediately was to aid Germany in its struggle. In 1813 the Grimms donated the proceeds of their latest publication to equip Hessian volunteers for the wars of liberation against the French. Later that same year Jacob was appointed Secretary of Legation to accompany the Hessian minister to the headquarters of the allied army. In 1814 he was sent to France to recover books looted from the Kassel library by the French. In 1815 he was officially present at the Congress of Vienna.

Their later careers can be quickly summarized. From 1814 to 1829 they worked at the city library in downtown Kassel. They were librarians and professors at the University of Göttingen[GE[31]] (even closer to their home in Kassel than Marburg, but in the state of Hanover; probably the most liberal university in all the Germanies, because of Hanover's connections with Britain) from 1829 until they were fired for a political protest in 1837. In that year the new ruler canceled the constitution, and they were two of only seven professors who had courage enough to protest, knowing it would cost them their jobs. By 1840 they had gravitated to the University of Berlin, still the educational center of German patriotism. In these years came an outpouring of major works, which dwarf and at the same time complement their collection of *Fairy Tales*; among them a two-volume collection of German legends, *A History of the German Language*, the main construction of the huge *Dictionary of the German Language*, and the four-volume *Teutonic Mythology*. An intense patriotism permeates the whole body of work. In an 1844 introduction to one of the volumes of *Teutonic Mythology*, Jacob Grimm concluded: "Having observed that her Languages, Laws, and Antiquities were greatly underrated, I was wishful to exalt my native land." Towards the end of his life, he summed up his work so:

> Nearly all my labors have been devoted, either directly or indirectly, to the investigations of our [German] earlier language, poetry, and laws. These studies may have appeared to many, and may still appear, useless; to me they have always seemed a noble and earnest task, definitely and inseparably connected with our common fatherland, and calculated to foster the love of it. [12]

The Grimms and the "organic" idea

The Grimms were caught up in the mysticism of the organic conception of history. They were convinced that a folk grew and flowered like a plant, and that the truer a nation was to its early principles, the stronger and

---

31. GE Layer 31 is a Placemark set on the campus of the University of Göttingen, just outside the north wall of the old city. Under the blue Pushpin icon is a Photos icon titled "Platz der Göttinger Sieben"—which translates as "Square of The Göttinger Sieben." The courageous stand of those seven professors back in 1837 is obviously still remembered.

more brilliant that nation would be. This is what drove them to devote their lives to a study of the Germanic past: if they could just capture the essence of the original German culture and revive it in their day, Germany would become free and strong again.

They ran into some snags in their research. The easiest way to study the past of most any people is to read what they have written about themselves. Until very late, however, the Germanic peoples had no written language. When they did get one, it was mainly used for magical purposes. This is the runic alphabet, in use from as early as the third century AD and surviving in remote fringe areas of the Germanic world down to relatively modern times. Runes were only used on formal occasions, and then cut in wood or stone. There were something like three thousand runic inscriptions left, and the information in them might be typified by the inscription on the seventh century Björketorp stone in Sweden:

> I have here the secret meaning of powerful runes. He who destroys the monument will forever be tormented
> by evil witchcraft. He shall die a treacherous death. I prophesy ruin.[13]

Interesting prose, and maybe you can use it the next time you play "Dungeons and Dragons," but it is not especially informative about the culture. It seems likely that some bronze-age people who spoke the ancestor of the German languages lived in northern Germany and southern Scandinavia, and sometime around 500 BC they gradually began to fan out to the east, south, and west. But as to what their culture was like, no runic histories, or diaries, or law codes were written to tell.

The Grimms then fell back to a second approach. They read what civilized writers in Mediterranean Europe had to say about the expanding German tribes. Even here, there were major disappointments in store. The classical Greeks did not know of the Germans, or at least no word of theirs on the subject survives; and even Roman references are sketchy. Julius Caesar brushed up against them in his Gallic wars in the 50s BC and mentioned them, and Augustus fought a dramatic series of wars with them a half-century later. Finally around AD 100 the Roman historian Tacitus wrote a little book called *Germany* apparently based on interviews with Roman veterans of the German wars. He dropped hints about their morals, dress, chieftains, the use of horses in burial sacrifices, and their worship of Mercury as chief god, but it was just enough to tantalize the Grimms. Then the classical sources went silent for a century, with only scattered glimpses of Franks pushing into Gaul and the Goths drifting into southern Russia.

In AD 375 the Roman Empire west of the Rhine and south of the Danube was in decline, and the German tribal groups across the river were growing in power. Suddenly this delicate balance was destroyed by the Huns. They appeared unexpectedly from the east and hit the German tribes with the effect of a cue ball hitting a rack of pool balls in a good break, setting whole peoples in motion. In the next century and a half, in what is usually known in English as the "Barbarian Migrations" but which is more aptly described in German as *Völkerwanderung* (literally the Folkswandering), the Huns and the German tribes such as Angles, Saxons, Vandals, Ostrogoths, Visigoths, Lombards crashed the Roman frontiers on Danube and the Rhine Rivers and destroyed the western half of the Roman Empire. The lamp of civilization was considerably dimmed, in terms of written records left after that, and in the medieval darkness that followed yet another Germanic wave flooded over the shores of Europe—the Viking invasions of the eighth and ninth centuries. They drove into England as Danes, into France as Normans, into Russia as Varangians. They conquered as far as Sicily, Africa, the American coast. What was the original, parent Germanic culture really like? The Grimms could not learn enough from written accounts, and so they invented a new kind of "history" that used unwritten sources.

The Model of Cultural Breakdown

The Grimms speculated that as much as two or three thousand years ago there was a living Germanic culture. By "living" they meant to say it had a unique religion, language, and social practice formed in harmony with the land. That culture underwent change because of contact with other cultures, particularly Mediterranean ones, so that the religion was no longer completely believed. As the culture further fragmented, the mythology broke up into separate epics, and the long epics broke up into shorter legends. The legends in their turn degenerated into smaller, less formal and increasingly changed folktales, and these spun off proverbs and riddles. The final level of fragmentation was reached in simple words, popular customs, and gestures. The point is, as the Grimms stood in their present of 1810 or so, they saw themselves surrounded by cultural bits of flotsam and jetsam, the scattered debris of a culture long disintegrated—something like a zillion-piece jigsaw puzzle. To give order to the past, all they thought they had to do was to reconstruct the puzzle, and fill missing pieces with probable answers. Wilhelm, the more poetic of the brothers, expressed this idea of the breakdown of an original pure culture leaving bits and pieces of the old religion preserved in traditional tales:

> Common to all fairy tales are the remnants of a faith which goes back to the most ancient times and which is expressed in the figurative conception of supersensual things. This mythic element is like little pieces of a splintered jewel that lie on the ground covered over by grass and flowers and only to be discovered by very sharp eyes. The meaning of the mystical element is long since lost, but it is still felt and gives the fairy tales their content while at the same time satisfying the natural pleasure in the miraculous; they are never just the ornamental play of idle imagination.[14]

As an example of this process of cultural breakdown, in classical Norse mythology there is a powerful episode concerning Odin, father of the gods, and his daughters, the Valkyries. These nameless, faceless "maidens of the slain" rode down to fields of battle and transported the souls of dead heroes to the Hall of the Slain (Valhalla), there to prepare for the great last battle of Ragnarok between the gods and their allies on one side and all the forces of evil on the other. It deals with the contact of the immortals with mortals, and presumably explained for its believers the meaning of existence. This part of the ancient religion evolved later into the famous medieval legend about Brynhild and Siegfried. Brynhild, favorite daughter of Odin (notice that she now has a name and a face) was flying down to earth one day to pick up a soul of a dead human hero, when she saw Siegfried, bravest and most handsome of mortal men, and fell in love with him. She was put to sleep by her angry father on a mountain ringed with fire for daring to fall in love with a mortal, and was later rescued and awakened by Siegfried (who didn't recognize her and gave her away to somebody else, but you can still see how the heart of the legend comes from the old religion). Part of that legend in its turn seems to have evolved into the popular Sleeping Beauty folktale recorded from storytellers by the Grimms themselves and included in their collection: the sleeping beauty and the prince are unnamed, but the awakening from enchanted sleep seems suspiciously similar. The folktale is probably descended from the ancient religion, a piece of the "splintered jewel."

Modern scholars have discovered that some of the key sources of the folktales collected by the Grimms were of French Huguenot descent, and that an occasional Grimms' Fairy Tale came straight from the original French *Mother Goose*. Even the Grimms' modern defenders say that the folktale collection was their earliest and most amateur scholarly effort.[15] But the Grimms themselves obviously believed them to be straight from primeval German culture. These folktales taken altogether convinced them that the original German culture was either part of the ancient Scandinavian culture or very closely related to it. This had real prestige value in the Grimms' day because of scholars' excitement over the Old Norse myths.

The *Eddas* and Old Norse Mythology

In the late 1700s European scholars recovered some old Icelandic manuscripts called Eddas (there is some speculation that the word *edda* meant "grandmother tale"; maybe, maybe not). Iceland, about halfway between northwest Europe and Greenland, amounted to a rugged and isolated frontier of Norway, an island shielded from continental change until very late.[GE32] The pre-Christian religion had long survived there. Fragments of a poetic *Elder Edda*, in the handwriting of the 1100s but possibly a copy of some document as old as the 500s, and a *Prose Edda* from the 1200s (the main purpose of which was to explain the *Elder Edda*) were found. They are still our best source of the Old Norse myths. This mythology was an awesome drama, essentially a

---

32. GE Layer 32 is a Placemark framing a view of Iceland between Greenland and Norway.

tragedy, and the excitement its study generated among university scholars was tremendous. Cruder than the Greek mythology, it may be more brilliant.[GE33]

According to Norse mythology there were several races of beings each living in their own corner of the cosmos: the gods in Asgard, the giants in giant-home, the elves in elf-home, the dwarfs in dwarf-home, and humans in "mith-gaard" or middle earth.

There were a dozen or so major gods. First among them was Odin Allfather, who had brought order out of chaos. He had swapped an eye for wisdom early on, and having a feeling something bad was waiting for the gods out there somewhere in the future, was ceaselessly traveling to find out what it might be. The Far Traveler he was also called, and the Grey Wanderer. He had a patch over one eye, a slouch hat, ravens on his shoulders and wolves trotting behind. There was the strongman god, Thor, whose beard flashed orange when it light-ninged and caused the thunder when he hit something with his magic hammer; Freya, goddess of love, beauty and fertility; her brother, Freyr, god of dwarfs; and Iduna, the custodian of the sacred youth-giving apples. Most interesting of them all was Loki, whose aspect was fire with all its potential for good and evil (his mother was a goddess, everybody knew, but rumor had it his father was the Wind Giant who blew through town one day).

All these and more were the Aesir, or Asa, and their cousins the Vanir, creators and protectors of mortal men made to some extent in their image (in this religion the first humans were carved out of ash logs and then imbued with life). The Aesir fought a ceaseless war with giants of frost and wind and rock, and to protect themselves determined to build a mountain fortress to be called Asgard, which translates as Fortress of the Aesir. But it was built on a broken promise to its giant builder, and thus from the beginning it was without perfection. Other strange and evil events gradually collected around it, many associated with Loki, and in the final day when the gods and their allies, the heroes of Valhalla (from each of 539 doors would come 800 great human heroes, went one numerate version) would march out to meet the enemy, they would be destined to lose. There would be three years without summer, and then this world-ending battle of Ragnarok. The rainbow bridge into Asgard would be shattered, the mid-earth serpent who lies in the oceans and causes tidal waves and Thor would kill each other, the Fenris wolf of anarchy who swallows the moon during eclipses would kill Odin and the frost giant would lay low Freyr. Fire would burn the world in this end of the age, as Loki showed his true self and went over to lead the enemies of the gods. Only a tiny glimpse of hope would remain—a human couple, hidden away earlier in a fire-proof wood by Odin, who might yet carry on the race in a new age with a new sun and moon. Modern readers are not sure where they stand in a reading of these fragments, before or after Ragnarok!

This drama captured the minds of some modern readers and movie-goers in just a hint of the way it held its believers a couple of millenia ago. The popularity of J.R.R. Tolkien's *Hobbit* and *Lord of the Rings* trilogy and the afore-mentioned and related "Dungeons and Dragons" game, with all their spinoffs and imitations and movie versions, stands witness. Tolkien, although English and a century younger than the Brothers Grimm, was remarkably like the Grimms in that he was a trained linguist with a deep love for the old patterns of thought, especially the Germanic, and these are the basic building blocks of his works. In the regular weekly meetings of the informal literary group of Oxford intellectuals called The Inklings (which included C. S. Lewis) in the 1930s, Tolkien insisted they all learn some Old Norse and then whipped them through the *Elder Edda* in the original.[GE34] All of the dwarf names in his fictional work—Fili and Kili, Oinn and Gloinn, Thorin Oaken-shield, etc.—came straight from the *Elder Edda*, as did "Gandâlfr," an elf by his very name. The Brothers Grimm were just as fascinated with the Eddas and their imagery as Tolkien, but were less concerned with ancient literature as a mine for modern fantasy works and more concerned with the history and attitudes hidden away in that literature. What would it have done to you to have suddenly discovered that your ancestors had

33. GE layer 33 is a Placemark referencing the Icelandic Studies building on the University of Reykjavik campus, where the Elder or Poetic Edda is one of the greatest treasures of the collection. It was in Denmark for three centuries before being returned to Iceland.

34. GE Layer 34 is a Placemark referencing a Panoramio icon titled "The Eagle and Child; J. R. R. Tolkien's and C. S. Lewis's pub," for a photograph of the pub where Tolkien and the other Inklings met to read unfinished works, and where in 1939 Tolkien took them through the Elder or Poetic Edda.

invented such a brilliant tragedy and partly preserved it in their speech and stories? And the Grimms, for all their "organic" mysticism, brought a new level of scholarly depth to Romanticism.

European discovery of the *Rigveda*

At this point, the narrative will seem to jump halfway around the world to a completely different topic; you'll have to trust the author that it really will make sense after awhile in the context of the growth of this new kind of patriotism in Germany. Plus, it will help out as background for a later chapter on the Grand Trunk Road in India/Pakistan/Bangladesh, a particularly huge topic to cover.

Just before 1800, scholars in the British army and administration moving into India "discovered" Sanskrit, the classical language of the Hindu inhabitants of India. It existed in spoken form as early as 1500 BC, and began to be replaced by varieties of vernacular languages from as early as 500 BC to the early centuries AD, in the same process by which classical Latin was gradually replaced by modern Romance languages. Its major works came down to modern times written in the Devanagari script, still the basic script of Hindi and many other South Asian languages. This discovery of Sanskrit opened up one of the most extensive of world literatures to European linguists. First to appeal to them were the youngest (the latest to be written) products of Sanskrit, compiled as late as 200 BC or so, among them the two great epics *Ramayana* and *Mahabharata*—both considered sacred scripture by Hindus.

Briefly, the *Ramayana* revolved around a love story between Prince Rama and Princess Sita. She was of divine origin, turned up in a furrow by a plow as a baby and given to the local king to raise as a paragon of beauty and wisdom. The king, now her adoptive father, said that only whoever could string a great bronze bow in his keeping could have her hand. Many tried and no one could even lift it, until Lord Rama came, picked it up, strung it, and pulled it back until the bow snapped. The powerful demon Ravana later kidnapped Sita from Rama's hometown of Ayodhya[GE35] and took her down to his home in Sri Lanka.[GE36] Rama raised an army of monkeys, led by the white monkey Hanuman, to fight the lesser demons while he took on Ravana. He rescued Sita and took her back north to their Ayodhya home; townspeople lit up the town for their return, and thus the origin of the great yearly Hindu festival of lights called Divali. The epic profoundly impressed western thinkers who first read it, including Henry David Thoreau.

Equally briefly, the *Mahabharata* (*maha* means great, and Bharat was the name of the legendary founding family of Hindu India), the world's longest epic, was the story of the Pandavas, five brothers and half-brothers led in warfare by the middle of the brothers, the great archer Arjuna, in their struggles with their more or less evil cousins, the 100 Kuravas. The Kuravas tricked the Pandavas out of their rightful throne for fourteen years, at the end of which time the two sides fought a titanic battle at the Kurufield about 100 miles north of modern Delhi.[GE37] This is the setting for the small piece of the *Mahabharata* that is possibly the most important single piece of Hindu literature, the *Bhagavad Gita* or "The Lord's Song." The Pandava and Kurava armies are drawn up for battle, and for some reason Arjuna, commander of the former, is being driven in his chariot by the god Krishna. Arjuna looks across the battlefield and, foreseeing the carnage to come, tells Krishna he'd rather quit and go back to the forest rather than have all that blood on his hands. Krishna's reply—and this is the Lord's Song of the title—is first, that Arjuna is of the warrior caste and that it is his *dharma* (duty by his caste) to defend his family's rights, so get on with it; but second and more powerfully, that if he, Arjuna, imagines he kills or is killed, it's all just his imagination: the soul is immortal and goes from body to body as it deserves from its past behavior. So the whole *karma* and reincarnation essence of Hinduism is summed up here in one short piece of scripture.

Drawn into Sanskrit literature by the power of these epics, European scholars probed for earlier works and found the *Panchatantra*, or *Five Essays*. It seems to date from around or before 400 BC, and is a collection of animal stories ingeniously arranged as a political science handbook. The framework of the story is of a wise man telling a king's three blockhead sons stories designed to make them intelligent rulers in six months' time.

---

35. GE Layer 35 is a Placemark referencing the city of Ayodhya.

36. GE Layer 36 is a Placemark referencing the island/country of Sri Lanka.

37. GE Layer 37 is a Placemark referencing the city Thanesar, general locale of the Kurufield.

One of the five "essays" is how to deal with powerful enemies, for example. My favorite story from the collection is "The Lion-makers," which seems as pertinent today as when it was first written down two-and-a-half millennia ago. Four Brahmins (religious leaders and wise men) had been childhood friends and decided to go off and seek their fortune. Three of them had great depth of scholarship but no common sense; one had less scholarship but lots of common sense. As they walked through a forest they came across the bones of a dead animal, and the first said, "I can assemble the bones correctly." And he did. The second said, "I can supply flesh, blood and hide." And he did. The third said, "I can bring it to life." But the fourth, the man of only common sense, said, "This is a lion; if you bring it to life, won't it kill us all?" And the third replied, "You simpleton; it is not I who will reduce scholarship to a nullity," which was a fancy way of saying "we know how to do it, so we're going to do it." And the fourth said, "Please wait while I climb this convenient tree." And so the third brought the lion to life and it killed the men of scholarship but no sense, and when the lion had gone away the man of less scholarship but more sense climbed down and walked on into town. What a valuable moral even for our times, except in these days of virtually unsupervised gene splicing there are no trees high enough to climb . . . .

Back behind the *Panchatantra*, around 600 BC, came the life and preaching of Gautama Siddhartha, the original *Bud-dha* ("enlightened one") with his "middle way" and "eightfold path." He left no writings, but the boys in his seminar did. Buddha preached, and this early Buddhist writing was done, in the context of and with reference to much older levels of Hindu literature. Scholars gradually uncovered the *Upanishads* that elaborated on the earlier *Sutras*; then the *Sutras* themselves, condensed manuals of religion; then the ancient *Bramanas* that underlay the *Sutras*; and finally the incredibly ancient *Vedas*. Oldest of them all was the *Rigveda*, a collection of some thousand hymns to the Hindu gods. It may have been composed not long after 2000 BC, before Sanskrit was even written down, and then passed down by memory.

Most of this literature is sacred scripture to Hindus, but European scholars applied secular scholarship to it. Western scholars just beginning to absorb Sanskrit literature were faced with a most interesting puzzle. A good many Sanskrit words looked like European words for the same things. The English *father*, the older Germanic *fadar*, and the Latin *pater*, for example, had their Sanskrit parallel *pitár*.[16] The English *two, three, is* (as in "he is"), and *serpent*, were in Latin *duo, tres, est*, and *serpens*, and in Sanskrit *dva, trayas, asti*, and *sarpa*—and there were hundreds more such parallels. Europeans had already learned to think about a European family of languages, because of the obvious kinship of such basic words as *mother* in English, *mater* in the Latin, *Mutter* in the German, *mat'*, or *matere* in one case ending in the Russian, *madre* in the Spanish, and so on. This scholarly breakthrough happened mainly in Calcutta (today's Kolkata), key city of early British control of India.[GE³⁸] The person most responsible for it was the brilliant British linguist William "Oriental" Jones, who had been sent out to India as a judge in 1783. In a 1786 work he argued that Sanskrit, Latin, and Greek all had the same roots. By 1813, a generation later, so many word parallels between Sanskrit and virtually all European languages had been found that scholars coined the word "Indo-European," meaning European languages plus Sanskrit languages. It remains the name of the language family to which English belongs even today.

The invention of philology

European scholars were fascinated by these long-lost linguistic cousins, but archaeology was still in its infancy and all they had to go on were the 1,027 hymns of the *Rigveda* itself. So they dissected every word, trying to learn about this ancient people. The language turned out to be rich in specialized words for livestock, but there were no "city" words, for books, libraries, two-story buildings, and such. Conclusion? These must have been nomads following the herds.

Linguistic similarities with ancient European languages were just the beginning. The more they dug, the more they found cultural similarities. The old Sanskrit word for wine brewed from honey was *madhu*; honey

---

38. GE layer 38 is a Placemark referencing Calcutta's (Kolkata's) famous Indian Museum (which was not created until 1814, but which grew out of enthusiasm for things India that "Oriental" Jones helped create). The cluster of Photos icons beneath the blue Pushpin Placemark icon have photographs of the museum, mainly of the interior courtyard.

wine was known all over old Europe by similar sounding words, including Beowulf's *mead*. These early Sanskrit-speaking people raced chariots around two marks, in a religion and/or sport looking suspiciously like the chief game of the Roman circus and the last and most popular contest of the Olympic Games of the classical Greeks. The most startling similarity of all was mention in the *Rigveda* of the Sanskrit people's early god of thunder and lightning, whose name was *Dyaus-pitar* or Sky Father. That had to be the Greek Zeus (*Zeus* or *Dios Pater*, Father Zeus) and the Latin Jupiter (from *Jus-Pater* or *Jov-Pater*, Father Jove): same name, same wielder of thunder and lightning. A consensus grew among scholars—one that still holds today, in the main—that the early Sanskrit people were culturally and linguistically once a part of an original Proto-Indo-European-speaking unit somewhere in the Near East or Central Asia maybe 5–6,000 years ago when the climate was very different. When the original unit broke up, most tribes drifted west into Europe (most European peoples have a legend about coming from the East), a few south into Persia and Mesopotamia, and one that turned southeast and sometime between 2000 and 1500 BC invaded the civilized river valleys (the Indus and its tributaries) of Pakistan and northwest India.[GE39] The *Rigveda* was apparently composed during or just after that conquest. Since the winners most often get to write the histories, these barbarian victors called themselves *Arya*, or noble ones, and evidently set up some social barriers between themselves and the dark-skinned civilized peoples they subjected. Watch for a variation on that word, *Aryan*, to reappear later in this chapter, used with all the arrogance of the original.

Here, now, after several pages of what must have looked like a major digression, is the link with the Brothers Grimm. This discovery of Sanskrit by the western world and the linguistic analysis of the *Rigveda* brought about the new science of philology. It literally means "love of words," but it might be more practically defined as comparative linguistics in the service of history. Jacob Grimm was one of the first and most remarkable of the philologists. He studied Sanskrit for access to the *Rigveda* and Old Norse for access to the *Eddas*; he knew Greek, Russian and French, Old High German, New Frisian and Old, Old Saxon, Danish and Swedish, and dozens more. It was claimed that he had a working knowledge of seventy—70!—languages and dialects. He became such a great linguist that he worked out a still-celebrated theory, "Grimm's Consonant Shift," for an overall pattern in the Indo-European world. Many consonants and consonant combinations come in pairs, one aspirated (which is a fancy way of saying done with a puff of air) and the second "unaspirated" (in which the mouth and tongue are in exactly the same position but there's no puff of air): t and d; k and g; ch and j; p and b. Try out these pairs for yourself, using "uh" for a vowel to follow each. Don't you find that the tongue and lips are in the same place, but the first has a little explosion of air and the second just sort of dies there? Jacob Grimm plotted Indo-European languages on a grid, from the British Isles in the northwest to India in the southeast, and showed that aspirated consonants in the northwest tend to evolve into unaspirated consonants (such as d, g, j, b) in the southeast. For example, the English word *two* with its clearly aspirated "t", for example, is softened a bit in the Dutch to *twee* (pronounced like *tvee*), and softened even more in German to *zwei* with its "ts" sound, and loses its aspiration completely farther to the east and south in Latin, Russian, and Sanskrit's *duo*, *dve*, and *dva*. By plotting early Indo-European languages on a grid, and working out patterns of vowel mutation, conjugation, and inflection, he was not only able to reconstruct a language no one had spoken for a thousand years (Gothic, easternmost of the early German languages), but he was able to write a plausible dictionary and grammar of the original Indo-European language itself. Jacob Grimm's scholarship in this new field of philology was truly impressive, and he took that new tool back to the study of the Germanic past, hoping to discover that supposed original Germanic folk culture from the "form-giving" time.

Jacob Grimm's *Teutonic Mythology*

His talents are best seen in the massive four-volume *Deutsche Mythologie* (1835), which has been translated into English as *Teutonic Mythology*[17] (though it probably ought to be translated *German Mythology* or at least *Germanic Mythology*). He states in the introduction that his object is "to set forth all that can now be known

---

39. GE Layer 39 is a Folder titled "Indus Valley civilization." Placemarks in it reference these two most famous city ruins, Mohenjo-daro and Harappa, both in today's Pakistan.

of German heathenism," by which he means pre-Christian Germanic culture, long buried by time and an over-lay of Mediterranean culture. Then he goes on to cover a brilliant array of topics.

In an early chapter on worship, for example, Jacob Grimm wanted to show that the horse had been the most important sacrificial animal. He quoted a scattering of ancient and medieval writers including Tacitus, but when he ran out of written sources he continued the demonstration with unwritten sources. He analyzed words in Germanic languages whose root is "horse." He cited legends and folktales, among them "The Goose Girl" folk-tale he had collected about a disembodied horse's head that solved a distraught girl's problem: what could this be, he asked, but a late folk memory of the sacrifice where the horse's body was eaten and the head hung up in a sacred grove of trees? He went into popular culture, into the aversion to horseflesh among many people of Germanic descent. Ever wonder why we in our culture generally don't eat horsemeat? It has roughly the same food value as beef. And is it any greater crime to kill a horse than a little brown-eyed calf for veal? Since the horse stood as the prime animal of pre-Christian sacrifice, Jacob argued, its use was especially offensive to new Christian converts, and our aversion to horseflesh today is a legacy of those times. This is his pattern, drawing proofs from ancient, medieval, and modern levels of the supposed cultural breakdown.

There are full chapters on the aspects and attributes of each of the major deities. There are chapters on what ancient Germans thought about giants, the creation, trees and animals, souls and death, magic, herbs, and how their attitudes survived in bits and pieces down to the present.

A couple of two-page arguments of his might be particularly interesting for native English speakers. One is on the English names for days of the week, which are not exactly like any other set of such names in other European languages. Second is the unique word for Easter in English.

Take the English names for the days of the week, with "day" tacked on to Sun-, Mon-, Tues-, Wednes-, Thurs-, Fri- and Satur-. Jacob Grimm squeezes lots of history out of these everyday—no pun intended—names. As background, you need to know that the Angles, Saxons and Jutes (from today's northern Germany and southern Scandinavia) successfully invaded Roman Britain from AD 449–520, and that already by the end of that time the English weekday names were set. You also need to know that the Romans had the original seven-day week in Europe—they had it from the Egyptians—with every day named after a god and/or heavenly body. If you can see parallels between the English and Roman days, it is surely evidence of Roman cultural impact on the Germans as of AD 500 or so. And there are striking parallels. Our Sunday was the Roman day of the Sun; our Saturday was the Roman day of Saturn. The middle five Roman days are still there in most Romance languages such as French, Spanish, and Italian: Monday is *lundi* or *lunes* or *lunedi*, obviously based on the Roman *Luna* or moon, so "moon-day" (which if you say really fast for 1500 years becomes Monday). Tuesday is *mardi* or *martes* or *martedi*, obviously the Day of Mars, god of war. Wednesday is *mercredi* or *mier-coles* or *mercoledi*, for Mercury, the messenger god. Thursday is *jeudi* or *jueves* or *giovedi*, Jove or Jupiter's day. Friday is *vendredi* or *viernes* or *veneredi*, obviously for Venus, goddess of love, beauty, and fertility. To crack the code of the English names for Tuesday through Friday, it's probably easiest to start with Thursday: it's from Thor's day, god of thunder and lightning—and in a parallel list of English and Roman weekdays there he sits, just opposite of Jupiter, god of thunder and lightning. Friday is next easiest: it's Freya's day, and there she sits, just opposite Venus, another goddess of love, beauty, and fertility. Tuesday is a little harder, but it's named for the war god Tyr, or Tieu, or Zio, depending on your dialect of German—and there he sits, right across from Mars.

That leaves Wednesday, with its crazy spelling, which the Grimms can now explain for you. The Germans were so profoundly impacted by Roman culture that they were trying to copy the Roman calendar, with its seven days, and its gods in order. But they couldn't leave out their chief god, and anyway Odin as far-traveller had a certain superficial resemblance to Mercury, Roman messenger god. Remember Tacitus' comment that the Germans worshipped Mercury? Well, not quite, but this was as close as Romans and Germans could get to describing each other's gods. The Angles and Saxons usually put a G or a W before the opening vowel of the god's name, as in Guoden or Woden, and so Wednesday is Wodan's, or Odin's, day. So despite that enormous cultural impact of the Mediterranean world, by AD 500 or so the Germans were still not Christian: four days of the week retained the names of Germanic deities.

Another interesting puzzle that is solved in a couple of pages in *Teutonic Mythology* is the English word *Easter*, when most other European names for the great Christian holy day were based on Passover. The Grimms traced the name back to *Eastre*, a minor Anglo-Saxon goddess whose rites were celebrated in spring, and back beyond that to *Ostara* in Germany; old people in the Grimms' day still called April Ostara-month. In the context of the slow Christianization of Anglo-Saxon England—cities first, towns later, the countryside much later—they saw a pre-existing pagan holiday get intertwined with an imported Christian festival. Did you ever wonder why Easter bunnies bring Easter eggs? Rabbits don't lay eggs, do they? The egg is a great fertility symbol, dry and hard, but just waiting to burst into a new life. And rabbits—need I say more? On the premier Christian celebration you have one old Germanic fertility symbol hopping down the bunny trail bringing a basket of others.

One of the richest chapters in *Teutonic Mythology* is called "Wights and Elves." In the minds of ancient Germans, these were a kind of separate race with a kingdom of their own, only induced by accident or stress to have dealings with people. In some way they are related to the gods, and have power to hurt or help humankind; in other ways they are awed by human strength and a little shy around people. Grimm found them tucked away not only in folk wisdom, but in the language. The Old High German "alp," plural "elbe," and the Anglo-Saxon "oelf," or "aelf," appear on many old maps. Alfred king of England was literally Red Elf; the Elbe in Germany the river of elves. Family names such as Elbenstein or Elphinstone show that they were thought to live in mounds or under stones. Medieval sagas describe ritual sacrifice to these elf stones. The race had a king, in German lands literally Elf-king, "Albericht." Grimm traces the evolution of the name as it gradually drifted west, from Alberon to Auberon to Oberon, Shakespeare's king of the fairies.

There were bright elves, near to the gods, and dim elves, and finally dark elves, or dwarfs. The dim elves were the home sprites, living in the barn and helping tame animals, or behind the stove and coming out to help with housework at night. On occasion they required a person's help, to assist she-dwarfs in labor, to help divide a treasure they quarreled over, or to borrow a hall for a wedding. Every favor was richly repaid. One of the only really bad things they did was to steal human children to take home and help continue their fading culture. They would substitute one of their own adults as an ill-formed "changeling" for the human child. Germanic peoples as a result had all kinds of formulas for guarding against changelings. In Hesse, the family was to cook a meal for a good many people in a single eggshell; the changeling was then supposed to sit up and exclaim, "Well, I am as old as the Westerwald, but I never saw anything boiled in eggshells." And having given himself away, of course he had to leave and bring back the real baby. Toward the end of the chapter, Grimm talked about people's conception of dwarfs and elves becoming less and less charitable over time. They were believed in pre-Christian days as half-gods, then they became familiar and benign household spirits, but century by century they grew smaller and had less to do with humankind. In some folktales the dwarfs themselves discuss the faithlessness of humans, about how they have ceased believing and have thus caused elves and dwarfs to dwindle in size.

A German reader of this sensitive and scholarly chapter would have certainly been convinced that the elves and sprites of German popular culture were descended from the high elves of the Icelandic *Eddas* and Norse mythology. Even a modern scholar, who knows so much more about diffusion of cultures all over the world than the Grimms did, and who has learned to think about Jung's "spontaneous origin of archetypes" (the human mind is so much alike all over the world that it sometimes independently comes up with some of the same characterizations and legends), cannot help but be impressed. This chapter, like the whole life's work of the Grimms, demonstrated to its contemporary readers the antiquity and vibrant imagination of Germanic culture.

And so the Grimms—while still appreciating the depth of other cultures—found dignified "roots" for German culture, their own. This gives a reader some idea of the impact *Grimms' Fairy Tales* had when it was published in Germany in 1812, during Napoleon's retreat across the continent from Russia. It was a statement of national pride, perhaps not so much for children as it was for citizens and scholars and statesmen. The elements of the German past rescued by (and frankly partly invented by) the brothers Grimm would be used in literature, music, painting, and politics in the next few generations as the main force in the transformation of German lands into the nation-state Germany.

Wagner's opera

A case in point is Richard Wagner (1813–1883). His major claim to fame is a series of operas he wrote between 1844 and 1874, all based on German legends or history (or as with the case of *Tristan* a Celtic legend retold by a thirteenth-century German poet): *Tannhäuser, Lohengrin, Tristan and Isolde, The Mastersinger of Nuremberg*, and the tetralogy called *The Ring of the Nibelungs*. These fascinate musicians because they mark a whole new phase in opera. Wagner's ambitions for opera were so great that once he became famous, he eventually had built a huge new setting at Bayreuth[GE⁴⁰] in Bavaria to stage them, especially the *Ring* cycle. His famous approach was in telling the story with recurring musical motifs as well as a beautiful poetry. In the *Ring* cycle, for example, Nature is a major chord rolled up and up, and the Rhine River is a variation on that; Siegfried has his own unique horn call, and when you hear it, he is about to come bounding on the stage, or he is dead and somebody is thinking about him. Wagner's genius at weaving these individual motifs together into harmonies make him not just an object of interest but almost a cult item in some circles in every generation. These same works tend to interest historians as one of the clearest links between *Grimms' Fairy Tales* and the concentration camps of Nazi Germany.

Wagner was born into a family of actors and actresses. He was born in May of 1813 at Leipzig, interestingly enough, where five months later the great battle that really destroyed Napoleon was fought (of which you saw the memorial earlier). Do you believe in birthmarking—a pregnant woman, frightened by a bat, gives birth to a baby with a bat-shaped birthmark, or some such? Maybe Wagner was "birthmarked" to be a German nationalist. He was educated in German universities at the height of the Romantic period. The supernatural was much in vogue, and when he was twenty he wrote his first opera on such a subject, *The Fairies*. His career after school was something less than an immediate success, more of a bitter and turbulent time of apprenticeship. He held short tenure as *capellmeister* (literally "chapel-master," but what it implied was the musical leader of choir and symphony and opera) at some rather obscure places in France and the Germanies, although he did manage to spend some time in Paris and was *capellmeister* in the important city of Dresden,[GE⁴¹] capital of Saxony, when the revolution of 1848 broke out. His frustration with the theater and society in general was intense, and in his own mind he began to connect the two. When his most cherished works got a lukewarm reception, he began to think his "music of the future" could only be recognized after society was shaken up by some sort of upheaval. That is part of the reason Wagner became a revolutionary in 1848.

But even more importantly he had encountered the idea of a German national theater, and this was fast becoming the goal of his work. In his time of loneliness, he buried himself in the past, in the newly popular antiquities of Germany and Scandinavia. It should come as no surprise that his chief inspiration was the work of Jacob Grimm. In Wagner's autobiography, roughly chronological as are most autobiographies, he prefaces his account of almost every new opera he was working on by talking about how he researched it in the Grimms' works. In fact, a systematic study of Jacob Grimm's *Teutonic Mythology* seems to have been the genesis of all his mature operas. In 1843, he says, he was taking the water cure at the Töplitz spa (today's Teplice)[GE⁴²] in company with his wife, his mother, and a sister. Nearly forty years later he still vividly remembered his encounter there with Jacob Grimm's major book:

> . . . it had been noticed that I was always carrying around a rather thick book, with which I sat down to rest together with my mineral water in hidden places. This was Jacob Grimm's *Deutsche Mythologie*. . . . I was firmly in the power of its strange enchantment: even the most fragmentary legends spoke to me in a profoundly familiar tongue, and soon my entire sensibility was possessed by images suggesting ever more clearly the recapture of a long lost yet eagerly sought consciousness. There rose up in my soul a whole world of figures, which yet proved to be so unexpectedly solid and well-known from earliest days, that when I saw them clearly before me and could hear their speech I could not grasp the source of the virtually tangible familiarity

40. GE Layer 40 is a Placemark referencing Wagner's home for his last years, courtesy of the admiring young King of Bavaria. Most of the Photos icons under the Pushpin Placemark icon contain pictures of Wagner's house "Wahnfried," literally "Delusion-Free." The Bayreuth opera house is just a quarter-mile northwest.

41. GE Layer 41 is a Placemark referencing the celebrated Dresden opera house, virtually new when Wagner conducted there. Choose any of the nearby Photos icons with "oper" as part of a word for a view.

42. GE Layer 42 is a Placemark referencing a cluster of Photos icons with photographs of classic European spas in Teplice, high architecture and all. Located in today's Czech Republic, but in Wagner's day still part of the Austrian Empire just across the Ore Mountains from Dresden and Saxony.

and certitude of their demeanor. The effect they produced upon my innermost being I can only describe as a complete rebirth, and just as we feel a tender joy at a child's first sudden flash of recognition, so now my own eyes now flashed with rapture at a world I saw revealed for the first time, as if by miracle, in which I had previously moved blindly though presentient, like a child in its mother's womb.[18]

Soul, rebirth, joy, rapture, revelation, miracle: Wagner had to go to the language of religious conversion to describe his experience. This cult of the German *Volk* was part of his personal revolution in 1848–1849. Only when the Folk, the German-speaking people, were free to express their character, out from under the privileged classes and bureaucracy, could a true German culture and society be born. He made radical proposals for a "folk-arming," and was actively involved in the revolution in Saxony.

It was during the 1848–1849 revolt that Wagner conceived of and began work on his masterpiece, the monumental *Ring of the Nibelungs*. It was only finished in 1874 and staged in 1876, towards the end of his life. Four operas it is, in one: *The Rhinegold, The Valkyrie, Siegfried,* and *Twilight of the Gods.* It combines the medieval Siegfried legend and the frame story of Old Norse mythology. From the building of Asgard to the Doom of the Gods, a simple promise evaded by Odin leads to ever greater problems. Odin's attempt to create a hero who would not be bound by law and morality is a strong ends-versus-means thread tying the whole story together, and there are two great love stories here, too, for the price of one. And carrying it all is an emotional cascade of music that listeners seem either to like very much or not at all.

There was a darker side to Wagner's philosophy, too, explicitly anti-Semitic and perhaps implicitly anti-Christian. He clothed his visceral hatred of Jews in the newest scientific language, since even racism was becoming "scientific" or at least pseudo-scientific in these days. Between 1853 and 1855 the Comte de Gobineau, an aristocratic French writer, wrote what may still be the Bible of modern racism, "Essay on the Inequality of the Races." Only the white race could produce civilization, he argued, and the "Nordic" strain was the purest and best of all descendants of Aryan culture. In 1859 the Swiss historian Pictet wrote a two-volume world history that identified all the great achievements of humankind as Aryan in origin. Thus Aryan became a code word for the supposed "purest" Indo-European descendants. Darwin's *On The Origin of Species* was also published in 1859. He was no racist himself, but his work became the starting point for the Social Darwinists. They proceeded to identify ethnic groups as sub-species well on their way to becoming separate species, and felt that those that were stronger were morally entitled to dominate the weaker: it was "survival of the fittest," and the writers just happened to be members of the currently technologically superior European cultures.

Wagner was a true believer in this new religion of race. He was friends with Gobineau. He claimed not to create his music at all, but that he was just artistically sensitive enough to feel it humming inside his German bloodstream and write it down. Jews, for Wagner, were of a lesser and alien bloodstream, with a secret plot to raise themselves up by leeching onto the superior race of Germans. No wonder the music of Richard Wagner was outlawed for the first fifty years inside of the modern state of Israel (1948–1998): after you read Wagner on what should be done with Jews, Hitler's "final solution" comes as no big surprise.

It is time now to go back to politics, having gotten a glimpse of the strongest emotional current running below its surface. It is a bit like steam, which before it begins to condense is invisible, but which provides the power to turn the heavy metal machinery of a motor and whatever the motor is hooked up to. Cultural nationalism is the invisible power that makes much of the heavy machinery of German politics move. Watch carefully for it from the early nineteenth century on, and you'll see wisps of it condense around the edges of wars and key political developments!

The Congress of Vienna

The Congress of Vienna, which met in the Imperial Palace or Hofburg[GE[43]] from September 1814 to June 1815, ended the Napoleonic era in Europe. Dominated by conservatives of the old school led by the Austrian

---

43. GE Layer 43 is a Placemark referencing the magnificent, labyrinthine Hofburg, and its dozens of associated Photos icons to explore.

minister Klemens von Metternich, the Congress turned the clock back as far as it dared. The monarchies of France and Spain were restored and the émigré nobles came flocking back to their courts for old positions of power. Some things, though, had changed beyond recall. The title of the newly-crowned Louis XVIII was now "King of the French," not the grander and more absolute "King of France." Napoleon's simplification of the German map, too, from several hundred political units to less than forty, was kept. Most of those had jumped on the anti-Napoleon bandwagon in 1814, and as winners of the war were able to keep their enlarged states intact.

Under the surface of the so-called "Restoration" at the Congress, moreover, some heavy wheeling and dealing went on. Prussia, the large northeastern German state, lost most of the Polish territory it claimed and in exchange was given the Rhineland, the westernmost slice of the Germanies.[GE44] This territory on the French border was awarded to Prussia in part to make sure Prussia had a stake in resisting if France ever became expansionist again. Prussia thereafter manifested a certain schizophrenia between its conservative agricultural east and its liberal industrial and commercial west. And unseen by any then, the Prussian west would by late nineteenth century become the heart of coal and iron production for the entire continent.

Napoleon had stripped Austria's Hapsburg monarchs of the title "Holy Roman Emperor" in 1806, after his smashing victories over the big German powers—*he* was now Emperor, and he did not want another one so close—and had taken some Austrian territory away. But the Kingdom of Austria as it was now known did well territorially out of the 1814–1815 negotiations.[GE45] In terms of modern states, it included all or virtually all six of today's independent countries: Austria, Czech Republic, Slovakia, Hungary, Croatia, and Slovenia. In addition in the west it had two of northern Italy's three major regions, Lombardy and Venetia. In the east, impressively, was a huge arc of territory made up of today's southern Poland, western Ukraine, the Transylvanian part of Romania (almost half the modern country), and the northern part of Serbia.

Austria's Metternich, whose shrewd plans dominated the Congress, had two general strategies in mind. First, he wanted Austria to gain control of all the Italian states and all the German states, and so become the superstate of Europe. It would reach from the Baltic to the Mediterranean, cutting Europe in two, and have Europe's largest population, at least seventy million people. To this end, he set up a series of institutions, especially the German Confederation (*Deutscher Bund*).[GE46] Made up of all 39 German states left at the end of the Napoleonic era, this make-believe state had its capital in the old free city of Frankfurt am Main. It was a bit like the old Holy Roman Empire: Austria held the presidency of the Confederation, and the borders were fairly similar. But this enterprise seems to have been designed to let Austria gradually swallow up the small German states. And Metternich almost pulled off the same thing in the Italies with his proposed "Lega Italica."

Metternich's second great ambition was to keep Liberal and national revolution from breaking out anywhere else. To this end he established the Congress System: anywhere revolution threatened, the five Great Powers (Russia, Austria, Prussia, France, and England) were to meet together in a new congress and delegate a force to put it down. It is one measure of Metternich's fear of revolution that France—just defeated in the war—was so quickly admitted back into great power politics!

As it happened, Metternich soon realized that his first and second ideas were contradictory. Creating a super Austria would mean a rather ruthless disregard of neighboring states and undoubtedly war with some of them. Keeping revolution down with a functioning Congress system, on the other hand, required good relations with these same neighboring great powers. Metternich eventually gave up on his first idea and concentrated on

---

44. GE Layer 44 is a Polygon titled "Prussia 1815," showing its new dimensions in red. In reversal of usual pattern, first double-click on icon symbol to frame view, then turn layer on.

45. GE Layer 45 is a Polygon titled "Austria 1815," showing its entire territory in black. With the "Borders and Labels" layer turned on at bottom left, you can sort out how many modern European states are either wholly or partially inside that 1815 Austria.

46. GE Layer 46 is a Folder titled "German Confederation 1815—mid-sized German states and outline." Don't turn the whole folder on, but open it and then turn on one layer at a time. The first layer in the folder is a Placemark with a white star icon for the supposed "capital" of this fake state, Frankfurt am Main. The first Polygon is a white outline of the whole *Deutscher Bund*. The following eight filled Polygons represent the eight largest of the total of 39 German states, not including the two giants Prussia and Austria, symbolized in the two previous layers.

the second. The Congress System worked smoothly, at least until the Greek war of independence in the 1820s. Inside the German Confederation, Austria and Prussia cooperated in "peaceful dualism," agreeing on policy and then enforcing that on the small German states.

The Age of Metternich, 1815 to 1848

Even though the conservative forces were temporarily dominant, the newer forces of the Reform Era in Germany refused to die. After 1815 the mainstream of this reform movement began to emerge as the Liberal-National movement. It did not crystallize as a political party until mid-century, but was already there in embryo by 1815. "Liberal" in these days means Classical Liberalism (written with a capital "L" hereafter, and in fact herebefore in this chapter), a very different use of the word than today's "liberal." First, it meant laissez-faire economics, free trade—more of a conservative plank in today's political platforms. Second, it included expanding the voting public to include all men of property and/or education, but not yet women and not the un-propertied or un-educated (the masses of farmers, and later of industrial workers). Thirdly, it meant U.S.A-style freedom of speech and assembly, the right to face your accusers before a jury of your peers, and written guarantees of that nature in a constitution. The "National" part is easier to define—a wish for a united state for all or at least most native speakers of German, or Italian, or Hungarian . . . . In these times, these two ideologies were linked: if you believed in one, you most likely believed in the other. Publicly supporting either one could get you jailed as a revolutionary in most any German state, in fact in any European state except perhaps Britain (and they jailed the Irish nationalists, come to think of it), from 1815 to 1848.

The newer business community and the professional classes (doctors, lawyers, university teachers and such) and their college-age children made up the bulk of these National-Liberals. Beginning in 1815 a good many university students joined a *Burschenschaft*. This translates literally a Youth League, but it really meant a nationalist student organization, a secret patriotic society for students; our old friend "Father" Jahn of the gymnastics league set up the first one in Jena. In October of 1817 there was a great rally of Burschenshaften at Wartburg castle. The occasion was the fourth anniversary of the Battle of Leipzig, and the three hundredth anniversary of Luther's posting of the 95 Theses, soon after which, with a price on his head, he hid in disguise at Wartburg castle where he wrote and translated.[GE47] The rally attracted considerable attention by building a bonfire out of conservative books and symbols. In 1819, when a deranged student inspired by these groups assassinated a conservative poet, Metternich counterattacked. Under his leadership the German Confederation passed the Karlsbad Decrees,[GE48] outlawing the Youth Leagues as well as Father Jahn's super-nationalistic gymnastic societies, and restricting civil liberties generally. The decrees were copied in virtually every continental European state.

So National-Liberal forces were suppressed, but they simply oozed out into less politically sensitive areas. By the early 1820s the first Germany-wide professional conventions of historians, economists, and other professionals began to meet. Many attendees had never been out of their home states before, and it gave them a new sense of Germany as a whole. As early as 1819 there was a drive to create an all-German economic union, abolishing customs duties between German states in what we'd call today a Free Trade Association. Its supporters couched their arguments in terms of improvement of local economies, but everyone knew that if true economic unity came about, political unity would not be far behind. The key name in this regard is Friedrich List.

List's economic nationalism

Friedrich List (1789–1846) was a professor from Württemberg who worked towards a U.S.-style government in a united Germany. In 1819 this south German was one of the founders of the North German Customs

47. GE Layer 47 is a Placemark referencing Wartburg Castle, overlooking the Thuringian city of Eisenach. Lots of Photos icons to peruse, if interested, plus nice collection of views at following website: http://www.sacred-destinations.com/germany/wartburg-castle

48. GE Layer 48 is a Placemark referencing Karlsbad, today's Karlovy Vary in the Czech Republic.

Union—the *Zollverein*, literally "toll union"—that would finally be complete in 1834. In the early 1820s his Liberal-Nationalism and incendiary speeches got him fired and in fact sentenced to jail. He fled to the United States and lived here for eight years, until President Andrew Jackson appointed him U.S. Consul at Leipzig. [GE[49]] There, under the protection of American diplomatic immunity, he created an excellent plan for a pan-German railroad system, and in general continued his advocacy of the Customs Union and the political unification to which he hoped it would lead.

In 1841 he published his most famous work, *The National System of Political Economy*. It was an attack on Adam Smith's pure free trade theory. Free trade inside a nation was indeed good, said List, but internationally it was not necessarily so. A young state with vulnerable industries needed to protect those industries with high tariffs, that is, taxes on manufactured goods coming in from outside. In the first volume List carefully set out the reasons for the economic power of every major western state or coalition of states from the Renaissance on in an attempt to prove that. The most important aspect of the book in the context of this chapter, however, is that a fiery nationalism permeates the whole argument. List chastised Adam Smith for his complete absence of consideration of national issues: List probably stressed "National" when he pronounced the title of his new book! The emotional heart of his book is a chapter called "Nationality and the Economy of the Nation." Here are key excerpts:

> Between each individual and entire humanity, however, stands THE NATION, with its special language and literature, with its peculiar origin and history, with its special manners and customs, laws and institutions, with the claims of all these for existence, independence, perfection, and continuance for the future, and with its separate territory; a society which, united by a thousand ties of mind and of interests, combines itself into one independent whole, which recognizes the law of right for and within itself . . . .[19]

Here in one sentence is Herder on everything from the "form-giving time" of a nation to the possibility of its ultimate perfection; here are the Bros. Grimm on national law, language, and literature; here is Fichte on the nation as a law unto itself. List continued, saying that a large population in a large territory was not enough. The nation must be complete—all German speakers united—and must achieve defensible seas or mountains for borders. In past times, he said, territorial deficiencies of states were remedied by hereditary succession the way England got Scotland, or by purchase the way the U.S. got Florida and Louisiana, or by conquest the way Great Britain got Ireland. In modern times, though, there is an important fourth option—free convention of states like his Zollverein. Then comes an amazing paragraph:

> By its Zollverein the German nation first obtained one of the most important attributes of its nationality. But this measure cannot be considered complete so long as it does not extend over the whole coast, from the mouth of the Rhine to the frontier of Poland, including Holland and Denmark. A natural consequence of this union must be the admission of both these countries into the German Confederation, and consequently into the German nationality, whereby the latter will at once obtain what it is now in need of, namely, fisheries and naval power, maritime commerce and colonies. Besides, both these nations belong, as respects their descent and whole character, to the German nationality.

The Danes, the Dutch and even the Swiss are to be induced or coerced to join a super German nation. A higher good and a higher destiny demands it, said Friedrich List, and a NATIONAL system of political economy will help it come about.

Growing unrest

In 1830 another revolution, the July Revolution, shook France and reverberated for a couple of years (Victor Hugo's famous 1500-page novel *Les Misérables*, written in 1862, is mainly set in the Paris of 1832, though with flashbacks to 1815 and looks ahead to the 1848 barricades). The tremors of this new French revolution

---

49. GE Layer 49 is a Placemark referencing Leipzig, an important city in Saxony (where earlier you saw the memorial to the great victory over Napoleon in 1813).

reached neighboring states as well. National-Liberal sentiments in the German states surfaced anew. In the Grimms' home state of Hesse-Kassel, an angry crowd ousted their capricious and arrogant ruler, and a professor from the Grimms' alma mater the University of Marburg wrote a Liberal new constitution for the country. Hanover and Saxony, which except for Prussia were the two biggest north German states, got new constitutions as well. Perhaps the most dramatic happenings were the meeting of nationalists and admirers of the U.S. political system at Hambach castle in 1832,[GE[50]] and a student-led attempt to capture Frankfurt and create a united and Liberal German state. Metternich again let public emotions die down a bit, and then (as he had back in 1819 with the Karlsbad Decrees) led the conservative counterattack on these upstart National-Liberals. His lead was followed by every major European state except England; all across the continent it was truly the Age of Metternich. A lid was firmly clamped down on political change, and yet huge new economic and technological changes were forcing changes in society. Continental Europe was a pressure cooker with no safety valve.

The progression of the original English industrial revolution was generally repeated in the German states, but everything was telescoped, happening faster in time. Huge numbers of farmers either emigrated (mostly to North America) or left an impoverished countryside for the cities. Railroads began to call into being great coal and iron works. Steam power was harnessed to textile plants. An upper-middle class of industrialists and financiers grew up, and at the same time traditional artisans were wiped out. The revolt of the Silesian weavers in 1845 was a classic reaction of handicrafters to methods of mass production: they tried to break up the new power looms that were taking away their jobs.

The new business classes and their allies in the professions thought the German governments did too little to aid new industry. The handicrafters and poor farmers who were being driven into the urban slums or into emigration thought governments were doing too much. Either way, the governments lost public support. Sensitive observers began to predict social upheaval. When a business crash in the mid-1840s coincided with the failure of the potato crop (most famous in Ireland, of course, but felt all across northern Europe), it triggered the revolutions of 1848.

The Revolutions of 1848

The 1848 revolutions started in France, in a Liberal rally on George Washington's birthday, and quickly spread to most of the cities of Europe. By this time the French lead in revolutionary affairs was taken for granted: "When Paris sneezes, Europe catches cold," ran the quip. The revolts did not spread to England, which had allowed considerable political change, and they had little impact in Russia, where the divine right monarchy still ruled without much fear of Liberals. Everywhere in-between, though, 1848 was important, and nowhere more than in the Germanies.

The two greatest German cities, Berlin and Vienna, exploded simultaneously in mid-March when they got word of happenings in Paris. Crowds of students, workers, businessmen, and professional people took to the narrow streets and blocked them off with barricades made of carts, furniture and paving stones. This is one reason, by the way, that European cities were later rebuilt with such broad major boulevards; it was partly for beauty and grandeur but partly also for future crowd control.

The Prussian king since 1840, Frederick William IV, was initially under the mistaken impression that his people loved him, and he withdrew his army from Berlin rather than prolong bloodshed.[GE[51]] The revolutionaries—National-Liberals, mostly, but also some Democrats and even Socialists—held the city all through the summer and fall. They thought they had successfully overthrown the state, but the Prussian army was intact and merely waiting for the king's orders to put down the revolution. In October of 1848 the orders came and the revolution in Prussia quietly expired. All that was left was a very limited constitutional monarchy.

---

50. GE Layer 50 is a Placemark referencing Hambach Castle, just on the eastern edge of the Palatinate Forest. Under the Placemark pointer are several interesting Photos icons to peruse; the article in Wikipedia on Hambach castle includes a period painting of the student rally there in 1832. The student national-unity flags for Germany were horizontal stripes of gold, red, and black—not coincidentally the color of the German flag today, though reversed top to bottom.

51. GE Layer 51 is a Placemark referencing Elstal, where the Prussian army was withdrawn, framing its location to show both Berlin and Elstal, about 15 miles due west of Berlin.

For Austria 1848 was a much more traumatic matter. A National-Liberal crowd led by a medical student took over Vienna; in that respect it resembled Berlin. But although Prussia had one significant ethnic minority with which to deal in the Polish, Austria was a multi-national state, as you saw in earlier mapwork. Every one of those nationalities fought for their own independent states. Hungary actually formed one, along with a good little army. Some of the most dramatic events occurred in northern Italy. In Milan's "magnificent five days" the people of the city rose up and drove a good Austrian army back into the Alps.[GE52] The Austrian state survived only because of some military help from Russia, and because it found a new style of political leadership that was radical and conservative at the same time; but more on that later.

The lesser German states also had their revolutions. We have already seen Wagner plotting revolution backstage in Dresden, Saxony. One of the strangest happenings was when the normally conservative south German state of Bavaria replaced its monarchy with a socialist government. Overshadowing all the particular German events, however, was the great united German event of 1848–1849, the Frankfort National Assembly.[GE53]

The Frankfurt Assembly

Immediately after the March revolutions, National-Liberal elements in every German state worked toward creating a constituent assembly that could set up the framework of a new German state. They were thinking in terms of the Continental Congress in the U.S. or the Estates General in the French Revolution. The German name translates literally "pre-parliament," and Frankfurt am Main, the old capital of the Confederation near the geographic center of Germany, was the obvious meeting place. Elections were held, and delegates first met May 18. Early sessions were euphoric; a new United States of Germany seemed in the making. But debates developed between Liberals and the more radical Democrats and Socialists, and also between supporters of the *Kleindeutsch* (small German, no other ethnic groups in the new Germany) and the *Großdeutsch* (great German, including all the Austrian Empire's ethic groups) solutions. Historians and lawyers made long speeches while momentum slipped away and conservative forces reassembled. Lack of any military power of its own doomed the Frankfurt Assembly to rely on the very states it was trying to replace. In the spring of 1849, in a last-ditch effort to keep the dream alive, the Assembly offered the crown of a united Germany—on paper a fairly Liberal constitutional monarchy—to Frederick William IV of Prussia—by this time a bitter hater of Liberalism in all its forms. When he refused it ("I refuse to accept a crown offered to me from the gutter"), the Assembly broke up and all realistic hope for a Liberal united Germany died. This seems to have been the high-water mark of Liberal Nationalism. Now a new sort of Conservative Nationalism would have its turn.

Austria vs. Prussia

Austria took a full year longer to recover from the revolution than did Prussia. In that year, from the fall of 1848 to the fall of 1849, Prussia tried to absorb the small German states through a plan known as the Union of Princes. The Prussian government announced that the small German rulers could help create a united but conservative German state by simply giving their states to the Prussian ruling house. Not many of them were inclined to do so, of course, especially those states such as Bavaria with older ruling houses than the Hohenzollerns of Prussia. But the huge Prussian army was a thinly veiled threat, and one by one the small states began to give in. The Union of Princes had almost succeeded when Austria itself recovered from the revolution.

This Austrian government was a new and different kind. Metternich had lost his position just days into the revolution, and his place had been taken by hard-nosed ministers more than willing to use army and secret police violence against citizens. Led by Prince von Schwarzenberg, they aimed to revive Metternich's abandoned plan for the empire of seventy million, absorbing all the German states and all the Italian states. War

---

52. GE Layer 52 is a Folder titled "The Austrian 'Quadrilateral' 1848–1849"; it shows the four fortress cities in the mountains that were built to control northern Italy, into which the Austrian army was forced to retreat after being driven out of Milan and Venice.

53. GE Layer 53 is a Placemark referencing Frankfurt am Main.

with some of their neighbors to this end was completely acceptable to them, and what unification Prussia was doing needed to be undone so that Austria could do it better for itself.

This was the setting for the "Humiliation" of Olmütz, as later German history texts put it. Prussia was invited by Austria (along with Austria's close ally Russia) to meet at a small town in northern Austria (known today as Olomouc, near Brno in today's Czech Republic)[GE54] to work out their problems. Prussia knew that it had been caught poaching and thought that all Austria wanted to do was revive "peaceful dualism" in German affairs. It was in for a shock. Austria and Russia issued a flat ultimatum, in insulting language, that Prussia abandon the Union of Princes, fire its prime minister, and rejoin the German Confederation of which Austria was head. It also absolutely refused to recognize Prussia as an equal leader of the Confederation. Prussia had no choice but to obey, but its government still did not really understand what was happening. The Prussians appointed a new ambassador to the Confederation at Frankfurt with instructions to cooperate with Austria. Such cooperation would have quickly destroyed Prussia.

Otto von Bismarck

The Prussian ambassador chosen to go to Frankfurt was Otto von Bismarck (1815–1898). He was, as the *von* in his name indicates, a *Junker* (of the service nobility), from the agrarian eastern side of Prussia.[GE55] He spent his early years on rural estates, which he fondly remembered in later years. In 1822 the family moved to Berlin, partly for the schooling of the sons. As an adult he was a large, slow-moving man, but with a quick, reactive mind. He had been something of a rebel in the gymnasium, the elite military high school for nobles, so upon graduation he chose the most Liberal university in all the Germanies—Göttingen, in Hanover (where the Grimms were teaching, incidentally)—for college. Here he discovered just how intrinsically conservative he was. After trying both the army and the civil service—in neither of which did he fit, being easily bored and almost incapable of taking orders—from 1839 to 1847 he went back to the country to run the family estates.

By this time Bismarck had the well-earned reputation of a wild young bachelor baron, and did not seem satisfied with any career or lifestyle. But in short order he experienced some sort of religious awakening, married, and got into politics. In March 1848, hearing that revolutionaries were taking over the streets in Berlin, he actually armed his peasants to go help put it down. Too late for this, he then won election as one of the very few conservative voices—outrageously, provocatively conservative—in the revolutionary parliament in Berlin. Two years later, when the king's ministers were casting around for an ambassador to the German Confederation who was both conservative and pro-Austrian, Bismarck was remembered. He was the one sent to cooperate with Austria, and in the whole story of German affairs that may be the irony of the century.

In Frankfurt Bismarck got along badly with the pompous Austrian ambassador. More than that, he seems to have been the first Prussian to realize that Austria was out to destroy Prussia and absorb the German states. Against the repeated instructions of his government he worked feverishly against the Austrian plans—including one for Austrian military command of united German armies and one for Austrian entry into (and probably domination of) the Zollverein, that North German Customs Union currently dominated by Prussia, either of which would probably have resulted in the Austrian Empire simply swallowing up all the Germanies, including Prussia. He barely succeeded, but the only reason he was not fired was that Prussian government was grinding to a halt because of the king's progressive mental illness. When Frederick William IV was finally removed from the throne a few years later in 1858, Bismarck was quickly removed from the ambassadorship at Frankfurt and transferred to the ambassadorship at St. Petersburg where his only real functions were social. He had been kicked upstairs, and he knew it. Pushing forty-five years of age, his unremarkable career seemed to be winding down.

---

54. GE layer 54 is a Placemark referencing Olmütz, today's Olomouc in the Czech Republic. To see how it relates to Prussian and Austrian territories, go back and turn on layers 44 and 45.

55. GE Layer 55 is a Placemark referencing the primary von Bismarck family estate of Schönhausen.

Kaiser William I

The new king of Prussia was William III. As a younger brother of the old king, he had not been raised to be king but to serve as an army officer (European royal families had learned through the centuries that if you raised all your sons to be kings, they fought each other in civil wars). He knew the army well, but had few insights into and little talent for politics. The one thing he wanted most to do was reform the army. During the first year of his rule, in 1859, when France fought Austria (in the war that created the nucleus of modern Italy), the Prussian army had mobilized to threaten France. Although the Prussian army had not actually gone to war, the mobilization had been so disastrous that a war might have been disastrous too. On more than one occasion King William went to the Prussian legislature for new taxes to reform the army—for expanding the term of enlistment to three years, for training new officers, for totally re-outfitting the army in terms of modern weaponry and equipment. The Liberal-dominated legislature, hating the huge army as the symbol of everything backward in Prussia, voted the proposed reforms down every time, even when they were attached as a rider to the total state budget.

In 1862 one of the king's counselors suggested he try Bismarck in the role of chief minister. At wit's end, the king called him in for an interview. There it seems that Bismarck reminded the king that he differed with the government's policy toward Austria, and the king told Bismarck he could do what he pleased in foreign affairs if he just accomplished the king's army reform.

And so, said one historian, both King William and Germany got their master. In 1848 Bismarck had been just a witty and provocative defender of *Junker* class rights and the conservative state institutions in which they were set—especially the monarchy and the elite army officer corps. But he had by now had eight years residence in Frankfurt am Main, a great commercial city with delegations from every single German state and many non-German ones, and three years in the capital of Russia, where he had made friends with Emperor Alexander II and the Russian foreign minister. He now emerged on the diplomatic stage as Minister-President of the Prussian state, about to become the most successful of all politicians in the nineteenth century—and that may even include Napoleon. No politician ever surpassed Bismarck in the accuracy of his evaluations of public opinion both in his own country and other countries, or in his ability to manipulate confused situations to his advantage.

First, as Minister-President of the Prussian state, he had to solve the king's army reform problem. He approached the legislature apparently seriously looking for a compromise. The legislature distrusted the "mad Junker" about as much as it is possible to distrust, and no progress was made. Bismarck thereupon turned political scientist and invented "Gap Theory." There is a gap in the constitution, said he: no specific provision for a stalemate between king and legislature has been made; so in this crisis the government must govern without the legislature, collect taxes as it sees fit, reform the army . . . . If Bismarck had been disliked before, now he was the most hated man in Prussia. This Gap Theory was not just a lie, but a big lie; the very reason for a constitution was to give the people's elected representatives the right to vote or to deny new taxes on themselves. But Bismarck convinced the king that this was a moral stand, and if the legislators chose to call the people out into streets as in 1848, this time the Prussian army would be using live ammunition. The Liberal legislators generally fumed and made noisy speeches, but the army was reformed and Bismarck got a free hand in foreign affairs.

Bismarck's creation of the German Empire

Bismarck's first claim to fame in the history books is that in about nine years, including three short, sharp wars that he started in cold blood, he engineered the creation of the German Empire—at its birth probably the strongest state in the world.

In 1863 Russia took eight months to crush the latest Polish rebellion. Almost all of Europe's leaders condemned Russia's actions; Polish freedom-fighters were the heroes of the hour. Bismarck was the exception. He closed Prussian borders to Polish rebels, and even offered the Prussian army to aid Russia, should they need it. It only confirmed his reputation as the new Metternich, arch-enemy of Liberals and Nationalists. Although for Bismarck it was mainly about self-interest (*raison d'état* for Prussia—any Polish state would create problems for Prussia with its own huge indigenous Polish population), it won for him the warm feelings of a Russian government grateful for a friendly voice. Russian neutrality would be important for Bismarck in the coming years.

In 1864 the little state of Denmark absorbed Schleswig and Holstein, two north German territories that had long been the personal property of the Danish king. It was a terribly confusing issue, complicated by ancient "Salic Law" about which territories could be inherited through the female line and which could not. In general, the smaller German states wanted Schleswig and Holstein to be independent of Denmark, and to join the German Confederation as their allies. Bismarck, with his extemporaneous diplomatic genius, went fishing in these politically troubled waters. He offered an alliance to his hated enemy Austria, saying that they should both war on Denmark, and one could then take Schleswig and the other Holstein. Austria, which had been posing as defender of small German state liberties against Prussian aggression, swallowed the bait, and had to drop that pose.

The war itself was never in doubt, with two heavyweights matched against a middle-weight. There was a surprising political turn in that war, however. Bismarck seemed to be using the war to impress both the small German states and the Liberal-Nationals in Prussia, and although Austria and Prussia were winning the war, most of the headline victories had been Austrian. Bismarck approached the army high command about his political need for a Prussian headline victory. The impressive fortress of Düppel (*Dybbøl* in Danish), anchoring the eastern end of the Danish defense line,[GE56] had already been successfully flanked, and there was no real military reason to tackle it head-on. Nevertheless for political reasons the Prussian army did just that, quickly reduced it, and won the most famous victory of the war. Prussian medals with the name Düppel were struck and liberally distributed. One thing this did was soften the Liberal-Nationals toward Bismarck: that formerly hated army was winning victories for the greater German cause.

And unknown to the public at the time, the general staff of the Prussian army used this war to evaluate its erstwhile ally Austria. Their surprising conclusion was that, one-on-one, the Prussian army could beat the larger, more prestigious Austrian army. It took Bismarck only two years after getting that evaluation to engineer a war against Austria.

The Seven Weeks War, 1866

This was to be to war for supremacy in Germany. The double trick Bismarck pulled off was (a) to make Austria fight a two-front war, and (b) to make it all look like Austria's fault so the other great powers did not intervene and the Prussian king would go along with it.

Italian affairs loom large in this war and the next. The nucleus of the modern Italian state had just been created from 1859–1861 when the monarchy of Piedmont had absorbed all of Italy except the northeastern province of Venice and the city of Rome itself. Bismarck now offered Italy a secret 90-day treaty, promising that if Italian troops joined him in an attack on Austria on the first day of such a war, that no matter what happened on the Italian-Austria front he would guarantee that Italy received Venezia. This gave them three months to start a war and make it look like Austria's fault, or at least enough of Austria's fault to keep the other great powers from joining their side. The Italian state then began to recruit ethnic Italians from Austrian territories into its army, and Austria, Italy, and Prussia saber-rattled and mobilized their armies. When the other great powers (and the Prussian king) leaned on Bismarck as supposed instigator of this, he agreed to de-mobilize his army if Austria would, too. Austria then agreed to de-mobilize, and the crisis seemed to be waning. Italy, however, refused to de-mobilize and continued to recruit. Austria felt it had to re-mobilize, and Bismarck was able to convince both his king and the great powers that he now had no choice but to fight these perfidious, promise-breaking Austrians.

The war itself was surprising. The Austrians handily defeated the Italians, but at the cost of having to split their army. It was the Prussian-Austrian front that was critical. A Prussian army no larger than the Austrian

---

56. GE Layer 56 is a Placemark referencing Düppel; the half-dozen Photos icons closest to the pointer of this Placemark are all of the Dybbøl *museet* (museum) recalling the 1864 campaign. The fortification obviously controlled access to the large Danish island of Als.

army took the war to Austria in the Bohemian plain and within three weeks won the crucial battle of Sadowa, or Königgrätz (today's Hradec Králové in the Czech Republic),[GE57] depending on where the news correspondents were writing. One important reason for their victory was that the Prussian army was really the first in the world to fully assimilate the industrial revolution. It moved by rail and communicated by telegraph. It issued every soldier a breech-loading rifle, the Dreyse "needle-gun," that could be fired perhaps eight times a minute from a prone position, compared to Austrian muzzle-loaders that had to be loaded vertically and could only get off one shot, maybe two, per minute. Artillery was a larger version of the same. And the Prussians thought up new tactics based on this new technology. While the Austrians were standing rank in front of rank, such a formation would have wasted much of that new Prussian firepower. They wanted to fan their troops out in a long arc, to concentrate murderous fire on concentrated enemy units. That, however, brought up the problem of communication. The Prussian answer was to educate every squad leader of a unit of ten or less ahead of time: certain movements on the battlefield no longer needed communication, it being understood how everyone would move in response.

Still, Sadowa/Königgrätz was not militarily conclusive—the Austrian army withdrew able to fight another day, with reinforcements coming up from the South—so much as it was politically conclusive. Bismarck now offered Austria very generous terms to end the war. Except for Venezia, promised to Italy, not a square inch of Austrian territory would be taken. But Austria had to agree to withdraw from German affairs and give Prussia a free hand there. That was why the war had been fought. Austria agreed, and within the year Prussia had absorbed its neighboring north German states and signed firm agreements with the major south German ones (Bavaria, Wurttemberg, and Baden), in a political unit called the North German Confederation. This was the first step toward the *Kleindeutsch*, or "small German," solution to the problem of modern German nation-building: the new Germany would be in essence an expanded Prussia. Liberal-Nationals began to forgive Bismarck, their Nationalism proving to be much stronger than their Liberalism.

Franco-German War, 1870

The third and greatest of Bismarck's wars was the war with France in 1870. His double trick was played again. The city of Rome and what was left of the Papal States, under more or less of a French protectorate, was secretly promised to Italy if Italy would once again make Bismarck's enemy fight a two-front war. And the occasion for the war—the less-than-earthshaking matter of who would be the new king of Spain—showed Bismarck at his improvisational best in starting a conflict and making it look like the other side's fault.

Spain in the nineteenth century was no longer of world-class importance. It had generally fallen into the French orbit in the past two centuries, and in 1870 was casting around for a new king. Such a king needed royal blood and Roman Catholic convictions, and it was assumed that France would have the final say in the choice. Now the royal Hohenzollern family of Prussia was mainly Protestant, but there was a junior branch which was Catholic. Bismarck secretly put up a name from this branch, and tried to usher it secretly through the Spanish parliament. Discovered by the French before it ever came to a vote, it quickly blew up into an international crisis. A French ambassador appeared before the Prussian King, who was vacationing at a spa called Ems (*Bad Ems*, in German)[GE58] and demanded withdrawal of the offending candidate. The Prussian king, mainly in the dark about Bismarck's machinations, agreed in embarrassment, and wrote Bismarck a sharp criticism of his actions. Then the French pushed further, sending the ambassador back to the king, demanding that he promise never in the future to so elevate one of his relatives. The king refused to so bind the fortunes of his family, but wrote a second telegram to Bismarck about this second public humiliation.

Bismarck suddenly saw possibilities in this telegram. He released a sharply-worded summary of "the Ems dispatch" to both the German and the French press, seeming to know that it would drive France to war, and

---

57. GE Layer 57 is a Placemark referencing Hradec Králové (Königgrätz). It is near the upper Labe (Elbe) River in today's Czech Republic.

58. GE Layer 58 is a Placemark referencing Bad Ems, some five miles east of the Rhine at Koblenz. Click on Panoramio icon under Pushpin icon, titled "Kaiser Wilhelm Denkmal in Bad Ems," and "Bad Ems–Kaiser Wilhelm I" for photographs of memorial statue.

that he could use that war and the matching explosion of German patriotism to unify Germany under Prussian institutions. And indeed, on this basis the hostility of the German people and the French people—not just Prussian and French citizens—blazed up, and both nations marched resolutely to war, Prussia (the North German Confederation, by this time) with some major German allies.

The military part of this war was even more shocking and decisive than that against Austria four years earlier. In the last months of 1870 one French army at the fortress of Metz [GE[59]] and another at Sedan [GE[60]] were surrounded and forced to surrender. Prussia even captured French Emperor Napoleon III. But a vicious and dirty guerrilla war dragged on, and the Paris Commune, in a socialist rebellion against the rest of France, provided a civil war within a foreign invasion.

On January 18, 1871, after a German victory parade in Paris through Napoleon's triumphal arch down the Champs Elysees, the German Empire—long hoped for by patriots—was proclaimed in the Hall of Mirrors at the palace of Versailles[GE[61]] outside Paris. William III King of Prussia now became Emperor (*Kaiser*, or Caesar) William I of the German Empire (*Reich*); Minister-President of Prussia Otto von Bismarck became its Chancellor; and the Prussian legislature was now expanded to become its *Reichstag*. This Empire included all the north and south German states except Austria. It was now the single most powerful mover and shaker in Europe.[GE[62]] France had been soundly defeated. Austria had lost its Italian territory in these last two wars—Lombardy and Venezia—and was so vulnerable to its multi-ethnic groups that it gave Hungary parity (it was the "Austro-Hungarian Kingdom" after 1867) and was being pressured to give it to Czechoslovaks. At its birth, then, the German Empire was the dominant power of Europe.

If you had been a typical German in those days—raised in a fragmented country, inferior in strength to France and looked down on by the French; awakened to your own cultural glories by the Grimms; frustrated by failure to unite in 1848; a listener to Wagner's music retelling the glories of the past; and finally an increasingly enthusiastic fan of Bismarck's spectacular political and military planning—how would you have felt? A flood of national pride resulted in a burst of energy. What a time to be a German. Now Bismarck himself was never so much a German nationalist as he was a Prussian particularist; nevertheless, Bismarck was not a man to restrain such nationalist energy, and he channeled it for his own purposes.

Bismarck's domination of world diplomacy

Bismarck's second claim to fame in the history books is that he dominated world diplomacy from 1871 to 1890, and that even after he was removed from politics in 1890 his basic diplomatic structures served as the framework for the coming of World War I.

The peace treaty with France was nothing like the quick and generous one with Austria four years earlier. It was designed to cripple France as a great power. All of Alsace and part of Lorraine, the two easternmost French provinces, were taken by Germany.[GE[63]] Alsace had some German-speaking population, but Lorraine was mostly French. But here were strategic mountain ranges, and important coal and iron deposits. An enormous indemnity of five billion gold Reichsmarks was levied on France, and France itself divided into five occupation zones, from west to east. As each billion marks was paid, the Germany army was to withdraw from one zone. If the debt should never be paid—which is probably what Bismarck intended—the German army would never withdraw. French national pride, of course, meant that they pledged the debt in one year and paid it off in two, but now that enormous amount of money went to the German government.

---

59. GE Layer 59 is a Placemark referencing Metz.

60. GE Layer 60 is a Placemark referencing Sedan.

61. GE Layer 61 is a Placemark referencing the Hall of Mirrors at Versailles.

62. GE Layer 62 is a Polygon representing Germany 1871–1914; main source is the map on p. 234 of vol. III of Hajo Holborn's *A History of Modern Germany 1840–1945*. Again, first double-click on icon to frame view, then turn it on.

63. GE Layer 63 is a Placemark that zooms in on Alsace (all of which was taken) and Lorraine (the northeast corner of which was taken); you need GE layer 62 (Germany 1871–1918) and your basic "Borders and Labels" layer in Google Earth, bottom left, turned on; provincial borders should show in white.

Bismarck's future diplomacy, then, was all underlain by his basic assumption that France would take the first opportunity for revenge. German diplomacy must isolate France. Germany by itself could handle France, maybe two Frances, but if France ever won a major land ally—Russia or Austria—Germany might be in trouble, having to fight a two-front war against two major powers. Bismarck's answer was to wrap both Austria and Russia up in a three-power alliance. By 1872 the *Dreikaiserbund* (Three Emperors' League) was in existence, with Germany as senior partner. From this basic triangle other alliances branched off—Austria's alliance with Italy, for example. Cartoons from the period show Bismarck as a fat spider in the middle of a complicated web of diplomacy, and France as alone and friendless.

The only thing that might go wrong with such an arrangement was friction between Austria and Russia. If one of these ever became angry enough with the other to go to war, Bismarck would have to choose sides, and in choosing he would lose: the other, in dangerous isolation, would sooner or later go to France. Now both Austria and Russia, having been reduced by mid-century events such as Crimean War and Austro-Prussian War to second-rate powers, were in a crisis of self-confidence. And it so happened that each saw the Balkans, the southeast corner of Europe, as their most important remaining area of "manifest destiny," to use an American term. Greece was already independent, since the 1820s, and so was little Serbia. All the rest of southeastern Europe, though, was held by the failing Ottoman Empire,[GE⁶⁴] and these mainly Christian subject populations were regarded by both Austria and Russia as potentially theirs. Austria was closer, although Russia had Slavic language ties with the whole area, and Christian Orthodox ties with perhaps the eastern two-thirds of it. From the day the Three Emperors' League was signed, the Balkans became the most important real estate on the globe. Small events there could expand into crises of world-class importance in a matter of days. Crisis after crisis happened there. Eventually, of course, World War I began here.

The first crisis to threaten Bismarck's basic triangle began in 1876 with a Turkish massacre of Bulgarian Christians. Serbia, with Russian volunteers in its forces, went to their aid but was defeated by the Turks. At this point Russia took the field, in the Russo-Turk War of 1877–78. After early stubborn Turkish resistance, the Russians swept around both sides of the Black Sea toward Constantinople, and in the spring of 1878, at San Stefano almost within sight of the capital,[GE⁶⁵] forced the Turks to a peace treaty. The most important part of this Treaty of San Stefano was the reorganization of most of the Balkans into a huge new Bulgarian state.[GE⁶⁶] Most everyone at the time believed that this new Bulgaria would be a satellite of Russia—Slavic in language, Christian Orthodox in religion, and with a common frontier with the Russian Empire.

Austria was enraged, and willing to go to war to win all or part of this area for itself. Bismarck, rather than see his two essential allies go to war with each other, took a page from Metternich's book: in the fall of 1878 he staged the Congress of Berlin with the same five great powers (if you count Germany as an expanded Prussia). His thinking seems to have been that Germany already had more territory than it could digest, and that as the strongest state in Europe it had a lot to lose and not much of value to gain in some general war. He was genuinely trying to satisfy all parties. So Bismarck laid his cards on the table: he didn't think the Balkans were worth the bones of "a single Pomeranian grenadier," but if others were going to fight over it, he had to sort it out. From his point of view, everybody that came got something. France got a promise to Tunisia,[GE⁶⁷] to go with next-door Algeria which it already had. Britain was given Cyprus.[GE⁶⁸] Austria got a thirty-year lease to

---

64. GE Layer 64 is a Folder titled "Balkans before 1878." The first three Polygons inside represent independent Greece (since 1829); autonomous Serbia (since 1830, or by one reading 1804); de facto autonomous Moldavia and Wallachia; the fourth Polygon is an outline in red showing the remaining area of active Ottoman Imperial control in southeastern Europe; finally there is a Placemark indicating Istanbul, the Ottoman capital. You can turn the whole folder on at once or explore it one layer at a time.

65. GE Layer 65 is a Placemark referencing San Stefano, today's Yeşilköy, just eight miles west of the heart of Istanbul—today the site of Istanbul's Atatürk International Airport.

66. GE Layer 66 is a Polygon showing approximate territory of the original Bulgarian state established in the spring of 1878 by the Treaty of San Stefano forced on Turkey by Russia in the wake of the Russo-Turk War.

67. GE Layer 67 is a Placemark framing a view of Tunisia (and Algeria, and France).

68. GE Layer 68 is a Placemark framing a view of Cyprus.

a western chunk of the Balkans called Bosnia-Herzegovina.[GE[69]] Nobody asked Tunisians, Cypriotes, or Bosnia-Herzegovinians; the big five were just wheeling and dealing to suit themselves. Russia, the fifth of the great powers, got to keep a much-reduced Bulgarian state.[GE[70]] This, at least, was Bismarck's view of things. Russia, however, saw it as a disaster and a dishonor. Russian soldiers had died to save the Christian population in the Balkans from the Turks, but it was Austria that had picked up most of the gains. Now enraged in its turn against Austria, Russia dropped out of the Three Emperors' League.

At this point Bismarck signed a firm military alliance with Austria, which read that if Austria were attacked by a third power (Russia, obviously), Germany would fight with Austria. On the surface this seems to be the choice he could not afford to make. His use of it, though, made all the difference: he leaked it to the Russian foreign office to shake them into their senses. Russia might beat Austria in a war, but had no chance against Austria plus Germany. Jolted and chastened, Russia agreed to rejoin the Three Emperor's League.

A decade later, in 1886, a similar crisis broke out in the Balkans and once again Russia dropped out of the Dreikaiserbund. There was a new Russian government now, so Bismarck had to play the same game again with Emperor Alexander III. He signed a firm military alliance with Austria, leaked it to Russia, and then was able to deal with a shaken Russian foreign office. This time, instead of trying to keep Russia and Austria in the same open alliance, he offered Russia a secret treaty, the Reinsurance Treaty of 1887. It read that if Russia or Germany should fight another power, each would be benevolently neutral towards the other in such a conflict; the major exception was that should Russia "attack" Austria-Hungary, all bets were off. Again, on the surface, it seems that in case of Austro-Russian war that Germany was obligated to fight on one side and be benevolently neutral to the other. In reality, Bismarck had ensured that each power would check in with him in Berlin before they went to war. They would each come to Berlin to ask if Germany agreed that they were the victim of aggression, and this would give him time to patch up relationships and avoid war. This secret Reinsurance Treaty of 1887, to be renegotiated every three years, was probably the high point of Bismarck's diplomacy.

William II and Germany's "Place in the Sun"

Emperor William I died in 1888, and his quite Liberal and pro-English son, Frederick III—who in the natural course of things should have ruled for a generation—was on his own deathbed. By year's end, his twenty-seven-year-old son, and William I's grandson, William II inherited the throne. He was poorly educated and yet headstrong and egotistical, and between him and the seventy-three-year-old Bismarck there was not just one generation gap, but two. Bismarck could not take the young man seriously, although the position of Chancellor was still the Emperor's to award.

Brilliant as Bismarck was in foreign affairs, in domestic affairs he was still the "mad Junker." In the 1870s he had more or less declared war on the Catholics of the Prussian part of Germany in what the government grandly called the *Kulturkampf,* or "Struggle for Culture." His persecution only strengthened the Catholics in their beliefs and improved their organization, while leaving a lasting suspicion of a national government that called them "enemies of the Reich." In the 1880s he had waged the same sort of governmental war on socialists, who were organizing into the largest of German political parties, the SPD (Socialist Party of Germany). They, too, thrived on his persecution. As Bismarck tried to solve the problems that made the socialists popular, ironically enough, Germany soon had the most extensive public welfare programs in all of Europe. It was over a domestic affairs issue in 1890 that William II fired Bismarck. In domestic affairs Bismarck's dismissal may have been a turn for the rational. In foreign affairs it was disastrous. There was a cartoon of the time in the British press showing a cocky William II with his arms folded, leaning on the rail of an ocean liner, watching

---

69. GE Layer 69 is a Placemark framing a view of Bosnia-Herzegovina. This was essentially today's Bosnian state, with its capital of Sarajevo, framed in center of this view. Go back and turn on layer 45, "Austria 1815," to see how snugly this fit into Austrian imperial plans!

70. GE Layer 70 is a Placemark framing a view of the modern state of Bulgaria that resulted from the Congress of Berlin. It had lost its original western territories and also its foothold on the Aegean seacoast (compare with layer 66, "Big Bulgaria").

portly old Bismarck walking down the steps. It was called "The Dropping of the Pilot," and so in foreign affairs it proved to be.

The very first action of the new German government in foreign affairs was to refuse to renew the Reinsurance Treaty with Russia, seeing this as inconsistent with their treaty with Austria. Russia, now desperately vulnerable should Austria decide to go to war and bring Germany in with it, turned to the other isolated great power. No matter that Russia was still ruled by an Emperor "by the grace of God," and that France was now working on its Third Republic; military survival was more important. Within a year a Russian-French military alliance was formed. Bismarck's nightmare was coming into being, and from his retirement out on his estate in Friedrichsruhe[GE71] he could see it happening. Europe had begun to choose up sides for World War I.

There was one other great power in Europe that was essentially non-aligned and up for grabs—Great Britain, with not much of an army but with the world's largest navy. Great Britain, historically at odds with France, was very anxious to join Germany in an alliance. Germany, in pride approaching hubris—that blind arrogance for which the gods take their revenge in classic Greek tragedy—threw this easy British alliance away in two ways.

First, Germany became very aggressive in colonial affairs. Bismarck had only had one brief spell of colony-building, in the 1883–1885 period, and he honestly tried to reassure England then that the German colonies in Africa, especially, were no threat because he had no intention of building a navy. He was content with Germany being the superpower of the supercontinent. For William II and his generation, though, colonies were a matter not just of economics and world-wide military position but also of status: a great power would have colonies. So Germany got in the colonial game late, as the most aggressive player, and there were lots of occasions of friction with the world's greatest holder of colonies, Great Britain. Sharp German criticism of the British in the South African Boer War of 1899–1902 did much to sour relations between the two.

Second and much more threatening to Great Britain, Germany launched a drive to build a major navy. Back when the first naval bill passed the Reichstag in 1898, it won favorable response in Britain: here was a potential ally against the combined navies of France and Russia. But then a second naval bill was passed in 1900, however, two years before the first even expired, and the justification for the bill—openly printed for all to see—all but named Britain as an enemy. The bill was justified by the "risk theory." It said that Germany, starting the naval race so late, was not trying to have the largest navy in the world; it should, however, have one so large that even the largest navy in the world would not risk fighting it. The instant British translation of this was that after a German-British naval war, the British might be the winners, but would have suffered such losses as to make them vulnerable to the French and Russians. From then on British foreign policy saw Germany as enemy number one: all Britain wanted was naval superiority over Germany in the North Sea, the country's defense and trade lifeline. Anybody else was a potential friend.

By 1904 Britain and France were negotiating together in a spirit of *entente cordiale*, "friendly intent," and the *Entente* quickly became a military alliance. Then France got its two allies, Russia and Britain, to sit down and settle their grievances, and by 1907 the Triple Entente, one of the teams which would fight World War I, was virtually complete.

Diplomatic crises that threatened to bring war between rival alliances began in 1905. Two of them were in Morocco. As part of the French and British solution of their colonial rivalries, Morocco was designated as potential French territory. In late March 1905 Kaiser William II showed up in Tangier in the royal yacht—the idea being to embarrass the French in their takeover and put enough pressure on this new Anglo-French alliance to split it.[GE72] The pressure backfired, and only strengthened the Entente. A virtual repeat of this would come in 1911. One of the greatest of the crises came in 1908. The Young Turk revolt in the Ottoman Empire was attracting a good deal of attention, and while it was going on Austria (whose 30-year lease to Bosnia-Herzegovina was supposed to run out that year) quietly annexed Bosnia forever. Serbia, which saw itself and Bosnia as the basis of a future South Slav ("Yugo-slav") state, was angry enough to go to war. The Serbians checked in with their fellow Christian and Slavic friend and protector Russia, and Russia in turn checked in with France. France said it was in the middle of military reorganization and could not afford war

---

71. GE Layer 71 is a Placemark referencing Friedrichsruhe, an estate given Bismarck for his service to country.

72. GE Layer 72 is a Placemark referencing Tangier.

yet, so Russia backed down and Serbia had to swallow its anger. When much the same scenario reoccurred six years later in the summer of 1914, France would be reorganized and ready and Russia would not back down.

Trigger for the war came on June 28, 1914, in an Austrian parade in Sarajevo (the Bosnian capital, in what patriotic Yugoslavs considered occupied Yugoslavia), on a Yugoslav day of national mourning. On that date in 1389, in the battle of Blackbird Field (*Kossovo Pole*) the Ottoman Turks had destroyed the original Yugoslav state. During the parade the heir to the Austrian throne, Franz Ferdinand (or Francis Ferdinand), was assassinated by Yugoslav patriots.[GE73] This was the last straw for Austria, which issued an ultimatum to Serbia that, if accepted, would have made Serbia a province of Austria. Five weeks of ultimata and response took place. Austria checked in with Germany (as Bismarck had ensured decades before) and the German government responded with its famous "blank check" for Austria to do as it pleased (which Bismarck would never have issued). Serbia on its side checked in with Russia, which checked in with France and Britain which both said they were ready, and on August 3 and 4 the sides declared war on one another.

Conventional wisdom in 1914 expected a short war, the way Bismarck's wars had lasted only weeks or a few months at most. Instead, World War I would last four and a half years, with unimaginable physical and cultural devastation. All over Europe, however, crowds gathered in the major squares that first week of August to shout their enthusiasm. War tension had been growing; at least now the tension was over and the time for action had come.

World War I

The framework of World War I was established by German war strategy. Ever since the creation of the German Empire, theorists there had had to consider the possibility of such a two-front war with France and Russia. The military problems, at least in a general way, were simple. In terms of geographic obstacles, the Russian frontier was wide-open and the French frontier was short with easily defended mountains. Taking an army north of those mountains involved invading the Low Countries, particularly Belgium, whose neutrality had been recognized by every major European country including Germany. In terms of speed of mobilization, the French army would mobilize only shortly after the Germans, while the Russians would take months. Simply splitting the German army into eastern and western halves was military suicide; experts agreed that a minimal holding force against one would make possible the wiping out of the other, and then they could turn a united army against the remaining foe. In Bismarck's day, the military planners had decided to place a small holding force on the easily-defended French-German border (the Rhine River on the southern part of the border, and rugged mountains on the northwestern angle of the border) and turn the bulk of the German army first on Russia.

By 1905, however, the German army was redirected in the "Schlieffen plan," named for the current chief-of-staff. He saw some basic flaws in the original plan. First, Germany would have to deal with the French army (which mobilized in three weeks or so) long before it had to deal with the bulk of the Russia army (which mobilized in two or three months). Second, nobody had ever knocked Russia out of a war quickly; Russia tended to withdraw and call out "Generals Distance and Winter." And so General von Schlieffen, in a plan of military brilliance but disastrous political naïveté, decided on small holding forces on both the Russian and French frontiers, and put almost 90 percent of the army on the Belgian frontier. The southern end of that army would be hinged to the top of the Jura-Vosges mountains, and five huge army corps in a great right wing would wheel through Belgium into northern France in a matter of weeks, and force the French army to commit in defense of Paris. The French army would then be crushed back against the French-German border as the nutcracker closed. Militarily it was an inspired gamble, risking even the occupation of Berlin by the Russian army in exchange for the crushing of the French army. Politically, of course, the violation of Belgian neutrality ensured that certainly the British and probably eventually the Americans would join the war.

By the time the plan was put in motion by later generals, the holding forces on the borders were beefed up a bit, with corresponding weakening of the great right wing. The result was brilliant performance on the eastern

---

73. GE Layer 73 is a Placemark referencing a Photos icon titled "WORLD WAR 1 DAY 0," with a photograph of the assassination memorial plaque. Several other nearby icons show the Latin Bridge where the assassination of the Archduke and his wife Sophie, Duchess of Hohenberg, took place.

front at Tannenberg and the Masurian Lakes,[GE[74]] where the Russian army did so badly that its chief commander committed suicide, and on the French border itself. But the performance of the great right wing was critical. It marched through Belgium in perfect order, right on time. Then as the five army corps, outrunning their supplies and very tired, closed on Paris, a gap opened up between the inner three and the outer two armies. The French and British armies exploited this gap, forcing the outer two German armies to close up to the inner three, thus missing Paris—along with its chance for a quick trapping of the main French (and British) army. [GE[75]] When the rival armies tried to turn each other's flanks, they pushed the "western front" to the English channel in northern France and down across eastern France to the Swiss border.[GE[76]] When Italy joined the Entente in 1915, the western front quickly extended from Switzerland east across northern Italy.[GE[77]] Machine guns and barbed wire were standard, but tanks were only in their rudimentary stages. The result was a surprisingly static war. The western front was so stable that a huge battle costing hundreds of thousands of casualties might only gain a half-mile of ground.

For four years no foreign armies were on German soil, and Germany won at least as many battles as it lost. The German army was spectacular, clearly the best army in the war. Austria, on the other hand, was a real disappointment to its German allies, as its non-German ethnicities either fought without enthusiasm or defected outright to the other side. This gave rise to the famous German quip, "We are shackled to a corpse." On the eastern front, every spring of the war, the Russians would invade Austria, Austria armies would go into retreat, and Austria would cry to Germany for help, and German armies would arrive and the Russian army would go into precipitate retreat, whereupon it was time for winter quarters. Even in 1917, when a million fresh American troops joined the Entente side, that seemed to be balanced by Russian withdrawal from the war because of the Bolshevik Revolution. With Russia out of the war Germany was now able to turn all its armies west in the huge summer offensive of 1918.

Imagine the shock to the German public, then, when the offensive stalled and Entente powers counterattacked in August, and the German army went into uncontrollable retreat. Like a sentry asked to stand one watch too many, that magnificent army simply cracked. Complete units began to surrender (not taking anything away from the famous American hero Sergeant Alvin York, but this is when his capture of dozens of German troops took place), and the German generals told the politicians that the war was lost.

There had been some international efforts in the past couple of years of the war to make a compromise peace. In Germany, however, the reigning generals Hindenburg and Ludendorff—and the public at large—were determined to accept nothing but a *Siegfriede*, a "Victory Peace," in which they annexed large parts of neighboring countries and imposed huge indemnities on them. Off and on the generals overcame the politicians and diplomats, for whom they had nothing but disdain, and introduced unrestricted submarine warfare. The most famous victim of the first phase of this was the British liner *Lusitania* sunk in May 1915[GE[78]] with the loss of 1200, including over a hundred Americans. American protests enabled the German politicians to get it lifted temporarily, but the generals reimposed it the next spring. When the unarmed channel ferry *Sussex* was sunk in April 1916, again with some U.S. loss of life, an American ultimatum again caused this unrestricted submarine warfare to be lifted again. On February 1, 1917, it was re-imposed, apparently for good. About this time a clumsy German diplomatic attempt to get Mexico into the war on its side—promising it recovery of Texas, New Mexico, Arizona, etc.—came to light. On April 6, 1917, the U.S. formally entered the war.

---

74. GE Layer 74 is a Placemark referencing a Panoramio icon under the Pushpin symbol, titled "Tannenberg Memorial AD 2007," for view of grassy field that was the site of a German memorial to the battle, since destroyed. The Masurian Lakes are sixty miles east-northeast.

75. GE Layer 75 is a Polygon showing in red the five armies, the outer of which just missed Paris. Link below is to BBC website, with an animated map sequence of the western front of World War I. The first two animation sections are the Schlieffen plan as it was meant to be, and troop movements as they actually happened; hit "launch the animation" button when site opens: http://www.bbc.co.uk/history/worldwars/wwone/launch_ani_western_front.shtml

76. GE Layer 76 is a Path showing (in black) the Western Front as it first stabilized in the wake of the failure of the Schlieffen Plan. The "race to the sea" was the northern movement of the front as each side tried to turn the other's flank.

77. GE Layer 77 is a Path showing the extension eastward from the Swiss border when Italy first joined the war in 1915.

78. GE Layer 78 is a Placemark referencing the Lusitania sinking site off southeast coast of Ireland.

German citizens were deluded by their generals, who took pains to hide any German weaknesses or reverses lest it weaken public support for the war. The German public was also blinded to the chance of disaster by decades of phenomenal German growth and success. Here too was the argument found at the end of every war when victory proves elusive, that if the country stopped short of victory the dead had died in vain. But extreme nationalism contributed most to this catastrophe of World War I that was increasingly of Germany's own making. Just before the war, a German writer talked about how when the first edition of the German medieval epic *Nibelungenlied* had been presented to Prussian King Frederick II in 1755, he had snorted that it was not worth a charge of powder. But now, said the writer in 1912, presumably with a great swelling of the chest, "it has become the pride of the Fatherland." For German super-nationalists the war in the east was to be the showdown for all time with the Slavs; in the west the hated folk enemy France must be broken forever. Pay no attention to ethical arguments or political calculations, said the extreme nationalists; it was all just a matter of resolute German will.

Weimar Republic and revolution

It was in early October of 1918 that General von Ludendorff, virtual military dictator of Germany the last two years of the war, sent an aide to brief party leaders of the German Reichstag on just how bad the military state of affairs was. He insisted that the government seek an immediate armistice. Parliamentary leaders, once they got over their shock, realized they were going to have to come to terms with a defeat, and U.S. President Wilson made clear in his communications with them in that month that the existing imperial-military government would have to go. In Berlin a new government was being worked out, one that would keep a limited monarchy similar to Britain's but make the military answerable to the parliament. But the Emperor left the capital for army headquarters in Belgium, and popular opinion that now desperately wanted to end the war saw his move as a threat to any new government and the peace process. In this tense atmosphere the November revolution of 1918 exploded.

We don't get into socialism or Russian history in detail until the next chapter, but suffice it to say here that the Bolshevik Revolution of November of 1917 had featured a rebellion of the navy (at the naval base of Kronstadt just off St. Petersburg), mass strikes of workers during which soldiers began to fraternize with them, meeting of representatives of every Workers' and Soldiers' Council (*Sovyet*, or *Soviet*, in Russian), and the formation of a Council of People's Commissars as a new government, or at least a parallel government to make sure the existing Duma (parliament or congress) did or did not do certain things. Now in Germany in 1918— exactly a year to the week later—remarkably the same progression of events happened, and every politically conscious person around recognized the parallels. The navy revolted on November 4, particularly at the key naval base of Kiel.[GE[79]] Soldiers began to fraternize with striking workers. On November 9 truly massive marches of workers and soldiers headed toward the heart of Berlin. The Spartacus League (*Spartakusbund*), Germany's controlling Communist group (which paralleled the Bolshevik party in Russia; both renamed themselves the Communist Party in 1918) called for the establishment of a revolutionary republic. A Council of People's Commissars was established to make sure the parliament did or did not do certain things.

But whereas Communist control in Russia the year before had spread from Moscow and St. Petersburg to smaller cities and towns, in Germany it did not spread much beyond Berlin. Even in Berlin a backlash was growing that included forces from the moderate socialists (SPD) to far right-wing "independent military units" (*Freikorpen*) that came streaming in from the Polish front. The fighting became especially bloody by January, and on January 15 the two key Spartacus League figures, Rosa Luxemburg and Karl Liebknecht, were killed, and the attempted Communist takeover crushed.

Looking back over events in Germany from October 1918 on, it appears that the old imperial generals and politicians stepped aside and let Liberals and some socialists take over the government. In part they did this so as not to have to sign and take any blame for what promised to be a brutal peace treaty. On November 8, 1918, a new democratic republic was named Weimar, in part after Goethe's old haunts—it had a good late-Enlightenment, early-Romantic ring to it. And in part they hoped to be able to say to the invading

---

79. GE layer 79 is a Placemark referencing Kiel, framing a view that shows the mouth of the Kiel canal.

powers—mostly republics (the U.S. and France, and although Great Britain was technically a constitutional monarchy, the Parliament there ran foreign affairs as in a republic)—"don't blame the sins of the old Empire on us; we're a Republic just like you." Three days later this new government signed an "Armistice" with the U.S., Britain, France, and Italy (today's Veteran's Day on November 11 used to be called Armistice Day, for this reason). It was not really an armistice, which is a temporary cease-fire between more or less equal forces; it was a total surrender just called "armistice" to sugar-coat this bitter pill and make it easier for Germans to swallow.

Versailles Treaty

It took over a year to hammer out the details of the Versailles Treaty, that part of the general Treaty of Paris which ended the war in Europe. The terms were no more brutal than the Germans would have insisted on had they won (in fact, had insisted on with Russia in March of 1918 at the Treaty of Brest-Litovsk), but brutal nevertheless. Consider the motivation of the four treaty writing powers. Only the U.S. was close to disinterested. We had a legitimate idealist, former Princeton professor Woodrow Wilson, for President. As a country we had profited enormously by trade as a neutral: we went into the war a debtor nation (having industrialized on British loans) and came out of it a creditor nation. Then we joined the war just in time to turn the balance of power. But the U.S. was consistently outvoted by the other three.

Although Russia suffered more dead, France had suffered more per capita dead than any other country in the war: a lot of U.S. soldiers came back with French wives because by the war's end there was no able-bodied local competition. Much of eastern France was a moonscape. Understandably, French patriots were of the opinion that war on French territory must never happen again; Germany must be crippled as a state.

Britain had more or less swapped places with the U.S. in the war, going in a creditor nation and coming out a debtor nation. Britain had become a second-rate power, and Germany would pay for having caused it. Lloyd George campaigned after the war on the slogan, "Germany is a lemon; we must squeeze it until the pips squeak."

Italy was the only country to humiliate itself in the war. Pledged to fight with Austria, it refused to honor that pledge, and when offered territory by the Entente, Italy joined that side—as a mercenary. And when it did fight it fought badly, as at the Battle of Caporetto [GE[80]] where Italians greatly outnumbered the Austrians and were still thrashed. In nations as in people, sometimes personal humiliation is taken out in anger on others. Italy's would be a shrill, punitive voice.

When the treaty was signed early in 1920, the hundreds of provisions could be summed up in four categories:

1. Military provisions reduced the German army of five million to a hundred thousand; that is, of every fifty soldiers, one could be kept and 49 were to be released. Germany was allowed no tanks, no aircraft, no heavy machine guns, no poison gas, no submarines, and no battleship over 10,000 tons (destroyer class, which eliminated traditional cruisers and battleships). The battleship fleet Germany had worked so hard to build was to be sailed to Scapa Flow and surrendered to the British.
2. Territorial provisions stripped Germany of Alsace-Lorraine, all of its aggressively won colonies, and even gave the Saar,[GE[81]] the richest heart of its iron-coal district, to France to administer temporarily. A newly-reborn Polish state[GE[82]] was given a corridor to the sea and the seaport of Gdansk/Dansig, thus cutting off East Prussia from the rest of the German state.[GE[83]] The Austro-Hungarian Kingdom

---

80. GE Layer 80 is a Placemark referencing Caporetto (today's Kobarid in Slovenia).

81. GE Layer 81 is a Polygon of the Saar, or Saarland; shown here in green, it adjoins Lorraine in France (the part of Lorraine Germany held from 1871–1914).

82. GE Layer 82 is a Polygon representing Poland 1920–1939.

83. GE Layer 32 is a Polygon representing Germany 1920–38.

simply disappeared in the war, and all that was left was a little German-speaking state, adjoining Germany[GE[84]]—but political unification of Germany and this German Austria was expressly forbidden.

3. Financial provisions were not quite ready when the Germans were forced to sign, so they were in essence forced to sign a blank check. But every tree cut down, every mine flooded, every man-hour lost was being carefully itemized, and the total would be astronomical.

4. Honor provisions were worst of all for the Germans. Article 231 of the treaty, for example, the famous "war guilt" clause, was read by Germans to say that Germany and its allies were guilty of starting the war, and that justified the entire treaty.

Germany had to sign this in total, without discussion of any single item, or begin the war again—which the provisions of the Armistice had made impossible, or nearly so. Germans called it the *Diktat*, the dictated peace. To say it was hated is not strong enough. Germans who signed it on behalf of the government, or who worked to pay those astronomical reparations, were assassinated by their fellow countrymen in the next few years.

The political structure of Weimar

The Weimar constitution was written in emergency times; perhaps this is why it had such a strong executive. The President, elected above party politics every seven years in a nation-wide vote, was given the right to rule up to one year at a time by emergency decree should no regular parliamentary government be formed.

The Chancellor and the ministers of various branches of government were no longer appointed by the executive the way they had been before the war. They now emerged, in the common continental European democratic fashion, from the legislature. Unlike the British and American winner-take-all electoral district systems, which tend to produce two dominant parties, in Weimar Republic Germany there was a nation-wide vote for parties, each of which had its list of candidates already drawn up. The more votes for a party, the more of their list was elected, so the total percentage of legislators for a given party in the Reichstag approximated the total percentage of its vote nationwide. Any coalition of parties totaling over 50 percent of the elected legislators could agree to form a government. They would decide among themselves who should be the Chancellor and the ten ministers. The Chancellor, it was usually assumed, would come from the biggest party of the coalition, along with perhaps three or four of the ministries, including such powerful positions as Ministry of Interior. Lesser parties in the coalition would have to be satisfied with the Ministry of Post Office or some such. Having once agreed to form a government, however, decisions in the Cabinet were made by a vote of those eleven, the Chancellor and the ten ministers. If the coalition ever splintered and so lost a vote in the Reichstag, it was time for new elections and a new government coalition.

The single biggest party in the new Weimar Reichstag was still the SPD, the Socialist Party of Germany. Despite its Marxist rhetoric—"workers of the world, unite!" and all that—in 1914 the party had firmly supported the German government in the war, and it was still very popular. It had, however, just enough true socialism about it to feel guilty about joining some bourgeoisie alliance in government, and so the SPD lent its voting strength to a center-left coalition without taking an active ministerial role itself. One of the more interesting parties was the small Catholic Center party: it tended to have maximum political flexibility, able to ally with any party that could accept its fairly specific religious and social goals such as support for parochial education.

---

84. GE Layer 84 is a Folder titled "What was left of Austria after WW I." It includes six Polygon layers—the first a white outline of Austrian borders in 1914, the other five colored areas representing the new states, or new frontiers, of Czechoslovakia, Hungary, Romania, Italy, and Yugoslavia. For best viewing, keep layers 80 and 81 turned on (Poland; Germany); turn Google Earth's "Borders and Labels" layer off, and then turn the six Polygons on one at a time. The tiny uncolored area inside the white outline is all that was left of Austria.

Culture and economics in Weimar Germany

The Roaring 'Twenties in the U.S. is a distant memory of speakeasies, dancing the Charleston, and the gearing up of Hollywood film studios. A good part of the motivation of these times was war release. The times roared even more in Europe, especially in Germany—they had so much more war from which to be released. This was the great modern era of pacifism, with Erich Maria Remarque's *All Quiet on the Western Front* preaching the same message as Hemingway's *Farewell to Arms*. It was a decade of serious disarmament, from the Washington Conference of 1921–22 to the London Naval Conference of 1930. It was a time of unusual intellectual ferment. Almost every major subject on American college campuses today can showcase key intellectuals who worked in that discipline in Germany in the 1920s.

To elaborate on just one impact this 1920s intellectual ferment in Germany had on the rest of the world, including the U.S., most modern American cities (at least the downtown skyscrapers) are enduring examples of *Bauhaus* architecture from 1920s Germany. Bauhaus, literally "the House of Building," was started by Hugo Gropius. In 1919, after recuperating from war wounds, he was invited to the city of Weimar to head up the Saxon School of Arts and Crafts there. He quickly transformed it into Bauhaus, which tried to integrate art and crafts and architecture with an eye to function, and which borrowed techniques of industrial building construction for the construction of offices and residences. In 1925 the school moved to Dessau, some seventy miles northeast and about halfway from Weimar to Berlin. After 1928 Gropius built whole Bauhaus neighborhoods in Berlin. Unwelcome in Nazi Germany, by 1937 he was hired as Dean of Harvard's School of Architecture. About that same time other Bauhaus figures established Chicago's famous Institute of Design.[GE[85]]

Economic turmoil during the Weimar Republic can go a long way toward explaining the victory of political extremism there by 1933. Weimar began in a Germany under economic blockade, continued in one obligated to pay enormous war reparations, endured the spectacular inflation of 1923, the modest boom times of 1924–28, and collapsed in the Depression of 1930 and after.

The great Inflation of 1923 really began during World War I. At the beginning of the war, for one U.S. dollar you could get 4.2 marks, and it had been that way for years. Inflation was probably not a term the average citizen knew; "civilized" countries had relatively stable currencies. But Germany alone of the countries in World War I was so confident of winning the war that, instead of raising taxes to pay for the war as it went, it relied almost solely on the sale of war bonds. This way it fought the war on what amounted to internal loans from its citizens, who were to be paid off by the spoils of war after a great victory. By 1918, with such a victory receding into the distance, one U.S. dollar could get 16 marks, which was considerable inflation. But the frightening inflation was just beginning. By January of 1923 one U.S. dollar would get you 16,000 marks, and by mid-summer it would get 4,200,000,000,000 marks—that's four trillion, two hundred billion. There were American tourists in Germany going hungry because no one could change a $5 bill U.S. Money was now worth only what the paper it was printed on was worth, and the economy reverted to barter. Part of the reason for this was that the German government was trying to demonstrate through the hardship of its own citizens that reparations ought to be suspended or reduced. And partly it was a government device to pay off its internal debts with cheap money. Two things resulted by 1924: (a) a German government with no internal debts, seemingly one of the best credit risks in the world; and (b) a bitter element of the population which had had its life savings wiped out, and had been driven down from white-collar ranks into blue-collar manual labor.

After 1924 it was boom times, as cheap loans mainly from the United States came flooding into Germany. The economy rose from the ashes like a phoenix, and millionaires were made every day (although among the lower economic classes unemployment was still in the millions). Then came the October 1929 Wall Street crash in the U.S. In general the small firms were wiped out that first year, and the large ones desperately called in loans to survive the crisis. Those short-term loans to Germany which had supported the whole boom were not renewed, and the German economy collapsed like a house of cards. The Great Depression showed that the economies of all of the industrial countries were now interdependent, but it was Germany that was hit first and hardest of all the European countries. It would only be rescued from Depression by the Nazi Party.

---

85. GE Layer 85 is a folder titled "Bauhaus sites." It includes Placemarks referencing a cluster of Panoramio icons relating to Bauhaus at Dessau, and also at Weimar.

Hitler and the NSDAP

In 1919, in a beer hall in a working class quarter of Munich, a small political party was put together—the National-Socialist German Workers' Party (*National-Sozialistiche Deutsche Arbeiter Partei*). It was super-patriotic and yet big on a sense of socialist community inside Germany; it was anti-big business; and it was anti-Semitic. Its most important figure thought Bavaria ought to secede from Germany, which made about as much sense then as any single American state seceding from the U.S. today. It was a tiny and hopeless little party, probably going nowhere, except that it was encountered by Adolf Hitler, who at the time was also apparently going nowhere.

Hitler was born in 1889 in Braunau-am-Inn,[GE86] a little town on the Austrian side of the Inn river, just across from southeastern Bavaria in Germany. His father was a self-made man, a local customs official, determined that Hitler should follow in his footsteps. The young Hitler wanted to be an architect, and they quarreled. Hitler later in life claimed that he was a good student until his early-teen conflicts with his father, but the school grade reports and comments show him as a struggling student and a loner from the first. He had a peculiar kind of intelligence, but it wasn't the kind that lent itself to academic success in the very structured German or German-Austrian school system. When his father died, he talked his mother out of his share of inheritance and went to stay with relatives in Linz,[GE87] the closest city of any size. Then he dropped out of high school completely and went to huge, multi-ethnic Vienna, the New York City of central Europe.

Here at age eighteen he first pretended to be a college student,[GE88] but soon drifted down into the working class slums. He lived a hand-to-mouth existence of part-time jobs and flophouses, apparently contracting syphilis at this time. He encountered ideals of socialism and the sometimes violent reality of union organization. He read the newly-scientific racist pamphlets and ran into a bewildering variety of ethnic groups, including the recent Orthodox Jewish immigrants from Russia (see next chapter and Chapter 10 for the circumstances of their immigration). In his *Mein Kampf* (*My Struggle*), written in jail some fifteen years later, he recollected his first encounter in Vienna with an eastern, Orthodox, ghetto Jew. His first question to himself was, is he Jewish? His second question was, is he German? Sunk in the slums of Vienna, without self-respect, he apparently found something to identify with by finding something to hate—a process, incidentally, that seems as possible with whole nations as it is with individuals. The psychological interpretation of those questions might run like this: Was that man with his strange dress and strange hairdo and strange accent Jewish? Yes, Hitler had heard about these immigrant Russian Jews. Was he German, like Hitler? His answer was emphatically no. In Hitler's veins, he understood from current racist literature, ran the blood of the master race. He may not have looked like much at the present, but blood would out: he, Hitler, was of the superior race. Already his favorite musician, for more than one reason, was Wagner.

At age twenty-two, Hitler got a draft notice from the Austrian government, and dodged across the border to Bavaria, to Munich.[GE89] He was no coward, as his later war record shows, but he had no interest in fighting for what he considered to be a polyglot mishmash like Austria. In Munich he lived the same hand-to-mouth life, but at least found satisfaction that he was in a thoroughly German culture. When war broke out three years later, Hitler enthusiastically enlisted in the Bavarian branch of the German army.[GE90] He spent four years on the western front as battalion runner, one of the most dangerous jobs of the war. He was wounded twice and

86. GE Layer 86 is a Placemark framing a view of the little river town of Braunau am Inn, and referencing the Panoramio icon under pointer, titled "Hitler's Birthplace."

87. GE Layer 87 is a Placemark framing a view of Linz, a substantial provincial capital on the Danube River. Once in power Hitler would try to make it the artistic capital of the Third Reich, the equal of what Florence museums were to Renaissance Italy.

88. GE Layer 88 is a Placemark framing a view of the University of Vienna, where there are a Wikipedia icon and a couple of Panoramio icons to explore.

89. GE Layer 89 is a Placemark referencing Munich, biggest city and capital of the Bavarian state of Germany, in a view that also shows the three previous Placemarks.

90. GE Layer 90 is a Placemark referencing Munich's Odeonsplatz, where a great crowd gathered to celebrate the declaration of the war. By chance a photograph of the crowd caught twenty-five-year-old Adolf Hitler near the front, eyes shining, mouth open; see image at website: http://www.firstworldwar.com/features/graphics/munich_hitler_1.jpg

gassed once and won the Iron Cross (second class in 1914 and first class in 1918), still Germany's highest war decoration a century after its invention in the 1813 campaign against Napoleon. Despite his heroism, he was only promoted one step, from private to corporal, during the entire four years. He was apparently still a loner not trusted by those around him.

Convalescing from a gas attack when the war ended, Hitler could not believe that all the German sacrifices had been in vain. Along with many conservatives he believed the myth that the army had really won the war but the Liberals had given it away, stabbing Germany in the back. Here is a passage from *Mein Kampf* describing his feelings of those days, which also illustrates the growing power of his rhetoric:

> And so it had all been in vain. In vain all the sacrifices and privations; in vain the hunger and thirst of months which were often endless; in vain the hours in which, with mortal fear clutching at our hearts, we nevertheless did our duty; and in vain the death of two millions who died. Would not the graves of all the hundreds of thousands open, the graves of those who with faith in the fatherland had marched forth never to return? Would they not open and send the silent mud- and blood-covered heroes back as spirits of vengeance to the homeland which had cheated them with such mockery of the highest sacrifice which a man can make to his people in this world? Had they died for this, the soldiers of August and September, 1914? Was it for this that in the autumn of the same year the volunteer regiments marched after their old comrades? Was it for this that these boys of seventeen sank into the earth of Flanders? Was this the meaning of the sacrifice which the German mother made to the fatherland when with sore heart she let her best-loved boys march off, never to see them again? Did all this happen only so that a gang of wretched criminals could lay hands on the fatherland?[20]

Then came the Versailles Treaty, reducing the German army to 2 percent of its former size. Hitler was one of the few kept: he was not fit for physical labor yet, and every army takes care of its Iron Cross (or Victoria Cross, or Congressional Medal of Honor, etc.) winners. He was stationed in Munich with light duties, as political information officer to investigate promising paramilitary organizations.

The *Reichswehr*, the German army, had been reduced to a glorified police force of one hundred thousand. Newly independent Czechoslovakia next door had five or six times that number; France still had millions in uniform. What would happen if Germany suddenly had to go to war again? So the German army began to build secret, illegal contacts with patriotic, paramilitary groups so that it could quickly absorb them at the start of some future war.

It was in this capacity, as a German officer in uniform, that Hitler went to a September 12, 1919, meeting of the struggling little NSDAP.[GE[91]] He was unimpressed by the meeting, but a few days later was invited to join the Party's "executive board." Some potential power in its makeup must have impressed him, because he committed himself wholly to the party—going so far in April of 1920 as to resign his commission in the army, one of the few safe jobs in a Germany still under economic blockade.

Most people have so many contradictory forces pulling on their lives that they appear relatively inactive, absorbed by the activity of daily life. Occasionally, however, for good or evil, total commitment to some cause aligns all those forces and there can be in a given individual some sort of power flow—as different as laser light from normal scattered light. Hitler, who had had few if any real friends, now developed the kind of personal magnetism called charisma that made even strong people around him want to do what he wanted done. Hitler, who had apparently never had a meaningful relationship with a woman, and who was not particularly handsome himself, now became attractive to women. Hitler, who could not string two sentences together in public, in about two years' time became the foremost speaker of the twentieth century. The author once had an older German friend who had been six years old in 1944, with Germany in ruins and the allies invading from both sides. He remembered his mother and father sitting by the radio in that year, listening to Hitler speak on his regular broadcasts, then crying and rededicating their lives to the cause. Later, as an adult, he could only put it down to demonic possession. That is not the author's conclusion, but it is adduced to show that something extraordinary was at work here. By 1921, this ethnic south German of Austrian

---

91. GE Layer 91 is a Placemark at the approximate location of the beer hall, Sterneckerbräu. During the Third Reich, the Nazis made a museum of it; the building is still there, but today it's a store.

citizenship, with a raspy voice, with little formal education or higher culture in a nation that valued both, was convinced he would lead Germany.

Who was attracted to the young Nazi party? First, it was always strong in rural areas. We think about most social violence being urban, but there is a rural violence that has some social respectability, and the Nazis gave this to the countryside. Second, it was always strong among the *Freikorpen*, or "free corps," those independent military units fighting an undeclared war against the new Polish state over on the eastern frontier from 1918 to 1920. Ernst Roehm, Hitler's commander of the brown-shirted Nazi street army called the S.A. (*Sturm Abteilung*, Storm Troop), was of this connection. Roehm both recruited Freikorp veterans into the Nazi Party and ensured that the Bavarian wing of the German army looked on the Party with a benevolent eye. Third, the Nazi party was always strong with the *déclassé*—those white collar workers being pushed down into blue-collar ranks by the great Inflation. Fourth, it attracted social radicals of the right, labor organizers who were also superpatriots. The Strasser brothers Otto and Gregor were of this persuasion, as was their lieutenant Josef Goebbels, who eventually deserted them for Hitler. Fifth, there were traditional intellectuals, such as Alfred Rosenberg, who wrote the *Myth of the Twentieth Century* which synthesized a century's worth of racist literature. In terms of individuals, perhaps the single biggest catch of the early Nazi party was Hermann Goering, greatest living German war ace, successor to the famed Red Baron. By career and marriage he had access to the wealthy and the well connected, and he had tremendous organizing ability.

Beer hall putsch

By early November of 1923 the inflation had taken a catastrophic toll on German society. When the German government defaulted on its payments earlier that year, the French had militarily seized the industrial Ruhr valley in retaliation. In sharp disagreement with the national government in Berlin, the state of Bavaria—under the ministry of Gustav von Kahr with support from the Bavarian branch of the Germany army under General Otto von Lossow—had all but broken with the national government and army headquarters. Von Lossow was close to Ernst Roehm of the Nazi S.A., who had been on his staff. Earlier Kahr, von Lossow, and the head of Bavarian state police Hans von Seisser had had some negotiations with Hitler from the NSDAP and with other right-wing nationalist parties about launching a takeover of the government, starting in Munich and heading to Berlin. Apparently the firmness with which German army headquarters replied to their feelers gave Kahr and von Lossow, at least, cold feet about it. Hitler sensed this, and decided to force their hand.

For November 8, Minister Kahr had organized a great patriotic celebration in the *Burgerbräukeller*, the big Citizen's Beer Hall somewhat southeast of the center of Munich, across the river Isar.[GE92] Most socially or politically prominent people from the city were there. Hitler, as leader of the small and almost completely Bavarian NSDAP, stopped the proceedings by firing a pistol at the ceiling, and asked for attention—which of course he got. He was leading a revolt against the government, he said, beginning with Munich. He claimed that the hall was surrounded by machine-gun carrying S.A., and asked everyone except Kahr, von Lossow and von Seisser to remain seated. These three were to accompany him outside, where while waving a pistol like a madman he explained his plans for a *putsch* (attempted takeover of state) to them. Meanwhile Hitler had sent a car off to fetch the famous World War I General Erich Ludendorff, whose friendship he had carefully cultivated, and who indeed joined them. They all verbally agreed, although Ludendorff—out of power since 1918— was apparently the only one to mean it. As soon as the active civic and army leaders were out of Hitler's sight, none of them replied to messages he sent.

By the next morning, Ernst Roehm and his troops were in occupation of the War Ministry on the Odeonsplatz, but were surrounded by troops loyal to the government. Ludendorff convinced Hitler they could salvage the situation by marching through the center of town to Odeonsplatz (Ludendorff was convinced that when the army saw him, it would answer to his commands, as of old). So Hitler, Ludendorff and company marched from the Burgerbräukeller, over the bridge to the Marienplatz where City Hall stood[GE93], and there turned right on

92. GE Layer 92 is a Placemark locating the Burgerbräukeller.
93. GE Layer 93 is a Placemark locating "New Town Hall" on Marienplatz.

the narrow street that led to Odeonsplatz a few blocks away.[GE[94]] There they found the police ranged across the end of the narrow street, barring their way onto the open plaza. Although Nazi forces were hundreds strong, they could not bring much of that power to bear in the narrow street. When shooting started, sixteen Nazis and three policemen were killed and the remaining Nazis scrambled for cover. Goering was seriously wounded. Hitler escaped briefly, with a dislocated shoulder. Ludendorff alone never broke stride—his famous person was untouched—and he pushed through the police to the square. It was as if General Eisenhower had joined a protest march in the first few years after World War II—what American police force would have shot at him?

But the putsch was broken, and the survivors, including Hitler, were rounded up and put on trial for treason. It was one of the biggest single happenings in the first five years of the Weimar Republic, next to the general inflation which triggered it. Every major German paper had a correspondent there.

It helps explain the verdict to know that, when the 1918 revolution had ended imperial Germany and established the Weimar Republic, the court system had remained essentially unchanged. These old imperial judges tended to be harsh on left-wingers and lenient on right-wingers. General Ludendorff, guilty of treason by any reasonable standard, was immediately acquitted. Hitler was smaller fry and anyway had obviously started the whole thing, so he would not be acquitted. The judge, though, gave Hitler freedom for several days to tell his side of things. It was priceless publicity: Jews are behind the banks; Jews are behind the Communists; Liberals sold out the German war effort; if Germans simply willed it, they could do what no economic expert believed possible; the Leader rises from the folk and presents himself to the people not through the ballot box but through force of will . . . . Hitler did, however, make one concession. He told the judge that although he did not believe in a Liberal, parliamentary state, that he would work legally to get 50 percent of the vote and then legally change the state. He was given a five-year sentence of which he served less than a year (at Landsberg prison about thirty miles west of Munich.[GE[95]]) Here he wrote *Mein Kampf* (*My Struggle*)—part autobiography, part the rawest and most naive kind of racism, and part the most devastating critique of the weaknesses of the democratic state of modern times and how to exploit those weaknesses.

When Hitler got out of jail in December of 1924, better economic times were upon Germany. In good times everywhere, middle of the road parties grow and extremist parties of left and right shrink: you don't need extreme answers because middle-of-the-road answers are working well. Hitler desperately tried to hold the party together, predicting a new inflation, but the Nazi party all but disappeared. It was only saved by the Depression. In hard times, conversely, middle of the road parties shrink and extremist parties grow, because middle-of-the-road answers are not working anymore.

In September 1930, in the first major German elections of the Depression, the Nazi Party jumped from a tiny south German party to the second biggest in Germany. By 1931 it was single largest, and in early 1932 it got 44 percent of the vote, a huge percentage in such a multi-party system. Hitler was the first major European politician to campaign by airplane, dramatically descending through thunderstorms in a silver Ford Tri-motor. Nazi poster art surpassed even that of the Bolsheviks. Their use of the brand-new radio was superb. To the ordinary citizen, it seemed that a war for the streets was going on between Communists and extreme Nationalists, and of the two, the Nationalists were preferable because at least they were patriotic. And Hitler's was one of the few self-confident voices left in all of Germany.

On into 1932, however, Nazi voting strength dropped a few points: they had saturated their market, and were evidently never going to get to the magic 50 percent. The S.A., several hundred thousand strong to the official German army's one hundred thousand, more and more strongly pressed Hitler for a new putsch. He resisted, but had nothing to show for all his electoral success. This was the setting for a devious but strictly legal backroom political deal.

No regular parliamentary government had been possible since the Depression hit. Conventional economic wisdom of the time was to cut governmental expenditures and balance the budget, and the SPD, speaking for workers, simply could not agree. President Hindenburg, now in his eighties, had ruled for four years, year after year, by emergency degree, and he looked for some sort of consensus with increasing anxiety. At this point clever leaders of the small Catholic Center party offered Hitler a deal. If he would join them in a center-right

94. GE Layer 94 is a Path showing the route of the march in red.
95. GE Layer 95 is a Placemark framing a view of Landsberg prison, still a functioning prison today.

coalition, he could have the Chancellorship while they and their allies kept a voting majority of the eleven-member cabinet; that is, they would give him the symbol of power but keep real power themselves, and mostly with his voting strength among the electorate. Desperate for something to show, Hitler agreed. On January 30, 1933, the new government was sworn in, and a parade was held through downtown Berlin on the main boulevard, *Unter den Linden* ("Under the Basswoods")[GE⁹⁶] to celebrate. The parade psychologically undermined both von Hindenburg and the Catholic Center representatives. Nazis came to celebrate from all over Germany, by train, car, bike, on foot. Their brown-shirted S.A. units marched by all afternoon, through dusk, and then into dark carrying torches. President von Hindenburg had looked for the voice of Germany all through the Depression, and here it apparently was, wearing brown shirts. He had never liked Hitler, but after the emotional experience of "the Torchlight Parade," neither he nor the Catholic Center party put up any resistance to Hitler's assumption of real power.

The Third Reich

Four weeks later, on February 27, the Reichstag—the German equivalent of our Capitol building—burned. [GE⁹⁷] Possibly a Nazi plan all along, it was pinned on an itinerant Communist, and in the emotional backlash that followed Communists were banned from the Reichstag. The Nazi Party and its allies were now more than 50 percent in the remaining legislature, and on March 24 in the Enabling Act the Chancellor was voted special emergency powers—the essential legal foundation of the Third Reich. Do you believe in obeying the law, all times, all places? Hitler came to power legally.

Are you proud of your country's "heritage"? The Nazis made an art of celebrating Germany's (with their own racist twist on it, of course). Folklore was declared a science, and pushed in the school system from universities on down as Folk Sociology, Folk History, Folk Geopolitics, etc. "Nationality and Homeland" courses were integrated into the national curriculum. It was as if "Turnvater" Jahn's 1810 wish, that "We should consider what a university can do for folklore, and that it may be built on folklore," was coming true.[21]

Political scientists tell us that in elections economic issues are most often paramount: we tend "to vote our pocketbooks." Do you vote your pocketbook? You might have voted for Hitler. Hjalmar Schacht, his economic wizard, turned Germany into a hothouse economy, saying that all trade and currency transfers with the outside world would be carefully managed by the government. When the government said the German mark was worth so much, it was; no foreign exchange would have a say. Unemployed people were put to dignified, paid work, primarily on the world's first superhighways, the *Autobahnen*. These four-lane, divided highways were laid out with military strategy in mind (the U.S. interstate system, incidentally, is named the Eisenhower system because as a general in WW II he was so impressed with the German system that he worked to build one here when he was President). The original German superhighways were not made of ordinary asphalt paving, though the Germans were as modern as anyone in technology; their foundations were lengths of cobblestone, set almost vertically side by side. It absorbed a lot of labor to chip out the needed millions of such blocks.

Almost no one in the Depression could afford a car. Car sales in 1929 were not matched again in industrial countries until 1949 or thereabouts. So Hitler set Ferdinand Porsche, the most famous automotive designer in Germany, to work on the world's finest mass-produced car. Just put five marks away each week, the German workers were told, and in four years each family will have a "Volkswagen." As it happened in fact, war production stole most of those promised cars, but confidence in their delivery was great. Every time you see one on the road, you ought to remember that—a Wagon of the Folk, state of the art, still a testimonial to the economic and psychological success of the Third Reich.

In 1936 the Olympics were held in Berlin.[GE⁹⁸] Former millionaires were still selling apples on the streets in New York and Paris, but Berlin was clean, new, and bustling with full employment. The Germans

---

96. GE Layer 96 is a Placemark located at the crossing of Unter den Linden and Wilhelmstrasse, where many government buildings were located. The view as framed shows some of the Tiergarten, Berlin's great park, the Brandenburg Gate (*Brandenburger Tor*) where the main road across the park enters the city and becomes Unter den Linden.

97. GE Layer 97 is a Placemark referencing the Reichstag building, just north of the Brandenburg Gate.

98. GE Layer 98 is a Folder titled "Berlin Olympics 1936." Its Placemarks reference the Olympic Stadium on the west side of Berlin, and the Olympic Village at Elstal, another fifteen miles west.

in their newfound confidence won their own Olympics. Not every event, mind you—Jesse Owens, an African-American and so not exactly your Aryan stereotype, won four gold medals in the running events—but that was an exception in what was generally a German gold medal parade. Are you proud of your nation's sports victories? You might have liked Hitler.

Second only to our pocketbooks in the way we vote, we are told, is how successful we feel our country has been in foreign affairs. Hitler inherited a Germany hobbled by the restrictions of the Versailles Treaty, with part of its west still occupied by the French, and with union with German Austria forbidden. He immediately rejected these military restrictions. He put Goering in charge of creating from scratch the German *Luftwaffe*, an air force that by 1939 would be the single best in the world. Army and navy construction was also resumed without regard to Versailles Treaty limitations. No allied action was taken in response.

In 1936 Hitler assembled the German army staff and told them the German army was going to march into the French-occupied Rhineland. The generals were horrified, knowing Germany was not yet prepared for a war and afraid of French resistance. Hitler, with his "sleep-walker's intuition," assured them the French would withdraw rather than fight. Indeed they did, and German generals never seriously resisted Hitler again. In the spring of 1938 Hitler added Austria to Germany. In September of that same year he blew up an international controversy over the Sudetenland, that strip of mostly German population in the mountainous frontier territories of Czechoslovakia. The major leaders of Western Europe agreed to come to an international conference at Munich, Hitler's home turf. Hoping to stave off war; they agreed to give Germany the Sudetenland, which included all of the natural defenses of the Czechoslovak state.[G99] Prime Minister Neville Chamberlain proudly proclaimed on his return to Britain that appeasement had achieved "peace in our time." The next spring Hitler simply took the rest of Czechoslovakia, showing that appeasement had achieved nothing. In the fall of 1939 he split Poland with Russia. Britain and France finally declared war but did nothing for six months; pundits called this the "sitzkrieg," in sarcastic comparison to the German "blitzkrieg" in Poland. Then in May 1940 one German army was left in front of the supposedly impregnable Maginot Line[GE100] as a decoy, while a second army swung north around it, through the Netherlands and Belgium in a newer, more successful version of the Schlieffen plan of World War I. France fell in six weeks, while the British evacuated what they could of their trapped army from the beaches at Dunkirk.[GE101] Then Hitler turned Goering's spectacular new air force (*Luftwaffe*) loose on Britain to soften it up for invasion. Do you find satisfaction in the successful activity of your country in foreign affairs? You might have liked Hitler, at least until World War II turned sour for Germany (when the British won that air war called "The Battle of Britain"; when the Japanese bombed Pearl Harbor and the U.S. joined the war; and especially when Operation Barbarossa, the surprise German invasion of Russia that had been launched on June 22, 1941, eventually stalled out before Stalingrad[GE102] by late 1942; and at the tank battle of Kursk in July of 1943[GE103], after which Russian units took the offensive away from the Germans).

The Nazis paid incredible attention to detail. The S.A. dagger was modeled on a Black Forest huntsman's knife from centuries back, elegant in looks, efficient in action. The Nazi party anthem, the *Horst Wessel* Song, was good marching music even by German standards. The Nazis, especially German officers, survive in American T.V. sitcoms and some old American movies as rigid buffoons; in fact they were so inspired and disciplined that they came perilously close to taking over the world.

After you have understood the enormous popularity of Hitler from the resurrection of the economy, the rejection of Versailles Treaty restrictions, the sports glories of the Berlin Olympics, the general celebration of German-ness, and what seemed to be a new era of law and order, however, a disturbing chant still ought to

---

99. GE Layer 99 is a Folder titled "Czechoslovakia: Munich Conference"; it includes three Polygons: the outline of 1938 Czechoslovakia, the area of the "Sudetenland" taken from western Czechoslovakia by Germany, and the area of eastern Czechoslovakia taken by Hungary. All in all, about half the original country, and almost all the mountain frontier defenses.

100. GE Layer 100 is a Path showing the most heavily fortified section of France's famous Maginot Line.

101. GE Layer 101 is a Placemark referencing Dunkirk.

102. GE Layer 100 is a Placemark referencing the Battle of Stalingrad, today's Volvograd. This battle, along with Kursk, will be covered in more detail in the chapter to follow.

103. GE Layer 101 is a Placemark referencing the Battle of Kursk.

remain in your mind: Dachau, Auschwitz, Buchenwald, Bergen-Belsen, Theresienstadt . . . the concentration camps, the annihilation camps. Hitler aimed to purge society of Jews, Gypsies, those with mental illness, those with genetic physical disorders, and homosexuals. Six million of Europe's nine million Jews were executed outright, or starved or beaten or worked to death. We know their hometowns and almost all their names. We have photographs taken by American soldiers who first entered the camps. We have captured Nazi film of some of the mass executions. We have powerful eyewitness accounts from survivors, from Elie Wiesel's *Night* to Victor Frankl's *Man's Search for Meaning.* People who insist this massacre of six million is untrue are as irrational as those who think the moon landings were faked in Arizona. There is even some evidence that Hitler's invasion of eastern Europe and the Soviet Union was planned first to destroy the large communities of Jews there, and only second to defeat the Soviet Union and get more *Lebensraum,* living room, for the German people. When it was a question of a military train going to the German army proper, or to one of the *Einsatzgruppen* ("Commando Groups") [GE104] charged with rounding up and disposing of Jews, it was more often the *Einsatzgruppe* that got the train, for example.[22]

After the war, it was difficult to find Germans who knew about the concentration camps. Those were secret wartime things, they said; we civilians never knew. But the camp system existed in embryo by 1937. By the laws of the Third Reich every citizen had to do an official genealogy: if a single one of your four grandparents was identifiably Jewish, you were by definition Jewish. Jewish families tended to disappear from your street suddenly, after visits from the State Police, the Gestapo. At Dachau,[GE105] a village so close to Munich it almost qualifies as a suburb, trains jammed with people rolled in every day, and empty ones rolled out. How could people not see what was happening? Apparently there was a psychological "not-seeing." If you ever allowed yourself to be conscious of exactly what was happening, you had a choice: you could protest and you and your family would be hauled off to join them, or you could admit that you were a coward without the courage of your convictions, not a pleasant way to live. With such alternatives, it was easier never to allow yourself to become conscious of what was clearly going on around you.

Philosophical asides

Well into the twenty-first century the modern world is still trying to come to grips with the enormity of the Holocaust of the mid-twentieth. Is civilization such a thin veneer that it can be so easily stripped off and the savage animal unmasked?

It is easy for non-Germans to criticize Germans for the Holocaust. Except for about three factors, however—Germany's strong military tradition of obedience to authority, its lack of clear and firm physical borders, and of course the cult of the Germanic folk—there are enough strong parallels between Germany and the U.S. to give an American reader pause for reflection. Both nations traditionally prided themselves on a mainstream Christian tradition. Both were proud of their technological developments and their industrial strength. Both had confidence that they were states where the great majority believed in rule by law. Both were proud of their higher culture in the arts and literature, which were especially strong in Germany. Given loss of a major war and then a buffeting by huge Inflation in addition to our Depression, perhaps we too could have accepted a Nazi government? As a society we seem warned against the extremes of socialism on the left, but perhaps we need to warn ourselves about the extremes of racism and integral nationalism on the right as well. Hitler himself saw our potential; he was an admirer of how thoroughly we had killed off the native Indians here for our own *Lebensraum.*

Are present-day Germans still to blame for the Holocaust, even though most of them were born since 1945? This author would argue that the question is analogous to asking whether present-day whites in America are

104. GE Layer 104 is a Folder titled "Einsatzgruppen, 1941–42." Inside are four Polygon layers, one for the branched path taken by each of the four main Einsatzgruppen, in the wake of the German army advance. The map is adapted from Lucy Dawidowicz, *The War Against the Jews, 1933–1945* (NY: Holt, Rinehart & Winston, 1975), p. 161 "The Einsatzgruppen, 1941–1942."

105. GE Layer 105 is a Placemark referencing the main gates of Dachau. Most of the Panoramio icons under the Pushpin pointer are of the main gates, with their infamous motto *"Arbeit macht frei,"* "Work makes free." Cluster of icons at top left of this view are of the crematorium.

still responsible for black slavery. My answer is that for almost all of us, no, not directly, but we ought to treat it like a family history of a certain kind of cancer: we have cultural tendencies this way and need regular check-ups of society and the body politic to make sure it hasn't recurred. So ought Germans, about the Holocaust.

Germans were so burned by the superpatriotism of the Hitler era that they are as cautious of it now as the Japanese are of nuclear weapons. You hardly see a German flag in Germany today (in considerable contrast to the post 9/11 United States, where the American flag is everywhere)—except when Germany is playing in world cup soccer, and then the German flag has no more political significance than the flag of St. George that blossoms in England during that same world's cup. In 2001 an American undergraduate student who had been studying language in a western German town joined the author's travel/study course in Berlin and environs, and told this story. Staying with a German family, she had sewed a small German flag on her backpack to express solidarity with her host country. Her warm and loving *Hausmütter* took her aside and asked her to take it off, with a "We don't do that here nowadays."

Friedrich Meinecke's look back

Just after World War II, a famous, elderly German historian named Friedrich Meinecke sat down to ponder what had gone wrong with his country—a country that had produced such high culture, that had been so concerned with human liberty, and that had been so advanced scientifically. He was eighty-four years old, living in a bombed-out, occupied Germany that was being torn in two between the U.S.S.R. and the western allies. His eyes were so bad that he could not do any new reading or research, but his memory was still sharp and the patterns of German history during his own life haunted him.

Think what he had lived through. Born in 1862, as a boy of eight he might have seen victorious troops marching back from France. As a young man he had been educated in Bismarck's Germany that dominated world diplomacy. His maturity had coincided with the enormous German growth in commerce and industry. As a mature historian he must have kept one eye on domestic issues such as the huge socialist party and on Germany's "place in the sun" foreign policy. He must have shared the short-lived but intense national unity when war was declared in 1914. He saw the "stab-in-the-back" theory invented by the right wing to escape responsibility for the war's loss. He had despaired over the shallow and selfish political maneuvering of the Weimar Republic, had seen it buffeted by the Inflation and then the Depression. He was horrified when Adolf Hitler came to power in 1933, and lost his job of forty years' standing of editing Germany's foremost historical journal. He had felt the repressive terror of Nazi rule gradually screwed down on the country, and then as an old man had suffered physically and emotionally during World War II (he had known General Beck who tried to assassinate Hitler in the bunker in 1944 and in fact had gotten hints of what was going to be attempted).

So what had gone wrong with his beloved Germany? In nineteenth-century Europe, said Meinecke, there arose two giant new ideological waves. The first was when people pushed toward democracy and then beyond that, in order to protect their standard of living, into socialism. The heaven-on-earth that socialism promised through revolution began to eclipse the goals of traditional high culture in the realm of art, literature, and the intellect generally. The second and even stronger wave was nationalism. It too had its origins in Liberalism, originally aiming to give individuals of oppressed ethnic groups their freedom. The desire for political power, however, gradually became its main motivating force, and extreme nationalism was as hostile to the goals of traditional high culture as was extreme socialism. These two waves flooded crossways, and where they crossed as nationalism-plus-socialism they sent up a tremendous peak that flooded everything around it. It is clearly there, coming first in the full name of the Nazi Party, a reader of Meinecke suddenly realizes: *National-Sozial-istische Deutsche Arbeiter-Partei.*

These waves were not uniquely German, of course, observed Meinecke, but Germany did have special susceptibilities to them. One factor was the old Prussian military tradition with its ideal of self-sacrifice paired with blind obedience. Bismarck's "blood and iron" solution later built on that, and Germany was well on its way towards the victory of Machiavellism and "might makes right" over morality and justice in foreign affairs, and towards the fading of higher culture in the striving for power. Second, said Meinecke, in a healthy individual or nation there needs to be a balance between reason and emotion. The modern age, especially in Germany, stamped such a rational, mechanistic character on the lives of its engineers and other university specialists that in middle age their starved emotional side tended to clutch about "wildly and intemperately" for a cause, any cause. Finally, in Germany in the nineteenth century the old ethical ties associated with family, custom, social class, and perhaps church had eroded, and nothing had filled that void. Middle class nationalism and working class socialism were hostile camps. In this context Hitler's idea of a folk community that did not depend on one camp destroying the other, but that claimed it could steer them around and educate them "to serve a community which included them all," was frankly very attractive to many Germans.

What then should a German in 1946 do or think? Remember the higher culture, said an older and wiser Meinecke; listen to the great German composers and read to each other the great German poets, and try to resurrect the old liberating themes that were once important threads of German history and that might be so again.[23]

From Napoleonic occupation, to a world superpower first under Bismarck and again under Hitler, then back to ruin and occupation—so did Fichte's 1808 wish for a "new binding tie" play out in the fantastic drama of modern German history. In many ways the explosive power of cultural nationalism in modern Germany is a good model for what happens in much of the rest of the modern world, as you'll see as you read more of this textbook. Just remember the progression: (1) identifiable cultural group; (2) negative stimulus; (3) cultural nationalism; (4) political nationalism; and (5) integral nationalism.

Endnotes

1. Johann Gottlieb Fichte, *Addresses to the German Nation.* Trans. R. A. Jones, G. H. Turnbull. (Westport, CN: Greenwood Press, 1922 (reprint 1979), p. 11.

2. From *Denkwurdigkeiten des Staatskanzlers Hardenberg*, ed. by L. von Ranke, 5 vols (Leipzig, 1877), IV, appendix, 7–9, as quoted in Geoffrey Bruun, *Europe and the French Imperium 1799–1814* (NY & London: Harper & Bros. Publishers, 1938), p. 174.

3. A reader can call up a version of "The Juniper Tree" at the following website: http://www.pitt.edu/~dash/grimm047.html

4. The author ought to confess at some point that, having been impressed by Bruno Bettelheim's argument in *The Use of Enchantment: The Meaning and Importance of Fairy Tales* (that traditional folktales help child work through the psychological problems of growing up through a powerful but non-adult logic); he read Grimms' tales to his own children.

5 Johann Gottfried von Herder, *Reflections on the Philosophy of the History of Mankind.* Abridged and with Introduction by Frank E. Manuel. (Chicago & London: University of Chicago Press, 1968.) See p. 45 for the "national fictions spring from verbal communications" passage, and p. 144 for Jews as "parasitical plants" passage.

6. Fichte, *Addresses to the German Nation*; see p. 138 for love of fatherland as supreme authority; p. 215 for separate language equaling separate nation that deserves independence; and pp. 268–69 for the "if you go under, all humanity goes under with you" passage.

7. Golo Mann, *The History of Germany Since 1789*, trans. from the German by Marian Jackson (NY: Praeger, 1968), p. 58. The author has tried to find another reliable record of this quotation and has failed; he includes it here on the shaky grounds that it's too good not to use.

8. As quoted in Matthew Bernard Levinger, *Enlightened Nationalism: The Transformation of Prussian Political Culture 1806–1848* (Oxford and New York: Oxford University Press, 2000), p. 106.

9. Karl von Savigny, *The Vocation of Our Age for Legislation and Jurisprudence* (Legal Classics Library, Div. of Gryphon Editions, Ltd., Special Edition, 1986), p. 27.

10. Murray B. Peppard, *Paths Through the Forest: A Biography of the Brothers Grimm* (New York: Holt, Rinehart and Winston, 1971), p. 25.

11. As quoted in Peppard, pp. 53–54.

12. Jacob Grimm, *Teutonic Mythology.* Vol. III, p. lv. (Gloucester MS: Peter Smith, 1976).

13. "Björketorp Stone." *Encyclopedia Britannica,* 2008. Encylopedia Britannica Online.

14. From an 1856 volume of annotations by Wilhelm Grimm, as quoted in Peppard (p. 50).

15. See Christa Kamenetsky's *The Brothers Grimm and Their Critics: Folktales and the Quest for Meaning* (Athens: Ohio University Press, 1992), a newer and more scholarly work than Peppard.

16. Stuart Piggott, *Prehistoric India to 1000 B.C.* (London: Cassell & Co., 1962), p. 248.

17. Jacob Grimm, *Teutonic Mythology.* Translated from the Fourth Edition by James Steven Stallybrass, in four volumes. (Gloucester, MA: Peter Smith, 1976.) In this edition, chapter XVII on "Wights and Elves" is the first chapter of volume II.

18. Richard Wagner, *My Life.* Andrew Gray, Trans., Mary Whittal, Ed. (Cambridge: Cambridge University Press, 1983), pp. 259–260. Originally published in German as *Mein Leben* (Munich: Paul List Verlag, 1963).

19. Friedrich List, *The National System of Political Economy.* Trans. Sampson S. Lloyd, with an Introduction by J. Shield Nicholson. (London: Longmans, Green and Co., 1922. The "Nationality and the Economy of the Nation" chapter, XV, begins on p. 141, where the "Between each individual and entire humanity" passage. The rightful inclusion of Holland and Denmark in a German state argument is on p. 143. E-version at the following website: http://oll.libertyfund.org/titles/list-the-national-system-of-political-economy. In Table of Contents click on Chapter XV: Nationality and the Economy of the Nation, and see second paragraph.

20. Adolf Hitler, *Mein Kampf* (Trans. Ralph Manheim; Boston: Houghton Mifflin Co., 1943), pp. 204–5.

21. See Christa Kamenetsky, "Folklore as a Political Tool in Nazi Germany," *Journal of American Folklore,* vol. 85, no. 337 (Jul.–Sept., 1972), pp. 224–25.

22. Lucy S. Dawidowicz, *The War Against the Jews, 1933–1945* (NY: Holt, Rinehart & Winston, 1975). Map of routes of Einsatzgruppen is on p. 126; commentary on who got the transport on pp. 140–44.

23. Friedrich Meinecke, *The German Catastrophe: Reflections and Recollections.* Trans. Sidney B. Fay. (Boston: Beacon Press, 1963; first published by Harvard University Press).

"The Socialist Fatherland": Socialism in Russia

"The socialist fatherland is in danger! Long live the socialist fatherland! Long live the International socialist revolution!"

(written by Lenin for the Council of People's Commissars, Feb. 21, 1918, to counter renewed German invasion towards end of WW I)[1]

"It is *we*, not our enemies [the Hitlerites], who are the real nationalists . . . exterminate every single German who has set his invading foot on the territory of our Fatherland."

(lines from a speech by Stalin during the battle for Moscow, WW II)[2]

CONTENTS

The heart of the matter—Introduction to the Russian language—Topography and texture of the land—Kievan Russia—The rise of Muscovy—The Romanov dynasty—Imperial Russia—*Natasha's Dance*: Romantic nationalism in Russia in the nineteenth century—Meanwhile, Western and Central European socialism—Herzen and the birth of *narodnichestvo*—The Reform Era of Alexander II—"What is to be done?"—Reaction and Russification—Karl Marx—Classical Marxism—Its strengths—Its weaknesses—The first Russian Marxists—Nicholas II—Lenin and the St. Petersburg Group—The "short, victorious war" and the Revolution of 1905—Stolypin's necktie, and his "wager on the strong"—Russia's side of World War I—The March (February, old-style) Revolution, 1917—The Dual Government—The "Great October Revolution"—R.S.F.S.R. and SOVNARKOM—War Communism—*The ABCs of Communism*—The NEP—Stalin's power base—Collectivization and industrialization—Kirov's assassination and the purges—Stalin and Hitler—World War II—Tehran, Yalta, and Potsdam—Beginnings of the Cold War—Korean War—Solzhenitsyn's judgment—The succession; Khrushchev—Cold War in Africa, beginning with Ghana—Cold War in the Mideast, beginning with Egypt—Cold War in Southeast and South Asia, beginning with Vietnam—Cold War in Latin America, beginning with Cuba—The Soviet system stagnates—Czechoslovakia, Poland, and Afghanistan—Gorbachev: the system dismantled—Failure of the August Coup—End of the Cold War—Lessons learned

The heart of the matter

After cultural nationalism and political nationalism, socialism is arguably the third most powerful ideology that has shaped the modern world. The Marxist school of socialism in particular, with its conscious analysis of the relationship between society, economics, and politics (and its subconscious emotional appeal), transformed the crumbling Russian Empire into the powerful Soviet Union, and the weak and corrupt Chinese Republic into the powerful Peoples Republic of China. By 1950 these two revived world powers allied in a bloc antagonistic to the United States, the one industrial power that had survived World War II with its industry intact. The confrontation between the U.S. and its allies and the two Communist giants and their allies was then the dominant political and military fact in the world. The Korean War (which we "drew" with the Soviet- and Chinese-backed North Koreans) was fought in this context. And even though the monolithic Communist bloc only lasted a decade, the Vietnam War (which we lost to the Soviet-backed Vietnamese) and the Afghanistan War (which the Soviet Union lost to the Afghanis and their supporters we backed) were all fought in this dualistic setting of Western democracies versus Communist states. Even today, with the Soviet Union long disbanded and "to get rich is glorious" an accepted government policy in "Communist" China, Marxism is still important for any serious student of modern world history to understand.

To put a face on it, as well as to extend our look at basic European political developments from World War II on up to 1991 when the Soviet Union dissolved, let's look at Russia—not just today's Russian state but the greater "Russia" of the Russian Empire and the Soviet Union. As usual, we'll start with a short introduction to language and the topography and texture of the land, and then the sweep of Russian history up into the nineteenth century. At that point we'll break and look at socialism—particularly Marxism—as it developed in central and western Europe and as currents of it came into Russia. From that point on, we'll trace that two-stranded braid—socialism and nationalism in Russian history—on down to 1991. Elements of socialism in general and Marxism in particular will crop up in the following three chapters on smaller European case studies of national development, and along most of our seven "world regional corridors" studies that constitute the last half of the book. Chapter 13 in particular, on China's Yangtze Valley corridor, will deal in some detail with China's Marxist transformation. But first comes Russia and the Soviet Union.

Introduction to the Russian language

Russian is in the Slavic language group, which itself is one of the main subdivisions of the Indo-European language family that includes English. Slavic languages are usually divided into West Slavic (Czech, Slovak, and Polish are the big ones), South Slavic (Bulgarian and all the languages of the former Yugoslavia—which translates literally "South Slavia"—including Slovenian, Croatian, Bosnian, Serbian, and Macedonian), and East Slavic (Russian, Belorussian or White Russian, and Ukrainian). As spoken languages go, the Slavic languages are even closer to each other than Romance languages are, but they are divided between two scripts—the Latin alphabet and Cyrillic alphabet. West Slavs use the former, East Slavs use the latter, and the South Slavs are split between the two. Historically this reflects the division between Roman Catholic and Greek Orthodox influences: the Latin alphabet was associated with the Catholic Church, and the Cyrillic alphabet was actually invented in the Greek Orthodox Church's missionary work among the Slavs. Saint Cyril, for whom Cyrillic is named, worked in the 800s in what is today the Czech Republic. The Greek-based alphabet he devised for Slavic speakers spread east, generally accompanying the conversion of East and Southeast Slavic peoples to Orthodox Christianity. Interestingly enough, the word "Slavic" is probably based on the basic word in Slavic languages for "word" (*slovo* in Russian, for example). It meant those who used intelligible words, versus those others who used words impossible to understand (*nemets*), so *Nemtsy* was ever after the Russian word for Germans, the major foreign language group immediately to the west of the Slavs.

The standard Cyrillic alphabet used in Russian, the Slavic language spoken by more people than any other, has thirty-two letters. It has more than in our Latin alphabet in part because of several single letters representing what for us are consonant combinations (one letter each for CH, ZH, KH, TS, and such), and because it has not one but two sets of vowels, hard and soft. Many Cyrillic letters are obviously drawn from Greek. A few are identical or similar to Latin letters, but beware of a handful of *faux amis*, false friends—letters that may look like Latin letters but are something different. Here's a quick run-through of the Cyrillic alphabet:

А, а (English equivalent A, pronounced ah)
Б, б (B—looking somewhat like the B in our alphabet, and coming where it should in the alphabet)
В, в (V—the first of our "faux amis," looking exactly like our B)
Г, г (G, the Greek *gamma,* Γ)
Д, д (D, a fancy version of the Greek *delta,* Δ)

Е, е (much like its Latin equivalent, E, though pronounced "Yeh," not "Eh")

Ё, ё (not counted as a separate letter, but when written with the two dots, pronounced "Yoh")

Ж, ж (ZH, the first of what would be in the Latin alphabet a consonant combination)

З, з (Z, though the capital letter in Cyrillic looks like the lowercase cursive z in the Latin alphabet)

И, и (I, though pronounced EE, as in many European languages)

Й, й ("short I," ending syllables as does the "y" in "boy")

К, к (like the Latin K)

Л, л (L, a variation on the Greek *lambda*, Λ)

М, м (like the Latin M)

Н, н (N, the second of our "faux amis"; Russian has no H at all)

О, о (O; when stressed, like long O; when unstressed, more like UH)

П, п (P, the Greek *pi*, Π)

Р, р (R, the Greek *rho*, P—a third false friend)

С, с (always pronounced S, a fourth false friend)

Т, т (T, as in Latin and Greek alphabets)

У, у (U, pronounced OO, from the Greek *upsilon*, Y; a fifth false friend)

Ф, ф (F, simply the Greek *phi*, Φ)

Х, х (a gutteral KH, which we don't really have in Latin, from the Greek *chi*, X)

Ц, ц (TS, another consonant combination)

Ч, ч (CH, another consonant combination)

Ш, ш (SH, probably from the Hebrew, ש)

Щ, щ (SHCH, as if one said "plush chair" and abstracted the middle sound)

Ъ, ъ (hard sign; not a letter at all, but indicating that the consonant before it is a "hard" one)

Ы, ы (another I, though a "hard" I—see list of vowels below)

Ь, ь (soft sign; again, not a sounding letter, but indicating that the consonant before it is "soft")

Э, э (another E, but pronounced "Eh")

Ю, ю (another U, but pronounced "You")

Я, я (another A, but pronounced "Yah")

There are enough *faux amis* to make whole fake words. American tourists in Russia who have not learned the Cyrillic alphabet pronounce *РЕСТОРАН* the way it looks, whereas those who have spent a couple of hours learning the Cyrillic alphabet know to transliterate it as "*RESTORAN*," obviously "restaurant," from the French (the three vowels all work, but all of the consonants except the T are false friends).

It may look confusing at first, but one way to simplify it is to see that there are two sets of vowels, one hard and one soft. The soft ones are palatalized, the tongue squeezed up against the palate to give them an initial "Y" sound.

Hard vowel:	Soft vowel:
А (ah)	Я (yah)
Э (eh)	Е (yeh)
Ы (yerry)	И (yee)
О (oh)	(Ё) (yoh)
У (oo)	Ю (you)

The Ы (yerry) vowel is the only one that has no real equivalent in English; it's almost as if you shaped your mouth for "U" and tried to say "EE," or started off saying "UH" and wound up with "EE." The soft sign ь palatalizes the consonant before it, and is usually transliterated as an apostrophe. The word usually transliterated into English as "Tsar" and into French as "Czar" is in the original Cyrillic Царь (tsar'), the soft sign telling you to flatten that R out against the palate instead of making it with the tip of the tongue.

One incentive for memorizing the Cyrillic alphabet is that it immediately gives you a two- to three-thousand word vocabulary in Russian. A few are basic Indo-European cognates, as in *брат* (BRAHT) = brother and *сестра* (ses-TRAH) = sister. Many others are either Greek-based words common to both English and Russia, or loan words from central and western Europe that came in over the centuries—*музыка* ("musika" = music), *физика* ("fizika" = physics), *гэография* ("geografia" = geography), *парк* ("park" = park), *фонтан* ("fontan" = fountain).

With the Cyrillic alphabet in hand you can not only look words up in a Russian-English dictionary, but solve the old problem of whether the traditional capital of Russia is pronounced Mos-COH or Mos-COW. The answer is neither. The Cyrillic spelling is *Москва*, with emphasis on the last syllable, which sounds something like "musk-VAH" (unaccented O is more like an UH). When it came west into German in the late Middle Ages, the V and the U were fairly interchangeable, but UA got quickly turned around into the more common German dipthong AU, so it came to be pronounced Mos-COW. When that -AU got to France, the French pronounced those two vowels together as a long O, so the word became Mos-COH. England first got the word from both the Germans and the French, hence the centuries-long argument about Mos-COH vs. Mos-COW.

As with Romance languages, Slavic languages have gender—that is, nouns (and their adjectives) are masculine, feminine, or neuter. One aspect of Russian language that makes it more difficult to learn than Romance languages is its noun and adjectival declension—endings tacked onto nouns and adjectives in six cases, or ways they are used in a sentence (whether the noun is subject, object, object of a preposition, etc.). But that gets way too complex for a short introduction!

With the current version of Google Earth, the names of Russian towns and cities are given both in Cyrillic and in Latin alphabets. Even the "roads" layer brings up roads labeled in the Latin alphabet. But for most everything else, some familiarity with Cyrillic can be a help. Here are some common map words you will see browsing through the Google Earth surface, including the labeling of Photos icons. Generally speaking little letters in Russian are recognizable diminutives of capital letters, but one major exception is the little version of *T* which is *m* (as compared with the real little *M*, which is *м*).

Water features: *Море* (MOHR-yeh) = sea. *Река* (reh-KAH) = river (often abbreviated simply *p.*). *Озеро* (OH-zye-ruh) = lake. *Остров* (OH-strof) = island. *Мост* (MOST) = bridge.

Buildings, roads, towns: *Кремль* (KREML') = fort. *Улица* (OO-lee-tsah) = street (often abbreviated *Ул.*). *Город* (GO-rot) = city (a D at the end of a word is pronounced more like a T). The suffix -*град* at the end of a word is just a contraction of *город*, since most towns came from fortified high spots. *Село* (sye-LOH) = village.

Religious buildings: *Храм* (KHRAM) = cathedral. *Собор* (Suh-BOHR) = also cathedral. *Церковь* (TSEHR-kov') = church. *Монастырь* (Moh-nas-TIR') = Convent or Monastery.

Miscellaneous: *Сад* (SAHD) = garden. *Лес* (LYEHS) = forest. *Памятник* (PAM-yaht-neek) = memorial.

Common adjectives: *Старий* (-*ая, -ое*) (STAR-ee, -ay-yah, - oh-yeh) = old. *Новой* (-*ая, -ое*) (NO-vuh-ee, -vah-yah, - oh-yeh) = new.

Common color adjectives: *Белый* (-*ая, ое*) (BYEL -ee, ah-yah, oh-yeh) = white. *Красный* (-*ая, ое*) (KRAHS-nee, -na-yah, nuh-yeh) = red. *Чёрный* (-*ая, ое*) (Chyor-nee, -na-yah, nuh-yeh) = black.

Now that you have at least a nodding acquaintance with Cyrillic, here is a quick illustration that Slavic languages are as close—and perhaps even closer—to each other than Romance languages are. Take, for example, the word for "bridge" in each of these sub-families of Indo-European. The Romance language words are fairly similar, and (with the possible exception of the Romanian) you can understand their common evolution from a Latin original, *pontus*:

French—*pont*
Spanish—*puente*
Italian—*ponte*
Portuguese—*ponte*
Romanian—*podul*

In Slavic languages the words for bridge are even more uniform. In ten of the twelve major Slavic languages it is identical—though written in two scripts: in Latin as *most* and in Cyrillic as мост or *мост* (transliterated *most*). The two exceptions are in the Ukrainian міст, fairly close, and in the Bosnian *ćuprija*, not close at all, although while Bosnia was part of Yugoslavia from 1918 to 1991 the word used was *most*. For a visual idea of the current distribution of these languages, the attached Google Earth file references Photos icons of various bridges (each labeled in the local language) in three groups: West Slav (Prague, Czech Republic; Bratislava, Slovakia; Warsaw, Poland), shown in yellow stars; East Slav (Moscow, Russia; Kiev, Ukraine; near Babrujsk, Belarus), shown in orange stars; and South Slav (Ljubljana, Slovenia; Zagreb, Croatia; Sarajevo, Bosnia; Podgorica, Montenegro; Belgrade, Serbia; near Tirnovo, Bulgaria; and Skopje, Macedonia), shown in red stars. Note also how the South Slavs are cut off from West and East Slavs by a band of German, Hungarian, and Romanian speakers (in the modern states of Austria, Hungary, Romania, and Moldova).[GE1]

Topography and texture of the land

The first time I went to Moscow I flew there from London by way of Warsaw. London to Warsaw, in east central Poland, was about 900 miles, and I imagined Moscow would just be a short hop east. That short hop turned out to be 720 miles more, like flying from Chicago-O'Hare to Newark. It was almost as long as from London to Warsaw (and almost exactly the distance as from Brussels to Warsaw). The point is that while western and central European distances are relatively small by U.S. standards, when you get over to Russia the distances are truly continental again. No wonder the inhabitants of the land (ever since Herodotus described "Scythian tactics" in the 400s BC), faced with invasion, could withdraw and withdraw, stretching out enemy invaders' supply lines to the breaking point.

Relatively late in Russian and Eastern European history, the Russian state reached some truly impressive mountains—in the south, the Caucasus Mountains that run down from the northern shore of the Black Sea to end in the Caspian Sea; in the southeast, the Tien Shan and related mountain ranges. But the original Russian culture and state took form in the low, rolling plains west of the Ural Mountains.[GE2] Slow Eastern European rivers radiate like crooked spokes off of the central land called in Russian the *mezhdurechie*, literally "between the rivers." These rivers, easily navigable, were key trade routes from the Baltic Sea (and later the White Sea) in the north to the Black Sea and the Caspian Sea in the south. During the Soviet Union and before it in the late Russian Empire, all of the lands coursed by these rivers were under a single government. Now, as you'll see by the international boundaries as we survey these river systems, there are three nation-states involved: Russia, Ukraine, and Belarus.

In terms of size, the Volga (Волга in the Cyrillic) system ranks first in European Russia.[GE3] Some cities on this system are important in the history to come.[GE4] Astrakhan is near the head of the massive delta on the Caspian Sea (which is 75' below world sea level, incidentally). Volgograd (formerly Stalingrad, and before that Tsaritsyn) is about 275 miles up the river, near its sharp bend. Samara is on the eastern side of the long eastern loop the river makes. Kazan is at the bend where the main Volga heads west as you move upstream, and not far from the juncture of the Volga and the Kama Rivers. Nizhny Novgorod ("Lower Newtown," and renamed Gorkii during the Soviet period), site of a famous medieval fair and market, is where the Oka, the main western tributary, meets the Volga proper. Historically the most important city on the upper Volga is Tver'

---

1. GE Layer 1 is a Folder titled "Bridge (most/мост) folder." "Fly" to each of the twelve Placemarks to explore Photos icons referred to there, then turn on Polygon (in black) representing German-Hungarian-Romanian language zone that cuts off South Slavs from West and East Slavs.

2. GE Layer 2 is a Polygon in green generally representing the Ural Mountains that supposedly define the Europe/Asia dividing line. It's not a very convincing argument, geographically: they're no more impressive than the Appalachians, and as they go south they dwindle to rolling wooded hills and then disappear completely. It is culturally that the Urals are more important as a dividing line.

3. GE Layer 3 is a Folder titled "Volga & tributaries." Open it and click on the rivers one by one to see general locations.

4. GE Layer 4 is a Folder with Placemarks for Astrakhan, Volgograd, Samara, Kazan, Nizhny Novgorod, Tver, and Moscow, key cities on the Volga river system.

(Kalinin in Soviet times). And just 100 miles southwest of Tver', on the Moscow River that is a tributary of the Oka, is the city of Moscow.

Moving from the lower Volga westwards across the southern plains, the next main river system is the Don (Дон), with its main tributary the Donets (Донецк in Russian, Донецьк in Ukrainian).[GE5] It makes a small delta as it enters the Sea of Azov, a sea which is almost but not quite cut off from the Black Sea by the Crimean peninsula (the Straits of Kerch are about two miles wide). On this set of waterways historically important cities are Taganrog, Peter the Great's first naval base that was up near the delta of the Don, and at the head of the delta itself Rostov na Donu, "Rostov on Don,"[GE6] hometown of the famous writer Aleksandr Solzhenitsyn. Notice that at one point the Don and the Volga are only forty miles apart. Although efforts to build a canal between the two began as early as the 1500s, the current Volga-Don Canal [GE7] was only finished in the years after WW II.

But of all these southern river systems, historically the most important of them all was the next major system to the west, the Днепр ("Dnepr"), usually anglicized as Dnieper (Дніпро in Ukrainian, and Дняпро in Belarussian, just to be thorough!).[GE8] The river comes out into the very northernmost corner of the Black Sea through the Gulf of the Dnieper; the big southern seaport Odessa is just thirty-five miles to the west.[GE9] Upstream, on the Dnieper's easternmost section, used to be great rapids or cataracts; today submerged in a lake created by a huge hydroelectric dam at Zaporis'ka, Ukraine (*za-porozhe* meant "beyond the rapids" in Russian, hence the "Zaporozhian Cossacks" of the lands along the river downstream from the rapids). The most famous city in ancient Russia, capital of today's Ukrainian state, was Kiev (pronounced something like "KEE-ef")— just below where the last major tributary river came into the Dnieper. Chernobyl', where nuclear reactors melted down in 1986 and released clouds of radioactivity, is a few miles up the western tributary Pripyat'. The far northwest tributary of the Dnieper is the Berezina, famous as the 1812 border of Russia that Napoleon on retreat crossed with only 20,000 left of his original 600,000-man invasion army.

To match these rivers that flow south into the Caspian and Black Seas, let's now take a quick look at those that drain north and west into the White and Baltic Seas. Again going from east to west, begin with the Northern Dvina system.[GE10] Notice how close the upper Northern Dvina is to the northern tributaries of the Volga. Arkhangelsk is the port town of the river, on the northeast bank at the head of the delta.[GE11] Iced in for eight or nine months of the year, it was from 1550 to 1700 the Russian state's only access to the world's oceans.

Moving westward takes us to a most interesting chain of rivers and lakes.[GE12] The Neva River (stress on the second syllable) is only forty miles long, but is a substantial river running from Lake Ladoga (stress on the first syllable) to the Gulf of Finland. Lake Ladoga is Europe's largest lake by far, 70 miles across and 115 miles in its long direction, with many rivers coming into it. Historically the most important of these was the Volkhov, which ran north to it from Lake Il'men 120 miles to the south. Smaller rivers (not shown) in turn entered the three corners of Lake Il'men. In modern history St. Petersburg/Leningrad,[GE13] located where the Neva enters the Gulf of Finland, is of course one of Russia's two great cities (for two centuries after its foundation in 1703 by Peter the Great, St. Petersburg replaced Moscow as the capital city). In early Russian history Novgorod, sometimes called "Great Novgorod,"[GE14] where the Volkhov exits from Lake Il'men, was second only to Kiev in importance.

---

5. GE Layer 5 is a Folder titled "Don & Donets," with a Path in aqua for each.

6. GE Layer 6 is a Folder with Placemarks referencing Taganrog and Rostov-on-Don.

7. GE Layer 7 is a Path representing the modern Volga-Don Canal as a blue line.

8. GE Layer 8 is a Folder titled "Dnieper River System."

9. GE Layer 9 is a Folder with Placemarks referencing Odessa and the other sites on the Dnieper listed in the paragraph above, including Kiev.

10. GE Layer 10 is a Folder titled "Northern Dvina River System."

11. GE Layer 11 is a Placemark framing a view of Arkhangelsk.

12. GE Layer 12 is a Folder titled "Neva & Volkhov."

13. GE Layer 13 is a Placemark generally framing a view of St. Petersburg.

14. GE Layer 14 is a Placemark framing a view of Novgorod.

And finally, one important waterway to the west of that was the linked Narva River, Lakes Peipus and Pskov, and Velikaya River system.[GE15] In early Russian history the town of Pskov, near the mouth of the Velikaya at Lake Pskov,[GE16] was an important rival of Novgorod.

Now pull back and look at the overall pattern of the rivers we just ran through.[GE17] A narrow wedge of territory constitutes the (not so) high ground between the northern and southern river systems, on average less than 600′ elevation. On either side of that watershed, especially the southern side, it is low, rolling country that travelers often likened to a great ocean—distant church domes slowly inching by, in travelers' eyes, like distant passing ships.

In terms of vegetation, you go from tundra in the far north to a belt of taiga (mainly pine forests) just south of that, based on soils called podzols that are mediocre at best for agriculture. Then comes a band of mixed hardwood and pine forests, with better soils for agriculture, and then tall grass "step," or "steppe," (from степ, meaning prairie) with its rich chernozem, literally "black earth" soils. But further south the decreasing rainfall is reflected in decreasing agricultural fertility—first short grass prairie, then semi-desert and desert. Tundra, taiga, podzol (literally "sub-soil"), and chernozem, incidentally, came into English in modern times courtesy of nineteenth-century Russian scientists. To simplify that north-south zonation, it's generally forest lands in the north and prairie lands in the south. Basic Russian culture originated in the former, and fought with and conquered the steppe cultures, but absorbed something in the process, you'll see.

In terms of climate, a Russian summer within a day's drive of Moscow would look familiar to most Americans east of the Rockies—mild mornings, hot afternoons with a chance of late-afternoon thunderstorms. In early summer there is even willow and cottonwood seed fluff blowing around Moscow. Apparently Stalin, meeting with President Truman towards the end of World War II, complained that the war had destroyed many of Russia's trees, so later Truman sent him some Missouri cottonwoods. Contemporary Russians whose air filtration systems get clogged with the stuff call it "Truman's Revenge." In the northern parts of European Russia, the government has tried to maintain fairly wide bands of forest around some of the major cities. Here Russians from spring through fall pursue mushrooms in what amounts to the great national outdoor pastime. Spring there is later, fall earlier, and winters long and very cold because of Russia's northern latitudes and continental climate (extremes of heat and cold not moderated by nearby open oceans).

The traditional architecture of the forest zone, resulting from a blend of climate, materials available, and cultural preference, can still be seen in some thousand-year-old "museum-cities" such as Suzdal' and Vladimir. [GE18] White-painted and golden-domed stone churches, humbler many-gabled wooden churches, and traditional peasant log cabin *izbas* with their light blue, gingerbread window frames .... In every city are still monumental memorials of the kind of art known as "Soviet Realism." Although architectural change is coming fast now with Russia's new prosperity, city architecture still features enormous monotonously-similar apartment buildings created by decades of central planning. In Russian primary school texts, дом (*dom*, meaning "home") is usually illustrated by a picture of an apartment building instead of a free-standing single-family house. It is American cemeteries that Russians would find monotonous; grave markers in Russian cemeteries are wildly innovative and creative, by U.S. standards.[GE19]

This brief attempt to survey the topography and texture of just the European part of the world's largest country may have been an exercise in futility, but hopefully it gave you a general outline and some points of relevance. Some particular locations will get more detailed treatment as we go along.

Now to the sweep of Russian history proper.

---

15. GE Layer 15 is a single Path showing a route through all four bodies of water.

16. GE Layer 16 is a Placemark referencing Pskov.

17. GE Layer 17 frames a view of a Path in the form of a thin, curving red wedge roughly showing the high ground between northern and southern river systems, the *mezhdurechie*. There's nothing as high as 800′ elevation and the average is probably in the 500′ range.

18. GE Layer 18 is a Folder titled "Museum-Cities." Inside are two separate Folders, one suggesting Photos icons in Suzdal' to explore, and the second for Vladimir.

19. GE Layer 19 is a Folder titled "Novodevichy Monastir cemetery," suggesting some Photos icons to explore in this most famous of Moscow cemeteries.

Kievan Russia

The glory days of the East Slavs were from AD 862 to 1239, with the rise and fall of Kievan Russia. The *Russian Primary Chronicle* says that the land was rich but disorderly, so they invited down a Rus (Viking) chieftain named Rurik to rule over them. The economic reason for being of the state was the trade route from the Vikings up on the Baltic to the Greeks in Constantinople on the Black Sea and also to some extent the Abbasid Arab capital of Baghdad on the Tigris River, using those slow Russian rivers and some short portages between the headwaters. The key northern city was Novgorod (literally "New City"),[GE20] located as you've seen just where the Volkhov River leaves Lake Il'men' on its 120-mile journey north to Lake Ladoga. There was a prince in every major city of Kievan Russia, along with his noble retinue (his *druzhina*, based on the word for friend, *drug*), and a fairly democratic town council. Kiev,[GE21] on the lower course of the Dnieper after the last major tributary comes in, was the key city of the Grand Prince. All winter he collected taxes in the form of furs or forest products, and after the river ice broke in spring he led a flotilla to Constantinople—*Tsar'grad*, they called it, "Caesar-City."[GE22] There they traded or made war, whichever seemed more promising, and there they eventually fell into the Greek cultural gravitational field.

Missionaries brought what would later be called Greek Orthodoxy and the basics of the Cyrillic script. The first Russian painters painted Greek-looking figures on icons, and the first Russian builders in stone built Greek-style churches. In the year AD 988 the Kievan Grand Prince known ever after as St. Vladimir decided that his whole country would be Greek-style Christian Orthodox (when the officially atheistic Soviet Union in 1988 allowed the millennial celebration of that, the world knew things were changing!). The Kievan state reached its apogee under St. Vladimir's son Iaroslav "the Wise," Grand Prince from 1019–1053. He systematized the law code known as *Russkaia Pravda* ("Russian Justice," or perhaps "Truth"). In terms of high culture, democratic political freedoms, women's right to property, and other modern western standards of civilization since the Enlightenment, Kievan Russia by this time was probably the second most civilized place in Europe after Constantinople. Rome had dwindled to a village, Berlin didn't yet exist, and in Paris and London the pigs were still sleeping in. When a daughter of Iaroslav the Wise married a French prince, she was the only literate one in the French royal family!

One important policy of Grand Prince Iaroslav the Wise, looking back, was not all that wise. To keep civil wars from happening among rival sons whenever a princely father died, he instituted a complex rotation system. The Grand Prince would hold both Kiev and Novgorod, the northern and southern ends of the key trade route, but the other cities in order of importance would be held by other sons in order of their age. When anyone died, everyone below him in the system was supposed to move up. What happened, within a generation or two, was not just occasional but perpetual civil war. In these wars of self-interest, the whole country weakened, and began to suffer more from outside invasions, particularly from the steppe nomads. Vladimir Monomakh, Grand Prince at Kiev from 1113–1125, is remembered favorably as an exception who worked unselfishly for the good of the whole—but overall the trend was clear. The Russian national epic, *The Lay of the Host of Igor'*, recounts an 1185 battle against the Polovtsy on the steppe east of the rapids of the Dnieper—a military advance that started well for the Russians but ended disastrously. As the anonymous bard sang:

> Thus it was in those battles and in those wars
> But no one has heard of this kind of war
> From morning till evening, from evening till dawn
> Fly tempered arrows, clang sabres against the helmets
> Crack steel spears, in an unknown field, amidst the Polovtsian land!
> Under [horses] hooves the black soil was covered with bones and saturated with blood
> And trouble came to the Russian land!

---

20. GE Layer 20 is a Placemark at Novgorod that references a Panoramio icon titled "Kremlin: High Point of View (Fortress) Novgorod," which has a good photograph of the ancient fort in this "New City."

21. GE Layer 21 is a Placemark at Kiev's Saint Sophia Cathedral (click on Panoramio icon under pointer, titled "Sainte Sophie," and nearby icons to explore); it was built by Iaroslav the Wise, one of the sons of St. Vladimir.

22. GE Layer 22 is a Placemark referencing Constantinople/Istanbul, framing it in relationship to Kiev.

Do I seem to hear a noise and ringing early before the dawn?
Igor is turning his troops back! He is sorry for his dear brother Vsevolod!
They fought one day, they fought another,
And on the third day around noon Igor's banners fell!
Here the brothers parted on the banks of the swift Kaiala
Here too the bloody wine ran out and here the brave Russians finished the feast.
(And got their guests drunk) and themselves fell in defense of the Russian land.
The grass wilts because of sorrow, And the tree bends down because of grief!

. . .

Now brother said to brother, "This is mine and that is mine also!"
And the princes began to argue about trifles as if they were great things
And they began to create discord among themselves!
And from all sides the pagans invaded the Russian land victoriously[3]

The last century or so of Kievan Russia is usually just called the Appanage period, as the power of the Grand Prince waned and the outlying principalities became more and more independent.[GE[23]] The death blow to the Kievan state came when the Mongols came storming through in the 1200s. The last years of Kievan Russia produced one last Russian hero—the young Prince of Novgorod, Alexander Nevsky. First, in 1240 the young Prince led Russian armies to victory over a Swedish invasion on the banks of the Neva, hence his honorific. Second, in 1242 at a famous battle on the ice at Lake Peipus, he defeated the crusading Teutonic Order, which had conquered Prussia and Livonia. But Alexander Nevsky recognized the Mongol armies as too strong to defeat, and counseled the paying of tribute to save the city of Novgorod.

The Mongols pulled back from the lands they overran to the west of Russia, but stayed in occupation of what had been Kievan Russia for two centuries. So Russia, which had been more "western" than the west, missed much of the Renaissance, the Reformation and Counter-reformation and the early Enlightenment and thus much of what made modern "western" civilization.

The rise of Muscovy

Surviving Russian cities fought for the right to collect Mongol taxes, adopting some Mongol military and social ways in the process. Tver', on the upper Volga River, was a chief contender. The other was Moscow, which had only been a small fort on the northeast frontier when first mentioned in 1147. Moscow won the battle, of course. One big step in its rise to power and prestige was when the Patriarch of what was now the Russian Orthodox Church moved there in the early 1300s. In 1380 its Prince Dmitrii Donskoi forced the retreat of the Mongol army at Snipe Field on the Don River (hence his name), although two years later Moscow had to resume tribute to the last of the great Mongol leaders, Tamerlane (Timurlana).[GE[24]]

Ivan III "The Great" and Ivan IV "The Terrible" finished off any Mongol control over Russia in the 1400s and 1500s, hence their lasting fame with the Russian people. It was Ivan III who in 1472 married the niece of the last Emperor of Constantinople (who had died fighting when the Ottoman Turks took Constantinople in 1453) and was the first to take the title "*Tsar*'," or Caesar (*Czar* is the French transliteration). The old Russian "Third Rome" belief really started here: Rome was the first great Christian city and it fell; Constantinople was second and it fell; Moscow was the third, but would never fall and was destined to bring an era of Christian rule to the whole world. Ivan III captured both Tver' and Novgorod and all their territories in the north, held his own with the Lithuanian state to the west, and blocked the last serious Mongol attempt to invade Russia from the east. By this time he claimed the whole Kievan state, though under a much stronger, centralized rule.

---

23. GE Layer 23 is a Polygon outlined in white giving the approximate boundaries of "Appanage" Russia before the Mongol invasions of 1223 and 1236–8.

24. GE Layer 24 is a Folder titled "Rise of Moscow," with three Polygons representing (a) the Moscow appanage around 1300; (b) its growth by the death of Dmitrii Donskoi in 1389; and (c) the territories added by Vasilii I and Vasilii II in 1462, when Ivan III inherited the throne. If you still have the white outline of Layer 34 on, you can see how this was taking shape in the extreme northeast of old Kievan Russian territory.

[GE²⁵] The Moscow Kremlin, Russia's most famous architectural complex, is mainly of his doing. The walls and towers are his, and with architects imported from Renaissance Italy he had the three cathedrals of Cathedral Square and also the Palace of Facets built inside the walls.[GE²⁶]

Muscovite absolutism peaked with his grandson, Ivan IV "the Terrible" (though the Russian word means more "the Awe-inspiring," as in "Augustus" Caesar). Born in 1530, his father died when he was three and his mother died—probably of poison—when he was eight. Much like Louis XIV in France a century later and Peter the Great in Russia a century-and-a-half later, for some impressionable years he was neglected and his life very much in danger, and it marked him for all time. In 1547, not quite seventeen, he married Anastasia Romanova and had himself crowned Tsar'. She was kind-hearted and apparently a good influence on him in this "good first half" of his rule. He reorganized the army, among other things inventing Russia's first professional soldiers, a force of musketeers (*streltsy*, from the Russian verb for "to shoot"). Ivan IV called assemblies of church leaders, and of government leaders; he produced a modernized law code in 1550 that actually gave more power to local leaders than they had had before. In 1552 his armies took Kazan near the great fork of the Volga (where the Kama River comes in from the northeast), and in 1554 they took Astrakhan down on the delta, breaking the "Mongol yoke" for all time.[GE²⁷] In 1553 the first English ships made port at Arkhangelsk, the beginnings of important commercial and intellectual exchange between the two countries. The great bell tower of the Kremlin—the tallest structure in the Kremlin and for a long time the tallest in Russia—is Ivan IV's, as is the Cathedral of St. Basil the Blessed (*Khram Vasilieva Blazhennova*) in Red Square, built to celebrate the taking of Kazan.[GE²⁸]

But in that same 1553 things began to change. Sick and thinking himself on his deathbed, Ivan IV asked key nobles (boyars) to swear allegiance to his line, and didn't get whole-hearted compliance. He slowly recovered, but in 1560 his beloved Anastasia suddenly died—poisoned, the Tsar' was convinced. In 1564 he simply abandoned Moscow for religious retreat in Alexandrov, about sixty miles northeast of Moscow, until crowds wound their way to him (powerfully recreated in Eisenstein's film *Ivan IV*) and begged him to come back. He returned to Moscow only on condition he be given an absolutely free hand in government. Then he set up a black-uniformed special police that terrorized the central third of the land of the Russian state. If there was logic to it, it was breaking boyar power, that aristocratic resistance to his rule; but there was surely madness in it too by this time. In 1581 he killed his own son in a fit of rage,[GE²⁹] and died in 1584 leaving a fractured, vulnerable state.

The Romanov dynasty

What resulted was a disastrous period of governmental breakdown and foreign invasion from 1598–1613. This fifteen-year long period came to be called "The Troubled Time." From this emerged the modern Romanov dynasty, related to Tsarina Anastasia of the fondly-remembered early years of Ivan IV. Church reforms of the mid-1600s, trying to bring the Russian Orthodox Church back into line with traditional Greek Orthodox practice, sparked a reactionary backlash called the Great Schism. Those who rejected the reforms—the Old Believers—also in part rejected governmental control. From then on they had a history of refusing to pay taxes and quickly joining peasant revolts (usually called *jacqueries*, from the French for the rebellion of all the *Jacques Bonhommes*, or John Does).

---

25. GE Layer 25 is a Polygon showing in red the general borders of Muscovy by 1505, the year of Ivan III's death.

26. GE Layer 26 is a Folder titled "Ivan III's Moscow." It includes a Polygon in red outline around the Kremlin walls, and a red Pushpin icon in Cathedral Square in the heart of the Kremlin, with text explaining which cathedral is which.

27. GE Layer 27 is a Polygon showing in red the general borders of Muscovy achieved by Ivan IV.

28. GE Layer 28 is a Folder titled "Ivan IV's Moscow." It includes Placemarks for his great bell tower inside the Kremlin walls and St. Basil's Cathedral just outside the walls in the heart of Red Square.

29. GE Layer 29 is a Placemark referencing the Tretyakov Gallery in Moscow, mainly as an excuse to embed a website with a picture of its famous nineteenth-century painting of this scene by Il'ya Repin; either click on the embedded link, or do a Google—Images search of "Repin Ivan IV."

Muscovy even as late as the early Romanovs was a poor state compared to the prosperity of the early modern West. Technologically far behind, it was obliged to purchase expensive western arms and military advisors. How did such a poor government compensate and win the loyalty of its highest civil servants and army generals? By giving them the only thing it had to grant, land with farmers already on it. So at almost the same time that serfdom (a kind of slavery where the serf is not supposed to be sold separately from the land) ended in western Europe, it began to grow in Russia. At first the farmers were free to take their families and move, but that was reduced to a two-week period after the harvest, and then that too disappeared. The final completion of legal serfdom came in the Law Code of 1649 under the second Romanov Tsar'.

This process explains the origin of the Cossacks, incidentally. They were ethnic Russians and Russian Orthodox believers who fled south to get away from serfdom. On the southern grasslands and river valleys they picked up a mounted lifestyle from the Kazakhs, and so got their nickname: "Cossack" and "Kazakh" are spelled the same in Russian, as if more settled Americans had called Daniel Boone and his frontier friends "Indians"—you'd have known which Indians—or Kazakhs—by the context. Later, as Russia continued to expand, these Cossacks faced a choice of joining Catholic Poland, Muslim Turkey, or Orthodox Russia. Because of the language they spoke and the religion they practiced, they chose Russia. They were allowed to keep their own style communities and their own lands, provided they would furnish the Russian army with cavalry. They became the ultimate shock troops of the Romanov dynasty. In 1917, when even the Cossacks began to fraternize with revolutionaries, everyone knew the government was doomed.

The Russian exploration of Siberia mainly took place in these last decades of old Muscovy and the first decades of Romanov rule. It might be interesting for Americans to compare it with the western exploration of North America through the St. Lawrence, since these were roughly contemporary processes and both were driven mainly by the fur trade. To briefly rehearse American events and dates, Jacques Cartier landed near what is today Quebec City in 1534 and as far upriver as Montreal the next year, but the real interior explorations inland began in 1615 with Champlain going up the Ottowa River to Lake Ontario and Lake Huron's Georgian Bay. In 1634 came the discovery of the Fox-Wisconsin portage between the St. Lawrence and Mississippi River systems, by 1673 travels on the upper Mississippi by Joliet and Father Marquette, and 1682 the exploration of the whole river to its mouth by Lassalle. Then after this century-and-a-half of exploration came a century's pause before routes all the way to the Pacific were blazed by MacKenzie and then Fraser for British Canada and of course Lewis and Clark for the young U.S.A.

Now look at the faster and more extensive Russian explorations of Siberia, as they progressed across the drainages of four great river systems flowing north—the Ob, the Yenisei, the Lena, and the Kolyma, and one flowing east, the Amur.[GE30] It was Ivan IV's conquest of the lower Volga from Kazan to Astrakhan in 1552–4 (about twenty years after Cartier's landing in Quebec) that opened up the Urals and beyond to Russian power. The Stroganov clan's rise really dated from this time, as they mobilized Cossack forces to attack a remaining Mongol khanate in Siberia. Yermak, leader of those Cossacks, captured the khanate's capital near Tobolsk in 1582 while Ivan IV was still alive, and supposedly gave those lands to him. Although the pace of exploration was slowed by the Time of Troubles, Turukhansk was founded on the upper Yenesei at the mouth of the Northern Tunguska, a major tributary coming in from the east, in 1607. In 1619 Yenesei Ostrog was founded at the mouth of the Upper Tunguska, another eastern tributary. Within the next decade fur traders made it to the Angara, the great tributary of the upper Yenesei that comes from Lake Baikal, and even over to the Lena River. In 1632 Yakutsk was founded on the easternmost bend of the Lena, and subsequent Russian explorations radiated out from there—the first Russian view of the Pacific (at the Sea of Okhotsk) by 1639, the first Russians to see both the Kolyma and Amur Rivers in 1644 (and take the Amur all the way down to its mouth), and the first Russians to go from the mouth of the Kolyma along the north coast and sail south through the Bering Strait in 1648. All that happened in less than a century, from Ivan IV's capture of Astrakhan in 1554—less than 40 percent of the time it took Europeans to explore the broadest part of North America sea to sea.

---

30. GE Layer 30 is a Folder titled "Siberian rivers and outposts." Each main river system has its own subfolder, with Paths for individual tributaries and Placemarks with dates for key outposts. You can either turn the whole folder on at once, or click on each river or tributary to see where it pops up. Look at the pattern of how the upper (more southerly) courses of these rivers and tributaries make, how close together and how short the portages between them were.

Imperial Russia

The single most important ruler in all of Russian history was Peter the Great, who lived from 1672–1725. When he was just ten years old, this healthy son of a second Tsarina was chosen as the new Tsar' over his sickly older half-brother. This meant in practice that his mother's family, the Naryshkins, came to power over the Miloslavskys, the family of the first Tsarina. But the educated and ambitious older half-sister of Peter, Sophia Miloslavkaya, manipulated the streltsy—by this time a decadent military force that lived in the Zamoskvorechie (on the south bank of the river, across from the Kremlin). They stormed the Kremlin, butchering Naryshkins while young Peter and his mother huddled against the wall and watched. Historians generally see a parallel between Louis XIV's childhood dangers in the Fronde about forty years earlier—a key factor in his decision to tame the nobility and move the court out of Paris to Versailles—and Peter's experience with the revolt of the streltsy. If anything, Peter's was the more traumatic experience, leaving him with a permanent tic and an occasional seizure, and, as you'll see, he moved the Russian court a lot further away from Moscow than Versailles was from Paris! At the time, Peter's older half-brother and he became co-Tsars, but everybody knew the real power was exercised by Sophia. In the Armoury Palace of the Kremlin you can still see the metal double throne the brothers sat on, with a little door that opened behind their heads so they could repeat to their audience what Sophia whispered to them to say.

Gradually retreating from court to a royal retreat a few miles out of Moscow that had been favored by his father, Preobrazhenskoe (close to the road that led northeast to the Trinity Monastery in Sergei Posad and beyond that to the city of Iaroslav on the Volga)[GE31], Peter played war with boys his age. He sent in occasional requests for uniforms and arms to Sophia, who, to keep him quiet and occupied out of the capital, sent them to him. With such resources and with Peter's enthusiasm for it, the war games got larger and larger; eventually a boy regiment 300 strong would be called the Preobrazhensky regiment, and a second one named for the village just south would be called the Semenovsky regiment.

With this came Peter's discovery of the "Foreign Quarter" (literally "German Quarter," *Nemetskaia sloboda)*, right on the road from Moscow to Preobrazhenskoe.[GE32] This is where all the Scottish, Irish, French, Dutch, and German officers and technologists lived, to keep them separate from the Russian Orthodox population by whom they were generally classified as heretics. Peter thrived on their life, and with their expertise he progressed from play war to serious military organization of the Preobrazhensky and Semenovsky regiments. Support from the Foreign Quarter was crucial in the 1689 showdown with his half-sister Sophia, whom he locked up in Novodeivichy Convent for life. In 1698 Peter took a huge embassy to the Germanies, England, France, and especially Holland. His object was to master western technological and military skills, either by training his people or by hiring the best instructors from abroad. He brooked no more opposition to autocracy than any Muscovite ruler before him, but he yanked Russia technologically into the modern world. Inherited position without capability was his pet peeve. He created a Table of Ranks of advancement, so that whoever was talented and hard-working enough to pass the eighth rung (of fourteen) was automatically ennobled.

With his tireless energy he assembled the military technology and organization it took to defeat the militarily brilliant Charles XII of Sweden, and Russia took Sweden's place as the superpower of the north. In 1703, with the Great Northern War still in doubt (the decisive victory of Poltava would only come in 1709), Peter founded St. Petersburg on the marshy delta of the Neva River at the eastern end of the Gulf of Finland. Modeled on Amsterdam, this city of canals was his "window on the west," and would remain the capital of Russia

---

31. GE Layer 31 is a Folder titled "Moscow & environs ca. 1682." It includes a Polygon outlined in red with a red wash fill showing the walls of Moscow circa 1682 (today's Garden Ring road is where the old walls ran), two smaller Polygons outlined in black representing the old royal retreat of Preobrazhenskoe and Semyonovskoe village just south of that, a Path symbolizing the Yauza River in aqua, and another Path symbolized in a broader purple line as the beginnings of the main highway to Iaroslavl as it left Red Square and headed northeast.

32. GE Layer 32 is a Polygon titled "Foreign Quarter."

until 1917.[GE³³] You can see the stirrings of modern Russian nationalism in these days: a first generation of Russian university scholars trying to explain away the Viking origins for the Kievan state, and after Peter's death in 1725 a strong reaction against a German element at court. From Peter the Great's time on, "Emperor" was the correct title for the ruling Romanov, rather than "Tsar'."

The Empress Catherine the Great, who ruled Russia from 1762 to 1796, was Russia's famous "enlightened despot." Originally named Sophia, from the ruling house of a small German principality, she was married to the immature future Peter III. She changed her name from Sophia to Catherine (the first of bad odor in the Russia left by Peter the Great, the second of good because it was the name of Peter's wife and successor), and formally converted to Russian Orthodoxy. When in 1762 the unstable Peter III became Emperor and threw away the Russian gains of the Seven Years' War because of his admiration for Frederick the Great, Catherine supported military units in the capital which overthrew and killed him. She celebrated Peter the Great not least by having a famous statue of him (Pushkin's "bronze horseman") facing the river just southwest of the Admiralty building.[GE³⁴] She and her favorite minister (and sometime lover) Potemkin captured the northern coast of the Black Sea from Turkey, and created both the great naval harbor of Sevastopol on the Crimean peninsula as well as the beginnings of the great commercial port Odessa not far from the mouth of the Dnieper.[GE³⁵]

Fascinated by the Enlightenment as a young woman, she enthusiastically corresponded with Voltaire and for a time hosted Denis Diderot—the great Enlightenment writer already introduced in Chapter 2—at her court, discussing human nature and governmental policies with him almost daily. Early in her reign she prepared a radical instruction for a National Assembly to use as a beginning point to reform society along progressive Enlightenment lines. Part of her long-term plan was to eliminate serfdom (and by then about 80 percent of all Russians were subject to some variety of that slavery). Then in 1774, however, came the greatest of all Russian *jacqueries*, the Cossack-led Pugachev Rebellion that burned its way up along the Volga River, and she gave up plans for changing the aristocratic fabric of society—on which her power ultimately rested, she realized. In her times the upper classes in Russia probably spoke more French than Russian, and the Hermitage (on the Embankment just up the Neva from the Winter Palace)[GE³⁶] got shiploads of priceless central and western European art. The social gap between lords and peasants yawned deeper than ever, and after 1789 all the liberal ideas of the younger Catherine were forgotten in the wars of the French Revolution.

Alexander I (who ruled from 1801–25), Catherine's imperially named grandson, developed his own rather liberal plans for the reform of Russia, but they were interrupted by Napoleon's invasion of 1812. General Kutuzov fought one great battle with Napoleon's armies at Borodino, seventy miles west of Moscow.[GE³⁷] Napoleon called it "the most terrible of all my battles." There were perhaps 200,000 troops on the French side and 150,000 on the Russian side, and around 65,000 killed or wounded. Nothing on that scale had ever happened in Europe (forty years before our Civil War, it was even bloodier than our bloodiest single battle, Gettysburg, with its 50,000 dead or wounded). Lev Tolstoi in *War and Peace*, a perennial contender for best historical novel ever (but in his own mind not so much a novel as a history and a corrective lesson for historians who believe individual leaders really change history!) presents Borodino as the mortal wound to Napoleon's army, even though the French held the field at the end of the day and even advanced to and occupied Moscow for a month or so. A great upsurge of Russian national feeling made this the "Great Patriotic War" in Russian parlance. Napoleon was popularly pictured as the Anti-Christ, and Cossack irregulars and an inspired peasantry cut his foraging parties to pieces. *Neopalen* ("the unburnt") was how his name was twisted in Russian, and the joke was that he may have come *neopalen* but left *opalen* ("burnt"). The Russian army followed

---

33. GE Layer 33 is a Folder titled "St. Petersburg." It has Placemarks referencing the Fortress of Peter and Paul on the north bank of the Neva and the Admiralty on the south bank, and Paths representing the major canals. Notice how three main roads radiate out from the Admiralty, including the most important road in the city, the Nevsky Prospect.

34. GE Layer 34 references the statue, and suggests a Panoramio icon to view.

35. GE Layer 35 is a Folder titled "Odessa and Sevastopol," with Placemarks for each.

36. GE Layer 36 is a Placemark referencing the Hermitage, part of the Winter Palace complex.

37. GE Layer 37 is a Placemark referencing Borodino.

Napoleon out of Russia,[GE38] and helped break his last real army at "The Battle of Nations" near Leipzig in October of 1813. That same Russian army wound up as the most important occupation army of Paris in 1814 and again, after Napoleon's return for the 100 Days, from 1815 to 1818.

High-ranking Russian officers of the occupation, whose French was already fluent, absorbed some of the goals of the French Revolutionary era. Upon return to Russia, having saved the world from Napoleon's tyranny, they found Alexander I now a mystical reactionary. These officers also brought back from western Europe the Masonic Lodge institution, with its generally liberal intentions and more importantly with its secret organizational structure of layers within layers of membership. A plot was hatched to overthrow the Russian government in 1826 in order to set up a liberal or even a Jacobin-type government. When Alexander I suddenly died on the shores of the Black Sea the first of December, 1825, two weeks of confusion (during which the oldest son Constantine renounced the throne in favor of his brother Nicholas) gave them an earlier opportunity. On Nicholas I's coronation day some military units in the capital revolted.[GE39] This "Decembrist revolt" was disorganized and easily put down, and counts either as the last of the old-style palace coups or the first sign of a new-style revolutionary movement. It was more a rebellion of officers than of enlisted men; soldiers instructed to shout for "Constantine and a Constitution" ("*Konstantin i konstitutia*") apparently thought they were championing Constantine and his wife! Five ringleaders were hanged, and dozens exiled for life to deep in Siberia. Infected military units were broken up and scattered, and Russia settled down to the rigid thirty-year-long rule of Nicholas I.

The slogan of Nicholas I's reign was "Orthodoxy, Autocracy, and Nationality." Real pressure was put on ethnic and religious minorities to assimilate. Censorship of the press was heavy-handed, and the universities were virtually occupied by the military. No Emperor ever worked harder than Nicholas I at being Emperor—fifteen-hour days and six-day weeks were common with him—but in his inability or unwillingness to delegate and insisting that everything come across his desk, he all but paralyzed the government. He built whole new layers of watchdogs to watch the watchdogs, most famously his new secret police called the Third Section.

In spite of the repression and censorship under Nicholas I, it was a silver age of literature and philosophy for Russia. Maybe writing in an age of heavy censorship requires more creativity of mind and pen, to get by the censors but connect with your intended readers? But the creative ferment may also have been caused by two new currents of thought coming into Russia from outside—Romantic nationalism mainly from central Europe, and socialism mainly from western Europe.

Natasha's Dance: Romantic nationalism in Russia in the nineteenth century

In 2002 Orlando Figes, a modern British historian of Russia, wrote an interesting cultural history of Russia called *Natasha's Dance*.[4] He took the title from a scene some 500 pages into Tolstoi's *War and Peace* in which a young and graceful countess, who learned French before she learned Russian, visits the country estate of a landlord gone native. When they hear the huntsmen strike up balalaika music in the back of the house, they go back to hear it, and Natasha, who has never danced Russian peasant dances before, strikes an attitude and then dances as if she had been born to it. Figes' argument is that this is just one example of Russian intellectuals inventing a Russian folk past for themselves.

It all came from Romanticism, of course, with its mystic belief that every "folk" group was born in a "seed-time" by magic interaction with a certain land, and then developed "organically," the way a plant grows true to a seed. By the turn of the nineteenth century currents of this European Romanticism were percolating into

---

38. GE Layer 38 shows the general route of Napoleon's 1812 invasion in white, and the retreat of his main forces in black. But there is a much more vivid map showing the dwindling of his army by the relative thickness of the lines. A simplified version of it is at the following website:

http://www.historywiz.com/russianinvasion.htm

All the cities shown as red dots on that map are reproduced in this Folder as Placemarks symbolized by red targets. Notice the bottom part of the graph that shows temperatures along the retreat. It starts with the French leaving Moscow October 18 with the thermometer at 0°C, 32 above on the Fahrenheit thermometer we generally use. Near Krasnoi on November 14 it was –26°C, or 15° below zero F. Just past Borisov on December 6 it was –38°C, –37°F.

39. GE Layer 39 is a Placemark referencing the square where the main rebellion took place.

Russia, primarily from the Germanies. Alexander Pushkin (1799–1837) is not the most popular of Russian writers for those who read Russian literature in translation; but he would be a strong contender for the title of "single favorite writer" as voted by a typical Russian-speaking audience. This is because he really created a new, direct, and earthy Russian written language, and the simplicity and clarity of his prose and poetry are only fully experienced by native Russian speakers.[GE40]

There was a dash of Orientalism in this new Russian self-awareness, mainly owing to the Russian conquests in the Caucasus and Central Asia that coincided with the high point of this Romanticism. As early as Catherine the Great's reign, the Christian kingdom of Georgia, south of the Caucasus, appealed to fellow Christian state power Russia for help against the Muslim Turks. For Russia, this eventually meant subduing the Muslim mountain tribes on the northern slopes of the Caucasus Mountains—which meant the building of a "Causasian line" of forts from the Straits of Kerch to the Caspian. Then it meant subduing the "Gortsy," the most independent-minded mountaineers in the high mountains as well—which meant building a Georgia Military Highway over the Caucasus from Vladikavkaz (a Russian fort whose name translates "Ruler of the Caucasus") to Tblisi.[GE41] The peoples of the Caucasus are amazingly diverse linguistically; every population wave that passed by for thousands of years seems to have left a remnant in some Caucasian valley. But the mountaineers were united by Sunni Islam and a tradition of Sufi-led religious orders, and it took Russia over a century and a quarter-million troops to complete their conquest. Shamil, a Muslim imam and guerrilla warrior extraordinaire, led the Russian army on a merry chase for close on thirty years, only being captured in 1859. And before the Caucasus were subdued, Russian armies began conquering the key fortified cities of Central Asia. The main campaigns were in the four decades from 1839 to 1881.[GE42] Western readers more familiar with the British Empire may remember this British-Russian rivalry over India's northwest frontier and Central Asia as "The Great Game"; the Russian name for it was "Tournament of Shadows." It is remarkable how many great Russian writers there were particularly in the Caucasus campaigns, and who wrote about it, including Lermontov in his famous *Hero of Our Times*, and Pushkin and Tolstoi themselves. In general in the first half of the nineteenth century more and more Russians experienced contact with the east; by the second half of the century more and more claims were made that key eastern elements had entered Russian culture and bloodstream itself, making it not just another European culture. Anna Akhmatova, one of the four or five greatest poets of the past century in the Russian language, was born in 1889 as Anna Gorenko. When her father said he wanted no poets in the family, she changed her name to her Tatar great-grandmother's name, itself said to come from the last Mongol ruler to whom Muscovy paid tribute.[5]

At the height of the Romantic period in Russia, a school of intellectuals calling themselves Slavophiles celebrated the uniqueness of Slavic culture, and took to wearing traditional country dress and championing traditional Slavic institutions. The most famous of them all was Sergei Aksakov, who lived in Moscow all his early adult life (including the French invasion thereof). He was the great friend and popularizer of the writer Gogol', and after his retirement from the civil service began to write himself. In 1843 he moved to the country estate of Abramtsevo at Sergei Posad, the town most famous for Trinity Monastery, the most important lavra (super-monastery) in all of Russian Orthodoxy. There he hosted major Russian artists and preached the value of Russian traditions. His most famous work, *A Family Chronicle*, was published in 1856, just about the time that Alexander Afanas'ev was putting together the classic collection of Russian fairy tales. By the 1860s this enthusiasm for things Slavic became political Panslavism, which arranged for international conferences calling for the creation of a super Slavic state led of course by Russians. Sergei Aksakov's two sons, Konstantin and Ivan, carried their Slavophile heritage on into this sort of Panslavism.

Beginning with the French occupation of Moscow in 1812 and the quick subsequent flight of the French from Russia, in the popular mind Moscow more and more stood for the virtues of heartland Russia. Someone needs to write a book on the chancy, dangerous, "sketchy" sides of European river cities—London's South

---

40. GE Layer 40 is a Placemark referencing Pushkin's statue outside the Russian Museum in St. Petersburg, usually awash in flowers on his May 26 birthday.

41. GE Layer 41 is a Folder titled "Conquest of the Caucasus."

42. GE Layer 42 is a Folder titled "Conquest of Central Asia." Turn on each sub-folder one at a time for a color-coded pattern of Russian military operations.

Bank where scandalous plays were put on in the Globe by the likes of that sly Shakespeare; Paris's *Rive Gauche* (Left Bank) with its bohemian university students forever protesting on the Boul'Mich; Rome's *Trastevere* (say "Trans-Tiber" for 2000 years and this is what you get) with its maze of narrow alleys and kaleidoscope of ethnicities . . . Moscow's version of that is the *Zamoskvoreche*, literally the "Beyond the Moscow River," the neighborhood across the river and directly south of the Kremlin (briefly noted earlier as where the riotous strelsy regiments lived, those who frightened the younger Peter the Great).

On into the nineteenth century land in the Zamoskvoreche was generally flood-prone but cheap, and attracted much of Moscow's early industry. Here grew up Russia's first textile factories, many of them owned by Old Believers of serf ancestry who by the last half of the nineteenth century were far wealthier than most aristocratic families. One such was Pavel Tretyakov, who used his great new wealth to begin collecting Russian art in the early 1860s. When his collection was willed to the city of Moscow in 1892—nucleus of today's famous Tretyakov Gallery—it had over a thousand pieces of art that had cost a million rubles.[GE43] Without his patronage the "Wanderers"—fourteen rebellious students who in 1863 walked out of the Imperial Academy of Arts in protest against the classic compositions and subjects taught there, preferring to use folk themes, rural subjects, and unconventional techniques—would probably never have economically survived to paint much of anything. They included Ilya Repin, Ivan Kramskoi, Grigorii Miasoyedov, and Vasily Surikov (a sampler of whose great paintings you can browse if you do a Google–Images search under "The Wanderers Russian painters").

An even more important merchant supporter of the arts than Tretyakov was Savva Mamontsev, though he was not from the Zamoskvoreche (his father, a wealthy Siberian railroad baron, bought the family a mansion in the middle of Moscow and they moved there when Savva was eight, in 1849). He got some university education in St. Petersburg, and when sent to Milan for health reasons, fell in love with Italian opera there. His father had to work hard to keep him in the family business and out of the arts, but eventually Savva excelled at both. In commerce, among other things he opened up the whole Don River coal basin to railroad connection, and built a huge wagon factory in Mytishchi, about twelve miles NNE from city center Moscow. As a personal artist, he was described as being a talented singer and good playwright and sculptor. But it was as a patron of the arts that he really impacted Russian history. In 1863 Moscow merchants led by the Mamontsev family had banded together to create the first Russian-supported (as opposed to foreign investor) railway line—from Moscow to Sergeiv Posad, location of the famous Trinity Monastery. It was in part commercial—the railroad ran through Mytishchi where the wagon factory was, after all—but partly political, emphasizing the Russian heartland, with what Orlando Figes calls this "spiritual center of old Muscovy" as its destination. In 1870 Savva and his well-educated, musically talented wife of five years, Elizabeth, bought the Aksakovs' old Abramtsevo estate in Sergeiv Posad, and in short order turned it into the most famous artists' colony in all Russian history.[GE44] This became the center of a revival of Russian folk crafts and folk-theme-inspired art, more popular and influential in Russia than William Morris and the Arts and Crafts Movement ever were in contemporary Britain.

Mamontsev's famous Private Opera got its start at Abramtsevo, before moving to Moscow in 1885, and as in painting and crafts it too stressed Russian themes and motifs. In the early 1860s, at just about the same time the Wanderers dropped out of the Imperial Academy of Art, a group of five young musicians coalesced in a similar folk-inspired rebellion against classical music. They would come to be known as "The Mighty Handful"—Balakirev, Cui, Mussorgsky, Borodin, and Rimsky-Korsakov. Balakirev, the only music professional of the five, rounded up this group of army and navy officers and one chemist/physician, talented musical amateurs, and directed them all down the road of creating a unique Russian national music. Orlando Figes notes that all of Rimsky-Korsakov's later operas, for example, were done at the Private Opera in Moscow, not at St. Petersburg's famous Marinsky (later Kirov) Opera. The unification of art, music, and dance later made world famous by Diaghilev was pioneered in Mamontsev's Private Opera.

---

43. GE Layer 43 is a Placemark referencing the Tretyakov Gallery.
44. GE Layer 44 is a Folder titled "Folk Cult from Iaroslavsky Station to Sergei Posad and Trinity Monastery."

Looking back, then, at the whole of the nineteenth century in Russia, the Romantic cult of the folk was just as important here as in the Germanies. It peaked in Russia, however, a bit later than in the Germanies, and more in parallel with that second great ideological current from outside, socialism.

Meanwhile, Western and Central European socialism

In the last chapter on Germany, socialism was talked about to some extent as a powerful nineteenth century movement, almost as powerful as cultural nationalism. This chapter aims to treat it a little more systematically, and then show the role of socialism as well as nationalism in modern Russian history. With Germany knocked from the ranks of the great powers by the end of World War II, the Soviet Union would become for the next half-century the great superpower rival of the United States. Most smaller conflicts and movements of the age happened in the framework of the Cold War between the two. In the same way that the German chapter was to sketch in major European events from 1815 to 1945, this chapter is intended to give a reader another angle on major European events from the early nineteenth century to 1945, and then some generally new coverage of European as well as world events from 1945 to 1991, when the U.S.S.R. finally broke up. First, though, comes the short course on the development of socialism in western and central Europe.

Although there is considerable debate about it, the author sides with those historians who believe that socialism as a modern ideology took shape in the 1820s. The Frenchman Charles Fourier, mainly in reaction to the huge growth in city slums and the ugliness of the early industrial revolution, dreamed up an ideal living unit he called a "phalanstery." It was to be a shade less than two thousand people—small enough so you would know most everyone, but large enough to have a good variety of talents and interests. Half your working hours there might be with machinery and technology, but half ought to be farming living plants and animals in the open air. Most striking, though, is that Fourier wanted to take the values that prevail in a typical healthy family—whoever has the health and is the right age does the heavy work and generously supports the rest—and apply those values to the larger unit. The socialist cliché for this would become, "From each according to ability, to each according to need." A tight-knit little town to which ideal family values have been expanded might express it best; he took the word "phalanstery" from "phalanx," the classical Greek military formation where shields were locked together. Sharing the wealth would mean that no one was rich, but that no one sweated fourteen hours a day in a smoky mill. And just maybe if these ideas spread all over the world, bellicose states and their armies and wars would disappear.

That was and is the goal of almost every branch of socialism (although Marxism, admittedly, gets into larger scale units). What divides socialism into rival schools, however, is how we are supposed to get to that socialist future. Fourier advertised for a millionaire philanthropist, saying that if just one of these phalansteries got set up it would be so successful that the model would spread all over the world. Anarchists such as Proudhon thought if you just knocked off the top governing level of existing states that the small-scale agricultural villages and artels of industrial workers on the lower level already existed, and would flower without governmental oppression. Syndicalists believed you could force governments to change with strikes, the ultimate being the general strike when absolutely everybody quit work to force a change. State socialists such as Lassalle thought you might convince government leaders of this future, and they would turn governmental machinery toward helping the wish come true; as a German he even held meetings with Bismarck to this end. Marx saw the sprouts of this future naturally growing out of the decaying body of capitalism—but more on this later; much more.

Is socialism workable or impossible, good or bad? Robert Owen, by the 1830s a wealthy British industrialist with views much like Fourier's, helped set up the phalanstery-like New Harmony in Indiana. It soon failed. Of course it failed, said the critics; if there are no incentives for people to work, they won't. Supporters talked about the wrong mix of people, poor financing and such—weak arguments. But when supporters asked the critics what their answer was for the horrific slums and low life expectancy of the industrial revolution, the critics had no good answers of their own. The socialists said that at least they were concerned and trying to do something. The critics told them to be sure not to throw the baby out with the bath water.

Approaching the revolutions of 1848 in Europe, then, which were to be mainly Liberal and national, there was also an undercurrent of socialism, and it seeped into Russia.

Herzen and the birth of *narodnichestvo*

Alexander Herzen was the illegitimate son of one of Russia's wealthiest aristocrats (his name has overtones of "love child" in German). As a baby in 1812 he was bundled out of a burning Moscow. About thirteen years old when the Decembrist leaders were hanged or exiled, he and a friend stood on the Sparrow Hills looking down on Moscow and swore to be loyal to their memory. He was around nineteen, in 1830, when the July Revolution in France and the Polish revolt against Russia both excited him greatly. He was for a time the most important of the "Westernizers," the most vocal opponents of the Slavophiles. Western Europe, the Westernizers believed, was leading the world into a new era, and Russia needed to go that direction, not back into the Slavic past as seen through rose-colored glasses by the Slavophiles. Herzen saw Fourier-style socialism as the last word from the West, and championing that idea got him arrested and sent to Siberia.

In the 1840s, however, there were two critical developments in his thoughts that changed him from a Westernizer into something else, something new. First, in 1844 the German traveler von Haxthausen (whose sister, incidentally, gave the Bros. Grimm some folktales for their collection) discovered that the old medieval commune was still very much alive in the Russian countryside. The *mir*—the communal village with periodic land redistribution, where planting and harvesting were done as a whole but each family got the produce from its strips of fields—was of course known by most Russians, but was generally seen as a sign of economic and social backwardness. Now here a sophisticated German writer was seeing it in a positive light, and some Russians, including Herzen, began to see it with new eyes, too. Second, by the time the revolutions of 1848 broke out in western and central Europe, Herzen had escaped from Siberia and was there to see for himself. He was terribly excited about the socialist future that seemed to be so quickly coming into being, and then equally terribly disappointed when the conservatives crushed it all by 1849. This is when he invented *narodnichestvo*, a native kind of Russian socialism.

The West must be too materialistic to lead the world into the new socialist future, Herzen decided. Russia's very backwardness, preserving as it had the medieval rural commune, would let it take a shortcut to the future. Russian intellectuals could go to the peasants of the *mir* for practical lessons in socialist living, and intellectuals could teach peasants the place of the *mir* in the coming transformation of the modern world. *Narod* is the Russian word for people, or folk, and the literal translation of *narodnichestvo* is simply "populism." That word has such specific overtones from American history, however, that let's continue to use *narodnichestvo* for the movement and *narodniks* for its practitioners instead.

The Reform Era of Alexander II

The Emperor Nicholas I died in 1855, in the middle of a losing war in which Britain and France were successfully invading the Crimean peninsula of southern Russia.[GE45] How was the world's super-power of 1815, just forty years later, not able to defend itself against a marine invasion of its own coast? The answer seems to be that Russia had missed the power lessons of both the draft army and modern industrial development. The Russian army and navy were no longer competitive on the battlefield. Some historians believe that the future Alexander II made his dying father a promise to reform Russia along western lines. We have no proof of that, but it seems the only way to explain both his dogged pursuit of reform as well as the half-hearted nature of the reforms that resulted.

The first and basic reform had to be emancipation of the serfs, symbol and cause of much of Russia's backwardness. As crown prince and princess, Alexander and his wife had read to each other the 1852 book by Ivan Turgenev called *A Hunter's Sketches*, with its rich three-dimensional portraits of serfs encountered by a fictional gentleman hunter. It did for perceptions of serfdom in Russia what *Uncle Tom's Cabin*, published the same year, did for slavery in the U.S. Within the first year of Alexander II's reign he announced to the Moscow nobility that it would be better to abolish serfdom from above than to wait for it to abolish itself from below—in bloody revolution, obviously. The nobility did not take the hint, so the Emperor himself chaired a committee to oversee it.

---

45. GE Layer 45 is a Folder titled "The Crimea in the Crimean War."

The upper classes and intellectuals generally, in government and out, split into two parties. The Planters (taking their name from southern U.S. examples) were not unwilling to give the serfs freedom, but in the south of the Russian Empire where the land was good they wanted to keep all the land, and in the north where the land was poorer they wanted a high ransom for the person of the peasant worker. The Reformers stressed the danger of a huge landless group unable to support itself: by this time there were something like sixty million Russians total, and fifty million of them were either private or state serfs. A complicated compromise was struck that left the peasants with more land in the north and less in the south, legally free but with a mortgage on their persons so heavy that by 1905 their collective debt would actually be higher than in 1861.

The peasants were emancipated from the landlord, but not from the mir. Even so, the imperial government had to invent local governmental institutions to replace the landlord, who after all had been in effect chief of police, head of draft board, justice of the peace, public roads commissioner, etc. The result was the *Zemstvo*, or Land Council. Finally put into place in the mid-1860s, after Alexander II began to turn more conservative, it gave the old landlords a third of the vote, the townsmen a third, and the common farmers a third. Despite its limitations, however, it was the most democratic local governmental process since the Kievan town assembly. The rudiments of public education, public health, and public works programs came from the *Zemstvo*, and within four decades enough people had become accustomed to this locally controlled government to create a national party, the Constitutional Democrats (KDs, or the "Cadet" party; saying K and D in Russian sounds like the French word), which modeled itself on the British system.

The courts were restructured, with locally elected Justices of the Peace and even trial by jury. Cities were given a degree of municipal self-government. The ultimate reform, however, came in 1874 with the institution of a German-style draft army. The Minister of War was the driving spirit behind the Reform party, he probably did more for public education in the army than the Minister of Education did for all of Russia outside the army.

"What is to be done?"

The 1860s in Russia was a decade of student unrest something like the 1960s in the U.S. Both the "Hippies" of the 1960s and "Nihilists" of the 1860s were nicknamed by opponents, and each soon embraced the name as a positive label. The head of the Russian Third Section, the imperial Russian security police, when talking about "an unwashed male or several such, living with an unwashed female or several such," could pass for a 1960s F.B.I. officer's comment on communally-living Hippies. A rich underground literature was circulating, including issues of Herzen's periodical *Kolokol* (*The Bell*), coming in from western Europe. A *narodnik* named Nicholai Chernyshevsky, jailed in 1862, there wrote a novel called *What Is to Be Done?* that drew many young educated people into the movement. It told the story of Vera, who rejected her own family's wealth and the marriage they had arranged for her and instead began a sewing circle of poor girls. This became an artel, an urban commune, run on the principle of "from each according to ability, to each according to need," and in the novel it was so successful that it spun off copies of itself in other cities. What was to be done? Go live the ideal socialist existence, in commune-ity, and so change the world. Chernyshevsky's book probably got more Russian young people to leave home for a new lifestyle than Bob Dylan's "Like a Rolling Stone" did American students a century later. And the idealism of the 1860s in Russia ended in tragedy (in something of the way the idealistic American 1960s ended with the student deaths at Kent State and the Manson murders), in the Nechaev affair. He was the leader of a small socialist cell in a Russian university who had another member of the cell who challenged his facts killed. An ordinary police investigation of the campus murder turned up the cell, making Nechaev's trial national news and sparking a revulsion against the Nihilists in the general public.

But the movement still percolated below the surface, and in the spring of 1874, several thousand college students—some that would have graduated in early summer if they had stayed in school—suddenly left their universities heading for the countryside. They told their friends they were going *v narod*, "to the people, to the folk." They were going to learn practical socialism from peasants living in the *mir*, and were going to try to teach the peasants a comprehensive intellectual socialism. It is sometimes called The Children's Crusade, or the Mad Summer of 1874: the suspicious peasants mostly just turned them into the police.

Increasingly frustrated with society as it was, and failing to change it peacefully, a remnant of the group turned to violence. "The People's Will" (*Narodnaya volia*) may not have had more than fifty core members, but in 1877 they opened a terror campaign to kill leading members of the government. It began when a young woman named Vera Zasulich shot and seriously injured the Governor-General of St. Petersburg for ordering the beating of one of her friends in prison (despite eyewitnesses, a jury acquitted her to save her life, and she quickly left the country before a military court could reverse the verdict). The ultimate goal became the assassination of the Emperor himself. His study in the Winter Palace was blown up, and then a train he was supposed to be on from the Black Sea was also blown up, though he was in neither place at the time. Then on March 1, 1881—during the parade in the capital St. Petersburg celebrating the twentieth anniversary of the Emancipation decree—Alexander II was assassinated by bomb-throwing student revolutionaries.[GE46] It was in hopes of precipitating a revolution, or in some way modifying government policies. Instead it resulted in the rule of Alexander III, the most brutal and reactionary Russian ruler of the century.

Reaction and Russification

The tutor of Alexander III, Pobedonostsev, was quickly made new Prime Minister, and he led an uncompromising attack on anyone and anything he saw as an enemy of the imperial system. That included ethnic minorities, against whom he launched a fierce campaign of Russification. The so-called May Laws (announced in May 1882) were a virtual declaration of war on the Jewish minority of several million. They publicly called for solving Russia's "Jewish problem" by killing a third of the Jews, exiling a third, and assimilating a third of the Jews. Before this time there had been sporadic pogroms, attacks on Jewish neighborhoods often around Easter time, but now pogroms were systematically organized from as high up as the Minister of Interior. So 1882 may be the most important date on the modern Jewish calendar, setting in motion a wave of Russian-Jewish emigration, mostly bound for western Europe and the U.S. but also a small stream towards Turkish Palestine that in two-thirds of a century would result in the modern state of Israel, as you'll see in more detail in Chapter 10 on the Mideast.

The universities were in essence occupied by the Russian army. Censorship became leaden. In the famine years that began in 1891 the government forbid any but governmental relief, and yet itself managed to give only token aid. In foreign affairs friction continued with Austria over the Balkans, and yet the awesome might of the German army required Russia to stay in the Three Emperor's League or face the consequences. It was a slowly failing government, losing public support year by year.

In the context of the new heavy-handed government treatment of students under Alexander III, consider "Sasha" (Alexander Il'ich) Ul'ianov, perhaps the best single student at the University of St. Petersburg in the mid-1880s. A brilliant biology student, he won the university's gold medal for his research. He participated in a student demonstration on campus, and when all the other demonstrators were expelled but he was not (as the faculty's fair-haired boy), his friends played on his guilt. Increasingly radicalized, he got involved in a plot to assassinate Alexander III. On March 1, 1887—the sixth anniversary of the assassination of Alexander II—he and some other students were caught with explosives on the Nevsky Prospect, the most important road in St. Petersburg, waiting on the Emperor's carriage to come along. His mother, respectable widow of a district school superintendent, came to plead with the Emperor for her son's life, and was told that if he showed any contrition the death sentence would be commuted. But Alexander, age twenty-one, told his mother that would be like shooting your pistol in a duel and then dishonorably refusing to let your opponent shoot back. He refused to make any apology, and was among the student revolutionaries hanged that same year. It was a postscript to the narodnichestvo violence from 1877–1881, but also of particular interest for one other reason. At the time of his death Sasha had a sixteen-year-old younger brother, "Volodya" (Vladimir), who idolized him and was himself radicalized by his brother's execution. This same Vladimir Il'ich Ul'ianov would later take the revolutionary name of Lenin.

---

46. GE Layer 46 is a Placemark referencing the Church of the Spilled Blood, built on the site of the assassination.

Karl Marx

Karl Marx (1818–1883) was not just a German, but a West German from the Rhineland, and writing about him in a chapter on Russia might seem at first glance to be a bit of a stretch. The reason, of course, is that the Russian government would be the first to embrace Marxism, and Marxism is arguably a good part of the reason that the Soviet Union became one of the two dominant powers of the last half of the twentieth century.

Most of the elements of Marx's philosophy already existed before Marx; his genius was in putting them together in a system. For this reason, a good many famous explanations of Marxism are essentially biographical: you can see Marxism take shape as you follow his life from childhood to about age thirty. This may be the easiest way to begin a study of Marx.

Marx's father was Jewish, though he converted to Christianity before Karl Marx was born. The father was a passionate admirer of the Enlightenment, as was the young Marx's next-door mentor the Baron von Westphalen. Many biographers assume that Karl Marx took in the basic beliefs of the Enlightenment—the essential goodness of humans, given good surroundings; belief in the continual progress of humankind—with his mother's milk. These are the foundations of his thought, below the level of his conscious mind, beyond question or even reexamination (though if you want to critique Marxism, probably a good place to start).

Then in college and graduate school Marx absorbed the ideas of Georg Wilhelm Friedrich Hegel (pronounced something like HAY-gul). Hegel had died in 1831, but his philosophy still saturated the university curriculum in German states (and their intellectual dependencies in eastern Europe, including Russia) for years after his death. The attraction of Hegel is mainly lost on modern historians: anyone who tries to prove that philosophically there can only be seven planets orbiting round the sun, as Hegel did, is assuming way too much for philosophy! Modern day political scientists and philosophers, however, as a group tend to be more positive. The summary below, take note, is from an historian.

Hegel is, as much as Herder, an example of the Romantic Age's love of history, as contrasted with the essentially anti-historical views of the Enlightenment (which had said just find out what human nature is, and change all institutions to fit it, no matter how old or how rich their evolution). He solved to his satisfaction relationships between several pairs of opposites: the spiritual and the material; what is and what ought to be; golden ages and dark ages; and "great men" versus ordinary mortals. There is supposed to be an underlying, all-permeating spiritual force unfolding through time that Hegel calls the *Weltgeist*, or World Spirit. Alongside it there is an unfolding through time of the material world of people and things and events, and this imperfect material world is more or less a reflection of the World Spirit at any given time. The Weltgeist, of course, is as pure and perfect as it can be at any given point. The material world is sometimes so good that it almost perfectly reflects the state of the Weltgeist, in which case it is a Golden Age when everyone succeeds at things without half trying. Then again, the material world sometimes lags so far behind the Weltgeist that it is a Dark Age where nothing succeeds and the times seem out of joint. What seems to happen is that the social and political forms of a Golden Age are retained long after the Weltgeist has moved on, and society in conflict becomes increasingly polarized between two hostile social classes, one more backward looking and one more forward looking. When tension gets unbearable, social upheaval and war results, and the outcome is a synthesis that comes close again to the perfection of the Weltgeist. This process of increasing tension and polarization of society and then the sudden snapping up to the level of the Weltgeist in social upheaval and war is what Hegel called the "dialectic" (the "di-" part meaning "two"). Great men are those who instinctively realize where the Weltgeist has gone. Having helped the world catch up to it, often by violating conventional morality, they tend to die young, shucked off history like a husk from grain. Somewhere in the future the Weltgeist will reach its predestined end, and the material world will catch up to it once and for all in a virtual heaven-on-earth.

Whether or not you agree with the religion/philosophy behind the Hegel's dialectic, it is a powerful historical tool. Just sitting down to find out for yourself what the two dominant socio-political forces were in any place and age has to be instructive. And if you are also a believer in the basic spiritual control and shaping of world history, the dialectic is probably all the more comprehensive and comfortable. So it was, at any rate, for most German intellectuals in the 1830s, including Marx, who were Christian.

The Hegelian answer to the age-old question, "Is what now exists what ought to be?," depends in part on where the Hegelian thinks we are in the current dialectical movement. If society and government and the whole of the material world pretty well reflect the Weltgeist at this moment in time, the answer is yes; if not, no. Hegel shows himself to us as a real conservative in thinking that the Prussian government of the 1820s was as free and good as government could be. His younger followers, the "Young Hegelians"—including Marx—came to disagree. They thought the Weltgeist had moved way beyond the current reality of German politics. How could their dream of social justice have ever been dreamed if the Weltgeist had not moved on and made it possible for them to conceive it? These young intellectuals were so radical in their criticism of government that they were blacklisted in their chosen profession, university teaching. Karl Marx—who had "future ivory tower research professor" written all over him—was going to have to find other employment or means of support.

In the early 1840s Ludwig Feuerbach, in his *The Essence of Christianity* and other works, converted most of these Young Hegelians to atheism ("materialism" is the more comprehensive philosophical term, meaning disbelief in any spiritual forces, not just deity). Someone arguing for materialism sooner or later needs to wrestle with the question of why most people, most times and places, are spiritualists. Feuerbach's answer was in a process he called "alienation." If humankind lived rich and fulfilled lives, he said, religion would be unnecessary. In times of less fulfillment, said Feuerbach in blasphemous reversal of most Christian belief, people create god in their own image: if horses had gods, they would look like horses; if triangles had gods, they would have three sides . . . . In the short, brutal, and dirty lives of workers in the industrial revolution, said Feuerbach, people took qualities they ideally should have seen in their own lives—power, beauty, the ability to do things of lasting importance—and in subconscious way projected those qualities into the heavens, fabricating the image of an all-powerful, all-knowing God and a beautiful heavenly host. He parodied Hegel's description of humankind's spiritual side by saying, "Man is what he eats." The "*Weltgeist*" was an illusion, he argued, just a word that summed up all the material phenomena of an age.

Classical Marxism

So Karl Marx moved into this brave new world of atheism. There was one catch, however: to disbelieve in spiritual forces was to erase the Weltgeist, the motor that drove the dialectic, and the dialectic was by this time Marx's key method of inquiry into society and politics—how they got to be that way and which way they were going in the future.

This is when, at age twenty-nine, Marx invented Marxism, formally known as "dialectical materialism." *The Communist Manifesto* of late 1847 was its first and still classic expression. Marx replaced the Weltgeist with a force that is purely material, one of the few things in human history that almost never stops and never goes backwards—the progress of technology. This became the "base" of his system; everything else about society and politics was more or less a reflection of it, called "superstructure." Social class, for example, was determined by a person's relationship to the technological base. If cutting edge productive technology in the year AD 1000 was a castle in the middle of five thousand cleared acres, yoked oxen pulling a wooden plow, the wine-press, and the clay oven in which to bake bread, then the controllers of that technology—the feudal class—were the dominant class and rightly so. Even ideology was dominated by them: the chapel was built into the castle, and the variety of Christianity preached there was naturally supportive of their social and political superiority.

But technology inevitably progressed, with longer distance trade, double-entry bookkeeping, and more efficient and larger-scale production of goods. It was the bourgeoisie (town dwellers) or middle class which controlled this technology. But the old feudal lords held onto the old structures of political and social power, and polarization and tension grew in society. Finally, in the French Revolution, it all exploded in social revolution and war, and the new synthesis that came about was dominated by the bourgeoisie. They fashioned new political and social institutions to fit their class, and rightly so, because they controlled cutting-edge technology at the time.

In the future, predicted Marx in the mid-nineteenth century, technology would progress, with ever bigger and ever more concentrated industry. The industrial workers, or proletariat, would become ever poorer, concentrated, and class-conscious. The remaining bourgeoisie would gobble each other up in capitalist competition. Last, in a simple but final revolution, the proletariat would take over the world, and rightly so, as the real possessors of the cutting-edge technology of the day.

The state, Marx believed along with a long line of western thinkers including Sir Thomas More, has always been a device that a minority used to control the majority. The state is thus "the expression of class conflict." When the proletarian majority takes over, after a brief "dictatorship of the proletariat," there will be only one class left and therefore no class conflict. The state with its armies and police will then have withered away, and be put in the museum along with the flint hoe and the bronze axe. People world-wide will live in harmonious communal groups where family values hold true, as in the agricultural communal golden age that once was, but now machines will serve humankind and the living will be easy.

Its strengths

What are the strengths of Marxism? The nineteenth century had more faith in science than we have today, in general. The new science of statistics was supposed to wipe out mental illness by mathematically describing where it would occur, for instance, and the environment could be changed before it ever happened! Marxism claimed to be scientific, and surfed on that swell of popularity. In addition, in the twentieth century, from 1917 to 1991, Communist Russia could be tapped by most any world Marxist group for financial and military support and personal expertise. These were both temporary strengths, however, and the author would like to get at the more intrinsic strengths and weaknesses of Marxism. And it still does have a power in the twenty-first century, even with the Soviet Union disbanded and "to get rich is glorious" the slogan in "Communist" China.

Marxism explores economics as the key link between the cutting-edge technology of a time (the "base") and a particular social class (of the "superstructure"). Don't tell me what you believe, Marx said; show me where you get your money, and I'll tell you what you believe. Even if you want to argue with Marx about society and government and where they are headed, you must ever after do it on economic grounds. He probably did more than any single person to put Economics in the curricula of business schools (even though Marxism is usually not very popular with business school profs!). At least partly because of him there are probably more key political advisors today who are Economists than from any other single discipline. And the Marxist approach is still a fruitful line of social science inquiry today. Want to sharpen your ideas on the near future? Just set yourself a course of self-study into how a certain aspect of cutting-edge productive technology (computer software, for example) is economically linked to a certain category of people (from Microsoft's Bill Gates down to the lowest paid Microsoft employee and the most marginal outside consultant), and what the social and political implications of that new "sub-class" might be, with its new economic clout. It would take a lot of self-discipline to do such a study, right? Marx had such discipline, in spades. He studied ALL the cutting edge technologies of his day, trying to find the exact pattern of social and political impact of each.

Secondly, Marx and subsequent Marxists have made the world's most detailed study of Movements and Revolutions. Seeing all revolutions as manifestations of a single underlying dialectical pattern, they have carefully categorized, compared, and contrasted them. If the situation is this, and the public mood is that, we can do thus-and-so and manipulate the public mood to this new level, says a Marxist—and the best of them have done it with some success.

Thirdly, Marxists are the world's best practitioners of guerrilla war. They have a long history of perfecting cell organization to keep out secret police infiltrators. They have a manual of operations with rich and fat chapters added by Lenin and Trotsky, Mao and Zhu De, Ho and Giap, Castro and Che. Well, not a real book, you understand, but some scattered writings and a coherent pattern of practice. In 1943, for example, newspaper correspondent Theodore White was among the first westerners to visit the Chinese Communist guerrilla base at Yenan, behind Japanese military lines (on which more later in Chapter 13). He had expected a base area like Detroit or Pittsburgh that provided arms, supplies, food, and support to the front, and was astonished to find that it shipped nothing to the front but ideas. It was an "idea factory," he said, where politics was supreme:

> Yenan was a continuing experiment in 'do-it-yourself' government, with people learning, as they do not learn in Poli-Sci I in any American university, how you go about choosing the proper men to govern other men—or improvising all the multitude of technologies needed to govern. How does one make paper to print books,

leaflets or money in a hill country? They were learning by themselves. What do you do after you dip buckets of oil from traditional oil pits and try to make kerosene out of it for lamps, and the badly refined oil sputters in the homemade lamps? How do you refine oil? How do you melt iron and make guns? How do you care for sick and wounded? How, after all, do you make a revolution and a new government without ideas? That was Yenan's main function; to cycle and recycle individuals through the base area and teach them to think in new ways.[6]

In 1972 Frances Fitzgerald, who had lived in and written about Vietnam in 1966 and who later studied with the great French colonial scholar Paul Mus for his insights into why the French had lost in Vietnam, wrote one of the most important books on the Vietnam War written by any American. It was called *Fire in the Lake* (from the ideogram for Revolution in the Confucian fortune-telling book *I Ching*). In the book she argues that the U.S. never understood either Vietnamese culture or the Marxist strategy of the National Liberation Front, with the result that we were really defeated before we ever substantially militarily engaged in 1965, and this in spite of our enormous technological superiority. Here's her take on the Marxist side of it all; if you understand her "politics" to mean essentially the same thing as White's "ideas," it's a remarkably similar evaluation:

During the course of the [Vietnam] war Americans wrote a great deal about the military strategy of the NLF and relatively little about its politics. The reason is simple. Most research on Vietnam was official research, and the official American line was that the guerrilla war involved no internal political issues, but that it was merely part of the attempt of the North Vietnamese to conquer the south. . . . The result was that even those Americans responsible for the conduct of the war knew relatively little about their enemy, for within the NLF politics was all: it was at the same time the foundation of military strategy and its goal. For the NLF military victories were not only less important than political victories, but strictly meaningless considered in isolation from them. Those few American officials who studied the NLF saw the political focus, but did not understand its significance. Had they understood it, they might have warned that it would be better to send the Saigon regime's army to fight without weapons than to send it to fight without a political strategy, as was the case.[7]

This kind of practical revolution was latent in Marx's original thought, and some of his own practical organizing was shrewd, as in his work with the International Workingmen's Association. In 1863 an Exhibition of Modern Industry was held in London, and a French delegation came that was about half what Marx would have called proletarian, and carried on serious talks with British trade unionists. Marx was called on to give some structure to the vague draft statements of worker solidarity. Structure it he did, by 1864, into a much more centralized and active body. It met in later years in other European cities such as Brussels and Geneva, and picked up more and more international support. Only when a rebellion led by the Russian Anarchist Mikhail Bakunin threatened to take it over did Marx in essence kill it by moving it to New York. But the institution was not forgotten, and would be reborn in 1889 as the Second International, and again in 1919 as the Third International, better known as the Communist International (Comintern).

To list one final item on the "strengths" side, Marxism still claims the original moral high ground claimed by the first socialists. If you won't let us attack injustices with our weapons, they say, then please tell us what your approach is; or are you not interested in injustice in the world? This would be a particularly powerful argument in the era of de-colonization after World War II. A whole generation of independence leaders—educated in western, often Christian schools that taught the values of Liberal democracy—would become Marxist or at least adopt much of Marxist social analysis and strategy.

Its weaknesses

And what are Marxism's weaknesses? Perhaps a third of Marx's criteria for a socialist order that he listed in *The Communist Manifesto* have come to be—graduated income tax, national banks, free public education, and such. But many of Marx's major predictions began to go wrong even during his lifetime. The workers did not keep getting poorer. The middle class did not cannibalize itself, but grew to be the largest group in all technologically modern societies. World revolution, at least as Marx described it, has not come about yet.

And the states where "Marxist" revolutions did eventually succeed—Russia, China, North Korea, Cuba, Vietnam—were anything but the advanced industrial states where the proletariat was strong and where the world revolution was supposed to begin. They all had rural majorities by a huge margin, and they all had a problem of land-hunger by farmers. What transpired in each of those nations was much more akin to an old-style French Revolution than a new-style Marxist one. The ideological twisting and turning Lenin had to do to justify Marxist revolution in basically agricultural Russia is eye-popping. In his 1916 *Imperialism: The Highest Stage of Capitalism,* he argued that the capitalist countries had saturated their own countries with capital investment, so that rates of return were driven very low. Then they had turned to the colonies to invest, soon saturating that market. Friction between them on some colonial frontier would soon result in the world war that would trigger the world revolution. Imperial Russia, he said, was an economic colony of France, and therefore qualified as a likely place for world revolution to begin . . . .

Most new Marxist rulers really believed that the communal way of life would be such a positive experience that if people could be enticed or forced into it, they would enthusiastically embrace it. The communes and super-communes of Soviet Russia and in China after 1949, however—the kolkhoz and Sovkhoz, and their later parallels in the Chinese communes and Agricultural Producers Cooperatives—were in fact a harsh form of slavery that bled the agricultural sector to support the industrial sector. Any time the heavy state pressures were lifted, most people escaped as soon as they could. The Israeli kibbutz is really the only modern voluntary communal experience of any size to last three or four generations, and even the kibbutz was arguably inspired as much by nationalism as by socialism, and even it is fading away as a truly communal institution in the current generation. Material incentives seem necessary for most of us to work hard; human nature may not be quite as good as socialists in general and Marxist theorists in particular would like to believe.

Some babies were indeed thrown out with the bath water. Junking the old systems, with all their inequities, also junked the few built-in safeguards. Stalin and Mao exercised more totalitarian autocracy in Russia and China than their "feudal" predecessors Nicholas II and the Dowager Empress ever dreamed of. The human rights record of Marxist governments is, in general, dismal. This too was implicit in Marxism from the very first, as even other kinds of socialists pointed out. What is to keep your temporary "dictatorship of the proletariat" from becoming permanent?, Mikhail Bakunin asked Marx in the nineteenth century and Rosa Luxembourg asked Lenin in the early twentieth. One of the hidden attractions of Marxism for the national independence leaders of the de-colonization era after WW II was that it justified their taking of power by force, and so avoiding all the time-wasting fuss of trying to rule by the democratic process enshrined in most new constitutions.

Finally there is another hidden aspect of Marxism that shows it to be at least as much an emotional experience as a rational, scientific exercise (listed here as a "weakness" because it undermines Marxism's claim to be scientific, though in terms of attracting people to Marxism it is a strength!). You can see this at work in the life of Marx himself and in a good many future Marxists. In the early 1840s, Marx became a journalist, editor of the *Rhineland Gazette* sponsored by some West Prussian businessmen upset with anti-business government policies. He was not yet a Marxist, and was calling for individual moral regeneration of people. Can't you see what some human beings are doing to a mass of other human beings in this industrial revolution, he said; won't you change your ways? In these days he wrote about human fulfillment:

> Let us assume man to be man, and his relation to the world to be a human one. Then love only can be exchanged for love, trust for trust, etc. If you wish to enjoy art you must be an artistically cultivated person; if you wish to influence other people you must be a person who really has a stimulating and encouraging effect upon others. Every one of your relations to man and nature must be a specific expression, corresponding to the object of your will, of your real individual life. If you love without evoking love in return, i.e. if you are not able, by the manifestation of yourself as a loving person, to make yourself a beloved person, then your love is impotent and a misfortune.[8]

Marx on love! The author would bet if he'd given this quotation to an American audience of a couple hundred and asked which famous modern intellectual wrote that, nobody would have gotten it right. This pre-Marxist Marx believed that one key thing that made humans different from animals was that they had to make things, physical or mental, and surround themselves with their creations. In the industrial revolution, unfortunately, workers were reduced to robots, with no creative work to do, and the product of their labor not even theirs to dispose of. The pre-Marxist Marx borrowed a word from Feuerbach to describe this, saying that the worker's product was "alienated" from him.

Marx's heartfelt articles produced no change in society and his frustration grew. His editorials became so shrill that he was fired. And just then he invented Marxism, dropping all those emotional appeals such as "alienation." Is it only a coincidence that the final end of the "scientific" system of Marxism is a utopia exactly like the one the young Marx would have chosen for the world? Marxism has always strongly appealed to people so frustrated with society that they devote their lives to changing it, but can see no evidence that they are changing it by their activity. Marxism subconsciously solves the frustration. You may not see the results of your effort, it says, but you are on the side of the future: while the polarization of the dialectic is growing, nothing seems to change, but soon it will change dramatically. Now if a person looked at this objectively, after being convinced by Marx that mere individuals can only speed up or slow down the dialectical process by a tiny increment, the obvious thing to do would be to go fishing or do something less dangerous than revolutionary activity. But it's not a purely rational thing; it is more an emotional search for justification of their activity. Marxism, like Calvinism in the age of religious wars, preached predestination but in practice attracted some of the most dynamic spirits.

The strengths and weaknesses of Marxism are, for this author, both beautifully represented in a book written in the fall of 1978 by Fred Halliday, *Iran: Dictatorship and Development*. Halliday, a British Marxist, brilliantly surveyed the modern history of Iran and carefully traced the economic connections between social class, technology (especially oil production), and government. He confidently and correctly predicted the Iranian revolution a few months later that caught most everyone else in the world off-guard. At the end of the book, however, Halliday interpreted all his evidence as pointing towards a new socialist Iran:

> If the left can evolve a practice and a programme that guarantees political freedom after the end of capitalism in Iran, then it may be able to rally a wide and ultimately victorious popular movement against the Pahlavi regime . . . . It is quite possible that before too long the Iranian people will chase the Pahlavi dictator and his associates from power, will surmount the obstacles in its way, and build a prosperous and socialist Iran.[9]

Conservative religious nationalism under the Ayatollah Khomeini, of course, swept not just socialists but liberals too from the field, and looking back most of us are amazed that anyone would ever have predicted a socialist state in Iran. All ideologies have their wishful thinking, the author supposes, but there is so much utopian wishful thinking in Marxism that it almost needs to be categorized as a religious faith.

The first Russian Marxists

Now, having possibly alienated both Marxist and non-Marxist readers, the author would like to push on to the intersection of Marxism and Russian history proper.

With all its strengths and weaknesses—some only clear with 20/20 hindsight—this new ideology began to be embraced by some Russian intellectuals. In 1883 (the year of Marx's death, coincidentally) a handful of former narodniks who had escaped from Russia regrouped in Geneva, Switzerland. One of them was Vera Zasulich, whose attempted assassination of Gov. Gen. Trepov you've seen. Another was Georgii Plekhanov, formerly a neatly dressed chemistry student by day and worker organizer by night. He is credited with having given the first socialist political speech in Russia, in St. Petersburg's Kazan Square[GE[47]] in December of 1876 to a couple hundred radical students and workers, and having successfully eluded the police after that. Having tried peaceful change, and violent change, and having achieved nothing either way, their frustration as you might imagine was intense. Under Plekhanov's leadership they became Marxists, and established what seems to have been the first Russian Marxist Party—which they called "Emancipation of Labor." It was a small hand-

---

47. GE Layer 47 is a Placemark referencing Kazan Square. It opens onto St. Petersburg's main street, the Nevsky Prospect, and is embraced by the curving arms of the Kazan Cathedral.

ful; Plekhanov joked once while they were on an outing on Lake Geneva that if the rowboat went down there went Russian Marxism. But in the context of Russian developments, it was a movement with growth potential, and Plekhanov's secretly circulated translations and Marxist analyses of Russian society, economics, and politics became an interesting new thread in Russian underground reading and discussion. It was not specifically called Marxism, but Social Democracy. Historically speaking it's a bit confusing, because a moderate strain of socialism was already known under that same name in Britain. Just keep in mind that in a Russian and eastern European context, a "Social Democrat" (an SD) was a Marxist.

Nicholas II

Nicholas II, who ruled from 1894 until the Revolution of 1917, embraced his father's autocratic ideology but lacked his autocratic character. His formal coronation wasn't until 1896, over a year after his father's death; but despite all the preparations for it, it was disastrous. He had retained Pobedonostsev as his chief advisor, and in an address just before the coronation—replying to requests from the Zemstvo organizations that they be allowed to form a political party and participate more in government decisions—he said this:

> It has come to my knowledge that during recent months there have been heard in some zemstvos the voices of those who have indulged in senseless dreams that the zemstvos might participate in the direction of the internal affairs of the state. Let all know that I shall devote my energy to the service of the people, but that I shall maintain the principle of autocracy as firmly and unflinchingly as did my father.

Then on the actual day of the coronation, when enormous crowds came out for the event (and the presents traditionally given out on the occasion), Cossack cavalry pushed the unruly crowds around to the extent that hundreds were crushed to death in some nearby trenches. Instead of showing any public concern about it, which was his first impulse, Nicholas listened to his hard-line advisors and went to the coronation ball that night as if nothing had happened.

There was some economic progress, albeit with harsh side effects. Nicholas II had inherited his father's Minister of Railroads, Sergei Witte, and he was such a get-it-done administrator that he was promoted to Finance Minister. Under him work on the Trans-Siberian Railway was begun in 1891, working from the Urals in the west and Vladivostok in the east to meet in the middle. The last stretch around Lake Baikal was finished in 1904.[GE48] In the 1895–1900 "scramble for concessions" in China, just defeated by a modernized Japan and assumed to be disintegrating by the major European powers, Russia got its share of the spoils—in 1896 the concession to build the China Eastern Railway shortcut across Manchuria to Vladivostok, and in 1898 the right to a spur line called the South Manchurian Railway down to the ice-free port of Port Arthur.[GE49] To attract the capital necessary for railroad and industrial development from European financial centers, Witte determined to put Russia on the gold standard, and achieved it by 1897. He left an impressive railroad grid and the real beginnings of modern heavy industry, but if anything the condition of the common farmers—still the great majority of the people—deteriorated. Americans may be reminded of William Jennings Bryan's "cross of gold" speeches at about this time, on the same issue, arguing that the gold standard was crushing the indebted farmers.

Lenin and the St. Petersburg Group

In the famine years of the early 1890s, radicals in St. Petersburg especially, a generation younger than Plekhanov, were turning to Marxism. They formed the "St. Petersburg Group of Emancipation of Labor." The dominant mind and personality among them was Vladimir Il'ich Ulianov, who would not be calling himself

48. GE Layer 48 is a Folder titled "Trans-Siberian Railway." It includes a Path symbolizing the railroad as a thick red line, and key cities along it with red pushpin icons. If you still have your Siberian Rivers folder open, you can see how many of these key cities are at major river crossings (or in the case of Irkutsk, a "touching" instead of a crossing).

49. GE Layer 49 is a Folder titled "Manchurian railways." It has Paths in red for both the CER and the South Manchurian Railway, as well as red pushpin Placemarks for the junction city of Harbin and for Port Arthur.

"Lenin" until 1901. He was briefly introduced at the end of the narodnichestvo section of this chapter as the grieving younger brother of the executed Alexander Ulianov, but it might be instructive here to trace his conversion to Marxism. Although it will be anachronistic, let's just call him Lenin from the first.

He was born in Simbirsk[GE[50]] in 1870, third child of a District Superintendent of Education and a surprisingly well educated (for Russia in those days) doctor's daughter. Summer vacations were spent at a country estate east of Kazan owned by his mother's family. By the time Lenin's older brother was winning gold medals for his biology research at the University of St. Petersburg in the mid-1880s, Lenin was performing at valedictorian level at the Simbirsk Classical Gymnasium. Then, when Lenin was in his mid-teens, came two sudden blows—the death of his father of a brain aneurism in January of 1886, and the execution of his brother in April of 1887. More than one biographer of Lenin has commented on the impact of the death of their father on the lives of Alexander and Vladimir, as if some behavioral restraint had been removed. Alexander of course became the bomb-builder in the plot to assassinate Alexander III. Later on a form asking for religion, Lenin wrote "Non-believer since age 16," the year when his devoutly religious father had died.

Lenin continued to do well with his studies, and moved—with his mother and younger siblings—to Kazan to enroll in the university's law school there in August of 1887. He lasted not quite a semester. He had sought out the company of some radicals trying to rebuild the old narodnik "People's Will" terrorist group, and in early December was one of the ringleaders in a student protest against the harsh new laws on universities being imposed by Alexander III's government. He was suspended from the university and sent under virtual house arrest to the family estate east of town. There he not only studied law but revolutionary literature, reading among other things Chernyshevky's *What Is To Be Done?* He was allowed to attend the Kazan University law school again in the fall of 1888, and seems to have read his first Marxist literature then.

He made it through that whole year without being suspended, even though he renewed his contact with the narodnik underground. His mother was obviously aware of all this, and desperate to remove him from radical circles, bought a small estate not far from Samara at the village of Alakaevka. They spent the summer of 1889 there, and Lenin did take some interest in rural life, especially the state of peasant consciousness. But he was obviously not going to make farming, even small-scale gentry farming, a lifestyle, so his mother sold the estate and they bought a house in Samara. He spent three years there. He was allowed, after his private study, to take the law exams from St. Petersburg University, and passed with what in the west would be called *summa cum laude*, and then he worked with public courts and private lawyers in Samara. But he also translated Marx's *Communist Manifesto* into Russian and began serious study of Plekhanov's Marxist analysis of Russian development.

Then in the fall of 1893, just twenty-three years old, he moved to St. Petersburg. He worked as assistant in a law firm and lived just across the Fontanka Canal from the heart of St. Petersburg. Just because his family name was Ulianov, he had immediate access into revolutionary circles; he seriously quizzed those who had known his brother about his habits, beliefs, readings. He quickly became one of the two or three most important leaders of the revolutionary community there. In a matter of months he moved in with Nadezhda Krupskaia, a like-mined young revolutionary. Later she recalled the first time she met him; it was at a meeting where someone was waxing eloquent on teaching the workers to read and write, and Lenin laughed sarcastically and said that if someone wanted to save the Fatherland through literacy, no one should stop him. There was already evident in his thought and work of a fusion of narodnichestvo and Marxism, an acceptance of violence if it furthered the cause.

In the summer of 1894 he was sent by the Marxist community in St. Petersburg to talk to leading SDs in central and western Europe, including Plekhanov in Geneva. In Paris he took time out to study the Commune of 1871; in Berlin he spent over a month researching revolutions in the state library. He came back to St. Petersburg late in the year with sharper ideas on waging the class struggle, especially including publishing literature. His more energetic organizing got him arrested and jailed for a year, then sentenced to three years in the heart of Siberia on the upper Yenesei River. Krupskaia in her turn was arrested later, and got her place of exile changed to his, where they were formally married in 1898.

---

50. GE Layer 50 is a Folder with Placemarks referencing Simbirsk, a provincial capital city on the west bank of the lower Volga, and other sites mentioned in the text to come, including the still-standing country house of his mother's family, his house in Kazan, the village of Alakaevka, the city of Samara, Shushenskoe in Siberia, and finally Pskov.

Once again Lenin used exile and house arrest as a time for reading and writing. He was particularly opposed to the 1898 book by Edouard Bernstein arguing for "evolutionary Marxism," gradual progress that required no World Proletarian Revolution. When his sentence was up in 1900, and he was allowed to come back to live in Russia but not in St. Petersburg, he chose Pskov, close to it by train. Here he began work on a revolutionary paper called *Iskra* (*The Spark*, obviously a spark to set a revolutionary flame). In 1901 he moved to Munich to publish it, soon joined there by Krupskaia. Then in 1902 came what might be called the first of his important writings, *What Is To Be Done?* The title was straight from Chernyshevky's book of exactly forty years before, but the message was not. Its central idea was that only a disciplined, tightly-knit Marxist party could effect real change. Until the central leadership of such a party decided an issue, members could take any stand on it they chose. Once it had been debated up through the ranks, however, and judgment passed on it by the highest level, everybody needed to fall into lockstep behind that decision. "Democratic centralism," is how it was later described. A larger, more open party, with easy access for police spies, would be only a "tendency," not a party for real change. Here you can already see Lenin's push for revolution as soon as possible. He was increasingly frustrated with Plekhanov's orthodox Marxist view that Russia first needed its bourgeois revolution, then a full historical period of development before it could have its proletarian one.

Back in March of 1898, nine Marxist-leaning activists had met in great secrecy in a house in Minsk[GE51] to create a Russian Social Democratic Party. They drafted a constitution and a manifesto, but it was frankly a party in name only, and most of the "delegates" were soon arrested by the Tsarist police. The real foundation of a Russian Social Democratic Party only came five years later, in August of 1903, with the "Second Congress" that met first in Brussels and then (with the encouragement of the Belgian police) in London. Here Lenin lobbied hard for his centralized party idea. When he won an early vote with Plekhanov's support, he began calling his faction, "The Majority-ites," or *Bol'sheviki*, and his opponents the "Minority-ites," or *Mensheviki*. Ironically, when Plekhanov fully realized what was being proposed, he voted against Lenin, and so it was the "Minority-ites"—now the majority—who were left in control of *Iskra*. Lenin thereupon walked out. He obviously would rather have a tiny but loyal group behind him than be part of the mainstream SD Menshevik "tendency." So at the real founding of a Russian national Marxist party in 1903, it immediately split!

The "short, victorious war" and the Revolution of 1905

Meanwhile back in Russia the political situation was deteriorating for the imperial government. That same 1903 was also the year when the Russian government renewed its war on its Jewish minority, beginning with a huge pogrom in Kishinev.[GE52] Playing the anti-Semitic "race card"—appealing to the lowest common denominator in Russia—was surely in and of itself a sign that the government was desperate to rally some support. And then in 1904 the Minister of Interior Count von Plehve convinced the government to arrange a "short, victorious war" to rally the people around the flag. Unfortunately for Russia (and von Plehve himself, who was assassinated that same year), they picked Japan for their target and the war was not victorious. The Japanese fleet surprised the Russian Far East fleet at Port Arthur,[GE53] and sunk it (and probably remembered the success of that surprise attack later in 1941 when they went to war with the U.S.). When the Russians sent their Baltic fleet all around the world to engage the Japanese, it was sunk on the day of its arrival in the Tsushima Straits between Korea and Japan.[GE54] Meanwhile the Japanese army pushed up along the China Eastern Railway, engaging the retreating Russians in three exhausting battles.[GE55] If the war had gone on for a matter of years, Russian size and weight might have told in the end. But the newly completed single-track Trans-Siberian Railway couldn't move the Russian military fast enough, and a losing war did the opposite of rallying people round the flag—it triggered the Revolution of 1905.

---

51. GE Layer 51 is a Placemark generally referencing Minsk, now capital of Belarus.
52. GE Layer 52 is a Placemark generally referencing Kishinev, today's Chişinău, capital of Moldova.
53. GE Layer 53 is a Placemark framing a view of the former Pt. Arthur.
54. GE Layer 54 is a Placemark framing a view of Tsushima Strait.
55. GE Layer 55 is a Folder with Placemarks referencing each of the three battles.

There was considerable revolutionary activity in Moscow in 1905. Government-loyal troops held the Kremlin and environs, but were hemmed in on the west, north, and south by a zone completely under the control of revolutionaries.[GE[56]] Only the arrival of reinforcements from the east broke the revolution. But it was St. Petersburg, the capital and major industrial city with a tradition of labor strikes, that was ground zero of the Revolution. In December of 1904 workers at the giant Putilov metallurgical plant south of the city[GE[57]] went out on strike, and soon tens of thousands of sympathetic workers at other plants joined them. An Orthodox priest who sympathized with the workers, Father Gapon, was working in a "police union" (a legal union that met at police headquarters so it could be kept under regular surveillance!). In these times of desperate food shortage, he called on workers to march from six rallying points around the city to Palace Square to deliver a petition to the Emperor. They marched without arms, on a Sunday, carrying icons. A few made it to Palace Square, but most were dispersed or even shot down by the police. Father Gapon's own group was fired on near Narva Gate in Court Square;[GE[58]] he himself was not hit but some forty workers around him were killed. In all perhaps a thousand died on what was known ever since as "Bloody Sunday." So within three weeks the Russian armed forces lost a major battle with the Japanese, and shot down a thousand unarmed civilians in the capital.

That summer the sailors on the Battleship Potemkin, of the Black Sea fleet based at Sevastopol, mutinied. Conditions for the common sailors in the navy were awful, and there were rumors they were going to be sent east into the Japanese war. Apparently sailors who found maggots in their meat protested, and were ordered to eat it or face execution. The sailors mutinied, killed half the officers and locked up the other half, and sailed into Odessa with some general thought about aiding the revolution there.[GE[59]] They lobbed a couple of shells at governmental buildings, and then when government-loyal ships began to gather, sailed out through them and then wandered rather aimlessly around the Black Sea until they ran out of fuel.

Everything came to head about October 20, with one of the most complete and successful general strikes in world history. After ten days of this, with no relief in sight, Nicholas II granted the famous October Manifesto. It established a constitutional monarchy wherein the Emperor would share power with a legislature, a *Duma* (from the Russian verb *dumat'*, "to think"—which is, come to think of it, a more hopeful title than Parliament, which comes from the French *parler* "to speak"). Despite the Russian title, it was clearly a western-style legislature; this was Russia's first real experiment with democracy. We'll follow the course of the Duma directly, but another institution of 1905 needs at least a word of introduction here, too. A "Council of Workers' Deputies," mainly metal workers, came into being as early as October, beginning with a few dozen delegates from unions and factories and soon growing to several hundred. It did not call the successful general strike of October 20–30, and when it tried to call one later it failed. But "Council" in Russian is "Soviet," so here is the small, seemingly insignificant origin of that word that was to take on such huge meaning in 1917, a dozen years later.

Stolypin's necktie, and his "wager on the strong"

The dominant figure to emerge in Russian government during the era of the first two Dumas, 1906 and 1907, was Petr Stolypin. Since 1902 he had been a remarkably successful provincial governor with a "carrot and stick" policy—a brutal police suppression of disorder, coupled with a real concern for the hardships peasants

---

56. GE Layer 56 is a Folder titled "Moscow, 1905"; it includes a Polygon in yellow showing the area around the Kremlin held by government troops, a Polygon in red showing the arc of revolutionary control, and a yellow pushpin Placemark icon showing Kazan Station, where pro-governmental troops arrived to turn the tide.

57. GE Layer 57 is a Placemark generally locating the Putilov works, today the Kirov factory.

58. GE Layer 58 is a Placemark referencing Narva Gate; click on Panoramio icon under pointer for one view of this famous 1814 triumphal arch. Narva is the town further west along the south shore of the Gulf of Finland (where Charles XII's army defeated Peter the Great's in 1701), hence "Narva Gate."

59. GE Layer 59 is a Placemark referencing the waterfront in Odessa, mainly used here as an excuse to embed a website with an old photo of the Potemkin. The famous scene in Eisenstein's film on the subject, of the Cossack attack on people at the steps leading down to the waterfront, may never have happened in reality.

faced. In particular, Stolypin's land reform policy was designed to help end those hardships by freeing the farmer from both the control of the commune and from the inefficiency of the strip field system. This was to be done by encouraging the creation of a unitary farm, a *khutor*, for as many individual farmers as possible. Give the small farmers some private property of their own, he reasoned, and they will tend to respect the private property even of those who own a good bit more of it. This was Stolypin's famous "wager on the strong," a bet that government support for the most successful individual peasant farmers would swing opinion in the countryside to support of the government. Emperor Nicholas II, impressed by Stolypin's successes, made him Minister of Interior in May of 1906, and two months later President of the Council of Ministers.

It was with Stolypin, then, that the Liberal and Revolutionary Duma leadership of 1906 and 1907 had to deal. He dismissed the First Duma of 1906 when it demanded control over land policy, and simply issued his own land reform policies by imperial government decree. And even though the Second Duma of 1907 was less revolutionary and more inclined to cooperate with the imperial government, when it refused to endorse his land reforms he dismissed it too, and then immediately ended Russia's first modern experiment with democracy by severely curtailing the voting franchise. The Third and Fourth Dumas would be "kept" bodies, debating societies with no real power to legislate anything. All through Stolypin's tenure as head of government (he was assassinated in September of 1911), he also wielded the stick: thousands and thousands of peasant "terrorists" were executed. So many were hung at his direction that the hangman's noose became known, with true gallows humor, as "Stolypin's necktie."

G. T. Robinson was one of the first great U.S. students of Russian history. While still a fairly young scholar, in his early 30s, he spent much of 1925–27 in the new Soviet Union. This eventually resulted in one of the best books on Russia ever written by an American—*Rural Russia Under the Old Regime*. As the title hints, Robinson was trying to sort out the role of the peasantry in the coming of the Revolution, and his collection of statistics and governmental policies and specific laws is impressive indeed. But as with all good historians there are flashes of personal insight to illuminate the prose. Such is his presentation of an encounter with one of Stolypin's khutors, some fifteen years and a Revolution after Stolypin's death:

> In the depths of this countryside, on a certain morning in the late Summer of 1926, the writer had himself jostled over several miles of country road from a river-town on the upper Volga (green bluffs, white walls, gold domes) to a village which was to serve as the first halting-place on a wagon-journey northward; and he had not spent an hour here, beside the samovar (drinking tea, eating carrot-cakes, and watching respectfully a large cockroach which scuttled several times across the table) when he learned that there was in the neighborhood of this village a curiosity which every traveller must see. Accordingly there was more joggling along the street with its double row of houses, then on through a motley of scattered strips of plow-land, and around the easy slope of a hill to a fence where the patchwork came abruptly to an end. Beyond the fence was a substantial and prosperous house of logs set down alone in the midst of unbroken fields—the special marvel of the neighborhood, an isolated peasant farm. If this *khutor* had been established here in accordance with some pre-plan to dramatize the double contrast between the individual and the collective, the well-off and the not-so-well, the thing could hardly have been better done.[10]

It was a rural scene any American would have taken for granted—a unified farmstead with the farmer's house on the property—but here such a rarity that locals urged travelers to go see it. As Robinson points out, "the establishment of the *khutor* was costly, the situation novel, the testing-period short," as well as being very incomplete. It seemed to pay dividends from 1906 to 1914, in terms of rural stability. After the assassination of Stolypin in 1911, however, no firm hand was on the throttle of the engine of government. And then in 1914 came the Great War.

Russia's side of World War I

You have already seen some of World War I from the German side, beginning with how the assassination of the Austrian heir-apparent by revolutionaries working for an independent Yugoslavia on June 28, 1914, triggered the declaration of war August 3 and 4. On the Russian side Nicholas II made several last-ditch efforts to avoid war, including offering to have the matter decided by the assembly at The Hague, an early forerunner of the United Nations. But finding it inevitable, on August 2 he spoke from a balcony of the Winter Palace to a huge crowd on Palace Square, repeating word for word Alexander I's oath back in 1812 that he would not make peace until the last enemy soldier was gone from Russian territory. There is a Russian word, *sobornost'*, which means the religious unity sometimes felt in a great cathedral, or at times when the community seems to be everything and the individual nothing. And although this was the same square that had experienced part of "Bloody Sunday" only nine years before, *sobornost'* was the general mood of the crowd that day. Looking back, perhaps the only way to have sustained this mood would have been continual victory in the war. Instead, facing over half of the single most powerful army ever yet assembled on the planet, Russia steadily lost.

The Russian strategic plan for the war was a major attack on Austria and a smaller one on Germany. The invasion of Germany's East Prussia was led by Generals Rennenkampf and Samsonov, who were not on good enough terms with one another to communicate well. Rennenkampf moved west very slowly, and Samsonov came north from Warsaw at speed, perhaps too fast for good exploration of what was ahead, through swamps and thickets. The German commander von Hindenburg threw everything he had at Samsonov's army near Tannenberg,[GE60] and killed or captured so much of this Russian army that Samsonov shot himself. Then Hindenburg turned on Rennenkampf and drove him back out of Prussia. The whole debacle cost Russia a quarter of a million casualties and the loss of priceless artillery. Meanwhile the major Russian attack in Austria had some initial success; they took Galicia and cost Austria more casualties than they themselves had suffered in East Prussia. But Hindenburg shifted his attack to southwest Poland and forced the Russians to deal with him instead of Austria. German troops could see Warsaw before the Russian defense finally held and dug in for the winter.

The spring campaign of 1915 opened promisingly for Russia. The British and French landed in the Dardanelles, and Italy joined the Entente and engaged Austria from the south. Russian armies moved again through Galicia and were almost to the Hungarian plains when Hindenburg hit the Russians in the greatest offensive yet of the war. He put pressure on them along a thousand-mile-wide front, and by July Russian armies were reeling back through Poland. Warsaw fell to the Germans in August, and even Belarus was being occupied by German armies. This is when the Russian losses of artillery of the year before showed up most in the war: on the retreat through Poland, Russian artillery was firing fewer shells a day than the Germans were firing a minute. Russian troops were going into battle in some places without rifles or boots, instructed to get both from dead comrades on the battlefield. In the United States we tend to hear most about the Western Front of World War I, but twice as many German troops were thrown against Russia as against France. By late fall of 1915, the German army had gone as far as current supply lines could support it, and the front stabilized. Russia began a frantic winter of re-grouping.

In 1916, the western powers of the Entente were desperate for help. The Dardanelles campaign had been a disaster; the Italians were being trounced by the Austrians at Trentino; and the slaughter at Verdun on the Western Front seemed about to crack France and Britain. So once again the Russian high command decided on an offensive to take some pressure off their western allies. General Brusilov mounted a pincer movement to knock Austria out of the war for once and all, and for the first time Russian troops had adequate artillery support. Russia took almost half a million Austrian prisoners and hundreds of artillery pieces. A simultaneous Russian attack on Germany took no ground but pinned down a good part of the German army. These two drives really bled Germany and Austria. They probably saved Italy, and took some pressure off French and British armies. But what they did to Russia! It cost Russia two million casualties and a third of a million prisoners.

Early in 1917 the Russian general staff once again assembled in Petrograd (the German-sounding name *Sankht Peterbourg* had been changed in 1914 to the more Slavic *Petrograd*) to plan the year's campaign, and once again decided on a spring offensive. But the government that made that pledge did not live to fulfill it.

By the winter of 1916–1917 the war was taking a major toll not just on the armies at the front but throughout Russia. The Emperor had gone off the year before to take personal command of the armies, which helped the armies not at all and left government essentially in the hands of the Empress Alexandra. Since 1908, she had fallen deeply under the influence of Rasputin, a Siberian faith-healer and fortune-teller. The fifth child and

60. GE Layer 60 is a Placemark referencing Tannenberg.

only son of the Emperor and Empress, Alexei, was hemophiliac and in danger of bleeding to death from ordinary cuts and bruises. Apparently Rasputin could so calm the boy with conversation and stories that the free-bleeding was alleviated. A model of humility and playing the part of representative of the "noble Russian folk" to perfection around the royal family, Rasputin was in his private life so licentious and corrupt as to sound almost unbelievable. With the ear of the Empress, who sometimes likened him to Christ, he made and unmade government ministers. All it took was bringing a good-looking woman around to stay at Rasputin's for a few days, or "buying" a pair of gloves from an artisan connected with him for fifty thousand rubles, or some such. Neither Alexandra nor Nicholas would listen to any complaints about him. The rank and file of the army simply assumed Alexandra was Rasputin's mistress. Governmental efficiency declined so much under Rasputin's influence that others thought Rasputin must be working for the Germans: the speaker of the Duma famously remarked, "Is this stupidity or is this treason?" Members of the extended royal family itself murdered Rasputin in late December of 1916, to try to salvage some respect for the imperial family, but it was too late.

Nicholas II's last decisive action, taken from the front in 1916, was to dismiss the current Duma and postpone its meeting time after time. When the Duma finally did meet in February of 1917, in the context of a general strike and food riots, its members met with a vengeance, determined not to be stepped on again.

The March (February, old-style) Revolution, 1917

In 1917 Russian history intersected Marxism in a big way, which perhaps justifies slowing down for a more careful treatment of events. It's important to note first that here were not one but two fairly separate revolutions, one in March (late February on the old Julian calendar; Russia didn't come over to the modern Gregorian calendar until February of 1918), and one in early November (late October, "old style"). In both revolutions Petrograd played the crucial role.

On March 7 (February 22 o.s.) the industrial workers at the giant Putilov plant south of the city came out on strike, as had happened back in the 1905 Revolution. But the real upheaval during the next five days, March 8–12 (Feb. 23–27 o.s.), originated mostly in the northeast section of the city—in the Vyborg district,[GE61] a mainly industrial and workers' housing area north and east of the northernmost channel of the Neva delta rivers, and in the part of St. Petersburg immediately south of that channel where the Volynsky and Preobrazhensky Guards regiments were stationed.[GE62] March 8, International Women's Day, was chosen by Vyborg District radicals for a protest march, ensuring a heavy female turnout that joined perhaps half of Petrograd's industrial workers out on strike. When the Petrograd garrison was called out to clear the streets, the soldiers refused to fire on the crowds. Ordered to charge, the Cossacks walked their horses gently through the crowds, winking as they went. By March 12 (February 28 o.s.) most of the Guards regiments had gone over to the crowds, bringing with them rifles and machine guns. Mobs broke into arsenals for arms, attacked public buildings, and freed all the political prisoners from the Peter and Paul Fortress. If there is a Russian Revolutionary equivalent for the Fall of the Bastille in the French Revolution, this is it.

Just as the fall of the Bastille (symbol of Paris rebelling against the royal government) had saved the National Assembly at Versailles, so on March 12 the revolutionary crowds in the Russian capital of Petrograd saved the increasingly radical Duma. On that day the Emperor ordered them dispersed, but they stayed in session. Probably on the model of the French National Assembly 128 years earlier, they formed a "Provisional Government," with the same two-fold mission: take care of pressing day-to-day problems of government, and come up with a new constitution. Even some of the characters look the same. Prince Georgii Lvov was elected President; he was a nobleman who sympathized with the commoners, the counterpart of a Mirabeau or Lafayette. The historian Pavel Miliukov, who preferred a constitutional monarchy on the model of Britain—as did most of the middle-class revolutionaries in France in 1789—was made foreign minister. Minister of Justice was the brilliant thirty-six-year-old lawyer Alexander Kerensky, of a bit more radical Social Revolutionary back-

---

61. GE Layer 61 is a Placemark framing a view of this "corner" of the upper channel of the Neva. The Vyborg district was named for the first town on the railroad northwest to Finland.

62. GE Layer 62 is a Folder titled "Volynsky and Preobrazhensky Guards barracks," with a Placemark for each in the (approximate) location.

ground, something like the Girondins of 1790–91. The Provisional Government telegraphed the Emperor at army headquarters, asking him to save the situation by appointing a cabinet with the nation's confidence (themselves, of course). There was no reply. Three days later they demanded his abdication. When Nicholas II did abdicate in favor of his brother the Grand Duke Michael, the latter refused the offer and declared his support of the Provisional Government. And so autocracy in Russia died with barely a whimper, and a new French Revolution seemed underway. The Provisional Government took as its headquarters the Marinsky Palace, on the southeast side of St. Isaac's Square and just across the Moika Canal,[GE63] and prepared to rule Russia from there.

The Dual Government

As Marx had seen in the nineteenth century, however, and predicted for the near future, society had changed, and there was yet another social element (Marx called it a class) around for this revolution—industrial workers who would make the course of this revolution somewhat different from the French Revolution. On that key March 12, some 250 delegates elected from factories and army units in Petrograd gathered at Tauride Palace[GE64]—not far from the main Guards barracks and just a short walk across the frozen Neva from Vyborg District—to organize the Council (Soviet) of Workers' and Soldiers' Deputies. It was not planned or carried into effect by any party, least of all the Bolsheviks. It was a spontaneous regeneration of a very popular institution of 1905, only twelve years before. Some members of the new one who had also been members of the original one remembered their failures earlier, and determined to seize the initiative this time. They set up emergency food commissions and a make-shift police force, and sent word to the Duma demanding to be admitted to government as an equal partner. Their immediate demands were for amnesty of all political prisoners, the right to strike, and freedom of press and assembly—and the famous Army Order Number One, published in the Soviet newssheet *Izvestiia* (*News*), abolishing officer control of men, doing away with the salute and insignia of rank. By the next day the Petrograd Soviet had 1,500 members, and double that in a week. And beginning with Moscow and the larger cities, Soviets took root throughout the country—some 400 by May, 600 by August, 900 by October. Dominated by the Mensheviks and the Social Revolutionaries early on, they would become more and more Bolshevik as the summer went by.

This March Revolution that began the Dual Government was accomplished with fairly minor bloodshed, as revolutions go. There were something over a thousand killed in Petrograd, and most of those were at the naval base of Kronstadt[GE65] where sailors killed many of their officers. The Soviets had the guns (and those willing to fire them!), when push came to shove. They were generally content to let the Duma do the day-to-day governing, but continually interfered to make policy, many times unpleasant for the Provisional Government.

The foreign minister and perhaps dominant personality of the Provisional Government, Pavel Miliukov, was still firmly committed to the war effort; after all, Russia had been secretly promised Istanbul and the Straits. This put him squarely at odds with Army Order No. 1 from the Petrograd Soviet, of course, and within two months he resigned in frustration.

Meanwhile, the brain and the organizer of the Bolsheviks was beginning to influence the situation. In one of his "Letters from Afar" in March, Lenin began to hint at immediate withdrawal from the "capitalist" war, and then starting a new "proletarian" revolution. This was received less than enthusiastically even by other Bolshevik leaders in Russia, and nothing much along these lines happened until Lenin came to force the action. This brings us to the remarkable chapter of the "Sealed Train." It had occurred to someone in the German foreign office that the Russian government could be critically weakened by injecting Lenin and friends back into

---

63. GE Layer 63 is a Placemark referencing Marinsky Palace, one of the most impressive buildings built in the reign of Nicholas I.

64. GE Layer 64 is a Placemark referencing the Tauride Palace (Tavrichesky dvorets). Prince Potemkin's great palace, it had been the meeting place of the original 1906 Duma.

65. GE Layer 65 is a Placemark framing a view of Kronstadt, the great naval fortress that takes up most of Kotlin Island; first fortified by Peter the Great in 1703.

politics there. So the German army got up a train for Lenin and thirty hand-picked revolutionaries, mostly Bolsheviks and their current allies the Left SRs, and sent it from Switzerland to Finland (including ocean legs across the Baltic to Sweden and then from Sweden to Finland). It was called "sealed" because only Lenin was allowed to get off at stations and buy supplies. He arrived at Petrograd's Finland Station[GE[66]], in the heart of the radical Vyborg District, on April 3, and two days later issued his *April Theses*. March, he said, had been the bourgeios revolution; the proletarian revolution could now happen any time. Here he coined the slogan that would do more than anything to bring the Bolsheviks to power, "Peace, Bread, and Land"—peace now at whatever cost, doing whatever it took to provide cheap and plentiful bread, and land to those who worked it. By May the real agrarian revolution began, as peasants began to seize land, and the upheaval continued for four more years.

It was mid-July, new style, when Miliukov and the KDs pulled out of government, and it triggered the so-called "July Days." What seem to have been spontaneous worker and soldier strikes and parades, the biggest on July 17, called for "All Power to the Soviets." This was reluctantly embraced by the Bolshevik leadership (Mensheviks and SRs were opposed). But the Provisional Government was still able to bring in some loyal troop units, and recover the allegiance of some others, and Lenin tried to call off the strike. Rumors flew that he was a German spy; that he didn't really want to lead but only destroy organized Russian opposition to the Germans. In this situation the moderate socialist Alexander Kerensky was elected Prime Minister, and he immediately called for the arrest of the Bolsheviks. Many of the leaders, including Trotsky, were jailed; Lenin slipped back across the border to Finland.

Kerensky's fatal step, looking back, was to order a new offensive against German and Austrian lines—a pincer movement aimed at Vilna in the north, and two separate drives west in the south.[GE[67]] When the troops involved became aware of preparations for the offensive, there were mutinies in the location of each planned drive.[GE[68]] Since June, General Lavr Kornilov had been commander-in-chief of the army. Between him and Kerensky there was some complicated discussion about how to restore military discipline. Kornilov may have felt that Kerensky actually offered to make him temporary dictator to achieve this; on his side, Kerensky was apparently frightened that Kornilov was going to do exactly that. So in early September, when General Kornilov launched a drive up by Pskov straight towards Petrograd, Kerensky publicly fired him and called for a national unity government to resist his advance. The Bolshevik leaders in jail were freed—in large part because the Bolsheviks had a 25,000-strong street army called the Red Guard. Railroad and telegraph workers, sympathizing mainly with the Bolsheviks, sabotaged the movement of Kornilov's army, and propaganda among the troops resulted in increasing rates of desertion. The drive stalled not far south of Petrograd, and then what was left of Kornilov's army retreated.[GE[69]]

The "Kornilov affair" undermined Kerensky; his importance had been as a compromise figure between Right and Left, and now the Right seemed discredited. The Bolsheviks quickly became the majority in both the Petrograd and Moscow Soviets.

The "Great October Revolution"

At a secret meeting on October 22 (n.s.) the Bolshevik leadership, including Lenin, made plans to take over the government in a little over two weeks. The date for the rising was fairly obviously determined in advance by the meeting of the "Third All-Russian Congress of Soviets" scheduled in Petrograd for November 7 (October 25 o.s.).

On the evening of November 6 Lenin slipped into town from Finland, through the Vyborg District, to Smolny Institute which the Bolsheviks had chosen as headquarters for the operation (not far from the Tauride

---

66. GE Layer 66 is a Folder titled "Sealed train, Finland Station." The square in front of Finland Station is still called, logically enough, Lenin Square.

67. GE Layer 85 is a Folder titled "Kerensky's planned offensive"; the four planned drives are shown as white outline Polygons.

68. GE Layer 86 is a Folder titled "Mutinies against the Kerensky plan," individual mutinies shown as red stars.

69. GE Layer 87 is a Polygon showing the Kornilov attack in white outline with a whitewash fill.

Palace where the Soviet had re-formed in March).[GE70] That night phase one of the plan went into effect, the occupation of the six bridges connecting the northern part of the city with the rest.[GE71] The next day, the official November 7 (October 25), they occupied the bridge going east from the Smolny Institute, the two bridges from the main part of the city to Vasilevsky Island, and the four train stations in the south of the city controlling access to Petrograd from the southwest, south, and southeast.[GE72] Later that day the cruiser *Aurora* (one of the few Russian ships to survive the Russo-Japanese War, currently in Kronstadt for repairs and there seized by revolutionary sailors) motored up the main channel of the Neva, hove to right off the Winter Palace[GE73] where the Provisional Government was meeting, and fired a blank broadside as a broad hint of what it was capable of doing. There was some military defense of the palace, but later that night it was overcome. Several hundred Bolshevik soldiers thereupon poured up the back staircase of the Winter Palace and arrested virtually the entire government (though Kerensky himself escaped).

Except for Kronstadt, where sailors butchered officers, it was a relatively bloodless undertaking. It was mostly "revolution by telegraph," with Trotsky telegraphing government facilities and telling them when Bolshevik forces would arrive so they could be gone by then.

R.S.F.S.R. and SOVNARKOM

A new government was set up, quickly, piece-meal and haphazardly—partly because it wasn't expected to last long, as the revolution was supposed to spread worldwide. The new state, in this supposedly short dictatorship of the proletariat, was called the Russian Soviet Federated Socialist Republic. Its constitution, like most modern constitutions, began with a ringing Declaration of Rights (of the Toiling and Exploited People). It included things Americans would find normal and not-so-normal: the separation of church from state, but also school from church; freedom of speech and assembly, but also the obligation of all to work. Supreme authority was vested in the All-Russian Congress of Soviets (separation of executive and legislative powers was denigrated as "bourgeios"), and when it was out of session, a body elected from it called the Central Executive Committee—which appointed the Commissars for day-to-day administration. So the functioning government was the Council of People's Commissars, or SOVNARKOM for short. Also as with the writing of most modern constitutions, there was a conflict between those who wanted more power for the central government (SOVNARKOM) versus those who wanted more power for local government (the hundreds of Soviets in the country's cities and towns). It's possible the local government forces may have won out, except for the emergency situations faced by the government. But because of that, the Bolsheviks—the most hostile of all political theorists to government power (except perhaps for the Anarchists)—found themselves defending the power of central government, a government that showed no signs of "withering away." Here's how it happened.

"Peace" was a key part of the slogan that brought the Bolsheviks to power in November of 1917, but peace remained a real problem. In an armistice arranged with Germany to talk about it, Germany insisted on keeping all it had conquered, including Poland and a good slice of western Russia. War Commissar Trotsky was outraged, and stalked out of the meeting calling for "no peace, no war." "No peace" was easy enough, but German armies simply resumed their advance. Lenin finally threatened to resign without a true peace, even an "obscene peace," as he called the terms of the Treaty of Brest-Litovsk (finally signed in March). It cost Russia half its industry, three-quarters of its iron production, over a million square miles, and over 60 million people[GE74]— but Lenin had learned the lesson of the Provisional Government, and won a few months' worth of relative breathing space to establish Bolshevik rule.

After peace with Germany, food for the cities was the most pressing problem. With the turmoil going on in both planting and harvesting seasons the year before, and with the best of the grain lands in Ukraine and the

---

70. GE Layer 70 is a Polygon outlining in red the buildings and grounds of the Smolny Institute.

71. GE Layer 71 is a Folder titled "Phase I, night of Nov. 6."

72. GE Layer 72 is a Folder titled "Phase II, early Nov. 7."

73. GE Layer 73 is a Polygon outlining in yellow the Winter Palace.

74. GE Layer 74 is a Folder titled "Treaty of Brest-Litovsk." It shows Brest itself as an orange Placemark pushpin icon, German territorial gains as an orange Polygon, and a Path in black symbolizes the new frontier.

Caucasus in German hands, no longer under Russian governmental control, there were desperate shortages. In the villages "committees of the poor" raided the stores of wealthy peasants, and eventually armed raiding parties from the cities were sent to scour the countryside for food. They got enough to avoid famine in the big cities, but the immediate future didn't look any brighter.

It was all complicated by the affair of the so-called "Czech Legion"—around 50,000 deserters from the Austrian army. After Brest-Litovsk, when Russia got out of the war, they were in the process of being evacuated east along the Trans-Siberian Railway so they could sail around the world and fight against Austria (and for an independent Czechoslovakia) on the Western Front. The western Allies tried to delay their departure, seeing them as a potential anti-Bolshevik force that would help get Russia back into the war. When War Commissar Trotsky tried to have them disarmed, they simply took over the whole Trans-Siberian Railway corridor. From 1918 to 1920 and beyond, all of Siberia east and south of Lake Baikal was its own independent republic. The SRs tried to establish a state at the bend of the Volga. The British navy on the Caspian and Black Seas supported "White" armies which invaded Bolshevik-held territory from the south and west. All told, the lands controlled by SOVNARKOM were squeezed down to roughly the size of Muscovy before the time of Ivan the Great.[GE75]

Under such pressures, there was a real shift in Bolshevik practice, and the first signs of it were visible in just a few weeks' time. Right after the November 7, 1917, takeover, Lenin had said: "We are reproached with using terror. But such terror as was used by the French revolutionaries, who guillotined unarmed people, we do not use and, I hope, shall not use." Just five weeks later, however, in mid-December, Trotsky said much the opposite in justifying the government's outlawing of the KDs:

> You protest against the mild terror which we are directing against our class enemies. But you should know that not later than in a month's time that terror will assume very violent forms after the example of the great French revolutionaries. The guillotine will be ready for our enemies and not merely the jail.[11]

One week after Trotsky's speech Lenin formed the *Cheka* (from the Russian first letters for Emergency Commission, ЧК), a special police to lead what amounted to a terror campaign against the new government's enemies. It quickly became one of the most brutal secret police organizations in the world. When in mid-February of 1918 the Germans renewed their military advance, the central government led by Lenin declared the "socialist fatherland" to be in danger (the first quotation that headed up this chapter), thus justifying the immediate arrest and execution of anyone thought to be an enemy agent, a speculator, or a counter-revolutionary agitator.

War Communism

In 1918 the Bolshevik Party that controlled the government changed its name to Communist Party. In what they called "War Communism" the banks were closed and the ruble in essence discontinued, since workers were supposed to be assigned housing and given food, transportation, and clothing free of charge. This of course generated a huge black market where things were bartered. Industry was seized by the government and turned over to the workers, who came and went as they pleased and paid themselves with raw materials or tools. The factories simply ground to a halt, and perhaps half of all industrial workers drifted back to the villages they'd originally come from. Sanitation systems broke down and cholera and typhus raged. Famine ravaged the countryside from 1918–1920. The Bolshevik solution was to draft labor armies for projects, send city raiding parties for food out to the countryside, and shoot deserters from these as they would in the newly-disciplined military.

In cultural terms it was an era of social radicalism. The family was seen as a relic of a bygone bourgeois era. As early as December of 1917 civil marriage was introduced, and soon all you had to do to get married was sign your names in a register, and all you had to do to get divorced was for one of you to erase your name. From 1920 abortions were permitted without restriction. Komsomol (short for Communist Soviet Youth), a

---

75. GE Layer 75 is a Polygon showing Bolshevik-led Russia at its smallest point.

new youth organization of the Communist Party, encouraged the denunciation of the old by the young. In universities professors were lectured by uneducated but solidly proletarian stock, instead of vice versa.

Religion was a particularly important target of the new Soviet government. Religion was, in Marxist terms, "the opiate of the people," "pie in the sky bye and bye," to keep the lower classes contented with their lot. And as in the French Revolution, the official church fought revolutionary rule, with the Russian Orthodox Church excommunicating known Bolsheviks. It was a courageous stand, but curious in that ever since Peter the Great the official church had been more a wing of the government and less the conscience of the people. When the new Soviet government arrested the Patriarch, deprived the clergy of civil rights, seized church property, and outlawed religious instruction, there wasn't much protest from the general Russian public. Churches were torn down or turned into gymnasiums and swimming pools; even St. Petersburg's great Kazan Cathedral was eventually made into a museum of atheism.

In Moscow in March of 1919 the International Workingmen's Association was revived, and called the Third International or simply the Comintern (Communist International). The President was Grigorii Zinoviev, one of Lenin's earliest co-workers, and his plans for setting up secret Communist centers in other states—particularly in Germany, thought ripe for Communist takeover—frightened many in the western world (for example the "Red Scare" in the U.S.).

But in basic domestic economic terms, War Communism was a huge disaster, a government-induced famine. The upshot was that protests and strikes against Bolshevik rule exploded in early 1921, with signs calling for "Peace, Bread and Land" and rebellions even in formerly hard-core Bolshevik areas such as Kronstadt.

The ABCs of Communism

It's especially clear in hindsight which way things were trending in terms of state power. And even then Bakunin's question to Marx back in the nineteenth century—"if your dictatorship of the proletariat takes over, what keeps it from becoming the permanent power of a clique or even of one strongman?"—began to haunt some of the more contemplative Bolsheviks. Nikolai Bukharin, generally recognized inside the Bolshevik Party as a Marxist theorist second only to Lenin, wrestled with this during the Civil War and War Communism period, and in 1919 and 1920 co-authored a book, *The ABCs of Communism*, to explain why the trend towards more governmental power was only temporary; he elaborated on it a bit later in his *Historical Materialism: A System of Sociology*.[12] Here's his argument.

In the class struggle, the working class is not uniform, and must be guided by the "most advanced," namely the Bolshevik Party. The Bolshevik Party itself is not uniform, in class consciousness, experience, or executive expertise, and so must be led by "more or less stable groups of individual leaders." So what is to keep those cliques from permanent dictatorship? Bukharin answers this way:

> But Communist society is a society with highly developed, increased productive forces. Consequently, it can have no economic basis for the creation of a peculiar ruling class. For this power will be the power of specialists over machines, not over men. How could they, in fact, realize this power with regard to men?

But Bukharin, if you control factories, don't you control people? No, he says; the "incompetence of the masses" will disappear under the new system. The educational monopoly will be abolished, and all the new technologists and organizers coming from the working class itself will nullify that "tendency" towards a ruling clique. So "in the society of the future there will be a colossal overproduction of organizers, which will nullify the stability of ruling groups." It's just a matter of getting folks to experiment with socialized life:

> The nationalization of small scale industry is absolutely out of the question: first of all, it is beyond our powers to organize the dispersed fragments of petty industry; and secondly because the Communist Party does not and cannot wish to alienate the many millions of small masters. Their adhesion to socialism will be quite voluntary, and will not result from their forcible expropriation.

We'll give those who experiment with cooperatives and communes financial aid, and disperse contracts for needed government supplies to them. We know that for a long time small-scale peasant farming will have to continue, but we will help them improve productivity by ending the strip field system, giving them quality seed and pure-bred livestock, and opening a new chapter in expert assistance and agricultural education. And it will all result in "a single, harmoniously constructed society," "a society of highly cultivated persons, conscious of themselves and others."

Well, Bukharin, I admire your dream, and in 1920 I might even have been your disciple. But if we meet in some reincarnation we've got to have a long talk about Stalin. By 1930 the forcible and violent collectivization of agriculture was underway, as 99 percent of Russian farmers were stripped of private property and thrown together in communes subject to the brutal taxation of the Soviet state. Every industry from the size of two potters' wheels and up was nationalized, and consumer industry was stripped bare to serve heavy industry. The Cheka proliferated into OGPU and MVD, an archipelago of prison camps holding millions was set up, and atop it all sat a dictator more powerful and brutal than Ivan the Terrible.

The NEP

So with ideas such as this "slow, gentle" way to Communism in the air, in the Communist Party Congress that met in March of 1921 (the tenth such Congress) Lenin backed off War Communism and called for a New Economic Policy, the NEP.

In the NEP, the state would keep transportation, foreign trade, and the largest factories under its direct control—the "commanding heights" of the economy—but everywhere else allow a limited capitalism to revive. Banks and the ruble were reinvented, and a graduated tax levied on peasant farmers, one that encouraged them to produce more since they would benefit by selling it. Fairs and markets re-opened all over Russia. By 1925 farmers even got the right to hire labor for their farms, a practice that was formerly anathema to the Communist leadership. It lasted from 1921 to 1927, and was fondly remembered later as a relatively peaceful time between the horrors of WW I and War Communism that had come before it and the horrors of collectivization, the purges, and WW II that came after it.

The most memorable picture of Russia during the NEP is not from a work of history but a hilarious work of fiction by two Odessa writers, Il'f and Petrov, titled *Twelve Chairs*. Their anti-hero is a con man named Ostap Bender, out to be a millionaire by whatever means. He marries a rich widow for her money and then has trouble escaping from her. He gets free passage on a ship down the Volga claiming he is an artist who can paint a beautiful woman on the bow, and when he reveals it at trip's end it is a crude monstrosity. In a river town he pretends to be a Moscow grandmaster of chess, willing to play dozens of people simultaneously for a certain entry fee. One game he loses at fools' mate, and quickly begins to lose others—whereupon he and an ex-nobleman colleague grab the entry fees, jump in a boat and row down the river with an angry mob of chess players following on the bank. The thread of the book is that the ex-nobleman's mother had hidden the family jewels in the bottom of one of twelve English chairs. At novel's end, in a socialist conclusion, they find the twelfth and last chair in a well-equipped worker's gym and social center—the jewels had been found in the chair and used to build it for the benefit of the people, of course. Its lasting value, other than the humor, is in its picture of the variety of occupations and personalities that brings the era alive.

The NEP was Lenin's admission that the Marxist future would be harder to bring about than the Bolshevik revolutionaries had ever dreamed it would be. His last two or three years must have been painful. On the one hand he couldn't admit that state bureaucracy was a necessary and lasting aspect of modern life, because that would destroy the beautiful emotional solution Marxism offered in the first place. On the other hand he could see no withering away of the state anytime in the near future. In May of 1922 Lenin suffered the first of five strokes that were to kill him by January of 1924. St. Petersburg/Petrograd was renamed Leningrad in his honor in that same year, and of course his embalmed body is still there in its mausoleum on Moscow's Red Square for the viewing (all dead things unburied make trouble for the living, one Russian remarked about it).[GE76]

To most Communist Party members at the time, War Commissar Leon Trotsky, creator of the disciplined new Red Army several million strong and Lenin's intellectual equal, looked poised to take over as a Russian

76. GE Layer 76 is a Placemark referencing Lenin's Mausoleum.

Napoleon. Partly because of this general fear of Trotsky, power was slowly taken by a Party functionary never accused of being overly cerebral—Josif Stalin.

Stalin's power base

Stalin was born in 1879, making him nine years younger than Lenin and the same age as Trotsky. He was born Josif Vissarionovich Djugashvili, an ethnic Georgian (names ending in *-vili* and *-adze* are typically Georgian) in the town of Gori.[GE77] His father was an alcoholic cobbler and his mother a cleaning lady. In his mid-teens he got a scholarship to the Orthodox Seminary in Tblisi, the provincial capital. He was a regular offender there in terms of being in possession of forbidden literature, and dropped out of seminary at age nineteen or twenty and moved straight into underground socialist work, particularly in Batum, a city dominated by oil workers. He was no great orator or writer, but he was a very efficient organizer. By 1904, when he was twenty-three or so, he was quoting Lenin's works, and apparently came to the notice of Lenin and Krupskaya in 1905. In 1907 he organized the robbery of a major Tblisi bank—which came off with considerable loss of life—to finance the revolutionary underground. Lenin, with wry admiration, called him the "last Mohican" of the Revolution of 1905.

His first revolutionary alias was Koba ("the indomitable"), after a Robin Hood character in a famous Georgian poem, but later he took Stalin ("man of steel"). As with so many other Bolsheviks, he was jailed and exiled to Siberia more than once. Escaping Russia, he became undeniably close to Lenin. Lenin coached him in the proper Bolshevik interpretation of the nationalities question, presumably because the argument signed by a member of a national minority would carry more authenticity. In the March Revolution of 1917 he was one of the senior Bolsheviks to be in Petrograd, and in the aftermath of that he leaned towards accepting Kerensky's policies, including continuing the war. When Lenin appeared on the scene in early April, however, preaching "Peace, Bread and Land" and power to the Soviets, Stalin quickly sided with him. From April to October, 1917, he personally shepherded Lenin on his quick escapes from Petrograd to Vyborg, across the Finnish border, and cautious returns back again.

After the Bolshevik Revolution, Stalin's first real base of power was as Commissar of Nationalities, which he ran from its creation in late 1917 to its cancellation in 1923. As Soviet Russia expanded, the nationalities fringe became more numerically important, and all the new nationalities' delegates to the Communist Party congresses were Stalin's men. His second institutional base of power, beginning in 1919, was as Commissar of the Workers' and Peasants' Inspectorate, a new division of government set up by Lenin to investigate abuses of power and delays caused by red tape. Looking back, it gave Stalin enormous power. But these were mere governmental positions, and Soviet Russia had become a one-party state, with the Communist Party "advising" the government at every level. So it was probably Stalin's Communist Party positions that were key to his power. Party Congresses, since before the November Revolution, elected the members of the smaller Central Committee for day-to-day operations. But even that was too unwieldy for Lenin, so in March of 1919 he set up a Political Bureau—henceforth Politburo—of which he was Chair and of which two of the five other members were Trotsky and Stalin. This was the committee to set policy. Then a second committee from the Central Committee—the Organizational Bureau or Orgburo—was set up to carry out that policy. The load on the Secretary of the Orgburo was so heavy that a second and then a third Secretary was added, and by 1920 the Secretariat had evolved into the third special committee of the CC, with the power to make decisions when the Orgburo was not meeting. Although on the Politburo Stalin was not really taken seriously, from March of 1922 when he was appointed General Secretary, he was the only CC member to be on all three bureaus. Lenin had his first stroke two months later. The Orgburo would fade away; the Secretariat (which controlled the agenda of the Politburo) would in Lenin's absence come to control the Politburo; and at every level the Party controlled the Government. So the history of Soviet Russia is fairly well summed up in a list of those four men who were First Secretary of the Communist Party for any length of time: Stalin, Khrushchev, Brezhnev and Gorbachev.

---

77. GE Layer 77 is a Folder with Placemarks referencing Gori, and also Tblisi (Tiflis) and Batum, key sites of Stalin's early life mentioned later in this paragraph.

Stalin seems to have been personally loyal to Lenin, but with Lenin's removal from the scene was not bound by any ideology. The intellectuals he out-maneuvered in the 1920s were committed to certain positions, and besides, had been taught by Lenin ever since 1902 that if you lost a decision made by the Party elite, you fell in lockstep with that decision. In that critical 1924, the year of Lenin's death, Trotsky was calling for a return to War Communism. Stalin countered with his *Socialism in One Country*, arguing for forgetting about world revolution for awhile and straightening things out in Russia first—a very popular alternative to the new sacrifices called for by Trotsky. Stalin teamed up with "leftists" Zinoviev and Kamenev (Trotsky's brother-in-law!) to keep Trotsky from power, removing his supporters in Party and government one at a time and then stripping him of his War Commissar post. Then Stalin deserted his leftist allies and joined Politburo "rightists" Bukharin and Rykov to politically destroy Zinoviev and Kamenev, removing them from Politburo and then Party. Then in 1927 Stalin embraced Trotsky's old program of fast, forcible industrialization and collectivization, and when this was opposed by the "rightists," he removed them from Politburo and Party too. By this time he was ruthless and had developed a cunning feel for political power. More than one biographer has compared Stalin's evolution to the Caucasus warlords he so admired as a young man—Robin Hoods who when they came to power so enjoyed its exercise that only some actions and some catch phrases from the good old days were remembered, and none of the original motivation of taking from the rich and giving to the poor.

Collectivization and industrialization

It was at the October 1927 Party Congress that the first of the famous "Five Year Plans" was adopted, to begin in 1928. It was to be industrialization the fast, hard way, by the government squeezing the consumer for every last kopek and getting its hands on the peasants' stashes of grain. During 1928 collectivization was gradual, but in 1929 it was greatly accelerated. All peasant property was "expropriated." Destruction of the *kulak*—the most prosperous 5 percent of peasant farmers, generally speaking—was an official government slogan. From two to six million kulaks were killed in what amounted to rural class war encouraged by the government, and another two million were deported. The remaining peasants were thrown into kolkhozes (from *kollektivnoe khozhaistvo*, collective economy), roughly village size, and into the super communes called Sovkhozes that might have 25,000 people, corresponding to nothing before in Russian history. Thirty million small farms suddenly became a quarter-million unfamiliar new units. In 1933 Machine Tractor Stations (MTS) were introduced supposedly to bring industrial efficiency to agriculture, but in practice they were just one more way to levy money out of peasants—kolkhozes had no choice but to contract with them.

It all took tremendous brutality to impose, and even then the peasants never really accepted it. They sabotaged the harvesting tractors by driving steel rods in among the wheat. They slaughtered their livestock and had a feast instead of turning it over to their new kolkhoz or Sovkhoz. When the German army moved into the Ukraine in 1941, the peasants there immediately re-marked their old land plots. In the course of the 1930s, agricultural production was probably actually lower than in the 1920s, but the government got a greater share of it. The cities got enough food to stave off famine, and industry got the rest.

Russia had gotten its first modern industry in the age of Alexander II, and a modest industrial growth under Witte around the turn of the century. But Russia only really industrialized in the 1930s under Stalin.

Industrial development on the Five Year Plans in Russia was learn as you go. Entire new industries—including chemical and electrical—had to be created. By the early 1930s a whole series of technical schools were set up to educate the workers. In 1935 Stalin made a speech saying "cadres [managers] decide everything." It was nothing less than the creation of a managerial elite, and the nucleus of what some would call a "New Class" in supposedly classless Soviet Russia. Entire industrial cities such as Magnitogorsk[GE[78]] and Karaganda in Central Asia[GE[79]] were created, and whole new geographic areas were industrialized, including

---

78. GE Layer 78 is a Placemark referencing Magnitogorsk, just east of the Urals.

79. GE Layer 79 is a Placemark referencing Karaganda, a prison-labor mining city.

the Kuznetz basin in western Siberia.[GE80] The Soviet government experimented with special awards and bonuses for workers who worked long hours or who "overfulfilled their work norms." It culminated with the Stakhanovite movement, named for one heroic miner of coal. The average worker disliked it, because it raised everybody's norm; a good many Stakhanovite award winners were murdered by their fellows. The prison system, recipient of tens of millions of those deemed criminal because they opposed governmental policies, amounted to a slave labor pool for special governmental projects. Overall in the 1930s Stalin's government laid the foundations for the Soviet Union to be one of the two greatest industrial powers of the twentieth century. For all the brutality it took, Russia would probably not have survived the Nazi onslaught in WW II without it. And there were many in Russia inspired by what one writer called the "stern but deeply felt romance" of the industrial revolution there.

Kirov's assassination and the purges

On December 1, 1934, state terror entered a new level with the murder of Sergei Kirov in Leningrad. Although Stalin still had the post of First Secretary of the Communist Party, a Second, Third, and Fourth Secretary had been added by the Central Committee—evidence some interpret as the Party beginning to buck Stalin's rule a bit. Kirov was Second Secretary of the Communist Party, and from Leningrad, where Stalin was generally unpopular. Although he was almost certainly murdered on First Secretary Stalin's orders, it was blamed on the counter-revolution and used to justify a massive roundup of intellectuals and officials of any independence. The "purge trials" of 1937–38 were the outcome of a national hysteria as intense as that in Salem during the witch trials. It resulted in an even wider sweep of imprisonments under the new head of state security, Yezhov, soon nicknamed "the bloody dwarf." For the sheer physical pressure of the Gulag, or State Camps, read Evgeniia Semyonovna Ginzburg's *Journey Into The Whirlwind*. Think yourself into solitary confinement for years at a time. Into calculated brutality on special Soviet days such as May 1st or the anniversary of Kirov's assassination when you were taken to the prison basement, hosed with cold water, put in a box for five days with no food or dry clothes. Into cutting timber north of Magadan, in the area zoned exclusively for forced labor camps,[GE81] at 30 degrees below zero in inadequate clothes. Something like twenty million people were executed or worked to death in the Soviet Union in the 1930s, in peacetime. Only those with the strongest physical constitutions and some degree of mental resilience—Ginzburg quoted poetry in her mind—survived the camps.

Even knowing the increasing use of torture, how do you explain the public confessions and self-criticism of people of the stature of Bukharin—knowing they were going to be executed anyway—in the purge trials? In the West it was hard for most of us to believe that Communist rule was not just a naked power grab by scheming Bolsheviks. It was not, but it was something more dangerous. Enthusiastic belief in bringing about a heaven-on-earth was even stronger here than in the National-Socialist movement in Germany. Lenin and Trotsky and company were true believers: new Soviet woman and man would emerge—communal, unselfish, well-fed, and well-educated—and the old state bureaucracy and habits would fade away. Although it was all couched in terms of scientific social studies—"dialectical struggle," "temporary contradiction"—the great unspoken belief was that these wonderful ends justified any means. Lev Kopelev, a Russian-Jewish scholar who was an expert on German language and culture and later himself a famous dissident, in his political autobiography talks about the self-righteousness of his own role as a young Communist leader commandeering grain in the famine of 1932–33. The Party could only move ahead if everyone moved in lockstep, Lenin had taught them since 1902; to be against the Party was to be against the future. In a revealing view of this idealism's impact even on private life, Kopelev recalls how his commanding officer in WW II got married back in those days:

---

80. GE Layer 80 is a Folder titled "Kuznetz Basin." It has Placemarks for Tomsk at its northwest end and Novokuznetsk at its southeast end, and a Polygon in red roughly outlining the basin. The gray slashes on the Google Earth surface are huge strip mines.

81. GE Layer 81 is a Folder titled "Magadan and the forced labor zone," with a Placemark for Magadan and a Polygon for the forced labor zone that took in the Kolyma River basin.

'For a long time,' he told me, 'I didn't have any—you know what I mean—personal life. Regional committee, inspection trips around the villages . . . . When I became secretary I was entitled to an apartment, but who was going to take care of it? I worked so hard I'd often go to sleep without taking my clothes off—sometimes just sitting at my desk. Even so, I was a young man. Girls all around. They know the secretary's a bachelor, so they stick to me like flies. But I couldn't screw around; I was a public figure, and you know how it is in the provinces—everyone knows everything you're up to. Then they appointed me first secretary in another region. I get there, and there's a whole house full of furniture, all for me. But I still eat in a hash house and sleep alone. I decided to get married. But how?'

'I didn't have the time for sprucing up and going courting. Besides, you can't marry the first girl that comes along—got to exercise political vigilance, right? But I was tired of my dog's life. So, the very first evening, I decided what to do. I stayed behind at the regional committee office and looked through the personal files of all the girls in the local Komsomol [Communist youth organization]. Well, you know, every file comes with a photograph, so I wasn't choosing blind. It didn't take me long to find what I was looking for. She was a typist in the producers' cooperative—belonged to the co-op cell. Resume suitable: parents were poor, family record spotless, recommendations good. And not bad looking, either.'

'The next day, I ask for her. She comes in, and I can see she's scared. Why does the first secretary want to see her alone, the very first day? I come clean, right away. That's how it is, I say, thus and so. I want to get married, I got all the facts on you, and now I see you'd suit me fine. I haven't got time, you understand, for all that love and romance stuff. I'm not forcing you into anything, of course—I'm putting it to you, comrade to comrade. Think it over. I'll wait until tonight. I'll stay here in this office until nine o'clock. If you decide yes, come.'

She did, and the next day they moved in together and went to get registered. They had two sons, he kept her up-to-date "culturally and politically," and she eventually joined the Communist Party. Kopelev concludes, "He recounted all this with barely concealed pride, as though to say, 'There, that's how real people arrange their personal lives.'"[13]

With this idealistic loyalty to the Party above self, all it took was one truly amoral, power-hungry person around the levers of power at the top of the Party to turn it all into his blindly obedient servant.

Stalin and Hitler

In foreign affairs in the 1930s, the single most important development for Soviet Russia was the rise to power of Hitler in Germany. As you saw in the last chapter, Hitler became Chancellor in January of 1933, rejected the military restrictions of the Versailles Treaty, and began building up what in six or seven years time would be the best army and air force in the world. And as was clear from the 1924 publication of *Mein Kampf* and his later speeches, he considered Slavs to be inferior to German stock, and their lands would be needed for German *Lebensraum*.

Given the realpolitik logic of things, and Stalin's ideological flexibility, he sought for allies in the liberal western European states, particularly France and Britain. In 1935 he reversed the Marxist axiom that liberals were a dangerous class enemy, and called on Communists worldwide to join Center-Left "Popular Front" coalitions to counter the Nazi/Fascist rise on the Right. Popular Front governments were indeed elected—most importantly in France and in Spain. A reaction to it in Spain, led by General Franco and the Falange (a super-nationalist Fascist-like party) led to a brutal three-year-long Spanish Civil War between the Center-Left "Loyalists" and the Right "Nationalists." The Loyalists got outside help from a stream of unorganized volunteers, including the so-called "Abraham Lincoln Brigade" made up of Americans; Hemingway's famous *For Whom the Bell Tolls* is the great English-language novel to come out of this. But Franco and the Nationalists got much more substantial and organized aid from the Italian and German states. Picasso's classic *Guernica* memorializes a Luftwaffe bombing raid in April of 1937 on this Loyalist Basque town in northern Spain,[GE82] one of the first aerial bombardments of a basically civilian population, with somewhere around a thousand killed.

---

82. GE Layer 82 is a Placemark referencing Guernica. Click on website link to go to the Picasso painting, or just do a Google—Images search under "Picasso Guernica."

From Stalin's point of view, the western European states were spineless in giving in to Hitler's threats. In 1936 the French army moved obligingly out of the Rhineland as the German army slowly moved in. In the spring of 1938 when Hitler annexed Austria, in clear violation of the Versailles Treaty, they did nothing. In the fall of 1938, when Hitler blustered about the Sudetenland at the Munich Conference, Britain and France gave him the mountain defenses of Czechoslovakia,[GE83] and when he took the rest of Czechoslovakia the next spring, took no action (more on this in Chapter 7). And meantime Nazi Germany and militaristic Japan had concluded the ominously-named "Anti-Comintern Pact." You can see why Stalin felt both isolated and threatened.

And so, on August 23, 1939—giving up on any chance of allying with the western European powers—he signed a "Non-aggression Pact" with Germany offered by Hitler (the so-called Molotov-Ribbentrop Pact, after the foreign ministers). A secret agreement of this Pact was that Germany and Russia would divide up central-eastern Europe between them, from Finland down through Romania. On September 1—just a week-and-a-half after the pact was signed—Germany invaded Poland in the first classic "Blitzkrieg." Stalin wanted to negotiate a similar understanding with Japan before he went to war, so the corresponding Soviet invasion was delayed until September 15. The Soviet invasion of Finland, which only began in late November, was blunted by a surprising resistance from this little country, in what was called the Winter War (on which more in Chapter 6). Soviet might finally prevailed by March.[GE84] And now the Soviet Union and the Third Reich shared a long north-south border, with no buffer states between.

World War II

Other than Lenin, Hitler may have been the only man Stalin ever trusted. Operation Barbarossa—Germany's full-scale invasion of the U.S.S.R. that began June 22, 1941—had been in the planning for at least six months, and the British had found out about it and tipped off the Russians. Stalin apparently didn't believe the warning, and ignored all the signs of military concentration on his western border. Having decimated his own officer corps in the Purges, and having made no comprehensive plans for defense, he almost lost the war in the first six months. The German army cut off Leningrad, and almost cut off Moscow. Stalin made up for it later, in his will to resist, that proved to be contagious. Whole libraries have been written on World War II, but here let's content ourselves with three crucial encounters on the Eastern Front—the Battle for Moscow from December 1941 to February 1942, the Battle for Stalingrad from mid-November 1942 to the end of January 1943, and the Battle of Kursk from mid-July to late August of 1943.

Operation Barbarossa was at first a spectacular success. In the south, Kiev was taken and the Dnieper River crossed. In the north, though it never surrendered, Leningrad was virtually cut off (for the famous "900 days"). But Moscow and the destruction of the Soviet army was Germany's main goal, and the Moscow defenses held, though barely.[GE85] Stubborn, virtual suicide resistance by surrounded Soviet armies west of the capital slowed the German advance. In early October the mud season began with early snows that melted. Still, a German pincer movement designed to encircle Moscow came so close to success that on October 15 Stalin had the government moved east, to Kuibyshev on the Volga. He himself stayed. With air superiority the Germans hammered Moscow, a lot of whose life went underground. By November temperatures were hitting minus 20 and below on the Fahrenheit scale, and the German soldiers weren't equipped for winter weather. Marshal Zhukov beat off the pincer movement, and then in early December blunted a frontal tank assault from the west. The German offensive ended December 5, and winter-equipped troops arrived from Siberia to strengthen the Soviet

---

83. GE Layer 83 is a Folder titled "Sudetenland." It includes a Polygon in red outline giving borders of Czechoslovakia in 1938, and filled Polygons showing lands taken by Germany in the west and Hungary in the east.

84. GE Layer 84 is a Folder titled "Soviet gains, 1939–40." In Finland the northernmost territory was to protect the road to Murmansk, and the southern territory, of course, to push the international border further from Leningrad. The band of other territories taken is continuous, down to northern Romania.

85. GE Layer 85 is a Folder titled "Operation Barbarossa." It includes a Path, symbolized by a heavy black line, showing the German advance by December 1941. A yellow pushpin icon shows the closest German approach to Moscow.

army enough to turn the tables in a counter-attack.[GE86] This defense of Moscow and then being able to push German Army Group Center back a bit was the first real Soviet success in the war, a real morale-builder.

Stalingrad probably became the next military focus for both German and Russian armies because of its name. "Tsaritsyn," it had been back in the Civil War, when Stalin was active there as one of the Red military leaders defending it from the Whites, and Stalin had later celebrated his role there by renaming the city.[GE87] German armies could have crossed the Volga more easily downstream from there, closer to Astrakhan, but Hitler too was apparently focused on the symbolism of the name as well. So German armies were poured into taking it, and the defenders were told to fight it out factory by factory, house by house. On November 19, 1942, when the surviving Soviet units held only a thin strip—a block or so deep and about ten football fields long on the bank of the Volga[GE88]—the first prong of a three-part Soviet counterattack was launched from the north. The next day a second came from the northwest, and the third day one came from the southeast.[GE89] They cut the German army in two across fifty miles of the Don River, thus turning General Paulus's besiegers of the city of Stalingrad into a surrounded, besieged force themselves. The street-by-street defense of the city and then the huge counterattack destroyed what one writer called the "flower" of the German army. Paulus—with 23 generals and over 200,000 troops—surrendered February 1. In these post-Soviet days the city has been renamed once again, "Volgograd," but there still stands one of the most impressive monuments to any WW II event, worldwide, a huge statue of *Rodina-mat'*, "Birthland Mother."[GE90]

The Battle of Stalingrad critically weakened the southern German front, and it took desperate measures from the German army in the spring of 1943 to shore it up. When the front stabilized again, roughly on a line from Leningrad to Rostov-on-Don, there was a great Soviet bulge around Kursk (or two German bulges north and south of Kursk, depending on your viewpoint).[GE91] This "Kursk salient" became the focus of the last major German offensive in Russia, called Operation Citadel. It was a planned enveloping movement from German-held Orel (some 90 miles north of Kursk) and Kharkov (about 115 miles south of Kursk)—blitzkrieg-style tank columns with air support—focusing on Kursk and designed to surround and so bag the Russian armies in that Kursk salient. The Orel attack kicked off on July 10, and the one from Kharkov on July 12.[GE92] But it had taken the Germans a long time to move the needed Panzer tank divisions across from France, and the Soviets got detailed intelligence about German plans from British and other sources well in advance. They set up not one but eight lines of defense in a zone 150 miles deep, sown with anti-personnel and anti-tank mines. By the time the German offensive opened, Soviet anti-tank guns outnumbered German tanks, their artillery was dug in and pre-sighted, their own tanks massed (and most of them dug in as well so as to present less of a target). The German drive from the north stalled in less than a week. The southern drive had more success, actually capturing a bridge across the Donets and occasioning some scrambling on the Soviet side to contain it at the battle of Prokhorovka.[GE93] Then with both German drives stalled, exhausted by the depth of the defense (of which they penetrated less than a third), the Soviets counterattacked on both Orel and Kharkov fronts.[GE94] Meanwhile the air war overhead went about the same way, swinging from German to Soviet superiority. The upshot of it all was that instead of the Germans flattening the front by taking the Kursk

---

86. GE Layer 86 is a Folder showing the main Soviet counterattacks as red arrows and the resulting new front as a thinner black line than the original front that ran so close to Moscow.

87. GE Layer 87 is a Path showing the German front near Stalingrad, what is today Volgograd.

88. GE Layer 88 is a Folder showing in red polygons the small remaining Soviet territory in Stalingrad, consisting of a few riverside factories and other buildings.

89. GE Layer 89 is a Folder containing Polygons in red for each of the three successive attacks, with smaller black lines for the new front lines—the main one further west, and Gen. Paulus' army cut off and surrounded in the vicinity of Stalingrad.

90. GE Layer 90 is a Placemark referencing a Panoramio icon with a good view of the great statue of Rodina-mat'.

91. GE Layer 91 is a Folder titled "The Kursk Salient." It shows the front as a thick black line, and has Placemarks for, from north to south, Orel, Kursk, and Kharkov.

92. GE Layer 92 is a Folder titled "German offensives," containing Polygons in black of the two German advances.

93. GE Layer 93 is a Placemark referencing a Panoramio icon at Prokhorovka with a good view of some battlefield memorials.

94. GE Layer 94 is a Folder titled "Soviet counterattacks at Kursk."

salient, it was the Soviets who flattened it by taking the Orel and Kharkov zones and thus moving the whole southern front westwards by the end of August. Their Kursk counteroffensive led to a general attack on the whole southern front, and by December 1 the Germans were driven back an average of 200 miles across the whole of it, basically to the line of the Dnieper River.[GE95] And so WW II turned decisively against Germany before 1943 ended, a good six months before the famous D-Day invasion of Normandy by the western allies that we westerners usually think of as the war's turning point.

In that same 1943, to shore up his alliance with the western allies, Stalin did two most un-Marxist things. First, he disbanded the Comintern (aimed at the overthrow of the governments of his British and American allies, after all). Second, he to some extent rehabilitated the Russian Orthodox Church, making joint speeches with the Patriarch, to turn WW II into a holy war in the tradition of Russian national defense against invaders. His pronouncements in defense of the Fatherland, or the Birthland Mother, even took on the religious phraseology of his seminary days. And his calling up of an older, pre-Marxist patriotism was welcomed by the general Russian public. Hedrick Smith, *New York Times* correspondent in the Soviet Union from 1971–74, recalled asking Russian friends in a private setting what was the best time they remembered. The rather surprising answer was World War II, because for all its danger, death, and destruction, "it was not *their* country then [the Communist leadership's], but *our* country." Smith wrote this in 1976:

> In an age grown skeptical of undiluted patriotism, Russians are perhaps the world's most passionate patriots. Without question, a deep and tenacious love of country is the most powerful unifying force in the Soviet Union . . . today nationalism has more magnetism and meaning for the overwhelming majority of Soviet people than does Marxist-Leninist ideology.[14]

It was the memory of that "shared ordeal and triumph" of World War II that Smith believed to be the primary source of that patriotism.

Stalin got—and deserved—a lot of praise for that. Comparing Hitler and Stalin as war leaders, Hitler demoralized the German officer corps with his sometimes brilliant but more often naive military insights, and especially with his refusal to allow retreat in the face of almost certain annihilation. Stalin impressed western experts who visited the Soviet Union during World War II with his detailed grasp of the military at all levels. Although he ruthlessly got rid of under-performers, looking back you can sense that he let the generals freely debate the options before he stepped in and picked one, or a combination. At those three crucial battles of Moscow, Stalingrad, and Kursk, he psychologically had Hitler's number, seeming to know just how he would respond.

Tehran, Yalta, and Potsdam

The post-war future could be seen taking place in three famous wartime conferences of U.S., U.K., and U.S.S.R. leaders—those at Tehran, Yalta, and Potsdam.

The first meeting between Marshal Stalin (note the new military title he gave himself during the war), President Roosevelt, and Prime Minister Churchill was in the Soviet Embassy in Tehran,[GE96] from November 28 to December 1 of 1943. The year before, these "big three" had essentially forced the first Pahlavi Shah of Iran, of pro-German leanings, to resign in favor of his son, Muhammad Reza, and Iran had become an important route for American supplies to the Soviet Union. The chief agreement reached here was that the western allies would open a second front in the west (the campaigns in North Africa and even in southern Italy had been disappointingly small, by Russian standards). The invasion of Normandy in early June of 1944 would be fulfillment of that promise.

The second meeting of the big three, fourteen months later, was from February 4–11, 1945, at the Livadia Palace in the southern outskirts of the Crimean resort city of Yalta.[GE97] President Roosevelt was in desper-

95. GE Layer 95 is a Path showing in a black line the front by December 1.
96. GE Layer 96 is a Placemark referencing the Soviet Embassy in Tehran.
97. GE Layer 97 is a Placemark referencing Yalta's Livadia Palace.

ately ill health, and with the Red Army closing in on Berlin, Stalin dealt from even greater strength here at Yalta. All agreed on an unconditional surrender policy vis-à-vis Germany. Germany was to be reduced in size by a quarter, with most of the lost land going to Poland (Stalin insisted that the Soviet Union would keep the Polish lands it took in 1939, but compensated the new Poland by shifting its western border further west). [GE[98]] The new, smaller Germany itself was to be divided into U.S., British, and Russian zones of occupation (when the U.S. and Britain said there should also be a French zone, the Russian response was that they should carve it out of their zones).[GE[99]] Austria was to be similarly portioned out, as were both capital cities, Berlin and Vienna. The states of Eastern Europe were to have free elections (although how that worked out after they were militarily occupied by the Soviet Union you'll see). The Soviet Union agreed to rejoin the United Nations—if it got a seat on the Security Council with the right to veto anything it pleased. The Soviet Union agreed to join the war on Japan within three months after Germany's defeat—if the western allies recognized its rights to the Manchurian railroads and Pt. Arthur.

The third meeting of the big three—though now FDR was dead and Truman was there for the U.S. (and Clement Atlee of the Labour Party was there with the Conservative Party's Churchill, since the British elections had been held but not yet decided), was at Potsdam's Cecilienhof, the former residence of the German crown prince.[GE[100]] It took place from July 17 to August 2, 1945—three months after Germany's surrender but just before the atomic bombs of August 6 and 9 finally brought about Japan's surrender. Again Germany and the Soviet-occupied lands of Eastern Europe were the primary issues (though the "temporary" division of Japanese-occupied Vietnam at 17° latitude would loom large later). German industry of any possible military use was outlawed, and much of it—including any in the western zones that might raise German living standards there above their neighbors'—was to be dismantled and sent to the Soviet Union.

Beginnings of the Cold War

With Soviet armies occupying most of eastern Europe, the NKVD (the "People's Commissariat for Internal Affairs," the name of the current state security machinery with its secret police and extensive prison labor camps) under Lavrenty Beria oversaw East Bloc countries' conversion to Russian-style Soviet states. "People's Republics" set up in Albania, Bulgaria, Hungary, Poland, Romania (and by way of variation on a name, "East Germany" and the "Czechoslovak Socialist Republic").[GE[101]] This is all long ago and far away for typical college-age students in U.S. today—but North Korea with its cult of the socialist leader, its goose-stepping military parades, its dismal consumer industry status and its numerous and brutal prison camps is still as of this writing a living reminder (Korea was occupied by Soviet troops at the same time as all those East Bloc countries; more in a minute).

President Truman from the beginning was more suspicious of Soviet ambitions than FDR had ever been. In early 1946 two key events happened on the side of the western allies, one secret, one public. The secret one was that George F. Kennan, with the U.S. mission in Moscow since 1944, was closely reporting on Soviet moves and plans, and encouraging drawing a line against Soviet takeovers—which would come to be known as Containment Policy. The public one was Winston Churchill's famous "Iron Curtain" speech at Fulton, Missouri, to great public resonance in the U.S. Early in 1947 the U.S. President publicly committed to helping Greece and Turkey resist Soviet domination, and by implication other countries as well. It was the beginning of the Truman Doctrine.

In that same 1947 it was increasingly clear that the Allied-occupied parts of Germany were not to be industrially stripped as generally agreed on in the major wartime conferences, but in fact built up again with the Marshall Plan and forged into a West Germany, a "Federal Republic of Germany." When a new German Mark

---

98. GE Layer 98 is a Folder showing German lands of the pre-Hitler German state that went to Poland and the Soviet Union; this is when Poland took its modern state.

99. GE Layer 99 is a Folder showing the four zones of occupation by colored Polygons.

100. GE Layer 100 is a Placemark referencing Cecilienhof, in Potsdam—Prussia's and then Germany's answer to Versailles.

101. GE Layer 101 is a Polygon in red showing that band of East Bloc countries generally under Soviet Union domination.

was introduced by the western Allies in June of 1948, Stalin ordered the land routes into Allied-controlled West Berlin closed, apparently assuming that the three air corridors guaranteed by treaty would be far too expensive for the western powers to use.[GE[102]] The Americans and British, however, had both a lot more experience with cargo aircraft from WW II than the Russians had (flying the "hump" over Burma to supply the Nationalist Chinese, for example), and invested the money it took for this largely symbolic opening event of the Cold War. In spring of the next year, 1949, the Soviets abandoned the blockade, partly because it had become such an unpopular thing in the Germanies and the world at large.

But in general the rival alliances slowly hardened. In April 1949 NATO—the North Atlantic Treaty Organization—was formed of nine western European states, the U.S., Canada, and Iceland. An attack on one was to be considered an attack on all, and there was some standardization along military lines based on U.S. military practice and equipment. It would only evolve its highest integration, however, in the context of the Korean War of 1950–53, and of course generate its opposite number, the Warsaw Pact of Soviet-dominated countries, in 1955.

Korean War

Fate gave Stalin a rather unexpected ace in his post-war dealings with his western opponents. By 1949 the Chinese Communist Party led by Mao Zedong—ironically enough with virtually no help or encouragement from the Soviet Union, as you'll see in Chapter 13—had successfully defeated the U.S.-supported Nationalist forces led by Chiang Kai-shek. Partly because they had little experience with administering cities, for most of a decade the Chinese Communists would accept Soviet aid and advice and generally recognize the Soviet Union as elder brother in this whole Marxist enterprise.

Korea had been occupied by Japan for half a century, from 1895 to 1945. With the Potsdam conference and the surrender of Japan in August of 1945, it was split (without prior warning to the Koreans) along the 38th line of north latitude between a Soviet sphere in the north and a U.S. sphere in the south.[GE[103]] As in Germany, two separate states would gradually emerge here, each suppressing elements sympathetic to the other in its zone. One of the great ironies is that the northern half of Korea was the traditional center of Christianity (a clear majority of the population) and in general of supporters of liberal western-style state and policies, and the big cities of the south, especially Seoul, had the greatest density of Communist intellectuals. If there was a division in the Korean population at the time, it was much more between those who had collaborated with the Japanese and those who hadn't. But now the U.S. and the U.S.S.R. were imposing their rivalry as champions of different ideological systems on top of all local issues.

The North Korean leader, Kim Il-sung, had checked in with Stalin once earlier about supporting a possible invasion of the south by North Korea. Stalin, occupied with rebuilding the Soviet Union and remolding the East Bloc, refused on the grounds he couldn't afford to get involved in a war directly with the U.S. Kim Il-sung returned, with a map showing the U.S. security zone drawn to shelter Japan and the Philippines but not South Korea. This argument apparently won Stalin's reluctant blessing, and on June 25, 1950, North Korean forces invaded South Korea. In response, the U.S. overnight redrew the security line across Korea's 38th parallel. We took the matter to the United Nations, proposing that it should intervene against the North Korean invasion. The Soviet Union could have easily vetoed this from its seat on the Security Council (having only joined the UN, you may remember, when assured a Security Council seat with veto power over any UN decision)—but at the time the Soviet Union was boycotting the UN, protesting China being represented in the UN by the remnant of the Nationalist Government in Taiwan instead of by the CCP government on the whole mainland. The U.S. 7th fleet was sent to shelter Taiwan from "Red China," and NATO armies, mainly U.S. forces, were sent to counter the North Korean invasion of the South. The Cold War had just gone hot.

In swift summary, UN and South Korean forces were pushed by the original North Korean invasion into the southeastern corner of the whole country.[GE[104]] But substantial U.S. supplies began to arrive, and massive

---

102. GE Layer 102 is a Folder containing three outlined Polygons representing those three air routes.

103. GE Layer 103 is a Path symbolized by a thick red line along the 38th parallel as it crosses the Korean peninsula.

104. GE Layer 104 is a Path showing the smallest area held by South Korean forces.

air bombardments of bridges and other military targets shored up the defense. An amphibious UN landing at Inchon (the western coastal town closest to Seoul) started a new front behind North Korean lines.[GE105] The southern forces pushed on across the 38th parallel, capturing the northern capital of Pyongyang in mid-October, and approached the Yalu River that was the border with China. The chief Chinese Communist diplomat, Zhou Enlai, went to talk to Stalin about intervening in the war. Stalin agreed to offer supplies and the use of the Soviet air force, but only over Chinese airspace. Two days after the southern forces captured Pyongyang, massive Chinese armies crossed the Yalu. As they drove south, back towards the 38th parallel, the Soviet Union agreed to extend its air force coverage to North Korea. After this very active one year of warfare, by the mid-summer of 1951 the front basically stabilized for the next two years. An armistice was finally declared, with a neutral demilitarized zone (DMZ) between the two sides.[GE106] The war has never officially ended.

Solzhenitsyn's judgment

Domestically, after World War II, there was little let-up of Stalin's pressure on society. In early 1946 he outlined a series of coming five-year plans that—amid the ruins left by the war—seemed wildly utopian. The Donbas coal mines were still flooded, agriculture was largely disrupted, and there were only three adult men left alive for every five women. Most every Russian prisoner of war and many of those who had lived behind German lines were sent to the camps. Whole peoples—the Crimean Tatars, the Ingush, the Chechens—were packed on trains and sent to carve out new homes in Siberia. Stalin made Politburo member Andrei Zhdanov chief censor for arts and literature, and his "Zhdanovshchina" was more repressive than anything from the reign of Nicholas I. Every major scientific breakthrough of the past two centuries was now ascribed to a Russian, giving rise to the sarcastic phrase (uttered only to good friends in private), "Russia, home of the elephant." In the xenophobia and paranoia, anti-Semitism flourished; "rootless cosmopolite" was the new bureaucratic euphemism for Jew. And in Stalin's very last years, he claimed to see a western-inspired "Doctors' Plot" against major Soviet figures, and the stage seemed set for a new era of purge trials and pogroms when he died in early March of 1953.

For a comprehensive wrestling with the Soviet experience under Stalin, perhaps the most complete writer and thinker was Alexander Solzhenitsyn. He was born in December, 1918, when his father had already been killed in WW I, and was raised by his mother, a typist, in Rostov-on-Don.[GE107] He wanted to be a writer even as a child, but wound up taking a degree in math at a local university, and graduated just days before Hitler's invasion of Russia. He was put in an artillery-position-finding unit on the front, and stayed there until his arrest in February 1945 because of sarcastic remarks about Stalin in his correspondence. He got eight years in the hard labor camps, but because of his math skills was sent to a special prison camp in a former church building on the outskirts of Moscow. In 1950 he was sent down to the labor camps again, and in 1953 upon Stalin's death was more or less put on parole. He almost died of cancer, getting to the point of not being able to eat or sleep, but was cured in a Tashkent cancer clinic. He was freed in 1956. His major writings come out of his experiences—*One Day in the Life of Ivan Denisovich* from the labor camps in Kazakhstan, *Gulag Archipelago* a documentary of the camps in general, *Cancer Ward*, one of his longer novels, from the Tashkent clinic days, and his masterwork, *The First Circle*, taking place in one week in 1949 in that special prison in the outskirts of Moscow when the hero Nerzhin (and Solzhenitsyn) both had their thirty-first birthdays.

The First Circle, in your author's opinion, is the most powerful novel from twentieth-century Russia, and that is making a tall claim. The overt message of the book is that the only place in Stalin's Russia where there was real mental freedom was among the prisoners of the Gulag. Underneath that, however, is an underlying anger at what Stalin deprived prisoners of and the reluctant admission that there was still life he could deprive them of yet. The framework of the novel is the story of a diplomat who calls a doctor, warning him not to give medicine to a foreigner (in a later edition it was atomic secrets). The secret police intercept the call, and search out the identity of the caller. But the main characters of the novel are three intellectuals and an uneducated, nearly blind janitor who have been thrown together in the special prison (the "first circle of hell," from Dante).

---

105. GE Layer 105 is a Folder showing the landings at Inchon and subsequent breakout.

106. GE Layer 106 is a Path showing the border and the demilitarized zone (DMZ) after the armistice.

107. GE Layer 107 is a Placemark referencing Rostov-on-Don.

Nerzhin is obviously mostly Solzhenitsyn himself, so much of the book is thinly disguised autobiography. Rubin, a burly, black-bearded Russian-Jewish linguist, is drawn straight from life: he is modeled on the Lev Kopelev quoted above, still a true believer in Marxism, defending it even while in prison. Sologdin is a brilliant engineer, handsome even though his hair had thinned and he had lost some teeth in the labor camps; he has secretly solved the key problem the whole camp was set up to solve, and is manipulating it in a way that will assure his freedom. He believes the masses are worthless and that only those rare individuals of dominating intellect and will make humanity worthwhile. The janitor Spiridon is from another world, a basically uneducated peasant farmer for whom all hand tools and raw materials are obedient. The interplay of these four is the occasion for much of the best substance of Solzhenitsyn's thought on Russian socialism and life in general.

Here is a scene to illustrate the rarefied intellectual atmosphere among the prison intelligentsia. Nerzhin has angered the camp commandant, and will soon be sent down to the labor camps. He is chopping wood on a frosty morning with the older Sologdin, who wants to give him a farewell gift. It can't be anything material, because there are full body searches before transport, so he gives him his theories of work. First, Sologdin tells Nerzhin, treat difficulty in work as if you had hit a box containing buried treasure, because the greatest personal growth can take place when you have maximum external resistance and minimal internal resistance. Good, strong, says Nerzhin, who admires Sologdin's abilities to solve problems. Wait, there's more, says Sologdin. When you have had the brainstorm and then done 90 percent of the work on a project, you are tempted to let down. But the Doctrine of the Final Inch tells you that in that final 10 percent of fine-tuning and polishing-off of any enterprise is a good half of its value; so not only must you not slack off, but on this final 10 percent must redouble your efforts.

Nerzhin begins spending more and more time with the janitor Spiridon. His two intellectual friends joke about this as his "to the people" quest, comparing it to the *narodnichestvo* movement of the 1870s. Nerzhin, having fought and worked alongside the common people during the war and in prison, has few Romantic illusions about them, but still finds something of value in their behavior and judgment that is lacking in the intelligentsia. The bewildering political shifts the janitor had made in his life, from working with Reds, then Whites, then Germans, finally make sense to him—they were all in defense of Spiridon's family. Then Nerzhin engages him in criteria for human behavior, standards of good and evil. It takes the janitor a while to understand what Nerzhin is asking, but when he does his face lights up, and he answers as matter-of-factly as if he'd been asked who the duty officer of the day was: "I'll tell you: the wolfhound is right and the cannibal is wrong." It staggers Nerzhin with its simplicity and insight. Wolfhounds were bred to hunt down their kindred; humans weren't.

Just before Nerzhin is sent off, his two friends Rubin and Sologdin get involved in a vicious personal and intellectual clash. Rubin defends Marxism, eventually saying that its goal of social justice justified any means used to attain it. Sologdin pounces on that, saying that in any enterprise the means used to achieve it always color the end. The higher your end, then, the purer your means better be! This may be Solzhenitsyn's ultimate valuation of how Marxism worked out in Russia under Stalin.[15]

The succession; Khrushchev

As one Russian intellectual said about the general shock in March of 1953 when the news of Stalin's death was announced, "We had forgotten that Stalin was mortal." It took two years for a tentative collective leadership to sort itself out, with Nikita Khrushchev emerging by 1955 as something more than first among equals. Here are the major accepted facts from the skimpy materials we have about his early life and career—facts that as you'll see are used very differently by different biographers.

Khrushchev was born in 1894 to ethnic Russian peasants in a tiny, poor village in the Kursk area.[GE108] His father became a metalworker, and migrated regularly 300 miles to the Donbas for work, and when Khrushchev was fourteen, moved the whole family there to Yuzovka ("Hughes"-ovka, named for the British industrialist who built the foundries here back in the reign of Alexander II, today's Donetsk). Here Khrushchev by his mid-teens became a metalworker in and around the mines. He was involved in workers' strikes, and in early 1917 was elected to workers' Soviet in an industrial district just a few miles away from Yuzovka. He apparently

---

108. GE Layer 108 is a Folder titled "Life of Khrushchev," with Placemarks for most of the sites mentioned here.

leaned towards the Mensheviks, not joining the Bolshevik/Communist Party until 1918. When the Germans took the area at the end of WW I and by the Treaty of Brest-Litovsk, Khrushchev went back to his home village for a time. By the end of 1918 he was a political commissar with the Red Army, and after the Civil War was a commissar with a labor detachment at his old Soviet.

He rapidly rose in the Ukrainian Communist Party apparatus, and by 1934 became head of the Moscow city Party apparatus. As such Khrushchev was in charge of the greatest showpiece of Soviet construction of these days, the building of the Moscow Metro (subway system), which opened in 1935.[GE[109]] He took an active public role supporting Stalin's purges in the Moscow area, and when in late 1937 Stalin appointed him head of the whole Ukrainian Communist Party apparat, the purges there intensified. In late 1939 when (in accordance with the Molotov-Ribbentrop Pact) the Soviet Union annexed a broad strip of western lands, Khrushchev was sent to work in the Ukrainian population in what had been southeast Poland. He was nearly caught in Kiev by the German offensive that surrounded and forced the surrender of a whole Soviet army. He was at Stalingrad for almost all of its defense, and also at the Battle of Kursk, something he was obviously very proud of later in life.

After World War II, as head of the Ukrainian Party, he was responsible for rebuilding a shattered land. During those five post-war years in Ukraine, Khrushchev dreamed up his *agrogorod*, literally a "farm-city"—an urban high-rise with apartments, a cinema, a library, and workshops in the middle of pastureland and plowlands. Only one was ever built.

Upon Stalin's death, Lavrenty Beria—Stalin's fellow Georgian and head of the NKVD—seemed to be the rising strongman. But fear of him united his opponents, and his proposals for normalizing relations with the U.S. and even allowing East Germany to reunite with West Germany gave them an excuse for a counter-coup. Six months after Stalin's death he was arrested and executed. Then for a time there was a two-person struggle between Georgy Malenkov, Premier of the Soviet Union (head of government) and Khrushchev, First Party Secretary. Khrushchev chose the risky field of Soviet agriculture in which to stake out new ground, opening his "Virgin Lands" program in northern Kazakhstan, and later expanding the program mainly in Siberia. [GE[110]] Irrigating the thin, semi-desert soils immediately produced bumper harvests, which did a lot to bring Khrushchev to sole power (even though after four or five years all the soil fertility was exhausted and the project collapsed in disaster). By February of 1955, almost two years after Stalin's death, the Kremlin had an acknowledged leader again.

It's amazing how oppositely historians have interpreted those generally-agreed-upon facts. The negative view is that this basically uneducated man joined the Bolshevik Party late, jumping on the bandwagon after its victory was assured. He succeeded in constructing the Moscow Metro by ignoring all safety precautions, and rose fastest in the Party during the Purges first in Moscow and then in the Ukraine. The only reason he won the power struggle after Stalin's death was that everyone underestimated this "loquacious, lowbrow, *enfant terrible* of the Kremlin." The positive view is that he lived in rural poverty, in as lurid labor conditions as could be described by any Marxist, in which it was a simple battle to merely exist. He engaged in humble but important Party work, far from Moscow, and his limited education at least gave him an introduction to Marxism-Leninism. As a non-intellectual he may have been more malleable in the hands of his superiors, but his life in the 1930s was not a hate-filled one but colored by the "stern but deeply felt romance of the industrial revolution in Russia." He could do things other Party leaders could not because he was more than willing to go out on the job and get his feet muddy, talking to the workers about exactly what was going right and wrong and why. The *agrogorod* was essentially Fourier's phalanstery in modern guise—and in this sense Khrushchev may have been the last true believing socialist to head up the Soviet Union. The Virgin Lands program showed him to be a daring, impulsive gambler. The execution of Beria was done to lift the threat of execution from Soviet leaders forever after. Each argument has its strong points and weak points, and the whole is brilliantly presented

---

109. GE Layer 109 is a Folder titled "Moscow Metro Stations; assorted views." Each station was to be unique; each was to be dazzling. You can also do a Google–Images search of "Moscow Metro Stations" for a duke's mixture of such photos.
110. GE Layer 110 is a Folder titled "Virgin Lands." It includes a Polygon showing the original Virgin Lands area of northern Kazakhstan, and a Folder of other areas added to it later.

in Khrushchev's grave marker in the Novodevichy Cemetery in Moscow, one side abstract white marble, one side abstract black marble, with a naturalistic bronze head in-between.[GE[111]]

In the public eye from 1955 on, Khrushchev's career is clearer. In February of 1956, at the famous XXth Party Congress, Khrushchev made a speech denouncing Stalin as a cruel, bloody tyrant, denounced the Purges of the 1930s, and castigated Stalin's cult of personality. Supposed to be a secret speech to a closed meeting, it soon leaked to the public. A "thaw" seemed underway, with new press freedoms. When it spread to the East Bloc, however, Hungary more or less revolted against Soviet rule, and the Soviet Union crushed the rising with tanks. Questions were raised about the stability of the new Party leadership, and Khrushchev actually lost a vote of confidence in the Presidium (the renamed Politburo). This would have ended his political career anytime earlier in the Soviet Union, but he took his case down to the Central Committee—by this time the body of several hundred that supposedly elected the Presidium—and, with help from a timely airlift of delegates courtesy of Marshal Zhukov, won that vote there, and with it went back to the Presidium (the renamed Politburo) and ousted those who had voted him out earlier—Kaganovich, Malenkov, and Molotov among them, now labeled the "anti-Party group." By March of 1958, an even five years after Stalin's death, he was head of Party and head of State, and unrivaled.

The hallmark of the Khrushchev era, however, is that once the leadership rejected terror of the Stalinist kind, support had to come from a broader stratum than before. Neither Presidium (later once again Politburo) nor Central Committee was afraid to vote against Khrushchev—especially when his ideas on consumer economics clashed with defense.

The Soviet government committed huge resources in the general defense area in Khrushchev's tenure, and it made for spectacular achievements. Missile technology was showcased by the 1957 launching of the world's first artificial satellite, *Sputnik* (one of the Russian words for satellite, literally a "traveler together with"), and in 1961 the first successful manned orbital flight that made Yuri Gagarin the first man in space—both of which caused consternation here in the U.S. as we realized how behind we had fallen in this critical military technology.

But Khrushchev also seemed to believe that standard of living would be the ultimate measure of the success or failure of socialism (and from the perspective of the twenty-first century we might conclude he was right?). He set in motion a crash course to build city apartment buildings—hurriedly and cheaply built, subject to "instant ageing," but at least housing where families could have a room to themselves. In 1958 he had the MTS disbanded and the tractors and other machinery sold to the local kolkhozes to use as they saw fit. He set up "Little Academic Cities" (Novosibirsk[GE[112]] was perhaps the most famous Akademgorodok) to brainstorm problems of production. "Guns versus butter" has been a real-world dilemma for most of the world's larger states, and this was true of the Soviet Union as well. One measure of Khrushchev's commitment to reviving the consumer economy is that he worked towards détente with the west, particularly with the U.S. In 1959 he visited the United States (and was pleased to be invited to visit Eisenhower's "dacha" at Camp David) and Eisenhower was to make a reciprocal visit to the Soviet Union later. But Eisenhower approved a resumption of our secret U-2 spy plane flights over the Soviet Union, and on May 1 of 1960 the Soviets brought one down and captured the American pilot—thus making President Eisenhower's visit to the U.S.S.R. impossible and derailing détente. The Cold War threatened to heat up again. In 1961 Khrushchev initiated the building of the "Berlin Wall"—Berlin with its four occupying forces being to that point one remaining avenue of escape from the East Germany of literally millions of generally well-educated Germans and East Europeans, a huge brain drain. And then in 1962 the U.S. and the U.S.S.R. came as close to all-out nuclear war as they ever would, in the Cuban missile crisis.

Before we take a more detailed look at that, consider how this new bi-polar power relationship was reshaping the world. You've already seen how in Stalin's last years the Cold War had split Europe, and how in East Asia the U.S.S.R. and the Communist People's Republic of China had split Korea with the U.S. and its NATO

111. GE Layer 111 is a Placemark referencing Khrushchev's grave in the Novodevichy cemetery; click on Panoramio icon under pointer, "Khrushchev," for a good photograph of the monument.
112. GE Layer 112 is a Placemark referencing the Novosibirsk Akademgorodok.

allies. During Khrushchev's tenure, Cold War tensions—often punctuated by little "hot" wars—spread to every other region of the world. Here's a sampler.

Cold War in Africa, beginning with Ghana

In 1957 Ghana became the first modern sub-Saharan African state to win its independence from its European colonial overlord—in the Khrushchev era and in the context of the Cold War—thus becoming a model for much of the rest of Africa to follow. The George Washington figure of the new state, Kwame Nkrumah (1909–1972), was a teacher there in his early adulthood, but came to the U.S. for his college and graduate education. He wound up with a theology degree, and with Masters degrees in Science Education and in Philosophy from the University of Pennsylvania, always one of our top-ranked universities. But even the best of western thought and institutions offered him fewer tools for achieving independence for the Gold Coast than socialism, apparently. Just after WW II he led groups demanding "independence now," and led huge riots in 1948 which got him jailed by the British colonial government. When the British experimented with some local self-government there in 1952, Nkrumah's party won in a landslide, and he was released from jail to begin a transition government. In 1957 he declared "Ghana" (named after the late, great medieval West African state, though no part of modern Ghana's territory overlapped that of medieval Ghana farther north!) independent, and became the most visible champion of Pan-Africanism, encouraging other African colonies to do the same and join in a united bloc. And socialism, particularly Soviet-brand Marxism, seemed to offer Nkrumah a more reliable route to permanent power than slow parliamentary democracy. He centralized the economy, taking over the great cacao plantations that had been the mainstay of the old colonial government. He nationalized the labor unions, ending their independence. In 1961 he visited the Soviet Union, and came back with a pocketful of aid and grandiose ideas for a "Seven-Year Plan" of crash industrialization. In 1964 he turned the government of Ghana into a one-party state modeled on the Soviet Union. Overthrown in 1966, partly for the economic chaos that had resulted, Nkrumah nevertheless had established a popular model for de-colonization in Africa. First, he had been intellectually awakened and excited by Marxist analysis of colonialism and its weaknesses; later, he was able to tap the resources of the Soviet Union to help build a new state and cement his own power.

Cold War in the Mideast, beginning with Egypt

Gamal Abdal Nasser, who ran Egypt from 1954 until his death in 1970, was the most charismatic Arab leader of modern times. Chief military architect of the overthrow of the Egyptian monarchy in 1952 (as well as remaining British colonial rule), by 1954 he was unrivalled and looked to by the major western powers as the potential leader of a Mideast anti-Communist bloc.

Nasser saw residual British colonial control, however, as a much greater threat than that of the distant Soviet Union, and like most Arabs was bitterly resentful about the western support that had allowed the emergence of an Israeli state in the Mideast in 1948–49 (on which much more in Chapter 10). When the Eisenhower administration would not give him the offensive weapons he needed to match growing Israeli power just to his north, he discovered that Khrushchev would. The U.S. administration, as punishment, withdrew our offer to support construction of the Aswan High Dam on the Nile, central to Nasser's modernization plans. Again, the Soviet Union offered cheap loans for the project. In 1956 Nasser declared the nationalization of the Suez Canal (and closed it to all Israeli shipping), planning to use the tolls from the canal to fund the High Dam. This triggered a war, Egypt being invaded by British, French, and Israeli forces—the second of four major Arab-Israeli wars. The Soviet Union generally supported Nasser, and probably partly because of the danger of a new world war over the issue, the Eisenhower administration put pressure on the invading powers to disengage. Nasser became a firm Soviet ally. With the formal opening of the High Dam in early 1964, the media was flooded with images of Khrushchev and Nasser side by side. Nasser would trigger the 1967 Arab-Israeli War (the Six Day War, the third major Arab-Israeli war), which resulted in the Israeli seizure of the Sinai peninsula from Egypt, the West Bank from Jordan, and the Golan Heights from Syria—of which the last two remain important unresolved problems of international importance all these decades later. Nasser's immediate successor triggered the 1973 Arab-Israeli War (the Yom Kippur or Ramadan War, the fourth major Arab-Israeli war in thirty-five years). It was only settled by U.S. Secretary of State Kissinger's shuttle diplomacy between the combatants, all done of course in the larger setting of the U.S.–U.S.S.R. Cold War rivalry.

Outside Egypt, Ba'athist ("Renaissance") political parties—combining Arab nationalism with Soviet-style socialist central planning and yet not being officially atheistic, given the strength of Islam in most of the Mideast—took over in Syria and Iraq. These countries would of course get a good deal of support from the Soviet Union over the years to come.

Cold War in Southeast and South Asia, beginning with Vietnam

In 1954 Communist forces in Vietnam led by Ho Chi Minh ended the French colonial rule of that country at the great battle of Dienbienphu. Just ten years later, in August of 1964, with Khrushchev still the recognized leader of the Soviet Union, we, the U.S., essentially went to war with the Vietnamese Communists when Congress passed the Tonkin Gulf resolution. The war lasted almost twelve years, and of the half-million U.S. troops committed over 50,000 were killed. Forty years later it still remains a divisive issue in American politics, to some extent an unhealed wound for those old enough to remember it. In terms of world history, it dramatically impacted every Southeast Asian country, and even had echoes in Indonesia, where Sukarno invented his "Third Word" movement, as you'll see in Chapter 12.

In brief background, by the end of the nineteenth century colonial "French Indochina" consisted of what is today Vietnam, Cambodia, and Laos. Some Vietnamese nationalists were in Paris for the treaties ending WW I, hoping that Woodrow Wilson-style "national self-determination" would be applied to Vietnam too, but in vain. These included Ho Chi Minh, French educated and with years of experience living and working in the U.S. and the U.K. At this point he became a founding member of the French Communist Party and turned to Moscow and the Comintern for help. By 1930 he helped fuse rival socialist blocs of Vietnamese into the Vietnamese Communist Party. When WW II ended and the Japanese pulled out of Indochina, a revived French government tried hard to renew its colonial regime in Vietnam. A decade of war with the Viet Minh culminated in 1954 with the all-out French support of their military base at Dienbienphu, opposed by an all-out Viet Minh attack on it. The French, cut off and ringed by Viet Minh artillery on all the surrounding hills, surrendered, and that same year in the Geneva Accords the French agreed to give up all claims to North Vietnam. Ho Chi Minh thereupon moved his government to Hanoi, and within a year a one-party state modeled on the Soviet Union was created there. In that same 1955 Khrushchev was emerging as the key post-Stalin leader of the U.S.S.R.

Although generally not supportive of continuing French colonial rule, the U.S. in the decade after Dienbienpu became more and more engaged in Indochina, and Vietnam in particular, trying to shore up a non-Communist government in the south. In was in part a version of the Containment strategy—there was a lot of talk that if we let the Vietnam "domino" topple, the whole region would quickly go Communist. There was also a general belief that because we were much stronger than France, and were not so much interested in creating an exploitative colonial-style government, that we would succeed. So from political and military advisors and the supply of military matériel, our involvement progressed to small clandestine units. In early August of 1964, with Khrushchev still in power in the U.S.S.R., a shadowy and confusing naval clash in the Tonkin Gulf (between North Vietnam, South China, and China's big island of Hainan) convinced the U.S. Congress to give the administration broad powers of military response. By early 1965 our presence ramped up steeply to the commitment of whole armies—eventually half-a-million troops—with massive air force and navy support. "Operation Rolling Thunder," a tremendous aerial bombardment of North Vietnam to break their support of the Viet Cong in South Vietnam, was carried on from 1965 to 1968. The war seemed to be turning our way: how could any government on earth withstand such awesome technological force? And yet in early 1968, in the so-called "Tet" offensive coinciding with the lunar New Year, the Communists overran dozens of even strongly held positions in the south. It was obviously not going to be a short war.

Anti-war sentiment in the U.S. grew, and by 1975 we ended our involvement. The Communist government of the north took over the south, renaming Saigon "Ho Chi Minh City," and imposing Soviet-style rule on the population. There was at least some regional domino effect. In that same 1975 Laos got a Communist government (which it still has). Pol Pot and a Communist government took over in Cambodia, and in an infamous campaign of governmental terror killed perhaps three million Cambodians and depopulated the cities.

India, by population and resources, was the most important country of South Asia from its creation in 1947 in the Partition of the old British Raj (on which much more in Chapter 11 on the Grand Trunk Road corridor). India's founding political leader, Jawaharlal Nehru, swapped visits with Khrushchev in 1955. Enamored by the Soviet system since a visit there in 1927 (before Stalin had total control), he established a generally socialist-style centralized control of the economy in India that would last down to 1991. Although formally non-aligned in the Cold War all of those years, India was closer to the U.S.S.R. than the U.S.

Cold War in Latin America, beginning with Cuba

When World War II ended in 1945, Fidel Castro was a nineteen-year-old Cuban just starting law school at the University of Havana. Radicalized, as were so many Latin American students, by a political system they saw as controlled by the wealthy in alliance with the Colossus of the North, us, the U.S.A., he got involved in attempts to overthrow U.S.-supported strongmen in Colombia and in the Dominican Republic. He was a member of a recognizably socialist group by 1947 and seriously reading Marxist literature by 1948.

In 1952 Fulgencio Batista (who had been h dominant military strongman and sometimes President of Cuba from 1933–44), took over Cuba again in a military coup. Justifying most of his actions as anti-Communist in these Korean War years, he ruled with an iron fist, with torture and executions being commonplace. On July 26 of 1953, Fidel Castro led a small revolutionary group in an attack on the army barracks at Moncado, hoping to get arms for his group and spark a national rebellion the way so many Latin American heroes of history had. It failed, and most members of the attacking group were summarily executed—Castro and his brother Raúl and a few others escaping for a while into the mountains. Finally captured and put on trial, Fidel managed his own defense and first became a really national figure in Cuba. Revelations at the trial of gruesome torture at the hands of Batista's police and the military occasioned some public revulsion against the regime, which probably resulted in a relatively light sentence for Fidel. He eventually served less than two years in prison, whereupon he and Raúl went to Mexico City.

Meanwhile Ernesto "Che" Guevara, a young Argentine doctor who had been working in Guatemala, had been similarly radicalized by the U.S.-aided overthrow of the Guatemalan government in 1954. He too wound up in Mexico City, and in 1956 joined the Castro brothers and some eighty other Cubans as they were instructed in guerrilla war tactics by a veteran of the Spanish Civil War. Later that year they chartered an old boat and "invaded" Cuba. It was almost disastrous—the boat was delayed by storms and the prearranged local risings had already evaporated; the boat grounded somewhat off the coast and was shot up by a Cuban naval vessel— but about twenty of the original guerrilla team made it into the mountains, and in classic guerrilla fashion won the support of the locals, defeating all the cumbersome government forces sent against them. It was a small, bearded force that attracted *New York Times* reporters and got romantic coverage in *Life* magazine. By January 1959 they entered Havana, and by February Fidel Castro was Prime Minister.

Early in 1960 major Soviet figures came to Cuba for consultation with the regime that, although not calling itself socialist, was appointing many socialists to high positions. In September both Fidel Castro and Nikita Khrushchev were in New York for a meeting of the UN, and hit it off famously. On April 15, 1961, a U.S.-sponsored invasion of Cuba by Cuban exiles, with unofficial air support by U.S. pilots, hit the beaches at the Bay of Pigs; plans for it had begun under the Presidency of Eisenhower, and been approved by the newly-sworn-in President Kennedy. As an invasion it was a military disaster, and Castro, riding the swell of popularity for organizing a successful defense, immediately announced that Cuba was now officially socialist. Waves of Soviet advisors and technical specialists arrived by summer, and the next summer Raúl Castro went to the U.S.S.R. to coordinate military plans—including the installation of nuclear-weapon-tipped missiles that could reach most any U.S. city.

On October 22 of 1962 Kennedy publicly announced the U.S. discovery of the missiles in the process of being installed, and instituted a naval blockade of Cuba to stop any Soviet or East Bloc ships. The world came as close to all-out nuclear war then as it ever has. The crisis ended when Khrushchev agreed to withdraw the missiles on two conditions: one, that the U.S. promise not to invade Cuba; and two, that the U.S. pull its own nuclear missiles out of Turkey. In the spring of 1963 Fidel went to Moscow for over a month, and was featured at the May Day celebration when Soviet military hardware was paraded by Lenin's tomb on Red Square.

So a Communist Cuba had been created and defended within ninety miles of U.S. territory, and Che Guevara personally carried Marxist-style guerrilla war training into several Latin American countries until he was killed in Bolivia. Cuban troops became Soviet proxies as far afield as southern Africa. Beginning in the 1960s there was even a Latin American strain of that "Christian Marxism" called Liberation Theology (more in Chapter 8 on Mexico's Veracruz-to-Mexico City chapter). Cuba was just the most spectacular early chapter of how the Cold War shaped events all over Latin America.

The Soviet system stagnates

Khrushchev probably had other motives than simple defense of Cuba in mind when installing the missiles. These short-range missiles cost a lot less than true inter-continental ones, so he could shelter some money for the consumer economy from defense interests. And he later remarked that the U.S. up to that point had never been serious about negotiating nuclear arms treaties because we—unlike the Soviet Union—had never really been under the gun. But his public backing down on missile installation in Cuba was something of an embarrassment to the country, and in October of 1964 he was "released from all Party and governmental positions because of advanced age and deterioration of health."

Leonid Brezhnev as head of Communist Party, and Alexei Kosygin as Prime Minister, effective head of government, were the key leaders of the U.S.S.R. for the next fourteen years. They had ousted Khrushchev in large part for his crazy improvisations and his scientific ignorance, but in most respects they continued his system. The Chinese Communists were disappointed that the new leaders made no move to return to Stalinism; Mao called it Khrushchevism without Khrushchev.

Hedrick Smith began his classic *The Russians*—published in 1976 after a good half-century of Communist rule (and quoted earlier on Russian memories of World War II)—with a Chapter titled "The Elite: Dachas and Zils." Lenin had begun the policy of rewarding a managerial elite with special goods and services, Stalin had hugely expanded it, and by the Brezhnevian '70s it was a camouflaged but permanent part of Soviet reality. Roughly a million people by this time were on the *nomenklatura*, the secret "list" of those with access to special stores, schools, hospitals, summer camps, and health spas—and even neighborhoods. West of Moscow, in a cluster about a dozen miles across and isolated by dense woods, are Peredelkino where famous writers of the Writers' Union (even dissident writers such as Boris Pasternak) had their country homes, and Nikolina Gora where the Academy of Sciences elites lived, and between them and most elite of all, Zhukovka, with its dachas for the Party and governmental *crème de la crème*.[GE¹¹³] Later, wealthy individuals such as the world-renowned cellist Rostropovich bought such estates from the widows of the original owners (Solzhenitsyn for a time lived in Rostropovich's gardener's house). Smith was puzzled by the recurring cliché that "Moscow is just a small village," until he understood that everybody who was important had their dachas in or near Zhukovka. Such a "new class" was particularly galling to Russian intellectuals without access to it, because it was such a mockery of the original egalitarian socialist principles of the founders of the Soviet Union. The Zil and Chaika luxury cars, that parked wherever they chose and scattered city pedestrians like chickens, behaved in the manner of the carriages of the aristocracy and governmental elites of Tsarist Russia. A Russian joke of the time had Brezhnev trying to impress his mother with his dozens of expensive foreign cars and his palatial dacha. His mother finally says, "Well, it's good, Leonid, but what if the Reds come back?"¹⁶

If you were among the great majority of those without such privileged access, it generally meant spending half your life standing in lines in stores with little in them and that of low quality. You learned the sizes of hat, shoe, and every item of clothing of all your close kin and friends, and carried a good bit of cash on a regular basis (along with a collapsible string bag called an *avoska*), so that if they "threw something out" you could immediately snap it up. You knew not to buy goods stamped as made in the last few days of the month, because that was when everybody was "storming" to try to meet the quota set by Gosplan, the government planning center. You swapped services for rare goods and became expert at bribery (dealing "on the left," in Russian

---

113. GE Layer 113 is a Folder with Placemarks for the three elite "villages."

parlance). The land of plenty, promised by the government for decades as "coming soon," was obviously not coming soon, and although there was general pride in the international power of the Soviet Union, very little of the socialist dream was left alive by Brezhnev's time. It was a technocratic elite ruling in its own interests, and justifying its actions by time-worn socialist clichés almost nobody believed anymore.

Czechoslovakia, Poland, and Afghanistan

In the Vietnam War from 1965–1975, Soviet military aid and especially air support for North Vietnam was a factor of some importance in America's defeat. It was an ideal situation for the Soviet Union—tying down the bulk of America's military might in a tremendously controversial and expensive war, while spending little of its own resources. But the Soviet Union was about to face huge problems of its own, and mostly of its own making.

In the East Bloc of Soviet-dominated states, Czechoslovakia was most restive because it was the most westernized. In 1968 its classically Stalinist hard-line leader was replaced by Alexander Dubček, a self-proclaimed Communist who, remarkably, began to give a new and liberal face to government there. Censorship was lightened and—despite warnings from Brezhnev to cease and desist—a few western-style economic reforms were introduced. It was called the "Prague Spring." On August 20, 1968, Warsaw Pact forces anchored by Soviet Union tanks rolled in and crushed it. There was little bloodshed only because the Czechoslovak forces had been told by their own government not to retaliate (more later in Chapter 7 on Czechs, Czechoslovaks, and the Bratislavan Lesson). The Soviet government's rationale was clear: such westernizing independence would destabilize the whole East Bloc, maybe the Soviet Union itself. But for a country arguing loudly that the U.S. was engaging in a colonial-style imperial war in Vietnam, the parallels were embarrassing.

Less than a decade later huge labor strikes broke out in Poland, and in 1978 the Polish Archbishop of Cracow became Pope John Paul II. He had been outspokenly against Soviet policies in Poland before this, and now he had a world-class platform. This resonated particularly well in Poland, where membership in the Catholic Church was often considered also as a vote against Soviet domination. By 1980 trade unions in a "Solidarity" bloc, headed by the fearless and charismatic Lec Walesa, were paralyzing the government. The Soviet Union supported a military coup inside Poland in 1981, but there was such resistance from the general public that even the military government had trouble governing, and with time itself showed signs of wanting national independence.

But the straw that broke the camel's back of the Soviet Union was probably Brezhnev's decision in the last days of 1979 to invade Afghanistan. As with the U.S. in South Vietnam, a friendly government was being subverted by opponents, and the Soviet Union committed major ground troops to its defense. We of the U.S., of course, were delighted to be able to provide military equipment to those opponents via the Pakistani border, doing to the Soviets what they had done to us in Vietnam (and not thinking much about the consequences of arming such people as Osama bin Laden). And as with the U.S. in the Vietnam War, the Soviet forces were never able to defeat the nationalistically- and religiously-inspired guerrilla-style forces arrayed against them. Bogged down in a war with no end in sight, the Soviet government tried to keep the body count secret but generally failed as it grew larger. When Brezhnev died in 1982, and his successor as First Party Secretary died in 1983, and <u>his</u> successor died in 1985—both old men of Brezhnev's generation—the stage was set for a basic change of direction for the first time since Stalin's death in 1953.

Gorbachev: the system dismantled

Mikhail Gorbachev was born in 1931 in Privol'noe, a village in the Stavropol *krai* at the northern base of the Caucasus Mountains.[GE[114]] One of his grandfathers was chairman of the first kolkhoz of his village, and his father was a tractor operator with the local Machine Tractor Station. At age fourteen, in 1945, Gorbachev was working a full summer shift at the MTS, as boys replaced their fathers who were off at the war. In 1949, Privol'noe had a surprisingly good harvest, and the eighteen-year-old Mikhail—already an active member of

---

114. GE Layer 114 is a Placemark generally locating Privol'noe in the context of the whole Stavropol krai on the northern slopes of the Caucasus.

Komsomol, the Communist Youth organization—came in for his share of the awards for it and joined the Communist Party proper. This gave him the momentum to apply for, and win, admission to the premier law school in the whole U.S.S.R., Moscow State University (MGU).

The law faculty was not housed in the fancy new buildings up on the Lenin Hills (now once again Sparrow Hills) with the science departments, but in the decrepit old wooden buildings not far from the Kremlin where literature, history, philosophy, and linguistics were taught. Four to a dorm room, one toilet for the hall, the average stipend just enough for two meals a day in the cafeteria—Gorbachev went home summers to make extra money to make ends meet. By his upper-class years, he had a better room and acquired a Czech roommate. There were a good many Chinese and Eastern European students here in those days, but only "trustworthy" Soviet students were allowed to room with foreigners, and Komsomol stalwart Gorbachev was obviously trusted. But there was an independent streak in Gorbachev even then; as the former Czech roommate wrote later, in 1952—in the rising hysteria of the Doctor's Plot—Gorbachev said to him: "Lenin did not have Martov arrested, he allowed him to leave the country."[17] When he graduated in 1955, he was transformed in looks, taste in western clothes, and had had the law curriculum's training in public speaking, training offered by virtually no other academic discipline at the time.

Almost all new law graduates joined the staff of some local Procurator—the prosecutors of Soviet law (the defenders of the accused were traditionally denigrated, ill-paid, and handicapped by the rules!). But Gorbachev went back to Stavropol and took a job in the management of the Komsomol. By the next year he was First Secretary of the Stavropol city Komsomol. By age twenty-nine he had an important position in the regional Komsomol organization, which got him on the *nomenklatura*, the list of the privileged elite, for the first time. Two years later—getting a bit old for Komsomol, probably—he moved on into supervision in the Party organs of the Stavropol district. As such he was in charge of all the famous health resorts and mineral water spas of the area,[GE[115]] and in making sure the stay of Party and government bigwigs there was good, made invaluable contacts with the whole Soviet hierarchy. By 1971 he headed up the Stavropol district and was a member of the Central Committee. In 1977 a computerized harvesting system debuted there, got in the harvest in record time, and won Gorbachev national recognition. In 1978 he became the youngest member of the Politburo, in charge of agriculture—a chancy position given the vagaries of the weather in Russia. Sure enough, four years of generally bad weather and increasingly bad crops made Gorbachev's position seemingly untenable by 1982; he was probably saved from being demoted by Brezhnev's death that same year. In 1983 he made his first extensive trip abroad—to Canada, source of grain imports to the Soviet Union and a place with parallel climate in which to study grain production. Weather and harvests improved 1983–1985, giving Gorbachev the inside track to the position of First Party Secretary.

He was officially inaugurated on March 11, 1985. In time-honored fashion, he began to move his people into the Politburo, the most visible being the Georgian Edouard Shevardnadze, who was appointed in July, and who also replaced Andrei Gromyko as foreign minister. All of Gorbachev's earlier rivals "retired" from key Party positions. And now the media was full of three words—*perestroika* (literally "reconstruction"), *glasnost'* (openness, built on the root word for voice, *golos*), and *democraktisatsiia* (literally "democratization").

Economically, almost nothing worked his first two years. There were huge budget deficits and growing inflation. An anti-alcohol campaign just boosted the homebrew industry to the point where all sugar disappeared from grocery store shelves. On April 28, 1986, there was a nuclear meltdown at the Chernobyl facility, up the Dnieper and the Pripyat Rivers from Kiev. It was met at first with traditional Soviet cover-up—Scandinavian scientists discovered it by the radioactive cloud that blew up their way. But then it was used by reformers around Gorbachev as "an opening into glasnost and a strong argument in its favor," and by summer the U.S.S.R. had press and speech freedoms unknown since 1917. Gorbachev's biggest miscalculation may have been that he thought such openness would strengthen the Soviet system. Instead it opened it up to questions it would have preferred not to answer—about health issues related to pollution in the environment, about privileged classes, about the war in Afghanistan. The result was the organizing of interest groups into formal organizations and political parties—Greens, Gay Rights advocates, Orthodox clergy, skinhead Fascists (Pamyat, strongest of the new far right parties, started as a historical preservation society!), even monarchists.

---

115. GE Layer 115 is a Folder titled "Stavropol spas and mineral water springs."

But of all the groups that coalesced in response to glasnost, most important were the nationalists—in both the Soviet Socialist Republics and the national minorities within the RSFSR itself. The Baltics began to break away as early as the fall of 1988 when Estonia declared its right to reject Soviet laws. Gorbachev tried personal visits and speeches; then he shut off oil to Lithuania; and in January of 1991 he sent the Black Berets, Soviet special forces, into Lithuania and Latvia, with dozens killed. There were parallel explosions and retaliations south of the Caucasus, in Georgia's "Bloody Sunday" in April of 1989, and with Armenian and Azerbaijani growing independence measured by their fight over the disputed Nagorno-Karabakh territory.

What really pulled the rug out from under Gorbachev in terms of exerting force on the breakaway national fringes of the U.S.S.R. was that he got no support from the RSFSR, the Russian Republic that made up more than half the country. Russian nationalism itself surged—in part because despite the favored position of the Russian language, the Russian part of the Soviet Union was poorer than many of the other SSRs. And the Russian part of the Soviet Union got a charismatic leader, Boris Yeltsin. A key reformer in Gorbachev's early years in power, Yeltsin was by 1987 head of the Moscow Party apparatus. When he vocally criticized Gorbachev for the slowness of reforms, Gorbachev in essence fired him. But in a remarkable comeback, over Gorbachev's opposition he was elected speaker of the Parliament for the RSFSR.

With the Soviet Union disintegrating, Gorbachev was now hit by a hammer blow—the East Bloc countries broke away from the Soviet Union. The key time was the fall of 1989, as Communists governments were swept out of power in Poland, Czechoslovakia, Hungary, Romania, Bulgaria—and East Germany. The fall of the Berlin Wall on the night of November 9 and the day of November 10, 1989, is surely one of the most significant dates of modern history. The process ranged from remarkably peaceful, as in Czechoslovakia where Vaclav Havel masterminded the "Velvet Revolution," to remarkably bloody, as in the vengeance the common people of Romania took on the brutal dictator Ceaucescu, his family, and supporters. The only way to have kept the East Bloc countries under Soviet control would have been to send in tanks, and Gorbachev's argument to the Soviet hard-liners who criticized him was that tanks couldn't be used forever. He accepted the independence of the East Bloc, even the reunification of the Germanies.

By the end of 1990 there were signs that Soviet conservatives were organizing against Gorbachev. In December a "Committee of National Salvation" from this conservative Soviet bloc called on Gorbachev to impose a national state of presidential emergency, suspend all political parties, and remove elected officials in the breakaway SSRs of the Baltics and the sub-Caucasus region. The conservative bloc's most visible spokesman was Col. Viktor Alksnis, who by early 1991 was calling for the removal of Gorbachev from office and for the KGB and Interior Ministry to take over government. In response to this pressure from the right, Gorbachev himself veered sharply right—at which point such key reformers as Shevardnadze abandoned him. When he resigned Dec. 20, 1990, Shevardnadze said: "A dictatorship is coming . . . No one knows what kind of dictatorship it will be and who will come or what the regime will be like . . . I am resigning . . . Let this be my contribution, if you like, my protest against the onset of dictatorship." The next month was when Gorbachev sent the Black Berets into Lithuania and Latvia.

In the Presidential elections in Russia proper in June 1991, Yeltsin won in a landslide. Unlike Gorbachev, he now had a popular mandate to govern. With great public fanfare Yeltsin resigned from the Communist Party, followed by his key administrators. He ordered the Communist Party excluded from factories and the armed forces. The hard-liners called this a move toward dictatorship.

Failure of the August Coup

On August 5, 1991, Gorbachev left for vacation in Yalta. At dawn on August 19, 1991, the eight members of a so-called Committee for the State of Emergency attempted a coup d'état. All eight had been appointed to their posts by Gorbachev (on his swings to the right!) and they had been meeting in a KGB "safe house" since August 7. The timing was decided by the scheduled signing on August 20 of a new union treaty that was to transfer most Soviet powers to the individual republics. Now an announcement went out that Gorbachev needed an extended stay in Yalta for his health, and that the Committee was taking over to end bloodshed and preserve law and order. Gorbachev was captured by a group of plotters, though he refused to sign on with any support. But the Committee, strangely, overlooked Boris Yeltsin—who immediately denounced the coup and rallied public opposition to it. Crowds circled armored vehicles, which stopped so as not to run over them.

Troops sent to disperse the crowds would not fire on them. Yeltsin's finest hour was standing atop a tank in front of the Parliament building of the Russian Republic—the so-called Russian White House[GE116]—calling for a general strike. Part of the army came over to him and offered protection. The mayor of Leningrad backed him. In response, the Committee declared a curfew, which was riotously ignored. When on the third day of the coup, the Committee ordered a morning attack of its tanks on the White House, and when the tank units refused, the coup collapsed. Gorbachev made it back to Moscow, and the coup leaders were either arrested or committed suicide. But the Soviet institutions that were Gorbachev's source of power had disappeared virtually overnight.

The last nails in the coffin of the Soviet Union were the overwhelming vote for full independence in Ukraine on December 1, and then a week later the December 8, 1991, meeting in Minsk of the Presidents of Ukraine, Russia, and Belarus, declaring that they no longer recognized any such entity as the U.S.S.R. Instead they announced the formation of a Commonwealth of Independent States (*Sodruzhestvo Nezavisimykh Gosudarstv*). Two weeks later at a meeting at Almaty, the biggest city of Kazakhstan, all five former Central Asian SSRs joined, and then Armenia and Azerbaijan (Georgia, absent, was caught up in civil war, and the three Baltics—only added to the Soviet Union in 1940, remember—abstained completely). On December 25 of that same 1991—just over four months after the coup attempt—Gorbachev delivered his resignation speech on TV, and then instructed that the nuclear weapons codes of the now-defunct Soviet Union be given to the General representing President Yeltsin. So it was on Christmas Day that the Soviet flag, which had flown over the Kremlin for seventy-four years, was lowered ceremonially for the last time. Russia got the UN Security Council seat. Gorbachev got to write his memoirs.

A good bit has been written on how the growth of the U.S. military made it impossible for the Soviet Union to keep pace, and so brought it down. While it may have played some role, I doubt it played a major role, remembering western military experts' surprise after the end of the Soviet Union at how sophisticated they found Soviet warplanes and MIRV-ed missiles to be, for example. Personally I'm convinced that the more important reason was the computer and bio-technology revolution in consumer goods coming from the capitalist world, especially those high-quality Japanese manufactures. This "Japanese shock" battered even our economy, driving U.S. manufacturers out of high-end electronics and automobiles for awhile—but this all hit the U.S.S.R., with its paralyzing central planning and hugely inefficient industrial plants, ten times as hard. Consider this excerpt of a Gorbachev speech to a congress of Komsomol (Young Communists) leaders on Nov. 15, 1989—a group he felt especially close to given his own rise through Komsomol, and a venue at which he had no reason to expect, or cater to, a western audience. He quickly runs through Soviet history, and then gets to what he called the era of stagnation (politely not calling Khrushchev and Brezhnev by name):

All this is not to say that during those years we did not tackle major economic and cultural tasks. During that time we scored impressive achievements in space exploration. We shouldn't underestimate the importance of the military parity we attained, although it placed society under enormous material and intellectual strain, and of course told on the implementation of the social programmes. In time, however, the inability of the command-and-administrative system to ensure modern scientific, technological and socio-economic progress became more and more obvious. Meanwhile, the industrialized capitalist states entered a new stage of the scientific and technological revolution, and made breakthroughs to new production methods. The revolution in micro-electronics, information science and bio-engineering has brought about radical changes in modern civilization, particularly in the production of foodstuffs and consumer goods, and in services and housing construction. In many industrial branches labour productivity has increased nearly tenfold, which has brought about colossal changes in the people's way of life. All of these changes only affected us in certain areas—mostly in space research and the military sphere. I think the worst mistake we made then was to underestimate the significance of the revolution in science and technology. As a result, in the context of general civilization, we have been left, so to speak, in a bygone technological age in a number of vitally important social spheres. The industrialized Western countries, meanwhile, have entered another age, an age of high technology and

116. GE Layer 116 is a Placemark referencing the Russian White House—due west of the Kremlin on the next upstream loop of the Moscow River. The embedded website shows a classic picture of Yeltsin atop a tank rallying the opposition.

fundamentally new relationships between science and industry, new methods of saving resources, new materials, and new ways of ensuring better living standards, including services. Therefore, the stagnation period can rightly be described as a time of lost opportunities which inflicted serious damage on our social progress and on socialism in general.[18]

Gorbachev, however much he worked to reform the system, remained a Communist. Today he couldn't even be elected dogcatcher anywhere in Russia, because the die-hard Communist ideologues think he gave away the store (Russia's position as one of the two great world powers, and dismantling the new Russian Empire that called itself the Soviet Union), and today's Westernizers, who want a more central and western European-style state, and who reject the whole Communist legacy. But history will probably deal generously with him; if one of the other candidates had been elected First Secretary of the Communist Party in March of 1985, there would probably still be a Soviet Union and a continuing Cold War.

End of the Cold War

As you saw earlier, from 1945 to 1991 events in Europe and in every one of the six other major regions of the world were generally framed by the Cold War rivalry between the U.S. and U.S.S.R. Since any given point of friction had the potential to cause nuclear war between the two superpowers, we both tended to suppress the interests of the merely local powers. After 1991, with such suppression generally lifted, there was a flaring up of many of these local interests—which should not have, but did, catch most observers of world politics off-guard.

In the spring of 1989 the new freedoms of Eastern Europe and the SSRs encouraged Chinese liberals to agitate for the same, and Tienanmen Square was filled with delegations from universities from all over the PRC. On June 4 hard-liners in the government militarily crushed the occupation, establishing the tone of life in China to this day—considerable economic freedoms, but absolute political control by the Chinese Communist Party (which has obviously abandoned anything Communist about it, except centralized control). In 1991 the Nehru dynasty in India with its generally socialist central government planning gave way to a free market wave. This has transformed India's economy, though India and Pakistan regularly test nuclear weapons and threaten each other with them. In the summer of 1990 Iraq invaded Kuwait, occasioning our invasion of Iraq in the First Iraq War of 1991. In the 1990s Yugoslavia messily and bloodily split up into its constituent ethnic parts. Inside Russia itself Chechnya revolted, achieving some independence in a 1994 war before being brutally suppressed again in a 1999–2000 war. On September 11, 2001—at the end of a decade of post-Cold War activity—the modern psyche of the U.S. was changed at a stroke with Al Qaeda's seizure of commercial aircraft and terrorist strikes on New York's twin towers and Washington's Pentagon. It occasioned our immediate invasion of Afghanistan and seemed to give justification to policy hawks calling for the full invasion of Iraq which came in 2003 with the Second Iraq War. The Arab Spring of more recent years—with the overthrow of Libya's Gaddafi, of Egypt's Mubarak, and the civil war in Syria that as of this writing threatens to overthrow Assad—has not gone according to the wishes of either the U.S. or Russia. It's a more complex world than the simple dualism of the Cold War, but understanding it well still takes knowing the historical process that brought it into being.

Lessons learned

Socialism, every bit as much as nationalism, was part of that Romantic reaction to the extreme individualism of the Enlightenment—they are both "groupisms." The idealism of nineteenth-century socialist visionaries was very attractive in a world trying to grapple with the pollution and disruption of society brought about by the industrial revolution. Especially in the Russian Empire, where intellectuals lived in a hothouse world of ideas in which it was impossible to test new living arrangements by experiment, socialism was invested with high-flown virtues that were going to be extremely difficult to live out in the real world (though Russian Jews would make a go of the *kibbutz*, Hebrew for "commune," for several generations, as you'll see in Chapter 10 on the Mideast). You've already seen the list of Marxism's considerable strengths, and some of its weaknesses were either well hidden or only revealed over time. The Bolshevik takeover during a disastrous war and a huge peasant land seizure proved much easier than effecting Marxism in Russia in practice. The idealism of the Bolsheviks made them easy prey for Stalin and the most ruthless dictatorship Russia was ever under. But the industrialization forced through by the dictatorship was a key element in the Soviet Union's survival of the German invasion in World War II, and arguably was the key factor that made the Soviet Union for half a century one of the world's two greatest powers—in essence a new Russian Empire even more powerful than the old one that defeated Napoleon.

Although in the long run socialism turned out to be the servant of political nationalism and cultural nationalism more than their master, it is still the third of those great modern-world-shaping ideas that, first, gave unprecedented power to European culture, and second, were tapped for their innate powers in the fight against European intrusion by the rest of the world. Before we get to the second part of that in the second half of the book, though, let's see how these great ideas shaped the modern history of three smaller parts of Europe, in the context of that great power politics already talked about. Chapter 5 deals with the Irish in the far west of Europe, Chapter 6 deals with the Finns in the north, and Chapter 7 deals with the Czechs in the east. Each of these subjects ought to give us more depth perception on modern history generally, and these great shaping ideas in particular.

Endnotes

1. Lenin Internet Archive (http://www.marxists.org/archive/lenin/works/1918/feb/21b.htm).

2. From Stalin's *War Speeches, Orders of the Day* (London, 1945), pp. 18–20, as quoted in Isaac Deutscher's *Stalin: A Political Biography* (New York: Oxford University Press, 1966), p. 489.

3. Basil Dmytryshyn, ed., *Medieval Russia: A Source Book, 900–1700* (New York, Chicago, San Franciso, Toronto, London: Holt, Rinehart and Winston, Inc., 1967), pp. 76–77. Some changes made in punctuation, capitalization, and line division.

4. Orlando Figes, *Natasha's Dance: A Cultural History of Russia* (New York: Metropolitan Books, Henry Holt and Company, 2002). The text immediately below this footnote draws heavily on Chapter 2, "Children of 1812," and especially Chapter 3, "Moscow! Moscow!"

5. Figes, *Natasha's Dance*, p. 361 and generally Chapter 5, "Descendants of Genghiz Khan."

6. Theodore H. White, *In Search of History: A Personal Adventure* (New York: Harper & Row, 1978), pp. 190–91.

7. Frances Fitzgerald, *Fire in the Lake: The Vietnamese and the Americans in Vietnam* (New York & Boston: Little, Brown and Co., 1972), pp. 140–41.

8. T. B. Bottomore, trans. and ed., *Karl Marx: Early Writings* (New York: McGraw-Hill, 1964), p. vi.

9. Fred Halliday, *Iran: Dictatorship and Development* (Middlesex & New York: Penguin Books; second edition 1979), p. 309.

10. Geroid T. Robinson, *Rural Russia Under the Old Regime* (Berkeley and Los Angeles: University of California Press, 1960, reprint from 1932 edition), p. 238.

11. James Bunyan & Harold H. Fisher, eds., *Bolshevik Revolution, 1917–1918; Documents and Materials*, p. 362. (books.google.com/books?isbn=0804703442)

12. Nikolai Bukharin and Evgenii Preobrazhenskii, *The ABCs of Communism* (1920; first English edition in 1922). The quotations in this section are all from *Historical Materialism: A System of Sociology,* from pp. 262, 306–315.

13. Lev Kopelev, *To Be Preserved Forever*, trans. & ed. Anthony Austin (Philadelphia & New York: J. B. Lippincott Co., 1977; first published in Russian in 1976), pp. 16–17.

14. Headrick Smith, *The Russians* (New York: Ballantine Books, 1976), pp. 403–4.

15. See Aleksandr Solzhenitsyn, *The First Circle*, trans. Michael Guybon (London: Wilson Collins and Harvill Press, 1968). Solzhenitsyn's later revisions of the book, unfortunately, took some of the punch out of these passages.

16. Smith, *The Russians*, first chapter generally.

17. Zhores Medvedev, *Gorbachev* (New York & London: W.W. Norton & Co., 1986), p. 38.

18. Mikhail Gorbachev, *Channel the Energy of Youth into Perestroika: Speech at the All-Union Student Forum, Nov. 15, 1989.* (Moscow: Novosti Press Agency Publishing House, 1989), pp. 9–10.

"Racy of the Soil": Ireland

And what have we got in their stead? We have got such foreign and fantastic field sports as lawn tennis, polo, croquet, cricket and the like—very excellent, I believe, and health-giving exercises in their way, still not racy of the soil but rather alien, on the contrary to it, as are, indeed, for the most part, the men and women who first imported and still continue to patronize them.

(Catholic Archbishop Thomas Croke upon accepting appointment as patron to the Gaelic Athletic Association, lamenting the fading away of traditional Irish sports)

CONTENTS

The heart of the matter—Introduction to the Gaelic (Irish) language—Topography and texture of the land—Legends, folklore, and early history—The three most important dates in Irish history: 1171, 1533, 1610—Puritan Revolution and aftermath—The Penal Laws and the "Protestant Ascendancy"—Impact of the American and French Revolutions—The Irish Rebellion of 1798—"The Counselor" and Catholic Emancipation—Young Ireland—Potato Famine—"My Mother, Mary Kelly"– The Ordnance Survey in Ireland—Irish Republican Brotherhood and Fenians—Michael Cusack and the Gaelic Athletic Association—Parnell and Gladstone—Irish literary revival and the Gaelic League—The Home Rule Movement Before WW I—The Irish Orange—Easter Rising 1916—The partitioning of Ireland— De Valera shapes the Republic of Ireland—The Troubles—The Good Friday Agreement and since— Final musings on nationalism and socialism

The heart of the matter

The island of Ireland, as most Americans will know, lies west across the Irish Sea from the even larger island of Great Britain.[GE¹] The shortest sea crossing is between lowland Scotland and northern Ireland, about a one-hour ferry ride today unless you take a hydrofoil. From either of the western points of Wales to the south-eastern coast of Ireland the ferry is about three times as long.

Traditional Ireland was made up of four provinces named for ancient kingdoms—Leinster in the east, Ulster in the north, Munster in the south, and Connacht (formerly usually spelled Connaught, and pronounced something like CON-nockt) in the west.[GE²] Most of the population and the biggest cities were and still are along that curve of its coast nearest Britain and the European continent: Ulster has Belfast, Leinster has Dublin, and Munster has Cork, but Connacht has always been too remote from the rest of Europe to support any city as big as these. The River Shannon angles down from northeast to southwest across the middle of the island,

---

1. Google Earth Layer 1 is a Placemark framing a general view of the two islands.
2. GE Layer 2 is a Folder titled "Four traditional kingdoms." Turn on the whole folder. Take a minute to locate the key port cities of Belfast, Dublin, and Cork.

and was at times in history an important political and even military boundary.[GE³] The four provinces in modern times contain thirty-two counties in all. Today six of Ulster's nine traditional counties make up the Northern Ireland part of the United Kingdom.[GE⁴] The other twenty-six make up today's Republic of Ireland.[GE⁵] How that came to be, and why hostility flares in Northern Ireland between Protestants and Catholics especially around Easter and in the July "marching season," is the story this chapter tells.

Ireland, then, is our first case study of how political nationalism, cultural nationalism, and socialism—identified in the last three chapters of the textbook as the major shaping forces of the modern world—worked out in one Ohio-sized place in western Europe in the context of modern great power politics. As you'll see, cultural nationalism was the strongest of those three shaping forces, both for the Irish Green and the Irish Orange.

Introduction to the Gaelic (Irish) language

The Gaelic language, today often simply called the Irish language, is a member of the Celtic branch of Indo-European languages. Celtic speakers occupied most of Western Europe between two and three thousand years ago; the Gauls conquered by Julius Caesar from 60–52 BC, for example, in what is roughly today's France, spoke a Celtic language. Over the last couple of thousand years, though, successive population waves out of the east pushed Celtic language speakers over into the western fringes of Europe, including extreme western France (the Brittany peninsula, where some Breton is still spoken), and into Cornwall, Wales, Scotland, the Isle of Man, and Ireland.

Irish (Gaelic) and Scottish Gaelic are both members of the Goidelic branch of Celtic. Today Scottish Gaelic mainly survives in the Outer Hebrides, that long chain of islands off the northwest side of Scotland; its closest living relative is the Irish spoken in Donegal, the northwestern-most county of Ireland.[GE⁶] There are many basic similarities between Irish and Scottish Gaelic, beginning with *mac,* meaning "son of," in both. Some of them have come over into English from both Scottish Gaelic and Irish: "craig," meaning "cliff," from *creag*; "whiskey" from the first word of *uisge beath*, meaning "water of life." More Irish speakers survived into modern times than those of any other Celtic language, perhaps because Ireland was westernmost of all and so least under pressure from later population waves.

Earliest written Irish, from roughly the time of the late Roman Empire, was in the Ogham script, which looks like sets of short lines scratched squarely or diagonally across a single long line.[GE⁷] But by the AD 500s "Old Irish" was already being written in a version of the Latin script. Today modern printed Irish uses recognizable Latin letters, and only eighteen of them. The consonants are b, c, d, f, g, h, l, m, n, p, r, s, and t (although sometimes with non-Gaelic words borrowed from other languages such as English they also have to "borrow" the other Latin consonants that go with them). The vowels are the typical a, e, i, o, and u, but it is really a double set, because an acute accent over each of these lengthens its sound (á, é, í, ó, and ú). What is called the Old Gaelic script, used from the Middle Ages until early modern times, is obviously just a fancied up version of selected Latin letters.

---

3. GE Layer 3 is a Folder titled "Shannon River and estuary." Turning it on shows the main course of the river as a Path in light blue and the estuary as a Polygon in blue wash.

4. GE Layer 4 is a Placemark framing a view of Ulster. If you have your basic "Borders and Labels" layer turned on, a bright yellow line indicating an international border takes in all of Ulster except the county of Donegal in the northwest and the two counties of Monaghan and Cavan in the south.

5. GE Layer 5 is a Placemark framing a view of Ireland as a whole. Turn off GE Layer 2, the four traditional kingdoms, and just leave present-day borders.

6. GE Layer 6 is an arrow-shaped Polygon pointing from the Outer Hebrides to Co. Donegal; it's a distance of a little over a hundred miles between them.

7. GE Layer 7 is a Placemark used as excuse to call up website showing Ogham writing on a stone in a churchyard in Tralee, County Kerry; with website below call up *Wikipedia* article on Ogham, see photo at top right: http://en.wikipedia.org/wiki/Ogham

Below is a poem written around 1830 by an Irishman homesick for County Mayo and his hometown of Killaden, imagining himself going cross-country from Leinster in the east into Connacht in the west:

THE COUNTY MAYO (sometimes titled *KILLADEN*)

Now, with the coming of the spring, the days will stretch a bit;
And after the Feast of Brigid I shall hoist my flag and go:
For, since the thought got into my head, I can neither stand nor sit
Until I find myself in the middle of the County of Mayo.

In Claremorris I should stop a night to sleep with decent men;
And then I'd go to Balla, just beyond, and drink galore;
And next I'd stay in Kiltimagh for about a month; and then
I should only be a couple of miles away from Ballymore!

I say and swear that my heart lifts up like the lifting of a tide;
Rising up like the rising wind till fog or mist must go,
When I remember Carra, and Gallen close beside,
And the Gap of the Two Bushes, and the wide plains of Mayo.

To Killaden then, to the place where everything grows that is best;
There are raspberries there, and strawberries there, and all that is good for men;
And were I only there among my folk my heart would rest,
For age itself would leave me there, and I'd be young again.

Here is the original printed version in classic Irish letters:

Cill-Aodáin.

Anois teaċt an earraiġ, beiḋ an lá dul ċun sineaḋ
A's tar éis na féil' Bríġde árdóċad mo ṡeól
Ó ċuir mé in mo ċeann é, ní stopfaiḋ mé ċoiḋċe
Go seasfaiḋ mé ṫíos i lár Ċonndae Ṁuiġeó.

I gClár Cloinne Ṁuiris a ḃéas mé an ċéad oiḋċe,
'S i mBalla taoḃ ṫíos de ṫosóċas mé ag ól,
Go Coillte-maċ raċad, go ndéanad cuairt miosa ann,
I bfogus dá ṁíle go Béal-an-Áṫa-ṁóir.

Ó fágaim le h-uaḋaċta go n-éiriġeann mo ċroiḋe-se
Mar éiriġeas an ġaoṫ, nó mar scaipeas an ceó,
Nuair a smuainiġim ar Ċearra a's ar Ġaillin taoḃ ṫíos de
Ar Sceaṫaċ-a'-Ṁíle nó ar Ṗlánṫai Ṁuiġeó.

Cill-Aodáin an baile a ḃfásann gaċ níḋ ann,
Tá sméara 's súġ-ċraoḃ ann 's meas ar gaċ sórt,
'S dá mbéinn-se mo ṡeasaṁ i gceart lár mo ḋaoine
D'imṫeoċaḋ an aois ḋíom agus ḃéinn arís óg.

Antoine Ó Reaċtabra.

Here is the first verse in Irish, with English translation phrase by phrase:

Anois teacht an earraigh (now coming of the Spring)
beidh an lá ag dul chun síneadh, (the day will be going toward lengthening)
Is tar éis na féil Bríde (and after the feast of Bridget)
ardóidh mé mo sheol. (I shall raise my sail)
Ó chuir mé I mo cheann é (since I put it into my head)
ní chónóidh me choíche (I shall never stay put)
Go seasfaidh mé síos (until I shall stand down)
i lár Chondae Mhaigh Eo. (in the center of County Mayo)[1]

In terms of general words you might encounter when perusing maps of Ireland, including the Google Earth surface, here is a short list with original Irish in italics, followed by one or more common anglicized forms, and then by the translation:

baile, bally = village
cill, kil = church (so "Kildare," from *Cill Dara*, just means "the church of Dara")
caraig, carrick, craig = rocky outcrop
cláir, clare = a plain
doire, derry = grove of oak trees
droichead, droghed = bridge (so "Drogheda" just means "bridge," or "bridgetown")
loch, lough = lake
trá, tra = beach
sliabh, slieve = mountain

Here are a couple of common human-made features that can feature in place-names:

caiseal, cashel = ancient circular fort of stone
ráth, rah, or rath = ancient circular fort of earth

Here is a pair of useful opposites:

beag, beg = small
mór, more = big (so "ballymore" just means "big village"; and there are "rathmores," places named for big circular earthen walls, in Counties Kerry, Kildare, Meath, Westmeath, Wicklow, Limerick, Cork, Galway, and Louth!)

Here are some common color words:

bán, bane, or bain = white
glas, glas = green
rua, roe = red

Topography and texture of the land

By continental standards, Ireland is not a big place. In area it is slightly smaller than the state of Ohio, and no place in the country is farther than seventy miles from the ocean. The coastline is so indented and convoluted that it is an enormous linear distance, however. For this reason, and for the fact that successive waves of invasion tended to settle near the coast, let's start with some coastal views.

The most important cities in Ireland are coastal, and they almost all are on rivers: Belfast on the River Lagan; Dublin on the River Liffey; Londonderry on the River Boyle; Cork fourteen miles from the seafront on the River Lee; and of course Limerick on the River Shannon,[GE8] plus many smaller coastal towns on smaller rivers. Typically these river and port towns are located where the first practical fording or bridging site for the river is, and also where the tidal flow can still move boats in and out from the town to the sea, minimizing effort—and these two conditions often coincide at the same place, of course. One of those smaller towns, Waterford (world famous for its crystal manufacture), sits at just such a juncture, as the name partly illustrates. [GE9] In a sense most of the coastal river port towns are "water fords."

One of the most picturesque parts of Ireland is the extreme southwest coast of Counties Kerry and Cork, with deep and narrow bays pushing inland for miles. The three longest bays are each named for their major port town: Dingle Bay, Kenmare Bay, and Bantry Bay, each running from twenty to twenty-five miles deep into the land.[GE10] These bays are a long way from Dublin, and during the late French Revolution might be a nice place to land a French army to help with an Irish rising . . .

----

8. GE Layer 8 is a Folder titled "River Port Cities." Turn it on, open it, and double-click on the city name icons (Belfast, Londonderry, Dublin, Cork, Limerick City) to frame view of each city with its attendant river.

9. GE Layer 9 is a Folder titled "Waterford & R. Suir."

10. GE Layer 10 is a Folder titled "Southwest Bays," framing a general overview of this southwest coast of Ireland. Inside the Folder are three Placemarks, one each for the towns of Dingle, Kenmore, and Bantry.

All around the coast of the Republic of Ireland, especially, a common pattern to see even today is a manor house or castle still owned by an English family, on hundreds or even thousands of acres of an estate including managed forests, with an impressive (Protestant, Anglican) Church of Ireland nearby, built by that same English family and typically attended by them and very few others.[GE11] Nearby will be small towns and small farms and much better attended Catholic churches of the Catholic Irish. As much friction as was involved in the separation of Ireland into two parts, there was obviously no sweeping seizure of large-scale Protestant land holdings in the majority Catholic Republic of Ireland.

"Emerald Isle" isn't much exaggeration; a lot of the landscape really is green. The west coast gets 100″ of rain a year, and going eastwards the total gradually dwindles until the east coast gets almost half that. And it usually comes in small patchy rains with sunshine between, not week-long gray deluges. Any given spring day, should you be driving or taking the train most anywhere across Ireland, ought to be good for at least two rainbows.[GE12] Ireland is so wet that its most famous vegetational feature may be the peat bog—a low area of poor drainage that has grown sphagnum moss layer on layer for hundreds of years. This peat was traditionally cut out with a long, narrow shovel for use as fuel. When dried it looks almost like coal.[GE13]

The mountains of the country are mainly around the coast, which makes for some bold cliffs and headlands[GE14] (though there are no mountains as high as 3500′). The mountains of Mourne, as in "Where the mountains of Mourne sweep down to the sea," are in the southeastern corner of Northern Ireland. They show up on Google Earth as a reddish patch on an otherwise green landscape, because although most of Ireland's landscape is limestone based, these are of a reddish granite.[GE15] The Wicklow Mountains, some twenty miles southwest of Dublin, figured in guerrilla-style warfare time after time over several centuries.[GE16] There is a cluster of mountains in Waterford and South Tipperary, showing up as brownish (heather?) and dark green (planted forests), contrasting with the light green of the plains.[GE17] Zooming in on the Comeragh Mountains reveals some interesting views.[GE18]

The central part is mainly a rolling plain. One way to sample this might be to follow the homesick poet who wrote *Killaden*, as he comes westwards into County Mayo. "In Claremorris I should stop a night to sleep with decent men. . .;"[GE19] "then I'd go to Balla, just beyond, and drink galore . . .;"[GE20] "next I'd stay in Kiltimagh for about a month . . .;"[GE21] "I should only be a couple of miles away from Ballymore!"[GE22]

---

11. GE Layer 11 is a Placemark referencing one such pair, Castle Townshend and its associated (Protestant) Church of Ireland; click on Panoramio icon under pointer titled "Castle, Church, Pier and Fish House." Most of the forest that lies in the one mile north of the castle is still part of the estate. On a hill there is a stone arch commemorating Nelson's victory over the French at Cape Trafalgar in 1805—the fleet came by this way on their way back to England. It has sustained some damage from local vandals presumably not pleased to see English victories celebrated on Irish soil.

12. GE Layer 12 is a Placemark referencing a Panoramio icon titled "Mountain," with a double-rainbow draped across the scenery.

13. GE Layer 13 is a Placemark referencing a Panoramio icon titled "Turf 'footings' at Coillnaughton."

14. GE Layer 14 references a Panoramio icon titled "Malin more," for a good view of the rocky headlands of County Donegal.

15. GE Layer 15 is a Placemark referencing a Panoramio icon of the Mourne Mountains, titled "Royal County Down Golf Club 16th Hole Towards the Mournes."

16. GE Layer 16 is a Placemark referencing a Panoramio icon, titled "Mountain Gateway, Co Wicklow, Ireland."

17. GE Layer 17 is a Placemark titled "Cluster of mountains, southern Ireland," framing such a view; you can zoom in on any set of mountains and explore Photos icons at your leisure.

18. GE Layer 18 is a Placemark titled "View in the Comeragh Mountains," referencing a Panoramio icon named "the hills are green."

19. GE Layer 19 is a Placemark referencing a Panoramio icon titled "Claremorris Church."

20. GE Layer 20 is a Placemark referencing a Panoramio icon titled "Balla Station (Disused) Working Westport - Dublin Line."

21. GE Layer 21 is a Placemark referencing a Panoramio icon titled "The Woods Kiltamagh."

22. GE Layer 22 is a Placemark titled "Near Ballinamore," referencing a Panoramio icon titled "Kiltimagh" that has a classic view of "the wide plains of Mayo."

Legends, folklore, and early history

Gaelic speakers undoubtedly conquered earlier occupiers, and probably absorbed much of earlier culture. The emotional point here, though, is that when written history picks up in Ireland, Gaelic speakers already occupied it and so have that claim to be the natives. By the beginning of the Common Era Ireland was already divided into those four traditional kingdoms of Leinster, Ulster, Munster, and Connacht. They were called "fifths" of Ireland, although there are only four of them, because the fifth "fifth" was a small central-east royal domain (today's County Meath plus a little more) where the High Kings presumably presided over it all from the Hill of Tara.[GE23] The "Stone of Destiny" (*Lia Fáil*) there is supposed to be where each High King was sworn in.

The Irish language brought down to modern times with it a remarkable folksong that for centuries has been famed throughout Europe, along with a unique instrumental music featuring the harp and the Irish pipes. Folktales also were borne along on the language, including those celebrated ones about leprechauns, and hero sagas and legends as well. The most popular cycle of the latter dealt with the life and times of Fiona MacCuchail, or Finn Macumhail (Scottish Fingal), a warlord and magician who is supposed to have ruled sometime in the first or second centuries AD. No matter if your wound was mortal, if Finn brought you water in his cupped hands for you to drink, you were magically cured. Finn's war band, called the Fianna, was a marvel. Potential warriors had to pass all sorts of remarkable physical tests to be allowed to join—outrunning two good runners through the forest, cracking no twigs as you ran, not disturbing your hair in its braids as you dodged through the trees and brush . . . . You even had to be able to compose music on the harp to the admiration of the Fianna.

Many of the stories in this cycle of tales deal with Finn's handsome son Oisin, or Ossian. One, called *Oisin and the land of Tir na nÓg*, has Oisin walking in a garden with other members of the Fianna, when a fairy princess from a magical land in the west rides up on a horse and asks him to be her husband and go back and rule Tir na nÓg with her. He says, in effect, can't you get down and talk about it for a bit? She says, no, I can't dismount and you have to decide in just a few minutes. He talks it over with Finn, his father, who is against it, and with his friends in the Fianna, and finally decides it is his destiny. They ride off together on the same horse, down to the coast, and without breaking stride off across the ocean—a twenty-four-hour ride, in which they see all sorts of backwards things such as rabbits chasing hounds (presumably to let you know you are in the land of make-believe). For three years they rule in great happiness, but he gets so homesick for Ireland then that she gives him the magic stallion to ride back again, but makes him promise he won't dismount. He rides back across the ocean to Ireland, discovers that 3 years in Tir na nÓg was 300 years in Ireland and Tara was a ruin and his father and the Fianna long dead and gone. Riding pensively back to the coast he sees a man being crushed by a big rock he had tried to roll out of the road, and leans down from the saddle to flip the rock off of him—but the saddle girth breaks, and he jumps to the ground and the stallion runs away. Having touched the earth, in 3 days' time 300 years of age came crashing in on him. But before he died they took him to St. Patrick to tell his story, so that I could tell it to you. . . .

St. Patrick was a Roman Briton who as a young man was captured by Irish raiders sometime around AD 400, and brought to Ireland to be a slave. He escaped, following a vision, but later in life another vision instructed him to return to Ireland and teach Christianity there. March 17 was the day of his death, ever since "St. Patrick's Day." Most of the sites associated with his life are in northern Ireland, including his grave.[GE24]

Sometime in the early 500s St. Finian founded Clonard Abbey (some thirty-five miles inland from present-day Dublin, which didn't exist yet).[GE25] Here he expounded the Bible for hundreds of students. Twelve of them became "the Twelve Apostles of Ireland," converting most of the country to Christianity. Perhaps the best known of them is St. Brendan, who sailed off west into the Atlantic in his leather coracle of a ship

---

23. GE Layer 23 is a Placemark referencing "The Hill of Tara." Earthworks here, visible in the Google Earth overview, go back to the Iron Age.

24. GE Layer 24 is a Placemark referencing the grave at Downpatrick; click on untitled Panoramio icon underneath Pushpin Placemark icon, and nearby icons for a view of the cathedral itself.

25. GE Layer 25 is a Placemark referencing Clonard, where the abbey was.

in the mid-500s, looking for the "Isle of the Blessed."[GE26] Some think he found North America, almost a thousand years before Columbus. In the next couple of hundred years it was mostly from Ireland that Great Britain was re-Christianized. A most famous visual reminder of this Christian culture in Ireland is the *Book of Kells*, today the single most famous book in the substantial holdings of Trinity College in Dublin. It is an illuminated manuscript of the Gospels in Latin, held for centuries in the Abbey of Kells some fifteen miles northwest of Tara.[GE27] Christian symbolism is intertwined—literally!—with traditional local motifs such as Celtic knots, and the colors a millenium or so later are still vivid.

In the last ("Russia and Socialism") chapter brief mention was made of the Varangian creation of Kievan Russia—Varangians being what Vikings were called when they came down into Russia in the 800s. In France they were called Normans, in England they were called Danes. They also raided and then invaded Ireland. From the late 700s on into the 900s any settlement near the coast was in danger. Interestingly enough, the Vikings seem to have brought more urban culture into Ireland than they found there. Dublin, Cork, and Limerick are among the towns they founded. They were more quickly absorbed into the Irish population than they were in Britain, where the Danelaw of the northeast of Britain was long separate from the Anglo-Saxon southwest.

An Irish historical figure named Brian Boru, who died around 1014, is traditionally seen to have fought off the Vikings by uniting the land against them. That's probably not true, since the Vikings by this time were fairly well merged with the older population. The round towers that are such a striking feature of the Irish countryside, built in this same general time of Viking incursions from the 800s to the 1100s, are popularly supposed to have been watchtowers or defensive towers against the Vikings.[GE28] Again, probably not; their main function seems to have been as bell towers (though there's still lots of debate about it).

Language, legend, and music—this mainstream culture absorbed Viking settlement and occupation, assimilating the thin crust of military conquerors the way the culture nearly did the English later.

The three most important dates in Irish history: 1171, 1533, 1610

The single most important date in Irish history may be the year 1171. One of the English King Henry II's barons, Strongbow, had begun to carve out an independent territory across the Irish Sea in Leinster. This worried Henry; after all, it was only a hundred and five years since the Norman conquest of England, and he was well aware how a dependent feudal lord could go to an island to the west and become an independent king! So to protect his western flank, he invaded those domains in Leinster himself. The English—or more properly at this stage of history, the Anglo-Normans—never controlled more than a small territory around Dublin. In the next few hundred years they so intermarried with the native Irish and swapped English common law for the local Brehon law as to be the despair of London. Nevertheless, England had just begun the conquest of its first overseas colony.

During those three-and-a-half centuries of gradual Irish assimilation of the resident English, there was an interesting pan-Gaelic event. In 1314 Robert the Bruce soundly defeated an English army at Bannockburn, in Scotland, in what is called The First Scottish War of Independence. Having offers from Irish chieftains to join them in a united front war against England, he actually came to Ireland in 1316 with an army and serious thoughts about creating a greater Gaelic kingdom. He was killed in a battle there in 1318,[GE29] however, and nothing long-term came of it.

---

26. GE Layer 26 is a Placemark referencing a Panoramio icon of a statue of St. Brendan in the town of Bantry; click on icon under pointer, titled "St Brendan in The Square, Bantry."

27. GE Layer 27 is a Placemark referencing Kells, site of the former monastery that traditionally held the *Book of Kells*. For a sample of the rich imagery of the book, do a Google–Images search on "Book of Kells."

28. GE Layer 28 is a Placemark referencing a classic round tower, which shows up on the Google Earth surface mainly by its long shadow. Click on Panoramio icon underneath pointer, titled "Monasterboice Round Tower," for one good view. An even better view is in the nearby 360 Cities (red and brown square) icon.

29. GE Layer 29 is a Placemark referencing the battle site of Faughart, in Co. Louth.

The second most important date in Irish history, 1533, is of an event that did not happen in Ireland at all. King Henry VIII personally was looking for one more divorce than the Roman Catholic Church would allow, and England and lowland Scotland generally were gravitating to the Protestant side as all Central and Western Europe chose up sides for the religious wars. In 1533, then, Henry VIII broke with Rome and invented the Church of England. Ireland stayed staunchly Catholic, so to a basic ethnic difference there was now added a religious difference. The results were really only felt in Ireland during the reign of Elizabeth I, but then came as hammer blows. The Desmond wars in the south of Ireland in the 1580s and the Tyrone wars in the north in the 1590s amounted to the second English invasion of Ireland, more extensive and harsher than the first. This "Elizabethan settlement" created what was called the English Pale—a broad band inland from the eastern coast where English law prevailed and where most of the land went to English lords.

Queen Elizabeth died without heir in 1603 and King James VI of Scotland now also became James I of England. Catholics in Ireland expected sympathetic treatment from him, given his own Catholic roots (son of the very Catholic Mary Queen of Scots, and at least baptized as an infant in a Catholic ceremony). They were to be bitterly disappointed. Frustrated by the resistance to rule from London by the remaining strong Irish lord (the Earl of Tyrone, Hugh O'Neill) in Ulster, James began flirting with the idea of a plantation in Northern Ireland.

By "plantation" in these years was meant setting up a colony that would quickly become self-supporting. American readers thinking of plantations in the reign of James I may think first of Jamestown, but the Ulster plantation that began in 1607 and peaked in 1610 dwarfed tiny contemporary Jamestown. Much of the Gaelic-speaking, Catholic-affiliated population of Ulster was simply evicted, and most any potential immigrant from Great Britain who was Protestant and willing to live under English law was given land. Land-hungry lowland Scots came flooding across the narrow sea to occupy the land. This is the origin of the Scotch-Irish, or as purists say, the Scots-Irish—generally Scottish by cultural heritage, mostly Presbyterian by religious affiliation, already English (though with Scottish accent) by speech, and Irish only by virtue of where they now lived. Their 1610 settlement is the nucleus of present-day Northern Ireland. The second most important town in Northern Ireland, after Belfast, is Derry/Londonderry. It was a late addition to the Ulster Plantation in 1613, this particular territory given by James I to immigrants coming from London, who laid out a whole new town and renamed it Londonderry.[GE30] Even today, what you call the town matters: to avoid possibilities of friction, call it Londonderry while talking with the Protestant Irish, Derry with the Catholic Irish, and with groups including both don't mention it. As of this writing, at least, Google Earth is trying to straddle the fence with a "Londonderry/Derry" label.

Puritan Revolution and aftermath

Some simplification was involved in the broad-brush sketch above. For example, the original English settlers, by this time called the Old English, remained Catholic. Plantation settlers of Ulster from the highlands of Scotland also tended to be Catholic instead of Presbyterian or Anglican. The Puritan Revolution, however, when sectarian feelings burned at white heat, tended to simplify everything by forcing people in Ireland (and Great Britain too) into one of two molds: Protestant and pro-Parliament, or Catholic and pro-king.

In 1641, as Parliament in England took power away from King Charles I, the Catholic Irish (and eventually the Old English there too) rose in revolt, especially in Ulster where memory of lands taken from them had festered for thirty years. Soon only Dublin was still held by a Parliamentary army. In 1649, Parliament under the radical Protestants led by Oliver Cromwell executed Charles I and launched the bloodiest invasion of Ireland to date. Somehow religious wars tend to be the most inhumane of all wars, and early in the war there were massacres of civilians and of garrisons that had surrendered under white flag. The first of these was at Drogheda,[GE31] where the main road north from Dublin crossed the first river of any size, the Boyne.[GE32] Cromwell massacred part of the garrison that had surrendered under white flag, and even those who had taken

---

30. GE Layer 30 is a Placemark referencing Londonderry/Derry.

31. GE Layer 31 is a Placemark referencing the town of Drogheda ("Bridgetown").

32. GE Layer 32 is a Path symbolizing the River Boyne in aqua.

refuge in a church—something not forgotten by the Catholic Irish hundreds of years later. Shortly thereafter he massacred almost as many civilians as soldiers at Wexford.[GE33] Protestant forces in Ulster rose to join him. The Catholic Irish and Royalists fought a defensive battle, retreating into Connacht, but Cromwell and his near-fanatical "Ironsides" army swept the field. Limerick City fell in 1651, and Galway City fell in 1652. It was all over by 1653. Catholics who could not prove that they had fought with the English were liable to death penalty or forfeiture of land or both, and even the few Catholic landowners who had sided with this latest English invasion were removed from Ulster, Leinster, and Munster and given land in the less-developed, more isolated west: "to hell or Connaught," as Cromwell so gently put it.

Cromwell died in 1658, and an England tired of extremism soon brought Charles II back from exile in France. He understood enough of political reality to coexist with Parliament, but his brother who succeeded him in 1685 as King James II did not. In 1688, increasingly at odds with Parliament, he baptized his infant son in the Catholic Church, and Parliament and the King were immediately at war. Parliament in essence fired James II and hired his older daughter Mary, who had been raised a Protestant and was now married to the Protestant standard-bearer of all Europe, William of Orange of the Netherlands. William and Mary, agreeing to Parliamentary supremacy in this "Glorious Revolution," came to England in 1688 (William becoming King William III of England). James II was forced to abdicate, but escaped and went to Ireland to raise royalist and Catholic forces as a first step in returning to power. In response, in 1689 armies of the English crown invaded Ireland—the fourth major English invasion in a century.

James II was based in heavily Catholic Dublin. All of Ireland except Ulster came over to his side. Protestant Londonderry withstood a three-months-long siege by his armies in 1689 (still celebrated by the "Apprentice Boys of Londonderry" clubs in summer parades today, since thirteen apprentices are supposed to have slammed and locked the city gates against James II). The Protestant settlers in Enniskillen[GE34] in southwest Ulster also held out. Then in late June of 1690 William III landed with fresh troops (mainly Protestants from the continent, not England or Scotland) at Carrickfergus,[GE35] ten miles northeast of Belfast on the northern shore of the Belfast estuary ("Belfast Lough").

Marching south along the main road from Belfast towards Dublin, William reached the Boyne River, where James had set up his defense, on July 11 (July 1, old style), 1690. It was a little over six miles inland from the sea, and only a couple of miles upstream from the river town of Drogheda. The ensuing "Battle of the Boyne"[GE36] was an early victory for the Williamites. King James II had set his 21,000 or so forces up south of the Boyne River, to use it as a key defensive line. William attacked with his 35,000. There were French troops on both sides—7,000 regular infantry sent by King Louis XIV of France, a full third of James's army, and on the other side *Huguenot* (French Protestant) forces recruited from those evicted from France with the 1685 Revocation of the Edict of Nantes just five years earlier. Initially troops of both armies lined the banks of the small river between them. William broke the deadlock by a flanking movement to the west, crossing the Boyne a few miles upstream. When James marched part of his army southwest to meet that threat, the remainder of his army was too weak to hold the Boyne fords against the main Williamite army. This battle was not as decisive as the Battle of Aughrim a year later, but as the first big victory of William and the Protestants, and marking the turning point of the struggle in Ireland, it retains a cherished place in many Protestant Irish hearts, as folksongs generally still attest. "The Boyne Water" is one such, and it was (is?) traditionally played by Unionist bands in Orange Order parades in Northern Ireland, partly just to infuriate listening Nationalists, which it did (does?).

---

33. GE Layer 33 is a Placemark referencing the city of Wexford.

34. GE Layer 34 is a Placemark referencing Enniskillen.

35. GE Layer 35 is a Placemark referencing Carrickfergus.

36. Hopefully you still have GE Layer 32, the River Boyne, still turned on. GE Layer 36 is a Folder titled "Battle of the Boyne." Open it and turn on the six Polygon layers one at a time—one each for the Jacobite and Williamite camps on opposite sides of the river, then a third for William's flanking maneuver, a fourth for James's counter move, a fifth for William's main force crossing the Boyne, and a sixth for James's retreat. Williamite positions and movements in orange (of course), and Jacobite ones in green.

By the following summer the Jacobites had generally retreated west of the Shannon River, trying to hold Connacht and northern Munster while waiting resupply and reinforcements to be landed on the western coast courtesy of the French navy. They set major garrisons at Limerick in the south, at Athlone on the upper course of the river, and—continuing the defensive arc north and west back to the coast—at Sligo.[GE37] Williamite armies broke through the middle of the arc at Athlone, and marched west towards Galway City. Less than twenty miles down the road they met the Jacobite army near Aughrim,[GE38] drawn up across the main road (the M6, the main east-west highway today, still runs right by Aughrim). The armies were fairly evenly matched, 20,000 or so on a side. The Jacobites had chosen the ground well, with a ridge and a bog worked into their defensive lines. It was the bloodiest engagement of the whole war, with about 7,000 dead, but the Protestant force finally prevailed. This was July 12 on the old Julian calendar, and is still the main parade day today (on July 12 of the modern calendar) of what Northern Irish Protestants call "the marching season." In the wake of this decisive battle, Galway City fell without a fight, and the last Jacobite force surrendered in Limerick city after a short siege.

The resulting 1691 Treaty of Limerick[GE39] allowed Catholic opponents to ground arms and leave the country, the origin of those "wild geese" of Irish folksong. Those Catholics who stayed faced life in a thoroughly subjugated country.

The Penal Laws and the "Protestant Ascendancy"

Smoldering Catholic bitterness and the threat of a French invasion drove the scared Protestant minority in the next four decades to create the so-called Penal Laws. Catholics lost the right to bear arms, to own a horse worth more than £ 5, to buy land, to lease land longer than thirty-one years, to have any public employment, or even to leave Ireland for purposes of getting a good education. By 1728 the few wealthy Catholics lost the right to vote for members of the Irish Parliament, and of course only Protestants were eligible to be Members of Parliament there. Dissenters (of Protestant denominations outside the officially established Protestant Church of Ireland, sister of the Church of England) faced some persecution too; but Catholics were deprived of virtually all political power and land. For most of the 1700s, then, there were two populations in Ireland. One lacked civil rights, was generally poor and uneducated and rural, spoke Gaelic and went to the Catholic Church. The other had civil rights (Anglicans completely, Dissenters partially), was economically middle- or upper-class and urban or landed gentry, spoke English and went to the Anglican or Presbyterian churches. "Protestant" and "Catholic" had come to be shorthand labels for two ethnic groups. Following the paradigm of nationalism introduced in the chapter on Germany, here was a classic "negative stimulus" for the Gaelic-speaking, rural, Catholic natives.

Interestingly enough, the immediate nationalist reaction that took England by surprise came not from the suppressed Catholics but from those Anglican rulers of Irish society so recently rescued from Catholics by William's Protestant armies. By the mid-1700s, there had come to be a general self-image among English settlers of Ireland that they were no longer purely English, but had been colored by land and local culture into a new ethnic group. Beginning with Jonathan Swift in the early 1700s, they called themselves "the Irish." By the 1760s there was real tension between "the Castle" (Dublin Castle,[GE40] seat of British administration in Dublin) and these Anglo-Irish "Patriots." In the long run the majority Catholics, who could more rightly claim the whole Gaelic cultural heritage, would wrestle that "Irish" label away from these "Irish" Protestants. But up

---

37. GE Layer 37 is a Folder titled "Jacobite defensive arc"; it has green Pushpin Placemarks and labels for Limerick, Athlone, and Sligo.

38. GE Layer 38 is a Placemark referencing Aughrim.

39. GE Layer 39 is a Placemark referencing the "Treaty Stone" where the Treaty of Limerick was supposedly signed; click on Panoramio icon under pointer, titled "The Treaty Stone," for view of same in foreground, and St. John's Castle across the Shannon River in the background.

40. GE Layer 40 is a Placemark referencing Dublin Castle; click on Panoramio icon under pointer, titled "Castillo de Dublín," for nice shot of same. The core of the Castle complex was built in the reign of King John, 1199–1216, just thirty years or so after the original English (Norman) invasion of 1169–71.

until the twentieth century the key leader of every important Irish political and cultural movement—with the exception of the Catholic civil rights movement under Daniel O'Connell—was to be Protestant: Henry Grattan, Theobald Wolfe Tone, Thomas Osborne Davis, Charles Stewart Parnell, Douglas Hyde, William Butler Yeats. Each one would enthusiastically ally with Catholics. They either did not foresee that a mass Catholic cultural and political resurrection would eclipse Protestant leadership and even threaten Protestant membership in such an Irish national movement, or they were emotionally driven there as the only possible resort given their ethics, their need for community, and their location.

As a hint of what is to come in cultural nationalism in the nineteenth century, from 1761 to 1765 the Scottish poet James McPherson published an old epic he said he'd found—the *Ossianic Poems*, supposedly written by Ossian (Oisin in the Irish version of Gaelic) about his father Fingal (Finn in the Irish). It impressed international scholars of the caliber of Herder and Goethe. It was of course extremely popular among Gaels, the Irish as well as the Scots, who seemed to have found their own *Iliad* and *Odyssey*, their *Chanson de Roland*, their *Tale of the Host of Igor'* here. Most scholars today think it was written by McPherson himself and so in the sense he claimed—that he had found a complete ancient epic—it was a forgery. But its popularity brought many into Gaelic cultural nationalism who never left it.

Impact of the American and French Revolutions

The American Revolution was closely reported in Ireland, and even the Protestant Irish shared many American colonial grievances: taxation without much in the way of representation, a prohibition on colonial manufacturing, and lack of *habeas corpus* (the right to face your accuser in trials), to name three. Britain, stretched thin by its world wars with France in general and by the French-supported American Revolution in particular, in 1779 allowed the calling up of volunteer militias all over Ireland to meet a rumored French invasion. The Volunteers soon contained armed Catholics as well as Protestants. The very existence of such a force further pressured the British into granting sweeping new rights to the Irish Parliament. This "constitution of 1782" made for a self-confident new Parliament. Its leader was Henry Grattan, who worked for Catholic civil rights and achieved some lightening of the penal laws. Catholics, still unable to buy land, were at least allowed to lease it for 999 years, ownership for all practical purposes. Nicknamed Grattan's Parliament, this would be a model for Irish home rulers for the next century.

Then in 1789 came the even more radical French Revolution. Exciting news from France and shocking ideas such as Tom Paine's in *Rights of Man* were in the air. One result was the formation in Belfast in 1791 of a secret independence-minded group called the Society of United Irishmen. As the name implies, it embraced Catholics, Presbyterians, and Anglicans, one of the last being Wolfe Tone, who emerged as its leader. Its founders had read Rousseau on the General Will and were particularly inspired by Jacobin policies in Paris. British attention drove the United Irishmen underground, and by 1794 they were negotiating with the French for troops to help with a rising. In December of 1896 a French fleet of almost 50 ships, carrying 15,000 troops, was to rendezvous at Bantry Bay[GE41] and effect a landing. But the weather worsened, not all ships arrived (including the French flagship), and some were actually sunk by the storm. The troop carrier commanders—just a biscuit toss from shore, as Wolfe Tone famously observed later, using the common sailor's phrase meaning very close indeed—called it off.

The Irish Rebellion of 1798

On May 24, 1798, the United Irishmen did rise, though the rising was not well coordinated. The main rallying point for the rebellion in Dublin was discovered by the British ahead of time, and they occupied it before the rebels could. The counties around Dublin did rise, but the British won several sharp battles there. One at the Hill of Tara[GE42] effectively prevented the rebellion from spreading northwards (later the *Lia Fáil*, the Stone

---

41. GE Layer 41 is a Placemark referencing Bantry Bay; the town of Bantry, you may remember, lies deep inland at the head of the bay.

42. GE Layer 42 is a Placemark showing the Hill of Tara in an overview that includes Dublin.

of Destiny, was moved to mark the graves of the hundred or so rebels who fell here). There were several battles in Co. Kildare, west and southwest of Dublin, generally won by the British. A guerrilla army held out in the Wicklow Mountains south of Dublin until October.[GE43] In the northeast, not far from Belfast, the Battle of Ballynahinch[GE44] on June 12 was one of the biggest of the war; the British victory there generally secured the north for them. The largest territory gained by the rebels was virtually the whole of the southeastern county of Wexford. A June 21 battle at Vinegar Hill,[GE45] in the middle of the country, effectively broke the rebel armies there.

French forces came in support, though too little and too late to make a success of the Rebellion. A French army of a thousand or so landed in Co. Mayo. Linking up with several times that number of Irish rebels, they had some initial success, routing a British army at Castlebar[GE46] and pushing on into the interior. They were defeated at Ballinamuck, in Co. Longford.[GE47] In October a somewhat larger French force—accompanied by Wolfe Tone himself—tried for a landing in the fjord that comes down into Donegal from the north, Lough Swily, but the British fleet trapped them deep in the Lough off the town of Buncrana[GE48] before they could ever land the troops. A few guerrilla units held out in the hills, but with this October battle the Rebellion was essentially over.

It was one of the bloodiest of all Irish risings, with upwards of 10,000 dead. There were massacres of disarmed troops or unarmed civilians on both sides, and mass executions by the victors. The British saw this as treason in time of war, pure and simple. The rebels saw it as a noble national and republican independence movement. Wolfe Tone said that he would not regret being shot like an honest soldier, but hated being condemned to be hung as a spy. He cheated his sentence by suicide. His gravesite in a village churchyard at Bodenstown, less than twenty miles from Dublin, would become a place for Irish nationalist pilgrimage.[GE49]

The British government on the last day of 1800 ended the Irish Parliament altogether by merging it with the British Parliament. This Act of Union was reflected in a cleverly designed new flag, the "Union Jack." It combined the red cross on a white background of the flag of St. George of England, the white X on blue of St. Andrew of Scotland, and now the narrow red X on white of St. Patrick of Ireland, and is familiar around the world as the flag of the United Kingdom.[GE50] What it meant at the time was punishment for the Irish Protestants who had triggered the rising. It was obviously designed to make Irish MPs a small and powerless minority in the much larger Parliament at London.

A postscript to the 1798 rising was Robert Emmet's rebellion in 1803. He was the younger brother of one of the founders of United Irishmen, and led a clumsy rebellion that amounted to little more than a street riot in Dublin.[GE51] His last speech before being hanged, however—asking that his epitaph not be written until Ireland was free—made him one of the most famous of Ireland's martyrs. His picture hung in patriotic nineteenth-century Irish homes like an icon.

---

43. GE Layer 43 is a Placemark framing a view of the Wicklow Mountains with Dublin in the distance, less than twenty miles away.

44. GE Layer 44 is a Placemark referencing Ballynhinch.

45. GE Layer 45 is a Placemark framing a close-up view of Vinegar Hill; zoom out to see its relationship to larger area.

46. GE Layer 46 is a Placemark referencing Castlebar.

47. GE Layer 47 is a Placemark referencing Ballinamuck.

48. GE Layer 48 is a Placemark titled "Lough Swily, Co. Donegal." placed in the Lough just off Buncrana.

49. GE Layer 49 is a Placemark referencing Wolfe Tone's grave and memorial in a country churchyard in Bodenstown, Co. Kildare, just a few miles west of Dublin.

50. GE Layer 50 is a Placemark referencing a Panoramio icon under pointer, titled "La casa de la Reina," for (distant) view of U.K. flag; though frankly the Placemark is just an excuse to embed the following website showing the evolution of the flag: http://blog.londonconnection.com/wp-content/uploads/2010/03/Flags_of_the_Union_Jack-fr.png

51. GE Layer 51 is a Folder titled "Emmet's Rebellion." It has a Polygon in green outline showing Thomas Street in downtown Dublin, the heart of the July 23 rising and the site of Emnet's execution on Sept. 20; an orange star Placemark locating Dublin Castle half a mile east; and a green pushpin Placemark on Thomas Street itself referencing a Photos icon of the memorial to him there.

Then, at least on the surface, Irish nationalism subsided in the economic depression of the Napoleonic Wars. Folksongs suggest its continuance in popular culture, as in the "Arthur McBride" ballad collected in Donegal some years later, that ends with some young Irish men beating up a British military recruiting team. It was given new popularity in 1973 by the Irish band Planxty on their album of the same name; it might be of interest to listen to their version at the following website: http://www.youtube.com/watch?v=0hV9fvhCmbw

"The Counselor" and Catholic Emancipation

In the 1820s Daniel O'Connell led what may have been the classic civil rights movement of all time, M. K. Gandhi and M. L. King included. The Penal Laws against Catholics had been softened by this time but not broken. Most noticeably, Catholics were still not allowed to be members of Parliament or government administrators at any level. O'Connell became the champion of "Catholic Emancipation." Born in 1775 in County Kerry[GE52] to a Catholic family which had managed to retain some land, he was sent to France and Belgium for his education by a wealthy uncle. When that was interrupted by the French Revolution, he went to England where the bar against Catholic lawyers had just been lifted. In British tradition lawyers are of two main kinds—the prestigious barristers who actually argue cases in court, and the less prestigious solicitors who do the research. O'Connell, a wonderful speaker with a shrewd legal mind, became a barrister. He masterminded three strategies for Catholic Emancipation.

First, he used the British law courts, where the Anglo-Irish had always had a home field advantage, to educate the public politically and to embarrass the British government. At times he would take a case he knew was unwinnable just to demonstrate the gap between British ideals of justice and the reality of British rule in Ireland. He won some of these technically "unwinnable" cases before juries by pure eloquence of speech.

Second, he tapped into the existing Catholic Church hierarchy, which of course already had a priest in every parish and a bishop in every city. Without full civil rights themselves, Catholic clergy in Ireland right up to the Archbishops were sympathetic to his cause. He asked even the poor Catholics for a penny a month, to be turned over to their priests and sent on to Dublin. The money was used to fund test law cases and defend Catholics in court. This "Catholic rent" was enthusiastically paid, often even when it mean giving up tobacco or alcohol.

Third, O'Connell staged what came to be called "monster rallies." This was Metternich's Europe, with property qualifications ensuring that only the wealthy voted; political parties were typically small, and political rallies of a thousand people were considered enormous. In this atmosphere O'Connell would borrow a farm from a supporter and stage a rally, and perhaps 100,000 supporters would assemble there. These rallies were peaceful, but the very numbers were a veiled threat to the Protestant Ascendancy and British rule. In 1829 the British granted Catholic emancipation. Every position in Ireland except that of Lord Protector and two other chief posts was thrown open to Catholics.

Despite the fact that O'Connell was a native speaker of Gaelic, there was almost no element of cultural nationalism in his program. He was a cosmopolitan intellectual speaking French and English, and English in his hands seemed to be weapon enough. And the Irish national cause was not his exclusive concern. He was perhaps even more a champion of Liberalism than he was of Irish nationalism; in the 1830s after O'Connell was elected to Parliament, Jeremy Bentham considered him his floor leader in the House of Commons for prison rights and for political democracy for other ethnic groups in Britain. But for the Catholic Irish, Daniel O'Connell—known to them simply as "The Counselor"—was more than human. He gave them belonging and dignity in addition to civil rights.

Young Ireland

The decade of the 1840s is the pivotal decade of modern Irish history. In it a promising independence movement was interrupted by disastrous famine, and politics thereafter took a turn for the extreme.

---

52. GE Layer 52 is a Placemark titled "Cahirciveen," referencing Daniel O'Connell Cathedral in that town. O'Connell was born in Carhen less than a mile away. Carhirciveen is a little bay port on the south side of Dingle Bay, opposite the town of Dingle.

Inside the British Empire, the first step towards independence was always "Home Rule." A colony with Home Rule might stay part of the British Commonwealth indefinitely, royally welcome King and/or Queen should they come visit, and side with Britain on key foreign policy questions—but domestic politics would be run by those who lived there. A movement called Young Ireland began to champion Home Rule and something more in the early 1840s. These "Young" movements, whose prototype was Guiseppe Mazzini's 1830s "Young Italy," had as their ideal a U.S.-style republic but based on a single ethnic group; they also included some consideration, if not creation, of an underground army.

Thomas Osborne Davis was Young Ireland's most famous name. Although he was born in Cork in 1814, his father died in Thomas's infancy and his mother moved to Dublin, where he was raised. He attended Trinity College. Although Anglican in religion and of Anglo-Irish background, he was "converted" to Irish cultural nationalism by reading German Romantic writers. The Gaelic cultural heritage, which Davis argued had rubbed off on long-time English settlers there, needed to become the mental and emotional common denominator of all Irish. With Davis, there was a typically Romantic celebration of the rural peasantry. Charles Gavin Duffy, the other pillar of Young Ireland, was a Catholic from the north, born in Monaghan Town[GE53] and educated in Belfast. He provided the vehicle, a journal called *The Nation*. In its pages modern political strategies rubbed elbows with translations of Gaelic sagas.

The ageing Daniel O'Connell, despite differences with these young radicals on the dangers of unleashing the masses in violence, joined Young Ireland in a campaign to repeal the Union and gain Home Rule. In 1843, as the movement built to a crescendo, he staged one of his classic monster rallies on The Hill of Tara itself, and it attracted upwards of half a million people. By 1845, with Protestant money and education, and with O'Connell assuring mass Catholic support, the movement seemed certain of success. Had Home Rule occurred in this year, the island of Ireland would be profoundly different today—most likely a politically unified island with a sizeable and generally respected Protestant minority, most likely with only a fraction of the violence of the past century and a half. Such Home Rule was doomed, however, by two things: first, the early death of its leaders (Davis, only thirty, of tuberculosis, in 1845, and O'Connell in 1847), and second and most important, the famine.

Potato Famine

In Ireland in the summer of 1845 some leaves on the potato plants yellowed early, and perhaps a third of the crop was spoiled by the American potato blight. It hit earlier in the season in 1846, and by 1847 farmers harvested less potatoes than they planted.

Today such a blight in America or Europe would be a minor problem in the whole scheme of things; in the 1840s in Ireland it was a catastrophe that takes some explaining. The "Irish" potato was one of those American Indian foods that revolutionized Old World diet, along with maize, the tomato, manioc, and such. Probably domesticated on the slopes of the Andes, the Irish potato could have been designed with cool and rainy northern Europe in mind. In Ireland it underlay a gradual population growth to upwards of eight million people; even a large family could be raised on a one-acre potato patch. They baked, boiled, fried, and stewed them, made a wicked homebrew called "poteen" from them, and fed them to pigs and ate pork. Upper classes had a more varied diet, but for poorer folks, the potato was the staple, like bread to the French in 1789: those who had it, lived; those who had it not, starved.

So in 1846 Ireland lost a million people of its eight or so million total, and in 1847 a million more, and although losses after that were not so dramatic, the population kept shrinking until 1865 when it hit some three and a half million, and it has never really recovered since (today's population of the whole island is a little over 6 million). Not all these missing millions starved or died of famine-related disease—perhaps only a million. Only a million, what a terrible phrase. Some parts of the country were hit harder than others; Skibereen,[GE54] not far west of Cork, lost 60 percent of its people dead. The other millions of lost population emigrated. They mostly went to America by indenturing themselves as servants for up to seven years. This is when the flood of Irish immigration hit the east coast of the United States. They were likely to be Gaelic-speaking with only rudimentary English and were largely without marketable skills. Like most immigrant populations they faced a

---

53. GE Layer 53 is a Placemark referencing Monaghan (city, in Monaghan County).
54. GE Layer 54 is a Placemark referencing Skibereen.

good deal of ethnic prejudice; many of them first felt truly Irish as a result of signs in American cities that said "No Irish need apply!" The one remarkable skill they brought as a group was a sophisticated understanding of Anglo-American politics and law, largely gained in their civil rights and Home Rule struggles. American readers will know how well the descendants of these Irish immigrants still exercise those skills in Boston and other eastern and midwestern cities.

The famine had two dramatic results in the development of Irish national consciousness. First, with massive losses of Gaelic language speakers and associated cultural practices, the whole Gaelic heritage so taken for granted by most intellectuals began to be seen as a priceless treasure in danger of being lost. Second, perceptions of British mismanagement of the famine caused a new bitterness that resulted in a more or less sustained terrorist campaign against British occupation.

Today for a modern industrial economy the shape that best models socioeconomic grouping is probably the diamond: a few very rich at the top, a great middle class in the bulging middle, and a few very poor at the bottom. For agrarian and pre-industrial societies, the usual model is a squat triangle or pyramid: an upper tip of rich landed gentry, a narrow band of middle class below that, and a huge foundation of poor subsistence farmers at the bottom. Ireland in 1845 is better modeled by the triangle. English was the language of landed gentry and much of the middle class, but although it was slowly percolating down through Irish society, it was still the minority language. Then came the famine, wiping out over half the population. Those who starved or emigrated came from the bottom of the triangle, since those above could afford some high-priced domestic or imported food. By 1865—in a single generation—Gaelic had become the minority language in Ireland. Language is one of the best indicators of culture, and disappearing with the native Gaelic speakers were the folksongs, the leprechaun tales, the Finn stories, the village superstitions, and so on.

"My Mother, Mary Kelly"

Folk culture always seems to be most appreciated just as it is disappearing, whether it is the Brothers Grimm collecting stories from the last generation of illiterate storytellers in Germany, or students working on the Foxfire project in northeast Georgia in the late 1960s collecting accounts of the lives of the last generation of self-sufficient Appalachian mountaineers. William Carlton, a popular Irish novelist writing after the worst years of the famine, came to a new appreciation for his mother Mary Kelly, and the cultural legacy she had carried. He had been told by some who heard her sing when she was young that if it was hinted she might be at wake, a festival, or a dance a crowd would come just to hear her sing:

> My mother, whose name was Kelly—Mary Kelly—possessed the sweetest and most exquisite of human voices. In her early life, I have often been told by those who had heard her sing, that any previous intimation of her presence at a wake, dance or other festive occasion, was sure to attract crowds of persons, many from a distance of several miles, in order to hear from her lips the touching old airs of their country . . . .

> She had a prejudice against singing the Irish airs to English words; an old custom of the country was thereby invaded, and an association disturbed which habit had rendered dear to her. I remember on one occasion, when she was asked to sing the English version of that touching melody 'The Red-haired Man's Wife,' she replied, "I will sing it for you; but the English words and the air are like a quarreling man and wife: the Irish melts into the tune, but the English doesn't"—an expression scarcely less remarkable for its beauty than its truth. She spoke the words in Irish.

> This gift of singing with such sweetness and power the old sacred songs and airs of Ireland, was not the only one for which she was remarkable. Perhaps there never lived a human being capable of giving the Irish cry, or Keene, with such exquisite effect, or of pouring into its wild notes, a spirit of such irresistible pathos and sorrow. I have often been present when she has "raised the keene" over the corpse of some relative or neighbour, and my readers may judge of the melancholy charm which accompanied this expression of her sympathy, when I assure them that the general clamour of violent grief was gradually diminished, from admiration, until it became ultimately hushed, and no voice was heard but her own – wailing in sorrowful but solitary beauty . . . .

> Many a time, of a winter night, when seated at her spinning-wheel, singing the *Trougha,* or *Shuil agra,* or some other old "song of sorrow," have I, then little more than a child, gone over to her, and with a broken voice and

eyes charged with tears, whispered "Mother dear, don't sing that song, it makes me sorrowful"; she then usually stopped, and sung some one which I liked better because it affected me less. At this day I am in possession of Irish airs, which none of our best antiquaries in Irish music have heard, except through me, and of which neither they nor I myself know their names.[2]

The Ordnance Survey in Ireland

Cultural nationalism usually starts with a handful of eccentrics and only later swells into a powerful movement. In this light, consider the Ordnance Survey in Ireland. In the first few decades of the 1800s, Great Britain and the entire British Empire were being surveyed by a branch of the army using state-of-the-art techniques. One result, incidentally, is that today a hiker in the British Isles buys an Ordnance Survey topographic map the way a hiker in the U.S. buys a topo map from the U.S. Geological Survey.

More to the point, though, is how the Ordnance Survey was carried out in Ireland. The 140,000 or so Gaelic place names were often a puzzle to British surveyors. So in 1832 a Department of History and Antiquities was formed within the Survey to help with correct spelling, translation, and probable origin of these names, as well as to note valuable architectural features of the countryside. Its workers took it much farther than its establishers ever dreamed. John O'Donovan, born in Kilkenny[GE55] in 1809, eventually became a good scholar of Middle Irish partly because of his work on the Survey. He followed the surveying teams for ten years into twenty-eight of Ireland's thirty-two counties, doing what amounted to an oral history and manuscript collection for the entire country. He recruited Eugene O'Curry, a native Irish speaker and scholar born in 1796 in Doonaha, in County Clare where the Shannon estuary meets the sea,[GE56] to do associated manuscript research. George Petrie, a Dublin-born older musician and artist who already had an established reputation and had made a huge collection of Irish folksongs, eventually joined the Department as its head. On one of those rare occasions when they all went in the field together, Petrie took down the notes to a beautiful unknown melody sung by a country girl while O'Curry got the Irish words, and every few miles it was "Petrie, out with your flute, and give us that air." It was Petrie & co., incidentally, who collected "Arthur McBride," the lyrics of which you may have listened to by the band Planxty if you went to that website given a few pages back.

Funding for the Department was canceled in 1842, but the trio simply shifted their cultural history and language work to the Irish Archaeological and Celtic society. The striking loss of folk culture during the famine gave their work a new urgency. In 1851 Petrie founded a folk music society, and did three more years intensive music collecting, "lest the unsaved portion of the people's ancient music be lost forever in the total extinction of their ancient language." O'Curry became Professor of Irish History and Archaeology at the newly formed Catholic University (a struggling, small institution but it soon merged with others to form the University College Dublin[GE57]). He and O'Donovan collaborated on a translation and analysis of Brehon Laws, the Irish common law. Among O'Donovan's major works was a grammar of Irish.

So the British Army quite unintentionally gave these scholars of the Gaelic heritage a home and a start. Elements of the folktales, legends, and sagas they unearthed and made accessible in collections would soon reach the threshold of the public mind, play a substantial role in a groundswell of Irish cultural nationalism, and eventually pose considerable difficulties for that same British Army.

Irish Republican Brotherhood and Fenians

All through the famine there was little in the way of relief from Britain, and in fact grain and cattle were actually exported from Ireland every year. "Laissez-faire" economics had gotten to be a fairly rigid dogma (as compared to its origins three-quarters of a century before with Smith and Turgot as a warm human response to immediate needs of the mass of people). Though there is no evidence for any kind of British plot to starve out the Irish, that came to be popular belief in Ireland itself. The 1848 revolution in France and much of the rest of urban Europe set a flame to this new bitterness. In the last week of July, some Young Ireland leaders fresh

---

55. GE Layer 55 is a Placemark referencing Kilkenny town, in interior southeastern Ireland.
56. GE Layer 56 is a Placemark referencing Doonaha.
57. GE Layer 57 is a Placemark referencing the general campus of UCD.

from the revolution in Paris came back to Ireland, bringing with them a new flag given them by some sympathetic French women—a tricolor modeled on the French flag but with green and orange on either side of the white. They landed in Wexford and proceeded inland, through Counties Wexford and Kilkenny, holding mass meetings in hopes of beginning a national rising. It ended in a town called The Commons[GE[58]] in the edge of County Tipperary where there was armed confrontation with several dozen police, and some fatalities. The British deported those Young Irelanders they could catch to Australia. Several, including John O'Mahony and James Stephens, escaped back to France.

By this time there was a huge Irish immigrant population in east coast cities of the U.S., generally bitterly anti-English and out from under the U.K. army and police force. Some of the scattered leaders who survived, including O'Mahony, regrouped in New York, knowing that "the Queen's writ did not run in Manhattan." By 1854 they were meeting regularly as "The Emmet Monument Association," with more than monuments on their minds. Here the Irish Republican Brotherhood was dreamed up, and more or less founded in 1858 in both Ireland (where James Stephens had returned) and the U.S. (organized by O'Mahony). It was O'Mahony who from his interest in the Gaelic past coined the label "Fenian" for I.R.B. men—after the Fianna, that legendary war band of Finn. Another early member was John O'Leary, who had been imprisoned back in 1848 for trying to break other Young Irelanders out of a Tipperary jail. Twenty years later he would convert the young W. B. Yeats to Irish cultural nationalism.

A Fenian rising in 1867 was not much more successful than the one in 1848. There were some ill-coordinated risings in the southwest, in County Kerry, and in the ports of Limerick and Cork cities. The closest the rebels came to Dublin was a rally on Tallaght hill, over five miles from city center, and that was quickly dispersed by police. But a low level of occasional bombings and armed attempts to rescue prisoners persisted. So an organized, armed underground with funding from abroad existed after 1858 as one more element on the political scene, and as evidence of one more step taken in the development of Irish nationalism.

Michael Cusack and the Gaelic Athletic Association

Athletics and physical fitness were co-opted by post-famine Irish nationalism as they have been by so many other national movements in the modern world. What "Turnvater" Jahn was to German patriots in 1813, Michael Cusack was to the Irish in the 1880s. A Gaelic speaker from County Clare, he had run a successful school preparing boys for British civil service exams. His twin passions of athletics—particularly the native field hockey game called hurling—and Irish nationalism moved him to organize Irish athletics for political purposes. In 1884 he was the main spark for the formation of the Gaelic Athletic Association, an institution whose ties with the Fenian "physical force" men were notorious. Cusack called himself "The Citizen," and in *Ulysses* James Joyce describes him under that name. Something of the force of his persona shines through Joyce's satire:

> The figure seated on a large boulder at the foot of a round tower was that of a broadshouldered deepchested stronglimbed frankeyed redhaired freelyfreckled shaggybearded widemouthed largenosed longheaded deep-voiced barekneed brawnyhanded hairylegged ruddyfaced sinewyarmed hero . . . .[3]

One of Ireland's four Catholic Archbishops at the time was Thomas Croke, a sportsman himself as well as a supporter of Irish nationalism. He was called on to be the patron of the G.A.A. In his acceptance letter he lamented the fading away of traditional Irish sports (in this quotation you've already seen at the head of the chapter):

> And what have we got in their stead? We have got such foreign and fantastic field sports as lawn tennis, polo, croquet, cricket and the like—very excellent, I believe, and health-giving exercises in their way, still not racy of the soil but rather alien, on the contrary to it, as are, indeed, for the most part, the men and women who first imported and still continue to patronize them.[4] [GE[59]]

---

58. GE Layer 58 is a Placemark referencing The Commons, in today's South Tipperary.
59. The big G.A.A. stadium in Dublin, Croke Park, is named for him. GE Layer 59 is a Placemark referencing it. Lots of Photos icons to explore—Croke Park empty, full, setting up for a U2 concert in 2009. . .

"Racy of the soil": that was a phrase that had been used earlier by Thomas Osborne Davis, and was now established in Irish nationalist thought. It is a clear Irish echo of Herder's voice from the origin of Romantic nationalism a century earlier, in his view that a folk group's character was established at the dawn of time by a magic interaction between a group of people and a particular landscape.

Parnell and Gladstone

Charles Stewart Parnell dominated Irish affairs during the 1880s the way O'Connell had the 1820s. O'Connell had been called "The Counselor"; Parnell would be simply "The Chief." Parnell was a Protestant and a landlord, though a model landlord who championed tenant rights. First elected MP of the Irish Home Rule Party in 1875, he won a reputation for brilliant tactics of obstructionism in the House of Commons. No MP in Commons had ever been silenced on any issue—that was one proud British claim for their democracy. So Parnell and friends invented what Americans would call a filibuster there, to paralyze Parliament until Irish demands were met, and Parliament had to respond with a cloture rule for shutting off debate. Parnell's message to the British was that if they continued to violate Irish rights, theirs would suffer as well.

By 1877 he was chosen head of the Home Rule Party. Social issues were suddenly more pressing, as the American transcontinental railroad was being finished and cheap American grain imports flooded in to hurt farmers all over Europe. What was called the "Land War" convulsed much of Ireland in the 1870s and 1880s. Tenants, increasingly hopelessly behind with rents because of the general agricultural situation, were being evicted. In 1879 a Land League to organize protests against this was set up by Michael Davitt, a former I.R.B. man. Parnell became the League's President, while still heading up the Irish Party in Parliament. The Land League was where the "boycott" was invented, and then popularized by Parnell. It began in 1880 with the ostracism of a hated landlord's agent of that name in County Mayo. Further, anyone who moved onto one of the farms from which tenant farmers had been evicted was ostracized. It was a powerful weapon in village Ireland, where everyone knew everyone.

Parnell also worked informally with a radical Fenian spin-off group, the Clan na Gael. He was a master of "constitutional" techniques, yet also able to threaten the British establishment with "physical force" allies. He set 1882—the centennial of Grattan's fondly-remembered Parliament—as the date for his "New Departure," and the political mobilization of Ireland was as intense as in the early 1840s. The government jailed Parnell and made the Land League illegal, but it didn't stop the boycotts, and the rural violence continued to build. There was associated urban violence as well, most spectacularly the 1882 murder of two important governmental figures, the Chief Secretary for Ireland and his undersecretary—stabbed to death as they walked in Phoenix Park just west of Dublin.[GE60]

Ironically, just a month before this, Prime Minister William Gladstone had made a deal with Parnell—a deal named for the Dublin prison where Parnell was at the time, the "Kilmainham Treaty."[GE61] He, Gladstone, would set in motion laws to reduce tenant indebtedness and end most of the evictions, and Parnell in turn would work to restore law and order. By 1885 Parnell scored a tremendous victory when Gladstone came over to belief in Irish Home Rule. Together Parnell and Gladstone narrowly lost an 1886 Home Rule bill, but by 1889 they were working on another and seemed unstoppable. Parnell was at the height of his power and charisma, pulling together the energies of Fenians, the Catholic hierarchy, Catholic tenant farmers, and the American Irish.

Then Parnell was named correspondent in a divorce suit. For some time he had been living with a woman long separated from her husband, but an ugly divorce trial now made sensational headlines. It undermined Parnell's credibility with his mainly Catholic followers, Catholics being in general much stricter on the divorce issue than Protestants. Parnell died in 1891, exhausted and disappointed, at the age of forty-five. Without him the second Home Rule bill that had seemed so promising went down to defeat in 1893. Irish hopes for inde-

---

60. GE Layer 60 is a Placemark generally referencing Phoenix Park, a green wedge of territory west of downtown Dublin and north of the River Liffey that runs through the city. It's a former royal deer park, still with a herd of deer within the park walls. The Dublin Zoo takes up its northern part today.

61. GE Layer 61 is a Placemark referencing Kilmainham Prison (Gaol). It is also on the west side of Dublin, just a few hundred yards south of Phoenix Park.

pendence, raised so high, were dashed. This is the background for what some have called "a literary Parnellism" that comes next.

Irish literary revival and the Gaelic League

George Bernard Shaw, James Joyce, and William Butler Yeats may be the three most famous names in turn-of-the-century English literature. Why this Anglo-Irish burst of talent if not primarily because of Irish cultural nationalism and the emotions it stirred? William Butler Yeats, for example, although born in Ireland, spent almost all of his childhood and youth in England. His introduction to Irish cultural nationalism on his return at the age of twenty-one came at the hands of old Fenian John O'Leary, who told him to immerse himself first in Irish folklore and mythology. In this way a poet of genius found his theme, however contradictory it might prove in his own life and politics. Yeats aimed to use Irish material so brilliantly in the English language as to win world renown. In 1891, after five years of steady writing, mining old Irish seams for his work, he helped found the Irish Literary Society of London, and then the National Literary Society in Dublin.

Douglas Hyde was a co-founder of these societies with Yeats, and how he came to be is an interesting story. Hyde was the son of an Anglican minister, but had learned to speak Gaelic as a boy from gamekeepers and farmers around his boyhood home in Frenchpark, Roscommon.[GE62] Late in life he remembered a small, almost accidental event of his young adulthood, in or about 1875, that was to have such consequences in his life. He was going out hunting "of a fine frosty day in winter," with his little dog at heel and his gun on his shoulder, when he heard an old man "at the door of his cottage and he singing sweetly to himself." The song was *Killaden*, or *County Mayo*, that you have already encountered as a poem in the introduction to language section towards the first of this chapter. Hyde asked the old man to teach him the song, and learned most of it by heart on the spot. Some fifteen years later, "poking among the old Irish manuscripts that are in the Royal Irish Academy in Dublin," he found the words to that poem and others attributed to a blind singer and fiddler named Anthony Raftery, Antoine Ó Reachtabra, who had died in 1835. Eventually Hyde pieced together a whole poetry/song book, collecting from singers, old manuscripts, and other folksong collectors (including one interesting 1834 piece transcribed in Latin letters from "a manuscript that one of the Hessians wrote phonetically"—one of the Bros. Grimm?). Before this time Raftery, this native genius of a poet and singer, was not even listed in the biographical index of the Royal Irish Academy.

It was from growing love and respect for the Irish literary tradition in the Irish language that Douglas Hyde and other Gaelic literary purists such as Eoin MacNeill soon moved beyond Yeats. They thought that true Irish literature could only be continued by relearning and writing in the Gaelic itself. There had been small Irish language revival groups since even before the famine, but by 1893 Hyde and MacNeill brought them all together in a nation-wide group called the Gaelic League. Douglas Hyde's 1892 lecture at the National Literary Society, the spark that created the League, presented the Irish language as the key to Irish nationality, and made "West-Britonism," a positive word earlier for Daniel O'Connell, almost a curse. Here is a long excerpt from that moving lecture:

When we speak of 'The Necessity for De-Anglicizing the Irish nation,' we mean it, not as a protest against imitating what is *best* in the English people, for that would be absurd, but rather to show the folly of neglecting what is Irish, and hastening to adopt, pell-mell, and indiscriminately, everything that is English, simply because it is English.

I shall endeavor to show that this failure of the Irish people in recent times has been largely brought about by the race diverging during this century from the right path, and ceasing to be Irish without becoming English. I shall attempt to show that with the bulk of the people this change took place quite recently, much more recently than most people imagine, and is, in fact, still going on. I should also like to call attention to the illogical position of men who drop their own language to speak English, of men who translate their euphonious

---

62. GE Layer 62 is a Folder titled "Douglas Hyde sites," with three Placemarks within ten miles of each other, all in Co. Roscommon. Castlerea is where he was born, Frenchpark is where he grew up, and a Photos icon at Kilnamanagh shows the countryside to advantage.

Irish names into English monosyllables, of men who read English books, and know nothing about Gaelic literature, nevertheless protesting as a matter of sentiment that they hate the country which at every hand's turn they rush to imitate . . . .

To say that Ireland has not prospered under English rule is simply a truism; all the world admits it, England does not deny it. But the English retort is ready. You have not prospered, they say, because you would not settle down contentedly, like the Scotch, and form part of the empire. "Twenty years of good, resolute, grandfatherly government," said a well-known Englishman, will solve the Irish question. He possibly made the period too short, but let us suppose this. Let us suppose for a moment—which is impossible—that there were to arise a series of Cromwells in England for the space of one hundred years, able administrators of the empire, careful rulers of Ireland, developing to the utmost our national resources, while they unremittingly stamped out every spark of national feeling, making Ireland a land of wealth and factories, while they extinguished every thought and every idea that was Irish, and left us, at last, after a hundred years of good government, fat, wealthy, and populous, but with all our characteristics gone, with every external that at present differentiates us from the English lost or dropped; all our Irish names of places and people turned into English names; the Irish language completely extinct; the O's and the Macs dropped; our Irish intonation changed, as far as possible by English school-masters, into something English; our history no longer remembered or taught; the names of our rebels and martyrs blotted out; our battlefields and traditions forgotten; the fact that we were not of Saxon origin dropped out of sight and memory, and let me now put the question—How many Irishmen are there who would purchase material prosperity at such a price?

The bulk of the Irish race really lived in the closest contact with the traditions of the past and the national life of nearly eighteen hundred years ago, until the beginning of this century. Not only so, but during the whole of the dark Penal times they produced amongst themselves a most vigorous literary development. The literary activity of even the eighteenth century among the Gaels was very great, not in the south alone, but also in Ulster—the number of poets it produced was something astonishing . . . . Every well-to-do farmer could read and write Irish, and many of them could understand even archaic Irish. I have myself heard persons reciting the poems of Donogha More O'Daly, Abbot of Boyle, in Roscommon, who died sixty years before Chaucer was born . . . . But it may be said, roughly speaking, that the ancient Gaelic civilisation died with O'Connell, largely, I am afraid, owing to his example and his neglect of inculcating the necessity of keeping alive racial customs, language, and traditions . . . .

When my father was a young boy in the county Leitrim, not far from Longford, he seldom heard the farm labourers and tenants speak anything but Irish amongst themselves. So much for Ulster and Leinster, but Connacht and Munster were until quite recently completely Gaelic. In fact, I may venture to say, that up to the beginning of the present century, neither man, woman, nor child of the Gaelic race, either of high blood or low blood, existed in Ireland who did not either speak Irish or understand it. But within the last ninety years we have, with an unparalleled frivolity, deliberately thrown away our birthright and Anglicised ourselves. . . . So much for the greatest stroke of all in our Anglicisation, the loss of our language. I have often heard people thank god that if the English gave us nothing else they gave us at least their language. In this way they put a bold face upon the matter, and pretend that the Irish language is not worth knowing, and has no literature.

I have no hesitation at all in saying that every Irish-feeling Irishman, who hates the reproach of West-Britonism, should set himself to encourage the efforts which are being made to keep alive our once great national tongue. The losing of it is our greatest blow, and the sorest stroke that the rapid anglicisation of Ireland has inflicted upon us. In order to de-Anglicise ourselves we must at once arrest the decay of the language.[5]

What a powerful argument: who would sell a cultural birthright for simple material improvements in lifestyle? From this time on, those dwindling places mainly in the southwestern and western Irish countryside where Irish was still the everyday language—the *Gaeltacht* [GE[63]]– were places of pilgrimage for intellectuals

---

63. GE Layer 63 is a Polygon showing in bright green the main Gaeltacht areas as they were circa 1926. The main ones are obviously along the western coast, from Donegal in the north to Kerry and Cork in the south. This map mainly based on website below: http://www.irish-society.org/home/hedgemaster-archives-2/places-artifacts/gaeltacht

caught up in the Gaelic language movement. The folk as purest bearers of cultural legacy, that old Romantic idea, was still very much alive in Ireland as the century turned.

This helps explain the controversy over Irish literary theatre from 1899 to 1907. Yeats's *The Countess Kathleen* and John Synge's *Playboy of the Western World*—both based on what Yeats and Synge thought to be genuine Irish legend or folktale—were shouted off the stage in their first performances by Gaelic-minded patriots upset at what they saw as ignoble stereotypes of the rural, Catholic Irish.

Meanwhile, the Gaelic League had its own newspaper and publishing wing; it sent "traveling teachers" out to set up Irish language schools. Hyde himself became first Professor of Modern Irish at University College Dublin. He remained as head of the Gaelic League until 1915—resigning then when he saw it being taken over by more politically-inspired groups such as Sinn Féin (more below in a minute). Looking even further ahead, in 1937, when a new constitution for the twenty-six counties of Ireland that had Dominion status created an office of President, Douglas Hyde was the popular choice, and served out his full term until 1945. When he died four years later he was given a state funeral, a Church of Ireland (Protestant) service in Dublin's (Protestant) St. Patrick's Cathedral;[GE64] but such had been his warmth for Catholicism expressed in his writings, that Catholics by the tens of thousands, including many governmental figures, stood outside the cathedral out of respect.

The Home Rule Movement Before WW I

In recent times *Sinn Féin* has been known as the political party that represents the underground Irish Republican Army, and the I.R.A. itself found certain elements of Marxist thought and practice useful in the mid- and late-twentieth century. The origins of Sinn Féin, though, are solidly anti-socialist. "Sinn Féin" translates loosely from the Irish as "We Ourselves," meaning "Ourselves Alone." It was a party, or at least a movement, set up in the late 1890s by Arthur Griffith, another veteran of Gaelic literary studies and organizations. His original political scheme was modeled on the 1867 Dual Monarchy of Austria-Hungary, with separate independent legislatures united only by the person of a king. Eventually what the name implied was at least a passive resistance to the British: the Irish were not to ask the British for anything anymore, but simply to begin to rule themselves through a shadow government. The British, ignored and irrelevant, would presumably pack up and go home. The original movement was also racist in the sense of being openly anti-Semitic. In spite of (or because of?) this darker side, Sinn Féin would eclipse the Home Rule Party in popularity by the end of World War I.

There was an important left-wing strain of Irish nationalism as well in these years. James Connolly was a socialist with labor organizing experience in Scotland and the U.S.; his first organizing efforts in Ireland in 1896 resulted in the Dublin Socialist Club. As the skilled and then even the unskilled workers organized in the early twentieth century, a new force was added to the Irish political mix. Strangely enough for a European socialist in these years, Connolly was both a devout Catholic and an Irish nationalist. He admired the Gaelic movement and even the "physical force" side of the independence movement. The name of his first political group hints at this blend: the Irish Socialist Republican Party. He would bring a secret labor army, the Irish Citizen Army, with him to the Easter Rising of 1916.

So the Home Rule movement in Ireland gathered allies and new momentum on into the twentieth century. The Irish Home Rule Party in the British House of Commons became the crucial swing vote there. In 1911, for example, this bloc refused to vote for the governing Liberals' budget unless they followed through on their promise to limit the power of the House of Lords, perennially hostile to Irish Home Rule. With help from King George V, the Liberals rammed through the Parliament Act of that year that stripped veto power from the Lords for all time. Early the next year, knowing the Lords could only delay but no longer veto, the Liberals introduced the third Irish Home Rule bill. Political analysts were all but unanimous about its chances for success: seventy years of Irish Home Rule agitation finally seemed to be bearing fruit. But they reckoned without Protestant backlash in Ulster.

---

64. GE Layer 64 is a Placemark referencing Dublin's St. Patrick's Cathedral.

The Irish Orange

Much of the chapter to this point has been about Irish efforts—at first Anglo-Irish Protestant and then increasingly Irish Catholic—to win a degree of independence from Britain. Some sketch of the Irish Orange is overdue.

In 1795 a secret "Orange Order" was established among Protestants in the north of Ireland, triggered by the arming of Catholics in these emergency times of the French Revolution. The color was of course from William of Orange, defeater of Catholic armies. The great day of their celebration was (and still is) July 12, anniversary of the 1691 Battle of Aughrim (and close enough to the date of the 1690 Battle of the Boyne to be confused with it), won by the armies of that same William. The Orange lodges bore general resemblance to Masonic lodges. All classes from highest to lowest were allowed membership, and there were circles within circles into which one was gradually given the secrets. They were most striking in Ireland for being rallying points for the ethnic Protestants of the north. The charter oath of one reads:

> To the glorious, pious, and immortal memory of the great and good King William, not forgetting Oliver Cromwell, who assisted in redeeming us from popery, slavery, arbitrary power, brass-money, and wooden shoes. May we never want a Williamite to kick the . . . of a Jacobite! and a . . . for the Bishop of Cork! And he that won't drink this, whether he be priest, bishop, deacon, bellows-blower, grave-digger, or any other of the fraternity of the clergy; may a north wind blow him to the south, and a west wind to the east! May he have a dark night, a lee shore, a rank storm, and a leaky vessel, to carry him over the river Styx! May the dog Cerberus make a meal of his rump, and Pluto a snuff-box of his skull, and may the devil jump down his throat with a red hot harrow, with every pin tear out a gut, and blow him with a clean carcase to hell! Amen.[6]

All through the nineteenth century the successes of the Catholic Irish were resented by the Orange Order. When Parnell's Home Rule Party allied with Gladstone's Liberals, many Protestant Liberals—Ulster businessmen especially—countered by allying with the Conservative Party. The members of this alliance now called themselves "Unionists." When the Third Home Rule Bill surfaced in 1912, petitions against it were signed by hundreds of thousands of Ulster Protestants, and Orange Order militias openly drilled. By April 1914 they had come together as the Ulster Volunteer Force, 25,000 rifles strong, daring the House of Commons to go through with Home Rule for all of Ireland. While Parliament agonized about the problem, World War I broke out and Home Rule was put on hold yet again.[7]

Easter Rising 1916

On the holiday Monday after Easter in 1916, proclamations of an independent Irish republic went up, and a not very well organized army of a thousand or so "Sinn Féiners" took over several sites in Dublin including the General Post Office. In six days, ending when enough of the British army and navy arrived to burn out the Post Office with incendiary artillery shells and surround the rest, something like 500 people were killed and 2,500 wounded. It was the single deadliest week of the past century or so in Irish affairs. It still colors things in the twenty-first century, and still makes Easter a jittery time in Northern Ireland.

The general setting, of course, was World War I. In 1913, a year before the war broke out, the (mostly Catholic) Irish Volunteers were founded as a counter to the (Protestant) Ulster Volunteers. Looking for a dignified front man, they persuaded Eoin MacNeill—co-founder of the Gaelic League with Douglas Hyde and since 1908 Professor of Ancient and Medieval Irish History at University College Dublin, successor to the 1854 Catholic University—to take the job. Unbeknownst to him, a full-scale rising was being planned by I.R.B. men inside the Volunteers.

In late July of 1914, just a week before the world war was declared, came "the Howth gunrunning." Irish Volunteer sympathizers had raised the money to buy almost a thousand old Mausers from Germany, and a private yacht had run them into the little port just ten miles from Dublin city center.[GE[65]] A British army unit found out about it, but got there too late to confiscate the shipment. As they marched back into Dublin

---

65. GE Layer 65 is a Placemark referencing the little port at Howth, less than ten miles from the center of Dublin.

empty-handed, a crowd jeered them; at Bachelor's Walk,[GE[66]] along the river near city center, stone throwing and then shooting commenced, with three dead and dozens wounded.

When the World War was declared on August 3 and 4 of 1914, many extreme Irish patriots saw Germany as an ally—on the age-old political theory that "the enemy of my enemy is my friend." Roger Casement, Irish-born former diplomat for the U.K., had good German diplomatic contacts from his time spent in the United States. During the war he secretly visited Germany, trying to work with German authorities to recruit Irish POWs in Germany for an Irish independence army unit, and of course to get German arms to support a revolution. By the spring of 1916, a year-and-a-half into the war, a small anti-war group of Irish republicans had been openly carrying arms for weeks: no fighting for freedom for others until the British give us ours, they said. The British government hesitated to crack down for fear of precipitating a mass Irish upheaval that might complicate Britain's life-and-death struggle with Germany on the Western Front.

But on Saturday before Easter, a German freighter with 20,000 rifles and a million rounds of ammunition for Irish revolutionaries was captured. The ship, disguised as a Norwegian timber-carrying ship, had come into Tralee Bay[GE[67]] with the arms, but a confusion of dates meant nobody was there to meet it and offload the arms. The British Navy soon took it under its guns, discovered the arms, and demanded that it sail to Cork harbor. There the captain and crew sunk the ship, rather than surrender the arms. At this point the British government reluctantly decided it had to move, and began to prepare plans for a crackdown. On the holiday Monday after Easter, however, the rebels moved first. Padraic Pearse and James Connolly, chief and deputy respectively of the Irish republican forces, caught army units in Dublin—and most of the rest of the population of Ireland—totally off-guard.

Pearse, who began the uprising and later organized the surrender, was a product of the Gaelic revival. He had been introduced to Irish nationalism by the Gaelic League, and in 1908 had opened a bi-lingual school in Dublin that stressed Irish culture. He also had a fascination for the heroic deed, and thought Ireland might be reborn through the blood sacrifice of just a few. In 1913 he was one of the organizers of the Irish Volunteers.[8] In his life many themes of the Irish national movement come together. You can see these same themes in the proclamation of independence itself:

POBLACHT NA EIREANN.
THE PROVISIONAL GOVERNMENT
OF THE
IRISH REPUBLIC
TO THE PEOPLE OF IRELAND

IRISHMEN AND IRISHWOMEN: In the name of God and of the dead generations from which she receives her old tradition of nationhood, Ireland, through us, summons her children to her flag and strikes for her freedom.

Having organised and trained her manhood through her secret revolutionary organisation, the Irish Republican Brotherhood, and through her open military organisations, the Irish Volunteers and the Irish Citizen Army, having patiently perfected her discipline, having resolutely waited for the right moment to reveal itself, she now seizes that moment, and, supported by her exiled children in America and by gallant allies in Europe, but relying in the first on her own strength, she strikes in full confidence of victory.

We declare the right of the people of Ireland to the ownership of Ireland, and to the unfettered control of Irish destinies, to be sovereign and indefeasible. The long usurpation of that right by a foreign people and government has not extinguished the right, nor can it ever be extinguished except by the destruction of the Irish people. In every generation the Irish people have asserted their right to national freedom and sovereignty: six times during the past three hundred years they have asserted it in arms. Standing on that fundamental right

66. GE Layer 66 is a Placemark generally referencing Bachelor's Walk, along the river not far from city center.
67. GE Layer 67 is a Placemark set in Tralee Bay. Roger Casement had been put ashore here by German submarine a few days earlier, but was quickly captured.

and again asserting it in arms in the face of the world, we hereby proclaim the Irish Republic as a Sovereign Independent State, and we pledge our lives and the lives of our comrades-in-arms to the cause of its freedom, of its welfare, and of its exaltation among the nations.

The Irish Republic is entitled to, and hereby claims, the allegiance of every Irishman and Irishwoman. The Republic guarantees religious and civil liberty, equal rights and equal opportunities to all its citizens, and declares its resolve to pursue the happiness and prosperity of the whole nation and of all its parts, cherishing all the children of the nation equally, and oblivious of the differences carefully fostered by an alien government, which have divided a minority from the majority in the past.

Until our arms have brought the opportune moment for the establishment of a permanent National Government, representative of the whole people of Ireland and elected by the suffrages of all her men and women, the Provisional Government, hereby constituted, will administer the civil and military affairs of the Republic in trust for the people.

We place the cause of the Irish Republic under the protection of the Most High God, Whose blessing we invoke upon our arms, and we pray that no-one who serves that cause will dishonour it by cowardice, inhumanity, or rapine. In this supreme hour the Irish nation must, by its valour and discipline and by the readiness of its children to sacrifice themselves for the common good, prove itself worthy of the August destiny to which it is called.

Signed on Behalf of the Provisional Government,

Thomas J. Clarke, Sean Mac Diarmada, Thomas MacDonagh, P. H. Pearse, Eamonn Ceannt, James Connolly, Joseph Plunkett[GE68]

The opening line is Irish for "The Irish Republic." The I.R.B. and the two openly-armed militias are named to lead the rebellion, with support from the American Irish ("exiled children") and Germany ("gallant allies in Europe"). Irish rights to sovereignty were never nullified by centuries of British control: in every generation the Irish asserted their rights in arms. Civil and religious freedom is to be given to all, overcoming division between majority and minority so carefully exaggerated by the British. In all, this is quite a powerful manifesto, and the seven signers are now famous.

Here, in brief, is the geography and chronology of the rising that ensued. When Eoin MacNeill—titular head of the Irish Volunteers—learned of the planned rising, he not only confronted Padraic Pearse and the other planners but did what he could to stop it. The planners went ahead with it anyway, but with the off-again, on-again confusion only about a thousand fighters actually showed up on that Monday after Easter—800 or so Irish Volunteers, 200 or so of the socialist Citizen Army. Given that relatively small number, their activity was remarkable. The rebels cut the telegraph wires, and tore up the main railroad tracks five to six miles out of the city, planning to and in fact seriously interfering with any quick British response. In general they threw a sophisticated web of military bases around Dublin Castle.[GE69] On Monday at noon the military staff and the revolutionary leaders took over the General Post Office,[GE70] a fortress-like stone building on the north bank just three short blocks from the river, on the wide boulevard called O'Connell Street. The Irish Volunteers were organized in four battalions, each with a specified base to take and use as jumping off point. The 1st Battalion occupied the Four Courts, the big law court buildings directly on the north bank of the river.[GE71] The 2nd

68. GE Layer 68 is a Placemark framing center city Dublin, but is mainly used here as an excuse for entering a website with a facsimile of the proclamation of independence of the rising: http://en.wikipedia.org/wiki/File:Easter_Proclamation_of_1916.png

69. GE Layer 69 is a Placemark (symbolized by an orange star) locating Dublin Castle.

70. GE Layer 70 is a Placemark (symbolized by a green star) locating the General Post Office. The facade of the 1818 building is essentially the same today as in 1916; lots of Photos icons to explore, particularly the 360 Cities one titled "Dublin City Center" located in O'Connell Street directly in front of the GPO.

71. GE Layer 71 is a Placemark in green locating Four Courts.

Battalion occupied Jacob's Biscuit Factory two or three blocks south of Dublin Castle.[GE72] The 3rd Battalion based itself in Boland's Biscuit Mills buildings, controlling the main road coming into town from the southeast. [GE73] The 4th Battalion went into South Dublin Union hospital complex,[GE74] near the terminus of the main railway from the west and the terminus of the Grand Canal coming in from the west. Part of the Citizen Army occupied St. Stephen's Green,[GE75] and part of it was at Liberty Hall, the union headquarters on the riverfront not far from the GPO.[GE76] The first real fighting of the day was when a small Citizen Army force charged the main doorway of Dublin Castle, trying and failing to take it, but occupying next door City Hall. Barricades went across the main roads; sniper posts behind sandbags were set up to defend the buildings. As the police were withdrawn from the streets, looting of stores began that first day and continued all week. By Tuesday government forces were arriving from Belfast, and they re-took City Hall. More and more troops arrived the next couple of days, with machine guns and artillery, neither of which the rebels could match. Heavy artillery was hitting the GPO by Wednesday; by Thursday the gunboat Helga had come up and moored in the River Liffey, in point blank range of Liberty Hall.[GE77] The blasted, burning GPO was abandoned Friday evening. On Saturday Pearse surrendered, and sent messages to all the remaining rebel-held positions to surrender.

The great majority of Irish people—at the week of the rebellion—detested the rebels. Irish constitutional leaders, including almost all the Irish Members of Parliament, thought they were throwing away a half-century of progress toward Home Rule. The downtown of Ireland's biggest city was gutted, with many casualties and many more people endangered by these fanatics.

What changed their place in the Irish history books was the character of the British response. "Treason in time of war," just as in Wolfe Tone's day, was the official response, even though important British officials in both Ireland and America warned against this policy. But the spring of 1916 was a desperate time on the Western Front; Saturday, April 22, two days before the Easter Rising began, saw the first German chlorine gas attack at Ypres. There was a strong British feeling that these Irish rebels had stabbed them in the back while they were engaged in a life-or-death struggle with Germany. And so secret military trial and quick execution was the order of the day for the British. Sixteen leaders of the Easter rising, including all seven signers of the Proclamation, were executed, and dozens more only reprieved when massive protests broke out. Conditions of the sentences slowly leaked out and affected public opinion. Many of the executed were young, with young wives and babes in arms. Connolly, wounded, was carried to execution on a stretcher. Joseph Plunkett was married in his jail cell just before being taken out and shot. Within months there was a cult of these young Romantic leaders. They had fought a clean war, as wars go, apparently with no expectations of winning. Sean MacDiarmada wrote on the day before his execution, "We die that the Irish nation may live. Our blood will rebaptize and reinvigorate the land."[9] They had hoisted the green-white-orange tricolor, the one designed for Young Irelanders by French women in 1848, over the General Post Office; the rising popularity of the rebels after their deaths meant that it would eventually be the flag of an independent Ireland.[GE78]

In another sense, too, the Easter Rebellion marked a new phase of Irish history. There were a few Protestants in important positions (Roger Casement, for example); not just the mass participation but the leadership was almost entirely Catholic. All seven signers of the Proclamation were Catholic Irish, and most of them were devout, practicing Catholics. In the words of one historian of Irish nationalism, "Nationalist Ireland had, at last, found its own leaders."[10]

---

72. GE Layer 72 is a Placemark in green locating Jacob's Biscuit Factory.

73. GE Layer 73 is a Placemark in green locating Boland's Mills.

74. GE Layer 74 is a Placemark in green locating South Dublin Union.

75. GE Layer 75 is a Placemark in green locating St. Stephen's Green Park.

76. GE Layer 76 is a Placemark in green locating old Liberty Hall.

77. GE Layer 77 is a Folder titled "British strongholds, later Easter week." Turn on the whole Folder; individual Placemarks will show as orange Pushpin icons and labels, including the mooring location of the gunboat Helga.

78. GE Layer 78 is a Placemark referencing a Panoramio icon showing the Irish flag flying atop today's refurbished GPO, and also used to embed a website—a YouTube video showing scenes from Dublin in 1916, set to patriotic music by the "wolfe tones" (would I joke about such a group title?): see website below:
http://www.youtube.com/watch?v=XjsoKMQNULc

The partitioning of Ireland

In the year after the Easter rising, Sinn Féin was reorganized, replacing the Irish Volunteers. It was a fairly marginal group until the early spring of 1918 when Britain finally felt it had to extend the draft to Ireland. At that point Sinn Féin gained great public credibility by leading a general strike against it. So when WW I ended for the British in November of 1918 they discovered that the guerrilla war in Ireland had not. From 1919 to 1921 they sent in a handpicked police force known as Black and Tans from their uniforms. Not particularly chosen for their brutality, they reacted to a hostile population—as most any military force would—with hostility of their own.

Some of modern Ireland's basic institutions date from this tumultuous period. Today the lower house of the Republic of Ireland is called the *Dáil Éireann*, literally the Assembly of Ireland. It got its start in January of 1919, when twenty-seven Sinn Féin delegates newly elected to the British House of Commons refused to go to London, and set up their own legislature in Ireland. Just begin to rule ourselves, the theory went, and the British will pack up and leave. By mid-1921, amid the increasing escalation of violence, Lloyd George of Britain was ready to sit down and talk with Éamon De Valera, a battalion commander in the Easter Rising of 1916 and now leader of Sinn Fein.

These talks shaped the Ireland all but the oldest of us have known. Twenty-six of Ireland's thirty-two counties were given Dominion status—de facto independence, as in Canada; the United Kingdom eventually kept six of Ulster's nine counties, a compact territory with a Protestant majority, inside the U.K. as "Northern Ireland."

This radical 1921 settlement, obviously, did not wholly settle the Irish question.

De Valera shapes the Republic of Ireland

Edward De Valera was a U.S. citizen, born in New York in 1882 to an immigrant Irish mother and an immigrant Spanish father. His father died before he was three years old, and he was sent to his grandmother's in Limerick, where he grew up. This was the Gaeltacht, and he grew up speaking Irish as well as English. He was a devout Catholic all his life. He was a rugby star in high school and played later in college. Most of his university education was in Dublin, and he became a math teacher. He never managed to win a full-time university teaching position in math, but was teaching part-time in a college in Dublin when World War I broke out. He had joined the Gaelic League in 1908, and somewhere along the way had begun signing his first name Éamon instead of the English Edward. There is no record of any involvement of his with Fenians, the I.R.B., or other radical political groups before the war, but he did join the Irish Volunteers in 1913, and was one of its key military leaders in the Easter Rising.

With the failure of the Rising he was tried and sentenced to death. That he was not executed was partly because he was the last of the Irish Volunteer battalion commanders to surrender and was put in a different prison, and partly because he was a U.S. citizen by birth and the British—trying hard to get the U.S. into World War I—didn't want to do anything to alienate us. De Valera went to jail for a year, and upon his release in 1917 was elected head of Sinn Féin, which he led to popularity in resisting the British draft. He was re-arrested and deported to England. Dramatically escaping jail there in 1918, he went to the U.S. to raise funds for the cause of an independent Ireland.

It was as President of the Dáil, after the truce of July 1921 with the British, that he sent Arthur Griffith and Michael Collins to negotiate a final settlement with the British. Griffith you will know as the original founder of Sinn Féin. Michael Collins, as Home Minister for the Dáil government, had really run government while De Valera and Griffith were in jail, and as chief of intelligence of the I.R.A. had masterminded the brilliant if bloody guerrilla war against the British.

The treaty, partitioning Ireland and requiring a loyalty oath to Britain even in the southern part, triggered a civil war, a real shooting war that lasted a year, between opposing groups of the mainly Catholic Irish nationalists. Collins himself was ambushed and killed in August of 1922, down in West Cork near where he was born, by anti-treaty republicans.

De Valera, who had sent Collins with special powers to negotiate such a treaty, didn't back him on the treaty he negotiated—which probably sealed Collins' fate. De Valera resigned the Presidency, and said he was with the anti-treaty side, but took little part in the fighting. Better than anyone since Parnell, he was able to appeal to both "physical force" and "constitutional" strands of Irish opinion. When the Sinn Féin party kept insisting on non-recognition of the new 1922 Parliament—through which De Valera gradually decided he could make progress towards truly independent Irish rule—in early 1926 he created his own rival political party, Fianna Fáil ("Fianna" you will know, "Fáil" was an old name for Ireland). It worked well; in the 1927 elections Fianna Fáil won nine times as many congressional seats as Sinn Féin. By 1932 De Valera was able to form a government a step further along towards complete independence.

At the same time on the physical force side, as a former commander in the Easter Rising (he was the Irish Volunteer battalion commander at Boland's Mill), his credentials were impeccable. He and Fianna Fáil members could and did march with the I.R.A. and Sinn Féin in their yearly parades to Bodenstown and the gravesite of Wolfe Tone.[GE[79]] In 1937 he set up a government that went beyond legality, pretending it was not in the British Commonwealth at all, attending none of its functions—very popular with nationalistic public opinion and winning grudging acquiescence from the British who knew it would be war again if they opposed it.

But something about being in power brought about a practical governing response from De Valera. He talked a good game about land reform, but reassured the large Protestant landowners he would respect private property. He was careful to court the Catholic hierarchy, and was seen as devout himself. In 1936 he actually outlawed the I.R.A., jailed its leader, and even ended the yearly Dublin-to-Bodenstown marches to Wolfe Tone's grave. De Valera was strong enough politically to keep Ireland neutral in WW II, even faced with the outcry against that policy from the U.S., usually in Ireland's corner. He had obviously not forgotten that Sinn Féin had come to popularity opposing the draft just twenty years before, and understood that his Fianna Fáil could lose popularity just as quickly by starting one. Overall, he never lost focus on the goal of an eventual independent Republic of Ireland, and that probably accounts for most of his enduring political popularity.

The Irish Free State pulled out of the British Dominion for good in 1949 and reconstituted itself as a Republic. The I.R.A. shifted virtually all of its attention to Northern Ireland.

The Troubles

All this time Northern Ireland remained an open sore, one of the world's seemingly insoluble political problems. Northern Ireland Catholics, a ghetto-ized minority there, demanded an end to British rule and unification with the rest of Ireland. Northern Ireland Protestants, afraid of persecution if they should be forced into a larger Catholic Irish state, demanded that the British army stay in place.

There were glimmers of hope for peace in Northern Ireland, off and on. The robust economy in the 1960s dampened political activity; some observers said that if everyone in Northern Ireland had a job, they wouldn't have as much time for the paramilitaries! In 1969, though, physical conflict broke out afresh. It was generally called just "The Troubles." It started in August with a huge, three-day-long urban riot in Derry/Londonderry called "The Battle of Bogside." The Unionist Apprenticeboys staged a parade between the old city walls and the Catholic neighborhood called Bogside.[GE[80]] An Irish nationalist crowd gathered to protest, and when the police tried to disperse it, it erupted into violence. About that same time the I.R.A. split, into an "Official" wing that was avowedly Marxist but claimed non-violence, and a "Provisional" wing of younger, proudly Catholic, terrorists/freedom fighters. These "Provos" spread their attacks to England by 1973. In 1974 they killed five people in a bombing of the Grand Hotel in Brighton where the Conservative Party was meeting, narrowly missing Prime Minister Margaret Thatcher, their chief target.

In 1979 the Provos assassinated Lord Louis Mountbatten, uncle of Prince Philip and a most famous British royal family member. One of the highest ranking and famous British officers in World War II, he was just after the war put in charge of dissolving the British Raj and presiding over the birth of modern India and Pakistan (more later in South Asia's "Grand Trunk Road" chapter).

---

79. GE Layer 79 is a Folder titled "Bodenstown-Dublin"; it includes a purple Pushpin icon for Bodentown and a Path in purple, seventeen straight-line miles and probably twenty or more as the boys marched.

80. GE Layer 80 is a Polygon titled "Walled Londonderry and Bogside Derry" that uses orange outline and orange wash fill to represent the old city; in the framed view Bogside is the neighborhood just beyond it.

The site and circumstances of the assassination encapsulate a good bit of Irish history. As a young man of twenty-two, in 1922, he had married into the family that owned the estate and castle of Classiebawn [GE[81]], in Connacht's County Sligo and just north of Sligo city. The estate itself dated back to the seizure of Connacht lands by Oliver Cromwell in the mid-1600s, when some 12,000 acres were given to an Englishman who thus became the first Viscount of Palmerston. Apparently neither the first nor the second Viscounts ever even visited their new Irish estate, being content with land rents sent to England by their agents in Ireland. The third Viscount was the famous Lord Palmerston of British government, indispensable Foreign Secretary and twice Prime Minister, in high government service from 1807 to 1865. He first visited his family estate in Ireland in 1808, according to local history, when he was twenty-four years old. He it was who had the stone harbor at Mallaghmore[GE[82]] built beginning in the 1820s, and who began the building of Classiebawn Castle on a little hill just half a mile away (though the castle was not fully completed until 1874, almost a decade after his death).

Lord Palmerston got a terrible reputation with the Catholic majority population thereabouts during the famine. He is remembered for evicting many farmers behind on their rents, and contributing more than his share to the numbers of destitute locals forced to emigrate to America. After his death in 1865, towards the end of the famine, the Ashley family inherited title and estate, and it was by marriage to an Ashley daughter that Louis Mountbatten eventually got the estates and castle. While not a permanent residence for his family, Classiebawn Castle was a regular vacation place, even after his retirement. He kept his 30' wooden boat in the Mallaghmore harbor and when there regularly went fishing in it. Beginning one such fishing trip in 1979, having just cleared the harbor, the boat was blown up by a huge IRA bomb secretly placed aboard the boat and apparently detonated by remote control from the nearby shore. It killed Lord Mountbatten and several others on the boat. He himself seems to have had some sympathy for the Irish cause, and may even have been in favor of eventual Irish unification. Speculation later was that Mallaghmore, being only a dozen miles from Northern Ireland (zoom out a bit in Google Earth to see yellow international boundary), and owned by a famous member of the British royal family, made an obviously tempting target for the I.R.A. The I.R.A. assassins would probably have said that it wasn't personal; to them Lord Mountbatten was simply part of an unjust system that could only be changed by violence. They blew him up, like they did Nelson's Column in downtown Dublin, and the great equestrian statue of Willliam III in front of Trinity College, as a symbol of that system.

The most famous name on the I.R.A. side during "The Troubles" was Bobby Sands. Born in 1954 in rural Northern Ireland, by age eighteen he was living in the projects in Belfast. About this same time he joined the I.R.A., and was arrested and tried for illegal possession of arms. He was jailed until 1976. The next year he was tried and convicted of serving in a Provisional I.R.A. attack on British forces, and sentenced to fourteen years in jail. He was imprisoned at Maze, a disused airfield about ten miles southwest of Belfast that the government had quickly converted into a jail.[GE[83]] In jail, apparently, Provo morale was high. They refused to accept treatment as common criminals, saying they were political prisoners—to the point of wearing blankets instead of prison-issue clothing. One reason morale was so high was they were generally considered heroes by the Catholic minority of Northern Ireland. In 1981 an MP in a rural Catholic district suddenly died, and Bobby Sands was put on the ballot to elect a replacement. He won, from prison. But the ultimate protest was a hunger strike he went on within weeks of that, in that same 1981. He died of starvation in early May, followed in death by several other hunger strikers. He was twenty-seven years old. His funeral attracted over a hundred thousand mourners.

There was equal and opposite intransigence and resolve on the Protestant side, coming from the paramilitaries associated with Orange orders and the Ulster Volunteer Force. The ambushing of Catholic and Protestant

81. GE Layer 81 is a Placemark referencing Cassiebawn Castle. For one view of the castle, click on Photos icon under pointer titled simply "Classiebawn." There are better nearby Photos icons, though they call the castle Mallaghmore.

82. GE Layer 82 is a Placemark referencing Mallaghmore harbor; for one view of the expensive stone harbor, the building of which was originally set in motion by Lord Palmerston in the 1820s, click on Panoramio icon under pushpin pointer titled "Mullaghmore Harbour Sligo."

83. GE Layer 83 is a Placemark titled "Maze Prison." In the view framed you can still see the building footprints of the "H-Blocks."

funerals by extremists of the opposite sides, bomb damage to buildings, cars set ablaze by mobs—this was the image of Northern Ireland during most of the lifetime of this writer.

The Good Friday Agreement and since

Two "peace women" of Ulster, Mairead Corrigan and Betty Williams, won the Nobel Peace Prize in 1976 for their work there. Brought together by their protest at three children being killed in the urban war—run over by an I.R.A. getaway car—these two Catholic women in their early thirties led huge marches against the insanity of a Catholic-Protestant civil war between two ostensibly Christian populations. They successfully buttonholed U.S. politicians of Irish descent such as Ted Kennedy to get them to use their influence to stop the flow of arms and money from the U.S. to the I.R.A. But their organization soon dwindled and the violence escalated again.

In the next twenty years almost the only contact between the two groups was in the workplace. And although "Catholic" and "Protestant" were still the ethnic group labels, going to church was not critical in this ethnic definition; both sides joke about "Protestant atheists" and "Catholic atheists." Ulster Protestants may still be united most by their anti-Catholic stance; public opinion polls in Northern Ireland show that Protestants are even more negative about intermarriage than Catholics. When Mary Robinson, President of the Republic of Ireland, visited West Belfast and shook hands with the leader of Sinn Féin in the early 1990s, the most bombastic of the Protestant leaders, Presbyterian minister Ian Paisley, denounced it as "Jesuitical conspiracy." But only two of Northern Ireland's six counties had a Protestant majority left, going into the 1990s. A general feeling seemed to grow that some radical departure from the past was possible.

Then in 1998 came a breakthrough for real peace in Northern Ireland. Former U.S. Senator George Mitchell, himself partly of Irish descent, was appointed "Special Envoy to Ireland" from the U.S. He brought an American peace offensive to bear, with help from newly-elected Labor Party Prime Minister Tony Blair of the U.K. They cajoled three key figures into serious negotiations: David Trimble, leader of the mainstream Protestant party in Northern Ireland, the Ulster Unionists; John Hume, leader of the mainstream Catholic political party, the Social Democratic and Labor Party; and of course Gerry Adams, President of Sinn Féin, the political wing of the IRA. The result was the "Good Friday" Agreement signed in Belfast in April of 1998. The peace process survived a bomb blast in Omagh that killed over twenty in August of that same year, and endured through successive July "marching seasons" (when some Orangemen are determined to march through Catholic neighborhoods on the anniversary of the William of Orange 1690–91 victories over Catholics, and some Catholics are of course determined that they will not). Looking back, it really was a watershed in terms of the reduction of physical violence in the age-old conflict. The IRA claimed in 2005 that it had totally disarmed.

Messrs. Trimble and Hume shared a Nobel Peace Prize for their work, although not Gerry Adams who had worked actively for cease-fire if not IRA disarmament. There is a chapter in Gerry Adams' political autobiography, *Before the Dawn*, where a (Catholic Irish) sniper thoughtfully ties a rag on a lamppost, steps off the couple of hundred paces back to his apartment, and later, knowing the exact range, efficiently and composedly picks off a British policeman who walks by it. It is presented as a piece of creative fiction, strangely out of place inside an otherwise purely factual book.[11] Your author thinks the Nobel Peace Prize committee may have wondered about that, too—if it was really a piece of personal history thinly disguised as fiction. Violence has been so successful on both extremes of this national divide, for so many generations, that some on each side see it as simply one more card to be played when the time comes.

The political art in Belfast and Derry/Londonderry is still fresh and vivid. Especially in working-class and lower-middle class neighborhoods where Loyalists (Protestants) and Nationalists (Catholics) live close together, such art is uncompromising, proud, and hateful on both sides. Start with the west side of Belfast, where Shankill Road runs west and then northwest, not far north of Falls Road which runs west and then southwest.[GE84] Shankill Road is classic Loyalist territory, where the modern paramilitaries, the Ulster Volunteer Force and the Ulster Defense Association, got their starts. Falls Road is its Nationalist opposite. Take a few minutes and zoom in along these roads, popping open Photos icons. Most of the photographs there are of the

---

84. GE Layer 84 is a Folder titled "Shankill and Falls Roads," containing within it two folders, one showing and labeling Shankill Road in orange, and the other Falls Road in green.

political murals—celebrations of the U.V.F., Queen Elizabeth II, William of Orange and Oliver Cromwell along Shankill, and of the I.R.A. and Bobby Sands and—since this was James Connolly socialist territory—celebrations of Che Guevara and denunciations of U.S. military actions, along Falls. Then go to Derry/Londonderry, and look at the Nationalist "gable wall murals" of Bogside, much of the art recalling scenes from the 1969 Battle of Bogside, and then switch to the other side of the old city walls, the Loyalist, or as one mural puts it, "the British side of Derry," for flags of St. George and such.[GE85]

George Bernard Shaw called the Irish race a hackneyed myth: "we are a parcel of mongrels, Spanish, Scottish, Welsh, English, and even a Jew or two." But in politics perception is always more important than reality, and the "Irish race"—Catholic in religious allegiance and with warm feelings toward Gaelic even if they don't personally speak it—on the one hand, and English-speaking Ulster Protestants on the other, are still the two dominant social categories of the island. Every year of relative peace makes future peace more likely, but ethnic group nationalism has deep roots, and enough terrorism from either side could still awaken it. The "physical force" side of the Catholic Irish independence movement worked, in a way, to keep Ireland from being absorbed into the United Kingdom, and an equal and opposite Protestant physical force kept the U.K. from quite quitting Ireland; yet both also fixed the cycle of violence there that is so difficult to break. Difficult, but not impossible, judging by the relative peace of the past few years. Maybe the best image to end on is a statue of reconciliation in that same Derry/Londonderry.[GE86]

Final musings on nationalism and socialism

Ireland, then, has been our first case study of how political nationalism, cultural nationalism, and socialism worked out in one small part of Europe, in the general context of great power relationships.

Socialism played some role in modern Irish group identification, particularly on the Nationalist side with James Connolly, but even for him the ideal of an independent republic for the Irish people was equally important. The modern I.R.A. embraced many Marxist tactics from guerrilla warfare, but was not seriously Marxist in social analysis or in belief in world revolution. Both political parts of Ireland today have generous social safety networks, and a well established place for unions—but nothing special in this regard in the context of western and central Europe. Socialism was clearly the weakest of the three "-isms," as modern history played out in Ireland.

Modern political nationalism from France (and the U.S.) reshaped the literate Irish political world view by the last decade of the 1700s; to be an Irish "republican" was ever more to believe in a state where free men and women, without monarchs or aristocracies, could govern themselves. It began with the Anglo-Irish first of all because they were much more literate, and coastal, than the Catholic majority, and therefore more in touch with that new current of Enlightenment ideas. By the 1920s it was becoming majority political belief. What was not agreed on was if it should be applied to the island as a whole or in two parts—which disagreement leads us to cultural nationalism.

Cultural nationalism left the strongest mark of all three of these modern "-isms" on Irish political behavior, coming in particularly from Romantic Germany and England. Again, it started not so much with the native Irish speakers such as Daniel O'Connell as it did with the Anglo-Irish who felt themselves no longer English. The twists and turns of these Anglo-Irish—alienated from Britain and conscious of British disdain of the Irish among whom the Anglo-Irish lived, yet far from sharing the life and language of those Irish—may be the most fascinating part of this whole story. Douglas Hyde, he of the Gaelic League, was by his native abilities in the Irish language and his ecumenical religious views the last step of that Anglo-Irish evolution. Especially with the independence of the twenty-six counties, free from the Protestant Scots-Irish and English-Irish ethnic group in Ulster, cultural nationalism was generally vested in the hands of the Catholic majority, to whom it came naturally. With partition they were no longer threatened by a more prosperous ethnic minority closely allied with

---

85. GE Layer 85 is a Folder titled "Bogside vs. Fountain," containing two Placemarks—one in green referencing "Free Derry Corner" in Bogside, center of its mural art, and the other in orange referencing the Fountain neighborhood on the other side of the old walled city, where the art is a bit more scattered but no less political on the Loyalist side.

86. GE Layer 86 is a Placemark referencing a Panoramio image titled "LondonDerry, N. Ireland."

the rule of Great Britain, and so could be a bit more relaxed both in cultivating their cultural uniquenesses and in warding off outside dangers that might threaten it. The celebrated Gaeltacht, where Irish is still the common spoken language, may still be shrinking, but because Irish is now a mandatory subject in schools in the Republic of Ireland, for the first time in a couple of centuries the percentage of fluent speakers is rising.

The opposite seemed to happen in Northern Ireland. Loyalists always had to fear absorption into a unified Ireland. On the other side Nationalists in Northern Ireland were by 1921 all of a sudden a very threatened minority, more than ever conscious of their economic inequality. The symbolism of the muralists—for Nationalists, for example, the use of Irish script, or the image of a gold harp on a green flag—celebrates separate cultural heritages, each feeding off the hatred of the other.

Here are some lessons the author of this chapter, at least, learned as he put this material together over the years.

The first is confirmation of the pattern identified in the Germany chapter, that any cultural group treated with disdain tends to develop a solidarity and eventually a countering pride. If that happens after its intellectuals get hold of Herder's Romantic ideas on folk culture, it yields cultural nationalism. The swapping of English names bestowed at birth for the equivalent in Irish will have its regular parallels in many other ethnic group nationalisms in modern history.

The second is that, to reach any kind of intensity, every cultural nationalism needs a threatening enemy. That, in turn, tends to force everybody into one or the other of two clearly defined camps.

But we have two more case studies in these modern "isms" before we leave Europe, so we'll see how general these lessons may be.

Endnotes

1. This translation by James Stephens is from the following website: http://www.public-domain-poetry.com/james-stephens/county-mayo-38041. A slightly different translation can be found in James Carty, ed., *Ireland From Grattan's Parliament to the Great Famine (1783–1850): A Documentary Record.* (Dublin: C. J. Fallon Ltd., 1966) 5th ed.; 1st edition was 1949, p. 12. For the phrase by phrase translation into English, see the following website: http://www.scoilgaeilge.org/t_na_t/TnaT_Marta2004.htm

2. James Carty, ed., *Ireland: A Documentary Record, From Grattan's Parliament to the Great Famine (1783–1850)*, 5th ed. (Dublin: C. J. Fallon, 1966), pp. 21–23.

3. James Joyce, *Ulysses* (NY: Modern Library, new ed. 1961), p. 296.

4. John Renelagh, *A Short History of Ireland* (Cambridge: Cambridge University Press, 1983), p. 153.

5. James Carty, ed., *Ireland from The Great Famine to The Treaty: A Documentary Record*, 4th ed. (Dublin: C. J. Fallon Ltd., 1966) pp. 100–3. The speech in its entirety can be found at the following website: http://www.gaeilge.org/deanglicising.html

6. Hereward Senior, *Orangeism in Ireland and Britain 1795–1836* (London: Routledge & K. Paul, 1966), pp. 2–3.

7. Michael Farrell, *Northern Ireland: The Orange State* (London: Pluto Press, 1980), pp. 15–20.

8. Alan J. Ward, *The Easter Rising: Revolution and Irish Nationalism* (Arlington Heights, IL: AHM Publishing Corp., 1980), p. 81.

9. Redmond Fitzgerald, *Cry Blood, Cry Erin* (NY: C. N. Potter, 1966), p. 79.

10. D. George Boyce, *Nationalism in Ireland* (Baltimore: Johns Hopkins University Press, 1982), p. 311.

11. Gerry Adams, *Before the Dawn: An Autobiography* (New York: William Morrow & Co., 1997).

Chapter Six

"Land of Heroes": Finland

CONTENTS

The heart of the matter—A quick introduction to Finnish—Topography and texture of the land—The step-children of Scandinavia—The Kingdom of Sweden and the Reformation—Mikael Agricola—Sweden as the local great power: The Thirty Years' War—Russia replaces Sweden as the local great power: The Great Northern War—The Fennophiles—Napoleonic wars and Russian control—The Turku Romantics—The freshman class of 1822: Runeberg, Snellman, and Lönnrot—Defense of the *Kalevala*—Russian imperial politics—Sibelius—War and Revolution—Baron Mannerheim—Independence—The Winter War—The "Continuation War"—Since

The heart of the matter

An old epic singer in rural Finland traditionally sat knee to knee with an apprentice, looking into his eyes and holding his hands (the gender is used advisedly here; in this culture the epic was almost exclusively in male hands). He sang his song a phrase at a time and the apprentice repeated:

I am driven by my longing, And my understanding urges
That I should commence my singing, And begin my recitation.
I will sing the people's legends, And the ballads of the nation.
To my mouth the words are flowing, And the words are gently falling,
Quickly as my tongue can shape them, And between my teeth emerging.
    Dearest friend, and much-loved brother, Best beloved of all companions,
Come and let us sing together, let us now begin our converse,
Since at length we meet together, From two widely sundered regions.
Rarely can we meet together, Rarely one can meet the other,
In these dismal Northern regions, In the dreary land of Pohja.
Let us clasp our hands together, Let us interlock our fingers;
Let us sing a cheerful measure, Let us use our best endeavours,
While our dear ones hearken to us, And our loved ones are instructed,
While the young are standing round us, Of the rising generation,
Let them learn the words of magic, And recall our songs and legends,
Of the belt of Vainamoinen, Of the forge of Ilmarinen . . . .[1]

So begins the *Kalevala*, the Finnish epic first published in 1835. If this rhythm and meter should sound familiar from American literature, it is probably because it was a German translation of the *Kalevala* that inspired Longfellow to write *The Song of Hiawatha* ("By the shores of Gitche Gumee, By the shining Big-Sea-Water, Stood the wigwam of Nokomis, Daughter of the moon, Nokomis. Dark behind it rose the forest . . .") The *Kalevala* is much more than just another long poem, however, to most modern Finns. More than one writer has said that without a *Kalevala* there would not be an independent Finland today. "Kalevala Day" on February 28 (the day of its publication in 1835) is still probably a bigger holiday on the Finnish calendar than December 6, the anniversary of Finland's actual independence day in 1917. And thereby hangs a tale, or at least a history.

A quick introduction to Finnish

Finnish is one of the few languages of Europe that is not a member of the Indo-European family of languages. It is fairly close kin to the Sami spoken by the Lapps in the very northern parts of Scandinavia and Russia, and to the Estonian that is spoken south across the Gulf of Finland, and some distant kin to Hungarian. Technically, these are all members of the Finno-Ugric group of what is today called the Uralic family of languages. Finnish is an inflected language, meaning that depending on the place of a noun, pronoun, or adjective in a sentence, it gets different endings. It is written in familiar Latin letters, but even veteran travelers in Europe, used to being able to work out some familiar cognates from other European languages, find few such parallels here in Finland.

In terms of pronunciation, the first syllable of Finnish words is almost always stressed. It has short vowels and long, but conveniently doubles the vowels in writing to indicate the long ones. The H is a gutteral, as in the Scottish "loch." An *umlaut*, two dots over a vowel, generally does what umlauts do in German. Only a very few Finnish words have come over into English: among them "pike" (the fish); and "sauna" (in dipthongs such as AU each vowel is pronounced, so the original pronunciation of this word would be SAH-oo-nah instead of SAW-nah). The following words might help in exploring a map of Finland, including the Google Earth surface.

Some natural features:

järve is lake;
joki is stream or river;
pää is head (so the town named *Järvenpää* means Lake's Head);
mäki is hill;
metsä is forest;
and *nummi* is moor, a heather-covered expanse.

Some man-made features:

kirkko means church (presumably a loan word);
linna is fort or castle (so *Olavenlinna* means Olaf's Castle);
silta is bridge;
kaupunki is town or city;
kyla is village;
puisto is park;
and *yliopisto* is university.

And finally:

Suomi and *suomen* are the Finnish words for "Finland" and "Finnish."

Topography and texture of the land

Finland is usually classed as one of the four Scandinavian states of northern Europe, the others being Denmark, Norway, and Sweden.[GE¹] The outline of the modern Finnish state looks something like a sitting rabbit as drawn by a kindergarten student.[GE²] It is about 325 miles across at its widest point, and about twice that north to south. It borders Russia on the east, the Gulf of Finland on the south, the Gulf of Bothnia and Sweden on

---

1. GE Layer 1 is a Polygon titled "Scandinavia, overview." It shows as a white outline drawn around the four main Scandinavian states (some include Iceland in the definition of "Scandinavian," but we're just dealing with the continent in this view). Take a minute to locate capital cities that Google Earth shows as white star icons with red centers—Oslo, Copenhagen, Stockholm, and Helsinki. Then turn layer off to keep view uncluttered.

2. GE Layer 2 is a Placemark framing an overall view of Finland; with the basic Borders and Labels layer turned on, the international borders show up in yellow. If you will go to View drop down menu, and turn on the Grid layer there, the Arctic Circle will show as a yellow east-west line. Note that the head and ears of the "rabbit" are above the Arctic Circle, meaning never any sun in the sky there in mid-winter, and a never-setting sun in mid-summer.

the west, and Norway on the north. Although Finland does not claim the northernmost point in Europe (obviously there is a band of Norwegian territory across the northern border of Finland), it can claim to be on average the northernmost European country, just edging out Norway. With its outline superimposed on Canada, but correct as to latitude, it is easy for an American to see just how northerly Finland is.[GE³] Finland's southernmost point would be over 600 miles north of Montana's northernmost point!

As recently as 12,000 years ago all of Finland was under ice. In the retreat of the glaciers since then, there were a couple of cold spells (centuries long) when the front of the glaciers was fairly stationary. The result is seen today in two lines of eskers, gravel ridges up to 300′ high left at the melting edge of the glaciers. They run west to east across southern Finland, and are called the Salpausselkä ranges. They look like mountain ranges only because the rest of southern Finland is a low granite shield ground flat by those same glaciers—so flat that you can rarely see beyond the closest trees.[GE⁴] They also left upwards of 50,000 lakes, more than Minnesota ever thought of. Notice how some of these lakes make chains of lakes in a generally north-south direction; at times in Finnish history, especially in wars with Russia, these would be important military defense lines.[GE⁵] Travel through the country in the early days was as much by water as by land, the way the Canadian voyageurs used long lakes and short portages between them. The further north you go, the more the countryside gets a hilly roll to it, and the very northern part of the country, where it splits into a rough Y (the ears of the kindergarten rabbit) is more rugged and mountainous.[GE⁶]

One interesting feature is the Aland Islands and the whole "Finnish archipelago," an absolute maze of islands, big and small, that constitute the southwest corner of Finland.[GE⁷] This area was not only settled early by Finnish stock, but being closest to Sweden always attracted a lot of attention from that direction. The narrow mouth of the Gulf of Bothnia is about twenty-five miles wide. And speaking of the southwest of Finland, just in case the foregoing has presented Finland as a completely rural country, this is the center of its important ship-building industry.[GE⁸] A good many of the cruise ships plying the subtropical waters of the Caribbean and Gulf of Mexico were Finnish-built on the shores of the cold Gulf of Finland.

The step-children of Scandinavia

The main stock of the Finns seems to have come into the land from the area of the Volga River sometime around the beginning of the Common Era, bringing the Iron Age with them. They gradually populated a band from the southern (Gulf of Finland) coast to about a hundred miles inland, and a narrower band on the western (Gulf of Bothnia) coast. Mostly farmers, they plowed the thin soil in the summer, often letting it go fallow and burning forest for new farmland the next year. The rest of the year they were free to fish and hunt, and the further north into the country they went, the more important a part of making a living that was. Dense northern furs brought good money or exchange with populations south of the Gulf of Finland. The Finnish word for money, *raha*, originally meant "fur," and is said to have come from these days.[2]

The Finns frankly began modern times as the step-children of Scandinavia. Danes, Swedes, and Norwegians all speak Germanic languages, while Finnish is not even an Indo-European language, as you've seen. This complicated communication between Finns and most of their European neighbors. Secondly, a glance at a map of Scandinavia reveals that the Finns had no immediate access, as did the other three, to the North Sea,

---

3. GE Layer 3 is a Polygon representing Finland in red, correct as to size and latitude but spun round the globe longitudinally and superimposed on Canada. First double-click on the Polygon icon to "fly" to pre-set view of North America, then turn layer on.

4. GE Layer 4 is a Folder labeled "South country views," with several Placemarks and Photos icons to explore.

5. GE Layer 5 is a Placemark titled "Finland's lakes," framing a view of the southern half of the country where most of the large lakes are.

6. GE Layer 6 is a Folder called "North country views," containing a few Placemarks referencing interesting Photos icons of the scenery.

7. GE Layer 7 is a Folder titled "Aland Islands & Finnish archipelago." It references a couple of interesting Panoramio icons, and frames a typical island-strewn square mile in a red Polygon.

8. GE Layer 8 is a Placemark referencing a Panoramio icon with a view of a shipyard near the city of Turku.

and therefore western Europe and points beyond. In addition, the Finnish coast was almost always locked in sea ice for from three to five months every winter; of the four modern countries, Finland alone had no all-weather port (at least before the age of icebreakers). Generally speaking, then, Finland's stronger Nordic neighbors were its gatekeepers in early modern history, and largely determined its fate for some 600 years.

The Vikings (and all the other names they were known by—Danes, Norsemen, Normans, Varangians, etc.)—came from the Germanic-speaking lands of Scandinavia. Their longships were of oak planks that were riven (split with the grain), not sawn, making them amazingly resilient. One of their major water routes was along the northern coast to the head of the Gulf of Finland, up the Neva River for forty miles and thus into the huge Lake Ladoga, along its southern coast to the mouth of the Volkhov River, and then up the Volkhov 120 miles to Novgorod.[GE9] Novgorod, as you saw in the Russia chapter, was the key northern anchor for the trading network "from the Varangians to the Greeks," Kiev being the key southern anchor. In the heyday of the Vikings in the eighth to tenth centuries, no major Finnish towns were built on or near the coast, such was the danger of raids. But the Vikings, influenced by patterns from further south in Europe, eventually settled down to "civilized" life themselves; Oslo, Copenhagen, and Stockholm, today's Nordic capitals, were all founded from the mid-eleventh to the mid-twelfth centuries.

Also coming up from the south of Europe, along with this new town life, was Christianity. For Finland, it presented a choice: Sweden had become the western, Roman style of Christian in the 800s, and at about the same time Kievan Russia had become the eastern, Greek style of Christian. By 1054 those two variants had crystallized as Roman Catholic and Greek Orthodox. Although Novgorod was a close and powerful exponent of the latter, the former spread along the southern coast of the Gulf of Finland and proved the stronger influence. In the 1100s and 1200s all of Finland except the extreme east, Karelia, was converted to the Roman Catholic faith. It worked to tie Finland to the rest of Scandinavia. In 1249 the Dominican order founded a monastery in the southwest of what is today Finland, at Turku[GE10]—the most important, and probably the first, of the new Finnish towns. The first fort there dates to about 1280 (destroyed by Russian attackers from Novgorod in 1318; quickly rebuilt; the main structure seen today dates to the 1500s). Turku's modern name in Finnish is Turun; the Swedes called it Åbo; watch for it in the narrative to come, because by whatever name it would play a key role in the development of modern Finnish nationalism. A Swedish campaign to forcibly convert Karelia, the eastern part of the Finnish population (that wrapped around the northern half of Lake Ladoga), resulted in the 1293 building of a fort at Viibori (Vyborg in the Russian),[GE11] at the head of a sheltered inlet near the end of the Gulf of Finland. It was fought over by Sweden and Novgorod for thirty years, before a treaty gave it to Sweden. Meantime a town grew up here, thriving on trade, and it quickly became the second city of the Finnish land after Turku. By the end of the Middle Ages six important coastal towns had been created; Porvoo[GE12] was probably the next most important of these, historically speaking.

Turku, logically enough, became the seat of the first bishopric of the Finnish region. From about 1370 on the bishops were all native speakers of Finnish, the Catholic Church hierarchy obviously seeing that to be an advantage in spreading the faith among the general population there. And Finland seemed to settle down contentedly with Catholicism; there was little of the irritation with it that convulsed much of central and northwestern Europe (more in the following chapter on such convulsion in Czech lands). That Finland became Lutheran is owing more to Swedish history than to Finnish history proper!

---

9. GE Layer 9 is a Path titled "A Viking trade/raiding route." Symbolized by a purple line, it runs along the northern short of the Gulf of Finland, forty miles up the Neva River to the Lake Ladoga (Europe's largest lake) and, in this version, up the Volkhov River to Novgorod. At the time, the Finnish-speaking population wrapped around the west, north, and east sides of Lake Ladoga.

10. GE Layer 10 is a Placemark referencing Turku in general and Turku Castle in particular; click on Panoramio icon underneath Pushpin icon, titled "Turku Castle / Turun Linna / Burg zu Turku."

11. GE Layer 11 is a Placemark referencing Viibori/Vyborg. Click on Panoramio icon under pointer, titled "Выборгский замок," for close-up of island castle guarding narrow river mouth.

12. GE Layer 12 is a Placemark referencing Porvoo.

The Kingdom of Sweden and the Reformation

Around 1400 it appeared that a single Scandinavian state might be coming into existence. It made some sense in terms of linguistic unity (except for Finland!); back then the Norwegian and the Swedish languages were very close, just different dialects, and Danish was not much different. The union of Denmark, Norway, and Sweden was seemingly effected in the Kalmar Union of 1397 (named for a castle on the east coast of today's Sweden[GE¹³]). It was brought about by the remarkable Queen Margareth I of Denmark, who by marriage, diplomacy, and war over about forty years created this sort of Scandinavian "United Kingdom"—separate in terms of local law and custom, united in foreign policy and monarchy. It even included Iceland and coastal Greenland settlements as well.

By this time Finland was tied closely enough to the rest of Scandinavia to be brought in as a part of it, despite its very different language. By 1460, the rising state of Moscow had taken over Novgorod. Facing this more dangerous enemy, which renewed Novgorod's old claims to Viibori/Vyborg, Finland more and more appreciated being in the Kalmar Union, which invested in Viibori's defense.

The Kalmar Union, however, lasted little more than a century. Communication difficulties over long distances, personal ambitions by regional figures, and finally the Reformation all combined to kill it. In the early 1500s Sweden would break away from the Union, and take Finland with it.

There had been unrest in Sweden since the mid-1400s, something of a backlash against Danish and German influence (and particularly against the Hanseatic League, an alliance of commercial cities which exercised a virtual regional trade monopoly on Europe's northern coast) in Sweden. Gustavus Vasa, from a family long opposed to the Kalmar Union, led the resistance. After 1517–1521 events in the Germanies with Martin Luther, there was a Protestant option in politics for any ruler in central or northern Europe faced with determined opposition from church hierarchy and/or social classes allied with that hierarchy. Gustavus Vasa, crowned King of Sweden in 1523, played that Protestant card in 1527, eventually making himself head of an independent national church (the way Henry VIII did about the same time in England). His personal embrace of Lutheranism may have been sincere, but it also enabled him to seize rich Catholic holdings. At first Lutheranism was only popular around his capital city of Uppsala, but in the remaining decades of his rule (to 1560) it spread widely. To his supporters he seemed firm of character; to his enemies he was a dictatorial tyrant. Undeniably he set in motion the modern Swedish monarchy—and pulled into its orbit what is today Finland as well. It was King Gustavus Vasa who in 1550 established Helsinki[GE¹⁴] as close to opposite Tallinn on the south shore of the Gulf of Finland as he could find a good harbor, hoping to steal its trade.

For most of the next three centuries, upwardly mobile Finns increasingly taught their children Swedish, the language of government and high society, and sent them to schools in Sweden. Swedish administrators came to live in the major towns of Finland, and of course those who could speak Swedish with them got preferential treatment. Soon upper- and middle-class Finns were denationalized, at least in terms of language.

Mikael Agricola

But there was a counter-current of the Reformation that, at the same time the Finnish language was being abandoned from the top of society down, began to establish it on new foundations. One theme of the Reformation—maybe the single most important, in terms of social transformation—was putting the Bible into the hands of everyday people. Such everyday people, not being able to read Latin, needed the scripture in the vernacular, and some quick lessons in how to read. A certain Mikael Agricola (1510–1557) embraced that as his lifetime task for the Finns.

A bright student from a family of well-to-do farmers near the southern coast, he was sent to Viibori/Vyborg for Latin school. While there he took the last name "Agricola," meaning "Farmer" in Latin. When he was eighteen—just after King Gustavus Vasa proclaimed an independent national church for the kingdom—he went to study in Turku, which by this time amounted to the capital of the Finnish side of the Swedish kingdom. When Agricola was twenty-six he was chosen by church authorities to go study in Wittenberg itself, taking classes

---

13. GE Layer 13 is a Placemark referencing Kalmar Castle, where the Union was declared.
14. GE Layer 14 is a Placemark referencing Helsinki, framing a view showing entire Gulf of Finland.

with Luther and Melancthon. In 1537 he began translating the New Testament into Finnish (on Luther's model, obviously; Luther had translated it into German while holed up at the Castle of Wartburg in 1521–22). Realizing that some elementary reading lessons needed to come first, Agricola published an "ABC Book" in 1543. Then came a Prayer Book in 1544, the whole New Testament in 1548, and the Psalms in 1551—all in Finnish and indeed the first works ever published in Finnish.

Mikael Agricola's motivation was primarily religious. He had no use at all for the great oral epics still being told in the countryside, seeing them as celebrations of the gods of a pagan religion. His work, however, had the effect of calling attention to Finns as "a linguistically *separate* people,"[3] which would be a foundation on which to build a later Romantic nationalism. He died on the south coast of what was then Swedish territory, but which since 1721 has been Russian territory.[GE[15]]

Sweden as the local great power: The Thirty Years' War

By the late 1500s Muscovy's star was sinking, with the irrational end of Ivan the Terrible's reign, and the civil wars and foreign invasions of the Time of Troubles from 1598–1613. Sweden's star was rising. There is still a good deal of physical evidence from this era in eastern Finland, the side that fronted Russian power. In the 1570s, for example, an important Finnish leader built a castle in Russian-claimed territory, Olaf's Castle (Olavenlinna),[GE[16]] often called the best preserved medieval fort in northern Europe and still a must-see on the tourist circuit of Finland.

Sweden's real coming out on the great power stage, however, was in the Thirty Years' War of 1618–1648, a complex war that involved much of Europe. Its main theme, overall, was a Protestant vs. Catholic struggle in the lands of the Holy Roman Empire. It began with a Protestant rising in Prague in 1618 that was quickly put down at the 1620 Battle of White Mountain near Prague (more detail in the following chapter). In 1625 Denmark entered the war on the side of the Protestants, but was defeated by 1629. Then in 1630 King Gustavus Adolphus II of Sweden, with an army of Swedes and Finns including the feared Finnish cavalry (and well funded by subsidies from France, a Catholic power supporting the Protestant side for its own reasons of international power balance), joined the war on behalf of the autonomy of north German Protestant states inside the Holy Roman Empire. The Battle of Breitenfeld[GE[17]] in 1631 was the first major Protestant victory of the war. The Battle of Lützen[GE[18]] in 1632 was also a Protestant victory, driving the Catholic forces out of Saxony, though the Swedish king was killed there. The long war drug on until 1648, but those 1631–32 battles that had protected the autonomy of the Protestant states in the north of the Holy Roman Empire fairly well set the tone for the Peace of Westphalia.

None of the Thirty Years' War was fought on Finnish territory, for which the Finns were undoubtedly thankful (some parts of the Germanies lost upwards of 50 percent of their population!). But there were some interesting developments in Finland during these years. Most Swedish administrators of Finnish parts of the kingdom were just there as part of a move up the chain of command, the desired apex of which was reassignment in Sweden proper, especially the capital at Uppsala (or nearby Stockholm, after it became capital in 1634). But an occasional Swedish administrator fell in love with the region and the people, and one such was Count Per Brahe, Governor-General of Finland from 1637–40 and again from 1648–54. He had been a respected field officer in the Swedish phase of the Thirty Years' War, and after the death of the King, became one of the most important political leaders. He launched a series of reforms in Finland, set up a postal system, and established new towns. Perhaps most important of all, in 1640 he founded the University of Turku (ancestor of today's University of Helsinki), ever more the premier academic institution of the land. From 1646 until his death in 1680 he served as its first Rector, or President. On a statue of him standing today in Turku is

---

15. GE Layer 15 is a Placemark referencing a photo of a memorial stone for Agricola; zoom out and notice how deep it is in today's Russia.

16. GE Layer 16 is a Placemark referencing Olavenlinna; click on Panoramio icon underneath pointer titled "Medieval Olavenlinna castle in Savonlinna" for one good view.

17. GE Layer 17 is a Placemark referencing the battlefield of Breitenfeld.

18. GE Layer 18 is a Placemark referencing the battlefield of Lützen.

engraved a phrase of his: "I was well pleased with the land, and the land was well pleased with me." He is even remembered favorably in the popular Finnish proverb, "To come in Count's time," meaning to arrive just when you should have come, perfect timing.

Russia replaces Sweden as the local great power: The Great Northern War

With the emergence of Peter the Great in Russia, beginning with his actual active ruling in 1692, the stars of Sweden and Russia reversed directions.

The Great Northern War of 1700–1721 you have already briefly seen in the Russia chapter. Denmark, Poland, and Russia declared war on Sweden, which was led by an eighteen-year-old, King Charles XII—presumably easy pickings. With lightning blows, however, this young military genius knocked Denmark out of the war, and in 1700 defeated a much more numerous Russian army at Narva[GE19], a key fort on the south shore of the Gulf of Finland. Then instead of trying to finish off Russia, by diplomacy or military power, Charles fought his way down through Poland and gave Tsar Peter I eight years to regroup. In 1703 Peter took the little fort of Nevanlinna (Neva Fort) in the swampy islands at the mouth of the Neva, just eighty miles east of Narva, and proclaimed the beginning of St. Petersburg there. In 1709 the main Swedish army was destroyed by the Russians at Poltava, deep into today's Ukraine. From Turkey and then the Germanies Charles XII tried to keep up the war, but late in 1718 he was killed by a bullet to the head, possibly from his own side. The larger significance of the war was that Sweden was replaced as the great power of the north by Russia.

For our story, however, an important part is what happened directly to Finland. In these times Sweden proper had a population of somewhere around a million, and Finland about half-a-million. More than a third of the soldiers of Swedish armies were Finns, marched here and there at Charles XII's whim, and almost never stationed in direct defense of hearth and home. After Poltava in 1709, Charles could have negotiated and saved much of Sweden-Finland, but he refused to do so. In 1710 the Russians conquered three key Sweden-owned port cities in the Gulf of Finland and nearby Baltic Sea: Tallinn (capital of Estonia today) and Riga (capital of Latvia today) on the southern shore, and Viibori/Vyborg on the northern shore—still the second city of the Finnish land after Turku. By 1713, with still no move towards peace by Charles XII and the war going well elsewhere for the Russians, the Russian navy landed troops near Helsinki and headed west along the coastal road. Everything east of Turku was abandoned by the Finns. When the Russians circled north through the interior, the Swedish-Finnish army put up a defense at Napue[GE20] to protect the coastal towns on the Gulf of Bothnia. It was a hard-fought battle, but the Russians eventually crushed the last army opposing them in Finland, and the few survivors fled up and around the Gulf of Bothnia to Sweden. Russia occupied all Finland for eight full years, until the 1721 treaty that formally ended the war. Finns called the occupation "The Great Wrath." Charles XII, for all that he threw away a commanding Swedish position in the north, is generally still remembered favorably by Swedes as a dramatic boy military genius of legendary bravery and endurance. Finns generally have no such positive memories; Finnish soldiers had died for his egotistical dreams, and their whole homeland suffered a brutal military occupation because of him.

In the treaty of 1721, territorial losses of Finnish-speaking lands included that Karelian band of territory that wrapped around the northern half of Lake Ladoga, plus the northeast coast of the Gulf of Finland, including the key port of Vyborg.[GE21] In 1741 Sweden inadvisably declared war on Russia again. The Swedish army was smashed in one battle, and in the 1743 peace signed at Turku a slice of coast and hinterland (adjoining the 1721 Vyborg and Ladoga slice) was taken by Russia.[GE22] Empress Elizabeth of Russia also hinted broadly that she wouldn't mind seeing Finland independent. Sweden tried to counter this by building new defenses, most spectacularly in 1748 with the construction of Sveaborg ("The Fortress of Sweden")[GE23] to

---

19. GE Layer 19 is a Placemark referencing Narva.

20. GE Layer 20 is a Placemark referencing Napue.

21. GE Layer 21 is a Folder titled "1721 Russian gains." It includes a Polygon showing in orange the territory taken by Russia in 1721, and a Placemark showing Viibori/Vyborg's place in it.

22. GE Layer 22 is a Polygon showing in rose the adjoining territory taken by Russia in 1743.

23. GE Layer 23 is a Placemark referencing Sveaborg, today's Suomenlinna ("Fortress of Finland!").

guard Helsinki. A cluster of six little islands a mile or so from the Helsinki waterfront were transformed into an impressive fortress, "The Gibraltar of the North."

If you were Finnish, however, it generally made for a new lack of security, knowing you could not really depend on Sweden for defense against Russia. With this came a corresponding growth in Finnish self-identity.

The Fennophiles

By the 1600s there were Finnish antiquarians and collectors who were gathering proverbs and legends, as there were in many other regions of Europe (since the word "folklore" had not been invented as yet, these were generally called "popular antiquities"). One of these Finnish collectors was Juhana Cajanus. Around 1674 he recorded some local legends dealing with the giant Kaleva and his twelve sons, whose achievements included the conquest of all Russia. Here Vainamoinen and Ilmarinen, later heroes of the *Kalevala*, were identified as two of these sons—not (pagan) gods, as Agricola had argued earlier.

Around 1700 the first real Fennophile, Daniel Juslenius, wrote a laudatory history of the Finnish capital, titled *Turku Old and New*. It argued that, among other accomplishments, Finnish culture had come first and had inspired Greek and Roman civilization. Any particular criticisms that had been made of Finns and Finland in the past, he proved, or claimed to prove, just the opposite. Juslenius was born in 1676 in Mynämäki,[GE24] less than twenty miles northwest of Turku, making him about thirty-four years old when this was written—old enough to know better! But he had apparently heard a Swedish-born professor at the University of Turku argue that all Finns ought to give up Finnish and adopt the Swedish language for the good of the realm, and *Turku Old and New* was a measure of how strongly he reacted against that argument. As ludicrous as his main argument was in 1700, he developed into a more serious scholar later in life. He mastered Greek and Latin as well as Finnish, and by his late forties became himself Professor of Languages at the University of Turku. He eventually rose to be Bishop. By 1745 he had created the first dictionary of the Finnish language.

The French Enlightenment had a clear impact on Finland, too, as regional studies dealing with practical matters of roads and trade but also history and folklore were published—in the same spirit as Diderot's *Encyclopédie* of 1757–1771. There was some patriotism in this; the studies were mostly by earnest young scholars trying to do something for the country.

Then by the 1770s the Enlightenment forces in Finland began to weaken as the first waves of pre-Romanticism arrived. British literature played some part, including MacPherson's "Poems of Ossian" (1760–65), and Bishop Percy's "Reliques of Ancient English Poetry" (1765) with its verses from old English and Scottish ballads. And just at this transition from Enlightenment to Romanticism stood the greatest Finnish scholar of the age, Henrik Gabriel Porthan (1739–1804). On the one hand he challenged the made-up, exaggerated claims of the earlier Fennophiles (some of them from his great-uncle, Daniel Juslenius!), but on the other he really admired folk poetry, and used it in historical reconstruction better than anyone had up to that time.

Porthan was born well inland, in the town of Vitassari.[GE25] He was attending Turku University by the time he was fifteen, and graduated in 1760. For a time he gave private lessons in elocution and rhetoric, but eventually was made university librarian, and put together the nucleus of what would become the Finnish National Library.

By Porthan's time the official classes were all Swedish speakers, and only the peasant farmers still spoke Finnish. Between 1766 and 1778 he wrote a series of articles (in scholarly Latin) called *De poësi Fennica*. "I consider it a shame," he said, "not only that a native Finn does not know our poetry, but also that he doesn't admire it." You can feel the Romantic quotient of his thought in this passage:

> Our peasants too particularly cultivate these [old poems], though they receive no help from literature; among our people this art is naturally much older than literature. What's more, from the best and most competent of these peasants' poems one can, as from a clear and unspoiled spring, and more accurately than from other sources, draw and distinguish the [people's] real ancient spirit, particularly since the peasants do not change and corrupt the indigenous nature of our poetry by copying foreign art and mixing it with their own. For these

---

24. GE Layer 24 is a Placemark referencing Mynämäki, framing a view to show its relationship to Turku.

25. GE Layer 25 is a Placemark referencing Vitassarari.

rustic friends of the Muses especially love those poems they have inherited from their forefathers; these they value, willingly listen to, learn, sing, and are themselves able to compose—merely with the aid of the enthusiasm of their own thought and own fertile imagination.[4]

One of the things that made Porthan different was that he did not only communicate with Latin-language scholars. He was a moving force in the Aurora Society, a group working to advance Finnish culture. In 1771 this group started Finland's first newspaper to spread its ideals.

Napoleonic wars and Russian control

Napoleon crowned himself Emperor in 1804, and soon imperial Napoleonic armies and Napoleonic diplomacy were setting in motion waves that would wash over Finland. In 1805 he destroyed the main Austrian and Russian armies at Austerlitz, and in 1806 destroyed the main Prussian army at Jena and Auerstadt, as you saw in the German chapter. But Napoleon's drive east had not ended there. In June 1807 the Russians opposed him again at Friedland,[GE26] and again they were sharply defeated. A few weeks later in July, on a raft in the Neman River near a town then called Tilsit,[GE27] he got a promise from Emperor Alexander I of Russia and from King Frederick William III of Prussia (who had only half a country left) to join him in a war on Sweden and Great Britain. Early in 1808 Russia launched an invasion of the Finnish half of Sweden-Finland. It was generally a replay of the Russian invasion and occupation of Finland from 1710–21, back in the Great Northern War almost a century earlier.

With most of the Swedish army withdrawn to protect Sweden proper, the Finns had to shoulder the whole burden of defense. Outnumbered by the Russians, they gradually retreated west. Sveaborg, the "Gibraltar of the North" that guarded Helsinki, was puzzlingly surrendered to the Russians with hardly a fight. A last-minute counterattack on the Russians near the Gulf of Bothnia coast forced the overextended Russian army to withdraw south for awhile—an attack at Lapua[GE28] fondly remembered by Finnish patriotic writers later—but Russian forces by this time were at least twice as numerous as the Finnish ones, and by winter the whole country was occupied. During the first two weeks of October of that same 1808, with the war all but decided, Alexander I met Napoleon again, at Erfurt in the central Germanies.[GE29] Here most of the terms of Tilsit were renewed, and here Napoleon formally agreed to what he had hinted before at Tilsit, that Russia should have Finland permanently. Given the waning fortunes of Sweden and the waxing fortunes of Russia over the past century or so, this probably came as no great surprise to informed observers. Still, for Finns, it changed many things both obvious and subtle.

So in 1809 Finland came into the Russian Empire, but with some autonomy. It was to be a "Grand Duchy" (including "Old Finland," the pieces of territory taken by Russia in 1721 and 1743—a generous gesture) with its own constitution, and the Russian Emperor himself would be the Grand Duke. He would appoint the entire administration, but local laws would continue in effect and a limited legislature would retain some power. There would be no attempt to do away with the official Lutheran church or Lutheranism. Alexander I summoned representatives of the Four Estates of Finland—the nobility, clergy, townsmen, and peasant farmers—and had them meet at Porvoo ("The Diet of Porvoo," it was officially called, diet being an old word for an assembly of elected representatives). Here the representatives took an oath of allegiance to him, and he in turn promised to rule Finland through the existing Constitution.

In the century or so of Russian control, however, there would be increasing pressure on Finland to "Russify" its culture. The Russian government believed that those upwardly-mobile Finnish families that had taught their children Swedish before would just switch to Russian. By this time, however, the yeast of Romantic nationalism had begun to work, and there was an attractive alternative.

---

26. GE Layer 26 is a Placemark referencing Friedland with a white star icon, framed in a general view of northern Europe.

27. GE Layer 27 is a Placemark referencing Tilsit, shown by a white Pushpin icon.

28. GE Layer 28 is a red star Placemark at Lapua.

29. GE Layer 29 is a Placemark referencing Erfurt, in the central Germanies that were now firmly under Napoleon's control; also shown by a white Pushpin icon.

The Turku Romantics

Porthan, Herder's close contemporary, had in parallel with Herder developed the idea that a nation grows organically, true to its original seedtime, and that folklore preserves the original genius of the culture best. The explosive element Herder added to that, however, was the idea that struggling modern nations (struggling because they had fallen away from their seedtime culture) could build future institutions of great strength on those old cultural foundations, and so revive themselves and flourish.[5] It was this full gospel of Herder now reaching Finnish intellectuals, plus the shock of transfer to Russian control in 1809, that triggered the strongest cultural nationalism to date.

It emerged at the country's primary university, the University of Turku, with four upper-class, Swedish-speaking students, all born between 1791 and 1796.[GE30] One of these four, Anders Johan Sjögren (1794–1855), had begun reading Herder's *Andreastea* in 1812 while still in prep school in Porvoo. In his diary he wrote that Herder's "writings held a magic charm for me . . . I shall never forget the impression it made on me."[6] It was suddenly obvious to him that Finland, like Germany, was trying to graft on to the root of its living culture a foreign top, and needed instead to return to its own innate life, its own language and folk culture. Two years later, by then an undergraduate at Turku University, he made a pact with like-minded fellow student Abraham Poppius (1793–1866):

> . . .they clasped hands and swore to collect from the Finnish folk the old songs and tales which would illuminate the life of ancient Finland and inspire their countrymen with a patriotic regard for their fatherland and a desire to work for its survival.[7]

Two other Swedish-speaking Turku University students answered the call of these first two to collect Finnish proverbs, folktales, legends, and such: they were Carl Axel Gottlund (1796–1875) and Adolf Ivar Arwidsson (1791–1858). In 1817–1818 these two and Poppius all attended Sweden's Uppsala University.[GE31] They were fascinated by the Romantic researches into the Gothic past of Scandinavia, though generally angered by the refusal of Swedish academics to see a similar rich past in the Finnish heritage.

Gottlund, in particular, stayed long in Sweden. He rediscovered and did folklore field work among the "Forest Finns" on field trips in 1817 to Dalarna,[GE32] and in 1820–21 to Värmland.[GE33] These were the descendants of Finnish farmers who had been encouraged to settle the forest frontier with Norway, to cement Sweden's hold thereof back in imperial days. Forbidden in later years to do their traditional slash-and-burn agriculture, they were a despised minority in danger of losing their land. Gottland became their champion, and only returned to Finland in 1834. Sometime during this period, he predicted that it would be possible to collect the folk poems and work them into a larger whole, and so create "a new Homer, Ossian, or Nibelungenlied" (the Ossianic forgeries from Scotland having not yet been detected as such). A poet himself, he is mainly remembered in Finland for his folk-based, Romantic poems.

Adolf Ivar Arwidsson, the fourth young intellectual, was the oldest of the group. Already attending the college preparatory school at Porvoo in 1809, he was actually a delegate to the Diet of Porvoo that year. He graduated from Turku University with a degree in philosophy in 1814, the same year Sjögren and Poppius vowed their famous vow, but stayed on working on his doctorate until 1817. He then became a Lecturer (Assistant Professor would be the closest U.S. equivalent) there. Ardwisson was the most strident of the four about a Finnish language revival—although all of them were still writing mainly in Swedish—and started a newspaper that hinted at political independence. This was the Age of Metternich in Europe, however, with its anti-nationalism

---

30. GE Layer 30 is a Folder titled "Lives of the Turku Romantics." Inside are four separate Folders, one each on Sjögren, Poppius, Gottlund, and Arwidsson, with Placemarks for birthplaces and other key sites of their lives. They all, of course, attended Turku University; three of them attended Uppsala University in Sweden in the year 1817–18; most of them went to a good college preparatory school in Porvoo, and Poppius and Gottlund were raised in the same small town, Juva. Explore as needed to illustrate the narrative of the next few paragraphs.

31. GE Layer 31 is a Placemark referencing Uppsala University.

32. GE Layer 32 is a Placemark at Dalarna, Sweden.

33. GE Layer 33 is a Placemark at Värmland, Sweden.

and anti-Liberal policies that we talked about in Chapter 3. In 1821 the government suppressed his paper and in 1822 Ardwisson lost his university position. Most of his life he spent exiled from Russian-controlled Finland. In the 1850s he was allowed to return, and on a nostalgic circle of the country he fell sick and died at Vyborg. The phrase he is best remembered for is this: "We're no longer Swedes, and we don't want to become Russians: so let's become Finns."

These were the "Turku Romantics", and they imbued the next generation with the mission of creating "a nation proud of its common heritage, speaking a common tongue, and producing once again a body of literature reflecting the national soul."[8]

The freshman class of 1822: Runeberg, Snellman, and Lönnrot

Three students who would collectively change the Finnish national consciousness came to the University of Turku as entering freshmen in the fall of 1822. They were very different by temperament and by achievements, which gave the nationalist agenda they pushed great breadth.

Johan Ludvig Runeberg (1805–1877) was born at Jakobstad, a northerly town on the Gulf of Bothnia. He went to school at two other towns on the same coast, and was seventeen when he entered Turku University. He was a gifted linguist, and for almost forty years taught Latin literature at the Porvoo Gymnasium. But by avocation—inspired of course by the Turku Romantics—he was a poet who celebrated the Finnish rural life. His most famous poem, written mainly in the 1850s about the 1808–9 Swedish War, was called "The Tales of Ensign Stål." The first section of it, "Our Land" (*Maame* in Finnish), later became the words of the national anthem.[GE34] "Thy blossom in the bud laid low, Yet ripened shall upspring," goes one line.

Johan Wilhelm Snellman (1806–1881) was born in Stockholm, son of a ship's captain, but when he was six years old or so the family moved to Kokkola, a coastal town well up into the Gulf of Bothnia.[GE35] At Turku University after 1822, he was early on converted to the Finnish language movement, saying that it was up to the educated elite to take the language of 85 percent of the country and turn it into a sophisticated language that could be used for any scientific or humanist endeavor. After graduation he taught at the university (now moved to Helsinki) until 1838, when the government removed him for his radical tendencies. He studied in Germany and in Sweden for a few years, but even after his return, the government still would not let him teach at Helsinki.

So Snellman took a modest teaching post at Kuopio, well up into the lake district of Finland, and became a modern publicist. In 1844 he started two newspapers, one in Finnish ("The Farmer's Friend") for the general public, and one in Swedish for the educated elite. The paper for intellectuals was suppressed in 1846 for its radicalism. By 1850 Snellman moved to Helsinki. With the death of Emperor Nicholas I in 1855, and the Great Reforms soon instituted by Alexander II, the atmosphere in Finland changed enough so that Snellman finally got his professorate at Helsinki University. For a time he was Finance Minister, and his work for a separate Finnish currency as well as language paid off, as you'll see.

Elias Lönnrot (1802–1884) became the most famous name of this generation, so let's follow his life in a little more detail. He was born (and died) in the little town of Sammatti,[GE36] and was sent some thirty miles southwest to the port city of Tamisaari[GE37] to study Latin and Swedish. He entered the University of Turku in 1822 as a medical student, but was quickly also attracted to folklore studies. He was still a student there in 1827 when the University's buildings burned (along with most of the city) and the whole school was moved to the new capital, Helsinki.[GE38] The next year he did his first folklore collecting in Karelia, the part of Finland

34. GE Layer 34 is a Folder titled "Life of Runeberg," with Placemarks for the various sites associated with his life; but the Folder seemed a good place to enter the YouTube website of the Finnish National Anthem, with words printed in Finnish and English: http://www.youtube.com/watch?v=RKRvD5i44Ko

35. GE Layer 35 is a Folder titled "life of Snellman," with Placemarks for the various sites associated with his life.

36. GE Layer 36 is a Placemark referencing Sammatti; surprisingly, there are no Photos icons relating to his life and death here. All these sites connected with Lönnrot's life are shown in light green, to let the pattern of his life show distinctly.

37. GE Layer 37 is a Placemark referencing Tamisaari.

38. GE Layer 38 is a Placemark referencing today's University of Helsinki.

next to Russia, a region especially rich in folksong.[GE39] In 1831, just before he left the capital to begin practicing medicine, Lönnrot and friends created the Finnish Literature Society to sponsor more fieldwork. In the summer of 1832 he crossed the border of the Russian Empire into East Karelia, expanding his collecting to Finnish speakers there, and found one village particularly rich in songs about the old epic heroes.[GE40] Late in 1833, inspired by the ability of folk singers to combine different songs about one folk hero into a longer whole, he began to scissor-and-paste together a super epic combining all the major folk heroes. On February 28, 1835, it was published: *The Kalevala, or Ancient Karelian Poems from the Ancient Times of the Finnish Nation.* After graduation from medical school, Lönnrot became district medical officer of the Kainuu region of central Finland, based in the town of Kajaani.[GE41] He continued his collecting from this base, with occasional forays east into Karelia. Younger collectors gave him more folklore material, and when he put out the second edition of the *Kalevala* in 1849 (the one in most libraries today) it ran twice the size of the first.

It may not have been pure invention, like MacPherson's Ossianic Poems (or Hanka's supposed Czech epics, as you'll see in the next chapter), but it was a "folk epic" only by the loosest of standards. Lönnrot shuffled not only verses but lines around, and since different parts of it were in different dialects, actually rewrote a lot of it to smooth out dialect differences. That mattered not a whit to young Finnish intellectuals. In the 1830s having an epic meant that you as a folk group had such a dignified heritage that you deserved a state of your own. They had just been given their own epic, the greatest gift they could have wished for, and were in no mood to examine it for shortcomings. Fifty years later another Finnish scholar remembered the impact that the *Kalevala* had on his generation:

> Let us imagine a poor, unknown boy raised in the wilderness, who steps out into the world with a burning desire to take part in mankind's great battle for the promotion of everything beautiful, good, and noble. But all look at him with amazement, laugh at his unfamiliar movement, ask with scorn who he is that he imagines himself able to stand beside so many highborn and experienced heroes and [ask] how he can prove his ability [to perform] such great tasks. And then a good spirit suddenly puts in his hand a beautiful, brightly sparkling sword, a legacy of his father, at the same time an unquestionable witness of his royal lineage and a powerful weapon for his own future heroic deeds. And . . . [then] the scorn and laughter change to respect [and] fascination, and the young man himself feels his shyness giving way to hopeful bravery. Let us picture all this; only then can we fully know what kind of gift Lönnrot has given to his people in the *Kalevala*.[9]

Publication of the *Kalevala* was an enormous spur to the teaching of the Finnish language. When in 1850 the Russian Empire decreed that no books were to be published in Finnish except those of religious instruction and those necessary for economic development, consciousness about Finnish was already such that it caused an outcry. There were secondary schools in it by mid-century, at least one grammar school where the teaching was in Finnish by 1858. Soon there were "folk schools" for young adults on the order of the Danish "folk high schools," using the vernacular language. In the year the epic was first published, 1835, there was a single Finnish-language newspaper in the country; on its fiftieth anniversary in 1885 there were thirty-one; on its seventy-fifth anniversary in 1910 there were eighty-six.[10]

Defense of the *Kalevala*

When the supposedly Celtic Ossianic Poems were discovered to be forgeries later, the *Kalevala* came under attack as well. It was emotionally too valuable for Finns to give up, yet the whole was so obviously a scissored-and-pasted creation of Lonnrot's that had never existed before 1835. The result was a brilliant new defense of the antiquity of its parts, a whole school of scholarship called "the historic-geographic method" mainly asso-

39. GE Layer 39 is a Path symbolizing in light green that first major collecting trip. It is based mainly on the map on pp. x–xi of *The Kalevala, Or Poems of the Kalevala District Compiled by Elias Lönnrot*, trans. Peabody Magoun, Jr. (Cambridge, MA & London: Harvard University Press, 1963).
40. GE Layer 40 is a Placemark referencing the village of Vuokkiniemi (Voknovolok).
41. GE Layer 41 is a Placemark referencing Kajaani.

ciated with Julius Krohn. Let us plot all the examples of a single folktale, said he, on a map. Then let us look for regional sub-groups of the tale and possible local explanations for these particular variations. If one sub-group of the tale is (a) most general, and (b) most widespread, then plausibly it is the oldest version of the tale. By the end of the century, so many variations of so many tales had been collected by enthusiastic Finnish folktale collectors that they outgrew the old Grimms' system of classification (referring to the motif "princess kisses frog who turns into handsome prince," as "see Grimms' Fairy Tale No. One," for example). Antti Aarne, the latest defender of the antiquity of Finnish folklore, came up with a whole new "type and motif" classification system for folktales and folktale elements that eventually ran to nine volumes! Finnish folk poetry was the purest statement of everything truly Finnish: to question that in Finland after mid-century was as if you questioned Holy Scripture in church.

Cultural nationalism was clearly at work in Finland during the nineteenth century; political nationalism lagged behind.

Russian imperial politics

Compared to Poland, Finland was a relatively tranquil piece of the Russian Empire in most of the nineteenth century. Even in 1848, for example, when much of central Europe blew up in Liberal-National revolutions, the only nationalist happening worth notice in Finland was the first public singing of what would become the national anthem (Runeberg's poem) by students at the University of Helsinki's spring festival. This was partly because for most of the century Russia gave Finland at least the trappings of autonomy.

When Emperor Alexander I made Helsinki the capital, he endowed it a magnificent governmental center. [GE[42]] North of a central "Senate Square" his chief architect planned a huge Lutheran Cathedral. Finally built in the reign of Emperor Nicholas I, it was named St. Nicholas for his name-day saint—but was Lutheran, not Russian Orthodox. A Senate building was on the east (Finns appreciated the designation; it meant something parallel to the Russian imperial Senate, not under it!), today's Government Palace. Then after the 1827 fire in Turku that burned university buildings and most of the city down, the country's premier university was moved to Helsinki, with its main building fronting the west side of the square.

In terms of infrastructure, the Saimaa Canal[GE[43]] was finished by 1856, connecting the great eastern chain of lakes with the port city of Vyborg. Timber exports brought a new prosperity to the whole country in the following decades. By 1860 Finland had been allowed its own currency (the Finnish mark began to circulate in 1865) and version of a national bank, separate from the ruble. In 1863 Emperor Alexander II himself visited a military encampment near Hämeenlinna, and made a public statement favoring making the Finnish language the equal of Swedish in all governmental offices. With Poland in full revolt that year, and Finland staying quiet, in September Alexander summoned the Finnish Diet to Helsinki to approve economic reforms he had drafted. It was the first meeting of the Diet since the Diet at Porvoo in 1809. A mainline railroad connected Helsinki with St. Petersburg by 1870. You can see the hand of J. V. Snellman in much of this, as well as the generally friendly attitude of Emperor Alexander II (whose statue still stands in the main square of Helsinki,[GE[44]] despite all the Finnish-Russian friction before and since).

A new and less harmonious phase of relationship with Russia, however, began in 1874 with Russia's adoption of the draft army. You have seen the logic of universal military conscription at work—in France, in the Prussian Reforms, and in Russia itself, in previous chapters, and will see it again in some future chapters (Japan got its draft army in that same 1874, for example). Everyman a patriotic citizen, every citizen a potential patri-

---

42. GE Layer 42 is a Folder titled "Senate Square, Helskinki." It includes three Placemarks, suggesting views of St. Nicholas Cathedral, the Government Palace, and the main university building; though there are many interesting Photos icons to peruse, including three Cities 360 ones scattered around Senate Square. On the east side was the main governmental building. On the west is the main building of Helsinki University.

43. GE Layer 43 is a Path in aqua symbolizing the Saimaa Canal. It is still a most active waterway, and apparently a favorite place for tourists and locals to take photographs; zooming in along the canal reveals lots and lots of Photos icons. Slightly less than half its approximately forty miles is in today's Finland.

44. GE Layer 44 is a Placemark referencing a Panoramio icon with a good picture of the statue; click under pointer on the icon titled "Statue of Alexander II - A foggy January day picture."

otic soldier: it gives a whole new power dimension to the modern state. But what of minorities that aspired to have their own states? If they accepted this it would make their own eventual absorption by the larger state much more likely. By 1878 Finnish leaders got Emperor Alexander II's government to agree to a compromise, a Finnish conscription army inside the army of the Russian Empire but with some autonomy—Finnish officers, shorter terms of army duty, and a changing of the wording of the law saying it was for defense of "throne and empire" to "throne and fatherland." The Russians could take "fatherland" any way they wanted, but Finns understood it to mean the Finnish part of the army would only be used to defend the territory of Finland proper.

With the assassination of Alexander II in 1881, extreme Russian nationalism began to be reflected more and more in government. Alexander III's regime secretly prepared a plan to dissolve the Finnish part of the army in the greater Russian army, though he died in 1894 before it could be put into effect. When Finland got the hard-line Russifier Nicholas Bobrikov as Governor-General in 1898, the situation there changed dramatically. A quick timetable was set up for Russian to become the language of administration and schools, and for the separate Finnish currency and import taxes to be abandoned in favor of total integration with the greater Russian economy. Then in February of 1899 Emperor Nicholas II signed a law scheduling the phasing out of the autonomous Finnish army. This hit Finland like a bombshell. In one week half a million signatures were gotten on a petition to the Emperor to reverse his verdict, and 500 of the most famous men in Finland hand-delivered it to St. Petersburg. The Emperor refused to see them.

When the army law actually went into effect in July of 1901, with of course the energetic leadership of Governor-General Bobrikov, the whole population of Finland split into "Constitutionalists," who said uphold the traditional constitution and resist unjust laws such as this one, and the "Compliants" who thought resistance would destroy the country. When a peaceful demonstration in Helsinki was dispersed by Cossacks with whips, public opinion began to shift towards the Constitutionalist side. Two-thirds of young Finnish men conscripted refused to serve. In 1903, when the Russian language was made the language of the Finnish Senate, Bobrikov himself took over as its chair. By this time Emperor Nicholas II had given him true dictatorial power, including the power to arrest and banish anyone for any reason or no reason.

By now the country was almost totally alienated from the Russian government. Finnish refugees in Sweden were trying to form a shadow government. Occasional bombs were going off near Russian offices in Finland. Then in June of 1904 a young man named Eugen Schauman, son of a former Senator, shot and mortally wounded Gov.-Gen. Bobrikov as he was entering the Senate house, and then turned his gun on himself. He is generally regarded as a martyr and national hero today in Finland.

By this time the Russian government had much bigger problems than Finland on its hands. Declaring what the government hoped would be a "short, victorious war" in 1904 on Japan, to rally patriotic opinion behind the failing government, had backfired; the war proved to be neither short nor victorious, and triggered the Revolution of 1905. Using this as leverage, Finns got a new constitution within a constitutional monarchy. It included a one-house legislature elected from all men and women age twenty-four and above, one of the most democratic institutions in the world in 1907. Then in 1910 Nicholas II abolished that constitution as well.

Sibelius

This new repression from Russia confronted a heightened sense of national history and culture. Finland's most famous composer, Jean Sibelius, was shaped by these decades. He was born in 1865, in Hämeenlinna,[GE45] into a Swedish-speaking family, but at age eleven was enrolled in the very first Finnish-speaking grammar school (in Hämeenlinna itself). Here he first got interested in the *Kalevala*. As a child he was also already something of a prodigy on the violin.

He enrolled in the study of law at the University of Helsinki in 1885, but soon switched over to the music school there, where he studied for four years. He studied in Berlin and Vienna in 1889 and 1890, but was back to Finland by 1891. All these years, his fascination with the *Kalevala* and the cultural tradition it represented to him grew. In 1892 he premiered *Kullervo*, the first of his many works to draw on the *Kalevala*. That same

---

45. GE Layer 45 is a Placemark referencing the place where he was born; click on Panoramio icon under pointer, titled "Composer Jean Sibelius was born (Friday 8.12.1865) here in Hämeenlinna," for view of carefully preserved house.

year he married into an influential nationalist family; his new father-in-law was a great advocate of Finnish language studies. In the 1890s, with the Russian government tightening its grip on Finland, Sibelius's music increasingly became a focus for patriotic feeling. In 1899, the year of the decree abolishing the Finnish branch of the army, he composed music for a pageant that was a rallying point for patriotic Finns. One of its numbers was *Finlandia*, perhaps his single most famous work despite the great symphonies he wrote in the twentieth century.[11] By 1903 he and his wife had built a house about twenty miles north of Helsinki near Järvenpää; it was named Ainola ("Aino's Realm") after his wife.[GE[46]] Here he enjoyed the natural world of birds and trees and winds with an unusual intensity. He was amazingly productive until about 1926, but then composed virtually nothing for the rest of his long life.

You can see this new national consciousness in architecture, too, about this time, in a style called "National Romanticism." Eliel Saarinen is a name known to U.S. architects because he immigrated here in 1923 and had a huge impact on design. Born in Rantassalmi[GE[47]] in 1873 and educated in Helsinki's University of Technology, he was just over thirty when he designed the famous Helsinki Railway Station. It hints at the age of Bauhaus and Art Nouveau to come, with a nod to Finnish folk woodcarving from the past.[GE[48]]

War and Revolution

When World War I broke out in August of 1914, Finland was not called on for troops; the Russian government remembered its passive resistance from 1901 very well. It was nevertheless a part of an Empire at war, with most of its international trade cut off and a general economic depression. Some Finns saw German help as their only chance for autonomy or even independence, as several thousand young men quietly and illegally went to Germany for military training to produce an anti-Russian Finnish military unit.

In March (new style) of 1917 the Romanov dynasty was overthrown, and for a few months the Provisional Government ruled Russia. It immediately released Finnish political prisoners and restored the constitutional autonomy of Finland. Many Finns had thought their only union with Russia was through the Emperor, and with no Emperor now, Finland logically should be independent. Alexander Kerensky, "the persuader-in-chief," came personally to try to convince the Finns to stay inside a Russian governmental framework. Then on November 7 (n.s.) the Bolsheviks took over the big Russian cities, and on December 6 the Finnish legislature declared Finland's independence—celebrated on that day ever since. It would be nice to report that Finland lived happily (and peacefully) ever after—but Russia was heading for a Red vs. White civil war, and so was Finland.

In the early twentieth century Finland had an active socialist movement, and even an active Social Democratic (read: Marxist) political party. Their center was the city of Tampere,[GE[49]] an industrial city that grew up around the water power of a steep rapids that ran between two lakes. By 1900 this single city ("Manchester of the North") employed a full half of all Finland's industrial workers. Back in the Revolution of 1905 Social Democrat "Red Guards" mainly from Tampere had led a week-long general strike in Finland. When elections were held for that new one-house legislature in 1907 the SDs got 80 seats of the 200 total—a full 40 percent. But even then they were so focused on working class solidarity they could not work with any of the middle class parties, and of course Nicholas II ended any chance of that in 1910.

In mid-November of 1917 Finnish Social Democrats led another general strike, protesting when the legislature's middle class parties voted to pursue independence without dealing with the new Bolshevik government emerging in Moscow. There was a good bit of street violence, with several dozen killed, some by

---

46. GE Layer 46 is a Placemark referencing a photo of Sibelius's home. Also embedded in it is the following website. Click on http://www.youtube.com/watch?v=XojVmivqDrA or do a Google-Video search on "Finlandia" for illustrated audio (approximately 8½ minutes). About 6½ minutes in, you should hear a very familiar melody.

47. GE Layer 47 is a Placemark referencing Rantassalmi.

48. GE Layer 48 is a Placemark referencing the Helsinki station; click on Panoramio icon under pointer, titled "Statues (by Emil Wikström) outside Helsinki Central railway station," for one interesting view.

49. GE Layer 49 is a Placemark referencing Tampere, today the largest inland city not just in Finland but all of Scandinavia.

assassination—generally poisoning future relations between the socialists and the "bourgeois" parties. But Bolshevik ideology held that every "nation" had the right to secede from Russia, carrying out its own revolution (before "finally returning to the fold as a member of the federation of Soviet republics"[12]). So on the last day of 1917, SOVNARKOM (The Council of People's Commissars) recognized Finnish independence. Complicating things a bit were the 40,000 Russian troops still stationed in the country.

Opposing the socialists, and especially opposing the Marxist and pro-Russian Social Democrats, were the pro-German nationalists. Germany for its part was more than willing to help build forces to work inside its enemies' borders (as you saw in the Easter Rising part of the Ireland chapter). So during the war several thousand young Finnish men had secretly made their way to northern Germany, where they were trained and formed into "the 27th Prussian Jaeger Battalion." One historian estimated that more Finns fought in the German army in World War I than in the Russian army.[13] In Finland itself, by the summer of 1917 under the Provisional Government, patriotic and anti-socialist organizations started forming paramilitary groups, disguised under labels such as sports clubs and fire brigades. Collectively these would become the "White Guard," ("Civil Guard," it would be, when adopted by the Senate) anxious and willing to fight the Red Guard.

On its side, by December of 1917 the Red Guard began transforming itself from a rather local institution based at Tampere into a country-wide machine. If, in looking at this general set-up, you think Finland's chances for a peaceful transition to independence were slim, you'd be right. From SOVNARKOM's December 31, 1917, recognition of Finnish independence to the outbreak of Civil War took twenty-eight days.

On January 28, 1918, the Red Guard took over Helsinki and proclaimed Finland a Socialist Workers' Republic. On that same January 28 General Mannerheim, from his base in Vaasa[GE[50]] over near the narrows of the Gulf of Bothnia, led his White Guard-based White Army south against Russian forces. So Finland's Civil War started six months before Russia's did. It ended differently, too, with a White victory.

Baron Mannerheim

Baron Carl Gustav Mannerheim, third son of a Count, was born in Askainen—not far northwest of Turku—in 1867. At age fifteen he was sent to the Finnish Cadet School at Hamina, but dropped out (as a Swedish speaker he learned a bit of Finnish language here, though mostly forgot it later). He lived in Russia for a time, learning Russian fluently. A stint at a college prep school in Helsinki prepared him academically enough to get accepted to the St. Petersburg's imperial cavalry school, and he served in the elite imperial Chevalier Guard. He fought in the Russo-Japanese War. From 1906–9 he went on an espionage mission through Central Asia to China, disguised as an ethnographic researcher. He steadily rose in military rank, and when WWI broke out he commanded an elite cavalry brigade. He himself won the Cross of St. George, Russia's highest war decoration. In the wake of the March 1917 revolution he had risen to be a lieutenant-general. Increasingly at odds with the ascendant Social-Democratic philosophy, he was relieved of command in September. By year's end he was back in Finland, where he was offered and took the post of Commander-in-Chief.

The war began with the Reds holding the southern coast, strongest in the cities of Helsinki and Viibori/Vyborg, plus the great industrial city of Tampere inland; the Whites held the upper Gulf of Bothnia coast ("Ostrobothnia) and the north.[GE[51]] On paper the Reds had the Whites both outnumbered and outgunned, but they lacked experienced military commanders. In February Mannerheim received the German-trained Finnish "Yaeger" unit from Germany, and made the most of them training officers for his raw troops. The Whites quickly mopped up Red pockets of resistance in Ostrobothnia, and got supplies and in fact some volunteer military units from Sweden. Germany agreed to mount a military drive from the southern coast towards Tampere, to match a drive from the north by Mannerheim's army. They were late arriving, but even without them Mannerheim's army took Tampere, after bitter fighting, on April 5. The Germans then came along the southern coast, moving from west to east, and on April 14 they took Helsinki. The combined White and German armies then drove the Reds out of Viibovi/Vyborg. This Finnish Civil War was just a little over three months long, but was as bloody and ruthless as most Civil Wars. Thousands of Whites died in the Red Terror of the first of the war, and thousands

---

50. GE Layer 50 is a Placemark referencing Vaasa.

51. GE Layer 51 is a Path symbolizing the military front of early 1918 by a thick red line.

of Reds died in an equally vicious White Terror at the end, before firing squads, or starved to death as prisoners in Helsinki's Suomenlinna prisons. It left emotional scars slow to heal in the following decades.

Independence

Finland came to independence about the same time as many former parts of the Austro-Hungarian and Russian Empires—the larger ones including Poland, Czechoslovakia, Hungary, and Yugoslavia. Like them, it tended to go a bit overboard in terms of self-celebration. In 1922 a purely-Finnish-language university was established in Turku. In 1923 a national law instructed the flagship university, Helsinki, to make the language of instruction in courses proportional to the number of speakers of each language in the current student body.

Finland celebrated every victory and time record of Paalo Nurmi, the Turku-born "Flying Finn" who won nine gold medals and three silver medals in the distance running events of the 1920, 1924, and 1928 Olympic games. He was probably inspired by Finland's new independence; there is no doubt that independent Finns were certainly inspired by him. Copies of a famous statue of him commissioned by the government in 1924 now stand at various places, including just outside Helsinki's Olympic stadium.[GE52]

Finnish history reflects many of the currents of European history in general, as you've seen in the age of religious wars, the Enlightenment, and the Romantic period. So it was after World War I, with the general liberalism and disarmament mood of the 1920s and then the re-militarization and Fascist groups of the 1930s. In the context of the last named, consider the Lapua movement. Lapua, you may recall, was the site of one of the few Finnish victories in the 1808 war during which Russia took over Finland, but a victory celebrated by the poet Runeberg in his works and therefore of lasting patriotic memory. So when in late 1929 a Communist youth group announced a public meeting there, local patriots attacked the meeting and wrecked the hall. Anti-Communist and super-patriotic leaders nation-wide, including some military officers and Lutheran pastors, coalesced around this. In the spring of 1930 they formed the "Lock of Finland" society, promising to rid the land of godless Communism. The government was swept along with it, and in clear violation of constitutional freedoms, the Communist members of the legislature were arrested. There was grandiose language about pushing natural Finnish and Estonian borders (the Estonians south of the Baltic being close linguistic kin to the Finns) east to the Urals! The world-wide Depression hit Finland at this time as well, encouraging extremists on both left and right. In 1932 a former chief of staff of the army, General Wallenius, began to arm and train Lapua recruits, creating a formal military force at Hämeenlinna. There was open talk of a coup, and in March some units actually began marching towards Helsinki. That was too much for the government, which said there should only be one army, and ordered it to disband.

In Germany, of course, a parallel Fascist movement led by Hitler took over the government in January of 1933, and led to a quick rearming of the country and a most aggressive foreign policy. Stalin's Russia, desperate for allies against this rising enemy, gave up on the old Marxist "no alliance with bourgeois parties" philosophy and in 1935 launched the United Front policy in which Communists were instructed to ally with any center-left parties who seemed willing to fight Fascism. When that seemed to produce no reliable allies, in August of 1939 Russia signed a "Non-Aggression Treaty" with Germany. By 1938 and 1939 Finland was caught in a most awkward place between these two super-powers.

In the spring of 1938 the U.S.S.R. began making inquiries of Finland about use or lease of some Finnish land and islands for Russian defense of the Gulf of Finland, and expressing the opinion that the Finnish border was too close to St. Petersburg, in case Finland should be taken over by "a third power" (Germany, of course). For over a year Finland turned away or replied with vague generalities to all such Russian inquires, but after the August 1939 Non-Aggression Treaty, Russian inquiries became demands. They were stiff: (1) the Finnish border to be moved back from its current twenty miles from Leningrad to some forty-five miles, and (2) the peninsula of Hanko, at the mouth of the Gulf of Finland,[GE53] given to Russia to fortify—all in exchange for

---

52. GE Layer 52 is a Placemark referencing the statue; click on Panoramio icon under pointer titled "Olympisch stadion Helsinki."

53. GE Layer 53 is a Polygon outlining in red Hanko peninsula and associated islands. Stalin had already gotten such an agreement with Estonia, on the south shore.

some less strategic territory elsewhere on the Finnish-U.S.S.R. border. Finland refused, saying that in such case it would no longer be considered a neutral. When demands became more pressing after Germany invaded Poland on September 1, beginning World War II in Europe, Finland still refused.

The Winter War

On November 30, 1939, the U.S.S.R. attacked generally all along the Finnish border, and bombed Helsinki. On December 1 Finnish coastal batteries sank the cruiser *Kirov*. All the Finnish units pulled back behind the fortified Mannerheim Line[GE54] on December 6. Finnish resistance was stubborn enough so that the German general staff downgraded its estimate of Soviet military power, but by early March Soviet weight told.[GE55] The Mannerheim Line had been broken at Summa, and in this unusually cold winter Viibori/Vyborg Bay had frozen hard enough for Soviet forces to drive across it. Finland signed a treaty leasing Hanko peninsula and surrounding islands to the Soviets for thirty years, and—in a line very close to the 1721 line drawn at the end of the Great Northern War—giving up Vyborg and its bay, and the part of Karelia that wraps around the northern end of Lake Ladoga.[GE56]

With the signing of the treaty March 12 there was mass immigration of Finns from Karelia into Finland proper. They had two weeks to evacuate, and so had to leave behind much of their property (the cattle were mostly slaughtered). The Finnish government had to launch an emergency land reform program to settle them all. Anger at Russia was such that in August of that same 1940 Finland allied with Nazi Germany.

The "Continuation War"

When Germany invaded Russia in June of 1941, Finland was in the war too, fighting for old 1939 borders and perhaps more. It was so soon after the Winter War that Finns just called it "The Continuation War." Newly equipped with heavy armaments from Germany, and led again by Marshal Mannerheim, the Finns enthusiastically drove their part of the frontier through Karelia.[GE57] But then no amount of encouragement from Germany could get them to attack Leningrad, or Murmansk. In November, just to appease Germany, Finland did sign the Anti-Comintern Pact at Berlin. Then, in a twenty-four-hour period on December 6–7, Great Britain declared war on Finland and the Japanese bombed Pearl Harbor, bringing the U.S. into the war on the allied side.

Finland, by now desperately dependent on Germany, ignored offers from Britain and the U.S. to—quietly—drop out of the war. Over the next two years the tides of war turned against Germany, with Stalingrad, and the great tank battle of Kursk, and the breaking of the siege of Leningrad. On June 9, 1944, the Soviets opened a huge offensive on the Karelian front, and Mannerheim saw the writing on the wall, calling this "Finland's black day." Vyborg fell June 20, and by September Finland agreed to Soviet terms. They included a return to the 1940 borders, a promise to pay a huge indemnity, and the commitment of the Finnish army to fight the still dangerous armies of Germany in the northern part of the country. With war's end, the political leaders who had allied with Nazi Germany were tried in a war crimes tribunal, and generally sentenced to terms at hard labor.

Since

After World War II, Finland made it a point to keep on good terms with its remaining Great Power neighbor. First signed in 1948, and regularly renewed time after time thereafter, an "Agreement of Friendship" with the Soviet Union pledged Finland not to join any organization that Moscow deemed was opposed to the U.S.S.R.

---

54. GE Layer 54 is a Folder titled "Mannerheim Line." It includes a Path symbolizing the fortified line in orange, and several Placemarks referencing Photos icons with interesting pictures of fortification remains.

55. GE Layer 55 is a Folder titled "six major Winter War battles," showing each as a purple line.

56. GE Layer 56 is a Folder titled "Soviet pre-Winter War borders." The eastern border of Finland was changed in three places. The northernmost rectification cost it access to the Barents Sea, but it was the southernmost, with all its Karelian population and those *Kalevala*-country associations, that hurt the most.

57. GE Layer 57 is a Path in wide orange line showing the farthest Finnish advance.

When the Soviet Union was dissolved in 1991, however, Finland was quick to apply for membership in the European Union, and was admitted in 1995; since 1999 the Euro has circulated there.

The country is still officially bi lingual, Swedish and Finnish, with perhaps 10 percent of the population speaking Swedish as a first language (the Aland Islands, for example, are still almost completely Swedish language-speaking). As in most of the rest of Scandinavia, college-educated people are virtually all multi-lingual, speaking one or more of English, German, French, or Russian.

Finland still economically makes much of its living from forest products, but it has gone well down the processing line from simple raw lumber and pulp. In many big U.S. paper mills, for example, the shell of the building may be U.S.-made, but the football-field-long, story-and-a-half high machine that starts with pulp and winds up with sheet paper dozens of feet wide shooting out the other end is altogether Finnish-built. With a smaller population than the average state in the U.S., it is an impressive, self-confident little country.

So here is our second "case study" of political nationalism, cultural nationalism, and socialism at work in a smallish European country in modern times. What are some lessons to learn from this historical experience? Socialism was a much more important force here than in Ireland, our last case study. The success of the Marxist SD party in 1905–7 and again in 1917 ensured that the independent Finnish state would not be a monarchy, but a republic. Even here, though, socialism came in a poor second as a political motivating device to nationalism. The Finnish example generally confirms the role of language in cultural nationalism, and puts an exclamation point on the place of a native epic in the development of modern national consciousness. Since 1945 there has been no war, and no pressure to speak of, on Finland, and nationalism has correspondingly relaxed somewhat. Since 1995 Finland has to some extent submerged its nationalism in the supra-national European Union, and joined the Euro currency bloc. The development of a Finnish national consciousness, however, is what kept it from being absorbed into the Russian state.

One more case study, thinks the author, and we can succinctly sum up the evolution of modern political behavior as invented mainly in modern Europe. Then we can turn to its impact on the rest of the world.

Endnotes

1. *Kalevala the Land of Heroes* trans. W. F. Kirby (London: J. M. Dent & Sons Ltd., and New York: E. P. Dutton & Co., 1907); volume I, pp. 3–4.

2. Eino Jutikkala (with Kauko Pirinen), *A History of Finland*, trans. Paul Sjöblom. New York: Dorset Press, 1988, p. 16.

3. William Albert Wilson, *Folklore and Nationalism in Modern Finland* (Bloomington and London: Indiana University Press, 1976), p. 6. The author read this book decades ago, and still finds it a brilliant presentation of the overall pattern. His argument suffuses this chapter, which hopefully stays just the right side of plagiarism.

4. Wilson, *Folklore and Nationalism*, pp. 20–21; his source was Edv. Rein's translation, *Suomalaisesta runoudesta*, in *Henrik Porthanin tutkimuksi* in *Suomalaisuuden syntysanoja*, 1, *Suomalaisen Kirjallisuuden Seuran Toimituksia*, no. 105 (Helsinki, 1904), p. 61.

5. See Wilson, pp. 22–23.

6. See John H. Wuorinen's *Nationalism is Modern Finland* (New York: Columbia University Press, 1931), p. 68. Some of the key sentences read: "The pages of *Andrastea* opened a new world to the young student. His attention was fixed upon Herder's ideas: a people in order to fulfill its 'destiny' must develop its culture; culture is the result of the workings not of individuals but of folk-character; language is the basic and most important expression of the folk-character."

7. Wilson, p. 3.

8. Wilson, pp. 33–34.

9. Julius Krohn is the writer; quoted in Wilson, p. 44.

10. Wilson, pp. 47–48.

11. "Sibelius," in *Grove Dictionary of Music*.

12. Jutikkala, p. 216.

13. Anatole G. Mazour, *Finland Between East and West* (Princeton: D. Van Nostrand Co., Inc., 1956), p. 36.

Chapter Seven

Ma Vlast ("My Fatherland"):
Czechs, Czechoslovakia, and the Bratislavan Lesson

"He [historian František Palacký] brought them back to life, gave them courage and belief in a forgotten or despised past, and proved to them that they had achievements in the moral and intellectual sphere of which any nation might be proud . . . ."

—from Hugh Seton-Watson, *History of the Czechs and Slovaks*

CONTENTS

The heart of the matter—Some introduction to the Czech language—Topography and texture of the land—Prehistory and early history—Foundations of a Bohemian/Moravian state: two golden ages—The life and times of Jan Hus (John Hus)—The Hussite Wars—Another defenestration, another decades-long war—Roots of the Czech national renaissance—Ideal patterns of cultural nationalism—The forerunners—The Slav Congress in Prague in 1848—The nationalist composers: Smetana and Dvořak—Sokol—*Budweisers into Czechs and Germans*—Inside the Dual Monarchy's Cisleithania—Count Taaffe's "Iron Ring"—The Budweis/Budějovice Compromise—World War I—Tomáš Masaryk and independence—The Third Reich and German ascendancy—Eduard Beneš and the assassination of Heydrich—In the wake of WW II—Inside the Soviet Bloc—Velvet revolution, velvet divorce—The Bratislavan lesson—General lessons learned about modern European social mobilization

The heart of the matter

Nation-states are almost always born of war. There was blood enough, and wars enough, in the creation of Czechoslovakia, as you'll see. That made it very interesting, then, when on New Year's Eve of 1992—the night before Czechoslovakia was supposed to split into totally independent Czech and Slovak Republics—they put up a sound stage on the border-to-be, had a concert, and split the next day without so much as a bloody nose.

This is the last of the "rise of European power" first half of the book. As usual, we'll give a nod to language and then a longer nod to the topography and texture of the land. Then we'll talk about early history, especially those unique parts that would be used by later nationalists to justify an independent nation.

When we come to the Romantic Era where modern cultural nationalism was born, you'll see a Czechoslovak cultural nationalism so classic that it will suggest ways to fine-tune our "paradigm of national development" whereby most modern countries are invented. In the century from 1848 to 1948 you'll see, in what is today the Czech Republic, Czech and German nationalisms become more and more rigid—from when city mayors were perfectly bilingual with nicknames in both languages, to a situation where everyone was forced to choose either German or Czech nationality. With Nazi support in the 1930s the Germans rode high, but with the Soviet Union's victory in World War II and subsequent domination of Czechoslovakia, the Czechs ended the see-saw battle with a sweeping victory, packing almost all of the remaining Germans on trains headed for a bombed-out Germany most had never even visited.

Finally, with the end of the Soviet Union and the relaxation of outside pressures, you'll see the breakup of Czechoslovakia into smaller units, and the possibility of further breakups. It should be a last lesson in the importance of what is going on <u>outside</u> the nation-state for its own self-image—a self-image that in the long run is the glue that holds it together.

Some introduction to the Czech language

Czech is a member of the Slavic sub-family of Indo-European languages, and so is close linguistic kin to the Russian language we talked about at the start of the Russia and Socialism chapter. To briefly recap, the Slavic languages are usually divided into three groups:

- ○ East Slavic (Russian, Ukrainian, and Belo-Russian being the main ones)
- ○ South Slavic (Slovenian, Croatian, Serbian, Bulgarian—"iuk" incidentally, or some similar version in almost all Slavic languages means "south," so "Yugoslavia" translates literally "South Slavia"
- ○ West Slavic (mainly Czech, Slovak, and Polish)

Compared to varieties of the Germanic sub-family of Indo-European languages (Norwegian, Danish, Swedish, German high and low, Dutch, Icelandic, English, etc.) and varieties of Romance sub-family (Spanish, Portuguese, Italian, French, Romanian, etc.), Slavic languages are much closer in terms of pronunciation and speaking. That fact is, however, disguised by a huge writing difference. The Eastern Slavic-speaking peoples, who got Christianity straight from Greece and the Orthodox Church, received with it a modified Greek alphabet called Cyrillic. Those Western Slavs who were in the Roman Catholic orbit wound up with minor variations on the Latin alphabet. This religious/script divide split the South Slavs right down the middle, East from West. So Russians, Ukrainians, Bulgarians and Macedonians use the Cyrillic script, and Czechs, Slovaks, the Polish, Slovenes, Croats and Bosnians use Latin letters, and Serbians use both!

You can see the similarities of basic words if you transliterate the Cyrillic letter words to match the Latin letter words: here are the results for "Good evening," "land," "sea," and "hundred" in some major Slavic languages:

- ○ in Russian: dobrii vecher, zemlia, mor(y)e, sto
- ○ in Polish: dobry wieczór, ziemia, morze, sto
- ○ in Czech: dobrý večer, země, moře, sto
- ○ in Serbo-Croatian: dobra večer, zemlja, more, sto
- ○ in Bulgarian: dobra vecer, zemya, more, sto

There are some minor differences in stress and spelling with Czech (and Slovak):

- ○ Czech almost invariably stresses first syllable of any word (in Polish the stress is usually next to last; in Russian there seem to be no rules for stress at all!).
- ○ Czech carefully distinguishes between long and short vowels with what looks like an "acute" e mark from French, or a stress mark in Spanish, but which is different from either. In the Czech word *dobrý*, for example, the stress is on the initial o since it is almost always on the first syllable, but accent mark doubles the length of the *y* (something like our i or ee) sound; it's almost as if you say the *y* sound twice, *DO-bry-y*.
- ○ Another common diacritical mark in Czech is the *hachek* (the little v or hook over certain letters), which in general palatalizes them. You can find them over *c, d, n, r, s, t,* and *z*. With the *č, š,* and *ž*, it's just a matter of adding an h to our pronunciation to make ch, sh, and zh sounds. The *ň* is something like the *ñ* in Spanish. It's a little more complicated with the *Ď* (little letter printed as *ď*) and *Ť* (*ť*), gen-

erally flattening them out against your palate. And with *ř* it's a combination of zh and a trilled r sound. When this *ř* stands between vowels, it's not too bad: this is what causes the name of the famous Czech composer Dvořak to be pronounced something like DVORR-zhak. But when the *ř* is next to other consonants—as in the important early Czech dynasty Přemysl—it's really hard for native English speakers to wrap their tongues around it!

❍ Finally, Js are pronounced like our Ys, as they are in German words.[1]

In looking over a map of the modern Czech Republic, as in browsing the Google Earth surface thereabouts, one common Czech word you'll find is *hora* (mountain) and the related word *hrad* (fort or castle) [Prague's ancient *Vyšehrad* is just the "high fort"]. *Český* or *Česke* is an adjective meaning Czech, as in the city *České Budějovice*, to differentiate the Czech town of that name from one in Moravia. The usual name for a city square or plaza is *náměstí* and for the city hall it's *radnice*. A church is *kostel* and a cathedral is *chrám*. A street is *ulice*. Watery features include *potok*, a brook or stream; *jezero*, a lake; *rybnik*, a pond or small lake; *most*, a bridge; and *lázne*, a spa usually built around some special mineral or hot water spring (which also often shows up as -*bad* in the German, as in *Mariánske Lázne* a.k.a. *Marienbad*).

Topography and texture of the land

The lands we're dealing with here—from west to east with decreasing focus—are traditionally called Bohemia, Moravia (these two make up today's Czech Republic), and Slovakia. The Czech Republic especially, unlike so many regions of Central and Eastern Europe, has fairly well defined mountain borders. If you look down on it from 300 miles up, you can see veins and patches of dark green; this is forest, usually on hill slopes or mountains.[GE1] This is especially marked on the northern, western, and southern borders of today's Czech Republic where the highest mountains are. In the northeast you have the Giant Mountains (in Czech, *Krkonoše*; in German, *Riesengebirge*, or the Sudetes Mountains), with elevations topping 3,000'.[GE2] In the northwest you have the Ore Mountains (*Krušné Horý*; *Erzgebirge*), over 4,000'.[GE3] In the west and southwest you have the mountainous Bohemian Forest (*Šumava*; *Böhmerwald*), also with many ridges and peaks over 4,000'.[GE4]

Smaller ranges of hills separate Bohemia from Moravia to the east, making of Bohemia an almost circular bowl. The northern part of the bowl, the lowest, is drained by the Labe (in Czech) or Elbe (in German) River. It gathers all the other rivers of Bohemia and then cuts its way northwest through a most scenic canyon into Saxony, and then continues that general northwest flow across Germany from Dresden to Hamburg and the North Sea.[GE5] One of its biggest tributaries in Bohemia and certainly its most important one historically is the Vltava (in Czech) or the Moldau (in German) River. It heads up in the Šumava down near the Austrian border, and after flowing southeast for a time, turns and runs generally north, through Prague, to its confluence with the Labe.[GE6] We'll do a little more with the Vltava when we get to the nineteenth century and full-blown cultural nationalism, but for now just remember that it is the river that goes through Prague.

---

1. GE Layer 1 is a Folder showing traditional Bohemia and Moravia as green polygons and traditional Slovakia in blue. After that is a Placemark that takes you to an eye altitude of approximately 300 miles up of the Czech Republic; you can see veins and patches of dark green all over the country, but especially along the borders. This is forest, usually on hillsides or mountains.

2. GE Layer 2 takes you to a representative Panoramio icon titled "Rückblick zur Labska Bouda."

3. GE Layer 3 references a Panoramio icon in the Ore Mountains labeled "Spicak - Spitzberg."

4. GE Layer 4 references a Panoramio icon labeled "Plesne jezero," a mountain lake in the Šumava as seen from a high vantage point.

5. GE Layer 5 is a Path representing the Labe/Elbe River in light green color.

6. GE Layer 6 is a Path representing the Vltava in light blue.

A traveler coming north from the Šumava sees the mountains flatten out more slowly than they do at the northern border.[GE7] Then comes the real Bohemian plain, flatter, intensively farmed,[GE8] and interrupted by only the occasional hill, often crowned with an old castle.[GE9]

Speaking of architecture, every town of any size seems to have a handsome town square, a city hall, and a church or cathedral. Outside virtually every fair-sized town is at least one castle/manor house from the days of power of the local nobility. Some towns have folk museums, "open air museums," as they are usually called in Europe, or "living historical museums," like our Colonial Williamsburg.[GE10] And lest I have given the false impression that the whole country is bucolic and agricultural, it has been known for its mining and heavy industry for centuries. Perhaps its most famous name in sophisticated heavy industry of the last century or so is Škoda Works based in the city of Plzeń/Pilsen,[GE11] that were as important to the Austro-Hungarian monarchy before WW I and to the Czechoslovak state after WWI as the Krupp Works were to Prussia/Germany. The iron and steel industry was dependent on mines, and both mines and heavy industry have left the modern Czech state with some problems with air and water pollution.[GE12] Strip mines, of course, show up best in aerial views.[GE13] A discontinuous band of them some eighty miles long lies in at the base of the aptly named Krušné Horý, or Ore Mountains.[GE14] Interestingly enough, almost all of Bohemia's famous spas based on hot or mineral springs—the most famous being Karlsbad/Karlovy Vary—are in or around this same eighty-mile long swath.[GE15] At Karlovy Vary a tourist can buy what looks and feels like a rusty iron flower—a paper flower that has been submerged in the mineral water springs for a couple of weeks, so saturated with minerals is the water.

Prehistory and early history

Bohemia got its name from a Celtic tribe, the Boii, which occupied the river valleys of what is today the Czech Republic in the time of the Roman Empire. It's a matter of some debate when the first Slavic tribes arrived from the east to settle modern Slavic lands, but it seems at least in the West Slavic-speaking lands of Slovakia, Moravia, and Bohemia that they gradually moved in after the German tribes such as Ostrogoths and Visigoths moved west across the frontiers of the Roman Empire in the *Völkerwanderung*, the Barbarian Migration talked about in the German chapter. Whatever the motivation for those Germanic migrations, it doesn't seem to have been population pressure: in several places we know of, including the original lands of Angles, Saxons, and Jutes in today's northern Germany and southern Scandinavia, travelers reported the land totally abandoned and depopulated after the migration. Slavic farming groups (in the fifth to seventh centuries still speaking what was essentially a single Slavic language) moved west in their turn to fill the void, occupying central Europe from the mouth of the Elbe down to the heads of the Adriatic and Aegean Seas.[2] Cosmas of Prague, a twelfth-century chronicler, tells the story of the Slavic tribal leader Čech who took the vanguard of the Slavs up to the summit

---

7. GE Layer 7 is a Placemark referencing Panoramio icon "View from Nezamyslice"; elevation is about 1630′.

8. GE Layer 8 is a Folder titled "Views of the Bohemian Plain"; it includes references to three Panoramio icons with representative views of the heart of the Bohemian plain.

9. GE Layer 9 is a Placemark referencing a Panoramio icon labeled "Hazmburk." Nearby Photos icons are either of the castle or the view from the castle hill.

10. GE Layer 10 is a Placemark referencing a Panoramio icon titled "Zurbnice skanzen." It is named, either in reality or in humor here, after the famous Swedish folk museum Skansen on the edge of Stockholm.

11. GE Layer 11 is a Placemark that points to Panoramio icon labeled "Škoda Main Entrance."

12. GE Layer 12 points to Panoramio icon labeled "Industrial Pollution in Northern Bohemia."

13. GE Layer 13 is a Placemark framing a general view of a 3 mile × 3 mile strip mine. As of this writing there are perhaps a dozen Photos icons to explore there; see in particular one titled "Mining Area."

14. GE Layer 14 frames a view from about 120 miles up of the band of strip mines along the southern base of the Ore Mountains.

15. GE Layer 15 is a Folder labeled "Famous Bohemian spas" that holds Placemarks for five spas famous since at least the nineteenth century: Karlovy Vary/Karlsbad, Mariánské Lázně/Marienbad, Františkovy Lázně/Franzensbad, Teplice/ Teplitz, and Jachymov.

of Mt. Říp to show them their promised "land of milk and honey."[GE16] This is surely mythical, since the author was writing six or seven hundred years after the supposed fact and we have no other source about this original Čech; but don't tell that to the Czechs, for whom Father Čech (in the words of a recent writer) "remains until today part of the Czechs' historical imagination, and immediately evokes recognition."[3] National consciousness, many writers have observed, has a lot to do with what people choose to remember (and what they choose to forget).

By the early 600s more reliable historical mention has the invading Avars as overlords of the Slavic population. A Frankish lord named Samo—perhaps only semi-legendary—led the overthrow of Avar rule and the creation of a Western Slav state. Charlemagne himself, shortly after his coronation as Roman Emperor in the year 800, won enough battles against the Czech tribes in Bohemia so as to force them to pay tribute, and his son Louis the Pious similarly pressured Moravia, just east of Bohemia. As part of this western pressure, Christian missionaries were sent from German lands into Western Slav lands, which were still polytheistic.

At this point it occurred to the current Western Slav leader, Rostislav of Moravia (as the same thought would occur about twenty-five years later to the more famous Vladimir, ruler of Kievan Russia), that he had better pick a monotheism for his country. Perhaps it was heartfelt conversion, but there were some obvious practical advantages, too: for one, it would take away an excuse for outside invasion from neighboring Christian powers; and for two, these early Christian institutions tended to strengthen the power of local rulers and introduce a new literacy and an urban culture. Rostislav's choice, geographically speaking, was really between Western and Eastern Christianity. Although Roman Catholics and Greek Orthodox had not yet formally split (that would come in 1054), there was already a huge difference in language and tone between them. Perhaps because the Germans and their Latin church were such an immediate danger, Rostislav chose to ask Constantinople and the Greek Church for some Slavic-speaking missionaries. So in 863 or thereabouts the brothers Constantine (later renamed Cyril) and Methodius from Salonika came to Moravia and the western edge of Slovakia to work, creating the ancestor of the modern Cyrillic script in their work. This caused such a huge backlash from the western German powers that the disciples of Cyril and Methodius were pushed on eastwards to work with the Bulgarians, and so the Bohemian, Moravian, and Slovak lands fell back into the orbit of the Roman church and the Latin script.

Then around 900, according to the nineteenth-century nationalist historian František Palacký, came "the greatest misfortune that has befallen the Slavonic world in thousands of years"—the Hungarian invasion.[4] These non-Indo-European speakers came out of the east, like so many invaders of Europe. A more correct name for them than Hungarian is Magyar (pronounced something like MAH-jar), for their semi-mythical tribal leader. They drove a wedge into the middle of the Slavic-speaking world, separating Eastern and Western Slavs from Southern Slavs.[GE17] They ravaged all the lands around for decades (the English word "ogre" comes from the twelfth-century French, connoting "fierce pagan" and is apparently a corruption for "ongri," which they called Hungarians;[5] it gives you some idea of their early reputation). And especially important for our chapter, the Magyars occupied present-day Slovakia for a thousand years, during which time it came to be called "Upper Hungary" and its people developed a degree of cultural difference with their former very close cultural kinsfolk the Moravians and the Bohemians.

Foundations of a Bohemian/Moravian state: two golden ages

A modern Czech state really began to take shape under the Přemysl dynasty, which lasted four centuries and more from the late 800s to the early 1300s. The shadowy, ill-attested but dramatic beginnings have a visionary noblewoman named Libuše—descended from Father Čech, of course—choosing a commoner named Přemsyl

---

16. GE Layer 16 is a Folder titled "Mt. Říp, location and views." It includes a Placemark referencing the mountain itself, not too far west of the Vltava-Labe river junction, plus some views of the isolated mountain from other places.

17. GE Layer 17 is a Placemark framing central and eastern Europe from an eye altitude of about a thousand miles in space. With the "Borders" layer of Google Earth turned on, notice how a west-to-east band of non-Slavic language states (Austria, speaking German; Hungary, speaking Hungarian; and Romania, speaking the Romance language Romanian) cuts Southern Slavs off from Western and Eastern Slavs.

for her husband to be first duke of the Czechs. Their descendants founded Prague by 885 or so, building a castle on the heights of Hradčany,[GE18] the Castle District. Some dukes in the succession chose to rule from a second castle a couple of miles upstream and across the Vltava River, Vyšehrad,[GE19] the High Fort or High Castle. Prague (*Praha* in Czech) grew up between these two fortified hills.

By 921 you have the first appearance in their line of rulers of one of the most evocative names in all of Czech history, Václav, which somehow got westernized as Wenceslas (as in "Good King Wenceslas," which he wasn't, really, still only a duke). In a huge reorientation of regional power, the Roman Emperorship set up by Charlemagne a century before had passed from the Franks eastwards to the Saxons. Václav recognized this shift in power, and sent tribute to the Saxon kings. For this he got their support, and the relics of a Saxon saint, St. Vitus, whose shrine he began in Prague castle. More importantly, Václav was murdered by his brother's men in an act that was possibly just about power, but that was increasingly seen by later ages as Christian martyrdom. In the memory of Václav the Czechs for centuries found unity, as in the words of a medieval chronicler relating a vision at a battle:

> Comrades and brothers, be valiant, for above the point of the holy spear I see St. Václav, who, seated on a white horse and wearing white robes, fights for us; you also behold![6]

In general the Přemsylid rulers hitched their star to the Holy Roman Empire, rather than trying to create their own independent states as some neighboring countries such as Poland and Hungary did. It paid off in 1085 when the Bohemian dukes were elevated to kings; and again in 1114 when the King of Bohemia was made "cupbearer to the Emperor," which among other things entitled him to be one of the Electors of any new Holy Roman Emperor. The strongest of the line was Otakar II, who ruled in the mid-1200s. He held not only Bohemia and Moravia but a huge swath of land south, for a time even including Austria.[GE20] Ironically, his very strength and expansionist moves made him enemies, and got Rudolf, Count of Habsburg, elected Holy Roman Emperor in 1273. Rudolf fought Otakar II over Austrian lands, and won. When Otakar II renewed the war in 1278, he not only lost again but was killed in battle. The last member of the dynasty was assassinated in 1306. But in that last century of Přemysl rule there had been tremendous change. Massive immigration of German townspeople set up urban centers, run according to German town law that gave the common people more freedom and provided the local lords more money. Especially under Otakar II, towns from Budweis/České Budejovice[GE21] on the upper Vltava to Nymburk[GE22] on the Labe were created. German expertise developed Bohemian mines, especially the huge silver strike at Kutná Hora,[GE23] which, while the mines were thriving, was the second most important town in the country after Prague. And German farmers settled the relatively empty and less agriculturally productive mountain frontier areas all around the fringes of Bohemia, leaving the Czechs the more productive lands of the Bohemian plain. Overall Bohemian and Moravian lands were closely integrated with western European culture in this period, as shows up particularly in the Romanesque architecture of the period. And even more glorious glory days lay ahead.

When the old Přemysl dynasty died out, the Czechs turned for a new king to John of Luxemburg. He was a knight-errant who was no particular boon for the kingdom, since he spent little time there and demanded of it money for his adventures. He was killed in 1346 at Crécy, one of the three most famous battles of the 100

---

18. GE Layer 18 is a Placemark generally referencing Hradčany.

19. GE Layer 19 is a Placemark generally referencing Vyšehrad. Zoom out to see relationship between the two fortified hills, and Prague generally between them.

20. GE Layer 20 is a Polygon entitled "The Realm of Otakar II"; see how his territory included what was then Upper and Lower Austria and lands almost down to the shores of the Adriatic.

21. GE Layer 21 is a Placemark generally framing a view of the medieval center of Budweis/České Budejovice, a locale we'll come back to extensively later in the chapter!

22. GE Layer 22 is a Placemark generally framing a view of the medieval center of Nymburk, a locale that will also show up later in the chapter.

23. GE Layer 23 is a Placemark referencing Kutná Hora, showing its relationship to the Labe and Vltava Rivers and to Prague.

Years War between England and France. But his oldest son was Charles IV, perhaps the single most important figure in all of Bohemian and Czech history. Charles was born in 1316 and raised in Prague until age seven when his father had him placed in the royal court of France and married (still at age seven) to a Valois royal princess. In 1333, about age seventeen, he was sent by his father back to Bohemia to run the heartland, and made Margrave of Moravia to boot. Charles found the country devastated, with not a single royal castle—even Prague Castle—intact enough to live in, and the nobles having all become tyrants or little kings in their parts of the land. Upon his father's death he became King of Bohemia as well as Emperor of the Holy Roman Empire. With the backing of the Pope (who just happened to have been his personal tutor earlier at the French court, small world), and the greatest diplomatic and administrative skills of his age, Charles IV put his stamp on Bohemia like no other single individual in history.

First, he extended his direct personal control from the Bohemian and Moravian heartlands of his personal realm on up north, eventually even including Brandenburg.[GE24]

Second, he made of Prague a royal city fit to be capital of the Holy Roman Empire; it is hard to imagine what it would look like today without his transformation of it. He rebuilt Prague Castle up on Hradčany ridge, and the magnificent St. Vitus Cathedral inside it. They dominate the skyline on the northwest side of the city even today.[GE25] He replaced the wooden bridge between Old Town on the east bank and Small Side (*Malá Strana*) on the west bank at the foot of the castle with the spectacular stone "Charles Bridge," with statuary all along its parapets.[GE26] At the eastern end of the bridge, the entrance to Old Town, he built a version of a Roman Imperial arch.[GE27] In Old Town itself he established Charles University—the only university in Central Europe and really one of only four in all Europe (along with Oxford, Paris, Bologna) in these years.[GE28]

Third, he dotted the Bohemian plain with royally-sponsored structures. Most spectacular are Karlštejn Castle, about fourteen miles southwest of Prague, which he built to house the records and treasures of the Holy Roman Empire,[GE29], and the magnificent St. Barbara's Church at Kutná Hora, the important silver mine city. [GE30]

Fourth—though this really doesn't show up as important until a couple of decades after his death—he brought in religious reformers to purify religious practice and behavior in the Western, or Roman Catholic Church.

The life and times of Jan Hus (John Hus)

Martin Luther (1483–1546) is often thought of as the beginning of the Protestant Reformation. In a very real sense, though, he was the end of much of the process: almost every stand he took, almost everything he did, Jan Hus had done a century earlier.

---

24. See GE Layer 24 is a Polygon entitled "the Realm of Charles IV." Then try this interesting experiment: turn on both Polygons for realms of Otakar II (GE Layer 20) and this one for Charles IV, and make sure you have the Borders feature of Google Earth Layers turned on. It's remarkable that the two Polygons have in common, almost exactly, the territory of the Czech Republic today, 700 years later.

25. GE Layer 25 references a Panoramio icon with a great view from Old Town on the east bank towards Hradčany and Prague Castle and St. Vitus Cathedral on the western skyline. Charles Bridge is in the foreground. Title of icon is "Prag_15."

26. GE Layer 26 references a Panoramio icon "Prague - The End of the Bridge (November - 1990) scanned." Pictured at the far end of the bridge Charles' triumphal arch through which visitors entered Old Town. On the bridge in the Google Earth screen there are also a couple of 360 Cities icons with wrap-around views into which you can "fly."

27. GE Layer 27 references a Panoramio icon titled "Old Town Tower."

28. GE Layer 28 is a Placemark locating the Carolinum in Old Town Prague, original site of Charles University.

29. GE Layer 29 references a Panoramio icon titled "Karlštejn Castle / Czech Republic." It is one of the most photographed places in all of the Czech Republic, as you can tell from the hundred or so Photos icons crowded together there.

30. GE Layer 30 references a Panoramio icon titled "Sv. Barbory," and there are dozens of others mainly at bottom right of this framed view in Google Earth. Despite the "chrám" or cathedral claim of these photo labels, it is a church and not the seat (cathedra) of a bishop.

Here's the general setting. By 1380 John Wyclif in England was translating the Bible into the common speech and encouraging an order of popular preachers to communicate it to the masses. He apparently thought the official church was so discredited by its wealth and political activity (*simony*, the buying and selling of church offices, was the particular focus of his criticism) that this would be a good way to replace it. His writings were of course banned, but spread anyway, including to Bohemia. In 1391 like-minded church reformers in Prague created Bethlehem Chapel in Old Town. The church authorities had approved a chapel, assuming it would be a fairly small place where Mass could be celebrated—but to their shock this "chapel" could hold 3,000 and was focused, not on the altar for Mass, but on the pulpit where public sermons were preached in Czech.[GE31] The whole Roman Catholic church administration was in disarray, to say the least, with competing Popes in France and Rome from 1378 to 1417. Locally, Charles IV's son, who like his father began his rule at age seventeen, was unlike his father a disaster of a ruler; in a few years he actually had the Holy Roman Emperorship yanked away from him for not being able to rule it. At Charles University in Prague trouble was brewing, because German language outsiders had three schools and three votes in university policy vs. the Czech language insiders who only had one school and one vote (though there were just as many Czech students as all the "foreigners" put together). Now enter Jan Hus.

He was born in 1372 or 1373 in the little village of Husinec ("Goosestown") down south near the headwaters of the Vltava River.[GE32] He got some elementary education at nearby Prachatice, a walled city that was something of a commercial center.[GE33] When he went on to the university in Prague in 1390, at about age eighteen, there were lots of Jans, or Johns, there, so he took his village name as a last name and later still shortened it to Hus. He became a brilliant student, and later what we'd call a graduate student and a professor, at Charles University there in Old Town Prague.

Like Wyclif before him and Luther after him, Jan Hus didn't set out to call for the destruction of the Roman Catholic Church. It's just that as he critiqued one abuse after the other, somewhere he crossed the line between thinking it was an institution that could be reformed and thinking it ought to be totally destroyed. Here are some landmarks of his evolution.

In 1402, at age thirty or so, he became the main preacher at this Bethlehem Chapel. In 1403, a German university prof at the university drew up a list of forty-five articles, presumably from Wyclif's writings, and had them condemned as heretical. One of the greatest heresies he pointed out was Wyclif's claim that the Scriptures were the only true source of Christian doctrine, not church administrative practice, not the College of Cardinals' decisions, nor those of the Pope. The non-Czechs at Charles University mostly supported the condemnation, and the Czechs mostly sided with Wyclif, but were of course outvoted 3–1. In 1409, a new Catholic Church council, held at Pisa, was trying to get down to just one Pope, AND reform the church as well. The reforms were supported by Czechs at Charles University, but denounced by Germans who of course carried the day 3–1. The King of Bohemia saw this as a challenge to his local rule, and so from Kutná Hora issued a decree named after the city that gave the Czechs three votes in the university and "foreigners" only one. This occasioned a mass exodus of those foreigners, mostly Germans.

Then in 1412 came a critical event, the sale of a new issue of indulgences in the Vltava River cities of Prague and Krumlov.[GE34] Jan Hus preached vehemently against it. The Bohemian king, however, who got a cut from the sale, supported it, so Hus lost the king's support. Hus voluntarily left Prague in October of 1412, and found refuge mostly in southern Bohemia in castles of his friends. He was for a while in Kozi, near mod-

---

31. GE Layer 31 is a Placemark referencing the Prague Old Town location of Bethlehem Chapel; click on Wikipedia icon under pointer, titled "Bethlehem Chapel," for picture of interior of the (reconstructed) chapel. Nearby Panoramio icons titled "Bethlehem Chapel" or "Betlémská kaple" have other exterior and interior views. This and the following sites associated with the life of Jan Hus are all in green, so as to show up as a separate pattern on the Google Earth map.

32. GE Layer 32 is a Placemark that frames the village of Husinec; click on Panoramio icon under pointer labeled "Husinec," which shows a statue of this hometown hero in front of the village church.

33. GE Layer 33 frames larger town of Prachatice; Panoramio icon at the pointer, "City Wall," shows a surviving part of the historic wall with an inset blockhouse. Other icons show the town set in its valley among the hills.

34. Prague you know; GE Layer 34 references the upriver town of Krumlov, about ninety miles due south of Prague.

ern Tábor,[GE35] and then in retreat at the castle at Krakovec.[GE36] His literary activity in this year or two was described as feverish, as he worked to finish his translation of the whole Bible into Czech, as well as writing articles explaining his side of the conflict.

Then came the great church Council of Constance, that opened in 1414 and only closed in 1418, that really did solve the problem of multiple Popes. It also set itself to deal with the theology of John Wyclif (now dead) and Jan Hus (still alive and making trouble). Hus wanted to go defend himself, confident of the theological soundness of his position and his own eloquence to present it, but individuals judged heretical could be given the death sentence. So he took the precaution of getting a safe-conduct pass from the Holy Roman Emperor, and set off for Constance.[GE37] When he arrived in late 1414 he was immediately jailed. Cries from crowds of commoners for his release only made him seem more dangerous to the church administrators. In mid-summer of 1415, after his supporters made enough noise so that he had to be brought out for public trial, he was condemned as a heretic. The Emperor was easily convinced that any promise to a heretic was null and void, so Jan Hus was burned at the stake.

Protestant/Catholic theological issues aside, Jan Hus did a good bit for the Czech language and Czech national consciousness. He was the heart and soul of the faction that "Czechized" the university. He promoted congregational singing in Czech and himself wrote many hymns in Czech. He wrote in a luminous and updated Czech that changed the use of language for all time, as well as Czech attitudes towards it. Jan Hus, in the carefully chosen words of one historian, "condemned in unmeasured phrase intermarriage with the Germans, as likely to endanger the purity of the Czech language."[7] Remember that this is still the early 1400s; Czech national consciousness is already closer to the national consciousness of the last century or two than that of most any other group in Europe. The Hussite Wars would only strengthen that.

The Hussite Wars

By 1418 the Council of Constance was over, having successfully replaced by this time not just two but three competing Popes with a single one. The only loose end left over seemed to be those pesky Hussites in Bohemia. The Council and the Emperor brought pressure to bear on the King of Bohemia to evict them from all church buildings, and although he drug his feet, the king did do some of this. As the Hussites lost church buildings, they began to hold services outside, especially on hilltops, which they called Tabors (after the strikingly situated Mt. Tabor which rises up in splendid isolation in the Jizreel Valley of Israel, and which had figured in Biblical warfare and is generally assumed by Christians to be the mountain where Peter, James, and John witnessed the transfiguration of Christ). There was an apocalyptic tone to all this, a feeling of end times and the absolute righteousness of holy brother- and sisterhood among them. In 1419, the storm broke. A popular Hussite preacher in New Town Prague led a crowd by City Hall, and the mob (some say responding to rocks thrown out of the window at them) stormed the building and threw the mayor and assorted city councilmen out upper-story windows to their deaths—the First "Defenestration" ("Out the Window-ing," literally, is its Latin meaning) of Prague. Then for seventeen years there was war between the Hussites of Bohemia and much of the rest of western Christendom.

As armies from all over converged on Bohemia, and then Prague, a military genius emerged among the Hussites. This was Jan Žižka, a sixty-year-old one-eyed soldier of fortune from the lesser nobility. He made war wagons out of farm wagons, to be pulled when needed into defensive squares, and he insisted on the rapid adoption of firearms. On July 14, 1420, on the hill of Vitkov just a mile east of the gates of the Old City gates of Prague, he led the victory over the first major crusading armies sent against the Hussites; today it is the hill

35. GE Layer 35 frames general location of his retreat at Kozi, near Tábor (which was itself founded around 1420 in the wars that followed the death of Hus).

36. GE Layer 36 is a Placemark referencing Panoramio icon below pointer, "The ruin of Krakovec castle."

37. GE Layer 37 is a Placemark framing a view of Constance (on border of Switzerland and southern Germany) in relation to Czech lands at top right.

of Žižkov, named after him.[GE38] On October 31 Žižka defeated another invasion force at Vyšehrad just south of the city. To make a long story short(er), for a full fifteen years the Hussites defeated all comers; but divisions gradually grew sharper within their ranks and fervor waned, and in 1434 the radical Hussites suffered a major military defeat. The Roman Catholic administration was also weary of the struggle, and so grudgingly allowed the Bohemian part of the church to have married clergy, and for the lay people to take the wine at Mass (the Chalice became the Hussite icon)—so you had what some have called the first recognized "separate confessional group" in the whole history of western Christendom to this point. These Hussite wars left most Bohemians with a feeling they were separate, set aside, with a special place in world history.

For the next two centuries there was a push and pull in Czech lands between Roman Catholic and Hussite forces, complicated by social struggles between nobles, townsmen, and peasants. On the one hand, in the 1400s the king and the nobles (like those in Russia at the same time who were creating serfdom) tried to freeze peasants to their estates, and to pile on *robota*, or draft labor days. On the other hand, in just these centuries king and nobles supported Bohemia's version of the Renaissance in the arts, architecture, and letters. The university in Prague, under Hussite control, was way too puritanical (if we can use that word before there were Puritans) to welcome the broad new Humanism of the Renaissance, so it was at Prague Castle and the royal court, not the university, that intellectuals such as Tycho Brahe and Johannes Kepler worked. In the first half of the 1500s, as you might well imagine, there was a huge and positive response in Czech lands to Martin Luther's Protestant rebellion against the Roman Catholic Church and the authority of both Pope and Holy Roman Emperor. After all, as Luther himself said, we (he and his followers) were Hussites before we ever realized it!

In this full-blown Protestant Reformation triggered by Luther in 1517 (as you saw briefly in the German history chapter), central and western European states chose up sides generally into a Protestant North (not including Ireland!) and a Catholic South. "Whose the reign, his the religion," went the formula from the 1555 Peace of Augsburg that amounted to a truce, not a lasting peace, in a century and a third of down-and-dirty religious warfare (the most uncompromising and brutal kind because, of course, God is always exclusively on your side). The Roman Catholic "Counter-Reformation" with its own internal reforms and new institutions such as Jesuits and the Inquisition emerged to reestablish its place in the world, and the Bohemian lands were a showpiece test case.

Another defenestration, another decades-long war

By 1618, with general support from the Holy Roman Emperor, Protestant churches in and around Prague were being systematically destroyed in the resurgence of Catholic power. In response, something over a hundred Protestant knights and noblemen invaded Prague Castle and—in conscious imitation of that first Defenestration of Prague back in 1419 almost exactly 200 years earlier—threw two of the king's councillors out of upper-story windows (by some accounts they landed on garbage or manure heaps, which broke their fall and saved their lives). A Protestant rising of virtually the whole country met to elect a Calvinist king. His armies immediately and rashly tried to capture Vienna, but were thrown back in disarray and then routed in 1620 at the Battle of White Mountain (*Bilá Hora*) just three miles west of Prague Castle.[GE39] In the larger sense, this Second Defenestration of Prague in 1618 began the Thirty Years' War that only ended in 1648, the last great religious war in European history. But in the local sense the Battle of White Mountain in 1620 was the great catastrophe, the end of any independent Czech or Bohemian state. For the next 300 years it was just a province of the Hapsburg Empire, ruled from Vienna.

The whole "Thirty Years' War" from 1618 to 1648 was particularly destructive in Bohemia, as armies from Denmark, Sweden (remember Gustavus Adolphus), Saxony, and Austria marched through and generally lived off the land. In terms of the Protestant-Catholic religious struggle that informed the wars, it ended with an overall Catholic victory, at least in this corner of Europe. The old "whose the reign, his the religion" formula was

---

38. GE Layer 38 frames a view of steep little ridge just east of Old Town Prague, where the July 14, 1420, battle climaxed; see Panoramio icon under pointer labeled "Vitkov—Jan Žižka from Trocnov."

39. GE Layer 39 is a Placemark, with pointer referencing a park on site of Battle of White Mountain. It's just about four miles from the Vltava River and less from Prague Castle (Hradčany); zooming out will show you the relationship.

applied here, too, and the ruler was Catholic. Perhaps a quarter of the whole population—mostly Protestant—emigrated (a few secret groups of Lutherans survived in the Bohemian hills, and a few secret Hussite groups survived in Moravia). Another quarter of the population died from war or disease. New Catholic nobles were brought in to take over the estates forfeited by Protestant exiles. The early nationalism that had developed with Hussite armies in the 1400s seemed to fade away, in a world limited to the interaction of landlord and peasant. Occasionally—usually after a peasant rebellion against the draft labor demanded by the lords—the Austrian central government in Vienna would send up a decree designed to mediate between lord and peasant, but by and large Vienna seemed far away and generally passive.

Roots of the Czech national renaissance

That began to change about a century later, as the Austrian Empire transformed itself in a way that would directly impact Czech and Slovak lands. It started abruptly in 1740 with the new Prussian King Frederick II's seizure of the rich province of Silesia[GE[40]] from the new Austrian Queen Maria Theresa. Two major multi-state, even world wars, resulted—the War of Austrian Succession of 1740–48, and the Seven Years' War of 1756–1763. At the end, Prussia still held Silesia, and was well on its way to first-class status as a European power—a story of which you have already seen the end in the Germany chapter. But in the struggle, even despite the loss of Silesia, Austria was strengthened too. This generally involved the Austrian central government taking away power and privilege from the great landlords—including a new taxation system by 1748 that paid for a 100,000-man army, a new state bureaucracy, and that even paid off the state debt. Maria Theresa's government also paid close attention to commerce and industry, and especially after the loss of Silesia, Bohemia led the Austrian Empire in the area of textile mill growth. By the 1770s the government had created a network of grammar schools, high schools, teacher training colleges, and even vocational colleges.

As progressive as she was in many areas, in that of religion Maria Theresa was not. She strongly supported the Jesuit order until the Pope ordered its dissolution in 1773. She expelled all of Prague's 20,000 Jews in 1745, and later widened it to include all the Jews in Bohemia and those of Moravia's major cities. But when she died in 1780 and was succeeded by her son, Joseph II, he brought the tolerance of the late Enlightenment to Austrian lands. Protestant and Orthodox Christians as well as Jews had virtually all restrictions on them lifted, and Joseph dissolved all the Catholic monasteries that administered no socially beneficial charities. In the first year of his reign he curtailed censorship, unleashing a flood of new newspapers. He also ended serfdom that first year of his reign, at least in name, replacing it with "moderate subjection" of peasant to lord. He seemed to be the classic "Enlightened Despot" called for by the Philosophes of the French Enlightenment. But protests from the landed elite slowed his reforms to a standstill by the last year of his life (1790), and after that the response to the armies of the French Revolution became the primary focus of the Austrian government.

In that 1740–1790 period ruled over by Maria Theresa and Joseph II, mother and son, you see the real beginnings of a Czech cultural nationalism. The first Masonic lodges in Prague were set up in 1742, and inside them aristocrat and commoner rubbed shoulders without distinction. By 1772 a Prague society for math, history, and natural history was set up; it would evolve into the "Royal Bohemian Society of Sciences." A "Patriotic Theater" for Czech-language works was built in New Town, Prague, in 1786. Czech-language newspapers and Czech-language publishing concerns, albeit short-lived, were established. Prague University got its first Chair of Czech Language and Literature in 1791. But before we get into full-blown cultural nationalism with the nineteenth century, there is one more thing we need to do, both for a fuller understanding of modern Czech nationalism, and for that of many others, too.

Ideal patterns of cultural nationalism

Let's now talk about the logic of patriotism built on a single ethnic group, but in a more detailed way than the four-step model (identifiable cultural group, negative stimulus, cultural nationalism, political nationalism)

---

40. GE Layer 40 is a Polygon showing Silesia in red, located just northeast of today's Czech Republic and over half its size; today almost altogether in Poland.

introduced in the German chapter. In particular, the author would like to expand on the critical "cultural nationalism" step, first offering an ideal model. In the state of Tennessee they have wonderful pictures of Tennessee Walking Horse champions that turn out to be composites of different photos—one that shows the raised foreleg best, one that shows the mane and the arched neck best, one with the tail blowing in the horse's slipstream best . . . . On that model, here is an ideal composite of championship cultural nationalism in modern Europe. Although it is a composite that was never fully realized in any single national experience, it is "true" in the sense that each part of it was realized somewhere, and in the sense that it all makes a coherent pattern.

A. **Language revival** is the first place to start. In most modern European ethnic groups, as of 1800 there was no single standard language—no standard Greek, or Czech, or Italian, or Finnish, or Irish, or Hebrew (for Russian Jews). Typically there was a classical language available in old manuscripts or perhaps archaic religious usage, and then there were widely varied regional dialects. These modern dialects tended to be less than sophisticated, because the sophisticated element of society spoke the local "world-class" or "imperial" language. There are at least four parts to this language-revival process:

    I.   First, a standard grammar has to be "harmonized" from the archaic classical language and the current dialects. Adamantios Korais did this for modern Greeks in the generation before the Greek independence movement of the 1820s.

    II.   A dictionary of the newly harmonized language has to be constructed. Making up this dictionary usually includes having to invent many modern words on the basis of ancient linguistic roots. Eliezer Ben-Yehuda did this for modern Hebrew, inventing even the word for "dictionary" in the process.

    III.   Some writer of genius has to commit to this newly created language. It can be a poet or a novelist or a translator, but the demonstration has to be convincing that here is a live language with no limitations. Chaim Bialik's early twentieth-century work in Hebrew is a good example here.

    IV.   An educational movement has to at least try to re-teach the mother language to intellectuals, first, and then all young people of the cultural group. The Gaelic League in Ireland, formed in 1893, was ultimately unsuccessful in reintroducing spoken Gaelic to the Irish masses, but it did ensure the political celebration of the Gaeltacht where it was still spoken and the presence of some Gaelic classes in the secondary schools. The Hebrew Youth Clubs of eastern Europe were more successful in their primary object.

B. **Literary recovery and new literature creation** closely follows language revival. There are three kinds of literature that seem to be of special cultural significance:

    I.   Collections of folktales must be made. The Brothers Grimm were the classic example of this, and every self-conscious European ethnic group soon wanted its own folktale collection. Afanas'ev, you've already seen, did this for the Russians around 1860.

    II.   Collections of legends needed to be made. The Grimms did this too; Yeats and the Irish Literary Society specialized in it.

    III.   The folk epic has to be dusted off and polished by professional study, if it exists. In a 1912 German edition of the *Nibelungenlied*, the editor said that when the original was given to Frederick the Great of Prussia back in the 1700s, the king remarked that it was not worth a charge of powder. Now, said the editor, it has become the pride of the Fatherland. If the folk epic is available only in fragments, these must be scissored-and-pasted together into a whole, as Elias Lönnrot did with the Finnish *Kalevala*. And if the ethnic group has no discernible epic, maybe some enterprising author needs to forge a plausible one, and hide the evidence of forgery as long as possible. The Scot MacPherson apparently did this with his once-famous Ossianic poems.

IV. In addition to the work with these three traditional forms of literature (or "orature"), some modern author needs to mine these three literary veins, and use the material to create popular modern works. Again, Yeats was a famous Anglo-Irish name in this regard.

C. **History recovery** is important as well.

I. First, the glory days of the cultural group (and every cultural group has its glory days) need to be written about from the point of view of an enthusiastic member of the group itself.

II. Then the whole sweep of history needs similar treatment.

III. Last, history ideally has to be shown leading inevitably to the present or future dominance of the cultural group. The Prussian historians Sybel and Treitschke in the mid-nineteenth century, with their historicism, are excellent examples.

D. **Music revival and creation** usually parallels that of literature:

I. The folksongs and dances have to be researched and popularized—easy enough to do while you are out there collecting the folktales anyway. But then sophisticated composers need to do two things to the admiration of their countrymen and foreign experts:

II. Use folk musical idiom—melodies, harmonies, rhythms, instrumentation—as a mine for modern works. Béla Bartók and Zoltán Kodály in Hungary are models in this regard.

III. Create musical tone poems around images of the nation's land or history. Richard Wagner did this in his German national opera after 1843; Jean Sibelius is the great Finnish exemplar.

E. **A cult of physical fitness** needs to be created. This really has two levels, one non-violent and the other violent:

I. Stress the physical fitness of the young people who must win an upcoming war or physical struggle with some domineering occupying power. If necessary, import outside techniques the way "Turnvater" Jahn imported Scandinavian gymnastics devices onto the German scene. Better yet, turn young people away from foreign games and exercises and back to those traditional in their own culture, as you've already seen Michael Cusack do in Ireland with the Gaelic Athletic Association.

II. Create a paramilitary organization with a cult of uniforms and physical fitness, as Vladimir Jabotinsky did with BETAR in the eastern European Jewish communities after 1923 (as you'll see in a later chapter). You've already seen how the G.A.A. was fertile recruiting ground for the Irish Republican Brotherhood.

The forerunners

Now, with the ideal raised foreleg and streaming tail of cultural nationalism fresh in your mind, consider how close the following figures from nineteenth-century Bohemia, Moravia, and Slovakia come to the ideal, in forging a "Czechoslovak" national mentality.

Josef Dobrovský (1753–1829) was born in Hungary because his father was stationed there as a soldier, but he was educated in schools in Bohemia. He first discovered and began study of the Czech language while in a college preparatory school in Německý Brod,[GE41] and later did advanced study at the Jesuit institution in Klatovy, south of Plseň. For a time he studied philosophy at Prague's Charles University. He joined a Jesuit monastery at Brno, in Moravia, but the whole Jesuit order was disbanded in 1772, when he was just nineteen years old. Most of his later life he alternated between the country seat of a Count who employed him, and academic institutions in Prague (in Prague he lived on Kampa Island, which anchors the western end of Charles Bridge). A superb linguist, he did detailed work on a Czech grammar and wrote a history of the Czech language, bringing

---

41. GE Layer 41 is a Folder titled "Dobrovský sites"; a reader can explore these at will, beginning with Německý Brod.

out the ultimate edition in 1818. This was all written in German, of course, since he was having to invent a harmonized Czech language himself. He also was fascinated by the use from the ninth to the eighteenth centuries of Church Slavonic in the branches of the Orthodox Church from Russia in the east to the Dalmatian coast in the west. Dobrovský saw this as one of the binding ties between the great majority of Slavs. The grammar of Church Slavonic that he wrote, then, had overtones of a broad Slavic cultural nationalism, and this former Jesuit came to regret the inroads his most Catholic order had made into Orthodoxy back in the days of the Counter-Reformation. Dobrovský was a major figure in the creation of both the Czech Academy of Sciences and the National Museum that was established in Prague in 1818. He died on a research trip to Brno, the biggest city in Moravia.

Josef Jungmann (1773–1847) was the first good writer to use Dobrovský's newly harmonized Czech language. He was from the little hill country village of Hudlice,[GE42] about twenty miles west and a little south of Prague. He taught high school for a time in the mainly German-language Labe River town of Litoměřice/Leitmeritz, but before he was thirty he moved to Prague permanently. He first taught Czech language at the grammar school in Old Town, but then finished up his doctorate in math and philosophy and gradually rose through the academic ranks at Charles University—actually winding up as President in 1840. He was, first, a tireless translator of great works of world literature into Czech, beginning with Milton's *Paradise Lost* in 1811. In 1825 he finished a massive *History of Czech Literature* based on extensive manuscript research and written in Czech. In his translations he found himself regularly having to invent words for which the Czech language had no real equivalents. This led him into decades more of work on a Czech dictionary that eventually ran to 4,500 pages in five volumes! He, like Dobrovský, had some Panslav overtones as well, thinking that eventually all the Slavs might pick a single alphabet and a single "middle" Slavic speech, and on that basis form a super-Slavic state that would dominate the world.

So together Dobrovský and Jungmann regenerated (and frankly sometimes created) the modern Czech language; and after philology came literature. By 1821 Jungmann could already see this Czech literary future in three young friends of his, writers just in their twenties—Kollár, Šafárik, and Palacký.

János Kollár (1793–1852) was the first good poet of the Czech language revival, even though he was by original culture and language a Slovak. He was born in Mosovce[GE43] in one of Slovakia's beautiful inter-mountain valleys, and lived with a cousin and went to school in the little town of Slovenske Pravno just five miles across the same valley. He went on to the big Danube River city of Bratislava for his advanced secondary education, becoming head of an orphanage there for a time. He went on to the University of Jena, over in the Germanies, and here drank deeply of Romanticism. Then for thirty years, most of his working life, he pastored a Slovak Lutheran church in Budapest. Like Bratislava, it was a big Austrian regional capital city on the Danube; but unlike Bratislava, it was overwhelmingly Hungarian. He wrote, said one author, as a Slovak who saw his nationality "threatened by Magyarization." His most famous work was *Slávy dchera* (*Daughter of Slava)*, a sort of epic of sonnets which was a love story on the surface, but with a longing for independence underneath. The hero of the epic wanders along rivers that were sites of former Slavic glory, but are now dominated by other peoples. It was Kollár's insistence on the "essential affinity" of Czech and Slovak languages that was most decisive in creating a "Czechoslovak" unity movement. Perhaps surrounded by fiery Hungarian cultural nationalists—the Hungarian language, after all, is not even in the Indo-European language family, much less Slavic—he may have found Czech and Slovak cultural differences insignificant by comparison.

Pavel Šafárik (1795–1861) was also Slovak, from the village of Štitnik[GE44] on the southeast side of today's Slovakia. As a young man he taught in the great Danube river city of Bratislava and became close friends with Palacký (see below). He wrote on Slavic language and literature, and gravitated to Prague by the 1830s. In 1837 he published a book on Slavic antiquities, which meant at that time not just things but cultural patterns. The book triggered intense new interest in the early history of the Slavs.

František Palacký (1798–1876) was the first really great historian the Czechoslovak national movement produced, and his work in history led him directly into national politics. Palacký was raised in an eastern Mora-

42. GE Layer 42 is a Folder titled "Jungmann sites"; its Placemarks begin with Hudlice.
43. GE Layer 43 is a Folder titled "Kollár sites"; its Placemarks begin with Mosovce.
44. GE Layer 44 is a Folder titled "Šafárik sites"; it begins with Štitnik.

vian village, Hodslavice,[GE[45]] where Hussite traditions were still secretly alive. Then he went to school in the Slovakian city of Bratislava—to the same Evanjelicke Lyceum (Lutheran prep school) Kollár had attended. Not many Czechs knew the Slovaks as well as Palacký did, and he liked them and sympathized with the oppression they lived under. When in 1823 he too moved to Prague, Dobrovský made sure he had access to key private libraries and was sheltered to some extent from government censorship. Palacký researched the glory days of Czechoslovaks, before 1620 when their last independence was lost at the battle of White Mountain. Hostile Austrian officials eventually cut him off from library sources, and his history ended in 1526. R. W. Seton-Watson, in his classic 1943 *History of the Czechs and Slovaks,* wrote that to a foreign reader a hundred years later there was nothing especially brilliant about Palacký's writings, unless you consider what he did in the context of his times. Only then could you understand why his history made him "the father of his people":

> . . . it was this achievement, whose full value can only be realized in the setting of an enslaved nation, a long-neglected language, a hostile Church and a denationalized middle class, that thrust upon him, with that suddenness which revolutions evoke, the political leadership of a new epoch.

> He brought them back to life, gave them courage and belief in a forgotten or despised past, and proved to them that they had achievements in the moral and intellectual sphere of which any nation might be proud . . . .[8]

By "denationalized middle class," of course, Seton-Watson meant those educated families of Czech-speaking background who raised their children to speak German, the official language of the Austrian state and the "cultured" language of much of central Europe.

At the time a fourth man shared the general reputation of the three above, although the luster has now gone from his name. Václav Hanka (1791–1861) was once the most famous collector of west Slavic epics. In 1817 he made a wondrous discovery in an ancient church tower in northern Bohemia of some ancient Czech poems, the oldest epic yet found from north and middle Europe. Joseph Dobrovský published it. Then, miracle to say, he found another epic in a castle in southern Bohemia. Even Dobrovský got a little suspicious at this point, and modern historians are virtually unanimous that Hanka forged them both. Excitement over the epics, however, probably brought many people to the Czechoslovak cultural nationalism movement who stayed with it even after the epics were shown to be fake.

The Slav Congress in Prague in 1848

By the revolutionary year 1848, Liberal Nationalism seemed as strong in Czech and Slovak lands as in German ones. František Palacký and company saw their future being debated at the Frankfort Parliament in terms of the *Kleindeutsch* vs. *Grossdeutsch* solutions to German unification (remember the argument over the "small Germany" limited mainly to German speakers vs. the "great Germany" that included all the populations of the Austrian Empire that we talked about in Chapter 3). In angry reaction they called a Prague Congress of all the Slavic nations inside the Austrian Empire, and also invited guests from major outside Slavic groups, particularly the Russians and the Polish. Pavel Šafárik made the ringing opening speech. But the Slav Congress, just like the German Parliament at Frankfort, was soon paralyzed by controversy. Mikhail Bakunin, a leading anarchist, was the most vocal Russian delegate, and left-right differences over politics were added to differences over how inclusive a Slavic nation might be formed. By June there were barricades in the streets, and the bitter Austrian commander Windischgrätz, whose wife had been killed by a stray bullet from the street fighting, shelled the city. The last gasp of a constitutional committee dominated by Palacký called for an eight-part federal Austria: (1) German Austrian districts; (2) Czech and Slovak districts; (3) Polish districts; (4) Illyria (the Slovene districts); (5) the Italian Tirol and Lombardy-Venezia; (6) South Slav districts; (7) Hungarian districts; and (8) Romanian districts. This federal compromise, however, never came to pass in Austria as political reaction swept the field.

---

45. GE Layer 45 is a Folder titled "Palacký sites"; it begins with Hodslavice.

The raising of nationalist hopes and the dashing of same in 1848 also seems to have been an important step in the century's Czechoslovak cultural nationalism. Karel Havliček (1820–1856), who got his secondary education in Německý Brod (today's Havlíčkův Brod, named in his honor),[GE46] is a good example. By age eighteen or so he had migrated to Prague. A radical Panslav by his early twenties, he went to Russia to teach, and cooled considerably in his admiration for Russia after his direct experience with the repressive rule of Nicholas I. Back in Prague, he became a popular satirical poet and journalist, founding his own newspaper in 1848. He hit on the idea of writing about Ireland's civil rights and home rule struggles to get around the censorship, and let his readers draw their own obvious lessons about how all this applied to Czech and Slovak lands under Austrian rule (this device worked very well, and that of course is concrete proof to your author that a single underlying pattern informs all modern national movements!). Havliček's nationalism was so radical that he was deported in 1851 to Austria's ethnic Italian lands and was only allowed back into his homeland years later when he was dying.

The nationalist composers: Smetana and Dvořak

It was Havliček's best friend who became the biggest name in Czechoslovak musical cultural nationalism. Born in Litomyšl,[GE47] on the Moravian side of today's Czech Republic, and growing up in the little town Jindřichův Hradec just over in the edge of Bohemia, Bedřich Smetana (1824–1884) was early on encouraged in music by his father, a good amateur musician. Sent to the prep school in Německý Brod, he and Karel Havliček became best friends and constant companions at school, until Havliček left for Prague in the late 1830s. Attracted by Havliček's description of what was going on in Prague, the fifteen-year-old Smetana transferred to a school there in 1839—the one led by Josef Jungmann. The musical scene there, however, was so lively and so appealing to him that he soon dropped school, aspiring to be a composer and concert pianist. His father was having none of that, however, and he was sent back to school, first with an uncle, and then with a cousin who was a school principal. In 1843 his father finally let him pursue a musical career. He went to Prague, made a living by teaching music to the children of a nobleman, and formally studied composition himself.

He was twenty-four years old in June of 1848 when the revolution broke out in Prague, and he was as caught up in urban insurrection as Victor Hugo's fictional young hero Marius in *Les Misérables*. He defended the barricades, and wrote revolutionary marches and a "Song of Freedom" for the occasion. After 1848 his finances were poor, and anyway life in the autocratically governed Austrian Empire was as depressing for him as for all those who wanted national independence. In 1856 he left to take a job in Gothenburg, Sweden. Here he taught piano, and added to his earlier enthusiasms for Mozart and Liszt a new enthusiasm for Wagner.

In 1859 Austria was defeated in a war with France, and Slavic nationalists in the Empire hoped they might take advantage of that to gain a measure of home rule. Soon Smetana left Sweden and came back to Prague to help create a Czech national opera. By 1866 he produced *The Bartered Bride*. In these years, no longer a young man, he worked hard to teach himself to speak and write Czech instead of his native German. For seven years he worked on a set of six symphonic poems called *Ma Vlast* ("My Fatherland"), and most of them, including the famous *Vltava*, were finished by 1875. This tone poem for the river running through Prague is frequently known to modern audiences, ironically enough, by its German name *Die Moldau* rather than the Czech *Vltava*. It ought to be required listening for all modern students of Czech and Slovak nationalism, but be careful: it is so sweet and powerful that it may convert you, too. You hear it rising as a small creek, then growing in volume and stateliness; hilltop castles, medieval dances and jousts are conjured up, and reflective, quiet reaches midcourse. The grand, dramatic part pictures your approach and entrance to Prague, and then the musical river gets

---

46. GE Layer 46 is a Placemark referencing Havlíčkův Brod.
47. GE Layer 47 is a Folder titled "Smetana sites."

quieter and is very quietly absorbed by the Labe (Elbe)—with a two-part exclamation point at the end for all the history and scenery you've envisioned. Try it out, in audio and video; the footnote explains how.[GE48]

Antonin Dvorak (pronounced something like DVORR-zhak, you may remember) may be more familiar to an American audience because he spent some time in the U.S. Born in 1841, he was fifteen years, almost a generation, younger than Smetana. Dvorak was born at Nelahozeves[GE49] on the Vltava River just twelve or thirteen miles above its confluence with the Labe. It was a typical medieval village complete with castle. The magnificent nearby Veltrusy mansion with its high architecture must have impressed him as a boy. His father, a butcher turned inn-keeper, taught Antonin enough violin so that by age five he could entertain the customers. The whole family moved to nearby Zlonice where his father ran "The Big Inn" there, until it went broke five years later. His father, worried that Antonin's German language was not good enough for any kind of professional career, sent him at age fifteen to Česká Kamenice (then Böhmisch Kamnitz) for a year to live where nothing but German was spoken.

The next year, when Antonin was sixteen, he convinced his uncle that he had made a serious commitment to a musical career, and the uncle financed his studies at the Organ School in Prague for two years. Perhaps the key public event of those two years was the 1862 founding of the Czech National Theatre. Up to this point there was only a German theatre in Prague, doing operas in German, French, and Italian. A Czech theatre, of course, aspired to perform Czech materials in the Czech language. Within a couple of years Dvorak moved into an apartment with four roommates and a piano, and began a lifetime of composing such work. For a time here in Prague he played viola in a Bohemian Provisional Theatre Orchestra conducted by none other than Smetana. Not much of Dvorak's earlier work has survived, but by the 1870s he was producing lasting works celebrating the Czech heritage. Among them were the operas *The Devil and Kate* (based on a play which was based on a Czech folktale) and *Rusalka* (a fairy tale opera about a human falling in love with a water sprite, performed in 1901 to great public acclaim in Prague). He is perhaps more famous for his nine symphonies, some of them commissioned by British and U.S. orchestras. By 1884 he had made enough money to buy some land from a brother-in-law near the mining town of Příbram and to build on it a little house. For the rest of his life, except when traveling, he spent summers there and winters in Prague.[9]

From 1892–1895 Dvorak was Director of the National Conservatory of Music in New York City. His secretary there talked him into taking his family to spend the summer of 1893 in Spillville, Iowa. As Dvorak himself wrote later, it was "a completely Czech village," with its own Czech-language school and its own St. Wenceslas church. The family spent over three months there, with most of Dvorak's afternoons spent interviewing the old-timers in town about their memories of the old country. From his New York days came the "From the New World Symphony"; from his Spillville summer came "The American Quartet" and "The Piano Quintet" chamber music. He died in 1904 in Prague and was buried in Vyšehrad cemetery.

---

48. GE Layer 48 is a Folder titled "Vltava/Die Moldau." It has forty Placemarks referencing and framing Photos icons from the very spring where the Vltava rises down to its merging with the Labe. Of course you need the music of "Vltava/Die Moldau" to go with it. One YouTube site available as of this writing is http://www.youtube.com/watch?v=kdtLuyWuPDs and it includes the whole piece by the Czech Philharmonic. But it is illustrated just with pictures of Prague itself. So use the music, but minimize the YouTube site and get back to Google Earth to go through my forty suggested Placemarks. "Fly" to each in turn by double-clicking on the Placemark icon, and while you are flying, turn it on by clicking in square at left (each is symbolized by a light blue pushpin icon). You can click on blue layer titles if you want to get additional information, but you can save time if you're under time pressure by just clicking on Photos icon under each blue pushpin icon. Look briefly at the photo that pops up, then click somewhere off the picture to turn it off, and finally double-click on the next Placemark icon to "fly" there. The music is about 11 minutes (660 seconds) and you have forty sites, so you need to average 16.5 seconds per site, including "flying" time between them. Go to Tools—then Options—then the Touring tab, and set "Time Between Features" to 10 seconds (any faster makes the countryside hard to see as it flies by!). This gives you 6.5 seconds to click open and briefly look at each photo, which should be enough. The last two loud notes of the tone poem—the musical exclamation point—should have you hitting a forty-first and last Placemark, "Overview," which zooms you out to a view that frames the whole river, where you started.

49. GE Layer 49 is a Folder titled "Dvorak sites." You can explore Nelahozeves and all the other sites mentioned in this and the next two paragraphs.

Sokol

In 1862 a gymnastics society called *Sokol* ("Falcon") was founded in Prague. Its distant inspiration was the German *Turnverein* from Napoleonic days, but it outgrew its model. Eventually its national assemblies (each called a *Slet*, or "flock" of falcons) would feature as many as 15,000 young athletes performing advanced gymnastics in unison. It had as strong political and even military overtones as the Gaelic Athletic Association in Ireland. During World War I, the President-to-be of the 1918 state, Tomáš Masaryk, had as one of his two key lieutenants the current president of Sokol. Towards the end of World War I the membership of Sokol became the de facto army and police force, and they fought Hungarians over Slovakia.

Budweisers into Czechs and Germans

A good many terms relating to beer come from what were in the nineteenth century the still mainly German-speaking towns of Bohemia. "Pilsner," from the city of Plzeň/Pilsen,[GE50] was a process developed there in the 1840s that produced a very clear, pale beer. The brand name "Budweiser" came from the Vltava river town of Budweis/Budějovice—today's České Budějovice[GE51]—about seventy-five miles due south of Prague. In the 1870s a modernizing faction gained control of the beer cooperative there and exported some to the United States. Disappointingly for them, international sales didn't really take off, and even worse, a couple of German-Americans in St. Louis named Eberhard Anheuser and Adolphus Busch appropriated the name Budweiser for their own beer and turned it into the first real nation-wide seller in the U.S. International lawsuits were apparently still in progress almost a century and a half later.

More to the point for our purposes here, however, is a history written about the people of the town, also traditionally called Budweisers: Jeremy King's 2002 *Budweisers into Czechs and Germans: A Local History of Bohemian Politics, 1848–1948*.[10] It is one of the best local case studies of European cultural nationalism (and political nationalism, and socialism) that your current author has ever read. In general it shows how the patterns of cultural nationalism generated in the intellectual community (as described above for Czechs and in an earlier chapter for Germans) "took" with the general public in one particular town—a good vantage point from which to look at this critical century. In the coming pages, as nationwide events are related, specific examples will be given of what went on in this one little Vltava River town. All of the local illustrations (and a few of the nationwide ones) come from King's book.

In the mid-nineteenth century, Budweis/Budějovice had a perfectly bilingual mayor (with a nickname in each language), and a mostly bilingual population which in general thought nothing special of whichever language they spoke most. The old nobility still called itself neither Czech nor German but "Bohemian." A good bit of the population was "Habsburg-loyal," and the pro-German and pro-Czech factions in politics were still embryonic. But in the course of this century from 1848 to 1948 modern cultural nationalism as an ideology tore that bilingual population apart—in Budweis/Budějovice in particular and in fact in virtually every town in today's Czech Republic in general. Virtually every individual was forced by circumstance (including new ideologies!) to commit to either an extreme German or an extreme Czech patriotism.

In just a word of background, Budweis/Budějovice was founded in 1265 under the last and greatest of the Přemysl kings, Otakar II. German colonists were allowed to set it up near the linguistic border between the mountain German speakers and the lowland Czech speakers. An island near the confluence of the Vltava and a smaller river was fashioned into a beautiful and functional medieval fortified city, still largely intact and worthy of an informed tourist's visit.[GE52]

50. GE Layer 50 is a Placemark referencing Plzeň/Pilsen, the big city of eastern Bohemia mentioned earlier as home of the famous Skoda works.

51. GE Layer 51 is a Placemark framing a view of České Budějovice, shown by yellow Pushpin icon, in relation to Prague and the Vltava River valley.

52. GE Layer 52 frames a view of the old medieval city, moated and walled. The central square, today's Náměstí Přemysla Otakara II, is named for the king who commissioned the town in the 1260s. When it was established by a German population it was called the Hauptplatz, or Main Square. The town hall (today's Radnice) is the southernmost building on the east side. A good many Photos icons scattered around the medieval city let you do a virtual tour.

Here is the (very brief!) summary of the first almost six centuries of the town. In the Hussite Wars it stayed loyal to the Catholic, Austrian side, withstood a siege by the Hussites, and with the ultimate 1620 Austrian (and Catholic) victory at White Mountain was rewarded for its loyalty by being made a "free royal town." German-speaking "burghers" monopolized political power and kept the town purely German speaking for almost two centuries thereafter. During the Napoleonic wars, however, Budweis/Budějovice was occupied by various armies for a time, and the German burgher monopoly faded. Czech-speaking immigrants began to move into town, of necessity speaking German in the town's business world, but still socializing in Czech. Jeremy King talks about the early "asymmetry" between the German and Czech languages in and around Budweis/Budějovice in those days. Anyone with a secondary education got it in German; it was the language of higher culture and administration. The Czech language was for country things—not without its charm, but with the image of being boorish or farmer-ish.

The Liberal-National revolutions of 1848, however, began to make the Czech language, at least in the ideal, the equal of German, and more of a symmetrical opposite to German. At one time there were three separate elections going on: (a) to the radical German Parliament at Frankfort, working to create a Liberal-National U.S. of Germany; (b) to the radical Czech national movement in Prague, calling for linguistic equality and the autonomy of the "crown lands of St. Wenceslas" and strongly opposing being put inside any new *Grossdeutsch* state; and (c) to a new and at least temporarily more democratic Habsburg legislature, which was actually given the authority to write a new constitution for "Bohemia." The German decision makers in Budweis/Budějovice were split between options (a) and (c). They created a "National Guard" to patrol the city for the emergency, and began to call themselves "true Bohemians" (meaning German speakers) as opposed to "Czechs" (Czech speakers). On the Czech side a Budweis/Budějovice chapter of the Prague-based "Slavic Linden Tree" society was created, demanding linguistic equality and of course opposing any inclusion in a German state.

The quickening growth of cultural nationalism first became visible to all about 1861, when after some fifteen years of reactionary repression the Austrian government moved towards constitutionalism and allowed a good bit more local decision making. Although upwards of 60 percent of the Budweis/Budějovice town population spoke German as a first language, a second Czech-speaking middle school was announced by the bilingual mayor, along with a request for a new schools inspector who would be truly bilingual. An "Ultra-German" faction angrily protested; although the school was built, the inspector who spoke only German was kept. In 1862 "Ultra-Czechs" demanded that the town choral society, the *Liedertafel* (literally "Song Table" in German) sing at least every third song in Czech. When the society refused, the Ultra-Czech members broke away and formed their own choral society, the *Beseda* (Czech for a "get-together"). When an important local politician died the next year, the *Liedertafel* sang in German at the church funeral, and the rival *Besesda* sang in Czech at the burial site.

Inside the Dual Monarchy's Cisleithania

In 1866, as you've seen in the Germanies chapter, Austria was defeated by Bismarck's Prussia and excluded from German (*Kleindeutsch*, "small German") affairs. The key battle, in fact, was in today's Czech Republic by the headwaters of the Labe River near the town of Sadowa/Königgrätz, today's Hradec Králové.[GE53] The next year Austria tried to solve its most pressing internal problem, a fiery Hungarian independence movement, by giving Hungary autonomy within an "Austro-Hungarian" monarchy. Habsburg domains were split in roughly half, connected only by the monarchy. There was "Cisleithania," or the "Austrian Empire" made up of the northern, western, and southwestern rim of the old realm;[GE54] and there was "Transleithania," or "Hungarian Kingdom,"[GE55] which made up of the rest. The cumbersome names Cisleithania and Transleithania,

---

53. GE Layer 53 is a Placemark, a red pushpin icon, locating the battlefield in relation to upper Labe River. Zooming in on the Placemark will reveal a good many Photos icons, mostly of battlefield memorial structures (in Czech, a "pomnik").

54. GE Layer 54 is a Polygon titled "Austrian Empire/Cisleithania," shown in red.

55. GE Layer 55 is a Path titled "Hungarian Kingdom/Transleithania," shown as a thick black line outlining the southern border. Everything in-between the black line and the red "Austrian Empire/Cisleithania" Polygon (and the little stretch of Adriatic Sea coast) is the Hungarian Kingdom.

incidentally, were named for the very small Leitha River[GE56]—more of a creek or brook, really—that was the border between the two halves of the monarchy on the road fifteen miles southeast of Vienna (in Latin "Cis" means this side of, "Trans" means across). The key point here is that from 1867 until the Austrian monarchy evaporated in 1918 at the end of World War I, a growing Czech (and German) patriotism took place in this Cisleithanian half of the monarchy, which had its own interesting policies on how to harmonize linguistic nationalism with the monarchy.

From the very beginning, increasingly self-conscious Czechs pressed hard to make it a trio instead of just a duo of autonomous states. Instead, in this Cisleithanian half of the Austro-Hungarian monarchy, German power actually increased for a few years. In 1867 the aldermen in Budweis/Budějovice canceled plans to build a Czech-language high school. In reaction, the local Czech-speaking Catholic bishop came up with the funds for a private school, and on the same day ground was broken for the school and a St. Wencelas church right next to it. Czech-speaking villagers converged on the place in their thousands, and turned it into a festival. Within two years the town had its own chapter of Sokol, the Czech gymnastics club. With the Prussian victory over France in 1871, and the creation of the German Empire, the Austrian government began working out a "trialism" government that would have given Czechs the same rights as Hungarians. It went all the way to the Emperor Francis Joseph's desk. He refused to sign it, however, and riots broke out all over Czech lands. In Budweis/Budějovice they morphed into a pogrom against the tiny Jewish minority there.

Over the next decade the German-Czech rivalry in Budweis/Budějovice only sharpened. There was some economic modernization: the medieval walls were razed, and gas lighting was introduced to the city center, for example, but it was all contracted out to German-speaking construction firms and set up to favor German-speaking neighborhoods. Budweis/Budějovice was gerrymandered into the smallest electoral unit in all Bohemia to keep German-speakers in charge there. When the German-speaking town government routinely vetoed proposals for Czech-speaking schools, the Czech-speakers invested heavily in private schools and other organizations. The *Beseda* got a magnificent new building with restaurant, ballroom, and smaller meeting rooms. German speakers in reaction built an even more expensive *Deutsches Haus* for their *Liedertafel* and other functions. They put the director of the *Turnverein*, the German gymnastics union, on the city payroll, and required German-style gymnastics in every public grammar school in town. In Jeremy King's view, the two language sides had by this time grown much more symmetrical: the German Liberals had become "more German and less liberal," and their opposites "more Czech and less Catholic."

Count Taaffe's "Iron Ring"

The next turn of the wheel of Cisleithanian politics favored the Czech-speakers. In 1879 the Austrian Emperor asked an old friend, the Bohemian aristocrat Eduard Taaffe, to create a government. Taaffe thereupon put together his "iron ring" of federalist, Slavic, and Catholic constituencies. By 1880 governmental directives ordered Bohemian offices to quit favoring German at the expense of Czech. Political representation was decided by the local proportion of language speakers. The choice was "German," or "Bohemian-Moravian-Slovakian," and voters could only pick one. There was no "Habsburg" choice, and the polarization of the population into Germans and Czechs proceeded. In the 1881 census, the number of people claiming to be Czech speakers in Budweis/Budějovice was a virtual tie with numbers of German speakers. From this point on, the German city government was on the defensive, fighting a rear guard action to try to stop or at least slow a Czech takeover.

The remaining German government in town put up a bust of Joseph II (who had wanted German to be the lingua franca of Habsburg lands) right in front of the *Beseda* building, guaranteed to provoke hostility. They created a "Union of the Bohemian Forest" from the German-speaking population in the hill slopes of the Šumava Mountains south of the city, with the object of replacing Czech-speaking maids and factory workers with German-speakers. Both sides worked to get their members to buy only from German-speakers or Czech-speakers, each eventually producing a directory of "correct" firms.

---

56. GE Layer 56 is a Path titled "Leitha" showing in light blue the relevant part of the course of the little Leitha River southeast of Vienna.

Both sides of the linguistic divide split into rival factions. A "folkish" German element emerged to challenge the Liberal one; a pure Aryan state of greater Germany must be created, it said—no compromise. On the other linguistic side, a Liberal "Young Czech" faction broke with the "Old Czechs," criticizing their reliance on the great landowners, the Catholic Church, and for their political conservatism. Another political group, socialism especially in the form of a Marxist Social Democracy, leaned towards the German-speakers (as its founders Marx and Engels had earlier). Up until 1895, however, only the last of these five, the Social Democratic faction, was anti-Austrian government. When Emperor Francis Joseph himself visited Budweis/Budějovice in that year, folkish and Liberal Germans and Old and New Czechs all staged demonstrations of welcome. The first sentence of the Emperor's short speech was in German, and the second in Czech. By this time every Budweiser had had to choose between being a German-speaker or a Czech-speaker, but they could still be roughly equal and loyal to the old dynastic state.

After 1895, however, polarization would grow to such an extent that one language group would have to become dominant—even to the extent of destroying the other—and have its own state.

The electorate had gradually expanded in the late nineteenth century. In 1882 the vote was given to the "five-florin" men—the shopkeepers and small craftsmen who paid as little as five florins in taxes. Then in 1896 all males twenty-four and over were allowed to vote in some elections. Looking back, this expansion of the electorate worked to increase the language group polarization. The elections of 1897 were a real turning point, in terms of the appearance of violence on a regional scale. The Social Democrats generally sided with the German speakers, thus enraging the Czech speakers, who immediately began to create their own Czech-speaking socialist workers party (one of the first chapters was set up in Budweis/Budějovice). The new Austrian prime minister tried to entice the Young Czechs into a coalition government, offering them a law that made it a requirement that every official in Bohemia speak German AND Czech. By the fall of 1897 German protesters were out in the streets of Budweis/Budějovice (and in larger force in Prague and even Vienna). Czech supporters of the new proposal came out to meet them in even larger numbers, and there were several days of rioting and property destruction in Prague and other Bohemian cities. In Budweis/Budějovice it never turned that violent in 1897, but in the next elections in early 1899 an enraged Czech crowd, convinced the elections had been stolen, rampaged through the city trashing German (and Jewish) buildings. Army units had to be brought in to help the police quell the riots.

All this affected—you may have guessed it—the beer business in Budweis/Budějovice. The original brewery, established back in 1795, had remained for decades a tightly controlled German monopoly. There were some 400 buildings large and small associated with it, and if you owned one, you "shared" to that extent in the enterprise. By the early 1890s Czechs were secretly buying into the monopoly through third parties. When the Czech faction was numerous enough to force a look into the books, they found that some leading German political families were making a killing selling fuel and material at inflated prices to the co-op, and of course raised a great public outcry. The greatest Czech coup came in 1895, however, with the establishment of a rival Czech brewery in town, the "Shareholders' Brewery." It was set up as a modern corporation, with stock in small enough denominations that most anyone could buy some. In the "Each to his Own" campaign, all Czech beer drinkers were encouraged to drink only Czech beer. In Jeremy King's words, "In hoisting a glass, they [shareholders] could quench their thirst, increase the value of their assets, and serve the national cause all at once." A howling success, Shareholders' Brewery by 1901 had 130 employees and outproduced the original German one.

The Budweis/Budějovice Compromise

Cisleithania was made up of more than a dozen "crownlands," of which Bohemia was the single largest and next-door Moravia one of the larger ones. From 1905 on there were experiments in many of these, cautiously sanctioned by Vienna, to create electorates of different nationalities instead of trying to divide the land between a pure group of one versus a pure group of the other.

The last and in many ways most interesting of these pre-war Austrian plans to harmonize language-group nationalism with the monarchy came from Budweis/Budějovice itself. In painstaking negotiations over seven years, from 1907 to early 1914, the two leading German and Czech politicians of the little town gradually hammered out a plan for such separate national electorates, or cadastres. Voters were allowed to sign up as Czech or German, and it turned out to be 56 percent Czech and 44 percent German. But thereafter they were not to compete as factions. The Czechs were guaranteed twenty city aldermen and the Germans sixteen by this proportion, and most budgets would be split accordingly. By May of 1914 all that was left was for the Bohemian legislature to vote on it, and for Emperor Francis Joseph to sign it. It would have been a most interesting local experiment, reducing the friction between nationalisms, with leaders who were still Habsburg loyal. Had it worked, it is probable that varieties of it would have been adopted all over Cisleithania. It was derailed, however, by white-hot nationalism elsewhere in and adjoining the Habsburg state.

World War I

On June 28, 1914, the Austrian royal heir apparent and his wife were assassinated in Sarajevo by Yugoslavian nationalists from Serbia. Five weeks of ultimatum and counter-ultimatum followed, and then World War I got underway on August 3–4 as the rival alliances declared war on each other. In the non-German population of the Austrian Empire—the majority population by far—there was little enthusiasm for the war. There were some Habsburg-loyal troops, and stories of mass Czech defections were probably exaggerated over the years—but indeed there were defections. You have already seen the tens of thousands of the "Czech legion" strung out along the Trans-Siberian Railroad in 1918, trying to leave Russia which had been knocked out of the war, and to sail from Vladivostok back to some European theater of the war where they could join forces fighting against Germany and German Austria. Many Czechs who nominally stayed in the Austrian army didn't really pull while in harness. In the early 1920s a Prague-born satirical writer, Jaroslav Hašek, wrote a book still much loved in the Czech Republic—*The Good Soldier Švejk*. The "good" soldier on the surface of things was a fiery Austrian loyalist, but who through supposed thickheadedness and simplemindedness cleverly never quite got anyplace dangerous in the war.

In January of 1918 President Woodrow Wilson of the U.S. gave a speech to a joint session of Congress in which he presented his famous "14 Points" about the sort of political world that should ideally come about after the war ended with an Entente victory. Point number 10 of the 14 specifically dealt with Austria: "The peoples of Austria-Hungary, whose place among the nations we wish to see safeguarded and assured, should be accorded the freest opportunity to autonomous development." This was a fancy way of saying that each of Austria's major ethnic/language groups had the right to form its own independent country. Since the U.S. was now a belligerent on the Entente side of the war, and an Entente victory seemed more and more likely, this was a very important sentence as regarded the future of the lands of Bohemia, Moravia, and even Slovakia. It became even more important in April, with the appearance in the U.S.—at President Wilson's side, so to speak—of the man Americans called "Thomas" Masaryk, the George Washington of the modern Czechoslovak state.

Tomáš Masaryk and independence

Tomáš Masaryk (1850–1937) was born in Moravia,[GE57], though his father was Slovak. A brilliant student, he began his studies in Brno, the biggest city in Moravia, at a German-language secondary school, and then moved on to the University of Vienna where he got his doctorate in philosophy in 1876. A few years later, in a post-graduate year at the university in Leipzig, he met and fell in love with an American girl, Charlotte Garrigue. When they married shortly thereafter he took her last name for his middle name—and so is universally known as Tomáš Garrigue Masaryk today. By age thirty-two he was Professor of Philosophy at the university in Prague.

Masaryk was something of a Czech cultural nationalist from early in his academic career, starting a periodical dealing with Czech culture, but he was not uncritical of its excesses. He thought the Hanka epics were forgeries, and said so publically in the face of much nationalist outrage. In classically Liberal terms he criticized anti-Semitism and the crude literature it quoted. He served three terms, off and on, in the Austrian par-

57. GE Layer 57 is a Folder titled "Masaryk sites"; it begins with Hodonín where he was born.

liament (first as a Young Czech party member) and up until World War I had still not called for an independent Czechoslovak state.

With the outbreak of the war, however, he threw all his considerable energies into just that goal. He spent 1915 in London, lecturing in universities openly, and secretly helping mobilize an intelligence network in central Europe for the Entente powers. By 1917 he was in Russia, one of the key organizers of the Czech legion there. When Russia left the war formally in the March 1918 treaty of Brest-Litovsk, he headed for the United States, arriving in April. He got a hero's welcome in Chicago, where he had briefly taught earlier, and where there were large Czech and Slovak immigrant communities. As the recognized leader of the Czech and Slovak movement, it was Masaryk who proposed territorial boundaries for a new Czechoslovak state to the western allies. These were accepted, and such a state was duly recognized by the western allies on June 3, 1918—a full five months before Germany surrendered in the Nov. 11 "Armistice." On November 18 of that same 1918, he was elected President, and re-elected every election thereafter until he voluntarily stepped down in 1935, at age eighty-five.

With the disintegration of the Habsburg state in 1918, "Habsburg-loyal" ceased to be a political option. Although Masaryk worked to defend ethnic minorities in the new state, Czech and German identities, more and more confrontational, were the two main remaining options. Germans nation-wide as well as in Budweis/ Budějovice found themselves an embattled minority in a new and enthusiastically "Czechoslovak" state. It also spelled the demise of the old Bohemian nobles. As late as the 1880s, 300 noble families such as the Schwarzenbergs, Lobkowiczs, and Thuns owned fully a third of the land—alternating stays at their magnificent country estates in Bohemia with their city mansions near the court at Vienna. They had made some effort to build contacts with both the German and Czech parties, but in 1919 the new Czech National Assembly declared a massive land reform aimed at these noble lands, and by 1938 the nobles had lost a full half of their lands.[11]

The Third Reich and German ascendancy

With the Depression and the emergence of Adolf Hitler in Germany proper, there was a corresponding new enthusiasm for the "folkish" side of German-speakers in Czechoslovakia. A new Sudeten German Party (the name originally from mountains north of the Bohemian plain, but generally applied to the German-majority hill country all around the plain), secretly funded by the Nazi government in Germany, got upwards of 60 percent of the German vote in 1935—in the town of Budweis/Budějovice and in Bohemia as a whole. In March of 1938 the German army moved into Austria, at which point Germany now threatened Czechoslovakia from the south as well as the north and west. The enthusiasm of these folkish Germans living in the Czechoslovak state, who longed for union with the Fatherland, reached new heights. That was especially true in Budweis/ Budějovice, which was only eighty miles from Hitler's hometown of Braunau am Inn.

In late September 1938 came the infamous Munich Pact, wherein the western European liberal states gave to Hitler's Germany the Sudetenland[GE[58]]—majority German speaking areas of Czechoslovakia and also the mountain ridges around Bohemia that were the country's key natural defense features. Budweis/Budějovice was close but not quite inside the Sudetenland; but that ceased to matter in March of 1939 when German armies took the rest of the country. Speaking from Prague Castle on March 16, Hitler declared a "Protectorate of Bohemia and Moravia" (the Slovakian part of the interwar Czechoslovak state went to Hungary). "Masaryk Square" in Budweis/Budějovice was renamed "Adolf Hitler Square" (and for a time a box was built around the statue of a recent local Czech leader there, and the box draped with banners with swastikas on them). The leading German-language newspaper in town wrote "We are free!" In early June an enormous Nazi rally was held there. The folkish Germans were riding high; the Czechs generally laid low; the remaining Jews in town were terrified, and with reason.

---

58. GE Layer 58 is a Folder titled "Czechoslovakia: Munich conference" (for review; you have already seen it in Chapter 3). A Polygon outlined in red shows the original state; a Polygon in green shows territory taken from the Czech and Moravian parts that went to Germany, and a Polygon in blue shows that taken from the Slovakian part that went to Hungary (Hungary got the southern mountains, the rest of Slovakia was a puppet state under Germany).

On Sept. 1, 1939, Hitler started the European phase of World War II by invading Poland, and to the German dictatorship was added the martial law of wartime. The quick German victory over France in the spring of 1940 further depressed most Czechs. The overall Nazi plan of evicting Czechs from the Bohemian plain so as to give Germans *Lebensraum*, "living room," was slowed somewhat by Germany's wartime needs for the output of Czech factories and Czech labor. Eventually the government set a 50 percent compromise goal of absorbing "the better stock" of Czechs. To get everything moving again, in September of 1941 Hitler made the extremely racist and vicious SS officer Reinhart Heydrich "Reichsprotektor" of Bohemia and Moravia. With a carrot and stick policy he tried to reward those Czechs who collaborated, though he publicly said all Czechs (the 50 percent who wouldn't or couldn't become German) would eventually have to leave Bohemia. Those who resisted his rule could expect torture and execution as a matter of course. Heydrich approached "the Jewish problem" with a brutal efficiency. In April of 1942, for example, a train of nearly a thousand Jews was sent from Budweis/Budějovice to Theresienstat (Terezin),[GE59] a concentration camp up near where the Elbe cut through the mountains to Germany proper. It served as a holding pen before prisoners were sent on to outright extermination camps such as Auschwitz. Virtually no one on the train survived the camps.

Eduard Beneš and the assassination of Heydrich

Meanwhile, Eduard Beneš was trying to get recognition for a Czechoslovak government-in-exile in London. It was a familiar role for him: as a brilliant young professor of law and sociology at Charles University, he had gone to Paris in WW I to do the same thing! Beneš was the first and only Foreign Minister of the interwar state, until 1935 when he succeeded Masaryk as President. Thus he was at the helm when the titanic shock of the Munich Pact stripped Czechoslovakia of the Sudetenland. In the wake of this he resigned (more or less forced to do so by Germany) and moved to London. He organized a government in exile there by 1940, but at first had little success in getting the major allied powers to recognize it.

In late 1941 Beneš made a fateful decision, to send in a team of Czechoslovaks to assassinate the hated Reinhard Heydrich in the name of the Czechoslovak government-in-exile. He did this knowing full well there would be terrible retaliation from Hitler. The assassination team attacked Heydrich's car on a hairpin curve on the road heading north out of Prague towards Dresden[GE60] on May 27, 1942, and he died of his injuries a week or so later. And the Nazi retaliation was indeed terrible—perhaps 3,000 people executed. Having some (perhaps incorrect) information that men from the village of Lidice[GE61] were involved, Hitler had the 200 adult males there shot, the adult women sent to the camps, the children of what was judged to be acceptable Aryan stock put out for adoption by German families, the other children gassed, and every structure in the village razed. Nazi authorities then broadcast news of this nationwide. In Budweis/Budějovice, for example, the names of all those executed were published by the local Nazi authorities, and both the synagogue building and the Jewish cemetery were totally obliterated.

Allied reaction to this brutal retaliation was exactly what Beneš hoped for—recognition of his government-in-exile, and a growing consensus that Germans should all be kicked out of a post-war Czechoslovak state.

By 1943 the war had turned badly against Germany, in North Africa and even more spectacularly at Stalingrad and at Kursk. In June of 1944 the western allies opened a new front with the Normandy invasions, and the handwriting was clearly on the wall. By the fall of 1944, German farm families who had settled on conquered lands to the east were pouring back into Germany proper through Budweis/Budějovice. The town was bombed by the allies for the first time in the war in March of 1945; over 100 people were killed by it. On May

---

59. GE Layer 59 is a Placemark referencing Terezin/Theresienstat.

60. GE Layer 60 is a Placemark referencing the Prague suburb of Libeň, giving the approximate location of the assassination attempt.

61. GE Layer 61 is a Placemark referencing Lidice. Click on Panoramio icon under pointer, titled "Memorial of Lidice children . . .," for view of monument there. Layout of memorial shows clearly in the aerial view framed by the Placemark; other heartbreaking monuments pictured in nearby Photos icons. Lidice is about ten miles WNW of Prague; zoom out to see relationship.

5, just a few days before Germany's unconditional surrender on May 9, Czech mobs stormed the town hall. The pendulum had swung again, and further than ever.

In the wake of WW II

With the end of World War II and the destruction of the Nazi state, a Czechoslovak state was quickly recreated. By summer's end 1945, by the Beneš Decree, almost all Germans had been rounded up and readied for eviction ("transfer" was the politically correct term) from the country, and most of their property confiscated. The newly reborn state was (unfortunately for Beneš) enthusiastically socialist, because Czechoslovaks remembered having their frontier defenses given away at the 1938 Munich conference by the western allies, and because it was Soviet armies that did most of the liberating of the country. At Potsdam on August 2, Josef Stalin, Harry Truman, and Clement Atlee formally approved the expulsion of Germans from Czechoslovakia (and Poland, and Hungary). Then the trains really began to roll, carrying German-speakers stripped of virtually all property to a bombed out Germany that most had never even visited.

What did it look like in the town now known simply as České Budejovice? The swastikas and Hitler statues were pulled down, and Tomáš Masaryk's name went back up in place of honor on the central square. The *Deutsches Haus* was renamed the Stalin House. In July 800 Germans who had been rounded up locally were put in a guarded camp in town, with the Czech words for "An eye for an eye, a tooth for a tooth" written on the gate. Of 4,000 Germans who appealed their sentence as disloyal citizens, only thirty-four cases were reversed. Seventy German-speakers from the town were executed for wartime crimes.[12]

In the century-long polarization and growing rivalry since the Revolutions of 1848, Czech speakers thus had the ultimate victory.

Inside the Soviet Bloc

By 1946 the "Iron Curtain" separating the sphere of Soviet domination from the outside world was isolating Czechoslovakia from the west. The U.S.S.R. kept any of the Marshall Plan aid from getting into the country. In March of 1948 Jan Masaryk, son of the founder of the state and current Foreign Minister, was found dead in the courtyard of the foreign ministry building, several stories below his bathroom window. It was perhaps a suicide, but more likely yet another "defenestration of Prague," part of the Communist takeover.

After a few years under Stalinism's heavy hand, of course, a good many Czechoslovaks changed their minds about things Russian and even about things socialist. Nationalization of industries down to those with a few dozen workers was the order of the day—including the famous Shareholders' Brewery in České Budejovice. A most heavy-handed censorship allowed no free newspapers, and insisted that fiction celebrate the heroes and heroics of socialism. On the Soviet model, transportation and housing were free and food was cheap—but there was not much of any of it, and the contrast of living standard with Austria, just across the border, was striking. In 1968 there was a famous attempt to give a new and liberal face to Communism in Czechoslovakia, led by Alexander Dubček. His father had been a Slovak immigrant to the United States who was so disappointed in capitalism U.S.-style that he went back to the Socialist Bloc to build socialism, and even put his son Alexander in Russian schools. Judging by later events, however, some non-Soviet element must have entered Alexander Dubček's mind. Under his leadership, for a hopeful few months in 1968—"the Prague Spring," they called it—censorship was lightened and some modest western-style economic reforms begun. It provoked a reaction from Brezhnev's Soviet Union, however, which moved in with tanks. A hard-line Communist was put in power: no bloody purges, but a stern regime in line with Soviet domestic and foreign policies leaving no doubt that "spring" was over.[GE62]

A Czech independence, however, still stirred beneath the surface. It showed up best in the Czechoslovak version of *samizdat,* the "self-published" secretly circulated hand-written literature. Perhaps the most famous

---

62. GE Layer 62 is a Placemark referencing Prague, though mainly as an excuse for embedding the following video site: http://www.youtube.com/watch?v=xbbxw3To02g

A YouTube video, the first half has photos of Soviet destruction to the background of the sung "Internationale"; the second half to a Czech protest song. Do a Google—Images search on "Prague Spring" for others.

of these authors was Bohumil Hrabal (1914–1997). He was raised in Nymburk,[GE63] a little Labe River town less than thirty miles east of Prague that in many respects resembles České Budejovice. Child of an unwed mother, he was "influenced by a highly talkative uncle who arrived for a two-week visit and stayed forty years."[13] He became a law student at Charles University in Prague in 1935, but only finished his degree in 1946 because the Nazis had closed the universities during their tenure in the land. He worked on the railroads around Nymburk during the war, then lived in Prague for a time, involved in the theatre and supporting himself by working at industrial jobs. He got married in 1956 and managed a small factory in southern Moravia for most of a decade, and then in 1965 he and his wife bought a little house in his old hometown of Nymburk. This 1965 was a big year for him; he published *Closely Watched Trains* (made into an Oscar-winning movie in 1967), a great tale of the humorous problems of youth though with a tragic ending, drawn from his own days on the railroad. Then came the Prague Spring of 1968, with which he was associated, and he was banned from publishing. He turned then to samizdat, including most famously his *Městečko, kde se zastavil čas* [*The Little Town Where Time Stood Still*]. The major characters are a boy, his step-father who is the manager of a brewery, his free-spirited red-haired mother, and a crazy uncle who came to town for two weeks and stayed forty years . . . . One of the most unforgettable scenes in a companion story, *Cutting It Short*, is when the mother and the uncle climb the handrails up the 200'-tall chimney at the brewery. It is told from the perspective of the woman, remembering her long red hair being lifted up by the wind like a flame. The chimney is still there,[GE64] across the river from the old town, and presumably the view from there as given in the novel is not much changed.

Hrabal's prose was not so much anti-socialist as it was non-socialist, and certainly about as far from "socialist realism" as a writer could get: a sensitive manager, an impulsive mother, a less-than-heroic young boy, musings about Czech and German national consciousness, all set in an atmosphere something like the "magical realism" associated with Latin American writers such as Gabriel Garcia Márquez. His take on the German strand of Bohemian history, from the middle of *The Little Town Where Time Stood Still*, comes in a passage discussing the abandoned Dominican monastery on the edge of town, where a few things from the botanical garden there had managed to adapt to local conditions and grow on their own:

> . . . so that now, two hundred years after the abandonment of that garden, there are still strange flowers and bushes growing in the area, the descendants of those plants whose seeds climbed over the fence and adapted themselves to the habitat. Altogether it was a kind of tradition in our area to adapt yourself and merge with new and different times. Under Maria Theresa the country round about was populated with German peasants, whole villages and farmsteads, but as time went by, not only did these Germans adapt, but finally they merged with the land and the language, just like those plants from the botanic garden, and so now there is not a trace of the original Germans in this area, only the German names, whose bearers speak and feel themselves to be Czech.[14]

Hrabal got to see the emancipation of Czechoslovakia from the Soviet Union; he died in Prague in 1997. A few years before he died, he was visited in his favorite Prague pub[GE65] simultaneously by the current Presidents Václav Havel and Bill Clinton.

Velvet revolution, velvet divorce

This heavy-handed Soviet domination of Czechoslovakia lasted until Gorbachev's reforms (twenty years after the Prague Spring) in the Soviet Union. In October and November of 1989, thousands of East Germans trying to get to the west jammed the West German Embassy in Prague. This, plus the fall of the Berlin wall in November, also set things moving in Czechoslovakia. October 28, the old national holiday celebrating the 1918 birth of the modern Czechoslovak state, was celebrated in 1989 as never before (or since!). Czechoslovakia eased

---

63. GE Layer 63 is a Placemark referencing Nymburk.
64. GE Layer 64 references the brewery chimney at Nymburk, recognizable mostly by its shadow.
65. GE Layer 65 references Prague's *U zlatého tygra* (At the Golden Tiger) pub.

out from under Russian control so smoothly, compared to other East European states, that it was called "the Velvet Revolution." Václav Havel, a Czech playwright and political reformer, was the man of the hour and became President of the country. Dubček, a Slovak, re-emerged from obscurity too, and as Speaker of the Parliament became a rival of Havel. Dubček, however, never repudiated Communism, and he faded fast. In 1990, as Czechoslovaks set about reconstituting their state, problems arose even over the name: To keep "socialist" in the full title? The answer to that was eventually no. To hyphenate or not to hyphenate? that was a thornier problem. The original 1918 state name, "Czecho-slovakia," had been hyphenated until 1920 in a similar debate called "the battle of the hyphen." Havel now proposed a compromise, "Czech and Slovak Federal Republic," and it was adopted. The state had a federal assembly but separate Czech and Slovak lower houses. The first elections in June of 1990 saw the former ruling Communists win less than a fifth of the vote (19 percent in the Czech part and 19 percent in the Slovak part, evenly split).

So the whole state had Havel for President, but now the Czech part had its own Prime Minister and the Slovak part another. Vladimir Mečiar, the new Slovak Prime Minister, had been a Communist until expelled from the Party back in 1970. A colorful former boxer, the forceful Mečiar was dramatic but less than subtle as a politician. Václav Klaus, the new Czech Prime Minister, was an economist who seemed a cold intellectual by comparison, but was probably the more sophisticated politician. These two disliked each other at first sight, and quickly got into a public prestige rivalry. Klaus may have had in mind from the beginning splitting the economically more progressive Czech lands in the west from the commercially more backward Slovak lands. There had already been considerable modernization and liberalization on the Czech side. The main factories on the Slovak side were still those monstrous Stalinesque armament factories; not only were they inefficient, but the Cold War was over and arms markets had fallen on hard times. Havel as President had announced that for humanitarian reasons he eventually wanted to cut out all arms sales. He agreed to a U.S. request to stop the sale of 300 tanks to Syria, and that hurt the Slovak side much more than the Czech side. In sum, unemployment on the Slovak side was something like 12 percent compared to the 3 percent on Czech (Bohemian and Moravian) side, and Slovaks blamed some of this on Czechs. An "independent Slovakia" party got started in the east, and then a rival Czech one in the west. In July the two Prime Ministers met in the Moravian city of Brno and agreed on separation. President Havel pleaded for keeping ties, and asked for a national referendum. Polls as late as November showed Czechs at just over 50 percent for keeping the union, and Slovaks as high as 65 percent, but the two Prime Ministers would have none of it, and never called one.

On New Year's Eve of 1992, while the world's attention was on the continuing turmoil in the former Yugoslavia and the former Soviet Union, Czechoslovakia quietly split up into a Czech Republic and a Slovak one. It was totally peaceful, a "velvet divorce." They put up a sound stage on what the next day would be the border, and had a musical festival to celebrate. A Czech Republic of some ten million created in the west, and a Slovak Republic of some 6.5 million created in the east.

Will they get together again? Not likely. The Czechs quickly learned to love a separate existence. They felt they had leaned over backwards for decades to subsidize the more rural Slovaks, to give them more than a proportional share of seats in the legislature, to almost always have a Slovak President. All this, they felt, and then the ungrateful Slovaks kicked them in the teeth. And without what they saw as the economic drag of Slovakia, the Czech leaders hoped they might quickly meet requirements for European Union membership, to which most of them aspired. They had a minority of 400,000 Slovaks to deal with, mainly living in the Sudetenland (where the more rural Slovaks had gone to farm when the Germans who lived there were evicted after World War II); but this ethnic minority was less than 5 percent of the population, and presumably the really passionate Slovak patriots among them would move next door to independent Slovakia.

The Slovak state of around 6.5 million, with Slovak ethnicity proudly enshrined in its basic documents, also has 1.5 million problems. Six hundred thousand are Magyars (Hungarians) living in a fairly compact unit, totally indigestible by the small Slovakian state and generally favoring union with Hungary. Another 600,000 are Romani people (Gypsies), who have had more success in avoiding political restrictions and boundaries than any people in recorded history. Then there are another couple hundred thousand Ukrainians, Russians, and Bulgarians; they may be Slavic but are certainly not Slovak.

As it worked out, the Czech Republic joined NATO in 1999 and the European Union in 2004, and Slovakia joined both in that same 2004. Once again Germans can buy land in old Bohemia, including lands their families may have lived on for centuries.

The Bratislavan lesson

With this overview of the rise and fall of Czechoslovakia, the question obviously emerges, what are Czechs and what are Slovaks? Are these truly distinct nations, or just states of mind? Was there ever really such a person as a "Czechoslovak"?

In the Hussite Wars and Protestant Reformation of the fifteenth and sixteenth centuries, there were the roots of a Czech nationalism stronger that almost any other national movement in Europe. In the late eighteenth and then the nineteenth century, you had a near-championship cultural nationalism developing in the lands of Bohemia, Moravia, and Slovakia, among the peoples who spoke the fairly closely related languages of Czech and Slovak. Yes, there were once millions of people who thought of themselves as Czechoslovak. The strong belief that they were a "unitary" folk became a self-fulfilling prophecy, creating the Czechoslovakian state of 1918. So what happened to that belief?

If you are a native of the Danube river city of Bratislava, the capital of Slovakia today, you presumably have at least the subconscious choice of your own political identity (and something about human nature seems to demand that each of us commit to some group identity short of "all humanity in the world"). You can picture yourself primarily as a Bratislavan, a West Slovak, a Slovak, a Czechoslovak, a Panslav, or perhaps an East European, a European of the EU, and finally, maybe, a Citizen of the Western World. After some decades of reflection on this general topic, this author has concluded that most people choose to be patriots of the smallest cultural unit of belonging that has a good chance of economic and military survival. After all, the smaller the unit, the more cultural commonalities there probably are, and the more comfortable and predictable life probably is for you. Why join a larger, less homogenous unit unless there are real or perceived dangers that force you to it?

In the nineteenth century, in the vicinity of Czechs, Moravians, and Slovaks, the regional superpowers were first the Austrian Empire and the Russian Empire, with the German Empire added later. In this context a "Czechoslovakia" made sense as the smallest unit with a good chance of survival, and cultural nationalism was pressed into service to prove that such a unit had always been there.

From the 1930s to the 1980s, however, the power exercised in the region first by the Third Reich and then the Soviet Union was an order of magnitude greater than that of those nineteenth-century empires. Even a Czechoslovak political unit was too small to survive in that geopolitical climate. Many Czechoslovaks active in the Prague Spring of 1968 were understandably disappointed when it was crushed by the Soviet Union. It is interesting that some of them wished out loud that they had put their energy into some larger, East European unit instead of "wasting" it in this unsuccessful effort to revive an independent Czechoslovakia.

But then in 1989 the Soviet Union pulled out of Eastern Europe and itself began to disintegrate. The Cold War was over. The only large new political structure on the European horizon was the benign new federation of the European Community, now the European Union. All of a sudden not only was a Czechoslovakian state again viable, but pressures were so reduced that separate Czech and Slovak states were possible as well. In today's climate, maybe even an independent Bratislavan city-state could make a go of it, with its city center on the Danube and a shallow agricultural band around it. And so "Czechoslovaks," who existed in their enthusiastic millions as late as 1989, are now virtually impossible to find. Václav Havel may have been the last one (and even he became President of the Czech Republic from 1993–2003, and thus arguably just a Czech, no longer a Czechoslovak).

General lessons learned about modern European social mobilization

Any group of people that faces scorn tends to react to that, and to appreciate leaders that re-instill self-respect. Political nationalism did that for the middle classes in a Europe dominated by aristocrats, cultural nationalism did it for the peasant masses facing middle class financial domination, and socialism did it for the industrial workers working for wealthy industrialists. In this book's first seven chapters, you've seen the invention of these patterns in small groups of intellectuals, and then their communication to the general public:

○ political nationalism in the French Enlightenment and Revolution and Napoleonic draft armies, evolving (with the help of the British industrial revolution, and British and U.S. political thought) into the classical Liberalism of the nineteenth century—free press, free speech, and other U.S.-style constitutional guarantees; representative assemblies determined by expanding the vote from the propertied to include the educated; free trade.

○ cultural nationalism that eventually made language the single best key to ethnicity, and "folkish" states based on a perceived pure cultural past from Herder's postulated form-giving period. It tended to cluster around the smallest cultural unit consistent with economic and military survival at any given time. It generally led to universal suffrage, though with a tendency on its "folkish" side to glorify physical force and destroy the checks and balances that the Liberal state had created.

○ and socialism, especially Marxism, with its use of economics to analyze class attitudes and behavior, and its techniques of political education, underground survival, and guerrilla warfare. It tended to lead the modern European state in the direction of social welfare, and in its extreme Marxist form was as hostile to the checks and balances of the Liberal state as the "folkish" cultural nationalists were, though attacking from the left instead of the right. Despite the Marxist belief in "workers of the world, unite," socialism almost everywhere in Europe became the servant of cultural nationalism, not its master.

Political nationalism, cultural nationalism, and socialism—these all motivated individuals to commit more of themselves to the state, especially the nation-state. Tapping into these energies is what gave European and Europeanized states great power over the rest of the world (along with the parallel growth in technology). So Europeans in the age of neo-imperialism of the late nineteenth and early twentieth century generally dominated the rest of the world, and carved up most of it to suit themselves.

Those very "-isms" that were the source of this new European power, however, turned out to be as exportable as guns or cotton cloth. The second half of the story of the modern world is how the non-European world learned them and used them to achieve national self-respect and independence, though in part by becoming partly "Europeanized" in the process. The next seven chapters deal with the process of European intrusion and local response in the rest of the world, region by region, by focusing on a key transportation corridor per region (two for East Asia). Each is intended to be a regional history in microcosm, so as to try to keep things at a personal level and reduce abstract generalizing to a minimum. And each will make more extensive use of GIS (Google Earth variety), on the assumption that American readers are generally less familiar with non-European parts of the world.

Endnotes

1. See Mario Pei, *The History of Language* (Philadelphia and New York: Lippincott Co., 1949), especially his chapter on the Slavic Languages. Hugh Agnew's fairly recent survey history, *The Czechs and the Lands of the Bohemian Crown* (Stanford: Hoover Institution Press, 2004) begins with an excellent short introduction to the pronunciation of Czech.

2. Jean W. Sedlar, *East Central Europe in the Middle Ages, 1000–1500* (Seattle & London: University of Washington Press, 1994), p. 423.

3. Agnew, *Czechs and the Lands of the Bohemian Crown*, p. 9.

4. R. W. Seton-Watson, *History of the Czechs and Slovaks* (Hamden, CT: Archon Books, 1965), p. 15. Original edition in 1943.

5. OED, "ogre."

6. Agnew, *Czechs and the Lands of the Bohemian Crown*, p. 23.

7. Seton-Watson, p. 54.

8. Seton-Watson, p. 178.

9. Hans-Hubert Schönzeler, *Dvořak* (London & New York: Marion Boyers, 1984), pp. 32–111.

10. Jeremy King, *A Local History of Bohemian Politics, 1848–1948* (Princeton and Oxford: Princeton University Press, 2002).

11. Eagle Glassheim, *Noble Nationalists: The Transformation of the Bohemian Aristocracy* (Cambridge, MA, and London: Harvard University Press, 2005), pp. 2–3.

12. King, *Budweisers*, pp. 189–205.

13. "Hrabal, Bohumil," *Encyclopedia Britannica.*

14. Bohumil Hrabal, *The Little Town Where Time Stood Still* and *Cutting It Short* (New York: Pantheon Books, 1993), the first paragraphs of chapter 11.

Part Two

THE RESPONSE OF THE WORLD

Chapter Eight

"Strengthening Devotion to Patriotic Symbols": The Veracruz-to-Mexico City Corridor of Latin America

"Programa de Fortalecimiento al Culto de los simbolos patrios; Ceremonia de arriamiento de la bandera nacional" [A program of strengthening devotion to patriotic symbols; a ceremony of striking the national flag]

—(wall poster in the central square of Xalapa, Mexico, advertising a January 6, 2000, ceremony; found by the author most regrettably only on January 7)

CONTENTS

The heart of the matter—Introduction to area languages: Spanish—Introduction to area languages: Náhuatl—SECTION A: TOPOGRAPHY AND TEXTURE OF THE LAND—From the coast to the crest of the Sierra Madre Oriental—The altiplano, the volcano La Malinche, and the Sierra de Tláloc—The Valley of Mexico—SECTION B: "FIRST NATIONS" AND THE SPANISH INVASION—Before the Aztecs—The Mexica—Cortés and the Spanish invasion—SECTION C: THE COLONIAL ERA, 1521–1810—Colonial institutions take shape: encomienda and repartimiento—Christianity and Church institutions—The founding of Puebla—The Virgin of Guadalupe—Fr. Sahagún and the Indian-Spanish honeymoon—The hacienda—Commerce on rival roads—Royal fairs, royal convoys, and the Bourbon Reforms—SECTION D: INDEPENDENCE AND INTERVENTIONS—Beginnings of the independence movement—Ideas in the air—The "Interventions": foreign invasions of Mexico—Santa Anna—The main U.S. invasion—Benito Juárez, the Liberal Reforms, and the Civil War—The French invasion and Maximilian—SECTION E: THE PORFIRIATO AND THE REVOLUTION—The Porfiriato—The coming of the Revolution— Revolution: the military phase 1910–1920—Revolution: the cultural phase 1920–1940—SECTION F: SINCE THE REVOLUTION—The era of World War II—1968, Olympic Games and politics— Fidel Castro and Che Guevara in the Valley of Mexico—Liberation Theology—NAFTA and immigration—Lessons learned

The heart of the matter

Although we in the United States share a hemisphere with Latin America, in general we know no more about it than regions of the world much further away. It's a bit of a puzzle: with its fascinating pre-European-contact civilizations, its turbulent colonial era, and its dramatic independence movements and subsequent state histories—and the fact that there's no jet lag traveling north and south!—you'd think as a culture we'd have been more interested in it over the years. Lately we have more incentive to learn about it, of course, with Hispanic immigration being one of the hottest of our hot button political issues, and with new economic power-houses such as Brazil coming on line in international commerce.

This is the first of the "corridor" chapters of the book. As briefly explained in the Introduction, it's a teaching technique that goes into detail about one small part of a region, on the theory that it's more educational to learn a smaller history that keeps things on the personal level than to learn a much more generalized summary of the history of the whole region. No corridor can be perfectly representative of the whole, of course, but hopefully it will introduce many of the great Latin America-wide historical themes as a particular version of them plays out on that more intimate stage.

The small geographic stage we've chosen to represent modern Latin American history is the Veracruz-to-Mexico City corridor of Mexico. The Valley of Mexico was the site of one of the greatest of New World civilizations. The conquest of the Aztecs by the small Spanish force under Cortés proceeded along this corridor, and once the Spanish made the old Aztec capital their capital of New Spain, the road to Veracruz (and by ship to Havana and Cádiz) was their colonial lifeline. Here the hacienda-pueblo system took shape around 1600, and new cities sprang up as forts or as the fulfillment of the visions of monks. In the convoy-trade fair system of the 1700s, all the yearly trade goods brought in by the Spanish fleet to Veracruz were trundled up to Xalapa, seventy miles away but above the unhealthy fever zone, and meanwhile all the goods from New Spain and even from Japan by the "black ship" (that came from Asia yearly to Acapulco on the Pacific coast) were trundled across what is today Mexico to that same Xalapa. The independence movement of 1810 began just off our corridor, but the armies of the revolutionary priests Hidalgo and Morelos mainly swirled around Mexico City. Santa Anna, key military and political figure of the first third-of-a-century of Mexican independence, was born, raised, and trained in military affairs on our corridor. It was along this corridor that we, the U.S., pushed the third and most powerful of our campaigns in the U.S.–Mexican War of 1846–48. Here occurred the most important events of the Mexican Civil War of 1858–60 as landed interests and pro-Catholic forces rebelled against the Liberal laws of Benito Juárez. It was along this corridor that the French pushed their powerful invasions of 1862–63, setting up Maximilian as short-lived "Emperor." Here ran the first railroad in the country, the Veracruz-to-Mexico City one finished by 1872. All along our corridor you can see the buildings built from 1876–1910, an era called the Porfiriato, as a brain trust of Stanford-trained economists tried to modernize and industrialize Mexico under the dictatorship of Porfirio Díaz. Here occurred the most dramatic events of the Mexican Revolution that exploded in 1910 and lasted until 1920, every bit as important in Mexican history as the Russian Revolution was in Russia. There's hardly a flat surface in a government building on our corridor that's not covered with a leftist political mural from the cultural revolution from 1920–40. Mexico City is where in the mid-1950s the Brothers Castro of Cuba first met Che Guevara, a radicalized Argentine doctor, and got training in guerrilla warfare on a farm not far out of town. Mexico City and Puebla on our corridor were key cities in the Liberation Theology movement that convulsed much of Latin America from the 1960s to 1984. The signing of NAFTA, the North American Free Trade Agreement between Canada, the U.S., and Mexico that went into effect January 1, 1994, triggered the Zapatista Rebellion in southern Mexico; the political ramifications of that radiated out to some extent along our chosen corridor.

Many of those events and movements have their parallels in other Latin American countries, and of course every Mexican you meet, there or here, is to some extent a product of that history. I didn't really get introduced to Latin American history and culture until I was forty years old, at least in terms of travel and language study. I wish I had "discovered" it earlier in life; Mexico in particular now seems to me to be one of the most fascinating places in the world. What follows, then, is a "read, travel," approach to our first representative world regional corridor—read the text, and let the Google Earth footnotes "fly" you throughout our corridor in a virtual way. If it interests you the way I hope, you'll go read better works and <u>really</u> travel there, if you haven't already.

Introduction to area languages: Spanish

Most of the words and phrases associated with the history and geography of this corridor are Spanish. Like Portuguese and French, to which we gave a nod in the first and second chapters of the text, Spanish is one of the Romance languages that evolved from Latin (the other main modern branches being Italian and Romanian). The French, in their 1860s invasions of Mexico, worked hard to popularize the term "Latin America," so as to get French included on an equal footing with Spanish and Portuguese as a "legitimate" major language in this part of the world.

For a non-native speaker trying to pronounce Spanish, one good thing about written Spanish is that you always know exactly which syllable is stressed. There are just two basic rules for normal stress: (a) if a word ends in a vowel, an -N or an -S, stress is always on the next-to-last syllable (the *penúltimo*); and (b) words that end in any consonants other than -N or -S are stressed on the last syllable. Any different stress requires an accent mark placed above the vowel to be stressed (as in how the word *penúltimo* is written, where you can see it over the third vowel from the end). But confusingly enough, another use of that accent mark is to distinguish homonyms—*sí* = "yes" versus *si* = "if," for example. You can get away without using accent marks in casual writing such as e-mail, but for anything formal if you omit the accent in an accented word you have misspelled it. So, as a Latin American historian friend of mine says, just make the effort and do it correctly. With word processing programs it is usually just a matter of Insert, Symbol, . . , only taking a few seconds. Native speakers and writers of the language will appreciate it; non-native speakers and writers will be impressed by your erudition!

The Spanish alphabet is almost exactly the one we use to write English, with a few exceptions: it has traditionally had four extra letters. CH written together like this is a separate letter, if you are looking words up in an older Spanish dictionary. LL is a separate letter, pronounced like our Y (even a Y going on J for some American Spanish dialects such as Cuban), so the South American cameloid *llama* is NOT pronounced like the word for a Tibetan Buddhist monk *lama*, but more like "yama." Spanish has an N like ours, but then also an Ñ as a separate letter, an N with the "tilde" on top that makes it an NY sound (Italians do this with a G before the N, so the Italian *signor* is pronounced much like the Spanish *señor*). RR is a separate letter, as in "Sierra"; for those who can do it, it should be rolled dramatically with the tip of your tongue vibrating against that ridge above your front teeth ("tip and trill," language books have it). Incidentally, in 1994 there was a linguistic revision in which the CH and LL were demoted from being separate letters, though they are never separated when dividing syllables. RR and Ñ are still separate letters even in recent Spanish-language dictionaries.

Spanish Js and Xs are pronounced much like our Hs. One interesting aspect of Mexican Spanish is that 500 years ago the Spanish invaders used their X to write down the Náhuatl sound of SH. In many Mexican Spanish words the Xs are still pronounced like SHs. The city and state of Tlaxcala on our corridor, for example, is still pronounced Tlash-CAH-lah. And even when the X in these old words has taken on its modern H sound—as in México (pronounced "MAY-hee-ko" in Spanish today), you can understand how they got that from the word the Aztecs used for themselves, pronounced "meh-SHEE-kah," which the Spanish at the time duly spelled "Mexica."

Vowels in Spanish are pronounced as in most European languages: A is usually like AH, as in father; E is almost like our long A; I is like our EE; O is our long O; U is OO as in "boo," not as in "yu."

Here are a few common Spanish-language place names you're likely to encounter in browsing through maps of Mexico, including the Google Earth surface: for watery features, *bahía* (bay), *río* (river), and *lago* (lake); for population centers, *ciudad* (city), *puerto* (port), and *pueblo* (village); for transportation features, *camino* (highway, road), *puente* (bridge), and *calzado* (causeway); for features of the landscape, *volcán* (volcano), *sierra* (mountain range), *cerro* (hill), *barranca* (a gorge or steep-sided ravine), and *llanos* (flood plain).

Introduction to area languages: Náhuatl

Even an elementary discussion of spoken and written language along our corridor in central Mexico brings us to the *Náhuatl*, the language that is often commonly referred to as the Aztec language. It was not the only native American language of our corridor. In what is today Mexico there were at the time of the Spanish invasion dozens if not hundreds of languages. Near today's Veracruz where the Spanish first landed, for example, a coastal Indian language called Totonac was the majority local language, and there are villages that still speak it today. But the common language of the high plains, radiating out from the Valley of Mexico from even before the time of the Aztecs, was Náhuatl, which made a fair bid to be Mexico's lingua franca (as Latin was in medieval Europe or "business English" is in much of the world today).

Náhuatl has had some impact on modern English, mainly through the medium of Spanish. It makes regular use of what is to us the unusual consonant combination of TL—as in the word *Náhuatl*, of course, but also in the word for spear thrower, *atlatl,* which has two sets of those TLs; in their word for a salamander that stays in aquatic form to breed instead of transforming into a terrestrial, an *axolotl*; but more familiarly in *tomatl, coyotl, xocolatl,* and *ahuacatl*. Spanish speakers almost 500 years ago apparently had as much trouble with that TL as modern English speakers do, so what resulted was the easier-for-them-to-pronounce TE, as in *tomate, coyote, chocolate,* and *aguacate,* and it was a short trip from there to the English words tomato, coyote, chocolate, and avocado. *Guacamole* is what resulted when some early Spaniard heard *ahuacatl* (avocado) and *molli* (sauce) from some speaker of Náhuatl. Some very common Náhuatl parts of existing place names that appear on maps of Mexico (including Google Earth) are the suffixes *-tépetl* or *-tépec,* meaning hill or mountain, and *-pan* meaning the place of.

SECTION A: TOPOGRAPHY AND TEXTURE OF THE LAND

From the Gulf of Mexico port city of Veracruz due west to the heart of Mexico City is almost exactly 200 miles as the crow flies (though the crow has to gain a mile-and-a-half of altitude on the way). If you were to draw a rectangle that takes in all of Mexico City and some of the coast around Veracruz, including the major roads and railroads connecting the two cities—roughly 215 miles by 75 miles—that is only 2 percent of the entire Mexican territory, and of course only a tiny fraction of all of Latin America.[GE1] But as you've already seen this corridor played such a huge role in Mexican history (and secondarily in Latin American history) that studying it and what happened along it over the last 500 years can yield valuable insights into why Mexicans (and to some extent Latin Americans, though there is a huge variety of experience here) are as they are today.

The basic idea here, as with the other "corridor" chapters to follow, is to begin by getting a feel for the topography and texture of the land before getting into the history proper. For anyone in the world, of course, the ups and downs of the terrain, the watery features and soils and vegetation and animals, and finally the local architecture, all go a long way towards what makes home, home.

From the coast to the crest of the Sierra Madre Oriental

So begin a trip in your own imagination along this corridor. Start with the Veracruz port facilities themselves, piled high with containers and bristling with cranes, that have recently grown out from the mainland to reach the old island fort of San Juan de Ulúa.[GE2] South of the main port facilities comes the downtown waterfront of government buildings, exclusive restaurants, hotels and businesses, the visual centerpiece of which is the Carranza Lighthouse.[GE3]

On either side of the port and city proper stretch the gray sand beaches,[GE4] reefs, and islands[GE5] of the coastline of the State of Veracruz. It can be muggy and oppressively hot here in the summer. Before medical

---

1. Google Earth Layer 1 is an aqua rectangle enclosing our VC-MC corridor; it is about 215 miles E-W and 75 miles N-S. This same rectangle will begin all the rest of the sub-chapters, too. Turn it on by left-clicking once in the square box at left of layer title, zoom into a framed view of the rectangle by left-clicking twice on the layer icon, a polygon, and pop open associated text by left-clicking once on the blue layer title. Turn off this text box by clicking the X in top right, or by clicking anywhere on the map screen outside the rectangle.

2. GE Layer 2 is a Placemark referencing a picture of a tall sailing ship in front of the old island castle of San Juan de Ulúa; behind the fort are all the cranes and containers associated with modern shipping. Click on Panoramio icon in foreground indicated by pointer, "Buque Español pasando enfrente el Castillo San Juan de Ulua, en Veracruz, México."

3. GE Layer 3 is a Placemark referencing the Carranza Lighthouse which visually dominates harborfront of Veracruz. Click on most any of the Panoramio icons under Placemark pointer for a view.

4. GE Layer 4 is a Folder titled "Seacoast near Veracruz." Its Placemarks reference Panoramio icons views of beaches, dunes, and waterfront shelters twenty miles north and south of the port city.

5. GE Layer 5 is a Folder titled "Coral reefs and islands off Veracruz." It frames a view of the reefs from about thirty miles up. The one Placemark in the folder references a photograph of the Isla de Sacrificios set against city in the background.

developments as of 1900 or so, this was the season for yellow fever; it killed about half of all new European arrivals within the year (the local name for it was the *vómito negro*, since victims tended to bleed internally and then throw up the blackened blood and die soon thereafter, cheery thought). Winters are still warm enough for swimming, making it a popular vacation spot for Mexicans from higher or more northerly parts of the country. The winter season is complicated a bit by the arrival of fifteen to twenty *nortes*, gale force winds from the north that can blow for days at a time, sometimes with rain and always with rough surf. Hurricane season there is generally the same as in the U.S. Gulf Coast, growing through the summer and peaking in September, then fading away as winter cools the waters of the greater Atlantic and especially the Gulf and Caribbean.

Just inland from the coast is a belt of dry and thinly vegetated sandy lands, several miles wide.[GE⁶] Today sugar cane fields, pastures, and groves of glossy, evergreen mango trees dominate the lowlands at the bottom of the slope. Then the coastal plain takes on a gentle roll and swell, and a traveler going west soon starts up the complicated slope of the Sierra Madre Oriental, the "Eastern Mother Mountain Range."[GE⁷] Most of it is green year-round because the moisture in the Gulf air gets squeezed out by the higher and cooler altitudes as it rises up the slope.[GE⁸] White water rivers drain this eastern slope of the Sierra Madre and even small ones have cut deep gorges, or *barrancas*, into the natural terraces of the slope.[GE⁹] This means that it is almost always easier to go up (west) or down (east) the slope than to travel across it (north or south). A barranca you could easily talk across without raising your voice might take hours to cross. Somewhere around 3,000′ elevation travelers start to see clumps of oaks. In the old days this was cause for rejoicing, meaning they had climbed above the yellow fever zone. Generally at this altitude, too, in well-watered zones you find coffee plantations. The coffee bushes, which may look to a U.S. native like straggly camellia bushes, do best when partly shaded. Pasture lands dominate the drier areas hereabouts. Bird life, to hint at zoology, is rich in both these zones and includes at least two dozen species of hummingbirds, half a dozen kinds of trogons, the whole range of neo-tropical parrots from macaws down to parakeets, and occasional colonies of *oropéndola*, those brilliant black and yellow oriole relatives the size of crows that collectively hang their suspended woven nests from single isolated trees. Mornings on the eastern slope are typically crystal-clear and chilly, but noon even in winter usually warms up to short-sleeve shirt weather, with the increasing humidity gradually reducing the long-range views with haze. By late afternoon the warm, wet air from the Gulf has often risen to meet the colder, drier air coming down off the *altiplano*, or high plains. This causes a weather phenomenon somewhere between fog and drizzle so common here that the people of the eastern slope have come up with a special name for it, *chipi-chipi*.

Even halfway up the eastern slope of this Sierra Madre Oriental travelers become aware of former volcanic action: an occasional miniature but perfect volcanic cone rises up out of forest or pasture, extinct now and green with tropical vegetation.[GE¹⁰] One such lush, truncated cone rises up out of the city of Xalapa itself; today it is a park and bird sanctuary.[GE¹¹] Higher, at 6,000′ to as much as 12,000′ in sheltered parts, comes a belt of

6. GE Layer 6 is a Placemark referencing a Panoramio icon at town of Cotaxtla, on a river of the same name. It is thirty miles southwest of the city of Veracruz, and still low country at about 140′ elevation.

7. GE Layer 7 is Folder titled "Paso del Macho and the barranca Atoyac." Double-click Folder icon to fly to framed view, read text there, and then open Placemark 7a. for interesting close-up view of a sort of open train tunnel hugging the side of the ravine.

8. GE Layer 8 is a Placemark set some forty miles inland (west) in the vicinity of Jalcomulco, a river valley town at about 1,100′ elevation with hills a thousand feet higher on either side. The indicated Panoramio icon shows general scenery, the promised lush green of the eastern slope of the Sierra Madre Oriental.

9. GE Layer 9 is a Placemark referencing a Panoramio icon of Teocelo waterfall, at just less than 4,000′ elevation. It creates a barranca narrow enough to talk across, but incredibly difficult to travel across, for miles below the falls.

10. GE Layer 10 is a Placemark referencing Panoramio icon underneath pointer, "Xico hill (Acamalin)." It is just one mile away from the Teocelo (Texolo) waterfall and barranca; green with vegetation, it is clearly of volcanic origin.

11. GE Layer 11 is a Placemark framing a view of Xalapa's Cerro Macuiltépec. Many of the Photos icons there are panoramic views of the city, though a few show the obvious caldera, or crater, of the little, long extinct volcano.

pines.[GE12] At the top of the slope stands a massive forty-mile-long volcanic ridge, with both ends rising well above the tree line.

The northern end of this volcanic ridge is dominated by the Cofre de Perote, a great shield volcano over 14,000′ high with what looks like an absurd little pillbox hat on its top. The first Spaniards to see it thought the square volcanic extrusion looked like the chest a church in Spain would use for storing holy relics, called a *cofre*, kin to the English word *coffer*. The city of Xalapa, capital of the State of Veracruz, is sited at from 4,500′ to 5,000′ elevation.[GE13] Xalapa is only about fifteen miles from the base of Cofre de Perote, of which it has a great view.[GE14] The peak itself is named for the town of Perote on the altiplano at the northwest base of the volcano.[GE15] In Náhuatl the name for the mountain is *Nauhcampatépetl*, possibly meaning "the mountain with something square."

On the southern end of the mountain range, at 18,400′ the snow-capped *Pico de Orizaba* stands as the highest point in Mexico and one of the highest in North America. On clear days (especially in winter when a *norte* blows in with cool, clear air) Orizaba Peak can be seen from Veracruz and even from miles out into the Gulf. [GE16] It is almost as symmetrical and beautiful as Mt. Fuji and half again taller.[GE17] As a traveler goes southwest from Veracruz through the cities of Yanga[GE18], then Córdoba, then Orizaba, and then little mountain villages north and west of Orizaba,[GE19] Orizaba Peak grows to dominate the horizon. It claims several lives a year, on average. Inexperienced climbers often assume that it is tropical, so how dangerous could it be? Hazardous indeed: it is part of Mexico's Frozen Land (*Tierra Helada*), the fourth and highest zone (after the warm, temperate, and cold *Tierra Caliente* of the lowlands, the *Tierra Templada* of the slopes, and the *Tierra Fría* of the high plains). The old name for Orizaba Peak in the Náhuatl is more poetic—*Citlaltépetl*, or Star Mountain: from a distance its snowcap seems to float unsupported in the sky. A lesser summit on the ridge near Orizaba Peak is the 15,000′ La Negra, where a Mexican-U.S. radio telescope has been built up in the high and clear.[GE20]

The brash Cortés, as we'll see later, crossed the sway-backed Sierra Madre in the middle between Cofre and Orizaba, where it dips to about 10,000′ at its lowest point—maybe to get a military officer's look at the lands beyond. Savvy later travelers generally avoided the whole ridge, either swinging north of the Sierra through the city of Xalapa (also spelled Jalapa, whence *jalapeño* peppers) and topping out at the town of Perote, or swinging south of the great ridge through the cities of Córdoba and Orizaba and topping out at the little altiplano town of Esperanza. The northern route through Xalapa should be slightly easier, being a few

---

12. GE Layer 12 is Placemark referencing Panoramio icon titled "LIGERA NIEBLA EN EL BOSQUE"; open for view of light fog in piney woods. As you can see from the framed Google Earth surface view, the forests are patchy here, but thicker and more continuous on the slopes of the higher Sierra.

13. GE Layer 13 is a Placemark framing a Google Earth view of the 40-mile-long crest of the Sierra Madre Oriental. The city of Xalapa, the capital of the State of Veracruz, is from 4,500′ to 5000′ elevation. It is fifteen miles east northeast from the peak of Cofre de Perote, the tallest point on the right-hand part of the skyline. On the left hand end (southern) end of the Sierra is Mexico's highest point, the Pico de Orizaba.

14. GE Layer 14 is a Placemark referencing a Panoramio icon under pointer, titled "cofre de perote"; it seems to be a telephoto view of the mountain from Xalapa.

15. GE Layer 15 is a Placemark referencing a Panoramio icon with a good view of the mountain from the west, from near the altiplano town of Perote which helps give it its name.

16. GE Layer 16 is a Placemark indicating such a view of the Pico de Orizaba, or Citlaltépetl, from the "Mouth of the River" estuary just south of the city of Veracruz, click on Panoramio icon underneath pointer, titled "Citlaltepetl Volcano From Boca del Río."

17. GE Layer 17 is a Placemark referencing a Panoramio icon titled "Pico desde Xico." The photographer was at or near Xico, a small town ten miles south of Xalapa, and at roughly the same elevation. The peak is about thirty miles away.

18. GE Layer 18 is a Placemark referencing a Panoramio icon titled "Citlaltepetl desde Yanga, Ver," for view of Orizaba Peak. Yanga is ten miles east of Córdoba, a much bigger city which shows just beyond the next dark green mountain ridge.

19. GE Layer 19 is a Placemark referencing a Panoramio icon titled "Pico de Orizaba por Carlos Peniche." Photographer is about 10,600′ elevation; mountain peak some four miles away

20. GE Layer 20 is a Placemark referencing the peak of La Negra. At 15,000′, La Negra is a subsidiary summit of Orizaba. Many Photos icons to explore here, of the joint U.S.–Mexican telescope array.

miles shorter on its way to Mexico City and having a more gradual ascent. The southern route up through Córdoba and Orizaba is more rugged. It is easy enough to get from the port of Veracruz to Córdoba, but between Córdoba and Orizaba is the *Barranca de Métlac*, a sheer-sided ravine some 900' across and 400' deep.[GE[21]] The city of Orizaba itself is fairly level, lying in the western end of a huge box canyon. It is one of the world's most beautiful sites for a city, with towering walls of eroded limestone and semi-tropical vegetation, a bit like the karst topography around the Li River in southern China long popular with Chinese painters. The road on up to the altiplano from Orizaba, however, is spectacularly difficult. It goes through the well-named *cumbres*, or peaks, cutting through ridges and tunnels, hanging precariously on steep slopes.[GE[22]] Nevertheless the new interstate toll road (the *autopista*) generally follows the main railroad from Veracruz to Mexico City along this southern Córdoba–Orizaba route, leaving lesser roads and railroads to serve the easier northern Xalapa route. Why they take this harder way will be answered later in the chapter.

The altiplano, the volcano La Malinche, and the Sierra de Tláloc

When travelers round either northern or southern shoulders of the Sierra Madre Oriental they leave the pine forests and come out onto the altiplano, experiencing the quickest and most dramatic change of scenery on the entire road to Mexico City. The rain shadow west of the Sierra translates into immediate semi-desert, a narrow southern extension of the larger deserts of northern Mexico that comes down across our corridor. Especially when rounding the northern shoulder on the Xalapa–Perote road, in as little as two miles a traveler sees the scenery change from thick stands of pines to sandy flats and stony hills. The dominant vegetation is prickly-pear cactus, Joshua trees (close kin to the yucca plants familiar from the American South and West, but here grown into fantastic, Dr. Seuss-like trees),[GE[23]] and *maguey* ("ma-GAY"), the giant agave or century plant [*Agave americana*].[GE[24]] The rows and fields of maguey that give some symmetry to the arid landscape are striking to a first-time visitor. The maguey provided fiber (*henequen*) for woven fabrics; a kind of fine paper; ready-made needles and thread from the spines at the tip of each leaf; building poles from its flowering spike; and sugary sap to make a kind of beer called *pulque* (and with later distillation, the whiskey-strong *mescal* and *tequila*). In 1804 the great Prussian scientific investigator Alexander Von Humboldt, having just spent a year in what is today central Mexico, said that everywhere the Náhuatl was spoken, there was the maguey. Today the maguey is known over virtually the whole world, at least in its warmer and drier parts, as *sisal*, though it is grown outside the Americas solely for its fiber.

The altiplano ("high plain") itself begins at about 8500' altitude at the western base of the Sierra Madre Oriental, and its valley bottoms slope imperceptibly down the next hundred miles to Mexico City's 7200' or so in elevation. If you have never traveled to this part of the Mexican altiplano yourself, begin by picturing a flat gray volcanic sand lake bed, as perfectly level as dry lake beds such as the Bonneville flats in the American West. Then add to that perfect flatness a pile of gray boulders here and there, catapulted out of the earth by some past volcanic eruption. Subtract an occasional volcanic crater blown in it, now with a salty lake filling the crater.[GE[25]] Then add thousand-foot-tall volcanic cones or parts of cones, and a few truly world-class volcanoes rising ten thousand feet above the already high plains. Finally, to these add enormous ridges and slopes crafted by lava flow or ash accumulation.[GE[26]] La Malinche (*Matlalcuéyatl*), a great snaggle-toothed

---

21. GE Layer 21 is Placemark referencing a cluster of Photos icons at east end of railroad and interstate bridges across this impressive gorge.

22. GE Layer 22 is a Placemark framing a view of the passage of the *autopista* through the Cumbres, or Peaks.

23. GE Layer 23 is a Placemark referencing a Panoramio icon of Joshua trees in rocky, desert habitat.

24. GE Layer 24 is a Placemark referencing a Panoramio icon with a photograph showing a maguey (and some prickly pear cactus) next to a car, for scale.

25. GE Layer 25 references a Panoramio icon at Lake Alchichica, about fifteen miles southwest of Perote. It is clearly a volcanic crater now filled with water. There are several other similar crater lakes within a five-mile radius of that one; you can see them by zooming out in the view.

26. GE Layer 26 is a Placemark referencing a Panoramio icon with an impressive view of the altiplano as seen from Amozoc, State of Puebla.

volcano 14,600′ tall and about fifty miles west of the Sierra Madre Oriental, divides the easternmost valley of the altiplano from its neighboring western valley, the Tlaxcala-Puebla valley.[GE27] Here travelers going to Mexico City face the basic choice of going north or south of La Malinche. Going south brings you through or at least close to today's Puebla, a sprawling city of over a million, the only real industrial rival of Mexico City on the whole altiplano (*Poblano* is the term for someone or something from Puebla, city or state; you see it a lot on menus in Mexican restaurants). Going north of Malinche brings you through the historically important city of Tlaxcala, the sleepy capital of the state of the same name, or through the important rail junction town of Apizaco.[GE28]

On the western side of this Tlaxcala-Puebla valley, only forty miles past Malinche, comes the great volcanic mountain range called the Sierra de Tláloc.[GE29] It is anchored on the south by two huge volcanoes each around 17,000′ in elevation: the still active Popocatépetl ("Smoking Mountain")[GE30] and next to it at Iztaccíhuatl ("Sleeping Woman," named for the shape of its long snow-covered ridgeline).[GE31] A little further north in the ridge comes the slightly lower and broader bulge of Tláloc itself, named after the old Aztec rain god. There are really only three choices a traveler has when going from the Puebla-Tlaxcala valley over into the Valley of Mexico: (a) the high, hard way up between Popo and Izta called the *Paso de Cortés* (mostly closed these days because Popo is so active);[GE32] (b) the Río Frío pass between Iztaccíhuatl and Tláloc (where the interstate or autopista runs);[GE33] and (c) the wide northern swing around the end of the Sierra de Tláloc. This last is flatter and so favored by railroads, but it also involves either hugging the rugged skirts of the mountains or building causeways over the floodplains (*llanos*) there.

The Valley of Mexico

Over (or around) this great mountain range lies the central valley of the altiplano, the celebrated "Valley of Mexico," the ancient *Anahuac* or Place of Waters. Much of it is taken up by today's Mexico City. It is ringed by mountains on the south and west as well as the Sierra de Tláloc on its east, with smaller volcanic ridges that almost close it off in the north, too. It was once a natural lake,[GE34] but today some small brackish lakes at Texcoco near the airport in the east of the valley,[GE35] and some small freshwater ponds and canals near Xochimilco in the southeast of the valley,[GE36] are all that are left of the single great lake of 500 years ago.

The high plains in general are dry and brown in the winter, spinning up pretty little dust devils daily and an occasional massive dust storm that can blanket the capital. It is much greener and agriculturally productive

---

27. GE Layer 27 references a profile photo of Malinche, or Malantzin, from a distance; see Panoramio icon under pointer.

28. GE Layer 28 references a sunrise photo looking back east over Puebla-Tlaxcala valley with La Malinche silhoutted on left and Pico de Orizaba and its lower companion peak La Negra in the center.

29. GE Layer 29 frames a view of the Sierra de Tláloc as climbers on La Malinche would see it. Popocatépetl is the volcano on the left, Iztaccíhuatl the volcano at center, and Tláloc itself the low green bulge out to the right. If you turn on your basic Roads layer, you see the autopista going through the Río Frío ("Cold River") pass between Iztaccíhuatl and Tláloc.

30. GE Layer 30 references a Panoramio icon with a view from small hill in city of Puebla, looking over western part of the city towards Popo and Iztaccíhuatl.

31. GE Layer 31 references a Panoramio icon with a good view of Popocatépetl and Iztaccíhuatl from about twenty miles away. The colors in the clouds above Popo are probably due to volcanic gas and smoke coming from summit.

32. GE Layer 32 has a view of Popocatépetl from the Paso de Cortés; see indicated Panoramio icon; photographer seems to have been at or above 12,000′, still in pine forests.

33. GE Layer 33 has a "Sunrise near Río Frío" photo under Panoramio icon indicated.

34. GE Layer 34 is a Placemark framing a view of the Valley of Mexico. Most of the basin was filled with a great lake 500 years ago; today there are only a few remnant small lakes left (a reconstruction of the original lake will appear in GE Layer 42, soon to come).

35. GE Layer 35 shows remnant saltwater lakes at Texcoco, near the main airport.

36. GE Layer 36 shows remnant freshwater lakes, canals, and *chinampas* at Xochimilco; see Panoramio icon "Amanecer en Xochimilco" and also others nearby. Google Earth resolution of this dark wedge of waterlands is good enough so that you can explore in detail, find some close-packed chinampas and canals remaining, others showing where they've filled in.

in the summer, especially once you get out of the rain shadow west of the Sierra Madre Oriental. Up on the altiplano no compass is needed for navigation (except maybe when immersed in Mexico City's smog, often trapped in its mountain bowl) because five or six tall volcanoes, each unique and recognizable at a glance, stand on the horizon like giant road signs. This whole plateau is often simply called the *Mesa Central*, that "table-land" so central to the culture. Geologists have a general term for it that carries more punch and movement—the *Zona Neovolcanica*.

Most of the old colonial churches of Mexico City, even the Cathedral on the main plaza (or *Zócalo*), have great cracks in their masonry or sit at drunken angles because they have settled further into the sand of the old lake bed with each vibration in the earth.[GE37] Earthquakes are so frequent and devastating here that California seems a stable place by comparison: a minimum of 10,000 people died in the 1985 Mexico City quake. Recently the lava has risen so high in Popocatépetl that orange light has been seen reflected off clouds hanging over it. And the world's most populous city lies thirty to forty miles away from it, twenty-two million strong at last count. Life there is not dull and apparently never has been. This Valley of Mexico had Mexico's densest population 500 years ago, too.

SECTION B: "FIRST NATIONS" AND THE SPANISH INVASION[GE38]

The scale and richness of the centers of Mexican civilization stunned many of the first European observers in the early 1500s. Bernal Díaz del Castillo, decades after the fact, still vividly remembered standing with Cortés and company in 1519 at the beginning of one of the causeways leading out to the Aztec island capital in the Valley of Mexico's great lake, and what they saw and thought at the time:

> And when we saw all those cities and villages built in the water, and other great towns on dry land, and that straight and level causeway leading to Mexico, we were astounded. These great towns and *cues* [pyramidal temples] and buildings rising from the water, all made of stone, seemed like an enchanted vision from the *Tale of Amadís* [one of the travel-fantasy books then popular in Spain]. Indeed, some of our soldiers asked whether it was not all a dream.[1]

The antiquity of civilization there impressed these first European adventurers just as much: no one living could really tell them who built the huge Teotihuacán complex just twenty-five miles northeast of the Aztec capital, or why.

Before the Aztecs

Five hundred years later now, archaeologists, linguists, and historians can tell us much more. As in the Old World, a Neolithic Age of village agriculture and pottery came before large-scale civilization. Corn (maize, *maíz* in Spanish), beans, and squash were the basic trio of food plants domesticated here, as important as the trio of wheat, olive, and grape for the Mediterranean area. From the coastal areas of Veracruz, to the riversides, to the edges of the Mexico City great lake, wherever there was enough freshwater they built and farmed *chinampas*. These were narrow flat-topped ridges of earth bordered by narrow canals, as you saw around Xochimilco earlier in the Topography and Texture section. Gardens planted there could be watered simply by splashing them with a paddle from a canoe, and a thin layer of new muck from the bottom of the canal spread on top of a chinampa would make it as fertile as virgin soil again.

Only the dog, the turkey, and the duck were domesticated here in Mesoamerica, a limited number compared with all the animals domesticated in the Old World (which was to have profound medical consequences, examined later). An interesting variety of dogs were bred, most famously the Chihuahua, but also a black-skinned, hairless hound-sized dog, still around in Mexico and popularly called the "Aztec dog." Bred over the

---

37. GE Layer 37 is a Placemark framing a view of Mexico City's main square, or Zócalo. The Metropolitan Cathedral is at top of view. Lots of Photos icons to explore, including a 360 Cities one in center of square, should you wish.

38. GE Layer 38 is a Polygon layer, the familiar aqua rectangle bounding our chosen Veracruz-to-Mexico City corridor. Click in box at left to turn it on and double-click on Polygon icon to have Google Earth center it in the view.

centuries partly to be a living hot-water bottle, its 102° skin hot to the touch, it was placed wherever an ailing person needed heat applied. The turkey was imported to Europe so early by European explorers that there is no lasting record of it; the animal later took the name of the state of Turkey, though genetics proves it to be of Mesoamerican origin. The domesticated duck of the Americas, usually called the Muscovy duck, is the green-, black-, and white-feathered, red-wattled common farm pond duck (other than the mallard) of much of the U.S.

Modern archaeology has tentatively identified the Olmec culture, which originated at the base of the Bay of Campeche—the very southern part of the Gulf of Mexico—as the first true civilization of Mexico. It is called Pre-Classic because it precedes three later, greater civilizations, but also because it gave them painted hieroglyphs and stone pyramidal temples (*cues* or *teocallis*), stone courts for a ceremonial ball game, carved jadeite figures in an artistic style already recognizably Mesoamerican, rectangular grids of streets and blocks, a sophisticated calendar, and the framework of a powerful religion. Unlike early civilizations in the Old World, the Olmecs developed no wheels (even for pottery), no draft animals to pull or carry heavy loads, no metallurgy to speak of, and most of what we call "cities" may have been ceremonial gathering places instead of permanent habitations around centers of commerce. But there is no other word for these sophisticated Olmec cultural centers than urban. Olmec civilization began around 800 B.C., and flourished for half a millennium before collapsing around AD 300. Olmec culture appeared earliest in the coastal lowlands a little south of the city of Veracruz and our corridor, but quickly radiated into it and eventually absorbed areas on as far away as the Valley of Mexico. The most striking visual reminders of the Olmecs are their colossal stone heads, from five to ten feet tall, helmeted and pudgy, on display in Mexico's anthropological museums.[GE39]

The spectacular Classic Mesoamerican civilizations that followed lasted a thousand years, more or less, from around 200 BC to AD 800. If mapped, a quadrilateral taking in the Yucatan peninsula, Belize, Guatemala, a little of eastern Honduras and across Mexico to just northwest of Mexico City contains virtually every important Classic site.[GE40] Two relationships show up in such a map: (a) the original Olmec culture is perfectly central, furthering the argument that it was the mother culture; and (b) our entire Veracruz-to-Mexico City corridor is included. The Mayans in the eastern part of this rectangle of Classic civilizations may have had more sophisticated mathematics and writing (enough of Mayan hieroglyphs can be read today that Mayan civilization can no longer be called "prehistoric"), and the Monte Alban civilization centered near the modern city of Oaxaca may have lasted longer, but Teotihuacán in the Valley of Mexico held a larger empire and built the most impressive urban center in the Americas.[GE41]

Teotihuacán in its turn was sacked and burned about AD 650, leaving smaller states to try for empire themselves and carry on that same general civilization. In the ebb and flow of warfare among these smaller states of these Post-Classic later centuries, warrior kings seem to have crowded out philosopher kings. Human sacrifice also seems to have become much more common. In these troubled times new peoples immigrated into the Mesa Central from the uncivilized north, an average of one invasion wave per century. They wedged their way into the crowded and productive Valley of Mexico by their military prowess, and then absorbed much of the local civilization—including, usually, the Náhuatl language—later building up their own empire until defeated by the next wave of invaders. Of the nine waves of invasion known to have happened after the fall of Teotihuacán in AD 650, each had left still recognizable ethnic enclaves around the lake when the Spanish arrived. The last of these waves were the Aztecs, or more properly the *Mexica*.

The Mexica

"Aztec" is a word that became popular in the nineteenth century, describing the supposed original Pacific coast island home of these last native rulers of the Mesa Central. But they called themselves Mexica (meh-SHEE-

---

39. GE Layer 39 is a Placemark referencing a Panoramio icon, titled "Cabeza Olmeca en el Museo de Antropología." This one is in the gardens of the Museum of Anthropology in Xalapa.

40. GE Layer 40 is a Polygon representing such an irregular quadrilateral; turn on layer, then double-click Polygon icon to frame limits of the quadrilateral.

41. GE Layer 41 is a Placemark framing a view of Teotihuacán against the mountain to the north. Turn Photos layer off to see the whole, then back on to explore a few views.

kah), or sometimes Culhúa-Mexica, after a former ruling city they absorbed. Their empire was still young when the Spanish invaded it, less than a century old, even though it stretched all the way to Guatemala and held points on both Gulf and Pacific coasts. Mexica traditions recalled their original attempts to settle the rich lakeshore sometime before 1300—how they were driven away and lived for awhile on the rocky little "Grasshopper Hill" (Chapultepec) on the western edge of the lake that had a big freshwater spring, and how in turn they were driven off that land.

Mexica annals record that they finally settled in their permanent home on the island of Tenochtitlán on or about AD 1325, in obedience to their sun god Huichilopochtli's command that they locate where they saw an eagle perched on a cactus growing from a rock emerging from a lake—ever more the symbol of the land and even on today's flag. The name of their island city, Tenochtitlán, comes from the old Náhuatl name for the prickly pear cactus, *tenochtli*. For at least another century, however, the Mexica paid tribute to stronger powers, notably Atzapotzalco, a city on the lakeshore about four miles northwest of the island of Tenochtitlán. Around 1430 they joined the cities of Texcoco on the eastern shore and nearby Tacuba on the western shore in a dominant triple alliance. By the time the Spanish arrived in 1519, Tenochtitlán was the leading power of those ruling three. The island capital itself was really a double city, Tenochtitlán having grown together with Tlatelolco, originally a separate island. In 1519 they were still separate administrative areas, each with its huge temple complex, each with its great public marketplace, like a double-yoked egg.[GE42]

Technically, then, it should be remembered as the Mexica empire, but we've all said "Aztec" for so long now that it's hard to change. The Empire stretched from the Pacific to the Atlantic coasts, and snaked one long arm southeast into today's Guatemala. On the altiplano, the only independent areas left were the neighboring states of Tlaxcala and Huejotzinco, in roughly what is today's state of Tlaxcala.[GE43]

To begin our "roads" theme, it should be clarified that the Aztecs maintained a network of trails, rather than true roads. With no wheeled traffic, these were more like footpaths and paid less attention to minimizing the ups and downs than wheeled traffic would later—although they did build stone bridges over ravines and small rivers. They had no beasts of burden, so human carriers called *tamemes* carried up to 100-pound loads. These low-caste carriers were directed by sophisticated international businessmen called *pochtetcas*, wealthy and of relatively high status. Like some businessmen on the frontiers of later European overseas empires, these pochtecas may have been an undercover source of government intelligence for the military expansion of the Aztec empire.

In terms of specific routes along our corridor at the time of the Spanish invasion, we know of one major trail running east from the Valley of Mexico to Cholula, an important religious and commercial site firmly under Aztec control, and continuing southeast toward Oaxaca and the Yucatan in the quest for such lowland products as cacao (source of chocolate, so important that cacao beans actually circulated as money among the Mexica), a kind of cotton, colorful feathers, gold, and jadeite. At least a minor trail went east from Cholula, down what would later be the Orizaba-Córdoba road, to the town of Cotaxtla not far inland from the later city of Veracruz, probably for ocean fish and salt. And another minor route also seems to have angled down across the difficult eastern slope of the Sierra Madre Oriental from the base of the Pico de Orizaba, winding up at Zempoala (sometimes Cempoala, especially in older sources) near the coast and the mouth of the Río Antigua ("The Old River," as the Spanish named it later).[GE44]

---

42. GE Layer 42 is a Folder titled "Valley of Mexico 1519." Double-click on folder icon to open all components, single-click folder title for explanation. Turn off folder by unchecking box to left of icon; then go through successive icons below, double-clicking to "fly" to the view, single-clicking layer title for explanation/instruction. Main components of this folder are 42a. The lake in 1519; 42b. Tenochtitlan/Tlatelolco island; 42c. Other islands; 42d. Causeways; 42e. Chapultepec aquaduct; 42f. Dike of Netzalhualcoyotl; 42g. Major Lakeside cities near Tenochtitlan; 42h. Other lakeside or island cities. Four of these are folders that can be opened further, if needed: other islands, causeways, major lakeside cities, other lakeside or island cities.

43. GE Layer 43 symbolizes the Aztec Empire as a red Polygon.

44. GE Layer 44 is a folder called Probable Aztec Roads. The first road (the first of three Paths inside the folder) to Oaxaca, is historically very well testified to; second continuing east from Cholula and Tepeaca to Cotaxtla is fairly sure; the third, angling across the eastern slope of the Sierra Madre Oriental to Zempoala, is not as sure. Having viewed it, turn this and the previous Aztec Empire layer back off to unclutter the screen.

As far as experts can tell, the major Aztec routes to the Gulf coast avoided what is today the Xalapa-Perote northern route around the Sierra Madre Oriental. This was probably because their closest, most bitter enemies were the allied city-states of Tlaxcala and Huejotzinco, in what is today the Tlaxcala-Puebla valley. For fifty years these two states had been virtually surrounded by Aztec power, deprived of important items of trade such as salt, and subjected to the regular "Flowery Wars" designed by the Aztecs not to gain territory but to procure the thousands of human sacrifices they thought were demanded by their bloodthirsty "hummingbird-of-the-left" war and sun god, Huichilopochtli ("wee-chee-loh-POCH-tlee").

The best scholars of Mexican history are careful to balance descriptions of Aztec violence with the orderly and peaceful aspects of Aztec civilization. The traditional modesty and politeness of Indian and Mestizo in central Mexico today, for example, are supposed to be one legacy of the Aztec rule of 500 years ago. And European observers early in the conquest were just as impressed by the ordered, peaceful side of life there as by the violent and bloody side. The marketplaces of the capital city were larger, richer, and better organized than anything they had seen in Spain, France, or Italy, according to Cortés's letters, Bernal Díaz's memoirs, and more than half a dozen other eyewitness or early historical accounts.[2] Diego Rivera's famous 1945 fresco in the Palacio Nacional in Mexico City, "La Gran Tenochtitlán," is a Romantic but plausible visual summary of these accounts. It shows a close-up of Tlatelolco, which was said to host 60,000 people on the most important market day. Neighboring Tenochtitlán is seen in the middle background, some of the lake is beyond, and Iztaccíhuatl and Popo on the Sierra de Tláloc itself serve as the far backdrop.[GE45]

But of the blood and violence required by Aztec religion, there is no doubt. We also have multiple eyewitness accounts of neat racks of human heads by the tens of thousands, of the obsidian knife stroke that removed the still-beating heart of the sacrificial victim, of the clotted blood in the uncut hair of the priests who presided over the sacrifices, of the *chacmool* sculptures of reclining stone figures with turned head and a stomach made into a hollow bowl to catch the blood. In common with many native North American religions, Aztec belief was that the world had begun and ended four times, and that their era was the fifth and final creation. Unlike most of the rest, however, the Aztecs believed that only massive quantities of human blood shed for the gods could postpone the end of this last creation. And frankly, too, this seems to have been an instrument of terror used to expand and maintain the empire. The very recentness and the continuing violence of the Aztec conquest, however, meant that any promising opponent who rose to challenge the Aztecs would have natural allies who still resented their own loss of power to the Aztecs—from Zempoala on the coast to Tlaxcala on the altiplano and even disgruntled, recently dispossessed, chieftains inside the Valley of Mexico itself.

Cortés and the Spanish invasion

In the spring of 1519, Fernando Cortés (which is the way he usually wrote it, although he has been more popularly known as Hernán or Hernando in English-language literature) came coasting north and then west along the Yucatan Peninsula and the Bay of Campeche with a small force of about 500 soldiers, 16 horses, and a few small cannon. With unbelievable luck, on the island of Cozumel he picked up a shipwrecked Spaniard who by now knew coastal native languages, and later in the Bay of Campeche, local chiefs gave the Spanish a group of women, including the marvelous linguist the Spanish came to call Doña Marina; she knew both coastal and interior languages and picked up Spanish quickly. As a base for launching their invasion of the interior the expedition chose the sandy island they called San Juan de Ulúa, first reached by an exploratory fleet the year before. Here began, incidentally, that Spanish double-naming process so common in Mexico of prefixing a new Christian name to an existing non-Christian one. "St. John of Culhúa," we suppose this name to have been—since the Spanish expedition which first landed there in 1518 did so on the day of the festival of St. John the Baptist, and since the locals already called the island Culhúa, perhaps because it was already claimed by the Aztecs ("Mexica-Culhúa"). This way the newcomers could put a Christian spin on the name and the locals would still know what place they were talking about. Bernal Díaz had been with that previous expedition in

---

45. GE Layer 45 is a Placemark referencing the National Palace on Mexico City's Zócalo. A link to an image of Diego Rivera's famous 1945 "La Gran Tenochtitlán" mural, done on the walls of the Palacio Nacional, is embedded in the Placemark. Rivera based it, or at least the details in it, on half-a-dozen eye-witness accounts.

1518; he remembered that soundings south of the island showed "good bottom," and "also that under the shelter of the island our ships would be safe from the northerly gales."[3]

What happened after Cortés landed was the most spectacular and tragic of all European conquests, almost all of it occurring precisely along our chosen corridor—one of the reasons it was chosen to begin with, of course.[GE[46]] The story is well-known, from exciting eyewitness accounts of Cortés and Díaz, from classic histories such as William Prescott's 1843 *History of the Conquest of Mexico*,[4] and even from Aztec chronicles of what was, for them, a holocaust.

First, the Spanish fortified the little island they called San Juan de Ulúa, and then landed on the beach opposite it (in today's downtown Veracruz). Next, they sent a party to the town of Cotaxtla, southwest of their coastal base, and then to Zempoala, on the coastal plain across the Antigua River, northwest of their base. The larger Zempoala, with its shining white buildings that looked to one excited Spanish soldier like silver, offered hospitality and the first alliance to the Spanish, especially after Cortés humbled an Aztec tribute mission that happened to be in town.[GE[47]] Then with Zempoalan guides (led by the "fat *cacique*" (pronounced ka-SEE-kay, a word for chief the Spanish had picked up in the West Indies) they went uphill some seventy miles to Xalapa (from *Xallapan*, "Water-on-the-Sands"), from there a little south across the slope to Xico (today's Xico Viejo), and then in a rugged climb over the saddle of the Sierra Madre Oriental (a strange and difficult way to go, unless to avoid Aztec-controlled main roads, or to get a high view of the land to the west of the Sierra). The Spanish, sleeping in armor they were afraid to take off at night, suffered from the unexpected cold after the muggy heat of the lowlands.

On the altiplano their Zempoalan guides led them roundabout, northwest and then southwest, to the city-state of Tlaxcala (the name means literally "cornbread," "maizebread"), home to the greatest enemy of the Aztecs left on the high plains. Three pitched battles resulted, two by day and one by night, until the older Tlaxcalan leaders led by the cacique Xicohténcatl decided on an alliance with Cortés against the hated Aztecs. At a stroke the Spanish gained thousands of bearers and thousands more warriors at their side.[GE[48]]

Against Tlaxcalan advice Cortés went south to Cholula, a firm ally of the Aztecs.[GE[49]] Here he forestalled a planned Cholulan attack. According to Bernal Díaz, Doña Marina was told of the attack by an old woman so that Doña Marina might marry her son after the Spanish were all killed, but Doña Marina relayed the message to the Spanish, who carried out a surprise massacre of Cholulan nobles in the city center. Then Cortés marched west, crossing the Sierra de Tláloc at the high pass between Popo and Izta that still bears his name (almost nothing else in Mexico bears his name, incidentally; although he is the single most important figure in all of Mexican history, many Mexicans seem to feel ashamed of him, or at least ambivalent about him, for his destruction of the Mexica civilization). From the pass his troops first saw the entire Valley of Mexico laid out below them. They were received peacefully at the southeastern causeway, running from the lakeside town of Iztapalapa to the island capital, by the reigning Montezuma II. He probably thought Cortés was the promised second coming of the god Quetzalcóatl, the "Feathered Serpent," in the foretold "year of one reed"—which 1519 just happened to be, by a one in fifty-two chance on the circular Aztec calendar. All told, Cortés had the mind of Machiavelli and the luck of the Irish to go with it.

Maybe it was also the thoughtful and intellectual nature of Montezuma that made him react so passively to the Spanish invasion force. Some earlier Aztec kings, less intellectual and more forceful, would have simply overwhelmed the Spanish and their allies with an Aztec army of several hundred thousand. The Spanish soon repaid this hospitality by putting Montezuma under house arrest, to the increasing anger of the general population.

The Spanish lusted after gold, of course, but perhaps the most important point of friction with the natives was religion. A famous exchange took place between Montezuma and Cortés atop the great *teocalli* of

---

46. GE Layer 46 is a Path, the approximate path the invasion took.

47. GE Layer 47 is a Placemark referencing the old historic Zempoala; a couple dozen Photos icons to explore. The temple standing alone at right still has traces of original color in its stuccoed crest, almost 500 years later.

48. GE Layer 48 references a Panoramio icon showing a statue of Xicohtencatl in downtown Tlaxcala, in a park named for him.

49. GE Layer 49 is a Placemark referencing the ruined mound of the teocalli at Cholula, some six miles from today's Puebla city. Several dozen Photos icons to explore.

Tlatelolco. Here Cortés so forcefully condemned Aztec religion in the presence of Aztec priests that Monte-zuma felt it necessary to stay and placate the gods, or at least the priests. Then, when Cortés rushed back to the coast to ambush a rival Spanish invasion army under Narváez, his second-in-command Alvarado massacred leading Aztecs assembled on the occasion of an important religious feast. Cortés arrived back just in time for the whole city to rise in revolt against him. In this June 1520 rising, Montezuma was killed, and his prestige no longer sheltered the invaders. The only chance for survival the Spanish had was to cut their way out of the city, and they decided to do so along the short western causeway to Tacuba. A portable bridge they designed to span the gaps where the Aztecs had destroyed the bridges got stuck in the lake bottom at the very first gap; later gaps they had to fill with their own bodies. They lost virtually all the treasure they had demanded for Monte-zuma's ransom—literally rooms full of golden objects—and so many Spaniards were killed or wounded in the forced retreat that they remembered this as *La Triste Noche*, The Sad Night. And their troubles weren't over. As they circled northeast around the lake and then east within sight of the pyramids of Teotihuacán, they had to fight yet another bloody battle at Otumba before finally finding shelter in Tlaxcala again.[GE⁵⁰]

By 1521 the Aztec capital had been thoroughly ravaged by Old World smallpox. By some accounts there were not enough living left to bury the dead. Cortés and company, refreshed at Tlaxcala and with Spanish rein-forcements, moved on Texcoco, which allied with them rather than continue fighting on the side of Tenochti-tlán.[GE⁵¹] Exploratory moves south around the lake found first Chalco and then Mizquic willing to join the Spanish side as well. This opened up the steep but quick road back east over the Paso de Cortés so that literally tens of thousands of Tlaxcalans and Huejotzincans could come in quickly as reinforcements. After major bat-tles the Spanish and their growing number of allies then conquered Xochimilco. When they pushed on north-wards, up the west side of the freshwater lake, to Coyohuacán, Tacuba, Azcapotzalco, and Tenayuca—all the remaining freshwater lakeside towns with causeways going to them—they found them deserted as the Aztecs had pulled back their forces to the island of Tenochtitlan. The Spanish broke the aqueduct from Chapultepec to deprive the capital of drinking water, and launched a combined fleet and army along the causeways to Tenochtitlán. Thirteen European-style warships, a small cannon in the bow of each, paralleled military units on the march on the causeways. The city desperately resisted, for days and days, but fell on August 21, 1521. Tlatelolco held out longer than Tenochtitlán proper against the Spanish attack on the island, but it too finally fell. A chronicler there wrote this lament about the holocaust:

And all these misfortunes befell us. We saw them and wondered at them; we suffered this unhappy fate.

Broken spears lie in the roads;
we have torn our hair in our grief.
The houses are roofless now, and their walls
are red with blood.

Worms are swarming in the streets and plazas,
and the walls are splattered with gore.
The water has turned red, as if it were dyed,
and when we drink it,
it has the taste of brine.

We have pounded our hands in despair
against the adobe walls,
for our inheritance, our city, is lost and dead.

We have chewed dry twigs and salt grasses;
we have filled our mouths with dust and bits of adobe;
we have eaten lizards, rats, and worms . . .⁵

50. Turn on GE Layer 50, a Path, for the (approximate) route of the Spanish retreat.
51. GE Layer 51 is a refresher view of the original lake from the earlier "Valley of Mexico 1519" folder.

*From "The Broken Spears" by Miguel Leon-Portilla. Copyright © 1962, 1990 by Miguel Leon-Portilla. Expanded and updated Edition © 1992 by Miguel Leon-Portilla. Reprinted by permission of Beacon Press, Boston.

Cuauhtémoc, last of the Aztec emperors, was captured by Cortés's soldiers as he tried to escape by canoe. And so the Spanish replaced the Aztecs as rulers of the empire. It had taken less than two-and-a-half years from their Easter week arrival at San Juan de Ulúa in 1519.

SECTION C: THE COLONIAL ERA, 1521–1810[GE[52]]

The Spanish, without much discussion about it, made the old Aztec capital their new capital. It was the great center of population and wealth in the country, and the lesson for their new subjects was simple: "You brought tribute to the Aztecs in Tenochtitlán; just bring it to us here now." That decision immediately made the Mexico City-to-Veracruz corridor the most important in the land for the next three centuries of Spanish rule, their lifeline to the closest coast and from there by sea to Havana and Spain.

The modern city of Veracruz took a little time to locate itself. Spanish ships had found anchorage in the southern lee of the island of San Juan de Ulúa, but found the sandy coast opposite the island not very conducive to settlement—plus they had to ford the Río Antigua on their way to Xalapa, and a flood there could hold them up for weeks. For awhile they landed their goods on the beach opposite the island, portaged them up the beach twelve miles and across the shallow bar at the mouth of the Río Antigua, and then up the northern bank of the river about three miles to the first high ground, where they tried to make their new port town. Today all that is left of this experiment is the little town of La Antigua, or "Old Veracruz," which still has a wall or two of a house once owned by Cortés, its major claim to fame.[GE[53]] But there was simply no shelter on the coast from those fierce north winds of the trading season other than the island of San Juan de Ulúa. Out of its lee, the coral bottom wouldn't hold anchor, but the coral reefs would wreck a drifting ship. So, around an old inn just across from the island, the modern city of Veracruz slowly took root.

Colonial institutions take shape: encomienda and repartimiento

To the conquerors went the spoils, or so they thought. It had worked out that way in Hispaniola and Cuba, as Spanish occupation of the New World progressed westwards, through a system called *encomienda*. As the royal government in Spain saw it, this is where the more important Spanish conquerors would be given responsibility for groups of Indians. The *encomendero* would be entitled to some tribute and labor from these groups, but he in turn would owe them sheltering and nurturing of a paternal kind. The royal government was a long way away from the New World, however, and in practice the encomienda system differed little from outright slavery. Cortés, used to the system from his years as a plantation owner in Cuba, began assigning Mexican encomiendas to his most important followers as soon as the military conquest of the Mexica ended. To himself, it will come as no shock, he assigned the most, at least twenty-two. He had an eye for good land and dense populations, and despite occasional royal efforts to limit his holdings, the populations and lands he held under encomienda eventually made him the wealthiest man in New Spain, maybe in all of Spain. His treatment of the natives that he held under encomienda was not quite as nurturing as the crown hoped for. He openly sold some of them as slaves and even had his Texcoco population branded on their faces, like livestock.

Encomienda faded away as a control device for several reasons. First, the Indians died like flies from European diseases, beginning with that smallpox epidemic of 1520 that came in on the wings of the conquest. Many, if not most, of the Old World diseases had first been contracted by humans who domesticated wild animals back in Neolithic times, and related diseases jumped between species (the chickenpox, cowpox, and smallpox complex that went back and forth between animals and people, for example, or the interchange between swine flu, avian flu, and human strains of flu that is still much in the news every year). Those susceptible to these new diseases died, but those more genetically resistant lived through it, so over something like 10,000 years Europeans, Africans, and Asians had gradually built up immunity, or at least reduced such illnesses to relatively

---

52. GE Layer 52 is the aqua rectangle enclosing the Veracruz-to-Mexico City corridor, familiar from previous sections of the chapter.

53. GE Layer 53 is a Placemark referencing several Panoramio icons with pictures of the ruins of the old Casa de Hernán Cortés in "Old Veracruz."

mild "childhood" diseases. But now all those Old World diseases associated with the Neolithic domestication of animals hit a medically unexposed population in the New World, and by 1600 only about 10 percent of the native population of today's Mexico was left. We don't even know exactly which diseases caused some massive die-offs, because disease in a virgin population can take different forms than in one with some genetic exposure to it. Estimates of the original population of Mexico generally run from twenty to thirty million at the time of the Spanish invasion, and eighty years later that was reduced to two or three million. That sentence may be just numbers on a page, but think how shattering 90 percent of the population dying would be to your culture, to any culture. Encomienda holders could only really make money out of dense, organized groups of Indians, and so the practice became unprofitable.

Other reasons for the decline of the encomienda system were criticism of the institution by missionaries (more in a minute); the fact that the conquistadores despised farming and were hopelessly footloose, chasing after the new treasure finds in Peru or the fantasy cities of gold and fountains of youth in the north; and finally that those Spanish not well connected enough to have gotten their own encomiendas were jealous, and called on the royal government for their share of the dwindling Indian labor force. This resulted, from around 1550 to 1625, in a new controlling institution called *repartimiento*—the rotation of what Indian labor there was left, directed by royal officials. If anything that made life worse for those who were so rotated, and they continued dying.

Christianity and Church institutions

Christianity and Catholic Church institutions, of course, came with the Spanish conquest. On the one hand, they came with the ethnocentric extremism of those centuries of "holy war" against the infidels in Spain (that had only ended in 1492 when the last of the Moors were conquered and all the Jews were expelled from Spain). The Muslims' original conquest of Iberia, from their crossing of the Straits of Gibraltar in AD 711, had been lightning fast: it was virtually completed a few decades later. It left one little Christian enclave, however, up in the mountains of the very northeast, today's Galicia and Asturias. The miraculous discovery of the body of St. James at what is today Santiago de Compostela (originally "St. James of the Field of Stars") provided the emotional focus for that Christian enclave to begin the slow but inexorable reconquest of Muslim-controlled lands. Santiago de Compostela in the Middle Ages became the third biggest site of pilgrimage in the entire Christian world (after Jerusalem and Rome), and "St. James and at them!" was still the battle cry of Cortés's troops 800 years later. *Matamoros*, "Death to Moors," translated effortlessly to *Mataindios* during the conquest of Mexico.

On the other end of the spectrum of Christian culture came intellectuals of the Church. Churches were established as the conquest of Mexico progressed: Veracruz had the first one, Xalapa the second, and so on to Mexico City. It was the Mendicant orders of monks (often called "regular" clergy because they lived under monastic rule, or *regula*), however, who had been touched the most by the Renaissance ideas of Christian Humanism, by the works of Erasmus and Sir Thomas More, who were most sympathetic with the Indians. The first and most important order in New Spain was the Franciscan. The so-called "apostolic twelve" of them came to New Spain in 1524, and established their first monastery (*convento*, in Spanish) that same year at Tlaxcala. [GE⁵⁴] Its gardens were the first real botanical laboratory of the conquest, experimenting with what European plants would grow there, and for what native plants Europeans might acquire a taste.

For these early Franciscans, the education and social reform of the natives ranked not far behind conversion. A Franciscan monastery was founded at Xochimilco in 1535, just southeast of Mexico City, where the Indian community remained the majority, working that chinampa-style semi-aquatic farming that Europeans never learned. As each of these first monasteries grew, it sent out "mission" monasteries, or dependencies. The main road from the port of Veracruz through Xalapa and Tlaxcala to the capital was first called "the missionary road" because of all these monasteries that sprang up along it. It was a Franciscan brother around 1530 who first introduced Spanish-style wagons pulled by teams of oxen, to the amazement of the natives who first saw

---

54. GE Layer 54 is a Placemark referencing the former monastery (*ex-convento*) at Tlaxcala. The oldest Franciscan monastery in the New World, its property was seized during Liberal Reforms, and the building was later a barracks, then a jail, and since 1981 a museum. Several Panoramio icons to explore.

them. Soon this wagon road (*camino de los arrieros*) ran from Veracruz to Xalapa to Perote, then passed north of the volcano Malinche and around the northern end of the Sierra de Tláloc into Mexico City.

The founding of Puebla

In 1531, just ten years after the final subjugation of the Aztec capital, the Franciscan brothers of the Tlaxcala valley envisioned (and it was literally a vision) a way of settling down the Spanish freebooters who were wandering around preying on now-defenseless Indian communities. Their answer? Set up a "Village of the Angels" (*Pueblo de los Angeles*) in the southern part of the valley in which Spaniards would be given substantial farms where they could grow wheat to make the European-style bread (for which most of the Spanish population in Mexico hungered). In the original conquest, a foot soldier (a *peón*, built on the root word for foot) was to have been given a little over ten acres of land (a *peonía*), and a cavalryman (a *caballero*, built on the root word for horse) was to get about fifty-five acres (a *caballería*). In practice the Spanish adventurers scorned these small foot soldier grants, and the word *peon* was soon used only for poor Indian or Mestizo farmers. But now the Franciscans laid out a town, and offered two *caballerías*—a substantial 110-acre family farm—to any Spaniard who would settle this planned city of Puebla, as the name of the town evolved.[6]

It turned out that growing wheat there required irrigation, incidentally. Wheat has about the same growing season as maize, but maize responds to the altiplano's rainy season which begins in March and peaks in June with a spurt of growth; after that it can mature with little rain. Wheat demands more constant moisture. Interestingly enough, our earliest record of Neolithic domestication of maize is from the Tepeacan valley of this same state of Puebla, about twenty miles south of the Orizaba-Puebla main road. Maize was obviously selectively bred in the context of the climate of central Mexico.[7] Conveniently, there were rivers running down off the eastern slopes of Popo and Iztaccíhuatl for the irrigation of such new wheat fields. And so as nearby Indian Cholula faded, the mostly Spanish Puebla six miles away grew quickly to be second in size on the altiplano only to Mexico City. As it grew it altered the road network somewhat, acting like a magnet to pull horseback and foot travelers from the road north of Malinche down to it (though the heavy ox- and mule-drawn wagons, trying to minimize ups and downs and distance, kept to the more level but less populated wagon road north of Malinche). Puebla quickly became a conservative center of Spanish culture, and later a hub of industry, though in the long run its treatment of nearby Indians probably would have disappointed its Franciscan founders.

The Virgin of Guadalupe

Coincidentally, also in 1531 (though our first written record of this doesn't come until the mid-1600s) was the miraculous appearance of the Virgin of Guadalupe just north of old Tenochtitlán. The visions of her were given to an Indian who had taken the Spanish name Juan Diego; the Virgin herself he described as brown-skinned and dressed in the fashion of an unmarried Indian girl. The place of the vision was a hill long sacred to a female Mexican deity named Tonantzin—all of which may have made Spanish clergy reluctant to credit the vision. When the Bishop reportedly asked Juan Diego for more proof, the Indian went back to the hill the Spanish had named Guadalupe and the Virgin had "Castilian roses" bloom for him, even though they were out of season. He cut them and carried them in his cape to the bishop, and then imprinted on his cape was found the image of the Virgin, with radiating gold lines all around the edge. A surge of popularity then (and now) overrode all other obstacles. A new church or basilica has been built there every century since, with the cape itself in place of pride. On or around December 12, the date of her last apparition in 1531, several million Mexicans come there on pilgrimage.[GE[55]] Her banner was carried in wars with outsiders and in revolts by Indians and Mestizos against the Spanish-blood upper classes. Her fiesta became the most popular religious celebration of the whole culture. Even today there are many Mexicans, nominally Catholic, who are cool to the Catholic label but positive about being called Guadalupano or Guadalupana. And just in this present century, in 2002, on that special December 12, Juan Diego was at long last canonized—formally recognized as a saint—at a service in

---

55. GE Layer 55 references the new Basilica there. Explore some of the nearby Photos icons of "La Nueva Basilica." Some have general views of the interior, with the Virgin's image displayed on a vertical golden shaft, ceiling lights in patterns of constellations on Dec. 12, 1531.

the Basilica of Our Lady of Guadalupe presided over by Pope John Paul II. It was an amazing service that lasted for hours, juxtaposing the highest of Old World church pomp and circumstance with dancers in Aztec costume who could have come straight from Mexico's flamboyant Ballet Folklórico. A featured dancer was in eagle dress, since Juan Diego's original Náhuatl name was *Cuauhtlatoatzin*, "the eagle who talks."

Fr. Sahagún and the Indian-Spanish honeymoon

Many of the early missionaries, especially the Franciscans, were bitter critics of how the Indians were treated under encomienda and repartimiento. Their most remarkable chapter was written in and around Mexico City. Consider Brother Bernardino de Sahagún, born in Spain in 1499, a graduate of the brilliant Salamanca University, off to New Spain in 1529 at about age thirty. He was the Franciscan who founded the Monastery of Xochimilco in 1535. Meanwhile other Franciscans in Tlatelolco had gathered fifty sons of local chiefs and begun their primary and secondary education in 1533. They progressed so fast that in 1536 the College of the Holy Cross was set up for them in Tlatelolco. Sahagún came to be their Latin teacher that year, taught for five years, spent another five years in various ministries in the Tlaxcala-Puebla valley, and in 1545 came back to the college in Tlatelolco. By this time he was well on his way to becoming the greatest European scholar of the Náhuatl language and of Mexica ethnology. Indian graduates of the college and his Latin classes wrote the most elegant Latin in the land, which stirred up some jealousy among those Spaniards who insisted on natural Spanish superiority. When another plague year came in 1546 and carried off many of Sahagún's Indian students and friends, he turned his remaining students' attention to medicine, hoping to find cures in the collection of local, traditional herblore. One result of this came in 1552, a beautiful illustrated herbal medicine guide of which a copy was sent to Emperor Charles V. Called the Badianus Manuscript, it was only rediscovered in the Vatican Library in the twentieth century. The plant dyes of the illustrations have lasted these four-and-a-half centuries and more better than modern commercial dyes would have; the organization and artwork by one Indian scholar is as scientific and sophisticated as any parallel work of the day in Europe; the translation from Náhuatl into Latin is done by another Indian scholar.[8][GE[56]]

This spirit of Indian-Spanish cooperation even colored the royal government in New Spain about this time. The viceroy Velasco, responding to the disastrous flood that hit Mexico City in 1555, asked the governors of Mexico, Tacuba, and Texcoco (exactly the three key towns of the Aztec triple alliance of thirty-five years earlier, if you translate "Mexico" as "Tenochtitlán") if they could round up the old writings and drawings for the process of flood control used by their ancestors. Once these were collected and studied, the original Indian solution was by and large adopted by the viceroy's government.[9] There was also a potentially healthy alliance between some of the Indian nobility and the leading Spanish families descended from the conquistadores. Tlaxcalans, especially, because they had allied with the invaders, kept the rights to carry weapons and ride horseback, and were exempt from taxes. They enthusiastically helped the Spanish build Puebla, and expected to be part of the leadership elite.

This promising spring of Indian-Spanish cooperation and respect was blighted, however, before 1600. The Catholic Church, in its struggle with the Protestant Reformation, defensively circled its intellectual wagons, and Christian Humanism of the late Renaissance style was a casualty of the Inquisition. The Mendicant orders such as the Franciscans gradually lost parish control to the secular clergy, who tended to share the common Spanish racial prejudice against Indians. The Spanish monarchy still feebly protested on behalf of Indian civil rights, but eventually was in such need of money for its European wars that it turned a blind eye to exploitation of the Mexican Indians, a source of much of that money.

---

56. GE Layer 56 is a Placemark generally referencing old Tlatelolco, today in the heart of Mexico City, but the Placemark is mainly used to contain a website with a good copy of a page of the herbal (Badianus Manuscript). Scroll down to the third image in the website. The plant on the left seems to be a species of narcotic Datura with associated ants shown at its roots.

The hacienda

The ultimate institution of control that began to emerge about 1600, successor to the unsatisfactory encomienda and repartimiento, was the *hacienda*. The word comes from the verb *hacer*, to make or to do (as does the *hecho* in "*Hecho en México*," Made in Mexico) so a fair literal translation of it might be "a creation; an enterprise." Curiously enough, in North American English "ranch" implies a much larger concern than "farm," but in Mexican Spanish *hacienda* means a grander spread, even an estate, and a *rancho* is merely a farm.

There is one hacienda in particular in our corridor that has been used (and will be so used later in this chapter) as a famous case study of land reform in the Revolution of 1910–20—the hacienda San Pedro Coxtocán. It was a couple of miles south of the little town of San Martín Texmelucan, straddling the road south to Huejotzingo, in the modern state of Puebla just across the border from the modern state of Tlaxcala.[GE57] We know something of how it was created. In general the Indians around Tlaxcala and Huejotzingo who had allied with the conquistadors against the Aztecs expected to become part of the ruling elite. Eighty years of European disease and growing Spanish racism against the Indians dimmed this dream. In the countryside the native survivors were rounded up from their shattered pueblos and combined into new villages, placed somewhere easy for the Spanish to control. The newly emptied lands were then claimed by Spaniards in violation of existing royal laws against seizing Indian lands. Soon custom gave the force of law to the seizure. San Pedro Coxtocán had such origins. In 1602 a land speculator petitioned the government for some 2,000 acres, and then sold it to its first *hacendado* later that same year.[10]

As the Indian population slowly rebounded later, it found that most of the good farmland, pastureland, and water was already claimed by such haciendas. A few Indians went to live and work on the local hacienda permanently. Most continued to live in a nearby pueblo, hiring out as the cheap, seasonal agricultural labor such an estate needed. There was even a benevolent air about the hacienda. Unlike the wandering or absent encomendero, the hacendado and hacendada were resident, aware of much community feeling; contributors to local church and fiesta; sponsors of bullfights; patrons for young couples getting married; godparents for new babies; dispensers of free medical care for their workers; and other such *noblesse oblige* activities. But the hacienda-pueblo system from the very first rested on a basic inequality of land and water—those privileged who had lots, and those villagers who had not enough of their own to make a living on. The explosive potential of such a set-up was always felt by the more thoughtful landlords themselves, as much as the explosive potential of serfdom and land hunger was felt by the more sensitive landlords in traditional rural Russia before the Revolution there.

Today many of the old haciendas are just romantic ruins.[GE58] On our corridor there is at least the nucleus of one show-piece hacienda that travelers can still explore today. It is El Lencero, about ten miles downhill from Xalapa on the old colonial *Camino Real*, or Royal Road, to Veracruz. It was completely refurbished as a museum of nineteenth-century furniture not long ago (and drew lots of Mexican visitors when it became the setting for a popular TV soap opera). It started life as a *venta*, or inn, on that "missionary road" of the 1500s, and was located just about where travelers came into scattered stands of oak, which meant they were out of the yellow fever zone. The name supposedly came from a former soldier in Cortés's army nicknamed Lienzero because he took in washing. By the 1700s it had become a classic hacienda and in fact served as one of General Santa Anna's chief residences in the 1800s. It has its own manor house of two stories, with different music rooms for different kinds of music; its own free-standing chapel with delicate *trompe l'oeil* painting inside; its own two-story dormitory; its own separate kitchen building; its own dam and lake and gravity-fed clothes washing basins. You can work out for yourself there the symbolism of the hacienda—the wicker chairs, the two-room bedrooms each hung with a framed version of the local Immaculate Conception icon, the carved headboards, the wall tapestries woven in nearby Perote, the everyday red-and-black pottery from Cholula

---

57. GE Layer 57 is a Polygon showing approximate boundaries of the old hacienda in red. Most of the nearby Photos icons are pictures of distant volcanoes, though some show the general scenery of the locale in the foreground.

58. GE Layer 58 is a Placemark referencing a Panoramio icon called "Hacienda en Atzizintla," a romantic ruin on the altiplano just south of Pico de Orizaba. If you spend much time exploring Photos icons most anywhere on our chosen corridor, you'll find dozens of hacienda ruins.

alongside the fancier porcelain pieces from China and Europe. Two enormous 400-year-old fig trees in the garden give a visitor some live scale of the depth of history the hacienda has seen. El Lencero looks generally east over a natural terrace a mile wide below it, and is served by a fitted-stone road of a kind called *calle empedrada*: beautiful, labor intensive, and little changed from its prototypes built under Trajan in the Roman Empire.[GE59]

Commerce on rival roads

Up and down this road in front of El Lencero came the life-blood of the colony. Even though there were no important mines on the Veracruz-to-Mexico City corridor itself, cinnabar (mercuric oxide) came into Mexico along the road to be used at the mines for extracting silver from ore, and silver bullion came down by the same road. No other export had such value, and when the silver mines languished after 1640, so did the whole colony. After silver in value were probably the dyestuffs: cochineal (*cochinilla*) for orange and bright red, made from the scale insect that lives on prickly pear (maybe 20,000 insects to the dried pound, brushed off by patient Indian women), and indigo plants cultivated for their blues and purples. There were steel tools and wine from Europe going up (even though lots of Mexico has that Mediterranean climate favored by wine makers, the crown frowned on local production to keep Spanish winemakers happy), hides and wool from the altiplano coming down. From the lowland came vanilla from vines and cacao from trees. The altitudinal band through Xalapa itself produced the Jalap medicinal root, plus tobacco, and later on coffee, bananas, and other fruits, that went both up to the altiplano and down to the coast for export. The one major cash crop that did not pass through Xalapa to any extent was sugar. The first major sugar mills in the country were set up in and around Orizaba in the 1530s. Later the huge amounts of sugar produced in the State of Morelos, south of Mexico City, tended to come out of the country that way, beefing up traffic on the Orizaba road at the expense of the Xalapa one. So many African slaves were brought in for the heavy work of cutting cane and working the mills that for a time just after 1600 Africans in Mexico may have outnumbered the Spanish. Escaped African slaves called *cimmarones* took to the rugged peaks above the city of Orizaba and under a charismatic African chieftain named Yanga fought the Spanish army to a standstill for years. When the Spanish finally did defeat Yanga's forces, his surrender was not unconditional; he was allowed to settle his people down in one place, in a town that was supposed to behave as a "normal" Spanish-Indian one. It is still there, on the road southwest from Veracruz.[GE60] The Spanish government formally recognized Yanga's town in 1618. The much larger city of Córdoba, in fact, really got its start about 1624 as a Spanish army base to ensure no further cimmaron guerrilla insurgency from Yanga; the authorities carefully placed it between the rugged roads of the Peaks in the west and the settlement of Yanga in the east.[11]

Gradually, then, there built up a rivalry between the cities of Veracruz and Xalapa on the one hand, and Mexico City, Orizaba, and Córdoba on the other. Veracruz was so unhealthy for Europeans that anyone of substance who was based there built a permanent home up in Xalapa, seventy miles away in the cooler hill country, at least as a retreat during yellow fever season. It was said that no Spanish woman who became pregnant in Veracruz ever gave birth there; she quickly moved to Xalapa. Most of the city leaders in Xalapa, then, had firm ties with Veracruz, and it was Xalapa, not the port of Veracruz itself, that emerged as the capital city of the modern state of Veracruz. The two roads had rival guilds of businessmen lobbying for their respective sides, with the *Consulado* of Mexico City strongly favoring the Orizaba road and the *Consulado* of Veracruz equally strongly favoring the Xalapa road.

---

59. GE Layer 59 is a Placemark generally referencing Hacienda El Lencero. The nucleus of the classic hacienda survives today, beautifully restored as a museum of furniture. Spend a little quality time exploring the couple dozen Photos icons here. It was once one of Santa Anna's haciendas, and for a while the famous Chilean poet Gabriela Mistral lived here.

60. GE Layer 60 is a Placemark referencing a Panoramio icon with a picture of a statue of "Negro Yanga," Black Yanga, in the town of Yanga.

Royal fairs, royal convoys, and the Bourbon Reforms

During the colonial era the Xalapa road was dominant. For most of the 1700s the *ferias,* or annual royal fairs, were held in Xalapa itself. The yearly Spanish *flota,* or fleet (a huge convoy to discourage pirates, first instituted back in 1551) would dock at Veracruz port, and then its trade goods would all—every single item—be carted up to Xalapa. There they would be exchanged for goods that had all been carted down from Mexico City and the altiplano, even Chinese goods that had come across the Pacific in the yearly "Black Ship" to Acapulco and then by road through Mexico City.[GE61]

The colonial economy was still sluggish, with so many guilds and other monopolies tending to strangle trade. Beginning in the 1760s, however, there was a sort of "Indian Summer" of Spanish Empire under the Bourbon dynasty. Spain (and France) had suffered such a disaster in the Seven Year War of 1756–1763 that King Carlos III's ministers decided on the virtual reconstruction of their American empire. They brought in proven French techniques of centralization under efficient civil servants called *intendants* (remember Turgot, *intendant* of Limousin before 1776, from the French chapter). In time they broke the power of the Mexican *consulados* and of the imperial government office that had held monopoly control of the trading fleets. It was a case of more centralized administration to allow for less centralization in the economy, and was supposed to result in freer trade.

Veracruz, oldest European city on the mainland of the Americas, had always been vulnerable. It was plundered in 1568 by the English raiders John Hawkins and Francis Drake. In 1683 a French pirate named De Gaff had captured it, herded the people inside the church, and looted the town at his leisure. By the 1770s and 1780s, however, huge European navies such as the British posed an even more formidable threat. So the Bourbon reformers instituted a new defensive plan for the whole Gulf coast of Mexico. You can see a good deal of the construction of those times even today. The island fort of San Juan de Ulúa was rebuilt using fossil coral blocks that would absorb the shock of cannonballs without shattering. San Carlos, a powerful new fortress, was built at Perote at the same time, for last-ditch defense of the altiplano heartland in case foreign invaders came up the Xalapa road. They rebuilt the Camino Real from Veracruz up through Xalapa and Perote. Remnants of it—10½ meters wide, magnificently graded and clearly once beautifully surfaced and curbed—still survive from these Bourbon decades. The magnificent *Puente El Rey,* later the *Puente Nacional* or National Bridge, solved the centuries-old problem of the difficult crossing of the Antigua River on the road from Veracruz to Xalapa; it was the keystone and final piece of this new and improved version of the royal road. Built between 1805 and 1811, remarkably, it still carries heavy traffic today over its seven massive Roman arches.[GE62] Ironically, the empire that built it collapsed about the time it was finished.

SECTION D: INDEPENDENCE AND INTERVENTIONS[GE63]

Beginnings of the independence movement

The independence of Mexico from Spain would probably have happened sooner or later even without the Napoleonic Wars in Europe. Just next door to the north, between 1775 and 1789 the United States had thrown off British colonial rule and established what for those times was a radical Republic. The lesson was not lost on Creoles (*Criollos,* Spanish by blood but American by birth) who were bitter that all the plum government jobs in the colony went to the Peninsulars (*Peninsulares,* those born and educated in the Spanish homeland of Europe's Iberian peninsula), and so had their own grievance about "taxation without representation." And then came the French Revolution overseas, which inspired several small conspiracies in New Spain itself.

---

61. GE Layer 61 is a Path approximating the original road from Acapulco to Mexico City. Right-click on the layer name and choose "Show Elevations Profile." Run the slide bar along it, noticing how getting over the volcanic ridges into the Valley of Mexico was the highest part of the journey.

62. GE Layer 62 is a Placemark referencing Mexico's "National Bridge," with a cluster of Photos icons with pictures of the classic seven-arched, Roman-style bridge.

63. GE Layer 63 is the familiar aqua rectangle bounding our chosen Veracruz-to-Mexico City corridor; turn it on if it's not already showing.

The final trigger for Mexican independence, though, only came when Napoleon invaded Spain in 1808. He captured the central part of the country and the Spanish king himself. Napoleon then made his own brother the king of Spain. In the long run a Spanish guerrilla war would force the French out of Spain (and this is really when the Spanish word *guerrilla*, "little war," became internationally popular), but in the short run, it meant a hard pill for Spanish in the Americas to swallow—Joseph Bonaparte as their new king. The current Viceroy of New Spain thought he had a good shot at becoming "King of Independent Mexico" if he led a Creole rising against this. Some Peninsulars got wind of his plans, however, arrested him, and sent him under guard to Veracruz city until they could ship him off to prison in Spain. Meanwhile, the colonial economy, still basically tied to Spain, went steadily downhill.

September 16, National Independence Day, is one of Mexico's greatest holidays. Any Mexican school kid can tell you that on that date in 1810 the radical Creole priest Miguel Hidalgo de Allende, whose part in a conspiracy to overthrow the government had been discovered, rang the church bells in his little town of Dolores at two o'clock in the morning to rally the population to rebel against the *gachupines* ("wearers of spurs," a phrase originally from the Náhuatl and by this time a sarcastic nickname for Iberian-born Spaniards). This has gone down in the Mexican history books as the "*Grito de Dolores*," the Cry or Shout of Dolores, a call to arms as famous there as Paul Revere's ride is here. Father Hidalgo's powerful but increasingly undisciplined mob of Indians and Mestizos grew until it threatened Mexico City. They got as close as the hills just west of the capital at Monte de Las Cruces, but were eventually defeated by March of 1811 and Hidalgo himself was executed that summer.[GE64]

So Father Hidalgo became the model of a modern tradition in Mexico of "the left-wing priest," *la cura izquierdista*, by leading troops himself. Three years later the same banner of revolt was raised by the Mestizo priest José María Morelos. In his turn he surrounded Mexico City with his armies, cutting it off from both coasts, but also in his turn he was finally defeated by Royalist forces and killed in 1815.[GE65]

These populist leaders and their armies, however, were defeated not so much by power from Spain as by other Mexicans. The suppressed anger of the land hunger of the have-nots had flared up in these revolts, frightening many holders of property into supporting the existing government. So this so-called War of Independence of 1810–1821 was really also a civil war, that most brutal of all kinds of war. The populist insurgents gradually lost the war to the propertied interests, not least those of the conservative Mexico City–Puebla axis of the altiplano. The conservative General Iturbide's Plan of Iguala of 1821[GE66] finally ended the conflict, at least temporarily. It promised to set up an independent constitutional monarchy, to make Catholicism the state religion, and to establish absolute equality between Creole and Peninsular (no such guarantee for Mestizo or Indian!). To back this up, an "Army of the Three Guarantees" was formed. What was established was indeed a state independent of Spain, but it was not so much a normal state that had an army as it was an army that had a state. In the next few decades the army absorbed 80 percent of government revenue, not counting payments on the national debt. Its officers had all once been young Royalist army officers fighting the Hidalgo-Morelos independence movement. They included the young Antonio López de Santa Anna, who would become the dominant figure of the first thirty-five years of Mexican independence.

---

64. The town is today named Dolores Hidalgo; it is about sixty-five miles NW of the NW corner of our corridor rectangle, past Querétero and San Miguel de Allende—all of these in the Google Earth gazetteer. GE Layer 64 is a Placemark framing a view of a canyon leading down to Mexico City from the west, near where Father Hidalgo and the officer Ignacio Allende won a battle near there called Monte de Las Cruces, but decided against attacking the city itself. The opportunity never presented itself again as royalist troops took the offensive against them.

65. Father Morelos was from Valladolid, a town about fifty miles west of our corridor rectangle, later named Morelia in his honor—as was the state of Morelos south of Mexico City and Puebla; Morelia is in the GE glossary, about two valleys over from Toluca valley. GE Layer 65 here is Polygon showing the widest extent of territory held by Hidalgo and/or Morelos; based generally on map on p. 293 in Meyer and Sherman's *The Course of Mexican History*.

66. GE Layer 66 is a Placemark locating Iguala, framed in a view that shows its relationship to our corridor—about thirty miles SW of the SW corner of our corridor rectangle.

Ideas in the air

Before we get to Santa Anna, however, let's pause and take stock of ideological forces developing in Mexico by the 1820s—on the general theory that things are played out in the world of ideas a generation or so before they happen in fact on city streets, in country towns, on battlefields, and in politics. The two most explosive ideas on the loose in Europe at this time were nationalism and Liberalism (the European part of this text, at least, has argued strongly for that!). It turns out they were also on the loose in Mexico. They either developed according to a logic of their own, or came in from Europe—probably both.

First, consider nationalism. A special sort of Creole nationalism had slowly grown in New Spain since the sixteenth century. You can see in this a parallel, maybe, for that Anglo-Irish variety of nationalism that you've already seen in the Irish chapter—people English by ancestry but culturally different from having lived in Ireland for generations, and yet still very apart from the lower class Gaelic-speaking Catholic Irish natives. In Mexico one element of that nationalism was the Creole claim that they were no longer simply Spanish, but had been changed by Mexican sun and land into a new culture, and so were the natural heirs of the Aztecs. It wasn't quite yet a full-blown cult of a native *Volk*, central European style (since Mexican intellectuals generally were not introduced to Herder and other German Romantics until later in the century), but it was a step down that path. Some philosophers at the time justified the Mexican War of Independence as the "restoration" of the Mexica Empire; and the name of the country, México, still reflects that.

There was also a religious element of this early Creole nationalism—the Quetzalcóatl-St. Thomas argument. The Thomas of the New Testament was supposed to have actually come to the Americas (Preach the gospel unto all nations, commanded Jesus, and part of this argument was that the command would not have been given if it had not been possible), and the memory of St. Thomas in Mexico and fragments of the Christian doctrine he taught had survived in the Quetzalcóatl cult of native religion with its belief in a second coming of a divine figure. In 1790, as part of the Bourbon Reforms, the re-paving of the Zócalo in Mexico City had turned up the magnificent "calendar stone" of the Aztecs.[GE67] This sophisticated work of art was rightly admired, clearly the work of a most civilized people, but it was also claimed by some at the time as a record of St. Thomas's first-century visit. Then there was the matter of the direct appearance of the Virgin Mary to an Indian at Guadalupe just a few miles (less than four, to be precise) away. The upshot of all this was a Mexican nationalist argument that the native civilizations of Mexico were not of the devil, and that the Spanish were not the first to bring Christianity to Mexico: St. Thomas had done this over 1,400 years earlier, and then the Blessed Mother herself had appeared with a more direct message in 1531. However one judges this argument in terms of absolute religious truth, politically it was implicitly anti-Spanish (anti-Peninsular, that is), and also tended to unite Criollos with Mestizos and Indios who were generally deeply involved in church and fiesta. Father Hidalgo, a Creole champion of Mestizos and Indians, in 1810 quite deliberately chose as his visual standard the banner bearing the image of the Virgin of Guadalupe.

Second, consider Liberalism—not today's liberalism, remember, but that classical Liberalism of the nineteenth century that had its roots in the Enlightenment. One of its basic beliefs was freedom from any official church with all of its property, legal power, and control of education. The one adjective that summed up this attitude, in nineteenth-century Mexico as in Europe, was "anticlerical." Another clear element is free trade, *laissez-faire* economics: Adam Smith's "invisible hand" will take care of all social needs. That is, if shoes are in short supply and therefore becoming expensive, someone will begin to manufacture more shoes so as to make money. Private greed leads to public welfare, runs this ideology, if you can just keep state and church from skewing the whole economy. The remaining communal lands of Mexican Indians, the *ejido* ("eh-HEE-do") lands (on which more to come later), by this same reasoning needed to be privatized and thus become subject to buying and selling, available to the invisible hand. In terms of form of government, Liberals tended to lean towards a Republic. They were strongly in favor of the extension of education, believing only the educated and propertied could vote intelligently. Free press was also important to them: with free access to information, they believed, educated citizens could intelligently rule themselves. The United States

---

67. GE Layer 67 is a Placemark that frames Mexico City's famous Museum of Anthropology, on the grounds of Chapultepec Palace; see Panoramio icon at very back of same, under pointer, for photo of the Calendar or Sun Stone. Many others available, of course, from a Google - Images search under "Aztec calendar stone."

form of government was the shining ideal of Mexican Liberals, just as it was for European Liberals before 1848.

Nationalism and Liberalism are two very different ideologies with points of disagreement, obviously, but in Mexico as in Europe they came together as Liberal Nationalism before mid-century.

The "Interventions": foreign invasions of Mexico

The nineteenth century is mainly remembered in Mexico as the century of interventions—foreign invasions, to put it more plainly. There are rooms in most Mexican history museums that memorialize these *intervenciones*, especially those along our chosen corridor, from the Naval Museum at Veracruz to Chapultepec Palace in Mexico City, and sometimes whole buildings as in the former monastery of Churubusco. The Spanish stayed in military occupation of the island fortress of San Juan de Ulúa for several years after 1821, periodically shelling Veracruz city and refusing to recognize Mexican independence. In 1829 they tried to reoccupy the country, beginning with the port of Tampico (halfway between Veracruz city and the Texas border). A "Pastry War" with France in the late 1830s that started over something as trivial as a baker's debt resulted in French occupation of Veracruz for a time. The two major ones were the U.S. invasion of 1846–48 and the French invasions of 1862–65, although this last had something of the character of a civil war as well as a foreign invasion. Add to all these some purely Mexican civil wars, frontier wars, and violent changes of leadership (some of which are discussed later), and you have a new state so caught up in war as to have very little breathing room to establish itself.

All these wars were terribly destructive of Mexican infrastructure, for example. You can see this clearly in travelers' accounts of the Veracruz-Xalapa-Mexico City road, called the National Road (instead of the Royal Road) after independence. After 1821 thousands of international visitors, mostly from France, Britain, the U.S., and Germany (one scholar recorded 377 in the single year of 1830) came in along that road, and perhaps one percent of them left memoirs or published accounts.[12] The universal picture is of an old colonial road network dangerously decayed and not repaired. Robbery was so commonplace that travelers were routinely advised, *"hay que armarse para viajar"*—you must arm yourself in order to travel. One of the most vivid accounts comes from the 1852 travels up the National Road of an American named Wilson, whose stagecoach was robbed right beside the National Bridge over the Río Antigua that you explored earlier. The driver, as was customary, remained neutral during the robbery. The chief robber, in mockery, went down on his knees before a bishop, one of the passengers being robbed, asking for his blessing and his valuables at the same time.[13]

Santa Anna

Another weakness of Mexico in these decades was the rule of generals. Each state was dominated by one military strongman or more; none could achieve a lasting rule. Every change of government among them drained the economy as the old rulers left with their spoils and the new ones came in looking for their own. The dominant figure of the age, the most influential among them, was Antonio López de Santa Anna.

He came from our corridor. His father had a mortgage banking business in the port of Veracruz and a primary residence in Xalapa, where Santa Anna was born in 1796. As a young Creole officer in the Spanish army he fought the forces of Hidalgo and Morelos, and in 1821 his adherence to the Plan of Iguala helped seal the end of Spanish rule in Mexico. Two years later he led the rebellion against the self-styled Emperor Iturbide and helped set up the Mexican Republic. He was in power as President and out a dozen times from then until 1855, and accumulated an unrivaled collection of haciendas on the Xalapa-Perote as well as the Córdoba-Orizaba roads. Most spectacular was the afore-described El Lencero, although the largest was the lowland cattle ranch called Manga de Clavo, "Spike of Clove," nearer Veracruz city.[GE⁶⁸] At one point he had upwards of 40,000 cattle under his ALSA brand (from his initials). He was a frontier warrior a bit on the model of his slightly older

---

68. GE Layer 68 is a Placemark locating the general vicinity of Manga de Clavo; view framed shows Veracruz City at right, Xalapa at upper left.

contemporary Andrew Jackson in the U.S. Both were fighters of unquestioned bravery, charismatic captains, and quick organizers of armies to meet emergencies.

Like Jackson, Santa Anna was a terror of an Indian killer. There is a persistent anecdote about him that no historian has ever been able to document, but it may deserve repeating because it so succinctly sums up Indian views of Santa Anna. Turned out of power at one stage in his career, he was supposedly trying to get from Mexico City to Veracruz in order to take ship to Havana and comfortable exile until his country needed him again. He was slipping along the back roads around Xalapa, his hometown, where he was not particularly popular at the moment. A village of Indians discovered him, the story goes. They trussed him up, put the biggest kettle in the village on to boil, filled it with the spices proper to making *tamales*, and gathered banana leaves big enough to wrap him in. They were just about to pop him in the kettle to make a giant *tamal* of him when the local priest appeared, rescued Santa Anna from death and sent him under guard to jail.

Unlike Andrew Jackson, however, Santa Anna represented no interest group in politics or even any coherent policy, other than to skim off the spoils and to veto any action he disliked. Winning power was an exciting game to him; administration was so boring he paid it little attention. And in military affairs, despite his brilliance, he came up just short in the critical engagements of two wars.

It was on Santa Anna's watch that the Texas situation came to a boil, and partly of his own doing. U.S. readers are already familiar with aspects of this story, of course. In brief outline, in the 1820s and 1830s, land was much cheaper in Texas than in what was then the neighboring U.S., and attracted lots of interest. On the Mexican side, implacably hostile Indian tribes, notably the Comanche, made life miserable for the few thousand Spanish speakers in all of Texas. So the Mexican government made this cheap land available to U.S. citizens if they were Catholic and willing to learn Spanish. Promises were made, often with crossed fingers, and by 1835 English-speakers outnumbered the Spanish speakers something like 20,000 to 7,000. Add to this cultural division along language lines a general resentment of arbitrary, dictatorial rules coming down from Mexico City, and you had the makings of a revolt joined by some prominent Spanish-speaking families.

When Santa Anna took the Presidency by force in 1833, Stephen Austin, the accepted spokesman for Anglo opinion in Texas, went to consult with him on affairs in Texas. Santa Anna jailed him in Mexico City until 1835. Upon his release and return, Texas formed a provisional government and then in early 1836 declared independence. Santa Anna responded with the famous two-week siege of the Alamo, the shell of an old Franciscan monastery in San Antonio, and a "kill them all" bugle call for the last charge. Less than a month later he had the hundreds of prisoners of Goliad who had surrendered under white flag executed. This enraged Anglo-Saxon public opinion north of the border, and enough volunteers bent on revenge enlisted under Sam Houston to enable him to slip up on the unwary Santa Anna in late April at the San Jacinto River, capture him and force him to agree to Texas independence.

Texas remained shakily independent from 1836 to 1845, partly because of chaos in Mexican politics. When in 1845 the U.S. decided to annex Texas outright, and at the same time to double its size by pushing its border south to the Rio Grande instead of the traditional Nueces River, no Mexican government could have resisted the call for war. Once again the country turned to Santa Anna, who was actually still in exile when the war began. He barely lost the critical battle of Buena Vista to Zachary Taylor's invasion force which had come up the Rio Grande valley and then down through the city of Monterrey. Then he had to rush south to meet an even larger American force under the overall U.S. military commander, General Winfield Scott, which was invading Veracruz and preparing to march on Mexico City, the capital.

The main U.S. invasion

Scott's invasion proceeded straight along our corridor, and close enough to Cortés's original route that William Prescott's popular 1843 history of Cortés's conquest of Mexico was brought out in new editions. Many American soldiers carried it and used it as a guidebook. Artists in the train of Scott's army (or who were given official sketches to work with by officers who had been there) have left us colored lithographs of scenes and famous battles.[14] Soldiers of both sides have left memoirs. This was the real training ground for almost all later U.S. Civil War officers of note, both North and South, and so has attracted a lot of attention from American historians. For all these reasons, let's slow down and examine this last and decisive phase of the U.S. invasion in more detail.

Scott landed his armies in early March of 1847 on the beaches south of the city of Veracruz, trying to get as far away as possible from the guns of the still-dangerous island fort of San Juan de Ulúa, by this time controlled by Mexico. Sand bag defenses were erected to protect the heavy U.S. artillery that hammered away at Veracruz city until it surrendered. There was very high cost of civilian life, Mexicans remember.

Meanwhile, General Santa Anna began his organizing and planning to meet General Scott's army. Nobody, but nobody, knew the terrain between Mexico City and Veracruz the way Santa Anna did. He had been born and raised in Xalapa, had lived much of his life on estates up and down the National Road, and had already fought over a good bit of it. In 1822 he had captured a whole unit of Spanish Imperial Grenadiers at Plan del Río, on the road between Xalapa and Veracruz. So he chose an almost perfect site to stop Scott: Cerro Gordo, just two miles from Plan del Río, where the main road from Veracruz first started steeply uphill, winding under steep ridges, on a half-mile-wide slice of ground protected on each side by deep barrancas. The Library of Congress preserves a to-scale plan of the battlefield, hand drawn by a promising young officer named McClellan. On it you can see the three-fingered ridge on the south side of the battlefield where Santa Anna set up artillery batteries, and on the north side of the road was a tall conical hill (El Telégrafo) for battle headquarters and a smaller hill in front of it for more artillery.[GE[69]]

Santa Anna had twelve days to prepare the battlefield, to dig his artillery in, and construct a canal to bring water down to the site. The Mexican army outnumbered the American one and was probably just as well-armed, though worn from forced marches to get there. It was another promising junior U.S. officer named Lee, however, who reconnoitered the northern, shallower barranca and found a weakness. Santa Anna had thought it impossible for troops to climb its sides, especially troops with artillery, but it proved otherwise and the two center hills were hit with a surprise American assault from the flank.

The assault collapsed the Mexican resistance and turned a close battle into a rout. U.S. troops pursued; at the hacienda El Lencero (ten miles away, halfway between Cerro Gordo and Xalapa) one of the formal wall pictures still has a rough checkerboard scratched on the back, courtesy of bivouacking U.S. soldiers. Then Santa Anna successively abandoned Xalapa, then Perote, even with its fortress of Don Carlos, and in fact then the whole Tlaxcala-Puebla valley. The U.S. army marched behind him, finding the fortress in Perote especially interesting because of stories about how Texan prisoners had been treated there. In the sullen but peaceful city of Puebla, General Scott stopped for a while to rest his army for the final showdown; he was now as cut off from reinforcements as Cortés had been at nearby Cholula in 1519. It was a mostly Protestant army of less than 10,000 soldiers in a mostly Catholic town of 80,000 civilians. Scott—to his personal credit but future political liability in the militantly Protestant U.S. of those days—made it a point to deal politely and directly with the Catholic priests in lieu of the departed government.

Then Scott marched out of Puebla and west along the National Road, through Cholula, Huejotzinco, through the little town of San Martín Texmelucan (undoubtedly crossing the hacienda San Pedro Coxtocan we talked about earlier), and then up and over the Río Frío pass in the Sierra de Tláloc and down into the Valley of Mexico. The quickest road to Mexico City was just a little north of due west from the Río Frío pass, but by this time it was heavily defended. To circumvent these defenses Scott turned southwest to keep Lakes Chalco and Xochimilco on his right between him and the Mexican army. But this brought him up against the five-mile-wide, twisted, hardened lava field called the *Pedregal* (a *malpaís*, or badland, you'd call it in the U.S. Southwest) seemingly impassable for any army. Again it was the surprising Robert E. Lee who reconnoitered the field and found a way through for the army. Next came some of the heaviest fighting of the war: first at Contreras; then around the old seventeenth-century former monastery of Churubusco and Molina del Rey, the King's Mill; and then most famously at Chapultepec, the ancient "Grasshopper Hill" where the Aztecs had lived for a time on their road to power. The Mexican version of our West Point military academy sat atop this 100-foot tall hill, and it was defended by its teenage cadets. A U.S. artillery barrage and then a hand-to-hand

---

69. GE Layer 69 is an Image Overlay of a U.S. Army map of the battlefield of Cerro Gordo, complete with Mexican defenses and U.S. lines of attack. Turn on basic roads layer: today's highway, shown in yellow, is essentially the same as in 1847; then tilt and spin view to get an idea of how well chosen it was for a defensive battle.

charge killed many of the Mexican youth, and six of those left alive, rather than surrender, jumped over the wall to their deaths on the rocks far below. One is said to have had the Mexican flag wrapped around him as he jumped. So, at least—pictured on the ceiling mural of the portico through which visitors now enter Chapultepec Palace—is one of the Mexican boy heroes, *Los Niños Héroes*, falling to his death beneath gaunt specters of U.S. cavalrymen riding up on the rim of vision. Interesting it is to be a U.S. tourist standing there among crowds of Mexican visitors.[GE70] At the base of Chapultepec hill there is an impressive nationalistic monument to the six boys, at one end of Mexico City's single most famous avenue.[GE71]

After Chapultepec, the U.S. army drove in the Belén gates of the city proper. Then the center of Mexico City fell, U.S. troops paraded in the Zócalo, and the war was lost for Mexico. By the Treaty of Guadalupe-Hidalgo signed in February of 1848 Texas (to the Río Grande, not the Nueces) was lost to Mexico for good, as well as the western slice of what is today Colorado, and all or most of California, Nevada, Utah, New Mexico, and Arizona—half of all Mexican territory! Five years later, amazingly, Santa Anna came back to power one last time. To raise money he sold the U.S. what is now southern Arizona and New Mexico, the so-called Gadsden Purchase, for 10 million U.S. dollars. That was his swan song, the last straw in a career most Mexicans now recognize as having been disastrous for the country.

Adding insult to injury, of course, was the discovery of gold at Sutter's Mill in California just months after Mexico lost it in that brutal treaty. For centuries the Spanish speakers, at least, had looked for that gold, and now the U.S. found it. It used to be a truism among Mexicans that if Mexico had had the gold in California, Mexico, and not the United States would have become the great industrial power of the western world. Probably not (as a Mexican acquaintance said, we already had silver and that didn't do it); but it helped color attitudes towards the U.S.

Mexicans everywhere were shocked at the scope of this disaster at the hands of the Gringos (which term generally believed to have come out of this war, from a Mexican understanding of the words of a popular song U.S. troops marched to, "Green Grow the Lilacs"). Every developing nationalism needs a clear enemy against which to rally, and here Mexico found its favorite—the Colossus of the North, the United States. Commitment generally grew to strengthen their own country even at the cost of personal sacrifice. In 1854 the Mexican national anthem was written, and you can see some of the new patriotic resolve in its words. There is lavish use of the always-capitalized *Patria* (usually translated Fatherland or Parentland) and what true patriots will sacrifice for it, as in this nineteenth-century translation:

> But should ever the proud foe assail thee
> And with insolent foot profane thy ground
> Know, dear Country [*Patria*], thy sons shall not fail thee
> Every one thy soldier shall be found.

The Mexican nation was beginning to take on ideal form in many minds. And for all the harm the U.S. invasion did Mexico, it at least did it one favor—it broke the spell of military control of politics for a generation or so. The Liberals were waiting in the wings; it was their turn in politics now.

Benito Juárez, the Liberal Reforms, and the Civil War

Benito Juárez was a full-blooded Zapotec Indian from the rural hill country of the State of Oaxaca, a hundred or so miles south of our corridor. Until age twelve he lived in a typical village and spoke no Spanish, only the local Zapotec language. Then he walked to Oaxaca City to stay with relatives, found sponsors for his education, and eventually became a brilliant law student and a successful lawyer working with what we'd call today poverty law or *pro bono* cases. This led him into politics, as he gradually realized how the legal dice were stacked

---

70. GE Layer 70 is a Placemark located near main entrance pavilion of Chapultepec Palace; click on Panoramio icon under pointer, titled "Murales del Castillo de chapultepec," for a photograph of the ceiling mural.

71. GE Layer 71 is a Placemark referencing the monument to Los Niños Héroes; click on most any Photos icon near pointer for a view.

against Mexico's poor. Arrested by the government of Santa Anna's last administration, he was exiled—escorted to Veracruz and put on the first foreign ship leaving port—and soon joined fellow opponents of the Santa Anna regime in New Orleans. By late summer of 1855 they had gained enough support in Mexico to drive Santa Anna out of power for good.

This change of government, unlike those of the last thirty-five years, was not just about personalities and which generals would skim off the spoils. It was led by dedicated, even doctrinaire Liberals who had educated themselves in European, especially French, political, and economic theory. What they did is simply called in Mexico *La Reforma*, "The Reform." The reformers were uncompromisingly anticlerical and absolute believers in free trade and Adam Smith's "invisible hand." The first of three famous (or infamous, depending on your politics) pieces of reform legislation was the Juárez Law; it strictly limited church and military courts, requiring most everyone accused of crime to stand trial in the government courts. The second great legislation was the Lerdo Law, which seized all church property other than church, seminary, and school buildings and put it up for public auction, proceeds going to the government. The Catholic Church in Mexico, like the Catholic Church in France in 1789, had tremendous holdings in lands and non-church buildings, the sale of which was designed to give the government tens of millions of dollars' worth of buying power as it had the leaders of the French Revolution with their *assignat* paper money. This law also required that communal Indian lands, the *ejido* lands, be privatized. In the long run this hurt Indian communities, since individual villagers had no choice but to sell their private land whenever they were in financial difficulty. The third great law was the so-called Churches Law; it outlawed the charging of fees for administration of church sacraments. Other laws took the registration of death, birth, and marriage away from the church and gave all this to the state. All the above was packaged in the new Liberal Constitution of 1857, and many Conservatives, especially the serious traditional Catholics, rose up in arms against it.

So in 1858, 1859, and 1860 Mexico had yet another civil war. When traditional elements of the army rose in the Conservative cause, captured Mexico City and declared the new government and laws cancelled, Juárez and the Liberal government moved their capital to Veracruz, a city almost always allied with the Liberal cause. The Conservatives held the altiplano, but could never take Veracruz. The war was marked by the brutality of most civil wars. Priests were executed by the Juaristas, and Liberal doctors and nurses were shot by the Conservatives in control of Mexico City. Rural Indios communities were split between admiration for their fellow Indian, Juárez, and concern about his privatization of their ejido lands. The tide of war finally turned with the emergence among the Liberals of some generals of genius, chief among them Ignacio Zaragoza (for whom one street seems to be named in every Mexican city). He it was who recaptured Mexico City for the Liberal government on January 1, 1861.

The French invasion and Maximilian

Then, instead of the breathing space hoped for by the Liberal government, came its most serious challenge. The church lands had been sold for just a fraction of their value by the hard-pressed Liberal government in Veracruz, and the virtually bankrupt government decided it must suspend payment on its foreign debt for two years. This (plus the fact that the U.S. was all of a sudden internally occupied with its own Civil War and unable to enforce the Monroe Doctrine) led Britain, Spain, and France to agree to occupy the port of Veracruz until payments on debts were resumed. It turned out that French Emperor Napoleon III had much more in mind than debt repayment. He wanted to occupy Mexico for the glory of France and the reestablishment of the Catholic Church. When Britain and Spain realized his ambitions, they pulled out of the whole enterprise. What was left was a French invasion of Mexico in support of the Conservative side.

This invasion, too, proceeded along our chosen corridor, beginning with the port city of Veracruz in early 1862 and progressing by the southwestern, Córdoba-Orizaba road up to the altiplano. The reason it went south around the Sierra Madre Oriental instead of by what had always been the main road around the northern end was that the railroad—the future *Ferrocarril Mexicano*—had chosen that route. In 1857 a wealthy Mexico City businessman who just happened to have major estates in and around Orizaba got the contract for Mexico's first real railroad, to run from the capital to Veracruz. By the time the French arrived five years later, track had been laid in the lowlands from Veracruz city as far as Paso del Macho, halfway to Córdoba. European armies were just learning to use the railroad for military transport, so naturally the French chose the partially finished railroad route.

By May of 1862, the first French invasion army was closing in on the city of Puebla. On the 5th, battle was joined right next to the city. To the surprise of the French and possibly even the Mexicans, the Mexican army with General Zaragoza in command and the brilliant young officer Porfírio Díaz in the field drove the French back from the city and down off the altiplano. This is the origin of a second great Mexican holiday, *Cinco de Mayo*. No matter that the French came back 30,000 strong the next year, 1863, and captured the stubbornly-defended Puebla and then Mexico City—Cinco de Mayo will always be celebrated as the first true Mexican victory over a major foreign invader.

French nationalism also got a shot in the arm in these years on this corridor, incidentally. In 1863 a unit of the fairly new French Foreign Legion, to its disgust, was assigned to support work along the road from Veracruz to Córdoba instead of to the front-line fighting for the Juárista stronghold of Puebla. But the small unit was discovered and engaged by a superior Mexican force. The Legionnaires took refuge in a ruined building at a place called Camerón, and gradually all their officers and most of the men were killed. Finally, out of ammunition, the remaining four Legionnaires fixed bayonets and walked out of the ruins in a suicide charge. The Mexican commander, moved by such bravery, spared their lives. And for years thereafter French Foreign Legion posts all over the world set aside one special day for the heroism of Camerón.[GE72] It was the French in these years of their colonial enterprise in Mexico, incidentally, who really popularized the term "Latin America." It was an obvious attempt to stress their Romance language kinship with the Spanish speakers and so legitimize their whole imperial project.

Meanwhile the French Emperor Napoleon III and his Conservative, Catholic allies in Mexico had decided that a member of the Hapsburg royal house, Maximilian, would make a proper Emperor for Mexico. Maximilian agreed to pay the salaries of the French troops, and he and his wife Charlotte—she would be Carlota to Mexicans—landed in Mexico in May of 1864. Maximilian seems to have genuinely tried to bring Conservatives and Liberals together, refusing to restore lands seized from the Church, for example. All this did was alienate some of his Conservative followers, while for nationalist Liberals he would never be anything but a foreign dictator propped up by a foreign army. When the U.S. Civil War ended in 1865, the U.S. government made it clear to France that it should withdraw its forces, and began not-so-secretly equipping Juaristas with arms. Emperor Napoleon III needed his army back home anyway for more pressing challenges, given the rise of Prussia/Germany next door. The last of the French army pulled out in early 1867, and Maximilian, who chose to go down with the ship, was captured by Juaristas and executed that same year (at Querétaro, a little over a hundred miles northwest of Mexico City). Romantic to the end, he handed out coins to the party of soldiers detailed to shoot him.

Signs of this imperial interlude are all along the Veracruz-to-Mexico City corridor. Chapultepec Palace was lavishly rebuilt as the chief imperial residence for Maximilian and Carlota. The Cathedral in downtown Xalapa dates to 1864, not only the building but the title. Maximilian helped the church achieve the status of chair to a bishop, and later lobbied with the Vatican to have Felipe de Jésus, a Mexican Franciscan martyred in Japan in 1630, declared the first Mexican Saint. Although in 1864 Maximilian went upcountry from his chilly reception in mostly Liberal Veracruz to warmer ones in mostly Conservative Orizaba, Puebla, and Mexico City (the French route of conquest, obviously), in 1867 his body was brought down through Xalapa where it lay in state awhile in the Cathedral he had helped establish. Along that southern Córdoba-Orizaba road Maximilian made provision for Confederate veterans who had survived the end of the U.S. Civil War. General Joseph O. Shelby had marched across the Texas border with a sizeable intact Southern army at war's end, rather than surrender, and he threw in his lot with Maximilian and the Conservatives in the Mexican civil war. Maximilian in turn gave him a plush hacienda two miles out of Córdoba, one formerly owned by Santa Anna. An entire Confed-

---

72. GE Layer 72 is a Placemark referencing Camerón. Click on Panoramio icon underneath pointer, titled "mausoleo camaron," for view of shrine that honors both French and Mexican dead. This joint Mexican-French centennial memorial to heroes of Cameron in 1863, was erected on the centennial in 1963. The Latin motto in the center, and the "Homage to the Combatants of Cameron" in both French and Spanish, reminds a viewer that it was the French who really popularized the phrase "Latin America" during these days of French occupation of Mexico!

erate town was set up a few miles away near the main highway and railroad tracks, and named "Carlota" in honor of the Empress. For two years the social center of the Rebel veterans was the two-story brick "Hotel Confederate" in downtown Córdoba. There were Confederate veterans living in Orizaba as well, and some enterprising ex-Confederate officers established a freight-hauling service between Veracruz and the capital. All this died a quiet death with Maximilian in 1867, as this remnant of the "Lost Cause" lost yet again.[15]

Benito Juárez's last term as President of the Republic began in 1867. He would have five years of peace (before his death of heart attack in 1872) to work his ideas into the stubborn fabric of Mexican history. He successfully pushed public school education, trying to bring free, compulsory education with an emphasis on math and the sciences to the entire population. He established a rural police force, the *Rurales*, to bring law and order to the roads; for a time they had the sort of respect Texas Rangers won on the southwest U.S. frontier. He revived the mining industry.

About the only thing that he and the Liberals, the Conservatives, the French, and Maximilian all agreed on was the importance of the Veracruz-to-Mexico City railway, the first railroad in the country. In 1864 Maximilian's government granted a concession to a British concern to build the railroad and reap profits from its operation later. Juárez later renewed the agreement and found new funding for it. The line finally opened in 1872, with the bridge over the Barranca de Métlac between Córdoba and Orizaba as the most spectacular achievement of the British engineers. The railroad from Orizaba up through "The Peaks" to the altiplano was on grades steeper and in more difficult terrain than any railroad in the world had yet achieved. Up on the altiplano, the going was easier again; the railroad angled north of Malinche volcano and then went around the northern end of the Sierra de Tláloc, only dropping a spur line down from the town of Apizaco to the big city of Puebla. Later on, the cities of Xalapa and Puebla, feeling left out, sponsored a second railroad from Veracruz to Mexico City to be called the Interoceanic. It went uphill through Xalapa, then from Perote to Puebla, then closely paralleled the existing Mexican Railway around the northern end of the Sierra de Tláloc into Mexico City—and proceeded on south to the Pacific port city of Acapulco, hence its name.[GE73] Finally, appreciative of aid the U.S. had given him in his war with the Conservatives, Juárez cultivated the friendship of the U.S. to the extent that American investment in Mexico soon surpassed British investment. The second generation of important railroads went north, to U.S. border towns.

SECTION E: THE PORFIRIATO AND THE REVOLUTION[GE74]

The Porfiriato

In 1876 war hero Porfírio Díaz of Cinco de Mayo fame launched yet another of his attempts to take power, and this one was successful. He campaigned in the name of term limits for politicians, and then ironically enough ruled Mexico directly or indirectly for the next thirty-four years. His object was to use foreign expertise and investment to build a modern economy and infrastructure, and he did it with considerable success—though not without some unfortunate side effects.

The fingerprints of the Porfiriato, as his era is called, are still clearly visible on the Veracruz-to-Mexico City corridor. In 1889 President Díaz hired the British contractor Weetman Pearson away from his work on the Hudson River tunnel in New York and put him to work on Mexico City's 350-year-old drainage problem. Remarkably, Pearson solved the problem in short order, using heavy dredging equipment to complete the twenty-nine-mile-long Gran Canal that had been worked on for literally centuries. He was then assigned to Díaz's pet project of rebuilding the dilapidated, yellow-fever-ridden port of Veracruz. With the help of imported

---

73. GE Layer 73 is a Folder called "19th century railroads—VC-MC." It has three Paths inside it: (a) the route of the first railroad, the Ferrocarril Mexicano or Mexican Railway; (b) the spur line dropped down from Apizaco, on the railroad, to Puebla (both these in yellow); and (c) the rival Interoceanic built a little later, going through both Xalapa and Puebla (in orange). For a less cluttered view of it all, be sure and turn the Roads basic layer off.

74. GE Layer 74 is the aqua rectangle enclosing our Veracruz-to-Mexico City corridor, familiar from previous sections of the chapter; turn on if not already showing.

Irish labor and British industrial efficiency, new breakwaters and piers grew into the whole central harbor you see today, and yellow fever was curtailed in the process. The new harbor was complete enough in 1902 for President Díaz and his entire Cabinet to come formally inaugurate it.

Between 1906 and 1909 the Mexican national government took controlling interest in every major Mexican railroad, beginning with the Mexican Railway and the Interoceanic that run along our corridor, integrating them into a truly national network. Power plants were built to provide electricity to many Mexican cities. A telephone network grew up. The government supported increasing petroleum production with enough success so that Mexico joined the world's top producers. This is when the port of Tampico (230 miles north of Veracruz, about halfway from there to the Texas border) where most of the oil was shipped out began to surpass the port of Veracruz in value of exports—for the first time in about four centuries, the economic primacy of Veracruz as a port city was challenged.[16] On our corridor, cotton textile mills were the greatest success story. Four towns in a rough line—Mexico City, Atlixco (fifteen miles southwest of Puebla), Puebla, and Orizaba—had most of the big mills in all of Mexico, with smaller ones in nearby Tlaxcala. Spanish investors controlled most of the mills in Puebla. French investors ran most of those in Orizaba, including the biggest mill of them all, the Río Blanco mills that had over two thousand workers by 1900. Almost half of all the new hydro power in Mexico, by this time, was being generated to run these huge, modern new textile plants. In all, the Mexican economy from 1893 to 1907 grew faster than the U.S. economy.

A downside of all this, however, was a good bit of irritating foreign presence in Mexico. Huge, long-term concessions were given to foreign companies, and foreigners in Mexico were usually paid much better than Mexicans doing, or capable of doing, the same jobs. And for all the visible progress and all the wealth that went to progressive landlords, industrialists, and businessmen, very few of the benefits trickled down to the poorer half of Mexican society. Small farmers, even those who lived close to the new railroads, could not afford the rates they charged. So the rich got richer, but the poor got poorer. In the century before 1910 rural wages remained static and the price of food more than doubled, much of this during the Porfiriato. Over time the dictatorship became more rigid, democracy was a farce, censorship was leaden, and the young intellectuals were more and more alienated. Porfírio Díaz was the fourth most important person in the shaping of modern Mexico, along with Cortés, Santa Anna, and Juárez, and Mexicans today would generally like to forget about all but Juárez.

The coming of the Revolution

The Revolution is one of the most complicated periods of Mexican history, but absolutely crucial to an understanding of modern Mexico. The challenge now is to sort out its various themes and illuminate them with specific happenings on our chosen corridor. Where to start?

In 1906, with really bad timing, Rosalie and Harry Evans bought a Mexican hacienda. She was an American citizen and he was British, and they were both in Mexico at least indirectly because of the railroad boom.

Rosalie Caden was the daughter of a Galveston, Texas, businessman and a New Orleans belle. Her father had done so well trading with Mexico (along the new Mexican and U.S. railroads that met at Laredo/Nuevo Laredo on the border) that he could afford to send his daughters to finishing school in New York. The whole Caden family moved to Puebla city in 1896 so Rosalie's father could be closer to his business interests. There she met and in 1898 married Harry Evans, son of a British employee of the original Mexican Railway. Born in Mexico and sent to England for his education, Harry had come back to Mexico as branch manager of a British bank in Puebla.

After their marriage Rosalie tired of life in industrial Puebla city. Harry talked her into staying near Puebla, but agreed to move to the countryside. Liquidating most of their banking investments, they bought a 2,000-acre hacienda some fifteen miles away. It cost them 300,000 silver pesos and they invested another 200,000 pesos in a sophisticated irrigation system for growing wheat. This was the hacienda San Pedro Coxtocán near the town of San Martín Texmelucan that was discussed earlier in the chapter—an estate created back in 1602, rich in land and water rights, with crowded nearby villages almost as old that were correspondingly poor in land

and water.[17] [GE[75]] What could be more legal, maybe even moral, than buying a piece of property whose land title went back over three centuries (is the deed to your family land that old, dear American reader?), improving the land, giving employment to nearby villagers, and making a decent living from it? The great Mexican Revolution that began in 1910 would test that belief, and eventually destroy Harry, Rosalie, their hacienda, and haciendas everywhere.

In Mexico, generally, in this first decade of the 1900s, Liberal opposition to the Díaz regime grew more vocal. By 1904 an opposition-in-exile had formed in San Antonio, Texas, and moved on to St. Louis the next year to be safer from Díaz assassins. Their "Liberal Plan" of 1906 called for basic freedoms of assembly, press, and speech and the most basic of labor reform—a six-day work week instead of all seven, and the outlawing of child labor, for example. Most interesting, in this same year that the Evans bought their hacienda, the Liberal Plan called for some land reform. State banks were to help fund acquisition of land by *peones*, for example, and by implication that land would come from those who had lots of it.

This land reform plan—government interference in economic processes, after all—would not have qualified as "Liberal" back in the mid-nineteenth-century, evidence of how the word was evolving, being pulled Leftwards along the political spectrum by the power of the latest successful "-ism," socialism. One surprise to most U.S. citizens who read Latin American history for the first time is in how much more responsive it was to currents of ideology in Europe than our own history has been. The strong attraction to modern socialism for Mexican intellectuals is a good case in point. In rural areas the pre-feudal "primitive communism" that Karl Marx talked about was identified with the *ejido* (communal) landholdings of the Indian villages. In the urban sphere Mexico City got its first textile worker organization in 1865, directly inspired by European socialist ideas. In 1871 and 1872, influenced by the establishment in London of the International Workingmen's Association, activists founded the *Gran Círculo de Obreros de México* (GCOM), "Great 'Circle' of Mexican Workers," that quickly spread out along the Puebla-Orizaba textile mill corridor. There were at least thirty textile mill strikes between 1881 and 1895, almost all along our corridor.[18]

Of much more immediate concern to the government than the Liberals' 1906 plan were the massive strikes in mines and mills of Mexico during the rest of that year and the next. It started and in a sense ended at the big Río Blanco mill in Orizaba.[GE[76]] In April of 1906 some workers there founded the "Great Circle of Free Workers," agitating against fifteen-hours-a-day, seven-days-a-week labor. The agitation spread to Puebla. Mill owners in Puebla, in response, created their own council. They brought in enough other mill owners so that on December 22 they could hold a nationwide textile mill "lockout," turning all workers away to show who had the power to do what. The Díaz government had to step in to mediate and get this important export flowing again—a mediation skewed towards the owners, it appeared to the workers. By government order of January 4, 1907, all the workers were ordered back to work. All obeyed, if reluctantly, except the Río Blanco workers, who stayed out on strike. Fighting started at the company store when some wives of workers' leaders were refused groceries. Federal troops were called in, and on January 7 they fired directly into the crowd. When workers came back later to claim the bodies of their friends, they were fired on again. In all, over a hundred were killed, and anger against the regime grew. There were similar tensions and smaller explosions in the textile plants of Puebla and Tlaxcala.

In 1908 President Díaz casually mentioned to a journalist that he might be stepping down in 1910. Francisco Madero, son of a wealthy hacendado in the north of Mexico, quickly emerged as leader of the "Anti-Reelection" opposition to the Díaz party. He had studied in the U.S. and traveled in Europe, and had returned to run some of his family's properties. Apparently genuinely touched by the poverty of his *peones*, he thought free elections would surely bring improvement to their situation by letting reformers such as himself come to power. In 1909 he published a book on the coming elections of 1910 and almost overnight became the favorite

---

75. GE Layer 75 is a Polygon representing San Pedro Coxtocán. This map is primarily based on information in Henderson's *The Worm in the Wheat*.

76. GE Layer 76 is a Placemark referencing the huge Río Blanco mills just up the river of the same name from downtown Orizaba. For those interested, a photograph of the mills made sometime before 1925 is in an article by Alice Foster, "Orizaba—A Community in the Sierra Madre Oriental," in *Economic Geography*, vol. 1, No. 3 (1925), pp. 356–372.

Liberal candidate. The city of Puebla played a considerable role in these 1910 events. A radical shoemaker there named Aquiles Serdán, a born organizer, used his "Light and Progress" club to turn out an estimated 30,000 participants for Madero's campaign visit there in May, not counting the crowds that lined the railroad tracks to wave at Madero on his way to Puebla.

Madero's popularity frightened the regime, and it turned out that seventy-nine-year-old President Díaz had never had any intention of stepping down. The Governor of the State of Puebla, one of the most corrupt and brutal governors in all of Mexico and an old crony of the President, began mass arrests in Puebla city the day after Madero left town. Madero's presidential campaign, in fact, lasted less than a month after he left Puebla. He was arrested and was still in jail on election day. The votes, counted by loyalists of the regime, of course, returned Díaz in a landslide. It came as no surprise to an increasingly cynical public. September of 1910 was supposed to see the greatest civic celebration ever all across Mexico—the Centennial of the Mexican Independence movement, and the eightieth birthday of the Beloved Leader. In Puebla the ceremonies were poorly attended, most of them with heckling from the crowd, some of them with only government employees in the audience. The Governor had obscenities shouted at him and things thrown at him on at least one occasion. When those rioters the police did manage to catch were pressed into the army or sent as virtual slave labor to southeast coastal plantations, the mood of the city turned even uglier.

Revolution: the military phase 1910–1920

In October Francisco Madero escaped to the U.S. and called for a Mexican-wide uprising against the Díaz regime to begin on November 20 of that same fateful 1910. Serdán, who had secretly joined Madero there, returned to Puebla to collect arms and organize an underground army to do its part in the coming rising. The rising had broad support, not just from radical cobblers. Big businessmen had contributed substantial funds, and the revolutionaries had Winchester rifles and ammunition straight from Texas. Then on November 18, Serdán's house was approached by a police search party. Serdán and twenty armed men had word they were coming, and waited inside. Serdán shot the police chief dead as he entered the door, and then in a three-hour gun battle the police killed Serdán and most of his followers. His death cost the Revolution a local leader but gained it a martyr. Similar smaller urban risings took place from Veracruz to Tlaxcala on our corridor, and when police tried to crack down in the cities, many rebels took to the slopes of the volcanoes where they proved harder to catch or control.

The headline events of the following months came from the northern provinces of Mexico, where Pancho Villa and Pascual Orozco invented their guerrilla war strategies. Orozco captured Ciudad Juárez, right across the river from El Paso, Texas, and in late May of 1911 President Díaz gave up the struggle and agreed to go into exile. Hostility to his government from the usually conservative altiplano heartland around Puebla, however, helped make up his mind to go. From March to May, rebel bands there grew from a handful to 20,000 strong, outnumbering government troops in the area by ten to one. By May of 1911 they held the entire state of Puebla except the cities of Cholula and Puebla itself.

So Francisco Madero now inherited power, though in a country falling further and further into civil war. He made some initial policy mistakes. One was trying to disband all revolutionary armies after Díaz left and retain the old federal army as the sole military force; another was not rewarding leaders of successful revolutionary armies with military appointments. But with the benefit of hindsight it appears his basic undoing was that he naively thought he could suggest land reform to the land-hungry *campesinos*, and then control the speed and quantity of that land reform or even suspend it once his political objectives were reached.

This brings us to Emiliano Zapata, perhaps the most famous name of the entire Revolution. He was from just inside the southern border of our chosen corridor, in the state of Morelos south of Mexico City. Truth be told, the corridor rectangle was "fattened" a bit just to include his home village of Anenicuilco, so important is he in the story of modern Mexico.

In many ways the state of Morelos was the real firestorm of peasant uprising in the Revolution. In the past few decades it had become Mexico's most important sugar-producing area. When the second-generation railroads came into Morelos in the 1880s (the main one a loop south from Amecameca near Mexico City around the base of the Sierra de Tláloc and back up through Atlixco to Cholula (already tied to Puebla city)[GE[77]]), rapacious sugar plantation owners first got control of all public lands, and then began to seize village and peasant lands and use the out-of-work farmers as cheap cane-cutting and mill hand labor. Under the plutocracy of the Porfiriato, in any confrontation between sugar hacienda and small farmer or village, the judicial and police structure bent over backwards to favor the hacienda and the export crop it would produce. Many pueblos were strangled to death and disappeared. In 1910, of the approximately 100 surviving pueblos in the whole of Morelos, there was probably not a single one that was not involved in a bitter legal dispute over land with a neighboring hacienda.

Emiliano Zapata was a sharecropper and mule-trader from the little village of Anenecuilco. In 1909, when he was only thirty years old, the village elders made him village head. They were worn out with the paperwork fight against government and local hacendado and thought a younger man would have more energy in the fight to save the pueblo. After the Díaz government tried to destroy the Maderista movement in Mexico City and Puebla in November of 1910, Zapata began to meet with a half a dozen leaders of nearby villages to plan a response. He was one of the formulators of their Plan of Ayala (Ayala is less than two miles south of Anenecuilco), which called for restoration to villages of wrongfully seized lands. In the rebellion of March, April, and May of 1911, he emerged as a formidable anti-regime warrior. He was extremely popular in the countryside, and by mid-May even captured the substantial city of Cuautla.[GE[78]]

With the fall of Díaz, Zapata assumed that Madero's new government would work for land reform, and proceeded to set that in motion in areas he controlled. Then, to his shock, not only was he ordered to disband his army, but Madero actually seemed to back the sugar planters' land claims. General Victoriano Huerta, an officer of the old regime known for his brutality, invaded Morelos in the name of the new government. It was his persecution of peasants in Morelos, says one biographer of Zapata, that turned moderate Maderistas into hard-line Zapatistas: the label first appears during Huerta's campaigns there. So Zapata took to the hills again, the classic guerrilla leader moving on land he knew well, among people who appreciated what he was doing, who supplied him and informed him of enemy movements. He slipped around Huerta's ponderous formal army and captured towns within fifteen miles of Mexico City.[19]

Luz Jiménez was an Indian woman from the little town of Milpa Alta ("High Cornfield"). The village was on the southern slopes of the Valley of Mexico, on the road from Mexico City and then Xochimilco that headed up over the mountains to the south, across the border of Morelos and down towards the cities of Tepoztlan and Cuernavaca. Born in 1897, she would have been thirteen or so when the Revolution broke out. Here is how, years later, she remembered Zapata and his followers:

> The men of Morelos kept passing through the village, and it was said they were on their way to Xochimilco. I do not know why they were against Porfírio Díaz.

> These men from Cuernavaca and Tepoztlan spoke our language. They were only peasants, and we did not know why the Federals were afraid of them.

> This was the first thing we heard of the Revolution. One day a great man by the name of Zapata arrived from Morelos. He wore good clothes—a fine broad hat and spats. He was the first great man to speak to us in Nahuatl. When all these men entered Milpa Alta, we understood what they said. Each of the Zapatistas carried pinned to his hat a picture of his favorite saint, so that the saint would protect him.[20]

In February of 1913 Madero was killed in a barracks revolt in Mexico City led by General Huerta. Mexico City, which had been before this time sheltered from the actual violence of the Revolution, now experienced its "Ten Tragic Days" of artillery duel and bloodshed. Huerta ruled as a military dictator for the next year-and-

---

77. GE Layer 77 shows the new railroad loop south around the Sierra de Tláloc in the context of existing Ferrocarril Mexicano (yellow) and Oceanic (orange) railroads to which it was tied.

78. GE Layer 78 is a Placemark titled "Anenecuilco & vicinity." It frames a view of Ayala and Cuautla and, under the Pushpin icon, Zapata's village of Anenicuilco. Click on Panoramio icon under Pushpin pointer, titled "Casa de Emiliano Zapata (Anenecuilco, Morelos)" for view of same.

a-half, sending armies to terrorize the cities of Morelos and driving more and more farmers into the ranks of the Zapatistas. Meanwhile he also tried to fight the three armies from the north of Mexico, the so-called "Constitutionalists" loosely allied under Venustiano Carranza, as they pushed south. The United States, in a clumsy effort to oppose Huerta and support Carranza, occupied the city of Veracruz. This only triggered old Mexican memories of the *Intervenciones* of the past century and made Huerta look patriotic. But Carranza took Liberal Veracruz for his headquarters in 1914 (as had Juárez in the late 1850s) and the northern alliance advanced on Mexico City—Obregón down the west coast, Villa down the center, Gonzalez against Monterrey and Tampico in the east. After Obregón took Mexico City for the Constitutionalists in July, 1914, however, Carranza (a large landowner himself) refused Emiliano Zapata's land reform conditions.

The next six years of this military phase of the revolution are complex, with shifting alliances and a bewildering number of figures. This paragraph is an attempt to sum it up! In late 1914 Emiliano Zapata and Pancho Villa put together a short-lived alliance against the Constitutionalists. They first met face-to-face on December 4, 1914, in Xochimilco (on the side of Mexico City nearest to Zapata's strongholds) and then jointly paraded to Mexico City's Zócalo where they had a banquet and their pictures made in the National Palace. [GE[79]] There Pancho Villa grandly promised Zapata some artillery pieces to help him besiege the city of Puebla. The guns were repeatedly delayed, however, and when they did arrive Villa had provided no trains to carry them to Puebla. They had to be hauled up over the Paso de Cortés by man- and mule-power. In mid-December Zapata was outside the city of Puebla waiting on the guns when he got word that his chief deputy in Mexico City had been killed by Villa's men. When the artillery arrived a few days later, the Carrancista defenders of Puebla saw them being wheeled into place and abandoned the city. But Zapata had lost faith in his alliance with Villa, and soon left Puebla and returned home to his beloved Morelos. Carranza's armies saw an opening here. General Obregón quickly retook Puebla, and then in April turned on Villa's army. Obregón had been studying World War I tactics in Europe, and his machine guns and artillery cut Villa's famous cavalry to pieces. Later, with Villa in retreat, the Constitutionalists turned an army against the Zapatistas down in Morelos and once again Zapata took to the hills in guerrilla war.

What made Emiliano Zapata so unusual a figure in the Mexican Revolution was his careful, un-ambitious use of power. In a sense he remained true to those village elders who asked him to be village chief back in 1909. Village chiefs were his original officers, and when Morelos finally got a period of peace beginning in the late summer of 1914, civil society there was reconstituted by village councils with a minimum of interference from Zapata's military headquarters. By contrast, the armies of the north like Villa's were virtual "military corporations" that lorded over conquered territory, and even Carranza's government insisted that every major decision be from the top down, including every single case of land reform.

There were small-scale Zapatas operating on the altiplano in our chosen corridor, too. Domingo Arenas was from a village in the state of Tlaxcala near where it bordered the state of Puebla. In 1910, while drilling rebels in anticipation of the rising called for by Francisco Madero, he was accidentally wounded and lost an arm as a result. The authorities held his wife and son hostage for a year, and threw him in the Puebla city jail for another year (May 1912 to May 1913). When he got out, he fought Huerta forces in the states of Tlaxcala, Puebla, Veracruz, Morelos, and México, and by early 1914 had earned a certain measure of fame as the one-armed general of the Xicohténcatl Brigade. When Zapata and Carranza went to war, Arenas sided with Zapata, and for a time his army was the dominant force of the whole Tlaxcala-Puebla valley. Once the Carrancistas had Villa on the run and their government was recognized by the U.S., they came back to the area in overwhelming force. Arenas retreated to hideouts high on the volcano slopes, and switched back and forth in his allegiance between Zapatistas and Carrancistas.

---

79. GE Layer 79 is a Placemark referencing the National Palace; a search in Google Images under the names of Pancho Villa and Emiliano Zapata will turn up several versions of the famous picture of the meeting of the two, a jovial Villa and an unsmiling Zapata with his huge hat on his knee. Two minutes of actual newsreel footage available is from YouTube by copying this link: http://www.youtube.com/watch?v=d_wAoEqeHKU (or clicking on it here or in GE folder).
About second 37 of the newsreel Zapata's horsemen, dressed in white, appear; notice the lead horseman carries banner of Virgin of Guadalupe.

Whichever side he was on, notes one historian, "he was bad news for the local landlords." In December of 1916, his headquarters was in the town of San Martín Texmelucan itself, just two-and-a-half miles from the Evans' hacienda, San Pedro Coxtocan. He was passionate about redistributing land to the peasants, and at least this time was backed by local government. One of his followers, interviewed years later in 1974, found these times too good to be true. Arenas's headquarters sent word, he remembered, that "those who wish to go on fighting, fine; those who don't, cultivate the land." Arenas was killed in August 1917 in a meeting with Zapatistas on the slopes of Popocatépetl. Carranza's government gave most of the land he had redistributed to peasants back to the original hacienda owners.[21]

The Revolution continued to consume its sons. Pancho Villa, enraged when the U.S. threw its support behind Carranza, raided an American town in New Mexico. The U.S. sent a force under Pershing across the Mexican border to catch him, though it never came close. Villa was eventually bought off in 1920 with the gift of a sumptuous hacienda, and when he threatened to come out of retirement in 1923 he was assassinated. Venustiano Carranza himself, the "First Chief" of 1914–1915, became president in May of 1917 and immediately showed himself unwilling to do much in the way of the land reform called for by the Constitution. In March of 1919 Zapata wrote him a bitter, open letter than included these paragraphs:

> It never occurred to you that the Revolution was fought for the benefit of the great masses, for the legions of the oppressed whom you motivated by your harangues. It was a magnificent pretext and a brilliant recourse for you to oppress and deceive . . . .

> In the agrarian matter you have given or rented our haciendas to your favorites. The old landholdings . . . have been taken over by new landlords . . . and the people mocked in their hopes.[22]

The following month in that same 1919, Carranza sent an assassin who killed Zapata. A year later, when Carranza tried to name his own successor to the presidency, his own chief general Obregón revolted against him. Carranza tried to escape but was killed. In this final struggle with Carranza, Zapata's surviving lieutenants threw in their lot with Obregón, correctly predicting that he would take land reform more seriously. When Obregón recaptured Mexico City in May of 1920, he made the Zapatista army the Division of the South, and gave them a free hand with land reform in Morelos.

So whatever happened to the Evanses and their hacienda? The whole focus of the rest of their lives after 1910 was protecting their ownership of the hacienda in which they had invested almost all of their money. Rosalie spent the winter of 1910–1911 in the States nursing a sick father, and Harry kept thinking the political disturbance in Mexico would pass. In the following spring, at night, the people in Puebla city and presumably those left in the hacienda San Pedro Coxtocán could see rebel campfires on the slopes of the volcanoes. On May 20 of 1911, revolutionaries raided the hacienda for money, rifles, and a horse. Most of the next year it was too unsafe for hacienda owners to live on their isolated estates, and the Evanses lived for a while in Puebla city and when it in turn became too dangerous they moved to Mexico City. They were probably there in February of 1913 for the Ten Tragic Days. In April 1914 when the U.S. invaded Veracruz, popular hostility towards the Spanish was replaced by hostility towards Gringos and Brits. Harry and Rosalie left the country, taking the train from Mexico City to Veracruz, including a mile-and-a-half walk over a destroyed section of the tracks. From Veracruz they sailed to Havana, and then to Europe for a time, and then spent the rest of 1914 in Maryland. All this time they bombarded American and British embassies and consulates with demands for rightful return of property.

In 1917, with the Carranza presidency's friendliness towards large landowners, Harry Evans returned to Mexico. He died of illness there in November, probably aggravated by the strain of trying to operate in conditions of the Revolution. Rosalie Evans then felt called to go and win the hacienda back herself, and set off for Mexico alone in January of 1918. She was a vivid personality, and a strange mixture of traits and beliefs. On the one hand she was convinced she could commune via Ouija board and séance with the shade of her departed husband, and was a virtual racist in her attitudes towards the "dark and degraded" Mexican peasants. On the other hand, she was well-educated, well-traveled, multi-lingual (she could recite Goethe in the original German), absolutely courageous, and a magnificent horsewoman. At times, armed only with a whip, she scattered villagers armed with guns who had dared "squat" on her lands. These villagers, of course, thought the lands had been rightfully redistributed to them. As government see-sawed in the Revolution—from attempts to restore law and order and defend land titles on the one hand (as under Madero in 1912 and Carranza in 1917) to serious attempts to redistribute land to those who needed more on which to make a decent living (as under the influence of Zapata in 1914 and Obregón from 1920 on, not to mention local warlords such as Arenas)—the hacienda San Pedro Coxtocan was alternately occupied by Rosalie Evans and her hired guns, and then by nearby peasant farmers. In 1924 she was finally shot and killed from ambush near the hacienda. Two years later her sister in the U.S. published her collected letters home, which became a famous testament of her struggles and a condemnation of what had gone on in Mexico.[23] But Mexican memories, most of a century later, are mainly sympathetic with those nameless peasant farmers. This is in part because much of the psychology of modern Mexico was created in the so-called "Cultural" phase of the Revolution after 1920.

Revolution: the cultural phase 1920–1940

And whatever happened to Luz Jiménez, the village girl of Milpa Alta whose memories of Zapata were quoted earlier? Her father and uncles were shot by Carrancistas, the village was virtually destroyed, and she and surviving female relatives eked out a living for a few years in Xochimilco. Then she was "discovered" as a model of Aztec beauty by the French-born artist Jean Charlot, who along with Diego Rivera and a Who's Who of revolutionary Mexican artists including Orozco and Siquieros explored the political potential of mural art (you have already seen one painting of her in Rivera's *La Gran Tenochtitlán* mural from the first of the chapter). The lasting visual image of the cultural phase of the Mexican Revolution is in such murals, filling most every flat space in the halls of government and the walls of university buildings all over the country, and certainly along our corridor. It is didactic art, every bit as propagandistic as the Soviet art of the 1920s and later, of which it was a left-wing ally, and as the right-wing Nazi art of the 1930s of which it was the enemy. It is a greater art than these, however, truly world class and deservedly famous.

The Mexican muralists were funded and given a national platform by President Obregón's Minister of Education, José Vasconcelos. In Vasconcelos the Creole nationalist ideology of a century earlier was replaced by a Mestizo nationalism of real mass popularity. He combined this nationalism with social revolution in a way that still colors Mexico's view of itself. In it, Indian heritage is celebrated as every bit the equal of Spanish heritage, and the *mestizaje*, or "mestizo-ness," that resulted in Mexico was a hybrid culture supposedly stronger than either parent. As in Orozco's famous mural of Cortés and Doña Marina seated side by side[GE[80]], Spanish and Indian cultures united to give birth to *la raza cósmica*, the Cosmic Race. When the foundations of Aztec *cues* were dug up in Tlatelolco next to the oldest Catholic Church in Mexico City, work was stopped and the whole declared "The Plaza of Three Cultures"—Aztec pyramid in the foreground, earliest colonial Spanish church in Mexico City behind it, high-rise apartment housing for the present-day Cosmic Race at the back of it all. Excited Mexican sports fans, even those living in the U.S., when pulling for the Mexican team in a contest still shout *"Viva La Raza!"*

From the Ministry of Education, Vasconcelos sent his "normal school" teachers, suitably caught up in this ideology, to new schools all over the country. By one count over a thousand new public schools were set up from 1920 to 1924. The initial mission was to fully incorporate the Indian masses into this single *mestizaje* ethnicity. The ideal inspired a generation of secular missionaries. Mostly young city intellectuals, they proved themselves willing to live for years in the most backwoods corners of the land, in bad conditions and for small pay, teaching children by day and adult literacy classes by night.

But in one sense Indians in Mexico were once again victims of "externally imposed categories," as one writer put it. Intellectuals could celebrate the Ideal of Indian Culture as equal, possibly superior, to European culture, while continuing to define real-world Indians in negative terms of what Indians lacked—education, spoken Spanish, shoes, soap, etc.[24] The superficiality of Mexico's flamboyant Ballet Folklórico which still survives

---

80. GE Layer 80 is a Placemark at the former Jesuit College of San Ildefonso a block or so away from Mexico City's Zócalo, location of José Clemente Orozco's 1926 mural *Cortés y La Malinche*. Several different photographs of it can be found by a Google–Images search for the mural title.

from those years looks much like the purported ethnic dance of Ukrainians, Georgians, Uzbeks, and other national minorities of the former Soviet Union, as it was staged and carefully controlled by the Soviet state.

Meanwhile, ethnic and political differences kept erupting in which one part of the celebrated Cosmic Race tried to kill off another. In late 1923, when the radical Plutarco Calles was chosen as in-coming President, a military rebellion of Conservatives and landlords under De La Huerta occurred in the north. It took the central government months to suppress the revolt and resulted in thousands of deaths. And then when in 1926 President Calles began enforcing the letter of the anticlerical law against Catholic institutions, the so-called *Cristeros* rebelled, and this religious civil war flared and smoldered on into 1928 with atrocities on both sides. In July of that year, Obregón, just reelected as President, was assassinated by a young Cristero before he could assume office. The revolt of the Cristeros, unlike the rebellion under De La Huerta up north, was strongly felt along our chosen Veracruz-to-Mexico City corridor. Puebla always had the reputation as being the "most Catholic" city in all of Mexico. An older generation still living in Xalapa, the capital of Veracruz state, remembers anti-Cristero mobs vandalizing the churches, and loyal Catholics trying to collect and preserve what relics and partially burned historical papers they could from the debris left in the streets. Daria Acosta, a martyr from the city of Veracruz, was shot point blank while carrying the Host in a church service in 1927.

After the death of Obregón, Calles became more and more a strongman. Even after his formal term was over, he chose and manipulated current presidents like so many puppets. Only in 1936 did President Lázaro Cárdenas send him packing. Of all the presidents of Mexico from 1910 to 1940, maybe of all time, Cárdenas evokes the most praise from Mexicans in general. His personal honesty was a role model. He distributed, peacefully, almost fifty million acres of land (mainly as *ejido* lands for villages so it could not be sold as easily as by one farmer down on his luck), a total of twice as much redistributed land as all his presidential predecessors of the last quarter century put together. This is when the Mexican hacienda really disappeared as an institution, after three centuries and more of existence. And in 1938 it was Cárdenas who nationalized the foreign-owned oil companies, creating a wholly Mexican-owned company called PEMEX (*Petróleos Mexicanos*). This was extremely popular across Mexico, the country putting itself in control of what had become its most valuable export. Big business in Britain and the U.S. fumed and called for sanctions, maybe even invasion, but U.S. President Franklin Roosevelt turned a deaf ear. Finally, President Cárdenas renamed and broadened the scope of the dominant political party. It eventually became the "Partido Revolucionario Institucional," or PRI (pronounced "pree"). Despite the seeming contradiction between "institutional" and "revolutionary" of its title (or maybe because of it?), the PRI would hold the presidency of Mexico continuously until the spring of 2001.

Again, most U.S. citizens first coming to this history are likely to be surprised at how tilted towards socialism Mexican institutions and controlling documents are, at least compared to those of the U.S.A. Article 123 of the 1917 Constitution recognized the right to unions, to strikes, to an eight-hour workday, to a minimum wage, and a whole range of social benefits for workers. In state after Mexican state, beginning with Puebla, union power in factories grew until it was actually the unions, not management, that had the right to hire new workers. By the time of Calles' presidency the person who headed the dominant federation of labor unions was named Minister of Industry, Labor and Commerce.

Socialist ideology still has much more appeal to the Mexican intelligentsia than it does to its U.S. counterpart, as the historical residue of those years. Interesting insight into the Bohemian life of the Left during the Revolution comes from the play and then movie *Frida* which came out in 2002. It is about the intertwined lives of Diego Rivera and Frida Kahlo, a brilliant painter in her own right, twice Rivera's wife and sometimes his mistress. Salma Hayek, the actress originally from the port city of Coatzacoalcos in the southeastern part of the state of Veracruz, dominated the English-language stage production and was the driving force in getting it to the screen, where she naturally enough played Frida.[25] It is tempting to conclude that the Mexican Revolution was as important there as the Russian Revolution was in Russia. In his last years in Mexico, before his death in 1940 at the hands of a Stalinist assassin, Leon Trotsky seemed to feel right at home there.[GE81]

---

81. GE Layer 81 is a Folder referencing Cultural Revolution sites in the Mexico City neighborhood of Coyoacán. This is about five miles south of the center of Mexico City, and formerly one of the towns around the Aztec dominated lake, "place of the coyotes." Placemarks in the folder reference the Diego-Kahlo house, Frida Kahlo's house & museum, and the Trotsky house, museum & burial site. Many views accessible under "Frida Kahlo house" search of Google–Images.

SECTION F: SINCE THE REVOLUTION[GE[82]]

The era of World War II

To the disappointment of the agrarian reformers of the Revolution who lived to see it, in most of the country the ejido (communal) lands gradually faded both as units of production and as social institutions that brought contentment to those who lived there. Population growth plus environmental degradation meant less land per average farmer every generation. Attractive manufactured goods they wanted to buy always edged up in price compared to the farm produce they had to sell. The more adventurous young people of the villages found the economic opportunities and excitement of the cities irresistible—common the world over since World War II—and the "best and brightest" of the villages began to drift away.

On the other hand, Mexican industry began to boom in World War II. Despite handsome offers from Germany, Mexico allied with the United States and the two countries enjoyed better relations than for a century. Wartime demand for goods built Mexican industry, and eventually over a quarter of a million contract workers called *braceros* came to work in the U.S. proper, first in agriculture and later in industry, to make up for the U.S. manpower off in military service. After the war there were Mexican government programs resembling the TVA programs in the U.S. One of them was the damming for flood control and electricity of the Papaloapan river system—the big river that enters the Gulf about forty miles southeast of the city of Veracruz, some of the headwaters of the system drain south from the Orizaba-Puebla stretch of road in our corridor.[GE[83]]

Despite a couple of ships sunk in World War II, in 1940 Mexico embarked on a quarter-century of real peace, something the country had not had since the Porfiriato, if then. Life was generally better for the whole nation, though not without its strains. Economic progress was slowed by Mexico's high birth rate. If the economy grows by 3.3 percent a year, but the population grows almost as fast, there can't be much gain in standard of living. Mexico's population in the twentieth century roughly doubled every twenty-five years, and the government was reluctant to launch family planning campaigns in what was still a majority Catholic country. The P.R.I. as a one-party government monopolized political power and, as one-party governments eventually always do, gradually shut off political debate. Corruption in government and police was ubiquitous.

1968, Olympic Games and politics

The most important year of the past sixty-some in Mexico was probably 1968. Mexico was hosting the Olympic Games that year, the first Latin American country ever to win that honor. Olympic buildings and stadiums were going up in Mexico City itself, the result of a lot of national energy and pride.[GE[84]] Mexican university students in that year, however—just like their anti-Vietnam War counterparts on U.S. campuses and the student marchers on the Boul Mich in Paris—were especially radical, and determined to embarrass the government until it changed policies. Demonstrations began to turn to riots in July, and in September army units occupied the campus of U.N.A.M. (the cockily named "Autonomous" National University of Mexico) in its brilliant, new 1950s campus out on the *pedregal* in the southeast of the city.[GE[85]] The real tragedy came on October 2, ten days before opening ceremony of the Olympic Games, at the Plaza of Three Cultures in Tlatelolco. A crowd of several thousand was listening to radical speeches when the riot police rolled up in armored cars and tanks. Shooting started: snipers from nearby buildings said the government; unprovoked riot police said the students.

---

82. GE Layer 82 is the aqua rectangle enclosing Veracruz-to-Mexico City corridor, familiar from previous sections of the chapter; again, turn on if not already showing.

83. You can see the big lakes created, just south of the eastern part of our corridor, in aerial view. GE Layer 83 is a Polygon encircling the huge double lake created by two dams on the Papaloapan River system; by zooming in you can pinpoint the dams themselves.

84. GE Layer 84 is a folder with three Placemarks locating key Olympic venues from 1968 that are still landmarks in the capital. One is the open-air Aztec Stadium, built especially for the soccer championships but which has since hosted everything from rock bands to Pope John Paul II; the other is the indoor arena called the Sports Palace, jewel in the crown of the Magdalena Mixhuaca Sports City complex; the third is the University Olympic Stadium at UNAM.

85. GE Layer 85 is a Placemark referencing UNAM's library building, designed by the famous architect Juan O'Gorman.

It was something like the Democratic National Convention in Chicago that same year, only with hundreds dead in the streets from heavy machine gun fire (the official government toll, which almost no one believed, was thirty-two). It was the greatest violence in Mexico since the Revolution.

Bombings marked the anniversary of the Tlatelolco massacre a year later. Kidnappings of major political figures or their relatives continued into the 1970s. Small leftist guerrilla bands roamed isolated hill country in Mexico for the first time since the 1920s. Most striking, in comparison to the United States, was that the revolutionary ideology on the campuses did not wane in the 1970s but if anything grew stronger. Even today, with the Soviet Union's breakup decades ago and the general discrediting of Soviet-style over-centralized planning and rigid control of people, the popularity of Marxist thought among Mexican intellectuals can come as a shock to a visiting U.S. citizen. How can you explain it? Partly it was the revered memory of serious revolutionaries from Father Hidalgo to Emiliano Zapata, of course, but partly it was what happened to Latin America in the Cold War.

Fidel Castro and Che Guevara in the Valley of Mexico

Again, we might start with a place and a happening on our corridor. In April of 1956, on a rented former dairy farm called Santa Rosas near the town of Ayotzingo, up in the hills on the Lake Chalco side of Mexico City,[GE86] eighty men began a sort of Berlitz course in guerrilla warfare under the instruction of a Mexican expert. There was map reading, night marching, weapons training, mountain climbing, and readings in and discussions of the theory of it all. They were all Cubans, although their young Argentinian doctor volunteered as a participant for the physical course as well.

The Argentine was Ernesto Guevara Lynch, a twenty-eight-year old known to friends as "Che." He had come to Mexico City from Guatemala a couple of years earlier under unusual circumstances. In 1954 this bright and idealistic doctor had gone to work with the progressive Arbenz government just elected there. The new government's program included serious land reform, including the projected nationalization of the several hundred thousand acres held by foreign companies—land that was then to be redistributed to landless farmers. The nationalization was to have been done with compensation to the owners, not simply seized. But this was the height of the Cold War between the U.S. and the U.S.S.R., when the whole world was pressured to choose sides. In that context, two of President Arbenz's decisions were guaranteed to bring down the wrath of Washington: (a) inviting Communists to join his unity government; and (b) including United Fruit Company lands in those to be nationalized.

The Eisenhower administration at the time was deeply influenced by the Dulles brothers, John Foster as Secretary of State and Allen as Director of the Central Intelligence Agency, and the Dulles brothers just happened to be major stockholders in United Fruit. In the larger political context, this was still the United States of the McCarthy era's "red scare." A C.I.A.-aided army overthrew the democratically elected Arbenz, and a shaken Che Guevara took refuge in Mexico City, an enemy for life of the United States. Here in 1955 he met the man who would be his best friend.

That man was, of course, Fidel Castro, the leader of those guerrillas-in-training. A year older than Che, he was famous (or infamous, depending on your circle) as the young revolutionary lawyer who had led the July 26, 1953, assault on the Moncado army barracks in Cuba. His basic motivation seems to have been Cuban nationalism, against a U.S.-sponsored regime and history of U.S. manipulation of Cuban politics. Imprisoned, he had educated himself in political theory (like so many other prisoners before him). In Mexico City his brother Raúl introduced him to Che, and the two talked revolution all through that first night until sunrise. Not yet a Marxist even in 1956 when his guerrillas were being trained outside Mexico City, Fidel Castro was nevertheless reading Marx and Marxists for tips on guerrilla war. Eventually, his tiny guerrilla army bought an old

---

86. Ayotzingo, or more fully Santa Catarina Ayotzingo, is in the Google Earth gazetteer; just look for it in the Search box. This GE Layer 86 is a Placemark there shown as a red pushpin icon, though the specific location of the Santa Rosas farm is not marked specifically (because not yet located by author!).

boat, limped to the Cuban coast and took refuge in the Sierra Maestra Mountains. There they survived, and were discovered and romantically celebrated by U.S. journalists. By 1958 they had accumulated enough arms and men to take the offensive against the Batista regime, and they captured Havana in January of 1959. Shortly thereafter the honeymoon with the U.S. press ended, as Fidel Castro formally announced his belief in Marxism and then his alliance with the Soviet Union. Che Guevara became the roving ambassador of guerrilla war, Cuban style, to the rest of Latin America.

The Mexican government was uncomfortable with the ideas and practices of these Cubans and this Argentine, but many educated Mexicans shared—and still share—(a) their patriotic Latino dislike of heavy-handed U.S. pressure periodically applied to the region, and (b) their faith that Marxism offered the fastest way towards a more equal distribution of resources in society.

Liberation Theology

For a couple of decades, at least, there was also an interesting link between Marxism and a sort of social gospel Christianity in Latin American generally, in Mexico specifically, and along our corridor most especially. Successful ideologies in any given era have a way of gravitating to each other and experimenting with combinations of their strengths, no matter how deep their original differences ("National Liberalism" from the nineteenth century and "National Socialism" from the twentieth, for example), and so it happened here despite the seemingly glaring contradiction between the official atheism of Marxism and the even more official theism of the Catholic Church.

In the 1960s there came to be some consensus on the political Left, worldwide, that First World prosperity was directly responsible for Third World poverty. The conclusion soon drawn from that premise was that the Third World needed to "liberate" itself from the First World. Meanwhile the Latin American Catholic Church generally was responding to the challenge of successful Protestant mission work by setting up *communidades de base*, those "base communities" of active lay people who were to work for community improvement and social justice. Both the political Left and part of the Catholic Church, then, came to focus on the lower classes—the famous "preferential option for the poor" that came to be the heart of Liberation Theology. By the late 1960s, a version of Christian Marxism had appeared (though definitely not known by that name!) that amounted to Christian social gospel plus Marxist techniques of social analysis and community mobilization. The clearest formulator of the idea was a Peruvian; the base communities were most visible in Brazil; and the first international conference took place in Colombia—but overall Mexicans took perhaps the leading role. The first Conference of Latin American Theologians, a key Liberation Theology group, met in Mexico City in 1975. The city of Puebla hosted the third general conference in 1979. The movement generated a good deal of socially valuable energy, but its conviction that violence had been "institutionalized" by current governments led its more radical proponents to justify a counter-violence; occasionally there was the image of a Liberation Theology priest saying Mass while keeping a loaded revolver on the altar.

It was undoubtedly because Puebla had the reputation as a center of the movement that Pope John Paul II, Polish by nationality and an opponent all his adult life of Marxism (presumably at least in part because of what the avowedly Marxist Soviet Union had done to his homeland), chose that city in 1984 in which to deliver the following remarks:

> The present Instruction has a much more limited and precise purpose: to draw the attention of pastors, theologians, and all the faithful to the deviations, and risk of deviations, damaging to the faith and to Christian living, that are brought about by certain forms of liberation which use, in an insufficiently critical manner, concepts borrowed from various currents of Marxist thought.[26]

Liberation Theology waned among the Catholic faithful after that rather direct critique.

NAFTA and immigration

In 1992 it was negotiated, and it went into effect January 1, 1994: the "North American Free Trade Agreement" between Canada, the U.S., and Mexico. It seems mainly to have been a New World response to the successful integration of the European Union in the Old World. But on that same January 1, 1994, not coincidentally, a so-called "Zapatista Army" occupied twelve cities in Chiapas, the extreme southern state of Mexico that borders Guatemala. A running battle with the regular Mexican army ensued.

NAFTA is a classically Liberal statement of economics. In general it says that all property in all three countries should be freely buy-able and sell-able. Technically that outlawed the ejido, communal lands of the Indian communities, and Chiapas, with some 75 percent Indian population (Mayan, mostly), is the most Indian of all Mexican states. A masked, romantic "Subcommandante Marcos" of these so-called Zapatistas popped up to give interviews to the press and then disappeared. For a while Zapatista armies led less mobile government forces on a merry chase. In the long run they could not compete with state security forces, but they brought to the political table the whole Mexican legacy that celebrates Indian culture, and the widely admired land reform heritage of the 1910 Revolution, whence the name Zapatista.

NAFTA benefitted Mexico less than Mexicans had hoped, despite the initial success of the *maquiladores*, industrial assembly plants just inside the Mexican border from the U.S. In terms of the world economy, Mexican salaries may have been a small fraction of U.S. ones, but Chinese salaries were a small fraction of Mexican ones.

The greatest single stream of Hispanic immigration into the U.S.—one of the current hot-button issues in U.S. politics—is from Mexico. A good bit of it is what the experts call "chain migration," meaning that immigrants from one locale in Mexico tend to come join friends and relatives in one locale in the U.S. In rural Mexico checks or packages home are often sent to the local radio station, which then announces their arrival on the air, and the telephone-less and rural-free-delivery-less relatives come retrieve it at the station. Getting into the States illegally is almost a rite of passage for a young Mexican male. It elevates him in prestige above those who took the slower, safer, legal way, at least in the eyes of his own age group.

Lessons learned

With or without NAFTA, and with or without "immigration reform," U.S. and Mexican destinies seem more and more intertwined, including the tragic drug wars going on as of this writing in Mexico, driven in part by U.S. demand and with guns supplied from U.S. dealers. Hopefully this chapter has helped characterize these people, so we can see them in part through their own eyes. Every country has its own civic mythology, more easily recognized by outsiders than by its own citizens, who hold those beliefs deeper than conscious thought. Mexico has its own, to some extent a psychological response to the tremendous pressure of centuries of poverty, race and class conflict, and foreign invasion: "We are not Spanish or even Aztec but Mexica, a vigorous hybrid cosmic race"; "Most of us are not so much Catholics as we are 'Guadalupanos,' creators and believers of a European-American religion unique in the world"; "If we had not lost California and all its about-to-be-discovered gold, today Mexico and not the U.S. would be the dominant country of the Western hemisphere." In today's more peaceful and prosperous times, Mexicans seem to be easing into a more post-national state of mind, like Europeans of the European Union. In 2001 the P.R.I. finally relaxed control enough to allow a non-P.R.I. candidate to be elected President, for the first time since the Revolution. But the old social divisions of Criollo, Mestizo, and Indio still remain and keep the country from the stronger unity coveted by many of its political leaders. In January of 2000, the author came across the following sign in downtown Xalapa, left over from a rally the day before which he sorely regrets having missed:

> Programa de Fortalecimiento al Culto de los simbolos patrios
> Ceremonia de arriamiento de la bandera nacional

This translates roughly as "A program of strengthening devotion to patriotic symbols; a ceremony of striking the national flag." It's something beyond the annual Fourth of July festivities in the U.S. when, as one wag said, "Today's conservatives celebrate yesterday's revolutionaries." It's a feeling that with more national unity Mexico could achieve more in the world.

Look back on the currents of Mexican history that ran along this Veracruz-to-Mexico City corridor for the last 500 years. The city of Veracruz, oldest city on the mainland of the Americas, is not where Cortés initially planted it, but it is exactly where he first set foot on the mainland. On the other end of the corridor, for the single site of Tlatelolco, you have Diego Rivera's mural image of the huge Aztec market seen by the first Europeans there; the stump of the *teocalli* atop which the famous quarrel over religion took place between Cortés and Montezuma; the place of the first College for Indians where Sahagún taught and the Badianus Herbal was created; where U.S. troops went sight-seeing in 1847; where the cultural phase of the Revolution celebrated the Three Cultures in the 1920s; and where student protesters were shot down in 1968 in the run-up to the Olympic Games. The "main drag" of Mexico City today is the six-mile long *Paseo de La Reforma*, named for the Liberal reforms of the Juárez era. It runs east-northeast from the base of Chapultepec (the "grasshopper hill" from which the early Aztecs were evicted) where the memorial to the Boy Heroes is, then up between the major temples of Tlatelolco and Tenochtitlan, and then angles north-northeast straight up to the churches and basilicas built for the Virgin of Guadalupe on a hill sacred long before 1531 to the Aztec goddess Tonantzin. [GE[87]]

Every Mexican you meet, there or here, is to some extent a product of that whole history. The twentieth century Mexican philosopher Leopoldo Zea said, "Our past has not yet become a real past; it is still a present which does not choose to become history."[27]

Political and cultural nationalism and socialism—Old World European exports as much as Spanish wine was—became the three dominant ideologies of this Veracruz-to-Mexico City corridor and much of the rest of the Latin American part of the New World as well. It will be a recurring theme in regional modern world history, you'll see.

Endnotes

1. Bernal Díaz, *The Conquest of New Spain*, translated with an introduction by J. M. Cohen (London: Penguin Books, 1963), p. 214.

2. See Charles Martin, *The Aztecs Under Spanish Rule*, p. 569, footnote 128, where he cites Cortés's *Cartas*, Díaz's *Historia verdadera*, Motolinía's *Memoriales*, Lopez de Gómara's *Historia*, Las Casas's *Apologética historia*, Sahagún's *Historia general*, and others!

3. Díaz, *Conquest of New Spain*, p. 38. Locals, natives, "First Nations" as they've said in Canada for years—this might be a good time to say I'm trying hard not to use the word "Indian," but it's an uphill battle since most of us have used it for a lifetime. Columbus made four separate trips to the New World, but never, ever admitted it was not the East Indies he had found. The word *Indios* stuck in the Spanish language—it's the one Bernal Díaz uses—and later its analogue in English. Just as with "Aztecs" instead of the proper "Mexica," I'm afraid that just from force of habit "Indian" will creep back into the narrative here and there as a general label for those people who were already here when the Spanish first showed up.

4. William H. Prescott, *History of the Conquest of Mexico*; Introduction by James Lockhart (New York: Modern Library, 2001).

5. Leon-Portilla, Miguel (ed.), *The Broken Spears: The Aztec Account of the Conquest of Mexico* (expanded and updated edition) (Boston: Beacon Press, 1992), pp. 137–8.

6. Charles Gibson, *The Aztecs Under Spanish Rules; a History of the Indians of the Valley of Mexico, 1519–1810* (Stanford, CA: Stanford University Press, 1964).

7. François Chevalier, *Land and Society in Colonial Mexico: The Great Hacienda* (Berkeley and Los Angeles: University of California Press, 1963), p. 51.

---

87. GE Layer 87 is a Polygon, a yellow outline around the whole length of Paseo de La Reforma and Reforma Norte. Zoom in and navigate along it to explore detailed views, Photos icons. Note particularly to whom particular squares along the Paseo are dedicated, and to whom they are not (Cortés, Santa Anna, and Porfírio Díaz among the latter).

8. Martín del Cruz (ed.), *The Badianus Manuscript (Codex Barberini, Latin 241) Vatical Library; Aztec herbal of 1552* (Baltimore: Johns Hopkins Press, 1940).

9. Gibson, p. 27.

10. Timothy J. Henderson, *The Worm in the Wheat: Rosalie Evans and* Agrarian *Struggle in the Puebla-Tlaxcala Valley of Mexico, 1906–1927* (Durham and London: Duke University Press, 1998, pp. 23–28).

11. See Jane C. Landers and Barry M. Robinson (eds.), *Slaves, Subjects, and Subversives: Blacks in Colonial America,* especially Landers' Chapter 4, "Cimmarón and Citizen." (University of New Mexico Press, 2006.)

12. Alfred H. Siemens, *Between the Summit and the Sea: Central Veracruz in the Nineteenth Century* (Vancouver: University of British Columbia Press, 1990), p. 3.

13. Robert Anderson Wilson, *Mexico and Its Religion* (New York: Harper, 1855).

14. Carol and Thomas Christensen, *The U.S-Mexican War* (companion to the public TV series, "The U.S. Mexican War, 1846–1848") (San Francisco: Bay Books, 1998). Eight full-color reproductions of the contemporary lithographs of major battles, all but the first along our corridor, are between pages 182 and 183.

15. See Andrew F. Rolle, *The Lost Cause; the Confederate Exodus to Mexico* (Norman: University of Oklahoma Press, 1965).

16. See Alfred Tischendorf, *Great Britain and Mexico in the Era of Porfirio Díaz* (Durham: Duke University Press, 1961).

17. Henderson, *The Worm in the Wheat*, pp. 27–28.

18. Jeffrey Bortz, "Mexican textile workers: from conquest to globalization," in *A Global History of Textile Workers, 1650–2000*, posted by the International Institute of Social History at www.iisg.nl/research/mexico.doc.

19. John Womack, Jr., *Zapata and the Mexican Revolution* (New York: Knopf, 1970), pp. 4–123.

20. Luz Jiménez, *Life and Death in Milpa Alta; a Nahuatl chronicle of Díaz and Zapata* (Norman: University of Oklahoma Press, 1972).

21. Henderson, *The Worm in the Wheat*, pp. 52–64.

22. Meyer & Sherman, *The Course of Mexican History*, p. 548.

23. *The Rosalie Evans Letters from Mexico: Arranged with Comment by Daisy Caden Pettus* (Indianapolis: The Bobbs-Merrill Company, Publishers, 1926).

24. Alan Knight, "Racism, Revolution, and Indigenismo: Mexico, 1910–1940," in Richard Graham, *The Idea of Race in Latin America, 1870–1940* (Austin: University of Texas Press, 1990), pp. 99–100.

25. See "The Many Faces of Frida Kahlo," in *Smithsonian*, Nov. 2002, pp. 50–60, for color reproductions of many of her paintings and a good summary article on her life.

26. See John Witte, Jr. et al., *The Teachings of Modern Christianity: On Law, Politics, and Human Nature*, vol. 2 (Kegan, Paul International, 2005), p. 180. The formal document is "Instruction of Certain Aspects of the 'Theology of Liberation,'" as issued in Sept. 1984 by The Sacred Congregation for the Doctrine of the Faith of the Roman Catholic Church.

27. As quoted on p. 430 of Peter Rees' *Route Inertia and Route Competition*.

Chapter Nine

"The Only Antidote to Foreign Rule and Modern Imperialism": The Durban-to-Pretoria Corridor of Sub-Saharan Africa

"The history of modern times is the history of nationalism. Nationalism has been tested in the people's struggles and the fires of battle and found to be the only antidote against foreign rule and modern imperialism."

—from Anton Lembede's Natal newspaper *Inkundla ya Bantu,*
as quoted by Nelson Mandela in his book *Long Walk to Freedom*

CONTENTS

The heart of the matter—SECTION A: SOME INTRODUCTION TO AREA LANGUAGES AND THE TOPOGRAPHY AND TEXTURE OF THE LAND—The Click languages of the Khoisan—Bantu languages in Southern Africa: Sotho/Tswana and Nguni—A few Portuguese linguistic survivals—From Dutch to Cape Dutch to Afrikaans—General geography—The Durban-to-Pretoria corridor—SECTION B: PRE- AND EARLY HISTORY—The rock art of the Khoisan—*The Abundant Herds*—Halfway to Java—SECTION C: THE BRITISH ARRIVAL, THE ZULU CRUSHING, THE GREAT TREK, AND NATALIA—British takeover—Zulu power and the Mfecane/Difaqane—The fate of the refugees—The Great Trek and its legacy—SECTION D: BRITISH DOMINANCE, THE ZULU WAR AND THE BOER WARS—The British in Natal—Xhosa tragedy—The growth of British Natal by 1850—Bushman raiders of the Drakensberg—Shepstone, the N.N.P., and the "barrier locations"—Langalibalele of the Hlubi—The Colensos and English liberalism—Lord Carnarvon's federation idea—Cetswayo and the Zulu revival—The Anglo-Zulu War of 1879—*King Solomon's Mines*—Dismembering the Zulu state—The Boer republics and the Anglo-Boer wars—The first Anglo-Boer War—Diamonds at Kimberley; gold on the Rand—The railroads to Jo'burg—Cecil Rhodes—Jameson's Raid—The Second Anglo-Boer War—The "concentration" camps—The Union of South Africa, 1910—SECTION E: CULTURAL NATIONALISM AMONG THE AFRIKANERS—The first voices—The *Broederbond*—*Die Tweede Trek* ("The Second Trek")—*Cry, the Beloved Country*—Instituting apartheid, 1948–50—SECTION F: AFRICAN CULTURAL NATIONALISM—Early civil rights struggle part one: Gandhi in South Africa—Early civil rights struggle part two: J. L. Dube—The Bambatha (Zulu) rebellion of 1906—Dube, the African National Congress, and the Native Lands Act—Nelson Mandela—Albert Luthuli—The P.A.C. and the Sharpeville massacre—Steve Biko and "Black consciousness"—The Soweto riots—*July's People*—Buthelezi and Inkatha—Desmond Tutu and the Truth and Reconciliation Commission—The current state of affairs, post-apartheid, and lessons learned

The heart of the matter

The corridor chosen to teach modern Sub-Saharan African history in microcosm is the one from Durban to Pretoria in today's South Africa. By rights, given Africa's size and diversity, there ought also be at least a west, an east, and a central African "corridor" as well, but the book is getting too long as it is, and many, many movements and events on this one southern corridor have their echoes and analogues in the rest of Africa. So Durban-to-Pretoria it is, and here's an introduction to the heart of the matter as seen along this corridor.

In the Boer War that began in 1899, man for man the Boers—farmers descended from Dutch settlers—outclassed the British, but the British simply overwhelmed them with tens of thousands of troops. The conventional war was over by 1900. To end the continuing guerrilla war, the British burned all the farmsteads, rounded up a hundred thousand Boer women and children and kept them in "concentration" camps where perhaps a quarter of them died from disease. By 1902 it was all over, except for a legacy of bitterness on the part of the Boers. It's not always true that the winners write the histories. With the Boers as with American Southerners after our Civil War and Reconstruction, the losers in the grip of memory of a lost cause transmuted it into a triumph of the spirit.

Three individuals in South Africa in these few years around the dawn of the twentieth century give you a clue to what was to come.

One was a young cleric and writer whose pen name was Totius. He was a Boer whose father and uncle were educators and publicists just beginning to celebrate Boer culture, which they now called Afrikaner. The language they spoke, they insisted, was not just a dialect of Dutch; it was its own unique language—Afrikaans—which justified an independent state for its speakers. Totius, just twenty-two, was a chaplain to the Boer armies during the year of conventional war, then went to Holland for his doctorate, returning in 1903 an ordained minister in the Dutch Reformed Church, the denomination of virtually every Boer/Afrikaner. By 1911 he was a Professor of Theology, and at the same time becoming the great Afrikaans-language poet proving to the world, and to Afrikaners especially, that their language was the equal of any other. In him you see fully formed the strong cultural nationalism that would take this 6 percent of the population of South Africa to rule over the whole, and to the full establishment of apartheid—the world's most rigid racial segregation—by 1948.

The second was Mohandas Karamchand Gandhi, a timid young Hindu lawyer from Gujarat who had come across the Indian Ocean to the seaport of Durban in 1893 on a one-year contract with an Indian Muslim business firm there. He had gotten his legal training in London, and they needed someone who functioned well in English language and who knew British law. Instead of one year there, though, he spent twenty-one years; and in his reaction to the white racism that severely limited Indian rights he developed his whole range of non-violent civil disobedience strategies (which he only later took back to British India). In 1904 he set up his first ashram, a communal religious retreat, about ten miles out of Durban. It was called Phoenix Farm, and it was to support an Indian civil rights newspaper called *Indian Opinion*, published in English and in Hindi.

The third was John Langalibalele Dube, son of the first American-educated Zulu Protestant pastor, and himself carried by American missionaries back to Ohio's Oberlin College (which had sponsored Booker T. Washington's Tuskegee Institute in Alabama) and perhaps even to Tuskegee itself. He returned to South Africa intending to establish a "Zulu Christian Industrial School" for boys. In a conflict with the authorities, by 1901 this had morphed into Ohlange Institute, which was set up to support an African civil rights newspaper called *The Sun of Natal*, published in English and in Zulu. Ohlange too was about ten miles out of Durban—and as it turned out only a mile-and-a-half from Gandhi's Phoenix Farm. There was apparently lots of coming and going between the two, and no doubt Gandhi originally chose his site in 1904 to be close to J. L. Dube's already going concern. In 1912 Dube was tapped to head up a new African civil rights movement, countrywide, called the African National Congress (named after the successful Indian National Congress formed in 1885). Nelson Mandela, who would lead the ANC to end apartheid by 1994, wasn't born until six years after the ANC was founded.

In these first years of the last century these three were working in the deep context of Khoisan (Bushman) and Bantu-language group history, including the sixty-year-long heyday of the Zulu kings; of Dutch settlement patterns from 1652 on; of British imperial expansion and African and Boer resistance, including the Great Trek; and of the diamond strikes at Kimberley and the world's greatest gold rush at Johannesburg. Looking ahead from their times, with the advantage of 20-20 hindsight, we can see the outlines of modern South African history that were already forecast by their beliefs and activity. Apartheid had to happen, supported by a fierce Afrikaner cultural nationalism. And apartheid had to be opposed, and eventually dismantled, by movements that had some black African cultural nationalism about them as well but which in the end were broader and more generous.

There are many intense human dramas in modern world history, but few are more intense than the one that played out—and of course is still playing out—in South Africa.

SECTION A: SOME INTRODUCTION TO AREA LANGUAGES AND THE TOPOGRAPHY AND TEXTURE OF THE LAND

The Click languages of the Khoisan

The Click language family is unique to Africa, and is today confined almost exclusively to the southern cone of the continent. Clicks—as when you would say "tsk, tsk" to an erring child, or the "kh-kh-kh" made between the sides of tongue and cheeks as when encouraging a horse, or the loud pop made when you suddenly pull your tongue off the roof of your mouth, and others—are as prominent in this language family as are vocalizations. Many older Americans got their first exposure to the way these Click languages sound in the 1985 South African film *The Gods Must Be Crazy* by Jamie Uys. The movie opens with a clever contrast between the regimentation of "civilized" Johannesburg and the supposed Garden of Eden somewhere in the bush in Botswana where it is always Tuesday, or never Tuesday, as you wish. Every major character is a humorous caricature, including a Cuban revolutionary who laments having to work with amateurs. Knowing the tragedy behind this comic film, however—the virtual destruction of most of the remaining Khoisan society going on while it was being made—makes going back to see it a bittersweet experience.[1]

The word Khoisan is a combination of San (formerly called "Bushmen," from the Dutch *Bojesman* meaning the same thing) and Khoi (formerly called "Hottentot," from an old Dutch word meaning stutterer, because of the clicks). The San were thought to be hunters and gatherers only, the pure Kalahari-desert-colored aboriginals. The Khoi, generally taller and darker but still Click-language-speaking, were supposed to be those who had learned the herding of cattle from the Bantu-speakers and added it to hunting and gathering. In practice scholars had such a hard time separating herders and non-herders—otherwise "pure" San who had taken to cattle herding; otherwise bonafide Khoi who had none—that the separation of the terms eventually seemed pointless, hence the word Khoisan.

Bantu languages in Southern Africa: Sotho/Tswana and Nguni

Bantu is the largest single African language family, with hundreds of languages and literally hundreds of millions of speakers. The prefix "aba" or "ba" signifies the plural in many Bantu languages, and "ntu" means person, so "ba-ntu" or "Bantu" just means "The People." It's like Greeks vs. Barbarians, or Jews vs. Gentiles, in that it generally means We Real People (who speak an understandable language) as opposed to Those Others Out There (who just babble things that nobody can understand and have strange social customs). Linguists and archaeologists conjecture that the proto-Bantu language originated in West Africa at least 2,500 years ago. The cultural complex associated with the spread of Bantu languages included intensive agriculture and the maintaining of herds of cattle, and also the working of iron for spears and hoes. This last was so important that blacksmiths sometimes even acquired religious positions in Bantu societies. The language family and the associated cultural complex slowly but powerfully radiated east and south. In southern Africa, which it probably invaded before AD 500, it developed mainly as the Sotho/Tswana languages of the high interior grasslands (the name of the modern state of Botswana comes from "ba" and "tswana") and the Nguni-speaking groups of the lower grasslands sloping down to the Indian Ocean.

It might be worth noting early in this language lesson that one difference between modern U.S. English and modern South African English is the use of the word "Bantu." It is still generally acceptable in South Africa when talking about languages, but not about the people who speak those languages—a result of how it was used so pejoratively by the apartheid regime in the decades after 1948. And "native" and "tribal," words generally embraced with pride by the historically original ("Indian"; "First Nations") population of North America, are in South Africa also tainted by the way colonial governments used the words over the past two centuries; "ethnic" is a preferable substitute for "tribal," at least.

The Nguni sub-family of Bantu includes Xhosa and Zulu, the languages spoken by the key African players in the colonial and civil rights eras of modern South Africa, so let's spend a little extra time on Nguni (pronounced something like "en-GOO-nee"). Most of the Nguni languages today are located along the six-hundred-mile-long stretch of South African and Swaziland coast that is tilted from southwest to northeast, in that roughly hundred-mile-wide band of territory between the Drakensberg escarpment and the Indian Ocean. From northeast to southwest the largest groups today are the Swazi (which is the Zulu word for them by which they are best known; they themselves use the word "si-Swati"), the Zulu and the Xhosa (who call themselves ama-Zulu and amaXhosa, technically). Close neighbors and allies of the Xhosa are the Thembu, the ethnic group of South Africa's first popularly elected President, Nelson Mandela. The Swazi are mainly in today's independent state of Swaziland. There are roughly seven million Zulus in today's KwaZulu-Natal province, and about six-and-a-half million Xhosa and Thembu in today's Eastern Cape province.[GE1] The southern half of our chosen Durban-to-Pretoria corridor, to be properly introduced in just a bit, cuts right through the middle of this Nguni-language strip.[GE2]

Exceptions to this lowland location of Nguni speakers are the Ndebele, a group of Nguni speakers on the high grasslands of the interior, and the Matabele of today's state of Zimbabwe who were sent spinning up north early in the nineteenth century in the Zulu Crushing and the Boer Great Trek, described later. Conversely, a smaller ethnic group called the Hlubi, who have a short but key role to play in the historical narrative later, are basically Sotho-speakers from the high interior who came to live among Nguni-speakers in the coastal strip between the mountains and the Indian Ocean.

Whether Swazi, Zulu, and Xhosa tongues are separate languages or not may be a political question. As the wry question and answer goes, "What is the difference between a dialect and a language? A language is a dialect that has an army." By purely linguistic standards these all might be considered dialects of a single Nguni language: the northeastern-most of the Swazi can understand almost everything the southwestern-most of the Xhosa say, and vice-versa. But these languages/dialects have clear differences as well. The Xhosa were the first of the migrating Nguni people to meet the Khoisan, as is clear from their language and from their place at the extreme southern end of Bantu-language speakers. Although Zulu itself has absorbed a good many clicks, Xhosa has about six times as many "click" loan words from the Khoisan as Zulu does. The word Xhosa itself, for example, as an English traveler said in 1801, begins with "a strong palatal stroke of the tongue on the first syllable"[2]—that is, the "X" stands for popping the tongue off the roof of the mouth, and then adding the vocalization "hosa" with no elapsed time between the two. Arguments are made that the Xhosa (and Thembu) population is upwards of twenty percent genetically Khoisan in makeup, having absorbed some of that population while pressing southeast. Some claimed to see in (President of South Africa 1994–1999) Nelson Mandela's face itself traces of that Khoisan heritage.

A few Portuguese linguistic survivals

The first Europeans to arrive were the Portuguese, and even though they made their permanent colonial settlements further north, they left some very common words to all of southern Africa. *Kraal*, meaning a rounded enclosure for cattle or for homesteads, came from the Portuguese into Cape Dutch, then Afrikaans and then English (in exactly the same way that the cognate *corral* came from old world Spanish into Latin American Spanish and on into North American English, incidentally). *Mealies* is what South Africans call corn, maize;

---

1. Google Earth Layer 1 is a Folder that includes Polygons showing, from northeast to southwest, the approximate boundaries of the Swazi, Zulu, and Xhosa/Thembu branches of Nguni languages.

2. GE Layer 2 is a Polygon in pink outline framing the key transportation corridor from Durban to Pretoria. It is about 125 miles wide by 400 miles long. Although the continent of Africa is so huge that it makes the rectangle look small, this Polygon is almost twice the length and width of the Veracruz-to-Mexico City corridor we worked with in the last chapter.

this probably comes from the Portuguese word for grain, *milho*, pronounced with a liquid, palatalized "l." The spear used in southern Africa came to be called an *assegai*; that was not a Bantu word, but one the Portuguese had brought down with them from northern Africa.

From Dutch to Cape Dutch to Afrikaans

The Dutch language is, very roughly speaking, about halfway between English and German. Seventeenth-century Dutch was spoken, naturally, by the seventeenth-century Dutch founders of Cape Town. It evolved into the Cape Dutch dialect, and that in turn evolved into modern Afrikaans. From that hundreds of basically Dutch words have come into South African English and even into African languages. In terms of understanding Dutch/Afrikaans place names in South Africa, including some on our chosen corridor, *klip* means rock, and *kloof* means a ravine, often overlooked by cliffs (so the popular modern sport of "kloofing" means exploring ravines). *Kop* means hill (*Spionkop* is Lookout Hill), and the diminutive *koppie* or *kopje* means little hill. *Laagte* means valley or low ground (*Elandslaagte* is thus Elands Valley). *Vlei*, which comes from the same actual root as the English "valley," in practice usually means a valley with some standing water in it. *Poort* means a narrow pass through the mountains; it comes from the old Dutch word for gate. *Spruit*, linguistic cousin to the English word "sprout," means a small creek, in the same way that "branch" is used in the American South and West; and *stroom* is a cognate for "stream." As with German, in Dutch and Afrikaans the Ws are pronounced like our Vs, and the Js like our Ys. The double-o as in *poort* or *kloof* or *stroom* is like the long o as in "Roosevelt," the name of a Dutch family well rooted in Manhattan from long before the English ever took it over.

How close is modern Afrikaans to Dutch? The distance apparently depends on which direction you go. Afrikaans, like English, has lost most of its noun and adjectival declension—all those case endings that depend on the function of a word in a sentence. So for Dutch visitors to South Africa the Afrikaans language is fairly easy to understand, a sort of unsophisticated "red-neck Dutch," as my Dutch-American friends who grew up in Holland say. For Afrikaans speakers, those Dutch case endings make for more difficult understanding. And of course they see their own language as being as sophisticated as anyone else's: *Die Taal*, literally "The Language," they proudly call Afrikaans.

General geography

Most of southern Africa is a raised plateau of surprisingly high average elevation, from 3,000 to upwards of 6,000 feet. This leaves an arc of mountain escarpments virtually all around the coast.[GE³] This arc surrounds the interior grasslands of the east (the *highveld*, mainly in today's South Africa, "veld" a word kin to the English "field" but meaning any open, undeveloped land, either grass or brush) and the Kalahari Desert of the west (mainly in today's states of Botswana and Namibia). The drop to the coast from the mountain arc is so steep and the rivers so small that, unlike in North America, there are no navigable rivers that lead into the interior—no Mississippi or St. Lawrence, not even any Hudson or James. The whole plateau tips slightly down to the west, so somewhat south of the Kalahari the Orange River cuts an impressive canyon through the mountains to the Atlantic coast. The upper Orange River and its tributary the Caledon drain the high mountains of the Malutis and the west side of the Drakensberg. The long northern tributary of the Orange called the Vaal (meaning "tawny," "dingy," or "gray," in the Afrikaans language) drains the highveld on the shallow interior slopes of the mountains which parallel the southeastern side of the country.[GE⁴]

Elevations in the Drakensberg (Dutch/Afrikaans for "Dragon Mountain") range, highest of these mountains, are almost 11,000 feet. The range has some impressive escarpments, especially on the eastern side: the

---

3. GE Layer 3 is a Path in red that roughly follows the crest of the dramatic escarpment along the south and southeastern coast of South Africa.

4. GE Layer 4 is a Folder with three Paths included in it, one that shows the Orange River in light blue, and its short and long northern tributaries the Caledon and the Vaal as thinner blue lines. The deep canyon cut by the lower Orange River makes a natural border between modern South Africa and Namibia. South Africa's other borders (not counting the oceans) are less naturally definitive.

falls of the Tugela River running east off the Drakensberg drop over 3,000 feet in just a quarter of a mile (pictures a bit later when we get to the main corridor). One interesting geographically-influenced feature on a modern political map is the surprisingly rectangular outline of the independent country of Lesotho (usually pronounced Leh-SOO-too), a country totally surrounded by modern South Africa.[GE5] That is because the high Drakensberg and associated Maluti Mountains themselves form a fairly regular rectangle, at least as mountain ranges go. That, with the addition of the Caledon River valley just northwest of the mountains, makes for a remarkably rectangular country (with a little help from historical processes later described).[GE6]

Between this mountain escarpment and the southern and southeastern coast is the mixed brush, acacia thorn, and grassland called the *lowveld*. On average this strip between the mountains and the southern and southeastern coast is a hundred miles wide. Dozens of short rivers run down to the sea at fairly regular intervals across it. Many would gain short-term fame as the temporary frontier for the expanding European colonial settlement and resulting wars.[GE7] The farther east along the coastline you go, the more the rivers begin to run southeast and then east. One of the biggest of these, and of greatest geographic relevance for our corridor, is the Tugela River system.[GE8] Then by the time you get to the Pongola, it flows almost due east and then makes a turn northeast so it empties into Mozambique's Delagoa Bay.[GE9] The Tugela, the Pongola, and those lesser rivers between them[GE10] would be famous as the setting for the Zulu "Crushing" and the later Zulu Wars.

Last, the very northern part of our corridor is drained by the Limpopo River. Water from the northern suburbs of Johannesburg helps make its headwaters. It makes a great arc to the Indian Ocean, part of which defines South Africa's modern northern borders.[GE11]

The Durban-to-Pretoria corridor

Now that you've surveyed the general lay of the land of southern Africa—its bones and arteries, so to speak—let me invite you to take a trip, through prose and pictures, from the coastal strip around the modern city of Durban on up to and beyond Johannesburg to Pretoria. We'll go on the major roads generally north and west through the valleys of central KwaZulu-Natal—with a short side trip west to the high eastern face of the Drakensberg and a look east into the edge of old Zululand—on up onto the highveld, to Johannesburg's *Witwatersrand* and a bit beyond to the hills around Pretoria. As in the Veracruz-to-Mexico City sampling of Latin America in the last chapter, the general idea is to let a reader visualize both lay of the land and texture of the land of this corridor. Once in mind, it should serve as stage setting for the remarkable drama of history that played out there.

The modern city of Durban, several million in population (including more than a million Indians), faces the warm Indian Ocean. It is roughly the same latitude (though south instead of north!) as St. Augustine, Florida, or a couple hundred miles down the Baja coast from San Diego. Palm trees grow along the waterfront; surfers jump off the amusement park dock, boards and all, to get a head start on the waves; beachcombers pick up live cowrie shells; resort-style hotels, both fancy and seedy, crowd the beach. Looking at the city from the

---

5. GE Layer 5 is just a Placemark framing the international borders of Lesotho; make sure you have your Borders layer turned on in Google Earth to view same.

6. GE Layer 6 references a Panoramio icon entitled "Maluti Mountain View." It is a photo of the Caledon River valley in the foreground and the Malutis of Lesotho rising in the background.

7. GE Layer 7 is a Folder named "Some lowveld rivers." Turning on the folder shows five such short rivers that run across the lowveld to the sea, from Sunday's River to the Great Kei River.

8. GE Layer 8 is a Folder named "Tugela River System." Turn the folder on, and then expand it by double-clicking on the folder symbol. Turn on and off the Paths for Lower and Upper Tugela and the major tributaries, one by one, to familiarize yourself a bit with this river system that is the setting for so much of the history to come.

9. GE Layer 9 is a Path showing the Pongola River; notice how it cuts straight across today's Swaziland and then angles northeast to Maputo Bay.

10. GE Layer 10 is a Folder with Paths in it representing, from west to east, the Mhlatuze, the White Mfolozi and the Black Mfolozi.

11. GE Layer 11 is a Path tracing the Limpopo River. Notice how for a way it forms the northern border of South Africa.

sea, there is a prominent bluff on the left (simply called The Bluff) and a sheltered harbor inside it. To the right of the harbor entrance is a spit of land called The Point, and then on to the right of that come the beachfront hotels with the main downtown business district behind them. Well back of the urban heart of Durban is a prominent ridge called the Berea. Until about 1935 it marked the city limits, but the city spilled over it and by now has run from ten to twenty miles inland. Zulus call the city *eThekwini*, meaning "at the bay."[GE¹²]

In his 1885 adventure novel *King Solomon's Mines*, the English writer H. Rider Haggard—who had made this trip himself shortly before, as you'll see later—described arrival by ship at Durban:

> At last, one beautiful evening in January, which is our hottest month, we steamed along the coast of Natal, expecting to make Durban Point by sunset. It is a lovely coast all along from East London, with its red sand-hills and wide sweeps of vivid green, dotted here and there with Kafir kraals, and bordered by a ribbon of white surf, which spouts up in pillars of foam where it hits the rocks. But just before you get to Durban there is a peculiar richness about it. There are the deep kloofs cut in the hills by the rushing rains of centuries, down which the rivers sparkle; there is the deepest green of the bush, growing as God planted it, and the other greens of the mealie gardens and the sugar patches, while here and there a white house, smiling out at the placid sea, puts a finish and gives an air of homeliness to the scene. . . .
>
> When we came up again the moon was up, and shining so brightly over sea and shore that she almost paled the quick large flashes from the lighthouse. From the shore floated sweet spicy odours that always remind me of hymns and missionaries, and in the windows of the houses on the Berea sparkled a hundred lights. . . . Altogether it was a perfect night, such a night as you only get in Southern Africa, and it threw a garment of peace over everybody as the moon threw a garment of silver over everything.³

Driving or taking the train into the interior from Durban—directly away from the ocean in a generally northwest direction—a traveler first goes through "the Valley of a Thousand Hills" whose name is just a hint of the dramatic rise and fall and rise again of the land to come.[GE¹³] Less than an hour's drive or train ride up this main road from Durban comes the city of Pietermaritzburg. Hills are even steeper here, and it is so well nestled down in its valley that city folk from larger cities such as Durban and Johannesburg sometimes call it "Sleepy Hollow." Locals usually just call it Maritzburg.[GE¹⁴]

Pietermaritzburg's elevation is about 2,100′. Just over twenty miles upcountry along the main transportation corridor to Johannesburg, alongside the road is the old ruined watermill at Caversham, and the elevation here is already 3,800′.[GE¹⁵] Another fifteen miles up the road you come next to the town and the river called Mooirivier (meaning "Beautiful River" in the Afrikaans).[GE¹⁶] Elevation of the town is 4,500′ or better. It is on the southern slopes of the Biggarsberg, which is something of a low eastern extension of the Drakensberg (the road going on north from Mooirivier over the Biggarsberg will climb to over 5,000′, then drop to 3,100′ at the Tugela River crossing before it starts to climb again up to the interior plateau of southern Africa).

If from Mooirivier you make a foray due west along the Biggarsberg, in less than an hour's drive you will go through the outliers and then come up against the highest escarpment of the Drakensberg, as at Giant's

---

12. GE Layer 12 is a Folder named "Durban, views." Open the folder and explore at your leisure framed views or recommended Panoramio icons of the Bluff, the Point, the waterfront hotels, upscale housing up the coast a bit, and the "squatter" housing next to the most modern of construction.

13. GE Layer 13 is a Placemark indicating a Panoramio icon titled "valley of a thousand hills."

14. GE Layers 14A and 14B are a set of paired Path and Placemark. The Path is the old highway from Durban to Pietermaritzburg, and the Placemark represents the city of Pietermaritzburg. Turning on the Path first gives you an overview of this part of the road north, and then the Placemark zooms you in to see the city. GE Layer 14C references a Panoramio icon with a good photo of the city center.

15. GE Layer 15 is a Placemark referencing a Panoramio icon showing a ruined mill and nearby scenery up-country from Pietermaritzburg; notice the elevation has climbed to about 3,800′.

16. GE Layers 16A and 16B is another set of Path plus Placemark; turn them on in sequence for overview and closeup. The only Panoramio icons near Mooirivier show new hilltop suburb or single buildings; there's not one to show the truly "beautiful" river and valley.

Castle. By six or eight thousand feet elevation this becomes remarkably green country, by dry South African standards, with trout streams (the trout were imported) running down steep grassed valleys amid huge rock outcrops. If the weather permits, you see the high Drakensberg looming above you to almost 11,000 feet. They are unusual mountains, made of relatively flat layers of rock instead of folded and tortured ones as in the Smokies or the Rockies of North America. Above a thick, fairly level layer of sandstone is a dark, eroded basalt cap from some huge and ancient volcanic flow. The Zulu name for this crest of the Drakensberg is *Ukhahlamba*, or "Row of Upward Pointing Spears."[GE17] After visually exploring these faces of the Drakensberg, you'll have a feel for the difficulty British administrators had in rooting out the "Bushman raiders" there in the mid-nineteenth century, and also the difficulty of stopping Langalibalele, chief of the Hlubi, as he escaped British pressure in 1873 by heading up into the high mountains.

Now let's go back to the main road up-country. If you continue going generally north from the town of Mooirivier on the main transportation arteries to Johannesburg by road or rail, you pass through the small cities of Estcourt on Bushman's River,[GE18] then Colenso near the crossing of the Tugela River,[GE19] and then come to the city of Ladysmith[GE20]—all names that may call Boer War battles and sieges to mind. Ladysmith is a key rail junction town; here one rail line branches northwest straight up the face of the (now lower) Drakensberg to the city of Harrismith.[GE21] The main line to Johannesburg, however, goes northeast through Elandslaagte to the twin towns of Glencoe and Dundee, only four miles apart,[GE22] and thence north to the administrative center of Newcastle[GE23]—rising all the time, with the country opening out into wider vistas.

Off to your right, just across the lower Tugela River earlier and by this time in your travels upcountry very close across its major northern tributary the Mzinyathi or Buffalo River, lies the original Zululand.[GE24] Here are the most famous battle sites from the nineteenth-century Boer-Zulu wars and the British-Zulu wars. Even in old Natal, west of old Zululand proper, color-matched herds of Zulu cattle are often seen on the move down the dirt and gravel side roads. They may seem to newcomers too few for the huge grassy fields, though the carrying capacity of that pasturage has no doubt long been expertly judged by its owners.

All along these latitudes and altitudes the male Widowbirds grow their extremely long tailfeathers for the summer courting season and flirt their tails over the tips of the tall grass. Here Red Bishops, fat and almost tailless puffs of feathers, fly up from the reeds looking comically like small, slightly-out-of-control, winged red-orange footballs. Long-legged Secretary birds like huge, fierce hawks stalk the grass to flush lizards and snakes. In fact all the classic African fauna an American might associate with the Serengeti plains in Kenya and Tanzania—elephants, giraffes, Cape buffalo, many species of antelope, plus lions, leopards, and cheetahs—used to roam right down to the southern coast. Now most of the survivors are in game parks; the closest one of those of any size to our corridor is some thirty miles east, the Umfolozi/Hluhluwe Game Reserve.[GE25]

---

17. GE Layer 17 is a Folder named "Drakensberg, views from the east" referencing some interesting Photos icons at the eastern base of South Africa's highest mountains. Open the folder, double-click on each pushpin icon to "fly" there, then open the Panoramio icon indicated. The views are generally arranged from north to south down the face of the mountain range.

18. GE Layers 18A and 18B are a Path and Placemark for Estcourt.

19. GE Layers 19A and 19B are a Path and Placemark for Colenso.

20. GE Layer 20A and 20B are a Path and Placemark for Ladysmith.

21. GE Layers 21A and 21B are a Path and Placemark for Harrismith.

22. GE Layers 22A and 22B are a Path and Placemark for Glencoe (and Dundee).

23. GE Layers 23A and 23B are a Path and Placemark for Newcastle.

24. GE Layer 24 is a Placemark framing a general view of the northeastern side of our corridor. Notice how the Buffalo/Mzinyathi River and the lower Tugela River make a fairly straight line parallel with the northeast side of our corridor. That was the critical Natal/Zululand border in the heyday of the later Zulu kingdom.

25. GE Layer 25 is a Placemark framing an area slightly east of our corridor. You see Ulundi, the old Zulu capital, at left. Now go down to the basic Layers part of Google Earth at bottom left, and expand the "More" folder. Turn on the first layer under it, "Parks/Recreation Areas." Green outlines of all the parks should appear on your screen. Zooming into different areas of this general Hluhluwe/Umfolozi Park will reveal a hundred or more Photos icons, some of them with general views of the park, but most of them with close-ups of the animals there. Although Hluhluwe Park is east of our corridor, most of these animals were common along our whole corridor until firearms became common there in the mid-1800s.

Clumps and rows of sisal—an old friend from Aztec Mexico, the *maguey* or century plant—show up occasionally; they are grown in Africa for their fiber and to serve as living fences, though apparently formerly more so than now. More typical of the countryside, especially in the drier and rockier lands, are the tree-like aloes native to this land.[GE26] Vistas here, as at the site of the Zulu massacre of a British regiment at Isandhlwana, are as remarkable as most anything in the American West: if more Americans only knew about the grandeur of this countryside, a great many would join the British as tourists here. The only landscape disappointments are the rivers, small and dingy for such a great country except when in their rare floods; there's nothing here like the Green River or the Colorado, no Missouri, no Snake.

Finally, climbing up past the last big hills of the escarpment—including, just off to your left, the Majuba Hill of First Boer War fame[GE27]—you top out at a beautiful mountain valley town named Volksrust, "People's Rest" in Afrikaans.[GE28] At the even older Afrikaner town of Wakkerstroom ("Awake Stream," a mis-translation of the original Zulu name into Afrikaans) some twenty miles east of Volksrust, large springs feed a reedy wetland preserve that is an oasis in this dry land. Here in summer are swallows that come from Russia to nest and kestrels that come from China to hunt them.[GE29]

Just a short drive north past Volksrust and Wakkerstroom and you are in South Africa's version of Big Sky country. Here the view usually stretches for miles over the gently rolling grasslands of the highveld. Cosmos, a flower originally from Argentina (an interesting story, that, for later) blooms here through early fall (March and April) along most every road and fence line, taller than a tall person. Here is some of the world's cheapest coal, lying just underground in flat, unfolded layers. Coal-fired generating plants, each built on its own coalfield, pump electricity towards Johannesburg. Each has one or more great incurved, truncated cones for cooling the water of the steam plants, and each produces its plume of pollution blowing on what would otherwise be pristine prairie. The scattered local population must feel about this what Navajos in the Four Corners region of the U.S. feel about nearby power plants that feed California cities.

The main road from Volksrust to Johannesburg goes through Standerton; this valley town on the upper Vaal River is still over 5,000' elevation.[GE30] From Standerton, if you travel along the north side of the Vaal you come to the important industrial cities Vanderbijlpark and Vereeniging, with satellite industrial townships such as Sharpeville between the two.[GE31]

Vereeniging would be famous as the site of final Boer surrender in the great Boer War, and Sharpeville infamous for a police massacre during apartheid.

Then, at about 5,800' elevation, higher than the "mile-high city" of Denver, comes the great city of Johannesburg itself.[GE32] Johannesburg was born from the *Witwatersrand*. Word-for-word translation from the Afrikaans yields "White Water Ridge," but there is no white water anywhere to be seen: the real meaning is "white watershed ridge." The great ridge lies east and west, and water running south off of it is gathered by the Vaal on its journey west to the Orange River and the South Atlantic; waters running north join the Limpopo on its great arc east to the Indian Ocean. The soil of the Rand is indeed light-colored, though more yellowish than white, especially the man-made piles of it. This is the place of the world's greatest gold strike and gold rush, where a "reef" of gold-bearing ore comes to the surface. The mines now go as deep as 12,000 feet under the

---

26. GE Layer 26 is a Placemark referencing the Panoramio icon titled "beautiful cacti in wilderness o=k." Technically speaking, cactuses are all American, new world, though they have their African analogues!

27. GE Layer 27 is a Placemark showing where the traditional main road from Durban to Johannesburg crested the escarpment; note Majuba Hill of Boer War fame at left.

28. GE Layers 28A and 28B are a Path to and a Placemark for Volksrust.

29. GE Layer 29 is a Placemark framing Wakkerstroom; click on Panoramio icon under pointer for view of "Wakkerstroom in winter."

30. GE Layers 30A and 30B are a Path and a Placemark framing a view of Standerton; just west of town is a modern reservoir where the Vaal River has been dammed.

31. GE Layer 31 is a Placemark framing a view of Vanderbijlpark and Vereeniging, both of which should be labeled in this view. Sharpeville was a black "township" lying directly between the two. Vereeniging is where a loop of the Vaal River gets the furthest north of any part of the river, and also where it runs closest (about 30 miles) to Johannesburg.

32. GE Layers 32A and 32B are a Path and a Placemark for Johannesburg.

earth here, down where temperatures are a brutal 130°F. for miners working there. Scattered all about Johannesburg, relics of over a century of intensive mining, are what look to be perfectly flat-topped yellow hills: these are "slimes' dams"—earthen walls in regular geometric figures into which watery mine sludge is pumped and allowed to settle and dry. Interspersed with them are irregular piles of rock and gravel, the solid refuse from those same mines. Melville in *Moby Dick* wrote that the wealthy houses of Nantucket had been "harpooned" from the world's oceans and dragged ashore; in Johannesburg the mansions of the Randlords in the same metaphorical way were blasted from the solid rock of the gold-bearing reef and hoisted to the surface. The wealthy, semi-rural northern suburbs of Johannesburg are generally known as the "mink and manure" belt—mink for wealth, manure to represent the horsey set.[GE33]

Though not right in the city, there are some famous diamond deposits nearby; one of them, Culinan, famously yielded the world's largest diamond.[GE34] The diamonds appear mainly where a sort of rock called Kimberlite comes to the surface in surprisingly tubular structures called "pipes."

Johannesburg is far and away southern Africa's biggest city. Soweto (from "South West Townships") alone has almost five million souls in some forty townships. Johannesburg still generates over a third of the economy of the whole of the African continent every year. "Jo'burg," it is familiarly known to English and Afrikaans speakers, "Jozi" to speakers of Bantu languages. The greater Johannesburg area is today the smallest of South Africa's nine administrative areas. The area is officially known as Gauteng (the initial "g" pronounced as a gutteral "h" or "kh") a word from the Sotho language that means "Place of Gold").[GE35] So when, before every Christmas and New Year's summer holidays, you hear that coastal cities from Cape Town to Durban are bracing for the seasonal "Gauteng invasion," you know they're talking about the rush of Johannesburgers heading for the beaches. Americans may think of African climate as either hot jungle or hot desert, but this doesn't hold for the continent's extensive highlands. The highveld of South Africa has mild summers—over 80°F is a very hot day—and winters where days may climb into the 60s but nights are with frost and sometimes freezing weather. Such weather is usually pleasant, but would make baking on the beach a nice change.

Before leaving this northern, interior end of our chosen corridor, a couple of other historically important towns deserve mention. Some thirty-five miles north of Johannesburg is Pretoria, older, quieter and almost provincial by comparison.[GE36] It was first the capital of the Boer republic of the Transvaal, then after 1910 of a unified South Africa proper, and even today is the administrative capital of the country (although since 1994 the South African legislature has met in Cape Town and the high judiciary in Bloemfontein). Beautifully set in a valley,[GE37] it blooms purple with jacaranda trees in spring (October and November), hence the city boosters' name "Jacaranda City."[GE38]

The second important city, some forty miles southwest of Johannesburg, is the university town of Potchefstroom. It is barely in our chosen corridor, but the author needs it to pair with Pretoria, like a span of matched

---

33. GE Layer 33 is a Folder entitled "Witwatersrand views," which has in it nine or so Placemarks and one Path. The one Path can be "flown" with the line representing it either turned on or off. For optimum viewing in Google Earth, go to Tools drop-down menu at top, then choose Options, then Touring, and then change the bottom three settings: (1) Camera Tilt Angle: set at 70°; (2) Camera Range: set at 4,000'; (3) Camera Speed, set at maximum, 1,000 (presumably m.p.h.), at which speed you can "fly" the path in less than ninety seconds. Just highlight the layer "Witwatersrand," and hit the right-facing arrow at the bottom right of the Places part of the legend at left.

34. GE Layer 34 is a Placemark referencing a Panoramio icon with a picture of the Cullinan big hole, "Cullinan - Une mine de diamants -l'entrée du cratère." About forty-five miles NW of Johannesburg.

35. GE Layer 35 is a Placemark framing a view of Gauteng. In Google Earth, make sure the "Borders and Labels" layer is turned on.

36. GE Layers 36A and 36B are a Path to and a Placemark for Pretoria.

37. GE Layer 37 is a Placemark referencing a view of downtown Pretoria from nearby hill; click on Panoramio icon under pointer titled "Pretoria - Sudafrica."

38. GE Layer 38 is a Placemark referencing a Panoramio icon entitled "Jacaranda Trees Blooming in Beckett Street," a hillside northern suburb of Pretoria.

oxen. Pretoria may have been the administrative capital of Afrikanerdom, but the university town of Potchef-stroom was its key spiritual and intellectual capital.[GE[39]]

And finally, just north of Pretoria and a bit further north of Johannesburg runs an interesting terrain feature called the Magaliesberg. From the surface it appears as a dramatic escarpment or what you'd call in Mexico and the U.S. Southwest a cuesta.[GE[40]] From a couple hundred miles up in space it shows up to the naked eye as a very visible wrinkle in the earth's crust, curving and then re-curving almost all the way across the top of our rectangle.[GE[41]]

So if a reader will keep in mind these general geographic features of southern Africa, and more specifically some present-day views of this Durban-to-Johannesburg corridor,[GE[42]] we can now rehearse the history that played out on this spectacular stage.

SECTION B: PRE- AND EARLY HISTORY

The rock art of the Khoisan

Apparently the San culture had tens of thousands of years acquaintance with southern Africa. Their knowledge of the environment was incredible, and even today the survivors are famous as some of the world's best track-ers. Later Bantu-speaking arrivals believed that the Khoisan could charm snakes and bring the rain.

Paleolithic (Old Stone Age; pre-agriculture) cave art is justly celebrated as humankind's first great visual art. Westerners probably think first of the caves of Lascaux in France or Altamira in Spain, with their brilliant multi-colored art from approximately twenty thousand years ago that was probably done as sympathetic magic to ensure a good hunt. All of Europe, however, has only a few dozen good examples of such cave art, when by contrast a single South African province might have 10,000 sites of "rock art" (because most are not so much in true caves as in sheltered overhangs), some of them with a thousand images each. Some of this art is thou-sands of years older than that of Lascaux and Altamira, but this same art in South Africa was still being done—by the same culture!—at a few sites into the mid-nineteenth century AD. Johannesburg's English-language University of Witwatersrand ("Wits" for short) has a wonderful collection of reproductions of that art. Among it is the Harald Pager collection. He was an Austrian artist who took black and white photographs of hundreds of rock art scenes, blew them up to life-size (still black and white) and then painted colors on them from the original. The favorite place for the Khoisan to do such art was at the base of that thick sandstone layer (the Clarens formation, it is called today) that crops out all around the Drakensberg.[GE[43]] This, in fact, was the setting for the one crucial European-Khoisan conversation that unlocked the meaning of many of those images for us today. It took place in 1873.

Joseph Orpen, a doctor's son from Ireland, had immigrated to Cape Colony in 1848 when he was twenty years old. He worked for awhile as a surveyor in the Orange Free State, one of the Boer Republics in the high-veld, but he proved to be so sympathetic to the southern Sotho with whom the Free State was at times at war that he was arrested and deported. By 1873 he had become the British Resident of a territory called Nomans-land, just south of the highest of the Drakensberg. In that year a Hlubi chief or king named Langalibalele, in a

---

39. GE Layer 39 is a Placemark framing a view of Potchefstroom, indicating two clusters of Photos icons of (a) at bottom, city center and (b) at top, the famous university.

40. GE Layer 40 is a Placemark referencing a Panoramio icon located at the base of the Magaliesberg. It is titled "'Green Leaves' with ridge of Magaliesberg."

41. GE Layer 41 is a Placemark framing such a view.

42. GE Layer 42 is a Placemark framing a view of the Durban-to-Pretoria corridor; instruction in Placemark calls for review of what's been seen.

43. For this Section B of the narrative, turn all layers in Section A off except Layer 2 (our corridor rectangle) and the main rivers (Layers 4 and 8–11). Then turn on and "fly" to this first layer of Section B, GE Layer 43. It is a Placemark referencing a cluster of three Panoramio icons with excellent pictures of typical San rock art at the Game Pass Shelter in the Kamberg, an outlier of the eastern Drakensberg. They are labeled "Migration of Spirit," "San Rock Art, Game Pass Shelter, Kamberg. Eland, Hunters and Shamans"; and "San Rock Art at Game Pass Shelter, Kamberg." For further reading and viewing, see Rock Art Research Institute site at: http://rockart.wits.ac.za/origins/index.php?section=46

dispute with Britain over refusing to register small arms, fled the area near Giant's Castle peak of the eastern face of the Drakensberg with most of his people and cattle. Remarkably, he took herds and people on foot up over the high Drakensberg where Europeans did not think it could be traversed, trying to find refuge with the BaSotho: the pass above Giant's Castle still bears his name. Orpen was ordered to accompany the police force sent to arrest Langalibalele. They were unsuccessful—Langalibalele eluded them, though he was eventually betrayed by a Sotho chief who got his cattle as a reward—but Orpen in the meantime made arrangements with a local Sotho chief to borrow the services of a San hunter named Qing who was in his employment. Orpen took notes over campfire talks with Qing. It was a complicated process, with Qing speaking not in his native Khoisan language but in sePhuti, a Bantu language somewhere between Southern Sotho and Nguni and then with a Sotho or Xhosa interpreter translating that into English. Qing talked about rock art as well as mythology, and fortunately Orpen had earlier made careful copies of some San rock art, including paintings of the large antelope called eland that are so prominent in such art around the Drakensberg. As the expedition explored the high mountains in search of Langalibalele, Qing took Orpen to nearby rock shelters he knew of and explained the art there.

Orpen spent December 13, 1873, in a rock shelter art gallery with Qing, who tried to explain for him three figures with human bodies but the heads of antelopes, and sticks in their hands. This is what came through the double translation: "They were men who had died and now lived in rivers, and were *spoilt* at the same time as the elands and by the dances of which you have seen paintings." These were apparently representations of shamans in trance dance, trying to achieve out-of-body experiences in which they were supposed to be able to cure the sick, cause rain to fall by capturing and killing the mythical rain animal, and cause herds of antelope to come to the hunters. In such a trance the spiritual potency in the shaman's stomach begins to "boil," as a shaman describes it, and as the stomach contracts in a painful knot the shaman is bent over and has to use sticks to continue his dance. As David Lewis-Williams puts it in his *Images of Mystery: Rock Art of the Drakensberg*:

> Some of the most wonderful Drakensberg paintings show that the San artists expressed their notion of death by comparing the behaviour of a person in trance with that of a dying antelope, especially an eland that is succumbing to the effect of a poisoned arrow. Both Shaman and animal tremble violently, sweat profusely, stagger, lower their heads, bleed from the nose, froth at the mouth, and finally crash to the ground.[4]

Qing's assertion that antelope-headed men had been "spoilt" at the same time as elands and by the dances makes sense in this context, the shaman in trance dance being paralleled to the eland in real death throes.

Orpen had a rare open-mindedness, for a nineteenth-century European, towards these technologically primitive people. Qing, who like most San had never seen white people except in battle, showed the same quality. The conversation between them was one-of-a-kind between the waxing European and the waning San cultures, never preceded or repeated in such depth. From it we get a Khoisan view of the shape-changer god /Kaggen, creator of all things. Qing, asked for the sort of prayer the San prayed to /Kaggen, said: "O /Kaggen! O /Kaggen? Are we not your children? Do you not see our hunger? Give us food!" And then, Qing said, "he gives us both hands full." "Where is /Kaggen?" asked Orpen. Qing's response: "Have you not hunted and heard his cry, when the elands suddenly start and run to his call? Where he is, elands are in droves like cattle." Eland, largest of Africa's antelopes (a bull can weigh twelve hundred pounds) still roam the Drakensberg. More than any other animal they populate the rock shelter art of the Khoisan—including literally hundreds of sites clustered on the eastern face of the Drakensberg in today's KwaZulu-Natal—in polychrome naturalistic detail and impressionistic beauty.

There may never have been more than two hundred thousand Khoisan at any given time, and possibly no more than twenty thousand of the original San, thinly scattered as all hunter-gatherer societies must be. They defended their South African lands, however, as fiercely as Comanches in the American southwest, and left both a wealth of place-names and substantial genetic legacy along with their rock art.

The Abundant Herds

The Nguni speakers traditionally lived off their crops and the milk from their cattle. With very rare exceptions they ate no fish—even to the point of preferring to starve to death rather than eat fish as a last resort—or wild game. The women farmed; the men worked with the cattle, which were so precious they were hardly ever killed (meat in the diet typically came from goats). The cattle came with the Bantu migrations from the north, and had been domesticated for at least two millennia. The herds somehow moved south through the tsetse fly belt that is usually deadly to domestic livestock, did well on the highveld, and absolutely flourished in the lowveld where the Nguni lived. All grass is not equal, nutritionally speaking. Grassland near the coast and in the highlands was called in Afrikaans *zuurveld*, literally "sour field"—meaning that the grass was nutritious when green but lost almost all nutrition when dried. In the valley bottoms of that hundred-mile-wide strip of Nguni habitation, however, sweetgrass grew that was nutritious even when brown and dry. In such a dissected country, river bottom was never far from the ridge tops, meaning that Nguni cattle could usually be brought back to the homestead every night—unlike the Sotho/Tswana cattle on the highveld that had to be kept in far-flung cattle camps and only occasionally brought in. The very heart of any Zulu or Xhosa homestead was a kraal where cattle were kept at night and brought into at noon for milking; the human dwellings were in a circle outside the cattle kraal, usually with another circular wall outside them. In all Bantu-speaking groups in southern Africa cattle were considered the most important form of moveable wealth, necessary for the "bride price" (*lobolo*).

Not long ago a book was published in South Africa that gives an outsider some insight into the Nguni fondness for their cattle. The book is Poland and Hammond-Tooke's *The Abundant Herds: A celebration of the cattle of the Zulu people.* The beautiful color patterns of the cattle with their mirror-image sides are shown in dozens of full-color paintings, and the fanciful Zulu names for such colorations are explained ("fish eagle" for a beast with white head and neck but dark behind that, pictured alongside a painting of a real fish eagle, for example). Horn shapes all had their names, as in a lyre-shaped set of horns that sweep backwards at the tips that are called "women repudiating the case"; you can just see a woman throwing up her hands and turning them backwards as the ultimate body-language rejection of some argument. The Zulu expression "time of horns" vividly calls up daybreak, when the sky is just light enough so that the horns of the cattle in the kraal are silhouetted above the horizon. In times of plenty, Nguni societies had the luxury and time to breed herds of matched colors or color schemes. In the sixty-year-long heyday of the Zulu kings from Shaka to Cetswayo, enormous color-matched royal herds represented power and wealth almost beyond imagining.[5]

Halfway to Java

The Portuguese were the first of modern Europeans to explore the Atlantic and Indian Ocean coasts of Africa. Bartholomew Dias rounded the Cape in 1488. Because of its frequent mountainous waves and howling westerlies, he named it the Cape of Storms. The Portuguese government with an eye towards public relations changed it to the Cape of Good Hope. Vasco Da Gama cruised by the Natal coast in 1497 on the first successful ocean voyage from Europe to India and back, naming it as he did so: "Natal" comes from the Portuguese for Christmas Day, because that was when Da Gama first sighted this coast, putting into the bay behind the Bluff at what is today Durban to fish and rest a bit from the rough seas. Although the Portuguese did not settle South Africa proper (though they did Angola and Mozambique), other Europeans got their first introduction to southern Africa from them, as still shows up in linguistic survivals listed earlier.

Hard on the heels of the Portuguese came the Dutch. The Netherlands, a union of seven Protestant provinces (which in English is also known as Holland for its most prosperous state), coalesced in 1587 as part of the Catholic/Protestant religious wars of the century. Within ten years small groups of (Protestant) Dutch businessmen were challenging the (Catholic) Portuguese hold of trade routes east. In 1602 the Dutch government insisted that these Dutch firms quit competing with each other and unite as one government-protected monopoly called the VOC, from *Vereenigde Oostindische Companie*, or United East India Company. Some economists call this the world's first real joint stock company: investors committed to the entire enterprise for a five-year term, not just to a single ship or a single trading voyage. Presided over by a board of directors called the Gentlemen Seventeen, the VOC spearheaded Holland's "Glorious Century." A half-century of virtually total domination not just of European trade but of Asian trade as well generated incredible wealth. That in turn supported the famous artistic renaissance associated with Vermeer and Rembrandt, and the scientific and intellectual developments associated with Leeuwenhoek and Huygens and with the persecuted foreign intellectuals who found shelter there, such as Descartes and Spinoza (the latter born in Amsterdam, though his parents were Jewish refugees from the Inquisition in Portugal).

The Spice Islands in the east of today's Indonesia were the original lure, and Indonesia would be to the Dutch what India was to the British, the crown jewel of its far-flung world empire (much more on this in Chapter 12 on Southeast Asia). It was an eight-month-long trip, on average, from Amsterdam to Batavia (today's Jakarta) on the island of Java. The vitamin-deficiency manifestation called scurvy—in which gums turn black, teeth fall out, and bleeding begins from body orifices, usually in that order and ending in death—meant that Table Bay near the southwestern tip of Africa became a popular halfway stopping point. For one, the 3,000′-tall flat-topped mountain behind the bay, giving it its name (*Tafelberg*, or Table Mountain) was an easy landmark to spot from far out at sea, and the bay itself gave shelter from the fiercest of the storms that came from the south.[GE⁴⁴] Here freshwater supplies could be renewed and fresh meat bartered from the local Khoisan (or taken by force, leaving the next ship's landing party to be the subject of their revenge).

On April 6, 1652, perhaps the most important date in modern South African history, the VOC officer Jan van Riebeeck established the first permanent European settlement in southern Africa here, and called it Cape Town (*Kapstadt*).[GE⁴⁵] Within five years he released some VOC employees from fort duty to become permanent farmers. They were called simply "farmer," which in Dutch was *Boer* (pronounced "boor," as in boorish of which it is the root word, although it has been pronounced "boe-er" so long in English that it is now a usual pronunciation). Just two years after this the first slaves were imported into the colony. Soon itinerant farmers called Trekboers (*trek* from the word meaning "to pull," as a covered wagon) were expanding the frontier of the colony, "pulling" into an area to homestead for awhile, grow a crop, shoot out the wild game, and move on. For them it was a strenuous but wonderfully independent life that was known in later centuries as the *lekker lewe* (usually translated "the good life," though even today in Holland someone who finds a dish surprisingly good says "*oo, lekker!*", so that "delicious life" or "sweet life" may be a better translation). The farming side of their livelihood, however, became more and more dependent on slave labor—slaves from West Africa, slaves from Indonesia, enslaved local Khoisan. Eventually these slave populations would merge and—with the addition of white blood from the slave-owners—become the so-called "Cape Coloureds" of later times (today about 9 percent of South Africa's population, mostly Afrikaans speaking, mostly still in the Western Cape).

The early European colonists were not altogether Dutch. In France in 1685 Louis XIV revoked the Edict of Nantes that had given toleration to French Protestants (Huguenots) for almost a century. Under extreme persecution they left France, and as early as 1688 some came to Cape Town, bringing with them wine-making skills to match this Mediterranean climate. An infusion of Germans also came. But canny VOC administrators scattered these minorities throughout the colony so they would gradually have to learn Dutch and become fully assimilated into the majority white society—and so it happened.

It took the descendants of the original European settlers some time, however, to make it over into our Durban-to-Johannesburg corridor. It was almost as if the Dutch colony was a plant obeying the old gardening rule of anything transplanted, appearing in the first season to sleep, in the next to creep, then in the third to leap. It took the half-century from the establishment of the original fort at Cape Town to 1700 for the European population to pass a thousand, still huddled closely around the fort.[GE⁴⁶] By 1750 the colony was still limited to the extreme southwest corner of Africa, having crept along a mainly coastal ten miles or so east of Cape Town.[GE⁴⁷] Then in the short thirty years from 1750 to 1779 the frontier of the colony leaped some 300 miles east along the southern coast to the Sunday's River. Here, however, the Boers ran head-on into the Xhosa and for a time all leaping ceased.[GE⁴⁸]

---

44. GE Layer 44 is a Placemark referencing a Panoramio icon titled "TableM2" with a nice picture of Table Mountain taken from the north. Today's Cape Town is at the foot of the mountain. When the mist pours off the flat-topped mountain, locals liken it to the tablecloth coming off.

45. GE Layer 45 is a Placemark framing the seventeenth-century fort, or castle, that was the heart and soul of the original Cape Town; explore some of the Photos icons nearby.

46. GE Layer 46 is a Folder with yellow Pushpin symbols of Dutch towns founded from 1652 to 1700; Cape Town is the star.

47. GE Layer 47 is a Folder with green Pushpin symbols of some Dutch towns founded from 1700 to 1750.

48. GE Layer 48 is a Path representing Sunday's River, just east of today's Port Elizabeth, in aqua.

For the Boers, war with the densely settled and well organized Xhosa was another matter altogether than war with the scattered Khoisan peoples had been. In the century from 1779 to 1878 there were nine separate wars between Europeans and the Xhosa, and the first three of them, between the Boers and the Xhosa, have been described as "raid and counter-raid between two fairly evenly matched opponents."[6] With guns and horses the Boers made up for inferior numbers with superior firepower and speed, but their raiding parties called "commandos" were only temporary affairs. A new level of European power, however, was about to be introduced into the South African arena.

SECTION C: THE BRITISH ARRIVAL, THE ZULU CRUSHING, THE GREAT TREK, AND NATALIA

British takeover

By the 1700s, British ships rounding the Cape outnumbered the Dutch. In their wars against the armies and navies of the French Revolution and Napoleon, the British worried about a possible French occupation of Cape Town. On this ground they took it temporarily in 1795, gave it back, and then in 1806 occupied it permanently. Since then in South Africa there have been not one but two main white minorities; this is the origin of the second, called simply the English after the language they spoke.

British rule of Cape Colony brought changes to Boer lifestyle. Some of it, from the Boer point of view, was positive—improved markets for trade and a permanent standing army in Cape Town among them. The next three wars between Europeans and the Xhosa were European victories, pushing the Xhosa from the Bushman's River to east of the Fish River, then the Keiskama River, and then the Kei River,[GE[49]] taking from them a good 125 miles of coastline and the land at least that far inside it for white settlement. Much more of the change brought by British rule, though, was in Boer eyes disastrous. In 1807 the British Government outlawed the importing of new slaves, which cut into the Boer way of life by driving up the price of existing slaves and free labor. British missionaries arrived, challenging the Dutch Reformed Protestantism of the Boers with other Protestant denominations' views, and in a generally liberal way championing African labor against Boer exploitation of it. In December of 1833 the British outlawed slavery itself for the whole of the British Empire. When word of that arrived in Cape Colony in 1834, it was for many Boers the last straw. This is what triggered the Great Trek of 1835–43 (1838 was the single biggest year for the migration), as wagon trains of thousands of Boers and their dependents headed east and northeast outside the borders of the British colony to re-establish their traditional style of life. What the trekkers ran into, however, first takes some explaining.

Zulu power and the Mfecane/Difaqane

Mfecane, often translated as "the Crushing," probably comes from the Xhosa word *ukufaca*, "emaciated from hunger." *Difaqane* is a Sotho word from the highveld; sometimes translated "the Marauding," it basically means forced removal. This whole sequence of Mfecane/Difaqane was an African upheaval that radiated out of what is today eastern KwaZulu-Natal and sent dominoes falling halfway west to the Atlantic coast and as far north in east Africa as Lake Victoria. It was a real Folkswandering, with some interesting parallels to the Germanic tribal movements triggered by the Huns that brought down the western Roman Empire. Many traditional communities were broken up forever. Some new ones also emerged from this crucible, but only those with remarkable leadership.

---

49. For this Section C, in Google Earth turn off everything in Section B, and in Section A all you need turned on is Layer 2, our corridor rectangle. Now turn on GE Layer 49, a Folder entitled "Frontier Rivers," with Paths inside for the lower parts of the Bushman's River, the Great Fish River, the Keiskamma River, and the Great Kei River.

The first phase of all this, the Mfecane, took place in the lowveld between the Tugela and Pongola rivers. [GE[50]] Two massive droughts helped set conditions for it. Other reasons are as yet unclear. Some credit the insatiable hunger for slaves of the trading stations in Delagoa Bay (what is today the Mozambican port of Maputo); some credit population growth and cattle pressure on the narrow sweetgrass valleys so important to the maintenance of the herds of Nguni cattle. No single reason seems fully satisfactory. Whatever the causes, between 1817 and 1819 two great Nguni kingdoms went to war, and in both the conduct of the war and in the mobilization of their societies they became more and more militarized and totalitarian.

These two kingdoms were the Mthethwa under the rule of Dingiswayo (in their core area between the Mhlathuze and White Mfolozi rivers), and the Ndwandwe under the rule of Zwide further north (centered just south of the middle course of the Pongola River). In past decades each had grown in size and power and by 1817 they faced each other—with no buffer states and with increasing hostility—on a front from the Drakensberg escarpment down to the Indian Ocean.[GE[51]] Although the Mthethwa were probably the stronger, Zwide by a ruse was able to capture Dingiswayo and put him to death. He then drove the leaderless Mthethwa back almost to the Tugela River and pillaged their lands.

The stage was now set for Shaka, one of the most famous personalities of African history. Head of what until then was the small Zulu chieftaincy inside the Mthethwa state, and a former military commander under Dingiswayo, he reorganized the army, rallied Mthethwa survivors, and in 1819 broke Zwide's army in a decisive battle on the banks of the Mhlathuze. He immediately followed up on this with an invasion of Ndwandwe lands, killing all the people he could catch, irrespective of age or sex, burning all the homesteads, capturing all the cattle. Now the dominoes began to fall. The desperate, surviving Ndwandwe, now cattle-less, fell on the Ngwane to their west, seizing all their cattle in the same kind of total war. In their turn the now-destitute Ngwane fell upon the nearest people to their west, the Hlubi. The Hlubi might serve as a good illustration of what happens to one particular group in this entire upheaval. They were the initial link between the lowveld Mfecane and the highveld Difaqane, for example, and their relocation led to relationships with the Boers and the British that were important decades later. First, however, Shaka's new-style rule and power need some elaboration.

The origins of Zulu power are not very clear: the first literate eyewitnesses only got to the Zulu capital in 1824. The name of the group comes from a shadowy earlier ruler, Zulu, whose name literally meant "the Heavens." Later the people, in their own language, were the amaZulu, "the People of the Heavens." They were a small clan who were near neighbors of the Mthethwa, and in one sense Shaka of the Zulus inherited power from Dingiswayo of the Mthethwa.

Dingiswayo, "the Troubled One," seems to have been a wounded refugee from royal power struggles in the Mthethwa house, and when he found shelter with the Hlubi who lived on the slopes of the Drakensberg he took that name to hide his real identity. Upon news of the death of the old king, he returned to claim the throne. In less than a decade he conquered or won by marriage perhaps a hundred clans. He kept peace between them, and they in turn sent recruits for what was becoming an imperial army. He initiated the practice, later perfected by Shaka, of turning the old village coming-of-age rituals for young men into a state-wide calling-up of age-group regiments.

Shaka, born around 1789, was only marginally from the Zulu royal house. He was the offspring of an illicit dalliance between the Zulu king and Nandi, daughter of a neighboring chief of a clan officially judged too close blood kin for marriage with the Zulu king. When she turned up pregnant and messengers from her clan came to inform the Zulu king—so that he could fetch her to install her as his third wife—officials at the Zulu court said it could not be a pregnancy, it must be swelling induced by the intestinal parasite called *iShaka*. Several

---

50. GE Layer 50 is a Folder entitled "Mfecane/Difaqane area: rivers and escarpment"; it includes the Limpopo, the Orange and the Vaal, and the Tugela river network that a reader has seen earlier, as well as the Pongola (that cuts east, squarely across today's Swaziland, before angling north to Delagoa Bay) and two of the main rivers between the Tugela and Pongola that figure in the Mfecane and the rise of Zulu power, the Mfolozi River (White and Black tributaries) and the Mhlathuze River.

51. GE Layer 51 is a Folder with Polygons and labels representing the Ndwandwe (in red), the Mthethwa (in yellow), the Ngwane (in green), and the Hlubi (in blue), as they were circa 1816 when the great war began.

months later when the baby was born, the messengers came back again and sarcastically told the king to collect his new wife and her iShaka. The king and his newest wife Nandi had a few stormy years together, then he dismissed wife and young son. She went back to her old clan, which she had embarrassed by her pregnancy to begin with and which now had to repay the bride-price of cattle, making its members no happier. In a famine year they in turn evicted Shaka and his mother. In short, his formative years were those of persecution and taunting, and his only ally was his mother. He grew from herdboy to tall, strongly built warrior, but the psychological damage was deep and lasting: he was probably impotent; his revenge against his earlier tormentors would be extreme; and his grief at his mother's eventual death would totally destabilize him.

Shaka was twenty-three when his age-group was called up by Dingiswayo to create the *iziCwe* regiment. His drive and intelligence quickly made him its leader. In terms of tactics, he replaced the usual throwing spear common to all Nguni—it could be thrown far but only once—with a short-handled, long-bladed stabbing spear. Like the Roman legions with their short stabbing swords, the idea was to accept some damage from thrown spears just to be able to close and do much more damage to an enemy at arm's length. Shaka taught his troops to sweep the enemy's cowhide shields to the left, thus exposing their left sides to this new stabbing spear (called *iKlwa*, supposedly for the sound it made when withdrawn from the chest cavity of a dying enemy). He made his troops shed their sandals to give them an edge in speed and footing, making them dance on thorns to harden their feet with scar tissue and prove capacity to endure pain. In terms of strategy, he scorned the traditional show-of-force that might cause an enemy to submit but that left it able to rally and fight another day. He much favored a brutal military crushing of any enemy, with the subsequent adding of the surviving remnants to his own army. He began to evolve the characteristic Zulu attack by dividing his force into three parts: a central part to engage the enemy and pin him down, and fast left and right wings that could race out to encircle the pinned-down opponent. Eventually this was likened to a bull's attack: the "chest" to engage the enemy (and behind it the "loins" as a reserve), and the "horns" to surround it.

In 1816 Shaka's father the Zulu king—who had taken no notice of him for years—died. King Dingiswayo of the much more powerful neighboring Mthethwa "suggested" to the Zulus that Shaka should be their new king, and released him from his military duties with the Mthethwa regiment. And now began the Zulu rise to prominence, as Shaka began to mold them the way he had the iziCwe regiment. He immediately killed those in the clan who had offended him earlier in life, including the uncle who had made that sarcastic *iShaka* remark. To symbolize a clean break with the past he had the royal kraal of his father burned and established a new one at the threateningly-named *kwaBulawayo*, "At the Place of He Who Kills—With Afflictions."[GE[52]]

In 1818 Zwide of the Ndwandwe killed the Mthethwa king Dingiswayo, and launched an initial invasion of Zulu lands that took almost all the Zulu cattle. In 1819, while Zwide collected a huge army to finish off this upstart Zulu power, Shaka rebuilt his own forces. When the Ndwandwe invaded, Shaka's smaller army kept in sight, but just in front of the invading army, harassing it at night. Having drawn it deep into Zululand, Shaka smashed the Ndwandwe in a two-day running battle. Zulu regiments then approached the Ndwandwe capital by night, singing an Ndwandwe victory chant; when the inhabitants turned out to celebrate, they were slaughtered. Zwide and his chief general escaped, but Ndwandwe power was broken forever. Zululand had been created, from the Pongola River to the Tugela River, and from the coast to the escarpment of the interior plateau. More importantly, the modern Zulu people had been created, as fragments of smaller groups, both enemies and friends, found a place within Zulu power and embraced the Zulu identity.[7]

Kingdom began to become Empire. Only Shaka could have a first-fruits ceremony, now; all lesser chiefs and kings had to forgo the practice. He turned the traditional burial place of Zulu chiefs into a venerated "Valley of the Kings."[GE[53]] The royal herds of cattle grew so large they had to have outlying cattle camps to protect them. Shaka's nation building included a conscious policy of having the Zulu language "slaughter" surrounding languages. And a magic royal symbol was created, or at least expanded –the *iNkatha*, a woven straw or grass coil of the kind placed on the head to carry heavy loads. A girl in his women's quarters prophesied that there was a kind of soul force in the "body dirt" of the people—debris from the paths, scrapings from

---

52. First turn off GE Layer 51—the way the war wiped the slate clean! Then turn on GE Layer 52, a Placemark at the location of Shaka's capital KwaBulawayo.

53. GE Layer 53 is a Placemark at the approximate location of the Zulu "Valley of the Kings," or eMakhosini.

everyday objects, particles from the bodies of enemy chiefs killed in war, pieces of their *iziNkatha*. The king's inkatha was imbued with that soul force, and it was usually kept in the innermost recesses of the royal women's quarters.[8] It was a sort of Zulu *fasces*, that Roman bundle of rods bound together with an ax handle, carried by the lictor as a sign of strength in unity. Towards the end of this chapter you'll see a revival of the use of that Zulu inkatha in the twentieth century, in the service of a more modern kind of nationalism.

Shaka reigned a decade in terrible power, ordering executions regularly and seemingly at a whim. Despite the great success of his earlier military undertakings, by 1828 his military orders seemed to lack any sort of logic, demoralizing and exhausting his armies. When his mother died that year, in a frenzy of grief he ordered the death of all pregnant cattle and women, that all might really feel the sort of pain he felt; perhaps five thousand people died in this terror. The terror only ended when Dingane and another half-brother killed Shaka at his current capital of KwaDukuza (later Stanger)[GE[54]] and Dingane became Zulu king in his place.

The fate of the refugees

Consider the fortunes of one ethnic group—the afore-mentioned amaHlubi—from the shadowy pre-Mfecane/Difaqane era, through that catastrophe itself, and on into the era of white control of Natal and the explosive 1870s when almost all remaining African military power in southern Africa was broken by Europeans.[9]

As mentioned earlier, the Hlubi were a Sotho-Tswana linguistic group that by the mid-1700s was settled among the Ngunis on the upper Mzinyathi/Buffalo river. By 1819 the war between the two super-powers, Mthethwa and Ndwandwe, had set the Ngwane in motion. Faced with starvation themselves, they moved westward towards Hlubi lands and caught the Hlubi in a surprise attack, killing their chief. Fragments of the Hlubi scattered in several directions, most of them rallying around some member of the ruling house. Some fled south and west into what became West Griqualand, in that first wave of *Mfengu* (later called *Fingoes* by the whites, and literally meaning "The Emigrants") that eventually moved on into Xhosa territory. Another group of Hlubi refugees sought refuge with Shaka under the protection of Zulu power; there were enough of these so that soon Shaka was able to create an all-Hlubi regiment named for their distinctive, very unZulu-looking hairstyle.

Several other small bands of Hlubi fled up over the Drakensberg into the highveld. The breakup of the central Hlubi chieftaincy allowed Mpangzita, a son of the left-hand house who had earlier challenged the paramount chief for power, a chance for independence. Failing to rally his people enough to defend his base near the present-day city of Newcastle from the Ngwane, he took them all up onto the highveld where in cattle-less desperation they fell on the Sotho-speaking Tlokwa. This was the first major link between the lowveld Mfecane and the highveld Difaqane, as the Tlokwa in their turn then desperately fell on other Sotho groups west and north.

In brief, this burst of Zulu power from 1819 on swept all but the most able South African leaders from the field. One of the few who survived it was one of the Sotho clan leaders, Moshweshwe. Taking refuge at Thaba Nchu on a natural fort of a flat-topped mountain northwest of the Drakensberg and Maluti Mountains, he rallied those Sotho who had not been driven northwest.[GE[55]] He built an alliance of chieftaincies by marrying into them. He gave tribute to powers stronger than he was, and in his turn raided the territory of those weaker. By the early 1830s he asked Christian missionaries to come there, probably not so much because of interest in the Christian religion but because they would now attract European power to the defense of his area, and hopefully give him access to European weapons. It worked like a charm; by the 1840s he had enough guns and horses to feel fairly secure—at least from African powers such as the Zulu kingdom.

The Great Trek and its legacy

Meanwhile, the tightening of British control over Cape Colony—especially the British decision to end slavery in its territories—had determined a minority of Boers to leave Cape Colony forever. In 1834 and 1835 small exploring parties of Boers went northeast into the highveld and even scouted out Natal, east of the Drakens-

---

54. GE Layer 54 is a Placemark at KwaDukuza/Stanger.

55. GE Layer 55 is a Placemark at Thaba Nchu, on the other side of the Drakensberg and Maluti mountains from Zulu power!

berg, thus hoping to circle north around the Xhosa who occupied all the land between the Drakensberg and the Indian Ocean. By 1837 covered wagon trains set out from the Eastern Cape in earnest, in a remarkable exodus of some 14,000 to 15,000 Boers that was very different from the old trekboer semi-nomadic lifestyle. They were called *Voortrekkers*, literally "front pullers," although "pioneers" would be a better translation into American English. The major wagon trains were formed up under the charismatic leadership of individuals such as Pieter Uys, Henrik Potgieter, Gerrit Maritz, and Pieter Retief. Despite their common dislike of British rule, each was jealous of his own authority, and they were also divided by different aims. Potgieter wanted to carve out a territory in the highveld and make contact with Delagoa Bay, while Retief had his eye on Natal. Potgieter beat off an attack from the Ndebele in November of 1836, but was later voted out of power by Maritz and Retief and their supporters. In 1837 the Boers defeated the Matabele at Mosega, convincing the Matabele—Nguni speakers from the lowveld originally set in motion by the Mfecane—to continue their movement north into today's Zimbabwe.

Then, having broken all their challengers in the highveld north of the Drakensberg, these Boer Voortrekkers split into two groups. One group decided to stay in the highveld itself, and here it would eventually carve out the Orange Free State ("Orange" because the House of Orange had been associated with the Dutch state from the first days of Protestant Dutch independence). The other main group decided it could flank the Xhosa by dropping down east of them into the less well protected parts of coastal Natal that had been virtually depopulated by Zulu raids. Pieter Retief, with his long experience as a frontier military commander in the Cape Colony, was elected leader of this group that planned to move down into Natal. The adventures and misadventures of these Boers coming down into the recently de-populated but Zulu-dominated Natal are perhaps the most dramatic events of the whole Great Trek.[GE56]

On November 12, 1837, Piet Retief's daughter Deborah painted his name on a rock on the Drakensberg escarpment during their descent into Natal; the inscription is still there today.[GE57] The Boers began to settle when land showed promise as farmland, roughly in a thirty-mile-wide band that slowly grew down southeast towards the coast. On November 24, 1837, the first Voortrekker child was born in Natal, and that same night three horses were taken by lions. The countryside then was almost totally grassland with hardly a tree anywhere around; the mile-long ridge the Boers later called Spionkop was originally called "Three Tree Hill," trees being so scarce that they were thus remarkable.[GE58]

Retief negotiated for land with Dingane, Shaka's killer and half-brother and now king of the Zulus. Dingane agreed, on the condition that Retief and the Boers help him retrieve some stolen cattle he thought were rightfully his. The Boers did so, and sat down on February 6, 1838, in a hopeful mood in Dingane's *kraal* to pursue negotiations for land. Dingane at this point had them all massacred, some seventy trekker men taken by surprise at the feast that was supposed to celebrate the newly signed deal. Shortly thereafter several hundred women and children waiting back in the wagon trains were also killed by the Zulus (origin of the present-day town and area name "Weenen," which translates "Weeping" from the Afrikaans).[GE59]

It was all-out war between the Zulus and the Voortrekkers for the rest of that year. In April Uys and Potgieter, in an ill-coordinated attack on the Zulu capital, were defeated, with Uys killed and Potgieter getting the reputation of heading the "Flight Commando," because of his precipitate retreat.[GE60] The Boers pulled back north to better defensive positions, and there were raids and counter-raids that did not do much to change conditions until December of that same 1838. At that point Andries Pretorius arrived from the west with sixty fresh men, and eventually rallied a commando of some 460 men and three cannon. On December 9, as their wagon

---

56. GE Layer 56 is a Folder labeled "Main Voortrekker Routes, Sept. 1834–Feb. 1838." Notice how they almost all originate in the Eastern Cape Colony, converge on Thaba Nchu (where they were welcomed by Moshweshwe as a counter-weight against the Zulus), and then fan out from north to southeast in search of good lands to settle.

57. GE Layer 57 is a Placemark locating the site of the inscription, with some Photos icons to explore.

58. GE Layer 58 is a Placemark framing a view of Spionkop, or "Lookout Hill."

59. Clear the map by turning off GE Layer 56, the Voortrekker routes. Then turn on GE Layer 59, a Placemark referencing the town of Weenen, "Weeping."

60. GE Layer 60 is a Placemark referencing approximate location of Battle of Italeni, April 5–6, 1838, in which Uys was killed and Potgieter's force got the name "Flight Commando."

train came down through Blauuwkrantz (Afrikaans for "Blue Cliff") near the site of the massacre of Boers earlier that year, Sarel Cilliers stood on a wagon and led a prayer for this staunchly Dutch Reformed Protestant group, a prayer asking God to give them the victory and a pledge that the Boers would keep the "Covenant" they felt they had made with God to practice the true religion.[GE61] A week later, on December 16, 1838—one of the most important dates in modern South African history—Pretorius and his commando met a Zulu army about twenty times their size on the Ncome River (a tributary of the Buffalo coming in from the east) in what came to be called "the Battle of Blood River." The Boers had rifles and cannon and good defensive arrangements of circled wagons (a *laager*) on high ground near the river, and in the battle they suffered not a single fatality while leaving three thousand Zulu warriors dead on the field.[GE62]

Then Pretorius, having weakened Dingane's forces, allied with Dingane's own brother, Mpande. Together they drove Dingane off the throne and eastwards to his death. Then this branch of the trekkers settled down in Natal, west of the lower Tugela and its northern tributary the Buffalo River. This line remained the border between Natal and Zululand for some time. The city they founded, Pietermaritzburg, was named in honor of Pieter Retief and Gerrit Maritz, two popular leaders among those Boers killed in the past year. "Maritzburg" became the capital of the Republic of Natalia, short-lived, but the first Boer experiment in self-government. And in downtown Pietermaritzburg, a city with an overwhelmingly African population today, you can still visit the Boer "Church of the Vow" that the Boers promised to build and maintain in their 1838 Covenant.[GE63]

For a century and three-quarters, that December 16 anniversary of the "Battle of Blood River" in 1838—known as the *Geloftedag* or Day of the Vow, or sometimes "Dingane's Day," meaning the day Dingane got his come-uppance—has been celebrated by many Afrikaners in a yearly renewal of the covenant. Defeats and setbacks, as in the Second Boer War, some explained by their having fallen away from this covenant they believed they had made with God. In 1980 the American writer James Michener, casting around for a title for his monumental work of historical fiction telling the story of modern South Africa, named it simply *The Covenant.* The Great Trek was the stuff of national mythology, and like Valley Forge to American patriots and the Long Walk to the Communist Chinese, it grew larger and clearer in national memory as time passed, not dimmer. The powder horn the Boers used with their muzzle-loading rifles in the Great Trek became the symbol of the Nationalist Party, an almost exclusively Afrikaner political party of the twentieth century.

SECTION D: BRITISH DOMINANCE, THE ZULU WAR AND THE BOER WARS

The British in Natal

What is today the city of Durban began life in 1824 as a trading station set up by a few Britons who sailed in from Cape Town. They lived there initially only on the sufferance of Shaka, and called it Port Natal. By 1839, after the Voortrekkers had broken Dingane's power, it was uneasily absorbed into the Boer Republic of Natalia which had its capital at Pietermaritzburg where the *Volksraad* (People's Council) met. But the British Colonial Office was concerned by what it saw as a less-than-humane Boer policy towards the Africans, and also seemed unwilling for there to be any independent Boer power touching the seacoast where it might contact and ally with some other great power. Whatever the sum of the reasons, in May of 1842 a British force was sent to take the fort at Port Natal.[GE64] A fierce Boer counterattack led by Andries Pretorius almost overran the small Brit-

---

61. GE Layer 61 is a Placemark referencing the town of Blaauwkrantz on the river of the same name, presumably the spot of the famous assembly and "covenant."

62. GE Layer 62 is a Placemark referencing the battle site of Blood River (Bloed Rivier; Ncome River). Metal replicas of the sixty-four wagons, in the D-shaped laager, can easily be seen, and explored through a few Photos icons nearby.

63. GE Layer 63 is a Placemark referencing the Church of the Vow in downtown Pietermaritzburg. The city was established as the Boer capital of Natalia immediately after the defeat of the Zulus; the church was built in 1841. A Voortrekker museum is on the site, along with Andries Pretorius's house.

64. Let's start anew with the Google Earth materials; close and turn off Sections A, B, and C, and then open Section D. First turn on Durban-to-Johannesburg corridor outline Polygon; next turn on the whole "River system" folder. Then open the Folder titled "British administration of Natal." GE Layer 64 is a Placemark referencing the ruins of the original Fort Natal. Today a park in downtown Durban, it still includes part of the 1842 wall.

ish force, which was saved—it was just about to surrender—by reinforcements summoned by an English Paul Revere (who swam across the bay to the Bluff, at night, with two horses, and whose ride in this case was about 600 miles!). By July of 1842 the Boer government acknowledged British supremacy; in 1843 Port Natal was renamed "Durban" (after the British governor of the Eastern Cape, Benjamin D'Urban); and in 1845 Natal was formally annexed to Cape Colony.[GE⁶⁵]

Pretorius and most of the Boer leaders initially decided to accept life in Natal under British rule, but a Boer woman named Johanna Smuts shamed them by saying she would rather walk barefooted back up the Drakensberg escarpment than stay under the very rule they had made the Great Trek to escape. The closest pass to the highveld from Natal is northwest towards today's Free State, the way the Retief party had originally come down into the country; and there in its rugged setting still stands a bronze statue of this "barefoot trekker woman."[GE⁶⁶] Her emotion was widely shared, and most of the Voortrekker families soon went north. Many followed Andries Pretorius when he left in 1847 to settle the "South African Republic," popularly known as the Transvaal. After some oscillation between hostility and accommodation, the British recognized the independence of the Transvaal in 1852 and of the Orange Free State in 1854.[GE⁶⁷] Pretorius himself died in 1853, just months after the recognition of the Transvaal. Its capital city, Pretoria—later capital of a unified South Africa—keeps his name alive.

Xhosa tragedy

Given the dramatic, and often traumatic, impact of this European expansion on African groups in the path of it, it is not surprising that there was an unusual psychological dimension of response on the African side during these decades. Although somewhat to the west of our corridor, one of the most moving of all of these perhaps deserves a word here.

In 1857 apocalyptic prophecies ran like wildfire through the Xhosa population, which by this time had been reduced and encircled by whites and was increasingly powerless to resist them. If the Xhosa had the courage to slaughter all their livestock and destroy all their field crops, said the prophets, the ancestors themselves would rise from the dead and wipe out the white invaders. Many Xhosa indeed had the courage, and in the resulting famine perhaps fifty thousand of them either died of starvation or were driven to emigrate outside the Xhosa state, mostly to find work in Cape Colony.

This fascinating but heartrending scene had its parallels all over the world, wherever inhabitants of some land saw in themselves no inferiority to European colonists in bravery, honor, or intelligence and yet they lost battle after battle. Eventually they would learn that most of the secrets of modern power lie in superior technology and new ways of social mobilization (thus the "nationalism" and "socialism" focus of this book), but their first psychological response—and this happened in movements as diverse as the Maji-Maji in German Tanganyika, the Boxers in China, and the Ghost Dancers among the American Plains Indians—was often to seek invulnerability to bullets or tangible help from the dead by way of religious ritual. Such a belief usually died along with many of its believers in the first major war thereafter.

The growth of British Natal by 1850

To get back to our corridor proper, we've already seen that by 1845 the British had formally annexed the Boer republic of Natalia, retaining Pietermaritzburg as its capital. British power pushed north, up-country, with the founding in 1848 of what is today Estcourt at the crossing of Bushman's River (the original town name was

---

65. GE Layer 65 is a Polygon showing the area of Natal claimed by Britain in 1845. Fly to a framed view of it by double-clicking the icon, then turn the layer on.

66. GE Layer 66 is a Placemark at the approximate site of the "barefoot trekker woman" statue at Voortrekker Pass. A good photo of this *Kaalvoet Vrou* is at the following website:
http://www.flickr.com/photos/the_steyns/5237375793/

67. GE Layer 67 is a Folder with Polygons representing the Orange Free State, the Transvaal (South African Republic, technically), and their capitals. The early borders were often imprecise and controversial; the maps shown here are by 1871 when things had solidified to some extent, plus the 1884 western addition to the Transvaal.

Bushman's River Drift, and it was built in part to deny the Bushman raiders use of the fords there).[GE⁶⁸] In 1849 the current Cape Colony governor, Sir Harris Smith, approved the creation of a town named for him—Harrismith—up in the high veld (in today's Free State), in part to try to get the Voortrekkers to stay under British rule.[GE⁶⁹] In 1850 the British took over the whole Boer "Klip ("Rock," in the Afrikaans) River Republic" that occupied the triangle between the upper Tugela River, the Buffalo/Mzinyathi River, and the escarpment of the high plateau.[GE⁷⁰] The Boer capital city of the republic, founded earlier that same year, was immediately renamed Ladysmith (after the Spanish-born wife of that same Sir Harry Smith).[GE⁷¹]

Bushman raiders of the Drakensberg

From the first entry of the Voortrekkers into Natal in 1837, and for the next thirty-five years on down to 1872, a last independent remnant of the San/Bushmen came down from the Drakensberg to raid the farms of the Europeans for horses, sheep, and especially cattle. From their point of view, of course, they had been driven to seek their last refuge in the inaccessible ravines of the eastern, highest face of the Drakensberg, and it was only right to seize food from those who had seized their hunting lands. With their matchless knowledge of the terrain and of animal behavior, a half-a-dozen San could make off with a hundred head of cattle and, with just a few hours' lead time, move through rough country fast enough to escape even mounted pursuers. Once they reached the steep and rocky ravines of the face of the Drakensberg, they were virtually impossible to catch. Interesting enough, there is a weather phenomenon in the foothills of the eastern Drakensberg called the "mist belt" that came into play here. From about 3,600′ elevation to 5,000′, especially in the summer months, a good ten days a month have heavy mist—heavy enough to make the vegetation in the mist belt a shade greener than higher or lower on the slopes. Such misty, foggy days and nights were a favorite of the San raiders.

This raiding probably played at least a minor role in the decisions of virtually all of the Boers to leave Natal. The British would not allow the Boers to hunt down the Bushmen in commando-style counter-raids, but they did not give the Boers much in the way of help, either. The farm of Andries Pretorius himself (in Edendale, six miles west of Pietermaritzburg[GE⁷²]) was hit by Bushman raiders at least twice, and he complained to the British authorities that he and his friends needed some help from the government with this problem. One can imagine Boer disgust when a small British force would arrive a week or two after a Bushman raid, with no tracking skills to speak of and a cold trail to boot. Pretorius' advice to the British governor was simple: "Let the males who may resist be killed, and let the others be placed in the service of the people that they may thereby be brought to civilization instead of subsisting by plunder and murder."[10] This was a distillation of almost two centuries of trekboer practice, and he probably spoke for the majority of the white population. Lest those of us Americans of European descent feel too superior to the simple brutality of Pretorius's advice, it might be well to reflect that on our own moving western frontier we generally embraced the first half of his advice towards the original owners of the land, although we preferred for the second half to bottle the surviving Indians up on out-of-the-way reservations rather than place them "in the service of the people."

Shepstone, the N.N.P., and the "barrier locations"

Theophilus Shepstone (pronounced as if it had no final -e) was perhaps the key administrator of British Natal in these formative years of the colony. He was only three when he came with his missionary father from England to South Africa, and he proved to have a great gift for languages, eventually speaking several Bantu languages (especially Xhosa and Zulu) fluently. As a rising young official in British Natal in 1847, he was charged with creating a native military force to be stationed high on Bushman's River to stop the Bushman

---

68. GE Layer 68 is a Placemark referencing Estcourt.

69. GE Layer 69 is a Placemark referencing Harrismith.

70. GE Layer 70 is a Polygon approximating the borders of the Klip River Republic.

71. GE Layer 71 is a Placemark referencing Ladysmith. Turn it on, and it may also make the map clearer from this point on by turning off GE Layer 65, "Natal in 1845."

72. GE Layer 72 is a Placemark at the approximate location of Andries Pretorius' farm.

raids. The force was to be mounted and armed with modern weapons, trained and captained by white officers. It was an experiment that began with a hundred men, so chosen that no single African ethnic/tribal group was predominant in the group. This was the origin of the Natal Native Police.

Many white colonists worried about giving Africans modern arms and training, but a similar experiment had seemed to work in the eastern Cape Colony, and since the Natal government was strapped for cash it was argued that this was the cheapest possible solution. The N.N.P. did do some patrolling of the base of the Drakensberg, though other military emergencies and alarms on other frontiers of Natal often called them away, and Bushman raids always resumed.

So in 1849 Shepstone carried through a more radical idea that had been talked about for several years. In addition to the Bushman raids, the fairly new (only a decade old, the oldest of them) white farms in Natal were facing what they saw as a plague of "squatters," as surviving members of African groups evicted from the area by the Mfecane began to surge back to their old homelands. Shepstone, to kill two birds with one stone, ordered the four biggest of these groups to settle on reserve areas he had picked out for them at the base of the eastern Drakensberg.[GE73] One look at the pattern of Shepstone's new settlements shows you the logic of the arrangement: they were placed in a line across the path of the Bushman raids down from the high mountains, buffers between the Drakensberg San and the lower country white farms. While these resettled African communities may not have had horses or European-style weaponry, as an anti-Bushman force they made up for it with tight-knit social organization and what a military writer might call "immediate response potential" when it came to recovery of any of their precious cattle that might have been rustled by the San.

Langalibalele of the Hlubi

This doesn't mean these groups were particularly happy about being pushed around the map, especially the Hlubi under Langalibalele. These were that part of the Hlubi who had stayed with the Zulu after Shaka's death twenty years earlier. Under the following Zulu kings Dingane and then Mpande, one Hlubi clan chief after another was executed or deposed, until twenty-one-year old Langalibalele ("The Glaring Sun") inherited rule. His disagreements with current Zulu leadership in 1848 caused the Hlubi to come streaming out of Zululand and into British Natal—one of Shepstone's "problems." It took a serious military threat from Shepstone to make Langalibalele and his Hlubi move to the new reserve at the base of the Drakensberg. Once there, however, the clan seemed to take root again.

Although this is jumping ahead a little, it was just over two decades later, in 1871 and 1872, that Langalibalele and the Hlubi would make headlines again. The Natal government, worried by firearms being brought back by Hlubi workers returning from wage-work in the new diamond fields, ordered registration (which usually meant confiscation) of same. When this was ignored, and then openly defied by Langalibalele in 1873, British military force was sent (in the course of which Joseph Orpen and Qing had that key conversation that unlocked some of the spiritual meaning of San rock art, discussed near the first of this chapter). Fleeing yet again, north into what was then Basotholand and is now Lesotho, Langalibalele temporarily escaped but was finally betrayed to the Cape police.[GE74]

The Colensos and English liberalism

If Theophilus Shepstone was one dominant and famous figure in British Natal, the other was John William Colenso, an Anglican minister. In 1853, about forty years old, he was appointed Bishop of the just-created Anglican diocese of Natal. Having never been to Africa, he made a whirlwind ten-week exploratory tour there, meeting everybody of importance from Shepstone to Langalibalele. Then he went back to England to order affairs and raise money for his future work in Natal. In 1855 he came to Pietermaritzburg with all his family,

---

73. GE Layer 73 is a Folder called "Shepstone's Barriers"; it includes four separate Polygons, each named after the leader of the group so settled. Note particularly "Langalibalele's Hlubi," the group characterized by the bright yellow Polygon.

74. GE Layer 74 is a Placemark indicating a Panoramio icon of "Langalibalele's Trail," as the path up the headwaters of Bushman's River towards the crest of the Drakensberg is still called.

and built a home (Bishopstowe) and a Zulu mission (*Ekukhanyeni*, Zulu for "Place of Light") about four miles east of the city.[GE[75]] The town of Colenso on the Tugela River, where the main road from Pietermaritzburg to Ladysmith crosses it, was founded in that same 1855 when the bishop moved permanently to Natal, apparently in a burst of local English pride that Natal now had its own Church of England bishopric.

Colenso himself was a Cambridge-educated scholar of classical languages and math, and his wife and soul mate Frances was a talented linguist and scholar in her own right. They quickly compiled a Zulu grammar and, within five years, a Zulu-English dictionary with over ten thousand entries. The family hit it off with the Shepstones, socializing together regularly, with the children of both becoming fluent in Zulu.

As a man, and as Bishop, John Colenso ("Natal," he now as Bishop signed himself) was fearless in living out his beliefs. In Anglican Church history he figures as the Low Church champion of the compatibility of a Charles Lyell–Charles Darwin-style science with Christianity, versus the more literalist High Church traditionalism and fundamentalism that rejected these new theories of geological time and biological evolution. His bitterest opponent was the Bishop of Cape Town who had originally recruited him for the job, apparently without inquiring too closely into Colenso's theology. Their confrontation wound up in legal suits in the civil courts (the Anglican Church still being the official Church of England). For a time there were actually two competing Anglican bishops in Pietermaritzburg, not on speaking terms. This generally liberal perspective carried over into Bishop Colenso's preaching and social work, not surprisingly, with his mission to the Zulus emphasizing what one author called "universalism and enlightenment over the conventional Christian message of darkness, division, and damnation."[11] The white population of the colony was split as well. Those worried about the threat posed by African powers such as the Zulu and the Hlubi to the small white minority in the land castigated Colenso as naive and dangerous as well as a theological radical. On the other hand, the Colenso family home at Bishopstowe attracted all the liberal, humanitarian spirits in the colony.

One of these was Major Anthony Durnford, who was assigned to Natal in 1872 at about age 42. He was a career British officer, long estranged and separated from his wife but unable to divorce and still keep his officer's commission. He was immediately attracted to the Colenso household, and became a regular there (and apparently fell in love with and was loved in return by Fanny Colenso, a younger daughter of the house).

In late 1873, when it was clear that Langalibalele was trying to leave British Natal and take all ten thousand Hlubi with him, Shepstone arranged for an army to pursue him. Durnford was made chief of staff. Two main units were to climb the Drakensberg through passes on either side of the Bushman's River pass, converge on the Hlubi and drive them back down the pass to where a smaller force under Durnford was to block their passage. Militarily, it was disastrous for the pursuers: one of the passes was never even found, and only Durnford's small force confronted the Hlubi—not managing to halt their flight. Personally, his actions were heroic, even though he had never seen action before. And it was physically punishing. He and his horse rolled down a sizeable rocky drop early in the campaign, dislocating Durnford's shoulder and breaking a couple of ribs; and later in the skirmish he got stabbed twice with an assegai, severing some nerves in his left arm. Parenthetically, the Fort Durnford you can still visit in Estcourt was built in 1874 in the wake of Langibalele's insurrection to control the fords and the bridge over the Bushman's River there. It is named for Anthony Durnford and was probably designed by him. [GE[76]] A few years later it was also Durnford who pushed for the creation of a Natal Native Contingent (N.N.C.) of local, mostly Zulu, troops, though his vision of them correctly armed and uniformed was reduced to a red headband (to distinguish "our" Zulus from the rest) and a firearm given to every tenth man.

When Bishop Colenso got word of atrocities in the campaign against the Hlubi, such as the killing of some who had surrendered under white flag by angry colonists who were there as irregulars, he confronted Shepstone with it. An angry Shepstone defended every action, and the two men's friendship of almost twenty years was immediately and permanently broken. Early in 1874 Langalibalele was hauled before a kangaroo court by Shepstone, and condemned to life in prison on Robben Island off Cape Town—an unprecedented sentence for any court in Natal and of dubious legality. One of Shepstone's relatives was prosecution lawyer. The defendant was not allowed to talk to a lawyer at all. Bishop Colenso brought this to the attention of London, and the conflict got resolved at a higher level.

75. GE Layer 75 is a Placemark at the approximate location of Bishopstowe.
76. GE Layer 76 is a Placemark framing the location of Fort Durnford on a bluff over Bushman's River in Estcourt.

Lord Carnarvon's federation idea

A major wild card in South African events all through the nineteenth century was the attitude of the British government offices in London (usually just called "Whitehall" for the street they lined). For the Colonial Office in particular the whole world was a chessboard, a setting for the world's largest empire, its friends and its enemies. Sometimes there was money to support action, and sometimes the treasury was so empty that there had to be retrenchment somewhere. At times the key decision makers thought the solution was a military expansion in some theater of the empire—with considerable British understatement this was called a "forward" policy—and sometimes the decision makers for financial or other reasons were resolutely anti-war. And the fall of a cabinet could change that Whitehall policy overnight. And so at this particular point in time, the Langalibalebe affair was not just about the civil rights of one African under British law, or even about relations between a major African ethnic group and the Natal Colony government. It seemed to be a key proof to the current London policy makers that the only way to reduce the friction in South Africa—friction that forever threatened to spill over into war—was to create a federation of all major units there. Lord Carnarvon, in his earlier term as head of the Colonial Office, had successfully created a federation of Canada. In his second term beginning in 1874 he intended to do the same with South Africa. The South African federation envisioned was of course to be under British control, and was to include the two Boer Republics and the Zulu Kingdom.

The Boer republics were approached first. A heavy British pressure campaign to get the Orange Free State to merge with Cape Colony was tried first, with no success. The Transvaal, virtually bankrupt (ironic, in light of the huge gold strike there soon to come) was easier for the British to manipulate. Shepstone himself—a champion of the federation idea who had helped sell it to Whitehall—visited Pretoria in 1877 and formally annexed it; there was so little public protest that a few months later the whole of the Transvaal was simply declared a British colony. And then, before taking on the Orange Free State again, the British decided to subjugate the Zulu Kingdom.

Cetswayo and the Zulu revival

Shaka, Dingane, Mpande, and Cetswayo: these were the four Zulu kings of the sixty-year-long heyday of the Zulu kingdom from 1819 to 1879. Cetswayo (the name properly done starts with a pop of the tongue off the roof of the mouth, followed by "ketch-WAH-yo") translates "the slandered one." He was Mpande's most capable son, though his father never firmly settled the royal succession. He found his father too meek and subservient towards the Europeans, and was especially angry at him for allowing Boers (who had helped Mpande defeat Dingane) onto the land. In 1856 in a brutal civil war won by Cetswayo, he defeated and killed his brother, and virtually all of his brother's followers irrespective of gender and age, at a battle on the east bank of the Tugela River near its mouth.[GE77] Mpande died in 1872, but Cetswayo was functioning as king years before that, and he intended to rebuild Zulu military power so as to protect the remaining Zulu territory.[GE78]

The Anglo-Zulu War of 1879

Rorke's Drift was a little trading post on the British side of the Buffalo/Mzinyathi River [GE79] where the road to the Zulu capital Ulundi, fifty-five or sixty miles to the east,[GE80] crossed at a shallow ford, or, to use the local term, a drift. It had been founded as a trading post by an Irishman named James Rorke. Rorke used to go hunting, European style with shotguns, with a friendly chieftain named Sikayo just across the river. By 1878

77. GE Layer 77 is a Placemark showing the historic location of the battle of eNdondakasuka, just across the lower Tugela River from Ft. Pearson—that is, still in Zululand, but within sight of Natal.

78. GE Layer 78 is a Placemark with general overview of Natal-Zululand border. Turn on Polygons for Klip River Republic (GE Layer 70, area now absorbed by Natal) and Natal (GE Layer 65) for best view. For thirty years this was the border.

79. Now collapse and turn off the Folder titled "British admin. of Natal" you just explored, and then open the Folder below it titled "British-Zulu War." Turn on and fly to GE Layer 79, a Placemark with a view framing Rorke's Drift.

80. GE Layer 80 is a Path approximating the road from Rorke's Drift to Ulundi, based mainly on a map following the introduction in Donald Morris's *The Washing of the Spears* (New York: Simon & Schuster, Inc., 1965).

this little frontier post had come into the hands of a Swedish missionary society. They had renamed the mountain behind the mission station Oskarberg after the current Swedish king.[GE⁸¹]

Although at Whitehall enthusiasm for war with independent South African states had waned, the current British administrators in Natal pursued it with vigor. They were frankly looking for some *casus belli*, some excuse to start a war with the Zulus in which they could break their power and add them to the federation—and, not just incidentally, transfer much of their territory to white farmers. One way seemed to be to exploit a local quarrel about land. In March of 1878, then, a land commission investigating claims sat at Rorke's Drift for five weeks. To the secret disappointment of British officials bent on war, the commission found in favor of the Zulu side. By the end of 1878, the British government made do with a much more transparent excuse for war, ordering Cetshwayo to: (a) disband his army, and (b) pay reparations for some supposed insults. They had set the ultimatum to expire January 19, brought armies up to the frontier; the invasion began the very hour the ultimatum ran out.

It was a several-pronged invasion, focusing eventually on the current Zulu capital, Ulundi. Lord Chelmsford, overall commander, headed the central column that crossed the border at that same Rorke's Drift. The army got across and camped the first night within sight of the drift. On the next day's march there was some needless devastation of Sikayo's kraals,[GE⁸²] and the army moved about eight miles east (seven as the crow flies) to camp at the eastern base of a curious little quarter-mile-long hill that was shaped like a sphinx. It was so like a sphinx that some of the British units who had a sphinx emblem on their insignia (for deeds done by the regiment back in the Napoleonic wars in Egypt) felt that this was spooky, and recalled later that it gave them a premonition of bad things to come. The name of the steep little hill was Isandhlwana.[GE⁸³] All in all, military experts have noted, it was a spot well chosen for defense. There was a creek behind the hill for water. Lookouts could be stationed atop the hill and easily heard from the base. The "sphinx" faces almost due south, and the road from Rorke's Drift to Ulundi ran underneath the face of the sphinx, through a saddle between it and a lower "stony koppie" or rocky little hill. The British set up camp squarely across the road just on the eastern side of the mountain.[GE⁸⁴]

Scouts brought Lord Chelmsford word they had sighted Zulus several miles east. Before dawn the next day he broke camp with two-thirds of his 5,400-man army and went in pursuit, leaving about 900 British troops and an equal number of African allies (including the Natal Native Contingent under our old friend Col. Anthony Durnford). They had the new, state-of-the-art Martini-Henry single-shot rifles, some field cannon, and a couple of Congreve rocket batteries. And Lord Chelmsford had in them the confidence that any modern western force so armed, however small, could defeat any pre-modern non-western force, no matter how large or well-motivated. That attitude, and what happened next, may remind an American reader of Custer's Last Stand that happened in another part of the world three years earlier, in 1876.

By mid-morning, Chelmsford's force was ten miles east, lost to sight among low hills, finding no Zulus. Around 11:00 a.m., a cavalry scouting force from the camp at Isandhlwana was about five miles east-north-east, riding carefully through the tall grass that hid numerous rocks and boulders. They came upon a deep ravine so suddenly that the foremost horses' hooves rolled rocks down in it, and there they saw the main army of 40,000 Zulu soldiers, sitting quietly by regiment. The panicky cavalry force loosed off several shots in the direction of the huge army, which was a lot like hitting a hornet's nest with a stick. The Zulu warriors, to the tune of the ululations of 5,000 Zulu women with them, came boiling up out of the ravine, running so fast they speared many of the cavalrymen out of their saddles before they made it back to camp. Enough did return,

81. GE Layer 81 is a Placemark with a view framing Oskarberg, behind Rorke's Drift.
82. GE Layer 82 is a Placemark giving approximate location of Sikayo's kraals, just north of the road.
83. GE Layer 83 is a Placemark referencing Panoramio icon "Durnford Donga to Isandlwana." This is a view from the east, opposite the way the British came, though the mountain has the same outline from either east or west.
84. Open the Folder entitled "Isandhlwana: British positions." Making sure the Folder is not turned on yet, double-click on the Folder icon to "fly" yourself to a pre-set view. Open GE Layer 84, a Folder titled "British tent areas," and click them open one by one.

however, to alert the camp. It had time to be well prepared in terms of positions, arms, and ammunition by the time the main Zulu army arrived.[GE[85]]

About noon the main Zulu force stood all along the crest of the Nqutu plateau northeast of Isandhlwana. The Zulu commander Chingwayo Kamahole Khoza, seventy-two years old, had fought in his youth with Shaka's armies, and had just run twenty-five miles in the last two days. From the plateau, slightly higher than the top of Isandhwana, he looked down over the field, and shouted, "We've got them; let's go."[GE[86]] Some of the few European survivors remembered that the Zulu armies running down from the crest of the plateau looked like oil from giant containers being poured down the slope.[GE[87]]

The unreliable, hard-to-direct Congreve rockets—probably more for "shock and awe" effect than real killing power—exceeded expectations, exploding in leading Zulu troop units. Murderous rifle fire from the British side forced the left wing of the Zulu attack to flinch and swing very wide, seeking cover in a shallow donga. [GE[88]] But Zulu speed, numbers, and willingness to take losses was such that by 1:00 p.m. the British forces had been driven back to the base of Isandhlwana, totally surrounded (except for a hundred or so "fugitives" who broke free to try to run back to Rorke's Drift).[GE[89]] An eclipse of the sun began at 1:10, and by the time it ended at 4:10 the battle was over too.[GE[90]] Every soldier on the British side of the battlefield was dead—800 Brits and about that many African allies. It appeared to later observers of the battlefield, as they tried to reconstruct it, that the very last of the fighting was where Anthony Durnford fell, around the wagons in the saddle between the stony koppie and Isandhlwana.[GE[91]]

Some in Chelmsford's force miles away claimed they heard gunfire, so an observer was sent to the top of the closest hill with binoculars. He could see the tents still standing at the base of the sphinx-like hill, and reported the fact, so all assumed everything was well: in case of an attack on a camp, it was a standing order that tents were to be leveled first thing for a clear field of fire. For some reason this was not done at Isandhlwana. Lord Chelsmford only learned of the disaster when his advance scouts on the return trip came back with the news. It was the single worst British defeat between the Napoleonic Wars and World War I.

Against Cetswayo's orders a young Zulu regiment pursued the fugitives[GE[92]] over the river into British Natal and attacked Rorke's Drift itself. It had been left with a garrison of a hundred or so, a third of them in sick bay. It survived attacks by some 5,000 Zulus the rest of that day and all that night. The British government handed out sixteen Victoria Crosses, the highest British war decoration, to veterans of that battle, which was only a postscript to Isandhlwana. While taking nothing away from the courage of all involved, we can say that this was obviously a British way of drawing attention from the greater disaster to the minor victory.

For Zulus, this campaign remains a bittersweet memory. At Isandhlwana alone they probably lost 3,000 dead, many more than the British side lost. And Isandhlwana (as with the Sioux victory at the Little Bighorn and the U.S. army) only convinced the British to bring in overwhelming force and militarily completely break the Zulus, which happened within six months after Isandhlwana. It culminated with the Battle of Ulundi with some 1,700 Zulu dead. Cetswayo was arrested and deported, and a nation of warriors, as one writer put it, was

---

85. GE Layer 85 is a Polygon representing "British units at 1:00." Double-click on the Polygon icon to "fly" to pre-set view, then turn layer on. The British apparently had warning enough to set up a fairly well-ordered defense.

86. GE Layer 86 is a Placemark indicating Panoramio icon titled "View of Zulu Commander, Isandhlwana." The photo and the framed view in Google Earth both show his view of British defenses.

87. GE Layer 87 is a Placemark referencing a Panoramio icon "Heights and Conical Hill," for British view of center of main Zulu attack.

88. Now open the Folder called "Isandhlwana, Zulu attack," without turning it on; just double-click on Folder icon to fly to pre-set view. Open GE Layer 88, a Folder titled "Zulu armies attack"; inside it click on each layer (one per main Zulu regiment, which will show as black, arrow-shaped Polygons) in turn.

89. GE Layer 89 is a Polygon layer showing in light blue the approximate Zulu positions between noon and 1:00 p.m.

90. GE Layer 90 is a Folder titled "Further Zulu attacks," showing final surrounding of British force. Open and click on layers as before.

91. GE Layer 91 is a Polygon shaped like an orange iron cross representing "Durnford's Last Stand."

92. GE Layer 92 is a Path representing the flight of the "fugitives" and their Zulu pursuers. Where they crossed the river (in one of its rare floods, and several drowned here) is still called "Fugitive's Drift."

on its way to becoming a nation of gardeners and houseboys. But it also has remained all these years a point of pride: Zulus were the bloodiest thorn in the side of the colonial conquerors. There is a small Zulu memorial at Rorke's Drift today, a leopard reclining on a pile of Zulu shields.[GE93] But there is a more impressive one on the northeast side of Isandhlwana, the direction from which the attack came: a massive replica of the kind of necklace, lion's claws included, given to exceptional Zulu warriors.[GE94]

American readers who enjoy old movies may be familiar with the 1964 film *Zulu*, which although filmed on-site romanticizes the battle of Rorke's Drift to the extent that it can't be considered very historical (the author suspects most of its fame is because it was Michael Caine's film debut). A less famous film but with more historical value is the 1979 *Zulu Dawn*. It sets the framework of the British ultimatum and focuses more on the great battle of Isandhlwana. The actor Burt Lancaster, incidentally, plays Durnford, and Peter O'Toole is Lord Chelmsford.

King Solomon's Mines

There is also a famous echo of these events in historical fiction that will be familiar to many American readers. In the spring of 1885, at home in England, twenty-nine-year-old H. Rider Haggard bet his brother he could write a book as gripping as the very popular *Treasure Island* that had been published a few years before. Six weeks later he finished the manuscript of *King Solomon's Mines*. Upon publication later that year, he seemed to win his bet, and the book has retained its popularity for a century and more (despite a series of truly awful films based on it). Narrator of the novel is a fifty-five-year-old elephant hunter from Durban, one Allan Quatermain, who recounts the supposed events of the last year or so. Opening scenes are shipboard from Cape Town to East London, then from East London to Durban (including the description of arriving at Durban by ship quoted near the beginning of this chapter) as the hints of the mystery are being thrown out in conversation.

The book is about following a treasure map north to, where else, King Solomon's lost but fabled mines. Gold was not to be discovered on the Witwatersrand until 1886, the year after the book was written, so the "unknown north" was nearer, then. A European party accompanied by a mysterious but noble African man makes its way from Durban, presumably up through Pietermaritzburg to the highveld and on across the Vaal river, and then through largely fictional, obstacle-strewn lands to the territory of the terrifying Kukuanas, with their "smelling-out" of witches and instant deaths meted out to those so smelt out.

The biography of the author explains much of the material of the book. When H. Rider Haggard was nineteen, in 1875, his parents prevailed on family friend Sir Henry Bulwer to take the young Rider with him when Bulwer took up his new post as Lieutenant-Governor of Natal. Rider duly arrived at Cape Town later that year, sailed up the coast to Durban (thus seeing it as did the fictional Allan Quatermain), and then went to Pietermaritzburg where the Lieutenant-Governor's office was based. Haggard started out as Bulwer's secretary. The landscape, the vibrant local society, and especially the Zulus fascinated Haggard. He learned to speak Zulu and recorded some of their stories and customs. As early as 1877 he published an article on "A Zulu War Dance" about a ceremony performed for one of the Lieutenant-Governor's "up-country" visits. The Kukuanas of his novel are essentially the Zulus as encountered by Haggard, and writ large. Even the "smelling out" of witches was based on contemporary Zulu practice, a sort of periodic government terror in which all were assembled, and witch doctors trained in detecting evil presences inside people prowled through the crowd. Those identified were killed in the way reserved for evil witches, with sharpened stakes driven up their rectums. The Zulu king inherited all their cattle, less a fee for the services of those who had "smelled out" the supposed evil ones.

In 1877 Natal's Chief of Native Affairs, the famous (and by this time Sir) Theophilus Shepstone, recruited Haggard to go with his small diplomatic mission to Pretoria. In front of "an armed, ominously silent crowd of Dutchmen," Haggard raised the British flag (in place of the *Vierkleur*, the "Four-color," as the flag of the South African Republic was known), and when the British reader of the proclamation became too nervous to go on, Haggard took the document and finished it for him—which had to be altogether an interesting experience for a twenty-one-year-old. Two years later he was still in the land when the British invaded Zululand with the ini-

---

93. GE Layer 93 is a Placemark referencing a Panoramio icon entitled "Rorke's Drift Zulu Monument."
94. GE Layer 94 is a Placemark referencing a Panoramio icon entitled "Zulu Memorial, Isandhlwana."

tial disastrous result of Isandhlwana (a battle fought largely during an eclipse, as is the key battle of his novel *King Solomon's Mines*, not coincidentally). And Haggard was still in Natal and the Transvaal, by this time as a circuit-riding judge based in Newcastle and hearing cases as far off as the courthouse in Wakkerstroom, when the first Boer War of 1880–1881 (on which more shortly) broke out. He served as staff officer for the British general killed at Majuba. Some of the negotiations for British withdrawal and renewed Boer independence for the Transvaal were actually carried out in the kitchen of Haggard's house near the border of the Transvaal and Natal. He sailed back to England later in 1881, not to return for decades. Those six years of life in South Africa, however, obviously stayed vividly in his memory.

Dismembering the Zulu state

The 1879 British military crushing of the Zulus was just the beginning of the destruction of Zulu power, not the end. Zulu territory was divided among thirteen Zulu clan leaders, hand-picked by the British so as to effectively take power away from the royal family—always the focus of Zulu nationalism. When Cetswayo was allowed to return from exile to Ulundi, and assembled the surviving princes and advisors of the dynasty, one of these British-supported clan chiefs attacked the whole gathering. This was in July of 1883, and the carnage was such that it was called the Second Battle of Ulundi.[GE95] Most of the important members of the royal house were killed, and Cetswayo himself barely escaped with a stab wound to the thigh. He took to the Nkandla Forest,[GE96] a traditional Zulu refuge, and died there in 1884. His son and chosen heir Dinuzulu was there for his death. In the wake of this, seven important Zulu leaders visited the British residency at Eshowe[GE97] in Zululand, testifying that Cetswayo had willed the succession to his son and asking for British recognition of that fact, to preserve some Zulu unity and center of gravity. Zulu unity was, of course, the very last thing the white settler population and the British administration wanted to see.

The Zulus had suffered another blow the year before, 1883, with the death of John Colenso, Bishop of Natal, almost their only champion in the local white population. His eldest daughter Harriette Colenso, who had functioned as his chief administrator for years (local Zulus called her his "staff") and whose Zulu was better than his, took on the burden—but without the platform of any office from which to speak, and with the handicap facing any woman aspiring to influence public affairs in the Victorian era. Hers was a remarkable life, recently rehearsed in a university-press biography called *The View Across the River: Harriette Colenso and the Zulu Struggle against Imperialism*.[12] She wrote volumes of letters to individuals and to the press. She stretched the meager family budget to go to England and try to mobilize British public opinion on the matter, speaking to hundreds of groups. She arranged for legal counsel for Zulus on trial, including Dinuzulu, and either served as interpreter or arranged for another. As compared to the self-serving rhetoric of much of the white population, especially Sir Theophilus Shepstone and his party, what Harriette Colenso wrote seems today clear-eyed, honest, and courageous, as in this extract from a letter written in 1886:

> The English and Dutch conspire together to crush the Zulu and divide the spoil. And, if the Zulus make an attempt to stand for their liberty, they will be mercilessly butchered by either or both of these civilized and Christian nations.

> And I want you to understand the real nature of the transaction and the cruel injustice of thus wiping out the national existence of the Zulu people, by robbing them of their country, whether the robbers are to be ruled in future by Dutch or English law.[13]

As early as 1888 she was speaking of the "Zulu national party."

---

95. GE Layer 95 is a Placemark locating Ulundi, about twenty miles east of our corridor; explore Panoramio icons under pointer for recreations of traditional Zulu dwellings.

96. GE Layer 96 is a Placemark framing the Nkandla Forest, just inside our corridor. It shows as the dark green patch in center of view.

97. GE Layer 97 is a Placemark locating Eshowe; it is about halfway between Nkandla Forest and Ulundi on the one hand and the seacoast on the other.

The one tragedy associated with the Colenso family's support of the Zulus was their reliance on white men who proved unreliable. Possibly the Colensos were so isolated from the larger white settler community that they welcomed anyone who seemed willing to help.

Towards the end of his life Bishop Colenso sent an acquaintance named John Grant to help the Zulu royal family in the wake of their 1879 military defeat. Grant proved to be as vain as he was incompetent, and in the name of the royal clan he negotiated with Boers for their help against their British-sponsored Zulu rivals—in the course of which he signed away two million acres of land to the Boers! This became the so-called New Republic with its capital at Vryheid ("Freedom").[GE98]

When Dinuzulu and two other Zulu leaders were on trial for their lives in 1888, Harriette Colenso talked the brilliant Durban lawyer Harry Escombe into taking the case. He managed the trial well, getting them off with temporary deportation to the island of St. Helena. But that same politically ambitious Harry Escombe agitated for "responsible government" for Natal in 1893 (meaning among other things to let white Natalians decide what to do with the non-whites, with no more interference from London), and as the first Attorney General for "responsibly governed" Natal in 1894 he stood firmly for an early version of apartheid. It was his Franchise Amendment Bill of that year, incidentally, to exclude all "Asiatics" from voting, that would trigger Gandhi's involvement in a movement to protect Indian civil rights.

In 1895–96 the rinderpest epidemic devastated the Zulu herds, killing something like 90 percent of all the cattle. Zulu men had little alternative but to go in increasing numbers to work on white farms or in the mines, in a pattern that meant they only visited their home villages a couple of times a year—with disastrous impact on their home communities. In 1897 a divided, impoverished Zululand lost the last shreds of its independence as its administration was merged with that of British Natal.

All that happened in just eighteen years after the Zulu pyrrhic victory at the Battle of Isandhlwana.

The Boer republics and the Anglo-Boer wars

After the British defeated the Zulu army in 1879, it was the Britain-versus-Boer Republics conflict that dominated the last two decades of the century. The larger setting was the off and on expansion of the worldwide British Empire, approaching its historical zenith, and the great mineral strikes in southern Africa—first diamonds and then gold. The local setting included some of the most vivid personalities of South Africa's entire history, especially Paul Kruger and Cecil Rhodes and their rivalry.

The Orange Free State and the Transvaal (South African Republic), founded in 1852 and 1854, were a lasting legacy of the Great Trek. The Boers had rifles and cannon on their side when they fought the Africans, but they thought God was on their side, too. The outnumbered Boers had covenanted with each other at the start of their trek, and in their own minds, at least, with God, that if He would give them victory over the current inhabitants of the land, they would be faithful forever in their worship of Him. That sentiment was not unknown on the American frontier around this same time, of course, as an occasional white patriarch killed local "heathen" Indians with the same religious self-righteousness. What was different in South Africa is that this was almost universally believed among the Boers, who were almost to a person members of one of three branches of the (Protestant) Dutch Reformed Church. It was not a simple parallel with the Hebrew conquest of Palestine, they were told from many pulpits; it was a re-enactment, with Boers as the newly chosen people of God. By the end of the century, this belief would come to full flower. Here, from his classic sociological study of civic religion *The Rise of Afrikanerdom: Power, Apartheid, and the Civil Religion*, is T. Dunbar Moodie's summary of *Om* ("Uncle") Paul Kruger's philosophy as President of the Transvaal in from 1883 to 1900:

> When the fathers sought a new land, the Lord in mercy enabled them to escape the oppressions of Europe. God led them by faith to this rich and beautiful place, a veritable land of milk and honey, where his Word could be clearly heard and strictly obeyed. The gift of the land, basic to the ancient covenants' understanding of salvation, carries with it solemn obligations: faithfulness to the God of the covenant and his laws. And, as

---

98. GE Layer 98 is a Folder called New Republic; it contains a Polygon representing the New Republic, and a Placemark representing its capital Vryheid ("Freedom").

in the conquest of Canaan and the post-exilic return to Judah, assimilation with the peoples living in the land is absolutely forbidden. As the Lord's gift of land to Israel entailed the military conquest of Canaan, including the subduing of the heathen, so too the Voortrekkers proved by God's grace to be mighty in battle. In sum, the deuteronomic interpretation of history which sees God's mercy and judgment in the triumphs and failures of his people is still valid as his eternal word.[14]

Paul Kruger was born in the northern Cape in 1825, and set off with his parents on the Great Trek at age ten. As a young man he was legendary for feats of strength and military prowess, and he was involved in most of the important political developments in the Transvaal from its original independence in 1852 on. After the British annexation of the Transvaal in 1877 he became the leader of the independence movement. He went to Britain in 1877 and 1878 to try to convince D'Israeli's Conservative government to grant such independence, but got nowhere. He at first hoped that Gladstone's new Liberal government would help, but by 1880 gave up on that. Late in 1880, on that special December *Geloftedag* (Day of the Vow), anniversary of the victory over Dingane's Zulus in 1838, he, Piet Joubert, and Marthinus Pretorius (oldest son of Andries) held a rally to begin a war of independence. They staged it at Paardekraal, not quite halfway from Pretoria to Potchefstroom. Every man there, without urging from the leaders, took a rock and placed it on a pile as a sign of renewal of the "vow."[GE[99]]

The first Anglo-Boer War

The war itself, beginning in that same December of 1880, lasted only four months and had only four major encounters. The five fairly new British forts in the Transvaal were all beseiged,[GE[100]] and two of them closely attacked; none were able to send supporting forces to the major British advance. The first of four major encounters was thirty miles east of Pretoria at Bronkhorstspruit, where on December 20 a British unit marched straight into an ambush of sharpshooting Boer commandos.[GE[101]] The next three battles were in a tight cluster just where the main road from Durban to Pretoria crested the escarpment: here the main British force under General Colley tried to force its way up to the highveld.

The Boers defended Laing's Nek, a narrow pass south of Charleston where the main wagon road came uphill. On January 28—high summer just over a year after Isandhlwana, with the British troops still wearing their wool redcoats—the British attacked in formation. British artillery had little effect on the Boers scattered through the rocks, and neither cavalry nor infantry charges could make it through Boer rifle fire. Results, seventy-three British dead, fourteen Boer dead, and a British retreat. On February 8, about ten miles south at Ingogo (or Shuinshoogte), the British supply lines were attacked by the Boers. Results: another seventy British dead, eight Boer dead, and a precipitate British retreat. Then came the most famous, or infamous, battle of the war, Majuba (from the Zulu *amaJuba*, "Hill of Doves"). General Colley had just been reinforced with 2,000 men including a cavalry troop and a naval brigade (with Gatling guns), and a couple of pieces of artillery. Learning that the Boers were camped at the northern base of Majuba Hill, he had most of his men climb the southern side of the hill at night. It was Hendrika Joubert, wife of the Boer General, who first spotted the troops atop the hill. Although they had the high ground, the British could not hold against Boer skirmish lines. General Colley was killed, and the retreat became a rout. Result: 92 British dead, 134 wounded, 59 taken prisoner, versus 1 Boer dead and 5 Boer wounded.[GE[102]]

---

99. First open the next Folder titled "First Anglo-Boer War." Inside it, turn on and fly to GE Layer 99. It is a Placemark referencing the monument built over the cairn in 1889; as is shown here in a cluster of Photos icons under pointer, most with some variety of "Paardekraal Monument" in their titles.

100. GE Layer 100 is a Folder called "British forts" containing a Placemark referencing each fort with a light blue Pushpin icon and a white Polygon outline connecting them.

101. GE Layer 101 is a Placemark locating Bronkhorstspruit.

102. GE Layer 102 is a Folder titled "Majuba area battles." Inside are layers representing General Colley's camp at Mount Prospect, his three attacks and their ill-fated ends, and an overview of the general area; turn on each layer and double-click each icon to "fly" there.

None of these were major battles, in terms of numbers of people taking part. The shock to the British, however, of having regular troops totally outclassed by an army of farmers, was considerable. The new Liberal cabinet under Gladstone had no heart for continuing the war, and instructed General Bulwer to make peace (the commission sat in house of Rider Haggard in Newcastle, the center of his circuit riding judiciary).

The lesson learned by Boers from this First Anglo-Boer War was simple: in any future conflict, strike quickly and bloody the British nose, and they'll back off. Looking back, that was not the only lesson they should have learned; they should also have taken note of how this peace rankled with a large part of the British population. The English settlers of Natal reacted to the peace by putting an effigy of Gladstone on trial for treason and staging a burial of the British flag with gravestone and all. Later in the Second Anglo-Boer War, the big one, as that same General Bulwer embarked at Southhampton with 47,000 men it was to shouts of "Remember Majuba, boys!"

In the short run, though, it was a Boer victory. And towards the end of the four-month-long war Kruger showed as much skill in diplomacy as he had in military affairs: Transvaal won control of its own domestic affairs, with just a vague line about British suzerainty. He was elected President of the Transvaal in 1883. [GE[103]] In 1884 and 1885 the British negated Transvaal claims to lands in today's Botswana and Zimbabwe, thus closing off Boer avenues of expansion north and west (more on this shortly), but at least Kruger got all mention of British control of the Transvaal removed in return.

Then came the 1886 gold strike which transformed the whole situation.

Diamonds at Kimberley; gold on the Rand

More than anything, it was the great new mineral strikes in Boer territories that brought intensive new interest in the Boer Republics from the British Empire.

In 1867 scattered alluvial diamonds were found in the western edge of the Orange Free State, and by 1870 the great diamond-bearing "pipes" were found, resulting in the new city of Kimberley.[GE[104]] British diplomacy successfully gerrymandered this great new diamond field away from the Boer Orange Free State and into the British-owned Cape Colony. These were the diamond fields where young men from Langalibalele's Hlubi came to work for cash, with which to buy guns—as you saw earlier. And these were the diamond fields where a young and ambitious Cecil Rhodes began his remarkable cornering of the diamond market there in the still-famous De Beers Company—more on him later.

In 1886, about thirty miles south of Pretoria on the Witwatersrand, gold was discovered on a couple of adjacent Afrikaner farms. According to one account, a sometime English prospector and miner stubbed his toe on a rock while walking across the veld to meet a friend, and recognized it as gold-bearing. Despite attempts to keep the news quiet, it quickly became evident that this was the world's greatest-ever gold strike, and it started the world's greatest-ever gold rush. Three government officials or surveyors brought in to settle conflicting land claims all had the first name Johann or Johannes, and the little town they laid out for the first rush of miners may have been named for one or all of them. Within three years Johannesburg had become the biggest city in southern Africa.

Many of the gold rushers were native speakers of English—Brits, mostly, but also some Yanks, Aussies, and Kiwis. Soon they outnumbered the Transvaal's native speakers of Afrikaans, who called them *uitlanders* (pronounced something like "ATE-landers") or foreigners. Although the total amount of gold in the "reef" boggled the mind, it was thinly dispersed in very hard rock and difficult to extract, especially as the mines deepened. The small prospectors were quickly gobbled up by the bigger concerns. Skilled white labor in these deepening mines got decent wages. Part of the formula for the mines' success from the first, however, was the very low wage traditionally paid to unskilled labor, most of it African.

---

103. GE Layer 103 is a Placemark referencing a Panoramio icon titled "Paul Kruger Standbeeld, Ou Raadsaal." It is the centerpiece of Church Square, in front of the Pretoria's Town Hall.

104. GE Layer 104 is a Placemark referencing Kimberley's "Big Hole," once one of the largest hand-dug holes in the world—though now being refilled, as you can see by clicking on the Panoramio icon under the pointer titled "DeBeers Mine refilling operation." Zoom out to see location of Kimberley in relation to our corridor.

So many different ethnic groups came to live in the mining camps—from all over South Africa and even neighboring countries to the north—that a primitive sort of language of the mines called *Fanakalo* evolved. The name comes from the basic Nguni-language word *fana*, "be like," plus the possessive particle *ka*, plus *lo*, meaning "this." The whole phrase meant "do it like this," the first thing a mine boss would tell a new worker at his new job,[15] so it's really the "Do It Like This" language. The mining camps had their share of ethnic violence, but also began to generate a rudimentary pan-African feeling.

The railroads to Jo'burg

In 1860 the first two miles of railroad track in South Africa was laid—in the city of Durban, from "the Point" (the harbor mouth opposite "the Bluff") to dockside in the sheltered harbor. By the 1870s, railroads were moving into the interior from most of the major ports. In 1885 the railroad from Cape Town towards the Transvaal had been built past Kimberley, and the railroad from Durban had reached the Transvaal border. Then gold was discovered on the Witwatersrand in 1886. Despite stumbling blocks to this unwanted railroad "progress" erected by the Boer leadership of the Transvaal, the Cape railroad first reached the Rand in 1892. The railroad from Durban only reached it in 1895, but slowly became the dominant carrier of Rand output since it was the shortest route to a good port.

The main rail arteries across Natal were like a "Y" with its bottom point at Durban, the top sides of the "Y" splitting at the important rail junction town of Ladysmith. From here the northwestern branch headed up the escarpment to Harrismith in the Free State, and the northeastern branch went up though Glencoe and Newcastle towards the Transvaal.[GE[105]] The railroad planners originally had this northeast branch topping out on the escarpment at the town of Wakkerstroom, but the city fathers wanted no such agent of change anywhere near. So the railroad was rerouted a few miles west and topped out in the valley called *Volksrust*, the "People's Rest"—so-called because the Boer armies had retired from their victory in Majuba in 1881 to rest and recuperate here. A town grew up there around the railroad station (and later a repentant Wakkerstroom had to petition for a branch line to come east to it from Volksrust). Since the left-hand top of the "Y" of tracks through Natal ended at Harrisburg, it was the right-hand top of the "Y" that carried the main traffic between Johannesburg and Durban. The railroad just south of Ladysmith and just northeast of Ladysmith would be the corridor for much of the fighting in the greatest of the Anglo-Boer Wars, from 1899 to 1902.

Cecil Rhodes

Cecil Rhodes came out to South Africa from England in 1870 when he was seventeen, to work on an older brother's cotton farm in British Natal. Both the brothers got diamond fever and moved to Kimberley by 1871. For most of the next decade Cecil split his time between Kimberley and going to university at Oxford (he was doing so well in the diamond business at Kimberley that Oxford tuition was presumably no problem). He graduated from Oxford in 1881. Within a decade his De Beers firm had taken control of something like 90 percent of all the world's diamond production, and he had also became a major player in the gold mining business on the Rand.

Rhodes was also a most passionate booster of the British Empire. For Africa his grand vision was a sort of British "drive to the north," towards completion of a Cape-to-Cairo railway. This initially seemed to be blocked by the Transvaal Republic's claims to Bechuanaland (today's Botswana), and also to Matabeleland and Mashonaland (today's Zimbabwe) further north, across the Limpopo River. Rhodes first successfully lobbied with the British government to declare of Bechuanaland as a protectorate, which it did in 1884. Then he inveigled

---

105. GE Layer 105 is a folder titled "Railroad 'Y' Across Natal." It includes Paths showing the main route from Durban to Johannesburg and the unfinished left top of the "Y" to Harrismith, as well as a Placemark showing the town of Wakkerstroom that initially rejected the railroad. Right click on the "Durban to Jo'burg" Path layer title, and then choose "Show Elevation Profile" in the menu that comes up. On the bottom half of your screen such a profile will pop up. If you slide your cursor along the profile from left to right, a corresponding red arrow will show you where you are on the railroad. Notice the Biggarsberg hump you must go over before going down to the Tugela crossing at Colenso, and then gradually back up, steepening sharply around Majuba.

the King of the Matabele into signing a document allowing mining concessions, and by 1889 turned that into The British South Africa Company—to which the British government gave rights much more sweeping than the Matabele king ever dreamed. What resulted, within a few years, was a sort of joint Cecil Rhodes/British government takeover of "Rhodesia" (today's Zimbabwe), Northern Rhodesia (today's Zambia), and Nyasaland (today's Malawi). The Boers were being encircled by the British Empire yet again.

In 1890 Cecil Rhodes was elected Prime Minister of Cape Colony. As such he more and more saw President Kruger of the Transvaal as the greatest obstacle to his dream of a British Africa. Kruger had stubbornly refused to give the uitlanders the vote, rightly foreseeing Boer loss of control of the Transvaal in that case; in that same 1890 he had proposed that they might get the vote once they had lived in the Transvaal for fourteen years—a proposal not well received by either uitlanders or the British government. Kruger had built a railroad east to the Portuguese port of Lourenço Marques (today's Maputo in Mozambique) to try to escape British encirclement.[GE106] He levied huge import taxes on goods coming in from the Cape and Natal, and then in 1894 and again in 1895 even "closed the drifts"—blocked the fords over the Vaal River—to incoming wagon traffic. Meanwhile the uitlanders in the Transvaal had organized a union to demand the vote; one of Cecil Rhodes' brothers was actually a member of it.

Jameson's Raid

Leander Starr Jameson was a very close friend of Rhodes, who had made him his chief administrator for Matabeland and Mashonaland—essentially today's Zimbabwe. In 1895 Rhodes funded him to invade Johannesburg from the west around Mafeking,[GE107] with a small force—around 500 calvary (mostly young and untried men from the British South Africa Company's Matabelaland and Mashonaland police), eight Maxim machine guns and three pieces of light artillery. Their thinking was that it would just take a small force to trigger an uitlander rising that would either overthrow Kruger or at least create a situation that would force Britain to intervene on the side of the uitlanders. As the December invasion date approached, it became apparent that the uitlanders in Jo'burg were not prepared to rise, at least at that point. Jameson was sent numerous telegrams, from Rhodes and others, to postpone the invasion. On his own he decided to go ahead with it anyway, and it was a disaster. Boer scouts shadowed them from their entry into the Transvaal near Mafeking. When Jameson found the road into Johannesburg blocked at Krugersdorp, he tried to go southeast around it. Encountering a superior force at Doornkop (at the western edge of today's Soweto),[GE108] he surrendered. Instead of making a martyr of Jameson, the Transvaal government simply publicly handed him over to an embarrassed British government. An even more embarrassed Cecil Rhodes resigned from all public office.

In 1896, a few months after Jameson's Raid, Mark Twain just happened through South Africa on a world speaking tour. In his *Following the Equator* (1897) he tried to explain it to his readers humorously about Jameson's attempt to continue the British policy of the First Boer War of marching in tight columns against hidden and well-entrenched Boers, and concluded:

> There is a story, which may not be true, about an ignorant Boer farmer there who thought that this white flag was the national flag of England. He had been at Bronkhorst, and Laing's Nek, and Ingogo and Amajuba, and supposed that the English did not run up their flag excepting at the end of a fight.[16]

Such humor was probably not seen as funny by most contemporary British; their pride had been touched. Jameson was treated as a hero by much of the public during his trial in London, and the failure of his raid just made some important British policy makers more intent than ever on a showdown with the Boer Republics.

---

106. GE Layer 106 is a Path representing Kruger's new railroad to today's Maputo.
107. GE Layer 107 is a Placemark showing Mafeking, near today's Botswana border.
108. GE Layer 108 is a Placemark locating Doornkop in relation to Krugersdorp and today's Soweto.

The Second Anglo-Boer War

The new governor of Cape Colony and high commissioner of British South Africa as of 1897 was Sir Alfred Milner. He was personally determined on war with the Boer Republics, and in a key position to influence the British government decision. In 1899 he went to Bloemfontein to meet with Kruger, with a demand that the uitlanders get the vote in five years. Kruger offered to compromise on seven years—which, if Milner had not already been decided on war, would have defused the issue. Since British troops were already being mobilized and boarding ships headed for South Africa, Kruger understood that Milner was just buying time to finish preparation for war. Kruger issued an ultimatum of his own: that British troops be withdrawn from the borders of the Boer Republics within two days. Quickly bloody the British nose and they'll back off; that had been the lesson he had learned from the First Anglo-Boer War.

Militarily, the British plan was to advance on the Boer Republics from the Cape and from Natal—and eventually that was done, though first it was the Boers who did most of the advancing. The war began on October 11, 1899 (as soon as the Transvaal could get the neighboring Orange Free State to commit and to mobilize its troops) and quickly resulted in stunning reverses for the British army. In what the British called "Black Week" of December 10-15 British armies were sent stumbling back towards Cape Town and Durban, with British garrisons cut off and under siege at Ladysmith, Mafeking (where Lord Baden-Powell famously created the Boy Scouts) and Kimberley (with Cecil Rhodes there among the besieged). Although the Boer armies never numbered more than 90,000, and the British eventually mobilized half-a-million troops, the Boers knew the countryside, were most of them hunters and marksmen from childhood, and had interior lines of communication. Moreover, they were well-armed. The gold mines had made the Transvaal a very rich government in a very short time and afforded the Boer armies the latest in Mauser rifles from Germany and Creusot artillery from France. All of a sudden entrenched companies of riflemen could be accurate to almost a mile, and in this new age of smokeless powder they were virtually invisible to the enemy.

The Natal theatre of the war was again the most dramatic.[GE[109]] The main Transvaal armies staged up at Sandspruit, about ten miles northwest of Volksrust near the Natal border. They opened the war when the ultimatum ran out on October 11, the main army under Joubert generally following the railroad south. Joined by an army from the Orange Free State, they took Newcastle on Oct. 14. On Oct. 19 two armies converged on Glencoe and Dundee, and on the next day important battles were fought on Talana Hill and Mt. Impati. Here Louis Botha emerged as young military genius of the war.

Meanwhile a third Boer army bypassed Glencoe on the west and hit the railroad line again about halfway between Glencoe and Ladysmith, at Elandslaagte. A British force from Ladysmith moved northeast up the line and engaged them. This Battle of Elandslaagte, part of which was fought in a huge rainstorm, was a British victory; in fact the commanding Boer general was killed. It made possible the retreat of the British garrison from Dundee to Ladysmith, though closely pursued. As other armies from the Orange Free State joined the Boers, however, the victorious British commander felt so exposed that he too withdrew to Ladysmith. There he sat for months until finally relief came, actually surrounded by fewer Boer soldiers than he had in his garrison.

The Boer armies commanded by Joubert and the brilliant young Louis Botha left Ladysmith under siege, crossed the Tugela River near Colenso and left its garrison under siege as well. South of Colenso, an unexpected bonus fell to the Boers—an armored train, with which the British were trying to keep touch with the

---

109. First turn off everything in the last Folder ("First Anglo-Boer War") except GE Layer 105, the railroad "Y" across our corridor. Then open the "Second Anglo-Boer War" Folder. GE Layer 109 is a Folder titled "Boer invasion of Natal Oct. 11 - Nov. 23 1899." Inside are some thirty Paths, Polygons, or Placemarks marking troop movements, battles, besieged garrisons, etc. A reader can follow the campaign described in the next three paragraphs of text, step-by-step, by turning on layers inside this folder when appropriate, or simply go to the last layer of the folder for an overview of the whole campaign. When you have done all that, with each layer still turned on, you might like to have Google Earth "fly" you through the whole campaign. First go to the Tools drop-down menu, then Options, then the Touring tab, and change two settings there: first, set the "Time Between Features" to 4 seconds; second, set the "Wait at Features" to 2 seconds. Then highlight the Folder 109 in the Places box, and at bottom right of Places box hit the little right-facing black arrow next to the small Folder icon.

Tugela crossing at Colenso from their garrison at Estcourt about twenty miles south. To quote Thomas Pakenham from his 1979 classic *The Boer War*: "Imprisoned on its vulnerable railway line, the armoured train was as helpless against field-guns in the veld as a naval dreadnought sent into battle with its rudder jammed."[17] So the Boers ambushed and wrecked it and captured its occupants—a young newspaper correspondent and officer named Winston Churchill among them. He was later taken to prison in the Transvaal, escaped out through Mozambique, and circled back in to the Natal theatre of the war through Durban, exploits which first brought his name to much of the British public. But at this point he, temporarily, and the armored train, permanently, were *hors de combat*. Botha's armies circled Estcourt and cut the rail line below it just outside Mooirivier. Some have speculated that even though by this time he was down to a couple of thousand men, he could have gone all the way to Durban had he so chosen.

When a few weeks later General Redvers Buller came up from Durban massively supplied and with tens of thousands of troops, the Boers withdrew to the line of the Tugela River and all the defensible hills and ridges along it. Three times Buller tried and failed to force the line, earning the name "Reverse" Buller in the British popular press. The most famous battle of these campaigns was probably Spionkop, or Lookout Hill, about twenty miles west of Colenso.[GE[110]] The British seized the high ground, but it was convex and so rocky they couldn't dig in. Boer sharpshooters from two lower but more defensible hills killed some 300 British soldiers there, the biggest single British loss any day of the war. The battle of Spionkop was also famous because three rather famous figures, looking back, were there on the same day: Winston Churchill, still in his dual role as correspondent and British officer; Louis Botha in command of the Boer troops; and M. K. Gandhi with his non-combatant medical corps, helping the British side.

By the fourth try Buller had solved the puzzle of this new-style warfare. He ground out his advance hill by hill, helped by the fact that one of the key Tugela hills was south of the river, on the British side, as a good anchor point for the advance.[GE[111]] The British also broke through Boer lines from the Cape side, and in short order British armies relieved all the besieged garrisons and captured Johannesburg and the Boer capitals of Bloemfontein and Pretoria.

And then, though the conventional war had been lost, part of the Boer forces went into guerrilla war mode. Under Generals De Wet, De La Rey, and lawyer-turned-soldier Jan Smuts they did hit-and-run attacks on British supply lines and isolated garrisons, disappearing when major British forces came up. Like all successful guerrilla armies, they operated on land they knew intimately well, among a sympathetic population that informed them and fed them. One of Smuts' raids went deep into the Cape Colony itself, getting to within fifty miles of Cape Town. Since Boers considerably outnumbered the English even in Cape Province, there was always some danger of their rising to join the surviving armies of the Boer Republics, which would have totally transformed the war.

By this time Lord Kitchener had been brought in by the British to mastermind the end-game of the war. [GE[112]] His strategy was two-fold. First, he intended to strangle pockets of resistance with chains of block-houses built within sight of each other and connected by fences of barbed wire.[GE[113]] Such a circle would be completed, then a smaller circle built within that. Second, he intended to scorch the earth so the guerrilla armies could no longer live off the land. British armies systematically burned Boer houses, barns, and crops in the field (bringing in feed for their own horses from Argentina, along with the seeds of those cosmos flowers you saw back in the "topography and texture of the land" section). The Boer women and children so burned out were to be gathered in "concentration" camps, and there to stay behind barbed wire until the last Boer army surren-

---

110. GE Layer 110 is a Placemark framing a view of Spionkop from the south, the side up which the British advanced.

111. GE Layer 111 is a Placemark framing a view of the Tugela River hills around Colenso.

112. GE Layer 112 is a Placemark locating Melrose House, the 1886 mansion commandeered as headquarters of British forces in South Africa after Pretoria was occupied in June of 1900; it remained as headquarters for eighteen months. Today a museum. Some of the Photos icons nearby have good photos of the house.

113. GE Layer 113 is a Placemark referencing a Panoramio icon below pointer entitled "Fort Harlech." This is a typical blockhouse from Kitchener's "end-game" strategy for the Anglo-Boer War.

dered. Women whose husbands had not surrendered got no meat in some of the camps—this to hurry along the men's surrender. Although for two years the Boers were sharply divided among themselves between "hands-uppers" and "bitter-enders," as they sardonically referred to each other, all the major parties signed a surrender in May of 1902 at Vereeniging.[GE114] Looking back, though, the concentration camps were a long-term political disaster for the British, one of those cases of turning a war completely over to the military and forgetting von Clausewitz's old dictum that "war is just the extension of policy by other means."

The "concentration" camps

In the 1930s Hitler and company, for their rounding up and genocide of European Jews, would borrow the name "concentration camp" from this British original in Boer War South Africa. The name was obviously chosen by them so as to blunt any British criticism of what the Nazis were doing.

The British eventually constructed over forty such "concentration" camps, scattered across South Africa but especially thick along our corridor, that collectively held close to 100,000 people.[GE115] There was a major difference with the Nazi camps, of course, in that the British intended no genocide. But the camps were tent cities in seas of mud in the cold and rainy season, so ill-supplied with food as to cause general malnourishment, and so casual about sanitation that diseases such as typhoid and cholera swept through and killed 27,000 Boer women and children. In a single year almost half the people in the camps died. A courageous English woman named Emily Hobhouse blew the whistle, and brought the scandal out in the open with her writing and tours. British sensitivity about this tragedy probably led them to give more generous peace terms to the surrendering Boers than they otherwise would have, and more respect for Boer wishes in the near future, when it came to terms of the Union of South Africa soon to be created. For the Boers suspicions always remained that it had indeed been a planned genocide. The scorched earth policy and the camps were something never to be forgotten, shallowly-buried coals of anger easily fanned into flame—a bit like Reconstruction policies for white American Southerners.

The Union of South Africa, 1910

So Milner had his war with the Boers, and the British won it—though at a cost in lives and money much, much higher than he had supposed. He confidently moved the center of British governance of South Africa from Cape Town to Pretoria, where magnificent new buildings were built for it.[G116] But his long-term plans for a British-dominated South African federation generally failed. Instead of the great flood of British immigration he had projected after the war, there was hardly any new immigration at all. Anger at his decree that English be used in the schools and courts—plus the bitterness left by the camps—galvanized the Boer population, and the main political parties in the land emerged under former Boer generals such as Jan Smuts, Louis Botha, and Barry Hertzog. In 1908–9 a constitutional convention met in Durban, and here the British High Commissioner and the major Boer leaders decided on a unitary state. The former Boer Republics were to keep their "whites only" voting and the Cape would, at least for the time, retain its broader franchise. A general principle of separating white and black lands was established. The British Parliament approved all this in 1909, and on May 31, 1910, the Union of South Africa was formally proclaimed.

---

114. GE Layer 114 is a Placemark referencing Vereeniging, a town on the northern bank of the Vaal where that river makes its closest approach to Johannesburg, about thirty-five miles north.

115. GE Layer 115 is a Folder titled "Concentration camps on our corridor." Turning on the Folder and double-clicking on the icon to "fly" there shows major camps along our corridor marked by red squares.

116. GE Layer 116 is a Placemark framing a view of the spectacular Union buildings. A couple dozen Photos icons are there to explore; pointer of Placemark indicates some with a view of the buildings across an expanse of lawn.

SECTION E: CULTURAL NATIONALISM AMONG THE AFRIKANERS

The first voices

Afrikaner thinkers, while appreciating aid from Holland and the equal place given "Dutch" in the 1910 Union, had already begun to think of Afrikaans as a unique language, justifying a unique political state for its speakers.

The Du Toit family was something of a dynasty in this regard. The father, S. J. Du Toit, was born and raised in the western Cape. A politically active pastor, he began publishing books in Afrikaans by 1875 and in 1879 created the *Afrikaner Bond*, or League of Afrikaners, a very anti-British party. In 1882 he was invited to the Transvaal to become its superintendent of education. His brother, D. F. Du Toit, started the journal *The Patriot*. But it was the son of the former, Jakob Daniel Du Toit, or simply Totius (his pen name) who became the most famous of the house.

Born in 1877, Totius had just passed his final exam for the Dutch Reformed Church ministry in 1899 when the second and greatest of the Anglo-Boer Wars broke out. He was a chaplain for Boer forces the first year of the war, and in 1900 when the conventional war ended he went to Amsterdam to study theology. By 1903 he had his doctorate and entered the ministry. From 1911 on until his retirement in 1949 he was Professor of Theology at Potchefstroom.[GE117] Potchefstroom was the old original capital of the Transvaal, founded in 1838 by the Voortrekkers in their first year across the Vaal River. Although the political capital had soon moved on to Pretoria, Potchefstroom was still home to this famous seminary where a strain of Dutch Reformed theology that stressed the uniqueness and continuity of nations (including and especially emphasizing the Afrikaner *Volk*) had its center, not least because of Totius. It might be worth reminding a reader at this point of the author's argument that the two most common sources of modern national identity are first, language, and second, religion; they are obviously very powerfully combined here. Totius produced major works of scholarship, translating the greater part of the Bible into Afrikaans by 1932 and compiling an Afrikaans psalter by 1936, one of the implications of this being "Who needs Dutch now?" But historically more important is how his combination of Afrikaner patriotism and South African-style Dutch Reformed Calvinism was communicated in his poetry, such as his 1915 *Trekkerswee*, or "Trekker's Grief." Here was the artist who more than any other proved that world-class literature could be created in Afrikaans.

Another early proponent of this linguistic nationalism, much the same age as Totius, was Daniel François Malan (whose French name came from seventeenth-century Huguenot settlers). Born in the Western Cape, he went from math and science into philosophy in local colleges. Then he went on to the University of Utrecht in Holland for his doctorate in divinity, which was awarded in 1905. Back in South Africa he was ordained a minister in the Dutch Reformed Church and stationed for his first six months or so in Heidelberg, just south of Johannesburg, as assistant minister. In 1906 he was one of the founders of the Afrikaans Language Union, and in 1908 he summed up its essence in a speech:

> A linguistic expert can no more create a living language than a chemist can create life in his laboratory . . . . A living powerful language is born from the soil of the People's heart [*Volkshart*] and the People's history [*Volksgeskiedenis*] and lives only in the mouth of the People [*Volksmond*] . . . . Peoples and languages are born together and die together . . . . Give the young Afrikaner a written language which is easy and natural for him, and you will thereby have set up a bulwark against the anglicization of our People [*Volk*]. . . . Raise the Afrikaans language to a written language, make it the bearer of our culture, our history, our national ideals, and you will raise the People to a feeling of self-respect and to the calling to bake a worthier place in world civilization . . . .[18]

---

117. First close the Folder "Section D: Zulu War . . . ," leaving turned on only the first two layers in it, a Polygon for our corridor, and the Folder with all the rivers. Then open the next Folder, "Section E: Afrikaner nationalism." Inside it GE Layer 117 is a Placemark framing the city of Potchefstroom. Four miles of Potchefstroom's oak-lined streets have been given "national monument" status in South Africa. The cluster of Photos icons in the south of town are mostly of quaint old government buildings and churches; the cluster in the north mainly have scenes of the university.

Herder-style "unique-culture-carried-in-language" and Fichte-style "every-*Volk*-deserves-its-own-state" had just fully arrived in South Africa. It would carry D. F. Malan far in politics, you'll see.

Then came World War I, and the renewed bitterness of Afrikaner fighting Afrikaner. Former Boer War Generals Botha and Smuts, whose alliance supported joining Britain in the war effort, had to put down some 12,000 troops of a *Rebellie* led by other former Boer War Generals De Wet and Kemp (which would have also surely included General De La Rey had he not been accidentally killed at a roadblock on the eve of the rebellion). Much of it happened on or near our corridor. Several towns in the eastern Free State including Heilbron, Reitz, and Harrismith were in rebel hands for awhile; Potchefstroom, in fact, was central to the plotting of the revolt. In the Transvaal, the Magaliesburg north of Pretoria was a rebel stronghold.[GE118] It provided "one last martyr" for the Boervolk/Afrikaner cause, Commandant Joupie Fourie: when he was captured by the official South African Defence Forces, and discovered never to have resigned his commission in same, he was court-martialled, convicted, and then executed on December 20, 1914. His eve-of-execution exhortation that Afrikaners remain faithful to the death to Religion, Language, and Volk sounds like something from Bobby Sands in Ireland, and provided similar motivation to his side of the conflict for years to come.

This awakened all the old friction from the last years of the Boer War, from just a dozen years before, between "bittereinders" and "hensoppers." In 1913, foreseeing this Botha-Smuts support of Britain in a coming war, Hertzog had broken with them and created the National Party. Although he did not militarily side with the rebels in 1914, he quickly built the dominant white party out of those who sympathized with them.

Die Stem van Suid Afrika, which translates "The Call of South Africa," was a poem written in Afrikaans in 1918 and set to music in 1921. Almost all older South Africans today know it; whether they loved it or hated it, it was the sole national anthem for most of their lives. One part of it, in English translation which undoubtedly loses something, goes like this:

> Ringing out from our blue heavens, from the deep seas breaking round
> Over everlasting mountains, where the echoing crags resound,
> Through the plains where creaking wagons cut their trails into the earth,
> Comes the calling of our country, of the land that gave us birth[GE119]

The *Broederbond*

Perhaps the key institution in this new Afrikaner nationalism was the *Afrikaner Broederbond*—the Band or League of Brothers—started in and around Johannesburg in 1919 by Henning Klopper. It was initially a way to get the Afrikaans language equal treatment with English, featuring regular home discussion meetings in cells of from five to twenty. In 1922—as its ambitions grew—it went underground, with candlelight initiations of promising young Afrikaner men sworn to secrecy and a life of dedication to the Afrikaner cause. It soon spread all over the country. Although the administrative center stayed in Johannesburg, the real ideological center of the Broederbond shifted to Potchefstroom, ground zero of this new cultural nationalism.

From its secret underground the Broederbond organized and undoubtedly funded a huge range of Afrikaner (and Afrikaans-language) institutions. Boy Scouts were replaced by "Voortrekkers" and Rotary Club by the "Rapportryers" (originally dispatch carriers in the Boer Wars). One of the Broederbond's key creations was in 1929, of the F.A.K. (Federation of Afrikaner Cultural Organizations), which was to give some order to the like-minded institutions now springing up all over South Africa. Within fifteen years the Federation had set up Afrikaans-language music competitions, published folksong collections, set up regular "culture days," and demanded equal radio time with English stations. But the greatest coup of all was its organization of the 1938 centennial of the Great Trek.

---

118. GE Layer 118 is a Folder with Placemarks (red Pushpin icons) marking centers of the *Rebellie* on our corridor.

119. GE Layer 119 is a Placemark framing a view of Oudtshoorn in the Western Cape where the author of *Die Stem* famously lived and worked. He was C. J. Langenhoven, a tireless translator and writer of Afrikaans whose collected works run to sixteen volumes. You can pull up a version on YouTube, or do a Google–Videos search for "Die Stem" and get some stirring versions

Die Tweede Trek ("The Second Trek")

In South Africa in the 1930s the dominant political party was the South African Party. Botha had died in the early '20s, and Smuts and Hertzog had joined forces under pressure of the Depression and against the emergence of this new and radical Afrikaner nationalism—which saw even Hertzog as too willing to cooperate with the British. In 1936 D. F. Malan rebelled against Hertzog's alliance with Smuts and retained (or re-created) the "Purified" Nationalist Party.

In South Africa's general elections in May of 1938, this exclusively Afrikaner Nationalist Party jumped from seven seats in the Assembly to twenty-seven. Even though this was only a fourth of the seats held by the Smuts and Hertzog United Party, it awakened expectations among the Afrikaner leadership. Just after the elections, Henning Klopper (still chairman of the Broederbond after almost 20 years) proposed a re-enactment of the Great Trek in this the centennial of its greatest year. Two oxwagon (*ossewa*, in the Afrikaans) teams were to start out from Cape Town in early August and go by historic Voortrekker routes to Pretoria, arriving over four months later on the December 16 anniversary of the Battle of Blood River. There speeches would be made and a foundation stone of a proposed Voortrekker Monument be laid. Afrikaner nationalism was to be raised to new levels and Afrikaner voters registered in the process.

This "Second Trek," or more formally "Memorial Trek" (*Gedenktrek*) succeeded beyond its organizers' dreams. Klopper sent the two wagons off with a speech made at the statue of Jan van Riebeeck in Cape Town. [GE[120]] At their very first stop, 20,000 Afrikaners gave the wagons a reception described as near euphoric, and the wagons were soon being met by huge crowds of Afrikaners dressed in Voortrekker-style clothes. Such was the enthusiasm that eventually seven other wagons were started out from other parts of the county. One only made a short loop out of Cape Town and back, but two were destined for the actual battlefield of Blood River and six were headed towards Pretoria. Most of the wagons were named for one of the Voortrekker leaders, including Andries Pretorius, Piet Retief, and Hendrik Potgieter, though two, Johanna van der Merwe and Magrieta Prinsloo, were named for women who though seriously wounded survived Zulu attacks, and one was generically called *Vrou en Moeder* ("Wife and Mother"). The nine wagon teams among them made over 500 formal stops on their collective ways.[GE[121]] Most of the wagons went through Vegkop, where the trekkers held off the Matebele in 1836, their first significant victory on the highveld in the Great Trek.[GE[122]] Two wagons ended their journey at the battle site of Blood River,[GE[123]], but the emotional peak came when the main group was met on "Monument Hill"[GE[124]] overlooking Pretoria by between 150,000 and 200,000 Afrikaners, most of whom camped out there all night. Three thousand Afrikaner children with torches walked down the hill to meet the procession. The foundation stone of the monument was laid by granddaughters or great-granddaughters of Pretorius, Retief, and Potgieter. D. F. Malan himself ended the ceremony with a speech (in Afrikaans, of course; by the end of the commemorative trek English-language speakers were not really welcomed on the stage), and the crowd sang *Die Stem*, "The Call of South Africa."[19]

---

120. First open the Folder titled "Second Trek." GE Layer 120 is a Placemark referencing the statue of Riebeeck in front of the City Hall in Cape Town, just a few hundred feet from the fort he established.

121. GE Layer 121 is a Folder that includes nine Paths, one for each wagon. Make sure the folder is turned off but open, and click "on" each Path one at a time. The straight-line distance from Cape Town to Pretoria is over 800 miles, so it is visually obvious what a huge undertaking this was.

122. GE Layer 122 is a Placemark referencing Vegkop ("Battle Hill"), where the battle between Potgeiter's 40-wagon caravan and 5,000 Matebele took place on October 16, 1836. The Voortrekkers circled their wagons near the base of the hill but clear of brush so as to have an open field of fire. Battle site approximately marked by white pushpin icon; red-roofed buildings left of it are modern museum complex. Three months after this the combined forces of Potgeiter and Gert Maritz ran the Matebele out of their home village. Some interesting Photos icons to explore.

123. GE Layer 123 is a Placemark framing course two the oxwagons took to Blood River.

124. GE Layer 124 is a Placemark framing the final course of six wagons to Monument Hill, overlooking Pretoria.

This dramatic hilltop shrine is a huge granite structure, a cube forty-one meters on a side that can be seen for miles.[GE125] A visitor walks up steps through an oval wall that surrounds the whole structure with sixty-four wagons carved on it in deep relief, the number of the original Battle of Blood River. Much larger than life statues of trekker leaders stand at the corners of the building. Scenes of the Great Trek are carved in white marble panels on the interior walls. In a sunken circle in the middle of the building, the sun's rays are designed to fall precisely at noon on December 16 through a hole in the ceiling on a grave-like memorial to Piet Retief, precisely on the engraved words *Ons vir jou Suid-Afrika* ("We for you, South Africa"), that last ringing phrase from *Die Stem*.[GE126] The Monument would be completed in 1949, one year after the Nationalist Party rode the mass nationalism and voter registration of Afrikaners begun by this "Second Trek" to total political power. Like many historical developments, however, that is much clearer in hindsight than it was at the time.

An Afrikaner organization even more radical than the Broederbond was the O.B., the *Ossewa Brandwag* (Oxwagon Sentinel, or Oxwagon Watch). It was founded in 1939 as an Afrikaner cultural movement, capitalizing on the wave of emotion from the Second Trek. One writer called it "neo-Fichtean," because of its emphasis on the Volk—a word which it used just as the Nazis did. The O.B. more and more drifted towards adulation of Hitler, flourished in the early years of World War II when the Nazis seemed to be winning, and was eventually destroyed as a force in South Africa by Hitler's defeat—leaving the field of extreme Afrikaner nationalism to Malan's National Party.

Cry, the Beloved Country

A very famous South African novel from 1948, still worth reading—*Cry, the Beloved Country*—was written by an author molded by our Durban-to-Johannesburg corridor. Alan Paton was born in Pietermaritzburg in 1903. He studied at the University of Natal and taught school for a decade. Then in 1935 he took a job directing the Diepkloof Reformatory, near Johannesburg, working with African delinquent boys from the cities. Just before the national elections of 1948 he wrote this moving story of a young white man and a young black man from the same part of the South Africa, their respective personal lives which crossed tragically, and then the interaction of their families in the wake of the tragedy. The novel held out hope that white South Africa—for simple reasons of justice and for its own long-term survival—would eventually allow democratic government. The irony of the timing is that those very 1948 national elections brought to power the National Party, and it took the country away from universal suffrage, not towards it.

Instituting apartheid, 1948–50

In 1948 the ruling South African Party approached the national elections complacently. They had won comfortably in the last elections in 1943 and were headed by one of the most famous statesmen in the world in Jan Smuts. But they, and almost all political pundits, were blind-sided by the results of Afrikaner voter registration and Afrikaner patriotism generated by the Second Trek. Smuts even lost in his own constituency in Wakkerstroom, and the underdog Nationalist Party came to power by the thinnest of margins. But power it was, and power they would use, to turn an already very segregated society into complete racial "apart-ness"—*apartheid*. It took about a year and a half to create the legal foundation for the new regime; the key laws were in place in 1950.

First and most basic was the Population Registration Act: every South African was to be classified as White, Coloured, African, or Asian. "Coloured" referred to the Afrikaans-speaking population usually called "Cape Coloured," a racially mixed population whose ancestry was European, Khoisan, African (including slaves brought in from East and West Africa) and Indonesian. Asians were almost altogether the Indians. "Africans" were the Bantu-speakers, Nguni and Sotho/Tswana. If the category of an individual was not clear to those judging, tests such as sticking a pencil in the person's hair and seeing if it stayed there, measuring the slope of

125. GE Layer 125 is a Placemark referencing a Photos icon titled "Voortrekker Monument 10/10" which has a distant view of the huge Voortrekker monument on a hill overlooking Pretoria. The structure is generally cubical, forty-one meters on a side.

126. GE Layer 126 is a Placemark framing a close-up shot of the Monument, with a good many Photos icons with photographs made inside and out.

the shoulders or the width of the nose were used. In all seriousness. And these categories were intended to be permanent—a Prohibition of Mixed Marriages Act and an Immorality Act made marriage and/or sex between persons of different categories illegal.

Second, the Group Areas Act stated that if an area was needed by whites, whole African towns could be relocated. And this immediately happened to such vibrant black settlements as Cape Town's District Six and Johannesburg's Sophiatown. Causing even more havoc in the African community was the policy of creating "Bantustans" that this Group Areas Act envisioned. Eight and later ten reserves (termed "national units" in apartheid-speak)—supposedly independent homelands but actually client states dependent on Pretoria for hand-outs—were established.[GE127] To some extent it split African opposition to this new policy, because the chiefs so empowered generally supported the system out of self-interest. For the South African "African" community as a whole, though, which was at least 80 percent of the whole population, it was a tragedy. Whole communities were trucked to a given area and unloaded there, often where there was no housing or infrastructure, sometimes in cold and rainy weather.

Third, the Suppression of Communism Act defined "Communism" so broadly that almost any resistance to the new government policies was included. It was not only a practical tool that legalized a brutal governmental crackdown, it was a propaganda coup in these early days of the Cold War when western capitals and especially Washington tended to see the world as "with us or against us."

D. F. Malan—he who made that ringing speech about the Afrikaans language forty years earlier in 1908—was the new Prime Minister at age seventy-four. But the driving force of the government quickly came to be Hendrik Verwoerd. A brilliant politician and a hard-line racist, he was Minister of Native Areas beginning in 1950, and then Prime Minister beginning in 1958. In 1966 Verwoerd was assassinated on the floor of Parliament by a "Cape Coloured," from whose population Verwoerd's apartheid policy had stripped the vote.

Apartheid was fine-tuned and remaining "loopholes" closed in the 1950s and 1960s. The "pass laws" of 1952 required black men over sixteen to carry an identity book at all times; black women were included in 1956. In 1970 the Bantu Homelands Citizenship Act assigned every black South African person citizenship in one of the Bantustans, no matter where they actually lived; any civil rights they could expect would be there, not in the 80 percent of the country—South Africa proper by the new legal definition—owned by the roughly 10 percent white minority.

As part of the opposition went underground and armed itself (much more later), the government responded with extreme repression. As opposition leaders went to neighboring states to continue the struggle, the South African armed forces pursued them there, crossing into the territory of every surrounding state. The biggest of the resulting wars was in Southwest Africa (today's Namibia) and Angola, with the Cubans (funded by the Soviet Union) helping organize African resistance. Increasingly an international pariah, the apartheid government of South Africa stubbornly rejected all outside pressures (and increasingly inside pressures, some from influential Afrikaner intellectuals and religious leaders) to change its ways. The military was built up into the strongest in Africa, and by the end of the 1970s had apparently tested its own atomic bomb.

But change was coming, and the deepest roots of that change were in the development of African nationalism.

SECTION F: AFRICAN CULTURAL NATIONALISM

Early civil rights struggle part one: Gandhi in South Africa

Mohandas Karamchand Gandhi, the future *Maha-tma* or "Great-Soul" to many Indians, came to Durban in the spring of 1893 as a failed young lawyer, too timid to cross-examine in court and a person of no obvious direction in life or influence on people. He came only because he had a year's contract to work for a Muslim firm from his part of India; he never intended to stay a day more. Dragged almost against his will into leading an

---

127. GE Layer 127 is a Folder titled "Bantustans, 1984," inside which are ten Polygon layers, one per "homeland." Open the Folder, then turn the layers on one by one. The map is based mainly on Map 10, "African homelands in 1984," in T. R. H. Davenport's *South Africa: A Modern History*, 4th edition (Macmillan Press, 1991). Turn off some earlier layers, especially GE Layer 121 with the wagon train paths, to see the pattern better.

Indian civil rights movement there, he wound up staying twenty-one years. Finally returning to India just before World War I, his skills in law, publishing, group-building, and consciousness-raising had become truly world-class. In South Africa he had also, not incidentally, fused his private and public lives and invented *satyagraha*, or "soul force"—a specifically Gandhian variety of non-violent civil resistance that would later transform India. And this all played out, almost exclusively, on our chosen corridor from Durban up to Johannesburg and Pretoria, in what were in those years the states of Natal and Transvaal.

A sizeable Indian community began to immigrate to Durban and vicinity by the mid-nineteenth century, at first mostly indentured labor of poor low-caste Hindus brought in to work the sugar and coffee plantations. Many stayed on as market gardeners or railroad workers after their indenture was up. This was cheap, tractable labor, no threat to established white commercial interests. After 1880, however, comparatively wealthy and sophisticated Muslim businessmen from Gujarat, north of Bombay, came in and competed to the disadvantage of white-owned businesses. Even their numbers seemed a threat: by 1894 Natal had 43,000 Indians as compared to 40,000 whites. By 1899 even the Transvaal had 17,000 Indians. Most of the white community, with the English increasingly making common cause with the Afrikaners, reacted to these "Asians" in these decades after 1880 with fear and hostility—not just with pejorative names like "coolies" for manual laborers, "Sammy" and "Mary" as scornful generic names for any Indian man or woman, but with laws aimed at restricting immigration and eventually evicting the entire group. In 1895 Natal put a heavy yearly tax of £ 3 on Indian laborers to slow or reverse immigration. In 1897 immigration was limited to those who spoke a European language (this to eliminate the Gujarati Muslim businessmen).

Enter Gandhi in 1893, the timid Hindu lawyer hired by the Durban branch of a Gujarati Muslim firm to help with its legal cases—in part because of his good English acquired during three years in London as well as his formal law degree. Less than two weeks after his arrival in the country, he boarded the train in Durban and settled down in a first-class car in preparation for the trip up to Charleston (near the border between Natal and Transvaal, which is as far as the railroad went then; the rest was by horse-drawn coach on to Pretoria). A white passenger complained to the conductor about this non-white in a "white's only" car, and when Gandhi argued that he had never been so discriminated against in England, he was physically thrown off the train at the next stop, Pietermaritzburg.[GE[128]] There he sat one long, cold, thoughtful night. Looking back later, he saw this as a major step towards his becoming an active worker for Indian equality within the British Empire.

Even in that first year in South Africa, Gandhi made friends with an unusually wide circle of people for someone who had grown up a caste Hindu. From the poor Tamil-speaking Hindu laborers to wealthy Muslim businessmen to European intellectuals, Gandhi cast a wide net and began to build a matrix of relationships. Even more unusual was the determination he developed that first year to let ethics permeate everything he did, privately and publicly. Within that first year he quit taking fees for public legal work. He refused to coach witnesses in their testimony before the trial. And in that first year in South Africa he read Leo Tolstoy's *The Kingdom Of God Is Within You*, ending any belief he had that violent means could achieve any untainted good in the world. Eventually, even when beaten up by a white mob in 1897, and beaten into unconsciousness by a Muslim mob in 1908, he would refuse to press legal charges.

In 1894, we've already seen, Natal passed the Franchise Amendment Bill to exclude all "Asiatics" from voting. This drew Gandhi into action, as co-founder and moving spirit of the NIC, the Natal Indian Congress (partly named as to seem to be associated with the Indian National Congress formed in British India in 1885). This was his school of hard knocks: here he learned that he needed to ask for regular subscriptions to finance political work, to keep good financial books on contributions and expenditures, and to make a moving public speech.

In 1904 came another key development, again exactly on our corridor. A European friend in Johannesburg gave him a copy of John Ruskin's *Unto This Last*. Gandhi started reading it on the train from Johannesburg

---

128. Turn off earlier Folders Sections A through E, except for the first two layers of Section D (the corridor rectangle and the rivers), and collapse them. Then open this last Folder F: "African Nationalism." Then open the first Folder there, titled "life of Gandhi." GE Layer 128 is a Placemark referencing Pietermaritzburg. A "Google–Images" search of "Gandhi Pietermaritzburg" will turn up half-a-dozen pictures of the Gandhi statue on Church Street there in Pietermaritzburg, and at least two pictures of the actual train station, now renamed "Mahatma Gandhi Station."

(the line had been finished in 1895) down to Durban, and was so captivated by it that he read it through on the whole twenty-four-hour journey. The result, in December that same year, was the founding of his first *ashram*, the Phoenix Farm. It was about ten miles north of Durban; the last wild elephant in the vicinity had been shot only six years before. It was a hundred acres with some fruit trees and a creek running through it. It was to become a spiritual commune, ecumenical in terms of religion, dedicated to the simplest of lifestyles where each was liable to his or her own share of manual labor—and a place to plan political campaigns and most immediately a place to produce a newspaper Gandhi had just founded that year called *Indian Opinion*. Tents were gradually replaced by masonry and corrugated iron buildings (destroyed in the 1985 ethnic riots described later, though today lovingly reconstructed). The name Phoenix, incidentally, came from the previous owner of the farm whose sugar cane crop had burned but who planted more in the ashes; Gandhi liked the name and kept it.[GE[129]]

Up to this point Gandhi seems to have been a true believer in the civilizing mission of the British Empire. His methods were models of legality, with formal petitions and court cases. There was little sign as yet of the universalism he showed later in life in defense of all oppressed groups, including Untouchables in India. It was the Natal Indian Congress of which he was counsel and secretary, for example, that instead of asking for all to enter public buildings by a single door, requested that there be three doors: one for whites, one for Indians, and one for Africans. His main complaint to the British, about the fact that Indians were forbidden access to first and second class train travel, was that they were "huddled together in the same compartments with Natives." He claimed to take the British at their word in the historic announcement of Queen Victoria as she became "Empress of India" that there would be no discrimination on grounds of race or religion in her Empire; how then could any fair-minded Briton object to Gandhi's work towards that end? He supported Great Britain in its hours of need. Having volunteered in a charity hospital an hour a day for much of his time in Durban, he knew some practical medicine. In the Second and larger Anglo-Boer War he organized and then worked in an 1,100-man ambulance and stretcher corps; so employed he was thus at Spionkop, bloodiest of Boer War battlefields. In the Zulu Rebellion of 1906 he did the same, again at considerable risk to his own life and limb.

Then came the political developments of 1906–7, perhaps the pivotal point of his whole life. The Transvaal government came out with an Asiatic Law in 1906; it excluded new Indian immigrants, and required registration, fingerprinting, and permanent passbooks for all Indians in Natal—more restrictive in some respects than applied to Africans. Gandhi and the Natal Indian Congress had some success lobbying with Britain in this matter, but all that did was to get the law delayed a year. In 1907 Natal won self-government, and made the law permanent. The shock to the Indian community was huge. In the Boer War the British had virtually promised Indians more civil rights, and now the attitudes of the defeated in that war were enshrined in law, more rigid than ever.

This same 1906 is when, as pressure on the Indian community in the Transvaal grew to seem the most serious danger, Gandhi moved his base of operations to Johannesburg. It was also in this year that he took vows of celibacy and poverty. When it was time for Indians to register by terms of the new law of 1907, he preached a non-violent but firm non-compliance, and first used the term *satyagraha*—backing off from western models and selectively taking from the Hindu heritage. On Aug. 16, 1908, at the Hamidia Mosque in Johannesburg,[GE[130]] he staged the burning of Indian passbooks (soaked in paraffin so as to burn long and brightly for journalists covering the event) in two cauldrons, his first decidedly illegal act.[20]

In 1910—the last year of Leo Tolstoy's life, by which time he and Gandhi were into deep correspondence—came the founding of the Tolstoy Farm, Gandhi's second and larger *ashram* twenty miles outside Johannesburg.

---

129. In this same "life of Gandhi" Folder, turn on GE Layer 129, a Folder titled "Phoenix Farm"; it includes a Polygon in red giving approximate boundaries of original farm, as it relates to Durban ten miles away, and Placemarks indicating Gandhi's house and the location of the printing press. Again, a Google–Images search of "Gandhi Phoenix Farm" will produce several photographs of structures there including his home (destroyed in 1985 ethnic riots, rebuilt since).

130. GE Layer 130 is a Folder titled "Hamidia Mosque"; turning it on will locate structure and show arrow pointing to Mecca, explaining angled orientation of part of the building.

[GE[131]] It was on a thousand acres provided rent-free by a European supporter and participant; families of those jailed in protests were welcomed here. By this time Gandhi's public and private lives were almost completely merged. He had mastered the use of symbols to unify his side, shame the opposition, and sway the undecided. In 1913, in the unified South Africa after the 1910 Union, the high courts dropped a bombshell: only Christian marriages were to be considered legal. At a stroke, therefore, all Hindu, Muslim, and Parsi marriages among the Indian community were illegal. Gandhi fought back in part by leading symbolic Indian "invasions" of the Transvaal from Natal, knowing that all, including women and children, would be noisily arrested at the border, jailed and deported back, with the news reaching London and Calcutta.

His fight for Indian civil rights in South Africa by the time he left the country in 1914 was only a partial success. The £3 tax on laborers was rescinded, as was the rule that only Christian marriages were legal. Other restrictions were unchanged, however, and some actually became worse. But the impact on the future of what Gandhi had achieved would not only show up in India after his arrival there, but in the future of South Africa itself. The Indian community there sustained much of its hard-won cohesion and consciousness through later decades. Its fight against the restrictions of apartheid that were imposed from 1948–50, for example, caught the attention and won the grudging admiration of the young Nelson Mandela, who up to this point had no sympathy at all for Communists or Marxists.[21]

Early civil rights struggle part two: J. L. Dube

A promising new school of studies of nationalism is the trans-national, stressing the give and take between developing nationalisms, and what they learned from each other. In that context, consider that just over a mile's walk from Gandhi's first ashram Phoenix Farm[GE[132]] was the Ohlange Institute.[GE[133]] It had been set up in 1901 by the Zulu teacher J. L. Dube. There was lots of going and coming between Ohlange and Phoenix, and it seems probable that Gandhi patterned some of his most important civil rights activities after this Zulu original, and in fact probably bought land in its vicinity on purpose. For that reason, and for the fact that J. L. Dube was chosen first president of the African National Congress (ANC) on its formation in 1912—the institution that more than any other won African civil rights by 1994—perhaps we need to spend some time with him.

Dube's father was the first Zulu Christian minister ordained by the American Zulu Mission in Natal. On the birth of his son in 1871 he named him John Langalibalele Dube—the given names being a Christian name (for the most independent of the four Gospel writers of the New Testament) followed by the name of the Hlubi leader (who was at that time bucking the British rulers of Natal on registration of firearms, as we've seen). In a way J. L. Dube's life would truly be a twining of two strains represented by those names, an American-style Protestant Christianity and a quest for equal treatment for Africans.

After grammar school in the northern edges of Durban, John Dube went to Amanzimtoti College (later Adams College), a Christian institution seventeen or eighteen miles down the coast southeast of Durban.[GE[134]] During his stay there the American headmaster was trying to comply with current government requests for "industrial education" for the Africans being educated there, and the school created programs such as bookbinding, map-making, blacksmithing, and printing. When he was sixteen, in 1887, an American missionary took him under his wing and brought him to the States to attend Oberlin College.[GE[135]] Oberlin was the center of the northern philanthropic circles that were supporting Booker T. Washington's industrial school in Alabama, Tuskegee Institute.[GE[136]] The young John Dube was powerfully impressed with this model, which he

---

131. GE Layer 131 is a Placemark indicating the approximate location of "Tolstoy Farm"; described as having been 35 km southwest of Johannesburg and 2 km from Lawley station. Link below, as of this writing, gives old picture of dwelling: http://de.academic.ru/pictures/dewiki/84/Tolstoy_farm.jpg

132. Open folder titled "Life of J. L. Dube." GE Layer 132 is a Path running the mile and a third from Phoenix Farm to Ohlange.

133. GE Layer 133 is a Placemark referencing Ohlange Institute.

134. GE Layer 134 is a Placemark framing a view of Adams College. Zoom out to see relationship to Durban.

135. GE Layer 135 is a Placemark referencing Oberlin College in northern Ohio.

136. GE Layer 136 is a Placemark referencing Tuskegee University in eastern Alabama.

visited, and in less than fifteen years would create something of a parallel institution in Natal. In a South African setting it would be a more radical institution even than in Alabama, and Dube was always more political in his demands for African representation than Booker Washington was.

By 1901, mostly by speaking tours in the U.S. and Britain, J. L. Dube had raised the funds to buy a couple hundred acres of land for his Zulu Christian Industrial School, later renamed the Ohlange Institute.[GE[137]] In 1903—the same year Gandhi began printing Hindi- and English-language *Indian Opinion*—Dube launched the Zulu- and English-language newspaper *Ilanga lase Natal, "The Sun of Natal."* The author wonders what role J. L. Dube's middle name, Hlubi for "The Glaring Sun," played in the choice of the paper's name.

The Bambatha (Zulu) rebellion of 1906

Earlier, in the wake of the British military crushing of Zulu power in 1879, we saw the destruction, or at least Balkanization, of Zulu power by 1884. The rinderpest epidemic of 1895–1896 killed 90 percent of all Zulu cattle, and a feeble, impoverished Zululand was handed over to Natal in 1897. White farmers, losing more and more cheap black labor to the mines, prevailed on the government in 1905 to levy a £1 poll tax: Africans would presumably have to work more for whites to get the money to pay it.

Bambatha kaMancinza was leader of a Zulu clan of some five thousand people who lived in the Mpanza valley near Greytown—on our corridor less than forty miles north-northeast of Pietermaritzburg.[GE[138]] He first tried to levy the tax, then vacillated, then fled for shelter to Dinuzulu's camp, and finally upon his return to the Mpanza valley discovered that the British had replaced him as clan leader. He then retreated to the famous Nkandla Forest (where Cetswayo was buried), about forty miles northeast of Greytown, as his refuge. [GE[139]] A major British force engaged him near there in a sizeable battle, and he was killed. Perhaps 4,000 other Zulus died in the battle and rebellion.

Gandhi's reaction to this, even though his non-combatant medical corps helped wounded Zulu rebels as well as pro-government forces on the field, was not his finest human rights hour. His *Indian Opinion* said this at the time: "It is not for us to say whether the revolt of the kaffirs is justified or not. We are in Natal by virtue of British power. Our very existence depends upon it. It is therefore our duty to render whatever help we can." Dube's reaction to the rebellion was mixed, but when he was called on the carpet by the governor of Natal for supposedly encouraging it, he apologized and blamed it on his youth. Non-violence for him was not the ethical imperative it was for Gandhi; the lesson of the Bambatha Rebellion he carried all the rest of his life was that violence from the African side was counter-productive, given all the power on the European side.

Dube, the African National Congress, and the Native Lands Act

In 1909, just back from another fund-raising trip to America, Dube attended a meeting of Africans opposed to the draft version of the Union of South Africa act, with its hard-line racial segregation. In 1912 he was chosen head of the South African Native National Congress (later the ANC, with the dropping of the first and third words). In 1913 came the Native Lands Act, which the Act of Union had made possible. Dube bitterly opposed it, correctly foreseeing massive loss of African-owned land to whites, and joined a 1914 delegation to London to protest it. Even though he lost the presidency of the ANC in 1917 because he was seen by others in the movement as too cooperative with the whites, he maintained a remarkably consistent position all of his adult life on the issues of equality and civil rights. In 1942, as head of the "Native Representative Council" of South Africa, he replied in this fashion to a government minister's presentation on the Atlantic Charter:

> You have reminded us that the Charter sums up the cardinal points for post-war reconstruction. They are freedom from fear, freedom from want, freedom from oppression. What do these words mean for us? Does free-

---

137. GE Layer 137 is a Placemark referencing Ohlange High School, as it is called today.

138. GE Layer 138 is a Placemark referencing Greytown.

139. GE Layer 139 is a Placemark referencing Nkandla Forest, which still shows as a dark green patch on the aerial photos of Google Earth.

dom from fear cover fear that our land will be taken away, fear that we are going to be transported to some other part of Africa, fear of the loss of our citizen rights? Does freedom from want mean that we can hope that our people will not starve in these coming months when mealies are kept from our Native areas, that our men get a living wage for themselves and their families? Does freedom from oppression mean that no white man dare hit me or my wife or my children, that no policeman dare break into my home and drive out my wife naked and break up my furniture? Does it mean that the abominable pass laws will be destroyed for ever? Does it mean that my people shall be respected when they move in public places, on the railways, in Native Commissioners' offices and elsewhere? For at the present there are many forms of oppression and many degrees of it.[22]

John Langalibalele Dube died in 1946.[GE[140]] He had twisted and turned his whole life to be true to his people's needs, and to Christianity as he believed it, trying to progress non-violently and by cooperating with at least the Liberal whites. Despite his courage and his decades-long effort, against the settler regime he had little success. More radical elements took the leadership of the civil rights and independence movement away from him in his later years.

Nelson Mandela

In 1994, the same year he was elected South Africa's President in the first democratic vote ever taken in that country, seventy-five-year-old Nelson Mandela published his autobiography, *Long Walk to Freedom*. It is a fascinating story, from his birth in 1918 in the Transkei into a branch of the royal family of the Thembu people of the Xhosa ethnic group, his education in Christian schools, his early aspiration to be a "black Englishman," his acceptance into the law program at the prestigious University of Witwatersrand in Johannesburg, his political activity and eventual activity as head of the armed underground of the African National Congress, his arrest and imprisonment for twenty-seven years, and then suddenly his release, election, and inauguration. That 1994 election which brought the ANC to power and him to the Presidency was the first in which he as an African had ever been allowed to vote. It seems to be a remarkably honest and self-critical book, as autobiographies go, and two important "passages" in the young Mandela's life—first, when he turned to black nationalism as the only possible solution to throwing off imperial control, and second, when he embraced elements, at least, of Marxism as a most efficient tool of a broader nationalism—bear looking at in some detail. The reader will recognize that the present author has spent much of the textbook to this point to explain the attraction of precisely those two -isms. Nelson Mandela and those he chooses to quote do it here with more precision, power and brevity.

First, in 1943 at age twenty-four or twenty-five, in his first year in the exciting city of Johannesburg and in the pre-law curriculum at Witwatersrand, Mandela met Anton Lembede, one of the small handful of accredited black lawyers in all South Africa. Lembede was preaching a philosophy he called Africanism—"black is beautiful," improve your self-image and your self-reliance, and determine your own destiny. As Mandela remembered it, Lembede had learned from his teaching experience in the Orange Free State the power of Afrikaner nationalism, and was consciously using it as a model for a competing African nationalism. Mandela quoted this passage verbatim from Lembede's *Indundla ya Bantu*, a newspaper in Natal for Africans, and his reaction to it:

> The history of modern times is the history of nationalism. Nationalism has been tested in the people's struggles and the fires of battle and found to be the only antidote against foreign rule and modern imperialism. It is for that reason that the great imperialist powers feverishly endeavor with all their might to discourage and eradicate all nationalistic tendencies among their alien subject; for that purpose huge and enormous sums of money are lavishly expended on propaganda against nationalism which is dismissed as 'narrow,' 'barbarous,' 'uncultured,' 'devilish,' etc. Some alien subjects become dupes of this sinister propaganda and consequently become tools or instruments of imperialism for which great service they are highly praised by the imperialistic power and showered with such epithets as 'cultured,' 'liberal,' 'progressive,' 'broadminded,' etc.

---

140. GE Layer 140 is a Placemark referencing J. L. Dube's house and memorial garden.

Lembede's views struck a chord in me. I, too, had been susceptible to paternalistic British colonialism and the appeal of being perceived by whites as 'cultured' and 'progressive' and 'civilized.' I was already on my way to being drawn into the black elite that Britain sought to create in Africa. That is what everyone from the regent [his guardian in early life] to Mr. Sidelsky [a liberal white lawyer for whom Mandela had worked] had wanted for me. But it was an illusion. Like Lembede, I came to see the antidote as militant African nationalism.[23]

The second critical passage in Mandela's political life occurred in 1950, when he would have been about thirty-one years old. The Nationalist Party, mainly representing the Afrikaners, had won the national elections in 1948 and in a year or so had rammed through the basic laws that instituted full apartheid, as discussed earlier. On May 1, 1950, Communists—some of whom were in the ANC with Mandela—declared a May Day strike and march. Eighteen of the marchers were killed and the government not only outlawed all Communists but made the mildest protests subject to the same ten-year imprisonment penalty. It was apparently around the June 26, 1950, National Day of Protest against these deaths and the new decrees that Mandela began to join ranks with the Communists, a group he had firmly rejected before. After what he had seen, he could no longer question their devotion and courage in pursuit of civil rights for all; and now he wrestled with their ideology as well.

In Mandela's systematic study of Marxist literature, he was positively struck by the parallel between the classless society it described and traditional, communal African life. Marxist economic and social analysis helped him "transcend" black-white relations and put South African struggles in a broader world perspective. Its call to revolutionary action "was music to the ears of a freedom fighter," he said, and the whole dialectic— that things don't seem to be progressing, but change will surely come suddenly—was very appealing. He also recognized that current Marxists and Marxist governments had a lot of very practical help to offer national liberation movements. The reader of the text in hand has already seen, in the chapter on Russia and Socialism, the author's evaluation of the strengths and weaknesses of Marxism. On the "strengths" side, it is all elegantly encapsulated by Mandela in these two or three pages of his autobiography: the warm ideal of a shared and communal life in both past and future; Marxism as a "scientific" and therefore supposedly verifiable system; subsistence wages paid by capitalists who keep the value-added increment of what is produced for themselves; the hope that believing change comes in revolutionary jumps can bring at a time when little seems to be happening; justification for immediate action to those already inclined to action; practical information for national liberation movements; substantive help from the Soviet Union. The next paragraph in Mandela's book, however, firmly places Marxism as secondary to his nationalism. His friends had suggested the Marxists were using him, but he replied, "who is to say that we [the African nationalists] were not using them?"[24]

Albert Luthuli

In these early 1950s Nelson Mandela was not yet the ANC's key figure; that was Albert Luthuli, a Zulu Christian twenty years his senior. Luthuli was born to a missionary father in Southern Rhodesia but sent back when he was ten to the family home in Groutville, in our corridor near the lower Tugela River.[GE[141]] He was educated in Christian schools in Natal, first in Edendale and then at Adam's College. He remained there as part of the staff from 1920–35. He was a professional educator, eventually head of the main African teachers' association, and an active (Methodist) Christian lay preacher. In 1935 he was chosen chief of the Christian Zulu community around Groutville, and came into much more direct contact with the white legal authorities. In 1945 he joined the ANC. By 1948 his horizons had expanded considerably with visits to a Christian conference in India and a nine-month-long Christian-sponsored tour of the U.S.

In 1952 the ANC and some others sponsoring a "Defiance Campaign" to the new apartheid laws chose April 6, 1952—the tricentennial of Jan van Riebeeck's landing so idolized by Afrikaners—for mass protests. Albert Luthuli was the leading light of the campaign, and he was ordered by the government to give up either his chieftainship or his membership in the ANC. When he refused to choose, the government chose for him,

---

141. GE Layer 141 is a Placemark referencing Groutville (near Stanger; both in GE gazetter).

firing him as chief. By the end of the year he had been elected head of the ANC. In March of 1954 the ANC and several other anti-apartheid groups met near his home so he could chair their joint meeting (he had been "banned," the South African government's version of restricting travel or in extreme cases virtual house arrest). The result of this meeting was a "Call" (satiric echo of *Die Stem*?) to a "Congress of the People" to be held June 26–27, 1955, at Kliptown, one of the "townships" of Soweto, near Johannesburg.[GE[142]]

Over three thousand people, of all races, showed up for the Congress. Both the Freedom Charter distributed there—a classic manifesto of civil and economic equality—and the meeting itself, looking back, were key civil rights consciousness-raisers. And when the police showed up in armored vehicles on the second day of the Congress, arresting some and seizing all papers to be used in future treason trials, and then evicting everyone at rifle-point, the hard edge of apartheid showed up in headline stories in newspapers around the world. The first of the great apartheid "show trials" was set in motion, a spectacle that would last four years. Over 150 were originally arrested for treason; by August of 1958 when the trial actually began ninety-one were actually charged. By November 1960 all but thirty had been released, and every one of the thirty was found innocent of the charge of treason by the Supreme Court in its final March 1961 decision.

The P.A.C. and the Sharpeville massacre

There were two ideological groups of protestors of apartheid that were less than satisfied with the Freedom Charter. One was the liberals, worried about implications for land redistribution and other future central government functions that they thought had the potential to be, if not dictatorial, then less than liberal. The other were the Africanists, mainly young black radicals who were disappointed that race was not mentioned more in the Charter, and who believed only Africans should lead the movement. By this time Nelson Mandela and other key players had emerged from the "Youth League" of the ANC to take over real leadership (Luthuli was only nominally head by this point). In 1958 this current leadership locked the younger Africanists—whose beliefs Mandela had shared back in his "Lembede" phase, ironically enough—out of a 1958 ANC meeting. By 1959 the Africanists had created their own rival organization to the ANC, the Pan-Africanist Congress.

It was this ANC-PAC rivalry that set the stage for the Sharpeville massacre of 1960. The ANC set March 31 as the date for nation-wide protests, among other demands setting a minimum daily wage of one South African pound (the "rand" was not introduced as South Africa's currency until the next year, 1961, when South Africa declared itself a Republic and broke with the Commonwealth). The PAC declared *their* day of protest March 21, and set a higher demand for minimum wage.

Meanwhile, racial tension had grown. The treason trial was still dragging on, and more immediately there were several notable clashes, especially along our corridor. In 1959 Durban's townships had rioted, and protest marches of African women had been broken up in Pretoria. In January of this crucial 1960, authorities had set up transit camps in the Cato Manor area of Durban, a "squatter" town about four miles from downtown.[GE[143]] The population was to be relocated to the KwaMashu reserve under the "homelands" strategy. Nine policemen were killed in riots there at Cato Manor.

Sharpeville[GE[144]] itself was an unremarkable township near Vereeniging, and several thousand protesters turned out there on March 21 in response to the PAC-declared mass resistance. They were not armed, and many had apparently come just to be arrested for burning their passbooks. But the small garrison of thirty police seems to have panicked, especially with their fresh memories of dead police at Cato Manor. They opened fire, and 69 of the protesters were killed and another 180 wounded—many of them women, most shot in the back. When news of that spread around the country, many other riots took place. Chief Luthuli burned his own passbook in sympathy on March 27, and on March 28 the government outlawed both PAC and ANC and began the arrest of some 18,000 suspects. Albert Luthuli won the Nobel Peace Prize for 1960 (it was awarded 1961), the first real heads-up of how strongly the outside world disapproved of apartheid.

---

142. GE Layer 142 is a Placemark referencing Walter Sisulu Square in Kliptown.

143. GE Layer 143 is a Placemark referencing Cato Manor area; totally rebuilt today.

144. GE Layer 144 is a Placemark referencing Sharpeville.

Mandela, whose "M-plan" had already tried to prepare the ANC for underground survival, himself went underground. He headed *Umkhonto we Sizwe*, "Spear of the Nation" or just M.K., the new military wing of the ANC. He led police on a merry chase for a year and more, occasionally popping up just long enough to give a provocative interview to a journalist; the press started calling him "the Black Pimpernel" (in comparison with the Scarlet Pimpernel, fictional hero of a popular British play who rescued French aristocrats from the guillotine in the Terror). Mandela was finally arrested (not far from Pietermaritzburg) on August 5, 1962.[GE145] A five-year jail term would stretch to twenty-seven, before his release in 1990.

The PAC also set up its own underground military, *Poqo* ("We Go It Alone," sounding a lot like the Irish *Sinn Fein*, "We Ourselves"). The sabotage targets of the MK were mainly material—electrical pylons, police buildings, etc. Poqo had less reticence about killing people. Both the MK and Poqo set up offices out of country, in London, in Tanganyika's (soon to be Tanzania's) Dar-es-Salaam, and eventually in other parts of Africa. They had little military success against the apartheid regime, which made military service compulsory for all young white males and invested heavily in the armed forces in general.

Steve Biko and "Black consciousness"

The next real shift in political consciousness in South Africa came not so much from the outlawed PAC and ANC as from the 1960s-era university radicalism seeping in from all over the Atlantic world (from Mexico's "Autonomous National University" campus in Mexico City to the Boulevard Saint-Michel in Paris)—and especially the Black Consciousness/Black Power movement coming from the United States. The most famous leader of this movement in South Africa was Steve Biko. A Xhosa, born in 1946 some 250 miles west of our corridor, he attended a famous Catholic mission school at Mariannhill[GE146] just outside Durban, and went on to the University of Natal in downtown Durban, just at the head of the Bay of Natal, to study medicine.[GE147] The med school there had only been established in 1950, a "black faculty" in a "white institution," remembered proudly by its website today as "synonymous with the struggle for democracy and racial equality." It was while in med school that Biko broke with an anti-apartheid group led by liberal whites and founded SOSA, the South African Students Association. By 1972 he was one of the founders of the Black People's Convention, and its work to represent black unions illegal under apartheid, and to get appropriate legal and medical expertise to black people, came to dominate his life: he dropped out of med school. He was "banned" by the government in 1973—effectively sent back to the Transkei where he had grown up—but his great leadership skills had already set the Black Consciousness Movement in motion. It was on a collision course with apartheid, since the first "homeland" or Bantustan was set to go independent in 1976, supposed to end forever any claim to civil rights by any African assigned to that unit anywhere except in that particular Bantustan.

The Soweto riots

It all came to a head in Soweto on June 16, 1976. A heavy-handed imposition of Afrikaans as the language of instruction in black schools drew a protest of high school students who marched on Orlando West. They were unarmed, but their general feeling was that their teachers and parents had failed, so they would do it themselves. Police fired into the crowd, and there were deaths and injuries. An iconic photograph was taken of a boy and girl running away, the boy with a dying friend in his arms—terror on their faces equal to that of the Vietnamese children running to escape an American napalm attack made in another iconic photo from another conflict just a few years earlier. The dying boy in Soweto was Hector Peterson, for whom a memorial is named

---

145. GE Layer 145 is a Placemark showing where Mandela was arrested, outside Howick some fifteen miles from Pietermaritzburg.

146. GE Layer 146 is a Placemark referencing Mariannhill, in the outskirts of Durban, though this may be the center of the neighborhood, not the school itself.

147. GE Layer 147 is a Placemark referencing the med school of the University of Natal, just at the head of the Bay of Natal.

there today.[GE¹⁴⁸] These few early deaths, and the turning of police dogs loose on the students, triggered a mass riot. Over 500 students were killed, just in Soweto, along with some whites who were killed by Africans just because they were white. Riots spread all over the country, peaking in November and December. The riots were fiercer than those that had followed Sharpeville, as were the reprisals. In 1977 Steve Biko was arrested and—it was suspected at the time and confirmed later—beaten to death by police.

From this time on, there was a background level of anti-apartheid violence the regime could not repress. The Dictionary of South African English defines the phrase "lost generation" as the name given to that generation of black people who left school at the time of the Soweto uprising of 1976, and either went into exile or got involved in the country-wide disturbances of the 1980s. One of the best modern histories of South Africa says simply, "To say that the Homeland policy was collapsing in disarray by the mid-1980s would be an understatement."²⁵ A broad world anti-apartheid coalition of nations grew up. The U.S. Congress, for example, passed a Comprehensive Anti-Apartheid Act in 1986 that forbade everything from the sale of computers to direct air flights to South Africa. It didn't just squeak by, it resoundingly passed, easily overriding a presidential veto from Ronald Reagan.

July's People

Nadine Gordimer, South Africa's first Nobel Prize for Literature winner, was born (in 1923) and raised in Springs on the eastern end of the Rand.[GE¹⁴⁹] As she said, "The natural features of my landscape were mine headgear and man-made hills of yellow sand from the mines." Her father was a Jewish jeweler from Eastern Europe who, although he had emigrated to escape racial persecution, seemed to be racist himself, at least in black and white matters. Illness kept Nadine out of school and isolated in her early teen years, and reading and writing were her solace: she had her first piece accepted by a magazine at age fifteen. She did spend a year at the University of Witwatersrand in Johannesburg,[GE¹⁵⁰] and when she was twenty-six or so moved to Johannesburg for good. Her house in the upscale northern business suburb of Parktown[GE¹⁵¹] was full of art and gatherings of talented people, an aspect of the intellectual vibrancy of Johannesburg. It was also a safe-house for black freedom fighters. Although she did not admit association with the ANC until 1990 when it became legal, she and her husband had supported the fight for African freedom from the 1960s.

Most of her fiction has an element of autobiography in it; her 1981 novel *July's People* was this way. The female lead, Maureen, came from a small mining town and when the main action picks up is living a comfortable life in Johannesburg with her husband Bam, both proud of their liberal attitudes towards racial equality. But the race war heats up, ground-to-air missiles shut down Jan Smuts Airport, and this "liberal" couple leave town in a yellow pickup truck with their middle-aged "houseboy" July to try to weather the storm in his village. Trying not to ruin the ending for those who have not yet read it, suffice it to say that here in the village they discover just how shallow their liberalism is, or perhaps how shallow liberalism's solutions for the racial divide are. And as in almost all of her work, Gordimer sharply inquires into gender roles; in the novel Maureen is much quicker to sense social realities than her husband. But the main point for this chapter is how utterly convincing the book is about the all-out race war bound to come, and soon, if the rigid defenders of apartheid in South Africa continued their ways.²⁶

Even the Nationalist Party saw the writing on the wall. In late 1989 it elected Frederic Willem De Klerk its new President. Although from an old Nationalist Party political dynasty, a Potchefstroom law graduate, and until recently a life-long supporter of apartheid, within days of his election he lifted the ban on the ANC, and shortly thereafter Nelson Mandela was freed. The first one-adult, one-vote election in the country's history took place in 1994. In those elections Mandela cast his vote at the Ohlange Institute in the outskirts of Durban. It

---

148. GE Layer 148 is a Placemark referencing the Hector Peterson Memorial in Soweto. A Google–Images "Soweto riots" search will turn up multiple copies of the famous picture. The girl is Hector's younger sister Antoinette; the boy was Mbuyisa Makhubo.

149. Open folder titled "Life of Gordimer." GE Layer 149 is Placemark referencing Springs.

150. GE Layer 150 is Placemark referencing "Wits" (U. of Witwatersrand).

151. GE Layer 151 is a Placemark generally referencing Parktown area.

was classic Mandela, paying homage to the first president of the ANC, as well as a tip of the hat to a Zulu figure by a Thembu/Xhosa in the current ethnically charged atmosphere.[GE[152]]

Buthelezi and Inkatha

The bad blood was mainly Xhosa versus Zulu, expressed as a clash between the Xhosa-dominated ANC and
the Zulu-dominated IFP or "Inkatha Freedom Party" of Mangosuthu Buthelezi. The Inkatha, you may recall,
was that woven grass coil that had became the spiritual symbol of the Zulu nation back in Shaka's day. In the
1920s, the current Zulu king, grandson of Cetswayo, Solomon kaDinuzulu, had used the name for a cultural
revival group. Buthelezi was a Zulu clan chief who in 1972, the year a fragmented Zululand was being constructed, pulled off the brilliant trick of getting the government to recognize his clan (which had provided political advisors to the Zulu royal family) instead of the royal clan itself as the responsible political voice of the
Zulus. In 1975 he formally revived the Zulu cultural movement as *Inkatha YaKwaZulu*, and it gradually became
a Zulu-based political party under his leadership.

By 1976 Buthelezi was close to Black Consciousness leaders including Steve Biko, and was trying to pull
together all the "Homelands" leaders into a sort of African national convention to stop the "divide and rule"
strategy of Vorwaert's Homelands policy. In that year Buthelezi formally proposed a "Federal Union of Autonomous States of Southern Africa," although events beginning in June of that year in Soweto eclipsed it. Inkatha
became more and more a Zulu nationalist party, with Buthelezi protective of his own power and Inkatha
increasingly intolerant of any other power in its own "territory."

In the mid-1980s, as was revealed by the South African government in 1991, Inkatha began to be heavily
subsidized by the government as a counterweight to the ANC. A series of bloody clashes between Zulus and
non-Zulus broke out in 1985, especially in KwaZulu-Natal. This is when "necklacing" as a term was invented
for the horrific act of putting an old tire filled with gasoline around a victim's neck and setting it afire. It was
in this year that the buildings of Gandhi's old ashram Phoenix Farm in the outskirts of Durban were destroyed
in such ethnic riots.

Desmond Tutu and the Truth and Reconciliation Commission

Many churches and other Christian institutions played a role in changing South Africa. One interesting sidelight shows up in a brief re-visiting of Rorke's Drift. In the apartheid era, under the Group Areas Act, little
Rorke's Drift had been declared a "white's only" area. But in 1963 an Evangelical Lutheran Church mission
moved into the abandoned buildings there and established an Art and Craft Center employing African craftsmen. It was constantly challenged by the government and lived a precarious existence. Recently its story was
told in a book titled *Rorke's Drift Empowering Prints: Twenty Years of Printmaking in South Africa*.[27] Most of
the prints shown are linocut; the stories of the administrators and artists of the center are equally interesting.[28]

The one last key figure in this drama is one who most famously represented Christian institutions: Archbishop Desmond Mpilu Tutu. He was born in 1931 in Klerksdorp,[GE[153]] about twenty-five miles west of our
corridor. The family moved when he was eight, when his father got a new teaching job, to Ventersdorp,[GE[154]]
just in the northwestern corner of our rectangle. But then a couple of years later the family moved again with
the father's teaching job, to the Johannesburg area. All of Desmond Tutu's really formative years were here,
on the Rand—in Roodeport, in Munsieville (the black township of Krugersdorp), commuting to Western High
School (the only secondary education available to blacks in the western Rand), school vacations with his grandmother in Boksberg, twenty months in a TB ward at the hospital in Rietfontein.[GE[155]]

---

152. GE Layer 152 is a Placemark referencing Ohlange, which you've already seen; a Google–Images search of "Mandela
voting" will yield at least a dozen photos of him casting his 1994 ballot.

153. GE Layer 153 is a Placemark referencing Klerksdorp.

154. GE Layer 154 is a Placemark referencing Ventersdorp.

155. GE Layer 155 is a folder titled "Tutu on the Rand & nearby"; it includes a Placemark for each of the towns or schools
named above, a visual illustration of how his growing up was thoroughly intertwined with the Rand.

He was in a way that new South African creation, the Pan-African: his father was Xhosa, his mother was Tswana and his maternal grandmother was Sotho, and he grew up speaking all three languages at home. A brilliant student with something close to a photographic memory, he routinely topped his classes at every level of his education. His original professional dream was to be a doctor, but medical school was impossibly expensive, given his family's finances. So he trained to be a teacher, attending the new "Bantu Normal School" just outside Pretoria. He then taught secondary school for four years, from 1954–58, in Munsieville beside his father's primary school. But in the spring of 1955 the government began to apply the Bantu Education Act, severely limiting the subjects Africans could study and financially strangling any schools that bucked the system. By 1958 Tutu in frustration gave up teaching, and switched career tracks to theological seminary and the ministry. He enrolled in St. Peter's, an "Anglo-Catholic" (Anglican, though operated by a Catholic-like monastic order) seminary at Rosettenville,[GE156] just south of Jo'burg.

Either in the ministry or as professor in theological schools, he spiraled his way up in the Anglican system, broadening his horizons with several years in London, with stints in Swaziland and Lesotho. The explosion at Soweto in 1976, in particular, seemed to galvanize him politically. Exploring the new currents of Liberation Theology coming in from Latin America, as well as Black Theology coming in from the wider Atlantic world, he became perhaps the most vocal critic of apartheid while still seriously preaching Christian non-violence—and forgiveness of one's enemies. In 1978 he moved back to Johannesburg as General Secretary of the SACC, the South African Council of Churches. This council (which did not include the Dutch Reformed Church) had been generally critical of apartheid, and that criticism sharpened under Tutu's leadership. He made it a point to live in Soweto.[GE157] In those intervals when the apartheid government allowed him to travel, he spoke widely in America and Europe about the importance of economically boycotting the South African state, comparing it to the Nazi and Soviet systems. When critics asked him if such a boycott would not hurt African workers, he replied that a short-term pain was acceptable to end a long-time evil. At the same time his marvelous sense of humor and his vision of a state based on a "rainbow nation"—his famous phrase—won over many white voters in South Africa.

The regime never really knew how to deal with him, especially after he won the Nobel Peace Prize in 1984, was made Bishop of Johannesburg (its first black bishop) in 1985, and head of the Anglican church for all of South Africa in 1986.

Five years after the event, he remembered how apprehensive he was on the eve of the 1994 first-ever democratic election in South Africa. Buthelezi and his Inkatha Freedom Party were threatening to boycott the elections and return to the bloody clashes of 1985.[29] But the elections came off fairly peacefully, the ANC won an absolute majority, and in 1995, within a year, the new President Nelson Mandela called for a "Truth and Reconciliation Commission"—which came to be headed by Bishop Tutu, logically enough, because it was basically his plan.

Between the extremes of black revenge for the brutality that was apartheid on one hand, and the "forgive and forget" advice on the other hand, the TRC said forgive, yes, but forget, no. The only way to heal a festering wound is to open it; then real healing can begin. The TRC called for amnesty of all but the most egregious of human rights violators, if they would only come clean before the commission. So for five years the Commission sat, and documented and judged, and published its findings in 1999 in five clearly written, powerful volumes.[30]

The Truth and Reconciliation Commission report is not only about white-on-black violence, but black-on-white and black-on-black. Winnie Mandela had gathered a "football team" of young thugs based at her house, and the report—over her indignant rejections of all the evidence—dealt with eighteen murders or disappearances connected with that group, many of them carried out in the back rooms of her house. ANC vs. IFP violence is detailed. Considerable time is spent exposing MK and Poqo violence against whites. But the great weight of the volumes accurately reflects the regime's violence towards its black opponents. The torture and

---

156. GE Layer 156 is a Placemark referencing Rosettenville.

157. GE Layer 157 is a Placemark locating Desmond Tutu's house on Vilikazi Street, famous as the only street two future Nobel Prize winners lived on (Mandela's house is just down the street). Explore Photos icons "Desmond Tutu House Soweto" for Archbishop Tutu's original home, and Photos icon "Mandela's house Orlando (Soweto)."

the tens of thousands of deaths remind a reader somewhat of Solzhenitsyn's *Gulag Archipelago*. The five volumes manage to communicate the enormity of the violence, and still illustrate with the smallest of vignettes that also turn out to be unforgettable: the harassment of the two school children in the photo with the dying Hector Peterson, one his sister, and the other the boy emigrating to Nigeria to escape it and last heard from in a letter to his mother in 1978 . . . .

The current state of affairs, post-apartheid, and lessons learned

Nelson Mandela, who could have been "President for Life" and dictator, chose the path of George Washington and in 1999 voluntarily stepped down as President after a five-year term in office. The ANC won 63 percent of the vote in that year, electing Thabo Mbeki as President, and in the next voting cycle of 2004 won 69 percent of the vote—over the two-thirds required by the constitution to change basic laws such as the President may serve no more than two terms. That has not happened to date, but Mbeki was high-handed enough to win Archbishop Tutu's sharp criticism. A European-trained economist, from 1999 to 2009 Mbeki generally kept the economic structure intact, but promoted such irrational government policies as refusing to recognize that HIV causes AIDS—and this in a country ravaged by it.

Crime against property and persons is what you would expect anyplace with 40 percent and upwards unemployment; many wealthy whites—and more recently some wealthy blacks—live in enclaves behind hurricane fences and guard dog runs. There is a new problem with poor whites, especially from the Afrikaner community which for forty-six years got virtually all the patronage jobs in government. Despite their very real plight, there is not much sympathy for them from the majority black population—which suffered at their hands and which still has a much larger poverty problem of its own.

South Africa is still, for a first-time visitor, a startling combination of first and third worlds existing side by side. Government offices and business firms looking for first world caliber black expertise are to a certain extent check-mated because of how successfully the government limited black education in those decades of apartheid, and yet with dramatically rising black expectations, white professional leadership is no longer acceptable.

What final lessons can be drawn about national belonging from the modern South African experience to date? Since 1800 or so, as you have seen in earlier parts of this text, by far the most common pattern has been building new nation-states on language (primarily) and religious (secondarily) units. This hasn't really happened in South Africa. Not even a Zulu nation-state came into being. Why not? There are perhaps ten million Zulus, fairly tightly grouped in what is today KwaZulu-Natal. J. L. Dube, in addition to heading up the original ANC in 1912, wrote the first novel in Zulu, and modern historians of nationalism are virtually unanimous that such literature creation is a key building block towards erecting the modern nation-state. Mangosuthu Buthelezi, as late as the 1980s, seemed fairly well on his way to creating a Zulu state with his political gifts and ruthless drive as demonstrated in the Inkatha Freedom Party. Yet in the last elections in South Africa the IFP was down to 3 percent or so of the national vote, with even the majority of Zulus voting for the ANC— proving that classic "tribal" nationalism, which seemed viable as recently as a few decades ago, is no longer so. This may in part be due to that old subconscious need to belong to a unit large enough for economic and military survival; perhaps even Zulus realized that even if they got an independent state of their own, it would always be second-class under apartheid.

Another reason this hasn't happened in South Africa, and much of the rest of Africa as well, is the nature of modern political borders in the continent. In Africa, political boundaries are still mainly those drawn on European diplomatic tables a century and more ago—straight lines and even arcs that paid no attention to ethnic lines on the ground, or along rivers whose basins often had common cultures on both banks. One example of the absurdity of such lines is the present-day border between Tanzania and Kenya. In the 1880s Germany and Britain agreed on a straight line from the coast to Lake Victoria to divide these as their respective colonies. On closer inspection the German delegation was piqued that it gave Britain both the high mountains of east Africa, Mt. Kenya and Mt. Kilimanjaro. The British obligingly drew a little arc north around Kilimanjaro to put it in the German sphere, and then continued a new straight line from the end of the arc on to the great lake. South Africa's borders, and the borders of the four traditional states of Cape Province, Natal, the Orange Free

State, and the Transvaal, are almost equally European determined. All sorts of vested interests grow around political units, and they take on a momentum of their own over time, even if they cut across basic ethnic lines of belonging.

Overall, it was a Tswana/Sotho/Xhosa/Zulu Pan-African nationalism—as modeled on Afrikaner nationalism—that has emerged as the dominant force in modern South Africa. Ethnicity was eroded in the mines, and Bantu languages were to some extent replaced by Fanakalo and even English. For almost half a century the "Bantu" 80 percent of the country suffered equally the punishment of apartheid, and in the process forged some Pan-African group unity. On the other hand the newer "rainbow nation" nationalism championed first by Desmond Tutu and latterly by Nelson Mandela—including Indians (perhaps 2 percent of the population), the Afrikaans-speaking "Cape Coloureds" (9 percent), and the whites (around 6 percent Afrikaner and 3 percent English)—is having a hard time cementing over the white-black racial divide. Since 1994 you have had the flight abroad of perhaps a third of the white population (including white-controlled wealth).

It may still be too early to tell if South Africa is heading towards a Robert Mugabe-style dictatorship as in next-door Zimbabwe, or a multi-racial society in which the components are generally respectful of each other, or something in-between. The success with which South Africa hosted the 2010 World Cup soccer ("football") match seems to augur well for the immediate future.

But overall what a dramatic landscape, and what an incredible human story has played out here, and is still unfolding.

Endnotes

1. See Mary Marshall Thomas, *The Harmless People,* Revised ed. (Vintage Books, 1989), especially its 1989 epilogue written thirty years after the first edition.

2. See *Oxford English Dictionary* entry.

3. H. Rider Haggard, *King Solomon's Mines* (Peterborough, Ontario: Broadview Press, 2002), pp. 60–61. Originally published in 1885.

4. David Lewis-Williams, *Images of Mystery: Rock Art of the Drakensberg* (Cape Town: Double Storey Books, 2003), p. 35.

5. Marguerite Poland and David Hammond-Tooke, with artwork by Leigh Voigt, *The Abundant Herds: A celebration of the cattle of the Zulu people* (Vlaeberg: Fernwood Press, 2003).

6. Kevin Shillington, *History of Africa* (New York: St. Martin's Press, 1989), p. 267.

7. This account is largely from one of the great books in the English language on South African history, Donald R. Morris's *The Washing of the Spears: A History of the Rise of the Zulu Nation under Shaka and Its Fall in the Zulu War of 1879* (New York: Simon and Schuster, 1965), especially his chapter called "The Rise of the Zulu Nation."

8. Patrick Harries, "Imagery, Symbolism and Tradition in a South African Bantustan: Mangouthu Buthelezi, Inkatha, and Zulu History," in *History and Theory*, vol. 32, No. 4, Beiheft 32: History Making in Africa (Dec., 1993), pp. 107–8.

9. John Wright and Andrew Manson, *The Hlubi Chiefdom in Zululand-Natal: A History* (Ladysmith: Ladysmith Historical Society, 1983).

10. John B. Wright's *Bushman Raiders of the Drakensberg*, p. 56.

11. James O. Gump, in his review of Guy's *The View Across the River: Harriette Colenso and the Zulu Struggle against Imperialism*, AHR.

12. Jeff Guy, *The View Across the River: Harriette Colenso and the Zulu Struggle against Imperialism* (Charlottesville, VA: University Press of Virginia, 2002).

13. Guy, *View Across the River*, p. 162.

14. T. Dunbar Moodie, *The Rise of Afrikanerdom: Power, Apartheid, and the Afrikaner Civil Religion* (Berkeley: University of California Press, 1975), p. 160. Moodie, a South African born in 1940, spent some years studying at Harvard where he became fascinated with the Puritan legacy thereabouts; he says it helped him see this Afrikaner "Puritanism" in a larger framework.(p. x)

15. Penny Silva (ed.), *A Dictionary of South African English on historical principles*. Oxford and New York: Oxford University Press, 1996.

16. Mark Twain, *Following the Equator: A Journey Around the World* (Hopewell, NJ: Ecco Press, 1993), vol. II, p. 308. Originally published in New York: P. F. Collins, 1897.

17. Thomas Pakenham, *The Boer War* (New York: Random House, 1979), p. 177.

18. T. Dunbar Moodie, *The Rise of Afrikanerdom* (Berkeley: The University of California Press, 1975), p. 47.

19. Albert Grundlingh and Hilary Sapire, "From Feverish Festival to Repetitive Ritual? The Changing Fortunes of Great Trek Mythology in an Industrializing South Africa, 1938–1988," *South African Historical Journal* 21 (1989), pp. 19–37.

20. Paul F. Power, "Gandhi in South Africa," *Journal of Modern African Studies* vol. 7 no. 3 (1969), pp. 441–455.

21. Judith M. Brown, *Gandhi: Prisoner of Hope* (New Haven & London: Yale U Pr, 1989); see especially Chapters 2 (South African Experience I: The Self-Taught Political Apprentice) and 3 (South African Experience II: The Satyagrahi).

22. Quoted in Shula Marks, "The Ambiguities of Dependence: John L. Dube of Natal," in *Journal of Southern African Studies*, Vol. 1, No. 2 (Apr. 1975), p. 166.

23. Nelson Mandela, *Long Walk to Freedom: The Autobiography of Nelson Mandela* (Boston: Little, Brown and Co., 1994), pp. 84–85.

24. Mandela, *Long Walk to Freedom*, pp. 104–5.

25. Davenport and Saunders, p. 487.

26. Nadine Gordimer, *July's People* (Penguin Books, 1982).

27. Philippa Hobbs & Elizabeth Rankin, *Rorke's Drift Empowering Prints: Twenty Years of Printmaking in South Africa* (Cape Town: Double Storey Books, 2003), pp. 4–5.

28. Philippa Hobbs & Elizabeth Rankin, *Rorke's Drift Empowering Prints: Twenty Years of Printmaking in South Africa* (Cape Town: Double Storey Books, 2003), pp. 4–5.

29. Desmond Mpilo Tutu, *No Future Without Forgiveness* (New York: Doubleday, 1999), p. 3. See also Shirley du Boulay, *Tutu: Voice of the Voiceless* (Grand Rapids, Michigan: William B. Eerdmans Publishing Co., 1988).

30. *Truth and Reconciliation Commission of South Africa Report*, 5 vols. (New York: Grove's Dictionaries Inc., 1999).

Chapter Ten

"To Create a New State": The Damascus-South-to-Water Corridor of the Mideast

"To create a new State is neither ridiculous nor impossible. Haven't we witnessed the process in our own day, among nations which were not largely middle class as we are, but poorer, less educated, and consequently weaker than ourselves?"

—Theodor Herzl, *The Jewish State,* 1896[1]

"A nation which has long been in the depths of sleep only awakes if it is rudely shaken by events, and only arises little by little . . . . This was the situation of Palestine, which for many centuries had been in the deepest sleep, until it was shaken by the great war, shocked by the Zionist movement, and violated by the illegal policy [of the British], and it awoke, little by little."

—Khalil al-Sakakini, *Palestine After the Great War,* 1925[2]

CONTENTS

The heart of the matter—SECTION A: LANGUAGE AND TOPOGRAPHY—A brief introduction to Hebrew and Arabic—Topography and texture of the "Damascus south to water" corridor—A word on climate, and especially the availability of water—A "fruit ladder" of traditional routes across the land—SECTION B: BACKGROUND OF THE MODERN STATE OF ISRAEL—Beginnings—Greeks and Romans—Diaspora—Ashkenazi Jews: the European settlement—Enlightenment and Haskalah—The closing of the doors—Zionism: a quick definition—Ben-Yehuda and the rebirth of spoken Hebrew—The First Aliyah—Theodor Herzl and the Zionist Congresses—*The Fiddler on the Roof*—Ahad Ha'am—The Second Aliyah—Manya Shochat—A. D. Gordon—David Ben-Gurion—Chaim Weizmann and the Balfour Declaration—World War I in the region—Massive Arab backlash—Vladimir Jabotinsky and the Jewish Legion—BETAR and Irgun—British policies in the last years of the mandate—Independence—Politics and the "Ingathering of the Exiles"—SECTION C: BACKGROUND OF MODERN ARAB NATIONALISM IN GENERAL—The last chapters of Imperial Roman rule—The glory days of Arabic poetry—The life of Muhammad—Muslim expansion AD 632–732—The Arab kingdoms—Invasion from west and east: Crusaders and Mongols—*The Arabian Nights' Entertainment,* or the *1001 Nights*—Ottoman rule—The pilgrimage road—The challenge of the West—Muhammad Ali and Ibrahim Pasha—Protestant mission schools and the Arab Awakening—Reform and Reaction: from Tanzimat to Abdul Hamid II—Young Turks, Sharif Hussein, and "Lawrence of Arabia"—From the Sykes-Picot Agreement to the Hashemite Kingdoms—SECTION D: MODERN PALESTINIAN NATIONALISM IN THE LARGER CONTEXT OF ARAB, MUSLIM, AND WORLD EVENTS—How Tanzimat ("The Reforms") worked out in Palestine—The Afula land transfer of 1910—World War I and the first years of the mandate: intellectuals "imagining" the community—The Arab Revolt and World War II—*Al-Nakba*, the Catastrophe—The rise of Egypt's Gamal Abdal Nasser—Yasser Arafat, *al-Fatah*, and the P.L.O.—From the Ramadan/Yom Kippur War to the Camp David Accords—"Outside" and "Inside": from the *Intifada* to the Oslo Accords—Palestinians, Israelis, and the U.S. in the Arab Spring—Final musings on nationalism

The heart of the matter

The Mideast in general, and our chosen corridor in particular—Damascus south to the Gulf of Aqaba and the Nile delta—is the main crossroads of the super-continent of Asia/Africa/Europe by both land and sea routes. Several cities there, including Damascus and Jericho, claim to be the oldest continually occupied city in the world, and one of them probably is. Judaism and Christianity both have their holiest sites here from the formative periods of those religions, and although the two primary historical sites of Islam, the cities of Mecca and Medina, are in southwestern Arabia some 700 miles away, Jerusalem ranks with many Muslims as a close third and Damascus at least a distant fourth. The world's first alphabet, the world's first glass-blowing, the world's first soap-making, all came along the strip of coast on the east shore of the Mediterranean. The pyramids at Gizeh, just outside Cairo and barely south of our corridor, are the last remaining wonder of the ancient world. On our corridor Jordan's Petra, Lebanon's Baalbek, and Syria's Umayyad Mosque should all be in a serious traveler's top 25 "bucket list" of world-class cultural sites.

Especially important for our inquiry is the pattern of how the modern states along this corridor have taken shape—or are still trying to take shape! Egypt, just south of our corridor proper, began to assume its modern form with the British-Turkish defeat of Napoleon's forces there just before 1800. That makes it by a century-and-a-half older than any state on our corridor, or even nearby Arab states such as Iraq and Saudi Arabia. Syria and Lebanon only emerged as modern entities under French rule from World War I until shortly after World War II, Lebanon more or less gerrymandered out of traditional Syria by France. Jordan (Transjordan, it was at first) was created soon after World War I, early in the British mandate. The remaining piece of our corridor, Palestine from the Mediterranean to the Jordan River, became increasingly difficult for the British to manage. When in 1947 the British turned the "Palestinian problem" over to the new United Nations—"Here it is, young UN, your first real hot potato"—the UN plan was to partition Palestine between a Jewish state and an Arab state. With all-out war breaking out the very day the British forces pulled out in May of 1948, Israel wound up with the lion's share of the territory, Jordan got the West Bank including old city Jerusalem, and Egypt held the Gaza strip. No Palestinian Arab state came about—not then, and not after the Camp David Accords that President Jimmy Carter brokered in 1978 between Egypt's President Anwar Sadat and Israel's Prime Minister Menachem Begin, and not after the Oslo Agreement of 1993–4 negotiated between the Palestinian Liberation Organization's Yasser Arafat and Israel's Prime Minister Yitzhak Rabin. Not as of this writing. It is a complex and intractable problem, a perennial possible source of the world's next big war, and of course an issue that deeply affects U.S. domestic and foreign affairs. It is covered with a veneer of sound bites that rival sides throw at each other—many true, but not the whole truth, or much attempt to balance competing truths. A careful historical examination can help you sort out this Israeli-Palestinian conflict (though maybe come no closer to a solution to it!), and it turns out to be a good place to test as well as to refine the model of cultural nationalism first introduced in the German chapter. In particular, it may come as a surprise to you—I know it did to me—to discover that the development of cultural nationalism among European and later Israeli Jews and among Palestinian Arabs was a remarkably similar and parallel process.

SECTION A: LANGUAGE AND TOPOGRAPHY

A brief introduction to Hebrew and Arabic

In the chapter on Germany we introduced the Indo-European family of languages, and at least hinted at the kinship of modern Indo-European languages and their evolution from a common "proto-Indo-European" ancestor. Some treatment of the Semitic family of languages, of which Arabic and Hebrew are the two most important modern forms, is probably overdue. The languages of the world's oldest civilization, the Mesopotamian languages of the 3000s and 2000s BC, were Semitic, and one of them—Akkadian—became the expanding civilized world's first real "lingua franca" or common international language from around 2300 to 1300 BC. Hebrew was being written as well as spoken as early as 1000 BC. By the time of the Roman Empire, the Hebrew spoken locally had evolved into Aramaic. The Persians, the Greeks, and the Romans successively ruled our corridor for about a thousand years, but not many of the locals picked up Persian (Farsi), Greek, or Latin, these rather foreign Indo-European languages. Then in the AD 600s, with the Muslim conquests radiating out of Arabia, came speakers of Arabic. Arabic was a fellow Semitic language, so close to Aramaic that basically all the Aramaic speakers on the western end of the Mediterranean—in what is today Syria, Lebanon, Jordan, and Israel/Palestine—gradually shifted over to it. There are just a handful of towns in the entire Mideast that still speak the Aramaic. Once the author was an academic tourist visiting in Malula, Syria, some thirty miles NNE of Damascus—a little town in a spot of green where a tiny waterway breaks through a mountain ridge in generally desert country.[GE¹] On the tour was an ancient Christian church, the altar of which dated to the early 300s or perhaps before. Knowing this village to be one of that handful where Aramaic was still alive, some Christians in the group asked our young tour guide if she would say the Lord's Prayer in Aramaic, the language Jesus would have spoken. She looked up inquiringly, saw the request was genuine, collected herself for a minute, and then did it; I still remember how breathy the consonants were, and the feeling of being transported back two millennia in time.

There are important non-Semitic languages in the area, of course. For four of the past five centuries Turkish was the language of the rulers of these lands under the Ottoman Empire. It was written in Arabic script, but represented neither Indo-European nor Semitic language families, but a third major family, Turkic. And finally, as a legacy of more recent European colonialism, there is still lots of French spoken in Syria and Lebanon, and lots of English spoken in Jordan, Israel, and the West Bank. But the main task of this section is to introduce the two key Semitic languages of the area.

Semitic languages are traditionally written from right to left, so Hebrew and Arabic books open from what to us would be the back, and Arabic and Hebrew digital script on the modern computer screen lines up on the right margin, and reads leftwards.

Here, for example, is the first sentence of the 23rd Psalm from the Hebrew Bible:

$$\text{יְהוָה רֹעִי, לֹא אֶחְסָר}$$

The main letters are all, or mostly, consonants; those little dots, dashes, and half-crosses above and below the main letters are vowel symbols. Interestingly enough, those vowel markings were only added around AD 900, some 2,000 years after the first Hebrew was written, making for some uncertainty (in English, for example, would DD be "dead," or "did," or "deed," or "dad," or "dud?" Sometimes you might be able to tell which by context, but sometimes not so much.). This script with the vowel markings is called Masoretic, from the word for tradition—that is, it was a scholarly attempt to come up with an authoritative, standard version of the Hebrew scriptures.

---

1. GE Layer 1 is a Placemark framing a view of the little town of Malula, Syria. Zoom out to see general surroundings.

So let's first puzzle out the basic letters. Here's the Hebrew alphabet with the Latin-letter equivalent for each letter:

א—(a, the *alef*, one of the two letters that pass for a in Hebrew; see note below)

ב—(v, though written with a dot inside, like this—בּ—it's a b)

ג—(g)

ד—(d)

ה—(h)

ו—(v or w, another v with no hint of b)

ז—(z)

ח—(h, but a gutteral h, as in ch or kh)

ט—(t)

י—(y)

ך—(k); כ—(final k)

ל—(l)

ם—(m); מ—(final m)

ן—(n); נ—(final n)

ס—(s)

ע—(a, the *ayin*, the other letter that passes for a in Hebrew)

ף—(p); פ—(final p)

ץ—(ts); צ—(final ts)

ק—(k or q, a harder k than the one above)

ר—(r)

שׁ—(s or sh; שׂ =s, שׁ = sh)

ת—(t, a little softer—the tongue flattened out a bit against the palate—than the other t; one pronunciation guide suggests this is as in "team," the other as in "town")

That list is 22 letters long. The only letters for which there is truly no Latin equivalent are the *alef* and the *ayin*, transliterated as varieties of the letter a, but described by some as "rough breathing" and "smooth breathing."

So here's your first sentence from the 23rd Psalm again. Ignore the vowel markings, and try working out your own transliteration of the basic consonants of the first word, writing down the Latin letter equivalents and then reordering them so they read left to right.

יְהוָה רֹעִי, לֹא אֶחְסָר

What you should have gotten for the first word is Y-H-W-H, the famous "tetragrammaton" or "4-letter word" for God. With different sets of vowels inserted, it would be Yahweh or Jehovah—and since it was traditionally considered too holy to pronounce, it's a real guessing game to provide the original vowels. The whole sentence transliterates from the full Masoretic script something like "*y'hwah roiy lo echshar*," and translates literally "Lord shepherd of me nothing I lack." The most famous translation of the Bible into English, the King James version, gets an A+ for poetry—"The Lord is my shepherd; I shall not want"—but a B− for translation accuracy; there's no future tense "shall" anywhere in the original.

Arabic, too, is written right to left, and although it looks very different from Hebrew, many of its letters have matching Hebrew ones. Here is a most famous Arabic sentence, the *Basmala* that begins almost every *surah* (chapter) in the *Qur'an*:

بسم الله الرحمن الرحيم

It's a bit more complicated than Hebrew, in terms of identifying letters, because most Arabic letters are written differently when written as stand alone, or as the first, middle, or last letter in a word! In the table below, the first column is the stand-alone Arabic letter; the second column (in parentheses) is the matching Hebrew letter, and the third and last column is the usual Latin-letter transliteration.

ا	(א)	'(the *alif*, like the Hebrew *alef*)
ب	(ב)	b
ت	(ת)	t
ث		th
ج		j, g
ح		h, kh
خ	(ח)	kh
د	(ד)	d
ذ		dh
ر	(ר)	r
ز		z
س	(שׂ)	s
ش	(שׁ)	sh
ص		sh palatalized, s with dot under it
ض		dh, d with a dot under it
ط	(ט)	th palatalized, t with a dot under it
ظ	(צ)	ts, z with a dot under it
ع	(ע)	ʿ
غ		gh
ف	(ף)	f, p
ق	(ק)	q
ك	(ך)	k
ل	(ל)	l
م	(ם)	m
ن	(ן)	n
ه	(ה)	h
و	(ו)	w
ي	(י)	y

So here's the Basmala again; see if you can decipher some of the letters:

بسم الله الرحمن الرحيم

It transliterates something like "*bismi-llahi r-rahmani r-rahim,*" and the traditional translation is "In the name of God, the Compassionate, the Merciful." You should be able to see the b (ب) that starts the first word, at least half of the s (س) that makes up the middle, and the m (م) at the end. The definite article "the" in Arabic, transliterated "r-" above, is really the two letters "al" (ال)—apparently "r-" is what has resulted over the centuries when trying to say "al" fast! In Arabic this definite article is written as part of the word, as if we were to write "Thecompassionate" as one word, and its two tall parallel strokes are easy to recognize. The last two sets of this ال in the Basmala are each followed sooner or later by a true letter "r" (ر).

As foreign as all this may seem to those of us who speak and read no Hebrew or Arabic, students of these languages say that once you get familiar with these strange-looking alphabets—which takes less time than you might think—that the written languages have aspects that are very logical and easy to understand and use. Many Semitic language words, for example, are based on a root "triliteral," or three-consonant basis. The SLM triliteral, for example, is the basis of the noun Peace (*Shalom* in Hebrew; *Salaam* in Arabic). *Mu-* as a prefix in Arabic means one who does something (the way the -er on the end of lots of English verbs means one who does something: dig, digger; view, viewer; etc). *Muslim,* then, means literally "one who peaces," or works for peace. The triliteral DRS in both Hebrew and Arabic is the root for to study, to inquire, to research. From it comes both the Hebrew *Midrash* (מדרש), that tradition of commentary and analysis of Hebrew writings, and the Arabic *Medressa* or *Madrasah* (مدرسة), the usual word for an Islamic seminary or just a school in general. The last two of the three names for God in the Basmala are both from the triliteral root RHM that means "to feel sympathy for." Or take the KTB root that generally deals with writing, and by extension things written and persons who write; in Arabic *kitab* is book; *maktabat* is library; *iktitab* is registration; *katabat* is she wrote— and so on for literally dozens of words. Once you have the pattern down, just by learning a new triliteral root you will have automatically learned dozens of words similarly formed on that triliteral!

Although much of the Google Earth surface in our chosen corridor is labeled in Latin letters, there is lots of Arabic and Hebrew there, too, sometimes in the place names and especially as titles of Panoramio and Cities360 icons. Here, for the more adventurous, are some common words first in Arabic, then in Hebrew (in parentheses; transliterations in italics):

Mountain (جبل) *jabal*; (הר) *har.* For example, the 9,000′ mountain at the southern end of the anti-Lebanon range, is:

(جبل الشيخ) *Jabal al-Shaykh*, or Mountain of the Elder/Chief/Religious leader

(הר חרמון) *Har Hermon*, or Mount Hermon

Valley (وادي) *wadi*; (עמק) *nahal.* For example, the Kidron Valley on the east side of old city Jerusalem, separating it from the Mount of Olives, is:

(وادي الجوز) *Wadi al-Joz*

(נחל קדרון) *Nahal Kidron*

Spring or **Well** (عين) *ain*; (עֵין) *ein.* Here's one example in Arabic, and another in Hebrew:

(عين العذراء) *Ain il a'dra* –The "Spring of the Virgin," or "Mary's Well," traditional site of the Annunciation, now beneath Orthodox Church in Nazareth

(עֵין גֶּדִי) *Ein Gedi*—"Goat Kid Spring" by shores of Dead Sea; David hid out here when pursued by King Saul, according to the Old Testament/Hebrew Bible

Sea (البحر) *al bahr;* (יָם) *yam.* For example, the Dead Sea is:

(البحر الميت) *al-Bahr al-Mayyit* (literally "The Dead Sea")

(יָם מלחה) *Yam ha-Melah* (literally "Sea of Salt")

One of the most common components of a town name on our corridor is the Hebrew or Arabic for "house"—also not uncommon in English and American place names as in White House, Newhouse, Rock House, etc. The Arabic is تيب, usually transliterated *Bayt*, and the Hebrew is בית, usually transliterated *Beit*. Bethlehem may be the most famous town of such "house" names, from "House of Bread" (בֵּית לֶחֶם or *Beit Leihem* in the Hebrew, or "House of Flesh," بيت لحم, or *Bayt Lahm* in the Arabic).

Finally, it's worth noting that most of the Js in place names along our corridor (as transliterated into Latin alphabet), that are traditionally pronounced as "hard" Js in English, are really Ys—probably because we got a lot of it through German-language scholarship. This will explain why Jaffa is better spelled Yafo or Yaffa, and Jerusalem is more correctly Yerushalayim, and Jericho is more correctly Yerikho. Once, deep in the Jordan Rift Valley, I was standing in a group facing west towards the mountain ridge atop which Jerusalem is located, listening to an Israeli guide describe the topography. Near us was a Latin-letter sign, "Yarden," and I asked the guide what it meant. Wordlessly, and with an "I don't believe this question" look, he pointed to the Jordan River just a few steps behind us . . . . So we should probably add this to the list of useful common words for geographic features:

River (نهر) *nahr;* (נהר) *nehar.* The Jordan River is:

(نهر الأردن) *Nahr al-Urdun;*

(נהר הירדן) *Nehar haYarden*

Topography and texture of the "Damascus south to water" corridor

First, this is the hinge of the Europe-Asia-Africa supercontinent.[GE2] Whatever geographers tell you, there are just two major continents—the old world of Europe-Asia-Africa, much the biggest, and the new world of the Americas. By land from Africa to Asia, this hinge is the only way. And by water from the Mediterranean to the Indian Ocean, the Red Sea almost goes all the way through. It ends in two Gulfs—at an angle of about as far apart as you can spread your index and middle fingers, try it—called the Gulf of Suez and the Gulf of Aqaba (with the Sinai peninsula between them). From the Gulf of Suez to the Mediterranean is less than 100 miles, and since 1869 the Suez Canal has completed the water connection.

In this general overview, just south of our corridor you can see some of the valley and all of the delta of the Nile, with its lush green shape (like the stem and flower of a giant lotus) in startling contrast to the yellow-white of the barren Nubian desert. The canyon averages 10 to 20 miles wide; the delta is 170 miles wide east to west and 100 miles deep north to south. Both have well-watered topsoils washed down through the centuries from interior Africa, and the population density there has to be seen to be believed. The delta is flat as a board, honeycombed with waterways, and averages a village every mile in most any direction and a sizeable town every four or five![GE3] Where the canyon meets the delta has always been a crucial juncture. Ancient Memphis was here,[GE4] with the pyramids of Gizeh just ten miles to the northwest, up out of the farmland on the desert upland.[GE5] Modern Cairo is about ten miles downstream from ancient Memphis, even closer to

---

2. GE Layer 2 is a Polygon in white outline that generally locates our "Damascus south to water" corridor. The overall view frames this "hinge" of the supercontinent.

3. GE Layer 3 is a Polygon in white outline shaped as a double-ended arrow, the points of which are five miles apart, superimposed on a typical piece of the Nile delta. Dark green is agriculture; darker gray is housing; lighter gray-brown patches mostly inside the gray are cemeteries, some thousands of years old.

4. GE Layer 4 is a Placemark referencing a Panoramio icon of an ancient sphinx, in its original site in ancient Memphis. Zoom out to see general location, just where the delta starts to spread out.

5. GE Layer 5 is a Placemark generally referencing the pyramids of Gizeh, those of Khafre, Khufu, and Menkaure.

the great pyramids. Our corridor proper stops just short of the Nile delta, but it was a key destination for most travelers and armies coming south along it, and of course for armies sweeping north out of it—New Kingdom pharaohs, Napoleon when still just a general, General Allenby in World War I . . . .

Mediterranean Sea currents sweep east across the mouths of the Nile and then north up the coast of Gaza and modern Israel, and over the eons have deposited so much sand that there are almost no good natural harbors. All up that coast man-made harbors have sea walls that go out to sea and then hook to the right (north) to create a shelter that boats can enter only from the northern end.[GE⁶] The only natural harbors were two— the little wrinkle on the coastline that sheltered Jaffa (Joppa, Yafo), today's Tel Aviv,[GE⁷] and the greater shelter from those southern currents afforded by Mount Carmel at Haifa.[GE⁸] Shortly north of that, roughly where the coast of Lebanon begins, the mountains come right down to the sea and make lots of good natural ports— Sour (ancient Tyre), Saida (ancient Sidon), Beirut (Bayrutus to the Romans), and Byblos.[GE⁹] The major ports average thirty to forty miles apart, apparently a one-day trading distance for coastal sailors. It's no surprise, then, that the ancient Canaanites and Hebrews were generally turned inland in their political and economic interests, and that the Phoenicians who lived in what is today Lebanon were the greatest sailors of the ancient world.

Just inland from the coast there is also a dramatic difference on our corridor between Israel/Palestine in the south and Lebanon in the north. From the eastern edge of the Nile delta up as far as Mount Carmel, and then from Mount Carmel north to the Lebanese border, there is generally a band of sand dunes a mile or two wide along the seacoast.[GE¹⁰] Behind the dunes is a plain ten miles wide in some places (just south of Mount Carmel it is the Plain of Sharon, as in "the rose of Sharon").[GE¹¹] Further inland from that is a band of foothills, from around 400' to 2,000' elevation, called the Shephelah (today all of it except a corridor due west of Jerusalem makes up most of "The West Bank" claimed by Palestinians).[GE¹²] Then comes what you might call "Jerusalem ridge," the Judean hill crest that runs south to north from Hebron at about 3,000' elevation, Bethlehem at 2,550', Jerusalem (Old City) at 2,450', Ramallah at 2,800', and Nablus at 1,780', falling off to Jenin at 500' as the ridge runs out further north.[GE¹³]

Jerusalem, by both ancient history and modern controversy the key city of the Judean mountain crest, deserves a closer look. It was built on two southward-projecting ridges and the valley between them. The narrow ridge on the east is Ophel, site of Solomon's Temple of antiquity and visually dominated by the Dome of the Rock since AD 700; the broader ridge in the west was called Zion. The "valley of the cheesemakers,"

6. GE Layer 6 is a Folder with Placemarks referencing such harbors, each Placemark usually suggesting a Photos icon to view.

7. GE Layer 7 is a Folder titled "Yafo/Jaffa & Tel Aviv"; it includes three Placemarks framing views, each with a suggested Photos icon to view.

8. GE Layer 8 is a Folder titled "Haifa, sheltered by Mt. Carmel." It includes four Placemarks framing good views, each with a suggested Photos icon to view.

9. GE Layer 9 is a Folder titled "Southern Lebanon ports & coast." Its Placemarks generally frame views of the rugged Lebanese coast, from the border with Israel to about twenty miles north of Beirut. Only in the first view is a Photos icon suggested for viewing, but in most of the views there are dozens if not hundreds for exploration on your own; Jounieh, or "Little Bay" somewhat north of Beirut, has some stunning ones.

10. GE Layer 10 is a Folder titled "Sand dunes along the coast"; its five Placemarks frame views and suggest Photos icons to explore along the Israeli coastline.

11. GE Layer 11 is a Folder titled "Coastal plain views"; each of its five framed views and suggested Photos icons (except the overview of Ben Gurion airport), mention in the title how many miles inland each view is.

12. GE Layer 12 is a Folder titled "Foothills views." Most of the five Placemarks reference an interesting Photos icon for this "Shephelah" country.

13. GE Layer 13 is a Folder titled "'Jerusalem Ridge,' Judean Hills." Turn the Folder on, and double-click on the Folder icon for a framed view of its light blue Pushpin icons representing Hebron, Bethlehem, Jerusalem, Ramallah, Nablus, and Jenin. For view of Jerusalem made from Mount of Olives, fly to and open yellow pushpin Placemark of that title, and click on Panoramio icon titled "Jerusalem."

mostly filled in over the centuries, is in-between.[GE14] An underground tunnel was cut to channel water from a spring just east of Ophel to the valley. The Kidron valley, where the two ridges end, runs south of the city, separating it from the Mount of Olives which is about 500′ higher than Old City Jerusalem itself and a perfect spot from which to view it.[GE15] The Old City is still defined by the Ottoman Turkish wall; the New City generally spreads west of that.[GE16] In the 1948–49 war that created the modern state of Israel (and didn't create a modern Palestinian state), Israel wound up in control of New City Jerusalem and the state of Jordan controlled the Old City. Less than twenty years later, in the 1967 "Six-Day War," Israel took the Old City and everything else west of the Jordan, usually called the West Bank—but this is getting way ahead of the story.

Mount Carmel is a spur of that long north-south "Jerusalem ridge" that takes off somewhere between Nablus and Jenin, angling northwest, and then noses over into the sea, as you've already seen, like the head of a gigantic whale.

Running inland from that ten-mile-wide bay north of Haifa, and heading generally southeast parallel to the long axis of Mount Carmel, is the wide, shallow valley variously called the Jizreel, the Esdraelon, or the Marg ibn Amir.[GE17] If the world's oceans, including the Mediterranean, were to rise 180′, water would pour through the Jizreel and fill up the whole Jordan Rift Valley. Notice how the valley is drained by the Kishon River (which would be a creek or a brook in the U.S., not a river!) running northwest through Haifa, and Harod Stream running east until it joins the Jordan River. The Jizreel plain proper is shown in the attached Google Earth folder in green outline, and you can see how ancient Megiddo dominated its southwestern side. In the northeast it ends abruptly at the foot of the steep, stand-alone Mt. Tabor.

North of the Jezreel come the scattered hills and ridges of the Lower Galilee; Nazareth sits on one such, commanding the Jizreel from the north.[GE18] North of that comes the upper Galilee, averaging 1,500′ higher than the Lower Galilee. Its most important city is Safed, which became a great center of Jewish learning with immigrants from Spain's eviction of its Jews in 1492.

Moving on north, the coastal strip of Lebanon is dominated by what is sometimes just called Mount Lebanon—though it's not so much a single mountain as it is a whole mountain range over a hundred miles long. Its crest averages 7,000′ feet with peaks to 10,000′, and parallels the Mediterranean shore as close to it as fifteen miles.[GE19] Depending on the season, you can go waterskiing on the coast and then drive thirty minutes inland (sharply uphill on twisty roads) and snow ski. The landscape tumbles down to the sea in steep hillsides and steep-sided little creek valleys. The only river of consequence, the Litani, drains some of the Bekaa

---

14. GE Layer 14 is a Path generally tracing the outline of the original narrow ridge of Ophel and the broader ridge of Zion; the valley of the cheesemakers lay between them.

15. GE Layer 15 is a Placemark referencing a Panoramio icon with a photo of such a view.

16. GE Layer 16 is a Folder titled Old City Jerusalem. It includes a Polygon showing in red outline the old Turkish walls, and a few Placemarks referencing Panoramio icons with good photographs of the walls, gates, and a few celebrated sites holy to three religions.

17. GE Layer 17 is a Folder titled "Jizreel/Marg ibn Amir." Turn the Folder layer on and double-click on the Folder icon to open it. The aqua Paths symbolize the Kishon River, heading northwest to Haifa, and the Harod Stream, heading a bit south of east towards Beit She'an and its junction with the Jordan River. An east-west line drawn just south of Afula is nowhere as much as 200′ elevation, meaning that a general ocean rise of 180′ or so would totally flood the Jordan Rift Valley. And file away Afula for future historical reference; one of the big early Zionist land purchases was there, sparking the first really noticeable Palestinian Arab reactions. Mt. Tabor, referenced by the green pushpin Placemark icon, rises sharply from a plain less than 500′ to over 1,800′. Site of important military engagements in the Hebrew Bible, it is also generally identified by Christians as the mount of the transfiguration of Christ (remember the "Mt. Tabors" celebrated in the religious wars in Czech lands).

18. GE Layer 18 is a Folder titled "Lower and Upper Galilee views." A wide black Path roughly separates the highlands of the "Upper" Galilee from the more dissected southern "Lower" Galilee. One Placemark references a Panoramio icon titled "Olivetrees" that is a good typical view of the Lower Galilee countryside. The other frames a view in Google Earth of Safed, an almost totally Jewish mountaintop city of the Upper Galilee that in the past few hundred years has been considered one of the four holy cities of Judaism (Jerusalem and Hebron you've seen; Tiberias you'll see in a minute).

19. GE Layer 19 is a Folder titled "Mt. Lebanon views."

valley east of Mount Lebanon and then cuts an impressive little canyon through it to the coast.[GE20] There is a Lebanese coastal road that makes its torturous way along the rugged Mediterranean coast with its steep hills and steep-sided little creek valleys, but historically it was always difficult to move armies and freight along it; ambush and defense were just too easy there.

East of the Mount Lebanon Range and "Jerusalem ridge" lies the long and complicated Jordan Rift Valley. In Lebanon it is a high (averaging 3,000′ elevation or so), relatively dry valley called the Bekaa (also transliterated Beqaa) Valley.[GE21] Easy to irrigate with streams coming off the mountains on both sides, it is very fertile, with fields of row crops, orchards, and even famous vineyards (since much of the population here is Lebanese Christian, for whom alcohol consumption is generally not prohibited by religion as it is for Muslims). Historically its most famous site is probably Baalbek—"the Baal of the Bekaa," named for an ancient Semitic deity—with its spectacular Roman ruins. The Bekaa is walled on its eastern side by the Anti-Lebanon mountain range, wider and more geologically complex than Mount Lebanon, on which more in a minute when we cover the eastern highlands of the area.

The Jordan River rises at the southern end of the Bekaa Valley, and running south drops into a long, narrow valley that is soon below sea level. The Jordan runs into the northern end of the Sea of Galilee (or Lake Tiberias, or Lake Kinneret, or whatever name successive rulers and times gave it). The Sea of Galilee is itself 700′ below sea level. It is about 7½ miles wide and 13 miles long, and is a freshwater lake because the upper Jordan runs into it at its northern end and the lower Jordan runs out again at its southern end. The city of Tiberias, midway along the western shore of the Sea of Galilee, was founded by a Roman client ruler in AD/CE 20, and was named for the current Roman Emperor.[GE22]

The lower Jordan then runs sixty-five straight line miles (though its course is anything but straight as it wiggles southward down the broad valley) from its exit at the southern end of the Sea of Galilee to where it loses itself in the Dead Sea, dropping from the Sea of Galilee's 700′ below sea level to the Dead Sea's 1,300′ below sea level—the lowest place on earth. Notice the flat and fertile farmland on the southwest and southern sides of the Sea of Galilee. The Jewish settlement of Deganyah there, dating to 1910, is often identified as the first kibbutz, that key Israeli institution. The Jordan's biggest tributary, the Yarmuk River, comes into it from the east just a few miles below the Sea of Galilee. The gorge of the Yarmuk is for a ways the border between Syria and Jordan. Further on south Jericho, built on some springs a few miles from where the Jordan enters the Dead Sea, is at 1,200′ below sea level the world's lowest city. It's probably also the world's most guaranteed frost-free city: atmospheric pressure is such that it never gets cold! Allenby Bridge, famous since its creation in World War I, crosses the Jordan just east of Jericho. The site traditionally identified as Bethany, where many Christians believe Jesus was baptized by John, is on the Jordanian side just a couple of miles downriver from that.[GE23]

No water leaves the Dead Sea except by evaporation, and it is much, much saltier than the ocean. Swallowing one mouthful of its water, full as it is of salts and bromides, is supposed to kill you. But anybody who gets close has to go in for a dip, newspaper in hand, because even skinny non-floaters float high here in its super-salty and therefore very heavy water (newspaper held up as if sitting in a recliner for the photo).[GE24] Its southern end is separated from the main sea by a peninsula called the Lizan. Masada, famous for its suicidal resistance in the Roman siege of AD 70, is a little mesa split off from the western cliffs within sight of the Lizan. South of the Lizan you can see Israeli and Jordanian evaporation ponds for commercially exploiting those salts and other chemicals.[GE25]

---

20. GE Layer 20 is a Folder titled "Litani River, course and view."

21. GE Layer 21 is a Folder titled "The Bekaa Valley."

22. GE Layer 22 is a Folder titled "Upper Jordan and Sea of Galilee."

23. GE Layer 23 is a Folder titled "Lower Jordan, including Jericho."

24. GE Layer 24 is a Folder titled "Dead Sea views"; it includes two Placemarks referencing Photos icons with pictures of bathers floating high, one on the Israeli side and one on the Jordanian side.

25. GE Layer 25 is a Folder titled "The Lizan and evaporation ponds."

Now take just a minute and let's review this Jordan River system—the Upper Jordan River, the Sea of Galilee, the Lower Jordan with its biggest eastern tributary the Yarmuk and its little western tributary Harod Stream draining the Jezreel, and finally the main Dead Sea, the Lizan narrows, and the shallow evaporation ponds south of that.[GE26]

Running south from the Dead Sea is the valley called the Arabah (from Arabic) or Aravah (from Hebrew) that only gets up to about 600' above sea level.[GE27] It runs almost exactly 100 miles from the southern tip of the Dead Sea down to the head of the Gulf of Aqaba, where two cities huddle in opposite corners today with no coming or going between them—the Israeli city of Eilat and the Jordanian city of Aqaba.[GE28]

This whole Jordan Rift Valley, beginning with Lebanon's Bekaa Valley, is just the northern end of a 5,000-mile long crack in the earth's crust that goes on down through Kenya and Tanzania.

All that's left to do now in terms of the topography and texture of our corridor is to explore the eastern highlands. Coming back north up the Arabah from the Gulf of Aqaba towards the Dead Sea, these highlands rise to your east as the Jordanian massif, up to 6,000' or twice as high as "Jerusalem ridge."[GE29] Petra may well be Jordan's single most famous historical site. A Nabataean Arab capital from 400 BC or so, and later remodeled by the Romans, it is reached through a mile-long slot canyon (perhaps the model for protecting someone "in the cleft of the rock," as described in the Hebrew Bible). The narrow, vertical-walled canyon ends with the so-called Treasury, a temple or tomb carved from the living rock. Nearby Jebel Haroun—Aaron's Mountain—is traditionally identified by Muslims, Jews, and Christians as the site of the death of Moses' brother Aaron. The ruins of crusader castles such as Karak and Shobak are strung out along the crest of this Jordanian massif, an average of twenty miles apart or a long day's march. Most of them are built on Mamluk foundations, which are on Abbasid foundations, which are on Umayyad foundations, which are on Byzantine foundations, which are on Roman foundations, which are on Persian foundations, which are on earlier Semitic culture foundations . . . . Amman, Jordan, is located in a dip in that highland, at roughly the same latitude and 2,400' elevation as Jerusalem. As you go north from there towards Damascus you cross fairly fertile lands called the Bashan in Biblical days, or the heart of the Decapolis ("10 cities") in Greek and Roman days. Jarash/Gerasa, with its unique oval colonnaded forum, is one of those in today's Jordan, and Bosra, not much further on in Syria, has what may be the best preserved Roman theatre in the world.

Then comes Damascus. The great Umayyad Mosque that dates from circa 700 AD/CE includes in its walls fragments of Byzantine churches on which the Greek can still be read, and stands within still visible ruins of the Roman Temple of Jupiter, which itself was built on the site of an earlier Semitic deity . . . .[GE30] For an American, naturally enough growing up believing that anything older than AD 1607 (Jamestown) is really old, the historical depth of culture in this "hinge of the supercontinent" is amazing.

A word on climate, and especially the availability of water

On our corridor—except on lava flows and other solid rock—usually when there is freshwater there is fertility, given the latitude and abundant sunshine. For our corridor as a whole, in general rainfall decreases from west to east (that is, as you go away from the Mediterranean Sea) and also from north to south—but topography plays a huge role in the distribution of rainfall as well.

---

26. GE Layer 26 is a Folder titled "Review of the Jordan River system." To give yourself a clean slate, turn on the white Polygon layer and double-click on the icon to "fly" to appropriate framed view, and then go to your basic Layers box at bottom left and turn off Places and Photos and any other layers that may be open. Now turn the remaining layers on sequentially, beginning with Upper Jordan River. When finished with review, turn the white Polygon off, and in your basic Layers box turn Places and Photos layers back on.

27. GE Layer 27 is a Folder tiled "Arabah/Aravah."

28. GE Layer 28 is a Folder titled "Aqaba and Eilat."

29. GE Layer 29 is a Folder titled "The eastern highlands, including Petra and Amman."

30. GE Layer 30 is a Folder titled "Damascus views," including an overview of the Old City and a close-up of the Umayyad Mosque.

In the Israel/Palestine south of our area, for example, the western face of that "Jerusalem ridge" gets reliable rains as the moisture-filled air from the Mediterranean Sea is pushed up, cooled, and squeezed of its moisture.[GE31] By the same principle, the far side of the ridge gets almost no rainfall. This is the Judean Wilderness, a rocky desert of scrub thorn, except where there's a spring.[GE32] In Biblical times the scapegoat was driven out the east gate of the Temple into this wilderness. Then, across the Jordan River and Dead Sea valley, the Jordanian massif reaches up in some places to five and six thousand feet and squeezes a little more moisture out of the clouds. It makes for a band of fertility along the crest perhaps twenty or thirty miles deep, gradually shading off into the great and terrible desert that separates the fertile Mediterranean coastal band from the ancient Mesopotamia of the Tigris and Euphrates rivers. As you've seen, that crest fertility shows up in Google Earth as a thin, greenish band. What that means on the ground is often more impressive, including orchards of almond trees in pink bloom in January.

Those same moist Mediterranean winds blow without much hindrance eastwards through the Jizreel and the lower Galilee, and over the eons have both watered and eroded the Bashan, those high plains in today's southern Syria that are the breadbasket of the whole Jordanian massif. A framed view in Google Earth shows the tongue of greener land that this creates in southern Syria, just north of the Jordanian border, that extends well inland.[GE33] Snowmelt and rainfall collected by the Anti-Lebanon range is what generates the spring-fed rivers that water Damascus, making it one of the largest oases in the whole Mideast.[GE34]

The other useable water comes from irrigation. For all practical purposes, the lower Jordan River is used up entirely; nearing the Dead Sea, there is often no flow left at all in the Jordan proper.[GE35]

Vegetation is just a remnant of what it was three and four thousand years ago. There has been massive deforestation, and sheep and goats have cropped the lower vegetation down to its roots, causing the soil to wash off the hills and ancient springs to go dry. There are only tiny remnant forests of the once-extensive Cedars of Lebanon in the Mount Lebanon range.[GE36] One clue to what it used to look like is in Neot Kedumin, a "Biblical Landscape Reserve" that the Israelis have built somewhat west and downhill from Jerusalem.[GE37] Their ambition there is to reforest the hills, and to grow as many of the plants mentioned in the Hebrew Bible as possible. A guide will take a fragile, rambling plant, crush it under the nose of an American tourist child; and the child will cry out "pizza" because it is wild oregano—the original hyssop of the Hebrew Bible and Christian New Testament. Here you can still see "sycomores" (*Ficus sycomoros*), formerly common in the low plains of our corridor such as the Plain of Sharon (and not to be confused with either the English maple or the American or Chinese plane trees called "sycamores") whose figgy fruits grow on tiny little limbs on the trunk and main limbs. But there are still blue cornflowers, in season, and of course lots and lots of commercially valuable olive trees, which shimmer when the wind turns up the silvery undersides of their leaves, and the fruit of which produces olive oil worth perhaps $600 a tree annually.

Zoology is remnant, too, though there are some spectacular bird migrations that stop at some of the wetlands, and there are still long-legged desert hyenas living on the slopes around the Dead Sea.

---

31. GE Layer 31 is a Placemark framing a Google Earth view of the front (west) face of that Jerusalem ridge.

32. GE Layer 32 is a Placemark framing a Google Earth view of the back (east) face of that Jerusalem ridge. Note the brown (dry) tones in this view as compared to the last layer.

33. GE Layer 33 is a Placemark framing a view in Google Earth of this fertile green "tongue" of land that extends west in southern Syria.

34. GE Layer 34 is a Folder titled "Waters of Damascus," including a view of the Barada River below al Figeh springs.

35. GE Layer 35 is a Placemark titled "Low flow in the lower Jordan."

36. GE Layer 36 is a Placemark framing a view of a remnant patch of Cedars of Lebanon, and referencing a Panoramio icon titled "Cédrusok 1. The Ceders of Lebanon."

37. GE Layer 37 is a Placemark framing a general view of Neot Kedumin, and referencing a Panoramio icon of the same name. Lots of other nearby Photos icons to explore.

A "fruit ladder" of traditional routes across the land

Now, with the general topography, the location of key cities, and an idea of where the fertile lands are all under your belt, the logic of the traditional road network ought to be clearer.

There were two main north-south roads. The one coming up from the Nile delta is generally called by the Roman name for it, the *Via Maris*, The Way of the Sea or just The Sea Road.[GE38] Notice how it came up the coast just inland from the sand dunes, crossed the Mt. Carmel ridge at Megiddo Pass, went across the Jizreel valley and wound among the hills of the lower Galilee, circled north around the Sea of Galilee and on up to Damascus. The second main north-south road, coming up from the Gulf of Aqaba, is called the King's Highway.[GE39] We have no idea what king it was named for, incidentally; it was an old road even when Moses asked to use it and was turned down! See how it quickly climbs up the Jordanian massif to Ras an Negeb, "Head of the Negev," and then generally runs the fertile crest of the ridge going northward, detouring east just enough to get around the eastern ends of the ravines and canyons. Between these two major north-south routes is that incomplete north-south road you saw earlier that runs that "Jerusalem ridge" from Hebron to Jenin; it is usually called "The Patriarch's Way."[GE40] And finally, in terms of north-south routes, east of the King's Highway from Amman on south is the Desert Way, or Maiden's Way, that was popularized in the Ottoman Empire for camel caravans heading towards Medina on the *hajj,* or Muslim pilgrimage—on which more later.[GE41]

Let's use the image of a fruit ladder—a ladder with its two rails coming to a point at the top for ease in pushing up into a fruit tree—with three rungs. The rails (somewhat crooked, admittedly) are the Via Maris and King's Highway, the two main north-south roads that meet at Damascus. The three rungs are the main west-east routes connecting or crossing them. Southernmost is the Gaza—Bersheeba—Wilderness of Zin—Lizan—Karak route.[GE42] Middle is the Jaffa/Tel Aviv—Jerusalem—Jericho—Amman route, looking short on a map but with lots of climbing and descending involved.[GE43] It's only fourteen air miles from Jerusalem to Jericho, but the elevation changes from plus 2,500′ to minus 1,200′, for a 3,700′ drop. The parable of the Good Samaritan in the Christian New Testament says he "went down" from Jerusalem to Jericho, and you can well understand the phrase once you've been on that road. The third and easiest west-east rung is along the Jezreel valley, beginning in the vicinity of Haifa, crossing the Jordan somewhere below the Sea of Galilee, and climbing up the gradual slope of the Bashan to and through the city of Irbid.[GE44] And we probably should also put in the traditional road from Beirut to Damascus as a fourth west-east route, although it's not really a rung . . . .[GE45]

These, then—with one or two minor routes we'll talk about later—are the roads geography encourages, in ancient, medieval, and modern times alike.[GE46] Human relations, however, always has a say in who can travel them, or whether they can be traveled at all.

---

38. GE Layer 38 is a Folder titled "Via Maris"; it includes a Path layer symbolizing the road, or a general approximation of the road over the centuries, in red, as well as some Placemarks framing representative views or referencing interesting Photos icons.

39. GE Layer 39 is a Folder titled "The King's Highway"; it is similarly symbolized as a wide, red line.

40. GE Layer 40 is a Path titled "Patriarch's Way," symbolized in red though narrower than that for the more important Via Maris.

41. GE Layer 41 is a Path titled "Desert, or Maiden's Way," also narrowly symbolized in red.

42. GE Layer 42 is a Folder titled "The southern rung," which includes a Path symbolized in purple representing the Gaza-Karak route.

43. GE Layer 43 is a Folder titled "The middle rung," with a Path similarly symbolized, representing the Tel Aviv/Yafo–Amman route.

44. GE Layer 44 is a Folder titled "The northern rung," with a Path similarly symbolized, representing the Haifa–Irbid route.

45. GE Layer 45 is a Folder titled "Beirut to Damascus," including a Path similarly symbolized, representing the Beirut–Damascus route.

46. GE Layer 46 is an overview of this traditional "fruit ladder" of routes.

SECTION B: BACKGROUND OF THE MODERN STATE OF ISRAEL

Beginnings

Of all the peoples of the ancient world, Jews are perhaps the best known to most Americans. These are the people of the Bible, worshippers of the one God. A lot of their history is found here in these scriptures, including the migration from Mesopotamia led by Abraham, the exodus from Egypt under Moses, and the conquest of the "promised land" of Canaan. The Hebrew name for this area transliterates *Eretz Israel*, *eretz* or *erez* meaning land and *Isra-el*, "Wrestles with God," being Jacob's new name after he wrestled with the angel. In roughly the hundred years between 1020 and 920 BCE ("Before the Common Era," BCE, is non-Christian substitute for the Christian customary BC, "Before Christ"; it's to say, "we agree to use this dating system because most everybody else uses it, not because we accept the divinity of Christ."), the three great kings Saul, David, and Solomon created a kingdom that took in most of the land at the eastern edge of the Mediterranean. It was David who captured Jerusalem and made it the religious and political capital of the state, and advanced the state's borders perhaps as far as the Euphrates. Solomon, David's son by Bathsheeba, built the original Temple, which became the focal point of the religion. But then the kingdom broke up into a northern part, Israel, and a southern part, Judah, and fell on hard times. First Assyrians destroyed Israel and made of Judah a satellite country. Then in 586 BC (BCE) the Babylonians captured and destroyed Jerusalem and carried the population of Judah off for resettlement on lands to the east. The bitterness of this Babylonian captivity can still be felt in Psalm 137:

1 By the rivers of Babylon, there we sat down, yea, we wept when we remembered Zion.

2 Upon the willows in the midst thereof we hanged up our harps.

3 For there they that led us captive asked of us words of song; and our tormentors asked of us mirth. "Sing us one of the songs of Zion."

4 How shall we sing the Lord's song in a foreign land?

5 If I forget thee, O Jerusalem, let my right hand forget her cunning.

6 Let my tongue cleave to the roof of my mouth, if I remember thee not; if I set not Jerusalem above my chiefest joy.

7 Remember, O Lord, against the children of Edom [the Babylonians] the day of Jerusalem; who said, "Rase it, rase it, even to the foundation thereof."

8 O daughter of Babylon, that art to be destroyed; happy shall he be, that repayeth thee as thou hast served us.

9 Happy shall he be, that taketh and dasheth thy little ones against the rock.

Already the word Zion, the name for the broader of the two ridges on which Jerusalem is built, was coming to stand for the whole land, religion, and culture of the Jewish people. The Babylonian empire was indeed destroyed as the psalm seemed to predict, and the conquering Persians freed the exiles. As many as 50,000 Jews made their way back to Jerusalem to rebuild Solomon's Temple and the city walls, and to enjoy at least some self-rule for a time.

Greeks and Romans

Alexander the Great and his successors invaded and ruled the area next, followed by the Romans. It is safe to say that no people enjoy foreign occupation, but Jewish monotheists were especially irritated by the Greco-Roman worship of many gods. In 170 BCE/BC a Greek ruler desecrated the Temple, causing a major revolt associated with the Maccabee family. Nero, a first-century Roman emperor, put his statue in the Temple to be worshipped as a god and so ignited the great rebellion of the year CE/AD 66. Jerusalem was recaptured by

Roman troops only in 68.[GE47] In the conquest the Temple was burned and the city virtually destroyed. The last spark of the rebellion was not put out for several more years. Masada, a fortress on a natural plateau down by the Dead Sea, had been captured by Zealots at the start of the revolt.[GE48] In it a desperate garrison of not quite a thousand, including women and children, held out against a Roman army until April of 73. When the Romans finally finished their great siege tower ramp and burned the walls of the fort, the remaining 193 defenders were found dead, having committed joint suicide rather than surrender. Their story, according to the contemporary historian Josephus,[3] was told by two women and some children found hiding in a water cistern. In the long run, the defense of Masada created a legend of resistance; from early in the modern state of Israel's existence soldiers in the Israeli army who had passed basic training were taken there to be sworn in, part of their pledge being "Masada shall not fall again." In the short run, however, the revolt was crushed, and the first half of Jewish history pretty well ended under oppressive Roman rule.

Diaspora

Many Jews had already been scattered outside Palestine by Assyrians and Babylonians. Others had left on their own looking for better conditions, mostly in northern Africa. But the final Scattering—in Greek that comes out *Diaspora*, kin to the English word "dispersal"—began with this Roman reconquest of Jerusalem in CE/AD. Books of religious history call this the Destruction of the Second Temple, but what it meant from a political perspective was the end of any Jewish state. From CE/AD 132–135 one last great Jewish revolt against the Romans, the Bar Kokhba Revolt, temporarily set up an independent Jewish state in the name of a self-proclaimed messiah. The Emperor Hadrian assembled even more massive armies than Vespasian had used some sixty-five years earlier, crushed the revolt at Jerusalem and then besieged and killed Bar Kokhba and his last followers at the nearby village of Betar.[GE49] At this point Hadrian determined to end this Jewish unrest once and for all by in essence outlawing Jews and Judaism in the land. This was the finalizing of the Diaspora. The Hebrew word for it is *galut*—exile.

In the first thousand years of the Diaspora the Jewish population spread as far west as the Atlantic coast of Africa to as far east as deep inside Central Asia. The separated Jewish groups met very different fates. Some places and times were fairly good, as in Spain under the Moors; some were bad, with great poverty and persecution. But in the Scattering as a whole one remarkable thing happened: even the most isolated and far-flung groups tended to cling to their religious and ethnic identity. By far the more common pattern in history is for smaller cultural groups to get swallowed up in larger surrounding ones over the course of a thousand or fifteen hundred years. I can name a few other examples. One would be the Gypsies, or Romani people, who started out as a wandering *jati* (sub-caste) in India, and spent enough time in Egypt to get their modern popular name. Another would be the Chinese business communities in Southeast Asian cities. But then I start to run out of examples. How do you explain this Jewish exception to the general rule?

Fundamentalists of the Christian religion as well as of Judaism itself tend to see this as evidence of God's continuing concern for "the chosen people"—they have been marked out for a separate role in history. Most secular historians stress cultural factors. The daily practices of Orthodox Judaism by their very nature make extended social contact with non-Jews difficult, and intermarriage all but impossible, even today. And each Jewish community, no matter how small or poor, surrounded a *rabbi*, a teacher, who was not just a religious leader but a cultural historian. As long as the religion was faithfully practiced, Palestine was well remembered. The religious calendar was set by ancient Palestinian facts of life; observant urban Jews in Russia 1,800 years after Nero still called on God to send the "former" and "latter" rains of ancient Palestine in due season. By

---

47. GE Layer 47 is a Placemark referencing the triumphal arch of Titus in the Roman forum; on one of its interior surfaces you can clearly see the great menorah of the temple being carried off as loot by the Romans. The treasure looted from Jerusalem, incidentally, was apparently the main source of money for Vespasian's Colosseum (built circa CE/AD 70–80).

48. GE Layer 48 frames a view of Masada, what out in the western U.S. you'd call a mesa, split off from the cliffs behind it. In the Google Earth surface and in the Photos icons you can see the Roman circumvallation wall and the diamond-shaped Roman camps along it, and the great siege ramp built up the side of the little mesa opposite the Dead Sea.

49. GE Layer 49 is a Placemark referencing Betar.

some interpretations of the Hebrew Scriptures, a messiah was to appear and lead a very physical return to Zion. This kind of religious Zionism flamed and flickered and never died in all the centuries of the Diaspora, as many a self-proclaimed messiah found it possible to gather followers in a revolt against the local authority.

Ashkenazi Jews: the European settlement

Even though Jewish communities did not generally fade into the larger societies around them, they did pick up some local language and custom. This, plus the fact that there was no independent center of communication, meant that each group developed a little differently. The greatest cultural split that grew up in the Diaspora was between the Sephardim, the Sephardic Jews of the Muslim cultural world, and the Ashkenazim, the Ashkenazi Jews of majority Christian Europe north and east of Spain. The Sephardic community was probably the higher civilization, at least in the early centuries of Diaspora: the Ladino that Sephardic Jews spoke developed into a true literary language. But to understand the modern Zionism that set up Israel, as well as the origins of modern western stereotypes of Jews (such as Shakespeare's Shylock demanding his pound of flesh), and that hatred of the whole Jewish population that goes by the name anti-Semitism, you ought first to study the Ashkenazi community of Europe.

The original large Ashkenazi settlement near the mouth of the river Rhine happened sometime before the year 1000. Here Diaspora Jews seem to have appeared first as international businessmen, invited in by local rulers who saw them as important in creating a modern economy. In coming to northern Europe, unfortunately, these Mediterranean merchants had moved into a much more primitive, even tribal, society. In the late 1000s a great panic ran through the Christian population here, a mostly irrational fear that Islamic armies were going to crush Christianity. It caused the preaching of the First Crusade in 1095. This was to be a religious war to the death against the infidels, literally "the unfaithful," in practice those other monotheists who denied the divinity of Christ. As German knights from the Rhineland marched out in 1096, it occurred to them that there were "infidels" closer to home than the Muslims in the Holy Land, and they massacred Jews as they marched upriver. In the atmosphere of the Crusades, which dominated the whole of the twelfth century and even beyond, the social status of Jews rapidly deteriorated. Economic sanctions followed, including the closing of the greater guilds to Jews and their exclusion from owning land. They were pushed more and more into the petty trades and into one of the occupations forbidden Christians of that day—moneylending, which to the medieval Christian church was the sin of usury. A pattern of expulsion from the cities and towns of western Europe forced a slow mass migration eastwards through southern and eastern Germany and then Poland. By 1795 the Russian Empire had conquered the bulk of Polish territory, and thus inherited this large Jewish minority. Inside the Russia Empire, Jews were restricted to these lands acquired from Poland and to a few others areas, mainly in the south along the Black Sea, that the Russian Empire wanted to colonize. This western slice of the Russian Empire came to be called the "Jewish Pale of Settlement."[GE[50]]

Inside the Pale most Jews lived in a Jewish quarter in some larger Polish or Russian town. The word *ghetto*, meaning the ironworks, originally came from the Jewish quarter in Venice, and then was generally applied to urban Jewish quarters all over Europe. A *shtetl* was a newer market town in the Russian Empire, midway in size between the cities and the farming villages. Most of the Jews in the Pale wound up in either shtetl or ghetto. Respected international businessmen no longer, they now survived as small-scale bankers, pawnbrokers, and small tradesmen, in the main. In some eight hundred years, then, the center of gravity of the whole Ashkenazi settlement was moved east, and most of its people were driven well down the socio-economic ladder.

If you looked at things from inside the ghetto, the old culture was alive and well. Every boy, at least, had to show he could read Hebrew by the time of his Bar Mitzvah when he was thirteen. And even though Hebrew had died out as a spoken language in the Ashkenazi community in central and eastern Europe, the Ashkenazim had gradually created their own spoken slang or argot, Yiddish (from the German *Jüdisch*, or Jewish), made up of German, Polish, and Russian as well as Hebrew—in a way, a historical record of their forced migration eastwards across Europe. But from the point of view of the larger Polish or Russian society that surrounded and dwarfed the ghettoes of the Pale of Settlement, here were outsiders who rejected the local religion, who stub-

---

50. GE Layer 50 is a Polygon showing the "Jewish Pale of Settlement."

bornly kept to strange social customs, who spoke a foreign language and who preyed economically on the larger Christian community. The counterpart of the miracle of Jewish cultural survival is a long-lived anti-Semitism. Ethnic prejudice has probably been around ever since the first two ethnic groups, but anti-Semitism is a deeper running, uglier strain than most. From the time of the Crusades on, popular anti-Jewish riots sporadically recurred in Europe. *Pogrom* (as used in English, the first syllable is usually stressed, though the original Russian is pronounced something like "poh-GROM," and since *grom* is the Russian word for "thunder," it should probably translate "rumble") in Russian originally meant any race riot, but so many anti-Jewish riots happened in Russia and Russian-Poland that in practice "pogrom" has come over into English to mean a riot against the Jews. Lots of them happened on or about Easter, when a Christian lynch mob would invade the local ghetto to repay "the killers of Christ." This hostility from outside, plus the real attraction of traditional Jewish culture and religion from inside, was enough to ensure that for centuries the energies and talents of these eastern European Jewish communities were directed inward. But the world outside still fascinated the younger and more adventurous, and the walls around the ghetto were about to crumble.

Enlightenment and Haskalah

The first real change in tone of European society toward Jews came with the eighteenth-century Enlightenment with its emphasis on the equality of all (men, at least, if not yet women) before the law. That included Jews, who up to this time were legally second-class. This new attitude became a tenet of the French Revolution and part of the law laid down in the Code Napoléon in 1804, as you saw in the French Enlightenment and Revolution chapter. In the course of the next fifty years that attitude gradually spread eastward through Europe, and by 1855 it got to Russia. As you may recall from the Russia and Socialism chapter, that was the year Nicholas I died, in the middle of a losing war with France and England in the Crimea. Despite his strict military-style rule for the past thirty years, Russia had somehow lost ground to western European countries. On his deathbed, Nicholas apparently made his son promise to change things, to copy some of the social and technological developments of western Europe. Alexander II responded with the Great Reforms of the first part of his rule—the emancipation of the serfs in 1861, then the Land Councils for local government, and by 1874 the modernization of the army. So it had taken Russia about eighty years to get the French *levée en masse* of 1793—a modern draft army based on a population of legally equal and hopefully patriotic citizens.

The effect of this liberal political nationalism on the Jewish ghetto was remarkable. No longer were Jews restricted to the slice of western Russia known as the Jewish Pale. For the first time they could enter Russian schools, including universities. They could own land and choose most any occupation. The new mood of tolerance is shown in the story (perhaps apocryphal, but still a good story) about Alexander II descending the palace steps one Easter morning in the early 1860s. To each member of the guard he would say in the Orthodox Christian ritual greeting, "Christ is risen," whereupon the guard would reply, "Yes, He is risen." Suddenly one soldier answered, *"Nichevo,"* which is to say, "Nope," or "Not at all." The Emperor froze, wondering who would deny the resurrection of Christ on Easter. The soldier swallowed hard, but went on to explain that he was Jewish, so of course he could not agree. Alexander II thought it over a minute, then slapped him on the back and complimented him on his courage, and proceeded on down the stairs.

Working parallel with Enlightenment ideas was a Jewish intellectual movement called *Haskalah*, from the Hebrew word for "enlightenment" (the root word is *Sekhel,* "mind," and one who is so "enlightened" is called a *Maskil*). In part this Haskalah called for increased Jewish participation in non-Jewish society. Never before had European ideas, institutions, and technology offered such power, or been so exciting, and this was a reaching out of sorts to that world. So the ghettoes of Russia had been softened up a bit toward the outside world, and many young Jews especially were ready to take advantage of the door opening into the Russian world. Soon the greater part of school-age Jewish kids went off to Russian-language schools, especially after the 1874 draft law limited the military service of those who had already graduated from high school. A Jewish press quickly emerged. Many small-scale Jewish enterprises went large scale, notably in railroads and finance. There was even some attempt to write modern European-style literature in Hebrew, though the classic Hebrew really lacked the vocabulary for it. Overall, here was a miniature Jewish Renaissance. For the first time in centuries, the energies of the ghetto were unchained.

The closing of the doors

For the more secular Jews, this was a happy turn of events. In fact, the leading intellectuals of this Jewish Enlightenment almost all agreed that the real solution for "the Jewish problem" in Russia was for Jews to assimilate into Russian society, to gradually take up the Russian cultural heritage and lay down their own. This, however, they were not allowed to do. The door of Russian society, so quickly thrown open to them, began slowly shutting again. Great anti-Semitic riots broke out, especially the 1871 pogroms at Kishinev and Odessa that left hundreds dead. The U.S. Minister to Russia reported on the changing mood with some uneasiness:

> Just after the emancipation of the serfs there was a general movement of the Russian liberals for the emanci-
> pation of the Jews. Now, since the spread of Slavophile and ultra-Russian ideas, it is not unusual to find strong
> liberals and democrats who are animated with the feelings of the Middle Ages toward the Hebrews . . . [*evrei*,
> Hebrews, was then the polite Russian for someone Jewish; *zhid* was considered derogatory][4]

Alexander II himself grew more conservative, and began to annul some of his own reforms. Student revolt grew into the first large-scale revolutionary underground in the 1870s as a reaction. In 1881 terrorists assassinated Alexander II during the parade celebrating the twentieth anniversary of freeing the serfs. As you saw earlier, the killing was in hopes of creating a mass revolution or at least bringing about a more liberal government, but instead Russia got Alexander III, who instituted a reign of repression. His new prime minister announced in public his formula for solving "the Jewish problem" in Russia: (a) assimilate a third of the Jews; (b) exile a third; and (c) kill the final third. At this point the Russian army actively began to organize pogroms instead of suppressing them.

Sponsoring anti-Jewish riots seems to have been a desperate attempt by the failing Russian government to win support by playing on popular racism, the lowest common denominator. The logic of cultural nationalism was working on the Russian side, too: this was a campaign of Russification aimed at every religious and ethnic minority in Russia, not just the Jews. For Jews that was little consolation. Their condition was unpleasant at best and dangerous at worst. Many escaped with what they could carry, mainly to Vienna (as you saw in the German chapter), to northern Italy, to London, to New York.

For those who remained, psychological reaction to this persecution ranged from despair and passive acceptance to rage and activism. Many of the younger, more emancipated Jews flocked to the underground of the Social Revolutionaries or the Social Democrats; there was even a special wing of the underground called the Jewish Socialist Bund, or League. The other great activist movement goes under the label Zionism, and needs to be discussed in some detail. Of all the Zionist leaders and thinkers talked about in the pages to come, leading up to the creation of the modern state of Israel in 1948, every single one except Theodor Herzl was born and raised in the Jewish Pale of Settlement in the Russian Empire. Even Golda Meir, America's great contribution to the Zionist movement and the state of Israel, was Russian born, and spent not much more than her teen years in Milwaukee, Wisconsin.

Zionism: a quick definition

Zionism is a surprisingly modern movement, just over a century and a half old. It is the movement sponsoring Jewish settlement in the land of Israel for political purposes—a very different thing than the small, primarily religious settlements that persisted in Palestine all through the Diaspora. To the author, it is clearly the mainstream form of modern Jewish nationalism (though many Zionists would disagree, seeing it as much too special a movement to be just another variety of nationalism). The movement falls into some clear-cut periods mainly determined by the different waves of Jewish population arriving in Palestine. These waves are customarily numbered, called the First Aliyah, the Second Aliyah, and so on, the word *aliyah* meaning literally "the going up." It is a value-loaded word: leaving Eretz Israel one descends to *galut*, or exile; going to Israel one ascends.

Ben-Yehuda and the rebirth of spoken Hebrew

Eliezer Perlman, born in 1858, was raised in a fairly typical Jewish community of the Russian Empire's Pale of Settlement (in what is today Belarus)[GE51]. With the new mood in Russia under Alexander II, he learned Russian and in 1877 graduated from a Russian high school. This was the year of the 1877–78 war between Russia and Turkey, Russia defending the right of the Christian, Slavic Balkan peoples to set up their own independent nation-states and in fact helping establish an independent Bulgarian state at war's end. The excited young student immediately saw the potential of such national movements for the scattered and disheartened Jewish people. If the Bulgarians could do it, why not the Jews? He and some like-minded young Jews conceived the idea of creating a Jewish cultural center in Eretz Israel, so Jews worldwide would have a focal point around which to rally and eventually create a new state. He prepared himself personally to immigrate to Palestine by going to Paris to become a medical doctor, so as to have a reliable occupation in what was then a backwater of the Turkish Empire. A case of tuberculosis convinced him he did not have long to live, so he dropped out of medical school and joined a Jewish teachers' training college in Paris that planned to open a school in Palestine. In articles he wrote for local Jewish publications he began calling himself *Ben-Yehuda*, which in Hebrew means Son of Judah. By 1880 he was arguing that Jewish writers writing in Hebrew did not use it in their everyday lives, and as a result it was stilted and artificial. Only a majority Jewish community settled in Palestine could revive Hebrew as a real, living language. In 1881 he made the trip, marrying on the way the Jewish girl from Russia who had tutored him Russian language a few years earlier, and promising her he would speak to her only in Hebrew when they set foot in Eretz Israel.

That was quite a job. Hebrew as an everyday spoken language had virtually died out in the European part of the Diaspora. It was little more than a classical language, written only by religious leaders and scholars and a few *maskilim*. Now Ben-Yehuda tried to use it for everything. How could you say things as simple as railroad? pocketwatch? electricity? As he set to work on a modern Hebrew dictionary, he had to create words from old Hebrew roots, including even the word for dictionary. His speech was full of pauses as he invented or modified ancient words, and must have been painful for others to listen to, at first. He named his first-born son Ben-Zion, and is said to have hovered over the child's cradle speaking and reading Hebrew to make the boy a native speaker. The child supposedly was late to speak, but he was indeed the first native Hebrew speaker of European descent in modern times.

As proof of the difference between this kind of Zionism and the older Jewish settlement in the land, look at Ben-Yehuda's relations with those residents. The existing Jewish settlement of perhaps 20,000, called the *yishuv*, included many devoutly religious people who came to spend their last days on holy soil. Ben-Yehuda was fascinated by their pronunciation, finding it more guttural and Arabic-sounding, and in his mind closer to purer, original Hebrew. He tried to get to know them better, and even adopted their costume. They did not reciprocate his overtures, being offended by his use of the language of the Scriptures for everyday matters. He in turn became openly anti-religious, and began to set up all sorts of modern European institutions that horrified the old religious community, especially his new school for girls. In 1894 they turned him into the Turkish authorities as a dangerous radical and had him imprisoned.

But friends got him free and his dictionary grew apace. In 1901 he took time out to translate *Around the World in Eighty Days* to show that even a modern novel could be presented in his new Hebrew. It was a remarkable achievement. This new Hebrew included the most up-to-date technological words, and yet was closer to the Hebrew spoken by Moses than even that of Roman times. An Israeli citizen today walking the land calls the hills and valleys by the same words as King David used, and somehow all the centuries in-between—including 1,300 years of almost exclusive Arab occupation—vanish. Ben-Yehuda's revival of Hebrew was a key to Jewish cultural nationalism.

51. GE Layer 51 is a Placemark referencing Luzhki, Eliezer Perlman/Ben-Yehuda's hometown.

The First Aliyah

Ben-Yehuda's success was made possible by a new audience, the 20,000 or so settlers of the first wave. Roughly the size of the old Jewish settlement, this first aliyah was more than a match for it in activity and direction. These immigrants came from 1882 to 1903 as a direct result of the great persecution that began in 1882 in Russia. Again, the best way to illustrate might be through the life of one individual, an organizer of this first aliyah.

Leon Pinsker (1821–1891), a Jewish physician in Odessa—the big southern seaport of Russia that had perhaps the largest Jewish community of any Russian city of the time—was one of the most enthusiastic "Enlighteners" of the 1860s. He founded the first Russian Jewish weekly and was a powerful writer for the cause of Jews learning Russian culture. The pogroms of 1871 shook his faith in all this and for ten years he retired back into the medical world. With the mass pogroms of 1881 his worst fears were confirmed. Up until this time Pinsker and most other Enlighteners had felt that more education would gradually do away with what they saw as the medieval survivals of ethnic hatred and race riots. Events of 1881–82 taught the more perceptive that a whole new era of anti-Semitism was dawning—one connected with folkish nationalism. So Pinsker joined the debate on what Jews could do to escape persecution. He toured Europe, anxiously talking with other Jewish leaders.

On his return in 1882, he wrote a book called *Self-Emancipation*. It began with the brutally frank assumption that everywhere Jews became numerous, they would be persecuted. Pinsker criticized those Jews in western Europe who had achieved civil rights and thought this storm would blow over. He saw its passive acceptance by the more religious Jews of eastern Europe as equally hopeless. His solution? Organize a new Exodus, preferably to Eretz Israel; set up a modern administration to organize it, and a treasury to fund it. From his base in Odessa, Pinsker tried to create such institutions, and became the acknowledged leader of the *Hovevei Zion* (Lovers of Zion) movement. Some colonies were actually sent out. When many of them foundered for lack of money and skills, Pinsker got the Baron Edmond de Rothschild, a French member of that fabulously rich clan, to take over their support. Pinsker's organization never generated enough funds to be much more than symbolic. And in his last years, even he began to doubt that an exodus to Palestine would work. The Turkish government tried to halt all immigration, and the Arab world showed its first signs of hostility.

Still, for good or ill, Zionism had just taken that giant step for any movement, one from the theoretical to the practical. In 1882 the first Jewish settlement established directly in Palestine by Russian Jews was set up and called *Rishon le-Zion*, "First in Zion."[GE52] Others of this first aliyah went to support *Petakh Tikvah*, "Gateway of Hope,"[GE53] a village that had been set up by Jerusalem Jews in 1878 but that was about to go under. An 1886 poem in Hebrew inspired by news of the founding of Gateway of Hope (and set to the tune of Bedrich Smetana's Czech nationalist musical tone poem *Vltava* or *Die Moldau*) became the anthem of these pioneers. Some of the original lines went like this: "our hope is not yet lost, the age-old hope; to return to the land of our fathers, to the city where David dwelt." Today it is the Israeli national anthem *Hatikvah*.[GE54]

Theodor Herzl and the Zionist Congresses

Meanwhile, back in Europe, this Zionism was going mostly unnoticed by the general public and was in fact being rejected even by most Jews who knew of it. But the man who was to make it popular was waiting in the wings—Theodor Herzl. He was from a wealthy, Germanized family of the Austrian Empire, and had been a casual law student at Vienna and something of a high society dandy.[GE55] In 1889, by the time he was twenty-nine, success had come almost too easily. He had become a well-known society journalist, one of the editors of a major Viennese daily paper, and had a handsome young wife and two small sons. Then life turned on him; his best friend committed suicide and his own marriage went on the rocks. By the mid-1890s, the mayor of

---

52. GE Layer 52 is a Placemark referencing Rishon le Zion. Zoom out for relationship to coast, Tel Aviv/Yafo.

53. GE Layer 53 is a Placemark referencing Petakh Tikvah.

54. GE Layer 54 is a Placemark generally framing a view of Israel, but used here as an excuse for embedding a website, the clicking on of which will yield Barbara Streisand singing *Hatikvah*.

55. GE Layer 55 is a Folder titled "Theodor Herzl's life: some sites." It begins with his hometown of Budapest.

Vienna was Karl Lueger, whose popular rhetoric was pro-Catholic and explicitly anti-Jewish (he was still going strong as mayor a dozen years later when he was admired there by a young Adolf Hitler). To get out of this depressing personal and public arena of Vienna, Theodor Herzl transferred to France as foreign correspondent for his paper. He got there just in time to cover the greatest political scandal of that generation, the Dreyfus affair.

Now the Dreyfus affair is complicated, but the outline, at least, is clear. French military secrets known only to the General Staff were being leaked to the Germans by someone who signed his letters with the initial "D." Military investigators quickly jumped to the conclusion that it was Captain Alfred Dreyfus, the first Jewish member of the General Staff of the French army. He was court-martialed, convicted, and sent to Devil's Island, the infamous French penal colony off the coast of French Guiana in South America. But secrets continued to be leaked, and open-minded investigators had to conclude that either Dreyfus was not the guilty party, or that he was the world's greatest spy, able to continue his work from Devil's Island! Some said he was obviously innocent and should be brought back and exonerated. Others argued that the Dreyfus case should not be reopened: the French army was in a desperate race with Germany and anything that shook the public's faith in the army would hurt France. To this last argument was added a nasty streak of anti-Semitism. Dreyfus was Jewish, wasn't he? If he hadn't sold these secrets, he would probably sell others. The argument leaked out to the public, and all France chose sides in a bitter public debate. It split up marriages, and there were brothers on opposite sides of the issue who never spoke to one another the rest of their lives. It generated a viciously anti-Semitic political party called Action Française. It was the biggest political event in France between the war with Prussia/Germany in 1870 and the outbreak of World War I in 1914.

There was Herzl, covering the affair. He would not have been much surprised by such virulent anti-Semitism in central or eastern Europe, but apparently understood that if this sort of thing could happen in liberal western Europe, it could happen anywhere. Being ethnically Jewish had never really been important to Herzl (his favorite composer as a young man was Richard Wagner!). Now, however, it seems that he was personally obliged to wrestle with being Jewish in a hostile Gentile world.

His first idea for a solution was strange: take all the Jewish children in Europe on some Sunday morning, dress them up, and walk them down to the closest Christian church to be baptized into Christianity. Voilá, no Jews, no Jewish problem. This was obviously crazy, and Herzl's chief editor told him so; it was not just a religious problem but a cultural one. Herzl's second idea, from 1895—not original, though he did not know it yet—was more powerful, and he must have felt he had the key to the problem, because he began a diary. For the rest of his life he was a man in the grip of a single idea, as you can see by the opening passage:

> I have been pounding away for some time at a work of tremendous magnitude. I don't know even now if I will be able to carry it through. It bears the aspects of a mighty dream. For days and weeks it has saturated me to the limits of my consciousness; it goes with me everywhere, hovers behind my ordinary talk, peers at me over the shoulders of my funny little journalistic work, overwhelms and intoxicates me.[5]

With this Herzl began the last whirlwind ten years of his life, asking the rich for financial help, the powerful for political help, traveling and talking to any group that would listen. In 1896 he wrote a pamphlet called simply "The Jewish State," setting out his plan. It is clear (from this same quotation used at the first of the chapter) that he was modeling its development on the other national movements of the century:

> To create a new State is neither ridiculous nor impossible. Haven't we witnessed the process in our own day, among nations which were not largely middle class as we are, but poorer, less educated, and consequently weaker than ourselves?[6]

All that was needed was title to some land somewhere, and a great exodus from Europe to it. A Jewish Society could organize the funding, plan the settlement of the country and direct it, step by step. A series of yearly Zionist Congresses would give guidance to the Jewish Society.

Now the outline of the plan was roughly that of Leon Pinsker's of fifteen years before; Herzl later said if he had known of Pinsker's work he would not have written his own. But this one, in the hands of a world-class publicist, "took," whereas Pinsker's remained an isolated Russian phenomenon. In 1897 the First Zionist Congress met in Basle, Switzerland, and all of a sudden Zionism was front-page news. In the enthusiasm of the hour Herzl wrote in his journal, "At Basle I founded the Jewish State." Maybe that was true, in the popular mind, but it was fifty-one stormy years yet to the creation of modern Israel.

By 1903, the practical achievements of Herzl's Zionism were these: the movement had grown dramatically, and had a sizeable treasury as well as membership. But the setbacks were dramatic, too. The Sultan of Turkey, after initially considering it, refused to sell any part of Palestine, and a debate on whether or not to accept the British government's tentative offer of Uganda (!) was splitting the movement. Herzl's own health was rapidly deteriorating, due to a heart condition and the fantastic pace he kept up. And yet conditions for European Jews were getting more desperate, especially with the new wave of pogroms that began in Russia in 1903.

The vision still haunted Herzl, and his last work dealt with the dream of what could be rather than what actually was. He wrote what we would call a science fiction or utopian novel, *Altneuland* (*Old New Land*) about what an independent Jewish state might look like twenty years after its founding. Some of his predictions were uncanny, as in the use of new technology to make the desert bloom. Some were incredibly naive, as in his view of the brotherly relations that would prevail between Arab and Jew as linguistic cousins. In 1904, the heart that had raced for ten years broke; but in this last decade of his life, Herzl had served as the catalyst for mass political nationalism among European Jews. The Zionist Congresses and the Jewish Agency would continue on as the greatest outside source of help to the growing Jewish settlements in Palestine. In 1948 when the State of Israel was proclaimed, a single giant portrait hung on the stage curtain of the auditorium in Tel Aviv: Theodor Herzl's.

The Fiddler on the Roof

What Herzl gave the great bulk of Russian Jews was encouragement and organization. Suddenly this famous and sophisticated Austrian journalist had joined their cause and made it world news. What Herzl lacked, though, was any feel for eastern Jewish culture, that majority Jewish culture of Europe. What did he know about Yiddish? He spoke neither it nor the new Hebrew; German was his language. Eretz Israel did not have the same meaning for him, either; he was willing to accept Uganda as the Jewish national homeland.

Eastern European Jewish folk culture revolved around the ancient religious observances and festivals and the ghetto and shtetl ways of making a living. It was a round of Sabbaths, matchmakings, weddings, of better-off young men studying the Talmud in the synagogue and peddlers doing business in a suspicious world of Christians, all punctuated by the occasional pogrom. Yiddish as an everyday dialect had absorbed the folk characters, the bitter satire, the humor-through-tears of life lived by a persecuted minority. Inevitably with the rising consciousness of being Jewish and proud of it came the celebration of Yiddish as an important part of Jewish culture. Shalom Aleichem (the Hebrew greeting "Peace to you" pen name taken by Solomon Rabinovich, 1859–1916) is the most famous of those who began to use Yiddish as a literary language. Between 1894 and 1916 he developed his most famous work, *Tevye's Daughters*, the basis for the internationally acclaimed musical and later a film of the 1960s, *The Fiddler on the Roof.* In the long run Yiddish could not compete with a revived Hebrew, but in the short run its celebration was an important consciousness-raiser.[GE⁵⁶]

Ahad Ha'am

More profound than Shalom Aleichem in his stress on eastern European Jewish culture was Ahad Ha'am (the "One of the Folk" pen name taken by Asher Ginzberg, born 1856, died 1927). Raised in a devoutly religious family, he nevertheless gave up religious belief altogether. In Odessa in the 1880s he was drawn into Pinsker's Lovers of Zion movement, but was critical of the new Jewish settlements. He saw them as premature and not connected enough with Jewish tradition. In 1891 he actually went to Turkish-controlled Palestine for a few months, and reported back that the fertile agricultural land was all long since occupied by the Arabs—

---

56. GE Layer 56 is a Folder titled "Shalom Aleichem sites." His final years were spent in New York.

demolishing to his own satisfaction the catchy, breezy, but ill-informed Zionist slogan that called Palestine "the land without people for the people without land."

Perhaps the single most brilliant Zionist writer, Ahad Ha'am saw national belonging as a natural biological emotion. In his view, Jews living in scattered minority groups were either so enslaved to the old writings that they had no creativity of their own, or were so impressed with European culture that they tried to quit being Jewish. Ahad Ha'am called for Jews to identify with their cultural heritage for its own sake. This man who did not believe in God defended the Orthodox practice of Judaism as a key part of the cultural heritage!

Overall, Ahad Ha'am created a sort of sub-nationalism for Jews of the Russian Empire, and found for them a whole new pride in their way of life. He integrated ancient and modern events, giving familiar historical labels to confusing contemporary happenings and familiar contemporary labels to confusing historical happenings. Regarding the destruction of the Second Temple in 68 CE, for example, he presented the Essenes as anti-political spiritualists, the Zealots as materialists who stayed on the walls sword in hand to defend the state to the last, and between these extremes, the Pharisees as realists who found the means for preserving the nation during the Diaspora. Ahad Ha'am made Zionism much more attractive to eastern European Jews than Herzl did. He disguised the fact that modern Jewish nationalism was inspired by, and to some extent a copy of, other European nationalisms. He built bridges between modern Zionism and ancient Jewish traditions.

The Second Aliyah

A whole new wave of pogroms in the Russian Empire in 1903 precipitated the Second Aliyah. The city of Kishinev in the extreme southeast of the Russian Empire (today's Chişinău, capital of Moldova) where the pogroms began had around 100,000 people, just about half of them Jewish.[GE⁵⁷] With the support of the highest local authorities and evidently even the Russian Minister of Interior, a huge anti-Semitic press campaign built to a crescendo by Easter weekend. Then two days of pillage and rape left around 50 dead, 500 injured, and 2,000 homeless. The Russian state had just renewed its civil war against its Jewish minority.

Chaim Bialik, one of the first really talented writers to commit to Ben-Yehuda's new modern Hebrew, was sent by the Jewish Historical Commission in Odessa to research the Kishinev pogrom. From his interviews with survivors came a celebrated poem variously translated "Town of Death" or "City of Slaughter." It is angry and agonized; but the anger is directed as much at Jewish fatalism and meekness as at Russian or Romanian rioters: daughters and mothers being raped in the presence of one another, husbands and brothers hiding and watching, husbands only coming out later to ask the rabbi if—now that his wife had been raped—it was alright to resume sexual relations with her . . . . It's a powerful poem that goes on for pages, and I'm sorry we couldn't get permission to use extracts here (see Endnote for website with text, as well as printed sources).[7]

This anger and sense of danger galvanized young people, in particular, into action. The Second Aliyah of 1904 to 1914 was twice the size of the First Aliyah—roughly 50,000 strong—and although it was also mainly from eastern Europe, it was very different in character. These confident young socialists created the first Jewish cooperatives and communes, the first Jewish labor party, and the first Jewish self-defense forces in Palestine. Of all the waves of settlement, the Second Aliyah was most important in the creation of (and character of!) the modern state of Israel.

Now socialism may originally have seemed a strange thread to weave into a story about national creation— we usually think of socialism as international in flavor, a challenger of nationalism instead of a supporter: "Workers of the World, Unite!," and all that. Having seen Hitler's "national-socialism" and Stalin's "fatherland socialism" earlier in this textbook, however, you should be somewhat prepared to see these two "isms" go together here. European Jewish intellectuals in particular were always conscious that most Jews were not laborers in the factory or on the farm the way most people of other ethnic groups were. As a result many of them were struck with special force by socialist ideas on the dignity of labor: Jewish manual labor might be a way to "normalize" the Jewish position in the world. In this light, consider a series of cameo biographies of these Second Aliyah pioneers and groups.

---

57. GE Layer 57 is a Placemark referencing Kishinev/Chişinău.

Manya Shochat

Manya Shochat was born in 1880 in western Russia, the eighth child of fervently religious Orthodox Jewish parents who also admired the Russian Emperor. The stress and strain of being Jewish at this time in Russia really shows in her own family. Three of her older siblings committed suicide. Another, influenced by Tolstoy, became a peasant laborer; one became a socialist who fled to the U.S. to escape arrest; and one became a Zionist who emigrated to Palestine. In the first twenty-seven years of Manya Shochat's own life, she went from sincere religious belief, to Russian narodnichestvo with a vocation in carpentry, to leader of workers' strikes in police unions, to terrorism, and finally to Zionism and agricultural collectivism with a feminist slant. In 1901 she helped establish the Jewish Independent Labor Party, and in 1903 when the Russian Minister of Interior von Plehve ended all police unions and renewed the war on the Jewish minority, she joined an underground group pledged to assassinate him. Her brother in Palestine, afraid for her life in Russia, wrote to her claiming to be sick and needing her help, and so tricked her into joining him in Palestine in 1904. By 1907 she engineered the set-up of the Sejera Collective, probably the first Jewish collective in Palestine.[GE58] Eighteen young men and women were its full membership, and Manya Shochat insisted that women have "equal duties and full membership."[8]

That was a really radical break with Jewish tradition. According to a contemporary Jewish immigrant to the U.S. from western Russia:

> In Russia, a [Jewish] woman was nothing. [But] a boy was very important in Jewish life for a lot of things. When my father used to pray in the morning with his prayer shawl, I used to hear him say in Hebrew, "Thank God I'm not a woman." A girl wasn't much.[9]

It was Manya Shochat and her Second Aliyah friends who originated that much-celebrated Israeli equality of the sexes.

In 1910, three years after Shochat set up the first collective, the first real commune (*kibbutz* in Hebrew) was established. Ten guys and two girls age 17–21 leased some land near the southern corner of the Sea of Galilee, promising to pay the rent out of the harvest. When they got there the cornflowers were in bloom, so they named it "Cornflower," *Deganya* in Hebrew.[GE59] The men began working the fields in two shifts of five, with the women doing the housework—but when they all got malaria anyone with the strength to pick up a hoe went to the fields and that old European Jewish sexual division of labor was further eroded. When one of the young men, Moshe Barsky, was killed in a clash with local Arabs, his young married friends Shmuel and Miriam Dayan named their baby boy for him, Moshe Dayan. For Americans who lived during the establishment and first years of the modern Israeli state, this courageous, one-eyed Israeli general with a passion for archaeology was the great visual symbol of the new state of Israel. One of the first children born in the first kibbutz, and named for its first casualty, he came by his uncompromising Israeli patriotism rather naturally.

At the end of that first year, Deganya paid off its rent out of the harvest with a little left over. It proved that young, hard-working immigrants could stake a claim to the land with no money down, and the institution quickly spread. These Russian-Jewish communes, or *kibbutzim*, never held more than 5 percent of the Jewish population of Palestine at any one time, but they had an impact all out of proportion to their size. First, an ideal of commitment and unselfishness took concrete form here. Second, the kibbutzim were to be the armed outposts on the fringes of Jewish expansion into the increasingly hostile Arab areas of the land.

A. D. Gordon

Aaron David Gordon was a generation older than most of these young pioneers, or *chalutzim*, of this Second Aliyah. He had been foreman of a major estate in Russia, and the only unusual aspect of his early adulthood had been his fascination with children's education. In that same year of 1904, at age forty-seven, he made his own personal aliyah to Palestine. Here he was going to work out his own personal redemption through labor.

---

58. GE Layer 58 is a Placemark generally referencing Sejera (today's Ilaniya).

59. GE Layer 59 is a Placemark referencing Deganya; note multiple campuses today—Deganya A, B, etc.

The intellect, he said, is like a flame illuminating the dark around a person the way nothing else could. But the flame burns on the oil of personal doing, physical doing, and too much emphasis on the flame without worrying about replenishing the physical oil impoverishes any person. Consider his words below:

> Whatever man creates for the sake of life is culture: the tilling of the soil, the building of homes, of all kinds of buildings, the paving of roads, and so on. Each piece of work, each deed, each act is an element of culture. Herein is the foundation of culture, the stuff of which it is made. Arrangement, method, shape, the way in which a thing is done—these are the forms of culture. What a man does, what he feels, thinks, lives, while he is at work and while he is not working, the conditions arising from these relations—these mould themselves into the spirit of culture. From these, higher culture draws its nourishment—science, art, beliefs and opinions, poetry, ethics, religion. Higher culture or culture in its restricted sense, the culture which we mean when we speak of culture, is the *butter* of culture in general, of culture in its broader sense. But is it possible to make butter without milk or will man make butter from the milk of others, and will the butter then be his very own?[10]

His "religion of labor" and the attractive gentleness of his character made his home in Petakh Tikvah a place of pilgrimage for many young Jewish pioneers.

David Ben-Gurion

Finally, take the case of David Grien, born in 1886 in a small factory town in Russian Poland.[GE60] His father had been a member of Lovers of Zion, and Grien grew up in this atmosphere. At age fourteen, he and some friends made up their own Zionist youth club, pledging to speak only Hebrew among themselves. Then at age seventeen he experienced the 1903 wave of pogroms that left Jewish dead in many towns. He promptly joined *Po'alei Zion*, Workers of Zion, a Jewish socialist organization with some Marxist class struggle ideas. Two years of underground activity in the Russian Empire did not satisfy him, and in 1905, not quite twenty years old, he made his own aliyah to Eretz Israel.

When David Grien landed at Jaffa and walked around Palestine, he was amazed and a bit turned off by the lifestyles of First Aliyah Jews. He was a young radical, a socialist deeply committed to living by the sweat of his own brow and not someone else's. It seemed to him that the older Jews were not workers at all, but landlords ("effendi" was the local term) or foremen of Arab labor gangs. "It was clear to me," he wrote, "that we could never achieve national rehabilitation that way. Between the land and the people, there had to be a bond of labor." The only true Zionism for these Second Aliyah pioneers was the working of the land.

Grien and friends carried the Workers of Zion organization with them from Russia, and it flowered in Palestinian soil. From Workers of Zion and the new collectives and kibbutzim grew *Ha-Shomer*, the Watchman, the first Jewish guard for these little agricultural settlements. These pioneers were contemptuous of urban Jews, scornful of Lovers of Zion, and suspicious of Herzl's brand of Zionism. The only important things in politics and society were Jewish labor unity and waging the class struggle in Palestine. In David Grien's commitment, he went through the name change so common in great emotional movements: in 1910 he signed an article for the party newspaper not Grien but Ben-Gurion, a Hebrew word with the same consonants but built on the word for lion. Thirty-eight years later, no longer young but still a socialist way to the left of anything on the modern U.S. political scale, David Ben-Gurion would be chosen first Prime Minister of the state of Israel.

Chaim Weizmann and the Balfour Declaration

Chaim Weizmann (1874–1952), the first President of Israel, explained the traditional Jewish passion for education this way: "The acquisition of knowledge was not for us so much a normal process of education as the storing up of weapons in an arsenal by means of which we hoped later to be able to hold our own in a hostile world."[11] Weizmann broke out of the Russian Pale[GE61] by means of his own scholarship, and eventually got

---

60. GE Layer 60 is a Placemark referencing David Grien/Ben Gurion's hometown of Plonsk, not far from Warsaw.

61. GE Layer 61 is a Placemark referencing Chaim Weizmann's hometown of Motal, near Pinsk in today's southern Belarus.

a first-rate education in chemistry at German and Swiss universities. For a time before World War I he was a world-class chemist at the University of Manchester, England, though that profession was gradually eclipsed by his activity in Zionism.

Weizmann lived through the 1881 pogroms at a tender age and seems to have been something of a Zionist from then on. He was attracted by Herzl's dynamic leadership in 1896, though he was always much more impressed by Ahad Ha'am. From him Weizmann seems to have gotten a concern for the cultural quality of the movement and more than the usual sensitivity to any wrong done victims of the movement. Weizmann soon broke with Herzl, seeing his purely diplomatic efforts as fruitless and shallow. In 1903 when the second wave of pogroms began in Kishinev, Weizmann abandoned his classes and returned to the Pale to organize self-defense groups there. When Herzl came visiting the reactionary Russian Minister of Interior von Plehve, in an obviously hopeless attempt to stop the pogroms, Weizmann was angered that any Jew would engage such a man in polite conversation.

Weizmann's immediate importance to the Zionist movement was in setting in motion forces that resulted in the establishment of Hebrew University in Jerusalem, and then in what after Herzl's death was called "synthetic" Zionism—trying to bring into the movement everybody from left-wing socialists to right-wing Orthodox Jews by emphasizing the broadest common denominators of Zionism. But his key contribution to the movement may have been as go-between with Great Britain.

When Weizmann arrived in Manchester in 1904, an obscure chemistry professor in retreat from a fragmented Zionist movement, he knew neither English language, customs, nor style of humor. He learned the first fluently and came to a real appreciation of the others, especially the individual freedom he saw about the English. In 1906 former Prime Minister Arthur Balfour interviewed him in an attempt to learn why Zionists had rejected the earlier British offer of Uganda. Weizmann's explanations captivated him and eventually affected even Lloyd George and Winston Churchill. In World War I, by which time Weizmann was both a naturalized British citizen and had achieved an important biochemical breakthrough in the production of acetone for the British explosives industry, Lloyd George was Minister of Munitions, Churchill was First Lord of Admiralty, and Balfour was Foreign Secretary. The upshot of this combination (and some other factors, discussed below) in 1917 was an official British policy known as the Balfour Declaration, quoted here in full:

> His Majesty's Government view with favour the establishment in Palestine of a national home for the Jewish people, and will use their best endeavours to facilitate the achievements of this object, it being clearly understood that nothing shall be done which may prejudice the civil and religious rights of existing non-Jewish communities in Palestine, or the rights and political status enjoyed by Jews in any other country.

The word "state" is not actually used, and the rights of Arabs are at least mentioned (though the Arabs are not named), but in effect the British government here put itself on record as favoring a Jewish political unit in Palestine. This was not an altogether altruistic policy. The British hoped in this way to do something about the huge and growing eastern European Jewish community in London, and perhaps also saw this as a way to stake an imperial claim to Palestine at the expense of the French. But the chief impulse does seem to have been humane. The British government was, generally speaking, one of the first in the world to understand and sympathize with the Jewish predicament in Europe. It would take the British government a few more years to come to the same understanding of the Arab condition in Palestine, but, once again, this gets ahead of the story.

World War I in the region

When war broke out in August of 1914, the Ottoman Empire was on one side and the British Empire on the other, and one of the fronts was the line between British Egypt and the Turkish Sinai Peninsula, a line that included the Suez Canal.

Most Jewish settlers of the First and Second Aliyahs left Palestine for the duration of the war; many of them rode it out in Alexandria, Egypt's big port city. By late 1917 the tide of war was turning against Turkey and its German allies. The British General Edmund Allenby, head of an Egyptian Expeditionary Force (EEF) based in the Nile delta, feigned an attack on Gaza—strongly garrisoned by the Turks, who had beaten off several British attacks there earlier—and in a surprise right hook took Beersheba, outflanking the Turkish defenses. Much of his campaign across Palestine, headed towards Damascus and points north, can be explained by the existing Turkish railroad network.[GE62] When Allenby's forces took Junction Station at Wadi Sara,[GE63] it broke the Turkish hold on the whole Jaffa-Jerusalem line, and Allenby—who had been charged with capturing Jerusalem by Christmas—entered the city on December 11. Then a British assault on Amman failed, and their drive stalled as manpower was drained off to meet the last serious German offensive on the western front. It wasn't until August that enough troops and supplies could be brought in to renew the advance. In mid-September 1918, a week-long "Battle of Megiddo" was the result. A left wing of the British army swept up the Plain of Sharon to the base of Mount Carmel, and a right wing fought for the Judean hill town of Nablus, but the main spearhead in the center went up and over Megiddo Pass in Mount Carmel, raced down the Jezreel Valley and then down the lower Jordan, crossed the Jordan River near Jericho and took Amman on September 25 ("Allenby Bridge"[GE64] remains as physical testimony). Damascus fell on October 1 (though Arab armies entered the city first; more later), and the Ottoman Empire surrendered by month's end.

The real importance of the Balfour Declaration was revealed in 1918 when the war ended. Britain was by then a victor with an army occupying Palestine, and in 1920 officially got Palestine as a "mandate territory" to rule temporarily and oversee its development. Seeing that the same power that called for a Jewish "national home" in Palestine now owned the country, not only did First and Second Aliyah pioneers return, but Jews from eastern Europe responded in an enthusiastic tide of immigration. This Third Aliyah of 1919 to 1921 was short but spectacular.

Massive Arab backlash

This narrative has tried to keep the focus on things Jewish, saving general Arab and specific Palestinian things for later. But this new wave of Jewish immigration, plus the failure in 1918 of the first mass wave of Arab nationalism, to be discussed in detail later, created a touchy situation in British-ruled Palestine that has to be mentioned at this point. The first mass Arab riots against Jews in Palestine exploded in 1921 and 1922. Winston Churchill, by this time head of the Colonial Office, showed a new British awareness of Arab aspirations in the "Churchill White Paper" of June 1922. First, he set up a purely Arab state in Palestine east of the Jordan (Trans-jordan, it was called), thus effectively limiting the Balfour Declaration to west of the river.[GE65] Second, the principle of "economic absorptive capacity" of the country west of the Jordan River for Jewish immigration was established: that is, no Jew could come in and knock an Arab out of a job. Nonetheless the next great Arab riots came in 1929, leaving over a hundred Jewish dead and massive property destruction. In May 1930 the "Passfield White Paper" of the British government suspended Jewish immigration altogether and sharply limited the authority of the Zionist Jewish Agency to acquire more land there.

It was not just the British who were becoming aware of Arab points of view. Many Zionists whose concern had been Russian pogroms or Turkish officialdom were now abruptly awakened to local political realities. In retrospect Zionist lack of awareness of Arab presence and attitudes seems unbelievably naive. At first European Zionists were simply ignorant of an Arab presence in Palestine. You've already encountered that late nineteenth-century Zionist phrase that called Palestine "the land without people for the people without land." And then having discovered there were Arabs there, many Zionists were confident for a time that Arabs would welcome a Jewish majority in Palestine, assuming that the material prosperity and European-style organization the Jews would bring would be more attractive to the Arabs than maintaining their cultural integrity. With the Arab riots of the 1920s, some key Zionists—especially Chaim Weizmann, who knew so many Arab leaders—began

---

62. GE Layer 62 is a Folder titled "RR network ca. 1914."

63. GE Layer 63 is a Placemark referencing Wadi Sara, the approximate location of the Junction Station.

64. GE Layer 64 is a Placemark referencing Allenby Bridge.

65. GE Layer 65 is a Placemark framing a view of the international borders of today's Jordan. Notice the indentation on the east side; since Churchill once claimed he had thought this state up over a brandy, that indentation is sometimes referred to as "Winston's hiccup."

to see the Arab side of it too. By 1931 Weizmann had backed away from insisting on a majority Jewish state in Palestine.

Vladimir Jabotinsky and the Jewish Legion

There was an important countercurrent in Zionism, however, that from the point of modern U.S. politics was as far right as Ben-Gurion and the mainstream Zionists were far left. It was created and led by Vladimir Jabotinsky. Born in Odessa in 1880, Jabotinsky was raised in a cosmopolitan atmosphere that included little Jewish tradition. He spent his college years in Swiss and Italian universities. Already a superb writer and a phenomenal linguist, he picked up fluency in languages the way most undergraduates pick up single courses. Jabotinsky's three years in turn-of-the-century Italy were crucial, as he wrote in his autobiography:

> If I have a spiritual homeland, it is Italy much more than Russia. From the day of my arrival there I became fully integrated into Italian youth, and its life I lived until I left Italy. All my views on problems of nationalism, the state and society were developed during these years under Italian influence . . . . The legend of Garibaldi, the writings of Mazzini, the poetry of Leopardi and Guisti have enriched and deepened my superficial Zionism: from an instinctive feeling they made it into a doctrine.[12]

Here the brilliant Jabotinsky absorbed the intellectual beginnings of that integral nationalism which later surfaced as Fascism. He came to believe that there was "no value higher in the world than the nation and the fatherland, there is no deity in the universe to which one should sacrifice these two most valuable jewels."[13] And so this Jewish student in Italy came to Zionism with the enthusiasm of a convert. Somewhat attracted by Marxist socialism before World War I, he became its enemy after the 1917 Bolshevik Revolution. His language came to be that of the nationalism plus socialism of his day, with an emphasis on military might and discipline, on why some races were naturally superior (European Jews and most other Europeans) and others inferior (Arabs, Bushmen, and most other non-European peoples), on the "will to power" and even the role of the Leader. He was fascinated by the mass rallies and ceremonials of early Fascism. Despite his brilliance, he seems to many in a later age something of a small-scale Mussolini who never came to power.

But Jabotinsky had hold of two truths that it took mainstream Zionists longer to learn or accept. He understood early on that the creation of a Jewish state in Palestine would necessitate violence and armed force against the Arab inhabitants of the land. Secondly, he was aware of the desperate position of Jews in central and eastern Europe (what he called "the zone of incurable anti-Semitism") before any other major Zionist leader. They were heading towards a general "Bartholomew Night," he said, likening what was to come to the great Catholic massacre of Protestants in France in 1572. No other major figure of his generation made such a chillingly accurate prediction.

The Jewish Legion was the first institutional fruit of his thought. In 1914 there were some 12,000 Jewish refugees from Turkish Palestine living in Alexandria, Egypt, behind British lines. Jabotinsky appeared, calling for a Jewish military unit to fight in Palestine under the British flag. Josef Trumpeldor, a one-armed Jewish ex-Russian army officer just Jabotinsky's age, enthusiastically agreed to lead such a unit. The British, a bit nervous about the diplomatic implications of this, offered a compromise—a transportation unit to be known as the Zionist Mule Corps. Now Jabotinsky was doing this not just for a place at the peace conference after the war, but for a little pride. Off he went in a huff—he was not pulling any mules around. Trumpeldor, however, recognized that transportation was just as important in modern war as front-line heroism, and that the principle of British recognition of Zionist institutions was still true. Under him the Mule Corps actually served in the ill-fated Gallipoli campaign of 1915.

By 1916, now in England and in temporary alliance with Weizmann, Jabotinsky won approval for a front-line unit to fight in Palestine. To his great embarrassment most of the huge Russian-Jewish community in London was not just neutral but actively hostile to the idea. Three Jewish regiments were slowly created, however, and in June 1918, with Jabotinsky himself as a simple company commander, they were transferred to the front line twenty miles north of Jerusalem. In September, in the wake of the Battle of Megiddo, Jabotinsky's company was the first unit of the British army to cross the Jordan.

Jabotinsky's activities surely had some role in encouraging Britain to issue the Balfour Declaration of 1917. After the war, though, Jabotinsky's militarism was rejected by the British and mainstream Zionists alike. His shrill calls for unleashing the remnant of the Jewish Legion against Arab rioters got a cold reception. By 1923 Jabotinsky and his ideas had been rejected by the key Zionist institutions and leaders as well as the British Mandate government. Frustrated and isolated, he retreated to the Jewish communities of eastern Europe.

BETAR and Irgun

In October 1923 Jabotinsky was speaking to Jewish students in Riga, the capital of Latvia which had only been independent of Russia since 1917 (and which would be again owned by the Russian-dominated Soviet Union from 1940 to 1989). Students listening to Jabotinsky's stirring speeches told him either to quit stirring them up or organize them. The result was *Brit Trumpeldor*—the Trumpeldor League. Josef Trumpeldor had been killed in 1920 when an Arab assault wave overran a Jewish village he was defending; he was one of the first famous martyrs among the Russian-Jewish pioneers. Jabotinsky's movement in his name—BETAR for short ("Betar" also to memorialize the town where Bar Kokhba fought to the death against Hadrian's armies)—was to "militarize the Jewish youth of Palestine and the Diaspora." It was to be a cult of physical fitness, uniforms, discipline, and elaborate titles (Jabotinsky himself was "Head of World BETAR"). There were armed bodyguards for meetings as was becoming the norm for socialist and nationalist parties all over continental Europe. Always the institutional apple of Jabotinsky's eye, BETAR grew to over 78,000 members in fifteen years' time, mostly in eastern Europe.

On the basis of this new support, Jabotinsky in 1925 created the Revisionist Party of Zionism. It was always distrusted by mainstream Zionists for what they called its fascism. Revisionists and BETAR-im were in these years the key sponsors of *Aliyah Bet* (the illegal, therefore "B-grade immigration" was the joke) to get around the quotas established by the British. Less visible at the time, but looming large in historical hindsight, were Jabotinsky's 1930s attempts to form a coalition of all non-socialist Zionists, including even ultra-Orthodox non-Zionists. It was to be an alliance between extreme nationalists for whom culture and religion were important only as they expressed national character and belonging, and Orthodox believers who were increasingly positive about a Jewish Palestine as pressures on the Jewish community grew in Europe.

After 1935 or so, with the desperate need to rescue Jews from Nazi Germany, many Zionist leaders came around to parts of Jabotinsky's earlier program. *Haganah*, the underground Jewish army in Palestine, grew more active, and illegal immigration got more popular support from the Jewish community.

But Jabotinsky, too, was pushed further ideologically by the Holocaust. By this time he was into eye-for-an-eye retaliation against Arabs, and into a certain degree of violence against the British who in his eyes had reneged on earlier promises. Jabotinsky's ideology became the touchstone for a minority group of Haganah officers. In 1931 and 1932 there had been rumblings of discontent; in 1937 a group of officers seceded from Haganah and formed the *Irgun Zevai Leummi*, or National Military Organization. Usually called I.Z.L. or simply Irgun, it was mostly made up of former BETAR-im. Changes in policy and top leadership went for approval, not to any institution, but to Jabotinsky alone.

In 1940 Jabotinsky died of a heart attack while inspecting a BETAR camp in New Jersey. Within a month of his death the Stern group, even more radical, splintered off of Irgun. By 1943 a fairly new Jewish immigrant in British Palestine was chosen head of Irgun. Born in 1913, he had been a key BETAR leader in independent post-war Poland, personally close to Jabotinsky by the time he was twenty. He lost almost all his relatives and friends in the Nazi dragnet that swept Poland in 1939, and on escaping to Russia himself was imprisoned for a year there. In 1942 this formidable and uncompromising disciple of Jabotinsky made his way to Palestine and led Irgun in one of the most spectacular series of violent acts the area ever saw, including the execution of British officers in retaliation for British execution of Irgun terrorists/freedom fighters and the 1946 bombing of the King David Hotel in Jerusalem that left ninety-one dead, including many civilians. His name was Menachem Begin.

So all the major Jewish players were on stage now for the climactic act of modern Zionism, the creation of the modern state of Israel. There were David Ben-Gurion and Golda Meir as leaders of the mainstream Zionist left, Chaim Weizmann the Anglophile chemistry professor in the center, and now on the right Menachem Begin as heir-apparent of Vladimir Jabotinsky. Left and right were worlds apart; Ben-Gurion and Begin and their camps despised one another.

British policies in the last years of the mandate

British policy for the Palestine mandate during World War II was increasingly opposed by terrorist tactics of Irgun and the Stern group and a new militancy in Haganah. Even after declaring war on Germany in 1939 and Italy in 1940, Great Britain did not ease its strict quota policy for immigration of Jewish refugees into Palestine. When interning illegal immigrants in camps did little to stop the flow, Britain decided on deportation. The *Patria* was to have been the first deportation ship from Palestine. Loaded with recent immigrants and ready to sail in November 1940, it was sabotaged by Haganah; they were only trying to disable it, but it sank in minutes with 250 drowned. In February 1942 the *Struma*, a refugee ship from Rumania, was turned back by a British blockade; it broke up in the Black Sea with the loss of some 800 lives.

Even after the war ended and the full horror of the Holocaust was revealed, Jewish survivors were kept from going to Eretz Israel. They were settled in "Displaced Persons" camps in Germany, Austria, and Italy. Many of these DPs were hell-bent on going to Palestine, and the Jewish community there was just as anxious that they come. The confrontation between ancient refugee ships and the modern British navy only got worse. The most celebrated incident in post-war years was that of an old freighter renamed the *Exodus 1947*. In July the ship from a French port arrived off Haifa with 4,500 Jewish refugees. The British government sent the ship back to France, but the refugees refused to disembark. The British thereupon sailed the ship to Hamburg in the British occupation zone of Germany, and forcibly evicted the passengers onto German soil—an irony that did not escape public opinion in Britain or Jewish Palestine.

That same year, 1947, Britain finally decided to cut its losses. Britain had found no way to satisfy both Arabs and Jews in Palestine, and had decided it could no longer afford empire (this was the same year it ended its rule in greater India, as you'll see in a later chapter), so it announced to the young United Nations that as of May 15, 1948, it was ending its mandate authority in Palestine and going home. The UN thus inherited one of its first major challenges. It acted quickly and responsibly, putting together a "Special Committee on Palestine" (UNSCOP) made up of eleven chiefly non-aligned nations—that is, countries not closely aligned with either the U.S.A. or the U.S.S.R. as the Cold War took shape. Since UNSCOP members found not a single Arab public figure who would allow even a Jewish autonomous unit within a Palestinian Arab state, they decided they must partition the land.[GE66] Basing their plan as closely as they could on existing settlement patterns, they assigned to the Jewish side a northeast chunk of the land around the sea of Galilee, a stretch of coast in the central west from Haifa down to Tel Aviv, and a southeast chunk—mostly Negev desert—to balance things out. It was to be a three-part state, the three parts touching at two points. The Arab state-to-be was assigned the northwest chunk of country, the central east, and the southwest part around Gaza—plus the Arab city of Jaffa, unconnected to the rest. That made it, too, basically a three-part state, meeting at the same two points! Jerusalem (and Bethlehem four miles south), although inside one of the Arab parts, was to be an international city garrisoned by the United Nations. What a crazy plan, but without moving people around by the trainload, perhaps it was the best anyone could have done.

The UN approved the plan on November 29, 1947. Huge Arab riots began the very next day, and on through the winter and spring an undeclared but bitter war for possession of territory developed. There were atrocities on both sides. On April 9 forces from Irgun and the Stern group attacked the Arab village of Deir Yasin,[GE67] not far from Jerusalem, and massacred several hundred civilians irrespective of age or sex. Five days later, Palestinian Arab forces ambushed a convoy of Jewish doctors, nurses, and teachers on their way to a Jerusalem hospital and killed seventy-eight.[GE68] The domestic phase of the war was well underway. The international phase was due to begin with the British pull out.

---

66. GE Layer 66 is a Folder with three Polygons: one for the three-part Jewish state, one for the three-part Arab state, and one for the International zone of Jerusalem and Bethlehem.

67. GE Layer 67 is a Placemark referencing Deir Yasin.

68. GE Layer 68 is a Folder titled "Hadassah medical convoy ambush." It has Placemarks for Hadassah Hospital and Hebrew University atop Mt. Scopus, and a third Placemark for the Arab village of alShaykh Jarah where the ambush and massacre occurred.

Independence

On the morning of May 14, 1948, as a bagpiper skirled the melancholy "Minstrel Boy," the last British Governor General of Palestine sailed from Haifa. That evening on the stage in a Tel Aviv museum Ben-Gurion read a proclamation establishing a Jewish state in Palestine, "to be called Israel." The name apparently came as a bit of a surprise; earlier speculation had been "Judea," and "Israel" had a more expansive ring to it. On the following day, the official May 15, every surrounding Arab state declared war on Israel—Lebanon and Syria backing it with token forces, Transjordan and Egypt with impressive western-trained armies.

In the first month of war, Jewish forces were hard put to it; it was rifles against tanks, and considerable Jewish territory was overrun. But fighting with their backs against the wall, in virtual suicide stands at places such as Yad Mordechai,[GE69] they slowed and then stopped the Egyptian and Transjordanian advances. The arrival of shiploads of war matériel from U.S. and European ports, plus superior organization, completely turned the tide of war. The besieged Jewish community of some 100,000 in new city Jerusalem was relieved. By January 1949 all of mandate Palestine was in Jewish hands except the tiny Gaza strip (taken by Egypt) and old city Jerusalem and what came to be called the West Bank (taken by Transjordan, which promptly changed its name to Jordan).[GE70] Considerable argument has been waged ever since as to whether Palestinian Arabs left voluntarily or were terrorized and forcibly evicted by Jewish military units. The facts seem to be that before May 15 the Arab exodus was mostly voluntary, perhaps in response to Arab leaders' calls to clear the field for military action so they could "drive the Jews into the sea." After May 15, another wave of refugees was removed at gunpoint by Israeli defense forces.

Although the final chapters of this all played out in the Mideast, scholars generally classify this Zionist/Israeli nationalist movement with similar movements in central and eastern Europe. Remember Herder's sneer, in the late 1700s, that European Jews had never been inspired with a dream for a state of their own? In the nineteenth and early twentieth centuries many European Jews indeed became so inspired, in the atmosphere of the cultural nationalism of the age and area. Ben Yehuda and Herzl were frank about their modeling of a nationalist movement on Bulgaria and other European states. Jabotinsky was obviously inspired by the intellectual roots of Fascism while in Italy. It's not just coincidental that the music for the national anthem, *Hatikvah*, came from the contemporary and parallel Czech national movement. The pioneers of the First and Second Aliyah took all this with them to the Mideast. This new state came into being almost 1,900 years after the Roman destruction of the last Jewish state in the area, and was clearly informed much more by the modern European ideologies of nationalism and socialism than by religion.

And so Israel, like many another modern state, was born of war. Unlike most other states, though, war has remained Israel's steady environment. The major Arab-Israeli wars are dealt with in more detail below, but here at least is a list:

—the 1956 war alongside Britain and France against Egypt over Nasser's nationalization of the Suez Canal;

—the 1967 "Six Day" war that crippled the Russian-supplied forces of Egypt and Syria and resulted in the Israeli capture of the Sinai Peninsula, the West Bank, and the Syria's Golan Heights;

—the 1973 "Yom Kippur" (or "Ramadan") war engineered by Egypt's Anwar Sadat that caught Israel somewhat off balance;

—and the 1982 invasion of Lebanon in pursuit of the Palestine Liberation Organization.

And these are just the major conventional wars. Linking them together are extensive Arab fedayeen attacks against Jewish targets, acts of Arab terrorism such as the killing of eleven Israeli athletes at the Munich Olympic games in 1972, systematic Israeli retaliation campaigns and one-shot rectification schemes such as the

---

69. GE Layer 69 is a Placemark referencing Yad Mordechai, referencing a picture of the war-damaged water tank left as a memorial.

70. GE Layer 70 is a Polygon showing the borders of the Israeli state that emerged by January 1949.

rescue of hostages from the Entebbe airport in Uganda in 1976 and the bombing of a nearly-complete nuclear reactor in Iraq in 1981, and, since 1987, the street battles with young rock-throwing Palestinian Arabs of the *intifada*.

For its size, the Israeli military has been spectacularly effective, preserving Israel in the face of a hostile surrounding Arab population. Mossad, the chief Israeli intelligence force, has become a legend, larger than life. The Mideast is full of stories about Mossad agents. There was a deaf-mute beggar in a southern Lebanese city who had been there living in squalor for twelve years; when the Israeli army invaded in 1982, they went straight to every nearby P.L.O. command post and arms cache, and the beggar was last seen riding off in an Israeli jeep with a major's insignia on his uniform . . . . Terms in the army reserve are long. The transition from civilian to military life is easily effected, through practice. Introspective Israelis themselves worry about a certain callousness engendered by it all—a sort of military toughness that would have surprised First and Second Aliyah pioneers (except perhaps Jabotinsky).

Politics and the "Ingathering of the Exiles"

The first election in the new republic was held November 8, 1948, before the first Arab-Israeli war was even over. A census listed 713,000 Jews and some 120,000 Arabs. There were half-a-million eligible voters who determined the makeup of the legislature. It was called Knesset Israel—both its name and its 120 membership were taken from the Great Assembly that formed after the return from exile in Babylon in the 500s BCE. On a system of proportional representation, Mapai, the mainstream socialist labor party, won a handy plurality of forty-six seats; Mapam, a more orthodox Marxist party, won nineteen (thus giving these two socialist parties a clear majority); the United Religious Front won sixteen; and continuing the Revisionist theme, Begin's Herut, or Freedom Party got fourteen. Chaim Weizmann was elected President, and he called on David Ben-Gurion to form the first cabinet.

The "Ingathering of the Exiles" was the first order of business for the new government: an independent Jewish state was now ready to shelter and give citizenship to any Jew in the world who wanted to come. By the end of 1948, the camps in Europe emptied and some 100,000 DPs came to Israel. These were Ashkenazi Jews; the holocaust had given Zionism a new meaning for them. But an even greater "ingathering" came from the Sephardic communities of North Africa and the Middle East where Zionism—in fact, most other European political ideologies—had been little known. Absorbing the ingathered, especially the Sephardic ones, was quite a problem. Seventy-nine new kibbutzim were established for them in the first year and a half. The majority, however, were predisposed toward the *moshav*, a less-communal cooperative where land was held in private. Foreign donations and loans, much of it from the U.S., helped out, and by 1952 a flow of German reparations began. Remarkable strides were made; by 1954 new immigrants were going straight from ship to settlement without spending time in temporary camps.

Friction between the pioneer leadership, mostly Ashkenazim, and the newer immigrants, mostly Sephardim, was evident from the first. Golda Meir, Minister of Labor in the early 1950s, was heard to remark after being angrily criticized by newcomers about housing and work, "Not one word of gratitude."[14] There were especial differences between the Ashkenazim, many of them non-observant and most of them socialist, and the Sephardim, almost altogether strictly Orthodox. The place of religion in public life was hotly debated, from general matters such as observance of the Sabbath to specifics such as allowing mixed swimming at the municipal pool in Jerusalem. Even today you can go from stretches of the beach at Tel Aviv that have topless bathing to neighborhoods a few blocks inland where you can be stoned to death for riding a motorcycle on the Sabbath.

The "labor alignment"—Mapai (the Worker's Party) and Histadruth (the Labor Federation)—dominated politics for almost thirty years in Israel. Ben-Gurion was Prime Minister off and on until 1963. His successor, Levi Eshkol, from Histadruth and also former Finance Minister, was Prime Minister until his death in 1969. Golda Meir was then Prime Minister until criticism of unpreparedness in the 1973 war saw her replaced with General Yitzhak Rabin. Then in the fall elections of 1977 came the most important turning point in modern Israeli politics. The immediate cause of the defeat of Rabin and the Labor party was a personal scandal: Rabin and his wife were found to have kept illegal bank accounts in Washington, not exactly a vote of confidence in Israel's future. But a deeper reason was the growth of the Sephardic community with its high birthrate until by the mid-1970s it outnumbered the Ashkenazi part of the electorate. Menachem Begin, continuing Jabotinsky's early policy of combining Revisionists and the Orthodox against the socialists and liberals, led to power a right-wing coalition of parties called Likud. Politically it was the direct descendant of Jabotinsky's institutions and ideology. When the Israeli state was formed back in 1948, the mainstream Israeli army had made it clear to Irgun Zevai Leummi that there was only going to be one Israeli army, and the IZL wasn't it. Begin at that point instructed Irgun members to lay down arms and re-mobilize as the Herut ("Freedom") Party. Herut was the nucleus around which the Likud political federation coalesced, and Begin was the head of both.

Domestically under Begin there was a quick turn to a free market economy. And despite the Camp David Accords negotiated in the late 1970s by Begin and Egypt's Sadat, Israeli foreign policy was more militant than before Begin became Prime Minister. In the West Bank (taken in the 1967 war), new Jewish settlements of obvious permanency began to mushroom. A 1982 invasion of Lebanon, to get at Palestinian bases there, was called by some observers Israel's first real "war of choice," as opposed to wars forced on it. Yet Begin's scrappy political maneuvering and the personal integrity of his austere, Orthodox lifestyle continued to appeal to many Israelis. It was only poor health and lingering depression over his wife's death that caused him to resign in 1984. Without his personal drive, Likud slipped back into a deadlock with the Labor Party, neither able to put together a majority government. For years they simply agreed to take turns running the government.

In 1993 and 1995, again under Labor's Rabin, Israel signed the Oslo Accords with Yasser Arafat representing the Palestinians (more to follow below from the Arab side). Beginning with Gaza and Jericho, a Palestinian Arab political unit was to be allowed by the Israelis in exchange for peace. But the next year Rabin was assassinated by an Israeli from the extreme right (after a Likud rally that had featured a mannequin of Rabin dressed as a Nazi), and Likud under Benjamin Netanyahu soon won national elections. One reason after another was found to keep from honoring the Oslo Accords, and the 1999 deadline for a Palestinian political unit passed. In 2001 the hard-line rightist General Ariel Sharon took a much publicized armed stroll on Temple Mount, or Haram es Sharif, site of the Muslim holy places in Old City Jerusalem—Al Aqsa Mosque and the Dome of the Rock. It triggered, as he must have known it would, the Second *Intifada* or Palestinian Arab uprising. It brought down the government, and profiting from the chaos Sharon emerged as head of the new one. Then later that year came Al Qaeda's sky-jackings and destruction of New York city's twin towers and part of the Pentagon in Washington, the U.S. war in Afghanistan, and by 2003 the U.S. invasion of Saddam Hussein's Iraq. Moves towards any sort of Palestinian independence were a casualty of a broader confrontation between fundamentalists of the Muslim world and the U.S. and Europe; nothing serious has happened on those lines in all the years since then.

The establishment and preservation of Israel is a bittersweet success story. Six or seven generations after Ben-Yehuda and Ahad Ha'am, much of the original idealism of Zionism has eroded away. But the reason for the state is still remembered. The one event in Israel's history that shows that best must be the trial of Adolf Eichmann. Eichmann, the chief operative in the Nazi plan to kill all European Jews, escaped the German collapse of 1945 and lived under an alias in Argentina. In 1961 he was kidnapped by Mossad agents and flown to Israel to stand trial. In May of 1962 he was found guilty of all major charges against him, and hanged. But for a year the old people relived the Holocaust, and young ones learned about it every day in school. When the country falls quiet on its yearly spring Holocaust Remembrance Day, its will to survive is clearly visible. Israel seems to be the immovable rock of the Middle East.

But opposing it is what seems to be an irresistible force.

SECTION C. BACKGROUND OF MODERN ARAB NATIONALISM IN GENERAL

The historical depth of this corridor, to repeat an earlier exclamation, is amazing. Hanan Ashrawi, literature professor, university administrator, and one of the major spokespersons for the Palestinian national cause in recent decades, recalls when she came to the United States for graduate work (Ph.D. in Literature, University of Virginia, 1971), she was shocked at how shallow was the depth of history in the U.S.—as if it was painted on the surface. She could dig down in her backyard in Ramallah through 4,000 years' worth of various civilizations, as well as feel their inherited constraints still all around her.

But since in this historical narrative to date we essentially left the Damascus-south-to-water corridor when the early Roman Empire evicted the Jews from Judea in the first and second centuries of the common era, and only returned to it with the migration of sizeable numbers of European Jews to it in the late nineteenth century, that's probably where we should pick up the general story, at least in outline. In those 1,700 or so years there were some momentous events and movements there.

The last chapters of Imperial Roman rule

There are classic Roman Empire ruins all along our corridor. You can still visit parts of the Emperor Trajan's "new road" down the old King's Highway, with its median, its crushed rock curved surface, and mile markers still identifiable. There's an almost perfectly preserved and still very useable Roman theater in the heart of Amman, Jordan.[GE71] Jerash in northern Jordan is one of the best preserved Roman cities in the world.[GE72] Baalbek in Lebanon has its massive Roman Temple of Jupiter and more intimate Temple of Bacchus with traces of colored plaster still showing [GE73]

In the early 300s Constantine became Emperor of Rome. He was both the first Christian emperor of Rome, and the emperor who developed Byzantium—renamed Constantinople, today's Istanbul—as a second capital of the Empire. In 325 Constantine tried to deal with the increasing divisions in the greater Christian community by calling the first church council at Nicaea,[GE74] which embodied its decisions in the Nicene Creed that is still recited by some branches of the modern Christian church. In the short run, at least, this Roman standardization of Christianity worked. The Coptic Christian church of Egypt and countries south and east was a fully integrated part of this Roman church through the rest of the 300s and some of the 400s. Constantine's mother, Helena, was a Christian and surely influenced his choice of religion, and after the Council of Nicaea in 325 and before his mother's death in 330 he sent her to what Christians usually call the Holy Land. Many of the sites traditionally identified with the life of Christ there were those so chosen by Helena and her team of scholars in her travels and investigations, and then of course got the full sanction of the Roman Emperor, her son. These include the Church of the Nativity in Bethlehem and the Church of the Holy Sepulchre in Jerusalem, perhaps the two most visited Christian sites in the world.[GE75] The mosaic map at Madaba, Jordan, formerly the floor of a Byzantine church and a practical guide for Christian pilgrims back then, is the oldest existing map of our corridor.[GE76]

As the western half of the Roman Empire declined and fell in the "Barbarian Migrations" (*Völkerwanderung*) of the 400s and early 500s, Constantinople not only survived but thrived. This Eastern Roman Empire, in which the language gradually became Greek, lasted a thousand years after the traditional "fall of Rome." In the mid-500s the great Emperor Justinian made a fair bid to reconquer the western half of the old Roman Empire, and did a complete reorganization and systematization of Roman law. It was Justinian who ordered the building of the Hagia Sophia, the Church of Holy Wisdom.[GE77] As impressive a monument as anything in the city of Rome itself, for centuries it was the central church of the Byzantine Empire and what came to be called the Greek Orthodox Church (and for centuries more after 1453 a mosque under the Ottomans, hence the surrounding minarets, and since 1931 a museum). By the late 500s and early 600s, this eastern Roman Empire in Byzantium was successfully defeating a revived Persian state in the east. But both the Persian state and this Eastern Roman Empire were about to meet a greater challenge than each other.

---

71. GE Layer 71 is a Placemark referencing the Roman theater at Amman.

72. GE Layer 72 is a Placemark referencing Jerash/Gerasa.

73. GE Layer 73 is a Placemark referencing the Roman temples at Baalbek.

74. GE Layer 74 is a Placemark referencing Nicaea, today's Iznik, Turkey, in a fertile valley at the eastern end of Lake Iznik. It was on the main road from Constantinople/Istanbul to our corridor.

75. GE Layer 75 is a Folder with Placemarks and views of those two Helena-identified "traditional" sites.

76. GE Layer 76 is a Placemark referencing the church and map in Madaba.

77. GE Layer 77 is a Placemark referencing this great building.

The glory days of Arabic poetry

Arabic was the Semitic language spoken in the Arabian peninsula at least as early as the early centuries of the common era, and probably for long before that. Among the Bedouin Arabs with their nomadic lifestyle, rocking back and forth from the temporary grasslands when the seasonal rains fell to the wells in the rockier brushy areas in dry season, poetry was the great portable art form of these mainly illiterate tribal people. The glory days of Arabic poetry were said to be the third and fourth centuries AD. But there were cities in Arabia, too. Three of them in or near the Hijaz mountains that run the SW coast of Arabia—Jiddah, Mecca, and Medina [GE[78]]—are especially important for our story, and were key to the sophisticated long-distance trade and literacy that was beginning to change society in Arabia in the 500s. Jiddah was even then an important Red Sea port city; Mecca was in a key pass through the Hijaz Mountains just inland from Jiddah; and Medina, a couple hundred miles north of Mecca, was a population center (including several Jewish groups) supported by a huge oasis. Mecca was not just a commercial center but a center of religious pilgrimage, with shrines to various gods worshiped by the desert tribes.

The life of Muhammad

This was the setting for the appearance of one of the most important figures in world history, Muhammad. He was born in Mecca in AD 570 or 571, of a poor family and orphaned early in life, but of the dominant one of four clans in the city, the Quraysh (Kuraish). A successful businessman in what today we'd probably call a long distance trading concern, he seems to have traveled on our chosen corridor as far north as Damascus, and while still a relatively young man he married the wealthy widow fifteen years his senior who owned the business. He didn't marry again until after her death.

Meditating in the desert outskirts of Mecca when he was about forty years old—in the year AD 610, in the month of Ramadan, on what Muslims call "the night of power"—Muhammad received what Muslims believe to be the first of a series of divine visits from the Angel Gabriel, who impressed poetry on his mind from God, with orders for him to go recite it to others (the Koran, *Al Qur'an,* translates "The Recitation"). Reluctant to do so, Muhammad was struck dumb until he agreed. Some family members and gradually others in a wider circle, supportive of this partly because they felt that the poetry he was bringing in from his meditations was beyond the capacity of any mere mortal to create, memorized it. One of the proud claims of Christianity is in just how many languages the Bible has been translated. That's not a claim Islam makes, or would want to make, for the Koran. For one thing, poetry is so embedded in the nuance and cadence of language that it never translates well. If you are an English speaker who doesn't know Arabic, in a mosque you might be given a Koran with the English translation—but on the opposite page will be the Arabic, on the assumption that to really feel the power of the original sooner or later you need to learn Arabic. The parts of the Koran were only formally collected and ordered about three decades after Mohammad's death. Its 114 *surah,* or chapters, are (except for the first short one) mainly arranged from longer to shorter. In contrast to the Hebrew Bible and Christian New Testament, which are generally chronologically arranged, the Qur'anic order is if anything roughly the reverse of their general chronological revelation. The longer revelations, mainly from the later Medina period of Mohammad's life, come early in the book.

Muhammad, most Muslims believe, was neither a divinity nor the founder of a new religion, just the latest (and probably last) prophet chosen by God to purify the monotheism earlier revealed to the world in Judaism and Christianity, into which errors of belief and practice had crept over time. There is a grandeur reminiscent of passages in the Bible's Isaiah in descriptions of the Day of Judgment, even in translation:

> When the sun ceases to shine; when the stars fall down and the mountains are blown away; when camels big with young are left untended and the wild beasts are brought together; when the seas are set alight and men's souls are reunited; when the infant girl, buried alive, is asked for what crime she was slain; when the records of men's deeds are laid open and the heaven is stripped bare; when Hell burns fiercely and Paradise is brought near: then each soul shall know what it has done.[15]

---

78. GE Layer 78 is a Folder titled "Three key Hijaz cities," with a Placemark for each city.

This monotheism was not generally welcomed in the polytheistic pilgrimage town of Mecca. The growing Muslim community was apparently viewed by the greater Meccan community as a lower-class cult, among other things bad for business. By AD 619 some Muslims were being roughed up, and some fled across the Red Sea for shelter in the Christian society of Ethiopia (the first *muzzein*, or caller to prayer, was Bilal, a freed Ethiopian slave). By 622 the Muslim community in and around Mecca mobilized itself to make a clean break, by emigrating to Medina—in part because Medina already had monotheist communities including some Jewish ones. This was the *hijra*, sometimes translated "the flight." This AD 622 date, the real beginning of a self-governing Muslim community, became the starting date for the Muslim calendar (such dates identified by A. H., meaning "After the Hijra"). It was in Medina that the community of these "emigrants" (*muhajirun*, literally "those who emigrated") and their local supporters, "the helpers," recognized Muhammad as political ruler as well as religious leader. This was the original Muslim theocracy still looked to by part of the modern Muslim community as the prime model for government.

After the AD 622 Hijra there were three pitched battles between this growing Muslim community and the city of Mecca, two won by the Muslims. In 630 Mecca agreed to accept Muhammad's authority, assured of a new pilgrimage (to the one God). In that year Muhammad made what is called the farewell pilgrimage, and then returned to Medina. There he died in AD 632, to the consternation of much of the Muslim community. Even the later revelations of the Koran, dealing with inheritance, marriage and divorce, criminal penalties, and other matters, amounted only to the foundations of a law code; apparently many disputes were still brought to Muhammad personally. But now his uncle and early supporter Abu Bakr took charge, famously saying "You who worshiped Muhammad, know that Muhammad is dead; you who worshiped God, know that He lives and will live forever." Abu Bakr became the first *khalifa*, or Caliph (literally "one who succeeds, or comes behind," sometimes translated "Deputy" of the Prophet).

Muslim expansion AD 632–732

At the time of Muhammad's death, the Muslim community was still confined to the Arabian peninsula. But all the energies of inter-tribal warfare were now gathered under one banner, and the Arabs, motivated by one great ideal, began one of the most spectacular conquests in world history. In 636 the week-long Battle of Yarmuk[GE79] broke Byzantine armies, giving all the countryside of the eastern side of the Mediterranean to the Muslim conquerors, including the great cities of Damascus and Jerusalem. The western wing of the expansion raced through Egypt and along the southern coast of the Mediterranean, jumped the Straits of Gibraltar in 711, and in short order conquered almost all of the Iberian peninsula, as you saw briefly in "The Rise of European Technological Power" chapter that began the book. The eastern wing of the conquest was even more remarkable, capturing ancient Mesopotamia (today's Iraq), ancient Persia (today's Iran), and by that same AD 711 planting a colony at the mouth of the Indus River, near Karachi in today's Pakistan.

So these relatively unsophisticated, tribal Arabs in the historical blink of an eye came to control some of the world's most ancient and sophisticated cities and civilizations. For almost thirty years the leadership was fairly unified; the four "rightly guided caliphs" had the support of virtually the whole Muslim community. In 659, however, there was a war in which the forces of Ali (nephew and adopted heir of Muhammad) defeated the forces of Aishah, Muhammad's irrepressible younger wife, now widow; and in 661 Ali was assassinated and replaced as Caliph by a member of the house of Umayyad. This began the first—and still enduring—schism in the Muslim world, the Sunni-Shi'a division. Ali was seen by Shi'ites (from *Shi'atu 'Ali*, literally "the followers of Ali") as the rightful heir of Muhammad, and the Umayyad house as an enemy that had earlier actually opposed the rise to authority of Muhammad himself. Doctrinally, the Shi'ites only accepted the spiritual authority of the Koran itself, whereas the Sunnis also accepted a body of traditions mainly based on Muhammad's personal behavior and sayings, the Sunnah. Ali's sons Hassan and Husayn were killed in the struggle later, martyrs to the Shi'a cause. According to Shi'ites, a rightful successor to Ali would appear in a millennial age—the seventh successor, said the Seveners or Ismailis; the twelfth successor, said the Twelvers. But in the short run, at least, the Shi'ites were defeated by the Sunni Ummayads, and their religious practice mostly forced underground.

---

79. GE Layer 79 is a Placemark generally referencing the Battle of Yarmuk locale.

The Arab kingdoms

The Ummayad dynasty of Arab kings ruled from 661–750. Until about AD 700 the language of administration was Greek, a legacy of the part of the Byzantine Empire that the Arabs had conquered. With Greek-speaking intellectuals—including more and more Arabs—came the Greek learning associated with the great library at Alexandria (though the library itself was destroyed in various Roman and then Arab invasions), which is why in the European Renaissance later good humanists had to learn Arabic as well as Latin, Greek, and Hebrew. The most famous of the Ummayad rulers was Abd al Malik, who reigned from 685 to 705. He had the famous Dome of the Rock built in Jerusalem,[GE80] and the year after his death his successor began the building of the Ummayad Mosque in Damascus,[GE81] the capital of the dynasty. At its greatest extent, the Ummayad Empire ran from southern France and Spain across north Africa and the heartland of the Middle East to Uzbekistan. [GE82]

The second of the great Arab kingdoms, the Abbasid dynasty (circa 750–950) moved the capital to Baghdad in 762. Roughly the same extent as the Ummayad Empire (though early on it lost Spain and Morocco), the Abbasid Empire was much more impressive culturally and especially scientifically. Baghdad became a truly international city, with Indians, Persians, Armenians, Turks, Jews, and Greeks living there in sizeable numbers, all increasingly speaking Arabic as their common language. The Caliph Harun al-Rashid ("Aaron the Wise"), the rough contemporary of Charlemagne, ruled an increasingly opulent court from 786 to 809, and his support of scholars was legendary. Caliph al-Mamun (ruled 813–833) made a comprehensive effort to collect and translate all the classical Greek texts on math, science, and medicine. He set up the House of Wisdom (*Bait al-Hikma*) with salaried Christians as well as Muslims to do this. The Christian scholars would get everything from Greek into Syriac (a written form of Aramaic familiar to many of them as a liturgical language in a branch of the Christian church), the Semitic language they knew best, and Muslim scholars would translate that into smooth Arabic. They did everything from Archimedes to Aristotle to Euclid to Ptolemy, and it jump-started an Abbasid Renaissance of thought and work.

Early in the Abbasid dynasty their armies had captured a community of Chinese papermakers, and paper quickly replaced fragile papyrus and expensive parchment (animal hide). Paper was relatively cheap, sturdy, and lasting, and it revolutionized the library business. Zero-based math drifted into the Arab kingdoms from its invention in the Guptan dynasty in today's India and Pakistan (more in a later chapter, but isn't it interesting that today we use "Arabic" numerals but the Arabs themselves have adopted "Hindi" numerals), and this eastern math interacted with Greek mathematical principles from Euclid and others. It was around 830 that one of the scholars in Caliph al-Mamun's House of Wisdom—al-Khwarizimi (whose name was later Latinized as Algorismi, hence algorithm)—wrote a book on adding and subtracting in "Hindi" numerals, and at the same time invented modern algebra (from *al-jabr*, literally "the bone-setting," his description of how the two sides of a formula matched across the equals sign). It took another 500 years for Europeans to: (a) find, and (b) get interested in his books, including his book on the astrolabe, which Chaucer had obviously read in translation by 1391 before he wrote his *Treatise on the Astrolabe*, as you saw in Chapter 1.

Invasion from west and east: Crusaders and Mongols

By 950 the Abbasid Empire was falling apart. Turkish tribes were pressing on the northern frontiers; independent rulers were claiming parts of the old empire. So it was that a weakened heartland of the Arab world faced unexpected invasions from both west and east.

The Crusades (from cross-ade, a Christian attempt to reconquer the "Holy Land") probably loom larger in the Western mind than the Mideastern one. It's a brief interlude of just over a century—mainly the twelfth century—in what as you have seen is a long and deep history. In the First Crusade of 1096–99, western

---

80. GE Layer 80 is a Placemark referencing the Dome of the Rock.

81. GE Layer 81 is a Placemark referencing the Umayyad Mosque in Damascus. Within it is a shrine containing the head of St. John the Baptist; incorporated in the walls, with Greek writing still readable, are fragments of a Byzantine church; it sits in Roman ruins of a Temple "To Jupiter," which themselves are within an ancient shrine to the Semitic gods . . .

82. GE Layer 82 is a Polygon representing the maximum extent of the Ummayad Empire.

Christian states and great secular lords, spurred to help the declining Byzantine Empire, sent armies that took Jerusalem and in fact all of our corridor. They set up various "Frankish kingdoms" in the land, and the Knights Templar (whose fortune was later at the disposal of the Portuguese prince Henry the Navigator, as you saw in Chapter 1, and also aided the Teutonic Knights who pushed German civilization east into Slavic-held lands, as you saw in Chapter 3). The rich trade of the King's Highway that lay on the far side of the Bekaa and Jordan valleys soon drew their interest, and the result was a series of Crusader's forts—an average of one every twenty miles or so—were built there, including Karak and Shobak.[GE83] Saladin, a Kurd born in what is today Iraq, led Muslim armies to victory over the Crusader Kingdom of Jerusalem's armies at Hattin in 1187.[GE84] This triggered the Third Crusade of two years later to try to recover the territory, though it was nowhere near as successful as the first had been.

While there were still remnants of the Crusaders in our corridor, it was hit with the Mongol invasion—the same one which transformed Russian history, you'll remember. In 1258 the Mongols sacked Damascus, destroying all the libraries in the city. They were stopped in their drive on Egypt by the Mamluks at the Battle of Ain Jalut (Goliath's Spring) in 1260, just up in the Megiddo Pass off the Jezreel valley.[GE85] The Mongols had come down from Baalbek, crossed the Jordan River south of the Sea of Galilee; the Mamluks had come up the coast to Acre, then turned down the Jezreel to meet them. The remaining Crusaders, understanding the Mongols as the greater threat, declared neutrality and allowed Mamluk armies free passage across lands they still controlled. Within thirty years of the Battle of Ain Jalut the last of the Crusader-held lands were retaken by local powers.

The Arabian Nights' Entertainment, or the *1001 Nights*

By the 1400s the general Arabic-speaking world was, in terms of literacy and higher culture, in decline—just when the Renaissance was quickening higher culture in Europe. It may not be coincidental: long-distance trade routes from Asia to Europe mostly moved north through Turkish lands (especially after the Ottomans captured Constantinople and renamed it Istanbul in 1453) and by century's end moved south as European traders learned how to sail south around Africa. Or it may have just been the age-old pattern of civilizations rising, flourishing for a time, and falling to more aggressive cultures on the rise. No historian in the world, incidentally, ever considered the rise and fall of civilizations more comprehensively than Ibn Khaldun (a native Arabic speaker born and educated in northern Africa and Spain) in his "Introduction" to world history written about 1375.

The glory days of the Arab world, however, lived on in popular folk tales where the past survived with a rosy and magical tinge. Sometime in the 1400s, some unknown scholar or scholars took a selection of those folktales and turned them into Arabic literature—*The Arabian Nights' Entertainment* or *1001 Nights* (just when scholars in China were beginning to turn street-corner storytelling tales into the traditional Chinese novels, interestingly enough, as you'll see in Chapter 13). A king, Shariar, embittered and deranged by the unfaithfulness of his wife, marries a new wife daily and executes her the next day. Scheherazade, daughter of the Prime Minister (Vizir, Wezeer), marries him and cures him by telling folktales, each of which grows out of its predecessor so that the king postpones execution day after day for a thousand days, and then lifts the ban entirely. It was first introduced to the European public by a French orientalist in the early 1700s, but the translation in 1840 by Charles Lane, who lived for years in Cairo, is still the classic English version.[16] The text runs to almost a thousand pages, and there are 300 pages of notes on everything from religion to social practices that are still fascinating to read. There are some Persian elements to the tales, but the nucleus are from the times of Abbasid rule at Damascus (lots of great accounts of Caliph Harun al Rashid moving in disguise among his subjects); from the Mamluk rule of medieval Cairo, where the Ali Baba cycle of tales originated; the Sindbad the Sailor tales from the Indian Ocean side of Arabia; and the Aladdin and the Lamp tales from Syria.

But faded glory was about all that was left to the Arabic speakers of our corridor. Its new reality was as a sleepy backwater of the rising Ottoman Turkish state.

---

83. GE Layer 83 is a Folder titled "Crusader Castles on the King's Highway."
84. GE Layer 84 is a Placemark approximating the location of the Battle of Hattin.
85. GE Layer 85 is a Placemark approximating the location of the Battle of Ain Jalut.

Ottoman rule

One way to get a simple handle on a huge and complex historical problem is to consider the expansion of Islam from the Arabian peninsula as a three-shelled one:

○ The inner shell is where Arabic, the language of the Koran and the original conquerors, became the common spoken language. This includes Africa north of the Sahara Desert, and everything west of Persia/Iran and south of Turkey/Asia Minor. The best quick definition of an Arab is still one who natively speaks Arabic, and the great majority of them are in this inner shell.

○ The middle shell is where the Arabic alphabet was adopted to write the local, non-Arabic languages. That included all down the east coast of Africa and some of central Africa, with Swahili (a Bantu language with some Arabic vocabulary). It included Turkey (although after WW I Ataturk switched it to the Latin alphabet), Persia/Iran, much of Central Asia, and even Pakistan (as you'll see in the South Asia/Grand Trunk Road chapter, the Urdu spoken in Pakistan and the Hindi spoken in India are really dialects of the same language, but Urdu is written with Arabic letters and Hindi is not).

○ The outer shell is where Islam became the majority religion, from Indonesia and Bangladesh in the east, to much of east, central, and even west sub-Saharan Africa.

So Islam spread and became, geographically speaking, the central religion of the super-continent of Asia-Africa-Europe. It moved far beyond the Arab speakers, and seemed to inspire a new vigor in terms of state creation on its expanding periphery. By the 1500s three great Muslim but non-Arabic-speaking empires had emerged as among the most powerful and civilized states in the world—the Mughals in today's Pakistan, India, and Bangladesh, the Safavids in today's Iran, and the Ottomans in today's Turkey and Eastern Europe. Ming dynasty China may have been their only contemporary equal; certainly no single European kingdom of the time, even Spain, matched the power of the early Ottoman Empire.

The Ottoman Empire occupied our particular Damascus-south-to-water corridor from the early 1500s to the early 1900s. It was the matrix from which the modern states there emerged, and so deserves serious consideration here.

As with Huns before and Mongols after, their linguistic kinfolk, the Turks drifted west from deep inside Central Asia. Unlike Huns or Mongols (at least in the west), however, they gradually adapted to city life and created lasting political structures. The Turkish drift west seems to have begun in the AD 700s, and by the 800s they were gradually converting to Islam. Fighters of reputation, whole units of them were hired by the declining Abbasid kingdom. Soon the frontier between Christians and Muslims was dominated by *ghazis*, a Muslim-world parallel for the contemporary crusading orders of knights in the Christian west. For both groups, the ideals of brotherhood, of religious unity, and of self-sacrifice were what they felt about themselves; suicidal fanaticism was what it often looked like to their respective enemies. As the Byzantine Empire weakened, the tribe of Osman emerged supreme among all the frontier Turkish groups, and oozed in to fill the power void in the northwest of Anatolia/Asia Minor. By about 1360 one of their first great "Sultans" (a regional word for whomever wielded the ultimate power, originally from the Aramaic) built a new-style military unit that became the most feared in Europe and western Asia. These were the Janissaries (from *yeni cheri*, "new troops"). They were recruited from conquered populations—mainly Christian boys who were taken from home early and raised to be devout Muslim warriors whose single focus was to do the Sultan's will.

With *ghazi* irregulars and *yeni cheri* shock troops, the Ottomans gradually conquered the countryside west as well as east of Constantinople and isolated it. It almost fell to them in 1402, but Tamerlane suddenly overran Anatolia in one last burst of Mongol energy, and delayed it a half century. A revived Ottoman Empire finally took the City of Caesars in a spectacular assault in 1453, not only with ghazis and Janissaries but with a huge new navy and the best and heaviest artillery of the age. The engineers who cast the cannon were European, but the vision to assemble it and the discipline and the money to make it happen were Ottoman. Imperial schools better than any western counterpart focused on military affairs and statecraft, and—except for the hereditary Sultan, of course—resulted in something close to a true meritocracy. Most European states were still paralyzed by aristocratic privilege, with incapable sons replacing capable fathers by right of inheritance. Before 1500 all of today's Bulgaria, most of Romania, most of Hungary, all of Greece, all of greater Yugoslavia, and all of Albania were taken. The Ottoman Turks were poised to invade Italy beginning at the heel of the Italian boot; even Vienna was beginning to feel jeopardized.

Most important for our story, though, is Ottoman expansion southwards. In the short reign of Sultan Selim the Grim (1512–1520), he defeated the new Safavid Shi'ite Muslim state in Persia that was challenging the Ottomans, sacking its western city of Tabriz and executing perhaps 40,000 captives as heretics. The Mamluk Sultans of Egypt, who had defeated the invading Mongols near Nazareth three centuries earlier, now made the mistake of sending armies against Ottoman forces in northern Syria. "By tradition and code of military honor," as one writer put it, the Mamluks used only lance, bow and sword.[17] The Ottomans overwhelmed them with artillery and Janissaries armed with handguns. In 1516 and 1517 the Ottomans stormed down through Beirut and Damascus, Gaza, Jerusalem (where Selim made a quick pilgrimage to the Dome of the Rock of Muhammad) and Amman, and then occupied Cairo and snuffed out Mamluk rule forever in a battle fought within sight of the great pyramids. So at about the time that Fernando Cortés—who had apparently trained in warfare in Italy against these same Turks—was beheading the Aztec Empire in Mexico, the Ottomans destroyed the Mamluk Empire in Egypt and absorbed all its dependencies. These included Mecca and Medina in southwest Arabia, holiest sites in Islam. Hereafter the Ottoman Sultan styled himself "Commander of the Faithful," claiming leadership of the Muslim world as caliph.

His successor Suleiman, who ruled from 1520 to 1566, was the most famous and powerful of all the Ottoman rulers. Militarily he led a massive Turkish army through eastern Europe to the gates of Vienna in 1529 that came within an ace of taking the city, dominated the whole eastern Mediterranean Sea, and presided over a wealthy country and a sophisticated court. Westerners called him "The Magnificent" or just "The Grand Turk." The Turks themselves called him "The Lawgiver," because he systematized and rationalized the entire law code the way Emperor Justinian had done (from the same capital city!) a thousand years before. He set up a free and public education system for Muslim boys; it was modeled on the liberal arts of the classical Roman tradition but far in advance of anything in contemporary central or western Europe. Architecturally he transformed Istanbul into one of the greatest capital cities of the world.

The pilgrimage road

A chief interest of the Ottomans in greater Syria was the *hajj*, the pilgrimage to Mecca that, if you have the wealth and the health for it, is one of the five basic commands for any Muslim (in addition to belief in God, charitable giving, daily prayers, and daytime fasting during the month of Ramadan). Before Sultan Suleiman, travelers from the north still generally went down Trajan's New Road, the imperial Roman version of the old King's Highway. Now Suleiman built a chain of hajj forts along the Desert Route somewhat east of the King's Highway.[GE[86]] By one account, his daughter made the hajj along the King's Highway and found the going so winding and with so many ups and downs that she insisted on coming back by the smoother Desert Route, so that it is sometimes also called "The Maiden's Way." This included huge new water cisterns spaced two days' march apart, and the appointment of a yearly Caravan Commander who in the pilgrimage season outranked all local governors. Over 300 years later, in 1876, when not many westerners had ever traveled that *Darb el-hajj* or Pilgrimage Road, the Englishman Charles Doughty got permission to travel with the hajj caravan from Damascus as far south as Petra. In his 1888 *Travels in Arabia Deserta*, he wrote: "The *Darb-el-Hajj* is no made road, but a multitude of cattle-paths beaten hollow by the camel's tread." The King's Highway, by contrast, he called a true road that would take little improvement to haul artillery along. Looking even further ahead, when the Ottoman Empire in its next-to-last decade built the Hijaz railway from Damascus to Medina (1900–1908), it would follow the Darb el-hajj and not the King's Highway for most of its route, and many of its stations would be based at the old hajj forts.

---

86. GE Layer 86 is a Folder titled "The Desert Route." It includes a Path generally tracing the route, and a couple of Placemarks referencing Photos icons of remains of the old Ottoman forts, or castles (often labeled Qalat, meaning fort).

In the early heyday of the Ottomans, its massive military drives into the heart of Europe gave Turks a fearsome reputation there, and mostly out of ignorance Europeans generally thought of them as culture-less barbarians. That may have been true when they came into Anatolia from the Central Asian steppes in the eleventh century, but it certainly wasn't true 500 years later when they conquered Constantinople. Sultan Mehmet the Conqueror (of Constantinople), in addition to the traditional scholarly knowledge of Arabic and Persian literature common to educated Turks, knew Greek as well. On into the 1600s the empire had a complex and efficient bureaucracy, including careful storage of voluminous records. Non-Muslims were subject to taxes and other legal discrimination that did not apply to Muslims, but they were not persecuted (the way Muslims and Jews were, for example, under Ferdinand and Isabella in Spain about this same time). In its *millet* system (from the Turkish word for peoples or nations) the Ottoman government recognized a separate religious law for Muslims, Jews, Armenian Christians, Orthodox Christians, and later Catholic Christians, a law to be determined not by the Ottoman state but by the religious hierarchy of that particular group—even if the leader of that group resided outside the Ottoman Empire! One dramatic proof of how good things were, compared to conditions in Christian lands immediately to the west of Ottoman lands, was the continual immigration of Christians into the Ottoman Empire—a trend that lasted on into the 1600s.

On our corridor in particular Ottoman rule made for a more secure and prosperous Arab population than the Egyptian Mamluk rule it replaced. Many of the Mamluk-era landlords were killed in the conquest. Their estates were redistributed as fiefs to Ottoman soldiers, but under the Ottoman system the new fief-holder was only entitled to a fixed revenue, and not to those broad "seigneurial rights" that Mamluk owners had held. As a result, farmers were much freer to farm their land as they chose, in fact, much freer overall. In addition, Ottoman law generally prevented both the division of the land into smaller and smaller plots, as well as the concentration of land into great estates in the hands of wealthy, absentee landowners—either of which results over just a few generations in the common farmer not having enough land on which to make a living.

The Ottoman Empire, however, was not immune to the general law of dynastic rise and fall. After Suleiman the Magnificent, sultans isolated and smothered in the comforts of the royal harem (the *seraglio*, as it was known to westerners) were the rule and not the exception, and the body politic rotted from the head. And the Ottomans had to contend with the rising power of Europe, not halfway around the world as it was from the Mughal Dynasty in India and the Qing Dynasty in China, but right next door. The Ottoman Empire could still marshal impressive forces on occasion. In 1673 they once again invaded Europe to the walls of Vienna, and in 1711 they trapped Peter the Great on his rash advance down the Pruth River in today's Moldova. From the time of Catherine the Great on, however, Russia won all the major Russo-Turk wars. The Ottoman bureaucracy became rigid, corrupt and inefficient, and in their frustration the leaders of the failing state began to lash out at ethnic and religious minorities.

The challenge of the West

Western power had been growing, relative to Turkish power, ever since the late 1500s, but it only really reached a tipping point with the French Revolution and the draft army—the real beginning of modern times, as was argued in the Enlightenment and French Revolution chapter. In 1798 the rising and ambitious General Napoléon Bonaparte, with some vague ideas of linking up with anti-British allies in India, took a French navy and army from the great French naval base of Toulon to invade Egypt. They eluded the British fleet, landed in good order in Alexandria on July 1, and in one battle near there and a bigger one near the pyramids defeated the local Ottoman forces. Scholars in the retinue of the French army, incidentally, collected the Rosetta Stone—the trilingual inscription that was later key to deciphering hieroglyphs—in the delta town that Europeans called Rosetta (Rashid).[GE87] The French scholars compiled extensive drawings, measurements, and cultural and natural history collections, while common French soldiers shot the nose off the sphinx in target practice.

---

87. GE Layer 87 is a Placemark referencing Rashid/Rosetta.

But on August 1, just a month after the French landing, the British fleet arrived in force, and in the Battle of the Nile (in Aboukir Bay just off Alexandria[GE88]) they destroyed the French fleet. This cut Napoleon and his army off from resupply or evacuation by sea. The Ottoman government was concerned with this French invasion too, of course, since Egypt was still part of the Ottoman Empire, and Turkish military forces were sent south to help defeat Napoleon. Napoleon decided to fight his way north by land. He took the best of his army up the coast on the old Via Maris (as had New Kingdom Egyptian pharaohs 3,000 years before him) through El-Arish, then Gaza, then Jaffa—where he infamously executed 1,500 defenders who had surrendered because some there had given their parole earlier not to fight—and then up over Megiddo Pass and down into the Jezreel valley, thus flanking and taking Haifa. Napoleonic forces took the hilltop fort at Nazareth and even the first great port in what is today Lebanon, Tyre.[GE89] But Acre, or Acco, on the northern end of that ten-mile-wide bay north of Haifa, remained untaken, and here Napoleon met his match when Turkish troops with the timely arrival of a British fleet beat off his desperate siege of the city.[GE90] By May of 1799 Napoleon had retreated with his remaining troops back down the Via Maris to Egypt. In late August, apparently having wind of a coup d'état in the making back in Paris, he left his army to die on the vine and slipped back to France in time to become First Consul in the Coup of Brumaire, and soon the only Consul, and soon Emperor . . . you know the end of that story. What you may not know is the chain of events that this French invasion set in motion in Egypt in particular and on our corridor in general.

Muhammad Ali and Ibrahim Pasha

Muhammad Ali was the real creator of modern Egypt, although he was not Arab or even Turkish, but an ethnic Albanian born in what is today Macedonia. He was sent down to Egypt as a military officer with Ottoman forces charged with evicting and replacing the remaining French. An effective if brutal military officer and a cunning diplomat, by 1805 he had so made himself the strong man of Egypt that the Ottoman Sultan had little choice but to recognize him as *Pasha*, or Governor, of Egypt.

Muhammad Ali was one of the first rulers outside Europe to appreciate European military power and its sources. In his pursuit of creating a French-style army and a British-style navy, he transformed the country. Hiring western experts and sending bright young Egyptians off to western schools was expensive, and Egypt was a dirt-poor agrarian country, most of whose people worked at subsistence agriculture, raising just enough to eat. So Muhammad Ali in essence nationalized all the farmland, and experimented with new cash crops that Egypt might sell on the world market to get the hard currency needed for his desired reforms. In this process long-staple cotton—in increasing demand in the industrial revolution's textile plants—was tried, and it did so well in the delta and the Nile valley that it became a standard for the world. He built a western-style educational system, from the top down under pressure of time—an engineering school, then high schools in the major towns to send graduates to it, then grammar schools to feed the high schools. As Egyptian military power grew, he sent his sons out with armies—one to conquer the Sudan south of Egypt, and his oldest and perhaps favorite son, Ibrahim, to drive the Saudi family with their strict Wahhabi brand of Islam out of Mecca and Medina (in which he succeeded by 1818).

By the mid-1820s Muhammad Ali had the best army and navy outside Europe, better even than his supposed boss, the Sultan of Turkey. The Sultan, mired down since 1821 with the Greek independence revolt, called on his Egyptian Pasha for help, and Muhammad Ali sent his new fleet and army north and proceeded to cut through the Greek revolt as easily as a knife through butter. But in 1827 several major European states—Britain, France, and Russia, whose leaders had all cut their intellectual teeth on the Greek classics and thought they saw the land of Pericles being reborn—sent a combined fleet to sink Muhammad Ali's new navy at Nava-

---

88. GE Layer 88 is a Placemark referencing Aboukir Bay; the Placemark is located at the approximate site of the battle. The French thought they had anchored so close to the coast that the British couldn't get behind them, but the British did just that, and attacked the French line from both sides with devastating results. This was Lord Nelson's second-most-famous victory; the other, that cost him is life, came off Spain's Cape Trafalgar in 1805.

89. GE Layer 89 is a Path in red showing the route of the main French army up to Sour (Tyre).

90. GE Layer 90 is a green star-shaped Placemark icon referencing Acre/Acco.

rino Bay.[GE91] Ottoman (including Egyptian) armies then had to pull out of Greece, and its independence was secured by 1829.

But now Muhammad Ali demanded of the Sultan compensation for loss of his navy. For some time he had had his eye on the Levant, that whole eastern end of the Mediterranean that is now Syria and Lebanon, Israel/Palestine and Jordan, and he said, I'll take that. When the Sultan refused, Muhammad Ali simply invaded and took it in 1832, and gave it to his dynamic son Ibrahim to rule as Governor. Ibrahim was Pasha of these lands—including our entire corridor—only nine years. In 1840 great European powers including Britain and Austria put pressure on him to give it back to the Ottomans, and he pulled out in 1841. But those nine years were crucial for the development of modern Arab nationalism.

Muhammad Ali spoke Albanian as well as his native Albanian parents did, Turkish fairly well, and Arabic never much at all. But his son Ibrahim, born in 1789, was still young enough to learn the language fluently when he was brought to Egypt by his father. As Pasha of those levantine lands (then called Greater Syria) as of 1832, trying to build up support for the house of Muhammad Ali and resistance to the Ottoman Turks, he began to celebrate the glory days of the Arab world. He spoke of himself as an Arab: "I came to Egypt as a child, and my blood has since been colored completely Arab by the Egyptian sun."[18] He established religious and civic equality, talked about national regeneration, and began to be welcomed as a liberator. His popularity plummeted a few years later when, in obedience to his father's orders, he raised taxes, introduced military conscription, and ordered the surrender to the government of all personal firearms. That last order was about as popular as it would be in the American South and West today, and revolts broke out in the cities such as Nablus and Hebron, and then in rural Jordan and Lebanon. Few tears were shed on his departure in 1841. Yet early in his rule he had set one other thing in motion that far outlasted him—western-style, and to some extent western-staffed, education.

Protestant mission schools and the Arab Awakening

In 1832, when Ibrahim first became Pasha of Syria, almost all education was narrowly religious, and often of an old-style where students came individually to work with a single teacher. Literacy rates were very low. Although Arabic printing presses had been set up in Istanbul in 1816 and Cairo in 1822, only a trickle of printed Arabic books was produced. A British diplomat looking for bookstores in Damascus in 1838 found not a single one. There had been a few western-sponsored Catholic schools in the area for two centuries and more, mainly Jesuit until the Jesuit order was suppressed, but the languages of instruction were Latin and French. It was the introduction of Protestant mission schools, mainly American, that really began to change things.

Eli Smith, a Presbyterian from a leading family in Connecticut, was the key early American figure. He visited Beirut, traveled up in the mountains, and began the study of Arabic in 1827. After various adventures and misadventures in Turkish Armenia, Georgia and northwestern Persia, Smith married Sarah Huntington—also of good Connecticut family—and in 1834 they made their permanent home in Beirut. From then until Eli Smith died in 1857 he immersed himself in Arabic language study, as well as regional geography and ethnography. With Eli Smith, as Robert Kaplan writes in *The Arabists: Romance of an American Elite*, "the meaning of what a missionary was began to change from a proselytizer and woefully ill-prepared traveler and explorer to a rarefied Orientalist and scholar-educator . . . ."[19] Smith was insistent that the American mission schools teach in Arabic. He set in motion an enterprise to create a new type font for a press, "American-Arabic," a font still used. The first students and the first local teachers were generally recruited from the existing Christian communities, though later some Muslim families began sending their children as well. Sarah Smith opened the first school for girls anywhere on our chosen corridor.

Ibrahim Pasha welcomed the new British- and American-sponsored mission schools as a real help towards his goal of achieving western-style power. When he was forced out of Syria in 1841, the Ottoman government returned and cancelled virtually all of his reforms—but not the Protestant mission schools, since it was mainly the British who had made the Ottoman return possible. These schools—which by 1866 included the Syrian

Protestant College, later renamed the American University of Beirut[GE92]—provided a safe haven for the growth of one of the strongest strands of modern Arab nationalism. You can see this in the life and work of two scholars in particular, Nasif al-Yaziji and Butrus al-Bustani, both from the Christian community in the Beirut area.

Nasif al-Yaziji was born around 1800 into a Christian Lebanese family that had known better days. He never learned any language but Arabic, but sometime early in life he discovered the glory days of the Arab kingdoms and their literature, and it became his great passion. He rooted out old manuscripts and books in private libraries, and copied them or committed huge passages of them to his remarkable memory. He began to write in an Arabic informed by the classical Arabic, and eventually wrote books on Arabic grammar and literature that became school texts. It was said that if you ever took his classes in Arabic literature, you thereafter had some of his love of the language.

Butrus al-Bustani was a generation younger, born in 1819, and was from a wealthy family. He had the best of private tutors and then a good education at the hand of Maronite monks, and is supposed to have had facility in five languages by the time he was ten. In Beirut in 1840 he met Eli Smith, and found in the American mission schools a real home. He actually became a Presbyterian. He helped Eli Smith finish his translation of the Bible from English into Arabic. More importantly for Arab nationalism to come, he began standardizing the language by making up a modern dictionary of Arabic—a huge one for scholars, an abridged one for students. His last project, which he was six volumes into when he died, was an encyclopedia of Arab cultural history. Even after the great Muslim massacres of Christians in the area in 1860, he founded a "National School" for Arabic speakers of all religions, and got Nasif al-Yaziji to teach Arabic there.

From these two and their friends and Sarah and Eli Smith and their friends came some interesting institutions. The first, in 1847, was the "Society of Arts and Sciences," a local academy of sciences with regular meetings and a journal. Most of the fifty members were Christian Arabs; there were no Muslim members. It seems to have been designed to introduce key Arab Christians to a wider world that included European scholarship. In 1857 al-Yaziji and al-Bustani created a new and much more significant institution, the Syrian Scientific Society. Its membership of 150 was drawn from every major religious group—Sunni and Shi'ite Muslims and Druze, and Orthodox, Maronite and Protestant Christians, and even Jews. The common denominator of members was spoken Arabic, with "a pride in the Arab inheritance their bond," in the words of George Antonius in his 1939 classic, *The Arab Awakening: The Story of the Arab National Movement*.[20]

In 1868 Ibrahim al-Yaziji, one of Nasif's sons, quoted a poem he had composed at a closed meeting of the Scientific Society. "Arise, ye Arabs, and Awake!," it began, and went on to call for the overthrow of Turkish rule. It was too dangerous to write down, but it spread rapidly by word of mouth. In 1975 five former students of the Syrian Protestant College in Beirut formed a secret society to work for Arab independence. Soon they had branches in Damascus and Sidon. There were only a couple of dozen members, and their first—and perhaps only—action was to put up posters in the dead of night denouncing Turkish rule. It was a very small step towards Arab national independence, but it was the first concrete step—always a watershed in any movement.

Do you remember the basic outline for the development of modern nationalism from the German/cultural nationalism chapter—(a) identifiable cultural group; (b) negative stimulus; (c) cultural nationalism; (d) political nationalism? In this case native speakers of Arabic, newly conscious of Turkish oppression, had begun celebration of Arabic language and culture and even taken the first small steps into political nationalism by 1875. By this time Arab nationalism was well ahead of modern Jewish nationalism on their parallel paths—Ben-Yehuda was still a high school student named Eliezer Perlman who had no idea that he would become Ben-Yehuda; the pogroms of 1881 and the 1882 pioneers of the First Aliyah were not even a blip on the radar scope. But in 1876 something happened to put the Arab national movement into a thirty-year-long sleep, during which modern Jewish nationalism stole a march on the Arab world. That something was the accession to the sultanate of Abdul Hamid II, affectionately known in Turkish history as Abdul the Damned.

---

92. GE Layer 92 is a Placemark referencing the University of Beirut; lots of local Photos icons to explore. It is located in what is generally the Muslim part of the city—probably by original design.

Reform and Reaction: from Tanzimat to Abdul Hamid II

The Ottoman Empire would be broken to pieces by the end of World War I, in much the same way as the Austrian Empire fragmented at the same time—both finally destroyed mainly by rising nationalism in various ethnic groups within those empires, and in the course of a losing war. To many contemporary scholars, looking back with a century's worth of experience in the often-violent workings out of these ethnic group nationalisms, both Ottoman and Austrian empires are more and more interesting as examples of supra-national states that once worked. We touched just a bit on the Austrian Empire in the "Czechoslovak" chapter. Here we need to say a word especially about the Ottoman reformers of the mid-nineteenth century.

There was a strong current of Western European-style reforming thought in Ottoman government since the time of Napoleon. It increased markedly about the time of the Crimean War (1854–56), when France and Britain made common cause with the Ottoman Empire against Russia. In 1876 the leading Ottoman minister favoring western-style reforms in government, Midhat Pasha, got the old Sultan deposed in favor of a young, and seemingly liberal, Abdul Hamid II. By year's end the new sultan had publicly announced a new constitution with an elected legislature and a cabinet system. It enshrined such classic liberal western reforms as freedom of press and civic equality before the law of all, whatever one's ethnic background or religious persuasion. Liberals in the country were ecstatic. But then came the Russo-Turk War of 1877–78—the same war that created a new Bulgarian state out of Ottoman territory and started Eliezer Perlmann thinking about the possibility of a reborn Jewish state—and Abdul Hamid II showed his true colors by using the wartime emergency to suspend the constitution indefinitely. In 1884 he had Midhat Pasha strangled, the traditional Turkish form of execution. Any hope of liberal reforms in the Ottoman Empire died with Midhat.[21]

In brief, Abdul Hamid II's policy towards the Arab territories controlled by the Otttomans—which no longer included Egypt and the rest of North Africa but which did still include all of our chosen corridor—was a carrot-and-stick one. The carrot was the flashy and public support of Islam with the refurbishing of Muslim shrines and a generous scholarship program for students of that religion. It was perhaps cynically political, since Abdul Hamid was not notably religious himself, but it played well in the majority Muslim community. The stick was his unleashing of an unusually brutal secret police. Anyone even seen talking to a known ethnic-group nationalist would be likely to be yanked off the streets to languish in an Ottoman jail. Abdul Hamid's policies were disastrous in the remaining Turkish holdings in Europe, and even in the heartland of Turkey itself; in his reign Turkish power compared to its western neighbors plummeted. But it worked well enough in the Ottoman-controlled Arab territories to put the rising Arab national movement to sleep. Nothing of real note happened in that regard until just before World War I.

Young Turks, Sharif Hussein, and "Lawrence of Arabia"

Sharif Hussein of Mecca was a key figure in the Arab part of the Ottoman Empire. "Sharif" at the time meant not only an elder with political oversight (in this case, of the holiest of Muslim shrines, Mecca and Medina in the Hijaz) but also someone of direct descent from the Prophet Muhammad. On the surface of things, Sharif Hussein was a loyal Ottoman administrator. In 1908, however, a clique of young, nationalistic Turkish army officers took power away from old Sultan Abdul Hamid II (young folks even in the U.S. impatient to change things are still called "Young Turks" from this event!). After a brief "honeymoon" between the new Turkish leadership and the Arab parts of the Empire generally, though, the Young Turks gradually began to impose a policy called pan-Turanism, a "Turkification" of things. It is a direct parallel for the Russification that went on in the Russian Empire under Alexander III that resulted in the "one-third" formula for Russian Jews you saw earlier in this chapter—that aspect of cultural nationalism that demands that everyone speak the same language and celebrate the same cultural heritage, so as to make patriotism stronger. You can imagine how this played in the Arab world, when Turkish was increasingly insisted upon as the language of administration, army, and school. Even before World War I broke out in August of 1914, Sharif Hussein was sending his son Abdullah to feel out the British Resident in Cairo about joining forces against the Turks: if Sharif Hussein and his family led a revolt against the Ottoman Empire, would the British help them create a pro-British Arab kingdom in the region? The pre-war British authorities evinced little interest, with a "don't call us, we'll call you" response.

Then came the world war, and with every available British soldier being sent to the crucial western front in Europe, the British in Egypt faced the Turks as close as the Sinai peninsula with few troops at their disposal. All of a sudden Sharif Hussein's proposal looked awfully good to the British. This is the setting for the whole "Lawrence of Arabia" chapter.

In Arab history books, T. E. Lawrence rates a footnote, no more, partly because his role in history has been exaggerated in the West, and also because of his grandiose claims later that he "drew tides of men" around by force of his own will. But because his life was the prism through which much of the West first began to see the Mideast, he's worth a paragraph or three in this narrative.

He was born in Ireland in 1888, son of an aristocratic Anglo-Norman father and the children's governess with whom he ran off. They moved every year of T. E.'s first eight years of life, but finally settled down in Oxford. T. E. was a precocious scholar, fascinated with Stone Age artifacts as a grade school student, and by high school days a good student of twelfth-century castles. He and a friend had visited and done to-scale plans of most of the Norman castles in England and Wales, and spent a summer in France doing many twelfth-century castles there. When he went on to college—Jesus College, one of the colleges that made up Oxford University—he was a home-town kid who didn't have much part in the social life. On an Oxford library card you could check out three books; he'd typically max out his and his father's card, come home and read—eighteen hours a day, his mother recalled. He studied history, and for what we'd today call an Honor's Project he decided to study the twelfth-century castles built by the Crusaders in the Holy Land, to measure what influence Mideastern military architecture had on the Norman tradition in western Europe. His major prof warned him against traveling alone, but that's the way he went—on foot, unaccompanied, gradually improving his spoken Arabic. He did a to-scale ground plan of over fifty such castles, including such giants as the Krak des Chevaliers in today's Syria, came back and wrote a brilliant paper arguing that the Crusaders brought much more military technology to the Mideast than they learned there. Upon graduation, facing that eternal question "Is there interesting, gainful employment after graduation?", his major prof got him a job working on archaeological digs in northern Syria. With his fluent Arabic, he was at first just to boss the gangs of Arab diggers, but soon he was the dig's chief stratifier of pottery as well as its chief photographer.

Just before World War I, he began working in the Sinai peninsula, with less spectacular archaeological sites to survey, but with Ottoman-held terrain close to the British-held Egyptian border to map. He was already secretly in the employ of British military intelligence. Soon after the war broke out in 1914, he was moved to Cairo, regional seat of British military intelligence. Here he wrote a regular internal newssheet on who was whom and what was happening in the Arab world. Its insights and information were such that it quickly came to the attention of his superiors. When the British decided to take Sharif Hussein up on his offer of joining them in a war on the Ottoman Empire, the British in general agreeing to support an Arab state in the region after the war (in the Hussein-McMahon Correspondence, Sir Henry McMahon, the High Commissioner in Egypt, being the responsible British official in the region), T. E. was the one chosen to be military liaison with the family of Sharif Hussein.

In his autobiographical account, *Seven Pillars of Wisdom*, he claims he was the one who picked Faisal ibn Hussein, the third son of Sharif Hussein, to lead this Arab revolt against the Ottomans. The long, thin, vulnerable Hijaz Railway, built by the Ottomans with major help from their ally Germany, had been completed from Damascus to Medina in 1908.[GE93] It was to be the focus of the revolt, beginning with cutting off and isolating the Turkish garrison at its southern terminus in Medina. With the British navy in the Red Sea to provide explosives and eventually a couple of armored Rolls-Royces, Lawrence and a few British technicians and Faisal's Arab guerrillas leapfrogged their way up the railway, blowing up the tracks in front of trains, strafing the wrecked troops and then disappearing into the desert. They took the city of Aqaba, at the head of the Gulf of Aqaba, with a totally unexpected attack from the land side, and actually beat General Allenby and the main

---

93. GE Layer 93 is a Folder titled "Hijaz Railway." It includes a Path symbolizing the route, and a collection of suggested Photos icons to open to sample views of remains of rolling stock and track, and even the still-existing terminus in Damascus.

British army to Damascus by a day.[GE[94]] There was euphoria in the Arab ranks as Faisal became King of Syria in the spring of 1918.

And then secret wartime deals between the great European powers began to unravel everything.

From the Sykes-Picot Agreement to the Hashemite Kingdoms

In 1915 a secret agreement between a British representative Sykes and a French rep Picot drew a line across the Levant, saying that after the war the French would have hegemony north of it and the British south.[GE[95]] The world first learned of it after the Russian Revolution in November of 1917 when the Bolsheviks threw open the Russian diplomatic archives to show the devious ways of pre-socialist states. When the French insisted on the terms of this agreement in 1918, the British made no protest, and a French army fought its way to Damascus. From this and other French military campaigns there in the '20s you can still see shrapnel holes in the metal roof over the famous Hamidiyya Souk, the famous covered shopping arcade that leads east from the Umayyad Mosque.[GE[96]] Faisal's term as king lasted a grand total of four months, as he was evicted from Syria by the French by mid-summer 1918. The high hopes of many of the Arabs on our corridor of an independent state were thus dashed, and the Third Aliyah of Jewish immigration came in from 1919–21, helping trigger the first mass Arab violence in 1921–22.

North of the Sykes-Picot line, modern Syria and Lebanon took shape under French tutelage. Lebanon was essentially the largest area that could be drawn with a majority Christian population, gerrymandered out of greater Syria to become a little France-on-the-east-Mediterranean shore. Beirut between the two world wars probably came to be more like Paris than Damascus, and even in Damascus, the French language as the key to the French *"mission civilisatrice"* (civilizing mission) was spoken by the elites. The separation of Lebanon from Syria meant that Damascus, capital of what was left, modern Syria, thus lost its natural port city, Beirut. Syria also lost what Arabs considered Arab lands at the northeast corner of the Mediterranean, which went to the new state of Turkey.

South of the Sykes-Picot line was now British turf. You earlier saw how British sympathy for the plight of Jews in eastern Europe had resulted in the Balfour Declaration of 1917, but how after that the British slowly began to sympathize with the Arab side of things, too—especially with the enormous Arab riots of 1921–22. By this time Winston Churchill was Colonial Secretary for the British government. He also had on his hands the family of Sharif Hussein which had perhaps not been directly lied to but certainly misled by the British about their support of a post-war Arab state. The result was the creation of three "Hashemite kingdoms" by the British—Hashem being the Prophet Muhammad's great-grandfather, and Sharif Hussein and his sons in lineal descent thus being Hashemite.

To the oldest son of Sharif Hussein, Ali, went the "Kingdom of the Hijaz" with those key cities of Jiddah, Mecca, and Medina. It was short-lived; by 1924 Ali lost it all to a clan from the interior of Arabia, the family Sa'ud known for its association with the reformist/puritanical Wahhabi sect of Islam.

To the second son, Abdullah, went the "Kingdom of Transjordan" with its capital of Amman. There is a curious wedge in its eastern border, and since Churchill once claimed he thought the state up one afternoon over a glass of brandy, it is sometimes known as "Winston's hiccup."[GE[97]] In the May 1948 to January 1949 war, as you've seen, Transjordan took the West Bank and old city Jerusalem and renamed itself Jordan. Abdullah was assassinated in 1951, but after a year of turmoil his grandson Hussein took the reins and ruled Jordan for almost half-a-century until his death in 1999. As of this writing his son Abdullah (son of King Hussein and

---

94. GE Layer 94 is a Folder titled "Final British and Arab advances, WW I," with some of the movements shown.

95. GE Layer 95 is a Folder titled "Sykes-Picot Agreement," in which are colored polygons representing planned French and British spheres of influence after the war.

96. GE Layer 96 is a Polygon outlining in green the Hamidiyya Souk, so named because it was built in the reign of the last of the Ottoman sultans, Abdul Hamid II.

97. GE Layer 97 is a Placemark framing a view of the sharply indented eastern border or Jordan (formerly Transjordan), known only half-jokingly as "Winston's hiccup."

his British Queen) is king. This all explains why Jordan—the only surviving one of the three Hashemite kingdoms—is, year in and year out, the most western-leaning of all the Arab states.

To Faisal himself, the third son, went the new "Kingdom of Iraq," consolation prize for his loss of Syria. Although not on our corridor, it might be worthy of mention that "Iraq," meaning "the well-founded," was an optimistic rather than an accurate description of the new state. Never before had the three great cities—Basra in the south, Baghdad in the center, and Mosul in the north—been together in such an independent state. Faisal died in 1933 and was succeeded by his playboy son who was killed in a car wreck in 1939. The state was western-leaning and in fact a key to U.S. diplomatic containment of Communism until a revolution in 1958, on which more later.

So all the modern Arab states on or near our corridor—Lebanon, Syria, Jordan, Saudi Arabia, and Iraq—began to take shape in the early 1920s. In all of the area covered by the Sykes-Picot Agreement, then, that left only British Mandate Palestine, where—despite Churchill's efforts to sort things out—the British increasingly had a tiger by the tail.

SECTION D. MODERN PALESTINIAN NATIONALISM IN THE LARGER CONTEXT OF ARAB, MUSLIM, AND WORLD EVENTS

So now we circle back to the Israeli-Palestinian issue, but this time we'll come at it more from the Palestinian Arab side. From this perspective, as you'll see, it's mostly a rising consciousness triggered by land loss—from the Arab reaction to the very first of the modern Jewish settlements such as Petakh Tikvah to recent news in which an Israeli settler group claims a new hilltop in the West Bank and in reaction a Palestinian terrorist/ freedom fighting group blows up a bus in Jerusalem. Much of the material below is drawn from two remarkable books by Rashid Khalidi, *Palestinian Identity: The Construction of Modern National Consciousness*, and *The Iron Cage: The Story of the Palestinian Struggle for Statehood*.[22] Professor Khalidi is a University of Chicago/Columbia University-caliber scholar, as well as a member of a family as politically connected to Palestine as Kennedys are to Massachusetts or Byrds to Virginia.

How Tanzimat ("The Reforms") worked out in Palestine

There was a bit of discussion earlier about the Ottoman *Tanzimat*, those mid-nineteenth century western-style reforms in many areas of government aimed at making the failing Ottoman Empire more competitive in a world increasingly dominated by European powers. One aspect of that, particularly important for our study here, was the Ottoman Land Law of 1858 that made it easier for recent immigrants to get deeds to land. This law would prove most important in three areas of today's Israel/Palestine—the coastal plain that extends south of Mount Carmel, the Jezreel (Marj ibn Amir) valley that runs southeast from Haifa to the Jordan, and the plains just east of the Sea of Galilee (which together on the map make a giant letter N).[GE[98]] Why? There are basically two reasons. First, these flatter lands were more conducive to large land holdings than the smaller hill-country holdings, and thus more prone to be held by absentee landlords. Second, when sold they had a social impact proportional to their area, which was, of course, large.

In most of this land the *fellahin*, the common small farmers of the Arab population, had had long-standing rights to farm the land, paying rents to those who currently owned it. But now the new Ottoman laws allowed certain individuals—in Rashid Khalidi's words, "village shaykhs, tax-collectors, and urban members of the upper classes, adept at manipulating or circumventing the legal process"—to register the land as personal private property with which they could do as they pleased.[23] So Ottoman law and administration, after centuries of preventing both the fragmentation of the land into tiny plots on the one hand, and on the other the concentration into great estates in the hands of a few wealthy and usually absentee landowners, now allowed these very things to happen—in a quest for modernization.

Petakh Tikvah, as you saw earlier in the chapter, was one of the very first Jewish settlements in Palestine. It was created in 1882, the first year of the First Aliyah, just inland from the sand dunes behind Jaffa, today's

---

98. GE Layer 98 is a Folder titled "The flatter lands," containing three Polygons making the rough letter "N."

Tel Aviv.[GE[99]] In a violent 1886 confrontation, *fellahin* (small farmers; peasants) from a neighboring Arab village killed one Jewish settler there and wounded several others, requiring Ottoman troops to put an end to the violence. It was the reaction of local Arab peasantry to the loss of their traditional rights to farm the land. Disturbances only subsided when local Arabs were hired back to work those same lands (you saw David Grien, not yet Ben-Gurion, observing negatively in 1905 that First Aliyah Jews were reverting to traditional European roles of foremen of labor gangs, instead of working the land themselves).

In 1899 the Jewish Colonization Society bought up 22,000 acres of land in the Galilee near Tiberias, mostly from the wealthy Arab business family of the Sursuqs who were based in Beirut—by far the largest Jewish land purchase in Palestine to date. In 1901 the new Jewish landowners proceeded to evict the traditional Arab laborers from the land, and there was serious trouble. The land surveyor was harassed, the Jewish land agent was shot at, and as late as 1904 a Jewish settler was killed over it. It again took Ottoman military power to suppress the uprising, and the upshot was that a good many Arab tenant farmers lost their right to farm the land. Most of them wound up in slum housing on the outskirts of Haifa.

But then came the Second Aliyah of 1904–1914, shorter but much more numerous and of very different character—young Russian Jews coming to live out the socialist religion of labor. With the fertile land already occupied, the alternative was still to buy land from absentee land owners, and then evict the occupants despite their claims of traditional rights to farm the land. The Ottoman government enforced the legal rights of new Jewish landowners, though mid-level Arab administrators tried to reverse the verdicts—one sign of the Arab Revolt to come. In 1908, when Sultan Abdul Hamid II lost power to the "Young Turks," there was for a time in Palestine a lifting of press censorship and a quick spread of Arabic-language papers. In this setting local Arab frustration with European Jewish immigration boiled to the surface, accompanied by more riots against these relatively new Jewish settlements. This was the context of the 1909 formation of *Ha-Shomer*, the Watchman, the first open Jewish self-defense force for the Galilee and predecessor to Haganah and the Israeli army, as you saw earlier. It was also the setting for the Afula land transfer of the following year, a real watershed in Palestinian history.

The Afula land transfer of 1910

In 1910 the fairly new Jewish National Fund bought (again from the Beirut Sursuqs) something over 3,000 acres in and around Afula (al-Fula).[GE[100]] Although only a fraction the size of some earlier Jewish land purchases, several changes in politics and public opinion made this a key event. For one, Palestinian Arabs had learned from the 1899–1901 purchase/eviction process around nearby Tiberias how permanent and successful such purchases could be, backed by Ottoman power. Secondly, this was in the more open press and speech time after the Young Turk Revolt (and before World War I, when it was shut down again). Thirdly, Afula was squarely in the middle of the extremely fertile Jezreel/Marg Ibn Amir.

Regional Arab officialdom generally sided with the dispossessed fellahin. A local registrar refused to hand over the deed to the Jewish National Fund, and sent a military force to evict a Ha-Shomer unit sent to secure the land. A local candidate for the Ottoman parliament campaigned on the issue and won big. A growing local newspaper and magazine press kept the issue in the public eye. Greater force from the imperial Ottoman government negated all the concrete moves, but in this whole affair you see some crystallization of a Palestinian national identity.[24] By 1911 there was a journal called *Filastin* ("Palestine") that featured anti-Zionist articles. This 1910–11 Afula period is when the black-and-white checked *khaffiyya*—the headdress of the common Palestinian farmer—began to be adopted by urban intellectuals as a symbol of the Palestinian cause. Anyone old enough to remember Yasser Arafat (b. 1929–d. 2004)—the city-born and university-educated leader of the Palestinian liberation movement for a half-century—will probably be unable to remember a single photograph of him without that Palestinian khaffiyya (and if you're not old enough, just do a Google—Images search on "Yasser Arafat" as proof). Note this coming together of what had been two very separate strands of resistance—

---

99. GE Layer 99 is a Placemark referencing Petakh Tikvah.

100. GE Layer 100 is a Placemark framing a view of Afula and environs, smack in the middle of the fertile Jezreel/Marj Ibn Amir.

on the one hand, uneducated farmers angry and frightened about losing their right to farm the land, and on the other, urban intellectuals aware of other patterns of resistance to European domination, and able to use letters, newspapers, and books to comment on it. It's a not uncommon thing to happen at the dawn of modern national consciousness creation; in Chapter 12 you'll see a remarkably close version of this same process and at about this same time in the Dutch East Indies, a process that did much to create Indonesian national consciousness, with a *kampong* (village) revolt inspiring response among Dutch-speaking, college-educated intellectuals.

World War I and the first years of the mandate: intellectuals "imagining" the community

The years from the British drive north out of Egypt in 1917 to early in the British mandate, say 1922 or 1923—are for Rashid Khalidi the "critical years" of the creation of modern Palestinian patriotism. It began with the reaction to the public Balfour Declaration and the revelation of the secret Sykes-Picot Agreement, both in 1917, and progressed through the return of First and Second Aliyah Jews in 1918 and the new tide of Third Aliyah Jews from 1919–21. It culminated with 1921–22 riots against that new Jewish presence, and Colonial Secretary Winston Churchill's creation of a purely Arab unit east of the Jordan and the rule that no Jewish immigrant could enter the country who would take a job away from an Arab. For Palestinian Arabs there were still competing loyalties both broader and narrower—pan-Arab feeling for their language group, majority Muslim feelings of one *umma* or body of believers (though on our corridor there was a large Christian minority), and local ties to village stronger than most modern Americans can imagine. But in this time Palestinian nationalism arguably became the majority sentiment of native speakers of Arabic in Palestine under the British mandate. You've already seen the second of the two quotations that headed up this chapter, written in 1925 by a noted Jerusalem writer and educator:

> This was the situation of Palestine, which for many centuries had been in the deepest sleep, until it was shaken by the great war, shocked by the Zionist movement, and violated by the illegal policy [of the British], and it awoke, little by little.

Most modern historians of nationalism would say, instead of "and it awoke, little by little" (which implies a complete pre-existing Palestinian patriotism), "and it was <u>created</u>, little by little." But created it surely was, and it was behind the 1926–29 turmoil which included riots over access to the Western Wall (holy for Jews as it is supposed to be a remnant of the original temple, important for Muslims as a foundation wall for the high platform containing the Al Aqsa Mosque and the Dome of the Rock, sites associated with the life of Muhammad).

For the British, it was one more lesson in the intensity of feeling on the Arab side of things in Mandate Palestine. In 1930 the current British colonial secretary issued the "Passfield White Paper" that said the British would uphold the rights of all groups there. From the Zionist side of things, of course, it was one more step away from the Balfour Declaration of thirteen years before, and occasioned a storm of protest from their supporters in the British Parliament and some governmental retreat from the Passfield White Paper criticism of Zionist institutions operating in Palestine. Prime Minister Ramsey MacDonald himself wrote Chaim Weizmann a long, complicated letter trying to explain how Britain could honor the Balfour Declaration and still protect Arab land-holdings in Mandate Palestine. Any solution, he wrote plaintively, "depends upon an understanding between the Jews and the Arabs." With the rise of Palestinian nationalism, reacting to and rapidly catching up with Zionist nationalism, such understanding was getting less and less likely.

The Arab Revolt and World War II

In November of 1935, the Haifa funeral of Shaykh 'Iz al-Din al-Qassem turned into the biggest Palestinian political demonstration of the whole British Mandate period, though the Shaykh himself had not been an exclusive Palestinian nationalist. Born in northern coastal Syria and educated in Egypt's most famous seminary, he had fought Italian occupation of Libya in 1912 and French occupation of Syria and Lebanon after World

War I. Chased by the French out of French Mandate Lebanon and Syria by 1920, however, he went to Haifa and put down roots. He was both the imam preaching at the local mosque and an impassioned social worker in the slum housing of the landless fellahin, mainly those dispossessed by Jewish land purchases in the Galilee and the Jezreel. By 1930 his frustration was such that he became, in Rashid Khalidi's words, "the first articulate public apostle of armed rural resistance" among the Palestinian Arabs. The main targets of his group of guerrilla fighters were the Jewish settlements, though to some extent British officials as well. In October of 1935 a British constable was killed, probably by al-Qassem's group, and the British launched a manhunt that cornered him in the mountains where Mount Carmel joins Jerusalem Ridge, and he was killed in the firefight. He was the first great martyr of the modern Palestinian cause, as was noted even by such perceptive Zionists as Ben-Gurion, who likened him to Josef Trumpeldor (the 1920 martyr whose sacrificial death had helped fire up the Zionist movement). Crowds of many thousands of mourners at al-Qassem's Haifa funeral brushed aside the British police trying to limit the event. This event more than any other sparked the Palestine-wide general strike of 1936 among Arabs, and the resulting 1936–39 "Arab Revolt." Al-Qassem was buried in the cemetery of the little Arab town of Balad al-Shaykh (today the Israeli town of Nesher), on the northern slope of Mt. Carmel.[GE[101]]

This Arab Revolt had two clear phases. The first, in 1936, was a general strike led by acknowledged Palestinian Arab public figures. The most important of them was Haj Amin al-Husseini, from 1921 to 1937 the "Grand Mufti" of Jerusalem. "Mufti" was an old Ottoman title from the millet system, recognizing the leader of a separate religious community, and the British took a page from Ottoman practice by appointing him "Grand Mufti" in 1921 under their Mandate Authority. He is a clear example of a Palestinian nationalist first, and only secondly a pan-Arab or a Muslim nationalist. In the spring of 1936 he brought together a Higher National Committee of notable Palestinians, and the Committee organized a general strike to try to paralyze the British administration and so win concessions.

The general strike failed, and in late 1937 a grassroots rebellion of the Palestinian fellahin attacked Jewish holdings and British administrative posts on a scale unprecedented during the mandate. British search and seizure teams began going from village to village. Forts connected by barbed wire were built on the Lebanese and Syrian borders to keep other terrorist/freedom fighters out, and a special prison for those captured was set up down in the isolated Negev desert. Haj Amin al-Husseini himself escaped, and found refuge in Mussolini's Italy and Hitler's Germany. Whether or not he himself was personally anti-Semitic has been debated, but his rhetoric certainly was. It may have been only the old logic of "the enemy of my enemy is my friend," but thereafter the British, along with most other Western Europeans and Americans, lost what enthusiasm they had had for Palestinian Arabs. Too, during this Arab Revolt of 1936–39, the British army had to some extent allied with Haganah, the Jewish armed underground, even while not officially recognizing its existence. It didn't augur especially well for future British support of a Palestinian Arab state.

The Arab Revolt in Palestine was crushed by 1939, and Palestinian Arabs went into the World War II era essentially leaderless. At war's end the British found themselves caught in the crossfire between Arabs and Jews in Palestine, and as you saw earlier in this chapter, in 1947 submitted the problem to the United Nations. The November 1947 UNSCOP plan for partitioning the land dissolved by May 15, 1948, into the all-out war that saw Israel take all the Mandate Palestine except the West Bank (and Old City Jerusalem) and the Gaza Strip. The loss of Haifa and Jaffa, the two most intellectually vibrant Arab communities, compounded the leaderless factor of Palestinian Arabs.

Al-Nakba, the Catastrophe

And so a Jewish state emerged in Palestine, but the Arab state proposed by the United Nations did not. For most Palestinians it was then, and remains today, *al-Nakba,* "the Catastrophe." Of something less than a million Palestinian Arabs total at the time, about three-fourths fled the fighting or were evicted. A third of these wound up as officially registered refugees in United Nations-sponsored refugee camps in Syria, Lebanon, Jordan (then

---

101. GE Layer 101 is a Placemark approximating the cemetery where al-Qassem was buried—on the lower slope of Mt. Carmel about four miles from Haifa.

including the West Bank), and the Gaza Strip.[GE¹⁰²] Another two-thirds of those refugees went mainly to those same neighboring lands, but found places to live other than the formal camps.

To jump ahead a bit, to 1967—just twenty-one years later—the Israelis in the greatest of their victories took among other territories the West Bank, setting in motion a second huge wave of Palestinian refugees, and thus a whole new set of refugee camps, mainly in Syria and Jordan.[GE¹⁰³] The traditional Israeli view, reluctant to recognize any such thing as Palestinian national consciousness, has been that they left, and should have no right of return. They are Arabs, after all, and should be easily absorbed by the greater Arab world. The view of the Syrian, Lebanese, Jordanian, and Egyptian governments is that absorbing them would destabilize their own countries, and anyway the correct solution for the problem is for them to be restored to their rightful lands.

So the refugee camps have existed in a sort of limbo, year to year, decade to decade, and seem to have become a permanent feature of the landscape. If by "Palestinian refugee camp" you envision a tent city, envision again. They may have started that way, but over the decades they have become very permanent towns, with concrete and masonry buildings for schools, businesses, mosques, even homes. About all that differentiates them from neighboring towns is their extremely crowded nature, as you can see by exploring one of them, the "Beqaa" camp not far from Amman, Jordan.[GE¹⁰⁴] Since the children of a Palestinian Arab father are by definition also legally Palestinians, the Palestinian population in the camps is now close to 1.5 million, several times as large as when they were founded (with another 3.5 million Palestinians scattered outside the camps), but on no more land than was originally allocated. And when you ask the younger residents where they are from, they don't say "Beqaa," or the name of whatever camp they were born in and have lived in all their lives, but "Jaffa" or "Bersheeba" or "Ramallah"—their parents' or grandparents' home towns that they themselves have never even seen.

Inside Israel proper are Arab Israelis—around 20 percent of Israel's total population of 8 million. They have the right to vote in the Israeli democracy and even to be members of the Knesseth, the Parliament, where indeed there is a small Arab Party. But they are not asked to serve in the military (except for the Druze, a religious and ethnic group somewhat distinct from the mainstream Palestinian Arab Sunni Muslims), and there are sensitive positions in the Israeli government for which an unwritten code rules out any Arab Israeli occupant. Those Arabs in the occupied territories, particularly in the West Bank, have no rights of citizenship and are subject to a variety of daily humiliations. Some decades ago a close friend of the author's worked for a while at the University of Birzeit, close to Ramallah and probably the flagship of Palestinian Arab higher education. [GE¹⁰⁵] West Bank Arab-owned car tags were blue, Israeli car tags were yellow—and, he said, twenty out of twenty times when we met an Israeli-owned car in a tight place we were the ones forced to back down or were run off the road.

But we've run ahead too far with the refugee camps and Palestinians under Israeli control, and to properly sort things out—including the final chapter of Palestinian Arab self-consciousness—now need to go back to Arab affairs in the early 1950s, just in the wake of "the Catastrophe."

The rise of Egypt's Gamal Abdal Nasser

Gamal Abdal Nasser, who ran Egypt from 1954 until his death in 1970, was surely the most charismatic Arab leader of the past century. We dealt with the outlines of his career briefly in Chapter 3, in the context of the growing confrontation worldwide that came with the Cold War. Suffice it to say here that he headed up a secret

---

102. GE Layer 102 is a Folder titled "Palestinian refugee camps from 1948–9 war." It has subfolders for Lebanon, Syria, the West Bank, Jordan east of the Jordan River, and the Gaza Strip. Camps are shown by red target-shaped Placemarks.

103. GE Layer 103 is a Folder titled "Palestinian refugee camps from 1967 war." It has subfolders for Syria and Jordan. Camps are shown by orange target-shaped Placemarks.

104. GE Layer 104 is a Folder titled "Beqaa refugee camp near Amman, Jordan." It frames a view showing downtown Amman and the Beqaa camp, and includes a Polygon in green outlining the camp along with several suggestions for Panoramio icons to view.

105. GE Layer 105 is a Placemark referencing the University of Birzeit, on a hilltop near a town of the same name, some four miles from Ramallah.

clique in the Egyptian army called the Revolutionary Command Center (RCC), and was chief military architect of the overthrow of the Egyptian monarchy and remaining British colonial rule in 1952.

By 1954 the handsome and articulate Nasser was unrivaled and looked to by the major western powers as the potential leader of a Mideast anti-Communist bloc. But he was bitterly resentful, as were most Arabs, about the western support that had allowed the emergence of an Israeli state in the Arab heartland of the Mideast in 1948–49. When the Eisenhower administration would not give him the offensive weapons he needed to match growing Israeli power just to his north, he discovered that Khrushchev and the Soviet Union would. You may remember from the Russia chapter that the U.S. administration, as punishment, withdrew our offer to support construction of the Aswan High Dam on the Nile, central to Nasser's modernization plans. In response to that, in 1956 Nasser declared that Egypt had nationalized the Suez Canal (and closed it to all Israeli shipping), planning to use the tolls from the canal to fund the High Dam. This triggered a war, Egypt being invaded by British, French, and Israeli forces—the second of four major Arab-Israeli wars. The Soviet Union generally supported Nasser, and probably partly because of the danger of a new world war over the issue, the Eisenhower administration put pressure on the invading powers to disengage.

The year 1958, looking back on his whole era, was the single most influential time of Nasser's leadership, capitalizing on his new popularity in the Arab world with a sophisticated pan-Arab political campaign that transformed the Middle East. In February 1 of that year he formally merged Egypt with Syria in a new entity called the United Arab Republic—hopefully the nucleus of a single great and powerful state that would include all Arabs. The modern Syrian state, established by the French in their image, had undergone a series of military coups and counter-coups from 1949 to 1954, and by this time had—like Egypt—also fallen into the Soviet orbit primarily because it seemed to offer help for the Arab national cause. Both the pan-Arab *Ba'ath* ("Renaissance") Party—technically the "Arab Socialist Renaissance Party"—and the Communist Party had grown in popularity in Syria since World War II, and they were the chief players on the Syrian side that arranged this UAR merger with Egypt. Soon after Yemen also joined,[GE106] and prospects looked good for other members.

Iraq in 1958 was still a western-designed and western-leaning Hashemite kingdom, and very important to the western powers as the anchor of the 1955 Baghdad Pact with Turkey, Iran, and Pakistan as a "containment" fence against expanding Communism. But Iraq's leaders were increasingly isolated as the Iraqi population rallied behind Nasser's calls for a greater Arab state. The immediate response of the Iraqi leaders to Nasser's UAR proclamation of February 1 was their own February 14 announcement of an Iraqi-Jordanian federation (Jordan being a fellow western-leaning Hashemite kingdom). It got little public support, and on July 14 a bloody coup by pan-Arab military officers in Iraq killed the king, the crown prince, and the prime minister. A revolutionary council reminiscent of Egypt's RCC took over government. Iraq pulled out of the Baghdad Pact and allied with the Soviet Union.

For western powers such as the U.S., the U.K., and France, this was all a disastrous turn of foreign affairs events. In Lebanon a civil war was breaking out between the western-leaning Maronite Christians and the Soviet-leaning Sunni Muslims who wanted Lebanon to join the UAR. In Jordan—supposedly independent but with lots of British military presence still in-country—the government was in real danger of being overthrown. On the day after the Iraqi coup, President Eisenhower authorized the U.S. navy to land troops in Lebanon and Jordan, and they stayed there until late October to protect their pro-western governments.

That year of 1958, however, proved to be the high-water mark for pan-Arabism. By 1961 even Syria pulled out of the UAR, sealing its fate.

Nasser had become a firm Soviet ally. With the formal opening of the Aswan High Dam in early 1964, the media was flooded with images of Khrushchev and Nasser side by side. Although Israelis launched the 1967 Arab-Israeli War (the Six Day War, the third of our major Arab-Israeli wars) with a surprise air strike, most observers felt Israel had little choice because of the war fever that was being whipped up by Nasser. But to the surprise of Nasser, and probably of the Soviet Union as well, this turned into the greatest of all the Israeli

---

106. GE Layer 106 is a Folder titled "United Arab Republic," with Polygons representing the three states that initially committed to it.

victories over Arab armies, resulting in the Israeli seizure of the Sinai peninsula from Egypt, the West Bank from Jordan, and the Golan Heights from Syria.[GE107]

Outside Egypt, those Ba'athist ("Renaissance") political parties—combining Arab nationalism with Soviet-style socialist central planning and yet not being officially atheistic, given the strength of Islam in most of the Mideast—remained the governments in Syria and Iraq. These countries would of course get a good deal of support from the Soviet Union over the years to come.

And what was the influence of all this Nasser-era pan-Arabism and Soviet alliance on Palestinian Arabs? It was enormous, like a strong magnetic field operating on a little piece of iron. On the one hand, it tended to dampen a rising Palestinian national consciousness in a temporary surge of pan-Arabism. On the other hand, it produced the pre-eminent leader of the whole Palestinian national movement.

Yasser Arafat, *al-Fatah*, and the P.L.O.

Yasser Arafat (1929–2004) was from a family with roots in the Nile delta as well as in Palestine; he was born in Cairo, and as a child lived both there and in Jerusalem. He got an engineering degree at what is today Cairo University in 1950, having taken time out from college to fight around Gaza in that first Arab-Israeli war of 1948–49. From 1952–56—those years from the RCC takeover to the emergence of Gamal Abdal Nasser as unrivaled leader in Egypt—Arafat was President of the Palestinian Students' Union in Egypt. After the 1956 war, he got an engineering job and later a teaching position in Kuwait, but politics—particularly the Palestinian cause—gradually squeezed out all other professional and personal interests in his life. In 1959 he and some Palestinian friends in Kuwait had founded *Fatah*, from the Arabic initials for "Palestinian National Liberation Movement."

In 1962, with the UAR broken up and pan-Arab momentum fading fast, Arafat and his group moved to Syria. Here they first began military training and launching raids into Israel, though halting and amateur at first. The shocking defeat of Soviet-supplied Arab armies in the 1967 war convinced more and more Palestinians to back Arafat's purely Palestinian focus. He himself was apparently working underground, inside the West Bank—newly occupied by the Israeli army—recruiting for Fatah's paramilitary within a week of the defeat. Nasser began to speak of him as the voice of the Palestinians. In 1968 Arafat moved Fatah headquarters to Karameh,[GE108] a Palestinian refugee camp in Jordan only a couple of miles from the Jordan River defense line now held by the Israelis, from which Fatah could more easily launch raids into Israel. When an Israeli school bus was blown up by what we'd call today an IED, probably set by Fatah, the Israeli army came across the border and attacked Karameh with a much more professional, well-armed force than the Palestinians could field. The other allied Palestinian groups in Karameh all retreated, but Arafat insisted that Fatah dig in and fight. Its resistance was stubborn, and when the Jordanian army moved in, in support of Fatah (surprising the Israelis who didn't expect it given the friction between the Jordanian government and the Palestinian refugees), the Israelis broke off the battle. Although many more Fatah fighters died than Israeli Defense Force fighters, it was a moral victory for Arafat, who got the devotion of a Palestinian Arab public starved for success after "the Catastrophe" of 1948 and the disastrous 1967 war. It also got him his first real international recognition—on the cover of *Time* magazine in a December issue. In 1969 he was elected Chairman of the Palestine Liberation Organization (hereafter PLO), an umbrella group that included everything from the Marxist "Popular Front for the Liberation of Palestine" to units on loan from the Syrian army.

In Jordan after the 1967 war, the Palestinian refugee population substantially outnumbered the native Jordanians. A confrontation between the newly self-confident PLO and the western-leaning Hashemite monarchy under King Hussain erupted in September of 1970 into a full-fledged civil war that lasted ten months. The Jordanians, with their western-equipped standing army, won, so for Palestinians it became "Black September." Many of the Palestinian refugees now sought new refuge in southern Lebanon, and the PLO leadership

---

107. GE Layer 107 is a Folder titled "Israeli gains in 1967 war," with Polygons for the Golan Heights and the Sinai gains of the war. The taking of the West Bank pushed Israeli control to the Jordan River, still the international border with Jordan today.

108. GE Layer 108 is a Placemark referencing Karameh (no longer the site of a refugee camp).

including Yasser Arafat decamped for Beirut. Many older Americans will remember the Munich Olympics of 1972, when Palestinian terrorists/freedom fighters stormed Olympic village and killed eleven Israeli athletes there. Skyjackings became commonplace, and guerrilla *fedayeen* ("men of sacrifice") raids into Israeli more destructive.

From the Ramadan/Yom Kippur War to the Camp David Accords

In Egypt, in the fall of 1970, Gamal Abdal Nasser died of a heart attack, and was succeeded by Anwar Sadat. Sadat inherited an alliance with the Soviet Union, though he apparently didn't get along well with his Russian advisors. Not taken seriously by either Israel or the U.S., this may be one reason he began the Ramadan/Yom Kippur War in October of 1973—the fourth major Arab-Israeli war to date. Although by war's end Israeli might had begun to tell, the war had caught Israel off guard enough to embarrass the government and cost Golda Meir her Prime Ministership. Henry Kissinger, National Security Advisor for President Nixon, engaged in some famous "shuttle diplomacy" between Israel and Egypt to keep the conflict localized and hopefully end it. Surprisingly, it resulted in a thawing of relations between the two, with Sadat beginning to shift Egypt's great power alliance from the Soviet Union to the United States.

In 1977 President Sadat—with the Egyptian economy and his own personal popularity going downhill—said in a speech that he would go anywhere, "even Jerusalem," in pursuit of lasting peace. The government of newly-elected Prime Minister Menachem Begin issued such an invitation, and Sadat visited Israel for three days and spoke before the Knesseth. In 1978 President Jimmy Carter built on that by inviting Sadat and Begin to a two-week retreat at Camp David. Amazingly—Sadat and Begin were barely on speaking terms—it resulted in a substantial agreement. Egypt would get back the Sinai peninsula lands taken by Israel and get substantial aid from the United States. Israel would get recognition as a legitimate state by Egypt—a break in the united front against it in the Arab world. A West Bank–Gaza Strip "Palestinian Authority" would be established, with "full autonomy." The word independence was not used, and Jerusalem was not mentioned—but a Palestinian state seemed to be in the process of being born. It was the closest to a lasting solution of the "Palestinian problem" that has happened in modern times.

But Carter lost his bid for a second term as President (and in large part because of another Mideastern crisis, the Iranian Revolution and American hostage situation). In January of 1981 the in-coming administration of President Ronald Reagan was more focused on the Milton Friedman-style free market reforms in Israel than on holding Begin accountable on the Palestinian autonomy issue. In October of 1981 Sadat was assassinated by an Egyptian army officer belonging to an Islamic group—perhaps partly because with no progress to show on a Palestinian state, all of Sadat's negotiations with Israel and the U.S. now made it seem as if he had sacrificed the Palestinian cause just to get the Sinai lands back for Egypt. Three current or former American presidents attended Sadat's funeral, but almost no heads of Arab states paid their respects, so unpopular was his recognition of Israel and his alliance with the U.S., chief international supporter of Israel. In 1982 Israel launched a full-scale invasion of Lebanon, right up to the Beirut-Damascus highway and into Beirut itself, to evict the PLO "state within a state" from the country. In alliance with the (Lebanese Christian) Maronite Phalange, massacres of Palestinian men, women, and children in the Shatila camp and nearby Sabra neighborhood of Beirut were carried out. It was so directly under Israeli Defense Minister Ariel Sharon's supervision that he lost his post as Defense Minister, though he continued in the cabinet.

"Outside" and "Inside": from the *Intifada* to the Oslo Accords

Yasser Arafat, meanwhile, continued to consolidate his position as primary leader of the Palestine national independence movement. Stung by the emotional backlash of the world in general to the Munich Olympic village killings, he forbid Palestinian guerrilla violence outside Israel/Palestine. In 1974 the Arab League recognized the PLO as the only legitimate organization representing Palestinians—and so implicitly Arafat as head of the PLO became the sole legitimate voice of the Palestinian cause. With the Israeli invasion of Lebanon in 1982, the PLO leadership moved to Tunis.

In 1987 the Palestinian situation was transformed by a spontaneous new revolt against Israeli authority, mainly from young Arabs in the West Bank and the Gaza Strip. They called it the *intifada*, or uprising. From this time on there was an "outside" in the Palestinian movement—the leadership in Tunisia, and other exiles— and an "inside," those Palestinians under Israeli authority.

Not far away, from 1980 to 1988, a Persian Gulf War had raged between Iran and Iraq—Iran under the Ayatollah Khomeini's new theocratic rule, and Iraq under the dictator Saddam Hussein. The United States armed Iraq and provided military intelligence. In 1990, apparently thinking he had the approval of the U.S. Ambassador to Iraq, Saddam Hussein invaded Kuwait. The single most vivid image the world had of the Palestinian reaction to this was of a great public embrace between Saddam and Yasser Arafat (even though some of Arafat's advisors told him privately that if he justified taking land by force, that justified all the Israeli land seizures). When Saddam refused U.S. and other demands that Iraqi forces leave Kuwait, in January of 1991 we, the U.S., invaded Kuwait and parts of Iraq, and imposed a "no-fly zone" that successfully restricted Saddam Hussein's influence to the central, Sunni Arab majority part of Iraq.

First under President George H. W. Bush, and then President Bill Clinton, came some promising Israeli-Palestinian negotiations that resulted in the first Oslo Accord of 1993. The story is best told from the Palestinian side by Hanan Ashrawi, native of Ramallah, Professor of Literature and then Dean of faculty of the University of Birzeit, and a member of the negotiating teams. Her title of her 1994 book, *This Side of Peace: A Personal Account*, seems to be a double entendre—this side of peace as in the Palestinian view of it, and this side of peace as in we haven't gotten there yet. From a Christian family background, and working in the traditional male preserve of politics in the region, Ashrawi had consistently worked for three goals in her life: gender equality, democracy, and Palestinian independence. She lays out for an American audience the human dimension of Palestinian life under Israeli control, among other things how it affected her two daughters, her housekeeper, and her relatives. A wordsmith in English as well as Arabic, she talks about the importance that Palestinians, and Arabs in general, attach to names:

> How does one console *Nasr* (victory) for a lifetime of defeat not of his own making? Who can convince *Khaled* (eternal) that immortality in this world is beyond his grasp? And how does *Ni'meh* (the gift of grace) understand the disgrace of discrimination deliberately exercised against her gender?[25]

She discusses her travels involved in the negotiations, from Cold War spy novel-style secret car rides to conferences in Amman and London and Madrid. From her book you get a good idea of both the respect almost all Palestinians had for Yasser Arafat, and for his extremely jealous protection of his authority. When the main negotiating Palestinian team had made some major breakthroughs, all of a sudden they learned that Arafat had gone behind their back and arranged the Oslo Accord—achieving less for the Palestinians, but enabling him to claim the breakthrough and keep everything under his control. In brief, the PLO recognized Israel's existence and right to exist, and vice-versa, and Israel promised to pull its defense forces out of at least parts of the West Bank and Gaza strip so that a Palestinian interim government would begin functioning—the Palestine National Authority, to be complete by 1999. Arafat was free to return to Palestinian territory.

The Israeli Prime Minister Yitzhak Rabin—a tough former Defense Minister known earlier as "The Bone-Breaker" by Palestinians—had put his authority behind the negotiations. But in 1995, at a public rally in support of an extension of the original Oslo Accord, he was assassinated by a right-wing Israeli. As you read earlier at the end of the second section, without Rabin's personality and commitment to the Oslo Accords, the 1999 deadline came and went without much in the way of achievement of Palestinian autonomy. Palestinian frustration, pushed over the edge by General Sharon's armed excursion around the Dome of the Rock and the al-Aqsa Mosque in 2001, boiled over in the "Second Intifada." This might have attracted some serious U.S. and other western power efforts to re-start negotiations—but the al-Qaeda attacks of 9/11/2001 tended to force everything into a Muslim fundamentalist vs. the Western world dichotomy. The Palestinian issue has been pushed way down the list, behind such things as invasions of Afghanistan and Iraq, both wars going on for over a decade as of this writing.

Palestinians, Israelis, and the U.S. in the Arab Spring

After Yasser Arafat's death in 2004, Mahmoud Abbas became head of Fatah, and functioning head of the Palestine Authority. Arafat had first made him Prime Minister in 1993, but then refused to give him control of the military—which Mahmoud Abbas said he needed to disarm Palestinian guerrilla fighters in compliance with the Oslo Accord. Abbas thereupon resigned, but with Arafat's death was the obvious choice to be his successor. Meanwhile, through the democratic vote, the Gaza Strip went heavily for Hamas—a Sunni Muslim political party that has not rejected violence against or accepted the existence of the Israeli state. Its paramilitary units are named for the 1935 martyr for the Palestinian cause—the Iz al-Din al-Qassem Brigades. So now there are two experiments going on in the quest for Palestinian independence. One is an armed one from Gaza, from which rockets and raids are launched against Israel with some frequency and into which Israeli reprisal raids are launched with approximately equal frequency. The other is Mahmoud Abbas's attempt in the West Bank to prove to Israelis that an independent Palestine under his government will be a peaceful neighbor, able to disarm its potential extremists in the interests of Israeli security.

In the past few decades the West Bank—potential nucleus of any Palestinian Arab state—has being slowly but surely balkanized by the Israelis, and the process is still on-going. Take a minute to explore the attached Google Earth folder of the remaining patches of the West Bank under today's Palestinian Authority.[GE109] You'll see outlined in a thick red line the "butterfly wing" of the West Bank, with Jerusalem at the indentation between the upper and lower wings (and East Jerusalem shown in yellow, captured by the Israelis in 1967 as well). What's left of the West Bank for the Palestinian Authority to control is shown as around 150 separate black polygons outlined in red. The corridors in-between are controlled by the Israelis, making any unified Palestinian government virtually impossible. Now explore the following Google Earth folder that shows a sample 7 × 10 mile rectangle of the West Bank somewhat north and east of Tel Aviv. The yellow salients driven miles into the West Bank over the original 1949 border represent the course of the new barrier (a 30′-tall concrete wall near urban areas; barbed wire fence and cleared zone in rural ones). The yellow pushpins represent the new Israeli settlements there, giving the approximate dates of their establishment.[GE110] Visually it helps you appreciate the comparison the Palestinian negotiating team at the original Oslo Accord made, between two men at a table negotiating over a wheel of cheese, one of the men being allowed to cut pieces of it and eat it during the negotiations . . . . For West Bank Palestinians, crossing the barrier at Israeli checkpoints often means standing in long lines and being treated without much in the way of respect. Such balkanization invites immediate comparison to the "homeland" policy of the apartheid government of South Africa after 1948. The Israeli response to that is, "it is necessary for our security."

This writing is being done during the "Arab Spring," the latest major development in the region. It began in the last weeks of 2010 in Tunisia, and spread to much of the Arab world in the next few years. Governments were overthrown in Egypt, Libya, and Yemen, and many other governments were shaken, from Morocco to the Persian Gulf. It affected our corridor, too. In 2012 there were major protests in the West Bank against the Palestine National Authority, mainly over the price of fuel oil and other goods. Israelis for their part worried aloud that Egypt would reverse its recognition of Israel and perhaps begin a new war in support of the Palestinian cause.

Is there any resolution to this "Palestinian problem" on the horizon? The most talked-about possible solution is still the "two-state" one. As recently as 2013 two-thirds of Arabs in the region—and a surprising 40%+ of Israeli Jews—supported a two-state solution for the "Palestinian problem," though fewer and fewer on either side thought it would actually happen.[26]

---

109. GE Layer 109 is a Folder titled "Arab-controlled parts of the West Bank," mainly based on a 2011 United Nations map.

110. GE Layer 110 is a Folder titled "Section of West Bank border." It explores a 7x10 mile rectangle, shows the new barrier/fence/wall itself as a thick yellow Path, emphasizes the 1949 cease-fire line as a thick red Path, and the new yellow Israeli settlements, with dates of their establishment, as yellow pushpins, and the old Arab villages and towns in green. The one black line is where the Israeli Supreme Court ordered the destruction of the wall there so as not to isolate one Arab village, though the project in general was approved by the court.

As interconnected as the modern world is, every one of the seven regional corridors dealt with in the second half of this book is importantly impacted by the United States, and every one of them has in turn some impact on us. But on this Damascus-south-to-water corridor we arguably have a greater impact than on any of the others (greater even than on the Veracruz-to-Mexico City so close to us), and it in turn has a greater impact on us.

The national consciousness reached by both Israeli Jews and Palestinian Arabs affects us here in the United States in ways both subtle and not-so-subtle. Not too many years ago I introduced an important American Jewish writer at a conference presentation, and before and after we had time to visit. He had been to a meeting earlier on the subject of the increasing friction between the Jewish-American and African-American communities. Both are essentially urban populations (except for a remaining rural black community in the South), and it was Jewish-Americans more than any other segment of white America who supported the African-American civil rights movement of the 1950s and 1960s. So what has poisoned relations between the two groups in the last few decades? The visiting writer's take was that most American Jews were afraid that any criticism of Israeli policies, or the withholding of any degree of American support for Israel, would endanger Israel's existence, and that most African-Americans increasingly saw the Palestinian struggle as one for civil rights against an apartheid-style rule. We rarely talk about it, he said, but it is the 800 lb. gorilla in any room that has both ethnic groups in it.

Without a two-state solution, Israel/Palestine and its neighbors will surely smolder and occasionally flare up in war for the foreseeable future, and all Israel has to do is lose one war to go out of existence. Without a two-state solution, there will continue to be little or no trust in the United States from the greater Arab and the even greater Muslim world, a continuing primary motivation for Arab nationalist and Muslim fundamentalist terrorist/freedom fighters.

The first question is, of course, could it work, with long-time security for Israelis and independence and dignity for Palestinians? If so, the next questions are, where are the risk-takers on either side willing to chance assassination to get it done (Sadat assassinated within three years of the Camp David Agreement; Rabin assassinated within two years of the Oslo Accord)? And where is the political will in those interested outside countries—especially the United States—to help it happen?

Many impartial observers who know the history of the area believe that one key condition necessary for such a peace is for Arabs of Palestinian origin to give up "the right of return." Israel probably can't exist as a democracy with a majority Arab population, especially an Arab population that hasn't had Israeli citizenship for years. Israel, in fact, may have its hands full as it is in integrating its current Israeli Arab population, growing in relative size compared to the Jewish population. But for Palestinian Arabs living outside Israel to give up the right of return—while from their point of view, ironically enough, all the Jews in the world have been invited to "return"—would mean accepting the permanent status of the refugee camps in Lebanon, Jordan, and Syria, or for those countries to fully integrate the Palestinian population into their own—a huge change, dangerous for all those governments. And if that doesn't happen, the refugee camps will continue to produce terrorists/freedom fighters working to reclaim lands their families lost in 1948 and 1967.

As regards Israel's necessary compromise, those same middle-of-the-road observers would say, if Israel wants to build a wall all along the old 1949 West Bank boundary, fine (though maybe leaving a road open to Gaza)—but all those walls driven as salients into the West Bank, and all the Jewish settlements there built in the last few decades, must be dismantled. For the Israel government to do this, of course, would bring about violent protest from conservative Israelis and especially the ultra-Orthodox. A Labor Party government might consider it, there still being more belief in the possible success of a "land for peace" deal on the left of the political spectrum in Israel. A Likud government, given its roots in Irgun and Herut and more recent history, would have to be forced to swallow such a bitter pill by the United States and other outside forces.

Where is the political will in the U.S. to back this, the only possible (but not guaranteed of success) long-term solution? We in the U.S. have a long history of concern for Israel; we were the very first government in the world to recognize the new state of Israel in May of 1948. As a nation we have a lingering guilt about not having done something about the Holocaust. Mossad has been and presumably still is a key source of our intelligence about the Mideast. To a certain extent, Israel has been a military proxy for us and other major western states—bombing the almost-completed nuclear reactor in Iraq in 1981, for example. As a country we have generally sympathized with small but plucky Israel, holding its own in the region though vastly outnumbered by Arabs. Want to carry the vote in the New York metropolitan area, whose Jewish population after all constitutes the world's largest Jewish city? Need to carry any of the "Bible Belt" South, the population of which generally doesn't recognize that the new Jewish state is much more inspired by nineteenth- and early twentieth-century European nationalism and socialism than by any Biblical model? Perhaps because the new state has the same name as the ancient one, many conservative Southern Protestants equate the two, and still hold literally to Genesis 12, verses 2–3, as here in the King James version:

> And I will make of thee a great nation, and I will bless thee, and make thy name great; and thou shalt be a blessing: And I will bless them that bless thee, and curse him that curseth thee: and in thee shall all families of the earth be blessed.

Ironically enough, the conservative Christian attitude in the United States that the modern Israeli state be supported in anything it does hurts the Christian population of Palestine, traditionally upwards of 20 percent, which is almost altogether Arab. But overall a political fact of life in the U.S. is that we are so much in the Israeli camp that any criticism of any Israeli policy is likely to be labeled anti-Semitic.

Final musings on nationalism

So it's a complex and intractable issue, though simple enough at base—two mature modern cultural and political nationalisms focused on one piece of land. The awakening of those nationalisms was roughly parallel, though two developments in particular determined today's mainly Israeli control of that disputed land.

First was how homogenous the new Zionist settlement of Israel was. As Rashid Khalidi points out, of the estimated 3.3 million Jews who emigrated from Europe between 1881 and 1939, the great majority made a conscious decision to avoid Palestine. Most came to the United States; less than a sixth went to Palestine—and the majority of those who did only went after the U.S. Congress in 1924 passed a law essentially limiting immigration to those from northwestern and north central European countries. Those Jews who did go to Palestine, and who stayed and sunk roots, were in the main "a self-selecting sample, united by the Zionist ideology."[27] Although Palestinian Arabs in this same time period also came to cultural and political consciousness, there were waves of pan-Arab, pan-Muslim, "Greater Syrian," and other competing group consciousnesses that weakened the focus on Palestinian Arab nationalism.

Second was the timing of the emergence of integral nationalism in Europe, particularly Hitler's fanatically anti-Semitic Naziism. The desperation of Jews under that pressure convinced even many Orthodox Jews—who up to this time had generally rejected the project of creating a European-style secular state—to support it as a refuge. The feeling of a need to help Jewish survivors of the Holocaust, felt by most people of good will in the western world, was disastrously opposed by the Palestinian mufti who openly allied with the Fascists and Nazis. Arabs would generally say that modern Israel was the solution of a European problem at the price of Arab lands. A more neutral metaphor is that of a man jumping from an upper floor window of a burning building, landing on a chance passerby; the man who jumped was relatively uninjured, but the chance passerby had both legs broken . . . .

And finally, today, all varieties of Arab nationalism, including Palestinian nationalism, are being to some extent submerged in a wave of Muslim fundamentalism the poster child of which is al Qaeda. Unfortunately— much as he'd wish to claim it is—it is not a phenomenon explained very well by the author's model of developing national consciousness.

Endnotes

1. Theodor Herzl, *The Jewish State* (New York: Dover Publications, 1988), pp. 92–93.
2. As quoted in Rashid Khalidi's *Palestinian Identity: The Construction of Modern National Consciousness* (New York: Columbia University Press, 1997), p. 158.

3. Josephus, *The Jewish War* (London: Penguin, rev. ed. 1970), in the final Chapter 23, "Cleaning-up Operations," pp. 393 ff.

4. Eugene Schuyler, *Despatches*, September 29, 1872 (U.S. National Archives, *Despatches from United States Ministers to Russia 1808–1906,* Microcopy No. 35, Washington, 1953).

5. Herzl, Theodor, *The Diaries of Theodor Herzl*, ed. & trans. by Marvin Lowenthal (New York: The Dial Press, 1956), p. 3.

6. See footnote 1.

7. See English translation of full text at follow website: http://faculty.history.umd.edu/BCooperman/NewCity/ Slaughter.html Printed versions in Chaim Nahman Bialik, "City of Slaughter," trans. Abraham M. Klein, in *The Complete Works of Hayyim Hahman Bialik*, ed. Israel Efros (NY: The Histadruth Ivrith of America, 1948), vol. 1, pop. 129, 133–34; copyright 1948 by Bloch Publishing Company. As quoted in Paul R. Mendes-Flohr and Jehuda Reinharz, *The Jew in the Modern World: A Documentary History* (NY & Oxford: Oxford U.P., 1980), pp. 330–31.

8. Shulamit Reinharz, "Toward a Model of Female Political Action: The Case of Manya Shochat, Founder of the First Kibbutz," *Women's Studies International Forum*, vol. 7, no. 7 (pp. 275–87), 1984.

9. Susan A. Glenn, *Daughters of the Shtetl* (Ithaca: Cornell University Press, 1990), p. 10.

10. A. D. Gordon, "Labour," from *Selected Essays*, trans. F. Burnce, rev. ed. (New York, 1973), pp. 54–55, as quoted in Shlomo Avineri, *The Making of Modern Zionism: The Intellectual Origins of the Jewish State* (NY: Basic Books, Inc., 1981), p. 156.

11. Chaim Weizmann, *Trial and Error: The Autobiography of Chaim Weizmann* (Jewish Publication Society of America, 1949), p. 18.

12. Zeev Jabotinsky, *Ktavim* [*Works*], vol. 1, p. 27, as translated and quoted in Shlomo Avineri, *The Making of Modern Zionism: The Intellectual Origins of the Jewish State* (NY: Basic Books, Inc., 1981, pp. 162–3.

13. Zeev Jabotinsky, *Ktavim* [*Works*], vol. 9, p. 110, as translated and quoted in Avineri, *The Making of Modern Zionism*, p. 167.

14. Amos Elon, *The Israelis: Founders and Sons* (New York: Penguin, 1983), p. 310.

15. From the surah titled "The Cessation," in N. J. Dawood's translation *The Koran* (London: Penguin Classics, 1956), p. 419.

16. Edward William Lane, trans., *The Arabian Nights' Entertainments—or The Thousand and One Nights* (New York: Tudor Publishing Co., 1927).

17. Donnan, *King's Highway*, p. 146.

18. George Antonius, *The Arab Awakening: The Story of the Arab National Movement* (Beirut: Librarie du Liban, 1969 reprint of 1939 original), p. 28.

19. Robert D. Kaplan, *The Arabists: Romance of an American Elite* (New York & Toronto: The Free Press, 1993), p. 27.

20. George Antonius, *The Arab Awakening: The Story of the Arab National Movement* (Beirut: Librairie du Liban, 1939); see especially Chapter III, "The Start: 1847–68," pp. 35–60.

21. William Ochsenwald & Sydney Nettleton Fisher, *The Middle East: A History*, 6th ed. (Boston: McGraw Hill, 2004); on p. 305 Fisher's sentence is: "Modernization through liberal political reform was killed along with Midhat."

22. Full citations for Rashid Khalidi's books are *Palestinian Identity: The Construction of Modern National Consciousness* (New York: Columbia University Press, 1997), and *The Iron Cage: The Story of the Palestinian Struggle for Statehood* (Boston: Beacon Press, 2006).

23. Khalidi, *Palestinian Identity,* p. 99.

24. Khalidi, *Palestinian Identity,* p. 101–3.

25. Hanan Ashrawi, *This Side of Peace* (New York: Simon & Schuster, 1995), p. 132.

26. Shibley Telhami, *The World Through Arab Eyes: Arab Public Opinion and the Reshaping of the Middle East* (New York: Basic Books, 2013), see pp. 83–94 on the Israeli-Palestinian conflict; quotation itself on p. 94.

27. Rashid Khalidi, *The Iron Cage*, p. 18.

"The Idolatry of Nation": The Grand Trunk Road Corridor of South Asia

Even though from childhood I had been taught that the idolatry of Nation is almost better than reverence for God and humanity, I believe I have outgrown that teaching . . . .

—*Rabindranath Tagore, 1917*

CONTENTS

The heart of the matter—SECTION A: LANGUAGE, TOPOGRAPHY, AND THE TEXTURE OF THE LAND—Spoken languages and language families of South Asia—Written languages—Hindi: the (very) short course—Topography and texture—The Grand Trunk Road, northwest to southeast—SECTION B: ANCIENT RELIGIOUS HISTORY—Historical geography of the *Mahabharata* and *Ramayana*—Indian origins of Buddhism—SECTION C: CLASSIC DYNASTIES—Mauryans—Ashoka—Guptans—Mughals—Babur—The great road of Sher Shah Surii—Akbar—Jahangir and Nur Jahan—Shah Jahan—Aurangzeb—A word on non-Muslim religious developments in Mughal times—SECTION D: WESTERN INTRUSION—The century of "John Company" rule, 1757–1857—Sepoy Mutiny/First War of Independence—SECTION E: THE RAJ—The manner of British control—Gandhi returns to India: the highlights—Bengali Renaissance—Hindu nationalist manifestations from elsewhere in British India—The Muslim response—Gandhi in deeper context—SECTION F: INDEPENDENCE—Partition—Kashmir—The new Pakistan—The Republic of India—India's new linguistic states—Nehru's economic development plans—Indira Gandhi—Babri Musjid/Ram Mandir—Revenge & reconciliation

The heart of the matter

For South Asian history, our case study is the Grand Trunk Road corridor that runs from the vicinity of India's Kolkata in the Ganges delta up through Varanasi, Allahabad, Agra, Delhi, and Amritsar, then crosses the current border into Pakistan and goes through Lahore, Rawalpindi, Taxila, Peshawar, and on into the Khyber Pass. The enormous length of the road, plus the density of populations and the depth of history along it, have made this one of the most difficult chapters in this textbook to craft—rivaled only by the Chang Jiang/Yangtze River corridor chapter still to come for East Asia. For this Grand Trunk Road corridor chapter I tried to get a little bit ahead in Chapter 3 on Germany and Romanticism, by discussing classic Sanskrit literature for the key role its western discovery played in sparking the new science of philology; hopefully the Ramayana and the Mahabharata are familiar to you now.

As with the other corridor chapters, a brief introduction to area languages is followed by a less brief look at the topography and texture of the land. Then come the high points of early history—especially those parts of it that helped shape ethnic group consciousness later. In the sub-sections on western intrusion and then on the Raj (direct British rule from 1858–1947), the focus may seem to be more on forces coming in from outside South Asia. But those outside forces, to quote Newton somewhat out of context, all had their equal and opposite reactions inside the subcontinent. This new European power was obviously dangerous in many ways to South Asians, but it had its attractions as well—among them new jobs and economic niches to explore, new religious comparisons to make, introduction to a new level of science and a truly global view of things. And when it was decided by South Asians—gradually and piecemeal, even within individuals—that this European occupation must be ended, there came the even more complicated process of deciding how it could be ended, and what should or could replace it. In this modern world history textbook as a whole it has been argued:

1. that nationalism/patriotism is the strongest force available to end colonialism and imperialism ("the only antidote," to quote the young Nelson Mandela's mentor Anton Lembede from the Durban-to-Pretoria chapter), with socialism allied with nationalism a distant second option (from the Russia chapter);

2. that nationalism/patriotism works best when based in a common language and a common religion different from those of your opponents (the "folk consciousness to nationalism" pattern of the Germanies, circa 1800 to 1945, in the German chapter);

3. and that to some extent nationalism/patriotism is a subconscious choice, with people usually opting for the smallest and therefore most culturally comfortable group consistent with economic and military survival ("The Bratislavan Lesson," from the Czech chapter).

Now in a subcontinent with dozens of major languages, and with the followers of the two main religions fairly thoroughly mixed, what are all the possible permutations of such possible patriotisms? Urdu-speaking and Muslim in religion? Tamil-speaking and Hindu? Punjabi-speaking and Sikh? Even combining the plurality language, Hindi, and the by far most numerous religion, Hindu, you get a Hindi language/Hindu religious minority group patriotism that is assured of little support from others. Add to that the concerns that ethical minds and spiritual natures had about an undiluted nationalism's destructive transformation of individual humans, and you get a complex situation indeed. But it was in wrestling with these issues that the modern shape and character of Pakistan, India, and Bangladesh were formed. Of these three we'll spend the most time with India.

SECTION A: LANGUAGE, TOPOGRAPHY AND THE TEXTURE OF THE LAND

Spoken languages and language families of South Asia

In terms of the spoken languages of South Asia, generally speaking the northern two-thirds or so speaks languages derived from Sanskrit (Urdu, Hindi, Bengali, Gujarati, Kashmiri, Marathi, Oriya, and Panjabi, among them). The southern third speaks languages derived from Dravidian (Tamil, Telegu, Kannada, Malayalam). This division probably dates to the "Aryan" invasion of India back in *Rigveda* times, as was generally discussed in the Germany chapter; Dravidian was apparently once the general language of the subcontinent, and has been forced down into a southern refuge (in much the same way Celtic languages in Europe were forced over to Europe's western margins by later population movements). In terms of other languages, English is a holdover from the British colonial era throughout South Asia, and there are some other languages in the mountains and what are called tribal areas. India alone has twenty-two official languages!

Along the traditional Grand Trunk Road corridor from the neighborhood of Kolkata (Calcutta), India, in the southeast, to Rawalpindi and Peshawar, Pakistan, in the northwest, the Hindi/Urdu spoken language dominates the center-west of the area. Together they used to be considered the single language "Hindustani." With the separation of India and Pakistan in 1947, however, the Arabic and Persian influence on Urdu was emphasized, and conversely there was an attempt in India to "purify" Hindi of those influences. Speakers of Hindi and Urdu still have little trouble understanding each other speak. But writing was always a different matter, with Urdu written in the Persian style of Arabic script, and Hindi written in what is called the Devanagri script.

Written languages

The Indus valley civilization of 2600–1700 BC is traditionally counted as one of the world's four cradles of city life. It had its own script, although that died with the Aryan invasions and unfortunately has never been translated since. It took a thousand years more for literacy to be reborn in India. This happened in or around the 700s BC, apparently sparked by Aramaic-language businessmen from the shores of the eastern Mediterranean. "Sparked" is used advisedly, because the Aramaic influence is both foundational and also slight. Only a few letters are the same, and Sanskrit is written left to right (as are most European languages), not right to left as with Aramaic (and most other Semitic languages including Hebrew and Arabic). It seems that the idea of writing came in from outside, but most of its development thereafter was local. The resulting script was called Brahmi. It in turn evolved into the "monumental script" of the Guptan Dynasty (circa AD 300–500), and by AD 1000 had more or less reached its modern form called *Devanagri* (or *Devanagari*)—the "sacred script of the city." This is the written script in which most Sanskrit works reached modern times, and is essentially still the script of written Hindi. Hindi, the language spoken in and around the capital city of Delhi, is the single most important of modern India's languages (though the jealousy of the writers of other regional scripts/languages has kept Hindi from being imposed as THE national language).

Hindi: the (very) short course

In this section, for a change, you don't need the local language to work with Google Earth. For whatever reason—probably the huge number of "official scripts" in India—local place names on the main map and in Placemark descriptions are in the Latin alphabet; only a few are in Devanagri as well. But in Wikipedia articles and lots of other places you will see Hindi in its normal Devanagri script. So let's go ahead with a quick introduction to it, in line with this textbook's general philosophy that language is a rich part of any culture, and that a serious student of that culture must eventually learn the language!

Here's a phrase written in Devanagri script (*satyameva jayate*, "truth alone triumphs," the Sanskrit phrase on the Indian national symbol). You can see why it's called a "hanging" script; the line generated by the top of the letters seems to suspend the letters below it:

सत्यमेव जयते

At first glance it looks as foreign as, say, Chinese, but it is really much easier for a reader of Latin-letter alphabets to decipher. Devanagri has forty consonants and consonant combinations, though seven of these are only used to spell foreign words. There are eleven vowels. It is something between an alphabet and a syllabary. When each consonant is written, it is assumed that the vowel after it is "a, pronounced "ah." Any other vowel is usually indicated by a diacritical mark above the line (for short i, long ī, [ee], e, ai, au, and o) or below the character (u and ū). Only in a few special cases—as when a vowel starts a word, or follows another vowel—is a vowel written as a regular "hanging" letter.

Here are the transliterations of the names of some key towns on our Grand Trunk Road corridor:

PATNA

In the city name of Patna, both in Hindi and in English, there are three consonants:

P = प
T = ट (well, <u>one</u> of the Ts in Devanagri!)
N = न

In the Devanagri, पटना, you see those three consonants plus a final vertical straight line, which adds another a (pronounced ah) to the word.

प = p(ah)
ट = t
ना = n(ah)ah

So more correctly it is Patnā (that dash over the a you see in a formal transliteration just means you double the length of the vowel)

DELHI

For the city of Delhi, you need a couple more consonants (just the D and the L; they don't use the H):

D = द, which when you add a short i (ih) is the syllable दि

L = a letter shaped like a sickle, pointing down, followed by a straight line. If you double the L, you omit the straight line after the first. To add the "ee" vowel, you add a straight line after the consonant, connected with a short loop above the line.

Delhi, दिलली, which is दि + ल्ली

दि = di

ल्ली = lli (ee)

So it should be transliterated as "Dillee," as in dilly-dally, instead of the more conventional "Delhi."

BANĀRAS

The city name Varanasi (in Sanskrit) is Banāras (in Hindi): बनारस

ब = b(ah)

ना = n(ah)ah

र = r(ah)

स = s

AGRA

Agrā, आगरा

आ = ah (it starts with a vowel, so you use the "hanging letter" version of the letter A)

ग = g

रा = r(ah)ah

KANPUR

Kanpur, कानपुर

Kaa + n + pu + r (the little hook at the bottom of the letter p adds the u vowel to it)

So more correctly Kānpur

MATHURA

Mathurā, मथुरा

Maa + thu + raa

AMBALA

Ambala, अम्बाला

A + m + baa + laa

SHIMLA

Shimla, शिमला

THE WORD "DEVANAGRI"

देवनागरी = devanāgrī

दे = deh (the left-leaning slash at top is the e—pronounced eh—vowel)

व = v(ah)

ना = naa, nā

ग = g

री = ri (long i = ee)

THE WORD "HINDI"

Hindi = हिन्दी or हिंदी,

In both, the first and last consonant/vowel combinations are:

हि = hi (short i) and दी = di (long i, pronounced as ee);

The "n" sound in the middle, which is just a hint of an "en," is done in the first way as half of the n = न, and in the second way as the dot over the initial consonant h which signifies nasalization = हिं

If you would like to pursue written and spoken Hindi beyond this brief introduction, there is a fairly user-friendly free website up and running as of this writing at:

http://www.unilang.org/course.php?res=69&id=hindi_0&pagenum=index

The whole syllabary, with a list of vowels and vowel combinations down the left-hand side, and the thirty-three consonants or consonant combinations to which those vowels can be added, is at either of these sites:

http://www.krysstal.com/writing_hindi.html
http://www.omniglot.com/writing/hindi.htm

Many other Sanskrit descended (and Devanagri derived) scripts are similar to Hindi. The city we used to know as Calcutta, now as Kolkata, is in the Bengali script কলকতা = Kalkātā. You can make out its similarity with Hindi letters, and presumably readers of one Devanagri-derived script can make out much of the others.

In terms of some final linguistic odds and ends, here are some Hindi things you might encounter on a map, including the Google Earth surface. A common city name suffix is –pur or –pore, in the Hindi –पुर, as you saw above in Kanpur. It comes from Sanskrit and Old Persian, and means "city." Another common city name suffix is –bad, or –abad, -बाद, as in Allahabad; it means abode, or home of.

In addition to the transliterations above, here are translations of some key geographic terms from Hindi:

setu = bridge

qila = fort (for example Lal Qila, Delhi's famous Red Fort)

bagh = garden

Pradesh = Province, State

sagar = sea, large lake

Finally, here are English translations of the numbers one through five in Hindi, most of which will come in handy in the chapter ahead:

ek (one);

do (two);

teen (three);

char (four); and

panch, or *panj* (five).

Such simple numbers can help with cultural understandings in ways both big and little. The British brought back from South Asia, for example, a drink called Punch. It came from the Hindi, and just meant "five," since it was originally a mix of five different ingredients, one of them alcohol.

Topography and texture

The Indian subcontinent includes today's India, Pakistan, Bangladesh, the Himalayan states of Nepal and Bhutan, with the island state of Sri Lanka just offshore.[GE1]. By U.S. standards it is remarkably tropical; the capital of India, New Delhi, although a relatively northern city of India, is about the same latitude as Orlando, Florida, and Matagorda Bay, Texas.[GE2] The southern tip of India is about 8° north latitude, parallel to where Panama joins Colombia.

It has been set off from the rest of Asia—physically and therefore to a great extent culturally—by ocean in the south and by rugged mountains in the north. The tectonic plate carrying this Indian subcontinent, geologists assure us, has been driving north into and under the Eurasian tectonic plate for some fifty million years at a breakneck (for tectonic plates) 6″ a year. In the process it has pushed up the Tibetan plateau and the Himalayas (from the Sanskrit words *hima alaya,* "snow abode"). The Himalayas make an arc some 1,500 miles long and as much as 200 miles deep, all along South Asia's northern border.[GE3] The Himalayas are compressed and narrowed to a single range in the south, or belly of the arc. Mt. Everest and its neighbors are right at their southern extremity. You have great views of them on the flight from Kathmandu, Nepal, to Paro, Bhutan, if you have "posh" tickets (supposedly from "Port Out, Starboard Home," the most expensive steamship cabins from Brit-

1. Google Earth Layer 1 is a Placemark showing a general overview of the Indian subcontinent.
2. GE Layer 2 is a Folder titled "India relative to U.S. & Mexico." It includes a Polygon representing India, correct as to relative size and latitude, but spun around the globe longitudinally, and a Placemark representing Delhi, the relatively northern capital. Turn on entire Folder, and double-click on Folder icon to "fly" to preset view.
3. GE Layer 3 is a Placemark titled "Overview of Himalayas" framing a view of the Himalayan mountain arc.

ain to Asia in the days of the British Raj and ever since the British euphemism for "the best money can buy," though no actual tickets stamped POSH have ever turned up).[GE⁴] The mountain chain widens and gets complicated at either end, in both form and name. In the west you can see how the main mountain chain splits in the vicinity of Kashmir.[GE⁵] The Himalaya range proper runs southeast of the valley, and the Karakorum range runs along its northeast side (including the world's second tallest mountain, K2). Where they come back together and then wrap around to the southwest the mountains are called the Hindu Kush. Notice how the Hindu Kush come down southwest through northern Pakistan and fan out in Afghanistan. The present border between Pakistan and Afghanistan—based on an imperial British line of 1893, you'll see later—fairly well follows a line of these mountains. So in general overview of South Asia what you have is this giant, irregular "M" of mountains, that with swamps and deserts continues to the coast, sheltering the Indian subcontinent from outside influence.[GE⁶] It's not impassable, but is hard enough to cross so that inside the "M" a very distinctive culture developed.

In terms of human civilization and history, the most important part of the South Asian landscape here is not the Greater Himalayas themselves, but the rich alluvial plains of eastern Pakistan, northern India, and Bangladesh.[GE⁷] These lowland plains have always supported the subcontinent's densest populations. They are drained and watered by two famous river systems. Running east-southeast into the top part of the Bay of Bengal is the Ganges ("Ganga" as in "Gunga Din") and its major southern tributary the Yamuna (formerly called Jumna), gathering other tributaries mainly from the Himalayas as it goes.[GE⁸] Running south-southwest into the Arabian Sea is the Indus River with its five eastward-lying tributaries (the "Punjab," from *panch-ab*, or *panj-ab,* "Five Rivers")—from west to east the Jhelum, Chenab, Ravi, Beas, and Sutlej.[GE⁹] The tongue of land between any two neighboring rivers that run together is called a *doab*, literally a "two-river" land. Historically speaking, whoever has controlled both the Ganges system and the Punjab has held world-class empire—on which much more later. The lower course of the Indus, after it has gathered all its tributaries, is called the Sind or Sindh (*sindhu* may have meant river in early Sanskrit, and minus the initial letter seems to have been the origin of the Greek "Indos," source of the modern Indus).

South of these Indus-Gangetic lowlands are east- and west-running rivers and small but rugged mountain ranges that to some extent divide the southern cone of India from the north. Most of the south is a raised plateau called the Deccan (literally "the South"). It ends in two-to-three thousand foot escarpments near both southwest and southeast coasts, called respectively the Western and Eastern Ghats ("steps"). Mumbai (formerly called Bombay), for example, is built on islands and lowlands, but to those going inland from there it means climbing a 2,500′ escarpment within about thirty miles of the city.[GE¹⁰]

---

4. GE Layer 4 is a Placemark titled "View of Everest & neighbors" framing a view similar to that out the window of a plane on the Kathmandu to Paro run, with some eight of the world's ten tallest mountains seen along the 250-mile-long flight.

5. GE Layer 5 is a Placemark framing a view of the junction of the Himalayas, Karakorums, and Hindu Kush. K2 is at the very center of the view, marked by the Pushpin icon.

6. GE Layer 6 is a Folder titled "Mountain arcs sheltering South Asia." It includes three Paths in thick red lines—the basic inner "M" of mountains, and its eastern and western echoes in secondary ranges.

7. GE Layer 7 is a Polygon with sharp white borders and a white wash inside, very roughly outlining these 200 mile by 1,500 mile alluvial plains. Notice that it takes in all of Bangladesh in the east, and most of the agriculturally fertile (green!) parts of Pakistan.

8. GE Layer 8 is a Folder titled "Ganga & Yamuna River System"; individual rivers or tributaries are shown as blue or green Paths.

9. GE Layer 9 is a Folder titled "Indus River System." Individual rivers or tributaries are shown as various shades of orange, purple, or pink Paths, to differentiate them from Ganges system rivers. You can turn on each of the "panj-ab," Punjab, or "Five Rivers" individually to get a better sense of their location.

10. GE Layer 10 is a Folder titled "The Deccan and its Ghats."

The transportation corridor that is the focus of this South Asian chapter is huge in comparison to the three already studied.[GE11] It runs from Kolkata (Calcutta), India, in the southeast, to the Khyber Pass in the northwest, passing Varanasi, Allahabad, Agra, and Delhi in India, and Lahore, Rawalpindi, and Peshawar in Pakistan, in the northwest—a rectangle approximately 1400 miles long and 250 miles wide. It includes most of the course of the Ganges and Yamuna rivers, and most of the Punjab. Along it runs the Grand Trunk Road, the name the British colonial government used for their mainline railroad from Kolkata to Lahore (and by extension, on to the Khyber Pass); but it was probably already the world's single busiest transportation corridor for 2,000 or more years before the British arrived. Now let's explore that corridor in more detail, beginning in the northwest with the Khyber Pass through the Hindu Kush mountains.

The Grand Trunk Road, northwest to southeast

The Khyber Pass has traditionally been the main invasion route from Central Asia to South Asia. It is not so much a simple gap in a narrow chain of mountains as it is fifteen-mile-long passageway, anchored mid-way by the town of Landi Kotal. If you "fly" through it on Google Earth, from west to east, you can see rather dramatically how the rich Indus-Gangetic plains opened to the armies of Alexander, Babur, and other famous invaders of India in history.[GE12] Peshawar is the first town of any size east of the Khyber, and so is generally considered the gateway to the pass.

A second though much more difficult pass goes north from this northwest corner of South Asia's great alluvial plains. Today it is called the Karakorum Highway, a main artery between China and Pakistan.[GE13] It turns north off the GT Road at the little city of Taxila,[GE14] which is less than twenty miles WNW of Rawalpindi. It follows the valley of the Indus up until the Indus valley turns sharply southeast (the exact point where the Himalaya, Karakorum, and Hindu Kush ranges meet!),[GE15] and then goes by smaller and smaller mountain valleys up to the 15,400' high Khumjerab Pass,[GE16] and thence down into extreme western China. The modern highway only dates to the 1960s, but this was a key transportation route for millennia before that; it was South Asia's main communication with the Silk Road that ran between China and the Mediterranean. [GE17] So Taxila—then called Takshashila—was already a key town when Alexander the Great came through 2,300 and more years ago.

Peshawar, gateway to the Khyber Pass, and Taxila, gateway to the Khumjerab Pass, are only about seventy-five miles apart on this northwestern end of the GT Road. In general, the Indian subcontinent exported much culture and religion through Taxila and the Khumjerab Pass into China (this is how Buddhism got into China after the collapse of the Han Dynasty circa AD 200, important to know for the Chapter 13 to come). On the other hand, more Central Asian, Persian, and even European religious and cultural influence came through the Khyber Pass than India sent out through it—mainly borne by invading armies.

---

11. GE Layer 11 is a Polygon titled "GT Road corridor." It is a rectangle outlined in white, about 1400 miles long and 250 miles across—much larger than any corridors we've looked at thus far in the book, rivaled in size—and historical complexity!—only by the Yangtze River corridor in the China chapter yet to come.

12. GE Layer 12 is a Folder titled "Khyber Pass & Peshawar." Turn it on and open it, and work with first layer, "Khyber Pass flight path" as instructed. Result should be interesting "flight" from west to east through the pass.

13. GE Layer 13 is a Path showing the Karakorum Highway in dark blue.

14. GE Layer 14 is a Placemark locating Taxila (ancient Takshashila), Pakistan.

15. GE Layer 15 is a Placemark at this junction; it references a Photos icon of a monument proclaiming this Himalaya-Karakorum-Hindu Kush intersection point!

16. GE Layer 16 is a Placemark locating Khumjerab Pass.

17. GE Layer 17 is a Folder with Paths and Placemarks showing at least one historical iteration of the Silk Road; its eastern terminus is Chang'an (present-day Xian), and then at the famous Dunhuang Caves (known for Buddhist art from AD 300 to 1300) it splits north and south around the Taklamakan Desert. Coming together again at Kashi (Kashgar), it immediately splits again in alternate routes around and through the Pamirs. Reuniting at Merv (Mary), it runs with less incident across today's Turkmenistan, Iran, Iraq, and Syria.

The Indus and all five eastern tributary rivers of the Punjab come out of the Himalayas. Most of the population is located in the valleys and plains between patches of hills. Since 1947 all but the very eastern edge of the Punjab has been in Pakistan. Because most of the Hindu and Sikh population of the area emigrated to India, temple ruins are a familiar sight in the countryside of this overwhelmingly Muslim country. Lahore, an old city on the east bank of the Ravi, was traditionally the dominant city of the Punjab, but the British put their biggest military base further northwest (towards the traditional invasion route) at Rawalpindi, familiarly "Pindi." The Pakistani military is still headquartered there, and the new planned capital of Islamabad was built in the 1960s just north of there. This left Lahore almost a frontier city, within fifteen miles of the Pakistan-India border. But the old GT Road, with the modern railroad alongside it, is still visible running through this slice of Pakistan. As it goes through Pindi it is known as the Mall.

Coming into modern India from Pakistan, the first major city on the old GT Road (now India's National Highway 1) is Amritsar. It is the holy city of the Sikh religion, centered on the Golden Temple. The next city on NH 1 is Jullundar, which dominates the doab between the Beas and upper Sutlej Rivers; it too has a large Sikh population. From Jullundar the main road runs south to cross the Sutlej, and goes through nearby Ludhiana. At this point it heads southeast towards Ambala, leaving the Punjab for the Ganges drainage.[GE18] Even at this divide between river drainages, the GT Road and these alluvial plains never get much above 900' elevation.

The border crossing between Pakistan and India, about halfway between Lahore and Amritsar, is quite a show today, given the generally bad relations between the two countries. Flashy changings of the guard and flag lowerings and raisings remind you of two roosters in adjoining pens displaying for each other.[GE19]

From Ambala the main road heads almost due south to Delhi, cutting diagonally across the great plains of the subcontinent (and our rectangular corridor). The silty fill from Himalayan runoff is in some places thousands of feet deep (as in the Mississippi delta), with only a few former hilltops protruding as weathered ridges. The soil is a light yellowish-gray, fertile if watered. Delhi and vicinity gets only about 25" of rain a year, almost all in the late June to September monsoon. That is not nearly enough for the heavy rice cultivation that goes on hereabouts. Irrigation with water from rivers running off the Himalayas provides the rest. So in a landscape that is generally as flat as south Texas a traveler will sometimes see with interest an approaching ridge, and then discover it to be only the fill from building an irrigation canal. Eucalyptus trees native to Australia are as common here along the roads as they are in the dry Mexican altiplano, and here too they have raised some environmental eyebrows for how much underground water they draw up. What seem to be circular or rectangular houses of straw scattered around the farmland are in fact carefully preserved blocks of animal dung, most of it to serve as fuel.

The palaces and forts of Delhi and Agra are the jewels of this stretch of the GT Road. Delhi's Red Fort and huge Jami Musjid, India's largest mosque, are part of its Old City (Shahjahanabad). "New" Delhi built by the British from 1911–1931 has an amazingly geometric layout, beginning with its basis on an equilateral triangle. Agra, a little over 100 miles SSE of Delhi, has the world's single most beautiful building in the Taj Mahal, the great Agra Fort, and a few miles out of town the abandoned royal city of Fatepur Sikri (perched atop the first rock ridge travelers from the north will have seen for 150 miles!). We'll explore most of these in more detail later.

At Agra the main road crosses the Yamuna, and runs through the doab (in the Ganges drainage, "doab" means that slice of land between the Ganges and Yamuna). The road swings a little north of east to Kanpur, an important Ganges River crossing city, and then down the south bank of the Ganges to Allahabad at the juncture of the Ganges and Yamuna. Here it crosses the Ganges, and runs along the north bank to cross it again at Varanasi (Banaras),[GE20] one of the holiest sites of Hinduism.

---

18. GE Layer 18 is a Folder titled "Punjab & Upper Indus"; inside are some eleven Placemarks to explore. Most of them are in the north along the GT Road; note that the last two, going eastwards, are across the border in the Indian part of Punjab.

19. GE Layer 19 is a Placemark framing a close-up view of the border crossing. Embedded in the Placemark is a link to short video of the evening sealing of the border ceremony: http://www.youtube.com/watch?v=n9y2qtaopbE

20. GE Layer 20 is a Folder titled "Yamuna and Ganges delta."

From Varanasi to Kolkata the main road runs almost straight, skirting the edge of hill country to the south, until it hooks sharply south into Kolkata proper. By this time a traveler is fairly entered into the great delta country of the Ganges-Brahmaputra drainage. The delta is huge, perhaps 200 miles across its seafront, as wide as the mouth of the Amazon River. Here in India's West Bengal and in the neighboring Bangladesh is the world's single greatest block of mangrove forest. Kolkata sits on the Hooghly (Hughli) River, one of dozens of delta rivers as the Ganges fans out towards the sea.[GE[21]]

Today's version of the Grand Trunk Road is, from southeast to northwest, India's National Highway 2 (Kolkata to Delhi), NH 1 (Delhi through Amritsar to the Pakistani border), and Pakistan's N5 (mainly through Pakistan's Punjab province, but also through narrow bands of the Northwest Frontier province and then the Federally Administered Tribal Areas).[GE[22]] It might also help at this point to know the modern Indian states that the GT Road runs through.[GE[23]] Learning this simple line of adjoining states will give you a basis for adding others that at least tangentially show up in this history later. Southwest of Punjab and Haryana, for example, is the huge state of Rajasthan, "Land of Kings," and southwest of that is Gujarat with its important ports (and Gandhi's hometown). Southwest of Uttar Pradesh ("Upper Province" in the days of the British Raj) is Madhya Pradesh ("Middle Province"). Going down the coast southwest from Kolkata is the state of Orissa. West Bengal of which Kolkata is the dominant city is "west" because the rest of Bengal became first East Bengal, then East Pakistan and finally today's Bangladesh.

Now with all the states, rivers, and GT Road layers turned on, take one last look at our long rectangular corridor. This is the stage setting where so much critical South Asian history played out—to be rehearsed in coming pages.

SECTION B: ANCIENT RELIGIOUS HISTORY

South Asians have always seemed more interested in their religious past than their secular past. The mainstream of that past goes by the name of Hinduism, and it is so complex a tradition as to defy easy description. There is no single key scripture that plays the role that the Bible does for Christians or the Koran for Muslims. So instead of starting traditionally with theology—with the trinity of Brahma the Creator, Vishnu the Sustainer, Shiva the Destroyer, their aspects and attributes, their consorts, their mounts, their manifold reincarnations, and such—for purposes of this textbook with its historic-geographic angle it might be better to show <u>where</u> key religious activities took or take place, and why. Let's start with two important early works that are still vital today; and that are placed by Hindus in still-recognizable places on our chosen "Grand Trunk Road" corridor. [GE[24]]

Historical geography of the *Mahabharata* and *Ramayana*

The *Mahabharata* (in Sanskrit महाभारत), the world's longest epic to literary scholars but sacred scripture for Hindus, was alluded to earlier in the Germany chapter, under the "European discovery of Sanskrit" topic. To recap, the Pandavas—five good-hearted brothers and half-brothers—were rivals of a hundred less good-hearted cousins called the Kauravas. Tricked out of their rightful throne in a crooked gambling game, the Pandavas retired to the forest for the specified twelve years and lived in seclusion a thirteenth. Then in the fourteenth year they came back in the great battle on the Kuru field (*Kurukshetra*) to defeat their cousins and resume their

---

21. GE Layer 21 is a Folder titled "Varanasi to the delta."

22. GE Layer 22 is a Folder titled "Modern GT Road (highways)"; with Paths in black showing the two Indian and one Pakistani highways. Simply turn on folder without opening for overview.

23. GE Layer 23 is a Folder titled "Modern Indian Provinces along GT Road." The Polygons representing the states are, from northwest to southeast, Punjab (light yellow); Haryana (purple); Uttar Pradesh (green); Bihar (orange); Jharkhand (light green); and West Bengal (hot pink).

24. Google Earth Layer 24. First turn off the entire first Folder on topography and texture, and turn on the second Folder titled "GT Road ancient religions." Now turn on Layer 19, the Folder titled "GT Road, corridor & rivers," which reintroduces the corridor rectangle, the two river networks, and today's interstate version of the GT Road. We'll do this at the beginning of each new Folder.

rightful rule. Yudisthira is the eldest Pandava brother in the epic; Bhima the uncomplicated strongman is second brother, and the great archer Arjuna is the third, but perhaps the central figure (they are Yudisthir, Bhim, and Arjun in modern Hindi). The five Pandava brothers are accompanied through thick and thin by their patient and loyal wife Draupadi. With this epic in mind, look with me at the key suture line of the Indus-Gangetic plains—the west bank of the upper Yamuna where the Gangetic plain adjoins the Punjab.

About 100 miles north-northwest of Delhi, over several square miles in and around the town of Thanesar, is the Kurukshetra. It is not so much a single field as it is a great collection of battlefields identified by Hindus as where the eighteen Pandava and Kaurava armies fought for eighteen days. Thanesar is on today's Indian National Highway Number 1, and yesteryear's GT Road. The Kurukshetra's most impressive site is the holy Brahma Sarovar ("Lake"), where Brahma is believed after ritual sacrifice to have begun the creation of the world. The lake itself is an impressive two-thirds of a mile long and one-third wide and fifteen feet deep—one of the largest lakes in South Asia and entirely hand-dug. It has the traditional steps, or ghats, going down into it, for those seeking purification in its waters, and is bordered especially on the north by temples of different Hindu sub-castes. Some three miles west of the big lake is Jyotisar ("Light essence"), the traditional site where Krishna as charioteer gave instruction (the *Bhagavad-gita*, or *Lord's song*) to Arjuna, the war leader of the Pandavas, when the latter was having second thoughts about starting the battle.[GE²⁵] Here is perhaps the clearest statement in Hindu scripture about how the immortal soul is reincarnated as it deserves to be from its behavior in past life (*karma*), and about duty by one's station, or caste (*dharma*). If this is all true, says Arjuna in the *Gita*, why am I not aware of it? Humans are blinded by greed and anger and lust, replies Krishna, and so can't see the immortal soul—"as a fire is covered by smoke, as a mirror is covered by dust." Hindu pilgrims by the hundreds of thousands (and strangely enough almost no foreign tourists) come to Kurukshetra today.

Twenty miles south of Thanesar, on the main road to Delhi, is the town of Karnal. It was associated with, and apparently named for, the King Karna who figured importantly in the Mahabharata.[GE²⁶] Another twenty miles south, still on the main road to Delhi, is Panipat. It would achieve its modern fame in AD 1526 when the invader Babur defeated the Sultan of Delhi there and so began the Mughal Dynasty, and minor fame from other key battles there in 1555 and 1761. Panipat's original name as used in the *Mahabharata* was Panduprasta, or "Five Cities," for the five cities held by the five Pandava brothers; over time the name just shortened with use to Panipat.[GE²⁷] The city of Delhi, capital of India today and on and off for the past thousand years, is believed to have been the capital city of the Pandava brothers; it was called Induprastha in the *Mahabharata*.[GE²⁸] South of Delhi by thirty-five miles, still on the main road (National Highway 2, as the GT Road is numbered south and east of Delhi), is the old town of Palwal; the name is said to descend from Apelava, a town in the Pandava kingdom.[GE²⁹] Eighty miles down the GT Road south of Delhi is the city of Mathura, claimed as the birthplace of Lord Krishna himself.[GE³⁰] Agra, another thirty miles down the GT Road, was in modern times a Mughal capital, and of course most famous for the Taj Mahal. Its modern name apparently comes from *agrevana*, "edge of the forest," as it was known in the *Mahabharata*. [GE³¹]

Now in Google Earth zoom out and look at the Placemarks you just turned on.[GE³²] They form an almost straight line up and down the west bank of the Yamuna, each of them on or very close to the modern Interstate

---

25. GE Layer 25 is a Folder titled "Kurukshetra." Inside are Placemarks to explore for the turnoff into Thanesar from NH 1, for the great Brahma Sarovar (Lake), and for the Gita site. About two-thirds through the *Bhagavad-gita*, Krishna gives Arjuna divine eyes to see his true form, which will destroy most everyone on the battlefield, indeed all temporal creation: "Time I am, destroyer of the worlds . . .," says Krishna. In 1945 Robert Oppenheimer, watching the first successful atomic bomb test, remembered the line this way: "Now I am become Death, the destroyer of worlds."

26. GE Layer 26 is a Placemark referencing Karnal.

27. GE Layer 27 is a Placemark at Panipat.

28. GE Layer 28 is a Placemark at Old Delhi (Shah Jahanabad).

29. GE Layer 29 is a Placemark at Palwal.

30. GE Layer 30 is a Placemark specifically locating temple complex in Mathura celebrating Krishna's birth; see several interesting Photos icons below Placemark. "Krishajanmabhoomi" translates "Krishna place of birth."

31. GE Layer 31 is a Placemark for Agra.

32. GE Layer 32 is a Placemark framing a general overview of the six Placemarks above.

that is today's version of the GT Road. This is some proof that century in, century out—and in India's case millennium in, millennium out—this line where the Gangetic plain faces the Punjab has been important.

In the other great Hindu epic, the *Ramayana* (in Sanskrit रामायण), the home town of Lord Rama (Sri Ram in modern Hindi) where the story both begins and ends, is Ayodhya. Here he is born. Here he marries the miraculously manifested Sita, after heroically stringing and breaking the great bronze bow, the test given to all her suitors. From here she is kidnapped by the demon Ravana. To the lighted city Rama and Sita return after he rescues her with the help of a monkey army led by the white monkey Hanuman. Ayodhya, on the River Ghagara (older name Saryu) that is tributary to the lower Ganges, is not a big town today. Absolutely everyone in India, Pakistan, and Bangladesh, however, knows it for the 1992 destruction of *Babri Musjid* (Babur's Mosque) by right-wing Hindu nationalists, and their continuing attempts to build there a *Ram Mandir* (rebuild, they would say, believing that a Hindu temple at Rama's birth site was torn down by early Mughals).[GE33] Remember the Mexican philosopher who said the past in Mexico was not only not dead, it wasn't even past? It's just as true in South Asia. "Ayodhya" as a word also appears as the province name Awadh and Oudh in modern times, associated with much friction between the British and the local population both early and late in the British Raj.

In terms of modern religious celebration, the largest religious gathering in the world is the *Kumbh Mela*, or Jar Festival. It takes places every three years, at places where drops of divine nectar were accidentally spilled in the Hindu creation account. Two of the four places are on our corridor, where the Ganges breaks out of the mountains at Haridwar ("Gods' Gate"), and where it joins the Yamuna at Allahabad.[GE34] Allahabad has the largest of these, every fourth Kumbh Mela or twelve years apart. In 2013, an estimated sixty million people came during the five weeks there, eclipsing even numbers for the famous Hajj to Mecca.

In Hinduism the opposite of these great Kumbh Mela gatherings are the little village and rural Hindu temples, with their typical curved, truncated towers flying red flags. Here Rama is venerated on Mondays, Hanuman on Tuesdays, and so on, with no single day of the week as important as Sunday to Christians, Sabbath to Jews, or Friday to Muslims.

In city or countryside (and India alone has 750 million villages!), caste and sub-caste are still important in Hinduism. "Caste" is not originally a Hindu word, it comes from the Portuguese *casta*. It is usually used to mean the four major divisions of society described in the *Rigveda*, the oldest scripture of Hinduism: Brahmins (religious leaders); Kshatriyas (warriors); Vaisyas (business classes); and Shudras (agricultural labor)—with "outcastes" below them at the bottom of the pecking order. "Sub-caste" is the usual translation of *jati*, a word meaning "birth," of which there are perhaps 1,500 divisions. Many last names in Hindu India are occupation groups inside of which one marries—a Shroff (banker) usually only married a Shroff; and the same with a Vakil (lawyer); a Gandhi (grocer); and so on. A given village or neighborhood might have only a couple dozen *jati*, and by last name alone everyone there would immediately be able to "place" a person as to caste and jati.

Indian origins of Buddhism

Even the shortest sketch of South Asian religious history has to include the life of the *Bud-dha*, the first "enlightened one." Though in the long run Hinduism virtually reabsorbed Buddhism in India, the Prince Siddhartha Gautama appeared in the greater Hindu world as a powerful critic of at least the more rigid aspects of the religion. There is much debate about when he lived, though the 500s BC seems the most popular answer among scholars. There is much less debate on where he lived, and the major happenings of his life. Look at the pattern of the four most famous places of his life, as it appears on our corridor.[GE35]

---

33. GE Layer 33 is a Placemark referencing Ayodhya, particularly locating the Babri Musjid/Ram Mandir grounds.

34. GE Layer 34 is a Folder titled "Kumbh Mela sites," including Placemarks for Allahabad, Haridwar, Ujjain, and Nashik. Turning on the whole folder will show you the overall pattern; zooming in to each Placemark should reveal some interesting Panoramio icons of religious pilgrimage and the water purification that traditionally goes on.

35. GE Layer 35—Turn on and open Folder called "life of Buddha," and then click on unnumbered Path of same name.

Lumbini is the traditional birthplace of the Buddha. It is in today's Nepal, but if "Nepal" conjures up mountain scenery for you, it's not that Nepal; it's in the low plains fifteen to twenty miles from the base of the closest hills.[GE36] If the world's oceans rose 450 feet or so, in fact, all four of these key sites of Buddha's life would be submerged. The second site, about 220 miles south-southeast of Buddha's birthplace, is Bodh Gaya, where Siddhartha Gautama achieved Enlightenment while meditating under the Bodhi tree. Here he found his "middle way" between asceticism and indulgence, and came to understand the Four Noble Truths: that there is suffering in life, that it is brought on by desire, that you can end the suffering by ending the desire, and that can be done by the Eightfold Path of life: Right View, Intention, Speech, Action, Livelihood, Effort, Mindfulness, and Concentration. The first temple on that site was built by Ashoka, greatest of the Mauryan Dynasty kings, who ruled in the third century BC, on which more later. The basic brick construction of the current one is from the Guptan Dynasty of the fourth and fifth centuries AD.[GE37] The third famous site, where the Buddha is believed to have preached his first post-Enlightenment sermon to five former disciples, is the Deer Park at Sarnath, just north of Varanasi.[GE38] Its massive stupa has similar Ashokan and Guptan foundations. Varanasi was, long before Siddhartha Gautama, one of the holiest cities of Hinduism. For the fourth and last of these famous sites connected with Buddha's life, tradition has him dying at age eighty in Kusinagar, modern Kasia. [GE39]

Another way to get at the geographic center of early Buddhism is to look at the key Buddhist councils held in the first few centuries after his death—councils much like those in Christian Rome that tried (and also eventually failed) to keep religious unity.[GE40] They are in a band some thirty to forty miles east of the main sites of the Buddha's life, still on or around the middle course of the Ganges River.

There are other ancient religions from these alluvial plains of South Asia. Jainism, for example, first seems to appear here about the same time as Buddhism. But in terms of their future impact on Asian history, Hinduism and Buddhism—two of the world's four religions that claim at least a billion followers each—stand head and shoulders above the rest. So perhaps we should leave it at this: if we wander off too deeply into South Asian religions we may never get back to politics!

---

36. GE Layer 36 is a Placemark referencing Lumbini, birthplace of Siddhartha Gautama. Most of the Photos icons at the bottom of this view, in the center of the circle, are photographs of the Bodhi tree (the same species under which he is supposed to have gained Enlightenment later) under which he was born. The tight cluster of icons near top of view expands to nine different Photos icons, including a Tibetan monastery, a Chinese-style temple, and Cambodian and Nepali-style stupas, all fairly recent constructions. As important as Buddhism was in East and Southeast Asia, in India it was virtually reabsorbed into Hinduism. This site was abandoned for a thousand years, and was only rediscovered and refurbished a century ago.

37. GE Layer 37 is a Placemark referencing Bodhgaya. The Panoramio icons in a tight cluster at right are almost all of the Bodhi tree there, or of the Mahabodhi Temple. The Panoramio icons in a looser cluster at bottom left of this view, roughly half a mile southwest of the Mahabodhi Temple, are of quite recent Buddhist temples constructed by Japanese, Bhutanese, Burmese, and Thais—once again a reminder of the influence of Buddhism in East and Southeast Asia.

38. GE Layer 38 is a Placemark referencing Sarnath. The Panoramio icon just left of this Star Placemark icon sits atop a massive stupa, a solid masonry structure that is 150′ tall and 90′ through at the base; three icons left of this are on this general subject too. Once again, the basic structure was built in the Guptan Dynasty as a reconstruction of an original monument set up by Emperor Ashoka of the Mauryan Dynasty seven or eight centuries earlier. A Panoramio icon at right of star is of temple memorializing ruins in which the Buddha sheltered from the rains. Two Panoramio icons at lower left are of pieces of a proposed modern monumental Buddha statue. The single icon at lower right is celebration of Buddha's sermon in a Japanese-style temple. A Panoramio icon at bottom of view is of the huge, ancient dome stupa on site where Buddha met his five former disciplines; the octagonal tower on top celebrates a visit by Mughal (Muslim!) ruler Humayan.

39. GE Layer 39 is a Placemark referencing Kushinagar. The Panoramio icon to right of Placemark Star icon shows a picture of a Buddhist monk walking at the base of the ancient Muktabandhana stupa that preserves cremated remains of the Buddha.

40. GE Layer 40 is a Folder titled "Buddhist councils." There may also have been one in Kushinagar, where Buddha died, just after his death. The others, averaging about one a century, are all just east of the sites of Buddha's life by some thirty or forty miles.

SECTION C: CLASSIC DYNASTIES

Whoever holds both the Punjab and the Ganges River system has a world-class empire. It happened three times in recorded history—four if you count the British Raj.[GE41]

Mauryans

The first South Asian dynasty known to hold the whole sweep of Indo-Gangetic plains was the Mauryan Empire. It seems to have been triggered in part by Alexander the Great's invasion. The Persian Empire defeated by Alexander had included holdings in the Punjab, and these northern plains of South Asia had a reputation for wealth. So in 326 BC Alexander sent half his army and all of his cavalry through the Khyber Pass, and himself took the other half of the army through rugged mountains to the north. His army crossed the Indus in the vicinity of Attock, and moved into the important city of Takshashila (today's Taxila, in Pakistan not far west of Islamabad). Here he made an ally of the ruler, thus adding troops and elephants to his army. His favorite horse, Bucephalus ("Ox-Head") died and was buried with honors on the banks of the Jhelum, and he fought the easternmost of all his battles on that same river. But his troops mutinied on the west bank of the Beas river—3,000 straight-line miles from Macedonia and a whole lot farther as the Greek soldier marched—and Alexander agreed to return to Greece. He moved his army back to the Jhelum and had it build a thousand boats. With columns marching on both banks, flanking the boats, he marched and fought his way down to the mouth of the Indus, receiving a serious wound in a fight near the junction of the Ravi and the Jhelum. He had crossed almost all of the Punjab, west to east, and his retreat left a power vacuum that was almost immediately filled.[GE42]

Meanwhile over in the east of our corridor (in what is today the state of Bihar) there had grown up a kingdom called Magada. Its capital was Pataliputra, present-day Patna, a city founded in the 400s BC. In or about 320 BC the ruling dynasty was overthrown by Chandragupta Maurya, founder of the Mauryan dynasty. He had emerged as a protégé of one of the most brilliant intellectuals in all of South Asian history, Kautilya, a Brahmin who was resident in Taxila when Alexander the Great came through. Kautilya is most famous for his *Arthashastra*, a book that translates "The Science of Profit," but is full of insightful—and sometimes ruthless— political and military advice. The title comes from the core argument that political power rests on economic prosperity. There is no appeal to any sort of morality; it is all about *realpolitik* practicality. Many have compared it to Sunzi's *The Art of War* from ancient China and even more to Machiavelli's *The Prince*. With Kautilya's guidance, in just a few years' time Chandragupta solidified his hold over Magada and added the Punjab to it. In 305 BC he defeated a major Greek invasion by Seleucus, one of Alexander's successors, and by his death in 297 BC Chandragupta had added much of the Deccan to the empire. This was probably the first time in history that the Punjab and Ganges systems had been held by a single ruler, and the capital reflected that wealth and power. Around 300 BC the Greek Megasthenes (Seleucus's ambassador) wrote that the palaces in Pataliputra were more beautiful than anything in Persia. He also spoke of Chandragupta's *Rajamarga*, or King's Highway. It ran from Pataliputra (Patna) west-northwest up the Ganges plain and then across the Punjab to Takshashila (Taxila). This was the prototype of the modern Grand Trunk Road.[GE43]

Ashoka

Chandragupta's grandson Ashoka (sometimes also spelled Asoka) ruled from around 268 to 235 BC and is the most famous of the Mauryan dynasty rulers. His rule, though grand, was unexceptional until the seventh year of his reign. In that year he walked a particularly bloody battlefield where he had just defeated the state of

---

41. GE Layer 41 is a Folder titled "GT Road corridor, rivers"; please turn the whole folder on to open the by now familiar corridor outline, along with the Indus and Ganges River systems.

42. GE Layer 42 is a Folder titled "Alexander the Great, Punjabi sites." It includes Placemarks of most of the sites mentioned in this paragraph, with some interesting Panoramio icons to explore.

43. GE Layer 43 is a Folder titled "Mauryan Empire." It includes a Placemark for the capital Pataliputra a(Patna) and a Polygon in light yellow approximating the Mauryan Empire at its maximum expansion.

Kalinga (in today's Orissa, on the southeast coast of India just south and west of Kolkata),[GE⁴⁴] and was apparently sickened by the carnage. He forswore war (though there would still be a strict governmental system of control, including punishment) and embraced Buddhism. He undertook an eight-month-long pilgrimage to all the important sites associated with the life of Buddha, and then returned to the capital Pataliputra to translate this to national and international scale. Throughout his own domains he had carved on rocks and on polished columns his new philosophy and correct rules of behavior.[GE⁴⁵] In one of these texts he claimed that 100,000 had been killed outright in the Kalinga war, and many more died later, and that 150,000 had been forcibly uprooted from their homes. His was not an exclusively Buddhist message; he apparently included Hindu Brahmins among those who were to enforce his rules for "right conduct." But he sent Buddhist missionaries to states as far away as the eastern Mediterranean, and his own son in that role to Sri Lanka. He gave Buddhism an impetus that lasted centuries. From the northwest of our corridor—the Punjab and upper Indus—Buddhism would spread up to the Silk Road and into western China around the first century AD. From southeast India and Sri Lanka it spread broadly into Southeast Asia. You have already heard of the "Third Buddhist Council" he convened. Next to the Buddha himself, Ashoka is the most important figure in the growth of Buddhism as East and Southeast Asia's dominant religion.

After Ashoka's reign, the Mauryan Empire declined fairly swiftly. The last Mauryan emperor was assassinated by his chief general in 184 BC.

Guptans

Almost exactly 500 years later Pataliputra, the old Mauryan capital, also became the capital of the new Guptan Empire (circa AD 320–547). Under the third and greatest ruler of the dynasty, Chandragupta II, the area controlled by the Guptans approached that of the Mauryan Empire half a millennium earlier.[GE⁴⁶] Among the eyewitness descriptions we have is that of the Chinese Buddhist monk Faxian. Around AD 405 he came to India in search of Buddhist manuscripts. After visiting the four major sites associated with the life of Buddha, he settled down for years in Pataliputra, which he described as a wealthy city and a city of learning. There's nothing to see of all that glory in present-day Patna; after the fall of the Guptan Dynasty, the site was abandoned for a thousand years. But many Indians today look back on the Guptan Empire as the true golden age of their culture—for its developments in science and math (including the invention of the zero and the decimal system), in Sanskrit language and the arts in general. The reputation of the most famous of all South Asian playwrights, Kalidasa, still remains from these days. Although only three of his plays survive (*Shakuntala* is the most famous), his mastery of mood so prized by Indian audiences set dramatic standards for Sanskrit languages for all time, the way Shakespeare did for English speakers much, much later.

In the next 500 years there were some short-lived successor dynasties which briefly and partially united the Indo-Gangetic plains. The Harsha, who ruled from circa 600–650, were one. They moved the capital west along our basic corridor to Kannauj.[GE⁴⁷] Closer to western India and well situated to control the main routes south into the Deccan (and west coast port cities), it remained the key city of the land for several hundred years.

Mughals

The Mughal Dynasty of more modern history reigned from 1526 to 1858, though the last century-and-a-half of that was in name only, and the first thirty years were only a prelude. The remaining century-and-a-half of actual Mughal rule (1556–1707), however, is of real importance in understanding today's Pakistan, India, and Bangladesh. It was an officially Muslim state but with a great majority of Hindu subjects. It brought in much

---

44. GE Layer 44 is a Placemark at Kalinga, in today's Orissa.

45. GE Layer 45 is a Placemark referencing one of the remaining Ashokan pillars, this one in Vaishali some twenty-six miles north of Patna, next to an enormous Buddhist stupa.

46. GE Layer 46 is a Folder containing three Polygons; one for the Guptan domains proper, and two for tributary areas. Red is the heartland, pink the tributary states.

47. GE Layer 47 is a Placemark at the city of Kanauj.

Central Asian culture (such as Uzbek, Afghan, and Mongol—of which "Mughal" is just an alternative spelling), Persian administrative and literary forms, and even Turkish practices from further west. Among other achievements, the Mughal Empire produced some of India's most famous architecture, including what may be the world's single most beautiful building, the Taj Mahal. In keeping with the ambition of this textbook to explore at least one aspect of the culture of each world regional corridor under discussion, imperial Mughal architecture presents itself as an obvious candidate—especially since the architecture of individual Emperors tended to reflect their individual ruling philosophies. Finally, understanding Mughal rule is important for understanding the subsequent British rule, or Raj, of India. The British East India Company, from small beginnings, would grow around the Mughal Empire the way a tropical strangler fig, starting as a little vine, grows up around a huge forest tree and eventually takes its place. For all these reasons, let's slow down now and spend some quality time with the Mughal Empire.

In just a word on the background of Islam in the subcontinent, Muslim conquerors had first settled in South Asia in the Sind, near the mouth of the Indus River, in AD 711. This was exactly the same year the Muslim commander Tarik crossed the Straits of Gibraltar (thus giving Gibraltar its modern name, *Jebel Tarik*, Tarik's Mountain) some 4,300 miles away on the other flank of the huge expansion of Islam in the century after Mohammed's death in 632. For most of the next 300 years, though, the Muslim Sind was an isolated outpost supplied only by sea. Much more important for the future of Islam in South Asia was the AD 997 overland raid by Mahmud from Ghazni, that great Afghan fortress city not far south of Kabul. This initiated two centuries of such raids that despoiled many of the Hindu temples and cities of the northern plains. Then after about 1200, especially in Delhi and vicinity, Muslim rulers began to build up permanent states. By that time, as historian Stanley Wolpert puts it, the sharper edges of doctrinal difference between Muslim and Hindu had been rubbed off,[1] making coexistence in such states possible. Most of the Punjab and Ganges plains came under control of one or another of these so-called "Afghan" Muslim rulers.

Babur

The founder of the Mughal dynasty, Babur (1483–1530), was a descendant of both Genghis Khan and Tamerlane (though Babur and his successors, unlike their famous ancestors, were now Muslims). Babur originally ruled the rich Ferghana Valley of today's Uzbekistan, lost it in a war, and then managed to capture Kabul in today's Afghanistan as his new power base. From here he attempted several invasions of the rich South Asian plains. In April of 1526, having crossed the entire Punjab, he met the army of the strongest of the plains rulers, the Sultan of Delhi, at Panipat some fifty miles north of Delhi. Babur had an estimated 12,000 troops to the Sultan's 100,000 (plus war elephants), but Babur on his side had Turkish artillery (which the Turks in turn had gotten from the Europeans) and a military expertise honed in those fierce Central Asian wars. The Sultan was defeated and killed. The next year Babur broke a huge federation of Rajasthani kings at Khauna, as they approached Agra from the southwest. In 1529 he defeated the Sultan of Delhi's brother, who had rallied support in the area of modern Bihar, at a battle where the Ghangara River joins the Ganges.[GE⁴⁸]

The Sultans of Delhi had ruled since 1517 from a fort in Agra, and Babur simply occupied their quarters and ruled his new plains empire from here. He was not just a military figure, but an intellectual. He was a poet of some repute, and a landscape architect: in 1528 he laid out the gardens in Agra that are today called Ram Bagh.[GE⁴⁹] Like his famous ancestors, he actually preferred to camp out in gardens rather than to live in permanent buildings, and built a string of such gardens, usually a day's march apart, between Agra and Kabul. The *char bagh* (literally a "four-garden"), a square garden of four equal quadrants and planted with tropical fruits, sugarcane, and shade trees, was for him a metaphor for rule—bringing order out of what he saw as Hindustani chaos.[2]

---

48. GE Layer 48 is a Folder titled "Babur's battles." It includes Placemarks for the Ferghana Valley, Kabul, Panipat, Khauna, and the Ghangara River battle.

49. GE Layer 49 is a Placemark referencing "Ram Bagh," as it is called today, across the river from the fort and the Taj Mahal.

There are only three buildings of Babur's that lasted until recent times—all mosques, in the cities of Panipat, Sambhal, and Ayodhya, three points in a line right down the middle of our corridor.[GE⁵⁰] The mosque in Panipat, built from 1526–28, was obviously in thanks for his victory over the Sultan of Delhi there. The other two were built on Hindu holy sites, apparently on purpose—Sambhal is revered by Hindus as the future site of Vishnu's tenth and final incarnation, and Ayodhya, as you've seen, was Rama's birthplace and hometown. This was confrontational rule with a vengeance. Babur called Hindus "kaffirs," unbelievers or pagans, and called his war against the Hindu kings of Rajasthan a *jihad*, or holy war.

It's not clear that Babur ever thought of himself as founder of the ruling dynasty of a great new South Asian state. He hated the hot plains, and always wanted to get back to his cool hills. Before he died in 1530 he left instructions that he was to be buried back in Kabul; and indeed after a short interment in Agra's Ram Bagh, his remains were taken to Kabul for permanent repose in his garden there.

The great road of Sher Shah Surii

Babur's son, Humayan, quickly lost control of his father's new South Asian territories to the brilliant "Afghan" ruler Sher Shah, from the latter's base farther east along our corridor in today's Bihar. Sher Shah was originally named Farid Khan, but as a heroic soldier for the Mughal-appointed King of Bihar he was given the honorific Sher, meaning Tiger (presumed source of Kipling's "Sher Khan" name for his villainous tiger in *The Jungle Book)*. Later becoming king, or shah, himself, he became known as Sher Shah of Sur. He defeated Humayan first in the east at Chausa in 1539, and then at Kannauj, the old Harsha capital on the Ganges, in 1540. In so doing he effectively drove Humayan back into Afghanistan and took Agra for his own capital. From here he ruled for five years, until he again dramatically changed South Asian history by getting himself killed in the siege of a mountain-fortress near the southern edge of our corridor, on the border between today's Uttar Pradesh and Madhya Pradesh.[GE⁵¹] This would eventually let the Mughals slip back into power.

But he left his mark on the country in just those few short years. Most people in Delhi and environs today know the major road through their part of India, in Hindi, as *Sher Shah Surii Marg*, or Sher Shah of Sur's Road. In Pakistan it is still called by Sher Shah's name for it in Urdu, *Sadak-e-Azam*, "the Great Road." In six years time or less he had rebuilt it into a truly royal road. Every *kos,* or about two-and-a-half miles, he had erected a thirty-foot-tall solid masonry tower faced with white plaster. A good many of these *kos minar* (minar from the Persian for tower, as in minaret), still stand, though most of them were probably rebuilt under later Mughal rulers such as Jahangir. You see them especially along the main road from Ambala through Delhi to Agra (today's Indian National Highways 1 and 2). At every five or six *kos* were based a horse, a rider, and a drummer to hustle royal messages along the royal road. Each had a stepped well or water reservoir, plus a police station. Around these official government posts there soon grew up inns and caravanserais.

Even today one of Delhi's important landmarks is the Old Fort, *Purana Qila*, which Sher Shah built in that same 1539 to 1545 period. It is supposed to be atop the ancient city mound that was once Induprastha, capital of the Pandavas back in *Mahabharata* times. To make sure that Humayan (or any other invader from the direction of the Khyber Pass) did not dare to re-invade South Asia, he built a truly massive fort at Rohtas, in today's Pakistan overlooking where his "Great Road" crossed the Jhelum River. Finally, Sher Shah's monumental tomb back in his hometown of Sasaram was the largest built in South Asia for centuries before this, and obviously presented a challenge to later Mughal rulers. He even built his rather low-ranking father and grandfather impressive tombs, to (retroactively) elevate the prestige of his family tree.[GE⁵²]

Humayan, meanwhile, had plunged back into those Central Asian wars from which his father had emerged. Seeing confusion among the heirs of Sher Shah in 1555, he came back into the plains after a fifteen-year

---

50. GE Layer 50 is a Folder titled "Babur's mosques." Its Placemarks reference all three.

51. GE Layer 51 is a Folder titled "Sher Shah victories & defeats," including Placemarks for his victories at Chausa and Kannauj and the battle of Kalinjar, in which he died.

52. GE Layer 52 is a Folder titled "Sher Shah legacies." It includes a Folder of kos minar views, and Placemarks referencing his Octagonal Tower in Delhi's Purana Qila (Old Fort), of Rohtas Fort in the Punjab, and his tomb back east in his hometown of Sasaram.

absence and captured Lahore, the key city of the eastern Punjab. In that year the greatest of his generals took on the general of Sher Shah's son—once again at Panipat, not quite thirty years after Babur's victory there. There the Sur dynasty's general, like Harold at the Battle of Hastings in 1066, went down with an arrow in the eye, causing the collapse of the Sur army. Humayan's forces then quickly recaptured Delhi and Agra. But in 1556 Humayan died of an accidental fall. Ironically enough, he died from falling down the steps in the Octagonal Tower built by Sher Shah in the Old Fort, a tower Humayan had turned into his library. The stage was now set for the most famous ruler of the dynasty, and perhaps all of South Asian history, Akbar.

Akbar

Akbar's rule (1556–1605) was almost exactly contemporary with that of Queen Elizabeth I of England (1558–1603). She was a young woman of twenty-five when she became queen, but Akbar became emperor when just a boy of fourteen. A war of succession broke out immediately upon his father's death, with a breakaway Hindu minister seizing Delhi itself. The Prime Minister was loyal to Akbar, however, and helped him successfully claim the throne. At age nineteen, in 1561, Akbar dismissed the Prime Minister and began ruling firmly in his own right. It was a rule that generally would have made Kautilya proud.

Geographically, the scope of Akbar's conquests is spectacular. In 1561 he struck south into the Deccan. Then with a policy as much of conciliation and intermarriage as war, he drove into Rajasthan, either conquering or making allies (albeit subject allies) of the rest. In 1573 he took Gujarat in the west, and in 1576 he took Bengal in the east—both with many ports and a lucrative trade. He took the beautiful mountain valley of Kashmir in 1586, the Sind in 1591, and the eastern slice of Afghanistan in 1595. He is the real founder of the Mughal Empire; without him, his grandfather Babur and father Humayan would be known only to historical specialists.

The key to the direct military strength of Akbar's state was that he stationed heavily-armored cavalry in the major towns and key forts. They were organized and maintained by noblemen, who were given rights to raise some local taxes, but who were mainly paid with money from the imperial treasury. And the money in the imperial treasury came from a most efficient new system of taxation. The most famous book from all the Mughal Empire was the *Ain-i-Akbari* (usually translated as *An account of the court and empire of Akbar*) by Abul-Faxl. It amounted to a sort of Domesday Book (put together for William the Conqueror after his 1066 conquest of England) for South Asia—saying exactly who owned what, what was taxable. Every Mughal governor got at his elbow, whether he wanted one or not, a finance minister to see to a standard collection and distribution of taxes. Finally, Akbar systematized ranks, giving government administrators the same hierarchy of titles the military noblemen had. You've already seen (in the Russia chapter) that Peter the Great did this same thing in Russia around 1700. In both cases it let the ruler move talented but non-noble people into the government, and in both cases it took a really strong personality to overcome aristocratic resentment.

Pervading all the above and making it possible was the much more open attitude of Akbar's officially Muslim government to the Hindu majority. Earlier Muslim rulers had imposed both a pilgrimage tax on Hindus, and a head tax they paid for not being Muslims; now Akbar lifted both of these. In 1579 he issued a declaration that on issues that affected ALL his subjects, it was the Emperor who could decide issues, not the Islamic judges. He was not a scholar, and possibly not even literate, but his acute intelligence and general curiosity about all religions resulted in a successful policy of universal religious toleration. This was the single greatest key to the power of the Mughal Empire. For example, the alliance he struck with certain Rajasthani ruling families (virtually all Hindu) was sincere, and they provided some of the greatest generals for his army.

Architecture! Akbar was the first great Mughal builder; the palaces, forts, and tombs from his reign are remarkable.

Humayan's tomb, built on the outskirts of Delhi, was Akbar's first major work. It was designed by 1562 and finished by 1571. It is impressive, a clear dress rehearsal for the Taj Mahal of some eighty years later that was to be done by Akbar's grandson. It was the first tomb to be set in a *char bagh*, one of those four-square gardens generally aligned with the four points of the compass. The whole compound was walled, with impressive arched entrance ways (the *pishtaq*, a straight-sided, pointed archway set in a high rectangular wall) that were much like those of the great religious buildings in Afghanistan, Uzbekistan, and Iran. The watercourses dividing the "four garden," however, seem to have been a Mughal invention. They appear to go under the central tomb, perhaps reflecting a Koranic verse about rivers running beneath gardens of Paradise. Domes of white marble were much like their Central Asian models, but the smaller domes of traditional Islamic architecture were here replaced by *chattris* (a section of a dome on pillars, from South Asian tradition), which gave a lightness to the whole structure. The major faces of the tomb were red sandstone with white marble detailing.[GE53]

At the same time, Akbar began work on several fortified palaces in northern India. The first, in Agra, was begun in 1565. Reminding one who has seen both of Moscow's Kremlin, at least in this basic sense, Agra Fort is a rough triangle with one side facing the river and the other two sides with moats, and about a mile and a half in circumference. Other than the massive walls and gates, the so-called Jahangiri Mahal, or palace, is the most remarkable building left from Akbar's time in Agra Fort.[GE54]

After a prophecy made by a nearby Muslim saint regarding the birth of a son came true in 1569 (and then giving it another two years to make sure the son was going to live awhile), Akbar began building a new capital near the saint's village of Sikri. In 1573 he named it *Fatehpur Sikri* ("Sikri the City of Victory") to celebrate his conquest of Gujarat. Fatehpur Sikri is atop a sandstone ridge some twenty miles west of Agra, the first ridge a traveler sees for a hundred miles coming down from the north across the great alluvial plains of South Asia. It has a massive congregational mosque, on the grounds of which is the beautiful little white marble tomb of the saint who predicted the son's birth. An intricate palace complex is dominated, at least in height, by the five-storey "Panch Mahal," a sandstone *trabeated* structure (vertical pillar and horizontal beam, instead of building with arches) crowned by a large chattri. Here you also find the "cusped" or "toothed" arch, usually attributed to southern India, incorporated in the architecture. There were workshops and a market on one end, and a caravanserai on the other. It was finished about 1576, but Akbar suddenly abandoned it in 1585 (many say from shortage of water; tourists who have visited on a 114°F summer day may think it was because that dark red sandstone trapped too much heat). It is one of India's most spectacular and romantic ruins.[GE55]

He then moved to Lahore, closer to the turbulent northwest frontier, where he built a third palace/fort. [GE56] The single largest fortress built in his reign was that of Allahabad, at the confluence of the Ganges and the Yamuna Rivers, dating from around 1583; it was a staging point to deal with disturbances in the eastern part of the empire.[GE57]

Akbar's architecture was in no small part built to impress, to announce the arrival of a new world power and to overawe any domestic rivals. Unlike the tombs and mosques of his father and grandfather, he also drew on local, South Asian architectural traditions, blending them with the Timurid (Tamerlane's) traditions of Central Asia. It's not just coincidental that he did the same thing in governing.

Jahangir and Nur Jahan

Jahangir (the former Prince Salim, but named Jahangir or "World Seizer" by his father Akbar for some modest military victories) ruled from 1605–1627. In the main he continued his father's policies, so together their three-quarter century period of rule can be counted as the consolidation of Mughal rule. He was a naturalist and a linguist, and although he is probably most famous in the arts for his support of poetry and painting, he was also a considerable builder. His first major architectural production was his father's tomb, just outside Agra

---

53. GE Layer 53 is a Folder, inside the unnumbered general folder "Akbar sites," titled "Humayan's tomb." It contains five Placemarks referencing different Photos icons. Turn Google Earth "3-D" layer on for interesting perspectives. The last Mughal "Emperor" would surrender to the British here in 1858, at the end of the great Mutiny/First War of Independence—interesting symbolism.

54. GE Layer 54 is a Folder (again inside "Akbar sites" general folder) titled "Agra Fort." In it are three Placemarks suggesting views, mainly of gates and walls.

55. GE Layer 55 is a Folder (still inside "Akbar sites" folder) titled "Fatehpur Sikri."

56. GE Layer 56 is a Folder (still inside "Akbar sites" folder) titled "Lahore Fort." Placemarks suggest Photos icons with good views of gates, walls.

57. GE Layer 57 is a Placemark titled "Allahabad Fort," referencing one Panoramio icon of a picture made from the river. There are not many Photos icons inside the fort walls; most of it is still an active military post where casual photography would be frowned upon.

beside the main road to Delhi. Like Humayan's tomb, it is centered in a walled, four-square garden, which is entered through a massive *pishtaq*-style archway. More white marble detailing has crept into the basic red sandstone structure, and instead of a great central dome on top, you have trabeated (pillar and beam) structures that remind a viewer of the Panch Mahal of his father at Fatehpur Sikri.[GE58]

The Iranian Begum (princess or queen) Nur Jahan was the widow of a Mughal nobleman when she was chosen by Jahangir in 1611 to be his wife. He named her first Nur Mahal, "Light of the Palace," and then Nur Jahan, "Light of the World." She became his favorite wife, and her brother and father did much of the practical governing later when Jahangir was deep into his cups or opium. She herself was a creative designer and if not an architect then at least a sophisticated director of architects. The so-called "Baby Taj" in Agra was built under her direction, from 1622–1628, as her father's tomb. Its more proper name is *Itmad ud Daula*, "The pillar of the state," a title Akbar had originally conferred on her father. The central building is almost entirely of white marble (formerly used only for Muslim saints' tombs), with semi-precious stone inlays—as in the later Taj Mahal. The tomb is placed in the middle of a small, walled four-square garden, with an impressive red sandstone entrance way and a front garden outside of that.[GE59]

Inside Lahore Fort the best preserved structures from Jahangir's time are in the "Jahangiri Quadrangle."[GE60] South of the walled city of Lahore is Anarkali's tomb, for one of Jahangir's wives; it is a basically octagonal structure of white marble.[GE61] Nur Jahan, Jahangir's favorite queen, is buried north of the same city. She outlived her husband by many years, and so was buried in the reign of Shah Jahan; but she apparently designed her own tomb.[GE62]

Jahangir, even more so than other Mughal rulers, loved to spend time in Kashmir. Shalimar Garden may be the most famous of all the Mughal structures there; it was constructed on the northeast side of Lake Dal, on fairly level land near the lake, but backed up to steep, green, rugged mountains. Jahangir ordered his son, the future Shah Jahan, to begin developing the dams and canals for its waterways; most of the remaining buildings were probably built by Shah Jahan.[GE63]

Jahangir was capable of artistic and romantic gestures, but also capable of great cruelty. In punishment of Hindu enemies, especially, he would do things as outrageous as have a cow slaughtered on a Hindu holy site. It was just a hint of things to come later in the dynasty.

Shah Jahan

As Prince Khurram, the favorite of his father and grandfather, he won most of the military victories of his father's reign. While still a Prince he showed a taste for building in his frontier stations. As Shah Jahan (ruling from 1628–1658) he was the most passionate builder of the dynasty. He built so much that in the long run it brought on a financial crisis; but under him the Mughal combination of resources and artistic sensibility reached its height in creations for the ages.

His father Jahangir had died on the way from Lahore to Kashmir. Shah Jahan brought his body back to a site just across the Ravi River from Lahore, and built for him the third monumental tomb complex of the dynasty. It is set in a by-now classic walled, four-square garden, with an imposing pishtaq-style entrance. Today

---

58. GE Layer 58 is a Folder (inside the general Folder titled "Jahangir & Nur Jahan sites") titled "Akbar's tomb." Seven Placemarks suggest Photos icons for different views, detail.

59. GE Layer 59 is a Folder (also inside the general Folder titled "Jahangir & Nur Jahan sites") titled "Baby Taj (Itmad ud Daula)." Five Placemarks suggest representative Photos icons.

60. GE Layer 60 is a Placemark showing Jahangir Quadrangle centered in this view, indicating a Panoramio icon titled "Lahore: Le Fort-La cour carrée de Jahangir."

61. GE Layer 61 is a Placemark titled "Anarkali's tomb"; click on Panoramio icon suggested for view of the octagonal structure.

62. GE Layer 62 is a Placemark referencing Nur Jahan's tomb outside Lahore, not far from her husband's. Stripped of its marble trimming, it has been recently restored. There are a couple of dozen Photos icons to explore here; some were made of the ruins before restoration, some since.

63. GE Layer 63 is a Placemark titled "Shalimar Garden, Kashmir." Not on our corridor, it still deserves a look.

the central tomb itself is an unimposing single story with no high features other than minarets at the corners, but originally there were carved marble screens all around the top.[GE64]

Inside both the Lahore and Agra forts, Shah Jahan tore down most pre-existing structures and rebuilt; much of what you see inside the walls in both places is his work, especially at Agra.[GE65]

His greatest single building project was a whole new capital city in Delhi, to be called Shahjahanabad, literally "the Abode of Shah Jahan," or less literally "Shah Jahan City"—so vast and impressive that Delhi became the natural capital of India from then until now. Much of it was made up of the *Lal Qila*, or Red Fort (not to be confused with Akbar's Agra fort, also sometimes called the Red Fort), a rough quadrangle with walls enclosing 6,400 acres. In the northwest corner of the grounds, in the area generally called Shah Burj (King's Tower), several beautiful marble structures survive, and the white marble private and public audience halls of the middle east part of the fort are also memorable.[GE66] On a hill just west of the Red Fort Shah Jahan built Delhi's great Jama Masjid (Congregational Mosque). The monumental main (eastern) gateway, or red sandstone, is approached by a high flight of stairs. Once inside, the mosque itself appears across the expanse of public prayer space. More white marble than red sandstone, its central doorway is a high, cusped arch, flanked by five smaller cusped arches on either side. Three huge white marble domes with dark vertical decorative stripes top the whole. Side entrances into the prayer space are almost equally impressive.[GE67]

But his single most famous structure was built back in Agra. Popularly known as the Taj Mahal ("The Crown of Palaces"), more specifically Mumtaz Mahal, it was a tomb for his beloved Iranian wife who died at age thirty-nine giving birth to his fourteenth son. Like Agra Fort, it was on the west bank of the Yamuna River, though just around a bend so you could see one from the other across the water (or in dry times the river bed) about a mile away. Western tourists often go steeled against a sense of possible let-down at something that has been talked and written about so much, but it almost always exceeds expectations. Visitors enter a walled forecourt from the eastern side, through a fairly narrow lane flanked by red sandstone arches. Then the main (southern) gateway appears to one's half-right. A classic pishtaq-style gateway, it is more impressive than any of those built before. Of basic red sandstone, it has broad white marble detailing that is richly inlaid with semi-precious stones. Corner towers are topped with large chattris, and a row of small chattris, side by side, tops both inner and outer entranceways. The vaulted central archway is beautifully veined. Entering the square building, usually from northern India's fierce sunshine, a visitor has to negotiate forty yards of darkness approaching black. At the other end, framed in the black-shadowed archway, shines the brilliant white marble tomb itself.

On entering the *char bagh*, or four-square garden, the single greatest difference between this tomb and other monumental Mughal tombs appears: the tomb is not central, but is set on the riverbank on the far (north) side of the four-square garden. The only architectural shakiness the whole exhibits is the strange little viewing platform and walkways at the garden's center, where usually the Mughal tomb itself would be. But then the main tomb building itself commands all attention—huge and yet wonderfully proportioned at the same time. It is elevated on a square white marble base, or plinth. Upon ascending to this level and approaching the main tomb, detail comes into focus in smaller and smaller layers—from giant Arabic script around the main archway and giant floral inlays in colored stone on the top of the archway, to beautifully inlaid stone flowers and delicately carved marble screens at eye level. A mosque and a matching false mosque for symmetry flank the central tomb on west and east, respectively. A marble railing on the riverside overlooks the Yamuna below.[GE68]

---

64. GE Layer 64 is a Placemark titled "Jahangir's tomb"; several Photos icons to explore, both of main (western) gateway and central tomb itself.

65. GE Layer 65 is a Folder titled "Agra Fort, Shah Jahan structures."

66. GE Layer 66 is a Folder titled "Delhi's Red Fort." It contains seven Placemarks recommending Photos icons to explore.

67. GE Layer 67 is a Folder titled "Delhi's Jama Masjid." It also has a number of Placemarks suggesting particular Photos icons.

68. GE Layer 68 is a Folder titled "Taj Mahal," that has ten or so Placemarks referencing Photos icons illustrating most of the aspects mentioned in the two paragraphs above.

For all the loveliness and artistic sophistication of Shah Jahan's buildings, they also reflected his political views. More and more formal and impressive, they announced an increased distance between the imperial and all other levels of society.

Aurangzeb

When Shah Jahan became very ill in 1656, his four sons began fighting for the succession even before his death. By the time he recovered a year later, Aurangzeb had won the war, and would rule from 1658 to 1707. He imprisoned his inconveniently-still-alive father in a palace in Agra Fort, a white marble one on the Yamuna River side with a good view of the Taj Mahal (where Shah Jahan was buried beside Mumtaz when he finally died in 1666).

In Aurangzeb's half-century rule the Mughal Empire, especially with its expansion into the Deccan, reached its greatest extent.[GE69] Under him, though, the Mughal Empire also went steeply downhill in terms of finances and security. Part of it was the stubborn military resistance in the Deccan, especially in Maharashtra. More basically, however, it was because Aurangzeb gradually returned to a narrower, if more orthodox Islam, and broke the unofficial deal his great-grandfather Akbar had made with the Hindu majority including those Rajasthani generals so important in Mughal control.

You can see this in architecture, in what Aurangzeb built and in what he tore down. Like Babur at the beginning of the dynasty, Aurangzeb really only left mosques and tombs as his building legacy. He intended to rule from the city of Delhi (Shahjahanabad) and its Red Fort, where he was officially made Emperor in 1858. Just after his accession to the throne, he had built inside Delhi's Red Fort his only contribution to its architecture, the Moti, or Pearl Mosque—an exquisite white marble, walled, intimate mosque that was more of his private chapel. The carved relief on the interior walls was ornate to a degree that under his father was seen only on palace walls.[GE70] His father had given Agra and Delhi large congregational mosques; from 1671–73 Aurangzeb did the same for Lahore in building the great Badshahi Masjid, or Emperor's Mosque—directly in front of the main gate of Lahore Fort. Architecturally much like his father's congregational mosque in Delhi, it was much larger, in fact it remained the largest mosque in the world for some 300 years.[GE71]

Aurangzeb destroyed a number of Hindu temples, usually as punishment for political and military disloyalty rather than in a frontal assault on Hinduism. In 1669, for example, to punish the rebellious Jat community around the city of Mathura, he destroyed the Keshava Deva, the temple built by Hindus to honor Krishna's birthplace. On the hilltop thus leveled he had built a massive red sandstone mosque especially for the celebration of Islam's yearly Eid festival.[GE72]

Aurangzeb left Delhi after fifteen years to be closer to the army in its campaigns in the Deccan. As a Prince he had campaigned there, and here his favorite wife had died in 1657. He had built for her there, by 1660 or so, a monumental tomb closely modeled on the Taj Mahal (his mother's tomb). As massive as the original, it nevertheless is artistically much cruder, seeming too vertically stretched and horizontally jammed together. [GE73] White marble on the inside, it was mostly burnished stucco on the outside, with none of the semi-precious stone inlay of the Taj. The treasury was already showing signs of strain.

---

69. GE Layer 69 is a Folder titled "Aurangzeb's empire, main roads." A light yellow Polygon shows maximum boundaries of Aurangzeb's empire; main roads in black radiate out of Agra.

70. GE Layer 70 is a Placemark under which a small white structure can be partially seen. There are perhaps a dozen nearby Panoramio icons to explore, including the one beneath the Placemark pointer titled "Moti Masjid mosque." Then explore nearby 360 Cities icon, showing the relatively ornate relief of the interior. The Moti Musjid was built from about 1658 to 1662.

71. GE Layer 71 is a Folder referencing a couple of Photos icons of Lahore's Badshai Mosque, built close up against the Fort.

72. GE Layer 72 is a Placemark referencing Aurangzeb's mosque in Mathura; notice how a new Hindu temple celebrating Krishna's birthplace crowds up against its southern side.

73. GE Layer 73 is a Placemark referencing Bibi Ka Mazbara, the Tomb of the Queen, in Aurangabad, down in the center of Maharashtra.

Outliving his wife by a full half-century, he left orders just before his death in 1707 for his own tomb in that same general part of Maharashtra. By this time, in his gradual shift towards a more conservative Islamic orthodoxy, he considered mausoleums on top of grave sites to be un-Islamic; his own tomb is a simple walled enclosure with earth open to the sky over the grave itself. And it is not next to his wife's tomb, but a dozen miles away next to the shrine to a Muslim saint.[GE74]

He died with the Marathas still undefeated and the imperial treasury empty. He had failed to pay or rotate regional rulers, turning what had been Mughal provinces to something more like independent principalities. He had ordered the execution of the Ninth Guru of the Sikhs ("Disciples"), but all that did was forge the Sikhs into a much more disciplined force, with all Sikhs changing their last name to Singh ("Lion") and promising to fight like that in battle (more on the Sikh religion in just a minute).

The Mughal Empire went into steep decline after Aurangzeb's death. In 1739 it was so weak and disorganized that an army all the way from Iran invaded and occupied Delhi for two months, thoroughly looting the place and carting off among other things Shah Jahan's Peacock Throne and the famous Koh-i-Nur ("Mountain of Light") diamond. Historian C. A. Bayley speaks of the "quiet" decline of the Mughal Empire, as cities such as Hyderabad in the south and Lucknow on our corridor became major centers of art and learning under virtually independent local rulers. Soon the Mughal "Emperor" controlled only Delhi and vicinity.

The Mughal dynasty had, however, given Hindustan a unity it had never had before, and another "golden age" of culture. We have only looked at the great imperial Mughal architecture, but nobles and wealthy commoners spread those same building styles and motifs throughout the empire. In a less visible way, Mughal habits of rule and culture had likewise spread. In the first great rebellion against British rule in 1857–58, a full century-and-a-half after the Mughal rulers had any real political or military power, the British were going to be astonished by what power was still in the name of the last Mughal Emperor to mobilize much of the subcontinent against them.

A word on non-Muslim religious developments in Mughal times

The Sikh religion, briefly mentioned above, is the newest of the world's major religions (if we define "major" as having twenty-five million or more believers). It emerged in the context of Muslim domination of Hindus of the Punjab. It was elaborated by ten gurus, or teachers, and "sikh" translates from the Punjabi as "learner," or "disciple." The first of the ten teachers was Guru Nanak, whose beautiful hymns to God were later collected and compiled in the sacred Granth, or Volume. The fourth guru, Ram Das, established formal congregational leaders, and centered the religion in Amritsar (the Golden Temple built there by the Guru Arjun in the late sixteenth century was originally called Harimandir, or "God's Temple" in Hindi). When the fifth guru was arrested and tortured to death by Jahangir's government, his son the sixth guru heeded his late father's advice that Sikhs should go armed. He also claimed secular power to go with his spiritual power. When Aurangzeb had the ninth guru executed in 1675, the tenth and last guru Gobind Singh forged Sikhs into the *Khalsa*, or "Pure" army, with every Sikh changing his name to Singh, "Lion." And so the Mughal Dynasty, after Akbar's era of religious toleration, had by religious persecution raised up a stubbornly militant enemy. This Sikh community would play a role in future South Asian history all out of proportion to its numbers. The Sikh ruler Maharajah Rangit Singh, for example, would hold the entire Punjab from the Indus to the Sutlej rivers in a powerful grip in the half-century from 1780 to 1839.

Looking back, the Mughals were a huge challenge for Hindu India, and Vaishnaism ("Vishnuism")—a much more broadly inclusive and eclectic kind of Hinduism—was one response. Some aspects of it tended towards monotheism, with such important divine figures as Krishna and Rama being seen as avatars (reincarnations) of Vishnu, not separate deities. The first of the ten Sikh gurus, Guru Nanak, had come out of this Vaishnava movement in Hinduism, for example. And the flexibility of traditional Hinduism was about to be tested again in at least as serious a way: the British were waiting in the wings.

---

74. GE Layer 74 is a Placemark referencing the general location of the tomb. As of this writing there are two Panoramio icons in the view; one is of the Muslim saint's tomb and the other is of the simple white-walled open gravesite of Aurangzeb.

SECTION D: WESTERN INTRUSION

Even before the beginning of the Mughal Dynasty in 1526 (and certainly before its more solid "re-beginning" with Akbar in 1556), there was some European presence around the edges of the Indian subcontinent. As you saw in the opening chapter on European maritime power, Vasco Da Gama had reached Calicut in a successful trading voyage in 1498. In 1509 at a key naval battle off the port of Diu in today's Gujarat, the Portuguese defeated a naval alliance of the rulers of Gujurat and Calicut, as well as the Ottoman Turks and the Mamluks of Egypt. In the wake of that critical battle the Portuguese quickly grabbed ports all around the coast of India and on through the Straits of Malacca, creating a virtual Portuguese monopoly of the lucrative Asian spice trade for about a century. The Portuguese commander Albuquerque, for example, captured Goa on the subcontinent's southwest coast for the Portuguese in 1510, and it would become the real capital of Portuguese Asia (as a parenthetical aside, a generation ago a plurality of Catholic priests in the author's mid-sized American city were Irish; today they are Indians from Goa!). There was a Portuguese station on the Hooghly River in the Ganges delta (about twenty miles north of today's Kolkata), by 1535.[GE75] All this, that looms so large in hindsight, was seen as trivial by the rising Mughals. The really dangerous invasions of the subcontinent had always come from the northwest through the Khyber Pass; the coast, they thought, could be safely ignored. The Chinese, as you'll see in a later chapter, made the same miscalculation about this historically unprecedented seaborne European power.

In the 1500s, the only serious naval rival of Portugal was Spain (and Spain actually absorbed Portugal in 1580, holding it and all its eastern bases until 1640). By 1602, however (as has already been covered to some extent in the South Africa chapter and will be covered better in the Indonesia chapter), the Dutch entered the field with the V.O.C., the Dutch East India Company. The Dutch blew the Portuguese and Spanish out of key ports all around Africa and India and the Straits of Malacca, and on into what is today Indonesia, which would largely take shape as a Dutch colony. As a result it was the Dutch who controlled the lion's share of the spice trade during the 1600s, including key points on the South Asian coast such as a trading post on the Hooghly near the old Portuguese one. By the early 1700s, with the Mughal Dynasty going into steep decline, the larger European powers competing for India were France and Great Britain, each with its own East India Company ambitious for trade, and if it proved possible, land. The British had a "factory" (read: trading post) in Surat, the key western Mughal port, by 1608. They were attracted on to the southeast coast by the trade in Indonesian and Bengali fabrics there, and by the 1660s were going straight to Bengal. The French likewise progressed around the peninsula and into Bengal. Together they eclipsed the Dutch in the India trade, but the stage was set for a showdown between them.

As late as the 1740s an outside observer probably would have bet on the French, led by the remarkable Joseph-François Dupleix. Born in 1697, he was the son of one of the directors of the French East India Company, who sent him to India for the first time when he was eighteen. Five years later he was helping run the big French trading post at Pondicherry.[GE76] By age thirty-four he was head of the French trading post at Chandernagore,[GE77] in Bengal, and at age forty-five he was a most successful Governor-General of the whole French network in India. It was Dupleix as much as any European who really invented what the British later called "the nabob game" ("nabob" coming from the common princely title more correctly transliterated "Nawab," originally meaning the Viceroy of the Mughal Emperor). The French would find two principalities at war, and offer to help one of them with modern European arms and tactics, with instructors and advisors. Then, in the process of helping this local power defeat the other, the French would gradually take over the government of the first as well (easy enough since they soon controlled the military).[3]

75. Turn off earlier Folders, and then open this "GT Road western intrusion" once and turn on the first, unnumbered subfolder, "GT Road corridor, rivers." Then open GE Layer 75, a Folder titled "Early European Seizures"; it includes Placemarks for Calicut (today's Kozhikode), Diu, Goa, and the Portuguese fort in the vicinity of what is today Hooghly-Chinsura, north of Kolkata. Diu Fort and Goa's Aguada Fort are worth some (virtual) exploring.

76. GE Layer 76 is a Placemark referencing Pondicherry (Puducherry); notice that much of the imperial action is beginning to shift to the east coast of India.

77. GE Layer 77 is a Placemark referencing Chandernagore—just a couple of miles south of the older Portuguese settlement of Chinsura and less than twenty miles north of what would become Calcutta.

In 1744, two years into Dupleix's Governor Generalship, a major European war broke out with France and Britain on opposite sides. By 1746 the French had conquered Madras (today's Chennai),[GE⁷⁸] and they also defeated two local armies allied with the British. Beginning in 1751, however, the tides of war turned against the French—in large part because of the leadership of Dupleix's opposite number in the British East India Company, Robert Clive.

Clive, born in 1725, was a generation younger than Dupleix, but he too was sent to India when he was eighteen years old—to the British trading post at Madras (Chennai), just about the time that Dupleix was appointed Governor-General for the French. In the war that broke out later he proved to be a remarkable military leader. By 1749 he was largely in charge of organizing supplies for the British forces (in which capacity he began his rise to great wealth, perhaps not coincidentally). The real turning point of the British-French contest was in 1851 when with just a few hundred men Clive seized Arcot,[GE⁷⁹] the base of a rival pro-French army, and then held it for seven weeks against a large besieging force.

Robert Clive returned to England in 1753, but was sent back to Madras in 1756 (the year the Seven Years' War broke out) with new troops intended to sweep the French from India. It was in Madras that he first heard that the Nawab of Bengal had swooped down from his capital at Murshidabad[GE⁸⁰] onto British commercial outposts in Calcutta (Kolkata)[GE⁸¹]—at this time perhaps the most important trading city in all of South Asia—and had smothered to death a hundred Europeans there in the poorly-ventilated dungeon later called "The Black Hole of Calcutta." Clive immediately set off with a relief force of some 2,500 men, and conquered the city in January of 1757. In June he destroyed the army of the Nawab at the Battle of Plassey,[GE⁸²] some eighty-five miles north of Calcutta. By 1759 he had defeated a Dutch move against him from their base in Hooghly-Chinsura, as well as an army led by the Mughal crown prince at Patna.

In just these few years Calcutta (with its rising Fort William) and Bengal in general became the most important British base in the subcontinent. And as for Robert Clive himself, he eventually returned to England with hundreds of thousands of pounds of sterling, was knighted (and titled "Baron Clive of Plassey"), became a Member of Parliament, and bought himself the magnificent estate of Claremont in Surrey which he grandly rebuilt.[GE⁸³] Many bright and adventurous young men from all over Britain were convinced by Clive's role model to risk the fevers and other uncertainties of Asia in pursuit of such fame and fortune.

The century of "John Company" rule, 1757–1857

The victory at Plassey in 1757 is usually taken as the real beginning of British control in India. By 1765 the Mughals were forced to grant the British East India Company the position of *diwani* (with its rights of tax collection) for all of Bengal. This was the heart of the original British rule—*The Bengali Bridgehead* is the expressive title of one of the volumes in the New Cambridge History of India series. In 1793 Lord Cornwallis (last seen by Americans surrendering to the French and Americans at Yorktown in 1781, but by 1786 Governor-General of India) introduced the "Permanent Settlement of Bengal," a land taxation system.

As Mughal control evaporated, the British moved into the power vacuum, annexing state after state and pensioning off their former nawabs with salaries worth a fifth of their former incomes. The most dramatic British gains were northwest, successive moves up along our chosen corridor. The biggest such state annexed was Awadh (another transliteration of Ayodhya) in 1801, which included the entire Ganges-Yamuna doab (land between those rivers). They occupied Delhi in 1803. By 1816 the British got the Himalayan foothill territory

78. GE Layer 78 is a Placemark referencing Madras (Chennai). Although Dupleix took the nearby city, he never was able to take Fort St. George, held by the British.

79. GE Layer 79 is a Placemark referencing Arcot.

80. GE Layer 80 is a Placemark referencing Murshidabad.

81. GE Layer 81 is a Placemark referencing Calcutta (Kolkata). The British had attacked Aurangzeb in 1686, and it had proven to be a military disaster for them. But out of it had come the founding of Calcutta in 1690, a deep water harbor on the east bank of the Hooghly.

82. GE Layer 82 is a Placemark referencing Plassey.

83. GE Layer 83 is a Placemark referencing Claremont, just fifteen miles southwest of London in Surrey.

that included Shimla, by winning a war with the Gurkhas of Nepal—though in the process gaining such respect for the Gurkha fighters that they regularly hired them from then on to fight for the British army! By 1818 actual British control reached the Sutlej, the easternmost river of the Punjab. When the great Sikh ruler Ranjit Singh died in 1839, and his state began to disintegrate in the hands of less-capable successors, the British were there to pick up the pieces. Lahore fell to them in 1846. They took Rawalpindi in 1849 and permanently garrisoned it in 1851. It became the Headquarters of the Northern Command, British India's largest garrison (and not coincidentally is the Headquarters of the Pakistani army today). By the 1850s the British rulers were claiming rights even the Mughals had not exercised: if a nawab had no male heir upon his death, for example, his lands were forfeited directly to the British East India Company.

In Delhi especially by mid-nineteenth century you could feel the new British presence. The "Resident," as the chief local head of the British East India Company was called, built and lived in a showy Palladian mansion called after himself the Metcalfe House (or *Jahan Numa*, "World Showing").[GE84] It was on the west bank of the Yamuna, a bit north of the Red Fort but close enough to invite comparisons. Even more pointedly, the Resident had a country house built south of Delhi (*Dilkusha*, "Delighter of Hearts").[GE85] It was a remodeled Mughal tomb of one of Akbar's noblemen, replete with *char bagh* ("four-square garden"). It was within 300 yards of the famous Qutb Minar, and close enough (half a mile!) to the Mughal country palace of Zafar Mahal[GE86] to invite comparisons here too.[4]

British social policy in this century of "John Company" rule reflected a good bit of the European Enlightenment. Suttee (*sati*), the ritual burning of Hindu widows, was outlawed by 1830, and a campaign against thugee (*thagi*), a cult of ritual murder, was carried out with success. But it also had economic and religious dimensions less enlightened. Land policy resulted in the strengthening of the rights of the local nobles, *zamindars*, and the weakening of traditional rights to farm the land by peasant farmers—this most probably because it made for a more efficient way for the British to get taxes in money. In general, the introduction of cheap British industrial manufactures (machine-woven cloth, all sort of metal tools, pots and pans, etc.) wrecked the South Asian village handicraft economy. In 1813 the British East India Company was forced by pressure from Britain to allow the entry of missionaries into lands under their control, and a vigorous, mainly Protestant campaign to convert all Hindus and Muslims to Christianity caused an indignant backlash in both those communities. Add to this a persistent backcountry folklore to the effect that foreigners would be thrown out after a hundred-year rule, and in 1857 all that was needed was a spark to set off one of the most famous rebellions against British colonial rule in history. The British called it the Sepoy Mutiny; South Asians today generally call it the First War of Independence.

Sepoy Mutiny/First War of Independence

A "Sepoy" was the common locally-recruited soldier of the British army in India (the word comes from the Persian *sipahi*, soldier). In 1857 the British issued the regular troops a new Enfield rifle, for which powder for each round was contained in paper cartridges greased to be waterproof—the ends to be bitten off and the powder poured into the chamber. Rumor had it (and despite much historical controversy over it, it probably was true) that the grease used was either beef tallow or pork fat. At a stroke both Hindus and Muslims were offended, Hindus because of the sacrilege of cow-killing, and Muslims because for them as for Jews anything

---

84. GE Layer 84 is a Placemark referencing the Metcalfe House. Today it houses part of the Indian defense establishment, hence no Photos icons nearby! For one view of the house, go to http://www.drdo.gov.in/drdo/labs/DESIDOC/images/house.jpg

85. GE Layer 85 is a Placemark referencing Dilkusha (the octagonal structure under the icon pointer) with several nearby Photos icons to explore; Qutb Minar, conspicuous by its shadow, shows up near top left of screen.

86. GE Layer 86 is a Placemark referencing Zafar Mahal, the summer palace of the last Mughal Emperor that is today located within the labyrinthine city of Mehrauli. There are no nearby Photos icons to explore, but a Google–Images search will yield several good ones. Note proximity to Dilkusha, chosen by the Resident as his summer retreat, just half a mile northeast.

pertaining to pigs is ritual filth. When Sepoys at Meerut, about thirty-five miles northeast of Delhi,[GE87] refused to handle the cartridges, British officers handcuffed the offenders and bundled them off to jail with long prison terms. On May 10 the Meerut garrison rose up, killed its British officers and freed its comrades in jail, and marched on Delhi. The Delhi garrison joined them in rebellion, and they proclaimed the last of the Mughal line, eighty-two-year-old Bahadur Shah II, active ruler of the country in place of the British.

From Delhi the Mutiny or War of Independence spread rapidly. It attracted Hindus as well as Muslims, in part because the old Shah—in a hint of a throwback to Akbar—was sympathetic to the Hindus (his own mother had been Hindu). A map of the major centers of mutiny shows its major sites from Kolkata in the southeast of our corridor to Peshawar at the northwestern end of our corridor, but as you can see the great preponderance of the outbreak was on the middle section of both corridor and the GT Road corridor.[GE88] It was bloody, with wholesale massacres of Europeans irrespective of age or sex, and some British parties such as those in Delhi who retreated to "The Ridge"[GE89] under desperate siege for months. But almost none of the local rulers of Indian states rose, and the British gradually brought in force from either end of the GT Road. They came up from Kolkata, which they held with Fort William and naval power, and down from the Punjab, with local allies such as Sikh and Gurkha forces. General John Nicholson, who fought his way down to Delhi from the northwest, and who was killed at its gates, in his personal courage, fierce aggressiveness, and absolute faith in the Christian righteousness of his cause, reminds this American author very much of the Confederate General Stonewall Jackson, his near contemporary. British ferocity in the process of their return—the fighting was over by July of 1858—was greater than that of the Sepoys, in terms of numbers executed, some tied over the mouths of cannons which were then fired. The last Mughal Emperor died in 1862, in British-imposed house arrest in Rangoon (Yangon), Burma.

In this context, a film that came out in India in 2005, called *Mangal Pandey: The Rising*, might be of interest. The Mangal Pandey of the title was a Sepoy officer who had became close to an English officer in the Afghan wars. He eventually led the rebellion, and was captured and executed by the British, for whom "Pandey" became the generic name for any rebel from that time on. The movie has a bit of classic Bollywood in it (Mangal Pandey's love interest and her friends get to do a group dance number, for example), but it nicely shows the complex web of social relations and the tensions.

SECTION E: THE RAJ

In the wake of the 1857–58 Mutiny/First War of Independence, the British government took over direct government of its South Asian holdings from "John Company," the British East India Company. India had become too important a source of revenue and manpower for the British Empire, and obviously too big a job for even a quasi-governmental business enterprise to deal with. This direct British rule is usually just called the Raj, from the Hindi word for rule (transliterated *rāj*, and coming from the same Indo-European root as the English "royal"). Today's Pakistan, India, Bangladesh, Sri Lanka (Ceylon), and even Myanmar (Burma) were all then just "British India." The Raj lasted only ninety years, a small slice of South Asian history; but a good bit of both its substance and its style survive in its successor states.

The western world still mainly knows the region and the times through the British prism, and particularly through the works of Rudyard Kipling (1865–1936)—he of "the white man's burden." For all Kipling's association with India, he only spent a dozen years of his life there, though they were crucial. He was born and raised in Bombay/Mumbai, through age six. His parents sent him back to England for what turned out to be a brutally unpleasant boarding school experience. Then in his late teens he came back to India to join his parents who had by now moved to Lahore. He became a journalist in Lahore and then Allahabad, and spent a prized summer month every year in the hills in Shimla, the British summer capital. Kipling's prose masterpiece *Kim*,

---

87. GE Layer 87 is a red Pushpin icon Placemark referencing Meerut, showing its central location in the "doab" between the Yamuna and the Ganges.

88. GE Layer 88 is a Folder titled "1857 centers of revolt." Red stars symbolize major outbreaks.

89. GE Layer 89 is a Placemark referencing Flagstaff Tower, where a party of Europeans held out on "The Ridge" during the rising. The Ridge is of modest elevation, less than a hundred feet above the surface of the Yamuna.

written in the 1890s at or near the peak of British power in India, is the great fictional presentation of Britain's imperial struggle with Russia over control of Central Asia and what those living in South Asia called "the northwest frontier." The British called the contest "the Great Game"; the Russians named it "the Tournament of Shadows." Ethnographic expeditions supported by royal/imperial geographic societies in Britain, Russia, and their allies tended also to serve as cover for spy movements. Except for a foray by the central fictional characters of *Kim* into Shimla and up into the high hills above it, the whole novel is set along the GT Road from Lahore to Banaras. The opening paragraph describes Lahore (where in real life Kipling's father was curator of the museum), with a street urchin named Kim playing King of the Mountain with other boys on a giant cannon in front of the museum:

> He sat, in defiance of municipal orders, astride the gun Zam-Zammah, on her brick platform opposite the old Ajaib-gher, the Wonder House, as the natives call the Lahore Museum. Who hold Zam-Zammah, that 'fire-breathing dragon,' hold the Punjab, for the great green-bronze piece is always first of the conqueror's loot.[5] [GE[90]]

Farther on in the novel a retired old soldier, one of the few who had stayed loyal to the British in the 1857 rising forty years earlier, takes Kim (and the wandering Himalayan lama Kim has befriended) from his village back to the Grand Trunk Road, with the words "And now we come to the Big Road":

> . . .—the Great Road which is the backbone of all Hind. For the most part it is shaded, as here, with four lines of trees; the middle road—all hard—takes the quick traffic. In the days before rail-carriages the Sahibs travelled up and down here in hundreds. Now there are only country-carts and such like. Left and right is the rougher road for the heavy carts—grain and cotton and timber, fodder, lime and hides. A man goes in safety here—for at every few *koss* is a police-station . . . . All castes and kinds of men move here. Look! Brahmins and chumars, bankers and tinkers, barbers and bunnias, pilgrims and potters—all the world going and coming. It is to me as a river from which I am withdrawn like a log after a flood.[6]

The Grand Trunk road became as central to British rule of South Asia as it had been to that of the Mughals, Sher Shah Surii, and even Ashoka. But more was going on than showed in Kipling's works, even on the British side.

The manner of British control

Indian affairs were directed by the Viceroy most of the year from his regular Government House in Kolkata[GE[91]] and, after Shimla was declared the summer capital of British India in 1864, his "Viceregal Lodge" there in summers.[GE[92]] There was a Supreme Council, which looked something like a legislature, though the Viceroy had absolute veto power over it. The Viceroy's decisions were implemented by a core of about 1,500 ICS (Indian Civil Service) administrators. They were chosen in a rigorous competitive exam, and then

---

90. In beginning this section on the Raj, turn off former Google Earth layers, and then open the Folder titled "Section E: the Raj." Turn on first unnumbered Folder on corridor, rivers. Then open GE Layer 90, a Folder titled "Zam-Zammah and Museum." The great cannon is still in front of the museum as it was over a century ago when Kipling wrote *Kim*. The first Placemark references the cannon, and the second references the front of the museum nearby; lots of Photos icons to explore for each.

91. GE Layer 91 is a Placemark referencing Government House (today's Raj Bhavan) in Kolkata's Fort William. It's off-limits to the general public as a military base, therefore no Photos icons to explore, but go to following website for views: http://www.wmcarey.edu/carey/wmward/Misc%20html/govhouse.html

92. GE Layer 92 is a Folder titled "Views of Shimla, summer capital." It includes some Placemarks referencing appropriate Photos icons explore, from the narrow-gauge railroad going up to the "hill station," to views of and from Shimla. One of these is of the Viceregal Lodge, which was only completed in 1888. As regards the train pictures, if in the basic Layers box in Google Earth you will open the "More" folder and turn on Transportation sub-layer, the railroad will appear as a thin black line.

spent time in London's School of Oriental Studies or at Oxford or Cambridge learning South Asian languages and administration and law codes. It was technically open to anyone, of any ethnicity (said Queen Victoria); but since in practice the exams were only held in Britain and were not given to anyone over age twenty-four, it remained almost purely a preserve of the British.

A special proclamation from the Queen in 1858 tried to defuse any future rebellion by reversing several policies that had helped cause the Mutiny. First, the new proclamation ended the seizure of the princely estates of any prince who died without male heirs. Second, it announced a formal government policy of non-interference in religious affairs, to allay South Asian suspicions that the British government was sponsoring Christian proselytizing. For the next thirty-five years not a single liberal, western social reform was enacted—in deference to traditional Hindu and Muslim religious preferences. The army was quietly restructured: the new one was slightly smaller, but it went from having less than 20 percent of British soldiers before 1857 to almost 50 percent in the new one. Too, very few "native" soldiers were taken from the populations that had opposed the British in 1857; most were from the "martial races" such as the Sikhs and the Gurkhas that had aided the British in their hour of need.

Economically the most spectacular single innovation of the British in South Asia was the building of a very extensive railroad grid. A purely colonial enterprise, railroads started in from the British-built port cities of Bombay, Madras, and Calcutta (Mumbai, Chennai, and Kolkata) in the early 1850s. Not surprisingly, our GT road corridor of rich alluvial plains drew the railroad along itself. The first long stretch of continuous track in South Asia, over 500 miles, was the Kolkata to Banaras run—the first section of The Grand Trunk Road proper—that was opened in 1862. Of the dozens of railroad companies formed, with the British government guaranteeing a minimum rate of return on investment of 5 percent, the one that had this GT Road concession was the only one to make money from the beginning. By the time WW I broke out in 1914, British India had 35,000 miles of track, almost all of the present-day grid. A glance at a railroad map of India some decades into the Raj, with broad-gauge double track trunk lines showing as wider lines, shows the primacy of the railroads along the GT Road corridor.[GE[93]]

All in all, as empires go, the British administrators of the Raj were an efficient lot, but were spread so paper-thin over South Asia that a second level of administrators would have to come from the local population. The British chose to rely for their second tier administrators on Bengalis, the South Asians they knew best because of their real start in Kolkata, and who moreover had an impressive tradition of literacy and commerce.

The catch in this sort of imperial gamesmanship is, of course, that these educated second tier administrators after awhile come to resent the glass ceiling under which they are forced to live. With excellent knowledge of the working structure of the Raj, they eventually turn against it and become dangerous opponents calling for independence. Enough of this had happened by 1905 that the British partitioned Bengal into a Hindu west and a Muslim east (the "Bengal" of 1905 was made up of today's Indian states of West Bengal, Bihar, and Orissa, plus the country of Bangladesh).[GE[94]] Partly this was due to legitimate "communal" concerns ("communal" is the understated British euphemism for religious groups and the frictions between them)—on which more in a few minutes—but more of it was simply *divide et impera,* as the Romans classically put it, divide and rule. It sparked a wave of nationalist resentment, especially in Bengal, with the growth of the *Swadeshi* ("of our own country") movement of boycotting British goods and institutions, even educational institutions. The British reunited Bengal in 1911 (to general Hindu approval and general Muslim disapproval), but simultaneously stripped Bengal of its power as administrative capital.

---

93. GE Layer 93 is a Placemark framing a view of South Asia, but mainly used here as an excuse to embed a website with a scanned (.jpg) view of British Railroads there in 1909:
http://en.wikipedia.org/wiki/File:India_railways1909a.jpg
Should a reader want to correctly embed ("georectify") this into the Google Earth surface, the Image Overlay tool is for this. The author would have done it for you, but incorporating such images quickly increases the size of the Google Earth folder/.kmz file, compromising its "e-mailability." But in either case, notice how dense the web of railroads is from Calcutta up to about Lahore, all along the GT Road corridor.
94. GE Layer 94 is a Polygon showing in purple the original, pre-partition Bengal.

This growing Bengali resistance helped determine the British to move the administrative capital of the Raj from Calcutta to Delhi—hence "New" Delhi. The formal decision to move, and the first of the building, took place in 1911, and it wasn't finished until 1931 (giving the British just sixteen more years to rule from there!). The center of power was put atop Raisina Hill, some three miles south and west of old Delhi. The hilltop was flattened for the Viceroy's house[GE95] (Rashtrapati Bhavan, the President's House, today), with a garden behind it in the west. To the east ran the main ceremonial road, the Kingsway or Rajpath. On either side of it were the South Bloc and North Bloc of square, charmless, but huge and powerful government buildings. The Rajpath ran on east to the India Gate monument.[GE96] The new city itself, as opposed to these governmental structures, was an amazingly geometric planned city, with roads radiating out of great circular plazas, or "circuses" in British traffic language, in triangular array. Connaught Place,[GE97] famous for its high end shops, is the great circus in the north. Roads running southwest and southeast of it to either end of the Rajpath make a perfect equilateral triangle, 1.5 miles per side.[GE98] From each point of the triangle, other roads go to the midpoint of the opposite side, like the proof of some plane geometry problem. There is virtually no concession to terrain, or to local taste; this is empire from the top down.

Gandhi returns to India: the highlights

General American public knowledge of the South Asian response to the Raj—especially the older generations of Americans—is largely shaped by David Attenborough's 1982 film *Gandhi*. And it is indeed a film still worth seeing these three decades later, though not without some point of view or bias (the portrayal of Ali Jinnah, head of the Muslim League and later first Governor-General of independent Pakistan, is, as one reviewer commented, "particularly poisonous").

The biographical film spends quality time with Gandhi's development of his version of non-violent civil disobedience in South Africa (as did this text earlier in the Durban-to-Pretoria corridor chapter, the author hopes you agree). The most powerful and interesting scenes of the movie, however, are after Gandhi's return to India in July of 1914, the month before WW I broke out. He was warmly welcomed by many independence leaders because of his Indian civil rights successes in South Africa. He traveled mainly by train around the sub-continent to get to know it after a twenty-one-year-long absence (this visual part of the film, with driving sitar music from Ravi Shankar to back it, is marvelous). He found the most important independence-minded institution, the Indian National Congress that dated to 1885, to be mainly an upper-class debating society with little contact with everyday South Asians, and so split between moderate and radical wings as to have little impact. In just a few years he remedied both. He got bright young scholars investigating the root causes of poverty and starvation in the countryside, tracing it directly not just to British excesses but to the basic colonial system. His *satyagraha*, or soul force movement, coupled with his broad embrace of all kinds of religions and religious sensibilities, for a long time made him the indisputable center of gravity of the Congress institution.

The film hits the high spots of those critical years between WW I and WW II—the Amritsar Massacre of 1919, the Chauri Chaura police killings of 1922, the Dandi Salt March of 1930 among them. This text needs to, as well (after which we'll go back in time for a bit deeper and broader look at the pattern of response). Two of these three events transpired on our GT Road corridor, and the third had a strong echo there.

During World War I Indians of the Raj generally stayed loyal to the British. A million Indian soldiers served on the British side, some as far away from home as the Western Front in France. They expected, and during the war the British hinted at, more equality and perhaps progress towards independence after the war. What they got instead in March 1919 was not more but less in the way of civil rights: the Rowlatt Act, an antiterrorist law applying to British India, allowed holding any suspect up to two years without trial. Gandhi led a major

---

95. GE Layer 95 is a Placemark referencing a Panoramio icon, the photo looking towards Raisina Hill.

96. GE Layer 96 is a Placemark referencing a Photos icon titled "India Gate"; click on Panoramio icon under pointer titled "Gate of India, New Delhi 1997" for interesting picture.

97. GE Layer 97 is a Placemark referencing Connaught Place; click on Panoramio icon under pointer titled "C P ND."

98. GE Layer 98 is an overview of New Delhi, with the equilateral triangle based on the Rajpath in the top center of the view.

"Rowlatt satyagraha" against it. It all came to a head in the northern city of Amritsar. Protest crowds had gathered and been fired upon; some Europeans had been assaulted. Then on a Sunday in April, in the walled Jallianwala Bagh[GE⁹⁹] just a few hundred yards east of the Golden Temple, a crowd of a couple of thousand had gathered on a Punjabi religious holiday either in ignorance of or despite the martial law forbidding public assemblies. Brigadier-General Reginald Dyer—a fifty-five-year-old veteran army officer, actually born in Murree (the British hill country station closest to Rawalpindi),[GE¹⁰⁰] and Urdu-speaking—brought about a hundred Gurkha and Sikh troops into the garden and ordered them to open fire. There was no warning given to the crowd of men, women, and children to disperse. The troops fired until their ammunition was low, with between 400 and 1,000 dead and many others wounded. Europeans in British India were generally supportive, considering that a rebellion had been nipped in the bud. Back in London the Parliamentary inquiry into the massacre was less positive, and looking back this may have been a key point when the British public began to be aware of the truth of one of Gandhi's assertions—that empire takes a lot of violence to impose, and always takes at least a low level of violence to maintain.

In February of 1922 Gandhi's "Non-Cooperation" campaign was having an impact truly Raj-wide. But in the town of Chauri Chaura [GE¹⁰¹](in today's eastern Uttar Pradesh close to the border with Bihar, a little over a hundred miles northwest of Patna), a major flare up of violence occurred. A crowd of at least two thousand was protesting in front of a liquor shop at the local market, and a police force that was ordered to disperse the crowd first fired overhead and then into the crowd, killing perhaps three. The enraged crowd chased the policemen back to their police station and set it afire, attacking those who tried to escape the flames, and thus killing in all twenty-two policemen. Gandhi's reaction was to call off the Non-Cooperation campaign and go on a fast of penance for his part in inadvertently causing such violence. The British government's reaction was hardnosed, with over a hundred jailed, many for life, and nineteen sentenced to death.

The famous Salt March, or Salt Satyagraha, of 1930 marked the mass renewal of Non-Cooperation. In 1929 Jawaharlal Nehru, rising young protégé of Gandhi and then President of the Congress Party, had symbolically raised a flag of independent India beside the Ravi River near Lahore, and in January of 1930 Congress declared it was working for full and complete independence. Gandhi's Salt March took place immediately thereafter. It was mostly in and around his home state of Gujarat. It started at Sabarmati Ashram,[GE¹⁰²] Gandhi's Phoenix Farm-style communal retreat near Ahmedebad, the state capital city, and went to Dandi on the coast.[GE¹⁰³]

Salt has always been an easy thing for governments to tax, especially near the tropics, and most especially in a mainly vegetarian society (carnivores get some salt in their meat)—you have to have it to live. At times in the British Raj revenue from the salt tax was the third most important source of government income (after land and, at least indirectly, profits from the opium that was key to the triangular trade between Britain, India, and China). Now Gandhi was going to lead hundreds of people to the Indian Ocean, the name pointedly emphasized, where Indians were going to boil seawater and make salt without paying British government tax. Designed for maximum publicity, the march lasted over three weeks and covered 240 miles. Journalists were thoughtfully invited along. When they made salt on the beach and the government did not respond, Gandhi kept on going south, at site after site—provoking the government until it had to respond or lift the salt tax. He had participants selling salt in Delhi, challenging the salt tax in the very capital of the Raj. In early May came the government's answer, as Gandhi readied a demonstration in front of a government salt works at Dharasana, [GE¹⁰⁴] fifteen miles down the coast from Dandi. It was a major crackdown, including Gandhi's arrest, a police lathi (club) charge against the demonstrators, and eventually some 70,000 jailed. There were no significant British concessions, but the numbers mobilized for the independence campaign by the Salt March and its

---

99. GE Layer 99 is a Placemark framing a view of Jallianwala Bagh, showing its proximity to the Golden Temple.

100. GE Layer 100 is a Placemark framing a view of Murree. The only major British hill-country station inside today's Pakistan, it is still used as a retreat by today's governmental and economic elite.

101. GE Layer 101 is a Placemark referencing Chauri Chaura.

102. GE Layer 102 is a Placemark referencing Sabarmati Ashram, today "Gandhi Ashram."

103. GE Layer 103 is a Placemark at Dandi Beach; click on Panoramio icon under pointer titled "dandi by jayeshdobaria98252 38277" for view of Gandhi memorial there.

104. GE Layer 104 is a Placemark at (or near?) the government salt works at Dharasana.

publicity campaign were convincing many Britons that the tipping point of public opinion was near. At some point several hundred million South Asians, motivated well enough, could make the position of the representatives of a country of several tens of millions, halfway around the world, simply untenable.

In many ways M. K. Gandhi is central to this whole drama of the end of the Raj, but his life and work took on added meaning for this author as he learned more about the whole pattern of South Asian response to the British. Go back with me now to earlier in the Raj, and even before that to the late 1700s under British East India Company rule, in search of that pattern of response.

Bengali Renaissance

The first place a response to British power dramatically showed up was in Bengal, the area which had the longest exposure to intensive British rule. Here occurred what came to be called the Bengali Renaissance, beginning with Ram Mohun Roy (1772–1833) and culminating with Rabindranath Tagore (1861–1941).

Ram Mohun Roy was born in Radhanagore, a town about thirty miles northwest of Kolkata.[GE105] Of Brahmin birth, as a young man he traveled widely in South Asia and even Tibet, learned a remarkable number of languages, and became a Pandit (a scholar of Sanskrit, especially the Hindu scriptures) of note. He was a sometime employee of the East India Company, and enthusiastically worked with Christian missionaries from Britain to emphasize the concept of monotheism—arguing that there was just one God being worshiped in Hinduism, if its origins were correctly understood. He quickly embraced a good bit of the western liberal heritage, and became a most vocal critic of *sati* (or *suttee*, the ritual burning of widows in Hinduism), and the lack of women's rights before the law. He was not uncritical of British rule: when press censorship was imposed by the East India Company in 1823, he fought it very publicly. By 1828 he and a few other Bengali Brahmin friends including Dwarkanath Tagore had founded Brahmo Samaj, the Brahma Society. They gathered Saturday evenings in north Kolkata to read from the Upanishads in Sanskrit, and then to read Roy's new translations of same in Bengali. It stressed the monotheistic interpretation of Hinduism and embraced a whole range of western-style liberal reforms. Roy was an educator of note as well, setting up the Hindu College and then the Vedanta College in Calcutta in the mid-1820s in pursuit of his reformed Hinduism/western liberal social practice. He was also a publicist who understood the modern power of the press. He went to England in 1829—ignoring the traditional view that a sea voyage would make a high caste Hindu impure—as a formal representative of the Mughal Emperor, and died there in 1833. A generation later Brahmo would become a religion of its own, separate from Hinduism, but its importance for our study is that in Roy's hands it was the first serious attempt to use Hinduism as a building block for a new kind of South Asian national consciousness.

Dwarkanath Tagore (1794–1846)—mentioned above as helping Ram Mohun Roy found Brahmo Samaj—was a wealthy landowner whose fortunes had flourished under British rule. His strictly-run estates and businesses, including western-style banks, mines, and insurance and shipping companies, made him one of the wealthiest individuals in all South Asia, and his lifestyle was so expansive as to win him the nickname "Prince." He too visited England and he too died there, in 1846. His son Debendranath Tagore (1817–1905) revived the Brahmo Samaj a decade or so after Roy's death. He was just as critical of *sati* and "idolatry" as his father's friend Roy had been, but was less and less interested in Christian parallels. A real spiritualist who won the title Maharishi ("Great Sage"), in 1863 he set up a rural religious retreat called Santiniketan, "Abode of Peace," that would later be made famous as an educational center by his youngest son, Rabindranath.

Rabindranath Tagore (1861–1941), who was born and who died in the old Tagore family mansion in Kolkata, was the true "Renaissance Man" of the Bengali Renaissance—a world-class musician, poet, essayist, and playwright, who in his old age even became a great artist. There are many scholars who have learned Bengali just so as to be able to read his works in the original! A precocious writer—he translated *Macbeth* into Bengali at age fourteen—he spent a few years in his teens studying in England. In 1891, at about age thirty, he was

---

105. GE Layer 105 is a Placemark referencing Radhanagore, showing its relation to Kolkata.

made manager of the family's estates at Shilaidah and Shazadpur in what is today Bangladesh.[GE¹⁰⁶] He was there for ten years, sometimes living on a riverboat on the Padma (Lotus) River, as the main channel of the Ganges River through the delta is known. Here in the countryside he found a cultural richness that seemed deeper to him than that of the urban culture he knew, and it helped shape his life and future work. Some of his finest poems and short stories are set in the rural life thereabouts.

In 1901 he settled at his father's old retreat, Santiniketan,[GE¹⁰⁷] to build an educational community that would integrate the best of traditional Bengali and modern western culture and practices. Some of Gandhi's Phoenix Farm people later stayed there awhile, and Gandhi himself was to spend time there his first year back in India in 1914–15. Poems Rabindranath wrote in that decade—some of considerable sadness, because of the death of his wife and two children—were collected and published in Bengali and English in 1912 as *Gitanjali* (*Song Offerings*). It was mainly this that won him the Nobel Prize for Literature in 1913; he was the first South Asian so honored. In 1915 he was knighted by the British monarchy.

Traveling the world widely in that decade, he was an ambassador for South Asian culture and a gentle spokesperson for South Asian independence. He was to some extent a South Asian patriot; in reaction to the 1919 Amritsar Massacres he very publically resigned his British knighthood. More famously, his Brahmo hymn, *Gana Jana Mana*, first sung at the 1911 Kolkata meeting of the Indian National Congress, is today's Indian national anthem:

> Thou art the ruler of the minds of all people,
> Dispenser of India's destiny.
> Thy name rouses the hearts of Punjab, Sind,
> Gujarat and Maratha,
> Of the Dravida and Orissa and Bengal;
> It echoes in the hills of the Vindhyas and Himalayas,
> mingles in the music of Jamuna and Ganges and is
> hanted by the waves of the Indian Sea.
> They pray for thy blessings and sing thy praise.
> The saving of all people waits in thy hand,
> Thou dispenser of India's destiny.
> Victory, victory, victory to thee.

(His own translation into English of the Bengali original)

But Rabindranath Tagore was never a whole-hearted nationalist. His essays on nationalism are extremely critical of "its fierce self-idolatry," as in these couple of sentences from his 1916 essay "Nationalism in India," written while visiting the United States:

> India has never had a real sense of nationalism. Even though from childhood I had been taught that the idolatry of Nation is almost better than reverence for God and humanity, I believe I have outgrown that teaching, and it is my conviction that my countrymen will gain truly their India by fighting against that education which teaches them that a country is greater than the ideals of humanity.[7]

In that same year of 1916 he wrote a short novel, "The Home and the World," that was later (1984) turned into a great film by the director Satyagrahit Rai. A young wife, content with her isolation in purdah, is persuaded by a progressive husband into coming out into the world. Instead of a moderate experience with the outside world, she has an affair and runs off with a flashy but shallow politician—perhaps an allegory express-

106. GE Layer 106 is a Placemark referencing Tagore Kuthibari, the lodge where Rabindranath lived most of the 1890s, and where he wrote some of his most famous poems. Click on Panoramio icon under pointer, titled "Art on Rabindrahath & Kuthibari," for one view.

107. GE 107 is a Placemark referencing Santiniketan. It evolved into a full-fledged college, Visva Bharati, the administration buildings of which are just a short walk east of Santiniketan.

ing Tagore's fears for how India would react to western "modernity." At the same time RabindranathTagore was very critical of Gandhi's exclusive focus on village life, which implied rejection of industrialism, international commerce, urban culture, and many attractive elements of modern western life.

Also from Bengal came other strains of modern nationalism. Surendranath Banerjea (1848–1925), also from a wealthy Brahmin family in Kolkata, and actually went to London to take the ICS exams which he passed—the second British Indian ever to do so. But he was dismissed from the ICS, dishonorably, in 1874 at the first transparent excuse. At this point Bannerjea became both educator and publicist, founding a college in Kolkata, and buying the newspaper *Bengalee* to make his case for national independence through representative government. In 1883 he hosted a meeting of the "Indian Association" in Bengal, two years before the birth of the similar Indian National Congress association meeting in Bombay (and later Bannerjea twice served as President of the Congress). After the partition of Bengal in 1905 he first led the Swadeshi movement, boycotting British goods and institutions, and in 1909 went to London to appeal for a return to a unified Bengal and for the lifting of martial law. But his insistence on following western parliamentary policies cost him all his positions of influence in South Asia by the mid-1920s, as more radical voices took the stage.

Hindu nationalist manifestations from elsewhere in British India

A Hindu reformer from Gujarat, Dayananda Saraswati, who had met some of the Bengali Tagores from Brahmo Samaj in the 1860s, began preaching his reform Hinduism in Hindi instead of Sanskrit. Agreeing with much of the liberal western reforms championed by the Brahmo Samaj, he differed with them by his belief in the divine origin of the Vedas. In Bombay in 1875 he established the more folkish Arya Samaj. For the next few years the Arya Samaj was close to, and almost merged with, the Theosophical Society formed in New York in 1875. The Arya Samaj was closely associated with the Cow Protection Movement in British India in the 1880s, aimed primarily at Muslims for whom cows were not sacred and who regularly slaughtered and ate beef. The friction between the two religious groups would explode in 1893 in Hindu-Muslim riots over much of the Raj.

Several important nationalist thinkers and actors came from Maharashtra, just south of Gujarat. Two of them were B. G. Tilak (b. 1856) and G. K. Gokhale (b. 1866), who despite remarkable personal parallels came to lead bitterly antagonistic factions in the Indian National Congress. In terms of the personal parallels, they were both from the same Brahmin caste. They were both graduates of Elphinstone College (the British college for the Bombay Presidency), and both for awhile were teachers of mathematics. In terms of differences, Tilak came to represent a more impatient, independence-now strain of Hindu nationalism, and Gokhale a more pro-British evolutionary strain.

Tilak was probably the most popular Indian nationalist before Gandhi. He joined Congress in 1890, and was one of its most radical voices. In that decade he started a patriotic Shivaji festival in honor of that great seventeenth-century Hindu warrior and Robin Hood who led a revolt against the Mughal Empire. It used familiar priests, images, and prayers, so as to appeal to Hindus who felt ill at ease in more anglicized, upper-class meetings. In 1893—perhaps motivated by the Hindu-Muslim riots of that year—Tilak started the modern Ganesh festival, in part to get Brahmins and non-Brahmins sharing experiences and discussing politics together.

Gokhale, though a decade younger, had joined Congress a year earlier in 1889. He was a great admirer of the British Liberal tradition, and especially John Stuart Mill. Having visited Ireland and having appreciated the Home Rule currents there, he actually got a British Member of Parliament from the Irish Party to come serve as Indian National Congress president in 1894. In 1895 Gokhale and Tilak were elected joint secretaries of Congress, but by 1906, a decade later, their differences about how to proceed towards independence had split Congress so badly as to cripple it as an anti-British force. Gokhale was especially close to Gandhi. He visited South Africa in 1912, such was his interest in Gandhi's civil rights movement there. In July of 1914 when Gandhi returned permanently to India it was Gokhale—called by Gandhi his mentor—who told him to take a year and get to know India again before he made any public pronouncements on matters there.

Gokhale's death in 1915 robbed Gandhi of a mentor, but enabled rival factions of Congress to bury the hatchet at the 1916 Lucknow annual meeting of Congress. There was at least a temporary rapprochement between mainstream Hindu and Muslim nationalists here too; it was called the Lucknow Pact, on which more later when we examine the Muslim response in more detail.

During these same WW I years, however, some of the more extreme strains of majority Hindu nationalism came together as the Hindu Mahasabha ("Great Assembly"), the first Raj-wide communal (read: religious) party. It glorified Hindu history, and resisted all Congress Party concessions to the Muslims. Gandhi's future assassin had once been a member. In 1925 the like-minded RSS had been founded (the initials of the Hindi words meaning National Volunteer Organization). It was a paramilitary group much like its folkish contemporaries of the right wing politics in many European countries, in this case sworn to protect the interests of the Hindu nation, as it saw it. Like some of the Afrikaner paramilitary groups we saw in an earlier chapter, during the '30s and early WW II it was attracted by Hitler's folkish ideology and ethnic cleansing practice. On the positive side, it had and still has some history of community organizing and social relief work.

Back on the Punjabi part of our GT Road corridor, you can see the effect of all this majority Hindu nationalistic thought on a single individual, Lala Lajput Rai. He was born in 1865, making him four years younger than Rabindranath Tagore and four years older than Gandhi. His birthplace was Jagraon,[GE108] squarely in the middle of India's current state of Punjab. In 1881, when he was just sixteen, he first came to Lahore (some eighty-five miles northwest of his hometown) to study law, and later practiced there. Although Hindu by upbringing, he had been somewhat attracted by Islam. His father, in fact, had all but converted to Islam (probably kept from doing so only by knowing his wife would have thereupon gone back to her relatives, taking the children with her), and had insisted that his son study Urdu, Persian, and Arabic. But the son's new Hindu nationalist associations in Lahore changed all that, as he later remembered in his autobiographical writings:

> When I came to Lahore [in the early 1880s], Islam lost its charm for me. The company I had in Lahore made my mind turn away from Islam and what is more important, I became attached to Hinduism and Hindus. This attachment was not so much theological or religious, it was nationalistic.[8]

In 1882 a great public debate blew up in Lahore about which of the two major northern written languages to use. The debate was a lot more interesting to Rai than his law studies:

> The Hindi-Urdu controversy taught me my first lesson in Hindu nationalism. My mind took a turn at this time and there was no turning back thereafter. Early training and parental teaching should have enlisted my support on the side of Urdu; that way lay personal gain for me, for I had spent years in the study of Persian and was fairly well acquainted with Urdu literature, whilst of Hindi I did not know even the alphabet. But as I became convinced that political solidarity demanded the spread of Hindi and Devanagri, I brushed aside all personal considerations and started propaganda for Hindi . . . .[9]

He was making public speeches in favor of Hindi and in opposition to Urdu before he ever even memorized the Hindi alphabet!

Rai read a biography of Giuseppe Mazzini of "Young Italy" fame, and was much impressed by his Liberal Nationalism from the 1830s:

> The profound nationalism of this great Italian, his troubles and tribulations, his moral superiority, his broad humanitarian sympathies, enthralled me. I began to translate his *Duties of Man* into Urdu.

The last chapter of Lala Lajpat Rai's life reflected this upsurge in Hindu nationalism. He sharply disagreed with Gandhi when the latter called off the Non-Cooperation campaign after the Chauri Chaura killings of 1922, thinking—as had Mazzini—that some violence, though hopefully a minimum, would be necessary to achieve independence. When in 1927 the British Government put together a commission (the Simon Commission, after its head) of seven British MPs to visit India and decide its future evolution—with not a single Indian voice on it—it was met with a Raj-wide strike and protest marches. When the Commission got to Lahore in 1928, it was Lala Lajput Rai who organized and led the protest marches against it. Club wielding police broke up the crowd and seriously injured Rai, who died of his injuries a few months later. Today a statue of him stands in the

---

108. GE Layer 108 is a Placemark referencing Jagraon, near the center of today's Indian state of Punjab. It's about ten miles south of the Sutlej River and twenty miles SW of the GT Road.

central square of Shimla. There is most emphatically not one in Lahore where the critical part of his life passed, because Lahore was to go to Muslim and Urdu-speaking Pakistan in the division of British India.

The Muslim response

The Muslim response to both the colonial British rule and to the Hindu majority nationalism growing up in the Raj has crept into this narrative in several places, and some treatment of it is overdue. It had pro-western and anti-western strains, over time, and in this way ran parallel to the Hindu community's spectrum of response to western presence. It also swayed back and forth from tending to unite with Hindus to forge a truly subcontinental alliance against the British, and with seeing the British as their real guarantor of Muslim rights in the face of some future majority Hindu nation.

One foundational figure was Syed Ahmad Khan, born in Delhi in 1817. His father afforded him a western-style education, and he began as a clerk with the British East India Company and progressed to a lower-level judgeship. Like Ram Mohun Roy and Dwarkanath Tagore on the Hindu side (though they were a generation older), he was very much a proponent of western liberal reforms, and tried to harmonize them with his own religious tradition of Islam. By mid-century he had set up schools and founded a Scientific Society, sounding much like the contemporary Syrian Scientific Society in Beirut we talked about in the last chapter. He stayed loyal to the British in the Sepoy Mutiny/War of Independence, and later wrote an essay, "Causes of the Indian Revolt," that assigned root causes for the rebellion mainly to the Hindus. It was apparently widely read in British officialdom.

Some ten years after the Mutiny, he was transferred to Banaras/Varanasi—just when a strong movement for replacing Urdu with Hindi was taking place there. The rhetoric and passion of the pro-Hindi (and mainly Hindu) side convinced him that the two religious communities had to have separate political futures. There might not be overt religious persecution, but Muslims were at the very least bound to be frozen out of top government jobs in a single state with a vast Hindu majority, he thought. The only way to keep that from happening was to begin a new sort of education among Indian Muslims as quickly as possible, preparing them for a transition to Muslim independence in South Asia. A trip Syed Khan made to England in 1874 gave him the idea of setting up a "Muslim Oxford or Cambridge" in India, and in 1875 he opened Aligarh Muslim University. [GE[109]] Aligarh was in the middle of "the doab," that slice of land between the Yamuna and Ganges Rivers that is central to the GT Road corridor; the city was about fifty miles north of Agra and seventy-five miles southeast of Delhi. This was at first a "public" school (in the British educational lexicon this word means what Americans would call an expensive, college-prep "private" school), but within two years he had raised the money to support university-level education there. It was designed to merge the best of western education (the language of instruction was English) with the best of the South Asian Islamic tradition.

Aligarh University was the intellectual nest where the future "Pakistan" was hatched. In the last quarter of the nineteenth century, says one historian, "Syed Ahmed Khan's Aligarh men toured India persuading Muslims to repudiate Congress."[10] By 1886 Syed Khan had organized an "All-India Muhammedan Educational Conference," trying to unite Muslim opinion across the Raj. He died in 1898 (in Aligarh, fittingly), but in the next ten years events happened that would have delighted him.

In 1906, in the wake of the 1905 British decision to split Bengal into a Hindu western half and a Muslim eastern half—wildly unpopular with the greater Hindu community, and setting in motion a huge boycott of British goods and even educational institutions—some thirty-six Muslim leaders (including Aga Khan III, the leader of the world's Ismaili sect of Islam, and a major supporter of Syed Khan's Aligarh Muslim University), asked for an interview with the current British Viceroy, Lord Minto. They assured him the Muslim community supported the partition of Bengal, refused to join the boycott, and in general supported the British rule. In turn they asked that the British safeguard them, a minority community. Lord Minto pledged to do this, no doubt in part because this gave him a new weapon to use against the majority Hindu nationalist groups. Within two or

---

109. GE Layer 109 is a Placemark referencing Aligarh and the university. The Pushpin icon is directly over the University Mosque; notice how the main quadrangle of the university, including Strachey Hall, is automatically oriented towards Mecca by being oriented to the mosque.

three years he was making good on his word, appointing Muslims to councils and representative bodies in numbers out of proportion to the relative size of the Muslim community. But the immediate response of the thirty-six is even more interesting: they were so encouraged by the interview with the Viceroy that they went from Calcutta (Kolkata) to Dacca (Dhaka), the biggest city of East Bengal and largely Muslim, and founded the Muslim League.[GE110] This was the institution that led the drive for an independent Pakistan, which would be formed forty-one years later.

It was not, however, a smooth, inexorable road from the 1906 Muslim League to the 1947 Pakistan. And the other key figure of modern South Asian Muslim nationalism at times in his life actually disagreed with the project! This was Muhammad Ali Jinnah, born in 1876 in Karachi, the big port city just north of the delta of the Indus River.[GE111] His father, a wealthy businessman, sent him to London for a law degree (where Gandhi had gone for the same reason, seven years before Ali Jinnah). Jinnah was apparently fascinated by the proceedings of the House of Commons, where the Visitors' Gallery has traditionally been open to the public to watch debate, and spent a good deal of time there. He was back in Karachi by 1896, about twenty years old, and then he opened a law practice in Bombay to recruit the failing family fortunes.

His first venture into national-level politics was in 1906 when he went to Kolkata for the yearly meeting of the Indian National Congress. He was far, far from being allied with the thirty-six Muslim luminaries who spoke with the Viceroy and then founded the Muslim League that same year. He was friends with the moderate Hindu leader G. K. Gokhale, and in fact aspired to be "a Muslim Gokhale." He did not join the Muslim League until 1913, and then in 1916 he led it into an alliance with Congress called The Lucknow Pact (Congress and the Muslim League had scheduled their yearly meetings at the same time and place, Lucknow, to facilitate this). [GE112] They agreed on demands for a constitution, thus presenting a united front to the British; and Congress in turn agreed to the idea of separate Muslim electorates.

Just after WW I a special issue for many Muslims in the British Raj was the fate of the Ottoman Empire and the Caliphate. The Ottoman Empire was the last substantial independent Muslim state in the world, and its fragmentation and disappearance was troubling to most Muslims. Compounding this, the Sultan of the Ottoman Empire had for centuries also claimed the title of Caliph, Deputy of the Prophet. By 1919 the Ottoman Empire was in danger of dismemberment at the hand of Britain and its allies, and the future existence of any Sultan or Caliph was much in doubt. For five years the "Khilafat" movement, as it was pronounced in South Asia, was a focus for Muslim antagonism to the British Empire. It only ended when in 1924 Kemal Ataturk declared the Turkish Republic to be a totally secular state, even changing the alphabet from Arabic to Latin.

Gandhi in deeper context

The pages above hopefully give a hint of the complexity of the situation Gandhi found when he arrived in India in July of 1914. G. K. Gokhale, as you have seen called by Gandhi his mentor, knew Gandhi was out of touch with the Indian situation from spending more than twenty years in South Africa, and encouraged him to make no public pronouncements for a year. In 1915 Gokhale died, leaving Gandhi mentorless. No one would have guessed then how quickly Gandhi was able to make himself the pivotal figure of events in the British Raj. His call for direct action to protest inequities was insistent and backed by a flood of publications and private correspondence. His requirement of non-violent behavior in confronting inequity was absolute. No one else in the Raj came anywhere close to combining those two, and Gandhi's call for a moral foundation for a resistance to imperialism had a strong appeal all across a subcontinent whose people's quest for spirituality went back thousands of years.

Gandhi honored Gokhale's request for his silence that first year back in India. He was content to be a social worker in his tiny corner of Gujarat, in the edge of Ahmedebad, which was fast becoming a city of factories. Then in 1916 and 1917 he broke onto the Raj-wide stage with his Champaran satyagraha. Champaran was the

110. GE Layer 110 is a Placemark referencing the palace of Ahsan Manzil, the palace of the Nawab of Dhaka that dates to the mid-nineteenth century. This is where the Muslim League was formed.
111. GE Layer 111 is a Placemark referencing Karachi.
112. GE Layer 112 is a Placemark referencing Lucknow.

very northwestern district of the province of Bihar, and as such is partly in and partly out of our rather arbitrarily drawn GT Road corridor. [GE[113]] Peasant farmers there were being forced to grow indigo as a cash crop by the large landowners, many of them by this time British, whose demands were backed by British forces. Famine and near-famine resulted, and there were major revolts in the towns of Pipra in 1914 and Turkaulia in 1916. Gandhi went there to lead mass non-violent protest, disobeyed a government order to leave, and established an ashram there to give it all his brand of spiritual leadership. He recruited dozens of bright young intellectuals to come live there as a base for investigating the causes of the famine—producing the kind of basic statistical research no open-minded Briton could ignore, and telling the story of the human tragedy unfolding there. This was the first, and in many ways, the model for a quarter-century of such satyagrahas launched by Gandhi. It was also one of the most successful, with the British backing off new tax rates and returning land confiscated from rebels.

In 1919 Gandhi successfully yoked together the mainly Hindu Swaraj (Self-rule) movement and the Muslim Khilafat movement. Key Muslim leaders pledged non-violence, and a united front was presented to the British that was so promising that Gandhi predicted Swaraj in one year. But in 1922 when Gandhi called off Non-Cooperation campaign in the wake of the Chauri Chaura police killings, many of his Muslim allies drifted away. And in 1924 the Khilafat issue became a dead letter, as Turkey became a secular state. For the next twenty years and more Gandhi desperately tried to find Muslims to represent in a united spiritual satyagraha. He found only a few, the so-called "Congress Muslims," not enough ever to make a convincing claim to a united spiritual front. Syed Ahmad Khan's "Aligarh men" had been too successful in working for Muslim unity and a future separate independence.

By 1920 Ali Jinnah had broken with Gandhi and resigned from Congress to focus on the Muslim League. He disagreed with Gandhi's mass protests, thinking it would lead to irresolvable Hindu–Muslim conflict. Apparently disgusted with politics, he moved to England and lived from 1931–36. Upon his return he seems to have quickly converted to the "Two Nation" theory. It argued that, in a South Asian context, for Muslims religion was more important than language or anything else in determining their ethnicity—and was the key ideological step in demanding an independent Muslim state.

On the Hindu side the Nehrus were one important family attracted early on into Gandhi's orbit. Motilal Nehru, a wealthy lawyer in Allahabad where the Yamuna and Ganges meet, became interested in Gandhi early in the latter's career. Motilal was a founder of the Swaraj, or Self-rule, Party. His son Jawaharlal Nehru was born in 1889, making him about twenty years younger than Gandhi. Jawaharlal had a series of private tutors, and then went on to the best of upper-crust English education: two years at Harrow, three at Cambridge University, and another two preparing for a law career at Inner Temple, London. Jawaharlal emerged with a degree in Natural Science and qualified as a barrister, though he turned out to be less interested in the practice of law and even more interested in politics than his father.

The younger Nehru first met Gandhi at the 1916 Lucknow meeting of Congress, the one that produced the Congress–Muslim League Pact. He was one of the key young intellectuals to join the Champaran satyagraha, and counted himself an enthusiastic disciple of Gandhi's by 1919, the post-war year of Rowlatt satyagraha and Amritsar Massacre. He threw himself into Congress work, first becoming General Secretary of the Congress in 1923. In the process he learned a great deal about the countryside, both in terms of personal experience and in terms of a close study of economic relations there. The year 1928 was something of a banner year for Nehru father and son. In 1928 the elder Nehru presided at the yearly meeting of Congress, this year in Calcutta. The younger Nehru was just back from a two-year tour of Europe, having been especially impressed by the young Soviet Union (still in the NEP and not yet in the grip of Stalin), and gave his "Nehru Report." It recommended Dominion status for British India (the status of Canada and other former parts of the British Empire, a step beyond simple Home Rule). It emphasized central government over local ones, and envisioned a free India replacing the British Raj as overlord of the princely states. It was Motilal Nehru who asked Gandhi to come out of rural retreat and help unify Congress and its possible allies in pursuit of these objectives.

---

113. GE Layer 113 is a Folder containing a Polygon showing Champaran, and two Placemarks for the towns of Pipra and Turkaulia.

There were two quick outcomes. One was that by 1930, with no appreciable British concessions, Gandhi decided that complete independence was the only proper goal. This is what determined him on a new wave of satyagraha, which included the brilliant Salt March. The other was that even more Muslims were driven away from Congress. The Nehru Report, with its insistence on central government authority, meant the end of any separate Muslim electorates. The Hindu-Muslim violence had been fairly well limited to cities in the early 1920s. By the later 1920s it spread to the countryside. Successful as the Salt March of 1930 was—and there were major anti-British disturbances in every province in the Raj related to it—it attracted almost no Muslim support. This was not a particularly good augury for any future united South Asian state.

Motilal Nehru died in 1931, and from this time on Jawaharlal Nehru, just forty-two years old at his father's death, was seen as Gandhi's chief lieutenant and political heir apparent. When the British Raj gave limited autonomy to the provinces in the mid-1930s, Congress dominated the elections. Many Muslims called this "the Hindu Raj," and were motivated to much political organization on their own part in these 1937–39 years. When World War II involved Britain in the fall of 1939, the current Viceroy committed British India to the war with no approval from, or even consultation with, these Congress-dominated provincial governments. Most Congress leaders, seeing Congress as a partner with the British in ruling, were enraged at not being consulted, and resigned their positions. Most Muslims were on their side happy to see this development, since it ended "the Hindu Raj." In 1940 in Lahore, at the first annual meeting of the Muslim League held after WW II began, the League passed a "Pakistan Resolution" calling for an independent state made up of the Muslim majority parts of the Raj. "Pakistan" means "Land of the Pure" in Urdu—a value-loaded word, wouldn't you say?

The British, hard put to it in the war, sent delegations with hints of self-government in the unspecified future, but Gandhi (no doubt remembering how similar British hints in World War I had been followed by the Rowlatt Act) insisted on immediate independence. In August 1942 he led the "Quit India" movement, his last satyagraha. The British government in response arrested every important Congress leader, Gandhi among them. They spent most of the duration of the war in jail. Some parts of the Raj were so rebellious they could only be subdued with bombing by British aircraft. Hindus in general were non-cooperative with the British during the war and Muslims were generally supportive of the British, which helps explain what happened next.

SECTION F: INDEPENDENCE

Partition

In June of 1945, with the war over in Europe and with Japanese forces being driven back to Japan proper and the end in sight, a conference of major political leaders was convoked by the British Viceroy in Shimla (naturally enough; it was still the summer HQ of the British government). Looking back, this was the last serious chance for a single state to come out of the British Raj. The general proposal set forth by the Viceroy was of a single state with separate Muslim electorates. Ali Jinnah and Jawaharlal Nehru could agree neither on the specific issue of how the Muslim congressmen would be chosen, nor on the larger issue of Muslim autonomy within a South Asian state. Important Congress leaders such as Vallabhbhai Patel saw the continuing attempts to compromise between factions as so much unnecessary delay of independence; let the Muslims have their part, and let us get on with ruling our part, he said.

Since Muslims were only in the majority in the west and the east, partition of the land—splitting the Punjab into a Muslim west and a non-Muslim (Sikh and Hindu, mainly) east, and splitting Bengal into a Muslim east and a Hindu west—was the only real alternative. In July of 1947 the British government sent Lord Mountbatten, a member of the British royal family with some famous World War II naval command and leadership experience, to India as its last Viceroy. He was charged with splitting the Raj into two independent parts at least by August 15, 1948. Mountbatten decided the quicker the better (at least for the British forces and population involved!), and gave boundary-drawing commissions in the Punjab and in Bengal a month—one month!—to finish drawing their two lines. There was bound to be some violence in any such partition, but this precipitate action guaranteed it would be horrendous.

Even before the formal independence ceremonies of August 15, 1947, the more far-sighted Hindus and Sikhs had begun selling out and leaving (future) Pakistan for India, and their Muslim counterparts were similarly leaving (future) India. But with the formal declaration of Partition in August of 1947 it turned into a panicky, bloody two-way exodus. It was one of the greatest short-term migrations in recorded human history. Perhaps twenty million relocated, passing each other going opposite ways on the same roads, and a million died, most of them violently.

The Partition transformed both ends of our GT road corridor, and even had surprising influence in the middle. Virtually all Hindus and Sikhs left the new West Pakistan, and most Hindus left East Pakistan. There were also huge Muslim migrations into West and East Pakistan, though in India there was not the almost total "ethnic cleansing" that occurred especially in West Pakistan: more Muslims stayed in India than left (even today India has some 200 million Muslims, more than either today's Pakistan with 190 million or Bangladesh with 170 million). The difference was mainly caused by the strong anti-communal, pro-secular state rhetoric and actions of Gandhi, Nehru, Vallabhbhai Patel, and others.

In particular this was Gandhi's last but finest hour. In December of 1947 he went to Kolkata, where the communal violence (religious civil war!) had started and was still raging, and went on a fast to the death to protest it. Such was the respect of Muslims as well as Hindus for his spirituality and his long service to the independence movement, that the newspaper headlines of rioting were gradually replaced by headlines about his deteriorating health. By month's end the city riots had subsided into peace. In January of 1948 he went to Delhi and began a new fast to protest communal violence there, as well as the new Indian government's freezing of US $50 million due to Pakistan. On January 18 the government relented and released the money. On January 30, 1948, Gandhi was famously assassinated, in New Delhi not far south of the Rajpath,[GE114] as he was being helped to prayers in his still-weakened state. The assassin was a Hindu nationalist with past associations with Mahasabha and the RSS. Gandhi's funeral attracted a million or more; his cremation site is a memorial garden still visited by hundreds of thousands of people yearly.[GE115]

The Punjab was in instant turmoil on each side of the new border. On the India side, hundreds of refugee camps were set up in East Punjab. The single largest refugee camp was in Thanesar, for Hindus the site of the beginning of the world's creation as well as for Krishna's revelations on the Kurufield to Arjuna recorded in the *Bhagavad-Gita*, you may recall. Built for 100,000, three times that many eventually crowded into it. So many Punjabi refugees settled in Delhi that they permanently changed the character of the city, becoming its dominant businessmen and local politicians. Whole new townships, such as Faridabad less than twenty miles down the GT Road from Delhi towards Agra, sprang up.[GE116] The Sikhs crowded into what was left of the Punjabi state in India. Bad blood between them and Muslims went back to late Mughal times, and they were not about to live in a Muslim state. Only a small part of the total population of the former Raj (perhaps 2 percent), they were nevertheless fairly concentrated, and were certainly ethnically distinctive and desirous of their own state. From their point of view the Hindus had gotten their state, the Muslims had gotten theirs, but they, the Sikhs, had not gotten theirs. And on the West Pakistani side of Punjab an approximately equal number of Muslim refugees came flooding in, mainly into the larger cities, particularly Karachi and Lahore, with similar refugee camps and chaos.

On the other end of our corridor the already huge city of Kolkata was swamped by a tide of Hindu refugees from East Pakistan. They overwhelmed the infrastructure, and in desperation the new shanty towns began creating their own unofficial governments and public works programs. In a sense they were worse off than the Hindu refugees in the northwest, where at least there was some productive land vacated by emigrating Muslims available for resettlement. And again you had the mirror image of the refugee problem across the border in East Pakistan, especially in the city of Dhaka, one of the most violence-prone cities of the whole Partition.

---

114. GE Layer 114 is a Placemark at the site of Gandhi's assassination; it is in New Delhi less than a mile south of the Rajpath.

115. GE Layer 115 is a Placemark at the cremation site; the Devanagri script on the memorial reads *"He Ram,"* "Oh Rama," sometimes translated "Oh God," Gandhi's last words.

116. GE Layer 116 is a Placemark referencing Faridabad, framing it in relation to Delhi.

Kashmir

Of all the residual problems left by the boundary-drawing commissions, Kashmir may be the longest-lasting and most intractable: what the Palestinian issue is to the Mideast, Kashmir is to South Asia. This Himalayan mountain valley of great natural beauty, with a Muslim majority as clear as 60 percent, was assigned not to Pakistan but to India. Perhaps it was because the landlords were mostly Hindu, or because of the maneuvers of the current "Prince of Jammu and Kashmir" who was faced with Muslim terrorist/freedom fighters who struck early there—whatever the original reasons, it has remained an open sore between Pakistan and India, a shallowly buried coal easily fanned into flames.[GE117] Three of the four Indo-Pak wars of the last seventy-five years were of this origin. As late as 1999 the two countries went to war in Kashmir, a war that closely concerned the whole world because Pakistan had just joined India as a country with nuclear weapons. Fortunately the war never became nuclear, or spread beyond Kashmir. The Kashmiri issue still smolders, however, and the nukes are still ready for launching, a sobering thought.

The new Pakistan

The two-part Pakistan that came into being in 1947 kept Dominion status with the British Commonwealth until 1956, at which point it broke away and became an independent republic, "The Islamic Republic of Pakistan." The original capital of the country in 1947 was Karachi, the port that was the country's biggest city. But by 1960 it was decided to build a new capital city, Islamabad, closer to the geographic center of the country and hard by the military headquarters of Rawalpindi. Rawalpindi is on the old Grand Trunk Road, and the center of Islamabad is only seven miles north; Rawalpindi and Islamabad, in fact, have virtually grown together as one urban area.[GE118]

The new state got off to a rocky start for both specific and general reasons. Specific reasons included sudden changes in leadership. Ali Jinnah died in 1948, and his former right-hand-man Liaqat Ali Khan, the new Prime Minister, was assassinated in Rawalpindi in 1951. The garden/park where he was assassinated was named Liaqat Bagh (this is where Benazir Bhutto, former Prime Minister, would in her turn be assassinated in 2007 upon her return to a Pakistan under the military government of Pervez Musharraf).[GE119]

From the very beginning there was friction between the mainly Bengali-speaking population of East Pakistan and the mainly Urdu-speaking population of West Pakistan. East Pakistan, originally with slightly more population than West Pakistan, still had a smaller allotment of legislative seats. West Pakistan's moves to make Urdu the official language and thus replace the local Bengali triggered riots and guerrilla war against the government. In 1970 two things happened. First, a protest party in East Pakistan won all but 2 of the 162 seats available. Second, an enormous cyclone (the regional name for what we call a hurricane) devastated the country, with not much in the way of efficient help from the West Pakistani-dominated government. The result was a civil war in 1971, which India entered on the side of East Pakistan—thus creating Bangladesh and thoroughly humiliating West Pakistan, now just Pakistan.

Another general reason for the rocky start, and the generally rocky road Pakistani governments have walked—and this is just for the former West Pakistan, today's Pakistan—is that there were serious independence movements from the Pakhtun (Pashtuns), part of whose forty million population lives in Afghanistan, and from Sindhis, and from Baluchis—all of whom resent what they think of as Punjabi dictatorship. Under the Raj even the whole weight of subcontinental British India had trouble controlling the Northwest Frontier, as you've seen, and the Punjabi part of Pakistan, populous and technologically advanced though it is, brings much less weight to bear.

General reasons also include what seems to be an unbridgeable divide in Pakistan between a part of the population that will only be satisfied with a theocratic Islamic state run according to Sharia law, and a very westernized part that feels it can only live in a progressive, secular state. When the Soviets invaded Afghanistan

---

117. GE Layer 117 is a Placemark framing a view of Kashmir. The red lines are disputed boundary claims; the orange line is the current military control line.

118. GE Layer 118 is a Placemark framing an overview of Rawalpindi and Islamabad.

119. GE Layer 119 is a Placemark referencing Rawalpindi's Liaqat Bagh.

in 1979, we in the U.S. were delighted to be able to do to them what they had done to us in Vietnam—provide sophisticated weapons to the insurgents and discomfit our rival without much danger to our own troops. Peshawar was the main launching point of such teams, mainly through the Khyber Pass. We armed the wealthy Saudi citizen Osama bin Laden and his group. The name Al-Qaeda, "the base," seems to have come from the computer "database" bin Laden used to keep track of all the allied groups. With the Soviet pullout in 1988 bin Laden shifted his goal to the next enemy of his fundamentalist brand of Wahhabi Islam, his former arms supplier the U.S., with the resulting destruction of large passenger aircraft, Manhattan's twin World Trade Center towers, and part of Washington's Pentagon on September 11, 2001. The equally fundamentalist Taliban had filled the power vacuum left in Afghanistan when the Soviets left, and gave bin Laden a home. With the subsequent U.S. invasion of Afghanistan, rival elements in Pakistan were so balanced that the state played a two-part game with the United States—on the one hand formal ally and key source of information, provider of land bases from which to operate, and on the other the home of very popular anti-American sentiment, with elements of the army and the ISI, Pakistan's version of the CIA, apparently giving aid and shelter to elements of both Taliban and Al-Qaeda. On May 2, 2011, U.S. special forces raided bin Laden's secret mansion outside Abbotabad—less than a mile off the main Karakorum Highway and just twenty miles north of our GT Road corridor[GE[120]]—and killed him. No word of the raid was given to Pakistani officials, lest it be leaked to bin Laden by sympathizers. Immediate emotions in Pakistan included anger at violation of sovereignty and humiliation at being so impotent in the face of U.S. power. It clouds the future of U.S.-Pakistani relations, and yet Pakistan as a nuclear power—to date the only majority Muslim state to be so—has to be taken into serious American policy consideration.

It also makes the civilian government more insecure. Whenever government seemed paralyzed by one or another of these dilemmas discussed above, the Pakistani military stepped in to take control: from 1958–69, from 1969–71, from 1977–78, and from 1999–2008—as of this writing roughly half of Pakistan's existence.

Population growth in Pakistan has been extremely fast, with the population virtually quintupling from 40 million in 1947 to today's 190 million. While not the poorest state in South Asia, the population growth there has soaked up much of the economic growth that might otherwise have gone to improvement in standard of living. In terms of economics, Pakistan started out as fairly private property- and free enterprise-oriented, but by the 1970s went heavily into national control of transport and manufacturing. Though there has been some lifting of state control, over half of Pakistan's economic output still comes from the nationalized sector of the economy. In a way this was the mirror opposite of Indian economic strategy, which was very state socialist, top down, from the very beginning until 1991, with a radical shift then to free enterprise.

The Republic of India

In 1950, after a three-year transition in which Lord Mountbatten still played a role as Governor-General, India formally became an independent republic and the world's largest democracy.

During that transition period one of the most pressing problems—and solution of same, if one's goal is modern national integration—was the new Indian state's dealing with the semi-independent principalities. About 40 percent of formerly British-controlled territory in the new "India" was made up of the "princely states," only half-absorbed by the Raj. They varied in size from the huge Hyderabad in the central south down to postage-stamp principalities. The basic agreement earlier forced on them by the British had been that local rule would be left to the princely families, IF they paid stipulated taxes to the British, and IF they gave control of their foreign affairs to the British. Now, with the British pulling out, many of them expected their own independence, independent of India (or Pakistan). With Mountbatten's support, Vallabhbhai Patel launched a brilliant carrot-and-stick campaign with the 565 princely states, appealing to the greater patriotism of the rulers, promising cash payments ("privy purses") for extended periods to the rulers if they would commit to joining

---

120. GE Layer 120 is a Placemark referencing bin Laden's compound; lots of recent Panoramio icons nearby to explore. The house itself was destroyed by the Pakistani government; use the historical imagery took with its time slider to go back in time to see it in aerial photos.

the new India, but holding out the threat of force if such decisions were not made voluntarily. It worked in all but a handful of cases, and Patel had no qualms about sending the army in to take over the largest holdout, Hyderabad.

Delhi was of course the choice as new capital city, as the new government inherited the almost-new "New Delhi" with its functioning government ministries and office buildings. Most of the power of Parliament in this new republic was vested in its lower house, the *Lok Sabha*, or Popular Assembly. It met, and still meets, in Parliament House, a colonial structure first opened for business in 1927 as a key part of building New Delhi. [GE[121]] Jawaharlal Nehru, chosen by Congress as India's first Prime Minister, chose as his residence in Delhi the Teen Murti mansion (the "Three Statues" house, because it was close to the World War I memorial of that name).[GE[122]] British-built as part of the creation of "New" Delhi, it had formerly served as the residence of the Commander-in-Chief of the British army.

India's new linguistic states

The Indian government had no sooner settled the princely state issue than the thorny issue of language states emerged. As far back as 1928, the Indian National Congress had organized itself along linguistic lines. In 1947, however, Congress looked at the chaos of redrawing the political map (on top of the Pakistan-India redrawing already done by the British!), and postponed its commitment to language-based states. For this, however, they suffered in the 1952 elections. Then a Telugu-speaking martyr from Madras/Chennai, Potti Shriramulu, starved himself to death in the cause of a Telugu-speaking "Andhra" (named after an ancient kingdom) state. Huge riots broke out, with millions of dollars of property values destroyed and some loss of life. Nehru had to capitulate. A central government commission worked on the exceedingly complex problem on into 1955, and in 1956 Nehru announced the "Reorganization of States," further dividing India into fourteen states and six union provinces. Most of these 1956 changes dealt with the south of India, including of course an Andra Pradesh. And the principle continued to work later. In 1960 Bombay was split into a Marathi-speaking Maharashtra and a Gujarati-speaking Gujarat. This linguistic principle changed the administrative shape of our GT Road corridor in 1966 with Punjab divided into a Punjab state proper with a majority of Sikhs, and a Haryana in the west (and a mountainous Himal Pradesh in the north that achieved full statehood in 1971). Further east on our corridor, in 2000 Bihar was split into a northern state of Bihar proper and a southern state of Jharkhand, not so much on linguistic lines as on ethnicity and terrain—the hill country tribal groups that had worked for separation from the mainly Hindu flatlanders for decades had their ambitions at least partly satisfied with Jharkhand.[GE[123]]

Nehru's economic development plans

Nehru may have shared with Mahatma Gandhi a passion for a state in which people of all religions were treated as equals. In terms of economic development ideas, however, they were worlds apart. Gandhi was, in terms of the modern world, an agrarian romantic who saw village life as the ideal. Nehru, given the modern choice between capitalism and socialism, leaned strongly towards the latter. He had visited the Soviet Union in 1927 at age thirty-eight, and been very impressed with the progress and fervent idealism in the system. The result was a state economic planning system that even included Soviet-style Five Year Plans for industrialization. One star attraction of this, the Bhakra-Nangal dam, is well inside our corridor.[GE[124]] In 1952 work began on what

---

121. GE Layer 121 is a Placemark referencing Parliament House; click on Panoramio icon under pointer titled "Parliament House on Republic Day" for lighted nighttime view.

122. GE Layer 122 is a Placemark referencing the Teen Murti house. There are no Photos icons with pictures as of this writing, as befits a private, guarded government building; but an Images search of "Teen Murti" in Google has a good many pictures, including one of the statue for which the house is named.

123. GE Layer 123 shows these modern GT corridor states as colored Polygons (a refresher from early in the chapter when they were introduced).

124. GE Layer 124 is a Placemark referencing the Bhakra-Nangal dam; it is on the Sutlej River well within our corridor.

at this date, and at almost 700′ in height, was the second-highest dam in the world. It was to generate lots of hydropower for industry and also to provide water for new irrigation canals (particularly for those refugees who had flocked in during Partition from better-irrigated lands now on Pakistan's side of the Punjab). It was opened by Nehru to great fanfare in 1954.

Indira Gandhi

To this point the headline names in this chapter have been almost exclusively male ones. With Prime Ministers Indira Gandhi in India, Benazir Bhutto in Pakistan, and Khaleda Zia in Bangladesh, that would change. These were women who came to power in large part because of the positions of fathers or husbands, but they became fully independent heads of government themselves.

Indira Gandhi, despite similarity of family name, was no kin to M. K. Gandhi. She was Nehru's only child, born in Allahabad in 1917. Her earliest memories were of the independence struggle—the burning of foreign items of clothing in the Swadeshi ("Self-help") movement, various family members going off to prison (her father Jawaharlal served a total of nine years in prison terms). When her mother Kamala contracted tuberculosis and was sent to a sanitarium in Switzerland, Indira went with her for a year. She did more secondary education back in India, and was sent by her father to a college prep school in Britain and then on to Oxford. Her mother died in 1936, when Indira was nineteen. In 1942, against her father's wishes she married a Parsi, Feroze Gandhi, and they set up housekeeping in Allahabad. Later that same year she was arrested for protesting British rule, and looked on it as her proudest hour: her grandfather, mother, and father had all done the same.

When India became independent in 1947 she became her father's secretary and hostess, and moved with her two sons to New Delhi. She traveled widely with him, everywhere from the U.S. to the U.S.S.R. Nehru nominated her to head the Indian National Congress Party in 1959. Upon her father's death in 1964, the new Prime Minister, Lal Bahadur Shastri, appointed her Minister of Information and Broadcasting. When Shastri had a heart attack in 1966, Indira became acting Prime Minister. In elections later that year she was elected in her own right: the third Prime Minister in India, and the second woman Prime Minister in the world. Over the next eighteen years she would be the most famous and powerful woman in the world.

She was still Prime Minister in 1971 when friction between East and West Pakistan turned into a civil war. When West Pakistan launched an air raid against the rebels in early December, it gave Indira the reason she needed to enter the conflict. She had set the stage beautifully with her diplomacy with other major countries in the world, and now the Indian armed forces performed very well. Pakistan's army in East Pakistan surrendered on December 16, and East Pakistan quickly became Bangladesh. In the long run this added to the (West) Pakistan–India hostility, but in the short run Indira Gandhi got the bounce in the polls that successful, short wars tend to bring.

Domestic economic ills and a tendency to authoritarianism were her undoing. Her immediate response to extreme poverty and food shortage was to declare a "national emergency" to control rioters in 1975, and soon added to it a heavy press censorship. Her son Sanjay championed a heavy-handed slum clearance program and an aggressive family planning program, both of which were public relations disasters, and she lost the 1977 elections to the Janata, or People's, Party. Janata lifted the emergency decrees, and launched investigations into suspicious Congress activity during Indira's term as Prime Minister, but it had no agreed positive program. When infighting brought the government down, Indira Gandhi and Congress Party came storming back to power in 1980 on a "Government That Works!" slogan.

In 1982 the dominant Sikh political party passed a resolution calling for a majority Sikh state, with Amritsar to get recognition as a holy city (such as Banaras/Varanasi already had). The Golden Temple gradually became a military headquarters, used by terrorists/freedom fighters as a safe house. By 1984 Indira Gandhi's government decided it had to take action. A Sikh general was put in charge of Operation Blue Star, an attack on the militants in the Golden Temple. It amounted to an urban battle that took four days in early June, with from 500 to perhaps 1,000 dead. There was also damage to the Temple, which many Sikhs saw as a desecration. On October 31 two of Indira Gandhi's Sikh bodyguards assassinated her in the garden of her Prime Minister's house in

New Delhi.[GE125] Several thousand Sikhs were killed in the riots that followed; even Delhi's famous shopping district Chandni Chawk was trashed by enraged mobs, with no interference from nearby police.

The Nehru dynasty seems as star-crossed as the Kennedy dynasty in twentieth-century U.S. history, but the family tragedies have different roots. Looking back, the two most dramatic events of Indira Gandhi's Prime Ministership—the civil war between East and West Pakistan in 1971, and the Sikh pressure for an independent state in 1984—were both connected to ethnic friction in South Asia. Looking ahead, Indira's son Rajiv Gandhi, who became Prime Minister after his mother's death, died because of another ethnic conflict, a Tamil separatist movement, in 1991. He was campaigning for the local Congress candidate in Sriperumbudur, an industrial town about twenty-five miles west of Chennai,[GE126] when a woman with a hidden suicide belt of explosives came up and detonated it. Indian national governmental reactions to secessionist movements, since independence, have been at least as severe as those by the British Raj. The fear must be that if one area of India ever successfully goes independent, others will then follow until "India" would come unzipped right down to the province level—in violence that would make the breakup of Yugoslavia in the 1990s look like a grammar school picnic.

Babri Musjid/Ram Mandir

In 1992 the American travel writer Jonah Blank published *Arrow of the Blue-skinned God: Retracing the Ramayana Through India.*[11] His idea the past couple of years had been to follow Rama's path from his hometown of Ayodhya down to Sri Lanka and everywhere between mentioned in the great epic, and interview people along the way. He hoped this would be a framework to help him understand modern India, including the importance of its view of the past. It is a fascinating book; among other things he interviewed actors playing divine roles in a TV serial based on the Ramayana—a serial that stopped work and play nationwide at that broadcast time for weeks, so popular was it and its subject.

But even Jonah Blank was probably stunned by how good his timing was in publishing the book in 1992. In December of that year a Hindu mob stormed Babur's Mosque (Babri Musjid) in Ayodhya,[GE127] and tore down the almost 500-year-old structure stone from stone. Whatever the facts, general Hindu belief was that in 1527 the Mughal conqueror Babur had destroyed a temple to Rama located at Rama's birthplace (Ram Mandir) and built his new mosque on the same site. Destruction of Babur's Mosque had been threatened by Hindu nationalist parties and groups for years, and the government guarded the site with troops and razor wire, knowing the "communal" violence that was bound to follow that if and when it happened. But in 1992 the Hindu mob brushed aside the troops and the razor wire and demolished the building, and indeed there was Hindu-Muslim killing in every major Indian city, not to mention renewed tension between Muslim Pakistan and India because of it. I remember having an Indian student from Mumbai in class that year; his parents told him over the phone there were 900 killed in the fighting there in just one week.

From 1947 to today, some three-fourths of a century later, there have been some other important changes in India. From around 500 million at independence, the Indian population has more than doubled to upwards of 1.2 billion people. The 1991 free market reforms—perhaps not coincidentally undertaken in the year the Soviet Union broke up—created an economic boom that India is still riding. *New York Times* columnist Thomas Friedman showed how impressed he was by it in the first paragraph of his 2005 book *The World is Flat*:

> No one ever gave me directions like this on a golf course before: "Aim at either Microsoft or IBM." I was
> standing on the first tee at the KGA Golf Club in downtown Bangalore, in southern India, when my playing

---

125. GE Layer 125 is a Placemark at the assassination site; click on the Panoramio icon under pointer, titled "Last steps of Indira Gandhi," for view of same. It is less than half-a-mile away from the site of M. K. Gandhi's assassination.

126. GE Layer 126 is a Placemark referencing the Rajiv Gandhi memorial at his assassination site in Sriperumbudur, with a dozen or so Photos icons to explore.

127. GE Layer 127 is a Placemark referencing a Panoramio icon, titled "Babri Musjid," with a picture of the mosque before its destruction; then click on Photos icon below and a bit to the left of that one, titled "Babri Musjid demolition," for a picture made during the actual 1992 destruction.

partner pointed at two shiny glass-and-steel buildings off in the distance, just behind the first green. The Goldman Sachs building wasn't done yet; otherwise he could have pointed that out as well and made it a threesome. HP and Texas Instruments had their offices on the back nine, along the tenth hole.[12]

Although this was in southern India, with Bangalore as the regional "Silicon Valley," it had its parallels in much of the rest of India, including our GT Road corridor. The Indian Institutes of Technology, the first of which were set up back in Nehru's day, have become India's premier educational institutions: if as an Indian science student you don't get into your choice of them, you might take MIT or Cal Tech as your consolation prize! Of the original seven of the IIT, four are on our corridor (underlined): Kharagpur, some seventy miles WSW of Kolkata, was the first of all to be established, in 1950; Mumbai 1958, Kanpur 1959, Chennai 1959, New Delhi 1961, Guwahati 1994, and Roorkee 2001.[GE[128]]

Revenge & reconciliation

European intrusion, and then the borrowing of those shaping European ideologies of political and cultural nationalism as well as socialism to win independence from European control, is clearly as vivid a historical pattern along South Asia's Grand Trunk Road corridor as in any region of the modern world. It explains much of what motivates the existing states there today, as well as festering problems that may result in future states—a Khalistan for the Sikhs? a Dravidian-languages state for the southern cone? A Pashtun nation-state carved out of Pakistan and Afghanistan? The kaleidoscope of languages and religions there makes for a bewildering variety of possible "identifiable cultural groups," to quote the first step of the J. Brown "paradigm of national development," ensuring that the future there will probably be as interesting as the recent past. It's a future of more than passing interest to us in America, not least because the two major states of South Asia have nuclear weapons and a history of bad blood between them.

Rajmohan Gandhi is a grandson of M. K. "Mahatma" Gandhi. A scholar who has taught in U.S. as well as Indian universities, he wrote a most thoughtful book in 1999 titled *Revenge & Reconciliation: Understanding South Asian History*. From *Mahabharata* times to the present, he finds a lot more revenge than reconciliation in the history of the Indian subcontinent; it is a book of soul-searching honesty about his own culture, such as I have never read about my own American culture and political history. In a way, though, it makes those rare but key reconcilers stand out more vividly, and might be a good place to begin future study of the region if your interest has been piqued by this chapter. He closes his book with this little wish, or prayer, stolen here to end this chapter:

> May the Good Spirit that quickens the rain and kindles the laughter, the eagerness, and the dedication, use willing women and men to reconcile South Asia's ingenious, impossible and lovable inhabitants![13]

Endnotes

1. Stanley Wolpert, *India*, 3rd ed. (Berkeley & London: University of California Press, 2005), pp. 40 ff.

2. This idea, as well as so many others in this passage, is from Catherine B. Asher's volume in The New Cambridge History of India series titled *Architecture of Mughal India* (Cambridge: Cambridge University Press, 1992), pp. 28–30. Later (p. 37), she puts it this way: "Babur introduced the *char bagh* garden, which for him was a visual metaphor for his ability to control and order the arid Indian plains and ultimately its population."

3. The "nabob game" is nicely illustrated in Kipling's short story "The Man Who Would Be King," and the movie of the same name based—albeit loosely—on it.

4. See William Dalrymple, *The Last Mughal: The Fall of a Dynasty, 1857* (New York: Vintage Books Random House, 2006), pp. 47–50.

5. Rudyard Kipling, *Kim* (Penguin Classics 1987, reprinted from Macmillan original 1901), p. 49.

6. Ibid., p. 105.

---

128. GE Layer 128 is a Folder with all seven IITs marked with green star icons.

7. Sir Rabindranath Tagore, *Nationalism* (New York: Macmillan Co., 1917), p. 127.

8. Lajpat Rai, *Autobiographical Writings*, ed. Vijaya Chandra Joshi (Delhi & Jullundur, University Publishers, 1965), p. 77.

9. Ibid., p. 79.

10. Judith Brown, *Modern India: The Origins of an Asian Democracy*, 2nd ed. (Oxford University Press, 1994), p. 191.

11. Jonah Blank, *Arrow of the Blue-skinned God: Retracing the Ramayana Through India* (Boston: Houghton Mifflin, 1992).

12. Thomas Friedman, *The World is Flat: A Brief History of the Twenty-first Century* (New York: Farrar, Straus and Giroux, 2005), p. 3.

13. Rajmohan Gandhi, *Revenge & Reconciliation: Understanding South Asian History* (Penguin Books India, 1999), p. 411; the commas after eagerness and dedication my additions.

"True Love of the Soil of Indonesia": Southeast Asia's Java Roads

"[Sukarno], what path are you taking? In [head of the Communist Party] Aidit's heart there is no romanticism about revolution, no true love of the soil of Indonesia, no belief in the five principles of Pantja Sila! He and his cadres would stamp out the ancient dreams which are the spiritual life-blood of the country. The myths would be perverted into propaganda, the life of the spirit stilled in the name of the full belly, and love of God made an offence. Islam would be extinguished, and so would joy."

—as spoken by Billy Kwan in C. J. Koch's historical novel *The Year of Living Dangerously*

CONTENTS

The heart of the matter—A brief introduction to the languages of Java and environs—TOPOGRAPHY AND TEXTURE OF THE JAKARTA-TO-SURABAYA CORRIDOR—Setting in Southeast Asia and Indonesia—The Wallace Line—Views along one road—PREHISTORY AND EARLY HISTORY: JAVANESE KINGDOMS AND RELIGIONS—Prambanan and Borobudur—The Pasisir and the Muslim Kingdom of Demak—The Sultanate of Mataram—Legacies of the Javanese kingdoms: the *priyayi* and the Alus Art complex—DEVELOPMENT OF THE DUTCH EAST INDIES— Jan Pieterzoon Coen, "the Butcher of Banda"—The erosion of Mataram—VOC administration of Java—Gov.–Gen. Daendals and the *Grote Postweg*—British interlude—The Java War—The Cultivation System—*Max Havelaar*—The "Liberal Policy" and neo-colonialism—The Ethical Policy—ROOTS OF INDONESIAN NATIONALISM—*Letters of a Javanese Princess*— Sarekat Islam—The creation of Bahasa Indonesia—The young Sukarno—Japanese occupation— INDEPENDENCE—Establishing the Republic—The Bandung Conference—"Guided Democracy"—*The Year of Living Dangerously*—General Suharto's New Order—Pramoedya reflects on the Great Post Road and the New Order—The author reflects on Pramoedya

The heart of the matter

The transportation corridor chosen here to represent Southeast Asia is the network of roads along Indonesia's Java—an island about 600 miles long and averaging about 100 miles wide—from the capital city of Jakarta in the west to the big port and industrial city of Surabaya in the east. The two cities themselves are right at 400 miles apart.

The other obvious Southeast Asian transportation network option was to do the north-south coastal and interior roads in Vietnam, from Ho Chi Minh City (Saigon) to Hanoi; but frankly, given all the residual baggage of Vietnam as it has exercised the American public since the Vietnam War began there over half-a-century ago, the author lost his nerve and decided on a topic less well-known to the general American public, and thus presumably safer. On the rational side of the choice, the country of Indonesia with a population approaching

250 million accounts for almost half of Southeast Asia's total of 600-some million souls; Vietnam and the Philippines, next in line in population, have less than 100 million apiece. Arguably, Americans should know more about such a country!

In terms of modern state creation, Indonesia today has almost exactly the same borders as the Dutch colonial holdings ("the Dutch East Indies"). Jakarta is the current capital mainly because it was the Dutch capital (named Batavia) from 1629 until the Japanese invasion of 1942. The young intellectuals of the 1920s—who first popularized the word "Indonesia" and who created the Indonesian National Party—had in common fluency in Dutch and familiarity with Dutch culture. With no common language for this huge area—Javanese was the plurality language but resented by every other language group, and Dutch was the language of the colonial rulers and therefore unacceptable—these young intellectuals took a simple coastal trading version of Malay and turned it into Bahasa Indonesia, "the language of Indonesia." It was a fascinating psychological process, and it produced Sukarno, the George Washington of Indonesia and the real inventor of the Third World at his famous Bandung Conference of 1955.

A brief introduction to the languages of Java and environs

A prehistoric wave of Melanesian-speakers, hundreds of whose languages are still spoken in New Guinea and islands southeast of there, washed in first from the western Pacific, across the islands of today's Philippines and Indonesia, going as far west as the Bay of Bengal. Later a wave of Austronesian-speakers came down from the north, probably originally from China, moving down by way of Taiwan and the Philippine islands. They had domesticated animals such as the pig, and displaced most Melanesians in the western islands or isolated them in interior parts of large islands. Robert Cribb, in his masterful *Historical Atlas of Indonesia*, argues that the Austronesians probably came in speaking just one language, but that over the centuries dialects gradually diverged into new languages. He reckons that in present-day Indonesia there are still 150 Melanesian languages and 200 Austronesian languages spoken.[1] One of these Austronesian languages was Malay, a simplified coastal trading language that made possible communication over this bewildering variety of languages in the huge archipelago. Another of these was Javanese, which at the beginning of modern times was spoken in eastern and central Java, with a small pocket around Banten in the northwestern corner of the island. A third Austronesian language, Sundanese, was spoken mainly in the western third of Java and on neighboring Sumatra. By fairly early in the Common Era there were scripts for these languages, mainly based on Indian Devanagri and its predecessors—the script that Sanskrit was written in, as you saw in the last chapter.

Javanese, the plurality language of the territory that became modern Indonesia, is a very hierarchical language. It has a formal level in which you speak according to your social level; an intermediate level as when you would talk to a stranger whose social level you did not know; and an informal level you would use with close kin and friends. One reason it did not become the official language of Indonesia is that the other language groups were jealous of this "Javanese imperialism." Another was that the hierarchical nature of Javanese didn't lend itself well to the democratic brother- and sisterhood of the new Indonesian nationalism of the 1920s.

Dutch, by far the most important European language used in Java in colonial times, you have already glanced at in the South Africa chapter; many of the Js are pronounced Ys, (so *prijaji* and *priyayi* are pronounced the same way); most Ws are pronounced as Vs . . .

The official language of the Indonesia of today, Bahasa Indonesia ("Language of Indonesia"), is a nationalistic invention of fairly recent history, which we'll save for later in the chapter—see sub-chapter "The creation of Bahasa Indonesia" below. For now, it might be good to know that Bahasa Indonesia is written in Latin letters, so there is no transliteration problem to deal with. In terms of pronunciation, about the only unusual wrinkle is that "ci" is pronounced "chi" (as in Italian). The modern city on Java's north coast, today spelled Cirebon, used to be spelled by the English "Cheribon," for example, and is still pronounced much like that.

Finally, here are some useful words to know when browsing maps of Java, including Google Earth:

pasar = bazaar, marketplace
kebun = garden

istana = palace (newer European style palaces, as at Bogor)

kraton, keraton = palace (particularly a royal family type court, as the Sultan's at Yogyakarta)

jalan = street or road

alun-alun = the open square common to Javanese villages and towns

medan = main square in a city (as in Merdeka Medan, Jakarta's Freedom Square)

pulao = island

jembatan = bridge

bengawan = Javanese word for river

gunung = mountain, in both Malay and Bahasa Indonesia; also applies to volcanoes

padang = plain

TOPOGRAPHY AND TEXTURE OF THE JAKARTA-TO-SURABAYA CORRIDOR

Setting in Southeast Asia and Indonesia

The whole mainland of Southeast Asia—today's Myanmar/Burma, Thailand, Vietnam, Kampuchea/Cambodia, Laos, and Malaysia—used to be called generally "Indo-China." It's a term that, one can assume, is not appreciated by any of the citizens of those current states because it ignores their original unique local cultures. Nevertheless, it has a certain validity, and the word order of the "Indo-China" phrase is fairly chronologically accurate too, with the Indian influence being older and deeper, the Chinese influence newer and (except perhaps in Vietnam) shallower.[GE¹] The concept though not the term also generally applies to the islands between Southeast Asia and Australia—mostly today's Philippines and Indonesia.

The word "Indonesia" is of fairly recent historical coinage (a British geographer made it up in the mid-nineteenth century from "India" and "*nêsos*," Greek for "islands"),² but it preserves the importance of ancient Indian influence. Its borders are essentially those of the colonial Dutch East Indies. Side to side, from the western tip of Sumatra to the line that runs north and south across New Guinea separating Indonesian Irian Jaya from Papua New Guinea, it is 3,200 miles—600 miles wider than the lower forty-eight states of the U.S. It includes something like 13,000 inhabited islands, big and small.[GE²]

One way to get a quick handle on this geographic complexity is to see Indonesia as a rough northern arc of islands and a smoother southern arc of islands. The rough northern arc begins in the west with Kalimantan (most of the huge island of Borneo); then comes Sulawesi, the former Celebes, that island east of Kalimantan that looks like a strange beast with its tail curved up over its back (the equator runs just below that tail, incidentally, making it a handy reference guide to latitude)[GE³]; then east of that a complicated patchwork of islands generally called the Moluccas, or Malukus (the original "spice islands"), and finally Irian Jaya, the western half of the enormous island of New Guinea. The smoother southern arc of islands begins in the west with Sumatra, after which comes Java, Bali, Lombok, Sumbawa, Flores, and then, at an angle like a comma tilted a bit too much, Timor.

That smoother southern arc of islands is very earthquake prone and volcanic, part of the "ring of fire" that generally runs around the Pacific Ocean. A deep-sea trench is about 150 miles south of this southern arc (it shows up in Google Earth), where one tectonic plate grinds down under another, by fits and starts. The enormous tsunami that crashed into the southwest coast of Sumatra on December 26, 2004, with such tragic effects,

---

1. Open the Google Earth .kmz file titled "Chapter 12 Southeast Asia," and then open the first sub-Folder, titled "Java Roads: Topo & Texture." Double-click on the Pushpin icon for Google Earth Layer 1, a Placemark generally framing a view of "Indo-China."

2. GE Layer 2 is a double-ended arrow-shaped Polygon showing the 3,200-mile-wide expanse of Indonesia. After you've viewed it, turn it off so as to not clutter the screen for other features.

3. GE Layer 3 is a Placemark titled "Sulawesi & Equator," framing a view centered on Sulawesi; in Google Earth, under the View drop-down menu, turn on Grid for lines of latitude and longitude to see Equator's place in archipelago.

was of this origin. Krakatoa (Krakatau), that blew up in 1883 in a volcanic explosion with shock waves felt round the world, sits in the Sunda Strait that separates Java from Sumatra.[GE⁴]

It turns out that all volcanic soils are not created equal. Some is acidic, poor for agriculture, and some is neutral to basic, much better for agriculture. In this regard, Java is the most favored island of the whole double archipelago.[GE⁵] Far from being the biggest island in Indonesia (in fact, it is only fifth largest), it supports over half the population of the whole country. Apparently it did in the past, too: it was always a center of higher culture and a contender for supreme regional political power, one of the reasons we have chosen it as our "Southeast Asia in microcosm" corridor. The long island has an irregular double row of volcanoes (eighteen active, seventeen dormant), lavender cones of 10,000′ or so rising up out of jade green rice paddy land and deeper green hillside tea plantations and remnant forests. Java is too close to the Equator to have typhoons, but this being Asia, the climate is dominated by the monsoon, or seasonal winds. From June to October, hot dry winds from the center of Australia blow in from the southeast. During our winter and spring the winds in Java reverse, coming down from the northwest, and from their longer run over water they pick up moisture that falls on Java in classic monsoon rains, especially on the mountain slopes facing northwest.

While you have this larger perspective, instead of the land, look at the pattern of the oceans. First, see how the narrow Malacca Strait (Melaka in recent transliteration) separates Sumatra from Malaysia: this is one of the most critical and historic waterways in the world, because it is the easiest way to get from Arabia and India to most of Indonesia, to the Philippines, to China, Japan, and Korea.[GE⁶] And then more generally look at the Java Sea that lies between the northern and southern arcs of Indonesian islands, and the larger South China Sea north of the northern arc of islands.[GE⁷] Some historians have likened these two together as Asia's version of the Mediterranean Sea in terms of importance in commerce, war, and general cultural transmission. Once again, Java is in a favorable position. From Java's northern coast, sailors in summer could ride the monsoon winds either northwest to the Andaman Sea and the Bay of Bengal or north to the South China Sea and the Chinese coast, and in the winter ride the reverse winds back again.

The Wallace Line

Charles Darwin, as a twenty-two-year-old outdoorsman and (rather uninspired) theology student, signed on with the exploratory voyage of the good ship *Beagle* for its world cruise from 1831–1836 as its naturalist. Though he did not then believe in the thesis of the book—that the world was millions of years old and that current earth forms could be explained by everyday forces such as erosion and deposition and earthquake over immense time—he carried Charles Lyell's new *Principles of Geology* with him. He saw the lush ecosystems of tropical Brazil, where the profusion of life was such that every living thing seemed to have a niche, or a gimmick, to survive. He found seashell fossils way up in the Andes. He saw the stripped-down isolation of the Galápagos Islands, with just a few life forms and their intriguing variation island to island. All this percolated with Lyell's *Principles of Geology* to produce in him the belief that all species evolved out of other species, mainly under the pressure of natural selection.

A slow and careful worker, some twenty-two years after his return Darwin had not published much on the topic and was still collecting evidence—from areas as diverse as the breeding of domestic animals, comparative anatomy, the comparative development of embryos—when he got the draft of an article from a younger naturalist named Alfred Russel Wallace, asking for his comments on it. Since the argument in the article was almost exactly what Darwin had come to believe, he was in a bit of an ethical quandary about what to do. He had been working on the topic longer, but Wallace had really written the first comprehensive statement of it.

---

4. GE Layer 4 frames a view of Krakatau, or more properly Krakatau's successor islands.

5. GE Layer 5 is a Polygon titled "the Java corridor," the outline of a white rectangle that takes in the whole island of Java, and generally frames a view of the Jakarta-to-Surabaya corridor that is the focus of this chapter.

6. GE Layer 6 is a Placemark framing a view of Sumatra in the southwest and Malaysia (and Singapore) in the northeast, with "Malacca Strait" between them.

7. GE Layer 7 is a Placemark titled "South China Sea, Java Sea," framing them in a view.

So Darwin consulted friends, among them by this time Charles Lyell, and in that same year of 1858 these friends arranged a joint presentation at a major scholarly conference of Wallace's article with extracts from a couple of Darwin's earlier works. By the next year, obviously spurred to finish a book-length treatment of the theory, Darwin published his *On the Origin of Species By Means of Natural Selection.*

Wallace had earlier spent four years in and around the Amazon River valley collecting specimens of animals and plants. His publications had impressed even Britain's Royal Society, winning him sponsors for further tropical researches in the Malay Archipelago. He had been there for four years when he sent Darwin the article, and would be there four years more (in all, from 1854–62). The term "Malay Archipelago" then included everything between mainland Southeast Asia and Australia—today's Indonesia, the Philippines, Papua New Guinea, and beyond. Wallace's collecting journeys there were remarkable. He identified a dividing line in the archipelago between flora and fauna that was generally Australian, and flora and fauna that was generally Southeast Asian, called ever since simply the Wallace Line.[GE8] It runs between Bali and Lombok in the smooth southern arc of Indonesian islands, and between Kalimantan (Borneo) and Sulawesi in the rough northern arc. He noticed it first in birds, with birds of paradise, bowerbirds, cockatoos, and cassowaries similar to those of Australia almost exclusively east of the line, and birds common to the Southeast Asian mainland, such as trogons, to the west of the line. Later he realized it applied to other animals as well, with elephants, tapirs, rhinoceroses, orangutans, and tigers west of the line, and marsupials such as bandicoots and cuscuses east of the line. The explanation for this that is generally accepted today is that the Sunda Shelf, now covered by shallow seas around the islands west of the Wallace Line, was high and dry as recently as 20,000 years ago in the last ice age, and the Sahul Shelf, shallow seas between Australia and New Guinea, was, too—but between them ran a deep-water channel that kept most life forms from the two sides from mixing with one another.[GE9]

This junction between two very different biological regimes and the transition zone between them in eastern Indonesia, plus the moisture and warmth of the tropics, helps explain the biological richness of Indonesia. In various ways, this would affect world history—not least in the European and Chinese demand for its spices. Cloves, for example, were in AD 1500 still confined to the Maluku islands.[GE10] Nutmeg and mace (both from the same small tree), were even more tightly limited to a tiny handful of six islands, the Banda Islands,[GE11] in an isolated patch of ocean twenty-eight miles east to west and eight miles north to south.

Java just in itself was a naturalist's paradise. Wallace spent three and a half months there during 1861. He landed in the port of Surabaya and made a foray up to Wonosalam on the slopes of the volcanic Mt. Arjuna (Gunung Arjuna) at almost 2,000' elevation, and then after a week came down to the lowland village of Japanan at less than 200' elevation.[GE12] It was too dry to take many insects, but he collected ninety-eight species of birds, some of them unique to Java; here is his enthusiastic description of one particularly rare bird, a relative of the wild ancestor of the chicken:

> I also obtained here a specimen of the rare green jungle-fowl (*Gallus furcatus*), whose back and neck are beautifully scaled with bronzy feathers, and whose smooth-edged oval comb is of a violet-purple color, changing to green at the base. It is also remarkable in possessing a single large wattle beneath its throat, brightly colored in three patches of red, yellow, and blue.[3]

---

8. GE Layer 8 is a Path in red reproducing the Wallace Line. Zoom in on Google Earth to see interesting undersea crustal features along its path!

9. GE Layer 9 is a Placemark framing a view of both the Sunda and Sahul Shelfs; they show up nicely as solid light blue areas. A complex transition zone—east of the Wallace Line and west of New Guinea (Irian Jaya)—shows up as a 180° arc of islands and underwater mountain chains.

10. GE Layer 10 is a Placemark framing a view of the Moluccas (Malukus).

11. GE Layer 11 is a Placemark framing a view of the Banda Islands, only six of which are of any size. The westernmost island of Run, or Ran (Pulau Run), would be fought over by the Dutch and British for decades.

12. GE Layer 12 is a Folder titled "Wallace around Surabaya," with Placemarks at Surabaya, Wonosalam, and Japanan, and one marking the summit of Gunung Arjuna. Double-click Placemark icons for framed views in direction of his travels.

After Surabaya he went by ship along the northern coast to Jakarta (then called Batavia, the capital of the Dutch East Indies). After a week spent preserving specimens here and sending them off, he headed south up through cool and forested Bogor with its botanical gardens, and southeast on over the Megamendung Pass to the town of Cipanas at the eastern foot of the volcanoes Mt. Gede (active) and Pangerango (dormant), both of which he climbed.[GE13] He said it was by far the most interesting of his experiences in Java—marveling at the butterflies, and at many of the 300 species of fern his host said grew there, watching with extreme interest how much akin to the flora of temperate Europe the flora on the Javanese mountains became at high elevation, and musing on why that might be so.

Views along one road

Now that in following Wallace we've at least generally located the northern port cities of Surabaya and Jakarta, about 400 miles apart, let's visually explore along one of the main roads connecting them.[GE14] We'll start with Jakarta and environs, from posh island resorts just off the waterfront, to the old colonial Dutch buildings, to the modern high rise office buildings. Then we'll go straight inland, due south—the way Wallace did—up to Bogor, the Dutch "hill station" at almost a thousand feet elevation that let the European colonial elite get out of the tropical heat and fevers of the lowlands. Then we'll diverge from Wallace's route and follow the longer but easier road that circles Mt. Gede on the south side and then goes east into Bandung—at 3,000′ the "Paris of Java," and perhaps deserving the title of the intellectual capital of Indonesia. Then we'll go a good way west and a bit south to the ancient cultural capital of Yogyakarta, on the Kedu plain at the foot of the sacred Mt. Merapi, perhaps the single richest agricultural zone in all Indonesia. From Yogyakarta we'll go just a bit (thirty-five miles) northeast to Surakarta, another old royal capital, and then on east and a little north to Surabaya, the greatest industrial city of Indonesia since the mid-1800s. Though there is probably no place in Java more than sixty miles from the nearest ocean, meaning that rivers are generally small and unimportant, there are two rivers in eastern Java that are bigger because of the way they twist and spiral: the Solo and the Brantas, both of which debouche near Surabaya.[GE15] Their valleys play especially important historical roles in Javanese history. And note that the island of Madura, that shelters the port of Surabaya, is so close to Java that for all practical purposes it is an extension of same;[GE16] at least once in the historical drama to come a power from Madura will be the critical factor in shaping Java's future. This leaves out a few important highlands, and the "Pasisir," the strip of coastal cities of north central Java, but these can be introduced later in the narrative. But for now, just open the Folder called "Views along the road," and familiarize yourself with topography, vegetation, architecture, and such, along one road connecting Jakarta with Surabaya. As well as giving you a feel for the geographic setting of the historical drama to play out, some of the pictures offer a sneak peek into the history to come.[GE17]

---

13. GE Layer 13 is a Folder titled "Wallace around Jakarta," with Placemarks at Jakarta, Bogor, Megmendung Pass, Cipanas, and marking the summits of Mts. Gede and Pangerango. Again, double-click Placemark icons for framed views in direction of his travels.

14. GE Layer 14 is a Folder titled "One Jakarta-Surabaya road." The first layer in it is a Path titled "Through the highlands" that follows main roads between the six cities. The next six Placemarks reference those cities with green stars.

15. GE Layer 15 is a Folder titled "Rivers of Eastern Java"; it includes Paths for the Solo and the Brantas Rivers symbolized in aqua. In the nineteenth century the Dutch cut a canal north to divert the Solo, partly to keep from silting up the port of Surabaya.

16. GE Layer 16 is a Placemark framing a view showing western Madura's relationship to Java. In the narrowest part of the Madura Strait, in three places the islands get from 1.5 to 1.8 miles of each other.

17. GE Layer 17 is a Folder titled "Views along the road," containing twenty-one such "views." To visually familiarize yourself with at least this slice of the country, turn on successive Placemarks, "fly" there, and open suggested Photos icons.

PREHISTORY AND EARLY HISTORY: JAVANESE KINGDOMS AND RELIGIONS

This fertile island has been home to humans, and hominids before that, for time out of mind. Fossilized bone fragments of "Java Man"—an estimated 1.8 million years old—were discovered at Trinil on the Solo River in East Java in 1891, one of the first finds worldwide of what is now called "Homo erectus."[GE18]

Without Javanese written records to go on, the origins of civilization there are shadowy. The earliest religions seem to have been Austronesian pantheism and animism. But by the second century AD Chinese sources speak of ocean-going Javanese ships that could hold 600 men, and apparently Hinduism and Buddhism had already arrived from India. Around AD 400 there was a Hindu state whose capital was at or near present-day Jakarta. In AD 640 a state on the north coast named Ho-ling (it is still known only by its Chinese name) sent tribute to Tang Dynasty China, probably to secure trade rights in return. Early in the 700s Ho-ling joined with a state named Mataram (a later state took the same name, you'll see later), which was based down in the Kedu Plain around present-day Yogyakarta. The new joint state alternated between Hinduism and Buddhism. In the 800s, in a remarkable burst of energy in one fifty-year period, Mataram built the largest Buddhist structure in the world AND the largest Hindu temple outside the Indian subcontinent. Each is within a few miles of Yogyakarta; each is a "must see" for any tourist to Java.

Prambanan and Borobudur

Prambanan, the Hindu temple or *candi*, is less than ten miles east-northeast from Yogyakarta, right beside the main road to Surakarta that you've already explored. On its central platform, Prambanan has major temples to Brahma, Vishnu, and Shiva, and minor ones for their mounts. Smaller temples and a wall surround the site. The stories of the *Ramayana* and the Mahabharata are carved in stone on the walls, the way Christian cathedrals in the Middle Ages had carvings in stone of the Christian story for the largely illiterate population to "read" there. [GE19]

Borobudur, the Mahayana Buddhist temple, is seventeen miles northwest of Yogyakarta, and just twenty-two miles from Prambanan as the crow flies. From a distance it seems to be a small hill, but upon closer view it turns out to be a man-made mountain of carved stone, at which point it becomes much more impressive. The view from directly overhead resembles a Buddhist mandala, and pilgrims can make a miles-long pilgrimage by going round all the terraces, starting with the square-ish ones at the bottom and continuing to the three circular ones at top. There are hundreds of panels carved in relief, and over 500 statues of the Buddha. On the circular terraces at top, surrounding a huge central stupa, or Buddhist reliquary, are seventy-two larger-than-life statues, each in its own bell-shaped stone latticework stupa, all beautifully carved.[GE20]

The most famous king from this first Mataram kingdom, Airlangga (who ruled much of the first half of the AD 1000s), came near the end of the kingdom. His father was king of Bali, his mother the daughter of the king of Mataram, and he united the two areas in his rule. A famous epic poem dates from his era; called "The Marriage of Arjuna," it echoes the *Mahabharata* but was also considered to be about Airlangga himself.

The most famous of the Hindu kingdoms of early Java was Majapahit, which got its start in the wake of Mongol/Chinese invasions of 1292 and which lasted to about 1500. It was named for its capital city in the Brantas River valley. About all that survives are some brickwork portals and a few temple ruins; but the level

---

18. Turn off and collapse the first, "Topo & Texture" Folder, and then open the "Kingdoms and Religions" Folder. Turn on the unnumbered Folder titled "Java corridor, rivers, original road." Then explore GE Layer 18, a Placemark indicating the general site of Java Man's remains. Click on Panoramio icon under pointer titled "Java Man diorama in Trinil Museum, Ngawi," and then zoom out to see general location relative to whole island.

19. GE Layer 19 is a Folder titled "Views of Prambanan" with Placemarks inside recommending representative Photos icons. In addition there are literally hundreds of such icons to explore at the general site, some with close-ups of statuary and scenes from the *Ramayana*.

20. GE Layer 20 is a Folder titled "Views of Borobudur" with Placemarks inside recommending representative Photos icons.

of workmanship is superb.[GE21] Alfred Russel Wallace passed that way on his way inland from Surabaya, and said he had never seen the equal of such precise brickwork. At its greatest extent in the mid-1300s Majapahit controlled much of today's Indonesia and Malaysia, though its original heartland was east Java, Madura, and Bali. One of the best known figures from this time was the Prime Minister Gaja Mada who presided over Majapahit's conquest of the whole archipelago. Today the main university in Yogyakarta is named for him.

The Pasisir and the Muslim Kingdom of Demak

In the 1400s there was a quickening of ocean-borne trade and exploration worldwide. In the initial technology chapter we took a look at the Portuguese side of that, and in the China chapter to follow this one we'll spend some time with the great Ming Dynasty fleets of 1405–1433. Both powerfully impacted Indonesian territory in general and Java in particular. But neither one was as important a transformative force as the Muslim merchant and missionary influence coming into Java from the lands around the Arabian Sea. Because of it, today Indonesia is the most populous Muslim country in the world.

It began in the *Pasisir*, that central stretch of the northern coast of Java that runs roughly from Cirebon in the west to Surabaya in the east.[GE22] The word Pasisir comes from the Javanese for "beach," and earlier in Majapahit Kingdom times it was used to emphasize that this was a less important, peripheral area, separate from the inland heartlands of the Kedu Plain and the Solo and Brantas river valleys. But now the Pasisir came into its own, with new wealth being generated by trade and a world of new ideas coming in. This is where Islam first took real root in Indonesia. The grave sites of the *wali sanga*, the famous "nine saints" who brought Islam to Java, are all here along the Pasisir. The first hard evidence of Islam in Java, for example, is a Muslim tombstone found in Gresik, today virtually a suburb of Surabaya, dated to 1420.[GE23]

It was the Pasisir-based Kingdom of Demak that first dramatically spread Islam in the Indonesian archipelago, and particularly in Java. The town of Demak itself, the capital, was about eight miles from the Java Sea. In 1479 it proclaimed itself an Islamic city, and that same year work began on the great mosque there—a very Javanese-looking building.[GE24] This Great Mosque of Demak was so central to the establishment of Islam in Java that popular belief in Indonesia equates seven pilgrimages there with one to Mecca. The city-state spread, especially along the northern coast, founding such ports as Cirebon and Banten, thus beginning its rise to a kingdom.[GE25] And so it was Demak that was the most important Javanese power when the Portuguese arrived, and it was a fairly well-matched struggle. Demak mobilized a fleet in 1513 to attack the Portuguese in their key outpost, Melaka (on the Malaysia side of Malacca Strait), but the Portuguese defeated the Demak fleet and killed the king himself. A few years later the Portuguese allied with the Kingdom of Sunda in the western part of Java, thus threatening the power of Demak. In 1527 a Portuguese armada rashly sailed into what is today Jakarta Bay, where some Portuguese merchants were already active, but it was immediately ambushed and defeated by a Muslim naval coalition organized by Demak. The Demak naval commander apparently then gave the newly-captured city its modern name, Jayakarta, or "Glorious Fortress." The Portuguese were impressed with the size of ocean-going ships built in Pasisir ports such as Rembang and Japara. The common name in Europe for large ocean-going ships in Asia, "junk," probably came from the Malay word for these, *jong*.

---

21. GE Layer 21 is a Folder titled "Majapahit sites." It includes one Placemark located in old Majapahit, today's Trowulan; click on Panoramio icon under Pushpin icon, titled "Candi Bajang Ratu Sebelum Di Pugar," for a view of what is believed to have been a major entranceway to a building in the capital of Majapahit. A second Placemark is of Sukuh temple ruin high on the slopes of Mt. Lawu and some eighty-five miles to the west.

22. GE Layer 22 is a Path in red making a bracket around the Pasisir; it ends in the west at Cirebon and in the east at Surabaya.

23. GE Layer 23 is a Placemark referencing Gresik.

24. GE Layer 24 is a Placemark referencing a Panoramio icon of the Great Mosque of Demak.

25. GE Layer 25 is a Folder titled "Kingdom of Demak 1500–1550." It shows the general area of military operation of the kingdom, including its capture of the heartlands of the Solo and Brantas River valleys, the Kedu Plain, and by 1524 Banten (Bantam) and its hinterlands over on the western tip of Java.

The next twenty years was at or near the peak of the Kingdom of Demak's power, during which it conquered all the main river valleys of east Java and much of the old royal heartlands of central south Java. But after 1546 civil wars between royal contestants sapped the kingdom; it swiftly declined, and lost all independence by 1586 to an even more impressive central Javanese kingdom, Mataram.

The Sultanate of Mataram

The capital of Mataram, also a Muslim kingdom, was near Yogyakarta. Earlier the Kingdom of Demak, holding the Pasisir and all its trade resources, had expanded south to take the interior heartlands; Mataram would do it the other way around. The founder of the kingdom, Senapati (who ruled from 1584 to 1601), consolidated the heartlands by about 1594, a territory only touching the northern coast near Demak.[GE26] He and his son following him generally fought down the Solo River towards Surabaya, though with not much success. Mataram's greatest ruler, Sultan Agung (ruling from 1613–1646), in the first dozen years of his reign expanded the state to include all of Java except the extreme southeastern corner, and Banten and Jakarta in the northwestern corner.[GE27] The Pasisir cities fell to him in the 16-teens, though Surabaya stubbornly held out until 1625. He built a new capital—the heart of present-day Yogyakarta[GE28]—a few miles from Kota Gede, his father and grandfather's original base. In 1645 he was buried in his hilltop tomb at Imogiri, some ten miles south of Yogyakarta; most later royalty of Mataram, from the two royal cities of Yogyakarta and Surakarta, were buried here, such was Sultan Agung's lasting prestige in the country.[GE29] The turning point of Sultan Agung's reign, though it only became clear in hindsight, was his 1628–29 attempt to dislodge the Dutch from their new holdings in Batavia/Jakarta. Although it came very close to success, it eventually failed—on which much more in a few minutes. Later rulers moved to an alternate capital at Kartosuro;[GE30] when it was devastated in a losing war to the Dutch in 1745 they moved about six miles east to present-day Surakarta, or Solo, near the banks of the river of the same name.[GE31]

Legacies of the Javanese kingdoms: the *priyayi* and the Alus Art complex

The Kingdom of Demak and then the Sultanate of Mataram grew so large they were hard to administer, given the state of transportation and communications. The administrators charged by the royal governments with ruling were an upper-class of literate intellectuals called the *prijaji*, or *priyayi*. They were an aristocracy something like European knights or Japanese samurai, with extreme codes of honor and elaborate feudal etiquette. Later Dutch rulers would adopt them as their second-tier administrators, in much the same way the British in India adopted the Bengalis. Eventually from these priyayi—as with the Bengalis in the British Raj—would come the beginnings of a nationalist, independence-minded movement, to be examined later.

At this point in the narrative, however—in keeping with this textbook's attempt to introduce one important cultural legacy per world region and corridor—let's turn to the "Alus Art" that came down to modern times mainly in the hands of the priyayi. *Alus* means refined, high-brow, in contrast to *kasar*, coarse or low-brow.

The Alus Art complex has six traditional elements—*batik*, *jogèd*, *tembang*, *gamelan*, *lakon*, and *wayang*. Of these, perhaps only the first will be known by most Americans. *Batik* is a wax-resist process of dyeing cloth, especially silk. Hot wax is artistically dribbled onto fresh, lustrous white silk, and when the cloth is dyed, no

---

26. GE Layer 26 is a Polygon showing Mataram by 1594 (mainly after map 3.21, p. 89 of Cribb, *Historical Atlas of Indonesia*).

27. GE Layer 27 is a Polygon showing the growth of Mataram by 1625, when Surabaya was taken.

28. GE Layer 28 is a Placemark titled "Yogyakarta kraton and mosque" framing a view of the central square, or alun-alun, of Yogyakarta. The buildings with red roofs just south of the square are the Palace Complex of the Sultanate, the court or *kraton*. The single large building to the west of the square is the Great Mosque of Yogyakarta. Many Photos icons to explore for both sites.

29. GE Layer 29 is a Placemark referencing Imogiri; interesting Photos icons to explore.

30. GE Layer 30 is a Placemark referencing Kartosuro (Kartasura).

31. GE Layer 31 is a Placemark referencing Surakarta/Solo.

dye "takes" where the wax is. Then the wax is melted off in a hot wash, and dyeing can commence again. Batik is one of the world's most famous styles of decorated fabric, and was for centuries an export in much demand from Java. *Jogèd* is a stylized dance, with a story being told in every twist of the wrist and roll of the eye. It has its parallels in every Southeast Asian country, and clearly reveals its ancient Indian ancestry. The *tembang* are poems done according to rules as strict as those for a Shakespearean sonnet. They can be sung as songs, a capella, or to the accompaniment of the *gamelan* orchestra. The *gamelan* (literally "ensemble") is a percussion band, with most of the instruments in the gong family, and sometimes a small female chorus attached. To the uninitiated western ear it at first sounds like wind chimes run amok; to Indonesians who grew up with the symbolism, of course, every song and the mood it conjures up is understood. A surprising number of modern Indonesians still play one or more traditional instruments in the gamelan. The *lakon* are story outlines or plots, mainly stories from the ancient Hindu epics *Mahabharata* and *Ramayana*. Those from the former are more numerous and popular; those from the latter are sometimes denigrated as "monkey stories."[4]

But it is the *wayang*, especially the *wayang kulit* (literally "shadow leather") that truly integrates gamelan and lakon. It is a shadow puppet play performed at night during the dry (our summer) monsoon. It is fading away somewhat today as it is replaced by other media, but it was the television of rural Java for hundreds, maybe thousands of years.

Here is the setting. A wealthy household has hired a puppeteer (a *dalang*) and a gamelan orchestra. By 9 p.m. or so the family members are on the veranda, facing a white sheet on which the shadow play is to be shown. On the other side sits the dalang, a coconut-oil lamp (today an electric light) behind him. In front of him, stuck into a soft banana-tree log, are dozens of flat leather puppets mounted on buffalo-horn sticks—puppets with moveable arms but nothing else. They are intricately cut and beautifully decorated with bright colors and gold leaf—but still the place to be is on the shadow side of the screen, the illusion side. In a semicircle behind the dalang are the instrumentalists of the gamelan orchestra. Behind them stand the non-paying on-lookers. The dalang does all the voices, and manipulates all the puppets, sometimes two in each hand. They fly, dance, embrace, fight. There are special puppets to set the scenery, for arrows that fly across the screen, a single complex puppet to represent a whole marching army. The dalang raps for attention with a kind of knocker. He calls for the next song from the gamelan, and the mood changes. The play goes on all night, until dawn. The monologue and dialogue is not memorized, as it is in a Shakespearean play, but extemporaneous within the overall outline of the play. If a plane flies overhead, there might be an allusion to the Garuda Bird of ancient Hinduism. If a particularly juicy political scandal happens to be occurring at the present, it may be hinted at in the play. The *wayang kulit* plays are traditionally divided into three parts—*Patet Nem, Patet Sanga,* and *Patet Manjura,* or Parts One, Two, and Three in the old Javanese language—and represent generally the childhood, adolescence, and maturity of an individual.

If you like your cultural history with a dose of theatre, you might like the book *On Thrones of Gold: Three Javanese Shadow Plays.* James Brandon, the editor, explains the wayang in an eighty-page introduction, and then integrates the dialogue of the plays with black-and-white photographs of the screen. Indonesia may be the world's largest Muslim country, but only a minority of Indonesians are strict ("Santri") Muslims. The majority seems to be able to treat religion as a sort of layer cake, with an ancient layer of animism at base, layers of Hinduism and Buddhism atop that, and Islam atop that. Here is the first paragraph of Brandon's version of the wayang play "The Reincarnation of Rama," where he is describing how the dalang readies himself for the presentation; look at the elements of all four religious horizons—animism, Hinduism, Buddhism, Islam—that appear here:

> Before leaving home the dalang begins to concentrate his senses upon the performance. He silently prays, "Om, May nothing give hindrance, O Spirits of this house, flying over the earth, Mother of Generations. Allah, assist me, fulfill my wish, gratify my intentions. Creatures, male and female, look at my work, be pleased, and love by God's will. Oh, Allah! Oh, Allah! Oh, Allah!" Holding his breath, he stamps three times with his right foot.

> On arriving at his host's home the dalang repeats the same prayer, requesting the help of the spirits of the host's dwelling. At about eight-thirty the fifteen to twenty musicians who make up the gamelan begin to play the Talu, or introductory music. As the Talu draws to a close, the dalang takes his place before the center of

the screen praying, "O Great Serpent who supports the earth, O Spirits all here, I ask your help. Let not the onlookers disperse before I have finished performing my art."[5]

The characters are also *alus* or *kasar*. One can be kasar and still basically on the good side, such as the powerful but impetuous and thoughtless Bhima of the Pandava brothers. The kasar characters have round eyes and bulbous noses. The alus types, such as Bhima's brother Arjuna, have almond-shaped eyes and sharp noses.

Before the rise of modern media, the wayang was probably a part of the consciousness of every Javanese. [GE[32]] Looking ahead in this history, Sukarno, the key figure of modern Indonesia, fell in love with the *wayang kulit* during schoolboy summer vacations around the time of WW I in his grandparents' village in east Java. In power he consciously thought of himself as the great dalang, balancing the right against the left. Sometimes a minister in his government would first realize he was being fired because Sukarno had a dalang include it in a play set in ancient times. The Mataram royal domains of Yogyakarta and Surakarta were formally divided in 1757, and Surakarta/Solo especially put most of its energy into the preservation and enrichment of the Alus Art complex. The new Dutch colonial overlords eventually picked Surakarta as the place to train Dutch administrators in local languages. In this way the Surakarta dialect gradually became the standard for all of Java, and the Dutch administrators who trained there learned to appreciate the Alus Arts.

DEVELOPMENT OF THE DUTCH EAST INDIES

In the capital cities of all European countries that had long-time colonies, their former empires have come home to roost in terms of neighborhoods of ethnic minorities who came from there—Algerians and Senegalese in Paris, Pakistanis and Indians and Gambians in London, Indonesians in Amsterdam . . . . And so the best Indonesian restaurants in the world, outside Indonesia, are in Holland. If you go as a tourist to Amsterdam, should you have time for a leisurely meal (after visiting Anne Frank's house and the great art collections of the Rijksmuseum), ask your way to an Indonesian restaurant and order *rijstafel*, literally "rice table." It consists of dozens of small portions of different Indonesian dishes, arriving in a succession of small plates or metal containers. It's just one legacy of over three centuries of Dutch colonialism in Indonesia.

As you've seen in earlier chapters, the Dutch came east, after spices, hot on the heels of Spain and Portugal—their mortal enemies in Europe's religious wars of those days. The first Dutch ships got to Banten on the northwest corner of Java in 1596,[GE[33]] filled up with spices, and made it back home. They had just broken the Portuguese monopoly of trade, and made themselves immense profits. In 1601 they actually captured the port of Banten from the Portuguese. As briefly covered in the chapter on South Africa's Durban-to-Pretoria corridor, in 1602 the Dutch government insisted that the Dutch merchants work together in face of the Portuguese-Spanish enemy: they were to join the United East-India Company (*Vereenigde Oost-Indische Compagnie*, or VOC). In exchange the government would grant this company of merchants a monopoly on the spice trade. The VOC, as you've seen, was really the world's first joint stock company; investors had to commit their money to the company for five years, not just to a single ship or voyage. The *Heeren XVII*, or "Gentlemen Seventeen," were the first real board of directors, and the VOC initials, cleverly linked together and pasted atop the Dutch flag, was the world's first corporate logo.[GE[34]]

---

32. GE Layer 32 is a Placemark referencing Jakarta's wayang museum; but it is used here mainly as a place to say that if you will do a "Google–Images" search of "wayang kulit," you will get a good many representative images. The single puppets shaped like fat spearheads are the kayons, or scenery-setting puppets. Notice which human-type puppets are alus or kasar.

33. GE Layer 33 is a Placemark referencing Banten (again); hardly any historical remains of that early European presence are left to explore.

34. GE Layer 34 is a Placemark titled "VOC HG, Amsterdam." Today it is a naval museum with a crowd-pleasing replica of a Dutch Eastindiaman; living history actors playing different roles, from the captain showing how to use the backstaff for navigation, on down to bawdy songs being sung before the mast. For a view of the VOC logo, do a Google–Images search of either "VOC logo" or "VOC flag," or just go to following website: http://undevicesimus.deviantart.com/art/United-E-India-Co-Grunge-Flag-c-1660-1800-422469106

*From *On Thrones of Gold: Three Javanese Shadow Plays* by James R. Brandon, Ed. Copyright © 1993 by James R. Brandon. Reprinted by permission.

South Africa was just a way-station for the VOC; the spice islands of eastern Indonesia were the destination. By 1605 the Dutch had captured the Portuguese fort at Ambon in the Malukus[GE35]—in the heart of the clove producing islands and not far from Banda's nutmeg. It was the headquarters of the VOC for the next decade or so. The original idea was simple: control the spices there, and send them back to Holland. But the third governor-general of the company had much bigger ideas.

Jan Pieterzoon Coen, "the Butcher of Banda"

Jan Coen first came to the East Indies as a twenty-year-old, in 1607. In a failed attempt to seize the nutmeg trade in the Banda Islands, the Dutch expedition's commander and fifty soldiers were killed—a fact usually used to explain Coen's later brutality towards the Banda Islanders. Upon his return to Holland in 1610, his report on trade possibilities in the East so impressed the Heeren XVII that they sent him back in 1612 as chief merchant. In the next five years he secured a Dutch monopoly on cloves in the Moluccas generally, and nutmeg in the Bandas specifically. For this he was appointed Governor-General of the VOC in Asia.

By this time he had set up a chain of forts throughout the archipelago, freezing out the Portuguese who were the first Europeans there, and trying to block the English who were attempting to start trade there. He also saw the possibilities of Holland taking over most of the inter-Asian shipping trade, the way the Dutch in his day were cornering the shipping market for much of Europe. If he just had some central shipping point (the fort at Ambon was too far east to be on the main shipping lanes) he could turn it into a sort of Amsterdam East. So he settled first at Banten (Bantam) in northwest Java, with the permission of the Sultan there, and then in 1619 to rid himself of the Sultan's controls, moved about fifty miles east to the first good harbor, the fishing port called Jayakarta or Jakarta which he immediately renamed Batavia (the name of a part of the Netherlands).

Coen ruled from Batavia with an iron fist. When in his eyes in 1621 the Banda Islanders were violating their monopoly trading terms with the Dutch, his VOC forces descended on the islands and killed perhaps 15,000 and deported the rest.[GE36] Relations with the English were complicated. In Europe, they were close Protestant allies, fighting the great Catholic powers. But friction between them in the East Indies came close to and sometimes crossed the line into war. In 1623 Dutch agents seized, tortured, and killed English agents on Ambon. Coen was back in Holland that year, but was blamed for the massacre, and probably rightly so, since it was clearly part of his general policy. Even more crucial for Batavia's survival were relations with the great Sultanate of Mataram. Obviously Coen had placed his base of operations in the northwest corner of Java, about as far as he could get from its center of power in the island. Nevertheless, in 1628–29 Mataram's Sultan Agung decided to get rid of what it saw as an alien challenge to his rightful rule of the whole island, and besieged the young Dutch city of Batavia. Mataram could field a huge army of 150,000 or more—but a combination of Dutch control of the seas, and primitive land transport on Java itself, meant that not enough supplies could be moved to support such an army. Batavia survived, though barely, and Sultan Agung pulled back his armies.

J. P. Coen himself died of disease during the siege, in 1629, age 42. Much of his vision for a Dutch East Indies, however, came true. With control of the big island Sri Lanka off India, and the almost equally big island Taiwan off China, and permission to be the only Europeans to trade with Japan, the Dutch for a century did indeed become the inter-Asian shippers, as well as monopoly holders of the clove and nutmeg trade with Europe. Batavia/Jakarta flourished at the center of that trade. It was never again so threatened by Mataram. It would be the capital of the Dutch East Indies from 1619 until World War II, three and a quarter centuries (with one short British interlude).

---

35. GE Layer 35 is a Placemark referencing the city of Ambon in island of same name. Zoom out for overview of Moluccas (Malukus) and Banda Islands.

36. GE Layer 36 is a Placemark framing a view of the six main Banda islands. The largest was carved up into plantations and given to important VOC operatives or supporters. The westernmost island, Ran or Run, was fought over by the British and Dutch for half a century. In 1667 a treaty finally gave the Dutch control over it if they would relinquish their claims to another disputed island—Manhattan!

The erosion of Mataram

The failure of Sultan Agung of Mataram to defeat the Dutch in their new base at Batavia/Jakarta emboldened rebels in southwest Java to throw off rule from Mataram. When cities in the Pasisir became restive, the Sultan dealt with rebellious cities by closing all the Pasisir ports in 1655—perhaps effectively crippling resistance there, but depriving Mataram itself of the economic resources of the international trade of those ports. Java began to slip into a sleepy isolation, and the power of Mataram retreated to its rural heartlands of the Kedu Plain and the Solo and Brantas River valleys.

When Sultan Agung died in 1645, and whenever most rulers died thereafter, at least one contender for the throne enlisted the aid of the Dutch in Batavia. For every such service rendered, the Dutch demanded territory or privileges or both. In 1676 a revolt against Mataram blew up in Madura under the leadership of Trunajaya (also transliterated Trunojoyo). He and a substantial army crossed to Java proper and conquered the whole Pasisir. In 1677 he actually occupied the current Mataram capital. The king of Mataram, and after his death his son, had to swallow their pride and ask the Dutch for help. The price was steep: (a) all revenues from the Pasisir port cities; (b) a trade monopoly in textiles, opium, and sugar; and (c) the right to build forts and shipyards wherever they chose in Java![6]

In 1746, just a century after the death of Sultan Agung, the current sultan actually granted the VOC sovereignty over what was left of Mataram. In a 1755 treaty, even this remnant was split into two, with capital cities near today's Yogyakarta and Surakarta. In 1813, each of these two was further split, resulting in four "princely domains" (*Vorstenlanden*).[GE37] All that was left of the once-great state of Mataram was the Kedu Plain and the headwaters of the Solo River, and even inside these princely domains the Dutch could do as they pleased. They probably "pleased" not to do much, just to keep the illusion of independent Javanese royalty alive—but see for example a Dutch fort built in Yogyakarta in the 1760s, ostensibly to protect the Sultan, but also close enough to train its guns on his palace.[GE38]

VOC administration of Java

Here is a general picture of how VOC control developed in the lands they gradually acquired from Mataram (and Banten in the west). Batavia, the new Dutch capital, was originally built on the model of a typical Dutch town, with canals, and typical tall and narrow Dutch waterfront houses. As it spread a mixed style of architecture emerged, as the airy comfort of local tropical housing gradually dawned on the Dutch. By 1744 the current Dutch Governor General established "Buitenzorg" ("Beyond Care") as a retreat up in the cool hill country south of Batavia; it would gradually become modern Bogor.

Much of the land around Batavia/Jakarta, the *Ommelanden van Batavia* ("Surrounding Lands of Batavia") [GE39] was under direct VOC rule. It became the private property of Dutch or, in a surprisingly number of cases, Chinese landlords, mainly growing cash crops for the international trade such as sugar, and garden produce for the city of Batavia.

The VOC had different relationships with other areas of Java, since the lands were acquired piecemeal. Their next acquisitions were generally called the *Bovenlanden*, the "Highlands" south and east of the "Surrounding Lands."[GE40] In general the VOC policy was to avoid direct control and instead work through local officials that the Mataram sultanate had called *bupati*, and that the Dutch would call "Regents." Often a land-tax was levied by the Regent, who got to keep a percentage of it for delivering the rest to the VOC. Sometimes the Regents created coffee estates for the VOC, which bought the coffee at half its market rate and gave the

---

37. GE Layer 37 is a Folder including Polygons for Yogyakarta, Pakualaman, Surakarta, and Mangkunegaran; mainly based on map 4.2 in Cribb, *Historical Atlas of Indonesia*, p. 114. (This map is the simplified version of the four states done after the Java War of 1825–30).

38. GE Layer 38 is a Placemark referencing Fort Vredeburg with a familiar arrowhead-shaped bastions that marked European forts since the time of the Italian Renaissance. Zoom out of view to see Sultan's kraton at lower left.

39. GE Layer 39 is a Polygon in dark orange showing the "Surrounding Lands of Batavia." This and the following two layers are based on map 3.30 in Cribb, p. 95.

40. GE Layer 40 is a Polygon in lighter orange showing the "Highlands" next acquired.

Regent 10 percent for his trouble. Later the Dutch added the interior territories of Cirebon to their "Highlands" system, but around coastal Cirebon the Dutch left local ruling families with some authority as Sultan of the area.[GE⁴¹] They in turn farmed it out to ruthless overseers, and by the late 1700s it was infamous for its famines and rebellions. In 1774 the Dutch got a slice of land from the Sultan of Banten just west of the "Surrounding Lands."[GE⁴²] As other lands in central and then eastern Java came into VOC hands, similar policies of indirect rule were generally followed there, too.[GE⁴³]

In contrast with the British colony growing up in India, there were many times the number of Dutch administrators per unit of local population. Another difference is that many of the Dutch, especially in the early days when there were few European women in the Dutch East Indies, put down roots and intended to make this their permanent home.

By the late eighteenth century, despite looking prosperous on the surface, the VOC was in bad shape. It was riddled internally with corruption, as VOC operatives skimmed off the cream in illegal private trading. The most recent Anglo-Dutch War of the 1780s was financially disastrous. All the new money invested in the VOC was going to pay dividends due older investors—the desperate last phase of any failing business. So, on the last day of the 1700s, December 31, 1799, the VOC was abolished, and its debts and property were taken over by the Dutch state. Thereafter the area of today's Indonesia was officially called "The Netherlands Indies."

A particular problem with this was that the Dutch state itself seemed to be in the process of disappearing under Napoleon.

Gov.–Gen. Daendals and the *Grote Postweg*

The Napoleonic Wars influenced events worldwide, as you have already seen in some of our earlier "roads" chapters, and they had an impact here mainly in the person of Herman Willem Daendals. Even before the French Revolution he was a radical champion of democracy and a military leader in Holland's Patriot Movement. As a refugee in France, he became a general in the French revolutionary armies, and not surprisingly was given special assignments in the Netherlands. In 1806 Napoleon made his own brother, Louis Bonaparte, King of recently conquered Holland. With the British making inroads on Java, the Netherlands' most important overseas holding, the new king of Holland made General Daendals the Governor-General of the Dutch East Indies.

Daendals made it to Java in 1808, and with tremendous energy quickly evicted the British from their land holdings there. He built new forts in Jakarta and Surabaya in place of out-of-date facilities. He built an arms factory in Semarang, the most important city on the Pasisir (central northern) coast between them. But his most lasting creation was the Great Post Road.

With the British in command of the ocean, and the usual coastal sailing voyages between towns impossible, the logic of the Great Post Road was to be able to communicate—and to move troops efficiently—the whole length of the island of Java. The new road ran from Anyer on the western coast of Java to Panarukan just thirty-five miles shy of the eastern coast of Java.[GE⁴⁴] To avoid the swamps east of Jakarta (Batavia), and also to go up through the highlands favored by European settlers, from Jakarta the road went south up through Bogor and then circled Mt. Gede on the south side and on into Bandung (as did the initial road we perused). In fact, this is when Bandung as a city was created, with Daendals ordering a local administrator to move his capital eleven miles north up to his new road, instead of making the road go south to his capital. Then the road angled east and a bit north towards the westernmost of those Pasisir ports, Cirebon.[GE⁴⁵] From here on east,

---

41. GE Layer 41 is a Polygon in even lighter orange showing Cirebon (Cheribon in the spelling of the time).

42. GE Layer 42 is a Polygon in light orange showing this slice of territory west of the "Surrounding Lands of Batavia."

43. GE Layer 43 is an overview of Java; if you still have your GE Layer 37 turned on (the four princely domains), and Layers 38–41 showing the original Dutch land acquisitions, it gives you a fair picture of the waxing Dutch power and the waning princely power towards the end of the 1700s.

44. GE Layer 44 is a Folder titled "Grote Postweg/Jalan Raya Pos"; it includes a Path in orange at least roughing in the whole route, and twenty-one of the more important cities on the route, including Anyer as the western terminus and Panarukan at the eastern terminus, symbolized with purple star icons.

45. GE Layer 45 is a Placemark titled "Postweg, Jakarta to Cirebon"; it frames an overview of this stretch of the road.

the last two-thirds or so of the route, the road went through coastal towns including Surabaya and ended at the port of Panarukan (no longer important today; it didn't even make it into the Google Earth glossary!). The only variation from the coast is when the road took a shortcut across the base of the one major northern projection of the Pasisir coast, going through the cities of Demak, Kudus, and Pati before striking the coast again at Rembang.[GE46] Post stations for changing stagecoach horses were on average twenty miles apart, with a smaller station (*pendopo*) for resting and eating in-between. Over two centuries later you can still see its pattern along this main road and smaller roads that radiate out of it—cities about twenty miles apart, smaller towns halfway between them. The Great Post Road itself, especially where it runs along the Pasisir, has become one continuous strip city. In the words of one study of the road, "One could call Java the longest city in the world with the Grote Postweg as its main transport and economic artery."[7]

Gov.-Gen. Daendals had no money to work with, so the road was built on appeals to local authorities, and when those failed, on draft labor. The great postal road in the long run did much to knit Java together as a community. It reduced the time of sending a letter from one end to the other from two weeks to six days. In the short run, however, it was built with the loss of thousands of Javanese lives, perhaps as many as 10,000. Daendals in his person echoes the progression of the entire French Revolution—beginning in a quest for individual freedom and dignity, ending in the brutal manipulation of power. He is still known to the Javanese as *Tuan Besar Guntur*, or "Mister Thunder," for his dictatorial style. As a postscript, Daendals was back in Europe by 1811, and led a Napoleonic army in the invasion of Russia in 1812. He ended his days at Elmina on today's Ghana coast, a key Portuguese holding you may recall from early in their maritime expansion but now held by the Dutch (like so many earlier Portuguese holdings!). He had great plans for doing with Ghana what he had done with Java, but died there of malaria in 1818. But for now remember Daendals' Great Post Road along the length of Java. Towards the end of this chapter we will see its building again, through the eyes of a most famous modern Indonesia writer and a good Dutch filmmaker.

British interlude

In 1811 it took the British only a month and a half to conquer the Dutch and French forces in Java, even though the Dutch waged a spirited defense from Daendal's new fort in Jakarta. The British Proconsul, Stamford Raffles, would now have four and a half years to put his stamp on the colony. Raffles had been in Southeast Asia for six years, and already spoke Malay. He moved up to Bogor, and kept the bulk of the Dutch administrators there. He outlawed slavery and curtailed the opium trade. He set up a new system of landholdings based on the advice of the most progressive Dutch voices in the area. He launched an expedition to Borobudur, a ruin long overgrown with tropical vegetation, to uncover it and research its past. He argued mightily with his superiors for keeping Java as a key British base in Southeast Asia, but it was returned to the Dutch at the end of the Napoleonic Wars. It was Raffles who then sold the British on the idea of putting a "wedge" into Malacca Strait to keep trade open—in 1819 he founded the colony of Singapore on a little island about four miles by seven miles, at the tip end of the Malay Peninsula and right across the Strait from the mid-point of Sumatra.[GE47] A key treaty shaping the area's future—the Anglo-Dutch Treaty of 1824—was the result of Raffles' confrontation with his equally aggressive Dutch counterpart in Java. It gave the British hegemony north of Malacca Strait, and the Dutch hegemony south of it. They swapped out ports, and proceeded on their merry colonial ways. This is the main reason why the southern tip of the Malay Peninsula and Sumatra, despite their proximity and great cultural similarities, are in different states today.

So by 1824 the Dutch had fairly well settled their problems with their main colonial competitor for the last two centuries and more, the British. Without that interference, in the next century they would unify their Dutch East Indies in a way that made its borders the logical choice for borders for a future independent state, today's Indonesia. But in the first few years of that period—the 1825–1830 period of the Java War—it didn't look especially promising for the Dutch.

---

46. GE Layer 46 is a Placemark titled "Postweg, Demak-Kudus-Pati-Rembang"; it frames a view of the Demak to Rembang stretch of the road.

47. GE Layer 47 is a Placemark framing a view of modern Singapore, a totally independent state since 1965.

The Java War

This war is also often called the Diponegoro War, after its key leader, Prince Diponegoro of Yogyakarta. After the Dutch return to power in 1816, the court at Yogyakarta was in turmoil. Land seizures by both Dutch and British in preceding years meant the royal family had no lands to offer its followers. In a financial crunch, they leased lands to Chinese and European farmers, reducing many Javanese farmers to the status of poorly paid hired hands. Natural disasters came unusually close together—a cholera epidemic in 1821, a Mt. Merapi eruption in 1822, and poor rice harvests about this same time. In Javanese folklore there is the concept of a Just Prince, *Ratu Adil*, who will appear in a time of chaos and return the Kingdom of Mataram to all its former glory.[8] By 1825 it was like dust in a mine or a mill, tinder set to go off with the right spark.

Diponegoro was indeed of royal blood, a direct descendant of Mataram's famous Sultan Agung. He was not brought up at court (and so was not blamed for its current policies), but by a grandmother who schooled him in both Islamic and priyayi traditions. A Dutch decision to run a road through his personal rice fields in Tegalrejo[GE[48]] was the last straw as far as he was concerned, sending him into open rebellion against both the Dutch and the royal government at Yogyakarta, which he saw as lackeys of the Dutch. The Dutch sent an army to capture him, but instead it was Diponegoro's forces that did most of the capturing. They advanced as far east as Madiun and even threatened Surabaya; for a time they surrounded Yogyakarta and cut off its food supplies. [GE[49]] It was a bloody war lasting five years, with something like 200,000 dead (including 8,000 Dutch soldiers). The Dutch were on the verge of giving up, when they decided on one last ruse: they invited Diponegoro to Magelang (north of Yogyakarta and just five miles from his home at Tegalrejo, and eventual site of the future Dutch school for administrators and the future Indonesian West Point)[GE[50]] for treaty talks—where he was captured by deceit.

So almost overnight the Dutch were transformed from probable losers in the Java War to big winners with no serious opponents to a wide new extension of colonialism. This extension would be both geographic in the whole archipelago, and more to the point for our corridor, greater in its intensity on their central holding of Java.

The Cultivation System

The first and most dramatic change was the 1830 imposition of the "Cultivation System" (*Cultuurstelsel*). In place of a land tax, one-fifth of all land (and labor) in Java was to go to cash crops specified for each area by the government. In practice this mean taking a fifth of the land out of rice cultivation, and devoting that land to coffee, indigo, sugar, tea, cinnamon, tobacco, and even cochineal (the little scale insects that grew on prickly-pear cactus and gave a valuable red-orange dye, an old friend transplanted from colonial Mexico!). Virtually every village in Java (*kampong, kampung*) was physically transformed in the process, from scattered farmsteads throughout the fields to a central walled village with just a few doors, and a thorn hedge planted around the outer field holdings of the village with only a few openings. Villagers were forbidden to move without permission. The designated cash crops were collected and processed by either the Dutch or the ethnic Chinese minority that generally flourished under Dutch rule.

In terms of the Dutch colonial economy, it was a howling success. Revenues for the 1830s, the first decade of the Cultivation System, were six times as large as those from the previous decade! It more than paid off the costs of the Java and Belgium wars. In the words of one author, it was these "profits from agricultural production in Java that built the Netherlands' railways, canals and military fortifications."[9] Although the Dutch had grown coffee in Indonesia since the 1600s, the efficiency and quality control of this era made "Java" (and its corruption "Joe") the American euphemism for a great cup of coffee.

---

48. GE Layer 48 is a Placemark referencing Tegalrejo, about twenty-five miles NNW of Yogyakarta.

49. GE Layer 49 is a Folder containing a Polygon representing the center of the rebellion (red outlined with white), and a multi-part Polygon representing related uprisings (just red areas). Based on map 4.1 in Cribb, *Historical Atlas of Indonesia*, p. 114.

50. GE Layer 50 is a Placemark referencing Magelang.

The impact of the Cultivation System on the Javanese farmers is still an item of debate among historians. At the least, some extra labor was imposed on virtually every man in Java. Since both the Dutch administrators and their Javanese counterparts got a percentage of the production, their personal interest was in maximizing that production, whatever happened to the farmers. Scattered famines over the next thirty years were probably owing to the new exactions, as the more sensitive of the Dutch administrators came to believe.

Max Havelaar

In 1860 a book came out in Dutch, in Holland, titled *Max Havelaar: or the Coffee Auctions of the Dutch Trading Company*. It was an expose of what the Cultivation System was doing to Java, written by one who signed himself "Multatuli" ("I have suffered much")—in real life Eduard Douwes Dekker. Born the son of a Dutch sea captain in 1820, Dekker first went to Java in 1838. He married there in 1846, and he and his wife had two children in the mid-1850s. In 1856 he rose to the position of Assistant Resident of Lebak, an area of southwest Java, and because of his policies and friction with his superiors he lasted only three months on the job.

The book itself is a mixed blessing. Narrator through a good half of it is an over-the-top caricature of a narrow, selfish drudge of a coffee merchant named Batavus Droogstoppel. The hero of the story, Max, is obviously the author writ large and noble. There are way too many asides to the dear reader. But some of the prose sparkles, as in the short story of Saijah and Adinda, the love story of a young couple doomed by the repeated seizure of the household water buffalo by the greedy local regent. And the collusion of Dutch residents and local administrators in the fleecing of the common farmers is vividly told by one who had seen it at work in its details:

> *Famine?* In rich, fertile, blessed Java—*famine*? Yes, reader. Only a few years ago, whole districts died of starvation. Mothers offered their children for sale to obtain food. Mothers ate their children . . .
>
> But then the Motherland took a hand in the matter. In the council-chambers of the people's representatives in Holland there was dissatisfaction, and the Governor-General of that day had to issue instructions that in future the output of what were called the *European-market products* was not to be pushed to the point of causing famine . . .
>
> I see I have been bitter. But what would you think of someone who could write such things without bitterness?[10]

The naturalist Alfred Russel Wallace, it may be recalled, spent three and a half months in Java in 1861, the year after *Max Havelaar* came out. He took great exception to the book—"a very tedious and long-winded story, full of rambling digressions, and whose only point is to show that the Dutch Residents and Assistant Residents wink at the extortions of the native princes." He thought that Dutch Java was the best colonial system in the world, but fairly well laid the brutal control system bare in his own analysis:

> The mode of government now adopted in Java is to retain the whole series of native rulers, from the village chief up to princes, who, under the name of Regents, are the heads of districts about the size of a small English county. With each Regent is placed a Dutch Resident, or Assistant Resident, who is considered to be his "elder brother," and whose "orders" take the form of "recommendations," which are however implicitly obeyed. Along with each Assistant Resident is a Controller, a kind of inspector of all the lower native rulers, who periodically visits every village in the district, examines the proceedings of the native courts, hears complaints against the head-men or other native chiefs, and superintends the Government plantations.

Wallace defended the Dutch Culture System on these grounds:

> Natives of tropical climates have few wants, and, when these are supplied, are disinclined to work for superfluities without some strong incitement. With such a people the introduction of any new or systematic cultivation is almost impossible, except by the despotic orders of chiefs whom they have been accustomed to obey, as children obey their parents.[11]

In general it looks to most modern readers to be a defense that justifies the original criticism.

The "Liberal Policy" and neo-colonialism

In a word, *Max Havelaar* left a lasting impression on the Dutch public, and some humanitarian scrutiny was brought to bear on Dutch administration in the East Indies. But there was also a less altruistic Liberalism at work, one that asked that more agricultural land be opened to Dutch purchasers in the name of free market potentialities. In 1870 both these pressure groups resulted in an Agrarian Law being passed by the Dutch parliament. Europeans could not buy land outright, but they were now allowed to lease it long-term—provided it didn't cut into village subsistence lands. A modified version of the Cultivation System stayed in place.

About 1870, too, an intensification of European colonialism took place virtually worldwide, perhaps because never before or since was Europe so technologically superior. It was called neo-colonialism, and it affected Holland and its East Indies as well. In the next forty years the Dutch intensively occupied all of what is today Indonesia (which is why Indonesia has the borders it does today), and part of that new wave of managers and bookkeepers and overseers and surveyors and teachers came into Java. In general many of this generation of Dutch, too, in their own minds came to stay, in contrast with British who came to India in this same time. This is a key reason there was a lot more effort on the part of Dutch residents of Indonesia after World War II to retain their colony than among their British counterparts in India.

In the nineteenth century the Pasisir ports revived under the Dutch. The port facilities at Semarang were built up to handle the export of goods coming overland from Surakarta and Yogyakarta, and it became a banking center of some note. Around 1835 the Dutch had designated Surabaya to be their major industrial city and port, and by mid-century it was already coming to be. Bogor had its famous botanical gardens established in 1817, the year after the British left. In the neo-colonial era, however, it became a real intellectual center. By 1880 it had a school of agriculture, pharmacological labs, and a matching library. In large part because of this, for example, the Dutch East Indies would corner the world production market of pure quinine by World War II.

Railroads have been a critical development in every one of our regional transportation corridors thus far; in the next two chapters they will be again along Japan's Honshu, between Kyoto and Tokyo, and will have attenuated effect in China's Yangtze Valley (because there the river system itself does some of the heavy lifting in terms of cheap transport). Look at the pattern of Dutch railroad building in Java in three increments: track built by 1888, by 1899, and by 1913—virtually all of Java's railroad grid built in a period of just thirty-five years.[GE51] One of the first lines to be built was from Semarang down to Solo and Yogyakarta. By 1913 there was not just one but two main lines connecting Jakarta with Surabaya, 400 straight-line miles away.

The Ethical Policy

By century's end, there were strong opponents of the Cultivation System in the Dutch parliament. One legislator argued convincingly that Holland had taken so much treasure out of the East Indies that the Dutch had incurred a "debt of honor." The least the Dutch could do now (now being 1901), he convinced a majority of his colleagues, was to give something back in terms of granting some local autonomy, and particularly in terms of investing in health, education, and agricultural improvements. There is still a lively historical debate on its achievements, but generally speaking Indonesia's indigenous population stayed on the subsistence end of the scale and Europeans stayed on the large agriculture–mills–rails–big business end. What did change was the exposure of a whole generation of Indonesian students to European ideas. If anything, that speeded up antagonism to Dutch presence.

---

51. GE Layer 51 is a Folder titled "Growth of Railroads." Open it, and then turn on each of the three Folders inside in turn, 1888, 1899, and 1913. Note that the first railroad to connect Jakarta and Surabaya was the one going through Bogor, Bandung, Yogyakarta, and Surakarta—the original road we visually explored at the first of the chapter. A main line along the north coast came later. No railroad ever tried to go down from Bandung to Cirebon the way Daendals' Jalan Raya Pos did.

ROOTS OF INDONESIAN NATIONALISM

Letters of a Javanese Princess

April 21 is a national holiday in Indonesia because it is the anniversary of the 1879 birthday of Raden (a title of nobility) Ajeng Kartini. She was born in Jepara, the Pasisir city that had been a major port for Demak and Mataram, and where her father was currently serving as local administrator under the Dutch. Because of his position, unusually, his daughter was able to go to a Dutch-language school through age twelve, where she learned to speak and read Dutch with fluency. Then for four long years she was confined in seclusion in her house in preparation for marriage, as was usual with upper-class families. During this time she struck up pen-pal relationships with Dutch girls and read voraciously. One of her local mentors afterwards was Mevrouw (Lady) Abendanon, the socialist and feminist wife of the Dutch Minister of Education and Industry (socialism, as you saw in the Russia and Socialism chapter, was the most friendly of all the major nineteenth-century "-isms" to gender equality). Partly under her influence Kartini opened a school for girls. In 1903 she married a fairly progressive Indonesian administrator in the territory of nearby Rembang, and brought her little school with her ("what a strange bridal dower," she wrote in one of her letters). She died there of childbirth complications a few days after the birth of her first child in September of 1904, age twenty-five. Her letters were published in Dutch in 1911; they generated enough support and sympathy for her ideal girl's school that one was established in 1916, and in 1922 her letters were translated into the new Bahasa Indonesia language. Full of personality and sharp insights into both Javanese and Dutch culture and history, they are a poignant record of a promising life cut off way too soon.[GE52]

Sarekat Islam

Today's Indonesia celebrates May 20 as "National Awakening Day" because of the formation on that day in 1908 of the "Noble Endeavour" (*Budi Otomo*) movement in Yogyakarta. The brainchild of a retired Javanese doctor, it began as nothing more than an attempt to raise academic scholarships for Indonesian students. It quickly gained the support of Dutch-educated students and the *priyayi*, and within a couple of years had ten thousand members. They talked and wrote a lot about combining the best of European and Asian cultures, so in this sense there was some cultural nationalism here—at least Indonesian culture was seen as having equal value. But its leadership kept it carefully non-political, and Budi Otomo soon lost the support of the younger, more radical intellectuals.

Many of these went to the new "Islamic Association" (*Sarekat Islam*), whose moving spirit was Omar Said Tjokroaminoto (1882–1934; often transliterated Cokroaminoto). He was born in Madiun[GE53] of priyayi stock, son of a district chief and grandson of a regent. By the time he was twenty he had graduated from the Dutch school in Magelang[GE54] that trained local civil servants. Working as a second-level civil servant under the Dutch had little appeal for him, and he wound up in the bustling city of Surabaya. His day job was in the sugar industry, but politics took every other waking hour. In 1912 he took a local organization of Indonesian merchants that had been set up the year before in Surakarta—the "Islamic Trade Association," originally set up to protest Chinese business monopolies in the batik trade—restructured it and dropped the "Trade" word, turning it into the first real mass national independence party in the Dutch East Indies.

Looking back at it, there were three important intellectual currents in Sarekat Islam—currents that soon diverged and tore Sarekat Islam apart, but that it powerfully introduced to the political scene. The first was Islamic modernism, the belief that a pure Islam was fully compatible with modern science and representative political forms (sounding much like Sayed Khan and his "Aligarh men" in British India, no?). The second was

---

52. GE Layer 52 is a Folder titled "Life of Kartini." It has Placemarks for her birth city of Jepara and for the village of Bulu in Rembang's administrative district, near where she died. The two sites are about fifty miles apart, and her whole life was compassed in this small area; but as Thoreau said, "I have traveled widely in Concord." The Letters are available in English as a public domain e-text, at this website: https://archive.org/details/lettersofjavanes00kart

53. GE Layer 53 is a Placemark referencing Madiun (you've seen it before, and will again!).

54. GE Layer 54 is a Placemark referencing Magelang (also of future importance).

a socialist, and particularly Marxist, analysis of colonial society and economics (reminding one of the young Nelson Mandela's later encounter with, and grudging appreciation of, Marxism). The third was the idea that the West had generally paved the way to the future ("colonialism" not being representative of the best of the West!), and that Indonesia could take a shortcut to that future by learning more from the western powers, including the Dutch (perhaps reminding a reader of this text of narodnichestvo, that homegrown Russian socialism of the nineteenth century).[12]

By 1919, the year after World War I ended, Sarekat Islam claimed a membership of over a million. It was the first real mass nationalistic organization, catching a wave of popular opposition to the Dutch rule. But it had little idea how to translate that into effective change, especially in the face of Dutch military power. When a colonial official was assassinated in 1919 the Dutch cracked down hard, sending hundreds to political prisons. Tjokroaminoto himself was jailed by the Dutch in 1921, effectively beheading the movement.

At this point the young nationalist intellectuals saw the need for spreading their ideas to a broader part of the population, and for building up their own institutions that couldn't so quickly be undone by a military crackdown.

The creation of Bahasa Indonesia

Language is usually a good, and often the best, key to modern national identity. In this survey of modern history, watching modern group identities develop consciousness and then political form, you have seen remnant languages preserved (Irish), single languages standardized out of many regional dialects and old manuscript or religious languages (Czech, Afrikaans, etc.), and even reinvented (spoken Hebrew). The creation of Bahasa Indonesia is at least as interesting as any of those.

For Indonesian intellectuals of the 1920s in the process of shaping a modern national identity, the need for a unifying language was obvious. The choice of which language, however, was not so obvious. Javanese was the plurality language, but would be seen as Javanese imperialism outside that island. Too, it was a very hierarchical language, with degrees of respect related to traditional classes; the self-consciously egalitarian young nationalist intellectuals had a problem with that. Dutch was the common language of all those with higher education, including almost all of the nationalist intelligentsia—but it was the language of the colonial overlords and as such was unacceptable as a new national language. This Dutch language common denominator of these young intellectuals, however, did play a role in choosing such a language. As Benedict Anderson says in *Language and Power: Exploring Political Cultures in Indonesia*: "Paradoxically, the spread of Indonesian as the national language was only possible once Dutch had become the inner language of the intelligentsia."[13]

What they settled on (in discussions in Dutch!) was Malay, the coastal trading language that had been the lingua franca of the island chain for hundreds of years. The first Dutch to visit what is today Indonesia, in the late 1500s, talked about how widely it was spoken, and the first European missionaries, including St. Francis Xavier who spent time in the Moluccas (Malaka), said it was the language everyone understood. As befitted a coastal trading language, it was fairly simple and easy to learn—but it could be added to and elaborated on endlessly, for other purposes. There were newspapers published in Malay as early as 1902, and Sarekat Islam (founded 1912, as you've seen) championed its use. This, then, was the vehicle chosen to carry the nationalism of the educated elite to the masses.

They called their "new-and-improved" coastal Malay "Bahasa Indonesia," "The Language of Indonesia." One of the first fruits of this movement was a 1921 poem published by a member of the liberal-national "Young Sumatra," titled "*Bahasa Bangsa*," or "Language, Nation"; it argued that "a feeling of solidarity" would come from having a common language with deep local roots.[14] The parallel and even larger "Young Java" group hosted a Youth Conference in Jakarta in 1926, and voted to use Malay at all of its future meetings. Study clubs were set up for its study and practice.

Changing your spoken language after adulthood is a tough assignment, and despite the enthusiasm for it, communicating in Bahasa Indonesia often remained the ideal, not the reality. It grew slowly in use through the 1930s, with some new journals written solely in it. And the Japanese inadvertently helped it along during their 1942–45 occupation. They outlawed Dutch, intending eventually to make Japanese the language of instruction. But in the short run, since Japanese was so hard for Indonesians to learn, they relied on Bahasa Indonesia, and actually set up a commission to standardize the language. In the 1945 constitution of the newly-independent Indonesia, Bahasa Indonesia was named the sole national language.

The young Sukarno

Sukarno was born in 1901 in Surabaya.[GE55] His father was a Javanese primary school teacher of aristocratic background, and his mother was Balinese (Sukarno would speak the local languages Javanese, Balinese, and Sundanese among the ten or so in which he would become fluent). His father sent him to a Dutch-language Middle School in Mojerkerto,[GE56] some twenty-five miles southwest down the main road towards Surakarta and Yogyakarta. Summer vacations he spent with his grandparents in Tulungagung,[GE57] about eighty miles southwest of Surabaya and near the Brantas River. Here he fell in love with the puppet theatre, the wayang kulit sung into life by the dalang and the gamelan.

In 1916 Sukarno came back to Surabaya for Dutch-language secondary school. He lived not with his family, but with Tjokroaminoto, who was obviously grooming this handsome, personable, and brilliant teenager for future service in the nationalistic cause. He talked politics with the young Sukarno, introduced him to local movers and shakers in politics and economics, and in 1920 gave him permission to marry his daughter.

In 1921, the twenty-year-old Sukarno entered Bandung Institute of Technology,[GE58] which the Dutch had just opened the year before. He majored in civil engineering and architecture, and upon graduation in 1926 he and a friend actually set up an architectural firm, mostly working with upscale private housing. But politics and the future independence of Indonesia from Dutch colonialism gradually came to be his all-consuming cause. In his university years he met, or claimed to have met, a peasant named Marhaen in southern Bandung ("marhaen" simply means "farmer" in Sundanese, then still the main language of western Java). The farmer was young, hard-working, and well intentioned but still poor—because of colonialism and unbridled capitalism. Sukarno envisioned millions of such Marhaens working together in self-help organizations, generally bound up in a national independence movement. He gradually developed this into a political philosophy—or at least an attractive political slogan—called Marhaenism.

Sukarno's chief rivals for leadership of the Indonesian national movement in the 1920s, including Mohammad Hatta, were Dutch-university-educated "Social Democrats," Marxist at least in terms of social analysis and economic philosophy. They thought Sukarno's political ideals were vague, romantic, and provincial (he had never even traveled outside the Netherlands East Indies). Sukarno for his part (like Mao Zedong in the same decade, as you'll see in a later chapter) knew that the majority of the poor in Indonesia were not proletarians but peasant farmers. His soaring popularity proved that he was the one with his finger on the country's pulse, not the returned students.

The year Sukarno graduated from Bandung Technical Institute, 1926, he set up a General Study Club. It was a political organization openly aiming at national independence, and within a year would morph into the PNI, the National Independence Party. The general setting was a fight between the new Communist Party and the older Sarekat Islam that was fast crippling both. Sukarno used his marvelous oratory to argue that working for national unity should submerge all other differences. By 1929 Sukarno's PNI was claiming a membership of 10,000, and the Dutch decided to crack down. Late that year Sukarno was arrested in Yogyakarta, and tried in Bandung. He was able to turn the trial into a platform for speeches on the evils of colonialism, but was sentenced to four years in jail (of which he served two). In 1934 he was arrested again, this time without trial so there would be no speeches. He was sent to Ende, Flores,[GE59] in internal exile. In 1938, he was transferred to Bengkulu, Sumatra,[GE60] and was still there when Japanese invaded the country in 1942.

---

55. First open the unnumbered Folder titled "The young Sukarno." Then go to GE Layer 55, a Placemark referencing his (approximate) birthplace, near the heart of today's Surabaya.
56. GE Layer 56 is a Placemark referencing Mojerkerto.
57. GE Layer 57 is a Placemark referencing Tulungagung.
58. GE Layer 58 is a Placemark referencing Bandung Institute of Technology, still one of Indonesia's premier universities.
59. GE Layer 59 is a Placemark referencing Ende, Flores.
60. GE Layer 60 is a Placemark referencing Bengkulu, Sumatra.

The Dutch probably congratulated themselves on once again neatly beheading the independence movement; with Sukarno off the political scene his PNI, and the national movement generally, virtually dissolved. But the Japanese were soon to transform the situation.

Japanese occupation

Japan went to full-scale war with China in July of 1937. In early December of 1941 it opened war with the United States and its western allies by catching much of the Pacific Fleet at anchor at its base in Pearl Harbor, Oahu, Hawaii. Part of the Japanese logic for war with the U.S. was that we had cut off supplies of oil and scrap metal to them to protest their aggression in China and vicinity. The Dutch East Indies had oil, and rubber, and quinine, and tin; to secure it—and add this Asian territory to its "new order" of things—Japan attacked the Netherlands East Indies in mid-January of 1942. The initial attacks were in the rough northern arc of today's Indonesia, particularly in Kalimantan and Sulawesi. Then came attacks on the smooth southern arc of islands—Japanese landings in Sumatra in the west, and the surprise taking of Bali, just east of Java. With the airport of Denpasar[GE61] in southern Bali, Japanese bombers were less than 200 miles from Surabaya. At this point—around February 20, 1942, two and a half months after Pearl Harbor—the only large island of today's Indonesia left outside Japanese control was Java. It was carefully targeted, and an invasion fleet of cruisers and transports put together north of the island.

On February 27 an allied naval squadron of U.S., British, and Dutch heavy and light cruisers attacked the invasion fleet, trying to sink the transports. The Japanese heavy cruisers proved superior, especially in their use of torpedoes; most of the allied ships were sunk and the last two retreated. This was the Battle of the Java Sea, mainly fought north of Surabaya. Java was now ripe for the picking. The first Japanese troops went ashore on the north coast on March 1. Surabaya fell March 7, and on March 8—a stunning one week from the first landings—the Allies surrendered at Kalijati,[GE62] roughly halfway between Bandung and the north coast. The Dutch were summarily interned in camps, where many died, and use of the Dutch language was outlawed. It was a blow to the image of European superiority from which the Dutch never recovered in this part of the world.

Leading Indonesian nationalists and intellectuals generally faced a choice—to oppose Japanese rule, or treat Japan as a short-term ally. Sukarno's decision was crucial. When a Japanese army delegation came to Padang, Sumatra, in 1942 to ask him for his help in administering the country if they would promise Indonesia eventual independence, he agreed.

Many of the Javanese had appreciated seeing another Asian people humiliate arrogant westerners, and were at first inclined to welcome Japanese power. The Japanese created some mass organizations in Java, in an attempt to "win the hearts and minds" of the people of this key island. One of them was PUTERA, set up on the first anniversary of the surrender of the Dutch. It was an acronym for "Center of People's Power," and was limited to Java. Ostensibly set up to help Greater Japan in the war effort, it probably had more lasting importance as a public relations platform for Sukarno and Muhammad Hatta and their message of Indonesian unity and coming independence.

But Japanese control was always by strict martial law. All political parties were banned. Java was hit particularly hard by Japanese economic policies. All western markets for its plantation economy—coffee, tea, sugar, rubber—were cut off, and many of these plantations were converted to products useable by the Japanese war machine (castor bean production for oils and lubricants, for example). The result by 1943 was economic depression more severe than ever under the Dutch. Two million forced laborers were impressed from Indonesia, mostly from Java, by the Japanese (through PUTERA, for which Sukarno later came in for much criticism). These included women to serve as prostitutes for the Japanese army. Many such forced laborers were taken far from home, and would be stranded there at war's end. Two years into the Japanese occupation, high government demands for rice began to create famine conditions, which triggered popular rebellion. In February of

---

61. GE Layer 61 is a Placemark referencing Denpasar airport in southern Bali.
62. GE Layer 62 is a Placemark referencing Kalijati.

1944 a peasant rebellion broke out around Singaparna, about fifty miles southeast of Bandung.[GE63] In February of 1945 troops of PETA, a Javanese auxiliary force created by the Japanese (and also organized by PUTERA), mutinied near Blitar in East Java.[GE64] Its leader, Supriyadi, escaped the brutal Japanese suppression and went underground, becoming one of the first folk heroes of the independence movement.

Only as the war turned against Japan did the Japanese government begin to consider Indonesian independence. In March of 1945 the Japanese allowed a committee of sixty well-known nationalists to meet in Jakarta to prepare for future independence. On a couple of major points there was general agreement: (1) the new state was to have the same boundaries as the old Netherlands Indies, and (2) be a republic. On a couple of other major issues there was much disagreement. The first of these was whether the new state should be a centralized federal system or a more de-centralized confederation. Sukarno's views eventually carried the day. For a quarter century he had worked for unity in the national independence movement aimed toward a unitary state. The second of the hotly debated issues was whether or not the new Indonesia should be an officially Islamic state. Here again Sukarno won his argument against formal declaration as an Islamic state, saying it would cause fatal disaffection from places such as Bali (by far majority Hindu) and islands in the east such as Timor (majority Christian since Portuguese colonial days). What he left unspoken was that the majority of Indonesia's Muslims were not strict Muslims. By June of 1945, in a characteristic stroke of brilliance, Sukarno papered over divisions on this issue (and others) with his *Pancasila*, or Five Principles:

1. nationalism—meaning every Indonesian should aspire to be a loyal patriot, supporting a strong federal union;

2. internationalism—a view of the world that recognized other countries of the world as independent equals, including current colonies of the imperial powers;

3. social justice—the state would be one concerned with the plight of its weaker citizens; unrestricted capitalism would not be allowed to run roughshod over the poor Indonesians (Marxists in and out of Indonesia generally translated this term "socialism");

4. democracy—representative democracy in the form of a republic;

5. belief in God—an unspecified deity of one's choice, easy for the majority Muslim community to identify as Allah, equally easy for other religions to apply to their own beliefs and not feel threatened by imposition of Sharia law on the whole body politic . . .

On August 6 and 9 the U.S. dropped atomic bombs on Hiroshima and Nagasaki, and on August 15 Japan surrendered unconditionally to the Allies. With the Japanese army units still intact in Indonesia, however, Sukarno was wary about announcing independence. Only when he and Muhammad Hatta were kidnapped by young radicals did he agree to declare independence, and this only after informing the Japanese commander in advance. On August 17 Sukarno read a declaration of Indonesian independence. This was in Jakarta; but there is a great statue memorializing the moment in Surabaya.[GE65]

INDEPENDENCE

Establishing the Republic

In Jakarta the new state seemed to take quick shape. The constitution that had been hammered out by the preparatory committee earlier that year was put into place. Government ministries were set up, with Sukarno being chosen President and Muhammad Hatta the Vice President. But word of the new government spread slowly, even on the island of Java, and when it did arrive there was some fighting between excited new crowds celebrating independence and the Japanese army. The first Allied troops to come into Java and replace the Japanese

---

63. GE Layer 63 is a Placemark referencing Singaparna.
64. GE Layer 64 is a Placemark referencing Blitar.
65. GE Layer 65 is a Placemark referencing the statues, in Surabaya's Heroes Monument.

were British and Indian units. They not only did not recognize the declaration of Indonesian independence (seeing it as some sort of Japanese trick to end western colonialism), they saw Sukarno as a fascist collaborator, a Quisling, who should be tried for war crimes instead of being named President. There was even more friction between nationalist Indonesians and these British forces than there had been with the Japanese. Most spectacular was "The Battle of Surabaya" in November when independent Indonesian military forces stubbornly held out for three weeks against British forces that included naval and air support. This "Battle of Surabaya" convinced the British they needed to cut and leave as soon as they could. It generally convinced the Indonesians they had to have a regular army.

For almost two years there was a curious sort of joint Dutch-Indonesian Republican occupation of Jakarta. In Java as a whole there were generally separate areas of Dutch and Republican control; the Dutch held a narrow corridor including Jakarta, Bogor, and Bandung, a small zone around Semarang and a larger zone around Surabaya.[GE66] The British, desperate to leave, pressured both sides to an agreement at Linggajati[GE67] in November of 1946. Its main provisions were that Indonesia was to become independent on January 1, 1949, but as a loose confederation—this last to favor pockets of continued Dutch presence. The two sides signed, but neither was happy with the agreement. All-out war broke out between the two from July 21 to August 4, 1947. In these two weeks the Dutch conquered half of Java—all the territory inside what came to be called the Van Mook Line, named after the current Lieutenant Governor-General.[GE68] In January of 1948 the United States arranged negotiations between the two warring parties on a U.S. warship anchored in Jakarta Bay. The resulting agreement recognized the Indonesian Republic, but also the current Dutch holdings. It was extremely unpopular with the Indonesian public.

On September 18, 1948, a civil war broke out between Indonesian factions. P.K.I. and leftist army units took over Madiun in eastern Java[GE69] and proclaimed a Communist government. After a month of hard and bloody fighting, the Republican forces suppressed the rebellion. This in turn triggered two things, one that in the short run hurt the Republic, but also one that in the long run helped it. The short-run event was a Dutch decision in December to take advantage of Republican weakness and kill it once and for all. A new military offensive captured a good bit of territory, including the current Republican capital of Yogyakarta and the persons of President Sukarno and Vice-President Hatta. But it did not totally break the growing Indonesia army on Java. The long-run development was a new U.S. appreciation of the Indonesian Republic; in the Cold War atmosphere of 1949 any power that suppressed any Communist entity was a friend of ours! Since U.S. financial aid was critical in rebuilding Holland after the destruction of WW II, the Dutch were in no position to bargain when the U.S. applied pressure. In December of 1949 they recognized the full independence of Indonesia under the Republican government.

There were a few later repercussions. In January of 1950 a Dutch commando leader named Raymond Westerling, operating in the Jakarta-to-Bandung corridor, led one last and unsuccessful rebellion against the Republic. On the Indonesian side, some army and irregular armed forces that were being disbanded thought that the Dutch still had too privileged a position in the new Indonesia. They formed an underground "Sick At Heart" brigade, and were strong enough to operate for awhile in the outskirts of Jakarta. Everything was complicated by a 1953 economic boom associated with the Korean War, and a quick bust of same the next year.

The Bandung Conference

Books of modern history and political science often speak of "the Bandung generation." They refer to the world-wide impact of the Bandung Conference, technically the Asia-Africa Conference, of April, 1955, masterminded and hosted by Sukarno. The five organizing states were India, Burma, Pakistan, Sri Lanka (these

---

66. GE Layer 66 is a Folder titled "Dutch holdings 1945–1947"; inside are Polygons shaded in red representing the Jakarta-Bogor-Bandung area, the small area around Semarang, and the larger area around Surabaya.

67. GE Layer 67 is a Placemark referencing Linggajati in western Java.

68. GE Layer 68 is a Folder titled "Dutch conquests June 21–Aug 4, 1947"; it includes two Polygons again symbolized in red, of the territory within the Van Mook Lines.

69. GE Layer 69 is a Placemark referencing Madiun.

four the main pieces of the former British Raj, all newly founded within the past eight years), and Indonesia. Twenty-nine nations sent representatives, who represented a virtually solid bloc from Libya across to China. This was to be a consciousness-raising gathering of The Third World, those rising nations independent of both the U.S. and NATO on the one hand, and the Soviet Union and the Warsaw Pact nations on the other. Sukarno coined one of his more famous neologisms here, NEFOS, for Newly Emerging Forces (as opposed to OLDE-FOS, Old Established Forces, or NEKOLIM, Neo-Colonial Imperialists). It was a Who's Who of the non-aligned, including Jawaharlal Nehru of India, Gamal Abdel Nasser of Egypt, and Zhou Enlai of China. And it seemed to be a movement with growth potential: sub-Saharan African colonies were just about to join Asian and Mideastern independent countries—Ghana would win independence in 1957 and by 1960 many more would join the ranks of the independents yearly. There were some differences of opinion, including much debate about the Soviet Union's role in Eastern Europe (the wording that finally emerged condemned colonialism "in all its forms"). Overall, however, it was a love fest. Presiding over it all, perhaps at the zenith of his world prestige, was Sukarno.

"Guided Democracy"

Although Sukarno was President, the position was not a very powerful one in terms of the constitution of the Indonesian Republic. The 1955 elections seem to have given Sukarno a green light to change things: his P.N.I. came in first; the modernist Muslim party everyone had expected to come in first came in second, and the PKI, the Communist Party, came in a surprisingly strong third. After this Sukarno interfered more and more with the constitutional government process. In 1956 his Vice-President and ally of the past ten years, Muhammad Hatta, resigned in protest. But Sukarno had a stronger ally who was just as intent as he was on changing the parliamentary system: General Nasution, the real creator of the modern Indonesian army back in 1945–46 and still its Chief of Staff, who believed in a stronger governmental role for the army. In 1957, with army support, Sukarno announced "Guided Democracy," of which the first word should be written very large and the second very small. Sukarno told the people that western-style liberal democracy, with its pernicious "50% plus 1" majoritarianism, just didn't fit the Indonesian personality, and that he was returning them to traditional village-style deliberations that resulted in consensus decisions. In fact, it was a bloodless coup d'état, with Sukarno now an executive whose power was only limited by the army. When the congress protested, Sukarno appointed a new one.

It was as if all the adulation from the Bandung Conference had gone to his head. His new foreign policy became stridently anti-western and adventuristic, to say the least. In protest at continuing Dutch occupation of Irian Jaya, Indonesia seized all Dutch property, including many large estates that were very profitable for the government. The army had to be used to manage the confiscated estates, there were so many of them—and the army got used to such management. Show and prestige projects—a new national airline, a fancy high-rise hotel in Jakarta, a huge new Merdeka (Freedom) Monument in Jakarta's main square—consumed much government revenue. Sukarno led Indonesia to host the Asian Games in 1962, requiring new stadiums and other facilities. The rupiah began to inflate with increasing speed. Regional famine and rice riots became more and more common.

Sukarno's answer to this was to try to distract public opinion and shift the blame. In 1963 he declared a policy of "confrontation" with the newly-formed, British-dominated Malaysia. With his great oratory he whipped the crowds up against the Chinese merchant communities, which suffered pogroms not unlike those against Jewish communities in Europe somewhat earlier. In January of 1965 he withdrew Indonesia from the United Nations.

The Year of Living Dangerously

By 1965 inflation was spiraling up out of control, the infrastructure was crumbling, and there were rice riots breaking out all over. In his Indonesian version of a yearly State of the Union address in August of 1964 Sukarno had named the coming year "the year of living dangerously." By this time he had taken a billion dollars in aid from the U.S. and the west bloc, and then thumbed his nose at the west, and had taken another billion in aid from the Soviet Union and its bloc. At this point he was now abandoning any Soviet ties and moving closer to the People's Republic of China ("Communist China") and their allies in Indonesia, the P.K.I. or Indonesian Communist Party.

There is an insightful historical novel by Christopher J. Koch, the title of which should now sound familiar, *The Year of Living Dangerously*. It is set in Java, mainly Jakarta, in this crucial 1965 year (the novel was written in 1978; Peter Weir's film based on it came out in 1982). A radio journalist from Australia (in 1965 author Koch himself was working for the Australian Broadcasting Commission) gets his first foreign assignment—to Jakarta. There is a love interest who works in the British Embassy, and a diminutive, brilliant but moody Chinese-Australian cameraman who brings them together (Linda Hunt won an Academy Award for this role in the film). The novel turns on an expected Chinese arms shipment to the P.K.I., because if and when it ever arrives, it will most likely trigger civil war with the largely Muslim army.

Koch crafts the novel like a wayang play, with its three parts labeled in Javanese *Patet Nem, Patet Sanga,* and *Patet Manjura*. The three principal characters he likens to Prince Arjuna, the headstrong but beautiful Princess Srikandi, and Semar, the misshapen god-dwarf-clown that seems to be a local Indonesian addition to the ancient Hindu characters of the *Mahabharata*.

In the novel, in the hot August of 1965 when everything was coming to a head, the Australian Broadcasting male lead goes to cover a P.K.I. "Long March" from Yogyakarta to Bandung (in honor of the original Chinese Long March of 30 years before, as you'll see in the next chapter). He caught up with the marchers near Tasikmalaya, about two hours drive east of Bandung.[GE70] There were never less than a thousand marchers in the group at any one time, being led in political song by leaders with bullhorns—including one "Crush Malaysia" poem set to the tune "Michael Row the Boat Ashore." The journalist was almost killed, and came back into the edge of Bandung having slept something like three hours in the last forty-eight—and was snared by a spectacle like a moth by a flame. It was a wayang kulit play:

> The *wayang* had been set up in a clearing beyond the last shop, its lit screen hanging in the dark like that of a drive-in cinema. Approaching, Hamilton heard the gonging of *gamelan* instruments, and the guttural cries of the puppets. When he came to the edges of the crowd, brown faces turned and studied him briefly; then, grave and intent, they turned back to the screen, re-entering their ancient dream of the Kingdom of Dwarawati, Gate of the World, Kresna's kingdom, whose mountains are highest, women most beautiful, soil most fertile, men most noble. This had been their cinema since the time of Java's ancient Hindu kingdoms, and it seemed to Hamilton to have a weird modernity: a video-machine from an unknown civilisation . . . .

Returning from historical fiction to history proper, the Chinese arms shipment did indeed arrive, and a P.K.I. coup attempt did occur on October 1. It was almost successful. The night of Sept. 30–Oct. 1, P.K.I. forces attempted the murder of seven key anti-Communist generals in their homes in Jakarta. Three were killed outright, and three were captured and later that night killed out near Hakim Air Force Base southeast of the city—the headquarters of the coup. Only one of the seven generals so targeted, General Nasution, escaped, and that narrowly. On the day of October 1 itself, the Communist coup took over three sides of Merdeka Square, and the coup leaders at Hakim AF Base—joined by 9:00 a.m. by Sukarno himself—proclaimed rule in the name of a Revolutionary Council. But on the eastern side of Merdeka Square was KOSTRAD, the headquarters of the Army Strategic Reserve Command, under Major General Suharto since 1961 (Suharto too was Javanese; he had been born near Yogyakarta, and served as head of military intelligence there as far back as the Japanese government). Here the Muslim generals took a stand, and enough military force rallied behind them that by the afternoon of that same day they took Merdeka Square, and Jakarta generally, back from the Communists without a shot being fired.[GE71]

---

70. GE Layer 70 is a Placemark referencing Tasikmalaya; if you still have our original road from Jakarta to Surabaya turned on, you can see it is on that road.

71. GE Layer 71 is a Folder titled "PKI coup Oct. 1 Jakarta." Turn on the whole Folder, and then double-click on the Polygon icon for Merdeka Square to see Communist (red) control of three sides, and Muslim general (green) control of the east. Then double-click on Polygon icon for Halim Air Force base to see relationship of this center of the Communist coup to Merdeka Square.

The other main center of the coup attempt was central Java. It was based at the important northern coastal city of Semarang, which fell to the putschists on the morning of October 1. So did Salatiga, Surakarta, and Yogyakarta, seemingly a band of successful revolution cutting Java in two. But Magelang, home of the Military Academy that is Indonesia's version of West Point, was also in that band, and it became the base for the Muslim generals' re-conquest of Semarang on October 2 and both Surakarta and Yogyakarta on October 4.[GE⁷²]

Lurid stories of the torture and killing of the generals out at the "Crocodile Hole" near Jakarta's Hakim AF Base further inflamed the anti-Communist forces in Java, and over the next few months Communists were hunted down and killed—by the hundreds of thousands, estimates ranging from 200,000 to a million—usually in up close and personal violence with machetes. Sukarno, compromised by participation in the coup attempt but still with the prestige of an Indonesian George Washington, was left with most of his titles and the palace at Bogor, but stripped of all real power. Even those were taken away in 1968, and he died of kidney failure in 1970. He was buried in Blitar,[GE⁷³] not far from where he used to visit his grandparents on summer vacations. Real governing power was in the hands of General Suharto and the military from October 1965 on.

General Suharto's New Order

The new government immediately ended the "confrontation" with Malaysia, and Indonesia rejoined the United Nations. In 1967, it was one of the founding members of ASEAN, the Association of Southeast Asian Nations—generally anti-Communist and focused on promoting trade. The Suharto government's willingness to simplify economic regulations, encourage private enterprise, and to open more of the country to foreign exploration for oil (though through Pertamina, the state oil monopoly) won Indonesia a rescheduling of foreign debts and in fact a financial aid package. The currency quickly stabilized, a dramatic happening after the hyperinflation of the last Sukarno years.

Interesting also is what the New Order kept from the Sukarno era—the political philosophies, or at least slogans, of Marhaenism and the Pancasila! Although the military clearly played an unusual role in politics and in the economy, Suharto took care to honor at least the forms of parliamentary democracy. There was not much in the way of freedom of press, and the government in a heavy-handed way manipulated political parties and pressured voters for a certain turnout and a certain vote. Critics argued that inequalities between rich and poor became worse—but the new stability was generally appreciated after the tumultuous years from 1942–65.

By the 1990s, however, the nepotism of the Suharto clan—all of his children billionaires, dominating transportation, large-scale building, banking, and communications because the government awarded them every contract they applied for—was beginning to skew the whole economy and attract lots of public criticism. Suharto's only response was to wrap himself in the banner of religion, in what some call his "late Muslim phase." He made the hajj in 1990, and took "Muhammad" as a first name. This did nothing to change the economic picture, and little to improve his popularity. In the summer of 1997 an economic crisis began in Thailand but quickly hit Indonesia even harder, in part because so much of the economy was dependent on short-term loans. In early May while Suharto was off to a conference in Cairo, university students demonstrating in Jakarta were fired on by the army, and some were killed. Enraged mobs then came out and clashed further with the army, in an urban war with at least a thousand dead. A great rally was scheduled at Monas (from *Monumen Nasional*) in the middle of Jakarta's famous Merdeka Square for May 20. When it was called off at the last minute, students went to nearby congressional buildings instead and occupied them. Much of the government resigned in sympathy, and the next day, May 21, 1998, Suharto himself formally resigned to end the crisis. He had presided over Indonesia for a third of a century.

Since then press censorship has been eased, and although particular governing coalitions have risen and fallen with speed, there has been no return to rule dominated by the army. These governments have had their hands full with secession movements in Sumatra, and Timor, and Irian Jaya, and with natural disasters including

---

72. GE Layer 72 is a Folder titled "PKI coup Oct. 1–4 Central Java." The four cities taken by the Communists are in red pushpins, Megalang is in green.

73. GE Layer 73 is a Placemark referencing the memorial. Click on Panoramio icon under Pushpin, titled "Makam Bung Karno (Ir. Soekarno cemetary)," for view of same.

tsunamis and volcanic eruptions. There was at least one minor "man-made natural disaster," when in 2006 exploratory drilling for natural gas in eastern Java, just south of Surabaya, triggered the eruption of a mud volcano, still flowing as of this writing[GE⁷⁴].

Pramoedya reflects on the Great Post Road and the New Order

In the last decades before his death at age eighty-one in 2006, Pramoedya (pronounced something like Prah-MUDE-jah) Ananta Toer was the most famous writer in all of Southeast Asia. A member of the radical generation that welcomed the Japanese invasion as preferable to Dutch rule, he worked and fought in the independence movement. Although an admirer of Sukarno, his left-wing criticism got him in trouble with the regime before 1965, and when the army came to new political power after the abortive Communist takeover attempt, he was repeatedly jailed and tortured. He spent fourteen years on the prison island of Buru. Even after his release, many of his manuscripts were seized and destroyed, and he was generally refused permission to publish his work.

In 1996, when Pramoedya was still living under house arrest in Jakarta after over thirty years of General Suharto's "New Order," some Dutch film-makers made a deal with him: they would film current sights and sites along Governor-General Daendal's "Grote Postweg" (the "Great Post Road" we dealt with earlier in this chapter, the 600-mile-long road along almost the whole length of Java built in 1808–1809), and Pramoedya would write a narrative text to go with the film, with room for autobiographical comments and some commentary on change and continuity over the almost two centuries that had elapsed. The result was a film by Bernie IJdis, *Jalan Raya Pos / Die Grote Postweg* (The Great Post Road), still well worth viewing.[15]

Pramoedya's hometown of Blora was not on the great road, but was less than twenty miles south of it. [GE⁷⁵] By age fifteen or so he was riding his bike fifteen to twenty miles north to Rembang and Lasem just to watch the great Semarang-to-Surabaya traffic roll by on this stretch of the old Great Post Road. When he was seventeen, the Japanese came ashore on the beach at Lasem, as he remembers it, with copies of the Dutch map "Tropical Holland" in their hands. The film footage of the road itself goes from west to east, beginning with the port of Anyer on the western tip of Java opposite Sumatra (and Krakatau) on the Sunda Strait, and ending with the sleepy little fishing village of Panarukan a hundred miles east of Surabaya, no longer the important port it was in Daendal's day. This road footage is cut with scenes of Pramoedya typing, reading from his manuscript, playing with his grandchildren, burning the garbage, talking on the phone; and often his voice is played to accompany road film.

Early in the film he reminisces about when he first learned about the Great Post Road, in grammar school: the teacher presented it as a wonder, the equal of the Amsterdam-Paris road of the same time. But throughout the rest of the film his argument is persistent and powerful—on the loss of Indonesian life in the construction of the road because Europeans generally and Daendals specifically had no respect for their lives, on the "indirect genocide" caused by Gov. Van den Bosch's forced labor Cultivation System in the wake of the extremely bloody 1825–30 Java War, and on how much like their rule General Suharto's rule is in the film's present. As the film-makers come into Jakarta from the western side, they film a grim prison where Pramoedya spent a year, and he reflects aloud on daily deaths there from gang warfare and general ill-treatment. A Jakarta taxi-driver explains the current toll road through the capital, close to the old Post Road, as the construction of a firm led by Suharto's oldest daughter in the extreme, perhaps world-championship-caliber nepotism of the regime.

Scenes of the road going through Bogor, including a shot of the great white summer palace, trigger Pramoedya's comments about the heroic though losing defense of the area to the Dutch colonists after the Japanese left, the road washed with the blood of Indonesian youth. The film-makers spend time around Cianjur with jolly women tea-pickers, and with less-jolly mechanics working on a broken-down bus in a heavy rain. Bandung, the nineteenth century's touted "Paris of Java," is remembered by Pramoedya as a military center of

---

74. GE Layer 74 is a Placemark referencing the Sidoarjo mud volcano. It is still flowing as of this writing, and shows in Google Earth as a generally circular structure about a mile across. Interesting Photos icons nearby to explore.

75. GE Layer 75 is a Placemark referencing Blora, his hometown. And if GE Layer 44, the Folder titled "Grote Postweg/ Jalan Raya Pos" is not still turned on, go back and turn it on.

the twentieth century. The old Concordia Club[GE76] on the Post Road through town is featured; with independence it briefly became the Freedom House, and then in 1965 a removal center for political prisoners. Film-makers follow a "Bandung-Cirebon" bus downhill. They stop at a detour site where a landslide had just obliterated the road, and watch the hand-labor (which is all the original road was built with in 1808–9, that and ox carts) try to clear away the mud from a huge slope above the road. Footage of the city of Cirebon triggers Pramoedya's memories of being a young army officer there in the first half of 1946, living on the *qui vive*.

When the film-making passes the great city of Semarang, and then the cities of Rembang and Lasem where Pramoedya first experienced the Post Road, it gets to the little port of Tuban with boats in the harbor right alongside the road. Hereabouts the film-makers film part of a *wayang kulit* play that actually features Gov. Gen. Daendals—a red-faced, bearded, uniformed, energetic puppet threatening and beating his way up and down his famous roadway in the voice of the *dalang* and with the gamelan orchestra in the background.

In the great port and industrial city of Surabaya, the film-makers are given a tour of the magnificent Hotel Majapahit, just in the last stages of construction (by a firm headed by another daughter of Suharto).[GE77] Film-makers go to a restaurant with a young member of the upper class, whose father was a key navy officer and member of parliament; the young man naively talks about how hard he had to work to "achieve" his wealth and status—and the film then cuts directly to workers riding on a sugar cane truck. Cameras go all the way to the eastern end of the road, though Pramoedya himself never got that far in his own life. The film closes with guests leaving by Pramoedya's front door; the camera wanders on to a kid flying a little tailless kite on the street, and then shows lots of such kites derelict, snared, and flapping on the power lines.

The author reflects on Pramoedya

For the author of this history text, at least, the "Great Post Road" film was a brilliant stitching together of the past couple centuries of Indonesian life. And he was left musing about the passionate criticism of European colonialism by this most Europeanized of Javanese: a Marxist intellectual working in the mental framework of one of the last and greatest of all-encompassing European philosophical schemes; a world-class novelist working in what is surely by origin a European genre of literature. It again confirmed the author in his biases, that the two great stories of the past 500 years are: (a) with new powers (in large part of social mobilization) Europe explored and conquered most of the non-European world; and (b) the rest of the world then fought back to regain its self-respect and independence, but in part by borrowing many of those new European tools.

Endnotes

1. Robert Cribb, *Historical Atlas of Indonesia* (Richmond, Surrey: Curzon Press, 2000), p. 31.
2. See Colin Brown, *A Short History of Indonesia: The Unlikely Nation?* (Crows Nest, Australia, Allen Unwin, 2003), p. 2.
3. Alfred Russel Wallace, *The Malay Archipelago, The Land of the Orang-utan, and the Bird of Paradise* (Singapore: Oxford University Press, 1986), pp. 118–19. First published by Macmillan & Company, London, 1869.
4. See Clifford Geertz, *The Religion of Java* (Chicago and London: University of Chicago Press, 1960), especially Ch. 18 "The Role of Classical Art," pp. 261–88.
5. James R. Brandon, Ed., with Pandam Guritno, *On Thrones of Gold: Three Javanese Shadow Plays* (Honolulu: University of Hawaii Press, 1993), p. 83. First published 1970.
6. Brown, *Short History of Indonesia*, pp. 58–9.
7. Peter J. M. Nas and Pratiwo, "Java and De Groote Postweg, La Grande Route, The High Military Road" (Leiden/Jakarta, 2001; until recently available in English from Leiden University at following website, unfortunately no longer: http://www.leidenunivlnl/fsw/nas/pdf/NasPrativo Postweg30-10-2001.pdf
8. Brown, *Short History*, pp. 58, 76–78; Cribb, *Historical Atlas of Indonesia*, p. 114.

76. GE Layer 76 is a Placemark referencing the old Concordia Club building, now the Freedom Building or Freedom House (Gedung Merdeka).
77. GE Layer 77 is a Placemark referencing the Surabaya's Majapahit Hotel.

9. Brown, *Short History of Indonesia*, p. 85.

10. Multatuli, *Max Havelaar: or the Coffee Auctions of the Dutch Trading Company* (Amherst: University of Massachusetts Press, 1982), p. 74.

11. Wallace, *Malay Archipelago*, pp. 105–6.

12. Cribb, *Historical Atlas of Indonesia*, p. 146.

13. Benedict Anderson, *Language and Power: Exploring Political Cultures in Indonesia* (Ithaca: Cornell University Press, 1990), pp. 136–7.

14. A. Teeuw, *Modern Indonesian Literature*, volume I (Riverton: Foris Publications, 1986), p. 10.

15. As of this writing still available, with English subtitles, from Peter van Huystee Films in Amsterdam.

Chapter Thirteen

"Against Foreign Imperialist Oppression":
East Asia I

"Because of the distinctive peculiarities in China's social and historical development and her backwardness in science, it is a unique and difficult task to apply Marxism systematically to China . . . for here in China the main section of the masses are not workers but peasants, and the fight is directed against foreign imperialist oppression and medieval survivals, and not against domestic capitalism."

—Liu Shaoqi, 1945, as quoted in William Hinton,
Fanshen: A Documentary of Revolution in a Chinese Village[1]

CONTENTS

The heart of the matter—Introduction to the Chinese language—SECTION A: GENERAL GEOGRAPHY; TOPOGRAPHY AND TEXTURE OF THE YANGTZE VALLEY CORRIDOR IN PARTICULAR—The Middle Kingdom—Three river systems—Mountains—The corridor of special focus: the Yangtze River Valley—The Jiangnan—The middle Yangtze—The three gorges—Sichuan's purple bowl—Mountains, some with pandas—Commodities that shaped the traditional life cycle, and the landscape—Traditional river transportation—SECTION B: PRE- AND EARLY HISTORY—"Dragon bones"—Confucius—Warring States and the "First Emperor"—The sensuous and dangerous South—All Rivers' Weir—Miracle Canal—The Han Dynasty—Three Kingdoms, Six Dynasties—SECTION C: CLASSIC DYNASTIES CIRCA 600–1900—Buddhism enters China—A reunited China and a grand canal: the Sui-Tang Dynasties—The perfecting of the civil service—Commerce and culture in the Song Dynasty—The northern nomads—The Southern Song Dynasty—Mongol conquest and the Yuan Dynasty—The Ming and Qing Dynasties—Traditional Chinese novels—SECTION D: WESTERN INTRUSION AND CHINESE RESPONSE—The Ming voyages vs. contemporary western explorations—Matteo Ricci and the Jesuits—The "Canton System," the Opium Wars, and the Unequal Treaty—Treaty port life—Heavenly Kingdom of the Great Peace—The "Ever-Victorious Army"—"Self-strengthening"—The Jiangnan arsenal—Rong Hong's educational missions—The Dowager Empress—War with Japan—The "Scramble for Concessions"—Kang Youwei and the 100 Days of Reform—"Righteous, Harmonious Fists"—Sun Yatsen and "Double Ten"—May 4, 1919, and the New Culture Movement—Chinese Communist Party formation, Shanghai—SECTION E: FROM THE NORTHERN EXPEDITION TO THE PRESENT—Chiang Kai-shek, the early years—The Northern Expedition—The Nationalist decade, 1928–1937—Mao Zedong, the early years—Mao's "peasant Marxism" and the Jiangxi Soviet—Encirclement—The Long March—The Xian Incident—World War II: Chiang's conventional war—World War II: Mao's guerrilla war—*Wei Qi, Xiang Qi,* and end game—Governance: "expert" vs. "red"—The "Great Leap Forward" and the "Great Proletarian Cultural Revolution"—*The Last Emperor* and the Tiananmen Square Massacre—The 2008 Olympics and the foreseeable future

The heart of the matter

As with India, it is probably a mistake to think of China as just another country of the world's 250 or so countries, even as the largest of those countries by population. A better comparison is with Europe as a whole. China has more people than all of Europe, and probably has had for the past 3,000 years. The single province of Sichuan, or "Four Rivers," a distinct bowl of reddish-purple earth surrounded by rugged mountains except where the Yangtze River (*Chang Jiang*, or "Long River") pierces them on its way through, has a population of 120 million. That is considerably larger than Great Britain, France, or even Germany—only Russia of all European states has more people. Were Sichuan in Europe, it would be counted a world-class country. Each region of China has its own spoken language, as distinct as Spanish from French or French from German. Each has its own foodways, and each at least until this century had its own dress styles, boat types, economic patterns, and folkways in general—as different from one another as European cultures were in every way except the written Chinese language (on which more shortly). Even the historical depth of China parallels that of Europe. From sometime before 1500 BC to about 1100 BC, a bronze-age kingdom called Shang flourished at the elbow of the *Huang He*, or Yellow River, and there are rumors of earlier kingdoms that archaeologists still pursue. This is not quite as old as the civilizations of Egypt or Mesopotamia of the ancient Near East, but is almost exactly the age of the bronze-age Achaean Greeks, whose civilization peaked around 1300 BC and who probably invaded Troy about 1180 BC. Indian civilization may be slightly older than the Chinese, but there is arguably much more cultural continuity in China than in India. The Indus Valley civilization lost its early literacy, for example, and only reinvented it with help from the Mideast in the middle of the first millennium BC. Chinese today can still read about a third of the Chinese characters engraved on the "oracle bones" of about 1500 BC, almost a thousand years before the roots of written Sanskrit. This Chinese cultural continuity is one reason we will spend more time than in the average chapter on the time before AD 1500; it simply makes modern times more understandable. Any word starting *Sino-* or *Sini-* means something Chinese, from the old Greco-Roman name for China that got handed down to us by the Arabs. So scholars of Chinese history speak, only half-jokingly, of "the law of Sinological regression." That is, you have to know about Confucius before you can ever understand Mao Zedong!

Finally, while there are indeed a few other parts of the world with equal or even greater historical depth than China, China is a unique experiment in modern nation-state creation just because of its size. The Chinese were probably already the world's largest ethnic group as early as 500 BC. Its great size didn't much change the character of western intrusion, which all but tore the country apart by 1900. But Chinese ethnicity itself was never really threatened with extinction—even the Japanese "burn all, loot all, kill all" campaigns of World War II in China didn't do that—and that mainly because of its size. As a result you'll see only a little of that folklore-to-nationalism pattern of cultural nationalism so common in Europe and indeed other parts of the world. On the other hand, you'll see many varieties of political nationalism, all aimed at increasing Chinese strength and the chances for independence. And by the early twentieth century, socialism, and particularly Marxism, became an important part of that response to the West, though in the end Marxism in China proved to be more the servant of nationalism than its master.

Introduction to the Chinese language

These days when people speak of the "Chinese" language, they are probably talking about the standard north China language, sometimes called "Mandarin," that is taught as the national language in the schools of the People's Republic of China. It is just one language in the Sinitic language family. This family includes dozens of languages in China proper—Cantonese, Fujianese, Hunanese, Sichuanese, etc.—and even Vietnamese.

On a technical note, your computer may or may not be set up to display Chinese characters (or Japanese, for the next chapter). You can quickly tell, by "flying" into China on Google Earth to see if cities appear with Chinese character names beside a Latin-letter transliteration of it, or only empty square boxes where the characters should be, or look up a Chinese term on Wikipedia and see if characters or those same empty boxes appear. If in either case you see no Chinese characters, you need the proper fonts installed on your computer.

(A) Spoken

All of the Sinitic languages sound "sing-song" to a western ear, because the individual syllables are indeed, to some extent, sung. Standard Chinese has four "tones"—that is, four different ways the same monosyllable can be said or pitched. The first tone is "high level," meaning you start the syllable somewhat above the average pitch of your voice and keep it on the same note. Second tone is "rising"; you start a little below mid-range of your voice and rise in pitch (the way most of us end a question). Third tone is "falling-rising," where you start about mid-range, drop way down, and then come back up to mid-range. Fourth and last is "falling"; start somewhat above mid-range and drop the pitch quickly. Take the single monosyllable "ma," for example. Pronounced in first tone ("high level") it means *mother*; in second tone ("rising") it means *hemp*; in third tone ("falling-rising") it means *horse*; and in fourth tone "falling" it means *to curse*. Even if you know the correct monosyllable for a word in Chinese, you can still get in big trouble by missing the tone!

For those who grew up speaking Chinese, this is no problem at all. They absorbed this as toddlers and are hardly conscious of it. If you are a non-Chinese trying to learn Chinese, and you ask native speakers what tone a particular word is in, they will likely have to stop and think about it a minute. Textbooks that aspire to teach westerners spoken Chinese, using the Latin alphabet to represent Chinese pronunciation (more on "transliteration" below), have to write a little number 1, 2, 3, or 4 over each syllable so we can know the correct tone. Some modern materials (Wikipedia, for one), use four accent marks over vowels to indicate tone of a Chinese monosyllable: for example, mō, mó, mǒ, and mò.

Vietnamese has five tones. Cantonese has from seven to nine tones, depending on what you count as a tone. The tones may have come about originally because most Chinese words are single syllables, making for many more homonyms (such as "reed" and "read") than in English, and the tones helped differentiate them. And despite the seeming complexity, it may have advantages. "The building is on fire! Please leave the classroom quickly but in an orderly manner!"—could probably be said in two-thirds the time in the average Sinitic language.

Native Chinese speakers who learn English after childhood have real trouble with Ls and Rs, which are not separate sounds in Chinese. We native English speakers look on this with what might be called amused pity. Native English speakers who learn Chinese after childhood have real trouble with several variations of the S sound in Chinese, which at first all sound alike to us. While trying to say them myself, I have seen that same look of amused pity on Chinese faces.

(B) Written

There's no alphabet in Chinese. How can you write without an alphabet? Let's talk just a minute about our "alphabetic" writing system, which goes back to the coast of Lebanon in the fourteenth century BC when the Phoenicians came up with a business shorthand for cuneiform. It was the end product of a three-stage development. First, there were pictographs—simple pictures—in which you could show objects very well, but not much in the way of verbs or more intangible qualities. In the West we have none of that original picture level left in our writing. Second, there were ideographs—literally "idea pictures"—that show relationships, and sometimes put one or more pictures together to yield a third idea. Our Arabic numerals are the only part of our writing that is ideographic. The number 1 is represented by one mark, the 2 was originally two marks, the 8 was two diamonds stacked point-to-point, or eight marks—very simple ideographs. Then the third and final stage of writing was the phonograph, literally a "sound-picture." The general technique was to take a picture of something you could draw, and use it for something pronounced the same way that you couldn't draw. Suppose someone drew a picture of a bee and right next to it a leaf: a fellow English-speaker would say, of course, "belief." Over time—lots of time—this resulted in our simplified list of twenty-six sounds that makes reading and writing fairly easy. You learn to sing "A, B, C, D, E, F, G—H, I, J, K, LMNOP . . . ." in kindergarten or before, and then learn the written symbol for each of the twenty-six. Such a brief list of phonetic symbols makes for easy literacy.

In written Chinese, by contrast, every word is a unique collection of strokes called a "character" (the fancy word for that kind of writing is *logogram*, from the Greek for "word" and "writing"). Literacy in it has never been a piece of cake, even for native speakers. Some traditional Chinese characters can have upwards of thirty strokes, and there are tens of thousands of characters. And in written Chinese, all three levels of the ancient development of writing are still there—the pictographic, the ideographic, and the phonographic.

Perhaps 5 percent of Chinese characters are still simple pictures. In earliest written Chinese, for example, the sun was a circle with a dot in it, and the moon was a one-eighth full, outhouse-door sliver of a moon. In Song Dynasty times a thousand years ago the script got squared up a bit, and the modern characters for sun and moon are written 日 and 月. The original written word for "tree" was a kindergarten "three roots and three branches" tree, which is still visible in the modern word 木. Mountains were three little triangle mountains side by side, the one in the middle a bit bigger; today it is still recognizable as 山. Water was a sinuous line with dashes for banks; it became stylized as 水, and one word for river was an even simpler banks-plus-water, 川.

Perhaps another 5 percent of Chinese characters are ideographs. The simplest ones are the words for the numbers one, two, and three: 一, 二, and 三. Another simple ideographic principle is to write two of the same pictures together to mean many, so that writing two trees together, like this, 林, makes a new word which means forest. "Middle" or "central" was originally just a circle with a line straight down through it, now squared up to this: 中. But you can do much more sophisticated things than this with ideographs. Here is a single character made up of the sun picture plus the moon picture: 明. What could that mean? A twenty-four-hour day, perhaps? But it is better than that—it means bright. Here are the two great objects of natural light shining at you off the page! It's pronounced "ming" (second tone), incidentally, as in the Ming Dynasty. The ideograph for east is the sun coming up behind a tree: traditionally 東, now simplified to 东. The ideograph for tranquility or peace is made up of two pictographs, a roof (on top) and a woman (underneath it): 安. This is art, like collage or montage, where juxtaposing two or more visual symbols conjures up a third meaning. There is a whimsy or sense of humor about some of these. For example, if 口 means "mouth," what would 回 mean? "Reply," or "return."

Finally, the great majority of Chinese characters are compound characters, made up of a phonetic (giving you a clue to its sound) and a radical (which tells you something about it).

For example, here is a character for "tall," pronounced *qiao* (second tone): 乔. In the examples to follow, it serves as a phonetic. Here is a typical compound Chinese character: 桥. The left-hand part of it is the pictograph for a tree, which is used here as the "wood" radical, meaning made of wood; the right-hand part tells a Chinese speaker it is pronounced "qiao." Ah, says the Chinese speaker, "bridge"—the only word in Chinese for something (originally) made of wood and pronounced "qiao." Here is another compound character: 侨. If you look closely you can see that the right-hand part is that same phonetic, "qiao," and the left-hand side is another radical, 人, meaning "to enter." Ummm, says the Chinese speaker again, "emigrate" or "emigrant"—the only Chinese word that fits both those clues as to meaning and pronunciation.

The examples below show how the water radical, 水, is used in two compound characters (the original character having been compressed into a shorthand):

Shui (水) (water) + *mo* (末) (branches) = *mo* (沫) (froth, foam).

Shui (水) (water) + *cha* (叉) (fork) = *cha* (汊) (branching stream).[2]

Achieving literacy in such a written language is a long, laborious process. This has some major drawbacks in the modern age with its need for quick literacy. How would you telegraph Chinese? Their first solution was to number common Chinese words from 1 to 6,000, telegraph the numbers, and then somebody with the same book decoded at the far end. How would you set newspaper type in Chinese? The early answer was to limit the words used in the newspaper to a few thousand, and then teach a typesetter where each of a few thousand little cubbyholes were that held the type for each character. How can you type Chinese? Well, you can, with modern computers and word processing, but it has taken some doing and usually requires the use of Latin letters as in Pinyin. What about a dictionary in Chinese? They had one 2,500 years ago, but it was and still is cumbersome. They organized the radicals into a standard list (189 in one version, 214 in another). Scholars had to memorize these radicals in a given order, like we do the ABCs—"enter," "wood," "mouth," "water," and so on up to 189. Underneath each radical, characters were grouped by how many brush strokes they took to write. You found that section and then searched until you found your word.

Why in the world in modern times didn't the Chinese just "Romanize" their writing and put everything phonetically in the Latin (or Greek, or Cyrillic, or Arabic, pick one) alphabet? The answer seems to be two-fold. One reason is the beauty of their written characters; calligraphy and painting were much more closely allied in traditional China than in the West. And secondly and perhaps more important is the visual power of their ideographs, which would have all been lost in doing things alphabetically. There is some notion that whereas in the western world prayers were usually spoken, in China they were more often written and then burned, so close was written Chinese to the thing. And historically, the Chinese writing style played an interesting role in developments. If you compare the heyday of Rome (last two centuries of the Republic, first two centuries of Empire) and the Han Dynasty, there are remarkable parallels. They both flourished from around 200 BC to AD 200. Both were huge empires for the time (Rome with about forty-five million, China with about sixty million). Both had sophisticated legal, administrative, and military systems, and both had great road networks and government building programs. Finally, both declined and collapsed in barbarian invasions, and in both the single spoken language evolved in a few centuries into different spoken languages that were mutually unintelligible (Latin into French, Spanish, Italian, Romanian, etc., and Chinese into Mandarin, Cantonese, Hunanese, Fujianese, Sichuanese, etc.). Because Latin was written in a phonetic alphabet, when the spoken languages evolving from it diverged, the written languages sooner or later diverged too. But written Chinese, in which the phonographic element is not the dominant one, did NOT change. So centuries later the speakers of Mandarin, Cantonese, Hunanese, etc., who could not understand each other when speaking, could still write to each other on a napkin in a restaurant, or read the same law code, or take the same civil service exam. And so, the argument goes, the Roman Empire was like Humpty Dumpty and never put itself back together again, but the Chinese Empire did, within 400 years, and is still together today . . . mostly because of the way they wrote.

Traditional Chinese writing, to conclude, was done in columns of characters, written from top to bottom, with the next column to the left of the first one. Older Chinese books, like Arabic and Hebrew ones still do today, open from what to us is the back side. Western influence in the last two centuries impacted China to the extent that much of Chinese printing is now mostly in lines from left to right, with the next line below that, the way we do it.

(C) Transliterated into English

Transliteration in this case is getting the sounds of Chinese words into our Latin alphabet. One complication here is that there is an old system and a new system for doing it, which gives us *Peiching* (*Peking* was the old French transliteration) vs. *Beijing, Shantung* vs. *Shandong, Canton* vs. *Guangzhou, Mao Tse-tung* vs. *Mao Zedong,* and hundreds of other such pairs.

The old system is "Wade-Giles," named after a couple of mid- and late-nineteenth-century British scholars and administrators in China. Their use of vowels is fairly straight-forward, but what they did with consonants! Do you remember the "aspirated" versus "unaspirated" consonants and consonant combinations from back in the Brothers Grimm section? Wade and Giles did everything in such pairs: T with an apostrophe after it was pronounced like a regular T, but when they wrote T without an apostrophe, that was the unaspirated half of the pair, to be pronounced D. Why didn't they just use a D? No one seems to know. But in the same way, K' was a regular K sound, and K was pronounced like our G; CH' was CH, but CH was pronounced like a J; P' was P, but P was B. TS' was pronounced TS (hard T), and TS was more like DZ.

For example, the Chinese name for their capital was 北京, "North Capital." The word for "north" in Chinese is pronounced "bei" (almost like "bay" as in a body of water); it's third tone ("falling-rising"), incidentally. And the word for capital is pronounced more like "jing" (with a hard J), in first tone ("high level"). Try it out; nobody's listening. Wade and Giles heard that and, according to their system, wrote it down "Pei-Ching." And many who saw it later obviously tended to pronounce the P as a P and the Ch as a Ch, not knowing that

P without an apostrophe was supposed to be pronounced B, and Ch without an apostrophe was a J, or in this case a little something else. One other little wrinkle in the Wade-Giles system is what they did with the "soft" SH sound in Chinese that we really don't have in English. It is pronounced something like SYEH; Wade-Giles uses "HS" for this (so the famous northwestern Chinese city, which might be written something like "Syee-ann"), was transliterated "Hsian" in the Wade-Giles system.

The second, more modern way of transliterating Chinese into English is *Pinyin*, literally "spell-sound." It was imposed in the mid-1950s, after the Chinese Communists had taken over all of mainland China. The Chinese government was trying to make the standard northern language the model for spoken Chinese in schools nationwide, and the letters of a modified Latin alphabet were adopted to stand for very specific sounds (the way our dictionaries have specialized symbols, one for exactly how the "a" in "father" should be pronounced, for example). That is, students would still write traditional (though somewhat simplified) Chinese, but would memorize these western symbols for standard pronunciation purposes. And, killing two birds with one stone, this also solved the problem the Chinese had in having to transliterate Chinese into Spanish one way, and French another, and English, and German, and so on. Now every language written in the Latin alphabet would get its Chinese transliteration in Pinyin, take it or leave it.

Take it we have; since 1980 or before it has become standard transliteration from Chinese used in our newspapers, journals, and books. It is generally an improvement over the Wade-Giles—none of that "aspirated T' versus unaspirated T which is really a D" problem, so if the ordinary American reader reads "Beijing" in Pinyin, it sounds a lot closer to the original than "Peiching" or "Peking" does. But there are a few unusual wrinkles. In Pinyin the letter Q is like our hard CH, so the *Qing* dynasty in Pinyin is the same as the *Ch'ing* dynasty in Wade-Giles. In Pinyin the ZH combination is pronounced like our J. X is the symbol Pinyin uses for that soft SH sound discussed above: the Chinese for "thank you" is, in Pinyin, *Xie-xie* (that's fourth tone followed by a sort of neutral tone, if you would like to try this out at a local Chinese restaurant)—which comes out "Syeh-syeh" or some such. The western Chinese city written in Wade-Giles as *Hsian* comes out *Xian* in the Pinyin. And in Pinyin the letter J stands for a Chinese sound especially difficult for westerners to say, a sort of ZH with an R in it (try pronouncing ZH and then curl the tip of your tongue up to get close). And sometimes, frankly, even the Pinyin system fails. For example, there are two adjoining Provinces in northern China—Shanxi (first tone, first tone; "West of the mountains"), and Shaanxi (third tone, first tone; "West of the pass"), that should both be transliterated by the Pinyin system as "Shanxi." The extra "a" was thrown into the transliteration of the second one as a make-shift patch, to make the system work!

In general, if you are reading history written before 1980 or so, you need Wade-Giles; for history written after 1980, you need Pinyin. The early life of *Teng Hsiao-p'ing* will be transliterated like this before 1980 or so; the later life of *Deng Xiaoping*, exactly the same person and same pronunciation, will be written like this in the Pinyin. Or *Mao Tse-tung* versus *Mao Zedong*. Or *Chou En-lai* versus *Zhou Enlai*.

You know it is a difficult language to learn when even a simple explanation of how to transliterate it into English takes a full page! But a fifth of the world's people use it; more of us have got to learn it.

Here are some fairly simple and common Chinese characters that may show up in browsing through a Chinese map, or in the titles of Panoramio icons you may find in Google Earth:

North 北 East 东 (formerly 東) South 南 West 西

One 一; Two 二; Three 三; Four 四; Ten 十; Twenty 廿

Big 大; Bridge 桥; Capital 京

And of course 长 (Long—also used for the "Great" Wall and the "Grand" Canal), and 江 (River, particularly the Yangtze).

SECTION A: GENERAL GEOGRAPHY; TOPOGRAPHY AND TEXTURE OF THE YANGTZE VALLEY CORRIDOR IN PARTICULAR

The Middle Kingdom

China's traditional name for itself is written 中國 (or in today's simplified characters 中国), and transliterated in the Pinyin *zhong guo* (first tone, third tone), and in the old Wade-Giles *chung kuo*. It translates Middle Kingdom, or perhaps Central Country. The shape of the modern country is likened by the Chinese themselves to a chicken. The head is the area generally called Manchuria; the breast is where central and south China bulge out into the China Sea, and the tail fans out broadly west into Central Asia, marked by the great brown oval of the Taklamakan desert.[GE[1]] It is 2,800 miles from the western edge of the "tail" to where the "breast" touches the China Sea. To give you a sense of scale, that's a hundred miles further than from Cape Mendocino in northern California across the lower forty-eight of the U.S. to Cape Hatteras in North Carolina. Even counting Alaska (and Hawai'i), total U.S. territory is not quite as big as China's. China's population is about four times as large as ours.

If you have an aerial view of China (or composite aerial views, as in Google Earth map surface), you can see that generally speaking the northwestern half of China (the tail, the back and the top of the head of the chicken) are brown, and the southeastern half is green. It's that green southeastern half that has 90 percent of the population.

Three river systems

One quick way to get hold of the geography of the country is to look at three great river systems that run across the eastern part of the country. Each generally runs from west to east.

In the north is the Yellow River, 黄河, *Huang He* in Pinyin, *Hwang Ho* in the earlier Wade-Giles, *he* being a north China word for river. It does a great upside-down "U" through the Ordos Desert, picking up the silt that gives it (and the Yellow Sea at its mouth) its name. It has been compared to the Missouri, so choked with silt as to be relatively useless for commercial navigation. At the end of the stretch of river that runs due south, it makes a sharp right-angle turn towards the ocean. Just at that corner it receives its last tributary, the Wei River, coming in from due west at the right-angle corner. It's not a large river, by Chinese standards, but was strategically important in Chinese history, as you'll see. Its valley was big enough to support a large population, but the only easy way in or out of the valley was at the mouth, making it very defensible.[GE[2]] From the right-angle corner on to the sea the Yellow River receives no tributaries because it is on a flood plain of its own making. For awhile it heads east, straight for the mountainous center of the Shandong Peninsula (that in geologic time was an island, before the Yellow River filled the ocean north, west, and south of it with silt). Today the Yellow River angles northeast of the mountains, but every century or so it bursts its dikes and flip-flops to the other side of the mountains, wiping out a million or so farmers along the way. The poetic name for the Yellow River is "China's Sorrow."[GE[3]]

The great central river of China, even more important than the Mississippi is to us, has traditionally been known to westerners as the Yangtze, or Yangzi, River. The Chinese usually just call it the Long River (长江, in pinyin *Chang Jiang* [second tone, first tone]). It heads up on the Tibet-Qinghai plateau, some 1,800 straight-line miles from its mouth near Shanghai on China's east coast, and half again as much as the river runs. The lower half of the river's course will be the corridor of special focus, described in more detail later. For now, look at how when it comes out of the mountains it runs along the southern edge of the Sichuan basin, cuts due

---

1. Open the East Asia I.kmz file, and then expand the first Folder, "Section A: Topo&Texture." Then turn on and "fly" to Google Earth Layer 1, a Placemark framing a view of all of today's People's Republic of China. If you have the basic "Borders and Labels" layer of Google Earth turned on, it will be outlined in bright yellow.

2. GE Layer 2 is a Folder containing Paths representing the general course of the Yellow River and its tributary the Wei (in light yellow). Either turn the whole folder on, or open it and turn both Paths on one at a time.

3. GE Layer 3 is a Folder titled "Yellow River Views;" it has Placemarks either framing certain views or recommending certain Photos icons.

east through the mountains (the famous "Three Gorges" run), and then does a gigantic "W" across east central China. Its most important tributary, the Han River, comes in at the middle top of the "W."[GE⁴] At the bottom corners of the "W" are great lakes that swell in the wet season and shrink in the dry season, each of them fed by a major tributary river coming up from the south. Historically the bigger of these two lakes (but no longer because of land reclamation), at the bottom left corner of the "W," is Lake Dongting, fed by the north-flowing Xiang River. The southeastern lake, Poyang, is similarly fed by the north-flowing Gan River.

It is Lake Dongting that gives two important central Chinese provinces or states their names: 湖南, *Hunan*, means "south of the lake" (literally "lake-south") and 湖北, *Hubei,* means "north of the lake." Stacked on top (north) of them are two more provinces, named for their relationships to the Yellow River: 河南, *Henan* means "south of the river" (*He* or *Ho* being a northern word for river), and 河北, *Hebei* means "north of the river." Then you can add two more provinces to make a sort of cross: 山东, *Shandong* (Shantung in the Wade-Giles), means "east of the mountains," and 山西, *Shanxi* (Shanhsi), means "west of the mountains."[GE⁵] If you ever want to try to learn all the province names in China—we'll add a few more shortly to the Yangtze valley corridor—the simple cross made by these six is a good place to start.

The West River[GE⁶] looks much shorter than the Yellow River, but in south China the rainfall it gathers is so great that it is nearer in volume to the Yangtze. Today its active mouths enter the South China Sea somewhat west of the Pearl River estuary. It is this seventy-mile-long bay that has at its head the great south China city of Guangzhou (Canton), and the key former European colonial possessions of Macao and Hong Kong on its southern extremities.[GE⁷]

Mountains

Decades ago, before I'd ever visited China, I drove a visiting Chinese scholar from North Carolina to Tennessee through the highest part of the Smoky Mountains. I was puzzled that he seemed so unimpressed. Later, touring some of the lower, eastern mountains of China with him in turn as guide, I understood why: there were patches of mountains all around that were much more rugged than the Smokies, and even the Rockies were insignificant compared to those mountain chains farther west in China. I had always assumed that the vertically elongated mountains of traditional Chinese painting were imaginary shapes, but in the Li River valley there they were—fantastic, maybe, but very real.[GE⁸] The Tibetan part of Chinese territory is the highest average land elevation of any plateau in the world, and its southern edge is the northern side of the Himalayas—some of the highest and most rugged mountain country in the world.[GE⁹] In general China is so mountainous that it has less than two-thirds of the farming area of the U.S.

---

4. GE Layer 4 is a Folder titled "Yangtze River System." It includes Paths giving approximate routes of Yangtze downstream from Yibin; then a Path each for its two main headwaters, the River of the Golden Sands and the Min River; four Paths for other Sichuan tributaries; one Path for the larger northern tributary the Han River; and finally two Paths for the southern tributaries Xiang and Gan that feed the two lakes at those bottom corners of the great W traced by the main river.

5. GE Layer 5 is a Folder titled "Six Provinces"; it includes, at least in general outline, Polygons representing the six provinces in different colors. Open folder, turn on each in succession.

6. GE Layer 6 is a Folder titled "West River System." It includes Paths showing routes of West River itself and its historically important northern tributary the Li River.

7. GE Layer 7 is a Placemark framing a view of the Pearl River estuary. Hong Kong is at lower right; Macau is at lower left—an hour's hydrofoil ferry ride away—and Guangzhou (Canton) sits at top left of the estuary system. Note active mouth of West River entering the sea just west of Macau.

8. GE Layer 8 is a Placemark referencing a Panoramio icon titled "View from Li River Cruise" for typical view of Li River scenery in and around Guilin (Kweilin). There are many more icons to explore on stretches of the river south of this. This is what geologists and geographers call "karst" topography—limestone country where the sinkholes have run together and just left spires of eroded limestone remnants.

9. GE Layer 9 is a Placemark referencing a Panoramio icon titled "NamchaBarwa." This Tibetan peak, at 25,500 or so feet, is not the tallest mountain in China (Tibet)—after all, they have the north side of Mt. Everest—but is 10,000′ taller than anything in the Rockies and 3,000′ feet taller than anything in the Andes.

The corridor of special focus: the Yangtze River Valley

For this chapter, the focus is on a single great river valley more than a road network as in the other six non-European regional chapters. It deals with the Yangtze, or Chang Jiang valley, from the edge of the western mountains where the two main headwaters of the river enter the great bowl of Sichuan, down to the river's entry into the China Sea near Shanghai.[GE¹⁰] There are two reasons for this. First, most of the academic exchange visits I personally spent in China were here. Just as important for me is Professor Lyman Van Slyke's 1988 book *Yangtze: Nature, History, and the River*.[3] He makes the case that, although China's most famous early civilization was in the north, by 1,500 years ago the Yangtze was already the main center of population and food production, and beginning to dominate the cultural realm as well.

To digress just a bit (starting at the headwaters of a tributary that will meander back into the main narrative at the end of this long paragraph), Van Slyke had been much impressed with Fernand Braudel's *The Mediterranean and the Mediterranean World in the Age of Philip II*.[4] Many of us in the history field have been impressed; in fact, among historians this would be a serious contender for "most famous history book written in the whole world in the last century," if there were such a contest. In brief, Braudel wrote 1,200 pages on the Mediterranean world in the last half of the 1500s, and he only got to politics about page 900. The first of the book carefully looked at geology and climate, at soils, at lifestyles all around the shores of the Mediterranean and Black Sea based on grapes, olives, wheat, and herding, the building up of larger trading networks, the slow emergence of states, at cycles of disease, and of economic production. But when Braudel did finally get to politics and military affairs, up to and including the 1588 Spanish armada and its defeat by the English, it was a much richer and more deeply rooted analysis for all the foregoing. Overall, Braudel brilliantly telescoped time (and several different academic fields)—from geology and climate, to soils and native vegetation, to early, middle, and late levels of human habitation—in the service of history. Van Slyke, Professor of History and Director of Stanford University's East Asia Center, decided to try the same thing in a smaller book on China's Yangtze River valley. It makes for a wonderful introduction to China, by focusing on the Long River. Some of the framework of the following treatment, and more of the best prose illustrations, come from this book (unfortunately out of print, at least as of this writing).

Now let's work up the great river, in terms of topography and texture of the land, from its mouth to its headwaters.

The Jiangnan

South of the great lower bend of the river is the Jiangnan (Kiangnan), literally the "South of the River" area. [GE¹¹] Not only does it tap the whole trade coming down the Yangtze River; it is a water world of canals and lakes and very fertile delta soils. Always rich, it supported famous historic towns such as Hangzhou and Suzhou, and of course today's Shanghai—biggest and richest city in modern China. When people from the poorer areas north of the river crossed over to work there, they were called Jiangbei, or "north of the river," people, and when Jiangnan people said it, it had a little of the ring of "Okies," or "Hillbillies."

Shanghai means "On the Sea"; it's about sixteen miles up the Huangpu River from the Yangtze, where Suzhou Creek comes in.[GE¹²] The city of Suzhou itself is right at fifty miles due west of Shanghai.[GE¹³] You can get there from Shanghai via the canalized Suzhou Creek, or you can continue south and west up the Huangpu River itself and get to Suzhou that way via various other canals. You can go almost anywhere in the Jiangnan by water, and some of the canals are thousands of years old.

---

10. GE Layer 10 is a Polygon, fairly rectangular in shape, about 1,250 miles long and 350 miles wide. It embraces the heart of the Yangtze Valley.

11. GE Layer 11 is a Folder titled "The Jiangnan." Click on the Folder icon to open it and frame a view of the general area. Right in the middle is the third biggest lake in China, Lake Tai (south of Wuxi, west of Suzhou), almost perfectly circular on its south and west sides.

12. GE Layer 12 is a Placemark generally framing a view of downtown Shanghai.

13. GE Layer 13 references Panoramio icon under pointer titled "Canales-Sozhou"; it's a good view of one of the networks of connecting canals in this famous old city.

The other big commercial seaport of the area is Ningbo, south across the Bay of Hangzhou from Shanghai by about 100 miles.[GE14] It figures into the political narrative of modern times, not least as the home base of Chiang Kai-shek.

Hangzhou itself, with its famous West Lake,[GE15] was for a brief time the capital of China. Northern tribes drove the Song Dynasty south in the early 1100s, and the government retreated there. One of China's great patriotic heroes, General Yue Fei, was a Song general who made the retreat south, but whose plans for recovering the north were subverted by an evil emperor. His temple and tomb is at West Lake under the four-character slogan associated with him, translated "Return my rivers and mountains."[GE16] The modern city rises up across the ancient causeways and lakeside temples.[GE17]

The Grand Canal, dating to about AD 600 (more later) and much of which is still in service, began at Hangzhou,[GE18] went generally north to Suzhou, and then northwest through Wuxi until it crossed the Yangtze River and went through the north bank city of Yangzhou—a key commercial city in the area ever since.[GE19]

And just upriver on the south bank is historically the most important city of east central China, Nanjing (Nanking), 南京, meaning "South Capital."[GE20] It is second only to Shanghai as a commercial city in the East China area today, and is historically much more important. Several times in Chinese history it was indeed the capital of all or much of China—under the first Ming rulers, of the Taiping Rebellion, of the Chinese Republic. At some twenty-five miles around, it has reputedly the longest city wall in world history; it was really too long to defend well, as you'll see later.[GE21] Nanjing is one of the famous "three furnaces" of the Long River—three big river cities known for their brutally hot and humid summers (the others are Wuhan in the middle stretch of the river, and Chongqing above the gorges in traditional Sichuan).

In terms of provinces crossed by our corridor, there are three associated with the Jiangnan that a beginning student of Chinese history ought to know: Jiangsu[GE22] ("River Revival") Province (capital Nanjing); Zhejiang[GE23] ("Bore River") Province (capital Hangzhou); and Greater Shanghai, one of China's four independent urban areas.

Finally, upriver beyond Nanjing is Anhui Province,[GE24] a sort of vague transition from Jiangnan to the middle Yangtze. Anhui got the first syllable of its name from the important river town of Anqing,[GE25] which is just a narrow extension of the Jiangnan. The second syllable, though, comes from the rugged hill country of

---

14. GE Layer 14 is a Placemark generally framing a view of Ningbo.

15. GE Layer 15 is a Placemark generally framing a view of Hangzhou's West Lake.

16. GE Layer 16 references Panoramio icon titled "Yue Fei/岳飞/岳飛" for view of Yue Fei's mausoleum/temple.

17. GE Layer 17 is a Placemark referencing Panoramio icon under pointer titled "A Far View of the City from Sudi Causeway."

18. GE Layer 18 is a Placemark referencing Panoramio icon titled "Night View of the Grand Canal of China" for view as described. The Grand Canal here is probably little changed from its Sui-Tang original from around AD 600, but oh has the scenery around changed.

19. GE Layer 19 frames a view of the Grand Canal going north from the bend of the Yangtze in lower part of framed view, to busy commercial city of Yangzhou at top of view, city center about seven miles from the Yangtze. Zooming in on Yangtze River at canal mouth will reveal amazing riverboat traffic.

20. GE Layer 20 is an overview of Nanjing; Purple Mountain shows up at right.

21. GE Layer 21 references Panoramio icon titled "南京明城墙之清凉门 (QingLiang Gate, NanJing Ming Great Wall)" for view of same. Nearby Photos icons show view of Ming Dynasty walls built on Han Dynasty wall foundations.

22. GE Layer 22 is a Polygon showing Jiangsu Province in a shade of orange.

23. GE Layer 23 is a Polygon showing Zhejiang Province in a shade of pink.

24. GE Layer 24 is a Polygon showing Anhui Province in a shade of rose. After looking at all three a minute, turn the Polygons off to clear the map; with your "Borders and Labels" basic layer on, you can still see their outlines in white.

25. GE Layer 25 is a Placemark locating Anqing, about 180 miles upriver from Nanjing.

Huizhou,[GE[26]] with its distinctive architecture.[GE[27]] Huizhou is where the salt merchants lived. One of the most famous tourist spots (and sources of tea!) for this part of China is the Huangshan, or Yellow Mountains.[GE[28]]

So in an overview of the Jiangnan and its transition zone upriver, you've got in all three Provinces plus the Shanghai urban area.[GE[29]]

The middle Yangtze

The middle stretch of the Yangtze, with the Han River coming in at the middle top of the "W," and the Gan and Xiang Rivers coming into the great lakes at the lower points of the "W," is in many ways the heartland of China. Each of these three tributary rivers is the focus of a traditional province.[GE[30]]

The Province of Jiangxi (Chiang-hsi, literally "River West") is almost perfectly the drainage system of the north-flowing Gan River.[GE[31]] The Province of Hunan ("South of the Lake"), just to the west of Jiangxi Province, is mostly the drainage system of the north-flowing Xiang River.[GE[32]] The Province of Hubei ("North of the Lake")[GE[33]] is generally centered on the Han River valley, though it also includes much of the middle course of the Yangtze River proper.

The capitals of each of these three provinces are all impressive cities. Nanchang, capital of Jiangxi, is where the Gan River makes a delta as it enters Poyang Lake.[GE[34]] It is a city of five million. Changsha, capital of Hunan, is on the Xiang River a little above where it deltas into Lake Dongting. It is a city of six million or so. Like Nanchang, it is right at eighty miles south of a bottom tip of the "W" made by the Yangtze River. [GE[35]] The capital of Hubei, Wuchang, is on the south bank of the Yangtze across from the mouth of the Han River. Today, however, most people just talk about "Wuhan," the great urban area made up of the triple cities of Wuchang and the north bank cities on either side of the mouth of the Han, Hankou and Hanyang. Total population of Wuhan approaches ten million, making it the major metropolitan area of this middle stretch of the Long River.[GE[36]]

In a general aerial view of this middle part of the "W," forested mountains show up as patches of dark green.[GE[37]] Between the mountains and the great cities, filling every little valley, is small town and village China here in the heartland. Mao Zedong came from one such, Shaoshan, just on the southern edge of our corridor.[GE[38]]

---

26. GE Layer 26 is a Placemark generally framing a view of the Appalachian-like Huizhou country; the dark green are generally forested hills.

27. GE Layer 27 is a Placemark referencing a Panoramio icon showing some of the local architecture.

28. GE Layer 28 is a Placemark generally locating the Huangshan; dozens of Photos icons posted mainly by Chinese tourists.

29. GE Layer 29 is a Placemark generally framing an overview of the Jiangnan. You might want to review the major cities and the province names; then turn off whole Jiangnan folder, to clear the decks for consideration of the Middle Stretch of the Yangtze to come.

30. GE Layer 30 is a Folder titled "The Middle Stretch"; it frames an overview, and includes several Placemarks to which to refer.

31. GE Layer 31 is a Polygon showing Jiangxi Province in a shade of blue.

32. GE Layer 32 is a Polygon showing Hunan Province in a shade of light yellow.

33. GE Layer 33 is a Polygon showing Hubei Province in a shade of green. Turn off the last three Polygons to clear the screen; provinces outlines will still show in white.

34. GE Layer 34 is a Folder titled "Nanchang views"; explore as you wish.

35. GE Layer 35 is a Folder titled "Changsha views"; explore as you wish.

36. GE Layer 36 is a Folder titled "Wuhan views"; explore as you wish.

37. GE Layer 37 is a Folder titled "Mountain views."

38. GE Layer 38 is a Placemark titled "Shaoshan"; it references a Panoramio icon titled "韶山——毛泽东同志故居（远拍" for view of Chairman Mao's old house, set back of the ubiquitous lotus pond of the central and south Chinese countryside.

The three gorges

West of the "W" of the middle Yangtze is a rugged band of mountains that stretch from top (north) to bottom (south) of our chosen rectangle.[GE39] All of the east-flowing rivers, including the mighty Yangtze, cut their way through this mountain barrier. It is the stretch of river running from west to east that holds the famous "Three Gorges."[GE40] Coming downstream, the first is Qutang Gorge. Only five miles long (compared to the two lower gorges, which are about thirty miles long each), it narrows the river the most—at one place to 350 feet, and in those five miles never wider than 500 feet. Approaching the ancient White King City (*Baidicheng*) from upstream, the river seemed to end in rocky cliffs, but abreast of the city you could see it turn sharply right between huge cliffs—the Kui Gate. Van Slyke quotes the famous Tang Dynasty poet Li Bai (Li Po) on the fast ride down from White King City to Jiangling, a city ninety river miles below Yichang, itself a city just downstream from the last gorge:

> Dawn gone from White King, all misty-hued,
> Down river to Kiang-ling [Jiangling], a thousand li a day.
> From both banks monkeys' screeching sounds
> Behind our boat, already, myriad folded ranges.[5]

The middle of the Three Gorges is the twenty-nine-mile-long Witches', or Monkeys' Gorge (Wuxia). With the steepest walls and most jagged peaks, it is the gloomiest and most forbidding of the three. Winds here, even more than in the other two, are either upstream or downstream. Van Slyke says that veteran travelers can name the six northern peaks and six southern peaks in this stretch, the most storied being a small rock formation called Goddess Peak—a goddess who is supposed to have helped the primeval flood-tamer god drain China and make it fit for human habitation. Last, going downstream, comes the Xiling Gorge. Less visually spectacular than its upstream neighbors, its shoals made it the most dangerous of all to shipping.

Sichuan's purple bowl

The third great population center strung along the Long River was Sichuan's [Schzewan's] great oval basin of reddish-purple earth, about 300 miles from end to end, and 200 miles across the big end of the "egg." It clearly shows up in aerial or satellite photos, such as the composite surface in Google Earth. With most elevations in the bowl from one to two thousand feet, and with latitudes from 28–32°, with fertile soils, and with human improvements (some to be discussed later in the history sections), today it supports something upwards of 120 million people.[GE41] That by itself, as noted earlier, is larger than any European country except Russia. Opening it up to ocean shipping is the main reason for the Three Gorges dams today, even more important than the hydro power generated.

In geological time the Sichuan basin was apparently an inland sea, perhaps more than once. This left behind reminders in terms of salt and brine deposits, and natural gas, on which more on their human exploitation later.

The two biggest cities of traditional Sichuan are Chongqing and Chengdu. Chongqing will be known to older Americans by the Wade-Giles transliteration "Chungking," the World War II capital of the Nationalist Chinese. Today it makes a fair bid to be China's Detroit, in terms of auto and related industries; in fact fairly

---

39. GE Layer 39 is a Placemark framing a view of the left-center part of our chosen rectangle; notice the dark green band that generally runs from top (north) to bottom (south) of the rectangle. It also references a Panoramio icon titled "Finger Rocks" for a view of typically rugged terrain.

40. GE Layer 40 is a Folder titled "Three Gorges." It includes Polygons outlining each of the three gorges, and Paths through them so a viewer can "fly" them, along with references to Photos icons with interesting photographs. They are generally organized to fit the text above; explore as you wish.

41. GE Layer 41 is a Polygon showing the approximate extent of Sichuan's oval "bowl"—before Chongqing was carved out of it in 1997 as the fourth independent municipality of China (after Beijing, Tianjin, and Shanghai). Notice how Chengdu, the capital of Sichuan, is located very near the eastern edge of the bowl near where the Min River breaks out of the mountains; it's not just coincidental, as you'll see later.

recently (1997) the Chinese government made it into a "municipality," the fourth independent urban area of the country (after Beijing, Tianjin, and Shanghai), carving out a small province of its own out of southeastern Sichuan. Chengdu is the current and traditional capital of Sichuan Province. It is located near where the Min River comes out of the high mountains, between the Min and Tuo Rivers.

Mountains, some with pandas

The Sichuan bowl was difficult to get into from other parts of China. Many Americans got their first insights into Chinese (and Chinese-American) culture from Amy Tan's 1989 novel, *Joy Luck Club*. One of the key passages of the novel is when a young Chinese-American woman learns for the first time that she has older sisters living in China—that her mother, evacuating the south China city of Guilin (Kweilin) to escape the Japanese by walking to Chongqing (Chungking), was forced to abandon them on the trek. It is about 375 straight-line miles from one city to the other, a daunting task trying to carry two babies even if it were level and straight. But if you take a close look at the terrain between them, you understand the impossibility of such a task by even the most dedicated mother.[GE42] Coming down into Sichuan from the northeast, as from the Wei Valley, was even harder. Famous "gallery" roads were fixed along the faces of sheer cliffs in some places—beams fixed into rectangular holes cut in the vertical rock face, boards fastened to the beams, no outside railing and hundreds of feet of drop. Li Bai, the famous Tang Dynasty poet already quoted earlier on the trip through the gorges, wrote this about it:

> Eheu! How dangerous, how high!
> It would be easier to climb to Heaven
> Than walk the Sichuan Road.[6]

West of the Sichuan bowl come China's greatest mountains, rising abruptly like a green wall. The remaining giant pandas—of which there may be 1,600 left in the wild—live in a patchy arc from eastern Sichuan to southern Shaanxi.[GE43] They prefer bamboo-covered mountain slopes of about 10,000' elevation, in the summer; in winter they come down those same mountains to 2,500'. With their striking coloration and slow-moving vulnerability to hunters, the inaccessibility of their remaining habitat is undoubtedly a reason some of these fascinating animals still exist.

Commodities that shaped the traditional life cycle, and the landscape

Having looked at the Yangtze River and its major tributaries, and the ups and downs of the landscape, let's now focus more on the texture of the land. Rice, tea, silk, tung oil, salt, lumber from managed forests—these were the main commodities that shaped traditional life and even the landscape in the Long River valley.

Rice. Lowlands along the river, from the Jiangnan up to at least the Three Gorges, and in Sichuan beyond, are China's "land of fish and rice" par excellence. Rice, of all the world's domesticated grains, provides more calories per acre than any other; only corn (maize) is a close competitor. Rice was probably first domesticated in the Yangtze Valley; recognizable domesticated rice found in caves near Lake Poyang have been dated to almost 10,000 BC. Its cultivation came to dominate the yearly cycle of life in areas where it was grown—and on our corridor that was pretty much wherever there was enough water and flat land (or land you could make flat by terracing). While seeds were germinating into seedlings, the rice fields are turned into paddies by plowing,

---

42. GE Layer 42 is a Path along a straight line between Guilin and Chongqing. Of course no traveler would walk such a straight line between cities, but it gives you an idea of how rugged the countryside generally is. Right-click on this Guilin to Chongqing layer title, and then choose "Show Elevation Profile." Give the profile a minute to clear up, and its sawtooth character (note highest point, 6,609', just overlooking Yangtze River valley) should be vivid illustration of how rough the terrain is.

43. GE Layer 43 is a Folder titled "Mountains with Pandas." It includes a Polygon showing (roughly) the range of surviving pandas, plus some Photos icons referencing study centers for pandas there.

raking, leveling, and flooding. When the seedlings are about 8″ high, they are bound into bundles and taken to the fields for transplanting. Workers side by side work backwards through the muck, planting several rows each before taking a step back, burying the roots of each seedling some 3″ deep. Then the rice grows in the water-covered fields for about 100 days. Most of its nourishment in terms of minerals and algae is taken in from the water by rootlets above the soil, so the soils were never noticeably depleted from year to year. Fresh-water fish and prawns can grow during that three months or so alongside the rice. Then when the seedheads are full, the fields are drained (strained for the small fish and prawns, of course), and the rice is harvested on dry land.

It is a difficult process to mechanize, and very labor intensive. Van Slyke notes that it was called the "four stoops": one to plant, one to transplant, one to weed, and one to harvest. But it was woven into the year, with ceremonies and festivals marking each stage. By AD 1000, new, faster-maturing variants of rice appeared (developed either in China or in Southeast Asia or both). This made it possible to grow two rice crops a year in the very south of our area, and for most of our area a crop of summer rice and then one of winter wheat on the same field.

Tea. Although tea cultivation spread widely through Asia (you've already seen it growing near the Grand Trunk Road in South Asia, and in Java, and will see more of it along Japan's Tokaido), it apparently began in the Yangtze Valley. If westerners learned about it from association with south China, they called it "tea" as in English, "thé" as in French, or some similar pronunciation, from the south coast Fujian dialect. If they learned about it from the north of China, they called it "cha" as in Japanese, "cha" and "chaya" as in Hindi, or "chai" as in Russian, from the northern Chinese pronunciation.

> Tea cultivation happened relatively late in the course of Chinese history—really after the collapse of the Han Dynasty about AD 200 and the rise of the Tang Dynasty about AD 600. There is some conjecture that it was sponsored by Buddhist priests (in this era of cultural breakdown and concerns about degraded morality) as an alternative to alcohol. However it started, it suddenly flourished. A local species of the camellia shrub, it grew well on hillsides in Yangtze Valley latitudes. Seedlings could be transplanted about a year old, and at as early as three years they produced enough leaf for picking. A mature field was usually picked four times a year, with the first picking the choice one. A good tea gatherer could pick enough leaves for about ten pounds of tea a day. Green teas are not fermented before heating; "red" or "black" teas are.[7]

The delicacy of the Chinese tea palate has been compared to the French wine palate. And the storage and shipping of the tea was a science of its own.

Silk. Whether you're in Uzbekistan or Cambodia, anywhere in the world you see rows of coppiced mulberry trees—trees cut down near the ground and allowed to grow new shoots—you know you're in silk country. Mulberry leaves are the only food of the silk moth caterpillar, in its thirty-five-day growing period, and it takes over eight pounds of leaves to raise one pound of silkworms. A single cocoon yields a thread 1,000 yards long, humankind's favorite natural fiber. It has the tensile strength of steel for its diameter, takes dye uniformly, is a great insulator, and has an attractive luster and what you can only call a "silken" feel.

It is clearly a Chinese invention. Although the first archaeological evidence is from around 2500 BC in northern China with widespread use there by 1500 BC, Van Slyke says that the center of silk production moved to the Yangtze Valley as early as 500 BC. The Jiangnan and the Sichuan bowl (and late in history, Canton and the Pearl River area) became its great production areas. This really gave these areas a world-wide influence. Silk was China's first great export commodity, giving its name to the Silk Road west, and doing its part to motivate the eastern movement of Alexander the Great's armies and spark a good deal of Roman interest.

Tung Oil. Tung oil, or wood oil, has been since antiquity the favorite Chinese sealer and finisher for wooden surfaces. Unlike western shellacs and varnishes, it doesn't darken over time, so it has gained a lot of popularity in the west as well. It was also used in China as a base for paint and the key ingredient in the caulking used to waterproof boats. The tree's name is an old Chinese word for heart, because of its heart-shaped leaves. It is a small tree that grows well on steep hillsides with poor soils; all it needs is lots of rain. It produces its oil-bearing nuts from as early as the third year, and then for up to twenty years more. Its range is as far south as Vietnam and as far north as the Wei Valley in China, but the hillsides in the Yangtze River drainage, from Anhui and Jiangxi provinces downriver to Sichuan province upriver, were its center of production; Hankou and Shanghai were always its main shipping points.

Salt. Salt, especially to people living on a largely meat-free diet, is a basic human necessity. With only two basic sources for the whole Yangtze drainage area—solar evaporation on the coast, and the brine wells of Sichuan 800 miles upriver—it was also a really easy thing for the government to tax. On the lower Yangtze, the wealthy businessmen famous for monopolizing the salt trade came not from the Jiangnan as you might expect, but from the Appalachian-like mountains of Anhui Province's Huizhou, just upriver. In the upper Yangtze valley the most famous salt-producing town was Zigong, on a branch of the Tuo River called, appropriately enough, Salt-well River. Guildhalls of salt merchants from Shaanxi Province (the Wei valley of the Yellow River) as well as local Sichuan salt merchants, dating from the early 1700s, have been preserved as museums there. Their size and rich ornamentation testify to the huge role of the salt trade in the economy.[GE44]

The technology of drilling brine wells as deep as 3,000' was an ancient Chinese invention. Tomb tiles dating from the first or second centuries AD showed the process. A wooden derrick held a metal drill head suspended by a woven bamboo cable (more on such cables in the section on boats to come). As many as a dozen men jumped on and off a board like a see-saw to jerk the cable and drill head up and let it fall by gravity onto the rock. Such a well was lined with stone rings its first hundred feet or so to keep out fresh ground water. Every so often the entire cable had to be brought up so that the debris could be excavated. The ideal locations also had wells of natural gas, much easier to use in boiling the brine down than charcoal or coal.

Traditional river transportation

The transport of all these goods, and more, shaped life along the Yangtze River system. It largely determined the location and size of cities. Westerners generally lump the larger traditional Chinese river craft together under the label of junks, and the smaller ones under the label of sampans. As late as the nineteenth century, every small river had its own style boats. Those familiar with the river could probably tell where each boat originated. Some were dramatically different. Van Slyke describes a "twisted buttock" boat unique to the Crow River (Wujiang), a Sichuan river that comes up from the south to meet the Yangtze at Fuling;[GE45] the stern was built at right angles to the rest of the boat, enabling the mounting of not one but two stern sweeps, or long projecting oars, to be worked to meet some particular navigation hazard on the Crow. Another Sichuan river, the Tuo (and its tributary the Salt-well River)[GE46]—which served the salt-making city of Zigong written about earlier—gave birth to a style of junk in which both bow and stern were built at an angle to the main hull of the boat. These junks carried twenty-five tons of salt apiece on their downstream runs, and apparently the twisted bow and stern, plus a singularly long projecting stern sweep, evolved to meet the challenge of getting by one killer rock in a fast river curve. As the junk was swept down towards the rock, it was close enough to the bank so that a braided bamboo rope could be handed to the boatmen aboard it. One end was fast to the bank, and the boatmen quickly threw three turns of it around a stumpy post, or bollard, and "surged" the boat three times (tightened the cable and then quickly loosened it as they let the rope run out). This just deflected the boat from a head-on collision with the rock, and then five men on the crooked stern made one mighty haul on the large stern sweep. If all was done well, the boat pivoted sweetly and raced by the killer rock unscathed, home free for the downstream run.

In 1943 a regional Chinese writer published a book of essays on his home area, *West Hunan*. In it he described the variety of boats at the waterfront of the city of Changde (Ch'ang-te) at the mouth of the Yuan

44. GE Layer 44 is a Placemark icon referencing a Panoramio icon titled "Shaaxi guild hall in Zigong," today a history museum. The richly ornamented building gives you an idea of the wealth connected with the salt trade.
45. GE Layer 45 is a Placemark framing a view of the Crow River (Wujiang) as it comes into the main Yangtze at Fuling.
46. GE Layer 46 is a Placemark framing Tuo River and tributary serving Zigong.

River just before it goes into the western corner of Dongting Lake. [GE⁴⁷] Here, he says, all the goods of not just western Hunan but eastern Sichuan and Guizhou provinces come downriver, headed for Hankou—tung oil, lumber, hides, opium, tobacco, mercury, etc. Goods headed upriver, the other way, arrived here at Changde to be off-loaded into smaller boats for the journey upriver—salt, dyed yard, cotton cloth, kerosene, flour, sugar, etc. The result was a river full of boats, all sorts of boats. But the "undisputed kings" of the water were the Hung River oil boats:

> Most of these boats have a square bow and raised poop. They are brightly colored, sometimes embellished with gold paint, and are fitted with a stern house for the master's family. Downbound, they can carry three or four thousand barrels of tung oil; on the return trip they load two thousand bolts of cotton cloth or a full consignment of salt. Manning the sweeps are anywhere from twenty-six to forty men, along with thirty to sixty trackers. They must wait for spring flood in order to get underway between Hung River [a town about 275 river miles farther up the Yuan] and Ch'ang-te. During the high water season, they can make three to five round trips, and the rest of the time they sit idle, moored in large flotillas—truly the monarchs of the river.[8]

And as Van Slyke says, Changde was just a minor port on a lesser tributary of the Long River; if you had that kind of variety of boats and waterborne commerce there, what did you have at a major river city such as Nanjing?

For anyone who spent much time on the Long River, it was the boat traffic through the Three Gorges that was most dramatic of all. Before motorized shipping and the use of modern explosives to blow up the most dangerous rocks and reefs, the gorges could only be run in a narrow band between low and high water (and water level could change 20 feet in a single day, and the highest recorded river rise was 275 feet!). The pulling of loaded junks upriver, sometimes against a 15 m.p.h. current, around ledges and treacherous sunken rocks, was something no one who saw it ever forgot. There were paths cut in the cliff faces for the trackers, the oldest of them going back at least to the early Han Dynasty of the first and second century BC.[GE⁴⁸]

Some of the best insights we Americans have gained into Chinese culture and history came from American "missionary kids" who grew up in China, learned Chinese as early or earlier than they learned English, and either stayed there or came back in their adulthood. Pearl Buck may have been the best of all these, with her translations and works of both non-fiction and fiction, most famously *The Good Earth*. Possibly the best book on the Yangtze River ever written by an American was John Hersey's 1956 *A Single Pebble*. He too was a missionary kid, born (1914) and raised in Tianjin, sent back to the U.S. for high school and college (Yale), then back out to China as a journalist in 1937. In that year the Nationalist government began retreating upstream in the Yangtze valley because of the Japanese invasion—much more later, from both Chinese and Japanese sides, trust me—and moving its capital to Chongqing (Chungking), above the gorges. The narrator of the novel is a young American hydraulic engineer, sent to scout upriver for places for dams. At Yichang, at the base of the gorges, he was warned that bandits were attacking western steamers, so he boarded a junk:

> The boat was a *ma-yang-tzŭ*, one of the great upriver junks, a hundred and two feet in length over all, nineteen feet in beam, made entirely of the tough cypress of the Wanhsien [Wan Xian] district, with a turret-built hull divided by strong bulkheads into fourteen cargo compartments, and carrying on deck abaft the mast its living quarters, a big shelter for the crew and a cabin for the owner on the stern: a craft well designed forty centuries ago.[9]

The chief figure of the story is Old Pebble, the head tracker. One result of reading the novel is to convince any reader that the wrestling of a 120-ton cargo ship through the sixty-five total miles of the gorges was a magnificent feat, one that maybe only the Chinese of all people in history could have pulled off. Thomas Blakiston,

---

47. GE Layer 47 is a Placemark referencing the Yuan River city of Changde and the Yuan River.

48. GE Layer 48 is a Placemark located at the beginning of the gorges, where the paths were cut. It is mainly used here to refer to the following website, which has good photos of the trackways: http://www.photosanxia.com/view.asp?id=5972

the first British naval officer up through the gorges (about 1861) said this about such traditional (pre-steam) navigation on the Yangtze:

> The Chinese seem to practice this river navigation to perfection, and it is amusing to observe the remarks about the "clumsy and awkward native boats," and the "primitive mode of navigation," which are often seen in print in England. I have seen something of boat voyaging in North America, where it is carried to great perfection, but I am free to confess that the inland navigation of China beats it, to use a trans-Atlantic expression, "all to pieces." The only way in which we can hope to overreach the Chinese on their inland waters is by the powerful agency of steam . . . ."[10]

Each junk headed up through the gorges carried two inch thick bamboo cables, the outside part of braided outer rind of bamboo, the inner part of the softer inner surface of the bamboo. The more the tension on the cable, the tighter the grip of the strong rind strips on the soft inner strips. Such a bamboo cable was considerably stronger than hemp rope of the same diameter—plus getting stronger when wet, not weaker—and in fact the bamboo cables had about half the tensile strength of steel cable of the same diameter. Gangs of from 50 to 300 trackers towed the big boats up through the rapids, sometimes fastening the upstream end of two cables to some anchor on the shore and letting the two capstans on the junks reel in the lines, pulling the junks a few inches at a time up through the swiftest of the rapids. It took amazing coordination between ship and gang; getting the bow caught in a downstream eddy could jerk a whole gang out of the trackway and into the river, dooming the junk as well.

Even today in China, with an ultra-modern system of interstate highways being built, the deep countryside has its rural river ferries,[GE[49]] and its small boats rowed, Chinese-style, standing up and facing forward.[GE[50]]

The Long River system was the watery heart of China. So now, with the geographic stage fully set, let's turn to what Professor Van Slyke calls "Eventful Time"—the historical events and processes that played out there.

SECTION B: PRE- AND EARLY HISTORY

"Dragon bones"

Around 1900 "dragon bones" began showing up in Beijing drugstores. They were mostly the shoulder blades of horses and the plastrons of turtles, really, really old, with primitive Chinese characters carved on them. The druggists were grinding them up and selling them as virility potions. Once scholars got hold of them, they turned out to be earliest written Chinese. They were fortune-telling devices; questions were written on them, and in some cases what seems to have been a hot poker was applied to them to make the bone crack. Where the crack ran helped determine the fortuneteller's answer, which was written on the same bone. Today they are often called "oracle bones."

About the same time beautifully cast bronze vessels, with the patina of extreme age, began to hit the antique market. They generated as much or more interest, and sleuths tracked down the source of all this by the 1920s—ancient, royal, cross-shaped burials from sites near from the elbow of the Yellow River to downstream, somewhat north and south of the present river. The town of Anyang, for example, has a clutch of these. [GE[51]]

---

49. For view of a rural ferryboat on a Sichuan river, GE Layer 49 is a Placemark that references a Panoramio icon titled "渡船."

50. GE Layer 50 is a Placemark referencing such a view under a Panoramio icon titled "危水."

51. First, close the Section A Folder, and open the next one, "Section B: Pre&EarlyHistory." Turn on the two unnumbered GE layers that come first, the Polygon named "Main Yangtze Corridor" and the Folder named "China Rivers." Then turn on and "fly" to GE Layer 51, a Placemark framing a view of the cross-shaped (cruciform) tombs of the royal Shang burials at Anyang.

This turned out to be the Shang dynasty, whose thirty kings and seven capitals had been talked about in traditional Chinese literature, but usually assumed to be legendary. It flourished from sometime before 1500 BC down to 1100 BC or so, gradually spreading its control and literate civilization as far as the Wei Valley in the west and to the coast in the east.

As Shang declined, a warring free-for-all developed, and the winner, the Zhou dynasty of kings, came from the Wei Valley. As mentioned in the topography section, this is one area of China that is large enough, and fertile, and well-watered enough, to sustain a sizeable population, but that really only has one easy way in and out, the river's mouth. Did you ever play the old "Risk" board game? On the whole board only Australasia has just one way in and out; the winner of the game may not come from there, but it almost always plays a role in the game way out of proportion to its size. So did the Wei Valley in times of central government breakdown in Chinese history.

Zhou rule lasted 900 years, from around 1122 BC to 221 BC. But it was not one long, unbroken succession. Around 770 BC a combination of northern invaders and Chinese rebels destroyed the capital, really ending the original dynasty. The new rulers moved the capital eastwards, so the last half of Zhou is called "Eastern Zhou." And even that is broken down into the "Spring and Autumn" period (named after a chronicle of events that survived), and from 453 (or 403, depending on your source) on, the aptly-named "Warring States" period.

Confucius

The "Spring and Autumn" period was the springtime of Chinese philosophy. Its brightest light was Confucius, China's most important contribution to the "Axial Age" of great philosophers across India, the Mideast, and Greece. Confucius is the Latinized version of *Kongfuzi* (K'ung-fu-tzu), the last character of which is an honorific usually translated "master." The dates traditionally given for his life are 551 to 479 BC. He was from the state of Lu, in today's Shandong province.[GE[52]]

Confucius never held any important governmental position, and only a few of his disciples ever did. Although elevated by later Chinese thought into a religious deity, he was not what most of us would call religious. Once when asked about the possibility of an afterlife (as is recorded in the *Analects*, some sayings of Confucius remembered by his disciples), he replied that he hadn't yet learned how to live correctly in this world; how was he to even think about the next? Of all the world's most influential philosophers, he was the most conservative, even reactionary. He saw, or thought he saw, back in early Zhou dynasty times, a harmonious society where everyone knew his or her place, in five key relationships: ruler to subject, father to son, husband to wife, elder brother to younger brother, and friend to friend (notice that only the last one is equal to equal). If he could only learn the formal rituals and rules of behavior of early Zhou, he believed, he could revive their practice in his day, and revive their ethical behavior in the process. The key word in his thought was *li*, which translates as both "ritual" and "virtue." So in his own lifetime, he mainly had a reputation as an antiquarian. When a hawk fell dead in his home state of Lu with a strange arrow embedded in it (every culture being known by the unique features of its arrows), he was able to identify the Central Asian tribe that originally shot the hawk because he had seen a bundle of their arrows in an ancient tribute package they had given the early Zhou kings. Later, when two rulers met to discuss peace, and one ruler unexpectedly gave a gift to the second, there was an awkward pause that jeopardized the proceedings because the other ruler didn't know how to respond. One of Confucius's disciples saved the day by whispering in the second ruler's ear the correct historic formula for the receipt of such a gift.

But Confucius also had the idea that the educated (in the formulas of antiquity) and the virtuous (in the harmonies he claimed to see in antiquity) should rule, and that idea spread and worked its way into the stuff of Chinese culture like yeast. It would bear temporary fruit in the Han Dynasty, and more permanent fruit in the great string of dynasties from Tang to Qing.

---

52. GE Layer 52 is a Placemark referencing the tomb of Confucius in the temple of Qufu. Click on Panoramio icon under pointer, titled "'Confucius' Tomb (孔夫子) Qufu," for view of same.

Warring States and the "First Emperor"

One of the half-dozen contenders for power in these wars at the end of Zhou was the state of Chu, which held the middle Yangtze Valley (the "W" proper), plus a good bit of territory north of that. Around 300 BC Qu Yuan (Ch'u Yuan) was a minister of Chu. He saw the rising power of Qin in the Wei Valley, and urged his king to lead a general alliance against it. The king listened to other advisors, and abused and dismissed Qu Yuan. When in 278 BC Qu Yuan got word that Qin armies had taken the Chu capital, he is supposed to have drowned himself from sorrow in the Miluo River,[GE53] not far from Lake Dongting. Every year, all over China and even Korea, on the fifth day of the fifth lunar month, "dragon boats" race each other as the centerpiece of a major festival. It is a reenactment of the townspeople rushing with their boats, though futilely, to save Qu Yuan from drowning. On the one hand he can be seen as the model of an aristocratic, "noblesse oblige" sort of attachment to a dynastic kingdom. On the other—and this is how Qu Yuan is celebrated today in the People's Republic—it is an interesting example of a pre-modern version of patriotism.

In 221 BC the ultimate victor was Qin, as once again the winner in a general war came from the Wei Valley. Its ruler now owned a territory much larger than any previous Chinese state—all of north China and now all of the Yangtze Valley. He gave himself a title heretofore used only for deities: *Qin Shih Huang Di* (Ch'in Shih Huang Ti), usually translated First Emperor. He ruthlessly imposed the Qin system on his wider holdings. On coinage. On weights and measures. On land tax. On axle-lengths. Even on philosophy. In 213 BC he carried out "The Burning of the Books," destroying all philosophic works and sometimes their authors, excepting only two approved strains of political philosophy that lent themselves to supporting his centralized, authoritative rule. As with Alexander the Great in classical Greece almost exactly a century before this, centralized rule brought the end of a rich variety of thought, but the strengthening of imperial power.

This "First Emperor" demanded that nobility from his empire come live in his capital city, which quickly became the world's largest city. It was this Qin capital of Chang'an, near present-day Xian (Hsian), that became the capital of China for over 1,400 years (by contrast, Beijing, the Mongol capital of the 1200s, has been China's capital city only half as long). Chang'an was a city planned from the ground up. Oriented north and south, with the imperial palace ("forbidden city") at the north to catch full southern sun, it was a rectangle 5 miles wide × 6 miles long. Arrow-straight major boulevards and minor streets crossed at right angles, with designated nodes for commercial centers at the major crossings.

It was this First Emperor who built, or at least connected all the pieces, of the first Great Wall (though most of its visible shape today came from a rebuilding under the Ming). The famous terracotta army of 7,000 life-sized soldiers,[GE54] each with individual facial features, guards his tomb in the valley outside Xian—one of four such armies, apparently, one for each of the cardinal directions. And the Chinese wait with incredible patience to open his mausoleum,[GE55] that according to ancient official writings has models of continents made of gold and silver, rivers and oceans of mercury, supposedly guarded by devilish defenses like something out of an "Indiana Jones" movie. The Emperor Qin (Ch'in) is the source of our word China, and indeed he may be the single most important figure in all of Chinese history, including even Confucius.

The sensuous and dangerous South

So far most of the history described has been well north of the advertised historical corridor of this chapter, the main Long River valley. Professor Van Slyke, in his *Yangtze: Nature, History, and the River*, argues that there is a real northern bias to the early sources. Chengdu and Chongqing in Sichuan, for example, had bronze age city-state civilizations as old as anything in the Wei Valley, but so few written records survived there that by default northern sources came to dominate the field. In literature there was a real northern nervousness about the state of Chu on the middle Yangtze—it was the attractive and fertile, but sensuous and dangerous South.

---

53. GE Layer 53 is a Placemark referencing the Panoramio icon under pointer titled "Miluo river with dragon boat (dragon boat racing festival originated from here) river."

54. GE Layer 54 is a Placemark referencing the famous terracotta army site.

55. GE Layer 55 is a Placemark locating the Mausoleum, and referencing a Panoramio icon titled "秦始皇陵墓道" for view of stone steps ascending the hill of the mausoleum.

Van Slyke emphasizes southern elements that contributed to Chinese culture—rice culture, most dramatically, so central to the production of food, was never a northern thing. And other scholars suggest that even in philosophy, the South contributed its share to the cultural fusion with Taoism.

Next to Confucianism, Taoism is probably the most important strain of Chinese philosophy. It comes from the word *dao* (Wade-Giles *tao,* pronounced like the Dow in Dow-Jones) meaning the Way, a spiritual Way. The oldest book about it is attributed simply to "Old Master," Laozi (Lao-tzu), who is supposed to have lived before Confucius. It is a variety of mystic appreciation that all things are relative and depend on their opposites: no beauty without ugliness, for example. Water is the key metaphor for proper living—the softest thing, smoothly going around obstacles, but patiently wearing away the hardest structures over time. Taoism is consciously opposed to the rituals and laws of Confucianism. It urges a return to primitivism, praising the peasant who carries water in buckets even though he knows about water wheels. It thinks the ideal life is lived in a state small enough so that people can hear the roosters crow in a neighboring state, but where they are so content that they never even go visit it.[11] *Wu wei* (both second tone) is the classic Taoist phrase; literally "not doing," it comes from the phrase "through not-doing all things are done."

Ever since, this has made for an interesting duality in the Chinese philosophy of life, the yang of Confucianism and the yin of Taoism. In the prime of life and in position of influence, one would tend to be Confucian—active, doing, writing; in old age or political disfavor and retreat, one would be Taoist—passive, blending into the background, quietly absorbing the mysteries of life.

All Rivers' Weir

Qin rule had its brutal side, but there was also great energy and technical expertise behind it. In the centralization under the Qin this had an immediate impact on the Yangtze Valley. Even before the 221 BC defeat of his last enemies, the Qin ruler sent an engineer named Li Bing down to arrange for the irrigation of some 40 × 50 miles—2,000 square miles!—of the Sichuan bowl. Li built the key part of his irrigation work just where the Min River—one of the two main sources of the upper Yangtze—came out of the mountains thirty-five miles northwest of Chengdu.[GE⁵⁶]

Li's first problem was to keep the same amount of water going into irrigation canals whether the Min was in flood or at low water. His second problem was to make it all permanent, so it wouldn't shift or get silted in. His solution was elegant—the most remarkable irrigation work of the ancient world, and in virtually continuous use for the last 2,300 years. Li called it 都江堰, *Dujiangyan (Tu-chiang Yen),* or All Rivers' Weir.

On a gentle right-hand curve of the river (looking downstream), Li improved a long curved island that split the channel. He permanently anchored the island, by armoring the upstream head of the island with rock ("Fish Snout," it is called; its armoring today is concrete), and building substantial walls of large stone blocks along the sides. The whole island he called "Diamond Dike."[GE⁵⁷] In the steep rocky left bank of the river, near the tail of the island, he cut a vertical slice just a few yards wide. This was called "Precious Bottle's Mouth," the opening for the irrigation water.[GE⁵⁸] On the other side of the island, up near the head, in low water times he would have a temporary dam built of log tripods weighted with stones and covered with mats; this temporary

---

56. GE Layer 56 is a Placemark framing such a view.

57. GE Layer 57 is a Placemark referencing Panoramio icon under pointer titled "千古名渠都江堰." It has a good picture of "fish snout," the armored upstream end of the curved island, that splits the river in two. Water in the channel nearest the viewer was being directed into mouth of irrigation canal network; the dam on far channel was to divert more water to near side in low water season.

58. GE Layer 58 is a Placemark referencing a Panoramio icon under pointer titled "都江堰 离堆 宝瓶口" which has a good view of Precious Bottle opening from upstream. Water at left is rushing into the irrigation network mouth; excess water is rejoining main river at lower right.

dam would force more of the water around to the irrigation side of Diamond Dike.[GE59] And finally, connecting the tail of the island with the riverside opening of Precious Bottle, he built an angled, low dam or spillway. It had two purposes: first, to keep the water level going into Precious Bottle's Mouth high, and second, to sweep the silt away from the base of the whole structure; it was called "Flying Sand Spillway."[GE60] Just a few hundred feet away the irrigation canals fan out in all directions east and south, the key to the fabulous agricultural production of Sichuan; food from here would eventually be exported as far as Beijing.[GE61]

Carved on a cliff along the river is hydraulic engineer Li Bing's advice to future would-be tamers of rivers: "Dig the channel deep; keep the dikes low." Raising the dikes but letting the bottom of the channel get higher and higher over the surrounding countryside is a contest the river will always eventually win. Li Bing and his son, who took his place and finished construction, have in death been elevated to kings; the "Two Kings Temple" dedicated to them, fittingly enough, sits overlooking All Rivers' Weir.[GE62]

Miracle Canal

In the same decade another engineer was charged by the Qin ruler with creating a canal link from the Yangtze drainage over into the West River drainage to the south—with an eye to future expansion of the state. The result was the Miracle Canal. Somewhat south of our chosen corridor, it still deserves some description; not only is it in its own way as impressive as All Rivers Weir, but this would be a key to modern military comings and goings between armies of the south and armies of the center of China (on which more later). Where the headwaters of the Xiang (Hsiang) River came generally north by the village of Xiangan (Hsiang-an), the river was split three ways by an angled spillway:[GE63] some water entered the northern, bypass channel, suitable for canal boats; some water entered the south channel, a contour transport canal[GE64] destined for the Li River a few miles south;[GE65] and excess water washed over the spillway into the old bed of the Xiang. Heavy supplies could now accompany troops over into the southern drainage.[GE66] Over Miracle Canal the First Emperor sent his armies as far south as Guangzhou (Canton) and even Vietnam.

The Han Dynasty

The exactions of the First Emperor—in armies, in city and wall building and irrigation, in suppression of popular philosophies—helped cause an explosion after his death in 210 BC. Within the year, a former Chu general led a revolt, in an attempt to reestablish the old Zhou system. In the civil war that followed, it was a general based in the Wei Valley—again—that unified the land by 202 BC. He set himself up as Emperor now, and took as his dynastic name Han, from the northern tributary of the Yangtze that ran in the valley just south of the Wei

---

59. Log tripods, weighted with stones and covered with mats, were built as a temporary dam every low water season to help divert more water into the irrigation canals. Here on "Diamond Dike" Island are reconstructions to demonstrate the process; GE Layer 59 is a Placemark referencing a Panoramio icon under pointer titled "都江堰（古代中国の知恵）" for good view of same. Today a permanent dam with floodgates over the non-irrigation half of the river has replaced the traditional tripods.

60. GE Layer 60 is a Placemark referencing a Panoramio icon titled "Đô Giang Yển_Yuzui_congnt," for a view of the "Flying Sand Spillway" in high water.

61. GE Layer 61 is a Placemark framing an overhead view of the fan of canals.

62. GE Layer 62 references a Panoramio icon under pointer titled "都江堰二王庙;" it's a view of entrance to Two Kings Temple, the same written in large gold characters in Chinese.

63. GE Layer 63 is a Placemark referencing Panoramio icon titled "Ling Qu, Guangxi, China 灵渠," for a good view of these angled spillways, the river being divided above the corner of the angle.

64. GE Layer 64 references Panoramio icon titled "[悠悠的灵渠]" for view of same. Two other nearby Photos icons also have views.

65. GE Layer 65 is a Path generally representing the contour canal that goes south to meet the headwaters of the Li River, the upper stretches of which were also improved to carry barge traffic.

66. GE Layer 66 is a Placemark framing a view of Xiang-Li Rivers connection of two drainages.

River valley. His dynasty would last 400 years, the first classic Chinese dynasty. Chinese still call themselves "people of Han" today.

It was during the Han dynasty that paper and the porcelain we call "china" was developed. The state went about half-way towards implementing Confucius's idea of the educated and virtuous ruling, beginning the creation of a civil service chosen by exam (in the Confucian classics, primarily). Militarily Han pushed south and added northern Vietnam to China, pushed north and added northern Korea to China, and pushed way out northwest along the Silk Road, extending the Great Wall out to the eastern tip of the Taklamakan Desert.

In 1972, in the eastern suburbs of the city of Changsha (capital of Hunan Province), excavators opened Ma Wang Dui, or "Horse King's Mound." It proved to be the tombs of the Marquis of Dai (the early Han Emperors left some pre-existing states semi-independent, hence the use of "marquis" in translation, from a similar era in European history), his wife, and another relative. It got worldwide attention. Lady Dai's body had been so well preserved inside multiple coffins of cypresswood, sealed with white clay and packed with charcoal, that the skin was still flexible and they knew what she ate the day before she died of a heart attack. Thousands of magnificent artifacts were in the burials. Her clothes were beautifully woven, and one of her gauze gowns weighed just forty-nine grams (less than two ounces). There was a complete lacquerware set of dishes, stunning in their decoration. In the Marquis's tomb the entire *I Ching* or *Book of Changes* was painted on silk. Surprisingly sophisticated medical and astronomical texts were, too. The Marquis died in 186 BC, a little over fifteen years into the new Han dynasty; his wife died sometime later.[GE67]

Like the Roman Empire to later centuries of European rulers, the Han dynasty was to later Chinese the prime model of what government was supposed to be.

Three Kingdoms, Six Dynasties

Already with the Han dynasty you could see the outline of a dynastic pattern, or cycle. A time of general war and social upheaval produced a new military ruler, who became Emperor. A lean, efficient government rebuilt the roads, dredged the canals, sent out armies that paid for themselves as they conquered. Most farmers owned their own land, and paid taxes (or gave periods of labor) to the government. But the frontiers eventually stabilized and the army had to be paid for, and taxes went up. Over time fewer and fewer farmers owned their own land. The government began to get into prestige building programs. Eventually corruption sapped the army, and horsemen on the north and west began to break through the frontier. A few wealthy landlords controlled all the land, and a starving peasantry decided death in rebellion would be less painful than slow death by starvation, and at least they had a chance to change things. Secret religious organizations in the countryside began to meet. Ambitious generals began to weigh their chances.

The year AD 184 was the beginning of the end for Han. Faith-healing Taoist sects predicted a millennial age starting then, with the forces of the spirit world mobilizing to destroy evil government. So many desperate people believed it, that it became a self-fulfilling prophecy. They were called the Yellow Turbans for the yellow kerchiefs their leaders asked them to wear. The frontier armies had to be brought home to suppress the rebellion, making the frontiers that much more vulnerable.

As the central government collapsed in the early 200s, three claimants to the throne emerged. Strongest was the northern state of Wei, whose leader, Cao Cao, was a brilliant strategist and of a Machiavellian turn of mind. Instead of "Speak of the devil," the Chinese even today say, "Speak of Ts'ao Ts'ao [Cao Cao] and there he is."[12] The state of Shu was centered in Sichuan, led by Liu Bei, who claimed descent from the Han ruling family (so sometimes this state is also called Shu Han). The lowest part of the Yangtze Valley, especially the Jiangnan, was the base of the state of Wu. Wei, Shu, and Wu are the three kingdoms of possibly the most dramatic and famous of all periods of Chinese history, called logically enough Three Kingdoms. Cao Cao seemed well on his way to uniting the country and becoming the founding Emperor of a new dynasty, when he walked

---

67. GE Layer 67 is a Placemark referencing the approximate site of the Mawangdui tombs. Most of the artifacts are in the Hunan Provincial Museum, also in Changsha. For websites with good visuals, do a Google or other search on "Mawangdui."

over-confidently into the Battle of Red Cliff on the middle run of the Yangtze River.[GE68] Even though Wu and Shu had allied, their forces were greatly outnumbered by Cao's Wei armies. But they sent fireboats down on Cao's fleet on a rare east wind, and then cut his armies to pieces on their retreat through swamps near the river. Cao escaped, but had lost his chance to unify the country. The country was briefly unified by a successor, but invasions of nomads from the north cancelled that. China suffered about 400 years of civil war and foreign invasion.

SECTION C: CLASSIC DYNASTIES CIRCA 600–1900

Buddhism enters China

In the centuries of turmoil after the breakup of the Han dynasty around AD 200, Buddhism spread over China as thoroughly as Christianity spread over the collapsing Roman Empire. In both places faith in secular structures had been deeply shaken, and religious answers of more surety were looked for. The form Buddhism took in China (and Vietnam, and Korea, and Japan) was Mahayana, or "Greater Vehicle" Buddhism, as opposed to the stricter Theravada ("School of Elders") or Hinayana ("Lesser Vehicle") Buddhism of Southeast Asia. Mahayana Buddhism evolved far away from the "godless religion" of the original Buddha. Boddhisattvas— beings that had attained enlightenment but chose to stay on earth and help others—became gods and goddesses. The Avalokitesvara of Indian Buddhism, which could be male or female, became the Chinese Mahayana goddess Guanyin (and later the Kannon of Japan).[GE69] In Mahayana Buddhism all humans—and even all animals—were destined for a sort of salvation. One reason Mahayana Buddhism prospered in China was its toleration of other religions and philosophies. Taoism it treated as a parallel, though lesser, search for religious truth. Confucianism it regarded as a practical political philosophy with which it could ally. Over time the three merged into what some have called "traditional Chinese religion." Visual evidence of the Buddhist strand of this triad, found in most every Chinese town and village, is the pagoda. These evolved from the Indian Buddhist stupa, a dome-shaped reliquary of artifacts associated with the original Buddha, with ornate, antenna-looking structures on top. In China the dome disappeared and the "antenna" evolved into stacked rooms with each roofline echoing the one below.[GE70] Buddhism is still very much alive in China. In 1996 a colossal statue of Buddha almost 300 feet tall was built on the shores of Lake Tai near Wuxi, in the heart of the Jiangnan. A model hand (forty feet tall!) left on the edge of the working site gradually became a focus of local worship, so much so that it was kept there even after construction was complete—all this in officially atheist "Communist" China.[GE71] There is at least one other colossal Buddha on our corridor. In the very western corner of the Sichuan bowl, on the Min River, the Leshan ("Happy Mountain") Buddha was carved out of the face of a mountain.[GE72] But this one was done early in the Tang Dynasty, about 1,300 years ago. It makes for interesting musing on cultural continuity.

---

68. GE Layer 68 is a Folder titled "Red Cliff campaign." It includes Polygons showing key army movements of Cao Cao's pursuit of Liu Bei, Liu Bei's juncture with Sun Quan's forces, and their return up the Yangtze to meet Cao Cao at the fateful Battle of Red Cliff, and then Cao Cao's disastrous retreat. There is debate and uncertainty about most everything illustrated (!), but this is more or less modern consensus.

69. Please collapse and turn off Folders for Sections A and B in this Google Earth unit, and open the Section C: Classic Dynasties Folder. Turn on the first two unnumbered layers for our corridor limits and the riverine network. On our corridor there are islands and towns named for Guanyin, and hundreds if not thousands of temples with her statue. For a view of one such, turn on and "fly" to GE Layer 69, a Placemark referencing a Panoramio icon in Wuhan titled "GuanYin Goddess (观音)."

70. GE Layer 70 is a Folder titled "Assorted Pagodas." It includes Placemarks referencing pagodas, all on our corridor except the first, in Xian, associated with the famous Buddhist pilgrim Tripitaka who went to India to bring back writings and relics (on which more later).

71. GE Layer 71 is a Placemark referencing the Lingshan Grand Buddha near Wuxi.

72. GE Layer 72 is a Placemark referencing the general location of the Leshan giant Buddha; dozens of Photos icons to explore.

A reunited China and a grand canal: the Sui-Tang Dynasties

In 589, again by a power from the Wei Valley, China was reunited. In an echo of Qin-Han, the reuniting Sui Dynasty demanded so much, so quickly, that revolts ended it after a generation and the Tang (T'ang) Dynasty took control by 617, reaping the rewards. It was a much more populous country, mainly because of the transformation of the Yangtze Valley lands through drainage, irrigation, terracing, and the like. Its rice culture now thoroughly eclipsed the dry field culture of north China. But rather than move their capital from the critical northwest frontier, the traditional route of invasions of China, the Sui decided to build the "Great Transport River." It was all about carrying rice from the Long River valley to Chang'an, the capital in the northwest.

This Grand Canal, as it became known in the west, was a building project that dwarfed even the Great Wall. It started at the important central China port of Hangzhou, went north to cross the Yangtze River at Yangzhou, which thus became one of the key trading cities in interior China. Then the canal crossed the Huai River drainage, where it acted as a dam to some extent. [GE73] There were some sophisticated hydraulics required to get Huai water east across it, though some of it got shunted south to the Yangtze proper. Then came the Yellow River floodplain. From Xuzhou, the original Grand Canal in the last half of its length then angled northwest to intercept the Yellow River in its east-west stretch, which was improved for barge traffic, and continued straight west on or along the Wei River to Chang'an. After Beijing became the capital in the 1200s, the northern half of the canal was rebuilt to feed it instead of Chang'an. In its last version it ran a thousand miles—700 straight-line miles, point to point—from Hangzhou to Beijing.[GE74]

Marco Polo was impressed by the Grand Canal's construction and its operation. In one passage he spoke of a town that supplied grain to the court of the Emperor:

> This place is in the line of communication with the province of Cathay [north China] by means of rivers, lakes, and a wide and deep canal which the Great Khan has caused to be dug, in order to pass from one river to the other . . . without making any part of the voyage by sea . . . . On its sides, likewise, are constructed strong and wide embankment roads, upon which the traveling by land also is rendered perfectly convenient.[13]

By Ming times around 350,000 tons of rice a year was going up this one-way transport system to the capital—a remarkable but easily interrupted and hugely expensive enterprise. Each transport boat carried around twenty tons of rice, with a crew of ten or twelve. The boats had a mainmast that would fold down. The mast could carry a sail, but was more often used as a tall fastening point for the ropes that the trackers pulled—that way the ropes cleared obstructions on the banks, such as moored ships. A populous guild of canal workers and sailors thrived on the trade in good times, and were explosive trouble in bad times—right on down to the twentieth century, as you'll see.

The perfecting of the civil service

By Sui-Tang, Confucius's old dream of the educated and the virtuous ruling took firm shape. It's a strange and remarkable idea, as if you limited every important position in government (except that of hereditary Emperor) to Ph.D.s in ancient literature and history and philosophy. Do you know any Ph.D.s in ancient literature, history, or philosophy? Doesn't it make you smile just to think about it? But the Chinese did it, with the world's first real Civil Service Examination.

The exams were in the Confucian Classics, works that were old even in Confucius's day. Part of the test was composing an "eight-legged essay"—a stylized poem—on a given topic. That would be the equivalent of me asking you to write something as specific as a Shakespearean sonnet on a surprise topic, say, the water fountain outside the building; quick, you have thirty minutes. The exams were at three levels, the Chinese version of county, state, and national. Passing the first—and only 1 or 2 percent passed at each level—only got you a shot at the second. Passing the second could get you a minor, local government job. But only those

---

73. GE Layer 73 is a Path generally representing the course of the Huai River down to its blockage by the Grand Canal.

74. GE Layer 74 is a Folder titled "Grand Canal." It contains two Paths, first of the later canal that went to Beijing, and second, the northeast half of the first canal that fed Chang'an out in the Wei Valley.

who passed the third exam became Officials, or Mandarins (the Chinese title was *jin shih*, "Presented Scholar," implying presentation to the Emperor). And they filled every position in government from country registrar on up.

They were the judges and heads of Confucian colleges. They were the administrators of roads and bridges and public buildings. They oversaw tax collection and military supply. In the course of their work they invariably became rich. About the only limitation on their power was the "law of avoidance," meaning that they were not to be stationed in their home province (nepotism being too likely a result). And instead of rising in one branch of government, as is usually the case in the U.S., they spiraled up through all the different branches, into higher and higher positions, often including the military. By the last half of their careers, as a result, they had a really broad view of the workings of the whole.

Early in a given dynasty, when the exams were honestly run, the system tended to work well. In times of dynastic decline, corruption would affect the system to the extent that the rich could bribe their way in. The exams were open to all (half, I should say, since it was for males only, given the Confucian hierarchical setting), though in practice about half of all new Mandarins were sons or grandsons of existing Mandarins. Wealthy and aspiring families would usually groom at least one son for the exams; this was the surest road to power and wealth in traditional China. The success of the civil service system produced by the exams is probably the main reason there were no big inter-dynastic gaps such as Three Kingdoms, Six Dynasties. The virtually unbroken Chinese government from 600 to 1900 presided over perhaps the greatest era of civilization humankind ever produced.

Commerce and culture in the Song Dynasty

The Song (Sung) Dynasty in China, from around 960 to 1279 (though driven out of north China after 1127) reintroduced the civil service exams and government by the scholar-gentry. While never as militarily successful as Tang, the Song Dynasty was its superior in most of the arts (except maybe the Tang lyric poetry of the Li Bai era). This remarkable cultural flowering was built on a commercial boom—as in the Renaissance in Italy a bit later. The abacus came into widespread use as a hand-held personal computer. Paper money began to replace metals. Moveable type, the "invention" of which is celebrated in the west, was invented first here, some four centuries before Gutenberg. The wealth generated, plus government subsidies, supported the arts.

Perhaps the most famous ceramics in all of world history are Song Dynasty porcelains. There were government-supported kilns just south of West Lake in Hangzhou (now a museum of pottery).[GE75] But the most famous of all Chinese porcelain came from the factory in Jingdezhen, which was in Jiangxi Province, some ninety miles northeast of the provincial capital Nanchang. It used a fine local white clay today called *kaolin* (from *gaolin*, "high hill," source of the clay in Jingdezhen).[GE76] Such clay works easily in a potter's hand, taking the finest and thinnest shapes. When fired at high heat, it almost becomes a kind of glass—waterproof even without glazing. A light green jade-colored glaze, generally called celadon, was usually applied to the kaolin body, and such Song "celadons" are the centerpieces of great museum collections all over the world. Not for nothing is the finest porcelain called "china." Later, especially in the Ming Dynasty, Jingdezhen became famous for its blue and white porcelains.

The northern nomads

In the chapter on Russia, we talked about the struggle between the forest and the grasslands to the south. In China a version of that was the clash between farmland and the grasslands to the north. From the beginnings of Chinese history, there was always a threat of invasion from armies of horsemen on the prairies north of farming country—especially in times of dynastic decay. By the last half of the Song Dynasty, this clash dramatically

---

75. GE Layer 75 is a Placemark generally referencing the location of the old Song Dynasty kilns near Hangzhou, today a modern museum of pottery.

76. GE Layer 76 is a Folder titled "Jingdezhen porcelain." Photos icons referenced are mainly bronze statuary commemorating the historic local pottery production in town square.

shaped Chinese history. Such mounted forces from the northern steppes would conquer northern China in the last half of Song (called "Southern Song," therefore), all of China under the Mongols in the 1200s (the Yuan Dynasty), and—after an interlude of local Chinese rule in the Ming Dynasty—conquer all of China again under the Manchus in the 1600s (the Qing Dynasty). These minority ruling elites were partly but never thoroughly Sinicized in their culture.

Jurchen tribes from today's Manchuria captured the Song capital in 1126. They conquered all of north China, but then their drive south stalled out, leaving the frontier roughly along Huai River (between Yellow and Yangtze Rivers, generally the border of rice cultivation). Their main capital became Yenjing (Yen-ching), site of today's Beijing and still a literary name for the city. The Mongols ran them out of Beijing in 1215, and destroyed their dynasty altogether twenty years later.

The Southern Song Dynasty

The most vivid reminders of Southern Song are in and around Hangzhou, its capital city, especially the park and temple district called West Lake. Earlier you saw the celadon porcelains produced there, and in the topography section you saw that one of China's great patriotic heroes, General Yue Fei (a Song general who made the retreat south, but whose plans for recovering the north were subverted by an evil emperor), has his mausoleum there under the slogan associated with him, "Return my rivers and mountains."[GE77] Southern Song had the most vibrant urban culture in the world in the century and a half of its life. Its painting strikes modern critics as thoroughly "modern," when compared to anything being done in Europe in the 1100s. But there were newer and stronger barbarians at the gates.

Mongol conquest and the Yuan Dynasty

Central Asian Turkic and Mongolian horsemen were probably the best mounted warriors in the world, but their expertise was rarely seen outside their own countries, as they exhausted their energies in intertribal warfare. Around 1206, however, a Mongol chief named Temujin united all the tribes and assumed the royal title Khan and the reign name Chinggis, or Genghiz. In a burst of power unparalleled in history, in seventy years' time the Mongols created the world's largest land empire, over a fifth of the world's entire land, from Hungary in the west to the Chinese coast in the east (we had occasion earlier to mention their conquest of Arab cities such as Damascus, and the whole of the medieval Russian state). It was the first time grassland nomads ever conquered all of China.

The Mongol conquest of China began with an attempt to flank the Southern Song territories on the west, with armies moving down through western Sichuan to Yunnan and even Vietnam. Chinggis Khan's famous grandson Khubilai became Khan in 1259 when his brother, the current Khan, was killed besieging a city in Sichuan. But the main Mongol conquest of central China proceeded down the Han River. Their siege of the key Song Dynasty fortress city on the river, Xiangyang, took five years, from 1268 to 1273.[GE78] When it finally surrendered, Mongol armies moved on down the Han River, then downriver on the Yangtze proper, entering the Southern Song capital of Hangzhou in 1276. The last remnants of Song fleet were defeated near Guangzhou 1279, the date usually taken for the end of the dynasty.

The Mongols rulers of China became partly, but only partly, Sinicized. They adopted those parts of the Chinese system that were profitable to them (having been convinced they could get more from traditional taxation than from sacking and looting). But they never did much with the Confucian exams and the civil service system of the Mandarins—which may be one reason their Yuan Dynasty collapsed so soon, in 1368, just one century to the year from when they began the siege of Xiangyang. They made Beijing their regular capital, but

---

77. GE Layer 77 references Panoramio icon titled "Yue Fei/岳飞/岳飛" for view of Yue Fei's mausoleum/temple. You've seen this earlier, but here it is in its correct chronological place.

78. GE Layer 78 is a Placemark framing a view of Xiangyang on the Han River where it cuts through an east-west range of mountains.

the Great Khans kept their summer capital north of the Great Wall, at Shangdu (Coleridge's "Xanadu").[GE79] They did effectively reunite the whole of China, and passed some of the strength of their centralized rule on to later dynasties. But the Chinese, especially the scholar-gentry, never really accepted them, considering them uncivilized barbarians to the end.

The Ming and Qing Dynasties

By the middle 1300s Mongol generals were fighting among themselves in the north, and virtually every part of the Yangtze Valley had seceded. There were independent states in Sichuan, along the Han River, in the Jiangnan and on the coast of Zhejiang province, and these also warred among themselves. The winner, and founder of the Ming Dynasty, was Zhu Yuanzhang, whose hometown was in Anhui Province just within the border of our chosen corridor.[GE80] He made Nanjing his capital, and in his thirty-year-long rule reassembled China under Chinese rule (so the Ming Dynasty is celebrated by modern Chinese patriots as a time when the "natural" order of things was reestablished). After the first Ming Emperor's death in 1398 the capital was moved back to Beijing. The Great Wall was rebuilt. And the most remarkable ocean exploration fleets in history were set in motion under Admiral Zheng He (on which a little more later). Visually, the traditional China most of us automatically think of is Ming China—the latest rebuilding of the Great Wall, the Imperial Palace, and famous Ming tombs.[GE81] Ming rulers reinstituted the exam-based civil service, and the Ming Dynasty as a result enjoyed a typical three-century-long run.

In 1644 Manchu tribes from the north ended mainland Ming rule (a remnant of Ming rule lasted in Taiwan for another forty years, until the magnetism of the mother culture on the mainland pulled it back again). The thin stratum of Manchu conquerors, whose chiefs were called "bannermen," tried to keep their culture separate from the Chinese, going so far as to dig a willow-lined ditch between Manchuria and China. But much more than the Mongols they adopted the Chinese way of doing things, including the exam system. Qing was probably the equal or superior of any preceding dynasty in numbers of people governed and in power. The most famous ruler of the dynasty was the Kangxi Emperor, who ruled sixty-one years from 1661 to 1722. He was the near contemporary of France's famous "Sun King" Louis XIV, who also began rule as a child (1638, but actually ruled from 1661 to 1715), but there was no comparison between the population and wealth of the country ruled, or between the military success enjoyed by the former and eluding the latter. But the Qing Dynasty later had the misfortune of meeting the western challenge, in the years of maximum western power relative to the rest of the world.

Traditional Chinese novels

At this point the author despairs that, in trying to cover this rich era of human history dynasty by dynasty, pointing out events and developments of special relevance to the Long River valley, he has told too little to give the flavor of things, but given too much unconnected material for a reader to take in. So he will abandon the attempt, and try to do it in microcosm by focusing on one particular cultural manifestation that cuts across all of the dynasties at least from Southern Song on down—the development of the traditional Chinese novel.

Much of traditional Chinese historical literature forces individual humans into ideal Confucian molds. It's like those uniform statues of Egyptian pharaohs all in the same pose, or a critique I heard years ago of an Alabama history textbook for the public schools, particularly its section on the nineteenth century: "one bearded

79. GE Layer 79 is a Placemark framing a view of Shangdu, the summer palace the Great Khans maintained north of the Great Wall, reflecting their ambivalence about Chinese culture. Footprint of palace clearly visible in the view framed here. Its reputation lasted down to the time of Coleridge: "In Xanadu did Khubla Khan a stately pleasure dome decree . . ." Shangdu was 170 miles almost due north of Beijing; zoom out of view to see relationship.

80. GE Layer 80 is a Placemark referencing a clutch of Photos icons near Fengyang, home of the Ming Dynasty's founder Zhu Yuanzhang. Most of the photographs are of the impressive rows of animals and human statues there.

81. GE Layer 81 is a Placemark referencing Ming tombs on Nanjing's Purple Mountain, with several dozen Photos icons on the north-south axis of the tombs to explore. Those who have seen Beijing's Imperial Palace ("Forbidden City") will recognize the art and architecture.

governor followed another and they all stood for progress." But there are six traditional Chinese novels that can quickly get you past Confucian stereotypes.

They were written from about 1400 to 1800, in the heyday of the classic dynasties, but they built on earlier storytelling. Perhaps by Tang times, and certainly by Song times, wandering storytellers were very common. They usually specialized in a certain type of story—ghost stories (literally "transmission of the strange"); love stories; war stories. They would pass the hat after every passage; those who had no money stood far off, and the storyteller made sure to whisper the punch lines so they couldn't hear. And every passage would end with an intriguing couplet hinting at what was to come, so paying customers would stay around.

As a profession it of course attracted apprentices. And as literacy became more and more common, some of the apprentices began to take outline notes on the stories. By 1400 or so such "story texts" were coming into the hands of scholars, the literati, and they began to turn them into novels. The early novels still have many oral storytelling devices: "To tell it is slow, but oh how quick it was in the doing," is a common phrase. And every chapter of the early traditional novels ends, like street corner storytelling, in a couplet hinting at what comes next. The last two novels especially, from the mid-eighteenth century, have a psychological depth rooted in the mind of a single author. The novel may have started with story-texts, but was independent of them at the end.

Romance of the Three Kingdoms 三國演義

The oldest and still the most popular and influential is the *Three Kingdoms Romance*. It is huge: 120 chapters and perhaps 1,500 pages in the average unabridged translation. As the title suggests, it is set in that famous time of central government breakdown at the end of the Han dynasty when three competing kingdoms were emerging: Wei in the north, centered on the Wei Valley but dominating the whole north and intent on moving south; Wu centered on the rich Jiangnan of the lower Yangtze; and Shu centered on Sichuan in the upper Yangtze valley. It starts with one of the most famous lines in all of Chinese literature: "Empires wax and wane; states cleave asunder and coalesce."[14] Early in the novel Liu Bei, a poor but honorable descendant of the imperial house, made a "compact in the peach orchard" with wealthy butcher Zhang Fei and noted warrior Guan Yu. They swore blood brotherhood to each other, and decided to raise an army to help sort out the civil war. The three later attracted to themselves a fourth, Zhuge Liang, whose political and military advice was always brilliant. The Machiavellian genius of the north, Cao Cao, plays a big role. When captured by an enemy he had once pardoned, for example, he said "You have been well, I trust, since we parted?", reminding him of the pardon. Later, when that same worthy's head was delivered to him, Cao Cao spoke those identical words, dripping with cold-hearted irony, to the lifeless head.

Here's a most famous passage from the novel. As part of the lead-up to the Battle of Red Cliff, a general jealous of Zhuge Liang ordered him to come up with a hundred thousand arrows in three days' time. Meanwhile the general secretly told the quartermaster to delay delivery of feathers, arrowheads, glue, etc., thinking he will now have an excuse to execute Zhuge Liang for non-performance of critical military duty. For his part Zhuge Liang secretly readied twenty ships, with blue cotton screens and bundles of straw lashed to the sides. One of his associates, Lu Su, asked what he was doing, and Zhuge Liang told him to come with him and see (Zhuge Liang is called K'ung-ming in the text and dialogue below; Cao Cao goes by his Wade-Giles equivalent Ts'ao Ts'ao):

> Then the twenty boats were fastened together by long ropes and moved over to the north bank. The night proved very foggy and the mist was very dense along the river, so that one man could scarcely see another. In spite of the fog K'ung-ming urged the boats forward.

> There is a poem on these river fogs:

> > Mighty indeed is the Yangtse River!
> > Rising far in the west, in the mountains of Omei and Min
> > Ploughing its way through Wu, east flowing, resistless
> > Swelled by its nine tributary streams, rolling down from the far north . . . .

The little fleet reached Ts'ao Ts'ao's naval camp about the fifth watch and orders were given to form line lying prows west, and then to beat the drums and shout.

"But what shall we do if they attack us?" exclaimed Lu Su.

K'ung-ming replied with a smile, "I think the fleet will not venture out in this fog; go on with your wine and let us be happy. We will go back when the fog lifts."

As soon as the shouting from the river was heard by those in the camp the two commanders ran off to report to their chief, who said, "Coming up in a fog like this means that they have prepared an ambush for us. Do not go out, but get all the force together and shoot at them."

He also sent orders to the soldier camps to dispatch six companies of archers and crossbowmen to aid the marines.

The naval forces were then lined up on the bank to prevent a landing. Presently the soldiers arrived and a legion and more men were shooting down into the river, where the arrows fell like rain. By and bye K'ung-ming ordered the boats to turn round so that their prows pointed east and to go closer in so that many arrows might hit them.

The drums were kept beating till the sun was high and the fog began to disperse, when the boats got under way and sailed downstream. The whole twenty boats were bristling with arrows on both sides. As they left, all the crews derisively shouted, "We thank you, Sir Minister, for the arrows."[15]

Along the Water Margin 水滸傳

The Chinese characters of the title translate literally "Water Border Chapters." Pearl Buck titled her translation *All Men Are Brothers*, taking a line from western Stoic philosophy, which seemed a nice parallel. In a land of official Confucian relationships, these men found a higher good in personal friendship. One hundred and eight outlaws—good men all, aggrieved by corrupt officials—have taken to the swamps in western Shandong under the leadership of one Song Zhang, "the opportune rain." It's sort of a Chinese Robin Hood and his Merry Men, and was Mao Zedong's favorite novel. The heroes are all seven feet tall and built like NFL linebackers, and in terms of character development are distinguished from each other by not much more than dress and weaponry. They drub lesser mortals in combat, and when one hero unknowingly meets another, they fight "fifty to seventy rounds" evenly matched, and then, appreciating each other for a fellow hero, they usually go off drinking together.

Let me take time to rehearse one story from the novel, partly because it is the jumping off point for one of the later novels. Wu Song is the handsome and strong younger brother of Wu the Elder, who is so slight and ugly he is called "Three Inch Nail of Leprous Bark Skin." By the luck of arranged marriage, Wu the Elder marries Golden Lotus, the most beautiful girl in town. She thinks little of her husband, and makes advances to handsome brother-in-law Wu Song, who of course, as a respectful younger brother, rejects them. He is sent to take treasure to the court of the Emperor, and on the way comes to the foot of the great Yellow Mud Ridge. The day was hot, and there was a wineshop with a sign bragging on its wine, "Three Bowls and You Can't Go Over the Ridge." Wu Song had several bowls of wine, and several catties (roughly, pounds) of flesh, then more, and then more. Upon rising to pay the proprietor, he was told that it was now afternoon and the road over the mountain was closed: a great slant-eyed, white-browed tiger was loose there, eating travelers by the score, and the imperial troops only guarded the road during mid-day. Wu Song, a bit dizzy with wine, thought the innkeeper was just trying to get him to stay and spend more, so he paid and left. But sure enough, at the top of the first pitch of the road was an official sign saying the same thing. "But if I go back now," thought our hero, "the innkeeper will think I'm no good fellow." So up the hill he went in the late afternoon son, the wine rising to his head. He sat down in the shade of a strange bluish boulder to rest, and what should jump out but the great slant-eyed, white-browed tiger of Yellow Mud Ridge. Wu Song dodged fangs and claws, but the tiger's secret weapon was a tail like an iron bar. It whipped the tail down on Wu Song, who parried it with his club, though the club was shattered. Then it was tooth against tooth and claw against fingernail, until Wu Song "pounded the tiger into a heap as it lay there like an embroidered cloth bag." Imperial troops heard the ruckus, and came to find that Wu Song had killed the supernaturally evil beast. They carried him down the other side of the mountain in triumph. And a full two months later, he came back to his hometown and his brother's house.

Meanwhile wealthy merchant and man-about-town, Ximen Qing, had been walking down the sidewalk when someone accidentally let an awning pole fall and hit him on the head. He turned around prepared to beat up the culprit, but when he discovered it was the beautiful Golden Lotus, "his anger fled as far from him as Java." With many a backward look he walked down the street, and turned into the nearby wineshop of the disreputable Old Lady Wang. He asked if Golden Lotus had ever been known to step out on her husband, and the she said no, but perhaps something could be arranged—and drew up a ten-step plan for the seduction of Golden Lotus. To make a long story shorter, an affair was arranged, and by the rules of human nature soon everyone in town knew about it except Wu the Elder, "three inch nail of leprous bark skin." When he finally found out and surprised the couple in the back room of Old Lady Wang's, Ximen Qing beat him until he was comatose, and they carried him home where he lay between life and death. So shameless were the lovers that they then smothered him with a pillow, and bribed the undertaker to say it was a natural death. Wu Song came home, soon ferreted out the truth, and arranged a celebration for his brother's death. There he killed Golden Lotus and then went looking for Ximen Qing, quickly finding him and killing him in a running fight. For this and his reaction to other injustices he then went to join the outlaw band.[16]

The outlaws of the novel had some real historical background, being active on the Huai River in the early 1100s, just before the Song government was driven south. Apparently the stories the novel was based on were told in and around Hangzhou, capital of Southern Song, as a reminder of the good old days when the Huai River area was not the border with a non-Chinese state.

Journey to the West 西遊記

Attributed to an author who lived in the 1500s, this novel has some slight historic basis in the journey of a famous Chinese Buddhist monk to India to study Buddhism at its source. But the monk is accompanied by Monkey, who is the incarnation of all human ambition, and a character called Pigsy, who is the incarnation of all human greed, and is carried by a horse that is a transformed dragon. It is a fantasy classic, with lots of magic and magical battles. Monkey seems to be the Chinese literary descendant of the Hanuman of the *Ramayana*.

Jin Ping Mei; Golden Lotus 金瓶梅

The literal title comes from three of the main female figures in the novel, but its dominant figure is Golden Lotus and that is often used as the title in English. This is the novel that grows out of the scene related above in *All Men Are Brothers*, with the twist that Wu Song never came home and discovered the lovers, and Golden Lotus became the fifth wife of Ximen Qing, wealthy merchant and man-about-town. Despite the good management of the stately and respectable first wife, Golden Lotus's shamelessness and Ximen Qing's greediness eventually wreck the household. This is the erotic classic of popular Chinese literature; older translations into western languages put many passages in Latin, so as not to corrupt the masses.

The Scholars; or, An Unofficial History of the Officials 儒林外史

Written in the eighteenth century during the mid-Qing Dynasty, this novel is set—possibly for the satirical author's safety—back in Ming. Its focus is the Mandarins, the scholar-gentry who by virtue of passing the third and highest exam entered the civil service and in due course became rich. Fairly early in the book a character named Fan Chin is introduced. He is fifty-four years old, a student who has never been able to pass the exams. He is poor and threadbare and abused by his father-in-law, the Butcher Hu. But Fan Chin passed the second exam, and some locals raised the money for him to go take the final exams. The examiner, Chou, had just been appointed to his position, after himself failing the exams for many years. He looked at the shabbily-dressed older student with a certain pity. When Fan Chin turned his exam in first, the examiner read it, and could see nothing of value in it. When nobody else turned in a paper, he read it a second time, with the same reaction. Then a supremely confident, well-dressed young student turned his exam in, and asked for a chance to compose classical poetry orally. Examiner Chou took offense at his cocky confidence, and had him driven from the hall with rods, later marking his exam last place. And then with time hanging heavy on his hands, he read Fan Chin's paper again:

> This time he gave a gasp of amazement. "Even I failed to understand this paper the first two times I read it!" he exclaimed. "But, after reading it for the third time, I realize it is the most wonderful essay in the world—every word a pearl. This shows how often bad examiners must have suppressed real genius." Hastily taking up his brush, he carefully drew thee circles on Fan Chin's paper, marking it as first.

Later, when imperial heralds came to Butcher Hu's house with the news, Fan Chin was at the market. When told of his success, he went crazy, and everyone said what bad luck it was. But one of the heralds had an idea, that they should get someone Fan Chin was afraid of to fetch him a blow and bring him back to his senses. Everybody around said, of course, his father-in-law, Butcher Hu. But now the butcher was afraid to hit him:

> "He may be my son-in-law," he said, "but he's an official now—one of the stars in heaven. How can you hit one of the stars in heaven? I've heard that whoever hits the stars in heaven will be carried away by the King of Hell, given a hundred strokes with an iron rod, and shut up in the eighteenth hell, never to become a human being again. I daren't do a thing like that."

> "Mr. Hu!" cried a sarcastic neighbour. "You make your living by killing pigs. Every day the blade goes in white and comes out red. After all the blood you've shed, the King of Hell must have marked you down for several thousand strokes by iron rods, so what does it matter if he adds a hundred more? Quite likely he will have used up all his iron rods before getting round to beating you for this, anyway. Or maybe, if you cure your son-in-law, the King of Hell may consider that as a good deed, and promote you from the eighteenth hell to the seventeenth."

So the butcher did, and Fan Chin recovered his senses. And soon an older local Mandarin arrived to pay his respects to Fan Chin:

> "Sir," he said, "although we live in the same district, I have never been able to call on you."

> "I have long respected you," replied Fan Chin, "but have never had the chance to pay you a visit."

> "Just now I saw the list of successful candidates. Your patron, Mr. Tang, was a pupil of my grandfather; so I feel very close to you."

And the older official gave him a bar of silver and pressed Fan Chin to take a fine unused house . . . .[17]

Dream of the Red Chamber 紅樓夢

This is the last and most sophisticated of the six traditional novels; the title is a bit suggestive in that the women's quarters were painted red. A young man of a wealthy household, supposed to be studying the Confucian classics for the exams, is spending his time with novels, serving girls, and two female cousins, one of whom he will marry. The family fortunes are declining, and even though a later author pasted a happy ending onto the unfinished work, it rings false.

It's interesting to compare this development of the Chinese novel with that of the western novel, especially since they appear at roughly the same time. Cervantes' *Don Quixote* from around 1600 is often cited as the first modern western novel, for example. More important for our study is the insight this literature yields into Chinese history and society. And it's a good test for "Chinese-ness," because the Chinese in general know their literature better than we Americans know ours. If someone claiming to be Chinese doesn't know about "the compact in the peach orchard," or Wu Song and Golden Lotus, you should be suspicious of their claims! The authors of most of them came from the lower Long River valley, or at least spent considerable formative time there.[GE82]

SECTION D: WESTERN INTRUSION AND CHINESE RESPONSE

The Ming voyages vs. contemporary western explorations

From 1405 to 1433 the young, strong Ming Dynasty sent out seven fleets—huge fleets of from 200 to 300 ships (many six-masted), with tens of thousands of sailors. Their purpose was exploration, diplomacy, and perhaps conquest of lands south and west of China, and above all to acquaint the world with the Middle Kingdom. They all left from Nanjing under the command of Admiral Zheng He (Cheng Ho), cruised down the lower Long River, turned south down the China Sea and then west through the Straits of Malacca into the "Western Sea" (Indian Ocean). The first of the seven fleets touched at Java, Sumatra, Sri Lanka, and got as far as Calicut on the southwest coast of India. The last four fleets reached the Arabian peninsula, including the Persian Gulf and Red Sea, and the East coast of Africa almost as far south as Madagascar. There is continuing speculation that they even rounded Africa and explored some of the Atlantic. These voyages of exploration may have been triggered by the new knowledge of things Mideastern that had come into western China with Islam; Zheng He himself was a Muslim who had made the pilgrimage to Mecca. Today there's a museum, a reconstructed full-sized "treasure ship," and a statue of Zheng He in Nanjing. They sit alongside the original dry dock canals—now 600 years old—that still exist.[GE83]

Although these were by far the biggest fleets of exploration ever sent out in the history of the world, in 1433 they stopped as abruptly as they had started, on imperial whim. They had brought back information for Chinese mapmakers, some small increase in international trade, and curiosities such as giraffes for the amazement of the Imperial court, but otherwise they brought no real change to China.

During this same general period, as we talked about briefly in the first chapter on technology, timid Portuguese voyages usually of a small ship or two went south along Africa; Ceuta, across the straits of Gibraltar, was taken by them in 1415. The Portuguese crossed the equator in the Bight of Benin around 1470, Bartholomew Díaz rounded the Cape of Good Hope in 1487, and Vasco da Gama made it to Calicut (just less than a century after Zheng He, and with much less of a splash) and back on the monsoon winds in 1498. But the enormous financial success of that last voyage brought more and more western ships east—like a trail of ants established after one ant finds something good to eat, thought many easterners. Gold (mostly to be made in the spice trade), people to enslave, people to convert to Christianity—these were the three main motivations, however contradictory they may seem to our age. There was indeed some governmental support (as you've seen with the Portuguese in the technology chapter, the Dutch in the Jakarta to Surabaya chapter, and the British in the Grand Trunk road chapter). In this western drive to the east, however, there was much more private motivation than in the Chinese explorations of the west. What started as a western trickle grew to the power of a firehose, which to push the metaphor would wash many traditional governments away.

---

82. GE Layer 82 is a Folder titled "authors of novels." In this unscientific but hopefully thought-provoking pattern, the authors of the six great Chinese novels—or suspected authors, sometimes—are Placemarked as to origins and sites of adult activities. Only one of the six novels (Golden Lotus, attributed to an anonymous author in Shandong) is exclusively from the north. Two are split between north and south, either in attribution or in life of author. Three are entirely southern, along or within striking distance of the lower Yangtze Valley, with Nanjing as center of gravity. For maximum effect, double-click on each Folder to frame view, and only then turn it on.

83. GE Layer 83 is a Folder titled "Zheng He fleets." It includes several Placemarks referencing Photos icons with photos of the statue, treasure ship, etc., on the Nanjing waterfront. One last Placemark in the Folder generally references a cluster of Photos icons containing different views of a temple to and statue of Admiral Zheng He (Cheng Ho, or Sam Poo Kong in one dialect of Chinese) in Semarang, an important city on the Jakarta-to-Surabaya corridor of Java we studied earlier. It was obviously established and celebrated by Chinese community in Indonesia.

The first Portuguese ship sailed into Guangzhou (Canton) in 1513, only fifteen years after Da Gama first rounded the tip of Africa. It fired a salute to the city from its artillery, as was western custom, and the city panicked thinking it was under attack. It was not an auspicious beginning for east-west naval contact.

Matteo Ricci and the Jesuits

The Jesuit order, founded in 1540 as a new institution of the Catholic counter-Reformation, has entered this history tangentially at several places already, especially in the fields of exploration and education. Its role in the relationship of the West with China is particularly striking in the 1500s and 1600s, and its key personality was the Italian Matteo Ricci (1552–1610). At age nineteen, already educated in the classics and law, he joined the Jesuits, and, volunteering for Asia, spent from age twenty-five to thirty in and around Goa, the Portuguese holding on the west coast of India. An older member of the order, Francis Xavier, had gone on to open a mission in Japan, and was trying to do the same in China. Ricci was sent to help him.

In 1557 the Portuguese had been allowed to establish a permanent trading post at Macau, a narrow-necked little peninsula in the Pearl River bay not far from Guangzhou.[GE⁸⁴] By the time Ricci arrived there in 1582, the Jesuit leadership in Asia had decided the surest long-term way to convert the Chinese to Christianity would be to begin with a study of Chinese language and customs. The brilliant Ricci dove into Chinese studies headfirst. Befriending Confucian scholars who were attracted by his personality and new—to them—knowledge of world geography and mathematics, he was allowed to live and study in Nanchang (capital of Jiangxi) for three years, and then in the greater city of Nanjing for two years. During this time a Confucian scholar who had become a good friend advised him to give up Buddhist dress (which the Jesuits had at first adopted as accepted local religious garb) and adopt that of the scholar-gentry. In 1601 this forty-eight-year-old Italian, wearing Mandarin costume, speaking and writing Chinese to the admiration of Confucian scholars, was invited to live in Beijing, and stayed there until his death in 1610.

The Cambridge scientist and later historian Joseph Needham ended his massive work on traditional Chinese science and technology with Matteo Ricci, because Ricci presided over so much translation of works in Chinese to Latin and vice versa that a level of awareness of the other reached a new level. And in Ricci's later life the reputation of Christianity among the Chinese literati was probably never higher; several important scholar-gentry converted to Christianity. But the Jesuit hope of converting China, or at least opening it up to easy conversion, by converting the Emperor was probably never realistic. As more than one student of China has remarked, for the Emperor—head of the Confucian rites—to have converted to Christianity would have been as difficult as the Pope becoming a Protestant and still remaining Pope.

The "Canton System," the Opium Wars, and the Unequal Treaty

Around 1800, with the Qing Dynasty still strong, the Chinese limited trade with the west to one office in Guangzhou. And westerners could only live in Guangzhou the few months of the "trading season"; the rest of the time they had to go back to Macau. Western states, including Britain and the still-young U.S.A., sent emissaries asking the Chinese to open to trade along western lines, and to join the western community of nations. Even on those rare occasions when accredited western emissaries made it to the court, they had a hard time with the *koutou*, the formulaic obeisance required before the Chinese Emperor that included nine kneelings and three total prostrations. The Chinese answer on into the 1830s was a firm no, sometimes accompanied by the imprisonment or even the execution of the Chinese translator. China was still the Middle Kingdom, self-sufficient and self-centered; if barbarians were intelligent enough to recognize Chinese cultural superiority, they would be allowed some trade. And no serious threat had ever come to China from seaward; the life-or-death invasions had always been from the north and northwest. But for the first time in thousands of years of Chinese history, that was about to change.

---

84. GE Layer 84 is a Folder titled "Views of Macau." It frames an overview of the narrow-necked peninsula, then zooms in to the famous ruin of St. Paul's Mother of God Cathedral (built from 1582–1610), the hilltop fort overlooking it, and Senate Square with its Iberian feel after almost 4½ centuries of Portuguese occupation (it went back to China in 1999).

In the opening chapter of this textbook, in the sampling of European technological developments, we talked to some extent about the 1839–1842 Opium Wars and in particular the role of that classic early gunboat, the *Nemesis*. Heavily armored and shallow draft, it towed much heavier battleships up rivers; it grappled and towed out of harm's way fireships sent downwind toward the British fleet. When it entered the Long River and threatened Nanjing (Nanking), the "South Capital," the Chinese sued for peace. The punitive 1842 Treaty of Nanking was the prototypical "unequal treaty" of modern imperialism. In brief listing, Britain got the island of Hong Kong, the opening of five "Treaty Ports" to British trade, guarantee of Most Favored Nation clause, of no tax greater than 5 percent on imports, of extraterritoriality in judicial claims, plus a huge indemnity to be paid in silver by the Chinese government. And of course the one thing not mentioned in the treaty was what started the war in the first place, opium—evil solution to the British balance-of-trade deficit for buying Chinese luxury goods.

A couple of these topics we need to explore a bit geographically. First, the island of Hong Kong (*Xiang Gang*, "Fragrant Harbor"), hugging the southeast corner of the huge bay opening out from Canton, went outright to the British.[GE85] It sheltered one of the best deep water harbors in Asia, its "roads" still busy with freighter traffic today.[GE86] Later it got the mainland peninsula of Kowloon and a long-term lease to the so-called New Territories just to its north, an even larger chunk of the mainland. Hong Kong would be the wrist of the western grasp of China.

The fingers of the grasp were the five treaty ports from Guangzhou to Shanghai (the northern two, Ningbo and Shanghai, on our chosen corridor).[GE87] For each city this included a territorial base, for business and defense forces, off-limits to Chinese authority. In Shanghai, this developed into the still-visible Bund, especially after 1844 when the U.S. and the French won virtually the same terms from China without a war (followed later by Japan and every major and some minor European states).[GE88]

Treaty port life

Treaty port life for the westerners—mostly male, at first—oscillated from frantic activity in the trading season to lethargy in the off season. These western enclaves were remarkably insulated from surrounding Chinese culture. Westerners mostly without access to the difficult written Chinese language found it easy to dismiss the local culture, and the Mandarinate retreated into its walled mansions with equal cultural contempt. Western contact with Chinese culture was mainly limited to interaction with Chinese nursemaids ("amah") hired by western households, and their servants, gardeners, errand boys, and such. Most of the communication was in "pidgin" English, pidgin being a local pronunciation of the English word "business"; it used a mostly English vocabulary with a mostly Chinese grammatical order. Treaty port life looked a lot like British enclaves in Indian towns, except that in China a race track usually replaced the polo field.

But the treaty port trade quickly dislocated the local economy of all of south and central China. Cheap western industrial manufactures—cloth, tools, containers, knives—hit the Chinese handicraft market hard. The continued trade in opium ate into Chinese culture, beginning with the wealthier classes, and the Chinese government was implicitly forbidden to interfere with it. The stage was set for one of the biggest upheavals of modern times in China, the *Tai Ping* ("Great Peace") Rebellion. It lasted from 1850 to 1864, roughly contemporary with the American Civil War but about three times as long. And it was on a much larger scale. There weren't more than about thirty-two million people total in the fractured U.S., counting noses on both north and south sides of the Civil War, with something less than 700,000 war-related deaths. At least twenty million people were killed or died of war-induced diseases in the Taiping Rebellion in China.

---

85. GE Layer 85 is a Placemark framing a view of Hong Kong.

86. GE Layer 86 is a Placemark referencing a Panoramio icon under pointer titled "vista do pico Victoria"; it's a good view of naval "Roads" tucked in-between what looks like several Manhattan Islands.

87. GE Layer 87 is a Folder titled "Treaty Ports" with five Placemarks, one each for Canton, Amoy, Fuchow, Ningpo, and Shanghai, as the cities were traditionally called by westerners.

88. GE Layer 88 is a Folder titled "Shanghai, the Bund," with several Placemarks referencing interesting Photos icons.

Heavenly Kingdom of the Great Peace

In another time it might have been the end-of-dynasty social rebellion that created a new ruling dynasty. It began with a secret religious organization, like Yellow Turbans or White Lotus, though with a modern, western twist.

To back up just a bit, the story starts in the Hakka community—a distinct ethnic group of northerners who had moved down into the hill country of southern China.[GE[89]] Hong Xiuquan (Hung Hsiu-ch'uan) was Hakka, born in 1814 some thirty miles north of Guangzhou (Canton). He was a bright younger son set aside by his merchant family to pass the Confucian exams, though he could never pass the second level. After one failure at the regional exams in Canton, he apparently had a nervous breakdown; at least he was carried home on a cot, raving. Upon recovery he was a calmer and more reflective person. He still couldn't pass the exams, but in light of some Baptist missionary tracts picked up in Hong Kong, he now interpreted his convulsions to have been the physical manifestations of spiritual struggle. He had been taken up to heaven, identified by the Christian God as the younger brother of Jesus, set all manner of tasks of which his earthly convulsions were an echo. He began to reveal this to relatives and friends, gained a few believers, and started the God Worshipper's Society.

But prophets have no honor in their home towns, and he soon went west, to Hakka communities in eastern Guangxi Province about 200 miles away.[GE[90]] Soon Hong and a key early convert, Feng Yunshan, moved north, deep into isolated Thistle Mountain. Here in a rugged, Appalachian-like area, they found a receptive audience in the local coal and silver miners and the hard-scrabble mountain farmers. Between 1846 and 1850, four little areas of Tai Ping control developed. Hong and Feng preached monotheism, the Ten Commandments, the evils of opium and prostitution and polygamy, and the imminent coming of a heavenly kingdom. There was a smashing of local idols, and an anti-Confucian edge to reforms. Visions, prophecies, and faith-healing spread to many in the growing community of believers, and were generally accepted by Hong. By late 1850 the Qing administrators were being called "demons," and these base areas in Thistle Mountain began to organize militarily. By year's end, they were attacked by government troops. Losing a key position, the leaders made a decision to break out north. Believers were asked to make the ultimate commitment by burning their houses. In September of 1851, they took the small fortified city of Yongnan, some sixty miles north. Here their administration and military organization took a giant step. Five "kings," one each for the cardinal directions plus a "Wing King," headed up various aspects of administration. They devised their own calendar. They established a communal treasury. There was a strict, even puritanical, moral order proclaimed, with summary executions for opium smoking and adultery. Here are the words of the no-looting order:

> Let no officer or soldier, male or female, enter into the villages to cook rice or seize food; let no one destroy the dwellings of the people or loot their property; also let no one ransack the apothecaries' or other shops, or the offices of the various prefectural and district magistrates.[18]

As the Qing massed forces in pursuit, on April 5, 1852, the Taipings carried out a carefully planned mass exodus. When Qing forces killed 2,000 of their rear guard, the Taipings turned around in revenge and killed 5,000 of them, leaving pursuit in disarray. Then the Taipings, about 40,000 strong, headed north through the hills, to the important Li River city of Guilin (Kweilin). In a month-long siege, they failed to take the city; but here they quickly adapted to water warfare and transport tactics—those fast amphibious attacks and retreats that so impressed western military observers later.

The Qing forces, incredibly enough, had left the Miracle Canal pass at Xiangan undefended. The Taiping, with stores of rice and many dependents loaded on barges, made a swift strategic retreat over it, into the headwaters of the Xiang River. As they were bypassing the heavily defended city of Quanzhou on the Xiang some

---

89. GE Layer 89 is a Placemark referencing a Panoramio icon titled "Fukien round house" with view of typical Hakka round house, a communal dwelling probably for group defense in the early days of immigration into south China.

90. GE Layer 90 is a Folder titled "Taiping route." With ten Placemarks and ten Polygon arrows it represents the route of the Taipings from Thistle Mountain to Nanjing. You can turn on the whole Folder at once, or open it and turn on Placemarks and Polygons showing movements as you come to them in the text. Adapted from Jonathan Spence, *God's Chinese Son*, p. 157, map "From Yongan to Nanjing."

thirty-five miles downstream from the Miracle Canal, a lucky shot from a Qing marksman mortally wounded Feng Yunshan, now one of the "kings," who was riding in his sedan chair. The Taipings stopped their advance, seized the city, and massacred its population—the first time this had happened.

Renewing their parallel advance by boat and road, but without taking their usual care to reconnoiter, the little Taiping navy was ambushed by Qing forces at Suoyi Ford not far below Quanzhou. They lost 300 boats and 10,000 people. The brains behind this Qing operation was a new kind of opponent for the Taipings, a Mandarin who in the confusion of the times was working in his own province (against the traditional "law of avoidance" designed to limit nepotism). He combined the resources of the Qing state with local contacts and great knowledge of local geography. His name was Jiang Zhongyuan, and soon he would successfully defend the provincial capital of Changsha as well.

The Taipings left the Xiang River for awhile, making an eastern swing through the countryside—bypassing towns that were too well fortified or prepared, taking over those that were not. Then they attacked Changsha, provincial capital of Hunan, from the east. Even in failure to take the great city, they prospered—collecting boats by the thousands, sweeping up people from the countryside by the tens of thousands into their ranks. When they passed the Dongting Lakes and struck the Yangtze, moving toward the undefined but fervently-believed-in earthy paradise, they were a much more formidable force than when they crossed the pass at Miracle Canal.

Hong Xiuquan directed them downstream to the Wuhan cities. They occupied the poorly defended two of the tri-cities on the north bank, Hankou and Hanyang, and put the walled, strongly defended provincial capital Wuchang on the south bank under siege. The miners in the Taiping armies made great sappers for undermining and blowing up city walls. The rivermen in the navy created pontoon bridges that they could float downstream with them, bouncing the armies from bank to bank with great skill, facilitating both retreat and surprise attack. When Wuchang fell, Hong moved into the governor's housing, his kingly retinue and luxuries growing, but his defense works around the city also superbly done. Wuchang was taken in January of 1852. Just over a year later, in February of 1853, Hong directed the whole Taiping force downriver—about 450 miles downriver!—to take Nanjing, the "South Capital." And in a brilliant siege it was done. It was the center of the "Heavenly Kingdom of the Great Peace" (Tianjing, they renamed it—"Heavenly Capital") for another decade.

During that decade corruption and disaffection ate into Taiping idealism. The monogamy preached by the movement turned out not to apply to the kings. Some of the surviving kings got divine exemption from abstinence from alcohol. The luxurious living and arbitrary behavior of Hong Xiuquan himself, and the ambition of one of the remaining kings, triggered a brutal civil war and massacre among the Taipings. As late as 1863 there were still some brilliant military actions. The Taipings slipped by Qing defenses downriver and took the rich city of Hangzhou; then when Qing forces weakened those defenses to try to relieve Hangzhou, the Taipings swept their original defenses away. But the Taipings also sent a huge army of 70,000 veterans north to take Beijing, and even though it made it to the outskirts of Tianjin, within sixty miles of its goal, in the end it was totally destroyed. The beginning of the end was a Taiping movement to capture the Yangtze to its mouth, including Shanghai, that came to disaster.[GE91]

Noteworthy in the context of our general quest for understanding the roots of modern nationalism, Taiping ideology had a strong strain of Chinese patriotism. It was anti-Manchu, celebrating the original founders of Han and Ming as pure Chinese people who had founded pure Chinese governments. After western Christian powers refused to accept the most recent divinely inspired words of God through Taiping mouths, it was somewhat anti-western as well.

The "Ever-Victorious Army"

In this Chinese civil war westerners in the treaty ports had to take sides. At first glance, you might think they'd be sympathetic towards a Christian-inspired, social reforming movement. But the variant of Christianity was

---

91. GE Layer 91 is a Polygon representing the greatest extent of Taiping control. Adapted from map on p. 217 of Jonathan Spence, *God's Chinese Son.*

decidedly non-orthodox, and had gotten fused with local Taoist magic, and when it came right down to it, most westerners really wanted a weak China in which they could continue to have maximum freedom of movement.

With the Taiping surge coming down the Long River towards them, western forces in the biggest of the international settlements, Shanghai, built a western-officered, western-trained army of Chinese troops—the "Ever-Victorious Army." Its first commander was the American Frederick Townsend Ward. On September 20, 1862, the Ever Victorious Army took on the Taipings in a struggle for Cixi (Tzeki), a walled town about seventy-five miles south of Shanghai and thirty miles northwest of Ningbo.[GE92] Though Ward was fatally wounded there, it was a resounding defeat for the Taipings. A British officer named Gordon—the Charles "Chinese" Gordon of the Khartoum massacre in 1885, so he had twenty-three years of fame remaining—took over leadership of the Shanghai army after Ward's death.

Even though western forces may have kept the Qing Dynasty in power by helping defeat the Taipings, there was a price the Qing had to pay them. What some have called a Second Opium War broke out in 1856, again beginning at Canton. Victorious westerners dictated the Treaty of Tianjin of 1858. When its terms were not followed, a western expeditionary force went to Beijing and burned the Summer Palace (about nine miles northwest of the Imperial Palace). [GE93] Among the results were the establishing of permanent foreign legations in Beijing, and the opening of eleven new treaty ports, Nanjing and Hankou among them. Most important for our corridor, western commercial shipping and warships got full access to the Long River and all its navigable tributaries. In 1861 the first foreign commercial steamer (American) made it to Hankou. That same year a British steam flotilla under the command of Thomas Blakiston set off upstream with the really ambitious program of going by water to Chengdu and then overland to India via Tibet. They made it upstream through the Three Gorges—Blakiston's etchings were the first good representations in print—and on to Chongqing and Yibin and a bit beyond. A combination of growing navigational difficulty and growing local hostility caused a re-thinking of goals, and the expedition turned around and made it downstream without incident. Just one year later, when Blakiston wrote his book *Five Months on the Yang-tsze*, he had this to say about the city of Hankou:

> When we visited it, not an European—excepting a disguised priest or two of the Romish church—was within hundreds of miles of it; now [1862, a year later], merchants and missionaries follow their avocations without secrecy, and a vessel of war lies off the town to remind the Celestials of the promise they made at Tien-tsin.[19]

"Self-strengthening"

More important to the survival of the Qing Dynasty than grasping western allies was the emergence of provincial Chinese armies loyal to the Qing. In this regard, the two most famous names are Zeng Guofan and Li Hongzhang. Both were Mandarins, and both in these emergency times were working in their home provinces, in spite of the traditional "law of avoidance."

Zeng Guofan (Tseng Kuo-fan) was from a small town in Hunan, some forty miles southwest of Changsha. He was born in 1811, and in 1838 at age twenty-seven passed the third national civil service exam so brilliantly that he was assigned to the Hanlin Academy in Beijing. In 1852 he came back home on leave of absence to mourn his mother's death, as was the custom. It was just in that year, from May to September, and just a few miles away, that the Taiping armies blazed down the Xiang River from the Miracle Canal to Changsha. As one local Qing army after another was defeated, Zeng got involved in raising new local forces and coordinating them. Although primarily a student of Confucian philosophy, Zeng was no hide-bound traditionalist; he showed a quick appreciation for western technology and techniques of warfare. As the main Taiping armies passed on, down the Long River, his new coalition gradually recovered the territory behind them in Hunan and Hubei for the government. Nothing succeeds like success, and a grateful imperial government gave him virtual dictatorial authority over Jiangsu, Anhui, and Zhejiang provinces, hoping he could do the same there.

Li Hongzhang was a younger protégé of Zeng Guofan. He was born in 1823 near Hefei, capital of Anhui Province. He too passed the exams so well that he was appointed to the Hanlin Academy, where he fell into

---

92. GE Layer 92 is a Placemark referencing the old walled city of Cixi (Tzeki).

93. GE Layer 93 is a Placemark framing a view showing the relationship of the Summer Palace to Beijing proper.

Zeng's orbit. Taking Zeng's lead in raising irregular forces in Hunan, Li and his father raised similar anti-Taiping forces in their home province of Anhui. It was Li Hongzhang who cooperated with Shanghai's "Ever-Victorious Army" with armies of his own, steadily using more and more western technology in his warfare. After Li's forces liberated Suzhou, Zeng Guofan made him governor of Jiangsu province.

In 1864, while Li and the western-officered Shanghai army pinned Taiping forces down in the Jiangnan, Zeng Guofan finally laid siege to and took Nanjing, the Taiping's "Heavenly Capital." The Qing Dynasty had been saved, at least in the short run, though the violation of the old "rule of avoidance" pointed to a day not too many years off when all China would be in the hands of local warlords—less Confucian, less respectable than Zeng and Li.

The defeat of the Taipings in 1864 was also in one sense the beginning of a broader story, the "self-strengthening" movement by which China was supposed to become competitive on the world stage again. "Eastern ethics, western science," Zeng and Li preached, would do the trick.

The Jiangnan arsenal

Under Li Hongzhang, as governor of Jiangsu with the full support of Zeng Guofan, China built its first modern arsenal and shipyard. Li chose as head of the enterprise the western-educated Rong Hong (also known as Yung Wing). A Yale graduate in 1854, he was in fact the first Chinese graduate from any American university. A convert to Christianity and married to an American, he was a most westernized Chinese. In 1865 Rong, under Li's direction, rented a big American machine shop in the British (International) section of Shanghai, and in a couple of years moved it down south three miles or so—along with many of its western engineers and supervisors—to the edge of the old (Chinese) town of Shanghai.[GE94] In firearms, this "Jiangnan Arsenal" started out producing muskets and howitzers and soon graduated to producing the more difficult-to-manufacture breech-loading rifles. On up into the 1880s the steamships built there, engines and all, were probably better than those being built in Japanese shipyards.

As a philosophical reflection at this point, the response of traditional non-western countries to the irresistible new western combination of ideological motivation and industrial technology usually proceeded on a recognizable pattern. The first response, all over the world, was to use traditional methods to expel the foreigners: "smash the barbarians whenever they come into sight," as you'll see in the next chapter the Japanese samurai in Choshu were saying about his time. Against this new sort of power from the west, however, that simply didn't work. The second level of response was to adopt western technology while trying to remain culturally unaffected. "Eastern ethics, western science," said Confucian scholar Zeng Guofan. And if at all possible, disguise the necessary borrowing as simply a return to your own past. Zeng and Li used the phrase *zi chang (tzu ch'ang)*, "self-strengthening," from the ancient *I Ching*, or *Book of Changes*, a surviving Confucian classic. Some progress is usually made in reducing the power gap by such technological borrowing, and this was the case in China. But the catch is that you can't have western science without borrowing a lot more of western culture, from which it emerges. It was the Jiangnan Arsenal itself that set up its own translation wing. With the help of a bi-lingual British missionary, it translated almost 200 western works on very practical things such as mining, metallurgy, engine construction, firearms construction. Foreign experts, however, are too expensive to keep hiring; and to create your own engineers and managers, admirals and generals, takes an entirely new level of immersion in western-style education. Engineering schools and military academies need high school graduates; high schools need grammar school graduates. Muhammad Ali of Egypt had learned this in the first third of the nineteenth century; the Chinese were having to learn it now.

---

94. GE Layer 94 is a Folder titled "Shanghai and origins of Jiangnan Arsenal." Turn the entire Folder on; it shows the International (British) concession in green outline, the French Concession in yellow outline, and the original Chinese city in red outline. The approximate location of the original American machine shop in the Hongkew section of Shanghai is Placemarked. For a view of the Americanized Rong Hong, probably from Yale yearbook, do Google Images search of "Yung Wing."

Rong Hong's educational missions

Rong Hong, over and above his creation of the Jiangnan Arsenal, worked tirelessly to create a Chinese educational mission to the U.S. In 1872, having gained the full support of Zeng Guofan and Li Hongzhang, he sent off the first class, thirty Chinese boys, to Hartford, Connecticut.[GE[95]] Here they were to begin the whole American educational experience and hopefully go on to advanced educational institutions such as Harvard and Yale, Annapolis, and West Point, and return to China with world-class skills. Suspicious conservative Confucian Mandarins insisted they be sent with traditional tutors, and they were right to be suspicious. Within the first year the Chinese boys were either cutting off their Manchu-required pigtails or winding them up under their baseball caps, as they began to become Americanized. Four classes of thirty boys were sent, one class a year, before the conservatives cancelled the whole expensive experiment. Those who returned with modern technical expertise were generally shunned by government officials, though they found quick employment in institutions such as the Jiangnan Arsenal. Their reception shows what an uphill battle Li Hongzhang was fighting to introduce western technology and practices, even in military affairs where they were desperately needed.

The Dowager Empress

The dominant political force in China from 1861 to 1908 was Cixi (Tzu-hsi), the "Dowager Empress." Her origins are shadowy; daughter of a Manchu official, she was probably raised in Anhui Province. It is certain that she became one of the current Emperor's concubines. Giving birth to his only son (in 1856) elevated her in rank to "Imperial Consort." Upon the Emperor's death in 1861, wielding her authority as mother of the child emperor, she skillfully changed alliances to maximize her power. When her own son died, she had her sister's son made Emperor, and remained the real power behind the throne. After a short flirtation with "self-strengthening" in terms of acquiring western arms and ships, by 1881 she had become a reactionary. It seems to have been her decision in that year to cancel Rong Hong's educational missions to the west.

After Zeng Guofan's death in 1872, Li Hongzhang was the main standard-bearer for Self-Strengthening, doggedly pursuing western industrial and military power. Anytime there was a crisis with an outside power, the government turned to him. In 1870 the "Tianjin Massacre" of French-oriented Catholics required his transfer to Zhili Province (the capital province that then included Beijing), where he remained for an amazingly-long twenty-five years—probably due to massive bribes given to the Dowager Empress. There he opened the Tianjin Arsenal on the model of the Jiangnan arsenal, built western-style land and sea forces, and massively rebuilt the Dagu forts defending Tianjin and the ones at Port Arthur (Lushun) and Dairen (Dalian) on the tip of the Liaodong Peninsula some 200 miles across the Bohai Sea that helped control entry to that sea. The matching forts at Weihaiwei in Shandong Province were the southern anchor of the Bohai Sea defences.[GE[96]]

War with Japan

Korea was the last tributary power to the Chinese Empire, regularly bringing tribute, allowing general Chinese orchestration of its foreign affairs, enjoying full trade with the Middle Kingdom. As such it was psychologically important to the Chinese, a last remnant of the "normal" diplomatic system. But a fast-modernizing Japan next door, which had always cast a covetous eye on Korea, meant problems for China. Pro-Japanese and pro-Chinese parties in Korea increasingly came to blows. In 1888 Li Hongzhang met with the key Japanese leader Ito Hirobumi to try to solve the "Korean problem" without a war. The Li-Ito Agreement wasn't to last long. In 1894–95 the Sino-Japanese War occurred, and China was thoroughly beaten. Japan won a series of

---

95. GE Layer 95 is a Placemark referencing Hartford, which is mainly an excuse for referring reader to a short article in Shanghai News that includes a picture of the first thirty boys made at Shanghai before their departure for the U.S.; see website at: http://images.google.com/imgres?imgurl=http://app1.chinadaily.com.cn/star/2002/0404/04-18-03.jpg&imgrefurl=http://app1.chinadaily.com.cn/star/2002/0404/cu18-2.html&h=154&w=200&sz=23&hl=en&start=12&tbnid=1PpP-1nl6s4pKM:&tbnh=80&tbnw=104&prev=/images%3Fq%3DYung%2BWing%26gbv%3D2%26hl%3Den

96. GE Layer 96 is a Folder titled "Northern Sea Forts." It includes Placemarks in red for the Dagu forts protecting Tianjin, Pt. Arthur, and Dairen on the Liaodong Peninsula, and Weihaiwei on the Shandong Peninsula.

land battles and invaded Manchuria. In a crucial naval battle off the mouth of the Yalu River (the traditional border between China and North Korea, just east of the Liaodong Peninsula) most of Li's new iron-clad fleet was destroyed. The Japanese took Pt. Arthur and the Weihaiwei forts from their landward sides, then used land-based guns to capture or sink the remnants of the Chinese navy bottled up in both. China didn't have much of a navy for a hundred years thereafter.

Terms of the treaty were brutal. Korea was recognized as "independent," meaning in fact that Japan was to have a free hand there. The populous island of Taiwan (Formosa, today's Republic of China) and the Liaodong Peninsula went to Japan outright. China paid Japan a huge indemnity in silver, and Japan got all the "unequal" privileges the western powers had already wrung out of China, including open access to the Yangtze River valley.

The "Scramble for Concessions"

The major western powers were convinced by the ease of little Japan's victory over huge China that the whole country was falling apart. This initiated the so-called "Scramble for Concessions," as each country tried to carve out its permanent sphere. The last five years of the nineteenth century were probably the lowest ebb for China in modern times. Like the Germanies under Napoleonic occupation, it seemed to be in the process of being torn apart, perhaps forever.

Russia, concerned that Japan might get Manchuria when that was already in Russia's plans, "advised" Japan to return the Liaodong Peninsula to China, then immediately "leased" it from China. Having already built the CER (China Eastern Railway) across Manchuria as a shortcut to Vladivostok, Russia then dropped a branch line, the "South Manchurian Line," down from Harbin to Pt. Arthur and Dairen. It obviously meant to stay.

France extorted Chinese concessions for mines and railroads in southern China, to add this area to its Indochinese (mainly Vietnam) holdings. Germany generally took Shandong (except for the naval base of Weihaiwei, claimed by the British) as its sphere of influence. Qingdao with its excellent harbor became the German administrative center (from which time dates one of China's famous beers, known by its old Wade-Giles transliteration *Chingtao*). Britain was mainly satisfied to take the Yangtze River valley, of a million square miles and a population of several hundred million.

And we of the U.S.A. were not all that innocent in this greedy scramble. The "Open Door" notes issued by Secretary of State John Hay in 1899 and 1900 are sometimes presented in American history textbooks as a pro-Chinese act. It was not; it was to keep U.S. interests from being frozen out of the growing spheres of influence of other countries. We wanted our share of the spoils as well.

Kang Youwei and the 100 Days of Reform

In this time of greatest modern crisis several key Chinese patriots emerged. In 1895, when the brutal terms of the treaty ending the war with Japan became known, a south Chinese named Kang Youwei was in Beijing. He had just passed the third-level, national exams, that were always held in the capital city. Now he immediately circulated a petition among fellow successful graduates there to protest China's acceptance of those treaty terms. Kang's version of national self-strengthening came partly from his Confucian studies; he claimed the Confucian classics as currently studied had been faked or drastically modified in Han times, whereas the real Confucius—had he lived in 1895—would have been an agent for change; *Confucius as a Reformer* (1898) was Kang's most famous work. Kang had been curious enough about western power to visit Hong Kong and the International Settlement in Shanghai, and was generally impressed with what he saw.

In 1898 he won an interview with the Guangxu (Kuang-hsu) Emperor. The Emperor, twenty-seven years old, had "reigned" most of his life although the real rule of the country had been by his aunt Cixi. Champing at the bit to rule, in fact, he bought into Kang Youwei's reform plans and announced his intention to rule personally. The canny Cixi temporarily retired from the scene. The result was a flurry of reforms from June to September, 1898, that called for massive change of the Chinese system in almost every area of life—westernizing the postal service and police and armed forces, medicine, farming, mining, schools, and the exams, just to list a few. The traditional officials at court, the Manchu bannermen, were most threatened, and by and large little of the reform package was carried out. Everybody was waiting to see what the Dowager Empress would do. On September 21 she suddenly had the Emperor arrested and a death sentence issued for Kang (who escaped to Japan). The last ten years of the Emperor's life he spent under house arrest on an island in a lake in an imperial park in Beijing. Suspiciously enough, he died one day before the Dowager Empress, in 1908.

"Righteous, Harmonious Fists"

From Africa to India you've already seen one psychological response to overwhelming western power, a retreat to traditional spiritual rituals. It happened in China, too. Beginning in 1898 in northern China, especially in Shandong under an aggressive German occupation, a popular anti-foreign and anti-Manchu revolution grew out of a religious sect distantly linked to White Lotus—a perennial secret religious society that had figured in the overthrow of some previous dynasties. Believing that certain military calisthenics could make them invulnerable to bullets, they called themselves the "Righteous, Harmonious Fists," which westerners shortened to "Boxers." Their original slogan was "Overthrow the Qing; destroy the foreigners." Even after the Imperial government brought out the army against them (in the month after the overthrow of the young Emperor and his advisor Kang Youwei), the movement continued to grow. The Dowager Empress, apparently impressed by their claims of invulnerability, then allied herself with the Boxers, adopting them as her official militia. She then encouraged the change of slogan to "Uphold the Qing; destroy the foreigners." Many Christian missionaries to China were killed, more for the fact that they were western than Christian, and thousands of Chinese Christians were killed because they had fallen into the orbit of westerners and gotten special exemptions and favors. By June 1900 Boxer armies had occupied all of Beijing except the main foreign legation compound, which desperately held out under siege. A first western relief force sent from Tianjin was turned back, and the obituaries of all the western diplomats in Beijing were famously published in the London *Times*. A second and greater relief expedition found them still holding out.

The uprising was fully suppressed by 1901, and old Li Hongzhang was brought out once again to deal with the foreigners. The Boxer Protocol was yet another brutal treaty. China was to pay 450,000,000 silver ounces (one ounce of silver for each of the estimated 450,000,000 Chinese, went the harsh logic). Cities where the rebellion had flared were deprived of the civil service exams to punish the local gentry. Ten governmental officials were executed. Dozens of Chinese forts were razed, and the International Legation quarter in Beijing, like the International Settlement at Shanghai, got the right to station troops there permanently. The Dowager Empress agreed to all this by 1902.

Sun Yatsen and "Double Ten"

A more important patriot and political reformer than Kang Youwei was his contemporary, and rival, Sun Yatsen. He lived from 1866 until his death of cancer of the liver in 1925. He is perhaps the pivotal figure in modern Chinese history. Today both the Nationalists in Taiwan and the Communists on the mainland claim him as the father of modern China (though they tend to celebrate different aspects of his work and philosophy).

His father was a tailor from near Macao,[GE97] and as a bright young boy Sun Yatsen was educated in Christian mission schools. He went to Honolulu (where his brother was a successful businessman) for his high school education, and came back to Hong Kong—seat of British power in China—for medical school. His major professor was Dr. James Cantlie, from England. But although Sun won his M.D. degree, and even practiced for a few years, it was in those med school years that he really got caught up in politics.

Biographers have looked for the roots of Sun's revolutionary activity. In his village growing up he had listened to stories of the Taiping Rebellion from participants. In Guangzhou and Hong Kong he had friends in the local Triad societies—secret anti-Manchu groups in the area that were something like a cross between the Mafia and the Freemasons. He had absorbed some Lincoln and Jefferson in his Hawaii high school years. He had contrasted British efficiency, as in medicine, with existing Chinese inefficiency. In 1894 he wrote a letter

---

97. GE Layer 97 is a Placemark referencing Sun Yat-sen's hometown.

to Li Hongzhang—probably never read—advocating reforms. Later that year he went to Hawaii to raise money in the Chinese community there for agricultural reforms.

The next year, 1895, at about age twenty-nine, when the Chinese government was losing a dramatic war with Japan and the future existence of an independent Chinese state was doubtful, he crossed the line into professional revolutionary activity. A local uprising failed, and for the next sixteen years he was an outlaw with a price on his head. He took the alias Zhongshan ("central mountain"), and when in hiding in Japan used its Japanese translation "Nakayama." His general aim was the overthrow of the imperial government and the establishment of a western-style Republic, and his succession of revolutionary societies culminated in the Guomindang (Kuomintang, or KMT), literally "Country of the People's Party," and less literally, "Nationalist Party."

Sun Yatsen sponsored dozens of attempts to overthrow the Qing government, but the one that finally succeeded, on October 10 ("double ten"), 1911, caught even him by surprise. He first heard the news while on a train out of Kansas City, on his way from the west to the east coast of the U.S., raising money among Chinese émigrés.

It happened squarely in the Yangtze Valley, from Sichuan to the Wuhan cities. The unlikely trigger was railroad finance. Major railroads had been projected from Wuhan south to Canton, and from Wuhan west to Sichuan; many wealthy locals had invested in it. Suddenly the Beijing government, which saw little progress being made, cancelled the existing contracts and awarded new ones to foreign concerns. Minor revolutions broke out in Sichuan in protest, and when troops were sent up from the Wuhan area to quell these, a bigger rebellion occurred in Wuhan, beginning on the celebrated October 10. Within just a few months the Qing government lost control of virtually the whole Yangtze valley and everything south of that.[20] A new government, calling itself a national government, was established in Nanjing, and Sun Yatsen was invited home to be its President. He got there on Christmas Day of 1911, determined to create a U.S.- or British-style representative government.

Despite the euphoria of those involved who saw a new age dawning, it didn't happen. The new republic had no military force to match that of Li Hongzhang's successor, Yuan Shihkai, head of the Northern Army. The ambitious Yuan now played the old Qing government off against the new Republican one in a bidding war for his power. Sun Yatsen agreed to give Yuan the presidency for his support. This was the death blow for the Qing government, but also, as it turned out, for the Republic. Within a year Yuan had Sun Yatsen's parliamentary leader assassinated, and himself was well on his way to becoming new Emperor or at least dictator. Once again Sun slipped off into exile, in danger of assassination.

But Yuan Shihkai himself had an insoluble problem. In these first years of World War I, when all real European power was called back to the home continent, the uncontested Japanese made "21 Demands" on China that would have made of China a satellite state. Yuan desperately tried to fend off the most extreme of those, compromising when he had to and for this losing the support of any patriotic Chinese. Trying to solve this insoluble problem may have hastened his death, which came in 1916. At this point central government completely broke down, into what is often called the "warlord decade." Former Qing officials, whether generals or provincial governors, or bandits who had gained large territories—these became the absolute rulers of small domains. Whichever army currently controlled Beijing claimed to be the government of the nation, but it was a fiction that deceived no one. It was a free-for-all that lasted through 1926.

May 4, 1919, and the New Culture Movement

China had officially declared war on Germany and its allies, just to gain a voice at the peace conference that would end World War I. But at Versailles in 1919 it turned out that secret U.S.-Japanese agreements took precedence over Chinese integrity: the "self-determination" preached by President Woodrow Wilson, which had gotten so many Asians excited, turned out to be limited to European groups. The news hit intellectual and business circles in China hard, and there were huge demonstrations beginning with Beijing. They started on May 4 at *Beida* (short for *Bei Jing Da Xue*, Peking University), and then spread to every major Chinese city. It was something more than the xenophobia of the Boxers; it was a new-style, mass patriotic Chinese response, including a huge anti-Japanese boycott.

From these May 4 riots grew the New Culture Movement with its argument for writing in the vernacular, not classical, Chinese. It also included a push for popular education of a western nature. Its most famous writer was Lu Xun (Lu Hsun), who came from the eastern end of our chosen corridor. He was born in 1881 in a Zhejiang Province village about 100 miles south-southwest of Shanghai and some 35 miles southeast of Hangzhou. [GE[98]] His family was traditional gentry; his father's father, in fact, had been a member of the Hanlin Academy, though the family had fallen on hard times by Lu Xun's youth. At about age eighteen he went to the School of Mines in Nanjing that was associated with the Jiangnan Arsenal, and then went on to med school in Japan. He read English, German, and Russian in addition to Japanese, and eventually became a writer and professor of literature at Beida. Here in May of 1918 he wrote *Diary of a Madman*, its title and some of the viewpoint taken from Gogol's short story. For awhile he edited the flagship journal of the New Culture movement, *La Jeunesse*, often translated *New Youth*. His masterpiece came out in installments in 1921 and 1922, *The Story of Ah Q* (the "Q" of the title was literally the Latin letter Q). The satirical view of a peasant who in his own mind made every humiliation into a victory, it is Lu Xun's personification of China's current view of itself. Look realistically at what is happening to us, he is saying; then let's take those realistic steps, including essential westernization leading to power, that we have to take. Just as important as the subject is that this collection of short stories was written in the vernacular, the first real work of genius in the common Chinese language. Lu Xun spent the last decade of his life living in Shanghai.[GE[99]] Here he wrote most of his mature essays. Although never officially a member of the Communist Party himself, he brought many young Chinese intellectuals a few steps leftwards towards it.

Chinese Communist Party formation, Shanghai

It was in the context of the enthusiasm of the New Culture Movement that a Chinese Communist Party was formed. The founding date was July of 1921, and a dozen young Communists met in an empty girl's dorm in Shanghai to do so. Of the dozen, two were from Hunan Province, and one of them—though of no special prestige yet even among the Communists—was Mao Zedong (Mao Tse-tung). Two Russian advisors were also there. In accordance with Lenin's current ideas that proletarian-style Marxism was premature in Asia, they would encourage alliance with "bourgeois" elements in their struggle with "feudal" ones.

After the death of Yuan Shihkai, Sun Yatsen came back to Guangzhou not once but several times to try to establish a Republican and Nationalist base here in the area of his birth. From 1917 to 1922, every attempt failed. He got no help from the U.S. or British governments, on which he wanted to pattern his own, and without any significant military force of his own he was always unceremoniously evicted by the local warlord. In his frustration, he turned to the latest successful European ideology, Communism, Soviet Union style. In October of 1923 the Comintern ("Communist International") sent him Mikahil Borodin, to advise him and to funnel him aid. Borodin was an original Bolshevik from 1903, but after the Revolution of 1905 he went to the U.S. for his university education, and in fact had lived there until 1917. He and Sun communicated in American English.

Borodin's advice, in a nutshell? First, establish a "centralized democracy," more like the Bolshevik, now Communist, Party. This was done in 1924, and the Guomindang (Kuomintang, KMT) took new, more disciplined form. Second, build your own military; send a promising young military type to learn from Trotsky how to build a Red Army. In that same 1923 Sun sent Chiang Kaishek, a young officer from Ningbo in Shanghai—who had stood by him in a military crisis in Guangzhou earlier—to Moscow. Immediately upon his return after almost four months in Russia Chiang set up the Whampoa Military Academy on an island just down the bay from Guangzhou. Of 3,000 enthusiastic applicants, Chiang as commandant accepted 500, the first class of sev-

---

98. GE Layer 98 is a Placemark at Shaoxing, Lu Xun's birthplace, in Zhejiang Province, about 100 miles south-southwest of Shanghai, and 35 miles southeast of Hangzhou. Click on untitled Panoramio icon under pointer for view of mural at his homeplace; three other Photos icons nearby show the rather prosperous family home.

99. GE Layer 99 is a Placemark generally referencing Lu Xun Park is in the Hongren section of Shanghai; click on the Panoramio icon under pointer, titled "鲁迅坐像 for view of statue of seated Lu Xun. The park is just a few hundred yards north of his residence the last decade of his life.

eral that would transform the military situation. Third, accept the new and rather small (a thousand or so members) Communist Chinese Party as an ally, and use it as a Fifth Force in infiltrating and then capturing other parts of China. And Sun Yatsen accepted that advice, too—though as you'll see Chiang Kaishek thought less of it.

With such aid and advice for the first time Sun Yatsen was able to build a stable, defensible base in and around Guangzhou. And then on the eve of a northern expedition to take over the whole country, he was suddenly diagnosed with cancer of the liver and quickly died, in March of 1925. His mausoleum, on Purple Mountain on the outskirts of Nanjing next to some Ming tombs, dwarfs any U.S. presidential monument or mausoleum, including those of Washington, Jefferson, and Lincoln.[GE100] For awhile the Nationalist forces had no accepted leader.

SECTION E: FROM THE NORTHERN EXPEDITION TO THE PRESENT

Historically, by far the greatest drama of twentieth-century China was the contest between the Nationalists under Chiang Kai-shek and the Communists under Mao Zedong. Even the massive Japanese invasion of China in World War II may be most important as a sub-set and modifier of this conflict. Both Chiang and Mao claimed to be heirs of Sun Yatsen's mission to free China from outside control. Both are from our corridor.

Chiang Kai-shek, the early years

Although Chiang Kai-shek is known by the Cantonese pronunciation of his name (the Pinyin is *Jiang Jieshi*), he was from Zhejiang Province near Ningbo.[GE101] He was born in 1887 to a family that had been prosperous in his salt merchant grandfather's time, but had come down in the world under his father. Thanks mostly to the sacrifices of his mother, he studied in secondary schools in Ningbo and in nearby Fenghua, his hometown. At age nineteen, in 1906, Chiang decided to go to a military college in Japan. When his mother argued against that, he cut off his pigtail (the Manchu-imposed "queue," as it was called in British English) and sent it to her as a symbol of his commitment to such study and future career.

Japan had defeated Russia in 1904–5, and mostly on northern Chinese territory. Lots of young Chinese were attracted to Japan to learn how an Asian country achieved that kind of power. Upon arrival in Tokyo in 1906, Chiang found out that he would only be eligible for the Japanese Military Academy if he first graduated from the official Chinese government military preparatory academy. He dutifully went to both introductory and advanced military prep schools in Baoding, in northern China, for the next two years, and then in 1908 was indeed accepted back in Japan. By 1910 he finished the special introductory and intermediate courses in Tokyo, ones designed especially for Chinese officer candidates. Then he was assigned to field training with active Japanese units.

But then in 1911, back home, came Double Ten. Chiang and most other Chinese officer candidates in Japan were given passage from Nagasaki in western Japan to Shanghai, arriving before October was out. Chiang had already met Sun Yatsen in 1910, and had been a member of at least one of his secret organizations for several years. He immediately got involved in a plan by Sun supporters to capture the Jiangnan Arsenal. It succeeded, and not only Shanghai but Nanjing fell to the quickly-formed revolutionary armies. This is what made possible

---

100. GE Layer 100 is a Placemark generally framing a view of the south side of Nanjing's Purple Mountain. To the left of the Placemark icon are Ming tombs, set in front of a mountainside lake. To the right, with dozens of Photos icons to explore, is Sun Yatsen's memorial. From fountains at the bottom, to flights of granite stairs and archways, to the mausoleum at the top, it is beyond impressive and going on overwhelming. The memorial was constructed by the Nationalist government in 1929; Sun had died in Beijing and his body was removed from there to Nanjing, which he obviously intended to be the country's capital.

101. As with other sections, close and turn off previous sections, and open the Folder titled "Section E." Turn on the first two unnumbered layers for corridor outline and rivers network. Then "fly" to and open GE Layer 101, a Folder titled "Early life of Chiang Kai-shek." It includes Placemarks referencing his hometown, downtown Ningbo not far away, Baoding military academy in northern China, the Japanese military academy in Tokyo, and the port of Nagasaki as framed between Tokyo and Shanghai. You can turn each Placemark on as you get to that section in the next few paragraphs of the text.

the invitation for Sun Yatsen to come to Nanjing and become President of a new Republic, by the first of January, 1912. Chiang Kai-shek was twenty-four years old and already promoted to regimental command level of KMT armies. He had begun to build a network of personal alliances that would be the key to his future power—beginning with fellow graduates of the Chinese military schools at Baoding, and of the special prep school for Chinese in the Japanese military academy. Sometime in this 1911–12 period he made a secret blood brotherhood pact with two other high-ranking KMT officers—shades of the "Compact in the Peach Orchard" from *Romance of the Three Kingdoms*!

In the 1912–1916 years, when Yuan Shihkai shouldered Sun Yatsen aside and tried to become new Emperor, Chiang Kai-shek alternately retreated to Japan, or visited Shanghai, Guangzhou, or other parts of China in KMT attempts to overthrow Yuan. In Sun Yatsen's repeated attempts to build a stable base at Guanghzhou, from 1917 to 1922, Sun repeatedly tried to get Chiang Kai-shek to come down and help. Apparently Chiang felt out of place there, a Zhejiang Province man amongst clannish Cantonese. It's still a mystery where he spent all of his time in these years. Some of it seems to have been in the Shanghai underworld, engaged in some shady money-raising schemes for the KMT. He apparently got to know key players in the "Green Gang," an unofficial but lethal mob that controlled Shanghai and a lot of the traffic on the Chang Jiang.

In June of 1922, Chiang was at his old homeplace in Fenghua in the traditional Chinese mourning on the first anniversary of his beloved mother's death. He got a terse telegram from Sun Yatsen, asking him to come quickly. Local warlord forces had surrounded Sun, and he was stranded on a gunboat in the Pearl River and in real danger of his life. Chiang immediately went south and joined Sun Yatsen on the gunboat. He stayed with him all through July and into early August, finally managing to get them both safely on a British ship bound for Hong Kong. Sun Yatsen's ties with Chiang were understandably closer after that. When Sun cut his deal with Comintern the next year, 1923, he made Chiang Kai-shek head of the KMT delegation to the Soviet Union. The delegation was in Moscow for September, October, and November of 1923. Chiang spent time with Trotsky and his staff studying the Red Army. He met with key members of both the Comintern (the third, or Communist International, set up by the Russian revolutionary government in 1919) and the Commissariat of Foreign Affairs. He came away with what one biographer called "a shrewd appreciation of the methods and potential strengths of the single-party state dictatorship."[21]

The immediate fruit of this mission was the establishment of the Whampoa Military Academy (named for Whampoa, or Huangpu, an island just ten miles downstream from Guangzhou[GE[102]]) in May of 1924. It was to train officers, in a crash course, for KMT armies. Chiang was its Commandant, and the graduates of the first three classes (entering respectively May 1924, August 1924, and January 1925) would be his single most important network of support in the future. Within a year they had decisively defeated local warlords. Sun Yatsen finally had his secure base, and Chiang was accepted as the key military figure of the KMT.

With Sun Yatsen's sudden death in March of 1925, however, Chiang was only one of half-a-dozen possible heirs to leadership of the KMT. With his Russian experience and with Borodin's support, by 1926 he had become first among equals. By July he was named Supreme Commander of the planned "Northern Expedition" in which the KMT hoped to conquer all of China. He was thirty-nine years old, at the height of his energy and on the verge of his greatest triumphs.

The Northern Expedition

Like the Taipings, the KMT struck north through Hunan, down the Xiang River. They captured Changsha by August, and soon cleared Dongting Lake and important railway junctions alongside the Chang Jiang. Again like the Taipings, their next targets were the Wuhan cities. The northern two, Hankou and Hanyang, fell to the KMT in September, and Wuchang followed in October (on Double Ten, fifteenth anniversary of the revolution that began at this same place in 1911!). Then, instead of following the Taiping example and moving straight on Nanjing, the Nationalist plan was a great right hook. Jiangxi Province to the east of Hunan was the next on the list; its capital Nanchang fell in November. The coastal Fujian Province, east of Jiangxi, was captured in December. As 1927 opened, KMT armies invaded Chiang's home province of Zhejiang. Hangzhou, the capital,

---

102. GE Layer 102 is a Placemark referencing Whampoa (Huangpu), today integrated into urban Guangzhou.

was captured on January 19. Some of the heaviest fighting of the whole campaign then happened along the railroad from Hangzhou to Shanghai. Behind the lines, Communist allies of the KMT took over inside Shanghai. When KMT armies arrived March 22, instead of gratitude for the "gift" of the city from the Communists, they indiscriminately killed the Communist forces, a hint of things to come. Last, but not least, KMT armies on both the north and south banks of the Chang Jiang drove upstream, and the encircled Nanjing was captured March 24, 1927. Chiang had arrived at his home turf, where his support and contacts were greatest—in Zhejiang Province, the great city of Shanghai, and in general the whole Jiangnan. That was the first phase of the Northern Expedition. It had taken about eight months.

Then came an interesting interlude. Chiang, presumably because he had lost Xuzhou in a tentative first drive north from the Yangtze valley, and because of infighting in KMT leadership, simply resigned. He left China in September 1927 for Japan.

In retrospect it seems to have been a move designed to prove that nobody else could unify the movement as well as he could. And besides, there were personal motives. He had proposed marriage to the young U.S.-educated woman Americans called Mei-ling Soong, of what one historian has called the "Soong Dynasty." Her father was the Vanderbilt-educated Charles Jones Soong, sponsor of the YMCA in China; her brother was the financial wizard T. V. Soong; one of her older sisters—Song Qingling—was the widow of Sun Yatsen; and the other of her sisters was married to H. H. Kong, the wealthiest banker in China and a lineal descendant of Confucius. Song Qingling, whose politics matched the later, leftist phase of Sun Yatsen, strongly argued against the match. But on December 1, 1927, back in Shanghai, Chiang Kai-shek and Mei-ling Soong were married in both Christian and Chinese services (the Christian one complicated a bit by the fact that Chiang already had a wife). Cai Yuanpei, former chancellor of Beida and the real elder statesman of the KMT, presided over the Chinese wedding. It was a sort of laying on of hands, making of Chiang Kai-shek the brother-in-law of the (deceased) Sun Yatsen and thus his heir apparent as leader of the KMT.

In early 1928 four KMT armies resumed the Northern Expedition; by June they took Beijing. The four main military commanders, with Chiang Kai-shek as first among equals, met at "Azure Clouds Temple" out in the Western Hills, about three miles west of the Summer Palace and twelve or so miles from Beijing.[GE103] It was a wonderful late-Yuan Dynasty structure, looking like something out of northern India; but they met there because Sun Yatsen's body was still being kept there (he had died in Beijing a little over three years before). From this and other talks Chiang emerged as President of the new Nationalist government in Nanjing. Beijing was renamed *Beiping*, "Northern Peace," to indicate it was no longer a capital.

The Nationalist decade, 1928–1937

In this decade of Nationalist (KMT) control, not a single year was without fighting—against warlords, against Chinese Communist units, against Japanese incursions. But in this decade there were remarkable developments in the Chinese state and army, and in western recognition of such western-style progress.

The Nationalist government, said one western journalist, rested on a "four-legged stool." The first and strongest leg was Chiang's military, the apple of his eye and the reason in the first place for his power. Second was the urban business community, which for the first time in living memory got a fair playing field on which to compete with foreign businessmen. Third was the professional class, the western-educated doctors, lawyers, engineers, and university professors who could practice their profession to the benefit of their country and make a good living at the same time. It was the fourth leg of the stool that was the rotten one, the agrarian one. On the books went some of the most progressive land reform legislation ever, but it never went into effect. The regime relied heavily on traditional landed interests, and never challenged them. When the peasant looked up from his plow, he saw the same old landlords that had always dictated to him. And the great majority of

---

103. GE Layer 103 references four Panoramio icons under the pointer; each have pictures of all or part of the *Biyun Si*, or Azure Clouds Temple. It looks like something from northern India, and was built in the waning years of the Yuan, or Mongol, Dynasty. If you zoom out of the framed view here you can see how the temple sits within the arms of the closest mountains to Beijing. This part of the Western Hills is called "the Fragrant Hills." Apparently a hat and suit of clothes of Sun Yatsen are still kept there, memento of the three years or so his body rested there.

Chinese were still peasants. Looking back, this rotten leg of the KMT was conversely the strongest aspect of Chinese Communism, Mao Zedong-style.

Mao Zedong, the early years

Mao was a nationalist long before he was a Communist. His adoption of Marxism, in fact, may have come when he decided that it would be the best avenue to national independence. He made short forays to Beijing in the north and Guangzhou in the south, but most of his early activity was within or just south of our corridor.

Mao was born in 1893 in a little Hunan town called Shaoshan, just within the southern edge of our chosen rectangle and about thirty miles southwest of Changsha.[GE104] His father, a small town farmer and business-man who had done well financially, took him out of school when Mao was thirteen on the grounds that he had all the schooling he needed for life running the business in Shaoshan. Mao promptly ran away to his mother's native village not far away to study in a junior high school there. Sometime in his mid-teens he walked to Changsha, the provincial capital. He was there, seventeen years old, when Double Ten broke out in the Wuhan cities. He immediately cut off his pigtail and joined a revolutionary army. In 1912 he went back to school, fin-ishing high school and doing a lot of his own reading on the side. In 1913 he enrolled in the most competitive teachers' training college in this big city. In 1915, when Chen Duxiu's *New Youth* journal came out, Mao was an early and avid reader. Two years later that journal published one of his articles, his first important published piece. It was called "A Study of Physical Culture," notable for what one biographer has called "its spirit of elemental nationalism."[22] Its proposal will look very familiar to those who know "Father" Jahn's gymnastics union, the Gaelic Athletic Association, or the Czechoslovak "Falcons"—it called for a cult of physical fitness that would lead to military heroism to achieve national independence.

By this time Mao headed up a Changsha student organization, and had become personally very close to some of his professors. When he graduated from the Teachers College in June of 1918, twenty-four years of age, he was urged to go to Beijing and study French, so as to be able to take advantage of a work-study pro-gram available in France. In the winter of 1918–1919 he audited some courses and worked in the library of Beida. In early spring he went down to Shanghai to help those students who had been chosen to go to France get underway (he visited Confucius's birthplace in Shandong, interestingly enough, on his way south). In April of 1919 he went back to Hunan to take care of his mother, who was terminally ill, and who died just a few weeks later.

He was in Changsha, then, for May 4 and the birth of the New Culture Movement, into which he threw himself. On July 14—a good revolutionary anniversary, students of French history would agree—he founded a weekly political journal called the *Xiang River Review*, which claimed to work for "democracy and new cul-ture." It lasted exactly five issues before the local warlord cracked down. In December, when Mao organized a general student strike, student publications and student associations of any kind were outlawed. Mao went to Beijing "for his health."

This was January of 1920, which was a critical year in many respects for Mao. That month he got to see a favourite old professor from Changsha (who died later that same month), and renew acquaintance with the pro-fessor's daughter Yang Kaihui (whom he married later that year). Here in Beijing he read the *Communist Man-ifesto* for the first time. In May of 1920 he went to Shanghai to coordinate the activities of Hunanese students there who opposed the Hunan warlord. In June, the warlord having been driven out of Hunan by competing factions, Mao went back to Changsha. He taught in the model primary school attached to his old Teachers' Training College, and ran a Marxist-oriented bookstore on the side. He said of himself later that by this time he had become in theory, and to some extent in practice, a Marxist. Bertrand Russell, the famous mathemati-cian and philosopher, came on a speaking tour to Changsha that year. In his speech he was very critical of the violent Bolshevik seizure of power in Russia. Mao publicly argued with him that political power should indeed be seized by force, if that is what it took to get it.

---

104. GE Layer 104 is a Folder titled "Early life of Mao Zedong." It includes Placemarks referencing Shaoshan, and also Mao's mother's village where he went to school, and finally Beida, Peking University.

This was the twenty-eight-year-old Mao Zedong who was one of two Hunanese delegates to the convention of twelve Chinese Marxists and two Russian Comintern agents in Shanghai in July of 1921 to found, formally, the CCP—the Chinese Communist Party. Mao immediately returned to Changsha to "grow" the Party. He proved to be a master at using traditional personalities and institutions for radical means. One society that fronted for a lot of Communist activity was the Wang Fuzhi Study Society. Wang Fuzhi had been a scholar-gentry in Hunan when the Ming Dynasty collapsed and the Manchu (Qing) forces came in. First he fought against the invaders, and later he hid out from them. All the while he called for higher taxation of the landlords and a policy of land redistribution to the less fortunate farmers. But had Wang Fuzhi been able to return to see, he would probably have been surprised to see what was done in his name in the early 1920s. By the end of 1922 Mao led successful strikes of railroad and coal workers, so successful that an order was issued for his arrest. In April of 1923 he quickly left for Guangzhou, again for his health.

Mao's "peasant Marxism" and the Jiangxi Soviet

In light of the extreme ideological campaigns of his later years, the young Mao was a most pragmatic, flexible Marxist. He got to Guangzhou just in time for the Russian-brokered deal that the CCP would yield labor organizing to the KMT, and become its peripheral Fifth-Column allies. Mao was such an enthusiast for joining forces with the KMT that he drew criticism from many other Chinese Marxists. The KMT tried to shunt Communists away from key positions—away from proletarian affairs and into such (to Marxists of that era) secondary areas as peasant relations. Between 1924 and 1926 this worked a real transformation in Mao. In 1924 he went back to Shaoshan to recuperate from an illness, and in his recovery spend a quiet, reflective time among the peasantry there. Upon his return to active work, he was given a high position in the propaganda department, and eventually edited the KMT's weekly political journal. It seems to have given him time to mull over and systematize what he had seen back in Shaoshan. By the end of 1926 he was publicly arguing—and to a Marxist audience it was a really hard sell—that the key issue of the national revolution was the peasant problem. It was almost as if he wove the classic Chinese end-of-dynasty peasant revolt into Marxism's promised proletarian revolution.

Then came Chiang Kai-shek's 1927 attempt to hunt down and kill all Chinese Communists. The CCP response, orchestrated from Moscow, was called the Autumn Harvest Insurrection. In essence it ordered regional Communist elements to capture the closest urban areas. Mao was ordered to take Changsha with his forces, and from September 9 to September 15 he tried. Against superior military force, however, he withdrew to save his remaining troops—and was punished by CCP headquarters by being removed from all positions of leadership. In October Mao took his surviving forces to the Jinggangshan, the rugged "Well Ridge Mountains" on the Hunan-Jiangxi border.[GE105] Here in April of 1928 he was joined by the remnant forces of the like-minded Zhu De (Chu Teh), who had been told to attack Jiangxi capital of Nanchang, suicidally, and who like Mao had realized the impossibility of it and pulled his forces back to the hills. Mao and Zhu now merged their armies into "The Fourth Red Army," with Zhu as commander and Mao as political commissar. The next year, in the face of Nationalist military pressure, they retreated east across the Gan River into the hill country on the Jiangxi-Fujian border. Here, in and around Ruijin,[GE106] they established the first Soviet in China. It lasted six years, and was the real root of the Chinese Communist experiment with governing.

Militarily, Mao and Zhu De took more from Sunzi's classical *Art of War* than any advice from Russian Communists. If Nationalist armies invaded territories under their sway, the forces of the Jiangxi Soviet would withdraw, making no attempt to defend their borders. Then sooner or later they would catch one part of the Nationalist army a bit separated from others, concentrate their force, and crush it—the main way they renewed their military supplies.

---

105. GE Layer 105 is a Placemark referencing the Jinggangshan, rugged provincial border mountains.

106. GE Layer 106 references the Jianxi Soviet headquarters in Ruijin; click on Panoramio icon under pointer titled "The Temporary Central Government of Republic of Chinese Soviet (TCGRCS) in Ruijin, Jiangxi Province, China" for photo of original building that served as headquarters.

In terms of building a government from nothing, the key to Mao's work was land reform—getting land into the hands of the poor peasants, the majority of the population. It was a complex problem, because the rich and middle peasants were the vocal ones, used to leadership. Poor peasants had learned over the centuries that if they attacked the rich, and if governmental forces favourable to the rich moved back in, they were toast. Mao's genius was to educate the poor peasantry in self-confidence; to put the wealthiest on public trial to expose the sources of their wealth; to encourage poor peasants to challenge their right especially to the land. It was a process called *shen fan*, literally "to turn the body over," or create a new mindset.[23]

It was amazingly pragmatic. There was no emphasis at all on collectivization of land ownership, the holy grail of socialism since the early nineteenth century, on the grounds that the peasants weren't ready for it. Mao was careful to disrupt patterns of life as little as possible. For example, it would have been easiest simply to seize all land, divide it into equal plots, and redistribute it, and Mao avoided that because of the instant and massive dislocation it would have caused. Only Communist administrators who could make local government work without alienating most people survived. This was all so different from Russian Bolshevism/Communism, whose first experience with actual government came only in November of 1917. The Chinese Communists learned local government and practiced it for twenty years, at least in rural areas, before they ever came to power.[GE107]

For the CCP leadership and their Russian advisors—Stalin was now taking control—this was close to a Marxist heresy. And even though CCP leaders newly back from Moscow were forced to go to the Jiangxi Soviet for safety, they still didn't understand the reasons for its success. Mao was voted out of positions of leadership—of his own Soviet!—and the Moscow clique insisted in righteous socialist pride that the territorial borders of the Soviet should be rigidly defended. Militarily it was a disaster, especially coupled with Chiang Kai-shek's masterful blockhouse-and-barbed wire encirclement.

Encirclement

To many outsiders, and indeed to many Chinese, the Japanese encroachments on Chinese territory seemed to be the most important danger facing the country. In 1928, during the Northern Expedition, Japanese army units in Shandong had come out to challenge the Nationalists; if Chiang Kai-shek had not pulled Nationalist forces west, there could have been a major war then. In 1931 Japan staged an incident near Mukden (today's Shenyang), the south Manchurian industrial city. A section of Japanese-controlled track was blown up, by the Japanese army itself, and then blamed on Chinese saboteurs. Japan thereupon proceeded to occupy all of Manchuria. In January 1932 there were serious military clashes with Japanese troops based in Shanghai.

But as Chiang Kai-shek famously argued, for Nationalist China the Japanese were only a disease of the skin, but the Communists were a disease of the heart. From 1930 right on through World War II, his consistent policy was to hoard all military aid he got from western powers—aid supposed to be used to fight the Japanese—so as to use it against the Communists. In 1928 he launched the first of what would be five encirclement campaigns against the main Jiangxi Soviet, although the first three of these yearly assaults were not too serious in terms of numbers of troops. In 1932 he moved his military headquarters to the Wuhan cities so as to focus on destroying those Communist bases in Henan, Hubei, and Anhui provinces. Having done that, in 1933 he moved the military HQ to Nanchang, capital of Jiangxi, to concentrate on destroying the Jiangxi Soviet itself. In 1934, the fifth of Chiang's five encirclement campaigns had a quarter of a million troops and expert German military advice. They slowly built ring after concentric ring of blockhouses and barbed wire fences around the Soviet, reducing its area, carefully letting no KMT unit become so exposed that it was vulnerable to Communist encirclement, and came close to strangling this key Soviet. And it did succeed in prising them loose.

---

107. GE Layer 107 is a Folder titled "Communist areas, early 1930s." Enclosed Polygon layers representing core "organized bases" are shown as dark red with white borders, and broader "zones of activity" as lighter red areas on the middle and lower Yangtze valley. The ones along the central Yangtze Valley are based on Map No. 5, Chinese Communist areas, early 1930s, in volume 13, *Republican China 1912–1949,* Part 2 of *The Cambridge History of China* series edited by John K. Fairbank and Albert Feuerwerker (London: Cambridge University Press, 1986), p. 184. Note how the areas are almost all on mountainous provincial borders.

The Long March

On October 15, 1934, the remaining 100,000 or so Jiangxi Soviet troops feinted east and broke out southwest. [GE[108]] Their misdirection was so good, and their night marching so invisible, that it was a good four weeks before the Nationalist armies really understood what had happened.

The march began with Zhu De in charge of the military, and with the cosmopolitan diplomat Zhou Enlai as political commissar. So many military reverses came from not following Mao Zedong's advice that a conference in the town of Zunyi—right on the southern border of our rectangle, some 125 miles south of Chongqing—voted the Moscow-educated clique out of power and gave overall command to Mao. It was a spectacle. Muddy troops about to enter Zunyi washed up, and came in singing a marching song, "The Three Main Rules of Discipline and the Eight Points for Attention":

> The rules:
> Obey orders in all your actions.
> Don't take a needle or a piece of thread from the people.
> Turn in everything you capture.
>
> The points of attention:
> Speak politely.
> Pay fairly for what you buy.
> Return everything you borrow.
>
> Pay for any damage.
> Don't strike or swear at people.
> Don't damage the crops.
> Don't take liberties with women.
> Don't mistreat captives.[24]

It sounded remarkably like the Taiping rules of eighty years before.

Over a year the Long March averaged twenty-five miles a day, with fighting on almost every day, and occasional unopposed strafing from Chiang's airforce. KMT armies kept the Jiangxi Soviet refugees from linking up with other Communist bases in Hunan and Sichuan. But they not only survived, they recruited to try to replace losses, they land-reformed on the way, and they dropped off agents to be hidden Soviet government agents behind Nationalist lines. Circling south and then west of Sichuan's red earth bowl, through some of China's most rugged mountains (including those with pandas), was the stuff of heroism. The crossing of the Dadu River at Luding—supposedly across an iron-chain suspension bridge from which the roadbed had been removed, into the teeth of machine gun fire—was the most famous single action. There are probably as many Chinese paintings and reproductions of that as there are American ones of Washington crossing the Delaware.

In October of 1935 Mao arrived at Baoan in the Shaanxi Soviet, which fielded about 7,000 troops, with his 8,000—less than a tenth of those who started—and then moved to Yan'an about forty miles southeast. It would be the main Communist headquarters during the coming 1937–1945 World War II.

Looking at an overview of China, what had happened to the Communists in the past year was seemingly a disaster. All those Yangtze River valley Soviets and zones of influence had been wiped out, 90 percent of their armies destroyed, and the remnant was in precarious survival way up in the sparsely populated northwest. But it was a proud and confident remnant, with the attitude that if you could survive the Long March you could survive anything. This was the Valley Forge of the Chinese Communist Revolution. And the Japanese were about to transform the situation to Chinese Communist advantage by invading China.

---

108. GE Layer 108 is a Folder titled "The Long March." There are Placemarks for eight particular sites along the route of the march, including Zunyi and Luding, discussed later in the text. The arrows representing the main path of the march are adapted from map of Chinese Civil War from U.S. Military Academy website: http://www.westpoint.edu/history/SiteAssets/SitePages/Chinese%20Civil%20War/ChineseCivilWar03.gif

The Xian Incident

As Japanese pressure on China increased in 1935, Chiang's anti-Communist focus became more and more unpopular. To the public, it seemed as if the Chinese Communists were more patriotically anti-Japanese than the "Nationalists." This was the general setting for the Xian incident. Two Nationalist generals stationed in Xian, charged with subduing the emerging Communist headquarters in Ya'nan a little further north, in effect made a gentleman's agreement with the Chinese Communists to fight the Japanese and not each other. In mid-December of 1936 Chiang Kai-shek flew to Xian to see why there was no progress in his war on the Chinese Communists. Suddenly he was arrested by his own generals and told to end the war with the Communists and focus on the Japanese, or else. His life was obviously in real danger. A delegation of Chinese Communists under Zhou Enlai arrived to negotiate. Although nothing was put into writing, Chiang obviously agreed to a joint national defence effort, and was freed on Christmas Day. When, less than seven months later, the Japanese invaded, they met at least for awhile a united front among the Chinese.

World War II: Chiang's conventional war

On July 7, 1937, the Japanese staged a supposed Chinese attack on one of their own units (the so-called "Marco Polo Bridge incident" west of Beijing),[GE[109]] and used it as an excuse for a full-scale invasion of China. [GE[110]] In general overview, in the first year of the invasion Japan occupied north China to the part of the Yellow River that runs north and south. In the Yangtze Valley they occupied Shanghai, the whole Jiangnan, Nanjing, and about 400 miles of the lower Yangtze River. They took most of the important coastal cities of the south coast as well.

Chiang Kai-shek's response to the Japanese invasion was at first slow and cautious, but he finally took a firm stand at Shanghai. Militarily, it was throwing Chinese bodies at overwhelming Japanese steel, but in terms of the country's morale, it shot Chiang Kai-shek and the Nationalist Party to a pinnacle of popularity. In frustration with Chinese resistance, when Nanjing fell to the Japanese army on December 13, 1937, the Japanese generals simply turned their troops loose in Nanjing. In about six weeks time something like 300,000 people were killed, not counting the widespread looting, burning, and raping that went on. It seemed to start out as an attempt to get at Chinese soldiers hiding among the civilian population, but quickly lost all military rationale. History books usually call it the Nanjing Massacre, but a more vivid and not inaccurate label is the Rape of Nanjing.

When the Nationalist government withdrew up the Chang Jiang to the Wuhan cities and refused to surrender to the Japanese, in the summer of 1938 the Japanese pursued them and took Wuhan, and beyond, as far as the base of the Three Gorges. The Nationalists thereupon withdrew up through the gorges to Chongqing. It was a retreat, but perhaps their finest hour. Steam boilers were taken apart and carried by boat and human porter, plate by plate, up to Sichuan. Students carried whole libraries of books and drove the blood stock of A&M colleges through the mountains. Chongqing would remain the Nationalist base from 1938–1944. The Japanese could occasionally bomb and strafe it, but the capital was secure from land assault.

After Pearl Harbor was bombed on December 7, 1941, and the U.S. entered the war, we embraced Chiang Kai-shek and the Nationalists as our main ally in Asia. From Chiang's point of view, it bore real fruit in both recognition of his leadership and in achieving Nationalist Chinese aims. In the 1942 celebrations of Double Ten, both the U.S. and the U.K. promised to end all the "unequal" rights such as extrality, held since the Treaty of Nanking a hundred years before. But with corruption and inefficiency reaching new heights in

---

109. GE Layer 109 is a Placemark referencing Lugouqiao, known to westerners as "Marco Polo Bridge," because of that author's admiring description of it. It is less than ten miles west southwest from the heart of Beijing; there are a couple dozen Photos icons to explore.

110. GE Layer 110 is a Folder titled "Japanese invasion of China, 1937–1945." It has five different Polygons showing expansion of Japanese control from July 1937 when the war began until August 1945 when it ended. Open each Polygon in turn, paying special attention to how it intersects our corridor. Central and southern part of map, especially of the Chang Jiang valley area, adapted from Map 8. "Japanese military occupation of China proper," on p. 549 of *The Cambridge History of China, vol. 13 Republican China 1912–1949, Part 2* (London: Cambridge University Press, 1986).

the Chongqing government, and neither the honeymoon with the West or Chiang's popularity with the Chinese would last.

President Franklin Roosevelt had appointed General Joe Stilwell—a brilliant military strategist and fluent in Chinese—as head of the CBI (China-Burma-India) theater of the war, and at the same time Chief of Staff under Chiang Kai-shek. Massive U.S. supplies began to arrive in Chongqing "over the hump," flown in over the Himalayas from India, and later a "Burma Road" was scraped out over the hills. But Stilwell became more and more disillusioned with Chiang Kai-shek as a leader, and was especially frustrated by his hoarding of military supplies that should have been thrown immediately into the war with Japan. There was also friction between Stilwell and Col. Claire Chennault, who had been in China since 1938 organizing the American Volunteer Group ("Flying Tigers") to serve the Chinese Nationalists as an air force. Chiang Kai-shek was enthusiastic about Chennault's claims that he could end the war early by bombing the Japanese home islands from air bases in interior China, such as the one at Guilin; this way he could continue hoarding his military supplies and armies. Stilwell sarcastically asked Chennault how he proposed to hold those airfields without a committed, newly-trained Chinese army. The Japanese proved Stilwell right with drives, including one to Guilin, to eliminate those airfield threats (see Dec. 1941–August 1945 yellow Polygon in Google Earth folder; the yellow extensions of Japanese occupation are thrusts out at those air bases).

World War II: Mao's guerrilla war

Although on the accompanying map the Japanese occupation of China is done in solid colors, that occupation was generally thin. There were just not enough Japanese soldiers to occupy the whole very effectively. And so, except for major towns and along major railroad lines, Japanese military presence was vulnerable to local resistance. The Chinese Communists from their base in Yan'an flourished in this situation, especially since the Japanese front sheltered them from any Nationalist forces. In Mao's hands, the strategies of land reform and *shen fan* were successfully translated into the very different cultures of the north. Young and brilliant military commanders such as Lin Biao paralyzed local Japanese garrisons, and starting with the villages, and then the small towns and larger towns, virtually the whole of north China came under expanding Communist control. Earlier, in the chapter on socialism (and Russia) we had occasion to speak of Yan'an as something very different from a World War II Pittsburg or Detroit, an interior city that produced uniforms, tanks, guns, aircraft. Yan'an produced virtually no "things." Instead, it gave the impression to western visitors of being an idea factory, where Communist managers and military leaders were cycled through to learn the latest successful techniques for manufacturing their own things and creating their own governments. Mao Zedong, a talented poet and one of the most gifted political writers/propagandists of all time, made Chiang Kai-shek's writings and speeches on China's future look shallow and trivial.

For three-and-a-half years there was some genuine Nationalist-Communist cooperation, although they were fighting two very different wars—a rear-guard conventional war in the Yangtze Valley and the south, and a guerrilla campaign behind Japanese lines in the north. Then in January of 1941 came the "New Fourth Army incident."[GE111] Something less than 10,000 Communist troops, in the part of Anhui Province south of the Chang Jiang, had agreed to move north of the river. Before they did, they were attacked by a Nationalist army of over 80,000. About 2,000 of the Communists broke out and escaped, but the rest were killed or captured. No substantial Communist forces were now left south of the river, but the two sides were openly at war, a civil war within the China-Japan war.

Wei Qi, Xiang Qi, and end game

The Chinese are as passionate about chess as are the Russians—but for two very different kinds of chess.

Xiang Qi (fourth tone, third tone) usually translates "Courtier Chess." It is recognizably kin to western chess; perhaps they share the same Central Asian ancestor (though Joseph Needham argued that the original was indeed Chinese). The board is eight squares by eight squares, with a river dividing the two sides that

---

111. GE Layer 111 is a Placemark locating the New Fourth Army Incident site near Maolin in Anhui Province.

amounts to a ninth row. Since pieces are placed not on the squares but on the intersections, that makes it a 9 × 10 board instead of our 8 × 8. There are recognizable pawns, though they can't strike diagonally. There are bishop-like pieces, though they can only move two intersections diagonally at a time. The chariot pieces are almost identical to western castles, in both placement and moves. The king and his closest guards are limited to a little square of intersections around the king. Perhaps the most interesting difference with western chess is that xiang qi has two artillery pieces per side (one side has "fire cannon," one has "stone cannon") that must shoot over one piece to make a capture. But like western chess, certain pieces are more powerful than others, and certain parts of the board—where the king stands, for one—are more critical than others.

The other kind of chess is called *Wei Qi* (third tone, third tone), or "Encirclement Chess." This is the same game the Japanese call *Go*. The board is a 19 × 19 grid (playing again on the intersections), and one side plays black stones and the other white stones. A stone surrounded by four enemy stones is captured. Square connections between stones of one color cannot be cut through by the opponent, but diagonal connections can. You can play anywhere; if you are losing in one corner of the board you can start in another. Every piece of territory counts the same; at game's end, all 19 × 19 = 361 points are totaled, and whichever side gets 181 or better wins. Interestingly enough, computers can now beat the best humans at xiang qi (as with western chess), but the seemingly simpler wei qi still has humans beating machines—perhaps because of the visual patterns that take shape during play?

In August of 1945, with the sudden Japanese surrender after the atomic bombs of the sixth and the ninth, there sat Chiang Kai-shek and Mao Zedong, armed to the teeth. On paper the Nationalists were overwhelmingly superior, and they had major help from the U.S.A. But corruption had sapped KMT popularity since the drama of the forced withdrawal up the Yangtze Valley early in the war. And in the conflict of the next few years Mao played wei qi to Chiang Kai-shek's xiang qi. Chiang invested heavily in holding cities and railheads; Mao would make him pay a heavy price for a territory—even Yan'an—and take two or three territories elsewhere. Chiang sent large numbers of troops loyal to him to occupy Manchurian cities, and lost them as those cities were strangled by the surrounding Communist countryside. Mukden, the most important industrial city in Manchuria, fell to the Communists on November 1, 1948. Growing Communist armies took Beijing and Tianjin, and then in the massive Huai-Hai battle around Xuzhou they broke the last good Nationalist force north of the Chang Jiang. By 1949 it was all over, at least on the mainland, as Chiang's dwindling government was driven from Nanjing to Chongqing to Chengdu, back up against Sichuan's far western mountains. On November 10, 1949, as Communist forces were moving in on Chengdu itself, Chiang Kai-shek and his entourage boarded a military plane and flew across what was now "Red" China to Taiwan.[GE[112]] Here a remnant of the ROC (Republic of China) faced—and still faces, as of this writing—the PRC (People's Republic of China) across the hundred-mile-wide Taiwan Strait.

Governance: "expert" vs. "red"

Late twentieth-century travelers in both the U.S.S.R. and the People's Republic of China were impressed with two things: how many ancient things the Russians had adopted from the Chinese (as examples, tea culture, including the samovar; the *kang,* or fire bed, a clay bed with the kitchen chimney running through it for warmth), and how many Soviet practices China had fairly recently adopted. In the Soviet Union, for example, in a typical store a customer had to stand in three lines to buy something: one to get a price; one at the cashier to pay for it and get a receipt; and a third back at the location of the object to turn in the receipt and get it (thus keeping all the money in one pair of hands). The Chinese adopted that too. And in the Soviet Union there were two currencies—the ordinary ruble which wasn't worth much and which could not be traded outside the country, versus the "Certificate Ruble" that Russians got when they earned foreign, "hard" currency. There were special stores only open to those with certificate rubles. China fully embraced this, with their ordinary currency the *renminbi*—of little value—versus the FEC, or Foreign Exchange Certificate, for which there were special

112. GE Layer 112 is a Path, in red, depicting Nov. 10, 1949, shortest possible flight path as Chiang Kai-shek flew from Chengdu to Taiwan. It had to be a most thoughtful flight for him, going as it did over Mao Zedong's home base of Changsha.

stores. As late as the 1990s Russian speakers visiting China could talk to many older administrators in most educational and other institutions, who had been educated in the U.S.S.R. back in the 1950s.

The one kind of governance the victorious Chinese Communists had no experience with was urban, and suddenly in 1948 and 1949 they inherited all China's great cities which the KMT had held as its last bastions. At this point Mao insisted China had to learn from the U.S.S.R., which, moreover, had substantial technological and managerial know-how to offer China. For the next year or two there was a Chinese policy that looked a lot like the 1921–27 NEP of the Soviet Union—the encouragement of a strong private enterprise sector of the economy, a drive to recruit intellectuals and urban workers into what was then an overwhelmingly peasant Communist Party. The aim seemed to be general economic development.

But in the fall of 1950 China joined the Korean War and directly engaged the U.N. (mostly U.S.) army. A "Resist America, Aid Korea" campaign eventually targeted private businessmen, managers, and state-owned businesses. In 1953 the first Chinese Five-Year Plan was approved, with utopian targets of production. Collectivization was pushed with the creation of the Agricultural Producers' Cooperative, nothing less than the Russian *kolkhoz*. For three years propaganda drives to get reluctant peasants to join were pushed hard by the government. By 1956 symptoms of the Soviet Union's excesses of imposed collectivization under Stalin are appearing—the slaughter of livestock by peasants; the hoarding of grain; the dramatic flow to the cities of refugees from the countryside.

If you look at the two paragraphs above as a pair, it is a seesaw from the dominance of those who favored expertise in the topic and a return to a more pragmatic, ordinary pattern of administration, economics, and politics, to the dominance of those who called for destruction of bureaucracy and embracing extreme ideological stances through which to achieve that which had never been achieved. Looking back from the vantage point of the twenty-first century, the ideologues were hopeless dreamers. But at the time, it seemed plausible. Hadn't Mao ideologically done with *fan shen* what nobody had ever done, in history? Why not more? And behind the scenes, the ideological side of the seesaw may have been Mao's way of taking power back—after the pragmatists had whittled away at his power. Look for that same "expert" versus "red" seesaw in Chinese politics down to Mao's death in 1976, and beyond.

The "Great Leap Forward" and the "Great Proletarian Cultural Revolution"

By 1956 a policy of slow, gradual collectivization was supreme at the Communist Party Congress. It was championed by Liu Shaoqi, a veteran of the Long March. He was helped by Khrushchev's attack earlier that year on Stalin's personality cult. In parallel with the "thaw" instituted by Khrushchev in 1956, China had the "100 Flower" campaign. It was named for an old phrase of Mao Zedong's, "Let a hundred flowers bloom, a hundred schools of thought contend"—though it seems clear that Mao wanted to continue fast, forcible collectivization. Instead of flowers, the Party got what it called "poisonous weeds"—a vigorous and direct criticism of what it was doing.

In 1957, in a turn to the ideological, the Party began to uproot these poisonous weeds. Intellectuals, state administrators, and even army officers were targeted as insufficiently ideologically pure, not in tune enough with Mao's thought. In 1958, with the Five-Year Plan up for renewal, a quantum leap in production was called for, and named "The Great Leap Forward." China had little capital to invest in industry, but the world's largest population; why not turn the people loose with steel production, for example? Backyard blast furnaces were encouraged by the government. In the long run, it may have spread some metallurgical knowledge among the general population, but in terms of production, it was disastrous. Again, it sounds a bit like Stakhaonovite production norms in the U.S.S.R. in the 1930s. Apparently food production fell off so much as to trigger a great famine, and the Great Leap was abandoned by 1961.

From 1961 to 1965 the pragmatists, led by Liu Shaoqi, rebuilt a more normal administration. Deng Xiaoping said it best for the pragmatists, "No matter whether cats are white or black, if they can catch mice they are good cats." It was a direct attack on the "redder the more expert" line of the Mao camp.

At this point Mao, demoted to positions of lesser power in the leadership, turned to the army. The brilliant young general of the Japanese War, Lin Biao, had become Minister of Defense during the Great Leap, and he now emerged as Mao's closest ally. A campaign of "Maoist democracy" was promoted in the People's Liberation Army. Soon army officers were being assigned to civilian political offices to combat bourgeois tendencies, on the grounds that three years of study of Mao's work had inoculated them against it. Older Americans will remember images of PLA troops marching while shaking copies of "The Little Red Book," a collection of Mao teachings and sayings.

In May of 1965 Mao began to organize the Red Guards of high school and college students. By summer they were attacking their own schools as too Rightist and bourgeois. Soon they were running a nationwide campaign to elect "true" Communists in the Party's lower levels. Mao then used that new backing to force a meeting of the Central Committee of the Communist Party, where against bitter opposition he rammed through a permanent revolution program. By some accounts he got the right to speak for the entire Communist Party. Liu Shaoqi was publicly humiliated. This really splintered the Communist leadership for the first time in thirty years, since the Long March.

Universities and many secondary schools more or less shut down during the Cultural Revolution; overall, China lost about ten years of formal education here. Most college intellectuals were sent to the countryside, or to ethnic regions in the far west of China, for re-education through manual labor. The greatest turmoil lasted for three years.

Then from 1969 to 1971 the seesaw rocked again, perhaps as the army asserted its independence of Mao (at least Lin Biao was presented as the heir-apparent of Mao). And in late 1971 fantastic stories circulated that one of China's ten jet transports had taken off suddenly, with a lot of the top brass including Lin Biao, and had either crashed or been shot down way out west. Suddenly secret meetings between U.S. and P.R.C. officials took place, apparently under supervision of Zhou Enlai. In February of 1972, President Richard Nixon formally visited China. Mao was still alive, but it was unthinkable that he was still in charge. He (and Zhou Enlai) died in 1976, and a revival of capitalism in the countryside almost immediately took place. Looking back, that 1976 to 1989 period was also the most politically open of any time in recent Chinese history.

The Last Emperor and the Tiananmen Square Massacre

In 1987, Bernardo Bertolucci made an interesting film in China, and mainly with Chinese actors. It was called *The Last Emperor*, and is worth seeing not only for its portrayal of Chinese history from 1908 to 1967, but for what it says about 1987. One of the major supporting roles was played by actor and translator Ruocheng Ying, who was then China's Vice-Minister of Culture. He played the head of a camp where, after the Communist takeover of the country, Rightists (including the last Emperor) were being reformed. At film's end his character was being shamefully humiliated by mindless mobs of Red Guards in the Cultural Revolution. It's hard to imagine such a film being done in China now, because of a sharp ideological turn taken by the Chinese leadership in 1989.

Do you know the venerable series of coffee table photography books with titles that begin with *A Day in the Life of*? On a given day dozens of native and outside photographers are set loose in a given country to blaze away with their cameras from dawn to dusk, and the best shots go into a resulting book. On April 15, 1989, dozens of Chinese and western photographers under contract to produce *A Day in the Life of China*[25] fanned out across the country, including up and down the Chang Jiang valley. They made pictures of sleeping children in child care centers as soon as there was enough light (one of these made the cover), and the last of the photographers were still clicking away after dark—when one of them took pictures of the first of the "big character" (protest) posters that went up on that very day at Beida campus. Hu Yaobang, perceived by college students as a liberal who had been forced out of the Chinese leadership a couple of years before by hard-line Communists, had died that day, and his death triggered that outpouring. Over the next month and a half, virtually all classes in all Chinese universities ceased to function as striking students walked out. All the major university student bodies throughout China sent permanent, rotating delegations to the huge square adjoining—and named for—the "Heavenly Peace Gate" (*Tian An Men*) of the Imperial Palace in Beijing. A famous white statue, reminiscent of the Statue of Liberty, was the showpiece of the huge, extended demonstration.[GE[113]]

Some half-hearted police and military measures were taken to remove the students, but troops were reluctant to fire or commanders to give the order to fire, or—and virtually all older Americans will remember this image—tank drivers refused to run over one student who blocked them with only white flags in his hands. But on June 4 the hard-liners brought in an army loyal to them. In the night they surrounded Tiananmen Square on four sides (as one analyst said later, that meant they intended to kill people: from Sunzi's Art of War on down, the Chinese tradition was to leave an enemy a way out), and began shooting. The crackdown had begun.

That day I was in a lower Yangtze Valley university town, as head of a faculty/student travel-study group from my university (there were about 2,000 of us Americans in China that day, it turned out). Within twenty-four hours Chinese students there—a seventeen-hour train ride from Beijing—were quietly showing my students color photographs of dead and dying Chinese students being carried away from Tiananmen Square by their friends. There was talk of civil war, and some analysts claimed to see opposite sides setting up for a tank battle outside Beijing. But what it amounted to in this Chang Jiang valley town were student demonstrations during morning and evening rush hours. Students marched in an orderly way, carrying white (the color of death) funeral wreaths, to paralyze traffic. And the urban 20 percent of China fairly well honored the demonstrations by staying away from work. But the 80 percent of the Chinese who were rural, who had prospered first from the opening of the economy and who were much less ideological, ignored it. And no military force joined the protest side. So it was not a civil war, or even a revolt; just a Movement. But there was an edge of bitterness about its suppression. As my group was being taken to a ritzy, government-controlled hotel complex to await a flight out, our bus eased around a street march in a central China provincial capital city. Two of the signs being carried read "Learn from Romania" (which proved to be the bloodiest of the eastern bloc anti-Communist movements that year), and "The blood of the martyrs of Tiananmen Square must be washed out by the blood of Li Peng" (the Premier of China who had ordered the military crackdown). In Hong Kong on our way out, a million and a half of the total population of six million were out in the streets in protest marches.

The 2008 Olympics and the foreseeable future

Despite the retrenchment on general civil rights after the 1989 Tiananmen Square massacre, in 2001 China was awarded the Summer Olympic Games for 2008. Partly it surely had to do with China's growing economic clout, as some years the GNP of the world's most populous country grew at the astounding rate of 16 percent per year. As with Japan in the 1964 Olympics, and Mexico's in the 1968 Olympics, this was to be China's coming out onto the world stage. And what a coming out. A reputed $US 300 billion was spent on the games, and as one commentator said, in terms of opening ceremonies the world might as well retire the award now—surely nothing will ever surpass it. Ethnic protests in Tibet and among the Muslim Uighurs were the only minor irritants for a proudly nationalist Chinese public.

The regime got in some not-so-subtle ideological licks on this occasion, too. Once the Olympic torch relay got to China, it not only went to big cities and famous tourist sites (such as Leshan with its great Tang Dynasty Buddha carved out of the living rock, Dunhuang with its caves full of Buddhist art, and Qufu, birthplace of Confucius); it made a pilgrimage to five small but hallowed sites of early Communist Chinese history you've just recently read about in this chapter, the first four on or just south of our corridor: to Shaoshan, Mao's native village; to the Jinggangshan, or Well Ridge Mountains, to his first rural base; to Ruijin, center of the Jiangxi Soviet created by Mao and Zhu De; to Zunyi, where Mao was chosen first among equals early in the Long March; and finally to Yan'an, the terminus of the Long March.

---

113. GE Layer 113 is a Placemark framing a view of the huge Tiananmen Square. It is partly an excuse to embed a website that has a photo of the Chinese "statue of liberty," at: http://static.squidoo.com/resize/squidoo_images/-1/draft_lens1380536module8607154photo_LibertyFaceOffChina.jpg1204995676

Socialism and nationalism are as closely intertwined in modern Chinese history as they are in Russian history, and arguably here too socialism was warped into the service of modern patriotism. World Revolution, Marxist style, is manifestly not a goal of most Chinese, even of the avowedly Marxist government. Collectivization of society has been abandoned. The chief popular goals were always national independence and the re-assumption of China's traditional international prominence. Because Marxism helped achieve that, the Communist party bosses in China are generally still not openly attacked for their perks and luxuries. As Chinese security in their independence and growing international status rises with time, however, and as expectations rise too, it has to happen in the not-too-distant future.

Endnotes

1. See William Hinton, *Fanshen: A Documentary of Revolution in a Chinese Village* (New York: Random/Vintage, 1966), p. 477.

2. Example adapted from Colin A. Ronan, *An Abridgement of Joseph Needham's Original Text* (Cambridge: Cambridge University Press, 1978), vol. I, p. 10.

3. Lyman P. Van Slyke, *Yangtze: Nature, History, and the River* (Menlo Park, CA: Addison-Wesley Publishing Co., Inc.), 1988; a Portable Stanford Book.

4. First published in France under the title *La Méditerranée et le Monde Méditerranean à l'Epoque de Philippe II* in 1949; published in English in 1972 by Wm Collins Sons Ltd and Harper & Row.

5. As quoted in Van Slyke, *Yangtze*, p. 30. No attribution, so presumably the author's own translation.

6. From Li Bai's poem "The Sichuan Road" as quoted from Anderson's *Masterpieces of the Orient*, p. 461. According to the editor it was Li Bai's reworking of a traveler's song.

7. Van Slyke, p. 101.

8. As quoted in Van Slyke, p. 111.

9. John Hersey, *A Single Pebble* (New York: Alfred A. Knopf, 1956), pp. 5–6.

10. As quoted in Van Slyke, pp. 156–7.

11. The imagery of the paragraph, as well as the suggestion that the Chinese South contributed Taoism to the fusion of cultures, comes from John K. Fairbank, Edwin O. Reischauer, and Albert M. Craig's, *East Asia: Tradition and Transformation* (Boston: Houghton Mifflin Co., 1989), pp. 48–49.

12. As quoted in Van Slyke, *Yangtze,* p. 140.

13. As quoted in Van Slyke, *Yangtze,* p. 73.

14. Lo Kuan-chung, *Romance of the Three Kingdoms*. Trans. C. H. Brewitt-Taylor (Rutland, Vermont & Tokyo, Japan: Charles E. Tuttle Company, 1959), vol. 1, p. 1.

15. *Romance of the Three Kingdoms*, vol. I, pp. 482–5.

16. *All Men Are Brothers [Shui Hu Chuan]*. Translated by Pearl S. Buck (New York: Grove Press, Inc., 1933), vol. I, pp. 391–465.

17. Wu Ching-tzu, *The Scholars*. Third ed. (Beijing: Foreign Languages Press, 1983), pp. 62–76.

18. From Franz Michael and Chung-li Chang, *The Taiping Rebellion: History and Documents*, vols. 2–3, as quoted in Jonathan Spence, *God's Chinese Son: The Taiping Heavenly Kingdom of Hong Xiuquan* (NY & London: Norton & Company, 1996.

19. From Thomas W. Blakiston, *Five Months on the Yang-tsze: with a Narrative of the Exploration of its Upper Waters, and Notices of the Present Rebellions in* China (London: John Murray, 1862), as quoted in Van Slyke, *Yangtze*, p. 156.

20. Edwin E. Moise, *Modern China: A History*. 3rd ed. Harlow, England: Pearson/Longman, 2008, p. 45.

21. "Chiang Kai-shek," p. 322, vol. I of Howard Boorman (ed.), *Biographical Dictionary of Republican China.*

22. "Mao Tse-tung," p. 3, vol. III of Howard Boorman (ed.), *Biographical Dictionary of Republican China.*

23. The most interesting description of this process in English came with William Hinton's *Fanshen: A Documentary of Revolution in a Chinese Village* (New York: Random, 1966), though it was in a north China village in 1947 after twenty years of practice.

24. As quoted from Harrison E. Salisbury, *The Long March: The Untold Story* (New York: Harper & Row, 1985), p. 117.

25. *A Day in the Life of China: Photographed by 90 of the world's leading photojournalists on one day, April 5, 1989* (San Francisco: Collins Publishers, 1989). See pp. 206–7 for photograph of "big character posters" at Beida, the last picture in the book.

Chapter Fourteen

"The Era of Patriotism Has Come":
The Kyoto-to-Tokyo Corridor of East Asia

"The era of loyalty is passed. The era of patriotism has come . . ."

– *observation of U.S. educator William Griffis, teaching in Fukui in 1871, on hearing that the feudal domains had been abolished and French-style prefectures established in their place.*[1]

CONTENTS

The heart of the matter—Introduction to the Japanese language—Some common Japanese place names—The four main islands and the Inland Sea—*Tokaido* and *Nakasendo*—Topography and texture of the corridor—Samples of folklore and legend from our corridor—Archaeology and prehistory—Shinto and the Ise Shrines—Borrowing from China—The imperial Age of Heian—*Tales of the Heike*—The Kamakura Shogunate—Japanese feudalism compared with European feudalism—*Zen in the Art of Archery*—"Divine Winds"—The feudal wars of the late 1500s—Statler's *Japanese Inn*—Tokugawa Ieyasu—The Battle of Sekigahara—Will Adams—"Alternate Residence" and the formalizing of the Tokaido—Engelbert Kaempfer's 1691 trip on the Tokaido—The affair of the 47 Ronin—Basho—Chikamatsu—Hiroshige's "53 Stages of the Tokaido"—Roots of modern cultural nationalism—Commodore Perry and the Unequal Treaty—Meiji Restoration—Westernization, Japanese style—Sino-Japanese War and the Heian Jingu Shrine—Russo-Japanese War—The "21 Demands" and the Kwantung Army—*Nashonarizumu*: State Shinto and rising militarism—Prince Saionji and Japanese Liberalism—World War II—Damage on our corridor—The legacy of imperialism—*The Chrysanthemum and the Sword*—General Douglas MacArthur, S.C.A.P.—"Japan, Inc."—The 1964 "coming out" party: the Olympics and the *Shinkansen*—Yukio Mishima—"Prudent nationalism?"

The heart of the matter

Japan's reaction to rising western power is one of the most fascinating chapters of modern world history. The Japanese feudal lords—military men, after all—were quick to appreciate western military technology and tactics; within twenty years of the first Portuguese landings in Japan in 1543 the Japanese had thoroughly integrated western firearms into their armies, and were beginning to build their first cannon-proof castles. Then around 1600 in the newly unified Tokugawa Japan, western forces including Christianity were deemed to be too disturbing to the Japanese order to tolerate, and Japan closed like an oyster to the outside world for over 250 years.

Inside Japan, this was one of the great eras of civilization and the arts in world history. Externally, however, Japan fell way behind in the world power game. The political nationalism that grew out of the Enlightenment and French Revolution, the transformation of warfare, economic production, and transportation that came with the Industrial Revolution, and finally the new cultural nationalism that grew out of Romanticism—Japan missed it all in those two-and-a-half centuries. So it proved to be remarkably easy for rising western power to pry the Japanese oyster open. It was led by us in the U.S.A., of course, in the person of Commodore Matthew Perry in 1853–54—demanding a classic "unequal treaty" of the style that had been forced on China a dozen years before in the Treaty of Nanking.

And then came the second transformation of Japan, just as quick but much greater than that of the last half of the 1500s. Less than fifteen years after Perry's fleet threatened the Japanese capital, a remarkable social revolution overthrew the government. It was disguised as a return to the past, the "Restoration" of the Emperors who had been puppets in the hands of frontier military figures called Shoguns for seven centuries. In brief, a decision was made by key Japanese institutions to tolerate western presence until the Japanese could learn from and copy that power. They went shopping for it in the western world—to Britain to learn how to build a navy, to Germany for an army, to France for institutions of local government, to the U.S. for business . . . . And the youngest of the Meiji reformers would live to see their dream of rising to a world power brilliantly fulfilled—defeating China in 1895 and Russia in 1905, and winning recognition of equality from such great western powers as Great Britain before World War I.

In remarkable parallel with late nineteenth- and twentieth-century Germany, however, extreme nationalism and militarism gradually poisoned Japan's relationship with its neighbors, especially those neighbors that it occupied by a supposed right of being "elder brother." The cultural roots of all this were very different from Germany's—State Shinto and Emperor worship instead of a cult of the Old Norse religion—but the arrogance of those who considered themselves superior to their neighbors was much the same. Japan, like Germany, was destroyed as a great military power by the end of World War II. There has been as much soul-searching in Japan about the correct role of patriotism in modern life as there has been in Germany, from those unapologetic extreme nationalists who rally at Tokyo's Yasukuni Shrine to those liberals still ashamed that in 1999 Japan re-adopted as its national anthem the *Kimigayo*, so closely associated with earlier imperial expansion.

Introduction to the Japanese language

A. Spoken

Even though some of written Japanese resembles written Chinese, the spoken languages are no kin at all; Japanese has none of that tonality, or sing-song, quality of Sinitic languages. Japanese does have a good many "loan" words from Chinese (about as many as Latin loan words in English), but spoken Japanese is no closer in structure to Chinese than English is. In fact, Japanese has no clear kinship to any known language.

There are various dialects of spoken Japanese. The most different are the Tohoku dialect spoken in northeastern Honshu, and, at the other end of the islands, the dialect spoken down in and around Okinawa. Across the main islands of Japan there are still remnants of four or five dialects that were almost separate languages. Only with the late nineteenth-century westernization of Japan was there a serious move to unify the spoken language—by using the Tokyo-area dialect as the standard to be taught in western-style public schools. In recent decades, television news and other Tokyo-based media have reinforced that standard; virtually everyone in Japan can both understand and speak it.

B. Written

The Japanese learned to write from the Chinese, and not surprisingly the earliest written Japanese (from the AD 700s) actually uses Chinese characters in their original pictographic or ideographic sense. This part of written Japanese is called *kanji* (*kan* is a Japanese word meaning Chinese, which probably originated from *Han* as in the Han dynasty; and *-ji* is a suffix that can mean "letters" or "characters," or more generally, "writing"). Kanji is still one key part of the Japanese writing system.

Within a century of that first writing, though, Japanese were also using Chinese characters (and their monosyllabic pronunciations) to stand for syllables pronounced that same way in Japanese. This syllable-writing was generally called *kana* or *gana*, and it developed in two main forms. *Katakana* (*kata* means incomplete, so a fair translation would be "incomplete Chinese characters") is based on formal, squared-up style of Chinese characters, or parts of them, while *hiragana* ("plain borrowed-letters") with its rounded look developed from the more cursive "grass" style of Chinese writing. The hiragana syllabary, for example, has 131 symbols (syllabaries usually have several times the number of symbols of alphabets; instead of just a simple set of vowels to match with individual consonants, for example, you'd need symbols for ka, ke, ki, ko, and ku for the letter k, ma, me, mi, mo, and mu for the letter m, and so on). Here is the city name Shimonoseki written first in basic Chinese characters, or kanji, 下関,市, and then in hiragana, しものせき; you can tell the second has five syllables, one symbol each for *shi-mo-no-se-ki*.

This means that many, many words in Japanese can be written—and pronounced—in two basic ways. One way is to use the original Chinese ideograph (for example 山 meaning "mountain"), and to pronounce it *san* (from the original Chinese *shan*). The other would be to use katakana or hiragana syllable-writing to represent the Japanese spoken word for mountain, *yama*—that is, one sign pronounced "ya" written together with a second sign pronounced "ma." Even the Japanese have trouble sometimes pronouncing the kanji, and there's a sort of double script that has the hiragana in little characters written beside or above the kanji. It's much used in high schools, though by the time you're in college you're supposed to have mastered it all.

This all should help you know why the country is sometimes called "Japan" and sometimes (especially by the locals) called "Nippon." The written Chinese name for Japan, older than the Tang dynasty, was 日本. The first character is a squared-up pictograph of the sun you've already seen in the last chapter; the second is an ideograph in which the root of a stylized tree is emphasized, thus meaning root or origin, so the whole name is "Sun Origin," or more poetically, "Land of the Rising Sun." The Chinese pronunciation was something like *Jih-pun*; Marco Polo around 1200 heard it *Cipangu*; and the Portuguese who came into Malaysia around 1500 heard it *Japan* from the Malays. But Japanese language pronunciation of those same two words "sun" and "origin" was *Nippon* or *Nihon*.

But in general kanji, hiragana, and katakana have separate uses. Kanji is used mainly for nouns and verb stems, hiragana for most of the rest (including grammatical endings), and katakana is used for international loan words or unusual "spellings" (something like the way we italicize or underline words to call special attention to them). Finally, in modern Japanese writing use is often made of Latin letters, called *rōmaji*, and Arabic numerals. So written Japanese is not so much a single script as it as a mix of three or four scripts!

Traditional Japanese writing was in columns, from top to bottom, then a new column to the left of that—just as with traditional written Chinese, which is of course where the Japanese got it. But a lot of Japanese writing since the Allied Occupation after World War II is now done in the traditional Indo-European way of lines left to right, the next line coming below that.

C. Transliterated

The only really unusual thing about Japanese as it is transliterated into our Latin alphabet is the dash sometimes written over a vowel. Japanese has both long and short vowels, and this dash tells you it's the long vowel that actually changes in pitch. The dash over the two "ū"s in Kyūshū, for example, indicates that the vowels get a bit more time in pronunciation, and that each "u" starts on one pitch and is dropped to a lower one (there's also a rising pitch "long" vowel in other words). So although the truly correct transliteration of these famous cities should be Tōkyō, Kyōto, and Ōsaka, most of us have used them for so long in ordinary "Tokyo, Kyoto, and Osaka" form that these and other commonly known words will be used without dashes in the text below.

Some common Japanese place names

All along the rugged coastline of Japan are place names that end in *-shima* or *-jima* (meaning island) and *-saki* (meaning point or small peninsula). One common coastal name is *tsu*, meaning harbor (and since *nami* is wave, *tsunami* means "harbor wave," a devastating wave that floods even sheltered harbors). Continuing the watery theme, *ko* is lake, *kawa* is river, and *hashi* (or occasionally *bashi*) is bridge. *Hama* is beach and *matsu* is pine, so *Hamamatsu* must be "Pine Tree Beach." Other common suffixes you might come across browsing through a map of Japan are *-ji* (temple), *–ya* (place of business, such as an inn), *-jo* (castle), and a pair you've already seen, *-san* or *-yama* (mountain).

The four main islands and the Inland Sea

Japan lies off the mainland coast of Asia a bit the way Great Britain lies off the coast of Europe—far enough away for defense, but close enough to learn from mainland developments. This happy circumstance helped both Japan and Great Britain have an impact on world history all out of proportion to their size.[GE[1]]

Of Japan's thousands of islands, there are four major ones that a beginning student of Japan should learn: Kyushu in the southwest, Shikoku in the south, Honshu (the giant of them all) in the center, and Hokkaido in the northeast.[GE[2]] These are sometimes called the "home islands." The first three of these islands almost surround a little piece of ocean called the Inland Sea, also historically important.[GE[3]] The islands of Japan are mostly on the so-called "ring of fire" that generally circles the Pacific Ocean, and Honshu is where not just two but three tectonic plates intersect.[GE[4]] Minor tremors can be a daily affair, and as recently as 1923 an earthquake and resulting fires virtually destroyed Tokyo. The most famous of Japan's many volcanoes, Mt. Fuji, last erupted in 1707 but is only dormant now, not dead.

This arc of islands spans almost exactly the same 30–45° of north latitude as the eastern coast of the United States, from south Georgia up to New England.[GE[5]] Japan has, correspondingly, roughly the same climate as the east coast of the U.S., except that temperature extremes in summer and winter are moderated somewhat by surrounding ocean, and for the same reason it's a bit wetter. But conditions are similar enough so that Japanese vegetation, domesticated and wild, tends to thrive in the eastern U.S.A. There are more acres of the southeastern U.S. under wild Japanese honeysuckle, for example, than even under Chinese kudzu or English privet hedge. On the plus side, Japanese magnolia, cherry trees, mimosa, chrysanthemums, and in fact a whole range of Japanese flowering plants thrive here, brightening gardens and lawns.

To continue the parallels in climate, the East Asian typhoon that often batters Japan is nothing but a hurricane occurring in the western Pacific Ocean (the word *typhoon* comes from the Chinese *tai feng*, "great wind"), in that same June 1 to December 1 season, both peaking in September. Even the indigo-blue Gulf Stream that shoots up between Cuba and Florida and grazes the Outer Banks of North Carolina has its parallel in the *Kuroshio*, or Black Stream, that drives up along Kyushu and Shikoku; Japanese bill fishermen seek it out with the same enthusiasm Ernest Hemingway had for the Gulf Stream.

Tokaido and *Nakasendo*

For most of the last thousand years the key transportation corridor in all Japan was from the old imperial capital Kyoto to the newer eastern frontier military capitals—which since around 1600 has meant Edo, today's Tokyo. A rectangle that includes the wanderings of the main roads that connect them, and that extends from

---

1. First open the "East Asia II.kmz" file. Google Earth Layer 1 is a Placemark titled "Japan's relationship with Asia." As with preceding chapters, turn the layer on by clicking in box at left; then "fly" to pre-set view by double-clicking on the Pushpin icon; then single-click on blue layer title to pop open text. To close text, click anywhere on screen away from the text to clear the screen for the next layer.

2. GE Layer 2 is a Placemark titled "the 4 main islands."

3. GE Layer 3 is a Placemark titled "the Inland Sea," framing a view of same. The transliteration of the Japanese is "Seto Naikai," which should show in blue print.

4. GE Layer 4 frames a view to show the three main tectonic plates; just turn on the Volcanoes layer (under the basic Gallery layer in Google Earth) to see the symbols for active volcanoes. Where they form lines almost always indicates the meeting of tectonic plates. It may take a few seconds for all the volcano symbols to materialize. When through, turn the Volcanoes layer off and collapse Gallery folder.

5. GE Layer 5 shows the four main islands of Japan superimposed on the eastern coast of the U.S., to same size scale and correct for latitude. It might be interesting for U.S. citizens to find where their particular latitude runs through Japan. Positioning the cursor over your hometown in Google Earth, you can read your latitude at the bottom of the screen; then spin the globe around to Japan, to the area of Honshu under discussion, and run the cursor up or down until it reads the same latitude.

Narita (Tokyo's International Airport east of the city), to Osaka on a short extension of the Tokaido west of Kyoto, is the corridor we'll use to examine Japanese history and culture.[GE⁶]

The military road connecting the two through the interior mountains was long ago called the *Tosundo*, or East Mountain Road, and later the *Nakasendo*, or Central Mountain Road.[GE⁷] But the major road, and probably the world's busiest road from 1600 to 1850—eclipsing even the Grand Trunk Road in South Asia for those two and half centuries—was the *Tokaido*, the "East Sea Road"[GE⁸] that generally runs along the southern coast. So let's just call this the Tokaido corridor, for short.

Topography and texture of the corridor

If Mt. Fuji, a volcano about 12,300′ feet tall, were tucked somewhere into the Cascade Volcanic Arc of the states of Washington, Oregon, and northern California, it wouldn't attract so much attention. Mts. Ranier and Shasta are each a thousand feet taller; Mt. Adams is about the same size; Mt. Hood is only a thousand feet lower. But Fuji stands without equal in Japan, clearly visible on Tokyo's western horizon and a dominating presence on the eastern section of the Tokaido. The current culture inhabiting northern California has had less than two centuries to admire Mt. Shasta; the Japanese have been gazing at Fuji-san, and writing poetry about it, for over a millenium. More recently, especially given the Japanese love affair with the camera, it may be the single most photographed object in the world.[GE⁹]

Just to the west of Mt. Fuji, generally running up and down the 138th degree of longitude, are the Japanese Alps, rugged mountains that get to almost 10,500′. The Northern Japanese Alps are mostly north of our corridor, but the Southern Japanese Alps, also known as the Akaishi Mountains, run squarely across the middle of our corridor.[GE¹⁰] It is these Japanese Alps and Mt. Fuji that geographically force the Tokaido to hug the south coast here in its middle stretch.

Those are just the highest and most rugged mountains. In terms of terrain generally, however, Japan is so mountainous that perhaps only a fifth of it is flat enough to farm. The few plains are precious commodities and support amazingly dense populations. In aerial photos the mountains generally show as dark green with forest, and the developed flatlands as gray. In our corridor rectangle, at extreme left (west) is the Osaka plain with its northeast extension that runs up to Kyoto, and the smaller Nara plain just east across a couple of small ridges from the Osaka plain. The Nagoya plain is the next most densely populated area. And then, beckoning the Japanese for centuries out on the eastern frontier, the largest farming area of all Japan, the plain of *Kanto* (literally "beyond the barrier"), on which urban Tokyo is steadily encroaching.

Where populated flatlands meet the hillslopes, golf courses show up in aerial views like linked strings of bacilli.[GE¹¹] Tea plantations, similar to those you've already seen in India, China, and Indonesia, seem especially manicured here in Japan.[GE¹²] Rice paddies compete for space with factories.[GE¹³]

---

6. GE Layer 6 is a Polygon, an outlined rectangle in light blue of the corridor we'll use to examine Japanese history and culture. It includes the wanderings of the Nakasendo and the Tokaido.

7. GE Layer 7 is a Path that shows the general route of the Nakasendo as a white line.

8. GE Layer 8 is a Path that shows the route of the Tokaido as a red line. If you turn the Roads layer of Google Earth on and off, on and off, you can see how closely today's road network goes along the same paths. The mountainous geography leaves a modern road builder, even with today's technology, with not many more choices than a road builder had a thousand years ago.

9. GE Layer 9 is a Folder titled "Fuji-san." Double-click on Folder icon, without turning it on, to both "fly" to pre-set view and open whole Folder. Placemarks inside indicate sample Photos icons to explore, many of them views made from the Shinkansen, or bullet train, as it runs along the old Tokaido.

10. GE Layer 10 is a Folder titled "Japanese Alps" with several Placemarks inside, each indicating an interesting Photos icon either in the Akaishi Mountains or the smaller Kiso Mountains just to their west.

11. GE Layer 11 is a Placemark framing a view of several such golf courses.

12. GE Layer 12 is a Placemark referencing a Panoramio icon titled "Chá" that shows such a tea plantation.

13. GE Layer 13 is a Placemark referencing a Panoramio icon titled "kurasawa tanada"; it has a view of small, terraced rice paddies being prepared for planting.

Japan's incredibly long and indented coastline has waterfront derricks and oil refineries, sand beaches and headlands, geometric blocks of land reclaimed from the ocean and remnant coastal swamps, and an amazing collection of futuristic bridges across coastal rivers and connecting mainland with islands. It really makes you think about Japan's relationship with the sea.[GE14]

Finally on our corridor are the great cities, from the flashy urban canyons of Osaka[GE15] and Tokyo[GE16] to the green, temple-strewn hills surrounding Kyoto.[GE17]

Many of the most important events in modern Japanese history played out along this Tokaido-Nakasendo corridor.

Samples of folklore and legend from our corridor

There are some wonderful folktales and legends that come from our corridor, particularly on or close to the Tokaido. One of the most famous is *"Hagoromo,"* or "The Feathered Robe." It is set on the Miho Hook of Suruga Bay, a curling spit of black volcanic sand where the pines (at least used to) grow close to the sea. It still offers what many have called the perfect view of Mt. Fuji, looking over ocean to foothills to the beautiful volcano beyond.[GE18] In this folktale, to be brief, a fisherman found a beautiful feathered robe hanging in a tree by the beach. An equally beautiful woman—an angel from the Palace of the Moon, some versions say—came to claim it, saying that without it she could not fly back home. The fisherman refused to part with the robe until she danced a heavenly dance for him. By one account as she danced she rose into the sky and disappeared; by another she married the fisherman, they had a child, and then she reclaimed the robe and flew off.

Another story every Japanese person will know, something between a legend and a folktale, is that of *Kintaro*, which translates "Golden Boy." It has a little of the flavor of the Pecos Bill folktale in America, or the Mowgli of Kipling's *Jungle Tales*, in that it features a lost baby boy raised by animals, able to talk to them, eventually master of all of their physical skills of running, swimming, and climbing, and then reintroduced into normal human society with these special gifts. Kintaro was supposedly raised on Mt. Kintoki, one of the Hakone mountains near where the Tokaido crosses the neck of the Izu peninsula as it leaves the Kanto Plain of today's Tokyo.[GE19] He was supposed to have lived about a thousand years ago. He was healthy and strong, and is always pictured with a reddish complexion. The famous clan leader Minamoto Yorimitsu (more on the famous Minamoto family later), going through a mountain pass in the Hakone Mountains on his way from the eastern lands back to his home in Kyoto, supposedly encountered Kintaro here and recruited him to be one of his four closest retainers. On "Boy's Day" *matsuri* (festival) in Japan, the fifth day of the fifth month ("Girl's Day" is the third day of the third month; there's a sort of East Asian fascination with double-numbered months and days) it is still customary in Japan to put a Kintaro doll into a newborn boy's bedroom. His strength and gentleness are thereby held up as a role model.

In Japanese folklore there are animal shape-changers—foxes and badgers among them. Foxes were connected in the Shinto religion with the fertility of rice, but they could also be evil trickster figures who had the power to lead people astray in the woods and cause other kinds of harm. Folklorists in general recognize some

---

14. GE Layer 14 is a Folder titled "Coastal Views" with several Placemarks inside referencing representative views.

15. GE Layer 15 is a Folder titled "Osaka views" with several Placemarks inside.

16. GE Layer 16 is a similar Folder titled "Tokyo views."

17. GE Layer 17 is a similar Folder title "Kyoto views."

18. GE Layer 18 is a Placemark framing a view of Miho Hook. There is a wonderful artistic picturing of this place from the early 1830s, pictured in #18 of "53 Stages of the Tokaido," Ejiri, in woodblock print artist Hiroshige's Hoeido series— see website following: http://www.dartmouth.edu/~ukiyoe/tokaido/hoeido/stations/19.html. Also click on Panoramio icon under pointer for a photograph framed much like this Google Earth view.

19. GE Layer 19 is a Placemark entitled "Kintoki-yama." If you go under the basic "Places of Interest" layer in Google Earth, and turn on the "Geographic Features" layer under that, mountains and lakes will be labeled. Notice that Kintoki Mt. is the northern wall of an ancient caldera, and the caldera itself holds Lake Hakone and Hakone Mountain, a secondary volcanic cone in the center of the caldera. Exploring some of the Photos icons near the summit of Mt. Hakone will yield pictures of smoking fumaroles, proof of its active volcanic nature.

deep-seated cultural or psychological needs met by these folktales—perhaps preservation of the environment by those who make wasteful use of it; perhaps warnings about becoming so individualistic and "wild" that you break important ties with the rest of human society. In living memory people in rural Japan, seeing a fox that might be a shape-changer, would wet their finger in their mouth and draw a little X on their forehead to make them resistant to its evil magic—the way many people in the U.S. are still reluctant to cross the path taken by a black cat.

In this regard, an old article in the *Journal of American Folklore* called "Japanese Folk Beliefs and Practices, Tule Lake, California," might be of passing interest.[2] The Tule Lake Segregation Center (in northern California just a couple of miles from the Oregon line), was the site of one of the best known concentration camps where ethnic Japanese were interned during World War II. Some 18,000 people were kept there behind barbed wire from 1942–1946.[GE20] The author of the article was the "community analyst" of the center, and his article talks about the revival of long dormant folklore elements in this community under the stress of concentration camp living. The first section of his paper is on *hidama*, literally a fireball, and supposedly the spiritual form taken on by wasted rice. If you saw one, it was supposed to mean bad luck and even death for you or someone near you. This kind of folklore apparently had been long forgotten by the *Issei* (Japanese born, generally the older parents and grandparents in the camps) and presumably had never been learned by the *Nisei* (American born, younger generations). But in the camp lots and lots of these fireballs were reported. There were also fast-flying rumors about people possessed by foxes, and sightings of badgers that were trying to bewitch people. Just four years later this same community analyst interviewed people who had been in the camp. Some made light of it like this: "Oh, those fox and badger stories back in the Center; well, people used to believe a lot of things in that Center they never believed before and haven't believed since!" And some of those who had reported sightings of hidama, or shape-changing foxes or badgers, had no recollection of it at all. The other major category of supernatural beliefs that flourished in the Tule Lake Center had to do with Japanese swordsmen, who in the depth of their discipline could supposedly become invisible, or transport themselves faster or farther than simple human muscles could explain. Part of the attraction of this was in talking about the powerful aspects of your own culture, when you were shunned and put in concentration camps just for being part of a given ethnic group. But part of it was whatever role that folklore has in giving life meaning in difficult times.

Archaeology and prehistory

The first signs of settled village life in Japan came around 10,000 BC, in a culture called *Jomon* ("cord-marked") because of its pottery style. It is some of the earliest pottery in the world, only fitting for a country with such a brilliant ceramics culture in historic times.[3]

Between 300 BC and AD 300 the pottery style changed dramatically into a style called *Yayoi*. Along with this you had metals being worked; a good many bronze mirrors, bells, and spearheads have been recovered. Perhaps the most important change of all was that in Yayoi rice culture moved into Japan—indirectly from China, directly by way of Korea. On our corridor there is a good Yayoi site called Toro, in today's downtown Shizuoka (a coastal city on the Tokaido).[GE21] It had raised wooden granaries, and houses with semi-sunken, oval foundations. The conical thatched roofs came right down to the ground, as you can see in reconstructions. When written history picked up a thousand years after the appearance of Yayoi cultures, the Japanese were in the process of pushing an aboriginal people called *Ainu* southwest to northeast across Honshu. Today's few remaining Ainu—on reservations up in Hokkaido—may be a remnant of the Yayoi culture.

The last level of Japanese pre-history (if you don't count some vague Chinese records as history) is the *Kofun* ("old tombs") period. The Nara-Kyoto-Osaka plains at the eastern end of the Inland Sea have dozens if

---

20. GE Layer 20 is a Placemark referencing the Tule Lake camp. Click on two Panoramio icons under pointer titled "Tule Lake Relocation Buildings" and "Tule Lake War Relocation Center" for photos of remaining buildings.

21. GE Layer 21 is a Placemark referencing the *Toro* archaeological site. Excavated oval house sites show up clearly in this close-up aerial view of a site in Shizuoka. Some of the nearby Photos icons show reconstructions of the original Yayoi culture dwellings.

not hundreds of these so-called "keyhole tombs." The most impressive of them is the Nintoku tomb, a half mile long, over a third of a mile wide, and with a central burial mound some 400′ high.[GE22] It is named after the semi-legendary Emperor Nintoku who supposedly lived in the AD 300s, though the tomb itself seems to date from the early 400s. Such moated tombs have a square front and a rounded back, and huge mounds over great stone burial chambers. Although the history of this period is shadowy, it obviously took considerable social organization to achieve one such monument, much less this whole array of them.[GE23] Good Chinese records by the year 552 (when China was beginning to pull itself back together, soon to be the Sui-Tang dynasty) describe a dominant Yamato clan with a power base in central Honshu, whose divine descent was attested by the *Shinto* religion.

Shinto and the Ise Shrines

Shinto translates "the Way of the Gods" (who are called *kami* or *gami*). These countless ancestral or nature spirits that could hopefully be enticed, with offerings, to places of unusual spiritual feeling such as waterfalls, tall rocks, sites of spectacular views of mountains or sea, even to a beach where sharks were plentiful. Temple buildings were not often necessary, but most shrines had wooden "gateways" made of two pillars and a cross-beam (often decurved), called *torii*.[GE24]

The Ise Shrines, chief of all the Shinto shrines of Japan, may be the most famous religious structures in all Japan.[GE25] They are across the neck of the Kii (or Nara) peninsula from the keyhole tombs on the Osaka and Nara plains. At each of the Inner and Outer Shrines, one of the paired main buildings at each site is less than twenty years old, and the other is less than forty, but in a way these four are the oldest buildings in Japan. Every twenty years the older one of each pair is torn down and rebuilt exactly according to an ancient religious blueprint. Quadruple walls, each in a different style, emphatically separate these sacred zones from the everyday world outside.

When the first Japanese chronicles were written in the 700s, the Ise shrines were already old. The Inner Shrine was dedicated to the Sun Goddess Amaterasu and the outer shrine to the God of Rice. The whole complex was associated with the ancestry of the imperial family. Twin primeval deities, Izanami and Izanagi,[GE26] were believed to have given birth to the Sun Goddess, to whom the Yamato rulers traced their lineage (in much the same way Anglo-Saxon royal families in England at this same time traced their lineage to Odin). For centuries, then, only members of the imperial family could enter the Inner Shrine. Later in feudal times when the Shoguns took real power away from the Emperors, imperial control over the shrines relaxed and they became a place of popular pilgrimage for common people. Pilgrims to Ise were common on the Tokaido in those days, and in later centuries. Oliver Statler in his *Japanese Inn* includes an early nineteenth-century print by Hiroshige showing three girls doing "the Ise dance" in a section on the pilgrimage to Ise.[4]

The Ise Shrines are somewhat south of the Tokaido proper, but perhaps the second most important of all Shinto sites is the Atsuta Shrine in Nagoya, right on the Tokaido. It holds the "Kusanagi sacred sword," one of

---

22. GE Layer 22 is a Placemark framing a view of the Nintoku tomb; pointer references a Panoramio icon titled "mormint antic japonez," an aerial photograph. Some of the Photos icon at bottom have photographs showing how high the central hill of the tomb is.

23. GE Layer 23 is a Placemark framing a view of more kofun near the Nintoku tomb. But if you set off east in Google Earth, across the Osaka plain and into the Nara plain at an apparent elevation of 10,000′ or so, dozens and dozens will come into view.

24. GE Layer 24 is a Placemark titled "Typical Shinto torii gateway," showing one standing in the shallow water of Lake Biwa.

25. GE Layer 25 is a Folder titled "The Ise shrines." Placemarks inside take you to both the Inner Shrine, sacred to the Sun Goddess Amaterasu, and the Outer Shrine, sacred to the God of Rice, or Agriculture. They are 2½ miles apart, and are connected by a pilgrimage trail.

26. GE Layer 26 is a Placemark referencing *Meoto iwa* ("Wedded Rocks"), on the coast near Ise, representing Izanagi and Izanami. Lots of Photos icons to explore. Notice small torii gateway atop larger rock.

the three imperial symbols of Japan, as in "mirror, sword and jewel" (the Inner Shrine at Ise has the mirror; the Imperial Palace in Kyoto has the jewel).[GE²⁷]

With the introduction of Buddhism later, there was some initial friction with Shinto. A compromise was soon worked out, however (the local Shinto gods were asked to bless the foundation of a new Buddhist temple, for example), and Shinto kept quietly alive in the countryside. It would play an interesting role later in Japan's unique form of modern nationalism.

Borrowing from China

In Asia east of the Himalaya mountain knot, there is one huge, central country and many smaller peripheral ones. In the context of East Asia, China's name for itself—*Zhong Guo* or "Middle Kingdom" as we discussed in the last chapter—is no brag, just fact. The Chinese perfected a new style of central administration (the Confucian system) in the Tang Dynasty, from roughly AD 600–900, and were the most civilized county on earth in most of the ways we measure civilization—numbers of books published, reign of law and order, scientific developments, sophistication of arts and crafts, and so on. Japan frankly borrowed all the major elements of its first civilization from China, mainly in those centuries, in a clear attempt to make of itself a faithful though small copy of the Middle Kingdom.

Beginning in the 500s, shiploads of young Japanese men of good family were sent to China to study, often staying from age sixteen well into their forties. When they returned to Japan, of course, they had become all but Chinese in culture. They wore silk and ate with chopsticks. From porcelain cups they drank hot water in which a caffeinated leaf of a certain shrub had been soaked (those countries that learned about it from south China called the beverage some variety of the southern Chinese pronunciation "tee"; those that learned from the north called it some variety of the northern Chinese pronunciation "cha" or "chai"—in Japan it came to be known *sa* or *cha*). They wrote the Chinese language using the Chinese characters, using Chinese brushes on Chinese paper, and signing official documents with a Chinese "chop" or stone block carved with their (Chinese) signature. They brought that uniquely Chinese mixture of Confucianism and Buddhism back with them. They also brought back the Chinese belief that one Emperor should sit at the top of the governmental and religious structure, and that a centralized governmental administration should take care of everything important.

Prince Shotoku Taishi (d. 622) was the key Yamato leader in creating Buddhist religious orders and the building of Buddhist temples. A generation after his death, around 645, came the *Taika*, or "Great Reforms," in which all the land was nationalized under central government control, on the Chinese model. The growing impact of such Chinese beliefs and behaviors on Japan can easily be traced in historical buildings.

Most famous of these is the *Horyuji*, which Prince Shotoku built in the first decade of the 600s, and which was rebuilt after a fire in AD 670. The main hall and the pagoda, sitting side by side, are the two oldest wooden buildings in Japan, maybe in all the world.[GE²⁸] In aerial photos, including the Google Earth image, you can actually see only the top roof of the pagoda, and it seems smaller and less impressive than the neighboring main temple building. Only its shadow gives it away as an impressively tall pagoda. The East Asian pagoda, incidentally, evolved from the dome-shaped reliquaries (called *stupas)* which were originally used in India to house artifacts associated with the Buddha. Each such dome was usually crowned with a futuristic antenna-looking structure. As Buddhism migrated east through China to Japan, the building underneath shrank and the antenna-like structure evolved into upper floors almost the size of the ground floor, and with matching roof styles for the layers of roof. This one at Horyuji is over a hundred feet tall, and its construction is magnificent. To someone interested in Japanese history it says that Buddhism was already very important there before AD 700.

Around 750 another famous Buddhist temple, the *Todaiji* ("Great East Temple"), was built to serve as the center of a network of Buddhist monasteries and nunneries. It was enormous—even today it is the largest

---

27. GE Layer 27 is a Placemark referencing the Atsuta Shrine in greater Nagoya city. It is generally considered the second holiest site of the Shinto religion, the supposed site of the sacred sword, as in "mirror, sword & jewel."

28. GE Layer 28 is a Placemark titled "Horyuji." This Horyu Temple complex has a large temple at right, and the smaller but taller (as you can see from its shadow) pagoda at left. Click on the Panoramio icon beneath pointer, titled "Horyuji Temple," for photograph that includes both buildings. The temple was built in AD 601; it burned and was rebuilt in 670.

wooden building in the world—because it was built to house an enormous statue of a variety of Buddha associated with the sun (as of course was the ruling Yamato clan, not coincidentally). Not much original of either building or statue is left, from wars and fires over more than twelve centuries. But even though it's a bit like the proverbial 100-year-old axe (the head of which had been replaced twice and the handle three times), it is impressive nonetheless. It is just on the east side of the Nara plain, backed up against the hills.[GE29]

So these "returned students" took over the Japanese court, and tried to re-make Japan in the Chinese mold. One of the most interesting survivals of this are the five Chinese-style capitals (each small but faithful models of the north-south grid of the city of Chang-an, capital of China from 200 BC to AD 1200). They were all built in a century-and-a-quarter, from 672 on; each new ruler feeling obliged to build his own.[GE30] Heian, or Heian-kyo—"Tranquility Peace Capital"—the last of these capitals (construction began 794), was fated to be more permanent. Most Americans will know it better by its newer name of Kyoto.

For the next three hundred or so years, then, Japan was ruled by the imperial court of Heian in what is called the Age of Heian. The original intent may have been to become a little China, but the Japanese subtly modified those things they took from China, making of them something authentically Japanese.

One of the most interesting books ever written by a non-Japanese about Japanese culture is by Kurt Singer, a German scholar who lived in Japan between World Wars I and II, when the Japanese and Germans were particularly close politically. In English translation it is called *Mirror, Sword and Jewel: The Geometry of Japanese Life*. In it Singer argues that China is the land of Space, with the full, stately symmetry of its painting and architecture—but Japan is the land of Time, with asymmetry in everything, and the most important arts achieved not in a measured, paced flow of time but in the tension of a waiting, waiting, waiting, then a sudden stroke and release of tension. He suggests that every element of Chinese culture the Japanese borrowed underwent this basic transformation, from the little and mundane (sharp-ended Japanese chopsticks for quick stabbing motions, as opposed to the longer, square-ended Chinese originals) to the spiritual (the development of the Zen Buddhism of Japan out of the meditative Buddhism that China got from India). The argument may be extreme, but it leaves a reader with a lasting sense that even though most elements of modern Japanese culture were borrowed, the resulting culture may be no less uniquely Japanese. Whatever the reason, the last shipload of Japanese students sent to learn from China was in AD 838. Tang Dynasty China was in decline by this point and not as attractive as earlier; and the Japanese had created their own cultural fusion of native and borrowed elements that was deeply satisfying.

The imperial Age of Heian

The palace center in Heian proper is today called the Kyoto palace complex. It is closely hemmed in by the city today, as an aerial view shows,[GE31] but has been carefully maintained for centuries as a symbol of one of the great eras of high culture of world history. Many famous temples and shrines, both Buddhist and Shinto, are built into the foothills in a rough ring around the city—products of centuries of imperial rulers living here.

In the Age of Heian, arts and letters of great sophistication flourished at the court of Heian. Some literary historians call *The Tale of Prince Genji*, the story of a Kyoto courtier, sportsman, and lover, written by the Lady

---

29. GE Layer 29 is a Folder titled "Daibutsu at Todaiji." Three Placemarks are included, one framing a general view of the site (and two referencing Panoramio icons with good photos of (a) the whole building, and (b) the great Buddha statue, or "Daibutsu").

30. GE Layer 30 is a Folder titled "Chinese-style capital cities, built 674–794." Turn Borders and Labels off to see location of all five on plains: Naniwa is on the Osaka Plain; Asuka/Fujiwara and Heijo are on the Nara Plain; and Nagaoka and Heian/Kyoto are on the Kyoto Plain. This map adapted from map on p. 72 of Colcutt et al., *Cultural Atlas of Japan*.

31. GE Layer 31 is a Placemark framing a view of the center of modern Kyoto. The two green spaces in this view are, bottom left, Nijo (the castle ordered built in the early 1600s by the Tokugawa shogunate), and top right, the modern Imperial Palace complex (home to the Emperor). In Heian times the original imperial complex was between these two, actually overlapping a bit with the current Nijo (castle) grounds. The architectural features of the modern Imperial Palace, which you can explore through Photos icons there, are probably much like their prototypes of a millennium and more ago. Certainly the north-south grid of streets here in the center of Kyoto dates from the original construction in 794.

Murasaki ("the Lady Purple") the world's oldest novel. Styles of poetry were set that have lasted a thousand years. A tour through most any major art museum in the U.S. or Europe will include something from Heian-era ceramics, paper making, calligraphy, screen decoration, or sculpture.

The power of the imperial family in Heian/Kyoto was slowly eroded, however, as ambitious clans sought to control it. The first challengers were the Fujiwara clan (Fujiwara translates "Wisteria Field," from a place where successful military plans were laid), famous for their manipulation of Emperors. More deadly to imperial power were the clans from both eastern and western Japan, the Taira and the Minamoto, who fought to dominate it, eventually leaving an "Emperor" in name only.

Tales of the Heike

Of the many chronicles from these struggles in early feudal Japan, the best-loved for almost a millennium is the *Heike Monogatari*, or *Tales from the Heike*. They are set in the 1180–85 wars between Minamoto (also known as the Genji) and Taira (the Heike of the title) clans, which the Minamoto eventually won. It's a bit like Froissart's Chronicles from the 100 Years' War between England and France, the sort of high chivalry where Romance meets War. Here is a sample; the Taira have been routed in a battle and survivors are fleeing, and the Minamoto warrior Kumagai engages a richly armored Taira warrior on a beach:

> . . . Kumagai at once engaged him in mortal combat. Quickly hurling him to the ground, he sprang upon him and tore off his helmet to cut off his head, when he beheld the face of a youth of sixteen or seventeen, delicately powdered and with blackened teeth [a custom of the court at Heian], just about the age of his own son, and with features of great beauty. "Who are you?" he inquired; "Tell me your name, for I would spare your life." "Nay, first say who you are"; replied the young man. "I am Kumagai Jirō Naozane of Musashi, a person of no particular importance." "Then you have made a good capture"; said the youth. "Take my head and show it to some of my side and they will tell you who I am."

> "Though he is one of their leaders," mused Kumagai, "if I slay him it will not turn defeat into victory, and if I spare him, it will not turn victory into defeat. When my son Kojirō was but slightly wounded at Ichi-no-tame, did it not make my heart bleed? How pitiful then to put this youth to death." And so he was about to set him free, when, looking behind him, he saw Doi and Kajiwara coming up with fifty horsemen. "Alas! look there," he exclaimed, the tears running down his face, "though I would spare your life, the whole countryside swarms with our men, and you cannot escape them. If you must die, let it be by my hand, and I will see that prayers are said for your rebirth in bliss." "Indeed it must be," said the young warrior, "so take my head at once."[5]

And Kumagai, though with sadness, did so, and, when stripping the armor off the body, found a flute—the music of which he had heard from outside the enemy walls that very morning.

But high chivalry or not, the toughened Minamoto armies from the eastern frontier region thoroughly extinguished the more cultured Taira clan.

The Kamakura Shogunate

The 1185 winner-take-all of these wars was Minamoto Yoritomo. He left the Emperor in his palace in Heian/Kyoto, but only as a puppet through which to rule. For himself he kept the title *Seii-Tai-Shogun*—"Barbarian-Subduing Generalissimo"—a title which in practice meant chief of armies on the eastern frontier. His headquarters, over 200 miles east of Kyoto at the coastal town of Kamakura, now became the real power center of Japan.[GE32] So began the Kamakura Shogunate, that lasted a century and a half. Other shogunates followed, and power oscillated back and forth between Kyoto and the east. Instead of following them one by one, however, it might be more interesting to take a general look at the feudalism that was developing.

---

32. GE Layer 32 is a Folder titled "Kamakura sites"; it includes Placemarks referencing the Hachiman Shrine and the Great Buddha of Kamakura.

Japanese feudalism compared with European feudalism

Some scholars (Marxists, for example) use "feudalism" very broadly to mean any pre-modern culture, but feudalism strictly defined really only happened two places, two times in all of world history. One was in central and western Europe from around the ninth to the eleventh centuries, and one was in Japan from the eleventh to the sixteenth centuries (or including Tokugawa's centralized feudalism, even down to the mid-nineteenth century). Since we in the West have some general familiarity with western feudalism—dukes and duchies, jousting knights, humble peasants—exploring this parallel offers some immediate insights into Japan. It is just an introductory device, unfortunately: the deeper you go into both histories, the more simplistic the parallel drawn below will seem.

Despite the fact that Japanese feudalism seems to pick up in time where western feudalism leaves off, there is no direct connection. Instead each of them seems to grow out of the same rare set of conditions, independently arrived at. Feudalism is historically rare because it is a hybrid between two opposing forces: (a) a general belief (the "norm") that there should be one centralized government run by an Emperor; and (b) the fact that real power is local, even tribal. In that state of tension between belief and practice, political power gets stretched out between Emperor and layers of feudal retainers below him, in a system of infeudation. This is where the client owes some loyalty, but not total, to his superior, and the superior owes some protection, but not total, to his feudatory—and so on down to the level of professional fighting men.

In Europe the "normative" belief in one central government came from the memory of the late, lamented Roman Empire; but in practice power was very local, in the hands of the Germanic tribal chiefs. Charlemagne had himself crowned "Roman Emperor" on Christmas Day of the year 800, for example, but scholars have joked that he was just an illiterate German tribal chief who pretended to be both "Roman" and "emperor." Because of these opposed beliefs and facts, the levels at which power resided were stretched out, like taffy. At the top sat the Emperor, supposedly ruler of all the world that counted. Below him were kings, who owed him some loyalty and who deserved from him some protection. In fact sometimes in this reborn "Roman Empire" there were kings stronger than the Emperor. The kings for their part were made stronger or weaker as they were served by more or less dukes, and the dukes—each of which owned a duchy, the territorial building block of the age—were made stronger or weaker as they could afford more or less armored knights. Knights, about 5 percent of European society in the feudal age, were the basic building block of society, the lowest rank of aristocracy. The other 95 percent of people (leaving aside such groups as churchmen, which don't fit our mold very well) were peasant farmers. They had no civil rights to speak of, being about as much property as pigs or cattle.

In Japan the belief in one central imperial government came from the brilliant model of Tang Dynasty China; but in practice every Japanese valley was controlled by its own clan, or *uji*. This similar opposition between belief and fact stretched the levels of power out in Japan, too. At the top, in Kyoto, sat an Emperor who supposedly ruled all of the world that really mattered, a good parallel for the often weak Emperor in feudal Europe. Controlling the Japanese emperor from behind the stage was a powerful frontier military figure called the Shogun, short for "Barbarian-subduing Generalissimo." This is admittedly not a very good parallel for European kings, but as we go down the levels of feudal power, the parallels pick up again. In Japan there were mid-level feudal lords called *daimyo*—at one point, for example, there were 265 of these—each of whom controlled a territory called a *han*. A Japanese daimyo and his han are fair parallels for a European duke and his duchy. And the daimyo was served by armored knights called *samurai*, perhaps 6 percent of the population of Japan, almost exactly the same proportion of society and playing the same role as the knights in Europe. In both societies these were professional fighting men, trained in the expensive weaponry of their day from childhood up. Underneath the samurai were the other 94 percent of the population (leaving aside the Shinto and Buddhist priests, who don't fit our mold very well), the peasants, who had no more civil rights to speak of than did European peasants under feudalism. If a peasant offended a samurai, the samurai could pull his sword and *kirisute*—"cut and leave"—and it was legal. That's roughly the way it worked in Europe, too—the feudal ages get way too good a press in romantic novels.

Here then is a table summing up this argument of European and Japanese feudal parallels:

	Europe 9th–11th c.	Japan 11th–19th c.
Belief in centralized Empire:	memory of Rome	model of China
	vs.	vs.
Practice of local, tribal control:	German tribal power	Uji (clan) power
Social class:	Emperor	Emperor
	Kings	(Shogun)
	Dukes	Daimyo
	Knights (5%)	Samurai (6%)
	Peasants (95%)	Peasants (94%)

To finish the parallel, let us talk about the ethic of each age, an aristocratic code of honor produced by the upper-classes of each civilization, in the context of their dominant religion. In Europe it was of course *chivalry*. The word comes from cheval-erie, *cheval* being the French (and late Latin) word for horse. "Horsery," it is literally—for the expensive horse and armor every knight had to have, for the life-long training in arms he got. It was roughly one-half the code of arms of a professional military figure, and one-half a kind of selectively chosen Christianity: none of that "turn the other cheek" stuff, but a noble quest for the Holy Grail, the chalice Jesus drank from at the Last Supper; the rescuing of damsels (upper-class only, mind you) from dragons, and so on. And so you get from this a French chevalier, an English cavalier, a Spanish caballero, etc., and their elevated code of honor, which applied to women and children of the aristocracy as well.

In feudal Japan the ethic of the age was *bushido*. *Bushi* means warrior, but *-do* we ought to talk about a little. The average American will already know some Japanese "*-do*" words, many from the martial arts: *judo*, *akido*, *taekwando* (well, this last one is Korean instead of Japanese, but an exact parallel for this "*-do*" concept in Japan). Karate, for example, is formally speaking "*ka ra te do*," where the *ka ra te* means open-handed method of defense. A typical American signs up for karate lessons to learn some mayhem, or to keep from having sand kicked in his/her face on the beach, and is apt to be surprised by the reverence shown to the *dojo* and all the spiritual ceremony involved—because we generally don't know what that "*-do*" suffix means.

There are many more "*-do*" words in Japan that have become popular with small groups of Americans. *Kendo*, for example, is the Japanese practice of fighting with tough bamboo substitutes for swords. It's a competitive sport played between many Japanese universities today, seven on a team, matching them one to one the way we match tennis teams. It translates in a dictionary as "fencing," and it wasn't always just a college sport. "*Ken*" indeed means sword, but "fencing" is a poor translation because it doesn't include the "*-do*." A particularly Japanese form of meditation based on use of bow and arrow is called *kyudo*, where "kyu" is bow; but "archery" is not a good translation. Flower arranging has been elevated by the Japanese to the level of meditation, too; the informal name is *ikebana*, but the more formal name is *kado*, with "ka" meaning flower. Tea drinking has undergone the same elevation. Often called "tea ceremony" in English, that at least is a little closer to the *sado* or *chado* of the Japanese original, though it still doesn't quite catch the meaning of "*-do*."

So what is this "*-do*" so crucial to understanding these Japanese meditations? It is a Japanese mispronunciation of the Chinese "*tao*" (pronounced "dow" as in Dow Jones because of that strange Wade-Giles transliteration system we looked at in the first of the China chapter), meaning not a literal road such as the Tokaido, but the Way, a spiritual Path or Road. It might translate "a path to spiritual enlightenment," and it is mainly associated with Zen, a uniquely Japanese development of Buddhism.

Buddhism originated in Nepal and northern India around 600 BC, as we've seen, when the original "buddha," or "enlightened one," found his middle path enlightenment while sitting in meditation. In Sanskrit such meditation is called *dhyana*. From India Buddhism radiated into Southeast Asia, and also into East Asia. The closest the Chinese could come to pronouncing *dhyana* was *chan*, and when the Japanese borrowed this meditative Buddhism from the Chinese, the closest they could come to pronouncing *chan* was *zen*.

Scholars are a bit puzzled as to how to classify Zen Buddhism; is it a religion or not? It has temples and priests, and every temple has a *zazen* room for disciples to sit in meditation and try to achieve whatever enlightenment it is that the religion aims to achieve. But in Zen there are no spiritual forces outside the worshipper, no heaven or hell, not even any ethics. You could conceivably use Zen to become the world's greatest humanitarian or the world's greatest assassin. But in addition to meditation as the main path to enlightenment, Zen also offers activities, but activities raised to the level of meditation to achieve that same enlightenment. All of them, of course, end in "-*do*." Look again at karate-do, for example: it appears in this light as to so thoroughly immerse yourself in this open-handed-defense training that it becomes a spiritual meditation leading to that religious enlightenment. And so on with judo, akido, kendo, kyudo, kado, sado . . . .

Bushido, now, although today usually translated weakly as "the way of the warrior," should appear as the Japanese analogue of European chivalry—about one-half the code of arms of a professional military caste trained in this from childhood on, and about one-half a carefully selected and developed Buddhism. Zen Buddhism and the samurai caste, it might be argued, invented each other during the slow collapse of the Heian Empire. Pride and honor are the cardinal virtues of aristocracies, said Aristotle. A dishonored samurai man was supposed to commit a ritualized suicide called *seppuku*, or more popularly, *harakiri*, by slitting the abdomen. A dishonored woman of this samurai caste was to cut her jugular vein.

Zen in the Art of Archery

Today perhaps no more than 5 percent of Japanese are serious Zen Buddhists, but it looms large in history and has fascinated westerners since Japan was pried open in 1854. One of the best introductions to it is a little book called *Zen in the Art of Archery*. It was written by another German scholar, Eugen Herrigel, who taught at the University of Tokyo in those same 1930s. As a philosopher, he had always wanted to delve into an eastern religion, but had been unable to achieve any basic understanding on his own. A fellow professor introduced him to a Zen archery teacher (a *kyudo* master), who reluctantly took him as pupil (reluctantly because Herrigel was a westerner with no instinctive feel for these things). Herrigel assumed he would do well in archery because he was a rifle expert who knew about sighting, windage, smooth loosing of the shot, etc. It turned out that such technical expertise only got in his way.

To explain a bit, the Japanese folk bow is made of laminated layers of bamboo, about an inch thick at the grip. It is perhaps the world's only asymmetrical bow, in that the length of the bow above the grip is twice the length of the length of bow below the grip—perhaps for ease in shooting from horseback. Whereas we in the west put the arrow on the left side of a vertically held bow; in Japan it's on the right. The thumb of the right hand actually locks around the bowstring, and in turn is locked in place by the other fingers closed over it, and the bow is held over the archer's head before it is drawn. As the bow is drawn, it lowers itself into position, with the archer's right hand somewhere behind the right ear. When the shot is loosed, the bowstring actually follows the arrow around to the right for a bit, and winds up on the target side of the bow (away from the archer). It all may sound cumbersome, but unlike in the west, the Japanese kept their traditional archery alive, and Zen archers are still shooting at dinner-plate-sized targets at eighty steps. The glove for the right hand is made of thick leather, and has a wrinkle at the base of the thumb for holding the bowstring. It is a thousand-year-old "slick release" device: once you start drawing, it's like a cocked gun ready to go off and you'd better be careful where you point it.

At any rate, the Master told Herrigel that he was not to shoot, but to wait and let the "It" shoot, to let the shot "fall by itself." In his frustration at being unable to do so, Herrigel hit upon the technical trick of sliding his right thumb almost out from under his fingers. The shot would then sometimes come unexpectedly. The first time he tried this new trick for the Master, the Master asked him to shoot again. Then the Master took his bow and turned his back, a sign that he had been released from the class.

His Japanese friend interceded for Herrigel with the Master, who agreed to take him back only if he'd try no more technical tricks. The Master encouraged him to begin breath control even before coming to lessons, and to work at controlled breaths for the draw, the hold, and the loose. Then once the Master shouted from across the archery grounds, "That time the 'It' shot," and Herrigel realized there had been a qualitative difference about that particular shot.

Still, when in a discussion with the Master about aiming—the Master claimed he didn't aim—Herrigel impertinently said that perhaps he unconsciously did. The Master gave him a sharp look, and invited him to his home. There they had tea ceremony, and went out to the archery range. It had a half shell over the shooter's platform, wooden walls along the sides of the range, and a half-shell over the target stand. It was night, and the Master stuck a lighted pine taper a few steps in front of the shooter's platform: in the bright glare Herrigel could not see the target stand shelter, much less the target. The Master, in Herrigel's words, "danced" the ceremony and loosed one arrow off into the darkness, and Herrigel heard it hit the target. He loosed a second, and asked Herrigel to retrieve the arrows. When Herrigel found the first arrow dead in the bullseye, splintered by the second arrow the head of which had lodged right beside the first, he carried the whole target back to the Master. With those shots, he said, the Master hit not only the target but me.[6]

"Divine Winds"

In the 1200s the Mongols conquered and militarily reinvigorated China. In 1274 and again in 1281 Khublai Khan (grandson of Genghiz, and now greatest Emperor of the Yuan Dynasty of China) determined to add Japan to his already massive empire. The 1281 marine invasion force in particular was supposedly the largest before World War II's D-Day invasion of Normandy. The Kyoto courtiers were all for surrendering to this massive outside force, but the Shogun and samurai were for fighting them on the beaches. They won, aided both times by timely hurricanes (typhoons) that wrecked the invasion fleets. In Japanese eyes, these storms were divinely inspired by the gods of Japan, and they came to be called *kami kaze*, or "gods' winds." Almost 700 years later, faced with another massive outside invasion force, suicide pilots would adopt the name and hopefully embody the same spirit forces in defense of the homeland.

The feudal wars of the late 1500s

Kurosawa Akira, Japan's most famous modern film-maker, made an enduringly popular black-and-white classic in 1954 called *Seven Samurai* (copied by Hollywood later in *The Magnificent Seven,* with relocation to the American Southwest). It was set in or around the 1570s or 1580s, in a simple village, in the course of those late feudal wars that convulsed all of Japan. Bandits are raiding the countryside with impunity in this era of the breakdown of any central authority, and in a stormy meeting villagers argue what to do. The leader of the war party is a young man whose wife has been kidnapped by the bandits; the leader of the peace party is the father of a beautiful unmarried girl he is trying to protect. On the advice of the oldest man in the village—who had lived through civil wars in his childhood, and had seen a single village left standing because it had hired samurai—the village decides to recruit samurai to defend it. The recruitment itself, which takes place in the closest town of any size, may be the most interesting part of the whole movie, just for its portrayal of the aristocratic samurai. The villagers successfully recruit six real samurai, but the seventh turns out to be a commoner who is just pretending to be samurai (as played by the great character actor Toshiro Mifune). It is still worth seeing, even with white subtitles at times impossible to read on a black and white background. The film is a good reminder that the feudal wars of the last few decades of the 1500s are as enduringly fascinating to the Japanese as the Civil War is to Americans.

In brief overview, in about forty years' time three great military leaders—Oda Nobunaga, Hideyoshi, and Tokugawa Ieyasu—unified what had been an increasingly fragmented feudal Japan, and reorganized it into what some have called "centralized" feudalism. One reason for this burst of activity was the introduction into Japan of western firearms (the first Portuguese landed in Japan in 1543) and western ideas of fortification, strategy, and tactics; all three of these leaders were in the forefront in adopting this new western military technology.

Oda Nobunaga was an undoubted military genius. From the Oda clan base, between today's Nagoya and Kyoto, he tenaciously and ruthlessly subjugated surrounding domains, even independent monasteries. For example, he besieged a militant order of Buddhist monks in their fort in Osaka for ten years, from 1570–1580, and then razed the whole fort. Nobunaga built the first of a new generation of super-castles at Azuchi, on the plain southeast of Lake Biwa near the junction of the Tokaido and Nakasendo—obviously to control access to nearby Kyoto.[GE33] By 1582 he had united all of central Honshu,[GE34] and was well on his way to unifying all Japan.

His assassination in 1582 by one of his own generals opened the door for rule by another of his generals, Hideyoshi, a commoner of such low origins that he initially had no family name. Ironically, it was Hideyoshi who did more to freeze social mobility than any other Japanese ruler, by declaring who was and who was not samurai. This is when the famous "sword hunt" was launched to gather up the weapons from all those who were not now officially designated samurai. On the ruins of the fort in Osaka he built one of the most magnificent castles in all Japan (which of course had to be bigger and better in all respects than the show castle of his predecessor at Azuchi).[GE35]. By 1587 he had conquered all his enemies in western Japan, including the main islands of Shikoku and Kyushu. In 1590 at the battle of Odawara[GE36] he destroyed his last strong enemy in the east, the Hojo out in the Kanto plain. This freed him up, in 1592, to try his long-cherished plan of invading Korea, and ultimately China. His armies made it as far as Seoul, but Ming Chinese and local Korean forces quickly drove him out. He tried again in 1597, with no more success. When Hideyoshi died in 1598 he left a five-year-old son whose fate was in the hands of a five-man Council of Regents made up of key daimyo. One of them was Tokugawa Ieyasu, probably the single most important name in all of Japanese history.

Statler's *Japanese Inn*

To break the narrative just a minute, one reason this chapter was interesting for the author to write is that this Tokaido corridor was introduced to him long ago by Oliver Statler's 1961 book, *Japanese Inn*.[7] As a U.S. soldier in the occupation army in Japan in 1946, Statler fell in love with a particular Japanese inn, the *Minaguchi-ya*. The little inn fronted right on the Tokaido itself, in the town of Okitsu on Suruga Bay.[GE37] In the book itself Statler presents Japanese history as it came up and down the Tokaido, in front of and sometimes into the Minaguchi-ya, beginning with a 1569 battle on the nearby Okitsu river in those wars of the last half of the 1500s. The last events described in the book happen in 1957, when the Emperor and Empress stopped at the Minaguchi-ya to spend the night and have dinner (actual menu included in the book). Statler is an engaging writer, with a great eye for personal detail and individual characteristics. He allowed himself a little fictional leeway, as when he invented dialogue between some of his characters. But as a long-time student of and also a great admirer of Japanese culture, he had a gift for letting an American reader see events more through Japanese eyes. This includes his sensitive take on the life of Tokugawa Ieyasu, from which some of the material below is taken.

---

33. GE Layer 33 is a Placemark referencing the general location of Azuchi Castle. Most of the Photos icons underneath the pointer are views of the ruins of Azuchi Castle. Begin with line of icons at bottom; as you work up them from top to bottom, you generally ascend the castle steps. For a most interesting Japanese site—good for its pictures even if you don't read a word of Japanese—open the Gallery layer in your basic Layers at left, scroll down and turn on the "Google Earth Community" layer, and a blue letter "i" will appear in the middle of the Photos icons. Click on it to open the site, then click on blue links until you get to the pictures part.

34. GE Layer 34 is a Polygon representing in dark red the area of Japan controlled by Oda Nobunaga at his death in 1582; map adapted from *Cultural Atlas of Japan*.

35. GE Layer 35 is a Placemark referencing Osaka Castle; it is a modern reconstruction, but authentic-looking and as impressive as the original from the outside. Obviously a favorite subject of photographers, with all the Photos icons from which to choose.

36. GE Layer 36 is a Placemark referencing the ruins of Ishigakiyama Castle. This was the stone fort "built overnight" by Hideyoshi in the hills above Odawara, controlling the Tokaido which he could use to supply his armies.

37. GE Layer 37 is a Placemark referencing modern Okitsu. The Seikenji (temple) complex is still visible, but Oliver Statler's Minaguchiya, unfortunately, no longer functions as an inn. A woodblock print view from the 1830s you'll see later shows the village in the distance clustered near the water, and then on the hillside above it, the roofs of Seikenji.

Tokugawa Ieyasu

He was born in 1543, the year the first Europeans arrived in Japan. His original name (Japanese historical figures often cycle through an amazing variety of names during their lifetimes) was Matsudaira Takechiyo. He was the son of a minor daimyo, of the Matsudaira clan whose home base was the castle in Okazaki.[GE38] The father, as head of a small clan vulnerable in the shifting wars of the century, allied with a more powerful clan, the Imagawa. One price he paid for this was to agree to send his son, age six, as a hostage to Imagawa clan headquarters at Sumpu Castle (in today's Shizuoka). But the Oda clan, blood enemies of the Imagawa clan, heard about it, and kidnapped the boy on his journey. He spent from age six to nine as a captive in the Mansho-ji, a temple complex in Nagoya. Then hostage swaps were arranged so that at age nine he went, as originally planned, to Sumpu castle[GE39], and he was in and around that Suruga Bay area until he was fifteen. Here as a hostage, but an aristocratic hostage, he was well treated and well educated. The old abbot of a Buddhist temple there was also the abbot of Seiken-ji, the Buddhist religious complex in Okitsu. He brought the young man there to study—both Buddhism and military affairs, since the abbot was one of those military monks of the times and who in fact had been a successful general for the Imagawa clan. Here the Matsudaira boy first fell in love with falconry, which in feudal Japan as in feudal Europe was a sport mainly reserved for aristocrats. Here in his mid-teens he first commanded military units under the Imagawa banner.

In 1560 the Imagawa daimyo was killed in a war with the rising Oda Nobunaga. Matsudaira Takechiyo took that opportunity to leave Sumpu and go back to his own small domain, which was now his to run because his father had died. He was seventeen years old. By age twenty-five he had wrested much of the Suruga Bay area away from its current clan leaders, and by 1870, still only twenty-seven years old, he moved his capital to Hamamatsu.[GE40] The Imagawa clan was dissolving under the inept leadership of its newest head, and Tokugawa Ieyasu (as he styled himself after 1566) was picking up the pieces. Now a rising, powerful daimyo, he controlled everything from his old hometown of Okazaki to the Hakone barrier in the mountain passes that led over into the Kanto plain.[GE41] But Oda Nobunaga and then Hideyoshi in central and western Japan had become stronger still, and soon Tokugawa Ieyasu moved his capital a bit farther east—further away from Hideyoshi's power base in Osaka—to that same Sumpu castle where he had lived as a hostage as a young man.

By 1589, when Hideyoshi had finished his conquests of Shikoku and Kyushu, there were only two other independent daimyo in all Japan: Tokugawa, his ally, whose domain was just east of Hideyoshi's, and the Hojo just east of that in the Kanto plain. In 1590 Tokugawa Ieyasu joined Hideyoshi in a successful war on the Hojo, culminating in the battle of Odawara mentioned earlier. The next year or so may have been the most dangerous time in Tokugawa Ieyasu's life, because if Hideyoshi had forced an all-out war between them, Hideyoshi had more resources than Tokugawa did. But Hideyoshi wanted to pursue his dream of conquering China, so he offered Tokugawa Ieyasu a deal: if Tokugawa Ieyasu would give Hideyoshi all of his current domain, Hideyoshi would support his takeover of the old Hojo domains of the Kanto plain, a larger and more productive area. The deal was accepted, and Tokugawa immediately moved his capital—lock, stock, and barrel—to the little fishing village called Edo, nucleus of today's Tokyo.[GE42] He invested incredible energy into building a castle there, providing a reliable water system, attracting merchants, training soldiers and officers and civil servants. By the 1630s it would be the world's largest single city, bigger even than any city in China or India.

When Hideyoshi invaded Korea, Tokugawa was not involved and profitably spent his time strengthening his own domain. In 1598, when Hideyoshi fell ill and died leaving the Council of Five Regents to care for his

38. GE Layer 38 is a Placemark referencing Okazaki castle; many Photos icons available for browsing.

39. GE Layer 39 is a Placemark referencing Sumpu castle site (today Sumpu "park," since the castle has long since been destroyed).

40. GE Layer 40 is a Placemark referencing Hamamatsu castle; several Photos icons to browse that show castle and teahouse.

41. GE Layer 41 is a Polygon approximating the area controlled by Tokugawa Ieyasa from 1560–1589 (it was virtually complete by 1570).

42. GE Layer 42 is a Placemark framing a view of Tokyo castle, with its elaborate, irregularly spiraling moat, and central buildings.

young son, Tokugawa Ieyasu was far and away the strongest of the five. In the power struggle that followed, the five-year-old son of Hideyoshi never had a chance. By 1600 rival alliances had coalesced around the rival figures of Tokugawa Ieyasu and Ishida Mitsunari, the regent who had grabbed Hideyoshi's magnificent Osaka castle.

The Battle of Sekigahara

The decisive battle between the two sides took place at Sekigahara on September 15 of 1600. It was fought just where the Nakasendo goes through the mountain ridges east of Lake Biwa.[GE43] It was fought on a huge scale; perhaps 160,000 troops were on the battlefield. In terms of numbers, the "eastern" and "western" armies were fairly evenly matched. But Tokugawa's armies were probably better trained, and he had secretly arranged for the defection of some of Ishida's key allies. When, in the heat of battle, the most important of these "allies" showed no signs of joining the battle on either side, Tokugawa made a brief attack on him to "encourage" his commitment.[GE44] When he then indeed committed to the Tokugawa side, the right wing of Ishida's main battle line collapsed. The last stand of Ishida's armies was back against the northern hills, right underneath his doomed command post.[GE45]

When Tokugawa Ieyasu moved, he moved swiftly and decisively, but his patience was legendary. Japanese folk wisdom, comparing the three unifiers, puts it this way: when faced with a caged nightingale that would not sing, Oda Nobunaga would kill the bird, Hideyoshi would force it to sing, and Tokugawa Ieyasu would wait for it to sing.[8]

So now, at age fifty-seven, Tokugawa Ieyasu effectively controlled the whole of Japan. Neither Oda Nobunaga nor Hideyoshi had ever claimed the *Shogun* title (since neither claimed descent from the Minamoto, a prerequisite), but in 1603 Tokugawa Ieyasu did. His "Tokugawa Shogunate" lasted most of three centuries, until 1868, and was a very different shogunate than any in the previous 500 years.

Will Adams

Arriving in that crucial year of 1600 was the first Englishman ever to set foot in Japan. He was William Adams, navigator for a Dutch fleet the last ship of which was driven ashore in south Japan battered and with its few survivors—only six could stand—riddled with scurvy. Adams and company were important to Tokugawa Ieyasu (a) because they were Protestant, able to challenge the Jesuit and Franciscan views and counterbalance the Portuguese and Spanish influence; and (b) they were a source of new knowledge about the world and especially shipbuilding, gunnery, and other naval affairs. Adams learned Japanese and served as translator for Tokugawa Ieyasu. He was eventually made both samurai and a special retainer of the Shogun, and given estates of his own (in today's Yokosuka, where the Miura peninsula forms the western side of the entrance to Tokyo Bay).[GE46] He lived until 1620, four years past the death of Ieyasu, and never did return to England.

"Alternate Residence" and the formalizing of the Tokaido

And so by 1600 Tokugawa Ieyasu had defeated all opponents. In his reign, and that of his son (Ieyasu "retired" in 1605 but, in what had become a Japanese tradition, ran things from behind the scenes), Japan was transformed. All the members of daimyo families, except the daimyo themselves, were ordered to come live perma-

---

43. GE Layer 43 is a Placemark framing a general view of Sekigahara.

44. GE Layer 44 is a Folder containing four Polygon layers; the first shows the general area of the battleground in gray; the second shows Ishida's forces in light blue; the third shows Tokugawa forces in red; and the fourth shows the "uncommitted" forces in yellow.

45. GE Layer 45 is a Placemark indicating an interesting Panoramio icon under pointer, titled "Sekigahara - Final Stage of battle site below Ishida's HQ." It has a picture of a battle memorial, and the hills beyond.

46. GE Layer 46 is a Placemark in Yokosuka. The harbor of Uraga, where he built ships for the Shogun, is at lower right. For Will Adams' 1611 letter home, describing landing and life in Japan, and especially relationships with Emperor: see following website: http://www.fordham.edu/halsall/mod/1611adams-japan.html

nently in the new capital Edo (today's Tokyo). The daimyo—there were between 250 and 300 of them at any given time—were ordered to spend every second or third year there. This was the politely named "alternate residence" system, but the daimyo families were in essence hostages to the Tokugawa shoguns for the good behavior of their lords. With all their servants and retainers, and the commercial demands they generated, they almost overnight made Tokyo the world's largest city, a title it only lost in the twentieth century.

The Tokaido had been a major road for hundreds of years before this, but at this point, as the most powerful Shogun ever, Tokugawa Ieyasu made traveling the Tokaido (and the lesser traveled Nakasendo as well) much more formal and convenient. Not counting Kyoto at one end and Edo (Tokyo) at the other, he established fifty-three official "stations" between them that had appropriate inns (one grade of inn for aristocrats, another for lesser mortals) and restaurants. At every seven or eight stops, on average, he maintained a castle so that the whole road was thoroughly dominated by the Shogun. This is when he built Nijo, the castle in Kyoto not far from the Emperor's residence, to overawe it and to house the Shogun should he come to town.[GE47] Since much of the population of Japan lived in the Kyushu and Inland Sea part of the country, most of these huge daimyo processionals would gather at Kyoto, and then make a more or less ceremonial trek of from ten days to two weeks east on the Tokaido, and finish their journey at Tokyo (Edo)—and the reverse when the daimyo retinues were traveling back to their feudal estates in the west.

Engelbert Kaempfer's 1691 trip on the Tokaido

Other policies that Tokugawa Ieyasu began (and that his successor strengthened) was to outlaw Christianity, and to close Japan to foreign visitors and also make it illegal for any Japanese to go abroad. To some extent that was an understandable decision, if you think about all the turmoil in the previous sixty years in Japan from when the first Portuguese set foot on Tanegashima Island just south of Kyushu! Christianity had become very popular especially in Kyushu, and daimyos there—brought together by their Christian practice and relations to Portuguese and Spanish—seemed to pose an organized threat to the shogunate. The only peephole these early Tokugawa shoguns left open on the outside world was a narrow-necked peninsula in Nagasaki harbor, called "Deshima Island,"[GE48] where a Dutch trading delegation was allowed to live, and where nearby there were small Chinese and Korean delegations as well. Once a year this Dutch delegation was obliged to travel to Edo and pay their respects. They would generally travel overland cross Kyushu, sail from port to port along the Inland Sea, and at the great commercial city of Osaka take the main highway to Kyoto where they would strike the main Tokaido.

In the year 1691 the Dutch delegation made that trip, accompanied by their German doctor, Engelbert Kaempfer. He took careful notes, and (illegally) drew sketches of buildings and bridges along the trip, labeling things in Arabic letters so as to avoid detection. His written descriptions are vivid and detailed, as in this description of the Tokaido proper:

> . . . lined on both sides with a straight and thick row of fir trees to provide shade and enjoyment for the traveler, except where cities and villages along the road prevent this. The ground is always kept clean and level; rainwater is channeled off to the low-lying fields in practical drainage channels, and the road rises up on one side toward a high, carefully constructed earthen bank to stop the rainwater from draining to that side. Thus at all times (except when traveling on loam in the rain) there is a pleasant and fine road to travel on. More so since the road is diligently maintained due to certain sharing arrangements between neighboring villages and headmen, and, like the floor of a farmhouse, is cleaned and swept daily. . . . The leaves and pine cones that drop down every day are raked up and used as fuel instead of wood, which is often in short supply.[9]

---

47. GE Layer 47 is a Placemark referencing Nijo (castle). Dozens of Photos icons available for browsing of castle and gardens.

48. GE Layer 48 is a Placemark at approximate location of fan-shaped island of Deshima (or Dejima), connected to the mainland in Nagasaki harbor by a narrow road; it is fairly well buried under modern construction. Click on Panoramio icon under pointer titled "Dutch factory, entrance to Dejima and museum" for view of some remains. Several other Photos icons around mention Dejima, or the "Hollander Slope," or other obvious Dutch holdovers.

*From *Kaempfer's Japan: Tokugawa Culture Observed* by Engelbert Kaempfer; Edited by Beatrice M. Bodart-Bailey. Copyright © 1999 by the University of Hawaii Press. Reprinted by permission.

He paid careful attention to the "Miyako" (Kyoto) to Hamamatsu, and then the Hamamatsu to Edo (Tokyo) halves of the route, and has good descriptions of the embassy's receptions in both the imperial capital and especially the shogunal capital. In Edo the Shogun sat behind a screen with the ladies of the court. On finding out Kaempfer was a doctor, he quizzed him closely on medical matters, and then—apparently for the women of the court—had the Dutch delegation demonstrate some of their strange cultural ways. As Kaempfer says:

> He had us take off our *kappa*, or ceremonial robes, and sit upright so that he could inspect us; had us stand up and now walk, now pay compliments to each other, then again dance, jump, pretend to be drunk, speak Japanese, read Dutch, draw, sing, put on our coats, then take them off again.

The affair of the 47 Ronin

In terms of Japan itself, this isolation produced one of the great eras of culture and orderly life in all of modern history. The single greatest disturbance of the peace in those two and a half centuries was not a war, or a rebellion, or a riot, and cost the lives of less than 100 people—though every Japanese now alive surely knows the story. In 1701 Lord Asano, a small daimyo whose han supported 300 samurai (home base was Ako castle, some seventy miles travel west of Osaka[GE49]) was rehearsing a ritual at the shogun's palace in Edo. Lord Kira, the court official supposed to be instructing him in the proper ritual, was miffed at having been given a present that was beneath his dignity, and refused to instruct him properly. The daimyo, outraged, drew his sword and wounded Lord Kira. But shogunal law said no swords were to be drawn in the shogun's capital, and Lord Asano was obliged to commit seppuku. Many expected his samurai to try to get revenge on Lord Kira, whom they blamed for his death. Indeed 47 of the 300 total samurai, under the leadership of one Oishi, dedicated themselves to revenge, though for over a year they pretended to drift apart so as to lull the authorities and Lord Kira to sleep. A year to the day later, they secretly assembled, attacked Kira's mansion by moonlight, cut off his head and cleansed it and presented it to their lord's death tablet. And for this the shogunate obliged all forty-seven to commit seppuku as well, which they did.[GE50] There were a few popular riots in their favor, but that was it—except for play after play over the three centuries since the event, celebrating their successful fulfillment of their moral obligation.

Basho

A flourishing of arts in this Edo to Osaka corridor from around 1680 to 1730 goes by the name *Genroku*, after a particular shogun's reign. It was a real golden age.

Japan's greatest poet, Basho, lived most of his life on our corridor.[GE51] He was born in or around 1644 in a town a dozen miles or so south of the western section of the Tokaido. He was born and raised samurai, but published his first *heiku no renga* (poetry of 5-7-5 plus 7-7 syllables) by the time he was eighteen. Sometime in his twenties, after the death of his lord, he moved to Edo and became fully involved in the artistic world of the capital. Although his fame grew and he attracted disciples (who built him a hut—*basho*, hence his literary name—under a banana tree), he became depressed there. In 1684, about age thirty-eight, he set off on the first of his famous trips. He went west generally along the Tokaido, stopping off at Mt. Fuji and his old hometown of Ueno on his way to Kyoto—enjoying poetry competitions and the fellowship of the road. On his return to Edo, he was in noticeably better spirits. In 1686 he wrote his most famous haiku (5-7-5, leaving a reader to guess at implied conclusion) of all time:

> *Furu-ike ya kawazu tobi-komu mizu-no-oto*
> Old-pond : frog jump-in water-sound[10]

---

49. GE Layer 49 is a Placemark referencing Ako Castle; click on Panoramio icon under pointer titled "Ako Castle 01" for one view of the castle. The icon next to it is of the Oishi shrine, Oishi being leader of the revenge part of 47 Ronin.

50. GE Layer 50 is a Placemark generally locating Sengaku Temple. It is some three miles south of the Edo palace complex, is the site of burial markers of the 47 Ronin. Click on icon under pointer for one view of gravestones. Several other Photos icons nearby in which to explore Sengaku-ji, and at least two others of graves.

51. GE Layer 51 is a Folder titled "Life of Basho." You can open it and explore sites as they come up in the text above.

Obviously inspired by travel, he made another trip in 1688 to his birth city. In 1689, he made his famous trip north, a walk with a disciple of over 2,000 miles, at the end of which he wrote his "The Narrow Road to Oku." This was the only foray of his life outside our corridor, but it was a beauty. In 1694 he left Edo for the last time, visited his hometown, and died the same year in nearby Otsu at the southern tip of Lake Biwa.

Oliver Statler in *Japanese Inn* recreates a visit of the famous Basho, on one of these trips, to the town of Okitsu on the Tokaido. One of his poems was immediately engraved on a stone in honor of the visit, but when the plague visited the town shortly thereafter, it was seen as less than good luck. Still too precious to the towns-people to give up, the stone was made into a bridge over a little waterway at Seiken Temple, but face-down!

Chikamatsu

Sometimes called the "Japanese Shakespeare," Chikamatsu was only about nine years younger than Basho. Born just north of the western end of our corridor, he came to be associated with the cultural flowering of the city of Osaka. He wrote his great drama for *bunraku*, or puppet theatre. The half-life-sized puppets are tradi-tionally manipulated by one, two, or sometimes three puppeteers dressed in black (only the master puppeteer's head is uncovered). His topics were usually the obligations to home and family versus the human pleasure of the pleasure quarters of the city; one of his greatest plays, *The Courier from Hell*, was written on one such theme in 1711; he died in 1725.

One reason the Japanese so quickly began to make great films in the mid-twentieth century is that they already had great theater to base it on—the ancient *Noh* plays with centuries of stylization, and the newer *Kabuki* drama that was especially strong in Edo during the Tokugawa era. But *Bunraku* (puppet) theater may have been the strongest of the three traditions. In the mid-twentieth-century film "Double Suicide," a pair of star-crossed lovers have decided to die together. The man makes a long, clumsy, and bloody job of killing his girlfriend with a sword. Then, trying to hang himself with a scarf from a nearby torii gateway, he can't keep the wind from blowing the scarf off the crossbeam. In an obvious repaying of debt to bunraku theater, the film-maker has puppeteers dressed in black show up with a ladder, get the scarf in place over the crossbeam of the torii gateway, and help ease the man out of the toils and snares of this world.

Hiroshige's "53 Stages of the Tokaido"

Even towards the end of the Tokugawa shogunate, the arts thrived in Japan. In the visual arts, western things and ideas such as the Prussian blue dye and perspective drawing seeped in, to mingle with Chinese-derived Japanese art.

The Japanese got the basics of the woodblock print—a flat hardwood block carved with knives that was then rolled with ink and pressed on paper to leave an image of all that had not been carved away—from China, as they got so many basic arts and customs. Over the centuries, however, the Japanese took this art and made it their own. It was first used to transmit Buddhist images and texts, but when it came to be used in the secular world, for beautiful geishas and famous actors, it came to be called *ukiyo-e*, "the floating world." That might be translated into English just as well as "the fleeting world," because it meant that this was art dealing with everyday subjects, not the spiritual ones associated with Zen art. By Tokugawa times the best artists could make a living by selling their prints. The ukiyo-e was something between individual art and mass produced art. The chief artist might carve the outlines and finer points and leave it to apprentices to carve out the rest. The blocks were inked each time, by hand, with either brushes or rollers; some prints required twelve or more separate inkings and pressings to finish, the paper carefully kept "in register" each time. By the 1820s ukiyo-e was being used to show famous landscape scenery. Its first great practitioner was Hokusai, whose "Great Wave Off Kanagawa" may be the single most recognizable artistic image from Japan.[GE52]

Hokusai's younger contemporary and rival Hiroshige was also a specialist in the landscape print, and it is to Hiroshige that Statler devotes a whole chapter in his *Japanese Inn* book, entitled "In which one of Japan's

52. GE Layer 52 is a Placemark framing a general view of the Kanagawa coast, Mt. Fuji in the background. Go to the fol-lowing website for a view of the Hokusai's classic "Great Wave Off Kanagawa": http://upload.wikimedia.org/wikipedia/commons/thumb/0/0a/The_Great_Wave_off_Kanagawa.jpg/300px-The_Great_Wave_off_Kanagawa.jpg

great artists visits the Minaguchi-ya." Much of it is based on Hiroshige's own diary, his quest for good food and company, his comic poetry, lots of his prints—and most of it is set along the Tokaido. His single most famous woodblock print series was his first "53 Stages of the Tokaido," that including Edo on one end and Kyoto on the other, totaling fifty-five prints.[GE⁵³] As well done as they are, the reproductions you can access in the previous footnote can't do total justice to the originals. They are a full 9″ by 14″ in area printed, and the colors as they are printed on that soft Japanese paper have an almost luminescent glow about them.[11]

It's a time travel: trying to find the old Tokaido today (which many travelers have tried) is a bit like trying to find the old stagecoach road from Boston to Washington, D.C., from a map drawn by a traveler thirty years before our Civil War. But with these 1830s images of the Tokaido, wonderfully vivid and with those "sweet distances" of the ukiyo-e, Hiroshige took a series of snapshots for us of the key road in all Japan that was just about to be transformed almost beyond recognition by western intrusion.

Roots of modern cultural nationalism

Much of the chapter to this point has been spent on what were uniquely Japanese events and institutions. It is the historian's way of building a foundation for understanding modern Japanese patriotism, which would celebrate much of this "heritage." But early in this Tokugawa period there was also a growing consciousness among a handful of Japanese intellectuals about the uniqueness of their history and culture. There was even a feeling that it ought to be celebrated. I don't think there was any way Herder's scholarship could have been known to them, but the parallels with pre- and early Romantic German thinkers are striking.

The intellectual school in which this took place in Japan was called *kokugaku*, which translates "national learning." It was a nativist reaction to the pro-Chinese culture mood set by the Tokugawa government in Edo. It celebrated the country people as bearers of a purer practice of morality. It celebrated the early Japanese language as a model for the present. And it called for a revival of Shinto as the "ancient way" (*kodo*). In 1765 a writer named Mabuchi wrote a book called *Consideration of the National Will*; its main thesis was, in the words of a modern writer, "to point out the archaic simplicity and purity of people in Japan prior to the importation of foreign learning" (foreign here meaning mainly Chinese).[12] File this away; it was a belief system that would be enforced later with a rigidity that might have dismayed even its inventors.

Commodore Perry and the Unequal Treaty

After two and a half centuries the Tokugawa dynasty, according to some old universal rule of dynastic rise and fall, gradually lost efficiency, power, and respect. Those feudal territories furthest from Edo, with old traditions of independence, began to be restless again.

Once again, however, events were precipitated by western intrusion. In 1839–42, as you saw in the last chapter, a British fleet accompanied by state-of-the-art steel gunboats fought China for the right to keep importing opium into China. In these so-called "Opium Wars" Britain humbled huge China and forced it to a humiliating "unequal" treaty. Britain got Hong Kong and the best deep-water harbor in Asia; got five "treaty ports" in which to base trade; limited Chinese tariffs, or taxes on imports, to 5 percent or less, and won the right to have British citizens accused of crimes in China tried by British law. And the Japanese saw (through their little peephole on the outside world at Deshima Island in Nagasaki harbor) what this medium-sized western power did to the giant power of East Asia. Discussion grew about the sources of western power and how to respond to it.

In 1853 the discussion became less theoretical when Commodore Matthew Perry of the U.S. steamed into Uraga Bay (where Will Adams had his estates early in Tokugawa Japan) with two steam-driven battleships,

---

53. GE Layer 53 is a Folder titled, coincidentally, "53 Views of the Tokaido." It has fifty-five Placemarks, one for each of the "stations" on the Tokaido, plus one each for the starting and ending points in Tokyo and Kyoto. In each Placemark is embedded the website for Hiroshige's first set of prints (Hoeido); from that image you can also open the image from his second (Reisho) set of prints of the Tokaido. These images are posted by the Hood Museum at Dartmouth College, which holds originals of all the prints. Turning the whole Folder on opens up fifty-five Placemarks in the form of red star icons; you can now click either on layer titles or on stars for views of the appropriate woodblock prints of the place.

each pulling a sailing battleship, all heavily armed.[GE⁵⁴] Perry was a big proponent of a new steam navy in the U.S. He had, incidentally, been in charge of the naval side of Winfield Scott's siege of Veracruz, and after Scott's army disappeared up the Sierra Madre Oriental heading towards Mexico City, Perry led in the capture of several other Gulf coast Mexican cities. Perry was sent to Japan on the orders of the U.S. President, to insist that Japan sign an agreement about several things. One was the treatment of shipwrecked sailors (mostly whalers; Melville's *Moby Dick*, incidentally, was written in 1851, about this time). One was to open Japan to U.S. trade, or at least permit the resupply of ships with provisions. One was to accept the establishment of an American consulate on Japanese soil. Looking back from today, it would seem right that if Japan had wanted to stay closed, it should have been left alone to do so. A combination of western technological power and cultural self-righteousness, however, made most western countries in the nineteenth century reach the opposite conclusion: those countries not yet members of the "modern" western system of international relations should be forced to join it. Although this does not take any of the blame off U.S. shoulders for the intrusion, a Russian fleet was preparing to go do the same thing when Perry beat them to it. Perry was told by the Japanese he would have to sail to Nagasaki, and communicate through the Dutch settlement there. When he refused and threatened to deliver his message by force, he was allowed to land. Perry left the U.S. demands, and also left word he would return the next year—with a bigger fleet—for the Japanese answer.

For the Tokagawa Shogunate, this all came with bad timing. The dying Shogun was childless, and a fierce struggle for succession was going on between a party supporting a child with close blood ties and a party supporting a capable adult with more distant blood ties. At this point, for the first time in Tokugawa history, the shogunal government asked all the daimyo what it should do. That in itself was a sign of weakness, and unfortunately for the Shogunate there was no clear response. The answers they got varied from "fully join the western system" to "smash the barbarians whenever they come into sight."

True to his word, Perry showed up the next year, in February 1854, this time with eleven ships. He anchored at Kanagawa (a second "great wave off Kanagawa" threatening Japan, metaphorically speaking), even closer to Edo than his first anchorage at Uraga. The next month the weak shogunal government accepted minimum western demands—a couple of minor ports opened to U.S. trade, with a U.S. consul at one of them (Shimoda[GE⁵⁵]) and better treatment of shipwrecked sailors. Quickly other major western powers joined the U.S. in such treaties, the way other western powers earlier signed similar treaties with China after the British muscled through the first one.

There was one last figure who might have saved the Shogunate. He was Ii Naosuke, who had been daimyo of Hikone since 1850, when he was only thirty-five.[GE⁵⁶] In 1858 he assumed the position of *tairo*, or chief counselor to the Shogun, that was usually only filled during emergencies. He was of the persuasion that Japan needed to join the western order, simply to learn the new sources of this new power. With his firm hand on the throttle, the shogunal government began to regain the initiative. Just two years later, however, he was assassinated; in domestic affairs he had sided with the child ruler and his backers, and the other side caught him in ambush when he was traveling to the Shogun's castle in Edo. After his death, the power of the Shogunate eroded quickly.

It was in 1859, during Ii Naosuke's brief tenure as tairo, that the U.S.—and quickly other western powers—got Yokohama as a trading base to go with the other two minor ports. It was to be much more important than the other two, because it was just around a little bay from Kanagawa, which itself was a station on the Tokaido.

---

54. GE Layer 54 is a Placemark referencing a Panoramio icon at Uraga Harbor titled "Perry monument. Uraga, Kanagawa, Japan." A good series of Japanese and western artists' paintings of Perry's ships is at following website: http://ocw.mit.edu/ ans7870/21f/21f.027j/black_ships_and_samurai/core_blackships.html.

55. GE Layer 55 is a Folder containing two Placemarks. The first indicates a Panoramio icon with a good view of little Shimoda Bay, titled "Shimoda Bay" down near the tip of the Izu peninsula. The second indicates a nearby Panoramio icon titled "Shimoda in Shizuoka" for large outdoor model of one of Perry's steamships. The second minor port opened to westerners was Hakodate, on the northern island of Hokkaido.

56. GE Layer 56 is a Placemark framing a view of Hikone Castle. Of the many old-looking castles in Japan, most are reconstructions. This is one of, if not the oldest remaining historically authentic castles, its keep dating to at least 1575. Lots of Photos icons to explore. Located on the Nakasendo, not far from Oda Nobunaga's original super-castle of the mid-1500s.

At first the small foreign settlement there lived within the *Kennai*, "Inside the Barrier"—a quarter literally surrounded by a moat. Later the foreign settlement grew and spread south, to what was called Yamate Bluff; the cemetery and many of the surrounding western-style houses are still there.[GE[57]] Yokohama was a classic Treaty Port resulting from an Unequal Treaty, like Shanghai in China. Westerners had "extrality," or immunity from Japanese law, and from the first this occasioned friction with the locals. In 1862, for example, three western gentlemen and a lady went horseback riding from Yokohama up to the nearby Tokaido, and encountered a daimyo processional there. Instead of dismounting and showing what the daimyo's samurai considered proper respect, they rode along the processional. One of the men was killed by the outraged samurai and the other two wounded; the woman alone escaped back to Yokohama. It was the shogunal government that then had to make restitution to the foreigners.[13]

Meiji Restoration

This new western intrusion and the virtual collapse of the Tokugawa Shogunate triggered the Meiji Restoration from 1863 to 1869 or so. It was a remarkable social rebellion disguised as a simple return to the past.

Two western feudal domains—Satsuma in the southern half of Kyushu, and Choshu on the western end of Honshu—took the lead.[GE[58]] They had been among the last of the independent han defeated by Tokugawa Ieyasu, and in the 260 or so years since their defeat, had nourished those bitter memories and kept them alive. In Satsuma there was a day of what amounted to mourning on the anniversary of the defeat, when the losing battle was rehearsed and then meditated upon by the samurai. In Choshu mothers still had their sons sleep with their feet towards Edo and the "tent government," as they called the Shogunate, as an insult. Both of these feudal domains were strong. Of all the 200-odd han, Satsuma was ranked number two in numbers of samurai it supported, with 27,000; Choshu was number four with 11,000.

With their latent anti-Shogunate feeling, these two were the first to call for the dismantling of the Shogunate and the revival of Imperial rule—especially after the Shogunate's caving in to western demands, as they saw it. Their slogan became "Revere the Emperor; Expel the Barbarians." Unilaterally Choshu declared the Straits of Shimonoseki (between the western tip of Honshu and the northeastern tip of Kyushu) closed to western ships. Satsuma tried to be more pro-Emperor than Choshu, outlawing western ships off its coasts. Western fleets simply hammered their coastal forts into submission.

A lot has been written on why China was so slow to respond to the sharp new western imperialism of the nineteenth century, and Japan was so fast. China's size, its centralized control from an interior capital, its tradition of seeing dangerous invasions come from inland and not the seacoast, and its self-conception of the "Middle Kingdom" as the source of all things good—these are all probably important factors. Japan was smaller, most of its cities on or near the coast; and it had a tradition of borrowing what it needed from other cultures. But not least among the factors that led to such a fast Japanese response to the new western imperialism of the nineteenth century was the quick and correct assessment by its leaders of western power versus their own. In 1863 and 1864 the radical samurai in Choshu and Satsuma learned this power lesson painfully but well. The "barbarians" could only be expelled once the secrets of their strength were learned. This made these young, radical samurai no less anti-Shogun and pro-Emperor; it just meant temporary acceptance of western presence while Japan mastered its sources of power.

In 1864 shogunal armies marched on Choshu, and seemed successful in putting the radical samurai out of power. But almost before their withdrawal, the radicals took over the government again. When in 1865 the Shogunate tried to mount another invasion of Choshu, Satsuma and some other radical han for the first time allied with Choshu. These new forces, claiming to fight for the "Restoration" of the Emperor after almost eight centuries of "illegal" shogunal rule, blunted the Shogunate's attack and then took the offensive themselves. In

---

57. GE Layer 57 is a Placemark icon framing a view in Yokohama of a green area which is the old western cemetery in Yokohama. The arc of Photos icons below and to right are almost all photographs of classic western houses, exteriors and interiors. It is amazing that so much survived (a) the 1923 Kanto earthquake and (b) U.S. bombing in WW II.

58. GE Layer 58 is a Folder titled "Choshu and Satsuma" containing Polygons representing the former in red and the latter in orange.

1868 they drove the shogunal armies out of Kyoto and proclaimed the "Meiji Restoration" ("Meiji" was the reign name just taken by the fifteen-year-old Emperor). Their armies then pushed up the Tokaido and in 1869 occupied Edo itself, chasing the remnants of the shogunal forces up into northeast Honshu and defeating them all.

But Edo had for so long been the real center of government that it now seemed more practical to bring the Emperor to Edo rather than move the whole machinery of government to Kyoto. And this meant that Edo must be renamed "To-Kyo," East Capital.

Although everything was done in the Emperor's name, his proclaimed divinity put him above politics, center of the Shinto religion that now had a revival. The real governmental decision-makers after 1868 were a group of comparatively young—age twenty-seven to forty-one—leaders whose ambitions were to make Japan a major world power in their lifetime. Remarkably, it worked. It was as improbably successful as the American Revolution in the hands of Washington, Jefferson, Franklin, and company.

The beginning of everything was to centralize power. The daimyo of Choshu and Satsuma voluntarily "returned" their domains to the Emperor, and he in turn appointed them governors at a salary of a tenth or so of their former estate income. Other daimyo could now do no less, and in just a few short years most of the major decision making in the land had moved to Tokyo. This chapter on the Tokyo-to-Kyoto corridor opened with a quotation from the American educator William Griffis in 1871, to the effect that the era of loyalty was past and that of patriotism had come. As the tutor for a Japanese student who had been sent to study at Rutgers University (more on Japan and the west in a minute), Griffis had been invited back to the Japanese domain of Echizen to build western-style schools. He was living in its castle town of Fukui[GE[59]], teaching full and enthusiastic classes. All of a sudden, as he said, the "thunderbolt" fell. The samurai assembled in the castle in full formal dress, preparing to go to Tokyo and acquiesce in the dissolution of the feudal estates—and implicitly, in the laying down of their own samurai status. His own school simply melted away:

> My best friends and helpers have left Fukui, and now my advanced students, their support at home being no longer sufficient, are leaving to seek their fortune in Yokohama or Tokio. My classes are being depleted. Fukui is no longer the capital of a prince. It is simply an inland city . . . .[14]

Within the year Griffis himself moved to Tokyo, center of the action, where his services were once more in high demand—but to a growing national government, no longer to a feudal lord.

Westernization, Japanese style

The West in general the Meiji reformers treated as a school for knowledge. Want to understand naval power and banking? Go to Britain. Want the best local government? Go to France and study the Napoleonic prefectures. Want the best in armies and a good model for a conservative, powerful central government? Go to Germany. Want the latest in business techniques? Go to the United States. Bring it all back home. Transform government and society.

The results were spectacular. Japan is still the only country in history (other than Britain which slowly developed the first industrialization) to industrialize without major foreign investment. We in the U.S., for example, were financed in our basic industrialization by British loans. The Japanese immediately took to some key aspects of modern capitalism; their individual savings rate—which is where banks get the capital to lend out—was from the first and is still one of the highest in the world.

Also unlike in the U.S., it was the new Japanese government itself that drove industrialization. It built heavy industry in the 1870s by either generously financing existing businesses, or by creating needed industries itself and then selling them off to the highest bidder. This was the real origin of those great modern Japanese financial combines called *zaibatsu*, with famous names such as Mitsubishi, Mitsui, Sumitomo, and Yasuda. No matter how a given zaibatsu started out, each eventually had its own banking system and its own production

---

59. Fukui is a town the center of which is less than a mile north of our corridor. GE Layer 59 is a Placemark referencing a Panoramio icon under pointer, "Rebuilt Castle Bridge." The moat survives, but only the foundations of the castle itself.

complex that went from raw materials to finished products. Sumitomo, for example, originated as an old Kyoto book shop early in the Tokugawa period. By 1690 the family had branched out into developing a rich copper field in Shikoku, and soon moved the business headquarters to Osaka to be closer to it. After the Meiji Restoration the Sumitomo family was nicely positioned to take full advantage of the government's willingness to swap money for industrial growth, and in the next few decades became a world-class financial combine. Sumitomo Bank was created in 1895; Sumitomo Electric in 1897 (copper wire and cable, its original basis); Sumitomo Chemical by 1913 (beginning with by-products of copper manufacture, such as sulfur and sulfuric acid); Sumitomo Heavy Industries in 1934; Sumitomo Metal Industries in 1935.

Technological modernization on the most current western lines occurred in many areas. Perry in 1854 had brought as a gift a ¼-scale working model of a steam train. By 1872 the Japanese had a full-scale version of it up and running from Yokohama to Tokyo. By 1889, just fifteen years later, a railroad ran the length of the entire Tokaido. It diverged from the traditional route in only two of its sections: it circled north around the rugged Hakone region, and from Nagoya it again went north, and then approximated the last part of the Nakasendo into Kyoto.[GE60] Steel mills, steamship construction facilities, collieries—the new government was determined to build them all.

Old Confucian schools were transformed into western-style universities, with the strictest of admissions standards based on competitive exams (which remain even today). Many of the new schools were in Tokyo, including the most famous public and private universities in the country. Tokyo (later "Imperial" was added to the title) University was redesigned and moved to its present Hongo campus in 1876.[GE61] Most of the best schools in the whole country were on that Osaka - Kyoto - Nagoya - Tokyo corridor, as those old daimyo towns of the Tokaido were quickly being transformed. Like the University of Berlin in 1810, these Japanese universities were to teach the technical skills necessary for modern state power, but also a broad new patriotism.

In 1872—a year after the Chicago great fire started by Mrs. O'Leary's cow—much of Tokyo, too, burned to the ground. The burst of architectural energy in the rebuilding that resulted in the "Chicago School" of architecture here had its parallels in Tokyo. This is when the Ginza, the famous upscale, western-style shopping center just southwest of the Imperial Palace complex, took shape. Most of the western-style department stores have since been replaced by newer high rise buildings; a few, such as the Wako Department Store with its famous clock, are left as historical reminders.[GE62]

The aristocratic structure of society was transformed into something resembling a modern western society by paying off samurai and daimyo with lump sums. Most of these former nobility sank into genteel obscurity (lots of Japanese you meet will have a samurai ancestor, as former samurai intermarried with former commoners), though a few used the lump sum to invest in those new zaibatsu when the government auctioned them off, and prospered.

The final level of modern western state power, of course, resides in the modern military. The logic of the French Revolution—that everybody near France had to learn or be defeated by it—is that every man, at least, should be made a citizen so that he can be a patriotic soldier. By the mid-1870s Japan had created its first draft army of commoners, trained according to western drill manuals and armed with modern western rifles and artillery. This was the setting for the 1877 last-ditch revolt of the samurai under the famous Saigo Takamori, one of the three key leaders of the Meiji Restoration a decade earlier. When a good half of the reform team had taken off for Europe and the U.S. to learn the sources of western power, he was the most important leader to stay home and mind the fort. The change in those who experienced western power firsthand may have begun the rift that took place on their return. When Saigo was voted down on his aggressive Korea policy in 1873, he withdrew from government. With the outlawing of sword wearing in 1876, he resisted, piling up arms and followers in Kagoshima, main port of Satsuma. The Meiji government had no choice but to enforce compliance.

60. GE Layer 60 is a Path in dark pink representing approximate route of 1889 Tokaido railway. Note departures from the old road over the base of Izu peninsula, and then from Nagoya northwest to Gifu, Tarui, Maibara, and down the southeast side of Lake Biwa. Adapted from map on p. 16 of Jilly Traganou's *The Tokaido Road: Traveling and Representation in Edo and Meiji Japan* (New York & London: RoutledgeCurzon, 2004).

61. GE Layer 61 is a Placemark locating present-day Tokyo University's main Hongo campus.

62. GE Layer 62 is a Placemark referencing a Panoramio icon titled "Wako Department Store."

The war in 1877 took almost six months, but in it the first modern draft army of commoners armed with rifles and artillery defeated 40,000 sword-wielding samurai of Saigo. A larger-than-life statue of him still stands in Kagoshima, in tribute to his early contributions to the Meiji Restoration and perhaps in memory of the tragedy of his later resistance.[GE63]

Sino-Japanese War and the Heian Jingu Shrine

One measure of the new Japanese power is that Japan defeated China in 1894–95 in the Sino-Japanese War, as you saw in the Yangtze Valley chapter. At the peace negotiations Ito Hirobumi said to Li Hung-chang, why no change to speak of in the years since our last discussion? Li responded that the Chinese system was so constrained by tradition. In the war Japan picked up real control of Formosa (Taiwan) and Southern Manchuria, and Dairen (sometimes also written Dalian, Pt. Arthur, Luda) on the tip of the Liaodong Peninsula until the western powers took it away and awarded it to Russia. Most important of all, China was removed from Korean affairs, giving Japan a free hand. The massive indemnity China was forced to pay was plowed straight into Japanese industrial and military development. When outside troops put down the Boxer Rebellion in China, the number of Japanese troops in the invading army matched the total of all the western states' soldiers. This really marked the entry of Japan into the club of major states. The unequal treaties were lifted in 1899, and in 1902 in the Anglo-Japanese naval treaty (partly a product of Britain's naval race with Germany, as you saw in the German chapter) was the first agreement of equality between a major western state and an Asian country in modern history.

In 1895, in the first flush of victory over the Chinese, the Japanese government built the Heian Jingu shrine in Kyoto. This was a replica of the original Heian palace from AD 794, begun on the 1,100th anniversary of the original.[GE64] Entrance to the complex is through a massive *torii* gateway that spanned a wide avenue. [GE65] It radiates muscularity and power, not the artistic delicacy of most traditional torii. Imperial Japan was beginning to flex its muscles.

Russo-Japanese War

Ten years later Japan fought and won—though the victory was much more difficult—a war with Russia. As you saw in the Russia and Socialism chapter earlier, part of this was a too-clever Russian government plan to rally their disaffected citizens in a "short, victorious war." The deeper conflict, though, was over Manchuria. Japan, in its victory over China in 1895, thought it had won the ports of Darien and Pt. Arthur on the tip of the Liaodong (Kwantung) Peninsula, just across the bay from Tianjin.[GE66] The great European powers not only demanded that these be returned to China, but in two years time Russia had won them in a grant from China. [GE67] Russia had already won from China the China Eastern Railway,[GE68] its shortcut across Manchuria for the Trans-Siberian Railroad; now it dropped another railroad down from Harbin to those two ports, calling it the South Manchurian Railway.[GE69] The war began with a surprise Japanese torpedo boat attack on the Russian Pacific Fleet at harbor in Pt. Arthur, and followed with a land attack that was a sneak preview of World

---

63. GE Layer 63 is a Placemark referencing the larger-than-life statue of Saigo in Kagoshima, key port of the han of Satsuma. Three Photos icons nearest Placemark pointer are all photos of the statue.

64. GE Layer 64 is a Placemark referencing a Panoramio icon titled "Heianjingu shrine." Photograph shows a group of students walking up to main shrine. Dozens of other nearby Photos icons to explore, including gardens, gateway shrine.

65. GE Layer 65 is a Placemark indicating the Panoramio icon under pointer titled "Heian mon." The photo is of the massive torii (gateway).

66. GE Layer 66 is a Folder titled "Liaodong ports"; it contains two Placemarks, one referencing Pt. Arthur and the other Dairen (today's Dalian).

67. The Russian Governor's house still stands; GE Layer 67 is a Placemark referencing a Panoramio icon titled "Dalian, Old Russian Govenor Headquater[sic]."

68. GE Layer 68 is a Path, colored orange, titled China Eastern Railway.

69. GE Layer 69 is a Path, colored red, titled South Manchuria Railway.

War I, with barbed wire, machine guns, heavy artillery bombardments. When the Russian fleet tried to slip out and run for shelter to Vladivostok, Admiral Togo Heihachiro intercepted them. The battle was not decisive, though the remnant of the Russian fleet that made it back into Pt. Arthur could not be repaired, and Japanese forces could. Eventually heavy land-based artillery sunk the Russian ships at harbor. The Russian Baltic fleet sailed completely around the world to join the action, only to be intercepted and destroyed upon its arrival by that same Admiral Togo in the narrows between Japan and Korea.[GE70] Both sides were near exhaustion. If the war had gone on longer, Russian weight might have been brought to bear. The Revolution of 1905, however, meant that Russia had to sue for peace. President Teddy Roosevelt, an admirer of these "plucky little Japanese," offered his good offices and Portsmouth, New Hampshire, for treaty discussions. In it Japan got a free hand in Korea, took over the Russian lease to Pt. Arthur and Dairen, most of the South Manchurian Railway, and when the Russians refused to consider paying any indemnity, Japan took the south half of Sakhalin Island, just north of Hokkaido.

By the time the Meiji Emperor died in 1912, Japan was reckoned the major Asian power and one of the great powers of the world. Its rise in those forty-four years since his "restoration" in 1868 had been stunning. [GE71]

The "21 Demands" and the Kwantung Army

World War I convulsed Europe from early August 1914. By spring of 1915, in the power vacuum left by the transfer of most European forces back to their home countries, the Japanese issued an ultimatum to China called "the 21 demands." U.S. and some British intervention got the most extreme provisions at least postponed, such as the Chinese government having to hire Japanese "advisors," and the demand for the control of major southern Chinese railroads by the Japanese. What was left, however, was a virtual takeover of Manchuria and part of Mongolia by Japanese interests, plus the domination of the Chinese coastal province of Shandong where Japan moved smoothly into the old German concessions.

During the 1920s—a great decade for disarmament in reaction to the blood-letting of World War I—Liberal thought predominated in Japan as well and some Japanese pressure on China was lifted. But during the 1930s there was a spectacular rise of militarization in Japan, accompanied by the political use of folklore and the Shinto cult that had some parallels with Germany's folk cult sponsored by the Nazi Party—on which a bit more shortly.

Meanwhile Japan's Kwantung Army occupied the Liaodong Peninsula (also called Kwantung, hence the army' name) and patrolled the railroads of Manchuria. It became the heart of the aggressive new chauvinism and militarism of twentieth-century Japan. The Kwantung Army was not really under central army control, and in fact elements of the army central control in Tokyo were not really under Japanese governmental control—a recipe for foreign policy disaster, because the Japanese government could not implement key agreements it made with other countries. It was elements of this army that murdered Zhang Zuolin (Chang Tso-lin), warlord of Manchuria, in 1928. In September of 1931 it staged the "Manchurian Incident" claiming a Chinese plot to blow up a train, and used that as an excuse to occupy all of Manchurian territory, not just the railroad corridors. In 1932, when the League of Nations demanded that Japan withdraw its troops, the military had such support that in 1933 Japan left the League. In 1934 Japan placed the Chinese figure known to westerners as Henry Pu-yi

---

70. GE Layer 70 is a Folder titled "Admiral Togo," containing two Placemarks. The first locates the approximate site of Battle of Tsushima. The second frames a view of the Japanese battleship "Mikasa" in a naval park between Kanagawa and Yokosuka, with a statue of Admiral Togo in front of the ship; this was his flagship in both major battles against the Russian Navy in 1905. Click on Panoramio icon under pointer titled "kouenn" for a good view of same.

71. The Japanese themselves are fascinated with the Meiji age. GE Layer 71 is a Placemark referencing the Meiji Shrine, about three miles west of Tokyo's Imperial Palace. Built in 1920 to "enshrine" the souls of the late Meiji Emperor (d. 1912) and Empress, the shrine is set in a huge park a mile long in its longest dimension—a remarkable dedication of space in crowded Japan. Its history museum is also a celebration of this era, in which Japan took a position of full equality in the world international order. Dozens of Photos icons to explore (buildings were mostly leveled by World War II bombing raids; rebuilt in the 1950s).

(the last Qing Emperor, who had reigned if not ruled as a child from 1908–1911) on the throne of "Manchukuo."[GE72] It was a transparent fiction; every key administrator was Japanese.

Back in Tokyo, on February 26, 1936, a plot of radical army officers to take over the civilian government was set in motion. Several important government officials were murdered, and the radical army units actually held the center of Tokyo for three days, plus the new Japan National Diet Building and Army Headquarters. [GE73] In one of the few examples of a modern Japanese Emperor directly entering politics, the young Emperor Hirohito defied them. The guard of the Imperial Palace repulsed the radical troops, keeping them out of the Imperial Palace complex. With Hirohito's public condemnation, the coup collapsed, and its leaders were soon arrested and quickly executed. But after a temporary lull, the radically expansive elements of the military came back stronger than before. If the Emperor had ever seriously bucked the military tide again, he would certainly have been one of those removed from the scene by a future coup. The divinity of the imperial institution may have been passionately celebrated by the militarists, but Hirohito himself as Emperor was a bit suspect. He had visited the West, and was a good student of marine biology. This hobby—which one would think valuable in any Japanese leader, given Japan's dependence on the sea for food—was sarcastically mocked by militarists, who said he should spend be spending his time in Shinto meditation.

Nashonarizumu: State Shinto and rising militarism

Modern nation-state creation, as hopefully has been shown many times in former chapters of this book, almost always involves creation of a new mindset—a new and more all-embracing patriotism. It shows up most clearly in those ethnic groups with no modern state. Even in Japan, however, with its long traditions of self-identity and self-government, social and regional divisions before Meiji were such that a new patriotism was required. The designers of this new Meiji experiment had gone to school in France and Germany of the 1870s and 1880s, in the atmosphere of such strong new nationalism. The word itself was taken straight into Japanese pronunciation from French and/or English as *nashonarizumu*. Shinto, a uniquely Japanese religion and moreover connected from earliest days with the Imperial house, now became obligatory for Japanese citizens: everyone had to register, if not worship, at a local shrine. In 1873 a National Holiday was established for February 11, celebrating the supposed founding of the nation in 660 BC by the original divine Emperor Jimmu. A new national anthem was written celebrating the new unity under the restored Emperor. Called the *Kimigayo*, "May Your Reign Last Forever," it was based on a poem from the Heian period, set to music composed in 1880 but composed to sound ancient. In the first enthusiasm of the movement, even Buddhism was the enemy, and Buddhist temples and priests were attacked. This waned somewhat after it became clear how deeply rooted in common culture Buddhism actually was.

One case study of this is the Yasukuni shrine in the heart of Tokyo,[GE74] just north of the moat that surrounds the Imperial Palace complex. It was first set up in 1869, along with dozens of others in the land, as a memorial for the heroes who had died fighting for the Meiji Restoration. One of the key designers of the new westernized Meiji armed forces, Masujiro Omura, was wounded by an anti-foreign ronin, and died of those wounds in 1869. Soon after that a bronze statue of him was cast and put on a pedestal there; it still dominates the entrance of the shrine. Within a decade, with the elaboration of a new State Shintoism, this particular shrine was elevated to the premier position in the country. The massive torii gateway into the shrine was named *Dai-ichi*, or "Great (Number) One." Yasukuni came to represent all those who died in service to country, from 1868 to World War II. Their souls were now considered to be kami that were localized there. As Japanese

---

72. GE Layer 72 is a Folder titled "Manchukuo." It has a Polygon representing the kindgom in yellow, and a Placemark locating its proclaimed capital, Changchun (renamed "New Capital" by the Japanese controllers of this puppet state).

73. GE Layer 73 is a Folder titled "Feb. 26, 1936, coup attempt." It includes Placemarks referencing Army Headquarters, the area of most governmental office buildings, and the National Diet Building. This last has a link to an interesting historical photograph of troops in front of it; see website: http://aboutjapan.japansociety.org/resources/category/1/7/6/5/images/BE068701.jpg

74. GE Layer 74 is a Folder titled "Yasukuni Shrine," referencing three Panoramio icons with pictures of different aspects of the shrine complex. One is "Huge Torii" with photo of gateway; one, titled "Yasukuni," has a nice photo of Masujiro Omura, an early martyr to the Meiji cause; and the third, titled "Yasukuni Shrine" has a good view of shrine itself.

militarism and imperialist sentiment grew, this was a prime place for its celebration. For some historians it has something of the flavor of the Nuremburg rallies of Nazi Germany.

Prince Saionji and Japanese Liberalism

For Americans who only know early- and mid-twentieth century Japan through the lens of Pearl Harbor, one of the best chapters in Oliver Statler's *Japanese Inn* deals mainly with the life of Prince Saionji Kimmochi. He was born in 1849 of high imperial nobility in Kyoto, and was a childhood playmate and later a friend of the Meiji Emperor. Saionji was one of the few Kyoto courtiers to believe imperial forces ought to join the anti-Shogunal armies, and did so himself in those wars of 1867–69. In the extraordinary "learn from the West" era that followed, he was perhaps Japan's outstanding intellectual talent. He lived in Paris from 1871–1880, particularly studying French educational and judicial structures; then he came back to Japan and arranged for the founding of a European-style law school (today's Meiji University).

Saionji's younger brother had been adopted into the Sumitomo family, and became head of this rich and powerful zaibatsu. It was Sumitomo money that financed Saionji's travels and political career. Saionji in turn gave Sumitomo a link with the government (the firm had been so closely tied to the Shogunate that after the Meiji Restoration it would have otherwise been frozen out of the huge new government subsidies).

In 1882, when chief Meiji reformer Ito Hirobumi set off on what turned out to be a critical trip for the study of the institutions of Bismarck's Germany on which to model Japanese ones, he asked Saionji to go with him. The rest of that decade Saionji stayed on to serve as Japanese minister to Austria, then to Germany, and then to Belgium. Saionji returned to Japan for good around 1890. He was probably more knowledgeable about European culture than any other Japanese leader, and was certainly its most Liberal politician, believing strongly in Parliamentary rule. He was Minister of Education for a few years in the 1890s, and after Ito's death (Ito was assassinated in 1909 by a Korean patriot) was twice Prime Minister. Both of these times Saionji's government was brought down by army generals.

He moved to the little seaside town of Okitsu in 1919, building a house on land given him by the owner of the local inn, the Minaguchi-ya. He was about seventy years old, and ostensibly in retirement. But by 1924 he was the only surviving *genro*, those greatly respected "elder statesmen" associated with Japan's Meiji transformation. As such, he alone could suggest to the Emperor which person to tap to be the next Prime Minister of Japan. On those infrequent occasions when he took the train to Tokyo, the townspeople in Okitsu knew there was some major crisis in government. He undoubtedly influenced the young Emperor Hirohito, who strongly condemned the attempted takeover of civilian government by young army officers in February 26, 1936, postponing total military control of Japanese policies by a few years. Saionji himself was on the assassins' hit list, but escaped. It may be no coincidence that the bombing of Pearl Harbor came in 1941, the year after Prince Saionji's death in 1940. But in general Liberalism in Japan, as in Germany, proved to be just too weak to stave off conservative nationalism and later integral nationalism with its militarism and quest for empire.

World War II

In 1936 Japan joined Germany in "the Anti-Comintern Pact"; and Fascist Italy joined soon thereafter. World War II itself really began in July of 1937 with the full-scale Japanese invasion of China in the wake of the Marco Polo bridge incident (initiated, of course, by the Kwantung Army). The European theater of World War II only began with Hitler's invasion of Poland in early fall of 1939, two years and two months later. The U.S. only joined after the Japanese bombing of Pearl Harbor in December of 1941, two years and two months after war started in Europe. That brief listing alone shows something of Japan's importance in the world during this era.

When the U.S. cut off oil and scrap metal sales to Japan, this set a limit to how long the Japanese navy, especially, could function. This gave Japan a fairly clear choice between moderating its foreign policy—meaning withdrawing from at least some of its imperial ventures—or going after the rich resources of East and Southeast Asian countries. Many of them were still colonies of western powers, but most western military forces were being withdrawn to Europe for the war there. The first choice seemed to many Japanese to be accepting second-class status again. In October of 1941, when Tojo Hideki was chosen Prime Minister, the deal for war was quickly sealed. He had been commander of the Kwantung Army in 1937 when it began the full-scale Japanese invasion of China, and was resolutely pro-war. Since the U.S. Pacific fleet had been moved from the West Coast to Hawai'i, a surprise naval attack—perhaps with the 1904 attack on Pt. Arthur still in memory—was set in motion.

It is a story that has been told many times (without World War II material, someone said, the History Channel would have to go off the air). But in brief rehearsal, the attack was supposed to destroy the U.S. fleet, and be the trigger for Japanese seizure of Hong Kong in South China, and the whole of Southeast Asia. The Japanese battle fleet, assembled around its aircraft carriers, came down from the Kurile Islands in radio silence, and the U.S. fleet was famously hammered at its Pearl Harbor base. In a matter of hours after that, the U.S. air forces stationed in the U.S.-occupied Philippines were caught on the ground and destroyed, and the British battleship *Prince of Wales*, pride of the British navy, was sunk along with its consort off Malaya. This spectacular surprise strike that began the Pacific phase of World War II was, militarily speaking, a mixed success. Three U.S. carriers based at Pearl were at sea, and so were not caught in the raid, and some of the sunken battleships were refloated and made seaworthy again. But as a trigger for the occupation of Hong Kong and points south and west, it seemed in the short run to work out well for the Japanese. Hong Kong fell by Christmas. The Philippines were attacked in force on December 22, and U.S. forces surrendered the fortress of Corregidor in May. Singapore was bombed the same day as Pearl Harbor and was taken by the Japanese in February. The Japanese took all of Indonesia (except a few of New Guinea's jungles). The key island of Java, as you've seen, was attacked by February 28 and western forces there surrendered March 12, less than two weeks later. General Stilwell's U.S. force was run out of Burma over into India, as was talked about in the Yangtze Valley chapter. In just a few months' time, Japan had carved out an empire 4,000 by 6,000 miles, an impressive chunk of the earth's surface, even if much of it was water.[GE[75]]

But just six months after Pearl Harbor—June 5, 1942—at the battle of Midway, the Japanese lost four irreplaceable aircraft carriers to one for the U.S. The naval side of the war had turned against Japan that quickly, and without control of the sea all those rich resources of Southeast Asian countries in particular were never going to make it to Japan. By the end of the war the Japanese were reduced to making an aviation gasoline substitute from pine tree stumps. Even pines along the old Tokaido weren't immune to wartime requisitioning.

Damage on our corridor

In April of 1942, just five months after Pearl Harbor, sixteen carrier-borne bombers of the Doolittle Raid took off on a one-way mission to bomb Japanese targets on Honshu, knowing in advance they'd have to bail out or crash-land the planes in China. Most of their targets were in Tokyo, Yokohama, and Yokosuka, although one bomber each targeted Nagoya, Osaka, and Kobe, further west. Some damage was done, but each bomber could carry only 2,000 pounds of bombs; this was mainly a morale-building raid for the Allied side.

In 1943 General Chennault's Fourteenth Air Force began more serious bombing operations from inland Chinese bases, targeting the home islands of Japan. Japanese ground advances in turn targeted the airfields, effectively removing this threat.

But by the end of July 1944 the Allies in their island-hopping advance took Saipan (just over a hundred miles north-northeast of Guam) in the Marshall Islands, and then the relatively flat neighboring island of Tinian, perfect for a set of long, parallel airstrips.[GE[76]] This was the first base from which B-29 bombers could reach Japan, and it was in turn out of reach of the Japanese. It became the busiest airport of the war (and would be the airport from which the *Enola Gay* took off with the atomic bomb destined for Hiroshima a year later). In the spring of 1945, as the Allied island-hopping campaign converged on Okinawa,[GE[77]] B-29s from Tinian devastated the big Japanese cities, adding civilian to military and industrial targets. On March 9 the firebombing of

75. GE Layer 75 is a Polygon, outlining the greatest extent of the Japanese advance in World War II.

76. GE Layer 76 is a Placemark referencing the WW II airfields on the northern end of Tinian Island. Zoom out of view for relations of Tinian to Saipan, Guam.

77. GE Layer 77 is a Folder titled "Allied Island-Hopping." It has sets of thick red arrows (Polygons) representing the progress of the island-hopping, the two main branches coming together at Okinawa, and thin white arrows (Paths) representing the bombing of the main Japanese islands from Tinian Island's airstrips. Map adapted from "World War II in Greater East Asia" map on p. 811 of Fairbank, Reischauer & Craig's *East Asia: Tradition and Transformation* (Rev. Ed.).

Tokyo (just a few weeks after the firebombing of Dresden, 5,600 miles away) resulted in 120,000 dead. Within a week and a half of that Nagoya and Osaka were similarly burned. On our corridor every big city except Kyoto (spared as a cultural center) was virtually destroyed. The Empire so spectacularly assembled was crumbling.

The legacy of imperialism

There was a ferocity about Japanese treatment of enemy combatants, especially westerners, that was unusual even by the standards of World War II. More than a third of all U.S. prisoners of war in Japan died, either killed outright, or beaten, worked or starved to death. The Japanese were at first welcomed by many other Asians, who were proud to see fellow Asians throwing off western colonial rule. But Japanese nationalistic conviction that they were the divine race merged with wartime desperation to end most positive relationships. Requisition of materiel and manpower from places such as Korea and Indonesia included "comfort women," forced into prostitution for Japanese army units. The Chinese were not among the Asians who welcomed the Japanese in World War II. China was too big for the Japanese to totally conquer or occupy, and the Japanese resorted to higher and higher levels of punishment to force submission—which never came. From the "Rape of Nanking" early in the war to the "Burn All, Loot All, Kill All" campaigns late in the war, China suffered at Japanese hands unimaginably. I don't think Chinese and Japanese relations have a chance to become really warm until the last Chinese dies who remembers it.

The Chrysanthemum and the Sword

The U.S. had no foreign intelligence service to speak of before World War II. But when the war broke out, the Roosevelt administration and particularly the armed forces recruited all the talent they could think of to help provide it. In late spring of 1945 the American Office of War Information asked the great American anthropologist Ruth Benedict to tell them about Japan: how would the home islands react to invasion? how would a government of occupation be most successful? what, after all, made the Japanese, seemingly so different culturally from us, tick? She had never been to Japan, and only had access to Japanese-Americans and prisoners of war, but otherwise had all the wartime government resources for research, travel, and interpreting of which most scholars can only dream. She did all of her "fieldwork" in the three or four months before the atomic bombs were dropped on Hiroshima and Nagasaki in early August. Her answers partly determined U.S. occupation strategies, and it's still an interesting read today (she published a fuller version of her report in 1946).[15] A couple million Japanese have bought copies of it, as one measure of its impact.

For starters, the title is excellent: the Japanese as the inventors of some of the world's most delicate arts, including the slow and patient love needed to develop some of the most spectacular flowers, and the Japanese as the creators of the world's most efficient sword, and a brutal cult of the sword to go with it. Early on she discusses major differences between Americans and Japanese. We went to war because we were attacked, and because states greedy for international power were violating their neighbors. Japan went to war because a world of totally independent nations was a world of chaos, and Japan (in which everyone understood their place in the social hierarchy) would have to fight to establish a proper hierarchy among the nations. We celebrated our material progress in the war. The Japanese, of course, produced war matériel as well, but when push came to shove, they believed the spirit was supreme. An anecdote went around Japan in the war concerning a Japanese air force captain who landed first, checked off all his pilots as they landed, took a report to headquarters, and then collapsed. His body was ice cold and there was a bullet in his heart that had to have been immediately fatal. Obviously, even to many educated Japanese, his spirit had seen his responsibility through even though his body was technically dead. Naming the suicide pilots "kamikaze" after the "divine winds" that saved Japan from Mongol/Chinese invasion in 1281 was not just a public relations device.

There has been much discussion of Benedict's categories of "shame" societies, in which she puts Japan, and "guilt" societies, in which she puts Americans. Virtually no Japanese soldiers surrendered in the first years of the war; almost all prisoners of war were captured because they were wounded or unconscious. She notes what a dangerous thing laughter was for American prisoners of war in Japan; in Japanese eyes their surrender should have caused them such shame as to make them beyond laughter forever.

In Benedict's perception, every Japanese was born with an indebtedness too great to ever pay off—first, to Emperor; secondly, to parents; and then lesser indebtednesses to those who granted one favors. Perhaps the most important of her conclusions concerned Japanese attitudes toward the Emperor. He was in some way the symbol of the Japanese people, and Japanese of very different ideologies all attributed their stands to him. Those prisoners of war who were still very much pro-war said they were doing it all "to ease the Emperor's mind." Those opposed to the war argued that it wasn't the Emperor who had started the war; in fact, he had been against it, and all Japanese should be, too, because of that. Virtually all Japanese were in agreement that if the Emperor said to fight on, the Japanese would fight to the last village, but that if he said surrender, "even the Kwantung Army" would lay down its weapons.

That undoubtedly influenced the U.S. decision to soften its "unconditional surrender" demand, agreeing that it would respect the Imperial institution. Even after the second atomic bomb was dropped (on Nagasaki on August 9), the top decision-makers in Japan were split 3-3 on surrender or keeping up the fight. For only the second time in modern history, the Emperor directly entered politics, casting the tie-breaking vote for surrender. When his voice was broadcast, quoting an old Buddhist sutra to the effect that the unendurable must be endured, it was the first time most people had heard his voice. And the whole country laid down its arms.

General Douglas MacArthur, S.C.A.P.

It was called the Allied Occupation of Japan, but it was mainly an American show, as the Pacific war had mainly been an American theater. General Douglas MacArthur, who had said upon being run out of the Philippines by the Japanese in 1942 "I shall return" (and who influenced the focus on the Philippines in that return), was from 1945 to 1952 the SCAP: "Supreme Commander of Allied Powers." He presided over the surrender ceremony on the deck of the U.S.S. Missouri in Tokyo harbor, and every day was driven from the U.S. Embassy [GE[78]] to SCAP headquarters in the fortress-like Dai Ichi Insurance building, overlooking the Imperial Palace, that had survived the firebombing.[GE[79]] He was the American version of the old Roman Proconsul, a military leader who also became the first governor of a newly-conquered province.

The first order of business was dismantling the Japanese military. Army and navy equipment was all seized; soldiers and sailors were all demobilized. That may have been the single biggest change in the Meiji system, which had been designed by its founders to put the military leadership beyond civilian control. A war crimes tribunal modeled on the Nuremburg Trials was set up. It met in "Ichigaya Court," the pointedly-chosen former Imperial Army Headquarters.[GE[80]] Seven, including General Tojo, were sentenced to death by hanging, and sixteen got life sentences. Two hundred thousand were at least temporarily barred from any role in government.

The second order of business was separating the Emperor from State Shinto, so closely tied to Japanese militarism and imperialism. Hirohito went along; his New Year's address for 1946 ended with some remarks about relations between the people and himself, which, he said:

> . . .do not depend upon mere legends and myths. They are predicated on the false conception that the emperor
> is divine and that the Japanese people are superior to other races and fated to rule the world.[16]

In 1947 a Constitution—written mainly by members of the SCAP administration—was adopted. In it the Emperor was a symbol only, without political authority. A two-house legislature (Diet) produced the ministry or cabinet. The famous Article 9 said that the Japanese "forever renounce war." Women got the vote, for the first time in Japanese history. Right-wing groups that had supported imperialism were disbanded. The zaibatsu

---

78. GE Layer 78 is a Placemark referencing the U.S. Embassy.

79. GE Layer 79 is a Placemark referencing the Dai-Ichi building. Click on Panoramio icon under pointer titled "GHQ" for picture of same.

80. GE Layer 80 is a Placemark locating Ichigaya Military Academy, which later became the Imperial Japanese Army's headquarters. This was also the site of Mishima's famous suicide in 1970, discussed later. Click on Panoramio icon under Placemark for view of central entrance, main buildings of this Japanese combination of West Point and the Pentagon. The whole complex is about a mile and a half northwest of Tokyo's Imperial Palace.

were so closely related to Japanese imperialism and militarism that they were also outlawed under the U.S. occupation. They were broken up into their constituent pieces in what amounted to anti-trust legislation.

One of the most successful of Allied reconstruction efforts was in the area of land reform. Almost all the land was owned by a third of farm families, and the other two-thirds were mostly tenants trying to survive on minuscule plots. The government limited the land a given family could hold (varying with quality and value of the land), bought up the rest for distribution to those with too little to make a living on. Local commissions were established to determine who was deserving. SCAP built on a tradition of Japanese reform thought from the 1930s in so doing.

Labor, under the MacArthur proconsulship, got the right to organize but, it turned out in practice, not the right to enforce its demands by shutting down everything in a general strike.

"Japan, Inc."

As in post-war Germany, Japanese burned out by ideological extremism and defeat put much of their energy into economic rebuilding. The roots of Japanese economic recovery came with a group that began to meet in Tokyo even before the surrender. After U.S. occupation ended in 1952, the zaibatsu at least partially reconstituted themselves. Carefully called "consortia" now, with parts labeled fully independent, they are still recognizable as zaibatsu today—though some nouveaux riches additions such as Honda and Sony have been allowed to join the elite club. American businessmen facing high-tech competition from Japan from the 1960s on complained about "Japan, Inc.," claiming that certain Japanese businesses got unfair support from the government, making true competition impossible. Maybe so, maybe not; the author doesn't have the economic expertise to tell. But historically speaking it was just the way the Japanese had learned to do industrialization and production in the first place. In the 1950s in the U.S. "Made in Japan" was synonymous with cheap and shoddy manufactures. By the 1960s a new quality was beginning to show, and by the 1980s high quality Japanese goods were virtually eliminating whole sectors of the U.S. electronics industry, and Japanese cars (along with German ones), were pushing American automobiles completely out of the high quality end. This was the "Japanese shock" that was even more devastating to the Soviet economy than to ours, that the author argued earlier was more responsible for Gorbachev's reforms than any military race with the U.S.

The 1964 "coming out" party: the Olympics and the *Shinkansen*

The year 1964 was sort of Japan's "coming out" party, onto the world stage. Tokyo was awarded the Olympics that year, the first non-western site ever for the games. Some new athletic arenas had already been built for the 1958 Asian Games there, but many more were designed and built just for the Olympics. The Nippon Budokan in the Imperial Palace grounds—famous these days as a concert stage for rock and other groups—was built for the judo competition.[GE81] A couple of miles west of the Imperial Palace an Olympic stadium was built for soccer and other competitions; it was sited between a covered stadium for wrestling, two baseball fields, and a rugby field.[GE82] The whole Olympics came off beautifully, in terms of facilities and organization, and in what had to be an expression of national pride Japan came in an impressive third in the gold medal count for the games (behind only the U.S. and U.S.S.R.). It was hard for international spectators to take in, that just nineteen years earlier Tokyo had been a bombed- and burned-out ruin.

Japan's first "bullet train"—the Tokaido *Shinkansen* ("New Trunk Line")—opened in October of 1964, just in time for the Olympics. The world's first dedicated high speed rail system, it had been talked about since the 1930s. Work on it was derailed by World War II, and in 1958 it got full government approval. The first bullet trains ran from Tokyo through Kyoto to Osaka at 130 m.p.h., and smoothly enough so as not to slop your tea out of the cup. Today much of the rest of the country has been tied into this high-speed grid, and sections of it run at 200 m.p.h. The Tokaido section still carries Japan's (and probably the world's) heaviest daily passenger

---

81. GE Layer 81 is a Placemark referencing the octagonal Budokan building. Notice it is actually within the Imperial Palace grounds, inside the moat. Click on Panoramio icon under pointer titled "Nihon-Budokan (日本武道館)" for one view.
82. GE Layer 82 is a Placemark generally locating an arc of gyms and stadiums associated with the '64 Olympics.

load, and the whole trip from Tokyo to Osaka can be done in two and a half hours. Amazingly, especially in a country prone to earthquake, to date not the first passenger has been killed in collision or derailment in the almost half-century of such high-speed operation.[GE[83]]

Yukio Mishima

On November 25, 1970, Yukio Mishima—one of Japan's most famous writers and actors, at age forty-five at the peak of his career—came to visit the Commandant of Tokyo's Ichigaya Military Academy (Japan's version of West Point, where officer candidates were trained; scene of war crimes trial discussed earlier). The Commandant knew Mishima, and welcomed him into his office even though he had four disciples with him and they were armed with swords.

Mishima had been born in Tokyo in 1925. A grandmother of daimyo descent had claimed him to raise, rarely allowing him out of the house and filling him with ideas of aristocratic honor and the degeneracy of modern democratic times. At twelve he was returned to his father's house, and his father tried in rough ways to toughen him. Among other things he was forbidden to write, already a great love of his. Although he did not fight in World War II (suspected of tuberculosis by the draft board), he was fascinated with the idea of honorable death and got a reputation as "Japan's Hemingway." He rehearsed seppuku, the ritual suicide of a samurai, in a famous film. In politics he was an outspoken critic of the U.S.-imposed constitution. In 1967 he founded the "Shield Society," a samurai-style military force of perhaps a hundred young Japanese men who followed Mishima's lead in learning hand-to-hand fighting and kendo. The group was sworn to protect the Emperor, though Mishima publicly said Hirohito should abdicate since he had renounced divinity, and allow a new, self-consciously divine Emperor to ascend the throne. In 1968, many believe, Mishima narrowly missed the Nobel Prize for literature that went to a fellow countryman.

So on November 25, 1970, the Commandant tolerantly welcomed the actor and his disciples into his office, used to his flamboyant ways. But Mishima had chosen to play out his final scene here. When the Commandant refused to go along with his plans for a coup d'état, Mishima demanded that he be allowed to address the assembled officer candidates. He harangued them from a balcony, calling for a revolt against the constitution, but was shouted down. Then he returned to the Commandant's office and committed seppuku, with one follower "taking his head" at the proper moment, and then committing seppuku himself.

While he represented no substantial interest group in Japan, it is nevertheless interesting that some twenty-five years after World War II, in a thoroughly democratic Japan, its most famous artist was so imbued with nostalgia for the feudal age. The feudal ages in the West still have a hold on our minds, judging by the stream of historical fiction set there that moves through our bookstores. In Japan the age of aristocratic honor and privilege was four times as long as in the West, and much more recent.

"Prudent nationalism?"

In 1999 the *Kimigayo* once again became the official national anthem of Japan. The Yasukuni shrine is as attractive to ultra-nationalists in modern Japan as the Voortrekker monument still is to many Afrikaners in South Africa. Prime Ministers and other government leaders who expect any votes from the far right are obliged to make public, annual visits to the shrine. For this, they are angrily criticized from Beijing, Pyongyang, Seoul, and Taipei, not to mention the liberal press in Japan. The shrine stands for glossing over any Japanese wrongs done to others in the imperial era; for overthrowing the U.S.-imposed constitution, especially Article 9 with its renunciation of war for all time; and for a rejection of the Tokyo tribunal that found imperial Japanese leaders such as Tojo guilty of war crimes. Many modern rallies there have featured Tojo's granddaughter, who has insisted that her grandfather's only "crime" was to love Japan.[17]

But in opposition to what one careful observer of modern Japan calls "resurgent cultural nationalism" is "prudent revivalist nationalism."[18] The great majority of Japanese—in a vibrant democracy under a Constitution

---

83. GE Layer 83 is a Placemark referencing a Panoramio icon with a classic view of the Shinkansen speeding by under the foot of Mt. Fuji.

that has lasted more than half-a-century now—seem to have embraced this "prudent" nationalism that modestly celebrates cultural uniqueness and economic progress, but is much more open to respecting that of other cultures and states too.

It's a hard balance to strike for people anywhere. It involves honest soul-searching of places in one's own cultural history where evil was done, not just a celebration of only the good and glorious side of one's history. It often leads to the painful acceptance that soldiers—sons and sometimes daughters of the folk, fathers and uncles and cousins—did indeed die in vain in struggles fought for misunderstood or selfish causes. It often leads to understanding that there were battles that should have been fought that weren't, and courageous individual stands that should have been taken but weren't. A real Japanese patriot would honestly work through that political and cultural history—for personal wholeness, and for the good of the country. Real American patriots should work through ours, too.

Endnotes

1. From William Elliot Griffis, *The Mikado's Empire* (New York, 1876), as quoted on p. 348 of Marius B. Jansen, *The Making of Modern Japan* (Cambridge, MA & London: Belknap Press of Harvard University Press, 2000).

2. Marvin K. Opler, "Japanese Folk Beliefs and Practices, Tule Lake, California," *Journal of American Folklore,* vol. 63, no. 250 (Oct–Dec 1950), pp. 385–97.

3. The dating scheme used here, and a good bit of the material, comes from Martin Collcutt, Marius Jansen, and Isao Kumakura, *Cultural Atlas of Japan* (New York & Oxford: Facts on File, 1988). See particularly their timeline on pp. 8–9.

4. See Statler, *Japanese Inn*, p. 173, as part of his chapter entitled "Which concerns the light-hearted pilgrims of the Tokaido."

5. From A. L. Sadler, *The Ten Foot Square Hut and Tales of the Heike,* trans. by A. L. Sadler (Sydney: Angus and Robertson, 1928), as quoted in G. L. Anderson (ed.,), *Masterpieces of the Orient* (New York & London: W. W. Norton & Co., 1977), pp. 685–86.

6. Eugen Herrigel, *Zen in the Art of Archery*. With an introduction by D. T. Suzuki; trans. by R. F. C. Hull (New York: Vintage Books, 1989).

7. Oliver Statler, *Japanese Inn* (Honolulu: University of Hawaii Press, 1961).

8. Collcutt, Jansen & Kamakura, *Cultural Atlas of Japan*, p. 134.

9. Engelbert Kaempfer, *Kaempfer's Japan: Tokugawa Culture Observed*. Ed., trans. & annotated by Beatrice M. Bodart-Bailey (Honolulu: University of Hawaii Press, 1999), pp. 248–49. Following quote from p. 364.

10. Anderson, *Masterpieces of the Orient*, p. 747.

11. The author appreciated the personnel of the Hood Museum taking most of a morning with him in May of 2008 going through both the Hoeido and Reisho series, print at a time.

12. Kosaku Yoshino, *Cultural nationalism in contemporary Japan: A sociological enquiry* (London & New York: Routledge, 1995), pp. 46–47.

13. Statler, *Japanese Inn*, p. 266.

14. Jansen, *The Making of Modern Japan*, pp. 348–49.

15. Ruth Benedict, *The Chrysanthemum and the Sword: Patterns of Japanese Culture* (Boston: Houghton Mifflin Co., 1946).

16. As quoted in Jansen, *The Making of Modern Japan*, p. 669.

17. See David McNeill, "Family Ties: The Tojo Legacy," an article republished from Japan Focus, in the *Asia Times*, Nov. 12, 2005, at website http://www.atimes.com/atimes/Japan/GK12Dh04.html

18. Kosaku Yoshino, *Cultural nationalism in contemporary Japan: A sociological enquiry* (London and New York: Routledge, 1995), p. 203.

CPSIA information can be obtained
at www.ICGtesting.com
Printed in the USA
LVHW062136090123
736814LV00027B/669